What Is Psychology?

ELLEN PASTORINO
Valencia Community College

SUSANN DOYLE-PORTILLO
Gainesville College

WADSWORTH

THOMSON LEARNING ™

Australia • Brazil • Canada • Mexico • Singapore • Spain •
United Kingdom • United States

WADSWORTH
THOMSON LEARNING

What Is Psychology?

Ellen Pastorino and Susann Doyle-Portillo

Publisher: **Vicki Knight**
Senior Acquisitions Editor: **Marianne Taflinger**
Development Editors: **Jamie Sue Brooks, Jim Strandberg**
Assistant Editor: **Dan Moneypenny**
Editorial Assistant: **Lucy Faridany**
Technology Project Manager: **Darin Derstine**
Marketing Manager: **Dory Schaeffer**
Marketing Assistant: **Nicole Morinon**
Marketing Communications Manager: **Laurel Anderson**
Project Manager, Editorial Production: **Catherine Morris**
Art Director: **Vernon Boes**
Print Buyer: **Judy Inouye**

Permissions Editor: **Joohee Lee**
Production Service: **Dusty Friedman, The Book Company**
Compositor: **Thompson Type, Inc.**
Text Designer: **Lisa Buckley**
Art Editor: **Lisa Torri**
Photo Researcher: **Roman Barnes**
Copy Editor: **Mary Anne Shahid**i
Illustrator: **Precision Graphics**
Cover Designer: **Katherine Minerva**
Cover Image: **Shoji Sato/Photonica**
Text and Cover Printer: **Transcontinental Printing/Interglobe**

© 2006 Thomson Wadsworth, a part of The Thomson Corporation. Thomson, the Star logo, and Wadsworth are trademarks used herein under license.

ALL RIGHTS RESERVED. No part of this work covered by the copyright hereon may be reproduced or used in any form or by any means—graphic, electronic, or mechanical, including photocopying, recording, taping, Web distribution, information storage and retrieval systems, or in any other manner—without the written permission of the publisher.

Printed in Canada
1 2 3 4 5 6 7 09 08 07 06 05

For more information about our products, contact us at:
Thomson Learning Academic Resource Center
1-800-423-0563
For permission to use material from this text or product, submit a request online at http://www.thomsonrights.com. Any additional questions about permissions can be submitted by email to thomsonrights@thomson.com.

ExamView® and ExamView Pro® are registered trademarks of FSCreations, Inc. Windows is a registered trademark of the Microsoft Corporation used herein under license. Macintosh and Power Macintosh are registered trademarks of Apple Computer, Inc. Used herein under license.

© 2006 Thomson Learning, Inc. All Rights Reserved. Thomson Learning WebTutor™ is a trademark of Thomson Learning, Inc.

Library of Congress Control Number: 2004117250

Student Edition: ISBN 0-15-507333-8

Paper Edition: ISBN 0-495-03210-7

Loose-leaf Edition: ISBN 0-495-03209-3

Thomson Higher Education
10 Davis Drive
Belmont, CA 94002-3098
USA

Asia (including India)
Thomson Learning
5 Shenton Way
#01-01 UIC Building
Singapore 068808

Australia/New Zealand
Thomson Learning Australia
102 Dodds Street
Southbank, Victoria 3006
Australia

Canada
Thomson Nelson
1120 Birchmount Road
Toronto, Ontario M1K 5G4
Canada

UK/Europe/Middle East/Africa
Thomson Learning
High Holborn House
50–51 Bedford Row
London WC1R 4LR
United Kingdom

Latin America
Thomson Learning
Seneca, 53
Colonia Polanco
11560 Mexico
D.F. Mexico

Spain (including Portugal)
Thomson Paraninfo
Calle Magallanes, 25
28015 Madrid, Spain

In memory of my parents:
Joan Cantelmo Pastorino (1933–2004)
Edward Thomas Pastorino (1930–1986)
for modeling strength, humility, compassion, a passion
for life, a sense of humor, and a love of learning.
I cherish all that you have given me.

Ellen Pastorino

For my husband, Eulalio Ortiz Portillo, for his love
and understanding—and for keeping the TV low while
I spent many of our nights and weekends "together"
working on the computer. ¡Te amo mucho!

Susann Doyle-Portillo

ABOUT THE AUTHORS

Ellen E. Pastorino (Ph.D., Florida State University, 1990) is a developmental psychologist who established her teaching career at Gainesville College in Georgia. As a tenured professor she created and developed the college's Teaching and Learning Center, working with faculty to promote student learning. For the past 8 years she has been teaching at Valencia Community College in Orlando, Florida. Here, too, she has worked with faculty in designing learning-centered classroom practices. She actively participates in many conferences. In January of 2005 she gave a talk at the National Institute on the Teaching of Psychology (NITOP) entitled, "Being Learning-Centered: The Inclusive Classroom." Ellen has won numerous teaching awards including the University of Georgia, Board of Regents Distinguished Professor, the NISOD Excellence in Teaching Award, and Valencia's Teaching and Learning Excellence Award. She has been listed four times in *Who's Who Among America's Teachers* and serves as a reviewer for the Journal on Excellence in College Teaching. Ellen has published articles in The Journal of Adolescent Research and Adolescence, but her main passion has always been to get students excited about the field of psychology. She is a member of APA's, Division II, Society for the Teaching of Psychology and a member of APS. Ellen has authored test banks, instructor manuals, and student study guides. While working as a consultant for IBM Corporation she developed numerous educational materials for teachers and students. Her current interests include assessment, inclusion, and reaching underprepared students. Ellen strives to balance her professional responsibilities with her love of physical fitness and family life.

A professor of psychology at Gainesville College for the past 11 years, **Dr. Susann M. Doyle–Portillo** earned her Ph.D. in Social Cognition in 1994 from the University of Oklahoma. Prior to her doctoral program, Susann earned bachelors degrees in engineering and psychology. This exposure to both the hard sciences and the social sciences helped to ground her firmly in the experimental tradition of psychology. She has published articles in Social Cognition and Contemporary Social Psychology, but the main focus of her career has and will always be teaching. During her tenure at Gainesville College, Susann has earned a reputation as an excellent, but challenging instructor. Her annual teaching evaluations regularly rank her performance as being "superior" and "excellent" and she has three times been listed in *Who's Who Among America's Teachers*. In addition to her teaching responsibilities, Susann is actively engaged in student learning outside of the classroom. One of her major goals is to help students learn by getting them involved in conducting original research. She has supervised independent-study student research at the two-year college level and is the founder of the Division of Social Sciences and Education Annual Research Poster Competition at Gainesville College. This innovative program encourages students to submit posters for competition of original research projects they've conducted in the social sciences. She is also the chair of the Scientific Review Committee/Institutional Review Board for the Gainesville College Engineering and Science Fair, a program that encourages junior and high school students from ten counties in Georgia to engage in original research.

BRIEF CONTENTS

CONTENTS

4 Consciousness: Wide Awake, in a Daze, or Dreaming? 156

5 How Do We Learn?   200

6 How Does Memory Function?   250

10 How Do Adolescents and Adults Change and Develop?   434

11 How Do Gender and Sexuality Impact Our Behavior?   480

12 How Do We Understand and Relate to Others?   522

13 Health, Stress, and Coping: How Can You Create a Healthy Life?   576

16 What Therapies Are Used to Treat Psychological Problems?   702

PREFACE

Together, we have over 30 years of experience teaching introductory psychology. We each teach 4–6 sections of Introductory Psychology each and every semester—it is our bread and butter so to speak. So, it's a good thing that intro psych is also our favorite course. Contrary to what many may think of professors teaching the same course over and over, it never grows old for us. Teaching intro allows us to touch on many different aspects of our fascinating field and to work with diverse students from all walks of life such that no two classes are ever alike.

The uniqueness of each class is just one of the challenges that keep us excited about teaching this course. There are others. Intro psychology classes are often full of students who are just beginning their academic careers—some are fresh from high school—others are returning, non-traditional students who've been out of the classroom for several years. They come to us with the desire to learn about psychology, but often they face serious obstacles. Some are overworked in their personal lives. Some have lingering academic deficiencies. And most expect learning to be easier than we know it to be. As such, a big part of our mission is to help students overcome these obstacles and obtain success.

Getting students to read their textbook in preparation for lectures and exams is one of the biggest problems we face as instructors. Like many professors, our experience has been that few students read assigned chapters prior to lecture, and some even fail to read the chapters by the time they take exams. For years, we have tried various methods of motivating students to read—pop quizzes, reading quizzes, test questions from material in the book but not covered in lecture, and so on. None of these methods seemed to have much of an impact on students.

Students' free time is, of course, in short supply. And when they do have free time, reading a textbook doesn't always seem like an attractive option. Students often find their texts difficult to read, boring, and full of content that is far removed from the concerns of their daily lives. One of us overheard students speaking before class the second week of the semester. One student asked those sitting around him if they had read the reading assignment—most replied they had not. He then said, "I read it, but man I have no idea what they were saying in that chapter!" If we want students to read their books, we will have to give them books that they will *want* to read, and that means giving them a book that they can understand and one that *they* find relevant enough to be worth the time it takes to read. That is why we've written this text. Our goal was to write an "untextbook" textbook—a book with a clean, non-distracting format that students would find interesting to read, easy to read, and memorable.

I loved this course! Dr. Doyle-Portillo is a great teacher who can take something that is complicated and break it down so that it can be easily understood. This has been one of my most favorite classes in my time here at Gainesville College.

Motivating Students by Making Psychology Interesting

Each chapter opens with The Big Picture, a real-life story of a person whose experience illustrates the concept of the chapter. For example, Chapter 2, How Does Biology Influence Our Behavior? opens with the story of Jean-Dominique Bauby, a man who became a prisoner in his own body after a stroke damaged his brainstem. Despite the fact that the stroke left him almost completely paralyzed and able only to blink his left eye, Bauby still managed to write a book. Students will find this inspirational story intriguing and hard to forget. And after reading of Bauby, they will want to know more about the content of Chapter 2—the brain and how it influences our behavior.

Another wonderful feature of the Big Picture stories is that the majority of them come from popular books that students can read to further explore the lives of these intriguing people. Professors interested in adding an interdisciplinary element to their course could also assign these books as supplementary texts.

Making Psychology Relevant for All People

There is little doubt that students learn best when they become personally invested in the material that they are reading and studying. However, for this to occur, students must actually find the material to be applicable to their lives. Given that today's college students are a diverse group of people, writing a text that is relevant to today's student means writing a text that embraces their diversity. We have written our book with this in mind. Throughout our text, we have used examples of real people, who reflect the diversity seen in our classrooms. Where applicable, we have cited and highlighted research that reflects many aspects of diversity, including gender differences, racial diversity, cultural diversity, and age differences. Even the subjects of the Big Picture stories used throughout the text were selected in part because they celebrate people from many walks of life. In all, we have referenced people from 85 countries and/or cultural groups (see p. xxxiv).

In addition to the diversity of the Big Picture stories and the research cited in the text, each chapter also includes a chapter box called It's a Diverse World that illustrates how psychology embraces diversity. For example, in Chapter 5, How Do We Learn? the It's a Diverse World box highlights a Japanese view of reinforcement theory that is very different from the traditional Western model of reinforcement. Because Japan is a collectivistic culture, their conception of reinforcement includes reinforcers that involve other people. For example, the Japanese term *uketome* means reinforcement that occurs when you reward someone else for your own behavior, such as shaking your professor's hand after earning an "A" in the professor's course. In Chapter 1, What Is Psychology? the diversity in gender and ethnicity among psychologists is highlighted as we look at the contributions that women and minority members have made to our field in It's a Diverse World: Gender, Ethnicity, and the Field of Psychology.

Because students are notorious for skipping over all boxed material when they read, our It's a Diverse World feature was designed to prevent this. Each chapter contains only one box that is embedded in the text of the chapter. The text guides the reader into and out of the boxed material. Therefore, the reader cannot skip the box because it is integral to understanding the text.

Making Psychology Accessible Without Dumbing It Down

Motivating a student to read the text is, of course, a primary concern of professors. But reading the text does no good if the student does not understand what he or she has read. The student comment we mentioned previously is very telling. He read the assignment, but he did not understand it. We doubt this did much to encourage him to

I truly enjoyed her class. She challenged my thinking. I would recommend her to anyone who really cares about learning. Dr. Pastorino knows how to speak to people and get them to understand the concepts of what she is teaching. It was definitely a lot of fun.

I really like the dry humor used to incorporate the material into the lectures. Dr. Doyle-Portillo is very clear and easy to understand.

read his next reading assignment! A major goal of this text is to bring psychology to the student by making it understandable and to do so without sacrificing content. We believe that it is not necessary to condescend to students to get them to understand. Rather, you just have to explain difficult concepts thoroughly and clearly.

Engaging Narrative Writing Style

Throughout the text, we have adopted an engaging narrative writing style that will not intimidate students. Difficult concepts (e.g., neural transmission, classical conditioning) are given extended description and many examples are used to illustrate and clarify our points. The language we use in the text strongly reflects the way we speak to our students during class. We attempted to use our prose to tell students the *story* of psychology, as opposed to a mere litany of theories and research findings. We believe we have succeeded. Throughout the process of writing this text, many faculty reviewers and students have consistently praised our writing style for its clarity and accessibility. One reviewer commented that it was obvious that this text was written by authors who have spent much time in the classroom in front of students.

Enhancing Motivation and Learning by Making Psychology Practical

A key point in getting students to read a text and retain what they've read is making the material applicable to their lives. When information is associated with the self, it becomes more easily retrieved from memory. So, when students can see how psychology relates to their personal lives, they are much more likely to find it interesting and a lot less likely to forget it. Throughout the text, we have made a concerted effort to use practical, everyday examples to illustrate the concepts of psychology.

Integrated Applications and Demonstrations

For example, in Chapter 5, How Do We Learn? we discuss how habituation can be used in physical therapies that treat people suffering from chronic vertigo or motion sickness. In Chapter 3, How Do We Sense and Perceive the World? we show students how to prove to themselves that the moon illusion is just an illusion caused by perceptual processes by having them look at the moon from an unusual vantage point. Places like these in the text that show how psychology applies to the real world or contain demonstrations of psychological concepts are noted with an Application or Demonstration icon in the margin.

Let's Review!

Another feature, Let's Review!, appears after each A-head section of the chapter. Let's Review! allows students to actively assess their learning by asking them to apply the material of the preceding section to answer several multiple choice questions. Most of the Let's Review! questions are application questions that apply the material to practical situations. For example, in Chapter 12, How Do We Understand and Relate to Others? we use the following question to test the student's understanding of attribution theory:

> Jasper was quick to assume that Susan was intelligent when he saw that she earned an "A" on her last psychology exam. However, when Jasper earned an "A" on his history test, he was not so quick to assume that he was intelligent. Which of the following biases in social cognition *best* explains Jasper's behavior?

a. the fundamental attribution error
b. the self-serving bias
c. the social desirability bias
d. the actor-observer bias

To answer this question, the student must not only understand the different attribution biases, but he or she must also be able to think analytically about them in applying these concepts to a very common student-oriented scenario.

Studying the Chapter: Are You Getting the Big Picture?

The last section of the chapter is entitled Studying the Chapter: Are You Getting the Big Picture? This section briefly reiterates some of the highlights of the chapter and explains how the chapter's material is relevant to professionals. This feature will help address a common student concern—"Why do I need psychology when I'm not a psych major?" We clearly show how psychology is relevant to many different majors and professions. For example, in Chapter 12, How Do We Understand and Relate to Others? we discuss the relevance of psychology to careers as diverse as law, law enforcement, telemarketing, helping professions, lobbyists, politicians, managers, non-profit organizations, and sales.

Applying Psychology

In the end-of-chapter material, we have also included an Applying Psychology question among the critical thinking questions. This short-answer question asks students to apply their knowledge to solving a problem—again emphasizing the usefulness of psychology. For instance, in Chapter 4, Consciousness: Wide Awake, In a Daze, or Dreaming? we include the following applied exercise:

> Keep a dream log for a week. Using the different theories on dreaming, interpret what your dreams mean. Which of these interpretations seems the most plausible, and why?

Enhancing Learning by Making Psychology Thought-Provoking

Another way to enhance learning is to get students to read in an active fashion. All too often students read in a very passive, in-one-ear-and-out-the-other mode. Students must be enticed to actually *think* while they are reading. To further enhance active engagement in the material, we have embedded thought-provoking questions in the text material. These questions appear in light green and are designed to spur students to engage in goal-directed reading. For example, in Chapter 12, How Do We Understand and Relate to Others? we pose the question, "So, where do our attitudes come from?" immediately before we discuss how attitudes develop. By reading in a goal-directed fashion, students are more likely to engage in elaborative rehearsal of the material and will better retain what they've read.

Critical Thinking About the Chapter

In the end-of-chapter material, we have included a feature called Critical Thinking About the Chapter. This section contains several short-answer questions that require the student to think critically about and integrate several concepts from the chapter. For example, in Chapter 1, What Is Psychology? one of these questions asks students to use their new-found knowledge of research methods to design an experiment that

I loved this course! Every Tuesday and Thursday I jumped out of bed ready to come to class. I was challenged, I was encouraged, and I did things I never thought I could. I had a ball and I'd do it again. Dr. Pastorino was approachable, honest, and cool! She was clear and went the extra mile to meet her students' learning needs.

This class helped me under-stand a great deal more about myself. I enjoyed this class everyday. You (Dr. Doyle-Portillo) are an amazing teacher, friend, and woman. Thank you for being a teacher.

Dr. Pastorino does an excellent job explaining key concepts and relating them to our own lives so we can better under-stand them. I feel she uses her own knowledge of psychology on her students to improve their memories and motivate them. I learned a lot this se-mester. I'm impressed by her teaching ability. She has been the best professor I have had.

tests the hypothesis that listening to rock and roll music facilitates studying and to ad-dress the ethics of their design. By asking students to think about how several of the concepts from the chapter relate to the same problem, we are helping to develop a *big picture* of psychology in the students' minds.

Concept Check

A Concept Check exercise also appears at the end of each chapter. These checks have several formats, including fill-in-the-blank and matching, and they are designed to be a self-check for the student. By completing the Concept Check, students can get a feel for their level of retention immediately after reading the text.

Making Learning More Permanent by Giving Students the Big Picture of Psychology

As instructors, one of our greatest frustrations has been that many students seem to learn merely for the moment. They come to class, do their assignments, take their exams, and then immediately forget the material they were just tested on. What a waste of energy! One of our goals was to write a text that would help prevent this common problem.

Linking Concepts Together

As we wrote each of the chapters, we were very conscious of the *story* we were telling students. Our purpose was to get students to see the *big picture* of psychology as op-posed to seeing the material as a mere collection of ideas and data. Within each chap-ter, we made a concerted effort to link the concepts together into an integrated whole by frequently making reference to concepts covered earlier in the chapter, by asking questions that touch on more than one concept, and by using examples that unify the material.

Cross-Chapter References

Likewise, we encourage readers to see that the different areas of psychology are not mu-tually exclusive or independent by making many cross-chapter references to relevant material. For example, in Chapter 5, How Do We Learn? we compare operant condi-tioning to natural selection, which is discussed in Chapter 2. To account for the fact that sometimes professors omit or rearrange the order of chapters in their course, we pro-vide page references when we reference out-of-chapter material. These references will also encourage students to go back and re-read sections that they may have forgotten.

Critical Thinking for Integration

To help students further develop a *big picture* of psychology, we include Critical Think-ing for Integration questions at the end of the chapter—a feature that was consistently praised by our many reviewers. These short-answer questions require that the student apply concepts from more than one chapter in solving a problem. Professors could also assign these questions as written assignments to keep students current on material from chapters covered earlier in the course. For instance, in Chapter 4, Consciousness: Wide Awake, in a Daze, or Dreaming? we include the following question, integrating material from Chapter 4 with information about the brain from Chapter 2:

Using Chapter 2 as a guide, draw a model of the brain and graphically represent where in the brain various psychoactive drugs have their effects. Also represent on this visual schemata the neurotransmitters that affect these areas of the brain.

Visual Summary

A Visual Summary of the chapter is also included in the end-of-chapter material to allow students to truly *see* the *big picture* of the chapter. In the Visual Summary, all the major concepts and theories of the chapter are brought together in a graphical format. This tool will be especially helpful to students who prefer to learn through visual means.

Distinctive Content by Chapter

Chapter 1

This chapter presents an overview of the field of psychology—both its past and present. We outline early approaches of psychology and explain how psychologists do research. We explain what psychologists do, how they think, and where they work. Our unique content in Chapter 1 includes the following:

- We start out in a dramatic way with the real-life story of September 11th so we can capture the students' attention. We then use 9/11 as a theme to illustrate how psychologists think and the diversity of subfields in which they work. Students will immediately be able to relate psychology to their experiences.

- Following the story of September 11th, the chapter immediately outlines what psychology is not. It dispels common student beliefs about the field of psychology, such as psychology is just common sense and not a science or the belief that psychology is all about mental illness. Such an approach prepares students for understanding the definition of psychology and its scientific nature.

- We have a more thorough explanation of how Darwin's theory influenced James's development of functionalism than competing texts. Students can apply something they often already know something about (Darwin) to the history of psychology.

- We discuss in more detail the education and training needed to pursue a career in psychology. Students who are thinking of pursuing a bachelor's, master's, or doctorate in psychology will learn the requirements for each degree and the job opportunities in the profession.

- Many introductory texts offer the names of several women and minorities evident in psychology's past. We extend this coverage by examining the current progress of women and minorities in the field from the APA research office.

- Our discussion on research methods and ethics is abundant with student-friendly examples. These examples help students discriminate the different research methods and help them understand how a correlation cannot be used to make cause and effect statements—a common student mistake.

Chapter 2

In this chapter, we discuss communication within the body via the endocrine and nervous systems. The structure and function of neurons is covered in detail. We discuss neurotransmitters, their function, and their relationship to certain diseases before moving on to cover the organization and function of the nervous system and the brain. A detailed section on technologies used to study the brain is followed by a discussion of natural selection, and genetics closes the chapter. Compared to competing texts, the unique content of our chapter includes:

- We have a more thorough biochemical explanation of excitation and inhibition, which completes the logic of how neurons are brought to threshold. Many texts simply define excitation and inhibition without explaining what happens in the neuron to make it more or less likely to fire an action potential. We find that treating the action potential vaguely or leaving out details only confuses students. So we've given them the details in a very clear but detailed discussion of neuronal transmission.

- We have a thorough discussion of sex differences in the brain—a topic that many texts ignore. We've covered the available findings on this issue in our It's a Diverse World box and discussed problems associated with interpreting these findings.

- We have an expanded section on technologies used to study the brain, including: MRI, fMRI, PET, SPECT, CAT, EEG, ERP, lesions, angiograms, brains stimulation, and single cell recording. We've included this information because at some point many of our students will encounter these technologies in their everyday lives.

- We have coverage of the septum and its possible role in the addiction process. Students always find discussions about drugs interesting and relevant. By introducing this material here, we pave the way for discussions about drug use in Chapters 4 and 8.

- We have much more coverage of the hippocampus and its role in memory, including the story of H.M. This serves to link biology to memory, which is covered in Chapter 6.

Chapter 3

This chapter on sensation and perception opens with a discussion of measuring sensation and perception. Then, we move on to cover theories of how vision, hearing, taste, smell, and the body senses work. Perception, perceptual constancies, and theories of perceptual organization are also covered. Throughout Chapter 3, we make use of practical examples and demonstrations of sensation and perception to help the reader see why this is such an important area of psychology. For example, we have an in-chapter demonstration students can do to see the effects of having an unequal distribution of rods and cones in the retina. And when we cover the visible spectrum, we also discuss various animals that are able to sense wavelengths that humans cannot perceive. In addition, Chapter 3 also includes the following unique content:

- A discussion of synesthesia is discussed in the opening Big Picture story of Michael Watson—a man who *tasted* shapes.

- The application of signal detection theory to measuring sensory thresholds is discussed, as is the application of signal detection to the real-world problem of eyewitness testimony.

- We discuss subliminal perception and the infamous Vicary study—a topic many of our competitors omit.

- Our discussion of the transduction of light is much more complete than our competitors'. We discuss the function of photopigments in vision very thoroughly and clearly, making strong connections back to Chapter 2 that help students see why understanding the brain and neurons is important to psychology.

- Our description of the anatomy of the ear and hearing is more complete than our competitors.
- We cover sex differences in vision, including cutting-edge research by Gerianne Alexander (2003) that looks at the ease of face perception for females and male facility in the perception of movement. We also discuss the implications of this research.

Chapter 4

This chapter provides an in-depth look at three altered states: sleep, hypnosis, and psychoactive drugs. Our reviews validate that we were able to relate the difficult concepts in this chapter to the students' lives. The opening Big Picture examines how Dave Pelzer's life was influenced by his sleep schedule and his parents' use of alcohol. We highlight how students' weekly schedules often disrupt their circadian rhythms. We relate the effects of alcohol on the brain to show how students feel when they have consumed alcohol. Our unique content for this chapter also includes:

- Coverage of sleep disorders that affect children, such as SIDS and enuresis. Students often know of someone who has experienced or been affected by these disorders and have questions about their occurrence, causes, and treatments.
- Unlike our competitors, we discuss gender differences in sleep. Up-do-date research presents gender differences in the amount of sleep, circadian rhythms, and in types of sleep disorders.
- Our discussion of how drugs work is more complete because it focuses on more than just the chemical effects of drugs. It allows students to see how psychological variables, such as culture and expectations, can influence the use and actual effects of drugs.
- We have a more comprehensive look at alcohol, including health effects, social costs, and the influence of genetics and ethnicity. This is important given the prevalence of binge drinking on college campuses. This content also prepares students for the discussion on destructive motivations in Chapter 8.
- We highlight the limitations of survey research on alcohol use and ethnicity in the United States because it does not differentiate subcultures within one ethnic group. For example, research often lumps all Hispanic American groups together and does not compile data on Hispanic subcultures such as Cuban Americans, Mexican Americans, and Puerto Ricans.

Chapter 5

This chapter on learning theory addresses how learning occurs through the processes of habituation, classical conditioning, operant conditioning, and social learning. Unique content for this chapter includes:

- Unlike our competitors, we discuss the learning process of habituation and discuss its adaptive nature. Understanding habituation is helpful to students because this simple form of learning does have real-world applications. For instance, we explain how habituation can be used in physical therapy to help those suffering from chronic vertigo.
- Compared to some competing texts, we have a more thorough discussion of the potential drawbacks associated with punishment.

- We discuss how classical conditioning can be used to treat disorders like alcoholism.

- We include a unique cross-cultural look at how Japanese psychologists conceptualize reinforcement from a more collectivistic approach. Japanese psychologists recognize forms of reinforcement that involve other people. For example, *Mitome* is a form of reinforcement in which you reward yourself when someone else engages in a desired behavior—you may feel proud if your child does well in school, and your pride may in turn also reward your child. This discussion helps students see how a fundamental difference in culture can impact how psychologists from different cultures view behavior.

- We more thoroughly discuss the pros and cons of token economies, common strategies used with handicapped learners who are mainstreamed into classrooms at ever increasing rates. Some texts fail to mention token economies at all.

Chapter 6

In this chapter, we discuss aspects of the encoding, storage, and retrieval of memories, including implicit and explicit memory, the three stages model vs. the working memory model of memory, organization in long-term memory, theories of forgetting, the reconstructive nature of memory, improving memory, and the biology of memory. Some of our unique content for this chapter includes:

- An expanded section on implicit memory that has a hands-on demonstration of implicit memory at work. This demonstration really drives home the idea that we are not always aware of our own memory processes.

- A more thorough comparison of the traditional three stages/short-term view of memory and the newer working memory model. Many texts muddle these concepts together in a way that only confuses students—leaving them unable to understand the differences between the three-stage model and the newer working memory model. We avoid this by taking students step by step through these models so the differences between them are clear and easily understood.

- Using the case of a brain-damaged man, K.F., we give a detailed view of the subsystems proposed in the working memory model (i.e., the central executive, phonological loop, and visuospatial sketch pad) and discuss how the working memory model explains certain aspects of K.F.'s case that the traditional three-stages model of memory cannot.

- To help students better understand the processes involved in reconstructive memory and eyewitness testimony, we first introduce the concept of schemata in great detail. By introducing schemata first, we give students the building blocks they need to really "see" schemata at work in reconstructive memory and eyewitness testimony.

- We include an interesting section on gender differences in emotional and autobiographical memory highlighting the work of Penelope Davis (1999).

Chapter 7

This chapter gives an overview of the important concepts involved in cognition, language, and intelligence. Topics covered include: thinking, problem solving, decision making, language acquisition, and the measurement of intelligence. Some unique features in this chapter include:

- A discussion of ill-structured and well-structured problems and how they relate to algorithmic and heuristic problem solving. A nice cross-cultural demonstration of an ill-structured problem is also given so students can see the importance of culture in our approach to solving life's problems.

- Unlike competing texts, we cover the processes of inductive and deductive reasoning—concepts that all students should be familiar with but many texts fail to cover. By understanding these types of reasoning, students may gain better insight into their own cognitive strengths and weaknesses and therefore know where they need improvements.

- We discuss the nature vs. nurture debate over the acquisition of language in humans to help tie this chapter's content back to the content of Chapter 2.

- Our It's a Diverse World box highlights the importance of language to everyday life when we tell the story of languageless deaf children in Nicaragua who have adapted by spontaneously creating their own language. This theme echoes the content of our Big Picture story of a deaf man who didn't know that language even *existed* until adulthood. These stories help us convey the importance of language to memory and cognition to our readers.

- We provide well-balanced coverage of the sensitive issue of racial and gender differences in IQ so that students can see what this debate is all about.

Chapter 8

This chapter begins with a discussion of the various ways psychologists have viewed motivation before diving into discussions of the specific motives of hunger, thirst, and destructive motivation. We end the chapter with a section on theories of emotion that includes the traditional historical theories as well as some more modern approaches to this topic. Some of the distinctive content in this chapter includes:

- Both historical and current approaches to understanding sources of hunger feedback are presented. We begin with studies that examine the role of the stomach in hunger and end with modern theories that look at leptin and cck. Students are always very interested and surprisingly well-informed about diet and weight. It is necessary to have a text that is cutting-edge in this area to avoid lagging behind what students learn in health/PE courses.

- We discuss destructive motivations such as abusing drugs and self-injurious behavior. This discussion allows us to link motivation with topics covered in other chapters—drug use in Chapter 4 and personality disorders in Chapter 15.

- In our It's a Diverse World box, we discuss obesity in Black and White teenage girls and explain how both culture and genetics can impact weight.

- We discuss the problem of prejudice toward the obese—a topic that links this chapter with Chapter 12. Many texts focus on the health risks associated with being overweight and ignore the social costs shouldered by the obese. Given the growing rates of obesity in the United States, we feel it's a mistake to cover only gender bias and racism in a text while ignoring the existence of this commonly held prejudice.

Chapters 9 and 10

Chapters 9 and 10 cover physical, cognitive, and social development from conception to death. Most introductory texts devote one chapter to human development—focusing on infant and child development and spending very little time on adulthood topics. We wrote two chapters on development, which allowed us to thoroughly discuss the life stages and challenges of the teen and adult years. We spend the majority of our lives in adulthood, and these are the stages that college students are likely to be in themselves.

If students are going to apply psychology to their lives, they need to be informed of and prepared for adulthood issues. For many students, this will be the only psychology course they take. Hence, we felt a separate chapter on adolescence and adulthood was needed in an introductory text. The unique content of these chapters include:

- An in-depth look at prenatal development that emphasizes the importance of a positive prenatal environment. With the highest teenage pregnancy rate in the industrialized world, female college students especially need to be informed on how their behavior during pregnancy can influence the development of their child.

- Many texts ignore the subject of miscarriage, although its incidence is quite common. We highlight the emotional effects of miscarriage on men and women in our It's a Diverse World box so that students may be better able to understand and cope with this experience in their lives and the lives of their loved ones.

- We have more up-to-date and expanded research on brain development and neural changes that occur in infancy and adolescence. Such findings debunk college students' common beliefs that no new brain cells are formed after birth and the reason behind why brain cells "die."

- To make attachment theory more relevant to students, we apply it to real court cases.

- Students often can see how their parents' behavior has influenced their personality and childhood experiences but don't often look at how they have influenced their parents' responses to them over the years. Detailing the interactive effects of child temperament and parenting style allows students to see how relationships are mutually influenced by both parties.

- Not all introductory texts discuss Vygotsky's theory of cognitive development. We provide side-by-side coverage of the cognitive theories of both Piaget and Vygotsky, enabling students to critically examine and analyze two approaches to cognitive development.

- We cover how lifestyle, culture, and gender impact aging so that students can examine how their current habits and their attitudes about aging may influence their physical abilities in middle and later adulthood. It also allows students to understand the physical abilities of their parents, grandparents, and other older adults.

- Unlike many texts at this level, we take the time to explain cognitive dimensions of teenage thought that result in youthful idealism. We outline differences in how adolescents and adults think. We cover how mental abilities change in adulthood and discuss the nature of wisdom and life expertise.

- We have a much more complete coverage of social relations in adolescence and adulthood than our competitors. For example, we devote a substantial amount of coverage to the process of gaining an identity and relate identity development to career choice. For college students, this is often a personal and relevant issue. We distinguish satisfying marital relationships from dissatisfying ones, discuss the adaptations to parenting that many students will face, and examine the role of being a grandparent.

- Many texts examine the father's role in attachment. However, few look at the culture of fatherhood as we do in our It's a Diverse World box. We cover how the cultural stereotype of men as breadwinners is very powerful and how being an involved father is associated with a high level of stress. We also examine the influence of marital status and income level on a father's role.

- We have an unusually comprehensive coverage of the world of work. We discuss how young adults make a career choice, the predictable changes they may experience in their occupational development, and the factors that will influence their job satisfaction. We've included this information because it is directly relevant to the reason why most students are in college—to establish a career.

Chapter 11

Because sex and gender issues face students every day, we have devoted a whole chapter to this vital area. Students also find much personal value in these topics. The public health of our nation is impacted by the sexual behavior of young people. In this chapter we have the chance to educate students not only on how their thoughts and behaviors influence their lives and others, but also clearly show how psychological topics have personal application. In this chapter we explore gender differences in cognitive abilities and personality, the sexual behavior and attitudes of college students and adults derived from numerous surveys, and we discuss sexual differentiation, sexual orientation, sexual coercion, sexual response, and sexual disorders. Some of our distinctive content in this chapter includes:

- Up-to-date research (e.g., Halpern, 2004) on the cognitive differences in men and women. More importantly, we highlight the wider discrepancy among ethnic groups than between the sexes in national average math and science scores, and college completion rates.

- We include data from the Pfizer Global Study of Sexual Attitudes and Behavior (2002). Ed Laumann, from the University of Chicago, conducted the survey on over 26,000 men and women between the ages of 40 and 80 in 29 countries representing all world regions. It is the most comprehensive, worldwide sex research ever done to date.

- We have a more thorough explanation of how hormones, thoughts, and our culture impact sexual desire. We link the biological role of the hypothalamus and the hormone testosterone (Chapter 2) to the sensory role of visual cues, scents, and reaction to touch (Chapter 3). Students also can see how cultural expectations as to what we think should be sexually arousing influence sexual desire. It helps reinforce the "Big Picture" of psychology to students.

- Students have been receiving information on the types of sexually transmitted infections since middle school. That is why we have focused more of our attention on the prevalence of STI's and who is at risk for an STI. Using current research from the Centers for Disease Control, we look at why STI rates are so high in the United States. We also explain why young people, young women, and certain ethnic groups are at higher risk for contracting STI's. We feel that this information may be of more benefit in reducing a college student's risk of infection.

Chapter 12

This chapter explores many different aspects of how we understand and interact with others in the social world. We cover topics that are relevant to students' lives, as well as to a wide variety of college majors, including attitudes and persuasion, social influence, prejudice, aggression, attraction, and helping behavior. Some of our distinctive content in this chapter includes:

- We have a more thorough discussion of attitudes, persuasion, and compliance than many of our competitors. In the interest of space other text books may combine concepts like persuasion with compliance or obedience with compliance in a way that seems to equate these processes. We do not. Instead, we clearly separate these concepts in our discussion so as not to leave our readers with false impressions of these processes. We feel that a clear understanding of persuasion, compliance, and obedience is very valuable to students because these processes are so central to many professions (e.g., trial law, law enforcement, management, sales, marketing, politics).

- Our discussion of aggression includes the rarely covered cognitive neoassociation model of aggression (Anderson & Bushman, 2002; Berkowitz 1990). This coverage updates this discussion compared to many texts and makes a crucial link between aggression and the cognitive processes that were covered in Chapter 6 (i.e., priming in memory). Our coverage of this theory will also help students appreciate how culture and television may impact aggressive behavior far beyond mere modeling influences.

- Our discussion of helping behavior is also more up-to-date than most texts, in that we take a look at a study by Mark Levine and Kirstien Thompson (2004) that shows that our willingness to help others is influenced by whether or not the victim is perceived to be part of our in-group. This study and its implications have great importance to all of us living in a world where we tend to categorize others as being either "them" or "us."

- We also include a discussion of stereotype threat and female performance in our It's a Diverse World box. This discussion shows the detrimental effects stereotyping can have on women in the professional world. Both our male and female readers will benefit from reading and thinking about how their attitudes and prejudices may affect others' perceptions of themselves as well as their performance.

Chapter 13

Chapter 13 examines how our thoughts and behaviors impact our physical health. The chapter opens with one author's personal story of her parents' struggle with cancer. We often find that such personal accounts make psychology relevant to students and confirm for students that psychologists are human and similar to them in many ways. The chapter details the nature of stress, our physical and emotional reactions to stress, and how our coping methods may help or harm us. Compared to our competitors, unique topics discussed here include:

- A discussion on the stress of discrimination is highlighted in the It's a Diverse World box. Most students know that prejudice and discrimination still exist in the world today, but they do not often understand the damaging effects it can have on people's lives. Presenting this issue also allows us to link the concept of stress with the topic of prejudice discussed in Chapter 12.

- Most texts simply define the nature of daily hassles. Yet, we present how our perceptions of daily hassles are influenced by gender, race, age, and socioeconomic levels. As a significant source of stress, it is important for students to realize that not all people interpret the daily hassles of life in the same way.

- We have more coverage on stress management techniques so that students can learn positive ways of coping with the stress in their lives.

- We have a comprehensive section on health-defeating behaviors pertinent to college students, including alcohol use, tobacco use, and unsafe sex practices. Such content reinforces and links together concepts and material presented in Chapters 4, 8, and 11.

Chapter 14

This chapter outlines the four main theoretical perspectives on personality: psycho-analytic, humanistic, social-cognitive, and the trait perspective. It also discusses behavioral genetics and the hotly debated issue of stability and consistency in personality. Unique content in this chapter also includes:

- We provide expanded coverage on the stability of personality from childhood to adulthood by examining up-to-date longitudinal studies by McCrae et al. (2002) and Shiner et al. (2003). We also discuss how cultural differences in the way we define ourselves influence our ability to measure consistencies in personality across cultures—a serious methodological issue that reinforces students' critical thinking about psychological research. The influence of gender and historical events is also covered giving students a "Big Picture" on the stability of personality.

- We present side-by-side coverage of two well-known social cognitive approaches: Albert Bandura's reciprocal determinism and Julian Rotter's locus of control. We use relevant examples to help students remember their core concepts. For example, we show how reciprocal determinism can be used to explain why many of us adopt the same child-rearing practices as our parents. We also apply locus of control to the students' test-taking expectations.

Chapter 15

Chapter 15 reviews the major perspectives used to explain behavior and then details the symptoms of major mental health disorders, such as anxiety disorders, mood disorders, and schizophrenia. The chapter opens with three stories on mental health. These people are often familiar to students and do not always fit their stereotype of a person with a mental disorder. We present these stories so students can reduce their negative labeling and become more sensitive to people with mental health disorders. Distinctive content in Chapter 15 also includes:

- The inclusion of sociocultural theories to emphasize the importance of looking at people's behavior in relation to their environmental context. Many texts mention these types of theories in Chapter 1 but do not highlight their usefulness when examining abnormal behavior. Students need to know that society and culture influence all behavior, including mental health disorders.

- Many texts simply give an overview of the types of anxiety disorders. Our section begins by outlining the physical, cognitive, emotional, and behavioral components of anxiety. In this way, students can understand the nature of anxiety before focusing on the different disorders.

- The material on all the different disorders can often be overwhelming to students. This is why we focus our attention on the anxiety, mood, and schizophrenic disorders in this chapter. However, we do provide a comprehensive table that lists the major categories of mental disorders with examples. Students can readily see that many of the disorders not covered in this chapter have already been covered in previous chapters. For example, substance-related disorders and sleep disorders are detailed in Chapter 4. Sexual disorders are discussed in Chapter 11.

- Unlike our competitors, we don't simply give the types and symptoms of mental health disorders. We address students' real interest—why people have these disorders. We present up-to-date research in an understandable way so that students can see how biological, psychological, and sociocultural factors influence mental health disorders. For example, Andreasen's (2001), Berry et al.'s

(2003), and McDonald & Murphy's (2003) research shed light on how genes and brain dysfunction play a role in schizophrenia. Barlow's (2002), Ursu et al.'s (2003), and Rosen's (2004) research provides current information on the psychological and biological dimensions of anxiety. Gibb et al.'s, (2004) research highlights cognitive factors in depression, whereas Heim et al.'s (2004) research suggests a relationship between early adverse experiences and major depression. Parker & Brotchie's (2004) and Steiner, Dunn, & Born's (2003) research examine the role of biology and hormones in explaining gender differences in depression.

Chapter 16

This chapter outlines the four main types of psychotherapy: psychoanalysis, behavior therapy, client-centered therapy, and cognitive therapy. It also offers an in-depth look at biological therapies, specifically drug therapy. Some of the unique features in this chapter include:

- A detailed section on who is qualified to give therapy. We include this information so that students can be more educated consumers if they or someone they know is in need of psychological services.

- We answer the often-asked student question—When does one need to consider psychotherapy? We also describe how no one therapy hits the mark for all people. Any specific therapy may be effective depending on that person at that particular point in time.

- Unlike other texts, we address the impact of culture on the success of therapy. Most clients are members of minority cultures, yet most providers of psychological services come from the majority culture. This section highlights the importance of clients finding a therapist with a similar belief and value system as their own.

Countries and Cultural Groups Referenced in *What Is Psychology?*

Africa	Czech Republic	Ireland	Puerto Rico
African Americans	The Dani of Papua New	Islamic peoples	Romania
Alaskan Natives	Guinea	Israel	Russia
Algeria	Danish	Italy	Setswana
American Navajos	East Africa	Japan	Seventh Day Adventists
Arab Americans	Egypt	Jewish peoples	Singapore
Argentina	El Salvador	Kenya	Somalia
Asian Americans	Eskimo peoples	Korean	South Africa
Asians	Ethiopia	Latin American	South America
Australia	Ethnic Hawaiian peoples	Latino	Southeast Asia
Austria	Europe	Malaysia	Spain
The Bashi of Africa	European Americans	Mayan peoples	Sweden
Belgium	France	Mexican Americans	Swiss
Brazil	Germany	Mexico	Taiwan
Britain	Great Britain	Morocco	Thailand
Canada	Greece	Native Americans	Turkey
Central America	Hindi peoples	New Zealand	United Kingdom
Chile	Hispanic	Nicaragua	United States
China	Hispanic-Americans	Pacific-Islander	Viennese
Chinese Americans	Hong Kong	Palestine	Western Europe
Croatia	India	Philippines	
Cuba	Indonesia	Portugal	

Acknowledgments

Writing a college textbook has been an exhausting yet rewarding experience. We are ordinary community college professors who teach four to six classes every semester, so we were often writing in whatever free time we have—weekends, nights, and holidays. We do not live in a "publish or perish" environment. Instead we are valued for our contributions to student learning and service to our institutions. Yet, we have grown so much as educators and psychologists in tackling this project. This would not have been possible without the support of many people who deserve our acknowledgement.

We would like to thank Dean Tim Grogan at Valencia Community College and Deans Kathy Fuller and Michael Stoy from Gainesville College for their administrative support and Bruce Everson and Carol Jones from the Library Resource Center at Valencia Community College who provided much valuable research assistance. We would like to thank Earl McPeek, Carol Wada, and Brad Pottoff, formerly of Harcourt Brace for taking a chance on two unknown psychologists and encouraging our vision of this book. Thanks also to Leslie Carr, Jamie Sue Brooks, and Jim Strandberg for reading numerous manuscripts and giving direction on how to make our writing clearer and more effective. Special thanks to Vicki Knight and Marianne Taflinger from Thomson Learning. You are amazing motivators. We appreciate all your efforts in giving this book the best chance to succeed in such a competitive market. We also would like to thank the following reviewers for their insightful comments and expert guidance in developing this text:

Mark Agars, CSU San Bernardino; Yuki Aida, Austin Community College; Rahan Ali, Penn State University; Margaret Armitage, Howard Community College; JoAnn Armstrong, Patrick Henry Community College; Ted Barker, Okaloosa-Walton College; Linda Bastone, Purchase College, SUNY; Saundra Boyd, Houston Community College System; Norma Caltagirone, Hillsborough Community College—Ybor Campus; Herb Coleman, Austin Community College; Perry Collins, Wayland Baptist University; Mary Coplen, Hutchinson Community College; Donna Dahlgren, Indiana University Southeast; Stephen Donohue, Grand Canyon University; Michael Durnam, Adams State College; Ray Eilenstine, Southeastern Community College; Thomas Estrella, Lourdes College; Michael Firmin, Cedarville University; Rita Flattley, Pima Community College; Jana Flowers, Richland College; Nancy Foster, Mississippi State University; Karen Freiberg, University of Maryland, Baltimore County; Robert Gehring, University of Southern Indiana; Stan Gilbert, Community College of Philadelphia; Kendra Gilds, Lane Community College; Frank Hager, Allegany College of Maryland; Kaira Hayes, Fort Hays State University; Debra Hollister, Valencia Community College; Jaye Johnston, Kingwood College; Bradley Karlin, Texas A&M University; Irina Khramtsova, Arkansas State University; Shirin Khosropour, Austin Community College; Matthew Krug, Wisconsin Lutheran College; Ernest Marquez, Elgin Community College; Anne McCrea, Sinclair Community College; Martha Mendez-Baldwin, Manhattan College; Glenn Meyer, Trinity College; Leslie Minor-Evans, Central Oregon Community College; Karen Mor, Cuyamaca College; Dean Murakami, American River College; Debbie Podwika, Kankakee Community College; Jeff Reber, State University of West Georgia; Tanya Renner, Kapiolani Community College; Edna Ross, University of Louisville; Patricia Sawyer, Middlesex Community-Tech College; Jeff Schaler, Johns Hopkins University; Jean Selders, Arapahoe Community College; Kimberley Smirles, Emmanuel College; Mark Stewart, American River College; Greg Turek, Fort Hays State University; Denise Valenti-Hein, University of Wisconsin, Oshkosh.

We would also like to thank our friends and colleagues at Gainesville College and Valencia Community College for their support and latitude over the past decade. We would especially like to thank the thousands of students we have worked with over the years. In your own way, each of you has helped us to become better teachers and better people. Our hope is that this book will touch many other students and foster an interest in and passion for psychology.

Finally, we would like to thank our families. Susann would like to thank her husband, Eulalio Ortiz Portillo, for his love and understanding—and for keeping the TV low while she spent many of their nights and weekends "together" working on the computer. ¡Te amo mucho! Ellen would like to thank Christian, Andrew, and Scott for playing quietly and tolerating the "Do Not Disturb" sign while she was writing. Ellen also would like to thank her WonderBoy husband, Dave, for his technical assistance, his tireless rereading of material, and his patience and support through all the frustration, deadlines, and apprehension. Love is indeed something that you do.

Available Supplements

Student Supplements

Study Guide: Written by Susann Doyle-Portillo specifically to accompany *What Is Psychology?*, the *Study Guide* offers students the following for each chapter:

- Learning objectives
- *The Big Picture* narrative chapter summary
- *Outlining the Big Picture* chapter outline
- A *Key Points of the Big Picture* list of important terms and definitions
- A *Seeing the Big Picture* visual overview of important concepts organized to show connections
- *Apply What You Know: The Big Picture in Action* activities designed to help students use the InfoTrac® College Edition database to locate applications
- *Self-Check* quizzes using fill-in, true/false, multiple-choice, short-answer, and diagram-labeling questions
- *Developing a Bigger Picture* essay questions that help students make important connections across chapters

PsychologyNow™: This interactive online resource is the most exciting, assessment centered learning tool ever offered for this course. Through a series of diagnostic Pre- and Post-Tests (written by Cheryl Stewart) that you can assign, as well as media-rich Personalized Study Plans, students discover those areas of the text where they need to focus their efforts. While students can use PsychologyNow™ with no instructor setup or involvement, an Instructor Gradebook is available to monitor student progress. Please see the inside front cover of this book for more information.

Book Companion Website: http://psychology.wadsworth.com/pastorino1e/ Students will have access to a rich array of teaching and learning resources. There are chapter-correlated study tools, such as tutorial quizzes, a glossary, flashcards, crossword puzzles, **InfoTrac® College Edition** activities, Internet activities, web links, and more.

Telecourse Guide: Telecourse Guide for Pastorino/Doyle-Portillo's *What Is Psychology?* by Dan Muhwezi, Butler Community College. This helpful guide correlates Pastorino and Doyle-Portillo's textbook to the acclaimed Annenberg/CPB video series, *Discovering Psychology*, Updated Edition. For each unit in the series, the guide provides learning objectives, video overviews, web links, and quiz questions relating to the videos, as well as questions that ask students to make connections between Pastorino and Doyle's *What Is Psychology?* and the videos.

Instructor Resources

Multimedia Manager Instructor's Resource CD-ROM: A Microsoft® PowerPoint® Tool Windows/Macintosh CD-ROM: This one-stop lecture and class preparation tool contains ready-to-use slides in Microsoft® PowerPoint® (written by Debra Schwiesow of Creighton University) and the Instructor's Manual and Test Bank in Microsoft® Word® format.

JoinIn™ on TurningPoint®: Thomson Wadsworth is now pleased to offer book-specific JoinIn™ content for response systems tailored to Pastorino's and Doyle-Portillo's text. This product enables you to transform your classroom and assess your students' progress with instant in-class quizzes and polls.

Instructor's Manual: by Diane Cook and Thomas Hancock, Gainesville College. A comprehensive resource, the Instructor's Manual contains tools for each chapter of the text.

Test Bank: by Mark Stewart, American River College; Ellen Pastorino; and Susann Doyle-Portillo. The Test Bank includes nearly 200 questions for each text chapter (multiple-choice, true/false, essay, and "making connections" questions that help students link concepts).

WebTutor™ Advantage: The ultimate in online course management! Available on WebCT® and Blackboard.® With the text-specific, preformatted content and total flexibility of WebTutor™ Advantage, you can easily create and manage your own course website! "Out of the box" or customizable, this versatile online tool is preloaded with content from this text, including sample syllabi, additional quizzing, InfoTrac® exercises, and more, organized by text chapter. Customize the content in any way you choose, from uploading images and other resources, to adding web links, to creating your own practice materials. Also available: WebTutor™ Advantage Plus. All the features of WebTutor Advantage with a complete electronic textbook!

InfoTrac® College Edition with InfoMarks®: Now you can easily create continually updated online readers! Available FREE upon request. Not sold separately. An access card for four months of FREE access to this world-class online library is available upon request to be packaged FREE with every new copy of the book. InfoTrac® College Edition offers a fully searchable database, including more than 20 years' worth of full-text articles (not abstracts) from 5,000 top academic journals, newsletters, and periodicals.

© Robert Essel NYC/Corbis

"This is Lin. I'm on United Flight 93. We've been hijacked. There are terrorists aboard and they have a bomb." Linda Gronlund's phone call to her sister, Elsa.

JERE LONGMAN, *AMONG THE HEROES: UNITED FLIGHT 93 AND THE PASSENGERS AND CREW WHO FOUGHT BACK*, (p. 157 New York: HarperCollins, 2002)

CHAPTER 1

What Is Psychology?

CHAPTER PREVIEW

"Some of the people who were directly involved, who ran for their lives, have been deeply traumatized ... while there is some return to normalcy, many of them state that they feel they may never again be the way they were prior to 9/11."

(Paige-Bowman, 2002, P. 283)

psychology the scientific study of behavior and mental processes

What Do Psychologists Study?

Welcome to the world of **psychology,** the scientific study of behavior and mental processes. For centuries people have been trying to understand the mind and behavior. Psychology is probably one of the few disciplines students come into believing that they already know much about the topic. We see psychologists and psychiatrists on talk shows (Dr. Phil) and listen to them on the radio. We frequently see them depicted on television (Frasier Crane) and in the movies (*A Beautiful Mind, Analyze This, Good Will Hunting*). Many of these portrayals are quite entertaining, but they do not always represent psychology accurately. As a result, the public image of this discipline tends to be distorted.

The purpose of this textbook is to help you develop a deeper understanding of psychology. In this chapter, we explain what psychologists do, how they think, and where they work. It is a general overview, or "big picture" of the field of psychology, an introduction to the more specific areas of psychology discussed in subsequent chapters.

Each chapter begins with a "Big Picture" section to help you integrate the chapter material into the broader field of psychology. This big picture incorporates accounts of real people and events. We hope that by reading these real-life stories, psychological topics will be easier to understand and you will be better able to apply psychological principles and concepts to your own life. To begin, let's consider the events of September 11, 2001.

On the morning of September 11, 2001, life in the United States changed drastically. In the space of one hour, two planes hit the twin towers of the World Trade Center in New York City, one plane smashed into the Pentagon in Washington, D.C., and another crashed in an open field in Pennsylvania. These were not invading bombers but hijacked U.S. passenger airliners. People all over the world watched in horror as first one tower, then the second crumbled to the ground. Thousands of people were killed—people who had simply gone to work in the morning and firefighters, police officers, clergy, and medical personnel who went to the World Trade Center to help after the first plane hit. All other airline traffic was grounded, a first in U.S. aviation history. In the bursts of flame and billows of smoke shown over and over on television news, it was clear that all aboard these planes had perished.

As the day unfolded, we learned that members of a terrorist organization had planned this attack. They had hijacked the planes and deliberately crashed them into U.S. symbols of capitalism and democracy. We learned that the plane that went down in Pennsylvania was probably heading for the White House or the Capitol building, and that passengers may have resisted the terrorists, steering the plane toward their own deaths, but away from even greater destruction.

In the weeks and months that followed, we heard the stories of those who had risked their own safety and lives to save or console others, and we saw an enormous upsurge in patriotism and national pride. The American flag waved from many storefronts, houses, and automobiles. People across the nation waited in line for hours to donate blood, and Americans donated millions of dollars to victims and their families, to health organizations, and to fire and police associations. We also witnessed misery as family members went to Ground Zero to search for loved ones, and walls and telephone poles in Manhattan were plastered with pictures of the missing.

Prejudice and hatred were evident too. In towns and cities across the United States, Arab Americans and other Muslims were threatened or harmed, and several mosques were burned. Anti-Muslim hate crimes jumped from 28 in 2000 to 481 in 2001, including at least three murders (Swanson, 2002). Police departments across the country responded with genuine concern and community outreach programs.

AP Photo/Kathy Willens

In the days following the September 11 attacks, many people waited in line for hours to donate blood. Such altruistic behavior is of interest to psychologists.

The events of September 11 and after reflect behaviors of destruction, madness, and misery, but they also highlight human resiliency, courage, and optimism. All of these behaviors, by both individuals and groups, are of interest to psychologists. September 11 richly illustrates the depth and breadth of the field of psychology.

In this chapter, we introduce you to psychology: what it is and what it is not, how it became a science, and what the field is like today. We also describe the goals of psychological research and how psychologists study behavior. As you read this chapter and those that follow, keep the events of September 11 in mind. Consider how psychologists might study these events and behaviors. By doing this, you will have started to think like a psychologist. This perspective will help you integrate the different areas of psychology into a whole and keep the big picture of psychology in your mind.

Correcting Common Misconceptions About the Field of Psychology

> > > >

LEARNING OBJECTIVE

Identify common misconceptions about the field.

When you think about the events of September 11, you might suppose that psychologists would be most interested in studying the terrorists: who they were, their organization, and why they were so intent on taking U.S. lives. Many people assume that psychologists usually study abnormal behavior. This is just one of many common misconceptions about the field of psychology. Let's look at some others.

"Psychology Is Just About Giving People Advice"

You are probably reading this book because you have enrolled in a general psychology course. Your expectations of what you will learn have been influenced by your general impressions of psychology. Much of the psychological information presented in the media focuses on practitioners, therapy, and helping others, and you may have the impression that psychology is all about how you feel and how you can feel better. It is true that many psychologists (around 55%) counsel or otherwise treat clients, yet most of these professionals hold a doctorate degree in psychology, which required that they study scientific methodology and complete a considerable amount of research.

Most of us believe that medical research is necessary. We want assurances that any medications we are prescribed or surgery we undergo will reduce our symptoms without creating any additional problems or side effects. The same is true in psychology. We want to be sure that the techniques and therapies clinicians use will reduce particular symptoms and not harm us in any way. So, psychology, like medicine, is rooted in scientific research. The information in this book is research based. Every idea put forward in the field is subject to scientific study. You will notice that many statements in this text are followed by names and years in parentheses, for example: (Pastorino, 2002). These text citations refer to the scientific studies that were used to make these conclusions. The complete research citations (Figure 1.1) can be found in the reference section at the end of the book.

"Psychology Isn't Really Science, It's Just Common Sense"

Few people would call themselves chemists without the appropriate training, yet we all, at times, fancy ourselves lay psychologists. We interact with people all the time, and we observe others' behaviors. Therefore, we might naturally think that we already know a lot about psychology. People often behave the way we think they will behave, so isn't psychology just common sense?

The answer is "No." We may easily overlook the examples of behavior that don't confirm our expectations. Psychologists systematically test their ideas about behavior using the prescribed methods and procedures of the **scientific method.** This is what makes psychology a "true science." Using the scientific method, psychologists make educated guesses or *hypotheses* about behavior. They then collect data and systematically test their hypotheses by applying objective checking procedures to these data. The data allow them to support or refute their hypotheses (Bunge, 1984). We will outline the specific steps of the scientific method later in this chapter. In the meantime, consider this question: Do you make and test hypotheses in your everyday observations of behavior?

In a famous social psychological experiment testing the nature of attitude change, a researcher had participants spend time engaged in a dull and boring task (Festinger, 1957). The researcher then asked the participants if they would be willing to convince the next participant that the task was actually quite fun and interesting. The researcher told half of the participants that he would pay them $20 (the equivalent of $120 today) for their assistance in "selling" the task as interesting and enjoyable to the next person in the study. The other half of the participants received $1 (about $6 today) for making the same effort. The researcher's goal was to measure which group would be more

scientific method a systematic process used by psychologists for testing hypotheses about behavior

Figure 1.1 **Reference Citations in Psychology**

The Reference section at the end of this book lists the complete source for each citation. Here is the APA style format for psychological references. The citation for this particular reference would appear in the text as (Snibbe, 2003).

> **APA Style:**
>
> **Author, A. A., Author, B. B., & Author, C. C. (2005). Title of article:**
>
> **Subtitle of article. *Title of Periodical or Journal*, 18, 122–134.**
>
> Example:
>
> Snibbe, A. C. (2003). Cultural psychology: Studying the exotic other.
>
> *APS Observer, 16* (1), 30–32.

likely to change their own attitude about the task—that is, come to believe that the task was indeed fun. What do you think he found? Were the participants who were paid $20 more likely to change their attitude and say the task was fun, or were those paid $1 more likely to change their attitude?

When we ask students this question, most think that the participants who were paid $20 would be most likely to change their attitude. Students reason that because these participants were paid more, they would be more motivated to change their opinion of the task. It seems obvious—common sense. In fact, the participants who were paid only a $1 were most likely to change their attitude, a finding that seems counter to our commonsense notions.

Consider another example. Who do you believe falls in love more quickly, men or women? Many people in our culture believe that women are more emotional, so you may assume that women would tend to fall in love more quickly. However, psychological research suggests that men are generally quicker to fall in love (Kanin, Davidson, & Scheck, 1970). Again, the commonsense conclusion is in error. Psychological findings do not always confirm our everyday observations about behavior. By objectively measuring and testing our ideas and observations about behavior, we can determine which ideas are more likely to stand up to scientific scrutiny.

© Douglas Kirkland/CORBIS

Who do you believe falls in love more quickly, men or women? Psychological findings do not always confirm our commonsense notions.

"Psychology Is Just the Study of Mental Illness"

Most students entering a general psychology class expect to focus on diagnosing and treating mental disorders. Although some psychologists specialize in mental illness, many others work in academic settings, in industry, in education, or in government agencies. Psychology is an extremely diverse field, and new specialties are appearing each year. Table 1.1 ◆ lists the divisions of the American Psychological Association, one of psychology's major professional organizations. As you can see, psychologists are interested in learning, memory, aging, development, gender, motivation, emotion, sports, criminal behavior, and many other subjects. We cannot cover every area of psychology in this textbook, but we will give you an overview of the main areas of psychological research.

So, What Is Psychology? > > > > > > > > > > > > > > > >

⌄ **LEARNING**
⌄ **OBJECTIVE**
⌄ Define psychology.
⌄

We defined psychology as the scientific study of behavior and mental processes, but what exactly does that include? Behavior includes actions, feelings, and biological states. Mental processes include problem solving, intelligence, and memory to name just a few. Psychology is a science because psychologists conduct research in accord with the scientific method. They analyze the behavior of other species as well as humans.

Psychologists Won't Always Agree on Why People Behave as They Do

If you asked 10 of your friends how to tell when pasta has been adequately cooked, you probably would not get the same answer from each person. Some may focus on how tender the pasta is; others may rely on how well the pasta sticks to the wall. Still others

◆ Table 1.1

Divisions of the American Psychological Association

The Divisions of the APA illustrate the wide diversity of interest in what psychologists' study.

Division Number*	Name
1	Society for General Psychology
2	Society for the Teaching of Psychology
3	Experimental Psychology
5	Evaluation, Measurement, and Statistics
6	Behavioral Neuroscience and Comparative Psychology
7	Developmental Psychology
8	Society for Personality and Social Psychology
9	Society for the Psychological Study of Social Issues (SPSSI)
10	Society for the Psychology of Aesthetics, Creativity and the Arts
12	Society of Clinical Psychology
13	Society of Consulting Psychology
14	Society for Industrial and Organizational Psychology
15	Educational Psychology
16	School Psychology
17	Society of Counseling Psychology
18	Psychologists in Public Service
19	Military Psychology
20	Adult Development and Aging
21	Applied Experimental and Engineering Psychology
22	Rehabilitation Psychology
23	Society for Consumer Psychology
24	Theoretical and Philosophical Psychology
25	Behavior Analysis
26	Society for the History of Psychology
27	Society for Community Research and Action: Division of Community Psychology
28	Psychopharmacology and Substance Abuse
29	Psychotherapy
30	Society of Psychological Hypnosis
31	State Psychological Association Affairs
32	Humanistic Psychology
33	Mental Retardation and Developmental Disabilities
34	Population and Environmental Psychology
35	Society for the Psychology of Women
36	Psychology of Religion
37	Child, Youth, and Family Services
38	Health Psychology
39	Psychoanalysis
40	Clinical Neuropsychology
41	American Psychology-Law Society
42	Psychologists in Independent Practice
43	Family Psychology
44	Society for the Psychological Study of Lesbian, Gay, and Bisexual Issues
45	Society for the Psychological Study of Ethnic Minority Issues
46	Media Psychology
47	Exercise and Sport Psychology
48	Society for the Study of Peace, Conflict, and Violence: Peace Psychology Division
49	Group Psychology and Group Psychotherapy
50	Addictions
51	Society for the Psychological Study of Men and Masculinity
52	International Psychology
53	Society of Clinical Child and Adolescent Psychology
54	Society of Pediatric Psychology
55	American Society for the Advancement of Pharmacotherapy

*Note: There are no divisions 4 or 11.

may just follow the package directions. Similarly, psychologists do not necessarily agree on why people behave as they do. Human beings are extremely complex. Many variables influence why a particular person in a particular place behaves in a specific way on a certain occasion. One psychologist may focus on possible external reasons for behavior such as the influence of others or the environment in which people live. That psychologist's explanations will differ from those of a psychologist who focuses on internal reasons for behavior, such as people's physical health, their degree of motivation, or how they feel about themselves.

A psychologist's explanation of a particular behavior is typically presented within the context of a theory. A **theory** is an explanation of why and how a behavior occurs. It does not explain a particular behavior for all people, but it provides general guidelines that summarize facts and help us organize our thoughts on a particular subject. For example, in Chapter 9 you will read about Lawrence Kohlberg's theory of moral reasoning. His theory, which continues to be tested, explains how children and adults make judgments about whether a behavior is right or wrong (Kohlberg, 1969). Subsequent research by other psychologists has suggested that his explanations, or theory, may be most applicable to men in the United States and may not really explain the moral reasoning of women (Gilligan, 1982) or people from non-Western cultures (Snarey, 1995).

theory an explanation of why and how a behavior occurs

Psychology Will Teach You About Critical Thinking

As you can see from the misconceptions we've poked holes in, psychology requires critical thinking, and psychological theories generally don't definitively explain the behavior of all people. To think like a psychologist, you must analyze and evaluate information. You must be able to distinguish true psychological information from *pseudoscience*. Pseudoscientific findings sound persuasive, but they are not necessarily based on scientific procedures. Their conclusions may go far beyond the scope of their actual data. To think like a psychologist, you must be skeptical rather than accepting about explanations of behavior.

Critical thinking makes you an intelligent consumer of information, and you will be encouraged to practice this skill throughout the book. Critical thinking involves analyzing concepts and applying them to other situations. To foster these abilities, "Let's Review!" sections at the end of each main topic offer several questions to test your understanding of the concepts just presented, as learning is easier when you can digest information in small amounts. The "Concept Check" at the end of the chapter helps you test your knowledge further. This is followed by "Critical Thinking About the Chapter," which asks you to integrate, analyze, and apply the chapter's contents. In Chapters 2 through 16 "Critical Thinking for Integration" extends your use of analytical skills to previous topics and issues. Integrating psychological information across chapters will not only help you develop critical thinking skills but will also help develop your big picture of psychology.

Because we all engage in behavior, much of the information in this text will have application to your life. We all dream, remember, like or dislike others, are motivated, lack self-esteem, enjoy high self-esteem, suffer from bouts of depression, behave aggressively, help others, learn, perceive, and use our senses. Consequently, we recommend that you apply the material in this text to your own behavior as much as possible. This will increase your interest in the text, and you will study more effectively.

Let's Review!

In this section we defined psychology and identified several misconceptions about the field. For a quick check of your understanding, answer these questions.

1. Which of the following statements is *true*?
   a. Psychology is just common sense.
   b. Psychologists only study abnormal behavior.
   c. Psychologists know why people behave the way that they do.
   d. Psychologists test ideas about behavior according to the scientific method.

2. Which of the following topics would a psychologist most likely study?
   a. weather patterns in Africa
   b. memory changes in adults
   c. causes of the Vietnam War
   d. all of the above

ANSWERS:

1. d; 2. b

LEARNING OBJECTIVE < < < < < < < <

Describe the origins of psychology and understand how historical perspectives paved the way for modern approaches.

The Origins of Psychology

How did psychology become a science? Psychology has been described as having "a long past but only a short history" (Ebbinghaus, 1910, p. 9). Although psychology did not formally become a science until the 1870s, people have always been interested in explaining behavior. The roots of psychology can be traced back to philosophy and medicine in ancient Egypt, Greece, and Rome. Philosophers debated whether the mind could be studied scientifically and discussed the nature of the mind and where it was located. Because of the mind's association with the body, much of what we consider psychology today was then part of the field of medicine. Hippocrates (460–377), the father of medicine, believed that personality was in part a reflection of the mix of chemicals in the body, and abnormal behavior was typically treated with medical procedures.

Continued debate in these disciplines throughout the Renaissance (1400–1500) and post-Renaissance (1500–1600) periods influenced early psychologists' attempts to formulate a science of the mind. Although not considered "psychological" issues at the time, these doctors and philosophers debated many of the issues that concern modern psychologists.

When did psychology become a separate field of study? Traditionally, psychology's birth is linked with the establishment by Wilhelm Wundt of the first psychology laboratory in 1879 in Leipzig, Germany. In *Principles of Physiological Psychology*, originally published in 1873, Wundt outlined the beginnings of "the experimental treatment of psychological problems" (Wundt, 1904, p. v). It focused on physiological and philosophical approaches to "investigate conscious processes" (p. 2).

Early Approaches: Structuralism, Functionalism, and Psychoanalysis

As you will see, some of the people who brought psychology into the scientific arena were trained as physicians; others were more philosophical in nature. Communication was much slower in those days, and psychology developed in different ways in different countries. Advances in psychology in one country looked very different from the study of behavior in other countries. However, the net effect of these differences resulted in a psychology that was broad and complex, with many avenues of exploration.

Wilhelm Wundt and Structuralism

For Wilhelm Wundt (1832–1920) the goal of psychology was to study conscious processes of the mind and the body. He wanted to know what psychological processes enabled us to experience the external world. In particular, Wundt attempted to detail the *structure* of our mental experiences. Like a chemist who questions what elements combine to create different substances, Wundt questioned what elements, when combined, would explain mental processes. For this reason, Wundt is often associated with a very narrow view of psychology referred to as **structuralism,** a term coined not by Wundt but by his student Edward Titchener. To identify this structure, Wundt used a process known as **introspection,** a self-observation technique. Trained observers were presented with an event and asked to describe their mental processes. The observations were repeated many times. For example, suppose you are presented with a potato. How do you know that the object is a potato? Does the object fit your visual image or memory of a potato? That is, does it look like a potato, smell like a potato, taste like a potato, and feel like a potato? Using these mental processes, you deduce that the object before you is a potato. From introspections such as this, Wundt and his students identified two basic mental processes: sensations and feelings.

Wilhelm Wundt (1832–1920) wanted to know what psychological processes enable us to experience the external world. His approach today is referred to as structuralism.

structuralism an early psychological perspective concerned with identifying the basic elements of experience

introspection observing one's own thoughts, feelings, or sensations

 Application

Wundt's research went beyond introspection and structuralism and encompassed a very broad view of psychology. He conducted detailed studies on color vision, visual illusions, attention, and feelings. He also influenced the field of psychology through his students, many of whom went on to establish psychology departments and laboratories in the United States.

William James and Functionalism

William James (1842–1910) was the first U.S. professor of psychology, and as such he was responsible for introducing experimental psychology to U.S. college students. He had visited Wundt's laboratory but did not share Wundt's focus on introspection and mental processes. Rather, James came to believe that psychological processes developed not from the structure of the mind but through the process of *evolution*, an idea that was then quite new. Evolution refers to the development of a species—the process by which, through a series of changes over time, humans have acquired behaviors and characteristics that distinguish them from other species. For James, the question was not what elements contribute to one's experience but rather what *function* does the event serve

William James (1842–1910) introduced experimental psychology to U.S. college students and is associated with functionalism.

functionalism   an early psychological perspective concerned with how behavior helps people adapt to their environment

Charles Darwin's theory of natural selection influenced the beginnings of psychological research.

for the organism. How does a particular behavior help an organism adapt to the environment and thereby increase its chances of surviving and evolving? James's perspective on psychology became known as **functionalism.**

Functionalism was the first major non-German school of psychology. Its focus on the mind's functions and the adaptive value of consciousness were influenced by the scientific community's interest in Charles Darwin's theory of evolution. Functionalism dominated psychology in the United States for some time. Darwin's theory speculated that certain behaviors or traits that enhance survival are naturally selected. According to James, if behavior is naturally selected, it is important for psychologists to understand the function or survival value of a behavior. James's first book, *The Principles of Psychology* (1890), and its abridged version, *Psychology: A Briefer Course* (1892), became the standard psychology texts in the United States and Europe. The popularity of functionalism, especially in the United States, was in part because James's theory had personalized psychology, making it more practical. Functionalism was less rigid and was not as bound to laboratory methods and experimentation as was Wundt's structuralism. However, just as Wundt did not restrict himself to structuralism, functionalism was not the whole of James's work in the young field of psychology. James suggested applications of psychology to teaching, created the field of *educational psychology.* The James-Lange theory of emotion, formulated by James and a Danish physiologist, Carl Lange, at about the same time, describes how physical sensations give rise to emotions (more on this in Chapter 8). In addition, he published books on religious experiences and philosophy. James's open-mindedness also influenced psychology when he became intrigued by the unorthodox ideas of a Viennese physician named Sigmund Freud in 1894.

Sigmund Freud and Psychoanalytic Theory

Think of a famous psychologist. Did Sigmund Freud come to mind? He is probably the best known historical figure in psychology, more familiar to students than Wundt or James. Did Freud have such a huge influence on the beginnings of psychology, or is his contribution overrated? Historians and psychologists continue to debate this issue, but there is no doubt that Freud's ideas about behavior were radical for that time. Even today many consider his ideas to be far from mainstream thought. When ideas are different, they stand out in our minds. When these same ideas have to do with sex, we tend to pay even closer attention. Freud's ideas permeate Western culture in music, media, advertising, art, and humor—a testament to his influence and importance.

As a European Jew, the only professions open to Freud (1856–1939) were law and medicine. Freud opted for medicine, focusing on neurology and disorders of the nervous system. He began seeing people with all kinds of "nervous" disorders such as an intense fear of horses or heights or the sudden paralysis of an arm. Freud became interested in the use of hypnosis and what was then referred to as "the talking cure" to treat these nervous disorders, yet neither worked as effectively as he had hoped. One day while treating a patient, Freud encouraged her to relax on a couch. She rambled on about her physical problems and about issues that appeared to be unrelated to her physical complaints. Suddenly, she had a revelation that left her feeling better. Freud theorized that encouraging patients to say whatever came to mind allowed them to recall forgotten memories that seemed to underlie their problems. This process, known today as *free association*, is one element of psychoanalysis, a therapy that Freud developed.

From these experiences, Freud came to believe that the unconscious plays a crucial role in human behavior. For Freud, the *unconscious* was that part of the mind that includes impulses, behaviors, and desires that we are unaware of but that influence our behavior. Until this time, much of psychology had focused on conscious mental processes. Freud's focus on the unconscious was unique and led to his formulation of

Sigmund Freud's (1856–1939) focus on the unconscious was unique and led to his formulation of psychoanalytic theory.

psychoanalytic theory. We describe Freud's ideas in more detail in Chapter 14, but some background here will help you understand Freud's contributions to the beginnings of psychology. According to Freudian theory, humans are similar to animals in that they possess basic sexual and aggressive instincts that motivate behavior. However, unlike animals, humans can reason and think on a higher plane, especially as they mature. Beginning in childhood, we learn to use these conscious reasoning abilities to deal with and to suppress our sexual and aggressive desires so that we can be viewed approvingly by others. Consequently, dreams, slips of the tongue, a joke, or an odd physical symptom are clues to these unconscious wishes and desires. For Freud these unconscious conflicts—the desire to strike someone in anger, for example—were key to understanding human behavior. Although his ideas were controversial, Freud, and later his daughter, Anna Freud, continued to elaborate on these ideas and to emphasize the importance of the unconscious for the next four decades, particularly in Europe. Freud visited the United States in 1909 along with several other psychoanalysts, but here his ideas were overshadowed by another external approach to understanding behavior called behaviorism.

> **psychoanalytic theory** Sigmund Freud's view that emphasizes the influence of unconscious desires and conflicts on behavior

Behaviorism: A True Science of Psychology

While Freudian psychology was going strong in Europe in the 1920s, in the United States functionalism was slowly being replaced by a school of thought referred to as **behaviorism.** A growing number of psychologists believed that in order for psychology to be taken seriously as a "true" science, it must focus on observable behavior and not on the mind. The mind was unobservable and its processes unseen. Behaviorists believed that only overt, observable behaviors could truly be measured consistently from person to person. One of the most vocal proponents of this school of thought was John B. Watson (1878–1958).

> **behaviorism** a psychological perspective that emphasizes the study of observable responses and behavior

John Watson's Behaviorism

Watson had been influenced by Russian physiologist Ivan Pavlov's studies of digestion in dogs. While measuring and analyzing the first process of digestion (salivation), Pavlov noticed that his dogs would start to salivate before he gave them meat powder. The salivation had initially occurred only *after* the dogs were given the meat powder.

To further study this curious response, Pavlov performed experiments to train the dogs to salivate to other nonfood stimuli. (You will learn more about Pavlov's classic experiments in Chapter 5.)

Pavlov's experiments were important to Watson as examples of how behavior is the product of stimuli and responses. To further his point, Watson and his associate, Rosalie Raynor, performed an experiment on a 9-month-old infant named Albert. Two months earlier, Watson had presented Albert with a white rat. Albert had played with the white rat and showed no fear of it. Knowing that infants do fear loud noises, Watson paired the two stimuli, first presenting the rat to Albert and then presenting a loud gong sound behind Albert's head. Albert reacted to the loud

John Watson (1878–1958) believed in behaviorism—that only observable stimuli and responses should be studied by psychologists.

History of American Psychology, U. of Akron, Akron, Ohio

Ivan Pavlov's studies illustrated how behavior is the product of stimuli and responses.

© Bettmann/Corbis

noise with the startle, or fear, response. Over and over again, Watson repeated the procedure of pairing the two stimuli—presenting the rat followed by the loud gong. Then, when Watson presented the rat to Albert with no gong, the infant responded with the startle response. Watson had conditioned Albert to fear a white rat, a rat that 2 months earlier Albert had played with without fear. This demonstrated for Watson that observable stimuli and responses should be the domain of psychology. Unfortunately for Watson, a personal scandal resulted in his dismissal as the chair of the psychology department at Johns Hopkins University, and he later became a psychological consultant to an advertising firm (Buckley, 1989). We probably could consider Watson the first consumer psychologist—think about how advertisers today associate certain stimuli with products to get consumers to purchase them. For example, young, beautiful people, laughing and having a great time, may be associated with a particular brand of beer.

B. F. Skinner and Behavioral Consequences

Although Watson was no longer within mainstream psychology, behaviorism remained strong in the United States, partially due to the work of B. F. Skinner (1904–1990). Skinner, like Watson, believed that psychology should focus on observable behavior. But Skinner added a dimension to Watson's framework: *consequences*. Skinner believed that one should look not only at the stimuli in the environment that cause a particular response but also at what happens to the organism after the response—what Skinner called the consequences of a behavior. To illustrate consequences, let's look at baby Albert's behavior from Skinner's perspective. Once Albert was afraid of the rat, how would he act when he saw the rat? If Albert moved away from the rat, his behavior had the effect of reducing his fear. Feeling less fear or anxiety is a good (positive) consequence, or outcome. Whenever Albert saw the fearsome rat again, he probably moved away even faster. Skinner asserted that positive consequences, such as the reduction of Albert's anxiety, would lead the organism (Albert) to engage in the same behavior again. Negative consequences, or outcomes that are not liked, would lessen the organism's desire to engage in the behavior again. We know these processes as *reinforcement* and *punishment*, topics that are explored further in Chapter 5.

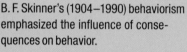

B. F. Skinner's (1904–1990) behaviorism emphasized the influence of consequences on behavior.

© Bettmann / Corbis

Beyond Behaviorism: Humanism and Cognitive Psychology

Behaviorism was a dominant force in American psychology until the 1960s. By that time, it became evident that this one theory could not account for all behaviors. This criticism, combined with the social climate of the times, opened the door for other views on behavior and a willingness to explore topics previously ignored.

The Humanists

humanism   a psychological perspective that emphasizes the personal growth and potential of humans

Discontent with behaviorism and the social upheaval of the 1960s led to a growing interest in an approach toward treatment called **humanism.** Many psychologists did not accept that humans were governed by stimuli and responses, with no will of their own to change their behavior. In the 1960s, societal values were rapidly changing, and the civil rights movement and the Vietnam War sparked widespread civil disobedience. Many young Americans were endorsing women's rights, free love, and free will. Psychology was changing too, and humanists emphasized that everyone possesses inner resources for personal growth and development. The goal of humanistic therapy, therefore, would be to help individuals use these inner resources to make healthier choices and thus lead better lives. Humanism stressed the free will of individuals to choose their own patterns of behavior. Two well-known humanists are Abraham Maslow and Carl Rogers. You will read more about their ideas and theories in Chapters 8 and 14.

Cognitive Psychology

While humanism was changing how psychologists were treating clients, changes also were occurring in research psychology. Researchers were becoming disenchanted with the limits of testing stimuli, responses, and consequences in the laboratory, and there was renewed interest in the study of mental processes, which had originated with Wilhelm Wundt. Research expanded to subjects such as memory, problem solving, and decision making. However, unlike the earlier functionalism and structuralism, this new study of mental processes was based much more on experimental methods. Acknowledging that mental processes are not directly observable to the eye, scientists believed that reasonable inferences about mental processes could be made from performance data. For example, in studying memory processes in children, a researcher can ask children what strategies or techniques they use to remember a list of items. If children using a particular strategy (Strategy A) remember more compared to children using a different strategy (Strategy B), then one can infer that there must be something about Strategy A that facilitates memory. This conclusion is reasonable even though we can't directly see the children use the techniques. Such reasoning led to much experimental research on mental processes, or *cognition*. By the 1980s the study of cognitive processes, **cognitive psychology,** was a part of mainstream psychology.

cognitive psychology the study of mental processes such as reasoning and problem solving

Modern Perspectives and the Eclectic Approach

How do psychologists explain behavior today? Given the historical sketch of psychology that we have just provided, it is probably no surprise to learn that modern psychology is a very broad profession. This diversity can seem overwhelming to the new reader of psychology. Not everyone agreed on how to explain behavior then, just as many debate the causes of behavior today. Many modern perspectives are an extension of the historical schools of thought. Here we discuss seven orientations or perspectives on behavior (Figure 1.2): biological, evolutionary, cognitive, psychodynamic, behavioral, sociocultural, and humanistic. An individual's training and personal views on behavior influence the perspective or perspectives a modern psychologist adopts.

Biological and Physiological Views

Psychologists who adopt a **biological** or **physiological perspective** toward behavior look for a physical cause for a particular behavior. For example, a physiological explanation of learning disorders in children may describe differences in brain processing.

biological / physiological perspective focuses on physical causes of behavior

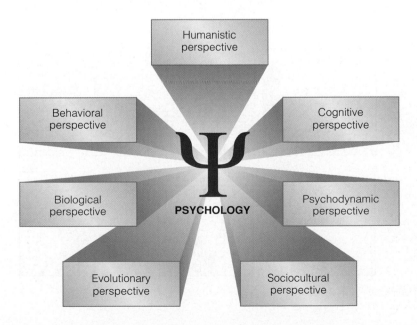

Figure 1.2 **Psychological Perspectives**

Just as a photograph or a piece of art can be examined from many different angles, so too can behavior. We call these angles perspectives. Each offers a somewhat different picture of why people behave as they do. Taken as a whole, these perspectives underscore the complex nature of behavior.

Genetics, chemical imbalances, and brain differences are often the focus of this perspective. (We discuss the physical processes of genes and the nervous system in Chapter 2.)

Evolutionary Views

evolutionary perspective focuses on how evolution and natural selection cause behavior

Very closely aligned to the biological perspective is the **evolutionary perspective.** This approach is similar to the biological approach in that the cause of behavior is biological. However, this is where the similarity ends. The evolutionary perspective proposes that natural selection is the process at work. Behaviors that increase your chances of surviving are favored or selected over behaviors that decrease your chances of surviving. Remember James's functionalism? One could say that James was an early evolutionary psychologist. Similarly, this approach analyzes whether a particular behavior increases the organism's ability to adapt to the environment, thus increasing its chances to survive, reproduce, and pass its genes on to future generations.

This approach often creates controversy because it seems to ignore environmental influences on behavior. An example will help illustrate this controversy. Both men and women can be jealous, yet psychological research has found that the type of jealousy exhibited by men and women is different. Men tend to be more jealous of sexual infidelity—that is, if their mate has sex with another person. In contrast, women report more jealousy over emotional infidelity—that is, if their mate establishes a close attachment to another woman (Buss, Larsen, Westen, & Semmelroth, 1992; Buunk, Angleitner, Oubaid, & Buss, 1996). Many argue that this difference stems from how boys and girls have been raised, an environmental influence. However, some psychologists have argued that this difference in jealousy stems from evolutionary forces. Men need to know that their offspring are in fact theirs, which is why sexual infidelity would be so upsetting to them. For women, help in child rearing requires a continued attachment with their mate. Consequently, emotional infidelity is more distressing to women. Keep in mind that not all psychologists support this particular explanation of gender differences in jealousy (DeSteno & Salovey, 1996; Harris & Christenfeld, 1996). It is one perspective among several for looking at and explaining this behavior.

Cognitive Views

cognitive perspective focuses on how mental processes influence behavior

A **cognitive perspective** explains behavior as the product of thoughts and interpretations that are based on memory, expectations, beliefs, problem solving, or decision making. A cognitive view focuses on how people process information and on how that process may influence behavior. For example, in explaining depression, a cognitive

For Better or For Worse © 1998 Lynn Johnston Productions. Dist. by Universal Press Syndicate.
Reprinted with permission. All rights reserved.

approach focuses on how depressed people think and perceive the world differently from nondepressed individuals. You will learn more about these cognitive processes in Chapters 6 and 7, when we discuss such topics as memory, problem solving, thinking, decision making, intelligence, and language.

Psychodynamic Views

The **psychodynamic perspective** is a collective term that refers to those assumptions about behavior originally conceived by Freud, which have been modified by his followers. The psychodynamic view focuses on internal, often unconscious mental processes, motives, and desires or childhood conflicts to explain behavior. For example, in the Columbine High School shootings in 1999, two students entered their school and shot at their teachers and classmates, killing themselves and 13 others. The psychodynamic view might suggest that the violent youths had some frustrated desires or unresolved childhood conflicts that erupted into hostility and anger that they unleashed on their classmates. These conflicts and frustrated desires also may explain why these teenagers were not able to control these hostile feelings—feelings that everyone has from time to time but does not act upon.

psychodynamic perspective focuses on internal unconscious mental processes, motives, and desires that may explain behavior

Behavioral Views

The **behavioral perspective** focuses on external causes of behavior. It looks at stimuli in the environment or at the consequences of a behavior that would influence an organism to maximize its rewards. This approach suggests that behavior is learned and is influenced by people or events in one's environment. We can look at study habits from the behavioral perspective. If a student studies and then aces an exam, that reward may encourage her to study again the next time. If she only gets an average score, merely passing the test may not be rewarding enough to encourage the student to study for future exams. This perspective stems, as you might guess, from Watson's and Skinner's behaviorist views (more on this in Chapter 5).

behavioral perspective focuses on external, environmental causes of behavior

Sociocultural Views

The **sociocultural perspective** adopts a wider view of the impact of the environment on behavior. It suggests that your society or culture influences your actions. Consider the fact that the United States has the highest teenage pregnancy rate among countries in the developed world. The sociocultural perspective would attribute this phenomenon to aspects of society such as sexual values, changes in family structure, or the lack of connectedness among people in neighborhoods and communities. Countries that have lower teenage pregnancy rates, such as Japan, may have experienced fewer or altogether different social changes. Sociocultural views will be evident throughout this textbook when differences due to culture, income level, or gender are highlighted.

sociocultural perspective focuses on societal and cultural factors that may influence behavior

Humanistic Views

The **humanistic perspective** explains behavior as stemming from your choices and free will. These choices are influenced by your self-concept (how you think of yourself) and by your self-esteem (how you feel about yourself). This view of the self and feelings toward the self direct you to choose certain behaviors over others. For example, if you see yourself as a low-achiever in school, you may be less likely to take challenging courses or to apply yourself in the courses that you do take. Humanistic views of behavior are explored in Chapters 8, 14, and 16.

humanistic perspective focuses on how an individual's view of him- or herself and the world influence behavior

The Eclectic Approach

Most psychologists do not rigidly adhere to just one of these perspectives but are likely to take what is referred to as an **eclectic approach** to explaining behavior. This eclectic

eclectic approach integrates and combines several perspectives when explaining behavior

approach integrates or combines several perspectives to provide a more complete, yet complex picture of behavior. Table 1.2 ◆ illustrates these approaches and shows how a combined approach gives a more expansive understanding of behavior than any single approach could.

◆ **Table 1.2**

Looking at Anxiety From Modern Perspectives

Psychologists can examine behavior from many different perspectives.

Approach	Perspective
Biological	Anxiety is related to chemicals in the body or to genetics (heredity).
Evolutionary	Anxiety is an adaptive response that prepares one to respond to potential threats in the environment. This response helps humans survive because it warns them of danger and thereby helps them avoid situations or people that may harm them. However, in modern times, these threats tend to be ongoing: traffic jams, crowding, and the hectic pace of consumerism.
Cognitive	Focuses on how anxious people think differently from nonanxious people. Anxious people may engage in more pessimistic thinking or worry that everything will go wrong.
Psychodynamic	Anxiety is the product of unresolved feelings of hostility, guilt, anger, or sexual attraction experienced in childhood.
Behavioral	Anxiety is a learned behavior much like Albert's fear of the white rat. It is a response that is associated with a specific stimulus or a response that has been rewarded.
Sociocultural	Anxiety is a product of a person's culture. In the United States more women than men report being anxious and fearful, and this gender difference results from different socialization experiences. Men in the United States are raised to believe that they must not be afraid, so they are less likely to acknowledge or report anxiety. Women do not experience this pressure to hide their fears, so they are more likely to tell others and to seek treatment.
Humanistic	Anxiety is rooted in people's dissatisfaction with their real self (how they perceive themselves) as compared to their ideal self (how they want to be).
Eclectic	Anxiety stems from various sources depending on the individual. One person may be prone to anxiety because many people in his family are anxious and he has learned to be anxious from several experiences. Another person may be anxious because she is dissatisfied with herself and believes that everything always goes wrong in her life.

Let's Review!

In this section, we discussed the early theories of psychology and the modern perspectives that grew out of them. For a quick check of your understanding, answer these questions.

1. Javier wants to know how aggression helps a person adapt to the environment. Which historical approach is Javier emphasizing?
   a. structuralism
   b. psychoanalysis
   c. functionalism
   d. humanism

2. Which modern psychological perspective emphasizes the importance of thought processes as the bases for understanding behavior?

   a. behavioral
   b. humanistic
   c. sociocultural
   d. cognitive

3. Which of these modern perspectives most emphasizes external causes of behavior?
   a. biological
   b. behavioral
   c. psychodynamic
   d. evolutionary

ANSWERS:
1.c; 2.d; 3.b

Careers in Psychology > > > > > > > > > > > > > > > > > >

Where do psychologists work and what kinds of work do they do? The complex history of psychology has resulted in a profession that has many subfields. Potential psychologists usually choose a subfield to specialize in during their education and training, and they may choose to focus primarily on research, teaching, or therapy.

≫ **LEARNING**
≫ **OBJECTIVE**
≫ Describe the training of a psychologist and discriminate among the different subfields of the profession.

Training to Be a Psychologist

What type of education and training do I need to become a psychologist? The majority of psychologists hold a doctorate in psychology—usually a Ph.D, sometimes a Psy.D. To obtain the doctorate, psychologists must first complete a bachelor's and a master's degree. The road to a doctoral degree is long, usually 5 to 7 years after the undergraduate degree. Most doctoral programs require extensive study of research methods and statistics, and most require that students do some form of research.

What if I'm interested in doing research? There are two general types of psychological research: basic research and applied research. **Basic research** focuses on uncovering the specifics about a behavior. An example of basic research is the work of a number of teams to pinpoint the chemicals in the brain that are involved in memory. **Applied research** seeks to solve a problem (possibly using the findings of basic research). Determining how to reduce aggression or prejudice is an example of applied research. Another example is testing which of two therapy techniques works better in treating depression.

basic research scientific study about the specifics of a behavior without concern for its application

applied research scientific study to solve a problem

What if I don't get a Ph.D.? Those who study psychology to the point of a bachelor's or master's degree aren't excluded from the profession. A bachelor's degree in psychology may qualify you to assist psychologists in mental health centers, rehabilitation and correctional programs, or to serve as a research assistant. Without additional academic training, the opportunities for advancement in the profession are limited (Appleby, 1997), but 20% of students who graduate with a bachelor's degree in psychology do find work in social services or public relations. The skills an undergraduate psychology major acquires are valued by employers in business, industry, and government (APA, 2000). As you can see in Figure 1.3, psychology is a popular degree among undergraduate students.

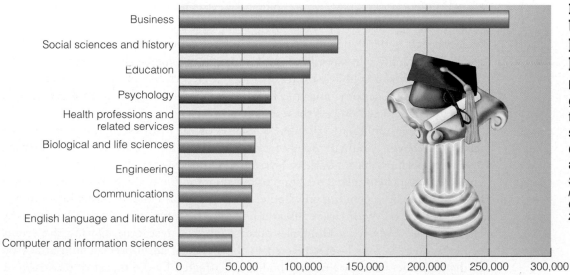

Number of Bachelor's Degrees awarded

**Figure 1.3
Undergraduate Degrees in Psychology**

Psychology is a popular undergraduate degree. It ranked fourth following business, social sciences and history, and education in number of degrees awarded in 2000–2001.

Source: Data from U.S. Department of Education, National Center for Education Statistics, 2003.

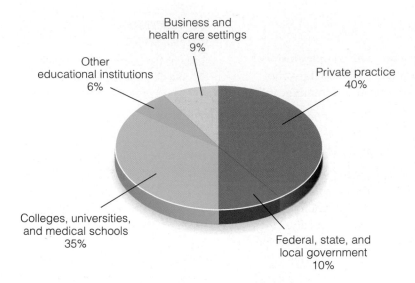

Business and health care settings 9%

Other educational institutions 6%

Private practice 40%

Colleges, universities, and medical schools 35%

Federal, state, and local government 10%

Figure 1.4 Work Settings of Psychologists

A large percentage of psychologists affiliated with colleges and universities teach and do research. Psychologists also work in school systems, hospitals, business, and government, or in private practice in which they see and treat clients.

Source: Survey of Doctorate Recipients, 2001. National Science Foundation. Compiled by APA Research Office, July 2003. Copyright © 2003 by the American Psychological Association. Reprinted with permission.

A master's degree typically requires 2 to 3 years of graduate work. Master's-level psychologists may administer tests, conduct research, or counsel patients under the supervision of a doctoral-level psychologist. In a few states, they may be able to practice independently. They may teach in high schools or community colleges, work in corporate human resource departments, or work as school psychologists.

A large percentage of psychologists affiliated with colleges and universities teach and do research. Psychologists also work in school systems, hospitals, business, and government; others are in private practice treating clients (Pion, 1991; Figure 1.4). Psychologists perform many functions in many different roles. Their job descriptions may include conducting research, counseling clients, and teaching college courses.

Major Subfields of Psychology

What are the different types of psychologists? In addition to the various approaches or perspectives psychologists take, they also study a range of different aspects of behavior, which correspond to the major subfields of psychology. But keep in mind that there are many subfields in addition to these (see Table 1.1). In each of these subfields some psychologists perform basic research, others conduct applied research, and some do both. Let's return to the events of September 11 to illustrate the types of behavior that psychologists might study.

Experimental psychology encompasses basic research in the areas of sensation, perception, and learning. (The term experimental psychologist is not just reserved for those who only do research. Many different types of psychologists conduct research.) The events of September 11 might interest experimental psychologists who study the different ways people perceive these events, or they may be interested in the worldview (perceptions) of the terrorists.

Developmental psychology is concerned with human development from conception to the end of life. Many developmental psychologists specialize further within this broad subfield. For example, some study infant development, others focus on adolescence or middle adulthood. Even within an age group, psychologists may study different aspects of development such as social development or the development of language. How children learn violence, aggression, or helping behaviors might be a focus of developmental psychologists investigating the September 11 events. Others might study the differences or similarities in how preschoolers, children, adolescents, and adults understand and process these events.

Biopsychology, another large subfield, focuses on the many biological processes that underlie behavior. Some biopsychologists may study how genetics and heredity influence a specific behavior such as depression. Others may study the behavioral influence of certain chemicals in the brain or hormones in the body. This research may be basic or applied, depending on whether the focus is on understanding how biology interacts with behavior (basic research) or on attempting to change a behavior by changing the underlying biological process (applied research). During the events of September 11, our bodies reacted to the shock of an unprecedented attack on civilians. Understanding how our bodies are affected by the threat of terrorism or other major catastrophes is of interest to biopsychologists.

Personality psychology deals with how people differ from one another in their individual traits. Personality psychologists may study how people develop personality, whether personality traits can be changed, or how these qualities can be measured. The events of September 11 call to our attention the influence of many personality variables in behavior: For example, how does one become a leader, or why are some people more helpful (or more aggressive) than others? Did Americans change in personality following the terrorist attacks? Research conducted 2 months after the attacks suggests that we did—showing increases in positive traits such as gratitude, hope, and kindness. Ten months later these positive traits were elevated to a lesser degree (Peterson & Seligman, 2003).

A developmental psychologist might study how video game violence influences aggressive behavior in children.

© Samuel Thaler / Index Stock Imagery

Social psychology is concerned with the ways we are influenced by others, whether in the classroom, on an elevator, on the beach, on a jury, or at a football game. The events of September 11 influenced how we interacted with others. Why did so many people donate blood or volunteer their time to help others? Who were the members of the "terrorist cells," and how did Osama bin Laden gain their blind obedience? How did the media coverage influence our responses to these events? These questions illustrate the focus of social psychologists.

Cognitive psychology focuses on mental processes such as decision making, problem solving, language, and memory. Cognitive psychologists might be interested in how the terrorists remembered all the details of the plan, solved the problem of how to bring down such huge buildings, or made the decision to do so. Similarly, prior to the September 11 attacks, many Americans held a mental structure or cognitive belief that they had a measure of control over their lives (called *illusion of control*). Cognitive psychologists study beliefs like the illusion of control, and the loss of this illusion, to see what effects they have on behavior.

Industrial /organizational (I/O) psychology looks at behavior in the workplace. Industrial psychologists may be studying applied issues such as increasing job satisfaction or decreasing employee absenteeism. Others may focus on understanding the dynamics of workplace behavior such as leadership styles or gender differences in management styles. Although it may not seem like the terrorist attacks have any relevance to workplace behavior, at least one organization was involved in carrying out the attacks; fire, police, and rescue organizations responded, as did hospitals and government agencies. The effectiveness or lack of effectiveness of these organizations, their structures, and how they operated, would interest industrial psychologists. Many businesses and agencies with offices in the World Trade Center lost employees, and many people changed their personal and professional priorities following the attacks. I/O psychologists would also address these issues.

Consumer psychology investigates consumer behavior. John Watson first brought his ideas about behavior to advertising. Similarly, consumer psychologists want to understand what factors influence people to buy or not buy a product. Is it the packaging? Is it where a product is placed? Is a product's popularity influenced by the age of the consumer or where the consumer lives? Following September 11, to woo back customers, airlines had to "sell" the idea that flying was safe and that newly installed security measures would protect us.

Forensic psychology deals with criminal behavior and the legal system. Forensic psychologists may study a certain type of criminal behavior such as rape or murder, or they may assist law enforcement organizations in conducting profiles of possible suspects for a crime. However, don't confuse the recent depiction of psychics on television with forensic psychologists. Forensic psychologists do not possess special powers that lead police to suspects. Forensic psychologists analyze research data such as crime statistics and suspect profiles to make scientific conclusions. The FBI, the CIA, and other intelligence agencies across the world use such data to identify and locate terrorists and terrorist cells.

Cross-cultural psychology looks at how culture influences behavior. Since psychology's formal beginnings in 1879, Western thought has dominated our understanding of behavior. For example, suppose that you are studying nonverbal communication patterns. In Western culture, one important feature of nonverbal behavior is eye contact. Typically, Westerners perceive a person who maintains eye contact during conversation as listening and paying attention. However, not all cultures perceive eye contact in this manner. Some cultures consider maintaining eye contact as rude, arrogant, and impolite, especially when directed at a person in authority. Knowing how people in other cultures behave in different as well as similar ways to ours can further our understanding of human behavior. Such research suggests cultural differences in reasoning styles, motivation, perception of color, and emotional expression to name a few (Marsh, Elfenbein, & Ambady, 2003; Snibbe, 2003). Many in the United States were shocked to see a news photo of Palestinian refugees rejoicing over the September 11 attacks. Many were equally shocked by the rise in hate crimes against Arab Americans and U.S. Muslims. To gain a better understanding of terrorist behavior, we need to know how we appear to others (Sanborn, 2003). Cross-cultural psychology looks at the cultural factors that contribute to behavior and at how our own cultural expectations influence our behavior.

Health psychology focuses on ways to promote health and prevent illness. Health psychologists want to understand issues such as why some people cope with stress better than others, what are the best ways to deal with stress, or what aspects of one's personality are more likely to lead to health problems. Health psychologists also are concerned with issues such as diet and nutrition, exercise, and lifestyle choices that influence health. September 11 would be of interest to health psychologists studying the health consequences of trauma, loss, war, and stress management.

Educational psychology encompasses how people learn and how variables in an educational environment influence learning. Educational psychologists also look at behavior on the teaching side. You probably recall a teacher from your past who you thought was very good. You probably also recall one you didn't like at all. Differences in their teaching methods or in their control of the classroom probably influenced your attitude and your learning. Days, weeks, and months after September 11, students continued to cope with changes in their lives, whether from loss of family or a more general fear and anxiety about their safety. These changes may have affected the student's ability to learn, and their teachers may have responded by changing their teaching methods and classroom behaviors.

As you can see, psychology is quite a diverse profession. But you're probably asking yourself, which types of psychologists do therapy? Aren't psychologists supposed to help people? Psychologists in these subfields do help people in an indirect way by furthering our understanding of some type of behavior even though they may not be working one-on-one with someone who has a problem.

Doing Therapy: Clinical and Counseling Psychologists

What psychology careers can I go into if I want to help others one-on-one? **Many** psychologists focus on directly helping people. In fact, one of the largest areas of psychology, *clinical and counseling psychology*, does just that. A clinical psychologist trains intensively in therapy and counseling techniques to treat people with mental health problems. Clinical psychologists also do research into mental disorders and mental health, but they don't hold a medical degree and generally cannot prescribe medication. (This is changing, as at least one state has passed legislation allowing clinical psychologists to dispense medication after undergoing additional training and supervision.) Counseling psychologists receive similar training but more typically do personal counseling with people who are experiencing life adjustment problems.

A related profession is *psychiatry*. A psychiatrist holds a medical degree (M.D.) and then specializes in mental health. A psychiatrist's graduate work includes a medical internship and residency, followed by training in treatment of psychological disorders. As medical practitioners, psychiatrists have extensive training in the use of therapeutic drugs, and they may dispense or prescribe medication and order medical procedures such as brain scans.

Clinical and counseling psychologists volunteered their time to help people cope with loss and grief following September 11. Five to eight weeks after the attacks, many people continued to show signs of trauma including depression, anxiety, sleeplessness, and fears of flying and of tall buildings (Galea et al., 2002; Grimsley, 2001). And after September 11, the New York Police Department mandated counseling for the entire police force (Fink & Mathias, 2002).

School psychologists work within the K–12 school system. They may do some individual or group counseling, but mainly they are responsible for testing or assessing students. The test results are then shared with teachers and parents to make decisions regarding the best educational placement for students. School psychologists assisted in many educational settings to help students cope with their grief and loss in the aftermath of September 11.

Sports psychology is a relatively new and growing subfield. Sports psychologists work with athletes as well as with athletic programs and teams. They may focus on injury recovery, which includes exercise, motivation, health, and illness. They may instruct an athlete in performance enhancement techniques. They also may study how other team members or fans influence athletic performance.

By now you are probably overwhelmed thinking about all the different fields of psychology. Just remember that this diversity stems from the complexity of behavior. Many areas of psychology have developed as psychologists focused on different aspects of behavior, but these subfields are interrelated. What a developmental psychologist studies is connected to and may have an impact on the work of social, clinical, and educational psychologists.

Clinical psychologists train intensively in counseling techniques to treat people's mental health problems.

David Buffinton/Getty Images

Women and Minorities in the Field of Psychology

Our review of psychology's past and present has shown the evolution of a professional field from one based on philosophy and medicine to one that has increasingly expanded and become more diverse in scope. Such a change can also be seen in the representation of women and minorities in the field of psychology. At one time, social constraints prohibited women and minorities from equal access to higher education, limiting their pursuit of careers in psychology. Societal changes in recent years have dramatically increased the number of women and minorities pursuing advanced degrees in psychology as the It's a Diverse World box highlights.

IT'S A DIVERSE WORLD

Gender, Ethnicity, and the Field of Psychology

In the early development of psychology, women and minorities were not allowed in many instances to receive graduate degrees despite completing all the requirements for a doctorate. Despite these constraints and many other societal hurdles, several women and minority individuals contributed significantly to the field. For example, Mary Calkins (1863–1930) became the first female president of the American Psychological Association in 1905. She studied at Harvard University with William James and performed several studies on the nature of memory. Christine Ladd-Franklin (1847–1930) studied color vision in the early 1900s. Karen Horney (1885–1952) focused on environmental and cultural factors that influence personality development (see Chapter 14). In 1894 Margaret Washburn (1871–1939) became the first woman to be awarded a doctorate in psychology (Furumoto, 1989).

Few degrees were awarded to minority students in the early 1900s. Gilbert Haven Jones (1883–1966) was the first African American to earn a doctorate in psychology—in Germany in 1909. Francis Sumner (1895–1954) was the first African American to receive a doctorate in psychology from a United States university (in 1920) and is known as the father of African American psychology. Albert Sidney Beckham (1897–1964), whose studies focused on the nature of intelligence, established the first psychology laboratory at

The first woman to be awarded a doctorate in psychology was Margaret Washburn (1871–1939).

an all-Black institution of higher learning, Howard University. The first African American female to be awarded a psychology doctorate was Ruth Howard, in 1934. George Sanchez was one of the first Hispanic Americans in the United States to be awarded a doctorate in psychology, in the early 1900s (Guthrie, 1998). Have times changed for women and minorities in psychology?

Women have indeed made great progress in the field of psychology. Consider that from 1920 to 1974, 23% of doctorates in psychology went to women (APA, 2000b). Currently, far more women than men earn psychology degrees. In 1997 nearly 75% of students doing graduate-level work in psychology were women, and 66% of the doctorates were awarded to women (Murray & Williams, 1999). Educational gains have in some ways been followed by progress in the careers of women in psychology. For instance, by 1996 the proportion of women in all but four subfields of psychology had increased to at least 50% (Sanderson & Dugoni, 1999). Yet despite the fact that since 1986 women have been awarded more than half of the psychology doctorates, in 1998–1999 only 39% of the full-time psychology faculty in 4-year institutions were women (APA, 2000b). Female psychology faculty are also less likely than males to be

Known as the father of African American psychology, in 1920 Francis Sumner (1895–1954) was the first African American to receive a doctorate from a U.S. university.

History of American Psychology, U. of Akron, Akron, Ohio (both).

promoted to the rank of full professor. In a faculty salaries survey conducted by the APA in 2000, women represented only 25% of full professors yet held more than 50% of the lower ranks of assistant professor and lecturer (APA Research Office, 2001). Only 30% of women faculty members are tenured compared to 52% of men (APA, 2000b). Consequently, although psychology has become more fully open to both men and women at the educational level, inequities at the professional level still exist.

Likewise, while the numbers of racial and ethnic minorities in psychology have increased, progress has been slow. Although approximately 25% of the U.S. population are minorities (U.S. Census, 2002), only 15% of applicants to graduate schools in psychology are minorities. Between

1976 and 1993, close to 8% of all doctorates in psychology were awarded to minorities (APA, 1997). By 2002 that number had increased to almost 19% (Hoffer, Sederstrom, Selfa, Wekh, et al., 2003). This means that more than 8 out of 10 psychology doctorates are granted to Whites, regardless of gender. Despite increases in advanced degrees awarded to minorities, they are still underrepresented as faculty in colleges. For example, in 1998 only 10% of all current psychology faculty members were minorities (Murray & Williams, 1999). The APA has established several programs to attract more minorities to the field of psychology. It is only through such efforts as these that the field will become as diversified in people as it is in scope.

Let's Review!

In this section we discussed the training that is necessary to be a psychologist and surveyed a number of the subfields of psychology. For a quick check of your understanding, answer these questions.

1. Which of the following professionals is most likely to prescribe medication for a mental health disorder?
   a. a clinical psychologist
   b. a psychiatrist
   c. a biopsychologist
   d. an experimental psychologist
2. Dr. Martinez is conducting a study on the nature of emotion. What type of research is Dr. Martinez doing?

   a. applied
   b. basic
   c. consumer
   d. preventative
3. A psychologist who studies individual differences in shyness is probably from which subfield?
   a. cognitive
   b. social
   c. developmental
   d. personality

ANSWERS:
1.b; 2.b; 3.d

Psychological Research ›››››››››››››››

The Goals of Psychology

Though psychologists in various subfields study and emphasize different aspects of behavior, they all share similar goals. The main goals of psychology and psychological research are:

- To describe behavior
- To predict behavior
- To explain behavior
- To control or change behavior

LEARNING OBJECTIVES

- Identify the goals of psychological research.
- Understand the steps of the scientific method and distinguish between predictive and causal hypotheses.
- Discuss the advantages and disadvantages of observational, correlational, and experimental research methods and the types of conclusions that can be drawn from each strategy.

Application

Description involves observing events and describing them. Typically, description is used to understand how events are related to one another. For example, you may notice that your health club tends to get more crowded in the months of January, February, and March. It seems you have to wait longer to use the weight machines or that there are more people in the kick boxing aerobic classes. This observation describes an event.

If you observe that two events occur together rather reliably or with a general frequency or regularity, you can make *predictions* about or anticipate what events may occur. From your observations, you may predict that the health club will be more crowded in January. You may arrive earlier for a parking spot or to get a place in the aerobics class. Another example is the relationship between standardized tests and college success. Many colleges use ACT or SAT achievement test scores as a criterion for admission. Why do they use these tests? Research shows that the scores on these tests and success in college are related (Hearn, 1984, 1990, 1991; U.S. Department of Education, 1995), therefore the tests reliably predict who will do well in college. Consequently, a student's scores on these tests often influence college admission personnel in deciding who will be accepted and who will not (Davies & Guppy, 1997). The more academically rigorous colleges tend to admit students who score very high on these tests because it is predicted that they will do better than those with lower scores.

Although it may be known that two events regularly occur together, that doesn't tell us what caused a particular behavior to occur. Winter months do not cause health clubs to become crowded. Performing well on an SAT test on an early Saturday morning does not cause an individual to perform well in college. These two events are related, but one event does not cause the other. Therefore, an additional goal of psychology is to *explain* or understand the causes of behavior. As stated previously, psychologists usually put forth explanations of behavior in the form of theories. A theory is an explanation of why and how a particular behavior occurs. We introduced seven explanations, or perspectives of behavior, earlier in the chapter. For example, how do we explain higher health club attendance in the winter months? Is it a behavior that is influenced by the environment? Perhaps health clubs are more crowded because the weather makes outdoor exercise more difficult? Is it a behavior that is influenced by our biology? Perhaps students with high SAT scores have better eyesight, so they are better able to read the course materials in college. As these ideas are tested, more and more causes and predictors of behavior are discovered. Some of these explanations or theories will be modified, some will be discarded, and new ones will be developed.

The purpose behind explaining and understanding the causes of behavior is the final goal of psychology, *controlling* or *changing* behavior. It relates to the goal of explanation because one needs to understand what is causing a behavior in order to change or modify it. For example, let's say that the weather is a factor in health club attendance. Health clubs could offer outdoor fitness activities beginning in mid-March to prevent declining enrollment. If eyesight is a factor in SAT performance, schools could offer vision testing to high school students to solve the problem. Many psychologists go into the field in the hope of improving society. They may want to improve child care, create healthier work environments, or reduce discrimination in society. Such sentiments reflect the goal of control and underscore the potential impact of good research. Figure 1.5 summarizes the goals of psychology.

The Scientific Method

The purpose of psychological research is to test ideas about behavior. As previously stated, researchers use a prescribed method or procedure to test ideas, called the scientific method. The scientific method is a set of rules for gathering and analyzing information that enables you to test an idea or hypothesis. All scientists adhere to these same steps even though they may use different techniques within each step. The decisions the scientist makes at each step of the scientific method will ultimately affect the types of conclusions that can be made about behavior. The steps of the scientific method are as follows:

1. *Define and describe the issue to be studied.* Psychologists decide what to study and then find relevant information on that behavior through observation or through studying previous research found in scientific journals.

2. *Form a testable hypothesis.* State what you expect to find in a way that can be objectively measured—that is, in a way that another person can come along and test the same hypothesis to verify or *replicate* your results.

3. *Choose an appropriate research strategy.* This step involves many decisions. You must decide how you are going to test the hypothesis or study the behavior. What research method will best test your hypothesis? (These methods are discussed in the next section.) You must also decide where your study will be conducted. Will it be in the field (the environment where the behavior naturally occurs) or will it be in a laboratory (a more controlled setting)? You must decide who or what you will observe in your study, in other words who you will use as *participants*. Will you use animals or humans? If using humans, how will these individuals be selected? If using animals as your subjects, what species will you use?

4. *Conduct the study to test your hypothesis.* Run the study and collect the data.

5. *Analyze the data to support or reject your hypothesis.* The type of research strategy that you have chosen will in many ways determine how you can analyze the data. Analysis of data is usually conducted using statistics, which enable you to support or reject your hypothesis.

Just as you have used the conclusions of other studies to investigate your idea (Step 1), the conclusions of your study may become a source of information for developing your next hypothesis or the hypothesis of another researcher.

Now that you are aware of the steps that psychologists follow when conducting research, you may be asking yourself, how can the scientific method be used to meet the goals of psychology? Let's say that you have an interest in understanding beer drinking among college students. You want to make some predictions (a goal of psychology) about beer drinking. You use the scientific method to test this idea as outlined in Figure 1.6 (page 26). First, you develop your hypothesis. You might hypothesize that college students who buy pitchers of beer tend to drink more than college students who purchase bottles of beer (a prediction). You want to see if there is a relationship between the quantity of beer consumed and the form in which the beer is purchased. The next step would be to select a research strategy, including who and what is to be measured and in what

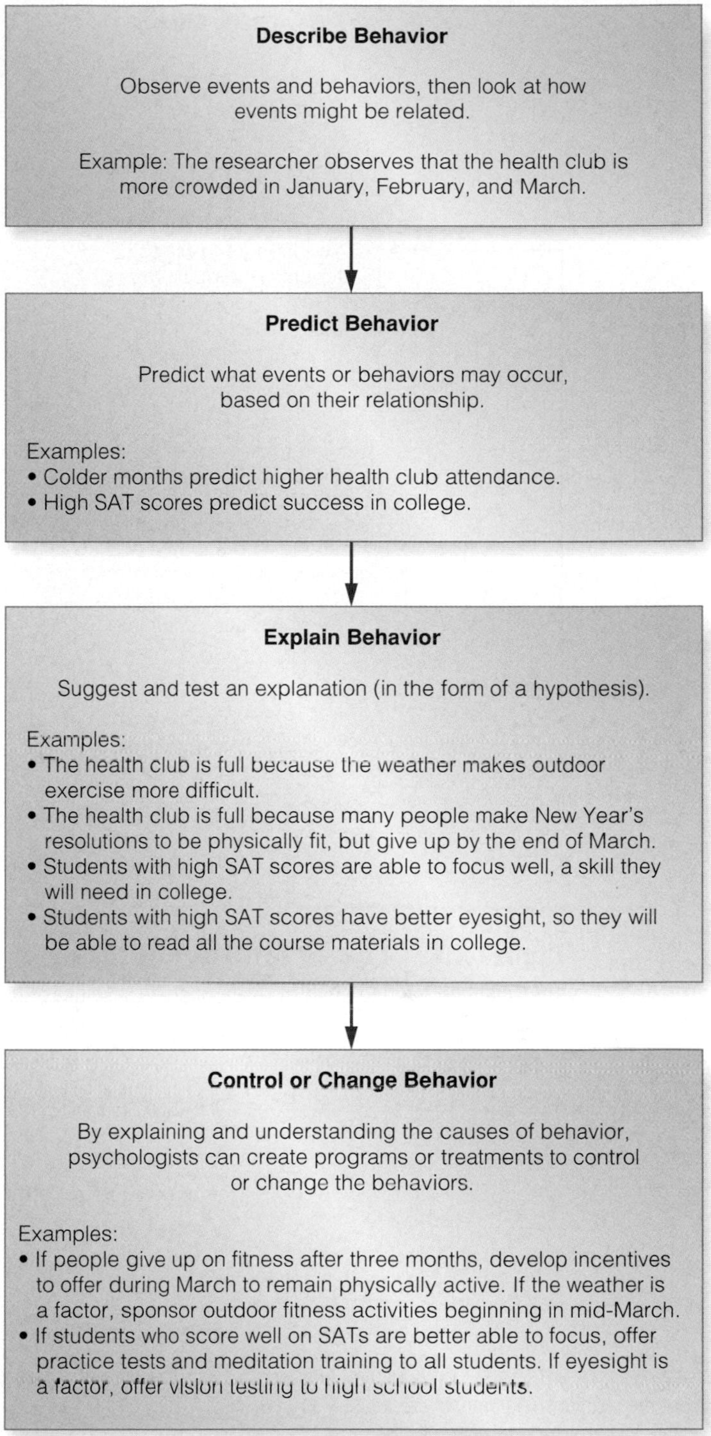

Describe Behavior

Observe events and behaviors, then look at how events might be related.

Example: The researcher observes that the health club is more crowded in January, February, and March.

Predict Behavior

Predict what events or behaviors may occur, based on their relationship.

Examples:
• Colder months predict higher health club attendance.
• High SAT scores predict success in college.

Explain Behavior

Suggest and test an explanation (in the form of a hypothesis).

Examples:
• The health club is full because the weather makes outdoor exercise more difficult.
• The health club is full because many people make New Year's resolutions to be physically fit, but give up by the end of March.
• Students with high SAT scores are able to focus well, a skill they will need in college.
• Students with high SAT scores have better eyesight, so they will be able to read all the course materials in college.

Control or Change Behavior

By explaining and understanding the causes of behavior, psychologists can create programs or treatments to control or change the behaviors.

Examples:
• If people give up on fitness after three months, develop incentives to offer during March to remain physically active. If the weather is a factor, sponsor outdoor fitness activities beginning in mid-March.
• If students who score well on SATs are better able to focus, offer practice tests and meditation training to all students. If eyesight is a factor, offer vision testing to high school students.

Figure 1.5   Goals of Psychology

Psychologists attempt to describe, predict, explain and, ultimately, control or change behavior.

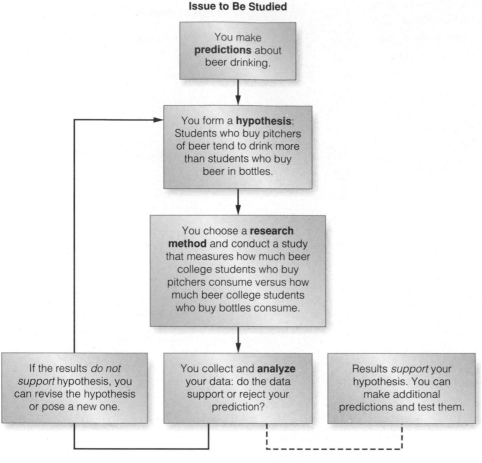

Issue to Be Studied

You make **predictions** about beer drinking.

You form a **hypothesis**: Students who buy pitchers of beer tend to drink more than students who buy beer in bottles.

You choose a **research method** and conduct a study that measures how much beer college students who buy pitchers consume versus how much beer college students who buy bottles consume.

If the results *do not support* hypothesis, you can revise the hypothesis or pose a new one.

You collect and **analyze** your data: do the data support or reject your prediction?

Results *support* your hypothesis. You can make additional predictions and test them.

Figure 1.6   The Scientific Method

The scientific method enables researchers to test ideas about behavior.

manner. So you design a study that measures how much beer is consumed by college students who buy pitchers versus the amount of beer consumed by college students who buy bottles. After collecting the data, you employ statistics to see if there is a relationship and whether support for your hypothesis was found. Geller, Russ, and Altomari (1986) actually included this prediction in a larger study on beer drinking among college students and found support for the hypothesis that buying pitchers led to larger amounts of beer being consumed.

No matter what goal of psychology you are addressing, the process is the same. The goal merely influences the decisions that you make when testing an idea through the scientific method. If your goal is description or prediction, your hypothesis will state what you expect to observe or what relationships you expect to find. Your research strategy then would be designed to measure observations or relationships, and your analysis of the data would employ statistics that enable you to support or refute your hypothesis. It is in this way that the scientific method allows one to test the ideas of psychology.

Hypotheses

What types of questions do psychologists ask when doing research? As you have seen, one of the first steps of the scientific method is to formulate a question or hypothesis about behavior. These hypotheses generally fall into one of two categories: predictive hypotheses or causal hypotheses.

Predictive Hypotheses

predictive hypothesis   an educated guess about the relationships among variables

Predictive hypotheses make a specific set of predictions about the relationships among variables. They are used to address two goals of psychology: description and prediction. The previous example on beer drinking and college youth illustrated a predictive hypothesis. Predictive hypotheses are made when the researcher measures the variables of interest but does not manipulate or control the variables in the study. For example, if we were to predict that people are more likely to experience nightmares after eating spicy food, we would measure the number of nightmares a person experiences, and then ask what he or she ate for dinner the night before. We then would see if a relationship existed between eating spicy food and having nightmares. Because the researcher does not control the variables, conclusions of research studies that test predictive hypotheses are limited. The conclusions can only state what was observed, or what variables appear to be related to one another. They cannot be used to make cause and effect conclusions. To do this, you must form and test a causal hypothesis.

Causal Hypotheses

In contrast to predictive hypotheses, **causal hypotheses** detail specifically how one variable will influence another variable. Causal hypotheses state our ideas about the causes of behavior and in many ways influence the theories that are formulated to explain behavior. Causal hypotheses can be tested only when it is possible for the researcher to control or manipulate the main variables in a study. The researcher sets up different conditions in a study and then observes whether or not there is a change in behavior because of the different conditions. For example, suppose a researcher has developed a new strategy to teach children how to read. The researcher hypothesizes that this program will cause greater gains in reading than the standard method for teaching reading. This is a causal hypothesis. Some students are assigned to the new reading program, and others are assigned to the standard program. The researcher then measures the children's gains in reading at the end of the year to see if there is a difference. As you will soon see, causal hypotheses can only be tested when an experiment is conducted. To test a causal hypothesis, a researcher must be able to conclude how one variable affects or causes a change in another variable.

causal hypothesis an educated guess about how one variable will influence another variable

Research Methods

Once you have stated a hypothesis, the next step in the research process is to decide on a research strategy. The type of hypothesis you make (predictive or causal) typically determines which research methods you can employ. You are more likely to use some research methods to test predictive hypotheses and to use other methods to test causal hypotheses.

What research methods are used to test predictive hypotheses? Several types of research methods are used to test predictive hypotheses. All of these methods are used when the researcher cannot control or manipulate the main variables in the study. Each method has its advantages and disadvantages. We will discuss three such methods: naturalistic observations, case studies, and correlational research.

Naturalistic Observations

Naturalistic observations are research studies that are conducted in the environment in which the behavior typically occurs. For example, Belsky, Woodworth, and Crnic (1996) collected naturalistic observations of parents and their toddlers around dinnertime on two occasions. Their observations enabled them to predict which families might be more troubled. The researcher in a naturalistic study is a recorder or observer of behavior who then describes or makes predictions about behavior based on what he or she has observed. Because the researcher doesn't control events in a naturalistic study, it is not possible to pinpoint the causes of behavior. Therefore, naturalistic studies are predominately used to get at the goals of description and prediction.

naturalistic observation observing behavior in the environment in which the behavior typically occurs

Suppose you want to observe and describe childhood aggression. Would this lend itself to naturalistic observation? Where might you conduct such a study? A naturalistic environment for observing childhood aggression may be a school playground. However, not all behavior lends itself to naturalistic observation. For example, if you want to study helping behavior in an emergency situation, it would be very difficult to conduct a naturalistic study. Where would you make your observations? You could go to disaster scenes, but these observations would be taking place *after* the emergency had occurred. Even if you decided on a place, you could be waiting there a very long time before an emergency actually occurred!

 **Application**

While naturalistic observation does allow a researcher to paint a picture of behavior as it normally occurs, researchers need to consider the influence of *reactivity*. Consider the example of studying childhood aggression by observing students on a

© Ariel Skelley/Corbis

A school playground could be an environment for naturally observing children's behaviors.

school playground. What might happen if you were to simply enter the playground, sit down, and start writing about what you saw? The children might behave differently due to your presence and/or due to the awareness that they are being observed, and your observations of aggression might not be reliable or true. Consequently, when conducting a naturalistic observation, researchers attempt to minimize reactivity. In this way, they can be sure that they are observing the true behavior of their participants.

Case Studies

case study an in-depth observation of one person

Case studies are an in-depth observation of one subject. The subject may be an individual, an organism, or a setting such as a business or a school. Every chapter of this book opens with a brief case study. As with naturalistic observation, in case studies researchers do not control any variables but merely record or relate their observations. Oliver Sacks, a neuropsychologist doing case study research, describes the behavior of people who have been affected by various neurological disorders in his book *The Man Who Mistook His Wife for a Hat* (1985). Case studies are used to detail unusual or rare circumstances. For example, much of what we know about dissociative identity disorder, formerly called multiple personality disorder, comes from case studies that have been turned into books and films such as *Sybil*, *When Rabbit Howls*, and *The Three Faces of Eve*.

generalizability how well a researcher's findings apply to other individuals and situations

Case studies are valuable because they provide in-depth information on rare and unusual conditions that we may not otherwise be able to study. However, the main disadvantage of the case study method is its limited applicability to other situations. It is very difficult to take one case, especially a rare case, and say that it applies to everyone. In other words, case studies lack **generalizability;** because of this, the conclusions that are drawn from case studies are limited to the topic being studied.

Correlational Studies

correlation the relationship between two or more variables

Correlational studies test the relationship, or **correlation,** between two or more variables: television watching and violent behavior, the presence of malls in a community and employment rates, or depression and gender, for example. Again, in correlational studies the researcher does not control variables but rather measures them to see if any reliable relationship exists between the two variables. For example, if we were to measure your weight (one variable), what other variable may show a relationship to your weight? Your height? Your calorie consumption? Your gender? Your age? Your life expectancy? If you were to measure all of these variables, you may find that all of them vary in relation to weight. These relationships are correlations.

Surveys, questionnaires, and interviews often attempt to establish correlations when tabulating their results. They measure many variables and then use statistics to see if any two variables are related. If you have ever filled out a questionnaire, participated in a phone interview, or completed a survey at the mall, you have participated in a correlational study. You were probably asked many questions such as your age, income level, gender, race, and what products you buy or how you feel about a particular issue or candidate. Your responses are then sorted by these attributes to see if, for instance, men are more likely to buy a particular product or vote for a certain candidate when compared to women.

Why bother collecting all these data and what are they used for? Such data are used to make predictions and test predictive hypotheses. Knowing which people are more likely to buy a product enables a company to market its product more effectively and perhaps devise new strategies to target individuals who are not buying its products. Similarly, knowing which behaviors are related to a higher frequency of illness enables a psychologist to predict who is more at risk for physical or mental illness.

The strength of correlations are measured through a *correlation coefficient*, which is a number that tells us the strength of the relationship between two factors. Correlation coefficients range from –1.00 to +1.00. The closer the correlation coefficient is to –1.00 or +1.00, the stronger the correlation, or the more related the two variables are. The closer the correlation coefficient is to 0, the weaker the correlation—that is, one variable does not reliably predict the other variable. For example, in a study on early parent–child relationships and the degree of later problem behavior in their children, Rothbaum, Rosen, Pott, and Beatty (1995) found a –.50 correlation between the mother's attachment to the infant and later problem behavior in the child. The correlation between the father's attachment to the infant and later problem behavior was –.15. The higher correlation found with mothers suggests that the mother–child relationship is a better predictor of subsequent problem behavior than the father–child relationship. Generally, the stronger the correlation is between two variables the more accurate our predictions are, but perfect (+1.00 or –1.00) correlations never happen in psychology. Human behavior is too complex for such perfect relationships to occur.

What do the positive and negative signs in front of the correlation mean? The sign before the correlation coefficient tells us how the variables relate to one another (Figure 1.7, page 30). A **positive correlation** means that as one variable increases, the second variable also tends to increase, or as one variable decreases, the other variable tends to decrease. In both cases, the variables are changing in the *same* direction. An example of a positive correlation is marijuana use and lung cancer. As marijuana use increases, so does the likelihood of developing lung cancer (Caplan & Brigham, 1990; "Marijuana as Medicine," 1997). Another example of a positive correlation is similarity in attitudes and attraction. The more similar two people are in attitudes, the more likely they are to be attracted to one another (Byrne, 1969).

In a **negative correlation,** as one variable increases the other variable tends to decrease in what is referred to as an *inverse* relationship. Notice that the variables are changing in *opposite* directions. An example of a negative correlation is exercise and anxiety. The more people exercise, the less anxiety they tend to experience (Morgan, 1987). Or consider the relationship between marital satisfaction and depression. As marital satisfaction increases, feelings of depression decrease (Beach, Sandeen, & O'Leary, 1990).

Application

Application

positive correlation   a relationship in which increases in one variable correspond to increases in a second variable

negative correlation   a relationship in which increases in one variable correspond to decreases in a second variable

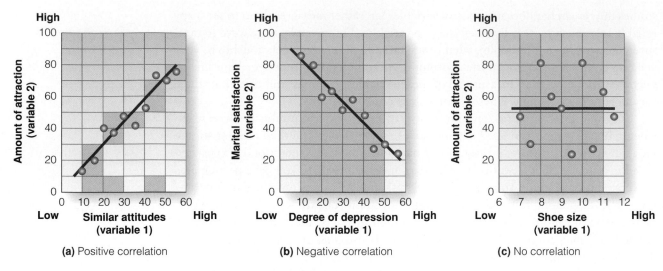

Figure 1.7 Correlation

Correlation, a research method used for prediction, shows how two variables are related.

As stated earlier, correlational studies enable researchers to make predictions about behavior, but they do *not* allow us to make cause and effect conclusions. This is a point often ignored by media reports of research results. For example, suppose you hear a radio announcer say that medical research has shown that people who eat bacon are less likely to have a heart attack. From these comments, you may incorrectly conclude that bacon *causes* the risk of heart attacks to decrease. However, the study yielding the results that bacon-eaters had fewer heart attacks was a correlational study. This type of conclusion cannot be drawn. Why? Researchers do not control the main variables in a correlational study; consequently, we cannot determine which variable causes the other. Perhaps more farmers than office workers eat bacon. Farmers may get more exercise than office workers. Hence, it may be exercise rather than bacon that is influencing the functioning of the heart.

An additional example will help underscore the point that correlations do not permit cause and effect conclusions (Figure 1.8). There is a positive correlation between academic achievement and self-esteem. Students who have high academic achievement also tend to have high self-esteem. Similarly, students who have low academic achievement tend to have low self-esteem. High academic achievement may cause an increase in self-esteem. However, it is just as likely that having high self-esteem causes one to do better academically. There may be a third variable, such as the parents' educational level or genetics, that actually causes the relationship between academic achievement and self-esteem. A correlational study does not tell us which of these explanations is correct. The only research method that permits us to make cause and effect conclusions is the experiment.

Experiments

What research method is used to test causal hypotheses? While several types of research methods are used to test predictive hypotheses, only one research method can test a causal hypothesis: the experiment. We will discuss several features of the **experiment,** including its advantages and disadvantages.

experiment a research method that is used to test causal hypotheses

Necessary Conditions for an Experiment Two main features characterize an experiment (Figure 1.9, page 32). First, the variables in the study are controlled or

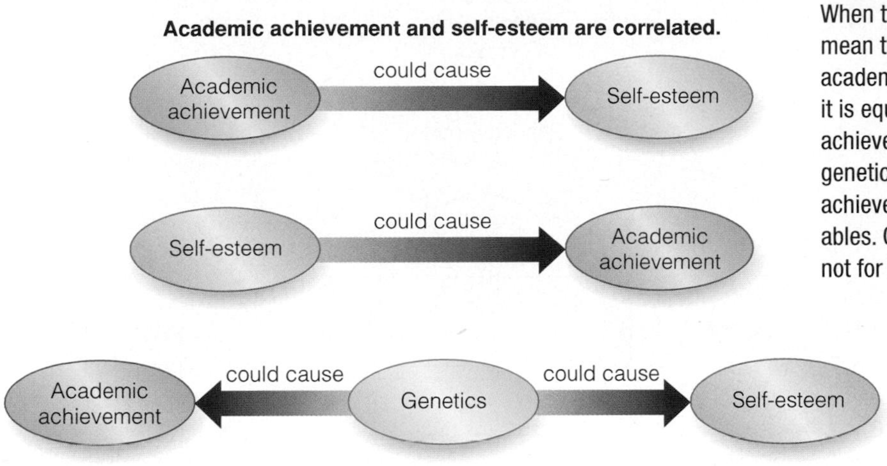

Figure 1.8   **Correlation Does Not Mean Causation**

Academic achievement and self-esteem are correlated.

When two variables are correlated or related, it does not mean that we know *why* they are related. It could be that high academic achievement causes high self-esteem. However, it is equally likely that high self-esteem causes high academic achievement. It is also possible that a third variable, such as genetics, causes both high self-esteem and high academic achievement, resulting in a relationship between the two variables. Correlation can only be used for making predictions, not for making cause and effect statements.

manipulated. Second, participants are randomly assigned to the conditions of the study. When these two conditions have been met, causal conclusions *may* be drawn. Let's first turn our attention to the issue of experimenter control.

The point of the experiment is to manipulate one variable and see what effect this manipulation has on another variable. These variables are termed the independent and dependent variables, respectively. The **independent variable** is the variable that the experimenter manipulates, and it is the cause in the experiment. The **dependent variable** measures any result of manipulating the independent variable, so it is the effect in the experiment. Suppose, for example, that we want to study the effects of sleep deprivation. Specifically, we hypothesize that sleep deprivation causes deficits in memory. This is a causal hypothesis that can be tested with an experiment. We decide to manipulate the amount of sleep participants receive to see if it has any effect on memory. In this example, the amount of sleep is our independent variable. Some participants will be allowed to sleep 8 hours per night for the week of our study. Others will be allowed to sleep only 4 hours each night. The experimenter has set, or controlled, the amount of sleep (the independent variable) at two levels: 8 hours and 4 hours. Each day of our study we measure the participants' memory (the dependent variable) by having the participants complete several memory tasks. At the end of the study, we compare the memory scores of those participants who received 8 hours of sleep with those who received only 4 hours of sleep.

To be sure that it is the amount of sleep affecting memory and not something else, we need to be sure that we controlled any variable (other than the independent variable) that may influence this relationship. These potentially problematic variables are called **confounding variables.** What variables might we need to control? Maybe age influences one's memory or how one handles sleep deprivation? If either of these is true, we would want to control the age of our participants. We also would want to make sure that participants had not used any substances known to affect memory or the sleep cycle prior to their participation in the experiment. Consequently, we would control for this variable too.

Both groups must be treated the same except for the amount of sleep they receive, so the researcher sets the conditions of the experiment to be the same for both groups. For example, every participant should complete the memory tasks at the same time of day, and every participant should complete the same memory tasks. The criteria for scoring the memory tasks must be the same as well. The instructions for completing the tasks must be the same. The lighting, temperature, and other physical features of the

independent variable   the variable in an experiment that is manipulated

dependent variable   the variable in an experiment that measures any effect of the manipulation

confounding variable   any factor that affects the dependent measure other than the independent variable

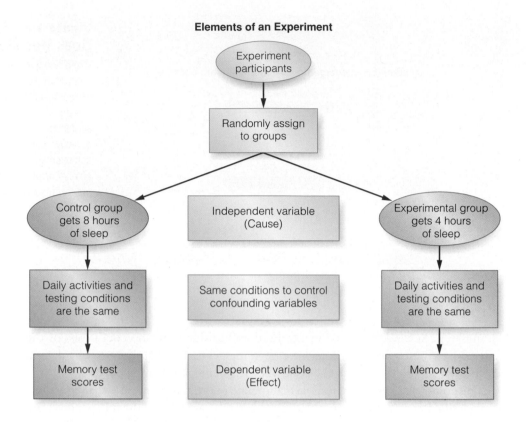

Elements of an Experiment

Figure 1.9 **Elements of an Experiment**

The two main ingredients of an experiment are (1) that the variables in the study are controlled or manipulated and (2) that participants are randomly assigned to the conditions of the study. When these two conditions have been met, causal conclusions *may* be drawn.

room in which the participants sleep and complete the memory tasks should be the same for all participants. Our purpose here is to design a study in which we manipulate the independent variable to see its effect on the dependent variable. If we control any potentially confounding variables that influence this relationship and find a difference in the dependent variable between our groups, it is most likely due to the independent variable, and we have proven a cause and effect relationship.

What if the experimenter does not control a confounding variable? We now have more than one variable that could be responsible for the change in the dependent variable: the independent variable and the confounding variable. When this occurs, the researcher is left with an alternative explanation for the results. The change in the dependent variable could have been caused by the independent variable, but it also could have been caused by the confounding variable. Consequently, causal conclusions are limited.

Let's not forget the second condition necessary for an experiment—how participants are assigned to the conditions of the independent variable. Just as we do not want any differences in the nature of our conditions other than the amount of sleep, we must be sure that there are no differences in the composition of our groups of participants. Psychologists eliminate this problem through the technique of **randomization.**

In the ideal experiment, researchers would include every person they are interested in studying. This is termed the **population of interest.** For a developmental psychologist who specializes in infant development, all infants would be the population of interest. It is impossible to test everyone, so researchers select a portion, or subset, of the population of interest called a **sample.** Because the sample will be used to make

randomization when all people have an equal chance of being selected to participate in a study

population of interest the entire universe of animals or people that could be studied

sample the portion of the population of interest that is selected for a study

© Charles Gupton/Corbis

By studying behavior in a lab environment, researchers are better able to control the variables in an experiment.

inferences or judgments about the entire population, the sample should reflect the whole population as much as possible; that is, it should be a *representative sample*. Random sampling of participants ensures a representative sample. In a *random sample*, every member of the population has an equal chance of being selected to participate in the study; thus, sampling bias is not introduced into the experiment.

Take a look around at your classmates in your general psychology course. Would this group qualify as a random sample of your college? Probably not. All of the students in the college did not have the same chance to choose the course. Registration typically is staggered such that students with more credits get to register earlier than students with fewer credits. So you are not a random sample. Would the group qualify as a representative sample of college students? Probably not. As a group, you may not represent the college student population in terms of age, race, income level, career major, geographic region, and so forth.

The more representative the sample is, the more the results will generalize to the population of interest. But random sampling is not always possible. Consequently, psychological research often uses *samples of convenience*, or groups of people who are easily accessible to the researcher. The students in your psychology course are a sample of convenience. In fact, much psychological research relies on using college students as their sample of convenience! In the United States only 24% of those over the age of 25 have college degrees, so these samples probably do not represent people from all walks of life (Snibbe, 2003).

Random sampling is ideal in research, but it is not a necessary condition for an experiment. It is always extremely important, however, that participants be **randomly assigned** to the conditions of the study. In our example on sleep and memory, assigning

 **Application**

random assignment   participants have an equal chance of being placed in any condition of the study

all the males in the sample to the 4-hour sleep condition and all the females to the 8-hour sleep condition would create a confounding variable. Gender differences may have an effect on memory scores. It may be that gender (the confounding variable) rather than sleep deprivation (the independent variable) is the cause of a difference in memory. To eliminate the influence of such confounding variables, experimenters randomly assign participants to conditions. Each participant has an equal chance of being placed in either condition. Males are just as likely to be assigned to the 4-hour condition as they are to the 8-hour condition, and the same is true for female participants. In this way, any participant variable that has the potential to influence the research results is just as likely to affect one group as it is the other. Without random assignment, confounding variables could affect the dependent variable. This is exactly what occurs in quasi-experiments.

quasi-experiment a research study that is not a true experiment because participants are not randomly assigned to the conditions of the study

A **quasi-experiment** is sort of like an experiment. The researcher manipulates the independent variable and sets the conditions of the experiment to be the same for both groups. However, the second condition necessary for an experiment—randomly assigning participants to conditions—has not been met. Quasi-experiments use existing groups of people who differ on some variable when compared to the other condition. For example, suppose you want to see if smoking cigarettes during pregnancy causes lower birth weight babies. For ethical reasons, you cannot assign some pregnant women to smoke and prevent others from smoking. Instead, for your smoking condition, you must select pregnant women who already smoke. These women may differ on other variables when compared to pregnant women who do not smoke. For example, their eating habits may differ. As a result, a confounding variable (the diet of the mothers) exists that could cause a difference in the dependent variable (the birth weight of the offspring) other than smoking. Consider another example. You hypothesize that couples living together before marriage causes divorce. You randomly select couples for your experiment, but you cannot randomly assign them to the conditions of your study. You cannot force some of them to live together. Those couples already living together would be used as one condition, a select group of people who may differ on another variable. As you can see, quasi-experiments do not meet the conditions necessary for a "true" experiment. Consequently, causal conclusions based on quasi-experimental designs should be made cautiously.

Advantages and Disadvantages of Using Experiments Experiments have several advantages. First, it is only through experimentation that we can approach two of the goals of psychology: explaining and changing behavior. An experiment is the only research method that enables us to determine cause and effect relationships. This advantage makes interpreting research results less ambiguous. It is in the experiment that we attempt to eliminate any confounding variables either through experimenter control or random assignment of participants to groups. These techniques also foster clearer conclusions of research results.

If experiments are so great, why don't we just use them all the time? First, experiments do not address the first two goals of psychology: describing and predicting behavior. These are often the first steps in understanding behavior, and naturalistic observation and correlational studies are quite useful for doing this. Second, in an attempt to control confounding variables, experiments conducted in laboratory settings may create an artificial atmosphere. It is then difficult to know if the same result would occur in a more natural setting. This may be another reason to conduct naturalistic observations or correlational studies. Third, sometimes employing the experimental method is simply not possible due to ethical and practical considerations. As we mentioned in the case of quasi-experimental designs, we cannot force people to be randomly assigned to a condition that would harm them (such as smoking) or that does not pertain to them (such as having high blood pressure). Psychologists must follow certain ethical guidelines and practices when conducting research. We turn our attention to this topic next.

Let's Review!

In this section we detailed the goals of psychology and outlined the steps of the scientific method. We distinguished between predictive and causal hypotheses and described methods of research. For a quick check of your understanding, answer these questions.

1. Theories are used for which goal of psychology?
   a. describe
   b. explain
   c. predict
   d. observation

2. When we know that two events regularly occur together, which goal of psychology can be met?
   a. predicting behavior
   b. changing behavior
   c. understanding behavior
   d. explaining behavior

3. Correlational studies test which type of hypotheses?
   a. predictive
   b. causal
   c. both predictive and causal
   d. neither predictive nor causal

4. As an educational psychologist, you might use naturalistic observations of college students in a test-taking environment to get at which of psychology's goals?
   a. change behavior

   b. predict behavior
   c. explain behavior
   d. describe behavior

5. In an experiment on attitudes, participants are given either positive or negative information about a speaker and then asked to evaluate the effectiveness of the speaker. In this experiment, which is the independent variable?
   a. the effectiveness of the speaker
   b. the type of information the participant is given
   c. attitude change
   d. the speaker

6. The more hours that students work, the less successful they are academically. This is an example of what type of correlation?
   a. zero
   b. positive
   c. perfect
   d. negative

ANSWERS:
1. b; 2. a; 3. a; 4. d; 5. b; 6. d

Ethical Issues in Psychological Research

> > > > > > > > > > > > > > > > > >

LEARNING OBJECTIVE

Describe the main ethical principles that guide psychologists as they conduct research.

Generally, psychologists affiliated with universities and colleges cannot conduct research unless their research proposal has passed review by an **Institutional Review Board (IRB).** The function of the IRB is to ensure that the research study being proposed conforms to a set of ethical standards or guidelines. This section details who sets these standards and what the main responsibilities are for psychologists who conduct research.

Institutional Review Board (IRB)   a committee that reviews research proposals to ensure that ethical standards have been met

Ethical Guidelines for Participants

Who sets the ethical guidelines for psychological research? The American Psychological Association (APA), one of the main professional organizations for psychologists, has taken the lead in establishing ethical guidelines or professional behaviors that psychologists must follow. These guidelines, the "Ethical Principles of Psychologists and Code of Conduct" (APA, 2002), address a variety of issues including general professional responsibility, clinical practice, psychological testing, and research. Here we look at the guidelines psychologists must follow when conducting research with humans and animals. The ethical duties of psychologists who treat clients are discussed in Chapter 16.

What is the Golden Rule for conducting research on human participants? One of the main concerns of the IRB is to ensure that the proposed research has met the ethical guideline of respect and concern for the dignity and welfare of the people who participate (APA, 2002). Researchers must protect participants from any potential harm, risk, or danger as a result of their participation in a psychological study. If such effects occur, the researcher has the responsibility to remove or correct these effects. In the experiment that Watson and Raynor conducted on 9-month-old Albert (see pg. 11), the fear that Albert developed toward white rats was never removed. Today the procedure for this experiment would be considered unethical. Watson caused harm to Albert and did not remove his fear at the end of the experiment.

informed consent   research participants agree to participate after being told about aspects of the study

A fundamental principle of ethical practice in research is **informed consent.** Researchers inform potential participants of any risks during the informed consent process wherein the researcher establishes a clear and fair agreement with research participants, prior to their participation in the research study (APA, 2002). This agreement clarifies the obligations and responsibilities of the participants and the researchers and includes the following information:

- The general purpose of the research study, including the experimental nature of any treatment
- Services that will or will not be available to the control group
- The manner by which participants will be assigned to treatment and control groups
- Any aspect of the research that may influence a person's willingness to participate in the research
- Compensation for or monetary costs of participating
- Any risks or side effects that may be experienced as a result of participation in the study

confidentiality   researchers do not reveal which data were collected from which participant

Prospective participants are also informed that they may withdraw from participation in the study at any time, and they are informed of any available treatment alternatives. In addition, the researcher agrees to maintain **confidentiality.** Personal information about participants obtained by the researcher during the course of the investigation cannot be shared with others unless explicitly agreed to in advance by the participant or as required by law or court order.

Can you trick participants in an experiment? It is not always possible to fully inform participants of the details of the research, as it may change their behavior. For this reason, psychologists sometimes use *deception* in their research. For example, suppose we wanted to research student cheating. If we tell participants we are studying cheating behavior, it will likely influence their behavior. If we tell participants we are investigating student–teacher behavior, we can measure student cheating more objectively. However, the use of deception must be justified by the potential value of the research results. Moreover, deception can be used only when alternative procedures that do not use deception are unavailable.

debriefing   after an experiment, participants are fully informed of the nature of the study

If participants have been deceived in any way during the course of a study, the researcher is obligated to debrief participants after the experiment ends. **Debriefing** consists of full disclosure by the researcher to inform participants of the true purpose of the research. Any misconceptions that the participant may hold about the nature of the research must be removed at this time. For example, suppose you volunteer to participate in a psychological experiment on attitudes toward your school. You arrive at the psychology lab at the appropriate time and are asked to wait in a room for a

Application »

moment with two other participants. While in the waiting room, the other participants start talking to you. One is very pleasant and kind, but the other is rude, negative, and overbearing. The researcher then arrives and escorts you to another room in which you complete a self-esteem questionnaire. After completing the survey, you are then told that the true purpose of the study was to investigate your reaction to the people in the waiting room. The researcher is exploring how positive and negative behaviors influence another person's self-esteem. The two people in the waiting room were not really participants but *confederates*, individuals who pose as participants but who are really working for the researcher. In such an experiment, you were not physically or psychologically harmed, so the deception and subsequent debriefing were ethical. This ethical standard was not always met in the past. Consider the following research study.

In the 1960s Stanley Milgram (1963) set out to determine if the average person could be influenced to hurt others in response to orders from an authority figure. (You will read more about Milgram's research in Chapter 12.) Participants were deceived into believing that they were participating in a research study on learning rather than on obedience. Participants were told that they would be playing the role of a "teacher" in the experiment. Participants were introduced to a "learner" who was then led to a separate room. The teacher's job was to administer electric shocks to the learner every time the learner made a mistake in an effort to help the learner better learn a list of words. In reality, the participant was not actually shocking the learner. The learner's responses were prerecorded on a tape, but the participants did not know this and believed they were, indeed, shocking the learner.

Despite the fact that participants believed the learner to be ill or worse, most of them continued to follow the experimenter's orders. A full 65% of the participants shocked the learner all the way up to 450 volts! During the procedure, Milgram's participants did exhibit many stress-related behaviors. Although Milgram debriefed his participants after the study, he still violated the ethical principle of psychological harm. He was criticized for exposing participants to the trauma of the procedure itself and for not leaving the participants in at least as good a condition as they were prior to the experiment (Baumrind, 1964). Because of these ethical problems, a study such as this would not be approved today.

We also must note that for years the primary focus in research was on white males. Women and minorities were not only discouraged from becoming professionals in psychology but also were largely ignored or neglected when studying psychological issues. Many minority and women psychologists as well as men have contributed to the field of psychology by addressing these shortcomings and designing research that looks specifically at the behaviors of minorities and women.

Ethical Guidelines for Animal Research

Animal studies have advanced our understanding of many psychological issues including the importance of prenatal nutrition, our treatment of brain injuries, and our understanding of mental disorders (Domjan & Purdy, 1995). Psychologists must meet certain standards and follow ethical guidelines when conducting research with animals. Psychological research using animal subjects must also be approved by an IRB. Less than 10% of all psychological studies involve animal subjects, and these consist mainly of rodents and birds (APA, 1984). Animals must be treated humanely and in accord with all federal, state, and local

Although Stanley Milgram debriefed his participants, he still caused them psychological harm. Such a study violates current ethical standards of psychological research.

Obedience © 1965, Stanley Milgram

laws and regulations. Researchers are responsible for the daily comfort, housing, cleaning, feeding, and health of animal subjects. Discomfort, illness, and pain must be kept at a minimum, and such procedures can only be used if alternative procedures are not available. Moreover, harmful or painful procedures used on animals must be justified in terms of the knowledge that is expected to be gained from the study. Researchers also must promote the psychological well-being of some animals that are used in research, most notably primates (APA, 2002).

Let's Review!

As a quick check of your understanding of ethical considerations in research, answer these questions.

1. Dr. Kwan is performing case study research. She should be most concerned with which of the following ethical principles?
   a. deception
   b. physical harm
   c. debriefing
   d. confidentiality

2. What is the rule for deceiving participants in a psychological study?
   a. Deception is never allowed in psychological research. It is against the law and you go to jail if you use it.
   b. Deception is allowed only when using animals as subjects; human beings are too intelligent for deception.

   c. Deception is allowed when alternative procedures are unavailable and participants are debriefed at the end of the study.
   d. Deception can be done under any circumstances since psychological research never harms participants.

3. Which of the following is *not* an ethical guideline psychologists must follow when conducting research?
   a. pay participants for their participation
   b. informed consent
   c. freedom from harm
   d. confidentiality

ANSWERS:
1. d; 2. c; 3. a

Are You Getting the Big Picture?

STUDYING THE **CHAPTER**

This chapter has given you an overview of the field of psychology and how psychologists do research. From its formal beginnings in Wilhelm Wundt's laboratory in Germany, psychology has emerged as a rich and complex field. Psychologists study all types of behaviors, from consumer buying, to how people develop attitudes, to love and aggression, and so on. Psychologists study these behaviors using the scientific method in the form of case studies, surveys, and experiments.

Psychologists don't always agree on why people behave as they do. Some look for the explanation in genetics whereas others look at internal cognitive processes. Still others look toward more external or environmental factors to explain behavior. We refer to these three main themes—biological, cognitive, and social processes—throughout the text to examine the complex nature of behavior and to help you integrate the information from each chapter into the big picture of psychology.

The big picture of psychology is relevant to many career fields. Advertisers and salespeople are more effective when they understand consumer behavior.

Educators and health care professionals benefit from understanding child and adult development. Video technicians and artists apply psychological principles of perception to their work. Consequently, no matter which career you are exploring, psychology will be of value to you.

In the chapters that follow, we will detail more specifically psychological research in the main subfields of psychology. In the next chapter, we start with the biological processes that underlie all behavior. Each chapter will prepare you for mastering the concepts of the next chapter, and we frequently remind you of concepts presented in earlier chapters to help you connect the information. We hope in this way, that the "big picture" of psychology is never far from your mind. A visual summary of the chapter's contents concludes this chapter. It will help you remember the topics and concepts that have been introduced and further your understanding of how these concepts relate to one another.

Key Terms

psychology (2)
scientific method (4)
theory (7)
structuralism (9)
introspection (9)
functionalism (10)
psychoanalytic theory (11)
behaviorism (11)
humanism (12)
cognitive psychology (13)
biological/physiological perspective (13)
evolutionary perspective (14)
cognitive perspective (14)

psychodynamic perspective (15)
behavioral perspective (15)
sociocultural perspective (15)
humanistic perspective (15)
eclectic approach (15)
basic research (17)
applied research (17)
predictive hypothesis (26)
causal hypothesis (27)
naturalistic observation (27)
case study (28)
generalizablitity (28)
correlation (28)
positive correlation (29)

negative correlation (29)
experiment (30)
independent variable (31)
dependent variable (31)
confounding variable (31)
randomization (32)
population of interest (32)
sample (32)
random assignment (33)
quasi-experiment (34)
Institutional Review Board (35)
informed consent (36)
confidentiality (36)
debriefing (36)

Test Yourself!

Concept Check

Test your knowledge of the chapter concepts by completing each of the following sentences with the correct term. For a more comprehensive review, visit the book Web site (http://psychology.wadsworth.com/pastorinole/) for online quizzes, flashcards, crosswords, and Internet links.

Psychology is the scientific study of (1) _____. Its birth is marked by the establishment of the first psychology laboratory in (2) _____ by Wilhelm Wundt. Wundt's view of psychology is referred to as (3) _____. Other early schools of psychology included the focus on an organism's adaptation to the environment, called (4) _____, and a focus on the unconscious, called (5) _____ theory.

Modern psychological perspectives also evidence diverse views. The (6) _____ perspective emphasizes physical aspects of behavior. The (7) _____ perspective focuses on how thinking processes influence behavior. The (8) _____ perspective emphasizes external or environmental causes of behavior.

These varied perspectives have resulted in a profession with many subfields. For example, (9) _____ psychologists perform basic research in the areas of sensation, perception, and learning. (10) _____ psychologists study how groups influence our behavior. Educational psychologists study (11) _____ whereas school psychologists focus on (12) _____.

As a science, psychology tests ideas about behavior by following a set of rules called the (13) _____. Our

ideas about behavior are referred to as (14) _____. We test these ideas with different research methods. For example, studies that test the relationship between two variables use the (15) _____ method whereas (16) _____ are in-depth observations of one subject. However, only the experimental research method can test (17) _____. Two main features characterize an experiment. First, the variables in the study are controlled or manipulated. The variable that is manipulated is called the (18) _____ variable. The second condition necessary for an experiment is (19) _____.

When conducting research, psychologists must follow ethical guidelines. For example, a researcher must get a participant's agreement or (20) _____ to participate in a study, and if deception is used, participants must be (21) _____ at the conclusion of the study.

Answers:

1. behavior and mental processes; 2. Germany; 3. structuralism; 4. functionalism; 5. psychoanalytic; 6. biological; 7. cognitive; 8. behavioral; 9. experimental; 10. Social; 11. how people learn; 12. testing students for educational placement; 13. scientific method; 14. hypotheses; 15. correlation; 16. case studies; 17. cause and effect relationships; 18. independent variable; 19. random assignment of participants to the groups; 20. informed consent; 21. debriefed

Critical Thinking About the Chapter

1. Suppose Wilhelm Wundt, William James, and Sigmund Freud had the opportunity to sit down and converse on the causes of behavior. What might this conversation sound like? On what issues might they agree? On what issues might they disagree?

2. Explain depression from each of the modern perspectives and using the eclectic approach. Use Table 1.2 as a guide if you need help.

3. Design a research study to test the idea that listening to rock music while studying facilitates learning. What type of hypothesis would you make? Could this idea be tested by

naturalistic observation? How could you set up a correlational study to test this idea? Could an experiment be designed to address this issue? What types of conclusions could you reach from these different research methods? What ethical considerations would you follow when conducting this study?

Applying Psychology. Explain how you can apply the scientific method to decide on a college major or a career choice. Could this method also be used as part of your decision-making process when purchasing large items such as a car or a house?

Chapter Study Resources

Suggested Readings

1. Susser, E. S., Herman, D. B., & Aaron, B. (2002). Combating the terror of terrorism. *Scientific American, 287*, 70–78.
   Discusses the psychological damage caused by the attacks of September 11.

2. Sacks, O. (1990). *The man who mistook his wife for a hat.* New York: HarperPerennial.
   Well-known neuropsychologist Oliver Sacks gives a compelling account of case histories of patients with neurological disorders.

3. Hock, R. R. (1995). *Forty studies that changed psychology: Explorations into the history of psychological research.* Englewood Cliffs, NJ: Prentice-Hall.
   Details 40 of the most influential studies that have shaped psychologists' understanding of behavior.

4. For additional readings, explore InfoTrac College Edition, your online library of archived journal articles and periodicals. Go to http://www.infotrac-college .com/wadsworth and enter the passcode from the card that came with your book. For this chapter, search using these keywords: gender differences in emotion, behaviorism, ethical decision in psychological research, pseudoscience, careers and psychology.

Web Links for Further Study

Additional information on chapter concepts can be found at these Web sites:

1. Time Management Tips with Personal Time Survey: Good suggestions on managing your study time, and a survey you can take.
   www.gmu.edu/gmu/personal/time.html

2. Marky Lloyd's Careers in Psychology
   www.psywww.com/careers/index.htm

3. American Psychological Association
   www.apa.org

4. History of Psychology
   www.unbf.ca/psychology/likely/headlines

5. Cyberlab: Links to tutorials, activities, and quizzes related to research in psychology
   faculty.frostburg.edu/mbradley/cyberlab.html

Student Study Guide

To help you organize your learning, work through Chapter 1 of the *What Is Psychology? Student Study Guide.* The study guide includes learning objectives, a chapter summary, fill-in review, key terms, a practice test, and other learning activities.

Psychology Now™

PsychologyNow is a Web-based, personalized study system that provides you with a pretest and a post-test for each chapter, quizzes you by chapter, and provides a personalized study plan, pointing you to elements in the text or in individual learning modules that will help you to achieve 80% mastery. Check out the learning modules that relate to this chapter: armchair psychology, experimental psychology.

PsychNow CD-ROM, Version 2.0

Go to the PsychNow CD-ROM for further study of the concepts in this chapter. The CD-ROM includes learning modules with videos, animations, and quizzes, as well as simulations of psychological phenomena. Each Explore module follows a consistent Explore, Lesson and Apply structure that allows you to experience the concept or principle, learn more about it, and then apply it. You and your friends can participate in a team-based Quiz Game that makes learning fun. Learning modules include:
1b. Psychology and Its History; 1c. Research Methods; 1d. Critical Thinking in Psychology.

What Is Psychology?

Psychology is the scientific study of behavior and mental processes. Contrary to popular misconceptions, psychology is:

- NOT simply giving good advice.
- NOT just "common sense."
- NOT limited to the study of mental illness.

To think like a psychologist, you must be skeptical about explanations of behavior, rather than accepting of them.

THE ORIGINS OF PSYCHOLOGY

- Although interest in explaining behavior dates back to ancient times, psychology did not become a distinct field of scientific study until the late 1800s.

- Wilhelm Wundt established the first psychology laboratory in Leipzig, Germany, in 1879. Wundt studied the elements that explained mental processes, and his approach is known as structuralism.

- William James was the first U.S. professor of psychology, and his focus was on how particular behaviors helped individuals adapt to their environment, which became known as functionalism.

- One of the most famous people to influence psychology was Sigmund Freud, a Viennese physician who believed the key to understanding behavior was uncovering unconscious motivations through a new technique known as psychoanalysis.

Wilhelm Wundt

- Skeptical of Freud's focus on the mind, a new group of psychologists, known as behaviorists, emphasized the need to study observable behavior in order to maintain psychology as a science.

William James

- John Watson was an important early behaviorist, but the most influential advocate of behaviorism in the mid-20th century was B. F. Skinner. Skinner studied how consequences—reinforcement and punishment—guide behavior, which is totally shaped by one's environment.

- In contrast to the environmental determinism of behaviorists, by the 1960s a new humanistic approach, led by Carl Rogers and Abraham Maslow, emphasizing free will and personal growth, became a significant force in psychology.

- Another modern approach that moved away from behaviorism is cognitive psychology, which conducts experiments to better understand key mental processes —such as memory, problem solving, and decision making.

- Other major forces in psychology today include biological psychology, which examines the physiological contributions to behavior; evolutionary psychology, which looks at how certain behaviors may be genetically programmed to help us adapt better for survival; and sociocultural psychology, which conducts comparative research of behaviors across ethnic groups and nations.

- Most psychologists today embrace an eclectic approach to study and understand behavior.

Sigmund Freud

B. F. Skinner

CAREERS IN PSYCHOLOGY

• Practicing psychologists and academic psychologists typically have a doctorate in psychology, which usually involves 5–7 years of postgraduate study and research beyond the undergraduate degree.

• There are dozens of subfields of psychology, including such diverse areas as developmental psychology (which studies child and adult development), social psychology (which examines ways in which we are influenced by others), industrial/organizational psychology (which looks at behavior in the workplace), forensic psychology (which deals with criminal behavior and the legal system), and health psychology (which focuses on ways to promote health and prevent illness).

• Clinical or counseling psychologists practice therapy to assist individuals with mental health problems.

• More serious psychological disorders are sometimes referred to psychiatrists. A psychiatrist holds a medical degree (M.D.) and then specializes in mental health. Psychiatrists are able to prescribe medications to treat mental disorders, whereas psychologists and other therapists generally are not.

• Women now make up nearly 75% of those pursuing graduate work in psychology, although they still lag behind men as a percentage of full-time professors at 4-year colleges.

• There has been an increase in the number of racial and ethnic minority students majoring in psychology, but their numbers are still far smaller than their percentage in the general population. The American Psychological Association has established a number of programs to attract more minority group members to the field of psychology.

Francis Sumner

Margaret Washburn

PSYCHOLOGICAL RESEARCH

• The goals of psychology are to describe behavior, predict behavior, explain behavior, and control or change behavior.

• To test their theories of behavior, psychologists form predictive and causal hypotheses, and then conduct research using the scientific method.

• To test predictive hypotheses, psychologists use naturalistic observation, case studies, and correlational studies. To test causal hypotheses, psychologists do experiments. When conducting experiments, variables are controlled, and care is taken to survey a true random sample of a population of interest.

• To assure humane conduct in experiments, the American Psychological Association has a strict set of ethical guidelines that must be followed. Key elements of the ethical guidelines include informed consent, confidentiality, protecting the participant against any potential harm, and debriefing to explain any deceptions used in the experiment.

• Ethical guidelines also govern psychological experiments on animals. Discomfort, illness, or pain must be kept to a minimum, or avoided if alternative procedures are available.

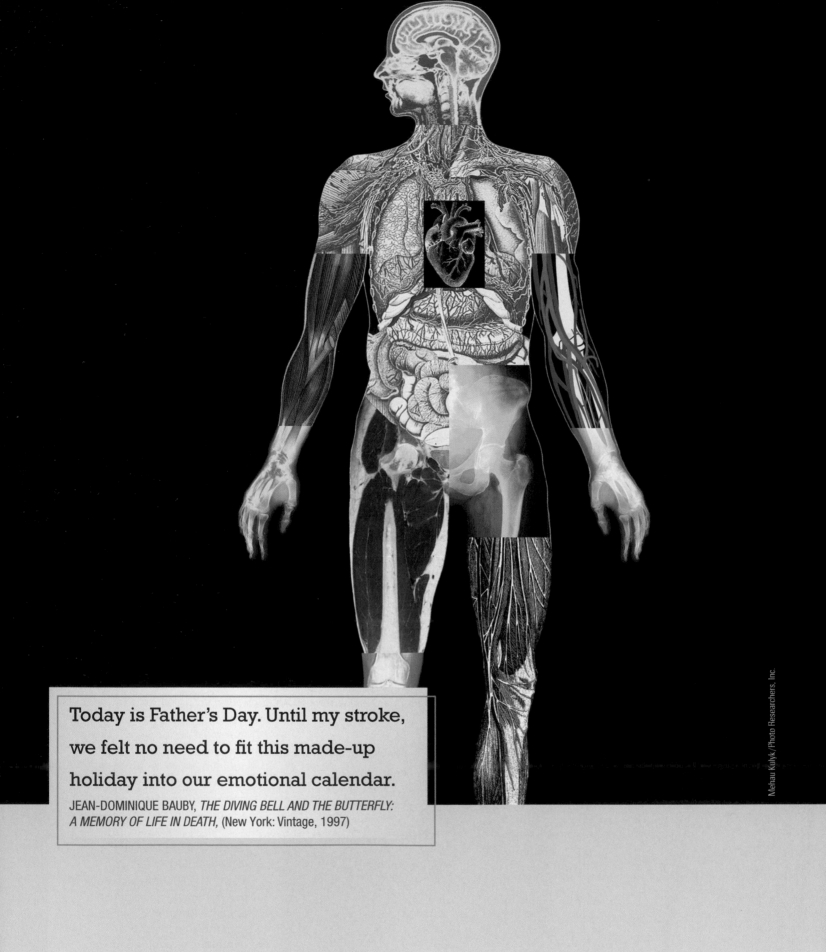

Today is Father's Day. Until my stroke, we felt no need to fit this made-up holiday into our emotional calendar.

JEAN-DOMINIQUE BAUBY, *THE DIVING BELL AND THE BUTTERFLY: A MEMORY OF LIFE IN DEATH,* (New York: Vintage, 1997)

Mehau Kulyk/Photo Researchers, Inc.

How Does Biology Influence Our Behavior?

CHAPTER PREVIEW

What Would We Be Without a Brain?

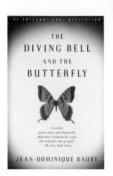

But today we spend the whole of the symbolic day together, affirming that even a rough sketch, a tiny fragment of a dad is still a dad.

(Bauby, 1977 p. 2)

When did you last stop to wonder how your brain works? For most of us, the answer to that question is probably "Never!" Most of us lead our lives without giving our brain much thought. Every day we go about our business, taking for granted our ability to move, speak, feel, and breathe. We seldom, if ever, stop to think about the amazing internal systems that allow us to accomplish these tasks. Sometimes the best way to gain an appreciation for things we take for granted is to see what life would be like without them. In the following case study, we see what life was like for Jean-Dominique Bauby when he suddenly lost much of his brain function. After reading his story, you will probably have more respect for your own brain and the abilities it gives you.

When Jean-Dominique Bauby began his day on December 8, 1995, his life was the essence of success. At age 43 he was editor-in-chief of the French fashion magazine *Elle*, the father of two loving children, a world traveler—a man who seemed to have everything. But all of this was about to change. That afternoon, as Bauby was test driving a new BMW in the company of his driver and his son, he suddenly began to experience unusual neurological problems. As he drove along, Bauby began to feel as if he were moving in slow motion. His vision began to blur and double, and familiar landmarks along the road seemed only vaguely recognizable. Realizing that he was in grave trouble, Bauby pulled off the road and attempted to get out of the car, only to find that he was unable to walk. He collapsed in the back seat of the car and was rushed to a nearby hospital where he lapsed into a coma that lasted nearly three weeks.

As you may have guessed, Bauby experienced a stroke on that December afternoon. Blood flow to the brainstem was disrupted, leaving Bauby with what physicians call "locked-in syndrome." Those with locked-in syndrome remain conscious but are almost completely unable to move or speak. They are essentially trapped or "locked" inside their bodies. When Bauby awoke from his coma, he was aware of his surroundings but unable to move any part of his body except for his left eyelid. He was also completely mute, half deaf, and because he was unable to blink his right eye, it had to be sewn shut to protect his cornea. Bauby lived the remaining two years of his life in this locked-in state, unable to move or speak but very aware of his surroundings and quite able to think and feel.

If Bauby's story ended here, it would certainly be a sad tale, but there was more to his life than this tragedy. There was also the remarkable triumph of an intelligent and resourceful man. Bauby gradually learned to communicate with others by doing the only thing he could—blinking his left eye. This ingenious system allowed Bauby to spell out words by blinking. An assistant would read off the letters of the alphabet in the order of their frequency of usage in the French language, with the most frequently used letters read first. When the assistant read the appropriate letter, Bauby would blink and the assistant would gradually compile words and phrases. In this manner Bauby was able to slowly and painstakingly communicate with those who were patient enough to go through this process. Through his ability to blink, Bauby was able to free himself to a small but meaningful degree from the prison of locked-in syndrome.

There is still more to Bauby's story. Not only did Bauby communicate with his family and friends, he also dictated a best-selling book. It is estimated that Bauby had to blink his eye more than 200,000 times to dictate the manuscript (MacIntyre, 1998). *The Diving Bell and the Butterfly* (Bauby, 1997), published in France just days after his death on March 9, 1997, recounts Bauby's struggle to cope with the infirmities he suffered as a result of his devastating stroke, as well as his musings on the life he lost that December day. It also serves as a testament to the awesome complexity and power of the human brain. We take for granted that our brain and nervous system will function properly and allow us to do just as we wish. Bauby himself wrote of how unaware he had been of the functioning of his brainstem until it failed him and he was locked forever inside his body.

In this chapter we explore many aspects of the biological processes that underlie our behavior. You will begin to recognize the amazing intricacy and precision with which the systems within our bodies influence even our simplest behaviors. Keep the story of Jean-Dominique Bauby in mind as you read this chapter. Be aware that right now, as you read this page, everything you are doing—reading, learning, holding the book, blinking, breathing, and so on—originates in your wonderfully complex nervous system. By the end of the chapter, you'll have a better understanding of how your nervous system makes all these behaviors possible.

Communication Within the Brain and Body

> > > > > > > > > > > > > > >

LEARNING OBJECTIVE
Explain the differences between the nervous system and the endocrine system.

As the case study of Jean-Dominique Bauby makes painfully apparent, we rely on our bodies to do everything for us. We do not question that our brain will somehow store the information we just learned in psychology class, and that on exam day it will retrieve that information. We take for granted that we will be able to walk, to talk, to play baseball, and to maintain a constant body temperature and a steady heart rate. But how are such everyday miracles accomplished? How does your brain know when you need to eat or sleep? How does your brain tell the muscles of your arm to contract so you can throw a baseball? In short, how does one part of the body communicate with another?

The Nervous System

The **nervous system** is one of the major systems of communication within the body (Figure 2.1). Its two main parts are the *central nervous system* (the brain and spinal cord) and the *peripheral nervous system* (the remainder of the nervous system). The nervous system consists largely of specialized cells called **neurons** that have the ability to convey information to one another. These cells use a sophisticated electrochemical system to conduct the signals that will ultimately allow us to guide the action and functioning of our bodies. When you touch a hot stove, neurons in your fingertips send information up your arm to your spinal column. In response to this possible threat, signals are sent back out from the spine to the muscles of your arm. The result is a quick, reflexive jerking of your arm away from the hot stove (Figure 2.2). Signals that indicate pain and possible damage to your body are then sent to your brain. As you can see from this example, actions of the nervous system tend to be quick and relatively short-lived.

nervous system an electrochemical system of communication within the body that utilizes cells called neurons or nerves to convey information

neurons cells in the central nervous system that transmit information

《 Application

The Endocrine System

A second major communication system, the **endocrine system,** influences such activities as sleep, eating, growth, and sexual behavior. In contrast to the nervous system, which is electrochemical in nature and fast-acting, the endocrine system is a chemical system that communicates more slowly and produces longer-lasting influences on the body.

endocrine system a system of communication in the body that utilizes hormones as chemical messengers

Figure 2.1 **The Human Nervous System**

The nervous system is divided into the central nervous system (shown in blue) and the peripheral nervous system (shown in red). Together the central and peripheral nervous system affect virtually all of our bodily functions.

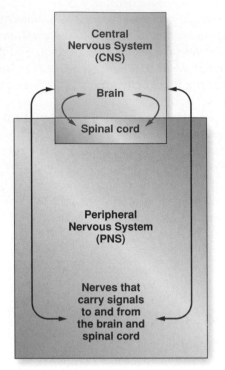
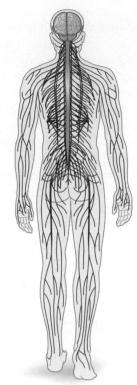

Central Nervous System (CNS)

Brain

Spinal cord

Peripheral Nervous System (PNS)

Nerves that carry signals to and from the brain and spinal cord

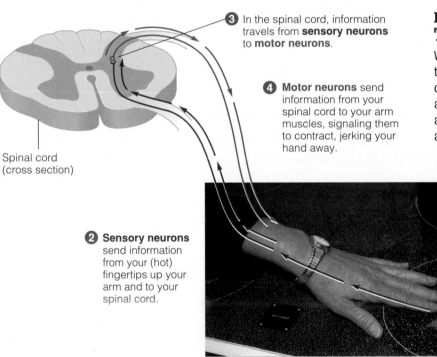

❸ In the spinal cord, information travels from **sensory neurons** to **motor neurons**.

Figure 2.2 **The Neurons Involved in a Reflex**

When you touch a hot stove, neurons in your fingertips send information up your arm to your spinal column. In response to this possible threat, signals are sent out from the spine to the muscles of your arm. The result is a quick, reflexive jerking of your arm away from the hot stove.

❹ **Motor neurons** send information from your spinal cord to your arm muscles, signaling them to contract, jerking your hand away.

Spinal cord (cross section)

❷ **Sensory neurons** send information from your (hot) fingertips up your arm and to your spinal cord.

Courtesy J. S. Brooks

❶ You touch the hot stove; the heat registers in your skin's sensory receptors.

Although the nervous system and the endocrine system function differently, and to some extent influence different aspects of our behavior, they are not totally independent. Later in this chapter, we discuss the endocrine system and the connections between it and the nervous system. For the moment, however, let's turn our attention to the functioning of the nervous system, which is arguably the most complex and influential system in the body.

Let's Review!

For a quick check of your understanding of the different functions of the nervous system and the endocrine system, answer these questions.

1. Which system in the body is *most* analogous to a computer?
   a. the nervous system
   b. the endocrine system
   c. the respiratory system
   d. the digestive system

2. Eduardo was just startled by a loud noise, which of the following systems in Eduardo's body *most* likely responded most quickly to this event?
   a. endocrine system

   b. nervous system
   c. nervous system and endocrine system would respond at exactly the same time
   d. neither system would have responded to this event

3. The cells in your brain are part of the _____.
   a. central nervous system
   b. peripheral nervous system
   c. endocrine system
   d. spinal cord

ANSWERS

1. a; 2. b; 3. a

Billions of Neurons: >>>>>>>>>>>>>>>>>>>>>
Communication in the Brain

It is estimated that an adult human brain contains roughly 100 billion neurons. Although 100 billion seems like a great many cells, our brains contain even more of another type of cell, **glia cells.** Glia cells provide support functions for the neurons of the brain. Appropriately, the word *glia* comes from the Latin word for glue. In some respects, the glia cells are what hold the neurons of the brain together. Without them, the neurons of the nervous system could not function.

Glia cells help maintain the chemical environment of the neuron, and they help repair neural damage after injuries. One of their most important functions is the production of **myelin.** Myelin is a whitish, fatty, waxy substance that coats portions of the outsides of many neurons. This protective coating insulates and speeds up neural signals. Much like rubber or plastic insulation on an electrical cord, myelin helps the signal get where it is going quickly. Myelinated neurons can conduct signals much faster than unmyelinated neurons. To appreciate what myelin does for neural communication, let's look at what happens when myelin is lost due to illness.

Multiple sclerosis (MS) is one disease that attacks and destroys the myelin insulation on neurons (Chabas et al., 2001). People with MS have difficulty controlling the actions of their body and have sensory problems, including numbness and vision loss. When myelin breaks down, neural signals are greatly slowed down or halted altogether. Initially, movement becomes difficult; as the disease progresses, voluntary movement of some muscles may become impossible. Sensory systems such as vision may also fail because incoming signals from the eye don't reach the vision processing parts of the brain. Life often becomes very challenging for people with MS as the "orders" sent to and from the brain are delayed or lost along the way.

Without myelin our nervous system cannot function properly—our neurons cannot efficiently carry information from one point to another in the nervous system. As psychologists, we are particularly interested in understanding how *healthy* neurons send signals throughout the nervous system. Before we can examine how neurons transmit

LEARNING OBJECTIVES

> Describe the basic structure of a neuron, including the axon, dendrites, and synapse.

> Explain what an action potential is, and describe how it moves down the axon and across the synapse.

> Explain what excitation and inhibition are, and how they occur at the synapse.

>

glia cells   brain cells that provide support functions for the neurons

myelin   fatty-waxy substance that insulates portions of some neurons in the nervous system

Actress Terri Garr suffers from multiple sclerosis, a disease that results in destruction of myelin. As the myelin is destroyed, patients may suffer from a variety of neurological symptoms including difficulty moving and sensory loss.

© Reuters/Corbis

signals, we must first examine the anatomy of neural cells and how they connect with one another in the nervous system.

The Anatomy of the Neuron

Like any cell in the body, the neuron has a **cell body** that contains a nucleus (Figure 2.3). The cell body is somewhat similar in shape to a fried egg with the nucleus being analogous to the yolk. Like the nucleus of any cell, the nucleus of the cell body contains the **DNA (deoxyribonucleic acid)** that directs the development of the neuron. Growing out of the cell body are branchlike structures called **dendrites** (from the Greek word for tree branch). The dendrites are the part of the neuron that receives incoming signals from other neurons. For ease of understanding, we will refer to the dendrite end of the neuron as the *head* of the cell.

Growing out of the other end of the cell body is a long tail-like structure called an **axon,** which carries signals away from the cell body. We will refer to the axon end of the neuron as the *tail* end of the cell. When a neuron is insulated with myelin, it is the axon that is covered, or *myelinated.* As you can see in Figure 2.3, myelin does not continuously cover the entire length of a neuron's axon. Rather, the myelin covers segments of the axon with a *myelin sheath.* Axons vary in length from a few hundred micrometers to many centimeters, depending on where in the nervous system they are located

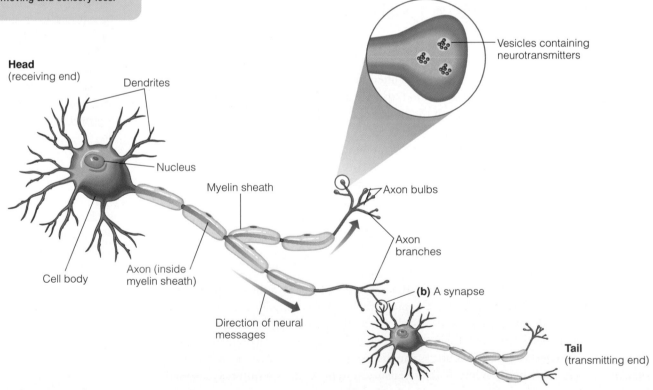

Figure 2.3 A Typical Neuron

The arrows indicate the flow of information from the dendrites on the head of the neuron to the axon bulbs at the tail of the neuron. Neurons may have many dendrites and axon branches, and some neurons are insulated with myelin, which helps speed up neural signals in the neuron.

From Gaudin and Jones, Human Anatomy and Physiology, *Fig 11.3a, p. 263. Reprinted by permission of the author.*

(Figure 2.4). Axons in the brain are typically very short (1 millimeter or less) whereas other axons in the body, such as those that extend down the legs, can be almost a meter in length (Purves et al., 1997).

The tail end of the axon splits into separate branches (Figure 2.3). At the end of each branch is an axon bulb, which houses small storage pouches or *vesicles.* These vesicles produce **neurotransmitters,** the chemical messengers that carry signals across the synapse. A **synapse** is the junction between two neurons where the axon bulb of one neuron comes in close proximity with specialized *receptor sites* on another neuron.

The neural structure of the brain is extremely complex, and synapses can occur at several places along a neuron (e.g., dendrites, axon, or cell body). However, for simplicity's sake we will discuss only a simple *head-to-tail* synapse. In this type of synapse, the axon bulb on the tail end of the first neuron comes in close proximity to specialized receptor sites on the dendrites on the head of a second neuron (Figure 2.5, page 8). You will notice that the first or *presynaptic neuron* does not physically touch the second or *postsynaptic neuron.* This physical space is called the **synaptic cleft.**

Humans have an extremely large number of synapses. Current estimates of the number of synapses range between trillions and quadrillions. Think about this for a moment. How is it possible for humans to have a quadrillion synapses but only 100 billion

cell body   the part of the neuron that contains the nucleus and DNA

DNA   The chemical found in the nuclei of cells that contains the genetic blueprint that guides development in the organism

dendrites   branchlike structures on the head of the neuron that receive incoming signals from other neurons in the nervous system

axon   the long tail-like structure that comes out of the cell body of the neuron and carries action potentials that convey information from the cell body to the synapse

neurotransmitters   chemical messengers that carry neural signals across the synapse

synapse   the connection formed between two neurons in the nervous system

synaptic cleft   the physical space between two neurons at the synapse

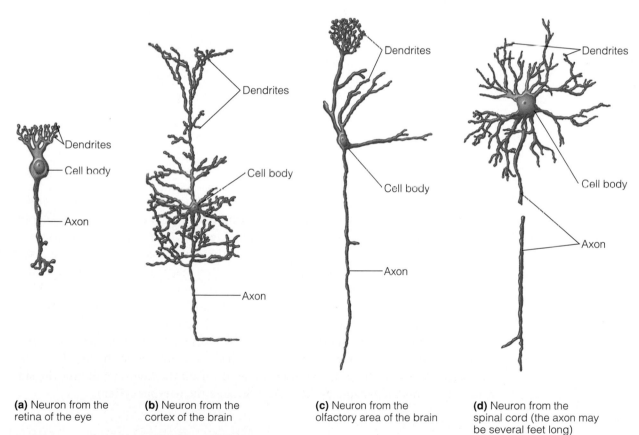

(a) Neuron from the retina of the eye

(b) Neuron from the cortex of the brain

(c) Neuron from the olfactory area of the brain

(d) Neuron from the spinal cord (the axon may be several feet long)

Figure 2.4 **Neuron Configurations**

Neurons come in many different configurations. Some neurons have many dendrites to receive input from many other neurons (**b** and **d**), whereas others may have relatively few (**a** and **c**). Likewise, some neurons have long axons to carry messages over long distances in the body (**c**), whereas others have relatively short axons (**a**). Regardless of the configuration of the neuron, all neurons tend to function in the same fashion.

From Gaudin and Jones, Human Anatomy and Physiology, *Fig 11.17. Reprinted by permission of the author.*

Figure 2.5 **Detail of a Synapse**

A synapse is formed when the axon bulb of one neuron comes in close proximity to the receptors on the dendrites of the post-synaptic neuron.

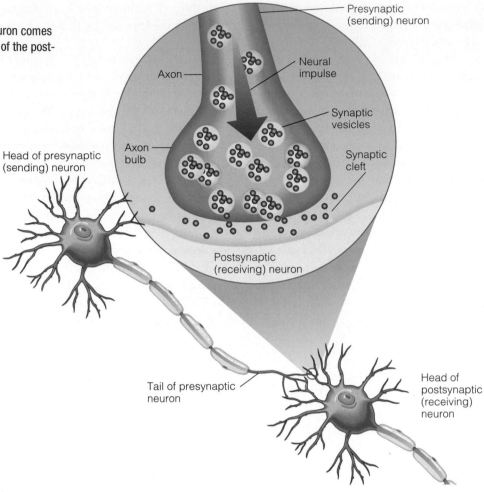

neurons? It's possible because the neurons of the brain do not synapse in a *one-to-one* fashion. Rather, each neuron can synapse with up to 10,000 other neurons (Bloom, Nelson, & Lazerson, 2001). Look again at the neurons in Figure 2.4. Synapses can occur at any place along any of the dendrites of these neurons. (Are you getting a feel for the complexity of the brain?) Keep in mind as you read the rest of this chapter that although we will describe simple one-to-one connections between neurons, this is merely for ease of discussion. The reality of the brain is much more complex: 100 billion neurons and trillions or quadrillions of neural connections.

This vast network of neurons and synapses gives our nervous system the ability to generate and send the messages that are necessary to govern our bodies. Let's take a closer look at how these signals are generated within the neuron and how the signals jump across the synapse as they travel through the nervous system.

Signals in the Brain: How Neurons Fire Up

To understand how these neural signals are generated within a neuron, we must first understand the electrochemical environment of the neuron. Brain tissue is made up largely of densely packed neurons and glia cells. Brain tissue is surrounded by a constant bath of body fluid that contains charged particles called **ions.** Some of the ions that play a particularly important role in neural signaling are sodium (Na^+), potassium (K^+), and chlorine (Cl^-).

ions   charged particles that play an important role in the firing of action potentials in the nervous system

When a neuron is at rest, meaning it is not actively conducting a signal, there is an imbalance in the types of ions found inside and outside the cell walls of the neuron. This imbalance is due to the fact that openings in the axon, called *ion channels*, only allow some ions to pass into and out of the neuron. Small ions such as K^+ can pass through the ion channels in the axon, but larger ions such as Na^+ cannot. Na^+ cannot enter the axon, so high concentrations of K^+ and CL^- are found *inside* the neuron and a high concentration of Na^+ is found *outside* the neuron (Figure 2.6).

Resting Potential

Figure 2.6 shows that this imbalance of ions causes an imbalance of electrical charges inside and outside of the neuron. Because the charge outside the cell differs from the charge inside the cell, the cell is said to be *polarized*. Look again at Figure 2.6. What type of charge predominates on the inside of the neuron? What charge predominates on the outside of the cell? The inside of the cell is more negatively charged than the outside because there are a lot of positive sodium ions (Na^+) on the outside and a lot of negative chlorine ions (Cl^-) on the inside of the cell. This polarization of the cell is called a potential difference, and the potential difference of a neuron at *rest* is called the **resting potential.** In mammals, the resting potential is about -70 millivolts (a millivolt, mv, is 1/1000 of a volt). This means that when resting, the inside of the neuron is about 70 mv more *negative* than the outside of the neuron. Even though the resting potential is a small potential difference, it is an important driving force in creating neural signals.

resting potential   potential difference that exists in the neuron when it is resting (approximately -70 mv in mammals)

The Action Potential and the Threshold of Excitation

When a neuron receives input from other neurons in the brain, these incoming signals enter at the dendrites and travel across the cell body to the axon. These signals have the power to make the inside of the cell more positive or more negative. If the incoming signals make the inside of the neuron more positive, the inside of the neuron may become positive enough to reach the neuron's **threshold of excitation** (about -55 mv in mammals). When the threshold of excitation is reached, the ion channels in the axon suddenly open and allow Na^+ ions to enter the cell. As Na^+ ions flood into the cell, the inside of the neuron becomes more and more positive. This is how a neuron fires. These neural impulses within the neuron are called **action potentials** (Figure 2.7).

All neural impulses are equally strong: If a neuron reaches threshold and fires an action potential, the neural signal will reach the synapse. A neuron firing an action potential is like firing a gun. You either shoot or you don't, and once the shot is fired, it's

threshold of excitation   potential difference at which a neuron will fire an action potential (-55 mv in humans)
action potential   neural impulse fired by a neuron when it reaches -55 mv

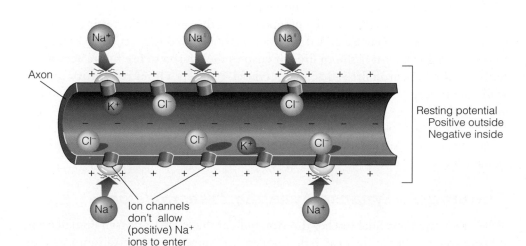

Axon

Resting potential
Positive outside
Negative inside

Na^+
Ion channels don't allow (positive) Na^+ ions to enter

Figure 2.6 **Resting Potential**

When a neuron is at rest, the ion channels do not allow large sodium ions (Na^+) to enter the cell. As a result of the high concentration of Na^+, the predominant charge on the outside of the neuron is positive. The predominant charge inside the neuron is negative due to the high concentration of chloride ions (Cl^-) found there. This difference in charge between the inside and the outside of the cell is called the resting potential.

Figure 2.7 **Action Potential**

The action potential shown here (**a**) occurs all the way down the axon and is how we send neural signals in our nervous system. As the action potential travels down the axon (**b**), the sodium channels close and potassium (K^+) channels open, allowing potassium to leave the cell. As the K^+ leaves the cell, the inside of the cell becomes more negative. Potassium will continue to leave the cell until the neuron has returned to its resting potential.

Source: Modified from Starr & Taggart (1989).

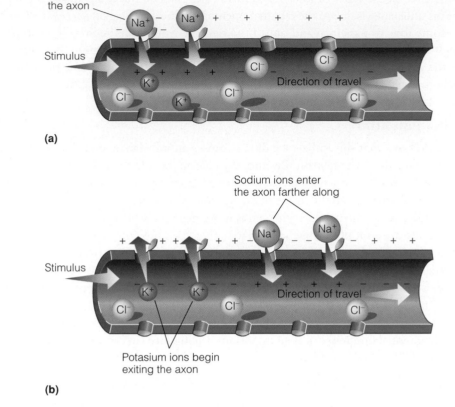

(a)

(b)

all-or-none fashion   all action potentials are equal in strength; once a neuron begins to fire an action potential it fires all the way down the axon

refractory period   brief period of time after which a neuron has fired an action potential in which the neuron is inhibited and unlikely to fire another action potential

not going to stop in midair! Because all action potentials are equally strong and because, once fired, they will reach the synapse, action potentials are said to fire in an **all-or-none fashion.**

The Refractory Period

As the action potential travels down the axon, the inside of the axon is becoming more and more positive as Na^+ floods into the neuron. Consequently, the potential difference inside the cell reverses, becoming more positive. At the same time, the outside of the cell becomes more negative because much of the available Na^+ enters the neuron through the ion channels. This change in the charges inside and outside the neuron will eventually reverse the flow of Na^+. As the outside of the cell becomes more negative than the inside, sodium will no longer be allowed into the cell. Furthermore, positive potassium ions (K^+) will be pumped out of the cell until the resting potential (-70 mv) is restored (Figure 2.7). This resetting of the resting potential is analogous to cocking a gun after it has been fired; it enables the neuron to fire future action potentials. After a neuron fires an action potential, it enters a brief **refractory period** while the resting potential is being restored. During this time, it cannot fire another action potential.

So far, we've looked at how a neural signal travels down the axon, but what happens when the action potential hits the axon bulb at the end of the axon? How does the signal get across this cleft?

Jumping the Synapse: Synaptic Transmission

When the action potential reaches the axon bulb of the presynaptic (sending) neuron, it causes the vesicles in the axon bulb to open and dump the neurotransmitters they contain into the synaptic cleft. The neurotransmitter molecules float in the fluid-

Just as one must cock a gun again after firing, neurons must also return to their resting potential before they may send more action potentials. The brief period of time it takes for the neuron to return to its resting potential is known as the refractory period.

filled synaptic cleft. Some of them will quickly drift across the synaptic cleft and come in contact with the tulip-shaped receptor sites lined up on the dendrites of the postsynaptic (receiving) neuron.

Each type of neurotransmitter has a specific molecular shape, and each type of receptor site has a specific configuration. Only certain types of neurotransmitters open specific receptor sites. Just as you must have the correct key to open a lock, a particular receptor site will only be activated by a specific neurotransmitter. When a neurotransmitter finds the correct receptor site on the postsynaptic neuron, it *binds* with the receptor site and causes a change in the electrical potential inside the postsynaptic neuron (Figure 2.8).

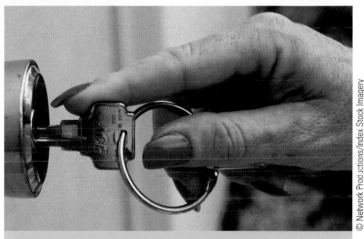

Just as we must use the correct key to open a lock, a neuron can only be stimulated when the correct neurotransmitter binds with its receptor sites.

Excitation

In some instances, the neurotransmitter will cause **excitation** in the postsynaptic cell. Excitation occurs when the neurotransmitter makes the postsynaptic cell *more* likely to fire an action potential. Think about what would have to happen to the electrical potential inside the postsynaptic cell to make it more likely to fire an action potential. In other words, what would have to happen to the resting potential of the cell? Would excitation cause the inside of the neuron to become more positive? Or would excitation cause the inside of the neuron to become more negative? If you said "More positive," you are correct!

In excitation, when the neurotransmitter binds with the receptor site, it causes Na^+ to leak into the cell, making the inside of the cell more positive and closer to the threshold of excitation (Figure 2.9a).

excitation when a neurotransmitter depolarizes the postsynaptic cell and it is made more likely to fire an action potential

Inhibition

Excitation is very important because it ensures that messages will continue onward through the nervous system after they cross the synapse. However, sometimes we need to stop the message from continuing onward. This process is called **inhibition**. Inhibition occurs when the neurotransmitter makes the postsynaptic cell *less* likely to fire

inhibition when a neurotransmitter further polarizes the postsynaptic cell and it becomes less likely to fire an action potential

Figure 2.8 **Neurotransmitters Carry the Signal Across the Synapse**

The neurotransmitter is carried to the presynaptic membrane in synaptic vesicles, which fuse with the membrane and release their contents into the synaptic cleft. The neurotransmitters travel across the cleft and bind with receptor sites on the postsynaptic neuron.

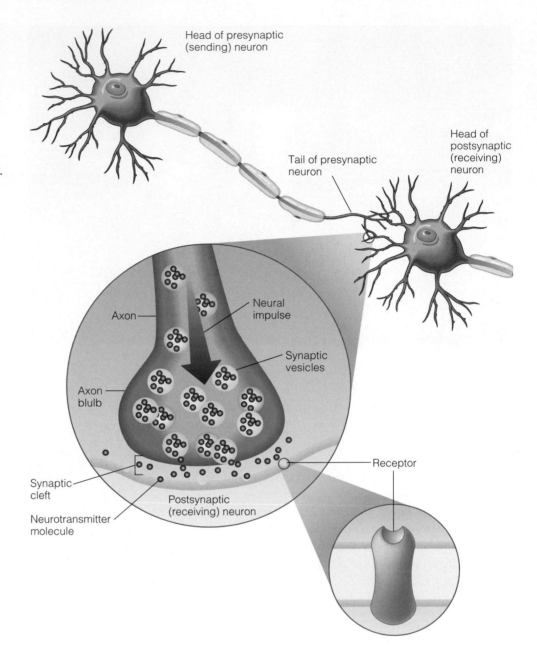

Head of presynaptic (sending) neuron

Tail of presynaptic neuron

Head of postsynaptic (receiving) neuron

Axon

Neural impulse

Synaptic vesicles

Axon blulb

Receptor

Synaptic cleft

Neurotransmitter molecule

Postsynaptic (receiving) neuron

an action potential. As you may have guessed, inhibition causes the inside of the postsynaptic cell to become more negative. Generally, inhibitory neurotransmitters cause chlorine (Cl^-) to *enter* the postsynaptic neuron or potassium (K^+) to *leave* the postsynaptic neuron. In either case, the net effect is to make the postsynaptic cell less likely to fire by making the inside of the cell more negative (Figure 2.9b).

Recall how we began our discussion of action potentials with the incoming signals at the dendrites of a cell? Inhibition and excitation at the synapse are where those signals originate! Inhibition at the synapse produces negative (−) signals that inhibit the postsynaptic cell's ability to fire an action potential. Excitation produces positive (+) signals that facilitate the postsynaptic cell's ability to fire an action potential.

How Excitation and Inhibition Interact

Because of the complexity of the brain, a single postsynaptic cell can simultaneously receive excitatory (+) and inhibitory (−) signals from a great number of presynaptic

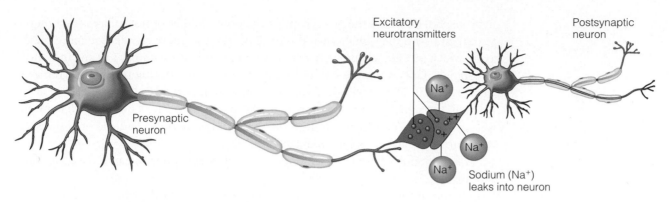

Excitatory
neurotransmitters

Postsynaptic
neuron

Presynaptic
neuron

Na+

Na+

Na+

Sodium (Na+)
leaks into neuron

(a) Excitation. The inside of the neuron is made
more positive; the cell **moves closer** to firing an
action potential.

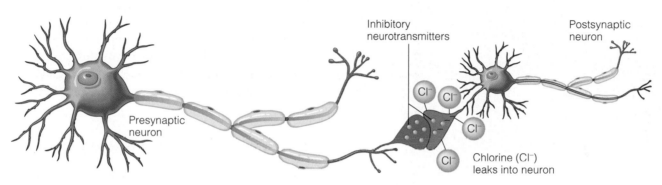

Inhibitory
neurotransmitters

Postsynaptic
neuron

Presynaptic
neuron

Cl−   Cl−

Cl−

Cl−

Chlorine (Cl−)
leaks into neuron

(b) Inhibition. The inside of the neuron is made
more negative; the cell is **less likely** to fire an
action potential.

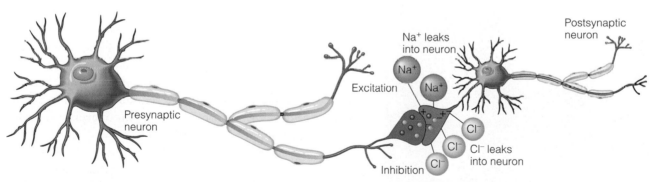

Postsynaptic
neuron

Na+ leaks
into neuron

Na+

Excitation   Na+

Presynaptic
neuron

Cl−

Cl−   Cl− leaks
into neuron

Inhibition   Cl−

(c) Neurons can simultaneously receive **both excitatory**
and **inhibitory** signals from other neurons. The cell will
fire an action potential only if it reaches threshold.

Figure 2.9 **Excitation and Inhibition in the Synapse**

Excitatory neurotransmitters cause sodium (Na+) to enter the postsynaptic cell **(a)**, making it more
positive on the inside and bringing it closer to firing an action potential. Inhibitory neurotransmitters
cause chlorine (Cl−) to enter (or potassium, K+, to leave) **(b)**, making it more negative on the inside
and moving it further away from firing an action potential. A neuron can simultaneously receive both
excitatory and inhibitory signals from other neurons **(c)**, but it will fire an action potential only if it
reaches threshold at −55 mv.

From Gaudin and Jones, Human Anatomy and Physiology, *Fig 11.3a, p. 263. Reprinted by
permission of the author.*

neurons. So, how does the postsynaptic cell know whether or not to fire an action potential and send the signal down the line? All the incoming signals converge on the axon, which acts like an adding machine, summing up the excitatory (+) and inhibitory (−) signals. Only when the sum of the signals moves the resting potential at the axon to threshold (−55 mv) will the neuron fire an action potential. If the threshold is not reached, the signal simply does not go any farther at this time. The axon will continue to sum up the incoming signals until the threshold mark is reached and only then will the neuron fire an action potential (Figure 2.9c).

The function of excitation in the nervous system is pretty clear. Excitation starts actions in the nervous system. But why do we need inhibition in the nervous system?

Application >>

Simply put, inhibition is required to slow down and shut off certain processes in the nervous system. For example, when you bend your arm, certain muscles must be contracted (excited) while other muscles must be relaxed (inhibited). If we only had the capacity for excitation, we would not be able to bend our arms and legs; we would only be able to stiffen them. Also, consider the inhibition of pain signals. If you hit your finger with a hammer, wouldn't you want a process in the brain that stops the transmission of pain signals? We discuss some of the numerous other applications of inhibition in Chapter 3.

Some everyday activities, such as lifting a weight, require both inhibition and excitation in the nervous system. Some muscles must be contracted or excited while others must be relaxed or inhibited to accomplish this feat.

© Network Productions/Index Stock Imagery

Cleaning Up the Synapse: Reuptake

When neurotransmitters cross the synapse to bind with postsynaptic receptor sites, not all of these floating neurotransmitters will be able to find available receptors with which to bind. What happens to the unused neurotransmitters left in the synaptic cleft? Unused neurotransmitters are recycled and returned to the vesicles of the presynaptic neuron by a process called **reuptake.** Reuptake accomplishes two goals. First, it resupplies the vesicles with neurotransmitters so that the next signal sent by the presynaptic neuron can also jump the synapse. Second, reuptake clears the synapse of the unused neurotransmitters, thereby ensuring that just the right amount of excitation or inhibition occurs in the postsynaptic neuron.

When neurotransmitters bind with receptor sites, they cause either excitation or inhibition. Afterward, the molecules either dislodge from the receptor site or are broken down by enzymes and cleared away. If reuptake did not occur, once the receptor sites were cleared out other unattached neurotransmitters in the synaptic cleft would bind with the sites, causing further excitation or inhibition. This duplication of signals could cause confusion or dysfunction in the nervous system. Therefore, reuptake is essential to healthy functioning of our brain and nervous system.

 Application >>

reuptake process through which unused neurotransmitters are recycled back into the vesicles

Later in this chapter, you will see that some beneficial drugs act on the body by altering this process of reuptake. In fact, most drugs have their effect in the body at the synapse. We look more closely at how drugs act at the synapse in Chapter 4. For now, let's turn our attention to the types of neurotransmitters and their basic influence on behavior.

Let's Review!

For a quick check of your understanding of how neurons generate and send signals, answer these questions.

1. Suki's dentist gave her a drug that froze the sodium channels along Suki's neural axons. What is the likely effect of this drug?
   a. Suki's neurons will fire more action potentials than normal.
   b. Suki's neurons will fire stronger action potentials.
   c. Suki's neurons will fire weaker action potentials.
   d. Suki's neurons will fail to fire action potentials.

2. Sabrina has contracted a disease that is destroying her myelin sheath. What effect would you expect this disease to have on the functioning of Sabrina's nervous system?
   a. It will speed up the neural signals traveling through her nervous system.
   b. It will slow down the neural signals traveling through her nervous system.
   c. It won't affect the functioning of her nervous system in any measurable way.
   d. Her nervous system will speed up and slow down in a random fashion.

3. The combination that you use to open a lock is most analogous to the _____.
   a. dendrites of a neuron
   b. receptor sites on the dendrites of a neuron
   c. neurotransmitters released at the synapse
   d. vesicles that hold the neurotransmitters in a neuron

ANSWERS

1. d; 2. b; 3. c

Neurotransmitters: >>>>>>>>>>>>>>>>>>>>> Chemical Messengers in the Brain

Well over 60 different chemical compounds have been identified as possible neurotransmitters (Bradford, 1987), and researchers will probably identify even more. A complete review of all known neurotransmitters is well beyond the scope of this text, but we will look at the ones that most influence our moods and behavior.

The First Neurotransmitter: Acetylcholine

Acetylcholine (Ach) was the first neurotransmitter discovered. Like many neurotransmitters, Ach is found at both excitatory and inhibitory synapses. In the early part of this century, Ach was found to inhibit the action of the heart and to excite skeletal muscles. Today, Ach is thought to play a role in our awareness or consciousness and to have a role in memory (Perry, Walker, Grace, & Perry, 1999). This hypothesized role in memory comes from the discovery that Alzheimer's patients suffer loss of Ach-bearing neurons during the course of their disease. Because Alzheimer's disease is associated with extreme dysfunction of memory and loss of Ach in the brain, it appears that Ach *may* help the brain store and/or process memory. Recall, however, that correlation does not imply causation. Just because the memory loss of Alzheimer's coincides with loss of Ach in the brain does not *prove* that Ach is needed for memory. More controlled experimentation is required before the exact role of Ach in the brain can be uncovered.

Parkinson's Disease and Schizophrenia: Dopamine

Dopamine is primarily inhibitory in the brain, but like most neurotransmitters it is also known to be excitatory. Dopamine appears to influence several processes in the brain,

LEARNING OBJECTIVE

List the major neurotransmitters, and describe the functions they may influence.

acetylcholine (Ach) neurotransmitter related to muscle movement and perhaps consciousness, learning, and memory

« Application

dopamine neurotransmitter that plays a role in movement, learning, and attention

Application >>

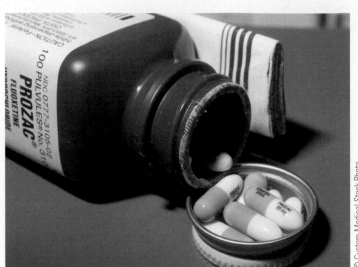

By inhibiting the reuptake of serotonin, Prozac increases the amount of serotonin activity in the synapse, which may reduce depressive symptoms in some patients.

© Custom Medical Stock Photo

including movement, learning, and attention. Parkinson's disease is associated with the loss of neurons in an area of the brain richest in dopamine. Drugs used to treat Parkinsonian symptoms work to indirectly increase the amount of dopamine in the brain. Care must be used in administering such drugs though, because too much dopamine in the brain produces some very troubling symptoms, in particular, symptoms similar to those of schizophrenia.

Schizophrenia is a serious psychiatric disorder (see Chapter 15). People with schizophrenia are unable to think clearly and are often troubled by hallucinations and delusions. Drugs used to treat schizophrenia block the action of dopamine at the synapse. Regulating brain chemistry is not simple. As you might imagine, prolonged use of dopamine-blocking drugs can cause Parkinsonianlike side effects. Think about it. Too little dopamine and one suffers from Parkinson's disease; too much dopamine and the result is schizophrenic symptoms. It appears that healthy functioning requires just the right amount of dopamine in the brain.

Playing a Part in Depression: Serotonin and Norepinephrine

serotonin   neurotransmitter that plays a role in many different behaviors including sleep, arousal, mood, eating, and pain perception

Serotonin is thought to play a role in many different behaviors, including sleep, arousal, mood, eating, and pain perception. It is primarily an inhibitory neurotransmitter and has received a great deal of media attention during the last 10 to 15 years. For the general public, serotonin is perhaps the most widely known neurotransmitter. Since the discovery of serotonin in the 1940s, an understanding of its function has become increasingly important to the understanding of human behavior and mental disorders.

Application   >>

Serotonin has been linked to several mental and behavioral disorders. These disorders seem to be related to having too little serotonin available in the brain. Drugs that increase the action of serotonin at the synapse by preventing its reuptake are called *selective serotonin reuptake inhibitors* (SSRIs). Prozac and other SSRIs have been used to successfully treat depression, eating disorders, compulsive behavior, and pain.

Norepinephrine (NOR) is also primarily inhibitory. It is thought to play a role in regulating sleep, arousal, and mood. Some drugs that alleviate depression have an effect on NOR as well as on serotonin. NOR may also play a role in the development of synapses during childhood and recovery of functioning after brain injury (Phillipson, 1987).

norepinephrine (NOR)   neurotransmitter that plays a role in regulating sleep, arousal, and mood

Inhibiting and Exciting the Brain: GABA and Glutamate

GABA (gamma amino butyric acid)   the body's chief inhibitory neurotransmitter, which plays a role in regulating arousal

Gamma amino butyric acid (GABA) is thought to regulate arousal. It is estimated that one third of all synapses and most inhibitory synapses in the brain use GABA as their neurotransmitter. Therefore, it appears that GABA plays an essential role in normal brain function. Loss of GABA in the brain can produce seizures, because without GABA's inhibitory effects, arousal levels become too high. Some anticonvulsant drugs work by lessening the effects of enzymes that destroy GABA molecules (Purves et al., 1997). Several classes of sedative drugs also work by acting on GABA. These include benzodiazepines such as Valium, barbiturates (Phenobarbital), and alcohol.

glutamate   the chief excitatory neurotransmitter in the brain found at more than 50% of the synapses in the brain

Although GABA is the chief inhibitory neurotransmitter, **glutamate** is the chief excitatory neurotransmitter in the brain. More than 50% of all synapses in the brain use glutamate as a neurotransmitter, and without it many brain processes would not

© Ron Sachs/CNP/Corbis

© Frank Trapper/Corbis

Actor Michael J. Fox and boxer Mohammed Ali both suffer from Parkinson's disease, a degenerative disease that results in decreased dopamine action in the brain, which causes tremors and other neurological symptoms.

take place. Ironically, glutamate can also be a deadly force in the brain. When physical brain damage affects glutamate-bearing neurons, glutamate molecules may be released in large quantities from torn vesicles. Large amounts of extracellular glutamate can cause brain cell death as the neurons literally become excited to death when the glutamate spreads to neighboring neurons and causes them to fire a frenzy of action potentials. It appears that in the brain too much excitation is a very bad thing!

Pain in the Brain: Endorphins and Substance P

Have you ever heard the term *endorphin*? If you have, what was the context? If you are like most people, your first exposure to endorphins was probably in the context of exercise or physical injuries. **Endorphins** are neurotransmitters that are chemically very similar to the class of narcotic drugs called *opiates* (e.g., opium, heroin, morphine, and codeine). Endorphins are released in the central nervous system during times of stress, such as physical exertion or physical injury, to protect us from pain. Endorphins work by blocking the action of another neurotransmitter, *substance P*, which carries pain messages in the central nervous system. When endorphins are released, we feel less pain and a mild sense of euphoria. This is the "runner's high" that long-distance runners often report experiencing. Recently, some evidence suggests that substance P may play a role in carrying signals of "emotional pain" in stressed guinea pigs and that chemicals that block substance P can actually alleviate depressive symptoms (Kramer et al., 1998). (Do you need another reason to begin an exercise program?) In addition to their role as painkillers, endorphins may also play a role in regulating eating behavior and cardiovascular functioning.

We hope that you now have a basic understanding of the actions that take place in your nervous system (see Table 2.1 ◆). Our next step is to take a look at how this neural signaling fits into the structure of the nervous system.

endorphins   neurotransmitter that acts as a natural painkiller

Exercise can lead to the release of endorphins, producing feelings of pleasure and well-being that are sometimes called a "runner's high."

© Mark Adams/SuperStock

◆ Table 2.1

Some Neurotransmitters, Their Functions, and Related Diseases and Clinical Conditions

Neurotransmitter	Functions	Related Diseases and Clinical Conditions
Acetycholine	Excites skeletal muscles Inhibits heart action Memory	Alzheimer's disease
Dopamine	Movement Learning Attention	Parkinson's disease Schizophrenia
Serotonin	Sleep Arousal Mood Eating Pain perception	Depression Obsessive compulsive disorder Some eating disorders Chronic pain
Norepinephrine	Sleep Arousal Mood	Depression
GABA	Chief inhibitor Regulates arousal	Some anxiety disorders Some seizure disorders
Glutamate	Chief excitatory neurotransmitter Many diverse functions	Neural death following head injuries
Endorphins	Suppression of pain Eating Cardiovascular functioning	Some indication of a link to mood
Substance P	Carries pain signals	Some indication of a link to depression

Let's Review!

We've described some of the major neurotransmitters and the roles they may play in our functioning. For a quick check of your understanding, answer these questions.

1. Lamont developed a disease that reduces the amount of serotonin in his brain. What symptoms would you expect Lamont to have?

   a. hallucinations

   b. trouble with his motor skills

   c. symptoms of depression

   d. seizures

2. A loss of which of the following neurotransmitters would *most* likely affect the greatest number of areas in the nervous system?

   a. glutamate

   b. GABA

   c. dopamine

   d. acetylcholine

3. Sasha has been drinking an herbal tea that she feels boosts her body's ability to manufacture acetylcholine. Why do you suppose Sasha is so interested in drinking this tea?

   a. She is trying to improve her memory.

   b. She is trying to treat her depression.

   c. She is hoping it will help her have more energy.

   d. She is hoping it will help her sleep better.

ANSWERS
1.c; 2.a; 3.a

The Structure of the Nervous System > > > >

Our nervous system is a vast, interconnected network of all the neurons in our body. Every single facet of our body's functioning and our behavior is monitored and influenced by the nervous system. The nervous system is arranged in a series of interconnected subsystems, each with its own specialized tasks. Because the brain acts as the command center of our nervous system, it along with the spinal cord is traditionally viewed as being a separate subdivision of the nervous system called the **central nervous system (CNS).** All other components of the nervous system are referred to collectively as the **peripheral nervous system (PNS).** We discuss the CNS in detail later in this chapter when we examine the brain. First, however, let's take a look at the parts of the PNS.

Messages From the Body: The Peripheral Nervous System

The functions of the PNS are twofold. First, the PNS must ensure that the CNS is informed about what is happening inside and outside our body. To this end, the PNS is equipped with **sensory neurons** that convey information to the CNS from the outside world, such as sights and sounds, as well as information from our internal world, such as aches and pains we may experience. Second, the PNS acts out the directives of the CNS. The PNS is equipped with **motor neurons** that carry signals from the CNS to our muscles. For example, when you see a juicy apple, the sensory neurons of your eye send this information upward to the part of the brain that processes visual information. Here the brain recognizes the apple, and you decide to eat the apple. The brain then sends signals downward to the motor neurons of your hand and arm, which, in turn, direct you to reach out and grasp the apple with your hand (Figure 2.10). In this fashion, the sensory pathways send sensory information *to* the spinal cord and brain, and the motor pathways carry "orders" *away* from the brain and spinal cord to the rest of the body. Because motor neurons and sensory neurons send messages in different directions, sensory neurons are often referred to as *afferent neurons* (sending information toward the CNS) and motor neurons are often referred to as *efferent neurons* (sending information away from the CNS). Neurons that process information locally but do not send messages to or from the CNS are referred to as *interneurons*.

Traditionally, psychologists and physiologists have further subdivided the neurons of the PNS into two subsystems: the somatic nervous system and the autonomic nervous system (Purves et al., 1997).

Reaching Out: The Somatic Nervous System

The **somatic nervous system** includes those neurons that control the skeletal muscles of the body (*soma* is Greek for body) and is therefore largely concerned with voluntary actions. Reaching for an apple is an example of a voluntary action that involves the somatic division of the PNS. The CNS made the decision to reach for the apple, then this "order" was sent downward, across efferent pathways of neurons, to the motor neurons of the somatic nervous system that control the muscles of the arm. The arm muscles then react to the orders from the CNS, and you reach for the apple. The functioning of the somatic nervous system enables us to control our bodies in a deliberate and flexible manner.

Although it is important to be able to control body movements, it is equally advantageous to have some processes in the body controlled automatically and involun-

LEARNING OBJECTIVE

Describe the major parts of the nervous system and what types of information they process.

central nervous system (CNS)   the brain and the spinal cord

peripheral nervous system   all of the nervous system except the brain and spinal cord

sensory neurons   neurons that transmit information from the sense organs to the central nervous system

motor neurons   neurons that transmit commands from the brain to the muscles of the body

 Application

somatic nervous system   branch of the peripheral nervous system that governs sensory and voluntary motor action in the body

Figure 2.10 **Afferent, Efferent, and Interneuron Pathways**

Reaching for an apple involves afferent sensory pathways (shown in red) as well as efferent motor pathways (shown in blue) and interneuron pathways (shown in green).

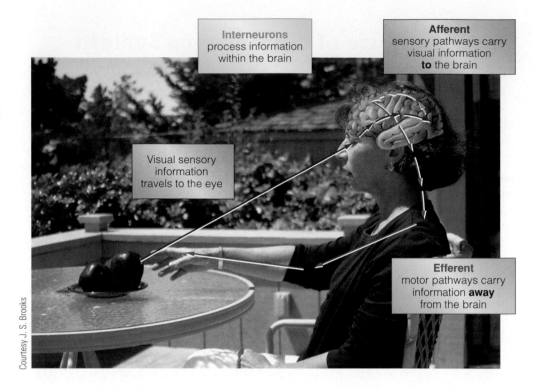

Interneurons process information within the brain

Afferent sensory pathways carry visual information **to** the brain

Visual sensory information travels to the eye

Efferent motor pathways carry information **away** from the brain

Courtesy J. S. Brooks

tarily. What processes in your body do you not have conscious control over? Did you think of heart rate, digestive function, and breathing? These are some of the processes that are controlled by the autonomic division of the PNS.

Involuntary Actions: The Autonomic Nervous System

autonomic nervous system branch of the peripheral nervous system that primarily governs involuntary organ functioning and actions in the body

The neurons of the **autonomic nervous system** control the smooth muscles of the internal organs, the muscles of the heart, and the glands. By automatically regulating organ functions, the autonomic nervous system frees up our conscious resources and enables us to respond quickly and efficiently to the demands placed on us by the environment. Imagine how hard life would be if you had to remember to breathe, tell your heart to beat, and remind your liver to do its job! You would have little energy and attention left for thinking and learning, let alone responding quickly to threatening situations. Thankfully, we have the autonomic nervous system to regulate our organ functions, and it is equipped with separate divisions to help us survive in an ever-changing and sometimes dangerous world. The **parasympathetic** division of the autonomic nervous system operates mainly under conditions of relative calm. The **sympathetic** division of the autonomic nervous system springs into action under conditions of intense stress.

parasympathetic nervous system branch of the autonomic nervous system most active during times of normal functioning

sympathetic nervous system branch of the autonomic nervous system most active during times of danger or stress

The Parasympathetic Nervous System

 Application

As you read this page, it is very likely (unless you find psychology terrifying) that your parasympathetic nervous system is primarily responsible for regulating the functions of your internal organs. When the parasympathetic nervous system is active, heart rate, blood pressure, and respiration are kept at normal levels. Under parasympathetic control, blood is circulated to the digestive tract and other internal organs so that they can function properly, and your pupils are not overly dilated. Your body is calm, and everything is running smoothly (Figure 2.11). But if threat arises in the environment, this will quickly change. In threatening situations, we must react—fast—to save ourselves.

© Renee Lynn/Corbis
© Dave Bartruff/Corbis 

Sympathetic (fight-or-flight response)		Parasympathetic (calmer, relaxed)
Dilates pupils, inhibits tears	Eyes	Contracts pupil, stimulates tears
Inhibits salivation (dry mouth)	Salivary glands	Activates salivation
Dilates bronchi, increases respiration	Lungs	Constricts bronchi, calmer respiration
Accelerates heart rate	Heart	Slows heart rate
Goose bumps; activates sweat glands	Skin, Sweat glands	No goose bumps; inhibits sweat glands
Inhibits activity	Stomach, Intestines, Pancreas, Gallbladder	Stimulates activity
Stimulates glucose release from liver	Liver	Release of glucose slows
Releases adrenaline	Adrenal gland	Stops releasing adrenaline
Contracts blood vessels	Blood vessels of internal organs	Dilates blood vessels
Relaxes bladder; inhibits elimination	Bladder, Bowels	Inhibits bladder; stimulates elimination
Promotes ejaculation and vaginal contractions	Genitals	Stimulates genitals

Figure 2.11 Functions of the Sympathetic and Parasympathetic Systems
The sympathetic and parasympathetic divisions of the autonomic nervous system have different functions on the organs of the body.

During times of stress, the sympathetic system takes over primary regulation of our organ functions from the parasympathetic system.

The Sympathetic Nervous System

The sympathetic nervous system evolved to protect us from danger. When it is activated, heart rate increases, breathing becomes more rapid, blood pressure increases, digestion slows, muscle tissue becomes engorged with blood, the pupils dilate, and the hair on the back of our neck stands up (like a cat confronted by a strange dog). All of these changes help to prepare us (and the cat) to defend our body from threat. For this reason, the actions of the sympathetic nervous system are often referred to as the *fight or flight* response (Figure 2.11). The increased cardiovascular activity quickly pumps oxygenated blood away from internal organs and to the muscles of the arms and legs so that the animal or person can swiftly attack, defend itself, or run away. Once the danger is past, the parasympathetic system resumes control, and heart rate, respiration, blood pressure, and pupil dilation return to normal. Because the sympathetic nervous system plays an important role in our response to stress, it also plays an important role in our health. We explore this connection in Chapter 13.

Let's Review!

We have described the structure of the nervous system, including the central and peripheral nervous systems. For a quick check of your understanding, answer these questions.

1. Juanita is hiking in the woods when she stumbles upon a rattlesnake. Immediately after she saw the snake, which branch of the nervous system was most likely in control of Juanita's internal organ functions?

   a. parasympathetic branch
   b. sympathetic branch
   c. endocrine branch
   d. spinal branch

2. Moving your arm is an example of a behavior that is governed by which branch of the nervous system?

   a. somatic nervous system
   b. autonomic nervous system
   c. sympathetic nervous system
   d. parasympathetic nervous system

3. Sensory is to _____ as motor is to _____.

   a. efferent; afferent
   b. afferent; efferent
   c. inter; efferent
   d. inter; afferent

ANSWERS
1.b; 2.a; 3.b

LEARNING < < < < < < < < <
OBJECTIVE
Be able to locate the hindbrain, midbrain, and forebrain, list their parts, and explain what they do.

hindbrain   primitive part of the brain that comprises the medulla, pons, and cerebellum

Application

forebrain   brain structures including the limbic system, diencephalon, and cortex that govern higher order mental processes

The Brain and Spine:
The Central Nervous System

Brain tissue is composed largely of neurons and glia cells. These cells form the brain structures that enable the brain to affect different aspects of physiological and psychological functioning. Ultimately, these seemingly discrete structures must work together to influence the actions of our body. Before we examine the specific functions of some different brain structures, let's look at how these brain structures are organized.

The structures of the brain are organized into three regions: the hindbrain, the midbrain, and the forebrain. The **hindbrain** sits directly above the spinal column and is named for its position at the bottom of the brain (Figure 2.12). The hindbrain is the most "primitive" part of the brain, involved in the most basic life-sustaining functions in the body. Recall that Jean-Dominique Bauby's stroke occurred in the brainstem. The term *brainstem* refers to a series of brain structures that are essential for life. The hindbrain makes up a good portion of the brainstem. In Bauby's case, the stroke damaged the hindbrain.

The **forebrain** resides in the top part of the skull and regulates higher order processes such as thinking and emotional control. It is the largest region of the brain and includes several subsystems that regulate many emotional, motivational, and cognitive

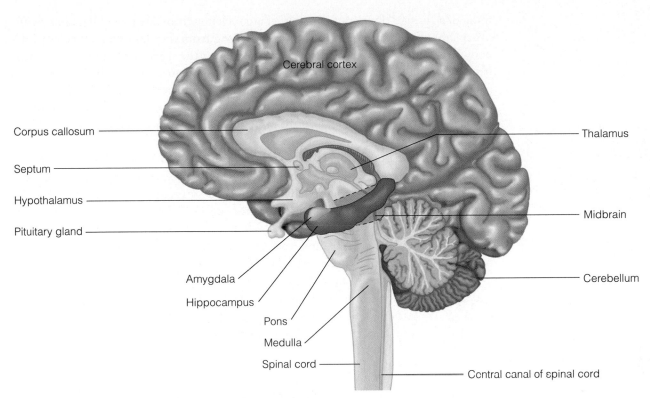

Cerebral cortex

Corpus callosum

Septum

Hypothalamus

Pituitary gland

Amygdala

Hippocampus

Pons

Medulla

Spinal cord

Thalamus

Midbrain

Cerebellum

Central canal of spinal cord

Figure 2.12 **The Brain and Its Structures**

This figure shows the cortex and the subcortical structures of the brain.

processes. Without such a well-developed forebrain, we humans would not have the mental abilities we do: problem solving, thinking, remembering, using language, and so on. Bauby's stroke spared his forebrain, and his "mind" was left intact—recall that he was able to think, feel, and remember. He was even able to write a memoir in his head!

Between the hindbrain and the forebrain resides the **midbrain,** which acts as a conduit between the more basic functions of the hindbrain and the higher order processes of the forebrain. Without the midbrain, the hindbrain could not supply the forebrain with the neural impulses it needs to remain active and to keep us conscious. Now that we have a feel for the overall organization of the brain, let's examine the components and functions of these structures.

The Hindbrain

Simply put, without the functioning of the hindbrain, we would die (Wijdicks, Atkinson, & Okazaki, 2001). The hindbrain consists of three structures: the medulla, the pons, and the cerebellum. The most crucial parts of the hindbrain are the medulla and the pons. The **medulla** sits at the top of the spinal column at the point where the spinal cord enters the base of the skull (Figure 2.12). The medulla regulates heartbeat and respiration, and even minor damage to the medulla can result in death from heart or respiratory failure. It also plays a role in sneezing, coughing, vomiting, swallowing, and digestion.

The **pons** sits above the medulla, where the brainstem bulges inside the skull (Figure 2.12). Like the medulla, the pons is crucial to life. The pons plays a role in respiration, consciousness, sleep, dreaming, facial movement, sensory processes, and the transmission of neural signals from one part of the brain to another. The pons is some-

midbrain   brain structure that connects the hindbrain with the forebrain

medulla   part of the hindbrain that controls basic, life-sustaining functions such as respiration, heart rate, and blood pressure

pons   hindbrain structure that plays a role in respiration, consciousness, sleep, dreaming, facial movement, sensory processes, and the transmission of neural signals from one part of the brain to another

thing of a "bridge" for neural signals that are traveling from one part of the brain to another. In particular, sensory information coming from the right and left sides of the body crosses through the pons before moving on to other parts of the brain. If the pons becomes damaged, the "bridge" is out, and serious impairments result. The pons was probably damaged when Bauby had his stroke. Cases of locked-in syndrome like Bauby's are most often associated with damage in the ventral (facing the throat) regions of the pons (Budak, Llhan, Ozmenoglu, & Komsuoglu, 1994; Gallo & Fontanarosa, 1989; Virgile, 1984).

The final part of the hindbrain is the **cerebellum.** The cerebellum is the large, deeply grooved structure at the base of the brain (Figure 2.12). Although not as crucial to survival as the pons and medulla, the cerebellum is necessary for balance of the body, muscle tone, and performance of motor skills (Seidler et al., 2002). It may also play a critical role in learning motor skills (Hikosaka, Nakamura, Sakai, & Nakamura, 2002). Damage to the cerebellum leads to loss of balance and coordination. Alcohol impairs the functioning of the cerebellum (as well as the functioning of some important forebrain structures), producing the familiar symptoms of staggering, clumsiness, and slowed reaction time. Police officers assess these behaviors when they give motorists a field sobriety test of balance, coordination, and reaction time. You can see why drinking and driving don't mix.

cerebellum   hindbrain structure that plays a role in balance of the body, muscle tone, and coordination of motor movements

RAS (reticular activating system) part of the midbrain that regulates arousal and plays an important role in attention, sleep, and consciousness

Application

The Midbrain

The midbrain structures connect the hindbrain with the more sophisticated forebrain. For psychologists, one of the most interesting midbrain structures is the **reticular activating system (RAS).** The RAS is located near the pons and is a network of neurons that extends from the hindbrain regions into the midbrain. The RAS primarily serves to regulate arousal levels (Kinomura, Larsson, Guiyas, & Roland, 1996). By regulating the arousal levels in the forebrain, the RAS plays an important role in attention, sleep, and consciousness. The RAS functions as a type of "on switch" for the high-level thinking centers of the forebrain. Additionally, the RAS appears to play a role in regulating cardiovascular activity, respiratory functioning, and body movement.

The Forebrain

The forebrain contains several groups of structures that function as subsystems. The structures of the **limbic system** govern emotional and motivational processes. The **diencephalon** contains structures important to sensory processing and motivation. Finally, the wrinkled and folded external surface of the brain, the **cerebral cortex,** governs high-level processes such as cognition and language. In Figure 2.13 you will see that the forebrain is divided into the right and left **cerebral hemispheres.** For the most part, forebrain structures are duplicated in the right and left hemispheres.

The Limbic System

Do you ever wonder why humans experience emotions? What is the value of feeling angry, afraid, or happy? One possible answer is that emotion helps us survive in a dangerous world. Fear may warn us of danger, and anger may help us fight to protect ourselves. Pleasurable feelings such as happiness and love can bind people together and foster cooperation. In this fashion, emotion functions as an early-warning system, and to some

Without the cerebellum we would not be able to accomplish tasks such as learning to ride a bicycle.

© Peter Hvizdak/The Image Works

extent it is a motivating force for our behavior. The series of brain structures collectively called the *limbic system* regulates some of our basic emotional reactions. Three limbic structures are located deep in the central region of the brain, above the hindbrain and beneath the cerebral cortex: the amygdala, the septum, and the hippocampus (Figure 2.12).

The **amygdala** is an almond-shaped structure located almost directly behind our temples. The amygdala governs the emotions of fear and aggression (Sah, Faber, Lopez De Armentia, & Power, 2003). Animal research has revealed that when certain parts of the amygdala are damaged, animals become very tame and impossible to provoke to aggression. When other areas of the amygdala are damaged, animals become extremely vicious. In a few cases, researchers have electrically stimulated the amygdalae of humans as part of experimental treatments for brain disorders. One early study found that electrically stimulating the amygdala in a female patient produced in her a nearly uncontrollable urge to attack the researcher (King, 1961).

More recent investigations have indicated that the amygdala may play a role in the way we perceive and respond to emotion-evoking stimuli (Adolphs, 2002; Isenberg et al., 1999). For example, surgical lesions were made in a woman's amygdalae in an attempt to lessen her epileptic seizures. As a result, she lost the ability to perceive the emotional tone of others' voices. She could no longer recognize angry and frightened vocal intonations although she could hear and comprehend spoken words (Scott, Young, Calder, & Hellawell, 1997). In another study, Adolphs and colleagues (Adolphs, Tranel, & Damasio, 1998) found that three subjects whose amygdalae had been destroyed could not make accurate judgments about others' mood states by looking at their facial expressions. Studies like these suggest that the amygdala may play an essential role in helping us size up social situations and, in turn, regulate our emotional reactions to these situations.

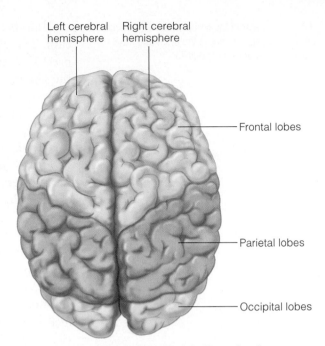

Left cerebral hemisphere   Right cerebral hemisphere

Frontal lobes

Parietal lobes

Occipital lobes

Figure 2.13 The Cerebral Hemispheres
The cerebrum is divided into the right and left hemispheres. The outside covering of the hemispheres, the cortex, is where the higher-order processing in the brain takes place.

 Application

The amygdala plays a role in emotions such as fear and aggression.

© Jose Luis Pelaez, Inc./Corbis

limbic system   system of structures including the amygdala, septum, and hippocampus that govern certain aspects of emotion, motivation, and memory

diencephalon   system in the forebrain that includes the thalamus and hypothalamus

cerebral cortex   thin, wrinkled outer covering of the brain in which very high-level processes such as thinking, planning, language, interpretation of sensory data, and coordination of sensory and motor information take place

cerebral hemispheres   right and left sides of the brain that to some degree govern different functions in the body

amygdala   part of the limbic system that plays a role in our emotions of fear and aggression

septum   part of the limbic system that seems to be a pleasure center in the brain and may play a role in addictive behavior

Another limbic system structure important to emotional functioning is the **septum.** The septum is above the amygdala, in the middle front region of the brain (Figure 2.12). Like the amygdala, the septum is thought to play a role in fear and anger, but the septum first caught researchers' attention for the role it appears to play in our experience of pleasure. When rats were rigged so that they could deliver a weak electrical current to the septal area of their brain by pressing a bar on the side of their cage, all the rats wanted to do was press the bar (Olds & Milner, 1954). The rats wouldn't eat, sleep, or have sex with other rats. They were only interested in pressing the bar. From the rats' behavior, Olds and others have concluded that stimulation of the septum causes pleasurable feelings. This could mean that the septum acts as a *pleasure center* in the brain, an idea that is consistent with the research that has been done on humans.

Humans seem to react similarly to rats to septal stimulation. Humans who have experienced septal stimulation report pleasurable feelings that resemble those felt during sexual arousal. In one case study, Heath (1972) fitted a patient with a device that enabled the patient to stimulate his own septum in an attempt to ease the symptoms of an emotional disorder. Once fitted with the device, the man quickly fell into a pattern of incessant self-stimulation, stimulating his septum more than a thousand times an hour. Eventually the researchers had to remove the device. Such animal and human studies intrigue researchers because the resulting behavior appears similar to the behavior of drug-addicted persons. Just as a crack addict loses interest in everything but smoking crack, both the animals and humans lost interest in everything but self-stimulating their septal regions. Research is now being done to see what role brain chemicals that act on receptor sites in the septum may play in addictions (Erdtmann-Vourliotis, Mayer, Ammon, Riechert, & Holt, 2001; Navarro et al., 2001).

hippocampus   part of the brain that plays a role in the transfer of information from short- to long-term memory

The **hippocampus** is the final structure of the limbic system that we will describe. Like the amygdala and the septum, hippocampal regions are found in both hemispheres of the brain. The hippocampus is a long, curved structure shaped somewhat like a sea horse (Figure 2.12). The word hippocampus comes from the Greek *hippokampos*, which means sea horse. The hippocampus appears to play a crucial role in the processes of learning and memory.

Much of what we know about the function of the hippocampus is from case studies of people who have suffered damage to the hippocampus as a result of disease, injury, or surgical procedures. One of the first case studies of such damage occurred in the early 1950s. Scoville and Milner (1957) reported the case of a young man named H. M. who had severe, uncontrollable epilepsy. H. M.'s epilepsy did not respond to medication and threatened his health as well as his lifestyle. In a last-ditch effort to reduce the severity of H. M.'s seizures, doctors decided to take the drastic measure of destroying part of H. M.'s brain with surgically produced lesions. The doctors cut neurons in the limbic system, hoping to check the rampant electrical current that occurs when an epileptic has a seizure. The surgery performed on H. M. destroyed his hippocampus.

The surgery did reduce the intensity of H. M.'s seizures, but it also appeared to produce some devastating and unexpected side effects. Shortly after the surgery, it became apparent that H. M. was suffering from *anterograde amnesia*, the inability to store *new* memories. H. M. could hold information in consciousness the way we briefly hold a phone number in mind while we dial, and his memory for events that occurred prior to the surgery remained intact. But H. M. was unable to form new memories for concepts and events. He would forget conversations seconds after they occurred. He was unable to learn new facts. Oddly, though, H. M. could store new motor skills (for example, he could learn new dance steps), but later he would have no recollection of having ever executed the new skill. Imagine waking up one day and knowing how to do a dance that you don't remember ever having danced!

© Corbis

London cab drivers, who must memorize complicated street patterns, have been shown to have larger than average hippocampal regions. More research is needed, however, to determine the significance of this finding.

It appears from H. M.'s case that the hippocampus plays an essential role in forming memories of concepts and events but that it does not play a necessary role in learning new skills. Should we assume that H. M.'s case proves conclusively that the hippocampus is needed for normal memory functioning? The answer, of course, is "No," because one case study proves nothing. Have other studies supported the findings of the H. M. case study?

Since H. M.'s surgery, a large number of subsequent case studies and controlled animal experiments have supported the hypothesis that the hippocampus is important to learning and memory. For example, one study used brain-imaging techniques to compare the hippocampi of London taxi drivers to those of normal control subjects. The study found that certain areas of the hippocampus were enlarged in the taxi drivers, but not in the control subjects. Furthermore, the amount of time a participant had been a taxi driver correlated with the size of certain areas of his or her hippocampus. This *might* indicate that certain areas of the hippocampus enlarge when we engage in memorizing complicated maps, such as a taxi driver would need to do (Maguire et al., 2000). Keep in mind, however, that this research is merely correlational in nature. Until we have conducted controlled experiments, it would be premature to conclude that the differences seen in the taxi drivers' hippocampi were *caused* by their experiences on the job.

The Diencephalon

The diencephalon consists of the **thalamus** and the **hypothalamus.** Their names are similar, but the thalamus and the hypothalamus have considerably different functions in the forebrain. The thalamus plays a role in the attention we pay to sensory stimuli (Michael, Boucart, Degreef, & Goefroy, 2001), and it functions as a relay station for information coming from our senses to the brain (see Chapter 3). Most of the input from our senses first travels to the thalamus before being sent on to the appropriate part of

thalamus   part of the diencephalon that functions as a sensory relay station in the brain

hypothalamus   part of the diencephalon that plays a role in maintaining homeostasis in the body involving sleep, body temperature, sexual behavior, thirst, and hunger; also the point where the nervous system intersects with the endocrine system

Application ≫

homeostasis an internal state of equilibrium in the body

the cortex for further processing. For example, when we look at an apple, our eyes take in the information and convert it into action potentials. These neural signals then travel to the region of the thalamus that handles visual information. The thalamus then relays the neural signals bearing the visual information to the back part of the cortex, which interprets the *meaning* of the visual information. Once the visual information finally reaches the cortex, we become aware that we are looking at an apple. So, what would happen if we suffered severe damage to our thalamus? We might be unable to make sense out of sensory input from the environment. Our eyes and ears would work, but we would probably be unable to interpret the meaning of these sensations because the neural signals would not reach the thinking parts of our brain.

Nestled below the thalamus is the hypothalamus (the prefix *hypo* means "below"). The hypothalamus maintains **homeostasis** in the body, a state of internal equilibrium across a variety of bodily systems. In maintaining homeostasis, the hypothalamus is responsible for monitoring and regulating body temperature, thirst, hunger, sleep, autonomic nervous system functioning, and some sexual and reproductive functions. The hypothalamus also serves as a point of connection between the nervous system and the endocrine system. We will have more to say about endocrine function in coming sections, but for now you should note that the hypothalamus can change hormone levels in the blood stream by communicating directly with the endocrine system. (We will talk about the hypothalamus again when we discuss motivation in Chapter 8.) To maintain homeostasis, the hypothalamus must ultimately motivate us to engage in certain behaviors. For example, when our body needs fuel, the hypothalamus motivates us with hunger. When we need sleep, the hypothalamus makes us sleepy, and we are motivated to go to bed. No other part of the nervous system plays a more central role in physiological motivation. Without the hypothalamus, we would not know when to engage in the behaviors that keep our bodily systems in balance.

The Cortex

The most noticeable structure on the external surface of the brain is the cerebral cortex, or simply the cortex. The cortex is the thin (approximately 2 mm thick), wrinkled layer of tissue that covers the outside of the cerebral hemispheres. It appears gray in color due to the absence of myelin on the axons of the cortex (Figure 2.14). The cortex is arguably the most sophisticated part of the brain and is responsible for the highest levels of processing: cognition and mental processes such as planning, decision making, perception, and language. It is the cortex that gives us our humanness. It is no coincidence that the human cortex is the most developed of all known creatures, and that we humans also have the most highly developed cognitive skills of all known

Figure 2.14 Cortex of a Human Brain and a Cat Brain

Note how much more convoluted or folded the human brain is compared to the cat brain. Many of the higher order processes that humans engage in (language, thinking, and so forth) are processed in the cortex.

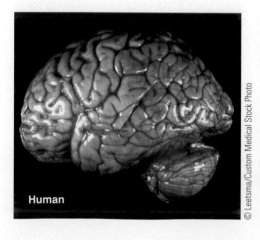

Human

© Leetsma/Custom Medical Stock Photo

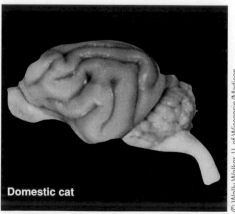

Domestic cat

© Wally Welker, U. of Wisconsin/Madison

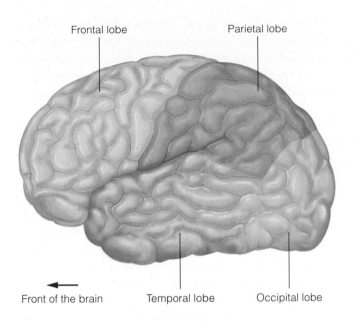

(a) Lobes of the brain (left hemisphere)

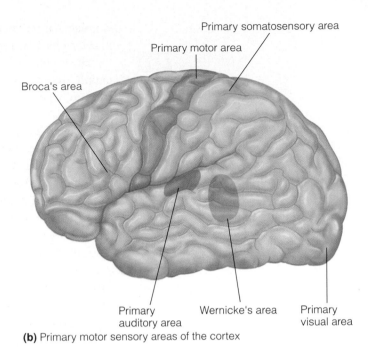

(b) Primary motor sensory areas of the cortex

Figure 2.15 The Human Brain

(a) The lobes of the brain. (b) The language centers of the brain are found in the left hemisphere. Wernicke's area in the left temporal lobe allows us to comprehend speech. Broca's area in the left frontal lobe allows us to produce speech.

From Gaudin and Jones, Human Anatomy and Physiology, *Fig 12.2, p. 294. Reprinted by permission of the author.*

species. Compare the photographs in Figure 2.14. Notice how the human cortex is very folded and convoluted, whereas the cat's brain is not very convoluted. The folds allow for more cortical surface area within the confines of the skull cavity. A cat has proportionately less cortical area than a human does, and this reduction in cortex translates into fewer cognitive abilities for the cat.

Lateralization and the Lobes of the Cortex

The human cortex is divided into four distinct physical regions called *lobes*. These are the **frontal lobe,** the **parietal lobe,** the **occipital lobe,** and the **temporal lobe** (Figure 2.15a). The lobes of the cortex are structurally symmetrical in both hemispheres of the brain, meaning that the brain has both right and left frontal lobes, right and left temporal lobes, and so on. However, the functions of the right and left lobes are often somewhat different.

So, isn't the brain a seamless whole? Functions are *lateralized,* or found in only one hemisphere of the brain, for a couple of reasons. First, the lobes of the brain tend to process information coming from and going to the opposite side of the body. Thus the right hemispheric lobes govern the left side of the body, and the left hemispheric lobes govern the right side of the body. Although *contralateral* wiring is the norm in the brain, some neural pathways carry information to and from the body to the same hemisphere of the brain.

frontal lobe cortical area directly behind the forehead that plays a role in thinking, planning, decision making, language, and motor movement

parietal lobes cortical areas on the top sides of the brain that play a role in touch and certain cognitive processes

occipital lobe cortical area at the back of the brain that plays a role in visual processing

temporal lobes cortical areas directly below our ears that play a role in auditory processing and language

The Left and Right Hemispheres

There is evidence to suggest that the right and left hemispheres process somewhat different types of information (Stephan et al., 2003). For example, most people process

Application ⟫

Wernicke's area a region of the left temporal lobe that plays a role in the comprehension of speech

Broca's area a region in the left frontal lobe that plays a role in the production of speech

language largely in the left hemisphere. Yet some people have major language centers in the right hemisphere, and some have major language centers in both hemispheres. For the average person, language is located in the left hemisphere. Because of this, when people suffer major damage to the left hemisphere (as from a stroke), their ability to use language often suffers. Two examples illustrate this hemispheric specialization of language.

When people suffer damage to **Wernicke's area** in the left temporal lobe, they are unable to understand spoken language. When damage is severe in **Broca's area** in the left frontal lobe (Figure 2.15b), patients are unable to produce understandable speech (Geschwind, 1975; Geschwind & Levitsky, 1968). When the damage is confined to the right side of the brain, patients usually remain able to understand and produce speech, but they have some difficulty processing certain types of spatial information (such as judging the distance between two objects). Differences in the linguistic and spatial processing of the left and right hemispheres once led scientists to broadly conclude that the hemispheres of the brain processed very different categories of information: they surmised that the left hemisphere processed verbal information and the right hemisphere processed spatial information.

However, more recent studies have suggested that the left and right hemispheres of the brain may not divide up their functions as neatly as once thought. In their review of the literature, Beeman and Chairello (1998) report that the right hemisphere seems to also process certain aspects of language. In particular, it seems to play a role in processing the subtleties of language. These include the phonological qualities of speech (the sound of speech), the visual details of printed words (the font they are printed in), and the unusual meanings of words (for example, the use of the word "dog" to represent an unscrupulous person instead of an animal). Newer research indicates that both hemispheres process different aspects of spatial information (see Chabris & Kosslyn, 1998, for a review). To sum up, we are coming to understand that the hemispheres perform complementary functions. Both sides of the brain work together to enable us to fully understand language and visual perception.

The Corpus Callosum

corpus callosum a thick band of neurons that connect the right and left hemispheres of the brain

Whether the hemispheres process different information or merely different aspects of the same information, they must have some means of coordinating the information they process. The **corpus callosum** is a dense band of neurons that sits just below the cortex along the midline of the brain (Banich & Heller, 1998; Figure 2.12). This band physically connects the right and left cortical areas and ensures that each hemisphere "knows" what the other hemisphere is doing. The corpus callosum passes information back and forth between the right and left hemispheres, allowing us to integrate these somewhat independent functions. Without the corpus callosum, the right and left cortices would function independently and in ignorance of each other.

Some studies of gender differences in the brain have suggested that certain areas of the corpus callosum may be larger in women than in men. Other areas of the brain have also been shown to differ for women and men. For an in-depth look at gender differences in the brain, read It's a Diverse World.

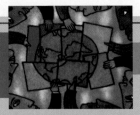

Male–Female Differences in the Brain

A popular belief is that men and women are quite different from one another. Indeed, you don't have to look too far to find authors and television personalities who speak as if men and women are from separate planets. Are we really all that different? Scientists, including psychologists, have been grappling with this question for many years: Does the brain of a man differ from the brain of a woman? As you will see, it has been difficult to conclusively show that male–female differences exist in the brain, and it has been even harder to say what, if anything, these differences mean when it comes to our behavior.

One of the most established gender differences in the brain is that men tend to have larger brains than women do. When men and women of equal body size are compared, the male brain is on average 100 grams heavier than the female brain (Ankey, 1992). Furthermore, evidence suggests that males have billions more cortical cells than females do (Pakkenberg & Gundersen, 1997). But the significance of these differences remains a mystery. No clear pattern of behavioral differences has been directly related to gender differences in brain size or number of neurons.

Another fairly well-established gender difference in the brain is seen in the hypothalamus. Certain regions of the hypothalamus tend to be smaller in females than in males (Swaab & Hofman, 1995). Again, it is too early to tell exactly how this translates to differences in male and female behavior, but some recent research suggests that this may play a role in sexual arousal. In one study, males became more sexually aroused by erotica, and this arousal coincided with significant activation of the hypothalamus. The female participants reported less arousal, and there was no significant activation of the hypothalamus (Karama et al., 2002).

The way in which the two hemispheres are connected may also vary somewhat with gender. The thick band of neurons that enables the hemispheres to communicate, the corpus callosum, appears to be somewhat different in male and female brains (Delacoste-Utamsing & Holloway,

1982). In particular, the back part of the corpus callosum, an area called the *splenum,* appears to be slightly larger in females than it is in males. However, this size difference is controversial because it is most likely to be found by researchers who correct their data for the fact that males tend to have larger brains (Driesen & Raz, 1995). In fact, some have suggested that this size difference may have less to do with gender and more to do with brain size itself. Smaller brains may tend to have larger corpus callosa regardless of gender. This could explain why many women tend to have larger corpus callosa (Leonard, 1997), but still not indicate a gender difference in the size of the corpus callosum. In other words, men with small brains may also have large corpus callosa.

A clearer picture is seen in another brain structure that allows for communication across the hemispheres. The *anterior commissure* tends to be larger in females, and this size difference is found even when researchers do not correct their data to account for the smaller brain size of females. Similarly, the *massa intermedia,* a structure that connects the two sides of the thalamus, also seems to be larger in women (Allen & Gorski, 1991). It appears that women may have somewhat more connections between the left and right hemispheres of the brain, but what does this imply about our behavior? To date we have no clear answers for what this difference means. Some speculate that because women have more connections between hemispheres, the functioning of the female brain is less lateralized, or more integrated (Reite et al., 1995). Others argue that increased communication between hemispheres may actually increase lateralization in the brain (Kimura, 2000).

Where does all this research leave us? We know that compared to the average male brain, the average female brain is smaller, has fewer cortical neurons, a smaller hypothalamus, and more connections between hemispheres in specific areas of the brain. We don't know yet how these differences translate into gender differences in behavior. Correlating brain structure with behavior is a tricky task at times.

The Split-Brain

Physicians have at times willfully disrupted communication between the hemispheres by destroying the corpus callosum in the human brain. Such a drastic measure is taken in cases where people suffer from severe, uncontrollable epilepsy. In severe epilepsy, aberrant electrical activity can build up in one hemisphere and spread across the corpus callosum to engulf the opposite hemisphere. This short-circuiting of both hemispheres produces a severe, life-threatening seizure called a *grand mal seizure*. If drugs cannot control the seizures, surgery may be performed to cut the corpus callosum and thereby contain the short-circuiting to one hemisphere only. The patient still suffers from seizures, but they are not as severe. Patients who have had this surgery are referred to as having **split-brains** because their hemispheres are no longer connected by neural pathways. Split-brain patients provide scientists with an opportunity to study the lateralization of the brain.

Working with split-brain patients, researchers have a chance to study the functioning of each hemisphere independent of the other. For example, split-brain research helped researchers conclude that the left hemisphere enables us to produce speech. Researcher Michael Gazzaniga (1967) briefly flashed pictures of familiar objects to the right and left visual fields of split-brain patients and asked them to identify the objects (Figure 2.16). When an object is briefly presented to our right peripheral field of vision, the resulting visual information is sent directly to the left hemisphere of the brain.

split-brain a brain with its corpus callosum severed; sometimes done to control the effects of epilepsy in patients who do not respond to other therapies

Figure 2.16 **A Typical Split-Brain Study**

In a typical split-brain experiment, an image is flashed to a split-brained person's right or left visual field, and she is asked to identify the object in the image. When the image is flashed to the split-brained person's right visual field, she is able to identify it; but when it is flashed to her left visual field, she is unable to identify it because the information cannot travel to the language centers in the left hemisphere.

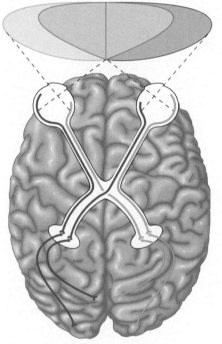

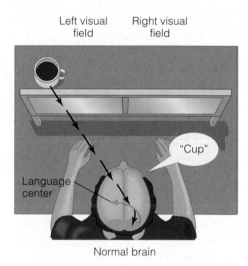

(a) Visual pathways in the brain

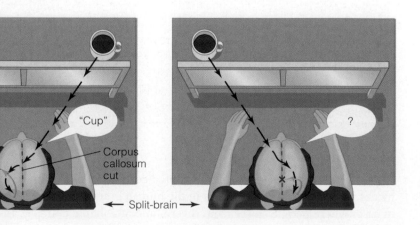

(b) Split brain

Because Broca's area is in the left hemisphere for most people, Gazzaniga found that the average split-brained person could verbally identify the object. But what about an object presented to the patient's left peripheral field of vision? When an object is briefly shown on our far-left side, the resulting visual information is sent directly to the right hemisphere of the brain. Recall that most people do not have a Broca's area in their right hemisphere. In a normal brain, the information travels from the right hemisphere across the corpus callosum to the language centers in the left hemisphere. However, in a split-brain individual this cannot happen. Without the corpus callosum, Gazzaniga's split-brain patients could not transmit the knowledge of what they were seeing to the language centers in their left hemisphere. The right brain knew what the objects were, but it could not inform the "speaking" left brain! Predictably, the split-brain patients were unable to name the objects they saw in their left visual fields. Split-brain research has helped us to begin sorting out the relative contributions that the right and left hemispheres make to everyday cognitive processes.

Within the different lobes of the brain there is also specialization. Let's take a look.

The Specialization of Function in the Lobes of the Cortex

About 25% of the total surface area of the cortex is dedicated to motor and sensory functions such as vision, hearing, movement, and tactile sensation. Specific motor-sensory areas can be found in all the lobes of the brain (frontal, parietal, occipital, and temporal). The remaining 75% of the cortical area is thought to be devoted to higher order processes that involve the integration of information such as thinking, planning, decision making, language, and so on. Collectively, this 75% is referred to as the **association cortex** because these areas are presumed to involve the association of information from the motor-sensory areas of the cortex.

association cortex   areas of the cortex involved in the association or integration of information from the motor-sensory areas of the cortex

We don't yet have a complete understanding of the functions of specific areas of the association cortex. Often, damage to the association areas produces general changes and deficits in behavior. However, stimulation of specific areas of the association cortex does not usually lead to specific, predictable physical reactions. It is thought that the association cortex plays a role in general cognition, such as planning and decision making. Where applicable, we will discuss the known functions of the association areas for the specific lobes of the brain.

The Frontal Lobe

The frontal lobe is the area of the cortex that lies closest to the forehead (Figure 2.15b). Much of the frontal lobe is association cortex. We know more about the association areas of the frontal lobe than any other lobes. Broca's area in the association area of the left frontal lobe is, as previously mentioned, involved in the production of speech. It also appears that the frontal lobe association areas play a role in cognitive processes such as problem solving, judgment, planning and executing behavior, and certain aspects of personality.

These cognitive functions are illustrated in a famous case study from the history of psychology. In 1848 a railway worker named Phineas Gage suffered severe trauma to his *prefrontal cortex* (the association area at the very front part of the frontal lobe) when a metal rod was shot through his head in an explosion. The rod entered his left cheek and shot out of the top of his head. Although he survived his injuries, they resulted in some dramatic personality changes. Whereas Gage had been a calm, responsible man prior to his injuries, he became impulsive, emotionally volatile, and irresponsible afterward. Because the prefrontal cortex is important for the regulation of emotion (Davidson,

Putman, & Larson, 2000), the damage to Gage's brain robbed him of his ability to control his emotions, make good judgments, and execute planned behaviors (Damasio, Grabowski, Frank, Galaburda, & Damasio, 1994). Phineas Gage was no longer himself, but he could still move and speak because the motor-sensory areas of his frontal lobe were undamaged.

motor cortex   a strip of cortex at the back of the frontal lobe that governs the execution of motor movement in the body

Application ⟫

At the back of the frontal lobe (behind the prefrontal cortex) lies the **motor cortex,** a narrow band of cortex that allows us to execute motor movements. The motor cortex on the right side of the brain affects movement on the left side of the body, and vice versa. Additionally, specific points along the motor cortex correspond to particular points on the body. Figure 2.17 is a rendering of a *homunculus,* or a humorous depiction of the mapping of body parts onto their appropriate motor and sensory cortical points. If stimulation were applied to these points along the motor cortex, the result would be movement of the corresponding body part. During brain surgery, surgeons may apply electrical stimulation to the brain before making incisions in the cortical tissue so that the patient's subsequent movements or other responses indicate where their instruments are located along the motor cortex (and other areas). Without such precautionary measures, a physician could accidentally cause paralysis in the patient with a misplaced cut along the motor cortex.

The Parietal Lobe

As with the frontal lobe, much of the parietal lobe is association cortex, but we know less about the specific functions of these association areas. One possibility is that parts of the parietal lobe may play a role in reading (Newman & Tweig, 2001). Damage to the

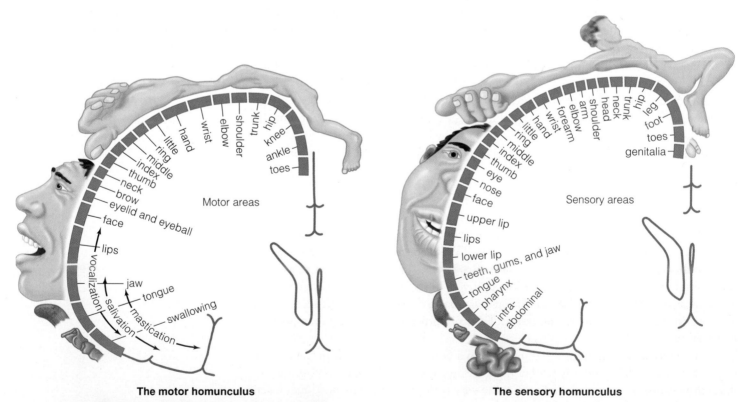

The motor homunculus   The sensory homunculus

Figure 2.17 **Motor and Sensory Homunculi**
Homunculi are humorous depictions of the localization of function on the cortex.

From Penfield and Rasmussen, The Cerebral Cortex of Man, © 1950 Macmillan Library Reference. Renewed 1978 by Theodore Rasmussen. Reprinted by permission of The Gale Group.

lower areas of the parietal lobe can be associated with deficits in reading ability (Diamond, Scheibel, & Elson, 1985). We have a better understanding of the role that the parietal lobe plays in sensation. A thin strip of the parietal lobe plays a role in our sense of touch, pressure, and pain. This strip, called the **somatosensory cortex,** lies directly behind the motor cortex, along the leading edge of the parietal lobe (Figure 2.15b). The somatosensory cortex is wired much like the motor cortex, and specific points along the somatosensory cortex correspond to particular points on the body (Figure 2.17). Damage to the somatosensory cortex often results in numbness of the corresponding body part.

somatosensory cortex   a strip of cortex at the front of the parietal lobe that governs our sense of touch

The Occipital Lobe

The occipital lobe of the brain is located at the very back of the skull, above the cerebellum (Figure 2.15b). Much of the occipital lobe is dedicated to processing visual information. The **visual cortex** of the occipital lobe is composed of layers of tissue that contain long axonal fibers. An action potential is stimulated in specialized cells of the visual cortex when our eyes see specific types of visual stimuli in the outside world. For instance, some cells only begin to fire when we see lines, and other cells only fire when we see circular shapes. Like a computer, our brain integrates all the incoming neural impulses from these specialized cells in the visual cortex to enable us to perceive what we are viewing. Without the operation of the visual cortex, our brain could not make sense of what our eyes see. Damage to the visual cortex can result in partial or complete blindness. In cases of visual cortex damage, blindness may occur even though the eyes are functioning properly. This would be like taking a photograph but not developing the film correctly. The camera (the eye) does its job, but we fail to develop the picture (the function of the cortex).

visual cortex   a region of cortex found at the back of the occipital lobe that processes visual information in the brain

The Temporal Lobe

The temporal lobe is in front of the occipital lobe and just below the parietal and frontal lobes—roughly behind our ears inside the skull. Not surprisingly, one of the major functions of the temporal lobe is the processing of auditory information or hearing. The temporal lobe areas devoted to hearing are the **auditory cortex,** located on the upper edge of the temporal lobe (Figure 2.15b). In addition to the auditory cortex, the left temporal lobe of most people contains Wernicke's area. As we've already seen, Wernicke's area is responsible for the comprehension of speech. Persons who have suffered major damage to Wernicke's area often cannot understand the meaning of spoken words. They hear the words, but they can't make sense of them.

auditory cortex   a region of cortex found in the temporal lobe that governs our processing of auditory information in the brain

The association areas of the temporal lobe are also very important to everyday functioning. The inner surface of the temporal lobes (the surface that adjoins the limbic system structures) appears to be very important to the processing of memory. This shouldn't be surprising because this area of the temporal lobe has direct connections with the hippocampus. Other association areas of the temporal lobe are thought to play a role in the integration of diverse sensory information. For example, the temporal lobe helps with the integration of the sight, texture, and sound generated as we bite into an apple (Diamond et al., 1985).

Now that you have learned about the structure and function of the brain, we hope that you are suitably impressed. We have merely begun to explore the function of our nervous system in this chapter, and scientists are far from completely understanding this amazing system. As research continues, scientists learn more about how our physiology influences our thoughts and behaviors. Luckily researchers have a great deal of modern technology to help them learn about the brain.

Let's Review!

This section dealt with the structure and function of the hindbrain, midbrain, and forebrain. The hindbrain is primarily involved in life-sustaining functions, and the midbrain connects the hindbrain with the sophisticated structures of the forebrain. The function of the cortex and lateralization of the cortex were also described. For a quick check of your understanding, answer these questions.

1. Damage to which of the following brain structures would be *most* likely to cause death?
   a. frontal lobe
   b. amygdala
   c. medulla
   d. hippocampus

2. Billy suffered a stroke on the left side of his brain. Most of his left frontal lobe was destroyed. What symptoms would you *most* expect to see in Billy as a result of this damage?

   a. Paralysis on the right side of his body and an inability to speak
   b. Paralysis on the right side of his body and an inability to understand speech
   c. Paralysis of his left leg, partial deafness, and stuttering
   d. Paralysis on the left side of his body and an inability to understand speech

3. Which of the following brain structures is most closely associated with the endocrine system?
   a. septum
   b. hypothalamus
   c. thalamus
   d. midbrain

ANSWERS

1. c; 2. a; 3. b

LEARNING OBJECTIVE < < < < < < < < <

Describe brain-imaging techniques and other ways we can study the brain, and explain their advantages and limitations.

Techniques for Studying the Brain

Psychologists have many methods for studying the brain. Some of these procedures are invasive (they require surgery), others are noninvasive. We begin by looking at the techniques used to examine living brain tissue. These techniques are often used in cases like Jean-Dominique Bauby's to diagnosis neurological problems. Many of these techniques are also very useful to researchers who wish to know more about the structure and function of the brain. We discuss eight such techniques: CAT scans, MRIs, PET and SPECT scans, fMRIs, angiograms, and EEGs and ERPs.

CAT Scans: Computer Imaging of the Brain

CAT scan (computerized axial tomography)   imaging technique that involves passing many X ray beams through the brain and measuring the intensities of the beams as they exit the head

A **computerized axial tomography (CAT) scan** is an imaging technique that involves passing many X ray beams through the brain and measuring the intensities of the beams as they exit the head. For a CAT scan, patients are placed in a machine with a revolving X ray camera that rotates around the circumference of the patient's head. As the machine rotates, it passes X ray beams through the head at regular intervals. The skull and brain tissue slow down the X rays. Because denser material will weaken the beams more than less dense material, the computer part of the CAT scan machine uses the exit intensity of the beams to determine the relative density of material that each beam passed through on its way through the head. The computer uses this information to create a picture of the brain (Figure 2.18). CAT scans are used to diagnose tumors, strokes, and other brain diseases. CAT scan imaging has been valuable to psychologists for correlating certain types of brain abnormalities with particular behavioral symptoms. By making these correlations, scientists have gained new understanding of the function of some specific brain structures (Raichle, 1987).

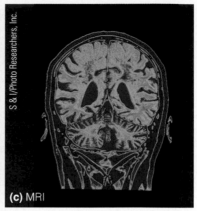
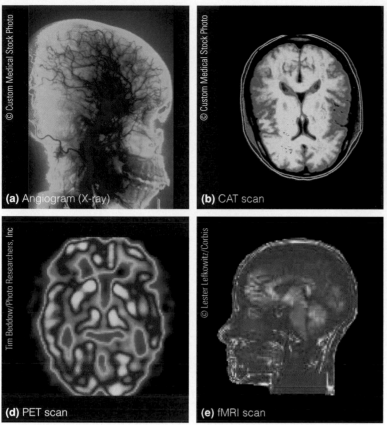

(a) Angiogram (X-ray)

(b) CAT scan

(c) MRI

(d) PET scan

(e) fMRI scan

Figure 2.18 Measuring the Brain
a. An angiogram shows the blood vessels of the brain.
b. A CAT scan shows the structure of the brain.
c. An MRI shows the structure of the brain in great detail.
d. A PET scans shows which areas of the brain are using the most glucose.
e. An fMRI shows which areas of the brain are most active.

MRI: Details of Brain Structure

Magnetic resonance imaging (MRI) scans are similar to CAT scans in that they yield a structural picture of the brain. The full technology behind MRI is extremely complicated and beyond the scope of this text. In brief, during an MRI, a patient is placed in a very strong magnetic field that excites the atoms in the body. When the atomic nuclei are excited, they emit specific energies that are then used by a computer to construct a very detailed picture of the body part being analyzed. Development of MRI technology has great benefits for medicine and brain research because the MRI yields extremely detailed pictures of the body. MRI images can identify structures in the brain that are as small as 1 to 2 millimeters (Raichle, 1994). Although MRI images are far superior to CAT scan images, CAT scans are used in cases where MRI is prohibited. (For example, people who have internal metal appliances, such as pins used to repair bone fractures, cannot have MRI due to the magnetic field involved.)

MRI (magnetic resonance imaging) a very strong magnetic field excites the atoms in the body, which emit specific energies that a computer converts into a very detailed picture of the body part being analyzed

 Application

PET Scans and SPECT Scans: The Brain in Action

Unlike a CAT scan or a standard structural MRI, a **positron emission tomography (PET) scan** can give researchers a picture of the brain in action. PET scans indicate which part of the brain is most active at any given moment in time. PET scan technology involves giving a patient an injection of glucose containing, or "labeled" with, a radioactive isotope. The radioactive glucose circulates throughout the body and the brain. Because the brain uses glucose as its major source of fuel, those areas of the brain that are most active should take up the largest quantities of the radioactive glucose. The computerized PET scanner determines which areas of the brain contain the highest levels of radioactivity and are thus the most active areas of the brain (Figure 2.18).

PET scan (positive emission tomography) measures the amount of a radioactively tagged glucose being used by the brain, allowing researchers to see which areas of the brain are active at any given moment in time

Application ▶ ≫

SPECT scan (single photon emission computerized tomography) indicates which parts of the body have absorbed an injected isotope and is used to indicate blood flow and organ activity in the body

fMRI (functional magnetic resonance imaging) shows the brain in great structural detail and shows which areas of the brain are active at any given moment in time by measuring the energy released by oxygenated hemoglobin cells

PET scans have been used to map the activity of the brain during visual tasks (Fox et al., 1986) and the processing of words (Petersen, Fox, Synder, & Raichle, 1990). For example, a researcher could give a study participant a list of words to remember, then use the PET to scan the brain while the participant is recalling the words. This allows researchers to see which regions of the brain are most active as the subject recalls the words.

Single photon emission computerized tomography (SPECT) scans are similar to PET scans. In a SPECT scan, the patient is injected with a radioactive isotope that is absorbed by specific cells or organs in the body. The SPECT scan equipment then indicates where the isotope has been taken up in the body, which (as in a PET scan) can be used to indicate blood flow or levels of organ activity.

Functional MRI (fMRI): More Detail, No Isotopes

One of the newest techniques for viewing the living brain is an extension of MRI technology called **functional magnetic resonance imaging (fMRI).** Like a PET scan, an fMRI can give researchers a picture of the brain in action. Using fMRI yields several advantages over PET scans. First, fMRI produces functional data and structural images that contain much greater detail and clarity than PET scans. Second, by examining the energy released by oxygenated hemoglobin molecules in the blood stream while the patient is in the strong magnetic field, fMRI can tell a researcher which neurons in the brain are most active at a given moment in time (Figure 2.18). Finally, fMRI is very safe and does not require injecting radioactive isotopes into the bloodstream or exposure to X rays (Raichle, 1994). Like PET scans, fMRI technology allows researchers to correlate behavior with specific brain activity (Menon, Mackenzie, Rivera, & Reiss, 2002).

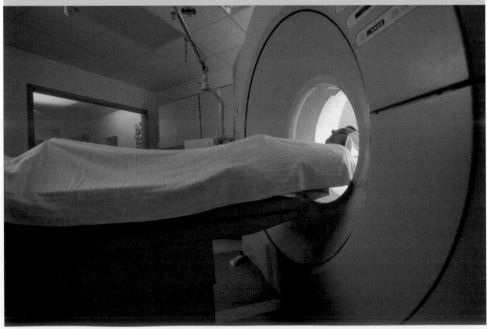

An fMRI scan can tell doctors and researchers which parts of the brain are active at a specific point in time.

© Corbis

Angiograms

Enhanced X rays, or **angiograms,** have also been used to examine the structure of the brain (Figure 2.18). For an angiogram, a dye or contrast is injected into the bloodstream to make certain structures show up better in an X ray. Angiograms are particularly useful for diagnosing blood-flow problems in the brain such as blood clots and arterial plaques such as those in stroke patients and those suffering with cardiovascular disease.

angiograms   type of X ray of the brain in which a radioactive dye or contrast is injected into the bloodstream to enhance the image of the brain

Measuring the Electrical Activity of the Brain

Several other techniques use measurements of the brain's electrical activity to study the living brain. By and large, these techniques are not as precise as those discussed previously, but they are still useful to researchers. **Electroencephalograms (EEG)** and **evoked response potentials (ERPs)** examine the electrical activity of relatively large areas of the brain. These techniques work by using electrodes to measure changes in the voltage between different points on the scalp. These changes are then plotted on graph paper or on a computer screen. Characteristic EEG wave patterns can give researchers an indication of the level of activity occurring in large areas of the brain at any given moment. The ERP technique is a derivative form of EEG in which successive EEGs are averaged to remove some of the electrical interference and background noise found in standard EEG tests. EEG technology has been particularly useful in the study of sleep (Endo, Roth, Landolt, & Werth, 1998) and in detecting gross brain function in brain injured patients. ERPs have been used to examine brain activity during specific cognitive functions such as memory tasks (Nelson, Thomas, de Haan, & Wewerka, 1998).

EEG (electroencephalogram)   measures changes in the voltage at points along the scalp, providing a gross picture of brain activity

evoked response potentials (ERPs) measurement technique in which successive EEGs are averaged to remove background noise and yield a clearer picture of the brain's electrical activity

 Application

Brain Lesions

To understand the brain, researchers may purposely destroy brain tissue, producing what is called a **lesion** (note that lesions are only used in humans when they may have some therapeutic value). By examining the behavioral effects of lesions made at specific points in the brain, researchers attempt to determine the function of particular brain structures. Why would anyone want to damage a healthy animal's brain on purpose? Many people and animals suffer natural damage from disease and accidents (like the case of Jean-Dominique Bauby). Can't researchers conclusively determine what the function of the brainstem is by looking at the symptoms someone like Bauby had as a result of the stroke? Unfortunately, the answer is "No." Bauby's case does not represent an *experiment*, and it is improper to draw *causal* conclusions when we have not conducted an experiment. It's possible that Bauby's symptoms were caused by some other unseen health problem and not by the damage to his brainstem. It may be unlikely, but it *is* possible.

lesion   specific area of damage intentionally produced in the brain to help researchers localize brain function

Recall also that we cannot generalize the findings of a single case study to the population at large. Could Bauby's brain have been abnormal in some way prior to the stroke?—Yes. Just because Bauby suffered locked-in syndrome as a result of the damage his brain suffered, does this mean that all other people would suffer the same fate if their brains were similarly damaged?—No. Although cases like Bauby's provide researchers with invaluable clues, they do not provide concrete *causal* answers to questions about the brain.

For this reason, researchers must conduct experiments to determine the functions of brain structures. For example, researchers have found that rats with intentionally induced lesions in an area of the brain called the medial septum were less likely to remember how to get through a familiar maze than control group rats without brain lesions. From this type of controlled study, researchers can conclude that the medial septum plays a role in a rat's ability to recall spatial information (Kelsey & Vargas, 1993). Experimentally produced lesions have been very valuable to researchers because they allow the researcher to directly manipulate the brain while maintaining experimental control over *extraneous variables* (the age, weight, and sex of the animal).

Brain lesions can also have therapeutic value. Recently, doctors have used lesions in the area of the brain called the thalamus to alleviate some of the tremors associated with Parkinson's disease. Some, like actor Michael J. Fox, have benefited from this type of surgery (Pfann, Penn, Shannon, & Corcos, 1998).

Brain Stimulation

Another technique that allows researchers to directly manipulate the brain is brain stimulation. In this technique, researchers insert a very fine electrode into the brain and deliver weak currents of electricity to the tissue. The brain is stimulated into action by the current, and the behavioral effects of this stimulation can be observed. Research studies involving brain stimulation are frequently conducted on nonhuman subjects. Brain stimulation may be used on humans only when it has some potential therapeutic value.

We've already discussed how Heath (1972) used electrical stimulation on the brain of a man in an attempt to alleviate his severe emotional problems. Although Heath was unsuccessful in treating his patient's mental illness, his research did suggest that the septum might play a role in pleasure and addiction—an idea that has also been investigated in experiments on animals (Figure 2.19).

Recording Individual Brain Cell Activity

Researchers can also measure the electrical activity of individual brain cells. The usual method is to surgically insert a device into the brain of an animal to measure the electrical activity of a cell. Then the animal is subjected to some form of stimulation, and the corresponding activity of the targeted cell is measured. This enables researchers to precisely correlate certain behaviors with the functioning of specific brain cells. Researchers have used this technique to investigate, among other things, the role certain brain cells play in visual processing in cats (e.g., Ferster, Chung, & Wheat, 1996). By presenting visual images to an animal and recording the resulting electrical stimulation in certain cells, researchers have been able to identify which brain cells are responsible for processing different types of visual stimuli.

The human nervous system is an impressive network, but it is not the only communication system within the body. We turn our discussion now to the other major communication network, the endocrine system.

Application ▶▶

Doctors also use brain stimulation to locate specific areas of the brain.

THE FAR SIDE®   BY GARY LARSON

© 1986 FarWorks, Inc. All Rights Reserved/Dist. by Creators Syndicate

The Far Side® by Gary Larson © 1986 FarWorks, Inc. All Rights Reserved. Used with permission.

"Whoa! *That* was a good one! Try it, Hobbs—just poke his brain right where my finger is."

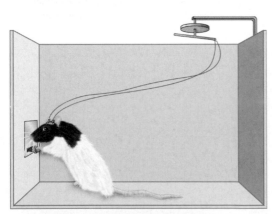

Figure 2.19 Self-Stimulation of the Septum of a Rat
This rat can stimulate its own brain by pressing the bar. Psychologists can learn about specific parts of the brain by observing how the rat's behavior changes when the bar is pressed.

Let's Review!

In this section we outlined some brain-imaging technologies. For a quick check of your understanding, answer these questions.

1. Which of the following techniques *cannot* indicate brain activity in an accident victim?
   a. EEG
   b. PET
   c. fMRI
   d. angiogram

2. Which of the following techniques would a surgeon use if she wanted to see the structures of the brain in great detail prior to operating on a patient?
   a. MRI
   b. angiogram
   c. EEG
   d. X-ray

3. Which of the following techniques would researchers probably be most reluctant to use on a human research subject?
   a. lesions
   b. EEG
   c. fMRI
   d. CAT scan

ANSWERS

1. d; 2. a; 3. a

The Endocrine System: Hormones and Behavior

> > > > > > > > > > > > > > > > >

LEARNING OBJECTIVE

≫ Explain how the endocrine system works, and list the endocrine glands.

We have seen that because of its electrochemical nature, the nervous system is especially good at quickly conveying information within the body. It is the speed of the nervous system that enables us to react quickly to changes in our environment. Messages are sent, decisions are made, and actions are taken—all accomplished with the speed of firing action potentials. At times, however, we require communication within the body that is slower and produces more long-lasting effects. In these circumstances, the endocrine system is called into action.

The endocrine system is a chemical system of communication that relies on the action of specialized organs called **endocrine glands** that are located throughout the body (Figure 2.20). When stimulated, endocrine glands release chemicals called **hormones** into the bloodstream. These hormones circulate through the bloodstream until they reach other organs in the body. Our internal organs are equipped with special receptor sites to accept these hormones. Some receptor sites are found on the outside surfaces of the internal organs, and other receptors can be found inside the organs themselves. When molecules of hormone bind with these receptor sites, they cause specific changes in the functioning of the organ (such as speeding up of the heart, uterine contractions, and so forth), depending on the hormone and the organ.

The endocrine system is considerably slower than the nervous system in relaying messages because it relies on blood circulating through the veins and arteries of the cardiovascular system to transport the hormones throughout the body. The stimulation created by hormones tends to last longer than the stimulation caused by action potentials at the synapse. Some of the bodily processes that are heavily influenced by hormonal activity include sexual activity, eating, sleeping, general physiological arousal, and growth.

Recall that there is communication between the nervous and endocrine systems through the hypothalamus and its connection with the **pituitary gland.** The pituitary gland is situated in the vicinity of the limbic system under the hypothalamus

endocrine glands organs of the endocrine system that produce and release hormones into the blood

hormones chemical messengers of the endocrine system

pituitary gland master gland of the endocrine system that controls the action of all other glands in the body

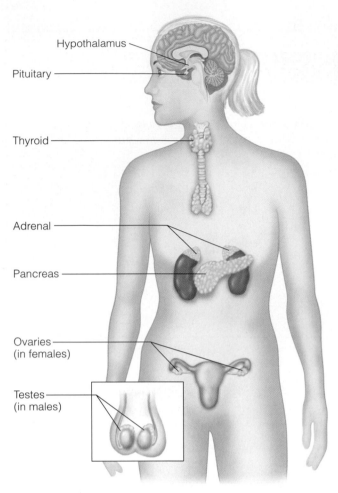

Hypothalamus

Pituitary

Thyroid

Adrenal

Pancreas

Ovaries
(in females)

Testes
(in males)

Figure 2.20
Major Endocrine Glands of the Body

The glands of the endocrine system make and release hormones into the bloodstream.

From Starr & McMillan, Human Biology, *2/E, p. 271, © 1997 Wadsworth. Art by Kevin Somerville.*

estrogens   a class of female hormones

androgens   a class of male hormones

adrenal medulla   center part of the adrenal gland that plays a crucial role in the functioning of the sympathetic nervous system

adrenal cortex   outside part of the adrenal gland that plays a role in the manufacture and release of androgens, and therefore influences sexual characteristics

Application

(Figure 2.20), and it is responsible for regulating hormone release in all the other endocrine glands. When the endocrine system is called into action, the hypothalamus sends a signal to the pituitary gland. The pituitary gland then releases hormones that travel through the bloodstream to the other endocrine glands of the body. The pituitary hormones stimulate these other endocrine glands to release the hormones they produce into the blood stream. These hormones circulate to their target organs where they affect specific changes in the functioning of these organs.

Our bodies are equipped with a great number of peripheral endocrine glands. We will concentrate our discussion on the endocrine glands that are of most interest to the field of psychology.

The ovaries and testes are probably the best known endocrine glands. The testes and ovaries are necessary for sexuality and reproduction. Ovaries are the female sex glands, located in the abdominal cavity. Ovaries are directly responsible for the production of female eggs (ova) and the release of female sex hormones, or **estrogens.** Testes are the male sex glands, located in the testicles. Testes produce male sex cells (sperm) and male hormones or **androgens.**

The adrenal glands sit just above the kidneys in both males and females and are important for regulating arousal and sexual behavior among many things. The inside of the adrenal gland, the **adrenal medulla,** is particularly important in sympathetic nervous system reactions. When the sympathetic nervous system becomes active during times of stress, the adrenal medulla releases norepinephrine and epinephrine (also known as *adrenaline*) into the bloodstream. When norepinephrine and epinephrine are released in the body outside of the central nervous system, they function as hormones. The sudden flooding of the bloodstream with these hormones causes the familiar sympathetic reactions of increased heart rate, blood pressure, and respiration.

The external part of the adrenal glands, the **adrenal cortex,** plays many roles in the endocrine system. Among other things, the adrenal cortex produces *adrenal androgens*, which are male sex hormones found in both males and females. These androgens control many aspects of our sexual characteristics and basic physiological functioning.

The thyroid gland is located in the throat, and it governs important aspects of metabolism. Dysfunction of the thyroid can lead to serious physical symptoms. *Hyperthyroidism*, or an overactive thyroid, is associated with increased metabolism, weight loss, bulging eyes, weakness, high blood pressure, and cardiac problems. *Hypothyroidism*, or an underactive thyroid, is related to lowered metabolism, obesity, sluggishness, thin brittle hair, menstrual abnormalities in females, and depression. The symptoms of hypothyroidism often mimic those of depressive psychological disorders. Prior to treatment for depression, a routine thyroid check should be done to avoid misdiagnosis.

The nervous and endocrine systems are nothing short of amazing in their intricate structure and function. The importance of these systems to everyday life is especially apparent in cases like Bauby's where damage has rendered part of the communication system useless. How did we develop such complex systems in the first place? Certainly the human nervous and endocrine systems are far advanced when compared to those of other species. Why are we so complex, and what accounts for the traits humans possess? These questions lead us into genetics and evolution.

Let's Review!

This section described the endocrine system and its relationship to the nervous system. For a quick check of your understanding, answer these questions.

1. Kerry has an overactive thyroid gland. His condition is also known as _____.
   a. hypothyroidism
   b. hyperthyroidism
   c. pituitary disorder
   d. dwarfism

2. A malfunction in which of the following endocrine glands would be *most* disruptive to the overall functioning of the endocrine system?

   a. thymus
   b. hypothalamus
   c. pituitary
   d. adrenal

3. Juanita was just frightened by a snake. Which of the following endocrine glands most likely played the biggest role in her response to danger?
   a. thymus
   b. thyroid
   c. ovaries
   d. adrenal

ANSWERS

1. b; 2. c; 3. d

Becoming Who We Are: > > > > > > > > > > > > > > > > >
The Influence of Genetics on Biology

One question that has plagued humankind for centuries is how we become the people we become. Each person is a unique collection of physical characteristics, personality traits, and abilities. What makes us different from one another? For example, Jean-Dominique

LEARNING OBJECTIVES

⋙ Give an overview of the nature versus nurture debate, and describe genetic and environmental factors in human development.

⋙ Give an overview of the theory of evolution, and explain how the human nervous system may have developed through natural selection.

The person on the left suffers from hyperthyroidism, a condition that leads to weight loss, bulging eyes, weakness, high blood pressure, and cardiac problems. The person on the right suffers from hypothyroidism, a condition that leads to obesity, sluggishness, thin brittle hair, menstrual abnormalities in females, and depression.

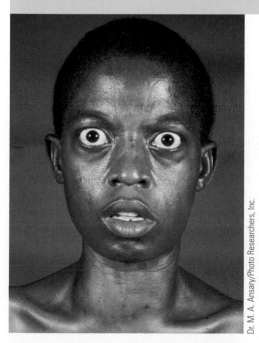

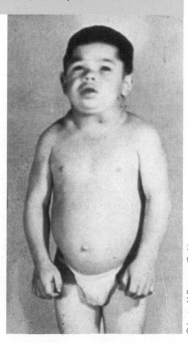

Dr. M. A. Ansary/Photo Researchers, Inc.

© Lester V. Bergman/Corbis

Bauby was, among other things, a gifted author, a courageous man, and unfortunately a man who was susceptible to a stroke. Why? Did Bauby become the man he was because of the environment he grew up in? Were Bauby's traits, abilities, and weaknesses predestined by the genes he inherited from his parents? To answer these questions, we look next at the relative contributions our genes and our environment make to our development.

Nature Versus Nurture and Interactionism

nature–nurture debate   age-old debate over whether we are mostly a product of our genes or of our environmental influences

Explaining how and why we develop as we do is the central issue in the age-old **nature–nurture debate.** Those on the nature side of this debate emphasize the idea that intelligence, kindness, athletic ability, and other characteristics are largely determined by one's genes and are not learned. Those on the nurture side of this debate tend to view behavior as being molded by environmental influences such as the way your parents treat you, the educational opportunities you have, and the TV shows you watch. From the nurture point of view, our traits and other characteristics are acquired totally by experience.

interactionism   perspective that our genes and environmental influences work together to determine our characteristics

What do you think? Are you a product of the genes you inherited? Or are you a product of your environment? If you are like most current psychologists, you probably answered "Both." Today, the dominant perspective on the nature–nurture debate is **interactionism.** Most psychologists now believe that genetic influences interact with environmental influences to produce our traits and behavior. For example, Bauby's amazing creativity was probably due in part to the genes he received from his parents and in part to the environments he encountered at home, in school, at work, and so on. Similarly, a child can inherit very "smart" genes, but if education is not provided, the child will not be as "smart" as he or she could have been.

Interactionism does not end the nature–nurture debate, however. Psychologists are attempting to understand the relative contributions of nature and nurture to specific traits. A psychologist may ask whether a trait such as intelligence is *mostly* genetic or *mostly* environmental. Psychologists don't ask these questions just to be difficult. If we knew that a particular behavior was due to nature or nurture, this would have a profound effect on our understanding of and ability to change behavior. For instance, what if we knew that alcoholism was the result of a particular gene? Could this knowledge lead to potential medical interventions?

Twin Studies

twin studies   comparing the relative similarity of identical and fraternal twins to ascertain the relative contributions of genes and environment to our characteristics

identical twins   twins that developed from a single fertilized egg and share 100% of their genes

fraternal twins   twins that developed from two separate fertilized eggs and are no more genetically similar than normal siblings

To answer questions about the relative contributions of nature and nurture, researchers often focus on **twin studies.** Twin studies compare specific traits between pairs of **identical twins** (twins who share 100% of their genetic code) and pairs of nonidentical or **fraternal twins** (twins no more genetically related than other siblings). If identical twins have a similar trait more often than fraternal twins do, a genetic basis for the trait is implied. In contrast, if identical twins and fraternal twins do not differ in similarity, there is less support for the existence of a genetic influence on the trait. Other valuable comparisons include comparing identical twins raised in different environments to identical twins raised in the same household. Dissimilarities between identical twins reared together and identical twins raised apart would be a powerful argument for environmental influence on the trait being measured.

In doing such comparisons, psychologists can isolate the influence of nature and nurture on the development of specific traits. The results of studies on intelligence indicate that genetics accounts for about 50% of the influence on one's intelligence. The remaining 50% of the influence comes from one's environment (Chipuer, Rovine, &

The twins on the left are identical, meaning they developed from a single fertilized egg and share 100% of their genes. The twins on the right are fraternal, meaning they developed from two fertilized eggs and share their genes only to the degree that ordinary siblings do.

Polmin, 1990). It appears that intelligence is truly a product of the interaction between nature and nurture.

The manner in which the environment affects our traits and behavior is discussed more fully in Chapters 5, 9, and 10 on learning and development. For now, let's turn our attention to the genetic, or nature, side of this debate.

Genetic Blueprint for Traits

There is little doubt that genes exert a powerful influence on the development of an organism. Development is not chaotic; rather, it usually happens in a predictable and orderly way. Where does this order come from? All living organisms develop according to a "blueprint" or plan contained in the genes that an organism inherits from its parents.

Genes are strands of deoxyribonucleic acid (DNA) that are found in the nuclei of all living cells. DNA directs the development of proteins within the cells of the body. By instructing a cell to make specific kinds of protein molecules, the genes direct the development of the different organs and systems of the body. We are human because our human genes direct our bodies to develop as human bodies. As individuals, we have unique characteristics because we inherited a particular mix of genes for specific traits from our parents.

At conception, we get half of our genes from our mother and the other half from our father. From this combination of genes, we develop our characteristics. The actual genetic code that we inherit for a trait is called the **genotype.** But recall that the genotypes we inherit only partly determine the traits we actually acquire. The environment plays a role as well. The actual trait or characteristic we develop is referred to as the **phenotype.** The phenotype is a product of the genotype an organism inherits and the environment in which it lives. For example, Siamese cats have a characteristic look because all Siamese cats share some common genes that are particular to the breed. However, the climate a Siamese cat is raised in affects the color of its coat. Siamese cats raised in hot climates tend to be light, whereas Siamese cats reared in cold climates develop darker fur (Gallagher, 1994). Inherited genotypes direct the cat to develop as a

genes   strands of DNA found in the nuclei of all living cells

genotype   inherited genetic pattern for a given trait

phenotype   actual characteristic that results from the interaction of the genotype and environmental influences

 **Application**

Siamese, but environmental influences produce further variations in the phenotypes that result. The same principle holds true for humans. The exact shade of your hair, the level of your intelligence, the speed with which you run—all are phenotypes, which are the expression of inherited genotypes and environmental influences.

Genetically speaking, the human species has done quite well. We are the most highly developed species on earth. Our cortex is more developed than those of other species. A direct consequence of this development is that we have many well-developed abilities that are lacking in other species. We use spoken language to communicate; we have well-developed self-concepts; we can imagine the future; and we are adept problem solvers, to name a few of our high-level abilities. We can thank our genes for these wonderful advances that separate us from the rest of the animal kingdom, but why are we humans genetically different from other animals? Why do different species exist? Many scientists believe the answer to this question is found in the process of *evolution*.

The Evolution of Species: Natural Selection

In 1859 Charles Darwin published *On the Origin of Species by Means of Natural Selection* (Darwin, 1859). In this text, Darwin outlined what has become the basis for modern theories of evolution, the process of **natural selection.** Natural selection is a simple but powerful process that can change, kill, or create a species over time. Natural selection states that for characteristics to be retained in a species, genes for these traits must be passed on to offspring. If an organism does not reproduce, its genes die with it. If a specific trait is *maladaptive* and tends to prevent an organism from surviving and procreating, then the genes for this trait are not as likely to be passed on to offspring. Over time, these maladaptive genes should die out in the species. In contrast, *adaptive* genes, which give rise to traits that help an organism reproduce, will be passed on to future generations. Over time, through *natural selection*, these adaptive genes will become more widespread in the species.

For example, a beaver born with a defective tail will likely be the young victim of a predator because it cannot swim well. If the beaver dies before maturity, it will not reproduce, and the genes it carried for the malformed tail will not be passed on in the species. A beaver born with a well-formed tail that enhances its ability to swim swiftly may elude predators efficiently and live to an unusually old age. Due to its expanded life span, this beaver will likely produce more offspring than the average beaver. Some of these offspring may carry the genes for the large, adaptive tail. The characteristic of having a well-formed tail will now have a chance of being propagated in the species. Over time, through this process of natural selection, subsequent generations of beavers may tend to have tails that are better suited to swimming.

The effects of evolution can also be seen in the human nervous system. As we've mentioned, human brains differ from nonhuman brains in some important ways. The most notable differences are seen when comparing the human cortex to the cortices found in other species. The human cortex is more highly evolved. Genes that supported such a highly evolved cortex were presumably selected in our species over millions of years of natural selection and evolution. Can you see how some of our cortical functions could have contributed to our ancestors' reproductive success? For example, how could the capacity for language have aided our ancestors? Could being able to communicate danger to

natural selection cornerstone of Darwin's theory of evolution, which states that genes for traits that allow an organism to be reproductively successful will be selected or retained in a species and genes for traits that hinder reproductive success will not be selected and therefore will die out in a species

BIZARRO

© Dan Piraro. Reprinted with special permission of King Features Syndicate.

© Niall Benvie/Corbis

Darwin's theory of natural selection predicts that characteristics that contribute to survival and procreation, like this beaver's tail, will remain in a species. Characteristics that hinder survival and procreation will die out in the species.

others have helped many of our ancient ancestors survive, reproduce, and safeguard their offspring? There is little doubt that having a large cortex and all the associated perks such as language, problem-solving skills, memory, and planning skills helped our species survive and flourish. We hope the knowledge about our amazing nervous system that you have learned here will help you realize just how kind evolution has been to us.

Let's Review!

This section described several aspects of the genetic bases for traits and behavior. For a quick check of your understanding, answer these questions.

1. I have brown hair. The exact shade of my hair represents my _____ for hair color.
   a. genotype
   b. phenotype
   c. gene
   d. all of the above

2. Genes that determine your eye color are made up of _____.

   a. DNA
   b. RNA
   c. phenotypes
   d. mitochondria

3. Dr. Jasper is a scientist who believes that our characteristics are primarily a function of the environment in which we are raised. Dr. Jasper's point of view is most closely aligned with the _____ perspective.

   a. evolutionary
   b. nature
   c. nurture
   d. interactionist

ANSWERS
1.b; 2.a; 3.c

Are You Getting the Big Picture?

In this chapter we have examined how our biology affects our behavior. Now that you have a greater understanding of how your nervous system and endocrine system work, we hope you have a greater appreciation for what these systems do *for* you. Together, the nervous system and endocrine system influence *every* action of your body—every movement, every biological process, and every thought. Psychologists, doctors, nuclear medicine specialists, nurses, and rehabilitative therapists are just some of the people who use knowledge of these systems in their work as they try to understand and help people with various physical, behavioral, and mental problems.

Because the brain plays a significant role in behavior, an understanding of the brain is crucial to your understanding of psychology. The knowledge you have gained in this chapter will help you to understand the rest of the material in this text. To truly understand why people do things like take drugs, eat, have sex, sleep, suffer from mental illnesses, fall in love, behave aggressively, suffer physical illnesses, have memories, and rise to the top of the social hierarchy, you must understand human biology. As you read the rest of this text, keep what you have learned about your biology in mind. In some respects psychology is a bit like mathematics; learning it is a cumulative process. What you learn in one chapter will help you learn the material in subsequent chapters. As you read, try to see the big picture of psychology. Look at how it all fits together rather than simply studying each chapter as a separate topic. If you do this, you will understand psychology better, and you will also find learning psychology easier.

STUDYING THE CHAPTER

Key Terms

nervous system (47)
neurons (47)
endocrine system (47)
glia cells (49)
myelin (49)
cell body (50)
DNA (50)
dendrites (50)
axon (50)
neurotransmitters (51)
synapse (51)
synaptic cleft (51)
ions (51)
resting potential (53)
threshold of excitation (53)
action potential (53)
all-or-none fashion (54)
refractory period (54)
excitation (55)
inhibition (55)
reuptake (58)
acetylcholine (Ach) (59)
dopamine (59)
serotonin (60)
norepinephrine (NOR) (60)
gamma amino butyric acid (GABA) (60)

glutamate (60)
endorphins (61)
central nervous system (CNS) (61)
peripheral nervous system (PNS) (61)
sensory neuron (61)
motor neuron (61)
somatic nervous system (61)
autonomic nervous system (64)
parasympathetic nervous system (64)
sympathetic nervous system (64)
hindbrain (66)
forebrain (66)
midbrain (67)
medulla (67)
pons (67)
cerebellum (68)
reticular activating system (RAS) (68)
limbic system (68)
diencephalon (68)
cerebral cortex (68)
cerebral hemispheres (68)
amygdala (69)
septum (70)
hippocampus (70)
thalamus (71)
hypothalamus (71)
homeostasis (72)

frontal lobe (73)
parietal lobe (73)
occipital lobe (73)
temporal lobe (73)
Wernicke's area (74)
Broca's area (74)
corpus callosum (74)
split-brain (75)
association cortex (77)
motor cortex (78)
somatosensory cortex (79)
visual cortex (79)
auditory cortex (79)
CAT scan (80)
MRI (81)
PET scan (81)
SPECT scan (82)
fMRI (82)
angiogram (83)
electroencephalogram (EEG) (83)
evoked response potentials (ERP) (83)
lesion (83)
endocrine glands (85)
hormones (85)
pituitary gland (85)
estrogens (86)
androgens (86)

adrenal medulla (86)

adrenal cortex (86)

nature–nurture debate (88)

interactionism (88)

twin studies (88)

identical twins (88)

fraternal twins (88)

genes (89)

genotype (89)

phenotype (89)

natural selection (90)

Test Yourself!

Concept Check

Test your knowledge of the chapter concepts by completing each of the following sentences with the correct term. For a more comprehensive review, visit the book Web site (http://psychology.wadsworth.com/pastorinole/) for online quizzes, flashcards, crosswords, and Internet links.

_____ **1.** A brain scan that can only show brain structure.

_____ **2.** The chemical messengers of the endocrine system.

_____ **3.** The connection between two neurons in the brain.

_____ **4.** A sensory relay station in the brain.

_____ **5.** The body's chief inhibitory neurotransmitter.

_____ **6.** The part of the neuron that receives incoming signals.

_____ **7.** A process that makes a neuron more likely to fire an action potential.

_____ **8.** A brain structure that may play a role in addiction.

_____ **9.** If you lost this part of your brain, you could no longer store long-term memories.

_____ **10.** Male hormones.

_____ **11.** The chemical messengers of the nervous system.

_____ **12.** This branch of the nervous system is most active during times of calm.

_____ **13.** This part of the brain allows you to speak language.

_____ **14.** The resting potential of a neuron.

_____ **15.** This brain scan shows brain function.

A. Dendrites

B. Neurotransmitters

C. Synapse

D. Excitation

E. GABA

F. Parasympathetic nervous system

G. Septum

H. Broca's area

I. CAT scan

J. PET scan

K. Hormones

L. Androgens

M. Thalamus

N. Hippocampus

O. −70 mv

Answers:

1. I; 2. K; 3. C; 4. M; 5. E; 6. A; 7. D; 8. G; 9. N; 10. L; 11. B; 12. F; 13. H; 14. O; 15. J.

Critical Thinking About the Chapter

1. Jean-Dominique Bauby was still able to think, feel, and remember the events of his life after a stroke left him in a permanent state of locked-in syndrome. Now that you know something about the brain, can you explain why he retained these abilities?

2. Dr. Martinez has just discovered a new substance that destroys glutamate in the brain. If a rat were injected with this substance, what would you expect to happen? Assume that a rat's brain functions similarly to a human brain.

3. What human traits do you believe to be adaptive at this point in our evolutionary history? If we assume that natural selection is still occurring, in a million years what would you expect humans to be like?

4. Your best friend is interested in what you are learning in your psychology class. He asks you to explain how the brain is able to control our behavior. What would you tell him?

Applying Psychology. Your best friend's grandmother has just suffered a stroke. This stroke has left her with an inability to speak, but she can still understand what others say to her. She also has paralysis on the right side of her body. Your friend wants to know what part of her grandmother's brain was likely damaged by the stroke. Based on your understanding of the brain, what would you tell your friend?

Critical Thinking for Integration

1. Design an *experiment* to test the hypothesis that the amygdala plays a role in the processing of emotional memories.

2. You want to test the hypothesis that low levels of serotonin are related to obesity in humans. Which type(s) of research design(s) would you *not* want to use? Why?

3. Discuss the ethical considerations involved in using invasive techniques for studying the brains of animals.

4. What questions would a developmental psychologist be *most* interested in asking about the nervous system?

Chapter Study Resources

Suggested Readings

1. Bauby, J. D. (1997). *The diving bell and the butterfly.* New York: Vintage.
The moving book featured in the case study.

2. Ramachandran, V. S., & Blakeslee, S. (1998). *Phantoms in the brain. Probing the mysteries of the mind.* New York: William Morrow.
Discusses numerous case studies of people with unusual neurological disorders.

3. Pinker, S. (1997). *How the mind works.* New York: Norton.
Takes a comprehensive look at what we know about the mind.

4. Veggeberg, S. K. (1996). *Scientific American focus: Medication of the mind.* New York: Henry Holt.
An excellent overview of neural transmission and drug action at the synapse.

5. For additional readings, explore InfoTrac College Edition, your online library of archived journal articles and periodicals. Go to http://www.infotrac-college.com/wadsworth and enter the passcode from the card that came with your book. For this chapter, search using these keywords:

    brain

    action potentials

    hippocampus

    myelin

    natural selection

    neurotransmitters

Web Links for Further Study

Additional information on chapter concepts can be found at these Web sites:

1. The Comparative Mammalian Brain Collections site has pictures of brains from a vast number of mammals. http://brainmuseum.org/

2. The Brain Explorer site has interactive information on the brain and its functions. http://www.brainexplorer.org/index.html

3. The National Institute of Neurological Disorders and Stroke site has information on neurological disorders and their treatment. http://www.ninds.nih.gov/

4. The Medscape site is a database of articles that deal with all aspects of medicine and is a great source for cutting-edge medical research and case studies. This site requires a free registration. http://www.medscape.com/px/urlinfo

5. The University of California at Berkeley's Museum of paleontology site has a wealth of information on Darwin's theory of evolution. http://www.ucm00berkeley.edu/history/evolution.html

6. The Whole Brain Atlas site has MRI and CAT scan images of both healthy and diseased brains. http://www.med.harvard.edu/AANLIB/home.html

Student Study Guide

To help organize your learning, work through Chapter 2 of the *What Is Psychology? Student Study Guide*. The study guide includes learning objectives, a chapter summary, fill-in review, key terms, a practice test, and activities.

Psychology ⬤ Now™

PsychologyNow is a Web-based, personalized study system that provides you with a pretest and a post-test for each chapter, quizzes you by chapter, and provides a personalized study plan, pointing you to elements in the text or in individual learning modules that will help you to achieve 80% mastery. Check out the learning modules that relate to this chapter: synaptic transmission, neural transmission, split-brain, genetics and evolution.

PsychNow CD ROM, Version 2.0

Go to the PsychNow CD ROM for further study of the concepts in this chapter. The CD-ROM includes the learning modules with videos, animations, and quizzes, as well as simulations of psychological phenomena. Each module follows a consistent Explore, Lesson and Apply structure that allow you to experience the concept or principle, learn more about it, and then apply it. You and your friends can participate in a team-based Quiz Game that makes learning fun. You can also participate in experiments such as: Brain Asymmetry, which is the same thing as lateralization in your book. Learning modules include: 3a. Neurons and Synaptic Transmission, 3b. Brain and Behavior.

Biology and Behavior

The nervous system is an electrochemical system that transmits information quickly throughout the body via action potentials. It is divided into the central nervous system (the brain and spinal cord) and the peripheral nervous system (the remainder of the nervous system).

The endocrine system is a chemical system that utilizes chemical messengers called hormones to convey information in the body. Generally speaking, the action of the endocrine system is slower and more long-lasting than the nervous system.

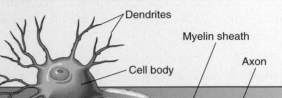

Dendrites

Synaptic terminals

Myelin sheath

Cell body

Axon

NEURONS AND NEURAL COMMUNICATION

- The nervous system is an electrochemical network that transmits information quickly throughout the body.

- Nerve cells are known as neurons, and they use electrochemical energy to generate action potentials that travel to the end of the neuron and cause the release of neurotransmitters.

- Neurotransmitters are chemical compounds that carry signals across neurons. Some of the key neurotransmitters are acetylcholine, serotonin, norepinephrine, GABA, and glutamate.

- Neurotransmitters play significant roles in regulating behavior and mood. For example, endorphins are natural opiates that block the sensation of pain, whereas too little dopamine is related to Parkinson's disease.

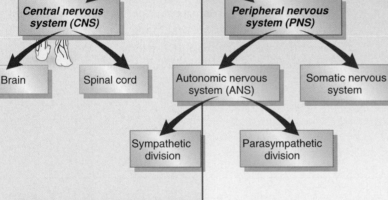

Nervous system

Central nervous system (CNS)

Peripheral nervous system (PNS)

Brain

Spinal cord

Autonomic nervous system (ANS)

Somatic nervous system

Sympathetic division

Parasympathetic division

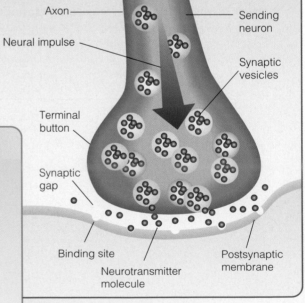

Axon

Neural impulse

Terminal button

Synaptic gap

Binding site

Neurotransmitter molecule

Sending neuron

Synaptic vesicles

Postsynaptic membrane

THE ENDOCRINE SYSTEM

- The endocrine system contains glands that release chemical messengers—hormones—into the bloodstream.

- Hormones travel through the blood and bind with receptor sites on bodily cells, affecting their function.

- The brain's hypothalamus controls the function of the pituitary, or master gland, of the endocrine system.

- The endocrine system plays a major role in the autonomic nervous system and in our motivational processes.

© Michael Keller / Corbis

THE STRUCTURE AND FUNCTION OF THE BRAIN

• Brain tissue is composed largely of neurons and glia cells that form basic structures that enable the brain to affect different aspects of physiological and psychological functioning.

• The brain is divided into many parts, but its three key regions are the hindbrain, the midbrain, and the forebrain. It is the forebrain that regulates higher-order processes like thinking and emotional control.

• The brain regulates our motor activity, our sensation and perception, our emotions, our ability to learn and remember, and all of the other elements of human behavior.

• The cerebral cortex is a thin layer of wrinkled tissue that covers the outside of the brain and is most responsible for the cognition, decision making, and language capabilities that are unique to humans.

• The brain is divided into right and left hemispheres. The left hemisphere generally governs the right side of the body, whereas the right hemisphere governs the left side of the body.

• To assist in studying the brain and its functioning, technology such as CAT scans, the MRI, the fMRI, PET, and SPECT scans are all important tools.

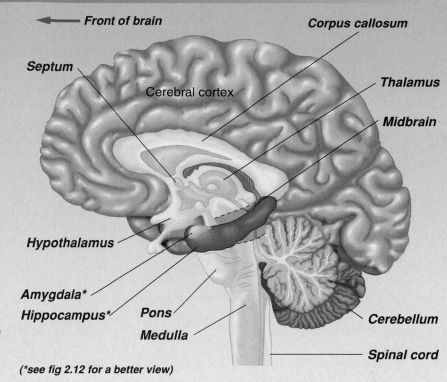

Front of brain

Corpus callosum

Septum

Cerebral cortex

Thalamus

Midbrain

Hypothalamus

Amygdala*

Hippocampus*   *Pons*

Medulla

Cerebellum

Spinal cord

(*see fig 2.12 for a better view)

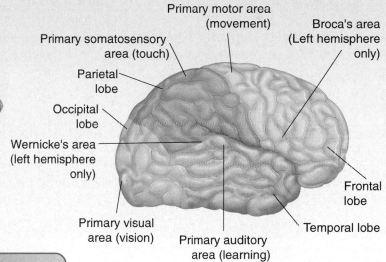

Primary motor area (movement)

Primary somatosensory area (touch)

Broca's area (Left hemisphere only)

Parietal lobe

Occipital lobe

Wernicke's area (left hemisphere only)

Frontal lobe

Primary visual area (vision)

Primary auditory area (learning)

Temporal lobe

Right hemisphere

THE INFLUENCE OF GENETICS ON BIOLOGY

• Our traits are the result of both nature (genetic) and nurture (environmental) forces.

• We inherit genotypes from our parents that are the genetic code for our specific traits. But our environment influences the ultimate expression of those genotypes, which are known as our phenotypes.

• Throughout the evolutionary history of a species, the selective process of natural selection changes the pool of genotypes that are possible within a species. Genes for traits that contribute to an organism's reproductive success tend to be passed on to future generations.

© Courtesy of Lisa Torri

"That's the problem," sighed Michael. "Nobody's ever heard of this. They think I'm on drugs or that I'm making it up."

FROM RICHARD E. CYTOWIC, *THE MAN WHO TASTED SHAPES: A BIZARRE MEDICAL MYSTERY OFFERS REVOLUTIONARY INSIGHTS INTO EMOTIONS, REASONING, AND CONSCIOUSNESS*, p. 4 (New York: G. P. Putnam's, 1993)

Richard Dobson/Getty Images

CHAPTER 3

How Do We Sense and Perceive Our World?

CHAPTER PREVIEW

How Do We Take It All In?

THE BIG PICTURE

At this moment, you are reading this textbook in an attempt to learn more about human behavior—and to ensure a decent grade in your psychology class. Take a moment to think about what is actually taking place as you read this page. Specifically, how do you get the visual information printed on this page into your brain where it can be stored for future use, such as on your next exam?

The obvious answer is that you *read* the information contained on this page. But what makes reading possible? To read this page, you must first focus your conscious awareness or **attention** on the page and be able to *see* the images printed on it. Seeing is an example of what psychologists call **sensation.** In sensation, sense organs of the body, such as the eyes, convert environmental energy, like the light that is bouncing off the book page, into *action potentials* that the brain can then process. Sensation, in this case seeing, is the first step to getting information into our minds. If you did not have sense organs such as your eyes, ears, tongue, nose, and nerve endings, you would not be able to accomplish **transduction,** or the conversion of environmental stimuli into a form that your nervous system can process. Without sensation, you would not be able to learn.

After sensation, the next step is **perception.** You must understand what the images printed on it mean. Perception occurs when you interpret the meaning of the information gathered through your senses. In this case, reading this page requires that you use your prior knowledge of the English language to help you perceive the meaning of the printed letters and words. Without this prior knowledge, your perception of this page would be drastically altered. Imagine what reading this page would be like if you had learned to read Spanish, but not English. You would still be able to see the letters and words on this page, but your perception of them would be very different.

What you already know about the world often helps you interpret your current experience. As you look around your room right now, what do you see, hear, smell, taste, and feel? To answer these questions, you must use your senses to take in information from your environment. Then you must use what you know about the world to help you perceive what you see, hear, smell, taste, and feel. For example, you recognize your textbook as a book because you have seen many books before. However, because perception depends in part on the experiences and knowledge we have, people do not always perceive things the same way. Look at Figure 3.1. What do you see when you *first* look at this picture? Some people see a bunny rabbit. Others see a chick. Whether you first see a rabbit or chick is due, in part, to the knowledge and experience you bring to bear when you interpret this stimulus. For example, if you were thinking about your pet rabbit right before looking at this picture, you may be more likely to first see a rabbit.

attention   our conscious awareness; we can focus our attention on events that are taking place in the environment or inside our minds

sensation   the process through which environmental energies like light and sound are transduced into neural impulses by our sense organs

transduction   the process through which our sense organs convert environmental energies into neural impulses

perception   the process through which we interpret sensory information

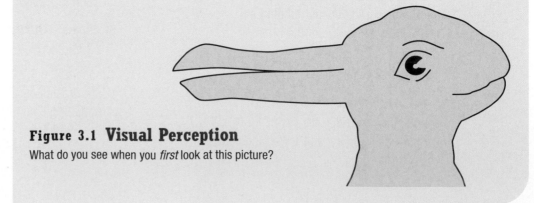

Figure 3.1 Visual Perception
What do you see when you *first* look at this picture?

Individual differences exist in *how* you sense things as well. Some people, like one of the authors (Doyle-Portillo), cannot see well without glasses. Some people have very acute hearing abilities, whereas others cannot discriminate well between different sounds—and some, like Michael Watson, have very unusual sensory and perceptual abilities indeed.

In 1980, neurologist Dr. Richard Cytowic attended a dinner party at the home of his friend Michael Watson. Michael, an artist and teacher, was also an amateur gourmet chef. Michael liked to develop his own recipes, and on this night he was trying out a new chicken dish on his friends. As the guests were mingling before dinner, Michael invited Richard into the kitchen to keep him company while he put the finishing touches on the supper. They chatted casually while Michael finished preparing the sauce that would cover the chickens that were roasting in the oven. Michael used taste to determine the appropriate amount of seasoning to add to the sauce. He dipped his spoon into the still-cooking sauce, tasted it, and uttered a phrase that would change the entire career of his friend: *"Oh, dear. There aren't enough points on the chicken"* (Cytowic, 1999, p. 3).

Richard's attention was piqued, and he asked Michael to explain what he meant about the *points* on the chicken. Michael became embarrassed. He had not meant to say something like that in front of another person, because it would give away a secret he had been living with his whole life. But, he had let the cat out of the bag, and now he would have to explain himself.

Michael explained that all of his life he had experienced sensations and perceptions differently from other people. When Michael tasted things, he also *felt* the sensation of certain geometric shapes. Michael had been hoping that his chicken recipe would taste *pointed* to him, but instead, it tasted *rounded.* When Michael tasted the chicken, he also had the sensation of feeling rounded shapes pressed against his body, especially on his face and hands. To Michael, this was a culinary failure, but for Richard the "rounded chicken" was the beginning of a long program of research with Michael as the primary research participant.

All his life, Michael had feared that he was imagining things or that he was "being silly," but Richard knew immediately what Michael was referring to as he described his odd sensations. Richard, a neurologist, recognized Michael's "secret" as an interesting case of a very rare condition, *synesthesia.* Synesthesia affects only about 10 out of every million people and is characterized by cross-linkages among the senses (Cytowic, 1999; Ward, 2003). When a person with synesthesia senses a stimulus with one sense, he or she experiences sensations in another sense. In general, the cross-linkage seems to be one-way. For example, hearing a sound may evoke the sight of a color, but the sight of a color does not evoke the hearing of a sound.

In Michael's case, taste invoked sensations of touch. Sometimes Michael felt the shapes over his entire body. Other times, such as when tasting sweets, he only felt the shapes in his hands. He felt most shapes in his face, hands, and shoulders. When Michael created a recipe, he was shooting for a particular shape. Adding certain ingredients would round the shape. Other ingredients would sharpen the dish's corners, make its lines steeper, or stretch its surface. On that night, Michael had not added the right combination of *pointed* ingredients to the sauce.

Richard was intrigued with Michael's unusual abilities and wasted no time in enlisting Michael to participate in some studies on synesthesia. Richard chronicled the results of these studies in his book *The Man Who Tasted Shapes* (Cytowic, 1999). As you might have guessed, Richard found that people like Michael do not process sensory information in the typical way. But what is the typical fashion? How does the average person's brain process sensory information? Answering these questions will be the focus of this chapter. As you read through this chapter, keep Michael Watson's story in the back of your mind. What must it be like to actually taste shapes?

"It's so perfectly logical that I thought everybody felt shapes when they ate. If there's no shape, there's no flavor."
(Cytowic, 1993)

The Man Who Tasted Shapes
Richard E. Cytowic, M.D.

© Jim Corwin/Picturequest

Measuring Sensation and Perception

LEARNING OBJECTIVE < < < < < < < <

Explain the concepts of absolute threshold, just noticeable difference (jnd), and signal detection used in measuring our sensation and perception.

psychophysics the study of how the mind interprets the physical properties of stimuli

Psychologists who study sensation and perception are most interested in understanding how we process stimuli. For instance, what occurs when you look at an apple? How does your mind interpret the color of the light bouncing off the surface of the apple? Why do some apples appear to be greenish-red and others appear to be deep ruby red? What makes the different notes of a musical piece sound different? What physical properties of a food make it taste sweet or bitter? Questions like these are the focus of the branch of psychology called **psychophysics.**

Psychophysicists seek to understand how the mind interprets the physical properties of sensory stimuli. Psychophysicists relate physical properties of stimuli to the psychological results they produce. For example, the wavelength of light corresponds to the color we see, and the frequency of sound waves relates to the pitch we perceive. As we examine the different senses, we will look at how the physical properties of different sensory stimuli affect our sensation and perception of them.

Absolute Thresholds

One of the fundamental questions psychophysicists have sought to answer concerns the limits of human sensory capabilities. In other words, how faint a light can humans see? How soft a tone can we hear? At what concentration can you first taste sugar dissolved in a glass of water? How intense a pressure must be placed on the arm for you to feel it?

Psychophysicists have conducted many experiments to establish the absolute threshold of each of the five senses. These experiments typically involve presenting stimuli of gradually increasing or decreasing intensities (along with some trials on which the stimulus is not presented at all). Participants are asked to report whether or not they can detect the presence of the stimulus. In theory, absolute threshold is defined as the *minimum* amount of stimulation required for a person to sense the presence of the stimulus. However, psychophysicists define **absolute threshold** *operationally* in a slightly different fashion; it is the minimum intensity of a stimulus that can be detected 50% of the time. This 50% mark is used because the level of the stimulus required for it to *just* be perceived varies from trial to trial and from person to person during an experiment.

absolute threshold the minimum intensity of a stimulus at which participants can identify its presence 50% of the time

For example, on one trial a participant may be able to *just* sense the presence of a teaspoon of sugar dissolved in 2 gallons of water. But on another trial, this same person may require 1.1 teaspoons of sugar in the water to taste its presence. This variation is, in part, due to changes in the subjective experience of sensation, which depends on the context in which the stimulus is sensed. If you drink a sweet soft drink right after eating a very sweet piece of candy, you usually find that the soft drink doesn't taste nearly as sweet as it does when you taste it after eating a non-sweet food such as potato chips. The sweetness of the soft drink does not change, but rather your subjective sensation of its sweetness changes with the context in which you taste the drink.

This girl can feel this insect only when its weight exceeds her absolute threshold for touch.

Another reason for variations in participants' reports of absolute threshold is changes in the individual's *response bias*, or tendency to report detecting the presence of the stimulus, whether or not the stimulus is actually present. It can be very difficult to tell whether or not we can actually sense stimuli when they are presented at very low levels so sometimes we tend to guess. Have you ever thought you heard the phone ring while you were in the shower, only to find that you were mistaken? Many of us have had this frustrating experience. Why does this occur? A simple explanation is that we are listening intently for the phone to ring. Because we *expect* the ring to be very faint over the sound of the shower, we convince ourselves that we hear a sound that simply isn't present.

The same thing sometimes occurs during laboratory experiments that examine absolute threshold. If you are listening intently to hear a very faint sound over a pair of headphones, you may think that you hear a stimulus when it isn't actually there. On another day, you may not make this same mistake. Your absolute threshold may appear to be moving around a bit. Thus the operational definition of absolute threshold accounts for variations in subjective sensation and response bias. Table 3.1 ◆ lists the approximate established absolute thresholds for the five senses, described in familiar descriptive terms.

Signal Detection Theory

Some theorists claim that the traditional absolute threshold measure is inadequate. Detecting a weak stimulus is a function of both the stimulus intensity and response bias. Therefore, some theorists propose that to get a true measure of the participant's sensory abilities, it is necessary to separate out the relative influence of response bias in a participant's judgments. **Signal detection** is a method of analyzing the relative proportions of correct judgments (*hits*) and errors (*false alarms*) that a participant makes in trying to detect a stimulus or signal. By applying statistical measures to these proportions, researchers can eliminate the effects of response bias and thereby get a truer measure of the participant's ability to actually detect the presence of the signal or stimulus (Parasuraman, Masalonis, & Hancock, 2000). Figure 3.2 illustrates the types of judgments you could make in a signal detection situation (like hearing the phone ring while you're in the shower) and the signal detection terminology for each possible response: hit, false alarm, miss, and correct rejection.

Signal detection has great significance in the real world. For instance, air traffic controllers monitor computer screens for unauthorized air traffic entering their airspace. In experiments on air traffic control, researchers can monitor participants' hit and false alarm rates for detecting intruding aircraft on a mock radar screen. Studies like these help researchers design radar screens and computer displays that will allow

◆ **Table 3.1**

Descriptions of the Absolute Thresholds for the Five Senses

Sense	Absolute Threshold
Vision	A candle seen from 30 miles away on a clear, dark night.
Hearing	A ticking watch that is 20 feet away in an otherwise quiet room.
Smell	One drop of perfume diffused in a three-room apartment.
Taste	One teaspoon of sugar dissolved in 2 gallons of water.
Touch	The wing of a bumblebee falling on one's cheek from a distance of 1 centimeter.

Adapted from Galanter, 1962.

signal detection   a method of analyzing the relative proportions of hits and false alarms to eliminate the effects of response bias in a participant's detection of a stimulus

 **Application**

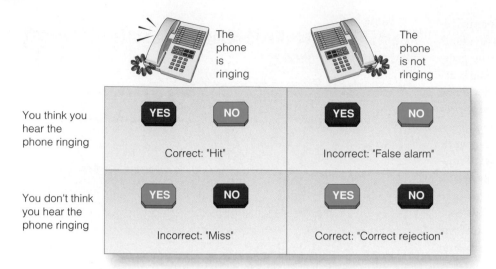

Figure 3.2 **Possible Judgments in Detecting the Presence of a Stimulus**

Imagine that you are expecting an important phone call, but you need to take a shower. While you're in the shower, listening for the phone, these are the possible situations that might arise and the judgments you might make in these situations. Signal detection theory uses the proportion of hits and false alarms that a subject makes to separate response bias from actual ability to detect the presence of the stimulus.

Air traffic control displays must be designed to maximize controllers' hits and correct rejections while minimizing their misses and false alarms.

air traffic controllers to maximize their *hits* while minimizing their *false alarms*.

Signal detection is obviously useful in improving job performance, but does it also apply to social situations? Researchers now believe that it can be applied to more complex situations in which people have to judge whether they have seen a person's face before, as in eye-witness testimony (Macmillian & Creelman, 1991; Podd, 1990). In this application a hit would mean correctly identifying a face you had seen before. A false alarm would be incorrectly identifying a face as one you had seen before that you had, in fact, not seen it before.

By applying signal detection to eye-witness testimony in controlled laboratory experiments, researchers study whether the average witness can reliably and accurately identify faces seen before. As we will see in this chapter and again in Chapter 6, many studies have shown that eyewitness testimony is often inaccurate. This, of course, has implications for our legal system, as well as for psychologists studying sensation and perception.

Just Noticeable Difference

In addition to establishing the absolute thresholds for the senses, psychophysicists have tried to establish the minimum *change* in the intensity of a stimulus that can be detected 50% of the time. This barely noticeable change in the stimulus is referred to as the *difference threshold* or **just noticeable difference (jnd)**. In the early 1800s, psychophysicist Max Weber discovered something very interesting about the jnd. Because sensation is subjective, the amount of change in the stimulus that is necessary to produce a jnd depends on the inten-

just noticeable difference (jnd) the minimum change of intensity of a stimulus that participants can detect 50% of the time

Weber's law a psychophysical formula used to predict the jnd for a given stimulus: $\Delta I/I = k$, where ΔI is the change in the stimulus required to produce a jnd, I is the original intensity of the stimulus, and k is a constant that varies for each of the five senses

sity at which the stimulus is *first* presented. For example, if you are holding a 10-pound weight, it will take more added weight for you to notice a change than it would if you started out holding just a 5-pound weight. After many experiments, Weber determined that he could express the relationship between the stimulus's original intensity and the amount of change in the stimulus that is required to produce a jnd, with the equation known as **Weber's law** ($\Delta I/I = k$). Weber's law says that when the change in a given stimulus (ΔI) required to produce a jnd is divided by the initial intensity of the stimulus (I), this produces a constant number (k). But this constant will vary for each of the five senses. Therefore, the k, or constant, for vision is different from the k for hearing, taste, smell, and touch. Table 3.2 ◆ lists the k values for the five senses.

If we know the particular k value for a stimulus, we can use Weber's law to predict the change in the stimulus that would be needed to produce a jnd in the average participant. For example, for candlelight, $k = 1/60$. Therefore, if you start with 180 lit candles in a room, Weber's law predicts that you would have to light 3 more candles for anyone to notice a change in the room's brightness. For taste, $k = 1/5$. So, if you begin with 5 teaspoons of salt in a pot of soup, you would have to add one teaspoon of salt to produce a jnd. Perhaps Michael Watson could have used this information the night his chicken recipe needed adjusting!

The same amount of stimulus change (DI) does not always produce a jnd. For example, if your soup originally contains 5 teaspoons of salt, adding 1 more will produce a jnd. If your soup originally contains 10 teaspoons of salt, you would need an additional 2 teaspoons of salt to produce a jnd. Weber's law clearly demonstrates the subjectivity of sensation and perception. One additional teaspoon of salt in a very salty pot of soup is not noticeable, but that same teaspoon of salt added to a less salty pot of soup is noticeable.

Research on absolute and difference thresholds deals with our ability to *consciously* perceive sensory stimuli—to be *aware* that we are perceiving the stimuli. But what happens when sensory stimuli are presented at intensities too weak to be consciously perceived? If we are not consciously aware of sensory stimuli, can they still affect our behavior?

Processing Without Awareness: Subliminal Stimulation of the Senses

In psychological terms, when sensory stimuli are presented at intensities that are too weak to reach absolute threshold, the stimuli are said to be **subliminal**. Subliminal perception became a topic of many debates in the late 1950s when a man named James Vicary attempted to use subliminal persuasion to convince moviegoers at a public theater to buy more popcorn and soda. Vicary flashed messages such as "Eat popcorn" and "Drink Coca-Cola" between the frames of a movie at a speed so fast that moviegoers did not have time to consciously perceive the messages. Because the messages were flashed so briefly, the moviegoers never consciously saw anything other than the movie.

Vicary reported that as a result of his "experiment," concession sales rose significantly. We should point out that Vicary did not conduct a true experiment. He had no control group and did not control for extraneous variables. Therefore, his "results" do not constitute scientific evidence for the usefulness of subliminal persuasion. Nonetheless, Vicary claimed that his subliminal messages had manipulated the unconscious minds of the moviegoers—increasing Coca-Cola sales by 18% (Pratkanis, 1992).

◆ **Table 3.2**

Weber's Law k Values for Five Different Sensory Stimuli

Sensory Stimulus		k Value
Candlelight		1/60 (Matlin & Foley, 1997)
Pure tones		1/333 (Engen, 1971)
Taste		1/5 (McBurney, 1978)
Weight		1/40 (Hunt, 1993, p. 114)
Smells		1/14 (Cain, 1977)

subliminal when the intensity of a stimulus is below the participant's absolute threshold and the participant is not consciously aware of the stimulus

There is no good scientific evidence to suggest that moviegoers can be coerced into buying refreshments through subliminal persuasion.

GDT/Getty Images

These claims sparked a great deal of public apprehension because of the possible implications of Vicary's "experiment." If advertisers could persuade us with subliminal messages, then we would be very vulnerable. Who knows what we could be talked into with such messages! In response, the Federal Communications Commission banned the use of subliminal ads on television and radio. However, the ban has not stopped some people from trying to use subliminal persuasion in print ads (Key, 1973, 1989). A modern approach to subliminal advertising attempts to create certain emotional states in consumers by embedding sexually suggestive messages in advertisements. Such attempts seem to have only a weak and indirect influence on consumers' attitudes (Aylesworth, Goodstein, & Kalra, 1999).

As it turns out, much of the fear sparked by James Vicary's "experiment" was unfounded. First, Vicary's so called experiment has been revealed to be primarily a hoax. In 1962, Vicary admitted that he had not really conducted the study as he had claimed. By his own admission, he had not collected data in a systematic manner, and the data that he did collect were so few that they could not be used for scientific purposes (Epley, Savitsy, & Kachelski, 1999; Pratkanis, 1992). Second, after Vicary's attempts at subliminal persuasion, researchers began to carefully examine the effects of subliminal persuasion both in the real world and in the laboratory. To date, it appears that subliminal persuasion in the real world does not have a significant effect on people's behavior (Aronson, Wilson, & Akert, 1999, p. 271).

In the laboratory, researchers have shown that subliminal stimuli can impact behavior in subtle ways. In one study, researchers showed participants a picture of a happy face, an angry face, or a polygon, followed by unfamiliar characters from the Chinese language. The faces and the polygons were flashed at a rate so fast that the participants could not consciously detect them. After seeing the Chinese characters, the participants were asked to rate their liking for the characters.

The results showed that the participants liked the characters that had been preceded by the happy face the most, followed by the characters that were preceded by the polygon. The characters that were preceded by the angry face were liked the least. It appears that the liking for the characters was directly influenced by the faces and polygons, none of which the participants could recall having seen because they were presented subliminally (Murphy & Zajonc, 1993).

Studies like this show that it might be possible to use subliminal stimuli to affect the attitudes of research participants. But these studies should not be generalized to what happens in the real world. First, even in the laboratory, subliminal persuasion cannot make people behave in a manner that goes against their own values (Neuberg, 1988). Second, in the laboratory, conditions such as lighting, distance of the participants from the screen, and distractions can be precisely controlled. Outside of the lab, these variables cannot be easily controlled, which most likely accounts for the failure of subliminal persuasion in the real world. For now, it appears that we do not have to fear hidden messages from advertisers and others interested in controlling our minds and behavior.

Now that we have a basic understanding of how psychologists measure the limits of our sensory abilities, we will examine how our bodies accomplish the process of sensation. Recall that sensation can be defined as the transduction (conversion) of environmental energy into neuronal impulses. Before we can detect the presence of a stimulus, our sense organs must first change the physical properties of that stimulus into a form that our brain can process, namely *action potentials* (Chapter 2). Our eyes, ears, tongue, nose, and skin are all equipped with specialized cells that allow transduction and sensation to take place. In the coming sections, we will examine what is known about how these special organs create sensations.

Let's Review!

This section has given you a quick overview of some important aspects of measuring sensation and perception—absolute threshold, signal detection theory, just noticeable difference, and subliminal stimulation of the senses. For a quick check of your understanding, answer these questions.

1. The minimal intensity of a stimulus that is needed for people to detect the stimulus 50% of the time is called the _____.
   a. just noticeable difference
   b. absolute threshold
   c. signal detection threshold
   d. stimulus threshold
2. Imagining that you hear your name called while you are waiting for your flight in a busy airport is an example of a _____.

   a. hit
   b. false alarm
   c. correct rejection
   d. miss
3. According to Weber's Law, who will *most likely* notice the addition of one more teaspoon of sugar in his or her glass of iced tea?
   a. Joni, whose tea has no sugar in it
   b. Bill, who has 2 teaspoons of sugar in his tea
   c. Sarafina, who has 3 teaspoons of sugar in her tea
   d. All of these people will be equally likely to notice the difference.

ANSWERS:
1. b; 2. b; 3. a

Vision: The World Through Our Eyes ⟩ ⟩ ⟩ ⟩ ⟩

Our eyes are at the front of our skulls, so you could assume that vision is a direct transfer from object to eye to brain. Vision is more complicated than that, however, and researchers have studied vision more than the other senses. To understand vision, we'll look at the properties of light that apply to vision, the anatomy of the eye, the layers of the retina, and how we process visual information in the brain.

How Vision Works: Light Waves and Energy

When we see an object, what we really see are the light waves that are reflected off the surface of the object. So a blue shirt will appear blue because blue is the only color of light that is reflected by the shirt. The shirt absorbs all other colors of light.

Measuring Light: Wavelength and Amplitude

Light is *electromagnetic energy.* Like all electromagnetic energies, light waves are characterized by their **wavelength** and **amplitude.** The wavelength of light is the distance

LEARNING OBJECTIVES

⟩ Describe the physical properties of light—wavelength, amplitude, and the visible spectrum—and how they relate to human vision.

⟩ Understand the anatomy of the eye and the layers of the retina and how they function.

⟩ Explain how we adapt to light and dark, how we see color, and how the brain processes what we see.

wavelength   a physical property of some energies that corresponds to the distance between the wave peaks

amplitude   a physical property of some energies that corresponds to the height of the wave peaks

hue   the color of a light

brightness   the intensity of light; it corresponds to the amplitude of the light waves

saturation   the purity of light; pure light or saturated light consists of a single light wave

visible spectrum   the spectrum of light that humans can see

between the peaks of each light wave. The amplitude of the light wave is the height of each wave peak. These distances are typically measured in nanometers (nm); (Figure 3.3).

Properties of Light: Hue, Brightness, and Saturation

The wavelength and amplitude of light waves determine some of the characteristics of the light we see. The wavelength corresponds to the color or **hue** of the light we see. Lower wavelengths correspond to cool colors like blues and purples. Higher wavelengths correspond to warmer colors like yellows and reds (Figure 3.3). The amplitude of the light wave corresponds to its **brightness**. The higher the amplitude of the light wave, the brighter the color we perceive.

One other characteristic of light, **saturation**, corresponds to the purity of the light. Light that consists of a single wavelength will produce the most saturated, or richest color. Light that is a mixture of wavelengths produces less saturated colors. For example, pure blue light is high in saturation, but a mixture of blue and white light produces a less saturated blue light. Figure 3.4 illustrates the differences in brightness and saturation for a particular hue of blue.

The Visible Spectrum of Light

The human eye cannot sense all electromagnetic energy. In fact, the **visible spectrum** of light is only a very narrow band of the electromagnetic spectrum that spans from about 360 nm to 750 nm. Figure 3.3 depicts the electromagnetic energy that is visible and invisible to the human eye. Although our eyes cannot sense much of the electromagnetic spectrum, we are capable of seeing millions of different combinations of hue, saturation, and brightness of color (Bornstein & Marks, 1982). As impressive as this is, other species can sense electromagnetic wavelengths that are beyond the human visible spectrum. Among snakes, pit vipers can sense infrared rays, allowing them to sense other animals by their body heat (Sinclair, 1985). Still other animals, such as fish, reptiles, birds, insects, and rodents, are able to sense ultra-violet rays (Matlin & Foley, 1997, p. 49). In some rodents, the ability to see ultra-violet waves may allow them to

Figure 3.3 **The Visible Spectrum of Light**

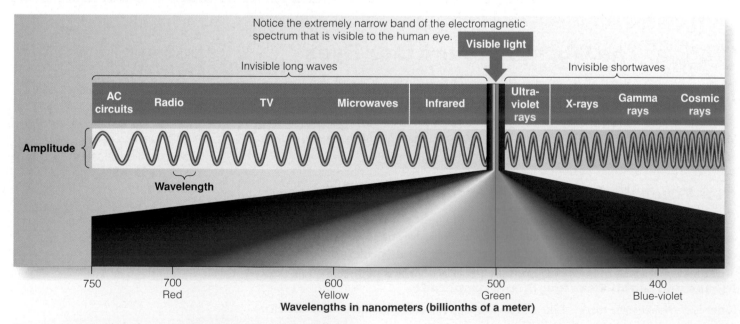

From *Psychology, 3/e* by Don H. Hockenbury and Sandra E. Hockenbury.
© 2003 by Worth Publishers. Used with permission.

a. Hue
Pure Saturated Blue

The hue (blue) corresponds to the wavelength on the visible spectrum. This blue is highly saturated—the purest blue.

b. Brightness
Brighter Intensity of the Same Blue

The higher the amplitude of the lightwave, the brighter the hue (blue) appears.

c. Saturation
Less Saturated Blue

Light that is from more than one wavelength—here, blue light mixed with white light—is less saturated than the pure blue in (a).

Figure 3.4 Brightness and Saturation for a Hue of Blue

see the urine markings of other rodents, because rodent urine strongly reflects ultraviolet waves (Pickrell, 2003). If you are hiking through the woods, keep in mind that certain animals may be able to see you before you see them!

For vision to occur, our eyes must be able to convert the electromagnetic waves of the visible spectrum into action potentials that our brains can process. In the next section, we will look at the anatomy of the eye to get a feel for how this conversion occurs.

The Anatomy of the Outer Eye

The process of vision begins with the parts of the eye we can readily see: the clear cornea that covers the iris, the colored part of your eye, and the pupil, the opening in the iris. From there, light eventually is focused on the retina at the back of your eye. The white part, the sclera, is a supporting structure that doesn't play a part in the processing of visual information.

The Cornea, Pupil, and Iris

When light enters the eye, the first structure it passes through is the cornea (Figure 3.5). The **cornea** is the clear, slightly bulged-out outer surface of the eye. It protects the eye and begins the focusing process. The light that is reflected off of an object in the environment must eventually be focused on the rear surface of the eye if we are to see the object clearly. As light waves pass through the material of the cornea, they slow down and bend—just as light waves bend as they pass through a camera lens. This bending of the light waves plays an essential role in focusing images on the back of your eye. A damaged cornea can make it impossible for a person to see clearly.

Directly behind the cornea is the **pupil.** This black opening in the center of your eye is not really a structure. Rather, it is an opening, or aperture, through which light passes into the center of the eye. Light cannot pass through the white part of the eye, or the **sclera.** Therefore, it must pass through the cornea and pupil to enter the eye. The **iris,** the colored part of the eye surrounding the pupil, is constructed of rings of muscles that control the size of the pupil. In dimly lit conditions, the iris relaxes to dilate the pupil, allowing the maximum amount of light into the eye. In brightly lit

Fovea. Point of highest visual acuity, cones, concentrated here.

Retina. Thin membrane lining back of eyeball, contains rods and cones.

Iris

Pupil

Path of light

Cornea

Lens

Optic nerve

Optic disk. Point where optic nerve leaves eye, no rods or cones in this part of retina creating a blind spot.

Figure 3.5 The Anatomy of the Eye

cornea the outer covering of the eye that protects the eye and begins the focusing of light

pupil the hole in the iris through which light enters the eye

sclera the white part of the eyeball

iris the colored part of the eye that consists of strong muscles that regulate the size of the pupil

conditions, the iris constricts to close the pupil, thus reducing the amount of light entering the eye so as not to overwhelm the light-sensitive cells in the eye. If you turn on a bright bedroom light in the middle of the night, you experience what occurs when the pupil allows too much light into the eye. Right before turning on the bedroom light, your pupil is fully dilated in the darkened room. At the instant you turn on the light, the pupil is still set for darkness. The light rushes through the dilated pupil for a brief time until your iris adjusts to the change in light levels. Although the iris reacts very quickly, for an instant our eye receives too much light. This type of overexposure to light can be painful. If the eye is exposed to intense light for prolonged periods of time, permanent damage can occur to the eye. This is also why we are repeatedly warned not to stare directly at the sun during a solar eclipse. The sun's light is so intense that the iris cannot constrict enough to protect the eye.

The Lens and Accommodation

Directly behind the iris and the pupil is the **lens** of the eye. The lens is a clear structure that is attached to the eye with strong **ciliary muscles.** The lens of the eye is somewhat analogous to the lens of a camera—its job is to bring the light waves entering the eye into sharp focus on the back of the eye. This analogy only goes so far because a camera adjusts by moving the lens in and out (by turning it) until the image is in focus. Our eyes focus light not by moving the lens in and out, but by changing the thickness of the lens itself. Unlike the rigid glass of a camera lens, the lens of the eye is somewhat soft and flexible. The shape of the eye's lens can adjust, or undergo **accommodation,** so that the image passing through it is focused properly.

When we look at an object that is far away (over 20 feet), the ciliary muscles stretch and flatten the lens. This way light waves passing through the lens bend very little and the image appears in focus on the back of the eye. On the other hand, when we look at an object that is close at hand, the ciliary muscles contract and push on the lens to make it thicker. In this state, light waves bend so as to focus the nearby image on the back of the eye. However, as we all know, the lens does not always focus light in an optimal manner. Why do some of us need to wear glasses?

Age is one factor. As we age, our lenses tend to become less flexible, which makes these accommodations more difficult (Koretz & Handelman, 1988). After age 40, many people find that they have difficulty focusing nearby images, a condition called **presbyopia,** or farsightedness. Reading glasses can correct for presbyopia.

For some, glasses will be a necessity even before middle age. For example, weaknesses in the ciliary muscles can cause problems such as nearsightedness, or **myopia,** which occurs when one can focus close objects but not distant ones. Another condition, **astigmatism,** occurs when the eye itself is misshapen, causing problems focusing certain images.

Glasses and contact lenses work to correct for these various accommodation problems by bending the light waves before they reach the lens of the eye. Myopic vision may also be corrected with a type of surgery in which a laser is used to resculpt either the shape of the cornea or the tissue underlying the cornea. As a result, the eye can better focus light on the retina. For some people, these procedures can reduce or eliminate the need to wear glasses or contact lenses.

The Retina: Light Energy to Neural Messages

Once the light waves have been focused on the back of the eye, transduction of light waves into neural impulses occurs in the **retina,** the surface that lines the inside of the back of the eyeball. In the retina are specialized cells, called **rods** and **cones,** that transduce, or convert, light into action potentials. Without these cells, vision would not

lens   the part of the eye that lies behind the pupil and focuses light rays on the retina

ciliary muscles   muscles that stretch and squeeze the lens to make it thicker or thinner as it focuses light on the retina

accommodation   the process through which the lens is stretched or squeezed to focus light on the retina

Application

presbyopia   an age-related deficit in vision in which the lens can no longer accommodate, causing one to become farsighted, or unable to see clearly up close

myopia   nearsightedness, or being able to see clearly up close, but not far away

astigmatism   a vision deficit caused by having a misshapen eye

retina   the structure at the back of the eye that contains cells that transduce light into neural signals

rods   the light-sensitive cells of the retina that pick up any type of light energy and convert it to neural signals

cones   the cells of the retina that are sensitive to specific colors of light and send information to the brain concerning the colors we are seeing

be possible. Before we look at how transduction occurs, it will be helpful if we describe the anatomy of the retina and the pathways through which visual information is processed there.

The Anatomy of the Retina

The diagram in Figure 3.6 shows a cross section of the layers in the human retina. The *ganglion cells* are on the surface of the retina, followed by successive layers of *amacrine, bipolar,* and *horizontal cells,* and finally the light-sensitive rods and cones. Look closely at Figure 3.6 and you will see that the light entering the eye must filter through all the layers of the retina before finally striking the rods and cones. It may seem counterintuitive to you that the light-sensitive cells of the retina are buried beneath several layers of cells, which is the reason the retina is sometimes referred to as "inverted."

Incoming light passes unimpeded through the transparent layers of the retina to reach the rods and cones, which transduce the light energy into neural impulses. These signals travel back out to the ganglion cells on the surface of the retina. Along the way, the horizontal, bipolar, and amacrine cells funnel and consolidate the neural information from the rods and cones so that we can see a unified, coherent image. The signals that reach the ganglion cells in the top layer of the retina are to some degree summaries of the visual information from the rods and cones.

Vision problems can strike at any age. Myopia is common at all ages, but presbyopia is more common after middle age.

The back of the retina, which lines the back interior surface of the eye

Rod (R) and cone receptors (C)

Horizontal cells (H)

Bipolar cells (B)

Amacine cells (A)

Ganglion cells (G)

Optic nerve fibers

Rods   Cones

Figure 3.6 A Cross Section of the Retina

Light rays entering from the outer eye

The top panel shows a schematic of the retina with the rods in pink and the cones depicted in purple. The side panel shows an electron micrograph of the retina with the rods and cones.

From "Organization of the Primate Retina," by J. E. Dowling and B. B. Boycott, in Proceedings of the Royal Society of London, 16, Series B, *80-111. Copyright © 1966 by the Royal Society.*

optic nerve   the structure that conveys visual information away from the retina to the brain

blindspot   the point where the optic nerve leaves the retina, where there are no rods or cones

fovea   the point on the retina that lies directly behind the pupil

The Optic Nerve and the Blindspot

Once the neural impulses reach the ganglion cells, they exit the retina and travel to the brain via the **optic nerve,** which is composed of the axons of the ganglion cells (see Figures 3.5 and 3.6). One consequence of having an inverted retina is that the optic nerve actually exits the retina on the *surface* of the retina; there are no light-sensitive rods or cones at the point where the optic nerve leaves the retina. With no rods or cones at this spot, each of our eyes has a **blindspot,** which is a point in our visual field that we cannot see.

Luckily, however, our blindspots do not pose much of a problem. For one thing, the blindspot is at the side of our visual field, where we normally do not bring objects into focus in the first place (see Figure 3.5). If the blindspot were located at the **fovea** (the point directly behind the pupil), it is possible that we would be much more aware of it . Another reason is that we have two eyes. Whatever part of the world we miss seeing due to the blindspot in our left eye, we see with our right eye and vice versa. This is because each eye receives a slightly different view of the objects we see. The image that hits our left blindspot is not the same as the image that hits your right blindspot. Therefore, if we have two functional eyes, we will not normally be aware of having a blindspot because each eye compensates for the other.

A final reason the blindspot is not troublesome is that our brain tends to "fill in" the missing information. In experiments that pinpoint their blindspots, participants do not report "seeing nothing" in their blindspots. Rather, they report that the missing image is replaced with some background image (Churchland & Ramachandran, 1996). Researchers are not yet sure how the brain fills in this missing information, but the evidence suggests that the brain plays a role in reducing our awareness of our blindspots.

Now that we have a picture of how the retina is constructed, let's turn our attention to a more careful look at how the rods and cones allow us to see.

The Rods and Cones

The rods and cones that line the inside layer of the retina play different roles in the process of vision. The rods, which are long and skinny, are sensitive to all colors of light, but they do not transmit information about color to the brain (see Figure 3.6). You can think of the rods as being black-and-white receptors. If you had only rods in your retina, you'd see everything in black and white. The fact that we do see the world in color is due to the presence of cone cells in the retina. The cones, which are shorter and fatter than the rods, are responsible for transmitting information about color to the brain.

Relative to rods, the cones of the eye require a higher intensity of light to become activated. Because of this, we do not have good color vision in dimly lit situations. Think about driving at night. When light levels are not very intense, it may be possible to see objects in the distance, but impossible to discern their color. You can see an oncoming car as it approaches, but you may not be able to tell what color it is. This is especially true if the car is a dark color like blue or black, which does not reflect much light. Under these conditions, you have a better chance of seeing a lighter color, like white or yellow, because more light is being reflected into your eyes. If the night is dark enough, you may not even be able to discriminate a white car from a yellow one.

In each eye, you have about 100 million rods but only about 5 million cones (Matlin & Foley, 1997). Having so many rods and so few cones in the retina indicates that perceiving shape and form takes precedence over perception of color. If you think about this for a minute, this arrangement makes sense. Which information would you need first: to see the shape of a car speeding toward you in the dark, or to see the color of the car? Your first concern would be seeing the car to avoid a collision!

Because cones require more light energy than rods, it can be difficult to discriminate among colors at night. Even though you can clearly make out the shapes of the oncoming cars, you may not be able to discern their color.

In addition to being differentially sensitive to light energy, the rods and cones of the eye are not distributed evenly across the surface of the retina, as Figure 3.7 shows. The highest concentration of cones is at the fovea, with fewer and fewer cones toward the peripheral edges of the retina. The density of rods follows the opposite pattern, with the highest concentration at the peripheral edges of the retina and fewer and fewer rods as you move toward the fovea. This arrangement means that our best color vision is for objects placed directly in front of us, whereas our color vision for objects seen out of the corners of our eyes is very poor. To demonstrate this for yourself, try this simple demonstration. You'll need a set of crayons, a chair, and the help of a friend.

Where's Your Best Color Vision? Close your eyes and have a friend hand you a colored crayon without telling you what color it is. Sit upright in a chair with the crayon in your hand, extend your arm directly out to the side so that your arm forms a 90-degree angle with your body (Figure 3.8). Fix your eyes directly in front of you and open your eyes. In this position, the crayon should be outside your range of vision.

Now slowly move your extended arm forward in an arc towards the front of your head. Don't move your eyes. Keep them fixed directly ahead. As you move your arm

Demonstration

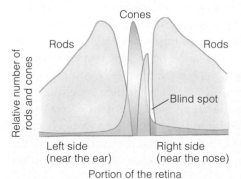

Figure 3.7 The Distribution of Rods and Cones in the Retina of the Left Eye

Cones (shown in gray) are concentrated in the fovea and rods (shown in yellow) at the periphery of the retina. Notice that no photoreceptors are found at the blindspot, where the optic nerve leaves the retina.

From Matlin & Foley, Sensation & Perception, *4/e. Published by Allyn & Bacon, Boston, MA. Copyright © 1991 by Pearson Education. Reprinted by permission of the publisher.*

Figure 3.8 **Color Vision and Position in the Visual Field**

When you hold a crayon to the side, you cannot perceive its color because there are no cones on the peripheral edges of the retina. When you hold a crayon directly in front of your eyes, the high density of color-sensitive cones at the fovea gives you the best color perception.

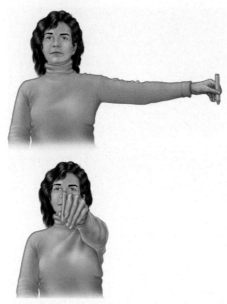

slowly forward, keep noticing whether or not you can see the crayon. When you can just see the crayon, stop moving your arm. Now, can you tell what color the crayon is? Don't cheat and move your eyes!

At this point, you should be able to see the crayon, but you should not be able to tell what color it is. This is because you are seeing the crayon on the edges of your retina, where you have only rods. The rods are good at picking up the image of the crayon, but they can't tell your brain the color of the crayon. Now, slowly move your arm forward again, until you can just perceive the crayon's color. You have now moved your arm forward enough that light from the crayon is striking some of your cones (closer to the center of your eye). At this point, your perception of the color should be washed out, because you are still seeing the crayon with mostly rods.

As you continue to move the crayon slowly forward, be aware of how the color seems to deepen and intensify. The closer to the front of your face you move the crayon, the more cones you are using, and the better your color vision becomes. When the crayon is directly in front of your eyes, its color appears most vivid. You are now seeing the crayon primarily with your cones because it is directly in front of your fovea.

Another consequence of the distribution of rods and cones is that our eyes are most sensitive to light away from the fovea, where we have higher concentrations of rods (see Figure 3.7). Recall that compared to cones, rods require much less light energy to become stimulated. Therefore, if you want to see an object under very dim light, it is best to look at it indirectly, more out of the corner of your eye.

Stargazers are familiar with this phenomenon. After seeing a faint star with their peripheral vision, many backyard astronomers have been frustrated to have it vanish from sight when they looked directly at it. The cones at the fovea are not able to pick up the faint light of the star that the rods at the periphery are able to sense. A veteran stargazer learns to spot faint stars using peripheral vision, and then amplifies this light using a telescope. The telescope enables the cones at the fovea to also sense a faint star.

Turning Light Energy Into Neural Messages

photopigments   light-sensitive chemicals that create electrical changes when they come into contact with light

rhodopsin   the photopigment found in the rods of the retina

The rods and cones of the eye are able to transduce light into neural impulses because they contain light-sensitive **photopigments,** chemicals that are activated by light energy. Human photopigments are composed of two chemical compounds, *opsin* and *retinal* (Stryer, 1987). To get a picture of the role they play, let's look at the photopigment found in the rods of the eye, which is called **rhodopsin.** When the rod is not receiving light input, the opsin and retinal molecules are joined together and the photopigment is stable. When light strikes the rod, the rhodopsin becomes unstable. Incoming light energy activates the rhodopsin and causes the opsin and retinal to separate (McNaughton, 1990). As these two compounds separate, they set off a complex chain of chemical reactions that ultimately change the electrical charge inside the rod.

As you learned in Chapter 2, changing the charge inside a neural cell causes either excitation or inhibition. Excitation and inhibition are the means through which our neurons communicate with each other. When the opsin and retinal separate, the resulting reaction is *inhibition*. This inhibition *reduces* the amount of neurotransmitter that is sent to the retina's bipolar and horizontal cells (see p. 111). As strange as it may seem, when we see a bright light, our rods *decrease* their rate of firing action potentials. This decrease signals to the bipolar and horizontal cells that we are seeing light. When we are in dim conditions, less of the rhodopsin breaks down, and the rods experience less inhibition. Therefore, the rods will actually *excite* the horizontal and bipolar cells more than when we are in bright light. After passing through the amacrine cells, the signals are sent via the ganglion cells to the brain. The brain receives the signals from the ganglion cells, and is informed that we have just seen a visual stimulus.

As we also saw in Chapter 2, after a neuron has sent a signal, it must return to its resting potential. The neurotransmitters must be taken back into the vesicles to prepare the cell to fire again. The same type of process must occur in the eye after the rods fire a signal. After the rod sends the neural impulse, the opsin and retinal recombine to form a new (stable) rhodopsin molecule. If we did not regenerate our rhodopsin, we would soon deplete our supply of photopigments and then we wouldn't be able to see!

Transduction in the cones is believed to occur in a fashion that is very similar to transduction in the rods. The photopigments of the cones also contain retinal and opsin, but the exact chemical nature of the opsin is different in the cones. We will see in an upcoming section that variations in the opsin molecule play a role in our ability to see color. But for now, let's use our understanding of how photopigments work to help us understand how our eyes adapt to light and dark conditions.

Adapting to Light and Darkness

Have you ever gone into a darkened movie theater in the middle of the day? It takes up to 40 minutes for our eyes to adapt to such low light conditions (Hood & Finkelstein, 1986). This type of adaptation is referred to as **dark adaptation.** It also takes our eyes a while to adapt to sudden increases in light brightness. As we mentioned earlier in the chapter, if you have ever turned on your bedroom light in the middle of the night, you most likely had the uncomfortable experience of being temporarily blinded while your eyes struggled to adjust to the bright light. This is called **light adaptation.**

Dark and light adaptation is, in part, accomplished by changes in our pupil size. As we have seen, our pupils contract and dilate to regulate the amount of light that enters our eyes. Unfortunately, the amount of dilation and constriction that our pupils can accomplish is limited. A cat's pupils can regulate light much better than a human's. Look at a cat's pupils and compare them to ours. A cat has vertical slits for pupils, which, when contracted, let in very little light. Under low light conditions, these slits widen to ovals that encompass much of the cat's eyes. Even at their most dilated, our pupils do not fill much of the surface of our eyes. This is one reason cats can see so much better at night than humans can.

Because our pupils are relatively limited in their ability to regulate the light that enters our eyes, they alone cannot fully account for the light and dark adaptations we experience. Another mechanism of adaptation is found in the photopigments themselves. If you were to enter a completely darkened room, no light would enter your eyes and no rhodopsin molecules would break down. After remaining in these darkened conditions for a period of time, the rhodopsin levels in your eyes would build up to high levels. This is what occurs when we sleep at night.

In your darkened bedroom, with your eyes closed, you do not use much of your rhodopsin, so your rhodopsin levels increase.

dark adaptation   the process through which our eyes adjust to dark conditions after having been exposed to bright light

light adaptation   the process through which our eyes adjust to bright light after having been exposed to darkness

The shape of a cat's pupil makes the cat's eye very efficient at regulating light. When dilated, a cat's eye takes in more light than a human eye. This is one reason cats can see well at night.

© Corbis

When you step out of the darkness into bright light, you may experience a flash of pain as the built-up rhodopsin in your eyes reacts all at once to the bright light.

With a large store of rhodopsin, your eyes are very sensitive to light. If someone were to suddenly turn on the lights in the bedroom, you would experience a bright flash of light and perhaps even pain. The light would cause the abundance of accumulated rhodopsin in your rods to suddenly break down all at once. It would take about one minute for your eyes to experience light adaptation, as the excess rhodopsin depletes to normal levels (Hood & Finkelstein, 1986).

The process of dark adaptation is the opposite of what occurs during light adaptation. Under normal daytime lighting conditions, we constantly use our rhodopsin to see our surroundings. This means that at any given moment during the day, a certain percentage of our rhodopsin molecules are broken down and temporarily inoperable. If you suddenly enter a darkened theater after being in the bright daylight, you will not have enough rhodopsin molecules stored to be able to see well. It will take up to 30 minutes for your rhodopsin levels to build again to allow you to see as well as you possibly can under the circumstances (Hood & Finkelstein, 1986). This is why you may have to stand, popcorn in hand, at the back of the darkened theater for several minutes before you can find your seat!

Recall that even if you stand at the back of the theater for several minutes, you may still find it impossible to pick out your companions from the rest of the crowd by the color of their clothes. This is because your cones will have trouble operating in the dim light of the theater. In our next section, we will examine how our cones allow us to see color when we are not in the dark.

How We See Color

As we already mentioned, like the rhodopsin found in the rods, the photopigments of the cones contain opsin and retinal. However, there is an important distinction between the photopigments in the rods and cones. All rods contain the same photopigment, rhodopsin. In contrast, there are three different types of cones, each containing a photopigment with a slightly different form of opsin in it. Why do we need three types of cones in our eyes? The answer seems to be that three different cones are necessary for color vision.

The Colors of Light

You may have learned in elementary school about three primary colors (red, yellow, and blue) from which all other colors can be made. But did you know that these primary colors refer to reflected colors (such as in paint or crayons) and not colors of light? When you mix paints together, what your eyes are actually seeing is the light that is reflected from the surface of the paint. Because your eyes are sensitive to *light energy*, your perception of color is due to the color of the light that enters your eye. When you see a surface that's painted blue, it appears blue because blue is the only color of light that is reflected by that surface. All other colors of light are being absorbed by the blue paint.

Mixing colored light is different from mixing colors of paints, crayons, or dyes. When colors of light are combined, you see the direct mix of light and not the light that's being reflected off of a surface. Therefore, the primary colors of light are different from those of paints, and thus the combinations formed by mixing primary colors of light are different from the combinations of similarly colored paints.

The primary colors of light are *red*, *green*, and *blue*. All other colors of light can be made from these three colors. If you mix all the primary colors of light together, you get white light. In contrast, what would happen if you mixed red, blue, and yellow paint together? You would get black paint. Mixing light is not the same as mixing paint (Figure 3.9). The eye senses only the light that is entering it. When we describe color vision and combinations of colors, remember to think in terms of light, and not in terms of paint.

The Trichromatic Theory of Color Vision

By now, we hope that some of you have made the connection between the three primary colors of light, and the three different types of cones in our retinas. Could it be that each type of cone detects the presence of a different primary color of light? This is the primary assumption of the **trichromatic theory of color vision.**

The exact origin of the trichromatic theory of color vision is not really known (Rushton, 1975; Wasserman, 1978). Most psychologists credit Hermann von Helmholtz (1821–1894) with proposing this theory in the mid-1800s. According to the trichromatic theory, we have three different types of cones in our eyes, each of which contains a slightly different photopigment that makes the cell particularly sensitive to a certain wavelength of light. Recall that a slightly different form of opsin characterizes the photopigment for each of the three types of cones.

One type of cone is particularly sensitive to long wavelengths of light (red), another is very sensitive to medium wavelengths of light (green), and the third is most sensitive to short wavelengths of light (blue). Notice that these colors correspond to the primary colors of light. These differentially sensitive cones give our brain a means of knowing what color of light we are seeing at any particular moment (Wald, 1964).

For example, if the brain receives input that the red cones are very active and the green and blue are not very active, the brain knows you are seeing the color red. This same logic can be applied to seeing the color green and blue, but how does it apply to seeing nonprimary colors? All colors of light are some combination of red, green, and blue light. So, the brain processes the relative proportions of red, green, and blue cones that are firing intensely to know what color you are seeing.

When you see a yellow light, your red and green cones begin to fire intensely, but your blue cones remain relatively inactive. This pattern of firing occurs because yellow light is made up of red and green light (see Figure 3.9). When the brain receives this combination of impulses primarily from the red and green cones, you perceive, or see, yellow light. Likewise, when the brain receives many signals from the blue and red cones, but few from the green cones, you would likely perceive purple light.

trichromatic theory of color vision
the idea that color vision is made possible by the presence of three different types of cones in the retina that react respectively to either red, green, or blue light

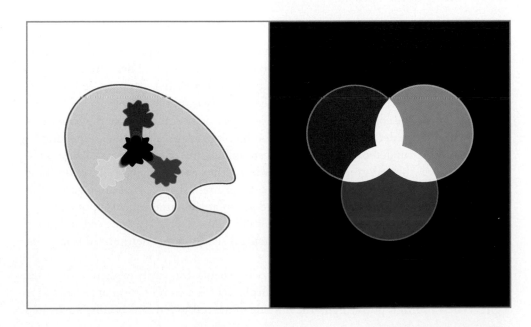

Figure 3.9 Primary Colors of Paint and Light
Mixing paint is not the same as combining colors of light.

If you were missing all of your cones, this piece of art would be perceived in grayscale instead of color.

color blindness   a condition in which one cannot perceive one or more colors due to the lack of specific cones in the retina

Demonstration

opponent-process theory   proposes that we have dual-action cells beyond the level of the retina that signal the brain when we see one of a pair of colors

Color Blindness

Does trichromatic color vision mean that all people have red, green, and blue cones? Curiously, research in the last decade or so suggests that some people with normal color vision may have more than three types of cones. The presence of additional types of cones may cause some people to perceive colors differently from others (Nathans, Merbs, Sung, Weitz, & Wang, 1992; Neitz, Neitz, & Jacobs, 1993). There is also abundant evidence that some people have fewer than three types of cones. **Color blindness,** or the inability to see one or more colors, is often the result of missing cones in the retina. A particularly common type of color blindness is red–green color blindness, a genetic disorder that occurs in approximately 1 out of 20 males in the United States (Neitz, Neitz, & Kainz, 1996) who are born missing either red or green cones. The red–green color-blind person has only blue and red cones *or* blue and green cones in his retina. The lack of red (or green) cones results in an inability to discriminate between red and green. At a stoplight, a red–green color-blind person must look at the position of the red and green lights, because the lights appear to be the same color.

Although trichromatic theory explains certain aspects of color vision, it does not explain all aspects of vision. Trichromatic theory cannot explain *negative afterimages.* To understand what an afterimage is, try this demonstration. You'll need Figure 3.10 in your textbook and a blank sheet of white paper.

A Negative Afterimage. Set the blank paper aside. Stare at the black dot in the center of Figure 3.10 without blinking or moving your eyes. Continue staring for 60 to 90 seconds. Then quickly move your gaze to the blank sheet of white paper. What do you see? You should see the image of a green shamrock with a yellow border on the blank sheet of white paper. The shamrock is a negative afterimage. Notice that the colors you see in the afterimage are different from the colors in the original.

Why would you see different colors in your afterimage? The trichromatic theory of color vision cannot explain this phenomenon. One theory that does so is the opponent-process theory of color vision.

The Opponent-Process Theory of Color Vision

The **opponent-process theory** proposes a different type of color-sensitive cell in the eye. An opponent-process cell is sensitive to two colors of light. There are thought to be three types of opponent-process cells in our visual system: red/green, yellow/blue, and black/white. The key to opponent-process theory is that these cells can detect the presence of only one color at a time. The colors *oppose* one another so that the opponent-process cell cannot detect the presence of both colors at the same time. For example, a red/green cell can detect either red or green light at any one time. If you shine a red light in the eye, the red/green cells tell our brain that we are seeing red. If you shine a green light in the eye, the red/green cells tell our brain that we are seeing green. But these red/green cells cannot detect red and green at the same time. Opponent-process theory is consistent with the finding that if we simultaneously shine red and green lights into your eye, you will likely see a neutral shade that is neither red nor green (Hurvich & Jameson, 1957).

Like trichromatic theory, opponent-process theory can easily explain how we see nonprimary colors of light. For example, purple light is a combination of red and blue light. When you view purple light, the red side of the red/green cells becomes activated and the blue side of the yellow/blue cells becomes activated. From this combination of input, the brain discerns that you are seeing the color purple.

Opponent-process theory can also explain the phenomenon of negative afterimages. Recall the demonstration you tried with Figure 3.10. After staring at the red and blue shamrock, you saw the green and yellow afterimage. Opponent-process theory proposes that as you stared at the red and blue shamrock, you were using the red and blue portions of the opponent-process cells. After a period of 60–90 seconds of continuous staring, you expended these cells' capacity to fire action potentials. In a sense, you temporarily "wore out" the red and blue portions of these cells. Then you looked at a blank sheet of white paper. Under normal conditions, the white light would excite *all* of the opponent-process cells. Recall that white light contains all colors of light. But, given the exhausted state of your opponent-process cells, only parts of them were capable of firing action potentials. In this example, the green and yellow parts of the cells were ready to fire. The light reflected off the white paper could excite only the yellow and green parts of the cells, so you saw a green and yellow shamrock.

Figure 3.10
Negative Afterimages
See text for instructions.

Trichromatic Theory or Opponent-Process Theory?

We've seen that trichromatic theory and opponent-process theory each explain certain aspects of color vision. So, which theory is correct? Both theories seem to have merit. It is generally believed that these two theories describe processes that operate at different places in the visual system (Hubel, 1995).

Trichromatic theory seems to best explain visual processing at the level of the rods and cones. The available evidence does indeed suggest that the photopigments in the cones of the retina are differentially sensitive to particular colors of light (Abramov & Gordon, 1994; Rushton, 1958, 1975). Trichromatic theory does a good job of explaining color vision at the level of the rods and cones.

Opponent-process theory best explains the processing of color vision beyond the level of the rods and cones. When we described opponent-process theory, we talked about opponent-process cells, but we didn't indicate where these cells are in the visual system. It turns out that some cells in the retina other than cones function as opponent-process cells, responding to pairs of colors (Gouras, 1991). Evidence suggests that the ganglion cells operate as opponent-process cells (DeValois & DeValois, 1975). When a ganglion cell receives input from the cones, it will detect only the presence of one of its two designated colors. For example, a ganglion cell designated as a red/green cell will detect signals that indicate the presence of red *or* green light. In true opponent-process fashion, the red/green ganglion cell cannot detect the presence of red and green light at the same time.

Opponent-process theory may also explain the action of the other layers of the retina—the amcarine, hortizontal, and bipolar cells. In fact, opponent processing may occur even after visual information leaves the retina and enters the brain (DeValois & DeValois, 1993; Masland, 1996). In the next section, we will trace the path that visual information takes as it leaves the retina and enters the brain.

The Visual Pathways of the Brain

Once the rods and cones of the retina transduce light into action potentials, this information begins its journey into the brain. Recall from Chapter 2 that the ultimate destination of visual information in the brain is the visual cortex of the occipital lobe (see p. 37). As visual information travels from the individual rods and cones of the retina to the visual cortex of the brain, it is continually processed and combined to ultimately give us a coherent perception of what we see in the environment.

As we have already discussed, the process of combining the input from the millions of rods and cones begins while the information is still in the retina. The bipolar, hori-

Figure 3.11 **The Visual Pathways in the Brain**

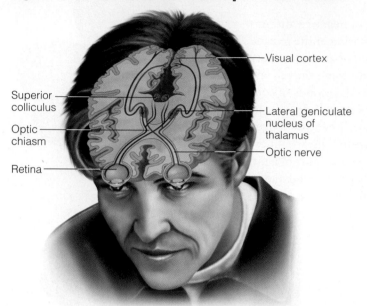

Visual cortex

Superior colliculus

Optic chiasm

Retina

Lateral geniculate nucleus of thalamus

Optic nerve

optic chiasm   the point in the brain where the optic nerve from the left eye crosses over the optic nerve from the right eye

lateral geniculate nucleus (LGN)   the part of the thalamus that processes visual information en route to the cortex

feature detection   a neurological theory of form perception that states that we have feature detector cells in our visual cortex that will fire only when we see certain visual features

zontal, and amacrine cells gather the information from the rods and cones and funnel it to the ganglion cells. The ganglion cells join together to form the optic nerve, which carries visual information into the brain (Figure 3.11).

The Optic Chiasm and Our Cross-Wired Brain

Visual information from the retina is processed *contralaterally* (or crosswise in the brain). Input from the right visual field travels to the left hemisphere of the brain, and input from the left visual field travels to the right hemisphere. Also note that each eye picks up information from both the right and left visual fields. If you were to lose an eye, the impact on your vision would be minimized. You would still receive information from the right and left visual fields, and this information would still reach both hemispheres of the brain.

As you can see in Figure 3.11, information from the rods and cones in the right and left visual fields of both eyes is gathered by the optic nerve and sent into the brain. The point at which the optic nerve from the left eye and the optic nerve from the right eye cross over is called the **optic chiasm.** From the optic chiasm, most visual information travels to the thalamus next. Recall from Chapter 2 that the thalamus is a sensory "relay station" (see p. 71). A portion of the thalamus called the **lateral geniculate nucleus (LGN)** is responsible for processing visual information. The LGN is thought to act as a filter for visual information coming from the retina. It also receives input from other areas of the brain (Kaplan, Mukherjee, and Shapely, 1993).

After leaving the LGN, visual information travels directly to the visual cortex, where specialized cells interpret the input. Many of these cortical cells function as **feature detectors** that fire only when they receive input that indicates we are looking at a particular shape, such as a line at a 45-degree angle, an edge, or colors of light. We have feature detectors for many different specific features of visual stimuli (Hubel, 1995). Additionally, regions of the visual cortex have been shown to be activated by the motion of an object (Seiffert, Somers, Dale, & Tootell, 2003) and perhaps its color (Conway, 2003; Hulbert, 2003; Xiao, Wang, & Felleman, 2003). The visual cortex and other parts of the brain gather information from our various feature detectors and combine it to give us a coherent picture of whatever it is we are seeing (Lumer, Friston, & Rees, 1998; Murray, Olshausen, and Woods, 2003).

Interestingly, studies have shown that certain areas of the visual cortex fire even when we think we see something that is not really there (as in a false alarm; Ress & Heeger, 2003). This indicates that the visual cortex goes beyond mere feature detection, or sensation, to also process aspects of perception.

Do Men and Women See the World Differently?

Recent evidence suggests that when it comes to processing visual information, men and women see things differently. Females tend to be better at discriminating one object from another (Overman, Bachevalier, Schuhmann, & Ryan, 1996), naming colors (Bornstein, 1985), and processing facial expressions (McClure, 2000). Girls also tend to show a preference for using many colors and seem to prefer warm colors to cool ones. Males tend to be better at processing moving objects and the spatial aspects of objects (Alexander, 2003).

Researcher Gerianne Alexander (2003) has argued that these gender differences in visual processing are neurological and that they have evolved to facilitate the performance of traditional male–female roles in society. In many societies, males have historically hunted for food, whereas women have gathered crops and nurtured their children. By being able to discriminate among objects and colors well, females are well suited to gathering food. For example, good color vision allows you to see a ripe fig among the green leaves of a tree. A preference for warm colors and faces may also predispose women to care for their young (many babies are pinker than adults). On the other hand, male superiority in processing movement and spatial information may have helped men perform hunting duties. According to Alexander, these visual differences may even explain why little girls prefer playing with dolls (faces), whereas boys prefer playing with trucks (moving objects). We'll have more to say about gender roles and gender differences in Chapters 9 and 11. For now, let's turn our attention to our other senses.

Let's Review!

In this section, we discussed vision, including the physical properties of light, the anatomy of the eye and the retina, how we adapt to light and dark, how we see color, and the role of the brain in vision. For a quick check of your understanding, answer these questions.

1. Jared was born with no cones in his retina. How will this condition affect Jared?
   a. He will be blind.
   b. He will not be able to see black or white.
   c. He will see the world in shades of black and white.
   d. His vision will not be affected.

2. Which theory *best* explains why Sarafina would see flashes of red light after eight hours of working on a computer monitor that has a green and black screen?
   a. The opponent-process theory
   b. The trichromatic theory
   c. The rod and cone theory
   d. The theory of red–green color-blindness

3. You have just returned to a darkened theater after a trip to the concession stand. Now you have a problem—you can't find your seat in the darkness. Knowing what you do about vision, which of the following would *most likely* help you to find your seat?
   a. Stare straight ahead at the seats.
   b. Search for your seat out of the corner of your eye.
   c. Go back out into the bright light and allow your eyes to deplete their rhodopsin.
   d. Cross your eyes and search for your seat.

ANSWERS:
1.c 2.a 3.b

Hearing: The World We Hear > > > > > > > > > > > >

Like vision, hearing is one of our most important senses; much of what we learn in life depends on these two senses. Additionally, hearing plays an important role in our ability to communicate with others. To understand hearing, we will describe the physical properties of sound waves, the anatomy of the ear, and how our brain processes sound.

How Hearing Works: Vibrating Sound Waves

As was the case with vision, hearing requires that environmental energy be transduced into neural impulses. In the case of vision, the energy is electromagnetic. In hearing, the environmental energy takes a different form. Sounds, such as a human voice, produce waves of compressed air that our ears convert to neural impulses. To demonstrate

LEARNING OBJECTIVES

- Describe the physical properties of sound and how they relate to what we hear: pitch, loudness, and timbre.
- Be able to locate the outer, middle, and inner ear, list their major structures, and describe their roles in hearing.

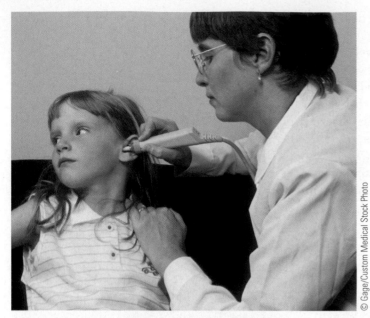

© Gage/Custom Medical Stock Photo

Figure 3.12 **The Vibrations of Sound**

This doctor is testing the patient's ability to hear sounds transmitted through the bones of the skull.

cycle   a physical characteristic of energy defined as a wave peak and the valley that immediately follows it

frequency   a physical characteristic of energy defined as the number of cycles that occur in a given unit of time

pitch   the psychophysical property of sound that corresponds to the frequency of a sound wave

Application ⟫

these waves for yourself, try the following: hold your palm about one inch in front of your mouth and speak in a normal tone of voice. Can you feel the waves of air hitting your hand as you speak? These waves are the stimuli that your ear transduces as you hear your own voice speaking.

Hearing depends on the vibration of some elastic medium as a sound wave passes through it. That medium is usually air, but this doesn't have to be the case. For example, we can also hear sound waves traveling through water and solid materials, like bone. Doctors sometimes test aspects of hearing by striking a tuning fork and placing the vibrating fork against the bone of the patient's skull, directly behind the ear (Figure 3.12). A patient with normal hearing will hear sound as the fork transmits sound waves directly to the patient's skull, which transmits these waves to the inner structures of the ear. Because most of the day-to-day sounds we hear are transmitted through the air, we will restrict our discussions of hearing to these cases.

Like light waves, sound waves have their own psychophysical properties. A sound wave has both peaks and valleys (Figure 3.13) that correspond to changes in atmospheric pressure as the sound wave travels through the air. A **cycle** is defined as the peak of the wave and the valley that immediately follows it. Counting the number of cycles in a given time frame allows us to determine the **frequency** of a sound wave. Traditionally, the frequency of sound waves is measured in hertz (Hz), or the number of cycles completed per second. A sound wave with a frequency of 1,000 Hz would complete 1,000 cycles per second.

The frequency of a sound wave corresponds to the **pitch** of the sound we perceive. The higher the frequency of the sound wave, the higher the pitch we perceive when hearing it. The average young adult can perceive sounds that range from a low of 20 Hz to a high of 20,000 Hz (Gelfand, 1981). We lose some of this range as we age, particularly our ability to hear high pitches. This condition is called *presbycusis*, and by late adulthood, as many as one third of us will suffer some impairment due to presbycusis (Whitbourne, 1985). Those of us who live and work in noisy environments may be even more likely to suffer hearing loss as we age. For instance, people who live

Figure 3.13 **The Amplitude and Frequency of Sound Waves**

The height, or amplitude, of a sound wave determines its loudness. The frequency or number of cycles per second determines the sound's pitch. The higher the wave's frequency, the higher the sound's pitch will be.

From Ellen R. Green Wood, Samuel E. Wood, The World of Psychology, 4/e. Published by Allyn & Bacon, Boston, MA. Copyright © by Pearson Education. Reprinted by permission of the publisher.

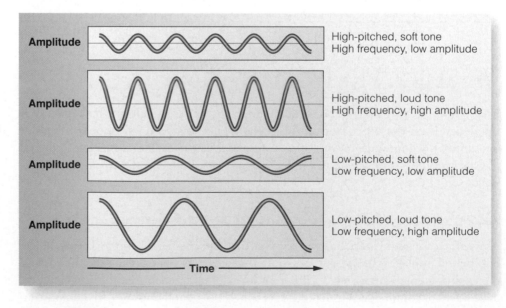

in North American urban areas suffer from presbycusis more than those who live in quiet, rural areas of Africa (Bennett, 1990). Luckily, most of the everyday sounds we hear fall well below the 20,000 Hz level. In fact, unless the gradual deterioration impairs our ability to hear sounds at 1800 Hz and below, our ability to comprehend speech should remain pretty much intact (Welford, 1987).

Like light waves, sound waves differ in amplitude (see Figure 3.13). The amplitude of a sound wave corresponds to the **loudness** of the sound we hear as well as the amount of pressure the compressed waves of air exert on the eardrum. The higher the amplitude, the more pressure exerted on the eardrum, and the louder the sound. Loudness is usually measured in **decibels (dB).** Table 3.3 ◆ shows the decibel levels for some common sounds. Note that the sensory threshold for sound in humans is defined as 0 decibels.

We also experience the psychophysical property of a sound's **timbre** (pronounced *TAM-ber*). Timbre corresponds to the quality of a sound. Most of the sounds we hear result not from individual sound waves, but rather from a complex combination of sound waves. Therefore, sounds of the same loudness and pitch can still sound different to us. An example of this would be to compare the sound of the A above middle C on a piano to the same note on a violin or a flute. The pitch is the same, but the sound is not. What differs across these tones are the additional sound waves, called *harmonics*, or *overtones*, that the instruments produce in addition to the fundamental frequency of the A note. Because a piano, violin, and flute produce different harmonics, the same A note will have a different timbre on each instrument.

Let's turn our discussion to the ear itself and how it allows us to transduce sound waves into neural impulses. As we did with the eye, we will begin by taking a closer look at the anatomy of the ear.

The Anatomy and Function of the Ear

We generally divide the ear into three sections: the *outer ear, middle ear,* and *inner ear* (Figure 3.14).

The Outer Ear

The very outside of the outer ear is called the **pinna.** It includes the part of the body normally referred to as the ear and earlobe. The pinna acts as a funnel to gather sound waves. The human pinna is stationary, but in some species, the pinna is free to rotate. For example, have you ever watched a sleeping cat? The slightest sound causes the cat's pinna to rotate in the direction of the sound. This allows the cat its best chance to perceive an approaching animal—even when its eyes are closed!

After being gathered by the pinna, sound waves are then channeled through the **auditory canal.** The auditory canal is specially shaped to amplify the incoming sound waves.

◆ **Table 3.3**
The Decibel Levels of Some Common Sounds

Decibels	Example
LITTLE OR NO CHANCE OF DAMAGE	
0	The softest detectable sound
20	A soft whisper
30	A quiet library
40	A quiet neighborhood
50	A refrigerator running
60	The average conversation
PROLONGED EXPOSURE CAN CAUSE DAMAGE	
70	A noisy restaurant
80	A loud radio
90	A lawn mower
100	Heavy traffic
120	A very loud thunder clap
SOUNDS OF THESE INTENSITIES CAN QUICKLY CAUSE DAMAGE	
140	A jet airplane taking off
160	*Extremely* loud rock music
180	The launch of a spacecraft

loudness the psychophysical property of sound that corresponds to the amplitude of a sound wave

decibels (dB) the unit of measure used to determine the loudness of a sound

timbre a psychophysical property of sound that corresponds to the quality or pureness of the sound

The pinna is much more than a place to hang an earring. It helps funnel sound waves into the ear canal.

© Ryan McVay/Getty Images

pinna the outside part of the ear that functions as a funnel that captures and channels the sound wave into the ear canal

auditory canal the passageway that runs from the pinna on the outside of the ear to the eardrum

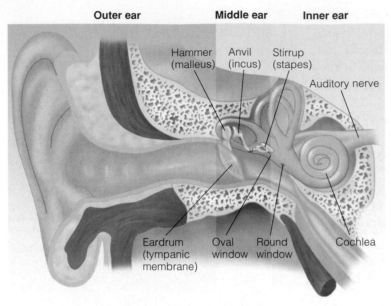

Figure 3.14 The Anatomy of the Ear

eardrum the thin membrane at the end of the ear canal that vibrates when struck by incoming sound waves

ossicles the bones of the middle ear that transmit sound from the eardrum and the cochlea

hammer the first bone of the middle ear

anvil the second bone of the middle ear

stirrup the third bone of the middle ear that connects the middle ear to the inner ear

oval window the point on the front edge of the cochlea where the stirrup of the middle ear transmits its vibrations to the cochlea

cochlea the curled, fluid-filled tube that contains the basilar membrane in the inner ear

vestibular canal the top internal duct of the cochlea

cochlear duct the middle internal duct of the cochlea that contains the basilar membrane; it is here that transduction occurs

tympanic canal the bottom duct of the cochlea

basilar membrane the structure in the cochlear duct that contains the hair cells, which transduce sound waves into action potentials

hair cells neurons that grow out of the basilar membrane and transduce sounds waves into action potentials

For example, a sound wave at 3,000 Hz may be amplified by as much as 10dB as it travels down the auditory canal (Gulick, Gescheider, & Frisina, 1989).

The auditory canal also protects the sensitive structures of the middle and inner ear from outside debris (Scharf & Buus, 1986). Because the auditory canal is about 1 inch long, foreign objects are not likely to come in contact with the internal structures of the ear—unless, of course, we purposely insert a foreign object, such as a cotton swab, into the auditory canal. Doctors strongly discourage this practice because of the damage it could cause to the membrane at the end of the auditory canal, the **eardrum.**

The Middle Ear

The eardrum, or tympanic membrane, is a very thin membrane that vibrates as the incoming sound waves strike it, much as the head of a drum vibrates when a drumstick strikes it. The higher the frequency of the incoming sound waves, the faster the vibration of the eardrum. If you were to damage your eardrum by puncturing it, you would experience serious hearing loss. The sound waves could not efficiently transmit their energy to the eardrum by making it vibrate correctly. If the head of a drum has a tear in it, the drum's sound is quite muted.

The three bones, or **ossicles,** of the middle ear that are directly behind the eardrum are the **hammer** (or malleus), **anvil** (or incus), and the **stirrup** (or stapes). These very small bones that rest against one another transmit vibrations from the eardrum to the inner ear. When incoming sound waves cause the eardrum to vibrate, this causes the bones of the middle ear to vibrate. The vibration of these bones amplifies the sound waves as they travel through the middle ear. As the sound waves travel from the eardrum to the inner ear, they may be amplified by as much as 30dB (Luce, 1993). Without the amplification that occurs in the outer and middle ear, our sense of hearing would be much less acute.

The middle ear connects to the inner ear at the point where the stirrup rests against the **oval window** (Figure 3.14). The oval window is found on the outer end of the **cochlea,** one of the major components of the inner ear. The cochlea is a coiled, fluid-filled tube of about 1.4 inches long that resembles a snail (Matlin, & Foley, 1997). The term cochlea is Latin for "snail." The transduction of sound waves to neural impulses occurs inside the cochlea.

The Inner Ear

If you were to uncoil the cochlea, you would see that it resembles a flexible tube that is closed off at the end. The inside of the tube is partitioned into three ducts, or canals, each filled with fluid. These are the **vestibular canal,** the **cochlear duct,** and the **tympanic canal** (Figure 3.15). The cochlear duct is sandwiched between the two larger ducts, vestibular canal on top and the tympanic canal on the bottom.

In our quest to understand how hearing occurs, we are most concerned with the cochlear duct because that is where transduction occurs. The floor of the cochlear duct is lined with the **basilar membrane.** Growing out of the basilar membrane are specialized **hair cells.** Hair cells are so named because they resemble the hairs that grow

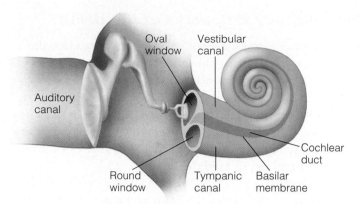

Figure 3.15 Enlarged Detail of the Inner Ear

This isn't quite how the ear works!

THE FAR SIDE® BY GARY LARSON

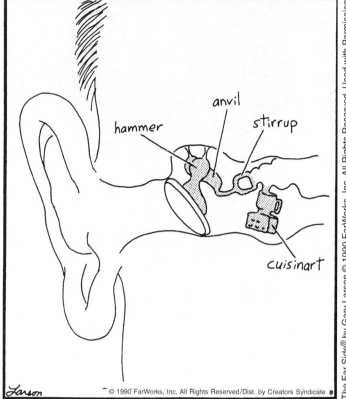

© 1990 FarWorks, Inc. All Rights Reserved/Dist. by Creators Syndicate

The Far Side® by Gary Larson © 1990 FarWorks, Inc. All Rights Reserved. Used with Permission.

Professor Harold Rosenbloom's diagram of the middle ear, proposing his newly discovered fourth bone.

out of our skin. It is the hair cells that transduce sound wave energy into neural impulses.

Recall our discussion about the transmission of sound waves through the outer and middle ears, and then look once again at Figures 3.14 and 3.15. Incoming sound waves cause the ossicles to vibrate. This vibration is transferred to the cochlea because the stirrup rests against the oval window. The vibration of the stirrup against the oval window sets up a wave action inside the fluid-filled vestibular canal. As this wave travels through the vestibular canal, the cochlear duct begins to ripple. Inside the cochlear duct, the traveling wave ripples across the hairs of the basilar membrane.

As the wave travels across the basilar membrane, the hair cells sway back and forth. To give you an idea of what the hair cells are experiencing, imagine submerging your right arm into a container of water. Agitate the water with your left hand. As the waves pass over your right arm, the hairs on your arm begin to sway. This swaying is analogous to what is occurring in your ears as you perceive a sound. The swaying motion of the hair cells stimulates the cells to send neural impulses. It takes remarkably very little movement to activate the hair cells. The wave moving through the cochlea's fluid may be quite small. Less than a billionth of a meter of movement is sufficient to allow hearing (Gutin, 1993).

When this traveling wave reaches the end of the vestibular canal, fluid is forced into the tympanic canal that runs underneath the basilar membrane. This increase in fluid causes increased pressure in the tympanic canal. The pressure must be released somehow, otherwise we would risk rupturing the cochlea. The cochlea is equipped with a pressure release valve, the *round window* (see Figure 3.15). As the fluid rushes into the tympanic canal, the round window bulges out toward the middle ear to relieve the pressure inside the cochlea. No damage to the system occurs—under normal conditions.

Given the nature of the cochlea and the hair cells, it is important to protect our ears from very loud sounds. Otherwise, the wave that is set up in the cochlea may be strong enough to damage this structure. Hair cells can actually be ripped out of the basilar membrane if the wave is strong enough. Hair cells, like most neurons, do not regenerate once they are destroyed. This damage can lead to permanent hearing loss. Such damage is one major reason that we may lose some of our hearing as we age. People who are repeatedly exposed to noisy environments are most at risk for hearing loss. Keep this in mind when you put on a pair of headphones or crank up the volume on your car stereo.

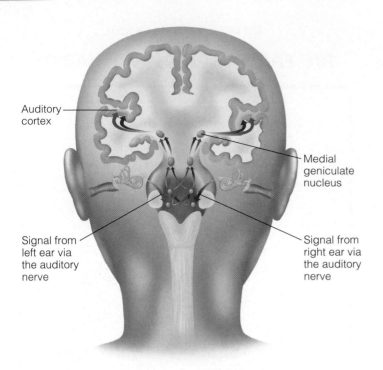

Auditory
cortex

Medial
geniculate
nucleus

Signal from
left ear via
the auditory
nerve

Signal from
right ear via
the auditory
nerve

**Figure 3.16 The Auditory Pathways
in the Brain.**

auditory nerve   the nerve that carries
information from the inner ear to the brain

medial geniculate nucleus (MGN)
the part of the thalamus that processes auditory
information en route to the cortex

place theory   proposes that our brain
decodes pitch by noticing which region of the
basilar membrane is most active

The Auditory Pathways of the Brain

Once the hair cells transduce sound into neural impulses, these impulses must be sent to the brain for further processing. Attached to the end of the cochlea is the **auditory nerve** (Figure 3.14). The bundled neurons of the auditory nerve gather the information from the hair cells to relay it to the brain. Figure 3.16 shows the path that auditory information takes from the ears to the brain. Notice that auditory information from each ear reaches both sides of the brain.

From the inner ear, the auditory information travels to several structures in the back of the brain in the *medulla oblongata* and *pons*. The information then travels to a section of the thalamus called the **medial geniculate nucleus (MGN)** for further processing. The MGN in the thalamus transfers the information to the auditory cortex of the temporal lobe. It is here that we decode the meaning of the sounds we hear—provided that we are not hearing *words*. Recall from Chapter 2 that in the special case of listening to speech, the auditory information travels to Wernicke's area (see p. 74) for further processing. Without Wernicke's area, we could still understand instrumental music and other nonverbal sounds, but we would be unable to understand the meaning of speech.

The auditory cortex has the power to decode the meanings of the sounds we hear. Our next task is to examine how the brain perceives, or makes sense of, the auditory information it receives from the ears.

Place Theory of Pitch Perception

Several theories have been proposed to explain how we perceive pitch. Hermann von Helmholtz, who is credited with the trichromatic theory of color vision, also studied pitch perception. Just as he made significant contributions to our understanding of vision, Helmholtz also contributed to our understanding of sound perception with his version of the **place theory** of pitch perception (Helmholtz, 1863/1930).

Place theory proposes that sounds of different frequencies excite different hair cells at particular points along the basilar membrane. Therefore, according to place theory, the brain receives information on pitch from the location, or *place*, on the basilar membrane that is being most excited by incoming sound waves. Evidence suggests that place theory may indeed explain some of our ability to perceive pitch.

In the early 1960s, Georg von Békésy conducted some important studies on pitch perception that eventually won him the Nobel Prize (Békésy, 1960). Békésy surgically opened holes in the cochleae of (nonliving) participants, to expose the basilar membranes. He then stimulated the cochleae with sound waves of different pitches and observed the resulting wave action in the basilar membranes. Under a microscope, Békésy could see where the different sound waves caused the most vibration of the basilar membrane. We know that movement activates hair cells. The point on the basilar membrane where the vibration is the greatest is also where the hair cells are most activated by the sound. In support of place theory, Békésy found that sounds of different pitches caused the most vibration at different points along the basilar membrane.

Békésy determined that low frequency sounds activate the far end of the basilar membrane the most. High frequency sounds cause the most activation at the front part of the basilar membrane, near the oval window. This makes sense in light of what we know about hearing loss due to damage. As we age, many of us lose some of our hearing due to wear and tear on the hair cells of the basilar membrane. It stands to reason that hair cells at the front of the basilar membrane are more vulnerable to damage because they experience the most intense vibrations coming in from the outside world. If we lose our front hair cells first and place theory has merit, this would explain why age-related hearing loss first affects our ability to hear higher pitches.

Although Békésy's research on place theory does describe some of our ability to perceive pitch, it does not fully account for our perception of pitch. One problem with Békésy's work is that he used only pure tones, or single sound waves without harmonics, in his experiments. Most of the sounds we hear are complex, made up of many separate pure tones. When place theory is put to the test using complex sounds as stimuli, it does not fare as well as it does in explaining perception of pure tones (Matlin & Foley, 1997). What other explanations do we have for our ability to perceive pitch?

Frequency Theory of Pitch Perception

Frequency theory proposes that our brain receives information about pitch directly from the frequency at which the hair cells are firing (Rutherford, 1886; Wever, 1949/1970). An incoming sound wave will cause the hair cells to fire action potentials at a frequency that is equal to the frequency of the sound wave. For example, a sound wave at 500 Hz would cause the hair cells to fire 500 action potentials per second; a sound wave at 750 Hz would produce 750 action potentials per second.

Frequency theory is a very simple concept, but it has a severe limitation. Hair cells can fire only at a maximum rate of 1,000 action potentials per second (1,000 Hz). Because we can hear sounds in the range of 20–20,000 Hz, frequency theory obviously falls short of explaining perception of pitches over 1,000 Hz!

frequency theory   proposes that our brain decodes pitch directly from the frequency at which the hair cells of the basilar membrane are firing

Volley Theory of Pitch Perception

Volley theory is an update of frequency theory that seeks to explain perception of sounds over 1,000 Hz (Wever, 1949/1970). According to volley theory "teams" of hair cells work together to give us the perception of sounds over 1,000 Hz. For example, let's say you hear a tone of 3,000 Hz. No single hair cell can fire at 3,000 Hz, but three hair cells, each firing at 1,000 Hz, can work together to tell your brain that you are hearing a 3,000 Hz tone. Three cells firing in turn at their maximum rate can send the signal as a group at 3,000 Hz. Hair cells that work together can accomplish what single hair cells cannot.

volley theory   proposes that our brain decodes pitch by noticing the frequency at which *groups* of hair cells on the basilar membrane are firing

Duplicity Theory: An Integration

Volley theory seems adequate to explain pitch perception, but we still have to deal with place theory, which also seems to explain some aspects of our perception. Recall that Georg von Békésy (1960) did find that different pitches excite different parts of the basilar membrane. Volley theory cannot explain why this would be the case. So, what is going on in our ears? Is it the place or the frequency of the excited hair cells that tell us what pitch we are hearing? It may well be that it is *both*.

Today it is widely believed that we perceive pitch through a combination of volley theory and place theory. This combination of perceptual processes is called **duplicity theory.** Researchers strongly suspect that frequency and place information work together to give us pitch perception, but we don't yet understand exactly how these two mechanisms work together.

duplicity theory   proposes that a combination of volley and place theory explain how our brain decodes pitch

Because we learn more through sight and sound than we do through our other senses, psychologists have put much of their effort toward understanding these two senses, and less toward understanding the remaining senses. Before we move on to discuss perceptual processes, we will briefly review taste, smell, and the skin's senses.

Let's Review!

In this section, we looked at the process of hearing: the psychophysics of sound, the anatomy of the ear, the brain's role in hearing, and theories of pitch perception. For a quick check of your understanding, answer these questions.

1. Jack is 58 years old and having trouble with his hearing. He has spent his life working around noisy machinery without any ear protection. Knowing what you do about hearing, what type of hearing loss is Jack *most likely* experiencing?
   a. Total deafness
   b. Deafness for low pitches
   c. Deafness for medium pitches
   d. Deafness for high pitches

2. Loudness is to _____ as _____ is to pitch.

a. amplitude; frequency
b. frequency; amplitude
c. wavelength; frequency
d. amplitude; wavelength

3. _____ theory proposes that pitch is perceived when the brain locates the region of the basilar membrane that is firing the most action potentials.
   a. Frequency
   b. Basilar
   c. Place
   d. Volley

ANSWERS

1. d; 2. a; 3. c

LEARNING < < < < < < < < <
OBJECTIVE

Explain the processes involved in taste, smell, touch, and the body senses.

Taste, Smell, Touch, and the Body Senses

For Michael Watson, whose story opened this chapter, the sensory pathways for taste are interconnected with his tactile, or touch, senses. Synesthesia only affects 10 people in 1 million, and Michael's form of synesthesia is one of the rarest. In this section, we'll review what is known about how the rest of us, as nonsynesthetes, experience the sensation of taste, smell, and touch, as well as what we call the body senses.

Taste: Information From the Tongue

Most of us will never experience taste as a tactile sensation, the way Michael Watson does. However, for us the senses of taste and smell are interconnected. These two senses are called chemical senses, because they require that certain chemicals come into direct contact with our sense organs. Vision and hearing don't require such direct contact, and you can perceive visual and auditory stimuli at a distance. But for taste, or **gustation,** to occur, certain chemicals in foods and other substances must be dissolved in our saliva and come into direct contact with the sense organ commonly know as the tongue. For smell, chemicals in the nearby air—from food or other substances—must come into contact with cells in the nasal cavity.

gustation our sense of taste

Properties of Taste: The Four—or Five—Tastes

Application

It is widely believed that humans are sensitive to at least four different types of tastes: bitter, sweet, salty, and sour (Bartoshuk & Beauchamp, 1994). It makes good sense that our tongues are designed to detect these tastes. They are associated with certain types of foods that have implications for our survival (Scott & Plata-Salaman, 1991). Sweet flavors are associated with organic molecules that contain hydrogen, carbon, and oxygen. Sugars are organic molecules, so our ability to taste sugars may ensure that we take in enough to fuel our bodies.

Salty flavors are associated with foods that release ions, or charged particles. As we saw in Chapter 2, ions such as sodium are crucial for normal functioning of the nervous system. Our ability to taste salts ensures that we take in enough of these critical ions.

Sour tastes are generally associated with acidic substances, and bitter flavors are often found in substances that contain nitrogen. Our ability to taste sour and bitter tastes may help us to regulate the level of acidity (pH) in our bodies. Bitter tastes are also often associated with toxic substances. Therefore, tasting bitterness may steer us away from certain poisons.

In addition to these four basic tastes, some researchers have proposed that humans may be sensitive to a fifth taste called **umami,** or glutamate (Rolls, 2000). Umami is a meaty, brothy flavor that is more common in Asian foods than it is in Western cuisine (MSG, or monosodium glutamate, is a common ingredient in Asian dishes). So, Westerners are not likely to be as familiar with umami's flavor as they are with the other basic tastes. Nonetheless, preliminary studies indicate that the ability to taste umami exists (Damak et al., 2003).

umami a proposed fifth taste, that of glutamate, or a meaty, brothy taste

The flavors we experience are most likely some combination of these four (or five) basic tastes. This makes taste perception similar to color perception. Recall the trichromatic theory of color vision, which states that all colors are some combination of red, green, and blue light. In taste perception, all tastes are thought to be a combination of sweet, salty, sour, bitter—and *maybe* umami. But, how does the tongue detect the presence of these basic flavors?

The Anatomy and Function of the Tongue

When you look at your tongue in the mirror, you normally see a bunch of little bumps lining its surface. We'll guess that you were taught to refer to these visible bumps as taste buds. This is incorrect—the bumps you see are the **papillae** of the tongue. Your **taste buds** actually reside in the pits between the papillae (Figure 3.17). Your taste buds are what transduce the chemicals in the foods you eat into the neural impulses that convey taste information to your brain. Most people have between 2,000 and 5,000 taste buds on their tongue (Miller & Bartoshuk, 1991). Unlike some types of sensory cells, taste buds can regenerate. This is important because we damage our taste buds on a regular basis. Have you ever eaten a very hot slice of pizza and as a result lost some of your sense of taste for a few days? You probably killed many of your taste buds with that molten mozzarella, and you had to wait for them to grow back!

papillae the bumps on our tongue that many people mistake for taste buds

taste buds the sense organs for taste that are found between the papillae on the tongue

We also permanently lose some of our taste buds with age. This may contribute to the diminished sense of taste that is often seen in older adults (Nordin, Razani, Markison, & Murphy, 2003). It might appear that one way to maintain an elderly person's appetite is a diet that includes many richly flavored foods. However, studies have shown that this strategy may not always work (Koskinen, Kalviainen, & Tuorila, 2003).

If we don't have much age-related taste bud loss and we haven't recently done in our taste buds with pizza, our several thousand taste buds should be sufficient to allow us to enjoy our foods. Many researchers believe that, like the cones of the eye, taste buds seem to be maximally sensitive to one of the four basic flavors (Shallenberger, 1993). According to this theory, we have "sweet taste buds," "sour taste buds," "salty taste buds," and "bitter taste buds." These buds can sense the presence of any of the basic flavors, but they are *most* excited by their particular designated flavor. For instance, a "sweet taste bud" may be also be sensitive to sour or salty flavors, but it is much more sensitive to the presence of sweet flavors.

You can see that taste perception on the tongue appears to work very much like color perception in the retina. If the brain is informed that the "sweet taste buds" are very active, we taste a sweet flavor. If the "sour taste buds" are most active, we taste something sour. If all flavors are some combination of sweet, salty, sour, bitter, and perhaps umami, the presence of four or five types of taste buds is sufficient to explain our taste perception. It's not quite that simple, though. A good deal of our ability to taste certain flavors depends on where on the tongue the substance is placed.

The different types of taste buds are concentrated in certain locations. This uneven distribution of taste buds results in differential sensitivities to each of the basic tastes at certain points along the tongue (Shallenberg, 1993). Over the years, there has

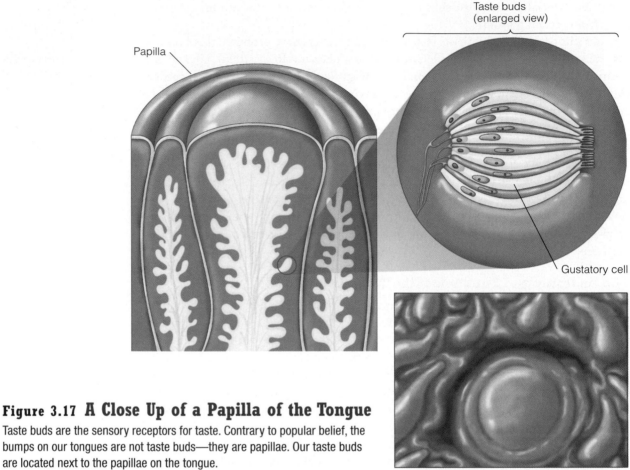

Figure 3.17 **A Close Up of a Papilla of the Tongue**

Taste buds are the sensory receptors for taste. Contrary to popular belief, the bumps on our tongues are not taste buds—they are papillae. Our taste buds are located next to the papillae on the tongue.

If you burn your taste buds with a slice of hot pizza, you will experience temporary loss of taste sensation until the taste buds grow back.

© Rolf Bruderer/Corbis

been significant disagreement as to where exactly these areas of sensitivity can be found on the tongue. Historically, some of these disagreements were among researchers studying sensory thresholds for tastes. For instance, some found that bitter flavors are detected best at the back of the tongue (Hänig, 1901), whereas others found that bitter tastes are more easily detected at the front of the tongue (Collings, 1974).

There is more agreement on the sweet and sour tastes. Sweet tastes are best detected at the front of the tongue, and sour tastes are best detected on the sides (Shallenberg, 1993). Salty tastes are thought to be detected best near the front of the tongue (Shallenberg, 1993).

You may be surprised to learn that the center of the tongue is lacking taste buds. You won't taste flavors that are placed directly in the center of your tongue. In a sense, this region of the tongue is like the blindspot in the eye—no taste sensation can occur here (Matlin & Foley, 1997). To demonstrate this for yourself, take a strongly flavored food, such as a small piece of orange flavored candy, and place it directly on the center of your tongue. Keep your mouth open so that your saliva does not dissolve the flavors and allow them to flow to other parts of the tongue. Can you taste the candy? You should not be able to, because the flavors are not reaching any tastebuds. Next, roll the candy to the side of your tongue. Now you should be able to taste the candy because you have plenty of taste buds on the sides of your tongue.

Of course, only after your brain has done its part can you become consciously aware that you taste orange candy. Next, we will very briefly look at the path of taste information in the brain.

Loss of taste buds may reduce our ability to taste as we grow older. A bland diet may only make this problem worse.

 **Demonstration**

Taste Pathways in the Brain

Each taste bud is connected to a neuron that receives input from the taste bud. These neurons join together to form three nerves. One nerve gathers input from the front of the tongue, another from the back of the tongue, and a third from the throat. These nerves travel to the medulla and the pons of the brainstem before conveying the taste information to the thalamus. Like most sensory information, taste information travels from the thalamus to the "thinking" part of the brain, the cortex. Most of the taste information ends up in the somatosensory cortex of the parietal lobe, but some of the information is diverted to the limbic system before reaching the cortex.

An interesting point is that some taste sensations may not require cortical processing at all. There is evidence of this from studying severely brain damaged infants, who are born with no cortex, but still seem to react to certain tastes. Apparently, these infants experience certain tastes despite the fact that they lack the "thinking" part of the brain (Keverne, 1982). In a similar vein, recall that Michael Watson's special sense of taste is linked to abnormal processing in the left limbic and left cortical areas of his brain. In Watson's case, his synesthesia seemed to coincide with a *reduction* in the activity of his left cortical areas and an *increase* in processing in his subcortical left limbic regions. In essence, when he "tasted shapes," the "thinking" part of his brain shut down on the left side.

Given that Michael Watson's sense of taste is far more unusual than that of the average person, it is likely that his food preferences were affected by his synesthesia. However, even for people with a normal sense of taste, food preferences can be a very individual thing. The choices we make when choosing foods may be a product of our genetics, learning, and even our culture.

IT'S A DIVERSE WORLD

What We Eat and What We Taste

How would you like to have a bowl of soup made with fresh iguana meat, onions, squash, and other vegetables? Sound good? It may surprise you, but to many it would! The spouse of one of the authors is from El Salvador, where iguana meat is considered to be a treat enjoyed mostly by the wealthy. In the United States, iguana is strangely absent from most restaurant menus! Around the world, taste preferences for food are as varied as the cultures in which they are found. Many Germans favor sausages made from pork brains (*Gehirnwurst*; Gade, 2000, p. 539). In East Africa, roasted camel blood might be one's meal

Whether or not you like jalapeños may be due to your genetic ability to taste certain flavors and/or your cultural background.

(Stephens, 2000, p. 474), but in Ethiopia and Kenya, fish are avoided in the diet (Newman, 2000, p. 1336). What accounts for such variations in taste?

It seems likely that several factors account for the diet of a particular culture. The availability of food sources dictates what a particular people *can* eat. Central Americans eat iguana meat today partly because their ancestors once ate the wild iguanas that roamed there. Every culture must take advantage of the food sources at its disposal. Ecological concerns also affect food choices. The use of camel blood as a food in East Africa makes sense because camels do not reproduce very quickly. If East Africans slaughtered their camels for meat, they might quickly deplete their stock. Bleeding the camels and consuming the blood utilizes the animals as a more sustainable food source (Stephens, 2000).

Religious values and traditions also shape cultural food preferences. Many of the world's religions include proscriptions and prescriptions that influence the diet of their followers. For example, Jews and Muslims will not eat pork, Hindus do not eat beef, and Seventh Day Adventists frown upon the use of chili pepper and black pepper (Grivetti, 2000).

Anthropologists and sociologists have studied the development of food preferences within cultures by examining these and other cultural factors that influence a people's diet over the ages. Psychologists, on the other hand, are much more interested in the biological and environmental influences that affect our *individual* taste preferences.

Just as we saw with cultural food preferences, many of our individual food preferences develop through learning—some of it very early in life. Research shows that the foods a mother eats can affect the flavor of her breast milk, and exposure to these flavors during breast-feeding can affect her child's later taste preferences (Mennella & Beauchamp, 1991). It has also been shown that being exposed to a variety of flavors in infancy tends to make infants more open to new and novel foods (Gerrish & Mennella, 2001).

Although the influence of learning on food preferences is strong, evidence also suggests that biological factors can impact our sense of taste. Prior to menopause, women's ability to taste fluctuates with hormonal levels, and after menopause it declines (Prutlin, et al., 2000). There are also some genetic variations in the ability to taste. Some people, called *supertasters,* have genes that

To some, this meal would be appetizing; to others, it would be disgusting. Our cultural background heavily influences the foods we like.

give them taste buds that allow them to strongly taste a bitter compound called 6-n-propylthiocuracil (PROP). In contrast, *nontasters* perceive very little or no bitterness from PROP (Bartoshuk, 2000a). This genetic difference can influence the foods that one consumes. Nontasters have been shown to eat a wider variety of foods than supertasters do (Azar, 1998; Pasquet, Obeerti, Ati, & Hladik, 2002). Compared to nontasters, female PROP tasters tend to eat more fat and less fruit in their diets (Yackinous & Guinard, 2002). Supertasters may avoid some foods that are rich in cancer fighting compounds but also have bitter flavors (e.g., Brussels sprouts). Therefore, our ability to taste PROP could be a significant health factor (Bartoshuk, 2000b).

Our sense of taste is not influenced solely by our taste buds, however. Our sense of taste is also heavily dependent on our sense of smell. If you ever tried to taste your food when you had a bad cold, you know that your sense of smell makes a significant contribution to taste. When you can't smell due to closed nasal passages, food loses much of its taste. You can easily test this effect in a simple demonstration. You'll need the help of a friend and some familiar foods.

« Demonstration

Gustation Depends on Olfaction. Have a friend cut several foods of similar texture into bite-sized chunks. Close your eyes and hold your nose while your friend places a chunk of food on your tongue. Can you identify it? Then try releasing your nose. Can you identify it now? If you are like most people, you will find it difficult or impossible to identify the foods without the benefit of your sense of smell.

Smell: Aromas, Odors, and a Warning System

As you can see in this demonstration, **olfaction,** our sense of smell, aids our sense of taste. Like our ability to taste, our ability to smell has adaptive value. Smells can alert us to danger. The ability to smell smoke could allow us to detect a fire long before we see flames. The rotten smell of spoiled food warns us not to eat it. Noxious fumes warn us to seek fresh air. Without such odoriferous warnings, we could easily find ourselves in harm's way. Interestingly, very recent research links declines in olfaction with an increased risk of developing Alzheimer's disease and other cognitive impairments (Schiffman, Graham, Sattley Miller, Zervakis, & Welsh-Bohmer, 2002; Swan & Carmelli, 2002). Although it's too soon to know the exact implications of these findings, they underscore the need for researchers to further understand olfaction. So, just how does olfaction work?

olfaction our sense of smell

© Bill Losh/Getty Images

The inability to smell also limits the ability to taste.

Like our sense of taste, our sense of smell is a chemical sense. Odors come from chemicals that are *volatile* and evaporate easily. When a volatile chemical evaporates, its molecules become diffused in the air. When these molecules are inhaled into our nose, we may experience smelling the substance. Our sense of smell is quite sensitive. Recall from our earlier discussion of sensory thresholds that we can detect the presence of a single drop of perfume in a three-room apartment (see Table 3.1). When it comes to discriminating between odors, we can detect roughly 500,000 different scents (Cain, 1988), and we can identify by name about 10,000 different smells (Lancet et al., 1993).

Of the half a million or so odors we can detect, some are decidedly pleasant, like apple pie, whereas others are decidedly unpleasant, like rotten eggs. Some olfaction researchers have attempted to catalog the basic odors that combine to make up the complex odors we smell (Amoore, 1970, 1977; Henning, 1916). Unfortunately these attempts have not yet met with much success, so there is no well accepted list of basic odors (Matlin & Foley, 1997).

Olfactory Pathways: The Limits of Our Knowledge

Researchers have also not been able to determine precisely how our sense of smell works. Of the senses we have described to this point, smell is by far the least well understood. What we do know is that we are able to smell due to a special piece of skin that lines the top of the nasal cavity (Figure 3.18). This special piece of skin, the **olfactory epithelium,** probably contains only a few hundred different types of odor receptors (Lancet et al., 1993). When we breathe in odor-laden air, the odor molecules reach the receptors in the olfactory epithelium and stimulate these cells. This stimulation accomplishes the transduction of odor into smell, but just how our brain understands what we smell is not well understood at this time (Matlin & Foley, 1997). One theory, **lock-and-key theory,** proposes that olfactory receptors are excited by odor molecules in much the same way neurotransmitters excite receptor sites on the

olfactory epithelium a special piece of skin at the top of the nasal cavity that contains our olfactory receptors

lock-and-key theory proposes that olfactory receptors are excited by odor molecules in a fashion that is similar to how neurotransmitters excite receptor sites

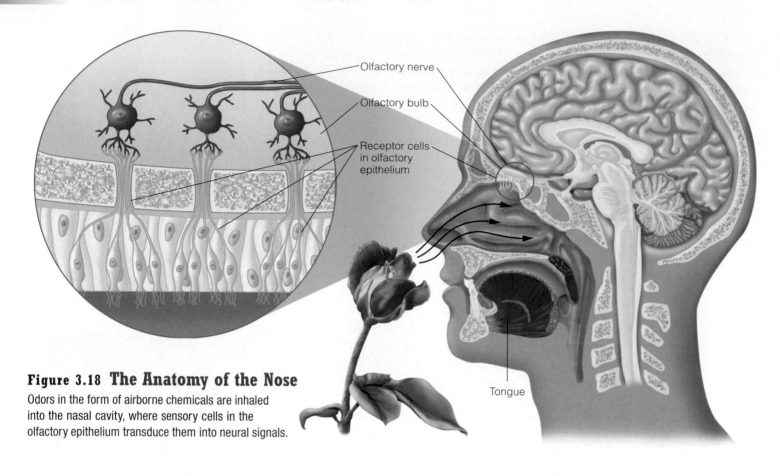

Figure 3.18 **The Anatomy of the Nose**

Odors in the form of airborne chemicals are inhaled into the nasal cavity, where sensory cells in the olfactory epithelium transduce them into neural signals.

postsynaptic neuron (Amoore, 1970; see p. 55). In lock-and-key theory, specific odor molecules have the power to "unlock" or excite certain olfactory receptors in the olfactory epithelium.

We have already noted that our sense of smell is closely linked to our sense of taste. When you place food in your mouth, some of the odor from the food rises up the back of your throat and into the nasal cavity. The resulting smell intensifies your experience of the food and its taste. Together taste and smell may work together to help us avoid dangerous substances. For instance, in addition to its odor receptors, the olfactory epithelium is also equipped with special cells that react to certain aspects of flavor and smell that may indicate danger. These cells cause our bodies to reflexively act in a protective manner when we smell a potentially dangerous substance, such as a caustic chemical like bleach (Holley, 1991).

Once the cells of the epithelium have transduced odor into neural impulses, these signals travel across the **olfactory nerve** to the **olfactory bulb** of the brain. The olfactory bulb is located just below the bottom edge of the frontal lobe of the brain (see Figure 3.18). The olfactory bulb processes incoming information before sending it on to other parts of the brain. Some olfactory information goes directly to the primary smell cortex, in the temporal lobes of the brain.

Other olfactory information is sent to both the cortex and the limbic system. Recall from Chapter 2 that the limbic system regulates emotional and motivational activity. The limbic system seems to be heavily involved in the processing of olfactory information. This may explain the strong emotional reactions we often have to certain smells. For example, one of the authors has a strong emotional reaction to smelling grease and gasoline odors. These smells always remind her of her deceased father, who was an airplane mechanic, and causes her to miss him. Are there particular smells that bring back emotionally charged memories for you?

olfactory nerve   the structure that carries olfactory information from the nasal cavity to the brain

olfactory bulb   the structure that sits at the bottom edge of the frontal lobe and processes olfactory information before sending it on to other parts of the brain

Application

Pheromones

Some researchers believe that humans have yet another sense somewhat related to smell. This sense, the *vomeronasal sense*, is well documented in animals (Doty, 2001). Many animals communicate with each other via airborne chemicals called **pheromones.** Pheromones are produced by glands in the animal's body and dispersed into the air, where other animals then inhale them. Such animals are equipped with vomeronasal organs that can detect the presence of inhaled pheromones. Perhaps you have seen a cat deeply inhale air through its open mouth—a process called cat's *flehmen.* The cat is passing pheromone-laden air over special organs, called Jacobson's organs, in the roof of its mouth. These organs can detect the presence of pheromones. Many mammals have been shown to have vomeronasal organs (Doty, 2001). The presence of such an organ in humans has been the subject of controversy, but at least one study has shown evidence that some people have vomeronasal organs in their nasal cavities (Won, Mair, Bolger, & Conran, 2000).

Certainly the evidence suggests that pheromones do impact certain aspects of human sexual behavior. For example, when women are exposed to pheromones in the underarm secretions of another woman, their menstrual cycle tends to synchronize with the other woman's cycle (Larkin, 1998; Stern & McClintock, 1998). When women are exposed to a pheromone (androstenol) that is released from men's hair follicles, they tend to increase their social interactions with males (Miller, 1999). Other pheromones found in men's sweat tend to improve a woman's mood state (Monti-Bloch, Diaz-Sanchez, Jennings-White, & Berliner, 1998). Current evidence, however, does not support the idea that pheromone-laden perfumes can make one wildly attractive to the opposite sex. It's more likely the case that the vomeronasal sense is just one of the senses involved in sexuality.

Touch: The Skin Sense

The sense of touch was the other half of Michael Watson's synesthesia. When Michael tasted a food, he felt geometric shapes pressed against certain parts of his body. This intertwining led Michael to describe foods in terms of the way they *felt* to him, hence the comment about "pointed chicken" that led Richard Cytowic to spend years studying synesthesia.

For most of us, our senses of touch and taste are not intertwined the way they are for Michael Watson. For us, touch has little to do with the flavor of a food. So, what role does touch play in our lives? Touch is associated with many of life's pleasurable experiences. Feeling a friendly pat on the back can certainly enhance our social interactions. Sexual activity depends heavily on our ability to feel touch. But our ability to sense with our skin also affects our survival. Through our skin we feel touch, temperature, and pain. The importance of touch is clearly seen in cases of people who are born without the ability to feel pain, or who lose that ability due to disease or injury. For such people, repeated, unnoticed injuries may be a serious problem and may lead to fatal infection (e.g., Melzack & Wall, 1988; Sternbach, 1963).

Aside from pleasure and pain, our sense of touch also contributes to our ability to function when our visual perception is impeded. If you head for the bathroom in the middle of the night without turning on the lights, you'll most likely rely heavily on touch to navigate. Luckily, we are very good at identifying objects by touch (Klatzky, Lederman, & Matula, 1985). This same ability allows those who are blind to read Braille.

Our keen sense of touch originates in our skin. Our skin is composed of several layers that contain touch receptors. The inner layer, the **dermis,** contains most of the

pheromones airborne chemicals that are released from glands and detected by the vomeronasal organs in some animals and perhaps humans

© Joe McDonald/Visuals Unlimited

Many mammals use pheromones to communicate with each other. This cat is passing pheromone-laden air over his vomeronasal organs in the roof of his mouth.

≪ Application

dermis the inner layer of our skin

Figure 3.19 **Anatomy of the Skin and Its Receptors**

Different types of skin receptors pick up different types of stimulation.

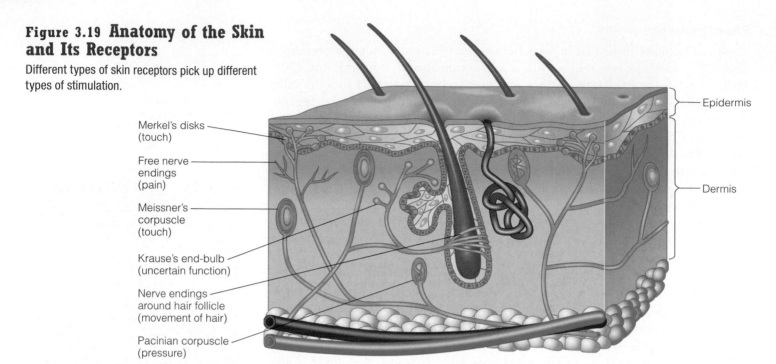

Merkel's disks (touch)

Free nerve endings (pain)

Meissner's corpuscle (touch)

Krause's end-bulb (uncertain function)

Nerve endings around hair follicle (movement of hair)

Pacinian corpuscle (pressure)

Epidermis

Dermis

epidermis the outer layer of our skin that contains our touch receptors

touch receptors (Figure 3.19). Our skin's outer layer is the **epidermis,** which consists of several layers of dead skin cells. The epidermis also contains touch receptors, especially in areas of the skin that do not have hair, such as the fingertips.

We have different types of receptors for touch, temperature, and pain (Figure 3.19). We know more about the function of the touch receptors than about the pain and temperature receptors. Pressure on the skin deforms the axonal membrane of the touch receptors. This causes a change in the axonal membrane's permeability to positive ions, allowing them to enter the cell (Loewenstein, 1960). As you recall from Chapter 2, as positive ions enter the cell, an action potential becomes more likely to fire. If the touch is intense enough to allow the receptors to reach threshold, neural impulses will be fired. These impulses travel to the spinal cord, and then to the brain. In the brain, the signals enter the thalamus and then go on to the somatosensory cortex of the parietal lobe. Some signals, particularly those indicating the presence of threatening stimuli, go to the limbic system in addition to going to the somatosensory cortex (Coren, Ward, & Enns, 1999). Once the signals reach the somatosensory cortex, our brain interprets the sensation and directs us to take the appropriate action.

The Body Senses: Experiencing the Physical Body in Space

So far, we have covered what are referred to as the five senses: vision, hearing, taste, smell, and touch. Do we possess other senses? The answer is "Yes," but we're not talking about a sixth sense, clairvoyance, or ESP. We are referring to the body senses, the senses that help us experience our physical bodies in space: kinesthesis and the vestibular sense.

Application

kinesthesis our ability to sense the position of our body parts in relation to one another and in relation to space

Kinesthesis

Kinesthesis refers to our ability to sense the position of our body parts in space and in relation to one another. As you walk, you are aware of where your arms, legs, and head are in relation to the ground. Kinesthetic sense is important to athletes, especially to gymnasts and high divers. It allows them to know where their bodies are as they execute their routines and dives. Our kinesthetic sense employs information from the muscles, tendons, skin, and joints to keep us oriented at all times. The information from these sources is processed in the somatosensory cortex and the cerebellum of the brain. (Recall from Chapter 2 that the cerebellum plays a critical role in balance and motor skill execution.)

The Vestibular Sense

Another important body sense is our sense of balance, or **vestibular sense.** Anyone who has ever felt sick after riding a roller coaster, traveling in a car, or otherwise spinning around, has been made keenly aware of the vestibular system. Normally, we are not conscious of the workings of our vestibular system. But when this system is overstimulated, such as on a roller coaster, we may feel dizzy, disoriented, and nauseous.

The vestibular system uses input from the semicircular canals and the vestibular sacs of the inner ear to keep us balanced (Figure 3.20). These structures are filled with a fluid gel that surrounds hair cells much like those in the cochlea. When your head moves in any direction, the gel inside of these structures moves in an opposite direction. The movement of the gel bends the hair cells and stimulates them to send neural impulses to the brain, which then uses these signals to determine the orientation of your head.

Rapid movements of your head, such as those you experience on spinning carnival rides, can overstimulate the vestibular system. Such movements can cause a violent wave action in the fluid gel of the vestibular system. When the gel crashes against the sensory cells, the result can be dizziness and nausea. There are individual differences in tolerance to vestibular stimulation. Some people can ride roller coasters all day long whereas others cannot ride in a car across town without feeling ill. Regardless of whether you enjoy intense vestibular stimulation, we all rely on this system. It allows us to do such everyday tasks, such as walking, driving a car, and bending over to pick up a pencil from the floor. Without our vestibular sense, we would simply topple over.

You now have a working knowledge of how our sensory organs transduce environmental energies into neural impulses. Our next topic is perception, or how we make sense of all of this sensory information.

vestibular sense   our sense of balance

Our vestibular sense keeps us balanced, and the kinesthetic sense allows this gymnast to perform intricate moves without falling.

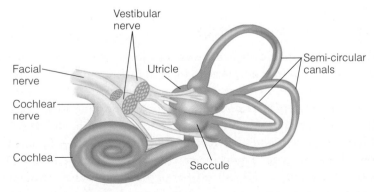

Figure 3.20 **The Vestibular Organs**

The vestibular system helps us balance our body by monitoring the position and acceleration of our head as we move. To accomplish this, a gel-like fluid in the semi-circular canals, saccule, and utricle presses against hair cells much like those found in the cochlea of the inner ear. When the hair cells of the vestibular system are moved, they signal the brain with information about the orientation of our head in three-dimensional space. *Based on S. Iurato (1967). Submicroscopic structure of the inner ear. Pergamon Press.*

Let's Review!

This section explained the chemical senses, taste and smell; touch; and the body senses, kinesthesis and the vestibular sense. For a quick check of your understanding, answer these questions.

1. Which of the following is *not* thought to be a taste for which our tongue has receptors?
   a. salty
   b. sour
   c. acidic
   d. bitter
2. Which of our body's senses functions in a manner that is *most* like how neurotransmitters fit into receptors sites at the synapse?
   a. taste
   b. touch
   c. smell
   d. vestibular sense
3. Which of your other senses would be *least likely* to be affected when you have a bad head cold?
   a. taste
   b. touch
   c. smell
   d. vestibular sense

ANSWERS
1.c, 2.c, 3.b

LEARNING OBJECTIVES

Understand top-down and bottom-up perceptual processing and explain the differences between them.

Give an overview of perceptual constancy theories and how we perceive depth.

Perception: Interpreting Sensory Information

At the beginning of this chapter, we defined perception as *the interpretation of sensory information.* That's it in a nutshell. When you look at your friend's face, light bounces off his or her face. This light strikes your retinas and the rods and cones transduce the light into neural impulses. Sensation is complete. But now your brain must interpret the meaning of the neural impulses so you will recognize your friend's face. The fact that you believe that you are seeing your friend's face and not, say, a dog or a cat, is the result of perceptual processes in your brain.

Likewise, for Michael Watson, once his tongue had transduced the flavor of the chicken dish, his brain interpreted, or perceived, that taste to be "pointed." Certainly most of us could have tasted the same chicken dish and had a different perception. We may have said that the dish was salty or spicy, but we wouldn't have perceived it as "pointy." Psychologists do have some understanding of how perception occurs for most of us, even if they don't completely understand Michael Watson's taste-related perceptions. In the coming sections, we will examine some of the theories psychologists have about the ways we perceive.

Using What We Know: Top-Down Perceptual Processing

top-down perceptual processing perception that is guided by prior knowledge or expectations

Top-down perceptual processing occurs when we use previously gained knowledge to help us interpret a stimulus. For instance, let's go back to the example of perceiving your friend's face. When you see a face that you recognize as a friend's, what leads you to this recognition? Your memory helps you understand the "meaning" of the face you see. You know that faces usually contain two eyes, a nose, a mouth, and so on. Furthermore, you know how your friend's particular eyes, nose, and other features look. This stored knowledge allows you to quickly perceive the face of a friend.

Top-down perceptual processing can also fill in parts of the stimulus that are missing from our actual sensation of it. For example, look at Figure 3.21. You cannot see the legs of the bride and groom or the groom's left arm, but you probably assume that they are there. Your knowledge of the human body tells you that the odds are slim that these people are actually missing the limbs you cannot see. Consequently, in perceiving this picture, you implicitly assume that the "missing" legs and arms do, in fact, exist. This effect is so strong that later when you recall this picture, you might even remember having seen the missing limbs! Unfortunately, this "filling-in" of missing details can sometimes lead to mistakes in perception. This can be a real problem in eyewitness accounts of crimes. One study showed that 75% of a sample of falsely convicted people were mistakenly identified as the criminal by an eyewitness (Wells & Olson, 2003). So, why is mistaken identity so common?

Sometimes your expectations about the world can *bias* your perception. For example, let's say that you are having lunch at a sidewalk café. Suddenly, your peaceful lunch is disrupted by a commotion at the bank across the street. You look up just in time to see someone run out of the bank. The person is dressed head-to-toe in black, wearing a black ski mask, and carrying a gun. The person is about 5'10" and about 150 lbs., but you have only a few-second glimpse before the figure pushes through the crowd and runs down the street. As you read this description, did you have a mental picture of this scene? If so, what assumptions did you automatically make? Did you assume that the bank robber was male? If you are like most people, you probably did. Furthermore, if you actually witnessed this event, you are likely to have told the police to look for a 5'10" male when, in reality, the robber could have been a female. After all, you never saw the robber's face!

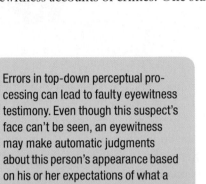

Errors in top-down perceptual processing can lead to faulty eyewitness testimony. Even though this suspect's face can't be seen, an eyewitness may make automatic judgments about this person's appearance based on his or her expectations of what a criminal is like.

© Novastock/Index Stock Imagery, Inc.

© Getty Images

Figure 3.21 Top-Down Perceptual Processing

When you perceive the image in this photograph, your knowledge of the human body leads you to have certain expectations about the people in the picture. Because of top-down processing, you do not perceive that the groom is missing an arm or that the bride and groom are without legs.

Building a Perception "From Scratch": Bottom-Up Perceptual Processing

So, what do we do when we have very little or no stored knowledge to help us perceive a stimulus? We use a different perceptual process, one that does not rely on stored knowledge or expectations of the stimulus.

In **bottom-up perceptual processing,** the properties of the stimulus itself are what we use to build our perception of that stimulus. Look at Figure 3.22. What do you see? With few clues about what this stimulus is, you cannot easily use your knowledge to help you perceive it. The stimulus is too ambiguous. Without top-down processing, you are forced to use bottom-up processes to perceive the stimulus. You build your perception of the picture by piecing together your perceptions of the many different components that make up this stimulus. You perceive the lines, curves, dots, shaded areas, and shapes. You then try to fit these components together to figure out what the drawing means. Most people find it very difficult to figure out what Figure 3.22 is using only bottom-up perceptual processes!

bottom-up perceptual processing
perception that is not guided by prior knowledge or expectations

Figure 3.22 **Top-Down Versus Bottom-Up Processing**

What is this picture? With no expectations to guide your perception of this picture, you are forced to rely mainly on bottom-up processes. Because this figure is ambiguous, bottom-up processes do not lead to a quick recognition of the stimulus in this picture. Turn to the solution, Figure 3.23 on page (142), to engage your top-down perceptual processes. After looking at Figure 3.24, you should be quickly able to recognize the figure in this picture because you now have expectations to guide your perception.

If you are ready to give up and try top-down perceptual processing, look at Figure 3.24 on page (142). Now, turn back to Figure 3.22. You will likely find that you can now readily perceive the image in Figure 3.22. You now have knowledge of what to look for, so perception becomes much easier. Your knowledge of what the picture is guides the way you piece together the components of the stimulus. When you switch to top-down processing, the picture of the cow becomes almost obvious.

In the course of a typical day, we probably use both top-down and bottom-up perceptual processes continually. We use bottom-up processes to piece together perceptions of ambiguous stimuli and top-down processes to tell us what we can expect to perceive in certain situations. Perception can be complicated in a three-dimensional world that is full of shapes and forms. To make perception even more complicated, our bodies do not remain stationary during perception. We move. The objects we perceive sometimes move. As a result, the information our senses receive from our world is highly variable. Our perceptual processes must be able to deal with these dynamic conditions. So, how do we organize and make sense of our perceptions?

Understanding What We Sense: Perceiving Size, Shape, and Brightness

When you see a tiny person, how do you know that he or she is actually far away? How do we develop an understanding of what the sensory data mean? One of the problems encountered in interpreting sensory data is that of perceptual constancy. When you look at a visual stimulus, the image it projects on your retina is highly influenced by the perspective from which you view the object. Yet your perception of the object is not as dependent on perspective as your sensation is. For example, if you view a friend from a distance of 3 feet, a certain sized image is projected onto your retina. If you move away and view the same friend from a distance of 6 feet, a smaller image of your friend is projected on your retina. Therefore, your *sensation* has changed, but you will not perceive that your friend has shrunk. If the image projected on your retina shrinks, why don't you perceive that your friend is also shrinking? Your brain appears to step in to correct your perception, to give you a *constant* perception of the objects that you see in the world. There is evidence that our brains correct not only for *size constancy*, but also *shape constancy, brightness constancy, and color constancy* (Figure 3.23).

Before we move on, think for a moment about how life would be if your brain did not correct your perception for constancy. Imagine what you would perceive as you walked around the room you are in right now. How would your perception of the shapes, sizes, and brightness in the room change from your perception now? Could you function well without perceptual constancies? Without perceptual constancy, your perception would be wildly distorted. Objects would appear to shrink and grow, to become dim and to glow, and to twist and change shape as you moved around. Thanks

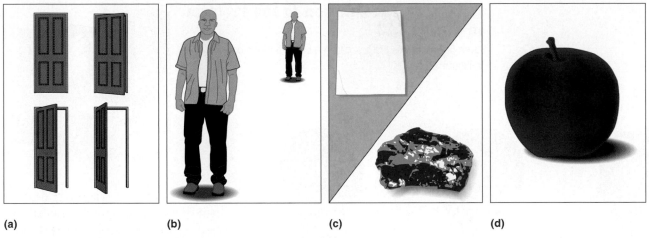

(a)   (b)   (c)   (d)

Figure 3.23 **Perceptual Constancies**

Panel A: The shape of the image this door projects onto the retina changes dramatically as the orientation of the door changes. Yet we still perceive that the door is rectangular due to shape constancy.

Panel B: Even though the size of the image this person projects onto the retina shrinks as he walks away, because of size constancy we do not perceive that he or she is shrinking.

Panel C: The coal may reflect more light in the sun than the paper does in the shade, yet we still perceive that the paper is brighter than the coal due to brightness constancy.

Panel D: Even though this apple is in the shade, we still perceive it as being red due to color constancy.

to perceptual constancy, you get a more accurate perception of the world. Objects do not appear to mutate as we move around.

Depth Perception: Sensing Our 3-D World With 2-D Eyes

Another perceptual challenge is that of depth perception. The world we view is three-dimensional, but the image it projects onto our retina is two-dimensional, like a photograph. Somehow, our brains must be able to determine depth from the information our eyes receive from the outside world. What makes this possible?

Binocular Depth Perception

One way that we perceive depth is through binocular depth cues. The term *binocular* means "two-eyed." As such, **binocular depth cues** rely on information from both of your eyes, specifically, information based on **retinal disparity.** Retinal disparity refers to the fact that each of our eyes sees a slightly different view of the world, because our eyes are set a few centimeters apart.

To check the disparity that occurs, look across the room and carefully note how your view changes as you close first your right eye and then your left. Notice that the view changes most for objects that are close to you, and less for objects that are distant (Figure 3.25). In short, the amount of retinal disparity we experience is a function of the distance from which we view an object. Our brain uses the amount of retinal disparity we experience to calculate how far the object is from us. In this manner, we perceive depth in the world. Figure 3.25 shows an example of retinal disparity for objects at two different depths.

Monocular Depth Cues

Binocular disparity is an important depth cue, but it is not the only way we perceive depth. If it were, we would be in serious trouble if we lost the use of one of our eyes. We also

binocular depth cues   depth cues that utilize information from both eyes

retinal disparity   a binocular depth cue that uses the difference in the images projected on the right and left retinas to inform the brain about the distance of a stimulus

Figure 3.24 **The Solution to the Problem in Figure 3.22**

After looking at this picture, can you easily find the cow in Figure 3.22?

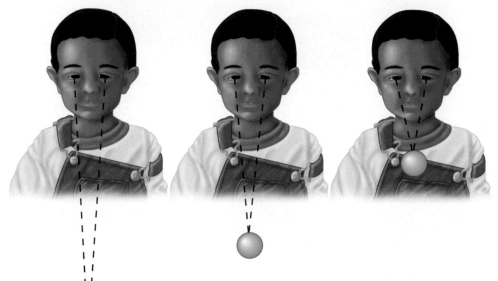

Figure 3.25 **Binocular Depth Cues**

The brain uses retinal disparity, or the degree to which the images projected on the right and left retinas differ from each other, to calculate how far away an object is. The farther away the object, the greater the degree of retinal disparity.

Application >>

monocular depth cues depth cues that require information from only one eye

would not be able to perceive depth in paintings or photographs. Luckily, we have another means of depth perception that requires the use of only one eye: **monocular depth cues.**

Many of you may have learned about monocular depth cues when you began drawing and painting as a child. You probably didn't realize then that you were learning about perception, but you were. A painter is faced with the challenge of representing the three-dimensional world on a two-dimensional canvas. A canvas has no depth; all parts of the painting are the same distance from the viewer's eyes. Retinal disparity cannot give the viewer the perception of depth in the flat painting. So, how do we perceive depth in paintings and photographs?

We use monocular depth cues, such as the relative size of the objects, that the artist has incorporated into the painting to give the illusion of depth. In the three-dimensional world, these monocular depth cues augment our binocular depth perception. We often first become consciously aware of these monocular depth cues when as children, we try to represent the world on a two-dimensional sheet of paper. Table 3.4 ◆ describes the monocular depth cues. How many of these cues have you used in your childhood (or adulthood) drawings? Look at Figure 3.26. Can you identify the monocular depth cues that the artist has used?

Perceptual constancy and depth perception are both important components of our perceptual processing. But how do we perceive the cylindrical shape of a soda can or the rectangular shape of a shoe box? To understand this level of perceptual processing, we will examine theories of form perception.

Perceiving Form: The Gestalt Approach

Gestalt approach a psychological school of thought originating in Germany that proposed that the whole of a perception must be understood rather than trying to deconstruct perception into its parts

One influential approach to understanding form perception is the **Gestalt approach.** Max Wertheimer, Wolfgang Kohler, and Kurt Koffka were the central figures in this movement, which originated in Germany in the years preceding World War II. According to the Gestalt approach, the whole of a perception is greater than the sum of its parts. In fact, the word *Gestalt* is German for "whole form." According to the Gestaltists, when you look at your friend's face, the resulting perception is not merely a sum of the angles, curves, shapes, and lines that make up the face; rather, you perceive

◆ **Table 3.4**

Monocular Depth Cues

Monocular Depth Cue	Description	Example
Interposition	More distant objects are partially hidden by closer objects.	© Robert Estall/Corbis
Height on the horizon	More distant objects are placed higher on the horizon than closer objects.	© Richard T. Nowitz/Corbis
Relative size	More distant objects are seen as smaller than closer objects of the same size.	© W. Cody/Corbis
Texture gradient	More distant objects have less texture or detail than closer objects.	© Corbis
Aerial perspective	More distant objects are hazier and blurrier than closer objects.	© Sylvain Grandadam/Getty Images
Linear perspective	Converging lines indicate distance or depth.	© Corbis
Motion parallax	More distant objects appear to move more slowly than closer objects as we pass by them.	© Steven Lam/Getty Images

Figure 3.26 Can You Find the Monocular Depth Cues?

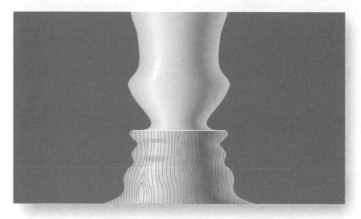

Figure 3.27 Figure-Ground

What do you see when you look at this picture? Depending on how you use the perceptual rule of figure-ground, you may see faces or a vase.

figure-ground   a Gestalt principle of perception that says that when we perceive a stimulus, we visually must pull the *figure* part of the stimulus forward while visually pushing backward the background, or *ground,* part of the stimulus

closure   a Gestalt principle of perception that states that when we look at a stimulus, we have a tendency to see it as a closed shape, rather than lines

proximity   a Gestalt principle of perception that states that we tend to group close objects together during perception

similarity   a Gestalt principle of perception that states that we tend to group like objects together during perception

the stimulus *as a whole.* In this case, you perceive a face because your mind has implicitly grouped all of the stimuli that make up that face into a coherent whole.

One of the major contributions of Gestalt theory is a series of perceptual laws that attempt to explain how our minds automatically organize perceptual stimuli together to produce the perception of a whole form (Wertheimer, 1923). One of the most important Gestalt concepts of perceptual organization is **figure-ground.** When you look at your world, you see a multitude of objects or figures that seem to stand away from the background. For instance, imagine you are in psychology class and your professor is standing at the blackboard. You perceive that your professor is in front of the board, and the board is seen as the background. As you look at her, you visually pull her *figure*, or form, to the foreground and push the image of the blackboard to the background, or *ground.*

Figure 3.27 shows figure-ground in action. You should have two different perceptions of this picture, depending on what you visually pull forward as the figure and what you push back to the ground. When you focus on the light parts as the figure, you see a vase. When you focus on the dark parts of the figure, you see two faces.

Another Gestalt principle is **closure.** When we perceive a stimulus, such as the one in Figure 3.28, we tend to mentally fill in, or *close,* the object. The stimulus is not a complete triangle, but nearly everyone will perceive it as complete. According to the principle of closure, we have a preference for viewing solid shapes as opposed to lines.

The Gestalt principles of **proximity** and **similarity** help explain how we group objects together. These rules state that we group together stimuli that are close to each other, or proximal, and also stimuli that are similar. What do you see *first* when you look at the pictures in Figure 3.29? Do you see 60 different objects in each of these pictures?

In Figure 3.29a, due to proximity, you probably perceive a group of four squares surrounding a white cross. In Figure 3.29b, due to similarity, you probably perceive alternating pairs of rows of shamrocks and diamonds. As you read this page, you are continually using proximity to discriminate between the words that

Figure 3.28 Closure

According to the Gestaltists, we tend to mentally fill in, or close, solid forms during perception.

Figure 3.29 **The Gestalt Rules of Similarity and Proximity**

make up the sentences. Without proximity, you would see a mass of letters, but you would not know where one word ends and another begins.

The final Gestalt principle that we will look at is **good continuation.** Good continuation states that our preference is to perceive stimuli that seem to follow one another as being part of a continuing pattern. For example, look at Figure 3.30a. How would you describe this stimulus? Many describe it as looking like the top of a castle wall. When we look at this stimulus, we tend to see the overall pattern as opposed to seeing a myriad of dashes on a piece of paper. Camouflage works on the principle of good continuation. Can you see the hidden animal in Figure 3.30b? This animal's very survival depends on its predator's use of good continuation!

Perceiving Form: Feature Detection Theory

Feature detection is a neurological theory of form perception. According to this theory, we have cells in our visual cortex that fire only in response to certain stimuli. Researchers have substantiated the basis for this theory with animal studies using electrodes to measure the activity of single neurons in the visual cortex. With an electrode in place, researchers presented the animal with a certain visual stimulus, such as a bar of light, then checked to see whether the neuron fired. Through a process of elimination, the researchers determined what particular stimulus was needed to cause the specific neuron to fire (Hubel & Weisel, 1965).

Using this approach, researchers found that some cells of the cortex respond to particular combinations of lightness and darkness, lines of differing thickness, location, and orientation (Hubel & Wiesel, 1979). The neurons that fire only when certain stimuli are seen may work as feature detectors. Presumably, the human brain also has feature detectors, and by noticing which of our feature-detecting neurons are firing, our brain determines the form of the stimulus we are viewing. The square in Figure 3.31 is made up of two horizontal lines and two

(a) Grouping based on proximity

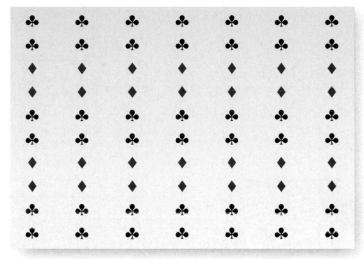

(b) Grouping based on similarity

good continuation   a Gestalt principle of perception that states that we have a preference for perceiving stimuli that seem to follow one another as being part of a continuing pattern

feature detectors   cortical cells that only fire when we see certain visual stimuli such as shapes, colors of light, or movements

Figure 3.30 **Two Instances of Good Continuation**

Good continuation ensures that we perceive continuous patterns in the world. This perceptual principle is vital to the survival of the animal in (b).

(a)

(b)

vertical lines. If each of these four lines is detected by four different sets of feature-detecting neurons, two detectors for vertical lines and two detectors for horizontal lines, then our brain can deduce that we are looking at a square.

Feature detection research holds much promise, but it is difficult to conduct (Hubel, 1990). Each neuron of the visual system has to be tested to determine what feature it detects. Mapping the entire visual system of feature detectors is likely to take a long time!

So far, we have looked at top-down and bottom-up perceptual processing, perceptual constancies, depth perception, and theories of form perception. These processes work hand in hand to allow us to understand our world. We take for granted that we will be able to process all the sights, sounds, smells, touches, and tastes we encounter in an average day. In our final section, we will briefly examine the issue of perceptual accuracy.

Figure 3.31 An Example of Feature Detection
Feature-detecting neurons fire for each of these four lines.

Let's Review!

This section described perception and perceptual organization, including top-down and bottom-up perception; ways that our brain corrects our perception to give us perceptual constancy; how our brain uses monocular and binocular depth cues to perceive depth; and a theory of form perception. For a quick check of your understanding, answer these questions.

1. Jamal was a witness to a bank robbery. Although he did not clearly see the robber's face, Jamal assumed that the robber was a man. What is the *most likely* reason for Jamal's assumption?
   a. Bottom-up perceptual processing
   b. Top-down perceptual processing
   c. Gestalt perceptual processing
   d. Faulty form perception

2. If you went blind in one eye, what would happen to your depth perception?
   a. You would not be able to perceive depth due to the loss of monocular depth cues.
   b. You would not be able to perceive depth due to the loss of binocular depth cues.
   c. You would still be able to perceive depth through monocular depth cues.
   d. You would still be able to perceive depth through binocular depth cues.

3. The idea that our visual cortex has specialized cells that fire when we see specific visual stimuli is the basis for which theory of perception?
   a. Feature detection theory
   b. Gestalt theory of perceptual organization
   c. Top-down perceptual processing theory
   d. Bottom-up perceptual processing theory

ANSWERS
1.b; 2.c; 3.a

How Accurate Are Our Perceptions? > > > > >

⟩⟩ **LEARNING**
⟩⟩ **OBJECTIVE**
⟩⟩ Describe some of the common
⟩⟩ perceptual illusions we experience
⟩⟩ and explain their causes.
⟩⟩

One of our students once had a frightening experience in which he misinterpreted a visual stimulus. He was driving in the mountains of northern Georgia when he passed a bear on a distant hillside. The bear was standing on its hindlegs, towering over the 20-foot tall pine trees that surrounded it. But the student knew that this was very unlikely, so he turned his car around and went back for another look. On closer inspection of the scene, he saw that all of the pine trees on the mountainside were newly planted saplings, about 3 feet high. The bear that towered over them was only an average-sized Georgia black bear! Our student was able to go back and correct his perception, but this is not always the case. We may never discover that we have misperceived a situation in the first place. Why do we sometimes misperceive our world?

Errors Due to Top-Down Processing: Seeing What We Expect to See

Why do you think the student misperceived the size of the black bear? The key to his misperception of the bear was in his misperception of the size of the pine trees. We would explain this in terms of top-down processing. When driving through the mountains, most Georgians do not expect to see hillsides of baby trees. It's more typical to see mountainsides covered with mature pine trees that can be well over 20 feet tall. Because this is the normal expectation, the student simply took for granted that the trees were a mature height. It wasn't until he saw the pine trees up close that he realized that his top-down processing had failed him. Because he misperceived the trees, he also misperceived the height of the bear.

Perceptual errors caused by misapplied expectations can lead us to think we have seen or heard things that we simply did not. There is ample evidence that expectations can strongly influence our perception of events as well as our memory for what we have seen, as in eyewitness testimony (e.g., Allport & Postman, 1947/1965; Loftus & Palmer, 1974). We will discuss this problem more in Chapter 6 when we discuss the accuracy of memory.

Errors Due to Perceptual Constancy: Tricks of the Brain

Errors that are caused by top-down processing relate to the knowledge and the expectations we have of our world. Misperceptions occur for other reasons, however we sometimes misperceive things when our brain's attempts to give us perceptual constancy go awry.

The Moon Illusion

Have you ever noticed how the moon appears to be much larger as it rises over the horizon than when it is directly overhead? Many people think it is because the earth is closer to the moon when it is at the horizon but this is not true. The answer lies in our brain's attempt to correct for what it thinks is a mistake in perception. The moon projects the same size image on our retina when it is on the horizon as it does when it is directly overhead. But when the moon is on the horizon, our brain is tricked into thinking that the moon is actually farther away than it is when it's overhead. When we view the moon on the horizon, there are many interposition cues, such as trees and buildings that stand between the moon and us that indicate distance to our brain. But when we view the moon directly overhead, there are no interposition cues to indicate distance. Consequently, our brain thinks the moon is farther away when it is on the horizon, even though

Due to top-down processing, it would take a long time to accurately perceive this laptop computer in the road. We simply don't expect to see laptop computers in the middle of the highway—therefore our perception is slowed down.

© Thinkstock/Getty Images

the image it projects on the retina is the same size as the one projected by the "closer" moon directly overhead. The logic involved is this: if the moon is farther away on the horizon, but it still projects the same size image on the retina as the moon overhead, then the moon on the horizon must be bigger than the moon overhead. The brain tries to *fix* the inconsistency by inflating our perception of the size of the moon on the horizon (Kaufman & Rock, 1989).

Demonstration ▶▶

The moon illusion occurs because our brain distorts our perception.

© Jim Wark/Lonely Planet Images

Undoing the Moon Illusion. Just in case you need convincing, try the following demonstration. You can stop your brain from trying to maintain consistency. Next time a full moon is rising, allow yourself to experience the illusion that the moon on the horizon is huge. Then turn so that you are facing away from the moon on the horizon. Bend over and spread your legs so that you can view the moon upside down between your legs. When you view the moon this way, it will look as small as it does when you view it overhead. When your head is upside down, your brain doesn't use its normal processes to correct for perceptual inconsistency, so the illusion disappears. When you stand up, turn around, and view the moon on the horizon from a normal position, it will again look larger.

The Ponzo Illusion

This same logic underlies the Ponzo illusion. Lines of equal length that lie across converging lines appear to be unequal in length (Figure 3.32). In the Ponzo illusion, linear perspective and height on the horizon cues tell the brain that the top line is farther away than the bottom. Yet, both lines project the same size image on the retina. In an attempt to maintain size constancy, the brain inflates our perception of the top line's length, thus causing the illusion that the top line looks longer than the bottom line. This illusion occurs even though we do not consciously perceive that the line on top is farther away (Gillam, 1980).

The Mueller-Lyer Illusion

Size constancy probably also plays a role in the Mueller-Lyer illusion (Figure 3.33; Coren, Porac, Aks, & Morikawa, 1988). In this illusion, our perception of the length of the vertical line segments changes, depending on the direction of the arrows at either end of the line. When the arrows extend away, the line looks longer.

Although researchers are not quite sure why the Mueller-Lyer illusion occurs, it is thought that the arrows serve as depth cues, much as we might find in the concave and convex angles of a building. If you look at panel C of Figure 3.33, you can see that this type of corner produces a surface that is closer to the viewer than the recessed corner in panel D. These depth cues may set off a process of compensation for size consistency that is very similar to those found in the moon illusion and the Ponzo illusion.

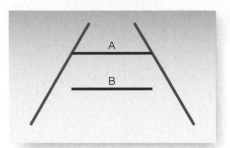

The Ponzo Illusion

Figure 3.32 The Ponzo Illusion
Line segments A and B are both the same length, but we perceive that A is longer than B.

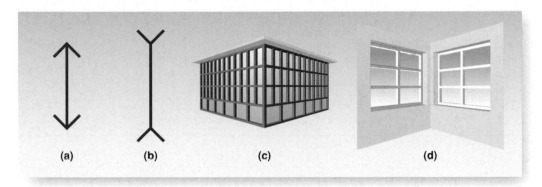

(a)   (b)   (c)   (d)

Figure 3.33 The Mueller-Lyer Illusion
Due to the Mueller-Lyer illusion, the line in figure A is perceived as being shorter than the line in figure B, even though they are of equal length. The Mueller-Lyer illusion is often seen in rectangular, "carpentered" buildings. The vertical line in the outside corner (figure C) looks shorter than the vertical line in the inside corner (figure D)—yet they are of the same length. Architects use the Mueller-Lyer illusion to create certain perceptions of their buildings.

Cultural Factors in Perception

As we've discussed, your beliefs and expectations of the world can influence your top-down perceptual processing. Given that culture and environment influence many of our beliefs and expectations (remember our student and the Georgia bear?), it stands to reason that culture and environment also impact perception. The Mueller-Lyer illusion is a good example of this type of influence.

People who live in "carpentered" environments where many of the buildings are wood-framed, rectangular structures have much experience with the architectural angles that produce the Mueller-Lyer illusion. Is it possible that these people also experience the Mueller-Lyer illusion to a greater degree than those who've lived their lives in "non-carpentered" worlds (where rectangular structures are rare)? This seems to be the case. The Bashi people of Africa traditionally live in round dwellings. When compared to Europeans, the Bashi are often found to be less susceptible to the Mueller-Lyer illusion (Bonte, 1962). A similar effect has been found among the American Navajos. When traditional Navajos who live in round homes called *hogans* were compared to Navajos who grew up in rectangular buildings, they were found to be less likely to experience the Mueller-Lyer illusion (Pedersen & Wheeler, 1983). These studies suggest that our perceptions are influenced by elements in our culture that prepare us to see the world in a particular manner.

Let's Review!

The material in this section deals with errors in perception and several common perceptual illusions. For a quick check of your understanding, answer these questions.

1. Which of the following is *most closely* related to errors in eyewitness testimony?
   a. Feature detection
   b. Top-down processing
   c. Figure-ground
   d. Perceptual constancies

2. Last night, Samantha noticed that the moon looked huge as it rose above the horizon. Later, when the moon was overhead, it did not look nearly as large to her. Which of the following is a primary cause of this illusion?

   a. Perceptual constancies
   b. Top-down processing
   c. Bottom-up processing
   d. Binocular depth cues

3. Which of the following is a primary cause of the Ponzo illusion?
   a. Monocular depth cues
   b. Binocular depth cues
   c. Top-down processing
   d. Subliminal perception

ANSWERS:

1. b; 2. a; 3. a

Are You Getting the Big Picture?

After studying this chapter, you should have a clear understanding of the processes of sensation and perception and how researchers study them. You should understand the difference between sensation and perception as well as how they work together to help us understand and respond to our world.

Such an understanding of sensation and perception is vital to many professions. For example, lawyers must understand how perception affects eyewitness testimony. Engineers design equipment, such as dashboard displays, so users can accurately perceive output. Designers of perfumes and foods must be aware of the sensory experiences caused by their products. Those who work with older adults or people with disabilities must be sensitive to their clients' special sensory capacities. Doctors use their knowledge of sensation and perception to evaluate patients' health and manage their pain. And advertisers use knowledge of perception to design product ads that will catch consumers' attention. We hope that after reading this chapter, you can see the roles that sensation and perception play in your life.

We also hope that this chapter has given you an appreciation for the variations in sensation and perception that people experience. The example of Michael Watson's synesthesia gave us a glimpse at an alternate reality created by the unusual way he sensed and perceived his world. Keep in mind that sensation and perception are filters through which we experience the outside world. Variations in sensation, such as color-blindness, our expectations, and illusions of perception can drastically alter our perceptions.

As you continue reading this text, remember to keep the bigger picture of psychology in mind. We will again call on your knowledge of sensation and perception when we discuss memory in Chapter 6. Your knowledge of top-down perceptual processing will also help you understand some of the issues, such as prejudice, that we will discuss in Chapter 12. Knowledge is cumulative. What you learn today will help you learn tomorrow!

STUDYING THE CHAPTER

Key Terms

attention (100)
sensation (100)
transduction (100)
perception (100)
psychophysics (102)
absolute threshold (102)
signal detection (103)
just noticeable difference
    (jnd) (104)
Weber's law (104)
subliminal (105)
wavelength (107)
amplitude (107)
hue (108)
brightness (108)
saturation (108)
visible spectrum (108)
cornea (109)
pupil (109)
sclera (109)
iris (109)
lens (110)
ciliary muscles (110)
accommodation (110)
presbyopia (110)
myopia (110)
astigmatism (110)
retina (110)
rods (110)
cones (110)
optic nerve (112)
blindspot (112)
fovea (112)

photopigments (114)
rhodopsin (114)
dark adaptation (115)
light adaptation (115)
trichromatic theory
    of color vision (117)
color blindness (118)
opponent-process theory (118)
optic chiasm (120)
lateral geniculate nucleus
    (LGN) (120)
feature detectors (120)
cycle (122)
frequency (122)
pitch (122)
loudness (123)
decibels (dB) (123)
timbre (123)
pinna (123)
auditory canal (123)
eardrum (124)
ossicles (124)
hammer (124)
anvil (124)
stirrup (124)
oval window (124)
cochlea (124)
vestibular canal (124)
cochlear duct (124)
tympanic canal (124)
basilar membrane (124)
hair cells (124)
auditory nerve (126)

medial geniculate nucleus
    (MGN) (126)
place theory (126)
frequency theory (127)
volley theory (127)
duplicity theory (127)
gustation (128)
umami (129)
papillae (129)
taste buds (129)
olfaction (133)
olfactory epithelium (133)
lock-and-key theory (133)
olfactory nerve (134)
olfactory bulb (134)
pheromones (135)
dermis (135)
epidermis (136)
kinesthesis (136)
vestibular sense (137)
top-down perceptual processing (138)
bottom-up perceptual
    processing (139)
binocular depth cues (141)
retinal disparity (141)
monocular depth cues (142)
Gestalt approach (142)
figure-ground (144)
closure (144)
proxmity (144)
similarity (144)
good continuation (145)
feature detection (145)

Test Yourself!

Concept Check

Test your knowledge of the chapter concepts by completing each of the following sentences with the correct term. For a more comprehensive review, visit the book Web site (http://psychology.wadsworth.com/pastorino1e/) for online quizzes, flashcards, crosswords, and Internet links.

(1) _____ _____ is defined as the least amount of stimulation that one can detect at least 50% of the time.
(2) _____ theory of color vision proposes that we have three different types of cones in the retina. Jose's eyes experienced (3) _____ _____ when he entered the darkened movie theater. The (4) _____ of the middle ear

rests against the oval window. Our (5) _____ cells are responsible for transduction in hearing. A supertaster is very sensitive to a chemical called (6) _____. Faulty eyewitness testimony can often be attributed to errors in (7) _____-_____ perceptual processing. Binocular depth perception is based on (8) _____ _____, meaning that our eyes see slightly different images of distant objects. The fact that the chalkboard in your classroom looks rectangular regardless of where you stand in the classroom is evidence of (9) _____ constancy.
(10) _____ is a body sense that helps you

remain balanced. (11) _____ _____ is a Gestalt principle of perception that explains why camouflage works. (12) _____ is the sense that is most closely linked to our sense of taste. The (13) _____ _____ contains odor receptors that allow us to smell. Visual information is processed in the (14) _____ lobe of the brain. The brain's (15) _____ acts as a relay station for sensory information.

Answers:
1. Absolute threshold; 2. Trichromatic; 3. dark adaptation; 4. stirrup; 5. hair; 6. PROP; 7. top-down; 8. retinal disparity; 9. shape; 10. Vestibular sense; 11. Good continuation; 12. Olfaction; 13. olfactory epithelium; 14. occipital; 15. thalamus.

Critical Thinking About the Chapter

1. Your younger sister listens to music at a very loud level on her Walkman nearly every day. What would you tell her to convince her to turn down the volume?

2. Your best friend wants to know how we see color. How would you answer his question?

3. Assume you work on the staff of a nursing home. Most of your clients are people in their 80s and 90s. How can you use your knowledge of sensation and perception to do your job better? In other words, what changes can you expect to see in your client's sensory and perceptual abilities, and how can you accommodate these changes?

4. You have been charged with determining the additional amount of sugar one would have to add to a cup of coffee that already contained 2 tsp. of sugar to produce a jnd. How would you go about determining this?

Applying Psychology. Find a picture of Vincent Van Gogh's painting *Starry Night*. What monocular depth cues are used in this painting?

Critical Thinking for Integration

1. Explain how top-down perceptual processing may affect the testimony of a person who has witnessed an armed robbery.

2. If Ali has a brain tumor in his occipital lobe, how might this affect his sensory and perceptual processes?

3. How might strongly held beliefs, such as racial prejudices, affect perception?

4. Design an experiment to test the hypothesis that people differ in their sensitivity to sweet tastes.

Chapter Study Resources

Suggested Readings

1. Cytowic, R. E. (1999). *The man who tasted shapes.* Cambridge, MA: MIT Press.
This book chronicles Michael Watson's synesthesia.

2. Goldstein, E. B. (2003). *Sensation and perception,* 6th ed. Belmont, CA: Wadsworth.
A comprehensive text on sensation and perception.

3. Keller, H. (1990). *The story of my life.* New York: Bantam.
The autobiography of Helen Keller, who was forced to live without sight or hearing for much of her life.

4. Mass, W. (2003). *A mango shaped space.* Boston: Little Brown.
This book chronicles a 13-year-old girl's life with synesthesia.

5. For additional readings, explore InfoTrac College Edition, your online library of archived journal articles and periodicals. Go to http://www.infotrac-college .com/wadsworth and enter the passcode from the card that came with your book. For this chapter, search using these keywords:

color vision

pitch perception

pain perception

perceptual illusions

vestibular sense

bottom-up perceptual processing

Web Links for Further Study

Additional information on chapter concepts can be found at these Web sites:

1. A page maintained by author Donald Hoffman that contains links to many different perceptual illusions. http://aris.ss.uci.edu/cogsci/personnel/hoffman/illusions.html

2. The Vischeck site contains links that simulate color-blindness for those with full-color vision. http://www.vischeck.com/

3. The Prevent Blindness America site has extensive information on sight, blindness, and blindness prevention. http://www.preventblindness.org/index.html

4. The National Institute on Deafness and other Communicative Disorders site has a wealth of information on hearing and hearing disorders. http://www.nidcd.nih.gov/

5. Just for fun, here's a privately maintained Web page listing companies that supply odd foods. Need to find a source of camel milk? Check out this page. http://www.kolvir.com/oddfood.htm

Student Study Guide

To help organize your learning, work through Chapter 3 of the *What Is Psychology? Student Study Guide*. The study guide includes learning objectives, a chapter summary, fillin review, key terms, a practice test, and activities.

Psychology Now™

PsychologyNow is a Web-based, personalized study system that provides you with a pretest and a posttest for each chapter, quizzes you by chapter, and provides a personalized study plan, pointing you to elements in the text or in individual learning modules that will help you to achieve 80% mastery. Check out the learning modules that relate to this chapter: hearing; vision.

PsychNow CD ROM, Version 2.0

Go to the PsychNow CD-ROM for further study of the concepts in this chapter. The CD-ROM includes learning modules with videos, animations, and quizzes, as well as simulations of psychological phenomena. Each module follows a consistent Explore, Lesson, and Apply structure that allows you to experience the concept or principle, learn more about it, and then apply it. You and your friends can participate in a team-based Quiz Game that makes learning fun. You can also participate in experiments such as Signal Detection. Learning modules include: 4a. Vision and Hearing; 4b. Chemical and Somesthetic Senses; 4c. Perception.

How Do We Sense and Perceive Our World?

MEASURING SENSATION AND PERCEPTION

- Psychophysics is the branch of psychology that studies how we process sensory stimuli.
- Psychophysicists conduct experiments to determine the absolute threshold of each of the five senses.
- Signal detection is a method of analyzing the relative proportion of correct judgments (hits) and errors (false alarms) that a participant makes in trying to detect a stimulus or signal.
- The difference threshold, or just noticeable difference (jnd), is the bare minimum change in the intensity of a stimulus that can be detected.
- Weber's law is the relationship between the original intensity of a stimulus and the amount of change that is required to produce a jnd.
- When sensory stimuli are too weak in intensity to reach absolute threshold, the stimuli are said to be subliminal.

VISION: THE WORLD THROUGH OUR EYES

- When we see an object, what we really see are the light waves that are reflected off the surface of the object.
- Light is electromagnetic energy, measured primarily by wavelength and amplitude. Wavelength= Hue; Amplitude= Brightness.
- The visible spectrum of light is the narrow band we are able to see. Some animals are able to see a much broader spectrum.

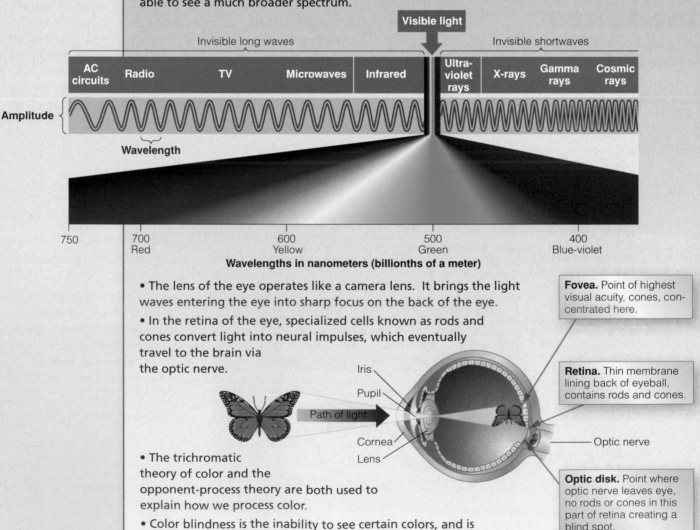

Invisible long waves · Visible light · Invisible shortwaves

| AC circuits | Radio | TV | Microwaves | Infrared | Ultra-violet rays | X-rays | Gamma rays | Cosmic rays |

Amplitude
Wavelength

| 750 | 700 Red | 600 Yellow | 500 Green | 400 Blue-violet |

Wavelengths in nanometers (billionths of a meter)

- The lens of the eye operates like a camera lens. It brings the light waves entering the eye into sharp focus on the back of the eye.
- In the retina of the eye, specialized cells known as rods and cones convert light into neural impulses, which eventually travel to the brain via the optic nerve.

Iris
Pupil
Path of light
Cornea
Lens

Fovea. Point of highest visual acuity, cones, concentrated here.

Retina. Thin membrane lining back of eyeball, contains rods and cones.

Optic nerve

Optic disk. Point where optic nerve leaves eye, no rods or cones in this part of retina creating a blind spot.

- The trichromatic theory of color and the opponent-process theory are both used to explain how we process color.
- Color blindness is the inability to see certain colors, and is often the result of missing cones in the retina.

HEARING: THE WORLD WE HEAR

- Sounds are produced by waves of compressed air.

- A sound wave has both peaks and valleys, with a cycle defined as the peak of the wave and the valley that immediately follows it. The number of cycles determines the frequency of the sound wave.

- Frequency= Pitch; Amplitude= Loudness.

- The eardrum, or tympanic membrane, is a very thin membrane in the middle ear that vibrates to incoming sounds, and begins transmitting that sound through small bones, to the hair cells in the fluid filled cochlea where neural impulses are generated.

- The auditory nerve carries sounds we hear into the brain.

- As we age, many of us lose some of our hearing due to the wear and tear on the hair cells of the basilar membrane.

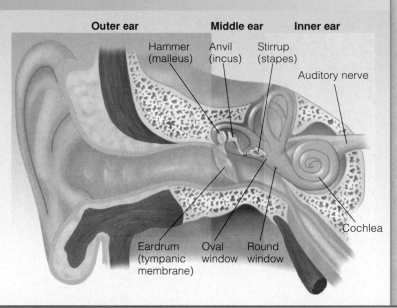

Outer ear | Middle ear | Inner ear
Hammer (malleus) | Anvil (incus) | Stirrup (stapes)
Auditory nerve
Cochlea
Eardrum (tympanic membrane) | Oval window | Round window

TASTE, SMELL, TOUCH, AND THE BODY SENSES

- Taste and smell are referred to as the chemical senses.

- Humans are sensitive to at least four different types of tastes: bitter, sweet, salty, and sour.

- The taste buds reside in the pits between the papillae on your tongue, and they transduce the chemicals in food you eat into neural impulses.

- The sense of smell operates by converting odors captured by a special piece of skin that lines the top of the naval cavity to neural impulses that travel via the olfactory nerve to the olfactory bulb in the brain.

- Many animals have a vomeronasal system that allows them to communicate with other animals via airborne chemicals known as pheromones. Some evidence suggests that humans also possess this sense.

- The sense of touch originates in our skin, with the inner layer—the dermis—containing most of the touch receptors.

- Kinesthesis refers to our ability to sense the position of our body parts in space and in relation to one another.

- The vestibular sense monitors the position of our head in space and helps us to stay balanced.

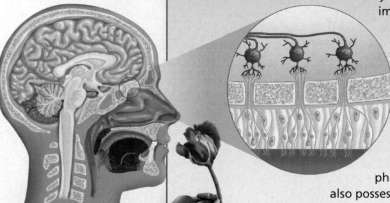

PERCEPTION: INTERPRETING SENSORY INFORMATION

- Top-down perceptual processing refers to using previously gained knowledge to interpret a stimulus to one's senses.

- Bottom-up perceptual processing refers to using properties of the stimulus itself to form our perception of a stimulus.

- Perceptual constancies, depth cues, and feature detection are among the mental shortcuts we automatically employ to assist in perceiving stimuli.

- Perceptual errors can occur due to a variety of reasons, and are often due to misapplied expectations that lead us to think we have seen or heard things we did not.

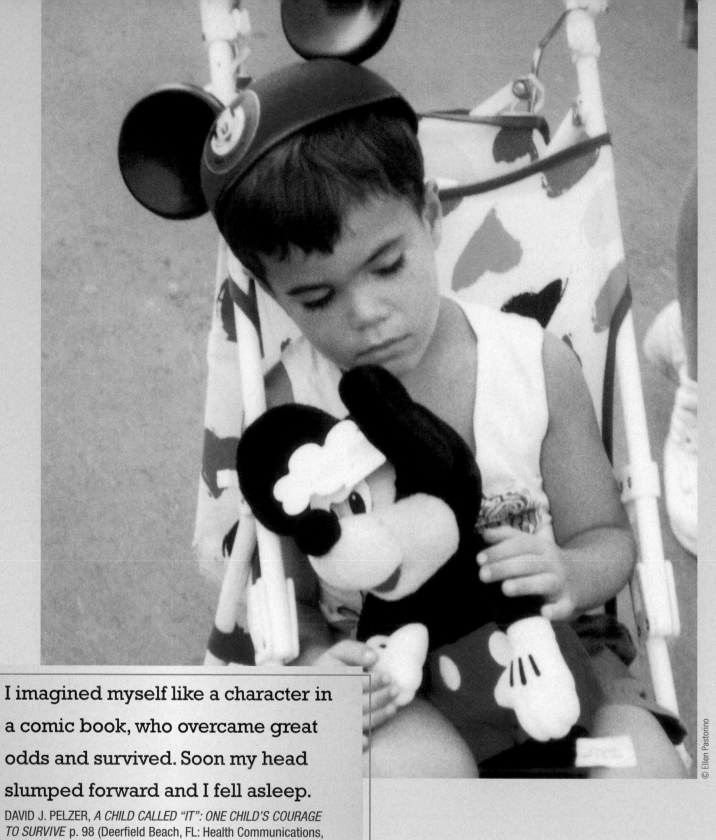

I imagined myself like a character in a comic book, who overcame great odds and survived. Soon my head slumped forward and I fell asleep.

DAVID J. PELZER, *A CHILD CALLED "IT": ONE CHILD'S COURAGE TO SURVIVE* p. 98 (Deerfield Beach, FL: Health Communications, 1995).

© Ellen Pastorino

CHAPTER **4**

Consciousness: Wide Awake, in a Daze, or Dreaming?

CHAPTER PREVIEW

consciousness   feelings, thoughts, and aroused states of which we are aware

"In my dream, I flew through the air in vivid colors. I was Superman."
(Pelzer, 1995)

WHAT IS CONSCIOUSNESS?

In previous chapters we examined psychologists' interests in the more biological domains of behavior—sensation, perception, the nervous system, and the hormonal system. For the most part these chapters focused on conscious behavior. **Consciousness,** in psychological terms, includes the feelings, thoughts, and aroused states of which we are aware. This chapter examines the levels, or gradations, of consciousness itself—when you are *not* fully awake, alert, aware, or perhaps of sound mind. For example, psychologists have done quite a bit of research in three areas: sleep, hypnosis, and the effects of various psychoactive drugs.

Today, conferences on consciousness draw everyone from quantum physicists to philosophers and everyone in between, and there is ample debate about what is unique about human consciousness. Yet changes in consciousness occur because of changes in the body and brain. In this chapter, you will see how brain functions and chemistry discussed in Chapters 2 and 3 actually operate and affect our awareness. The case story in this chapter powerfully reflects the intimate connections between biology, consciousness, and behavior. As you read David Pelzer's story, think about how states such as sleep and dreaming or the use of certain drugs might affect his behavior and the behavior of those around him.

David Pelzer had endured brutal physical, emotional, and mental abuse from his alcoholic mother, starting when he was in kindergarten. He was closed in a bathroom and forced to clean it with a toxic mixture of ammonia and bleach. He slept in the garage on a cot and was fed very little—just enough food to survive. His father, also an alcoholic, sat by and watched the abuse, as did David's four brothers, many of his teachers, and numerous friends and neighbors. David's life is an example of how one state—intoxication from alcohol—had serious consequences for this family. At times, the abuse was so bad that David would sink into himself and attempt to shut out the pain and torture. For self-preservation, he would alter his own consciousness to an almost numb state. He would mentally block out the sound of his mother's voice as she yelled insults at him. He would imagine his exhaled breaths warming his body as he shivered on the worn-out cot in the cold garage. He would imagine himself as Superman to prepare himself for when his mother beat him. David's behavior is characteristic of what many victims of abuse, rape, or trauma do to escape emotional or physical pain. Such changes in consciousness are similar to what happens under hypnosis—another state of consciousness that can be used to relieve or reduce pain.

After being rescued by child welfare authorities at age 12, David spent his teenage years in foster care. David lived in numerous foster homes, then came to rely on, accept, and love two people on whom he bestowed the titles of Mom and Dad. However, his traumatic childhood left him plagued with questions. Why did his mother abuse him? Why did she not abuse his other brothers? Why didn't his father defend him? Did his parents love him? These questions often caused David insomnia. When he did sleep, David often experienced nightmares about the abuse he had endured.

David's later career choice compounded his sleep problems. He joined the Air Force and was sent to the Middle East to fight in the Desert Storm campaign. Shift hours at work, along with the anxiety of war, made sleep even more difficult. He joined the military to fulfill his dream of becoming an Air Force pilot. Yet David became so anxious and excited before any flight that he could not sleep. And when he did manage to sleep, his nightmares continued.

David's nightmares all had a similar theme. His mother would be like a statue, as he stood in front of her, helpless. Then her eyes would open and her hand would raise a carving knife. As he attempted to flee, he would stumble and fall. He would look to his mother for mercy, but her eyes just danced with laughter as she flung the knife toward him. What, if anything, did these nightmares mean? Do dreams have any connection to reality? What do psychologists know about the state of dreaming?

David married, but unfortunately his wife abused alcohol and drugs. David's married life was chaotic. He attempted to understand his mother and reconcile their relationship but with little success. After many years, David did receive word that his father was in a hospital dying of cancer. David went to visit him and could readily see the physical toll that alcohol had taken on his father. He was only a ghost of his former self. His alcoholism had eventually cost him his job, his house, and his family. Alcohol also took its toll on David's mother. She had frequent memory lapses, denied much of the abuse, and had become bitter in her later years.

You may not feel that David's story has any relevance to you, let alone to psychology. But it does—David experienced several altered states of consciousness. He experienced "numb" states during his childhood beatings, and his sleep in adulthood was marred by nightmares. The behavior of his parents, and then his spouse, was altered by psychoactive drugs. You and I also experience altered states of consciousness: when we sleep, daydream, or if we meditate or drink alcohol or caffeine. We also may witness altered states in the lives of those we love. By closely examining these states, we may better understand our behavior and the behavior of those around us. We will start with the altered state we all experience—sleep.

David Pelzer's life experiences illustrate the influence of altered states of consciousness on behavior.

© Shannon Wilsey

Sleep, Dreaming, and Circadian Rhythm

Many of us never question what goes on in our bodies and minds as we sleep. But sleep offers plenty of behaviors for psychologists to explore. First, we will look at *why* we sleep, or the benefits of sleep. Then we will discuss what occurs in our brains and bodies as we sleep. We will explore the purpose of dreams and whether dreams have meaning. We will conclude by describing different types of sleep disorders. We caution you that just reading about sleep can make you drowsy!

Functions of Sleep: Why Do We Sleep, and What If We Don't?

What does sleep do for us? What would happen if you tried to stay awake? William C. Dement, a pioneer in sleep research, actually tried this experiment himself. As we will see, Dement's lack of sleep made him a danger to himself and others, but he did not die. Eventually he fell asleep. In the same way that you cannot hold your breath until you die, you cannot deprive yourself of all sleep. Sleep always wins. We drift into repeated microsleeps (Goleman, 1982). A **microsleep** is a brief (3–15 second) episode of sleep that occurs in the midst of a wakeful activity. We are typically unaware of its occurrence unless we are behind the wheel of a car or another similar environment. In such circumstances, microsleeps could cause a disaster. Yet, microsleeps appear to help us survive by preventing total sleep deprivation.

Sleep ensures our continued physical and mental health in several ways.

- *Sleep restores your body tissues and facilitates body growth.* Sleep allows your immune system, nervous system, and organs time to replenish lost reserves and energy and to repair any cellular damage. This prepares the body for

LEARNING OBJECTIVES

- Discuss why we sleep and what factors influence the amount of sleep we need.
- Describe the sleep stages we progress through during a typical night of sleep.
- Contrast Freud's theory of dreaming with the activation-synthesis theory on dreaming.
- Describe and distinguish among sleep disorders, including insomnia, narcolepsy, sleep apnea, sleepwalking, night terrors, and enuresis.

microsleep brief episode of sleep that occurs in the midst of a wakeful activity

action the next day and ensures the continued health of the body. Sleep also activates growth hormones, which facilitates physical growth during infancy, childhood, and the teen years. The same hormone also controls your metabolism (Pekkanen, 1982). Consequently, not getting enough sleep can be damaging to your body's metabolism and physical growth. David's lack of sleep in childhood (and his near starvation) contributed to a lack of body growth. He developed into a scrawny boy who appeared far younger than he was because of his size. Lack of adequate sleep can also affect energy levels by disrupting metabolic functions.

■ *Sleep increases your immunity to disease.* During sleep, the production of immune cells that fight off infection increases. Therefore, your immune system is stronger when you receive the appropriate amount of sleep (Beardsley, 1996; Born, Lange, Hansen, Molle, & Fehn, 1997). When you deprive your body of sleep, your natural immune responses are reduced. This is in part why you are encouraged to sleep and rest when you are ill. This occurs after as few as two days of total sleep deprivation or even several days of partial sleep deprivation (Heiser et al., 2000; Irwin et al., 1996; Ozturk et al., 1999; Rogers, Szuba, Staab, Evans, & Dinges, 2001). For college students, this may mean you are more susceptible to colds and flus at midterm and final exam time. You are more likely to sleep less at these times, thereby decreasing your immune system's ability to combat illnesses. Fortunately, after a night or several nights of recovery sleep, your natural immune functions return to normal (Irwin et al., 1996; Ozturk et al., 1999). Sleeping truly is good medicine.

■ *Sleep keeps your mind alert.* When people do not get enough sleep, they are more likely to be inattentive and easily distracted (Jennings, Monk, & van der Molen, 2003; Koslowsky & Babkoff, 1992). Sleep makes your body more sensitive to norepinephrine—the neurotransmitter that keeps you alert during the day—as we discussed in Chapter 2 (Steriade & McCarley, 1990). The Chernobyl nuclear reactor accident in 1986 and the Exxon *Valdez* oil spill off the coast of Alaska in 1989 were attributed in part to errors made by sleep-deprived workers. It is estimated that in the United

Application ▷ ≫

It is estimated that over 24,000 deaths occur annually in accidents caused directly or in part by drowsy drivers.

© Tom Carter/PhotoEdit

States, more than 24,000 deaths occur annually in vehicle accidents caused directly or in part by drowsy drivers (Dement & Vaughan, 1999).

■ *Sleep helps you process memories.* When you sleep, information that you have reviewed or rehearsed is more likely to be remembered (Karni, Tanne, Rubenstein, Askenasy, & Sagi, 1994). Does this mean that you can learn while you sleep? No. Chapter 6 offers an in-depth look at memory processing, but a few simple statements here will help you understand the connection between sleep and memory.

Memory involves three distinct processes: encoding, storage, and retrieval. In order to get information into your memory, you must encode it, or do something to remember the information. For some of you, this may mean repeating the information over and over again. Other encoding methods include visualizing the information or associating it with a personal experience or a particular person. When information is thoroughly encoded, it will be transferred to storage, or long-term memory. Information stored in long-term memory can be retrieved later.

So, back to the question of learning while you're sleeping. Information that you process during sleep must be well encoded while you're awake in order for memory to benefit from sleep. Sleep allows you to better assess what material was actually processed (that is, encoded well enough) during studying. Information that you can't readily retrieve in the morning probably wasn't encoded well enough, and you will need to study it again. You can see the advantage of a good night's sleep before an exam.

 Application

David Pelzer's academic problems might have resulted from his lack of sleep. He was easily distracted, forgetful, and had difficulty concentrating at school. Sleep's connection to memory processing also may explain why problem solving seems to improve after a night's sleep. You may repeatedly think about a problem during the day, frustrated by your inability to find a solution. The next day you awaken with a solution in mind. This suggests that pertinent details about the problem are processed during sleep. The phrase "sleep on it" really does have merit.

 Application

■ *Sleep enhances your mood.* Sleep activates many chemicals that influence your emotions and mood. Consequently, if you are deprived of sleep, you are more likely to be irritable, cranky, and unhappy, in addition to being tired (Boivin et al., 1997).

Research also suggests that sleep may have evolved as a necessary behavior for humans (Hirshkowitz, Moore, & Minhoto, 1997; Webb, 1983). When humans lived in caves, it was dangerous for them to go out at night to hunt for food because they had very little night vision and were relatively small compared to other species. If they did go outside at night, they were likely to be the food for larger predators. Consequently, humans who stayed inside the cave at night were more likely to survive and produce offspring. Over time, these offspring may have adapted to the pattern of nighttime sleeping and daytime hunting and gathering.

As you can see, sleep is a necessity, not a luxury. Sleep offers many benefits to our functioning and ensures that we will be healthy, alert, and happy.

How Much Sleep Do We Need?

How much sleep do we need to stay alert and healthy? Is there an optimal number of hours of sleep (6, 8, or 10) that each of us requires? Unfortunately, there is no definitive answer. People show differences in the amount of sleep they need. Some people brag about how little sleep they need. Yet research shows that although the amount of sleep we need depends on several factors, many of us are not getting enough. Forty-three percent of adults in the United States are chronically sleep-deprived (Maas, 1998). Some sleep factors and facts:

- *Age.* Who sleeps more, the young or the old? The older we get, the less sleep we need (Figure 4.1). Babies require a lot of sleep, between 16 and 18 hours a day. Preschoolers require less sleep, about 10 to12 hours a day, typically including a midday nap. Teenagers and young adults need less sleep than children, but they still require 8 to10 hours of sleep a night. On average, college students sleep 6.1 hours—2 hours less than they need—each night (Maas, 1998). Although sleep problems among college students have not been widely studied, one study of 191 undergraduates found that the majority exhibited some form of sleep disturbance (Buboltz, Brown, & Soper, 2001). According to sleep experts, most adults and teenagers require at least 8 hours of sleep a night. Yet according to the Sleep in America Poll (Sleep Foundation Organization, 2001), on average, adults sleep 7 hours a night on weeknights. However, when adults are allowed to sleep unhampered by alarm clocks and schedules, most will sleep 8 to 10 hours a night (Coren, 1996).

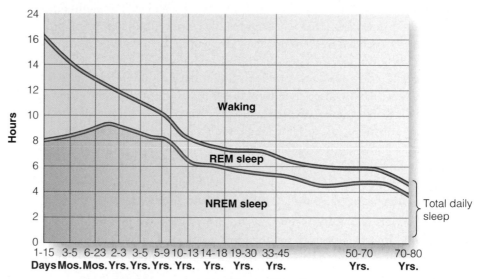

Figure 4.1 **Age Differences in Sleep Needs**

Newborns sleep an average of 16 hours a day. Preschoolers require less sleep, about 10 to 12 hours. Most adults and teenagers require 8 hours.

From "Ontogenetic Development of Human Sleep-Dream Cycle,"
by H. P. Roffwarg, J. N. Muzino, and W. C. Dement, Science, *1966, 152:604–609.*
Copyright 1966 by the AAAS. Reprinted by permission.

- *Lifestyle (Environment).* Our lifestyle habits and our environment also influence the amount of sleep that we need or get. If you were raised in a home in which everyone was up early on the weekends to do chores, you adapted to a different sleep schedule than someone who slept until 10 A.M. or noon on weekends. Stressors and responsibilities change as we get older. Job responsibilities, parenting, or living on one's own also brings about changes in our sleep schedule. Recall how David Pelzer's Air Force career affected his sleep schedule.

- *Genetics.* Genes also may play a role in the amount of sleep that each of us requires. For example, studies that measured the sleep patterns of identical twins compared to fraternal twins found more similar sleep needs among identical twins (Webb & Campbell, 1983). Additional research also suggests that genes may influence our propensity to be either "night owls" or "early birds." Some people may be genetically predisposed to getting up early in the morning and going to bed earlier, whereas others may prefer getting up later and going to bed later (Guthrie, Ash, & Bendapudi, 1995; Tankova, Adan, & Buela-Casal, 1994).

Circadian Rhythm and the Biological Clock

Our cycle of sleep also is greatly influenced by our biological clocks. For example, if you were put in a cave and had no cues as to time—no watches, light, or clocks—your body would exhibit a natural rhythm of sleeping and waking that closely resembles a 25-hour cycle. This phenomenon is referred to as **circadian rhythm.** This circadian rhythm is programmed by a group of brain cells in the hypothalamus called the **suprachiasmatic nucleus (SCN).** The SCN works very much like an internal clock—signaling other brain areas when to be aroused (awake) to start the day and when to shut down (sleep) for the day.

How does the SCN know when it is time to be awake or asleep? The SCN is very responsive to light changes and takes its cues from your eyes. When your eyes transmit light to the SCN, they are in essence telling it whether it is light or dark outside (Figure 4.2). The light information helps the SCN direct the release of **melatonin,** the hormone that facilitates sleep. Melatonin regulates your circadian rhythms and helps you get to sleep. As darkness increases, so does the production of melatonin in your body (Brzezinski, 1997). It is known as the "Dracula hormone" because it comes out at night.

We stated that the SCN functions on a 25-hour cycle. But our days are 24 hours long. Each day we ask our SCN to reset the clock by one hour. It does this automatically and without much consequence to our functioning. Yet when we try to reset the clock by several or more hours, we disrupt our body's natural circadian rhythm. We lose the benefits of sleep we discussed previously.

circadian rhythm   changes in bodily processes that occur repeatedly on approximately a 25-hour cycle

suprachiasmatic nucleus (SCN)   a group of brain cells located in the hypothalamus that signal other brain areas when to be aroused and when to shut down

melatonin   hormone in the body that facilitates sleep

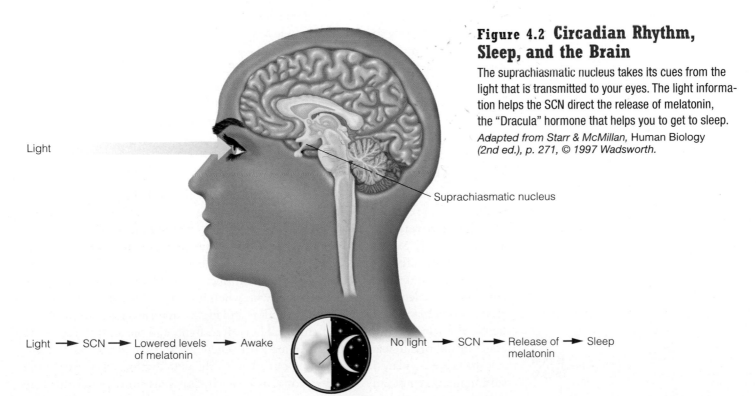

Figure 4.2 **Circadian Rhythm, Sleep, and the Brain**

The suprachiasmatic nucleus takes its cues from the light that is transmitted to your eyes. The light information helps the SCN direct the release of melatonin, the "Dracula" hormone that helps you to get to sleep.

Adapted from Starr & McMillan, Human Biology *(2nd ed.), p. 271, © 1997 Wadsworth.*

Light

Suprachiasmatic nucleus

Light → SCN → Lowered levels of melatonin → Awake

No light → SCN → Release of melatonin → Sleep

"Weekend Lag" and Jet Lag

Application

Many of us disrupt our circadian rhythm on a weekly basis. We attempt to maintain a routine sleep schedule on weekdays, going to bed around the same time every night so that we can get up in the morning for work or school. Then the weekend comes, and what do we do? Many of us stay up *later* and "sleep in" on the weekends, allowing our SCN to operate closer to its 25-hour pace. Then Sunday night arrives. We may have the best intentions—getting to bed at a decent hour so that we'll get enough sleep to meet the demands of our Monday schedules. But instead, we toss and turn, look at the clock, and wonder when we are going to fall asleep. When Monday morning comes, we feel tired. We may hit the snooze button several times, oversleep, or take a long shower to help us wake up. Why? Because we just asked our internal clock to reset itself by three, four, or more hours! Disrupting our circadian rhythm to this extent makes us irritable, tired, less attentive, and moody.

© 2000 Tribune Media Services, Inc. Reprinted with permission.

How does a time change affect our circadian rhythm? This rhythm must be reset to adapt to the one-hour time change that takes place in the fall and spring in most parts of the United States and in many other countries. It must also be reset when we travel to different time zones, hence we may experience jet lag as we adjust. On average, for each hour of time change, it takes one day to reset our circadian rhythm. However, you can minimize the effects of jet lag when you travel to other time zones. Some people start adapting their sleep schedule to the destination time zone before they depart. Others adapt to the new time zone as soon as they arrive. For instance, one of the authors took a 14-hour flight from Los Angeles to Auckland, New Zealand, arriving at 8:00 A.M. New Zealand time. Although she was tired, she went to the hotel, ate breakfast, and toured the city. She went to bed a little earlier than her usual bedtime and awoke the next day feeling refreshed and energized. Her jet lag symptoms were minimal.

Application

Working the Night Shift

Our body's circadian rhythm also has implications for shift work. In many professions (police work, firefighting, airline piloting, medical care, and the military), people may be assigned to work 8- or 12- or even 24-hour shifts, at varying times on different days. When you work Sunday and Monday nights, but Tuesday through Thursday mornings, it is more difficult for your body to reset its circadian rhythm. This disruption can impair your thinking and your health. For example, one study found that air traffic controllers made the most mistakes at 5 A.M., when it is most difficult to stay awake (Luna, French, & Mitcha, 1997). Airline pilots and flight attendants may also have difficulty resetting their biological clocks. They often fly in and out of different time zones in addition to maintaining changing work schedules. If late night or early morning shifts are regular, then your body can adapt to the new rhythm. However, if the shift hours are constantly changing, your circadian rhythm is disrupted, and your sleep

Application

benefits diminish. Hence, you may be less alert, easily distracted, and more prone to mental errors.

Stages of Sleep: What Research Tells Us

Not only do our bodies show a rhythm in relation to sleeping and waking, there is also a biological rhythm to the way we sleep. Using electroencephalogram (EEG) technology, sleep researchers have identified five stages of sleep. Recall from Chapter 2 that EEGs examine the electrical activity of relatively large areas of the brain. This technique works by using electrodes placed on the scalp and body that measure changes in brain activity, and the related physical responses of the body. These changes, often called brain waves, are then plotted on graph paper or a computer screen. The patterns the brain waves create give researchers an image of our brain activity when we are awake and when we are asleep. Brain waves vary in terms of the height of the wave (amplitude) and the number of waves per second (frequency). Brain-wave patterns are usually categorized as alpha, beta, delta, or theta waves (Figure 4.3).

When we are awake and alert, our brain (as measured by an EEG) emits *beta* waves. Beta brain waves are rapid, with a high number of cycles per second. This indicates frequent impulses of electrical activity in the brain. When we are awake but relaxed, our brain emits *alpha* waves. Alpha waves are somewhat slower and less frequent than beta waves. As we sleep, our brain-wave patterns change in a predictable sequence.

If you watch someone sleep, you will notice that at times the person's eyes move under the eyelids, showing rapid eye movement (REM). At other times during sleep, however, such eye movement is absent. From such observations, researchers have identified two distinct sleep patterns: **non-REM sleep** and **REM sleep.** When your eyes do not move during sleep, it is referred to as non-rapid eye movement, or non-REM

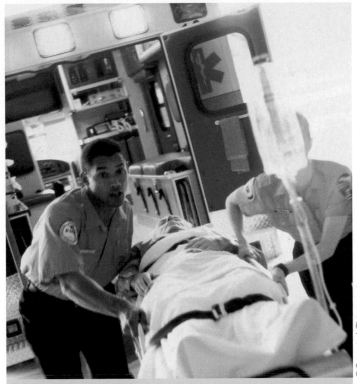

Shift work may interfere with normal sleep patterns, affecting job performance.

non-REM sleep   relaxing state of sleep in which the individual's eyes do not move

REM sleep   active state of sleep in which the individual's eyes move

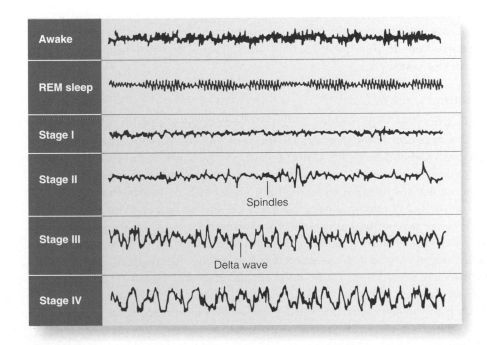

Awake	
REM sleep	
Stage I	
Stage II	Spindles
Stage III	Delta wave
Stage IV	

Figure 4.3 Brain Activity During Wakefulness and the Various Stages of Sleep

Electroencephalogram technology records brain-wave activity during wakefulness and the various stages of sleep. When awake yet relaxed, the brain emits alpha waves. Brain activity during non-REM sleep progressively slows from theta waves (stage I), to sleep spindles (stage II), to delta waves (stage IV). REM sleep is characterized by rapid and fast brain waves.

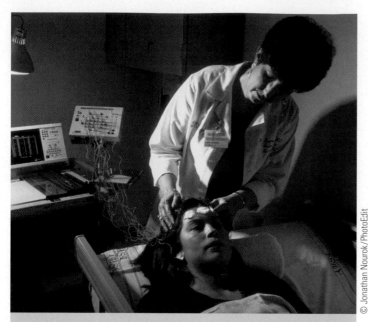

EEG measures brain waves to determine state of sleep.

© Jonathan Nourok/PhotoEdit

sleep. The state in which our eyes do move is called rapid eye movement, or REM sleep. As we will see, during these two states of sleep our bodies and brains are experiencing very different activities. Non-REM sleep is a progressively relaxing state of sleep. In contrast, REM sleep is very active. During a night of sleep, our bodies and brains move back and forth between states of relaxation and excitation until we wake up in the morning (Armitage, 1995; Dement & Kleitman, 1957). Our nights begin in non-REM sleep.

The Four Stages of Non-REM Sleep

When we fall asleep at night, our bodies and brains progress through a series of four stages of non-REM sleep:

- *Stage I sleep* is a light sleep and is characterized by *theta* waves. Notice in Figure 4-3 that theta waves are slower and less frequent than beta or alpha waves. During this stage, your breathing and heart rates slow down. You may experience sensations such as falling or floating. You can easily awaken from stage I sleep, which typically lasts from 1 to 7 minutes.

- *Stage II sleep* is characterized by *sleep spindles* and lasts approximately 20 minutes. Sleep spindles (Figure 4.3) are a pattern of slower theta waves sporadically disrupted by bursts of electrical activity. During stage II sleep, breathing, muscle tension, heart rate, and body temperature continue to decrease. You are clearly asleep.

- *Stage III sleep* is transitional: you begin showing *delta* brain-wave patterns. Delta waves (Figure 4.3), are large, slow brain waves. When a consistent pattern of delta waves emerges, you have entered stage IV sleep.

- *Stage IV sleep* is referred to as deep sleep. The body is extremely relaxed. Heart rate, respiration, body temperature, and blood flow to the brain are reduced. Growth hormone is secreted. It is believed that during this deep sleep, body maintenance and restoration occur (Porkka-Heiskanen et al., 1997). For example, your proportion of deep sleep increases after a day of increased physical activity (Horne & Staff, 1983). It is difficult to awaken people from deep sleep. When they are awakened, they may be disoriented or confused.

REM Sleep: Dream On

After approximately 30 minutes of deep sleep, your brain and body start to speed up again. You cycle back through stages III and II of non-REM sleep, then enter REM (rapid-eye-movement) sleep. REM sleep is a very active stage. Your breathing rate increases and your heart beats irregularly. Blood flow increases to the genital area and may cause erections in males (Somers, Phil, Dyken, Mark, & Abboud, 1993). Figure 4.3 shows REM brain wave patterns that are similar to beta and alpha waves. Your brain looks like it is awake while you sleep! However, your muscle tone significantly decreases, leaving the muscles extremely relaxed and essentially paralyzed.

REM sleep also is intimately connected to dreaming. Although you can dream in some form in all sleep stages, dreams during REM sleep are more easily recalled. Over 80% of people awakened from REM sleep report dreaming (Hirshkowitz et al., 1997). The body paralysis that occurs during REM prevents you from acting out your dreams.

However, in rare instances, people do not experience the paralysis that normally accompanies REM sleep. This is referred to as **REM behavior disorder.** These people may thrash about while in REM sleep, sometimes causing harm to themselves or others (Plazzi et al., 1997).

Why do we have REM sleep? Its purpose is constantly being questioned. Some studies indicate a connection between REM sleep and memory processing. People who are deprived of REM sleep and dreaming are less likely to recall complex information learned earlier in the day compared to people who were not deprived of REM sleep (Chollar, 1989). REM-deprived people also report having difficulty concentrating when they awaken. These findings have led researchers to speculate that REM sleep—and perhaps dreaming—facilitate the storage of memories as well as mental strategies that are useful to us. At the same time, REM appears to help us to "discard" information that is trivial or less important to us (Crick & Mitchison, 1995; Smith, 1995). Other research shows no relationship between time spent in REM sleep and memory problems (Siegel, 2001). The exact connection between REM sleep and memory continues to be investigated.

Another curiosity of REM sleep is referred to as **REM rebound.** When people lose REM sleep due to medications, drugs, or sleep deprivation, they make up for it on subsequent nights by spending more time dreaming (Dement, 1960). Before we look at theories and research on dreaming, let's review what happens during a typical night of sleep.

REM behavior disorder a condition in which normal muscle paralysis does not occur, leading to violent movements during REM sleep

REM rebound loss of REM sleep is recouped by spending more time in REM on subsequent nights

A Typical Night's Sleep

A typical night of sleep consists of cycling through non-REM stages and REM sleep (Figure 4.4). We progress through stages I, II, III, and IV of non-REM sleep. We revisit stages III and II of non-REM sleep. We then enter REM sleep. After a brief period in REM sleep, we begin the cycle again, starting with the non-REM stages. The pattern repeats throughout the night. One complete cycle of non-REM and REM sleep takes about 90 minutes. But notice from Figure 4.4 that as the night progresses we spend less time in deep sleep and more time in REM sleep. This means that the body-restoring function of deep sleep takes place early on, during the first few cycles of sleep. After these early cycles with longer non-REM sleep, we spend longer in REM sleep as the night progresses. If you are not getting enough sleep, you will miss out on the longest period of REM sleep. On average, we spend around 20% of our total sleep time each night in REM sleep. If you sleep 8 hours a night, you spend roughly 90 minutes of that time in REM sleep. That means each night you spend approximately 90 minutes having REM dreams. These dreams occur at intervals during the night. Why do we dream, and do our dreams have meaning? Let's find out.

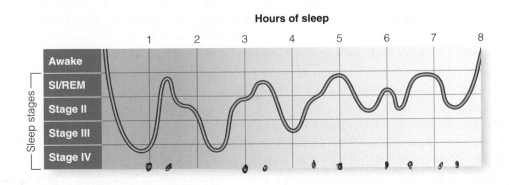

Figure 4.4 A Typical Night of Sleep
As the night progresses we spend less time in deep sleep and more time in REM sleep.

Fred Basset   By Alex Graham

Fred Basset © 2000 Alex Graham. Reprinted with permission of Universal Press Syndicate. All rights reserved.

Dreaming: The Night's Work

Do you remember your dreams? Although not everyone reports remembering their dreams when they awaken, everyone, regardless of culture, progresses through dream states during sleep. Dreams do show some similarities in content from one culture to another. For example, dream themes that focus on basic needs (sex, aggression, and death) seem to be universal. Other content seems to be specific to its presence in a culture. For instance, today's Alaskan natives may have dreams that include snowmobiles, but their ancestors of 100 years ago obviously did not. Kenyan herders and Wyoming dairy ranchers both have dreams about cattle. People dream about what they know, which is influenced by the culture in which they live (Price & Crapo, 2002).

Sigmund Freud's *Interpretation of Dreams*

Psychologists, along with other scientists and philosophers, have had a longstanding interest in the purpose and reason for dreaming. One of the most controversial and well-known theories of dreaming is Sigmund Freud's. In his *Interpretation of Dreams* (1900/1980), Freud called dreams "the royal road to the unconscious." According to Freud, dreams allow us to express fears and sexual and aggressive desires without the censorship of our conscious thought processes. Having straightforward dreams about these "unacceptable" desires would cause us anxiety. Instead, we dream in symbols that represent our unconscious desires. For example, a young girl may dream of coming home from school one day to find the house deserted. She runs from room to room, looking for her parents or some sign that they will be returning soon. Such a dream among children may signify the anxiety of being left alone, deserted, uncared for, or unprotected.

For Freud, dreams contained both **manifest content** and **latent content.** The manifest content of a dream is what you recall when you awaken. The latent, or hidden content, of the dream is the symbolic interpretation. For example, suppose you dream of riding a rocket into outer space. Recalling this image in the morning represents the manifest content of your dream. The latent content, according to Freud, is your internal, unconscious desires, expressed through the symbols of the rocket, the ride, and outer space. This dream might reflect an unconscious desire to engage in uninhibited sexual activity.

manifest content   according to Freud, what the dreamer recalls on awakening

latent content   according to Freudian theory, the symbolic meaning of a dream

Dreams as Coping, Housekeeping, or Just Biology at Work

Many psychologists and psychiatrists have challenged Freud's excessive emphasis on sex and aggression. Some have proposed alternative explanations for why we dream. Coping theory suggests that dreaming is a way we cope with daily problems and issues. We dream about everyday experiences and current concerns in an effort to resolve these issues (Cartwright, 1993). In this view, dreams are not as symbolic as Freud suggested. Memory theory suggests that dreams are mental housekeeping. They serve as a way to consolidate information and to get rid of trivial details in our memories (Porte & Hobson, 1996). From this viewpoint, dreams represent a function of memory.

A biologically based theory is the **activation-synthesis theory** (Hobson & McCarley, 1977), which suggests that dreaming is just a consequence of the highly aroused brain during REM sleep, when the brain shows activation of millions of random neural impulses. The cortex of the brain attempts to create meaning out of these neural impulses by synthesizing the neural impulses into familiar images or stories based on our stored memories. These images and stories may reflect our past, our emotions, our personal perspectives, and information accessed during waking (Hobson, Pace-Schott, & Stickgold, 2000), but they have no hidden "Freudian" meaning. However, because we are the ones who integrated these images into a plot, the story line may provide us with insights about ourselves (McCarley, 1998).

Recall David Pelzer's nightmare from our opening case study. How would these different theories interpret his dream? A Freudian perspective would suggest that his mother, her laughing, and the knife in her hand symbolize David's unconscious desire to kill his mother. Coping theory would suggest that David's nightmare reflects his continued efforts to deal with the abuse his mother inflicted on him. Memory theory and activation synthesis theory would both suggest that David's nightmare has no hidden meaning, but rather was merely a by-product of memory processing or brain functioning during REM sleep.

So, What *Do* Dreams Mean?

Two of these theories suggest that dreams have some meaning; others do not. What do you think about the meaning of dreams? Does your position take into account that many of us experience similar dream themes? Have you ever been chased in a dream? Have you ever had the experience of flying in a dream? Have you ever had a recurring dream? Have your dreams ever made you feel anxious, worried, or fearful? You are not alone. Others' dreams share these themes and emotions (Merritt, Stickgold, Pace-Schott, Williams, & Hobson, 1994; Van de Castle, 1994). Why do many of us experience thematically similar dreams if dreams represent our personal issues and concerns? What about age as a factor in dreaming? Infants spend significantly more time in REM sleep, and therefore more time dreaming, than do older people. What psychological issues would infants be resolving through their dreams?

All mammals experience REM sleep. But do they dream? Watching your pet dog or cat run or cry out during sleep would lead you to believe that they do dream. What is the purpose of their dreams? Do cats and dogs have unconscious psychological issues to resolve as well? Obviously, our understanding of the purpose and meaning of dreaming is incomplete. Dreaming and dreams offer plenty of research opportunities.

Dreams aside, sleep research indicates that not everyone always gets a good night's sleep. Some of us exhibit sleep disturbances, our next topic of discussion.

Sleep Disorders: Tossing and Turning—and More

Not everyone goes to sleep in the predictable pattern of stages described previously. Some people have a **sleep disorder,** or a disturbance in the normal pattern of sleep. It is estimated that 95% of Americans suffer from a sleep disorder at some point in their lives, and 60% of Americans suffer from a persistent sleep disorder (Dement & Vaughan, 1999).

Insomnia: There Is Help!

The opening story about David Pelzer offers a good example of insomnia, the most commonly reported sleep disorder. **Insomnia** is the inability to get to sleep and/or stay asleep. Occasional insomnia is quite common, with as many as 50% of adults reporting insomnia at some time in their lives (Nowell, Buysse, Morin, Reynolds, & Kuper,

activation-synthesis theory   suggests that dreams do not have symbolic meaning, but are the byproduct of the brain's random firing of neural impulses during REM sleep

 Application

sleep disorder   a disturbance in the normal pattern of sleeping

insomnia   a sleep disorder in which a person cannot get to sleep and/or stay asleep

Application >>

1998). Insomnia is caused by a multitude of factors including stress, coping with the loss of a loved one, a change in sleep schedule, chronic pain, drug abuse, or depression.

There is help for the insomniac, however. Non-drug treatments focus on following several guidelines that have evolved from our study of how we sleep (Bootzin & Rider, 1997):

- Establish a regular sleep-wake cycle to work your body's circadian rhythm. Go to bed at the same time every evening and wake up at the same time every morning. Even if you have difficulty falling asleep at night, continue to get up at the same time each morning.

- Avoid long naps during waking hours. Naps can disrupt your circadian rhythm. Why do children take daily naps, and why do adults use "power naps," or siestas? Children's naps and siestas typically occur at the same time every day and thereby work with, rather than against, our circadian rhythm. Power naps tend to be short periods of rest (15–20 minutes) that are relaxing. Any form of relaxation (yoga, meditation, a bubble bath) can reenergize the body and mind.

- Don't use your bed for anything other than sleeping. For example, insomniacs should not eat, study, work, or watch television in bed. The bed should be associated only with sleeping.

- If you can't get to sleep after 10 minutes, get up and do something you think will make you tired enough to get to sleep, like reading (but not in your bed). Then try again to fall asleep.

- Avoid sleeping pills, alcohol, cigarettes, and caffeine. These are all drugs and can interfere with your natural sleep cycle by disrupting REM sleep. A glass of milk before bedtime, however, may be helpful. Milk helps the body produce serotonin, a neurotransmitter that facilitates sleep (see Chapter 2).

- Exercise during the day can promote good sleep. But avoid physical workouts within an hour of bedtime. Your body should be relaxed prior to sleeping.

Insomnia may be treated medically using antianxiety or depressant medication. However, long-term use of these drugs (discussed later in this chapter) may lead to dependence and serious side effects, including memory loss, fatigue, and increased sleepiness. Consequently, chronic insomnia is best treated with a combination of medication for a limited time and following the sleep guidelines we've described.

Narcolepsy and Cataplexy

narcolepsy a rare sleep disorder in which an individual falls asleep during alert activities during the day

Narcolepsy, a rare sleep disorder, occurs when a person falls asleep during alert times of the day. This is not the same as a microsleep, though. The person with narcolepsy experiences brief periods of REM sleep that may be accompanied by muscle paralysis, a condition called *cataplexy*. Cataplexy occurs in about 70% of people with narcolepsy (American Psychiatric Association, 2000). People with narcolepsy may fall down or otherwise injure themselves during these episodes. If you have ever seen what are called fainting dogs or fainting goats, you have seen (at least in animals) the nature of narcolepsy. Narcolepsy is thought to stem from a neural problem in the control of the sleep-wake cycle. The root of this problem is unknown, but genetic factors may play a role (Mignot, 1997). Those with the condition typically take stimulant drugs to prevent falling asleep during daytime activities (Mindell, 1997). An increasingly popular wake-promoting drug for narcolepsy treatment is modafinil. In clinical trials, modafinil therapy significantly improved the health-related quality of life of narcoleptic patients. They also reported less adverse side effects with modafinil than with typical stimulant drug therapy (Becker, Schwartz, Feldman, & Hughes, 2004; Gallopin, Luppi, Rambert, Frydman, & Fort, 2004).

Sleep Apnea and SIDS

Sleep apnea is a disorder in which a person stops breathing while sleeping. This typically occurs during stage IV, the deepest sleep. In an attempt to get air, people with sleep apnea often emit loud snores or snorts that may awaken them or their partners. This pattern may occur hundreds of times during the night. People afflicted may feel sluggish, tired, irritable, or be unable to concentrate the next day because of the nighttime sleep disruption (Naegele et al., 1995). Obesity and the use of alcohol or sedatives increase one's chances of developing sleep apnea (Ball, 1997). Once diagnosed, treatments for sleep apnea vary. If obesity is a factor, weight-loss programs are the first treatment. In addition, nasal masks that blow air into the nose can be worn at night. Wearing mouth retainers can help in some cases. In severe cases, removing the tonsils or surgery to alter the position of the jaw can be performed (Saskin, 1997). Because apnea often occurs in subsequent generations, researchers suspect there is a genetic factor in this disorder.

> **sleep apnea** a sleep disorder in which a person stops breathing during stage IV sleep

Sleep apnea also has been suggested as a cause for *sudden infant death syndrome (SIDS)*. Over 10,000 apparently healthy babies die annually in the United States while they are sleeping. They stop breathing for reasons that are not yet understood. Known as "crib death," SIDS affects babies whose average age is 4 months old. African American and Native American babies are at greater risk than White or Hispanic babies, and the risk is higher for males than females (Lipsitt, 2003). The U.S. practice of laying babies on their stomachs to sleep puts them more at risk for SIDS (Hirshfeld, 1995). Consequently, a 1992 recommendation by the American Academy of Pediatrics encouraged parents of newborns to lay babies on their sides or on their backs to sleep. Parents and caretakers are also advised to remove large stuffed animals or heavy coverings such as blankets or pillows from cribs. This ensures that the infant's mouth and nose are not obstructed. This simple change in parental behavior has reduced the incidence of SIDS to half of its previous rate (Task Force on Infant Sleep Position and Sudden Infant Death, 2000).

Sleepwalking: Wake Me Up!

Sleepwalking, or somnambulism, is another non-REM stage IV sleep disorder. People with this disorder get up and walk around during deep sleep, perhaps performing actions that make them appear to be awake. They may cook, eat, open doors, or engage in minimal conversation. Should you awaken someone who is sleepwalking? Yes, if you can. Because sleepwalkers are asleep, they may potentially injure themselves or others. Wake them up or guide them back to bed. They may be initially disoriented or confused, but you will not freak them out or do them harm by awakening them. Are sleepwalkers acting out their dreams? Remember that most dreams occur during REM sleep, which is accompanied by body paralysis (unless one has REM sleep disorder). Walking and moving during REM sleep would not be possible.

> **sleepwalking** a sleep disorder in which a person is mobile and may perform actions during stage IV sleep
>
>  **Application**

Night Terrors and Enuresis

Night terrors also occur during non-REM stage IV, or deep sleep. Although night terrors can occur anytime in one's life, they are more commonly reported in children between the ages of 4 and 12. During night terrors, children awaken in an apparent state of fear. Their heart rates and breathing are rapid, and they may emit a blood-curdling scream and sit up in bed, wide-eyed with terror. This often frightens parents more than

> **night terror** a very frightening non-REM sleep episode

it does the children, who are actually in deep sleep (even though their eyes may be open). Children rarely recall the incident in the morning (Hartmann, 1981). An attack may last 5 to 20 minutes.

Why night terrors occur is still a mystery, although the disorder does tend to run in families (Guilleminault, Palombini, Pelayo, & Chervin, 2003) and is associated with various neurological and cognitive disorders such as Parkinson's disease and elderly dementia (Abad & Guilleminault, 2004). Such findings suggest a complex interaction of genetic involvement and key brain structures. Keep in mind that people who are having night terrors do not know what is occurring. You can simply reassure the person that everything is all right and to go back to sleep. Night terrors are different from *nightmares*. **Nightmares** are brief scary dreams that typically occur during REM sleep, and are often recalled in vivid detail in the morning.

Enuresis is bedwetting, but it does not refer to the occasional nighttime bedwetting that is common among young children. Enuresis is diagnosed when a child who is at least 5 years old wets his or her bed or pajamas at least twice a week over a three-month period (American Psychiatric Association, 2000). Fifteen to 20 percent of 5-year-olds are enuretic at least once a month, but typically, by adolescence the prevalence of enuresis decreases to about 1 percent. Enuresis is more common in males, and tends to run in families. Approximately 75% of children with enuresis have biological relatives who had the disorder (Ondersma & Walker, 1998). Such a high percent suggests that enuresis may be inherited. However, the behavior also may occur during times of stress such as when a new sibling is born or when familial conflict is high, and may accompany night terrors.

Enuresis occurs during deep sleep when the child is extremely relaxed. He is unaware that he is wetting the bed, and he is not engaging in this behavior to purposely or subconsciously frustrate and annoy his parents. Parents frequently ask, "Then why doesn't he wet the bed when he spends the night at other peoples' houses?" The answer is that when children aren't at home, they do not sleep as deeply—and are therefore not as relaxed—so the bedwetting does not occur. Scolding or punishing a child seldom has any effect on the bedwetting. In fact, scolding can potentially damage the child's self-esteem and the parent-child relationship. Several treatment methods are available, and most children outgrow the behavior.

Gender Differences in Sleep

Sleep research also has investigated the degree to which gender influences sleep. The Sleep in America Poll (Sleep Foundation Organization, 2001), conducted on over 1,000 adults, found that although both men and women report getting an average of 7 hours of sleep on workdays, women are more likely than men to sleep 8 hours or more. Yet there were no differences in the hours males and females slept on the weekend. Women were more likely than men to report daytime sleepiness whereas men were more likely than women to report that they have driven while feeling drowsy and/or dozed off while driving. One research study (Adan & Natale, 2002) also has indicated potential gender differences in the circadian rhythm of males and females. In the area of sleep disorders, two consistent gender differences have emerged. Insomnia tends to be more frequent in women (Voderholzer, Al-Shajlawi, Weske, Feige, & Riemann, 2003), and snoring and sleep apnea are more common in men (Jordan & McEvoy, 2003).

In summary, sleep is a state of consciousness that is as necessary to our survival as is food and shelter. Sleep refuels our bodies and minds, preparing us for the challenges of the next day. It includes a variety of behaviors such that during sleep we may be relaxed, excited, or dreaming. However, when we skip sleep, change our sleep cycle, or experience disturbances in our sleep, we may feel irritable, less alert, and tired the next day.

nightmare a brief, scary REM-dream that is often remembered

enuresis a condition in which a person over the age of 5 shows an inability to control urination during sleep

Let's Review!

This section described why we sleep, what influences the amount of sleep we need, and the stages we progress through on a typical night. We outlined several theories of dreaming and described some common sleep disorders. For a quick check of your alertness, answer these questions.

1. Ronnie has a dream that he is being chased by a golden goose. He is told that this reflects his anxiety about impregnating women. This analysis represents the _____ of his dream.

   a. manifest content
   b. latent content
   c. activation synthesis
   d. mental reprogramming

2. Maria falls asleep during alert daytime activities. Maria is most likely suffering from which sleep disorder?

   a. narcolepsy
   b. insomnia
   c. sleep apnea
   d enuresis

3. Which of the following is not characteristic of REM sleep?

   a. rapid eye movements
   b. paralysis of body musculature
   c. shortening periods as the night progresses
   d. increased heart rate

4. Hap is at a workshop and falls asleep. He is relaxed and his brain-wave pattern would show long waves—but not delta waves—interrupted by short bursts of electrical activity. Hap is in what stage of sleep?

   a. stage I
   b. stage II
   c. stage IV
   d. REM

5. Which of the following statements about sleep is false?

   a. Sleep patterns change with age.
   b. Everyone needs at least 8 hours of sleep a night.
   c. Some people are night owls whereas others are early birds.
   d. Circadian rhythms influence the sleep cycle.

ANSWERS

1. b; 2. a; 3. c; 4. b; 5. b

Hypnosis: Real or Imagined? > > > > > > > > > > >

What is hypnosis? Can anyone be hypnotized? Is hypnosis fake? Are all psychologists hypnotists? Can a hypnotist make you do something outrageous like squawk like a chicken or get naked in a room full of people? Students often ask these questions about hypnosis. This section will describe the experience of hypnosis, explain several ideas about how hypnosis occurs, and delineate what hypnosis can and cannot do for you.

LEARNING OBJECTIVES

≫ Detail the experience of hypnosis and explain several theories about how hypnosis occurs.
≫ Distinguish between what hypnosis can and cannot do for you.
≫

The Hypnosis Experience

Not all psychologists are hypnotists, and not all hypnotists are psychologists. **Hypnosis** is a method used by researchers and psychologists (and hypnotists) to create a state of heightened suggestibility in others. Typically, if you are undergoing hypnosis, you are asked to close your eyes and mentally focus on an object, image, or the hypnotist's voice. For several minutes, you are told that you are getting sleepy and becoming more relaxed (Druckman & Bjork, 1994). You don't fall asleep—though EEG brain-wave patterns of hypnotized people show an increase in alpha waves—and this isn't followed by the non-REM pattern of sleep stages discussed earlier (Graffin, Ray & Lundy, 1995). Once induced into this relaxed hypnotic state, the hypnotist makes suggestions to you about what you are seeing, feeling, or perceiving. For example, one suggestion may be to lift your left arm over your head. A more complex suggestion might be that your eyelids feel like they are glued shut and you cannot open them. Although accounts vary widely, many hypnotized people report that they feel like they are floating or that their bodies are sinking. They are not faking. Under hypnosis, they remain in control of their bodies and are aware of their surroundings (Kirsh & Lynn, 1995). David Pelzer engaged in a form of self-hypnosis as a means to protect himself from his mother's harsh beatings.

hypnosis   a state of heightened suggestibility

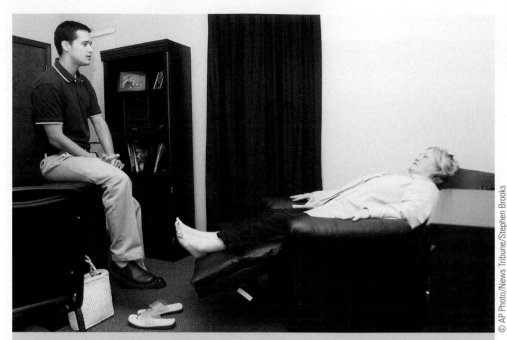

Not everyone can be hypnotized. You have to want to be hypnotized and believe it will work for you.

© AP Photo/News Tribune/Stephen Brooks

Hypnotic Susceptibility

Hypnotic susceptibility is the ability to become hypnotized. Some people have a low degree of susceptibility—they cannot easily be hypnotized. Others have a high susceptibility, meaning that they can easily be hypnotized. One well-known standard test for measuring the degree to which people respond to hypnotic suggestions is *The Stanford Hypnotic Susceptibility Scale*.

Contrary to what you may see on television or in the movies, research using such measures has found that not everyone can be hypnotized. The critical factor appears to be whether you want to be hypnotized and is not related to the skill of the hypnotist (Kirsch & Lynn, 1995). About 10% of adults are extremely difficult to hypnotize (Hilgard, 1982).

Can you be hypnotized against your will? No, you cannot be hypnotized against your will. Those people who are easily hypnotized tend to be better able to focus their attention (Crawford, Brown & Moon, 1993), have vivid imaginations (Silva & Kirsch, 1992; Spanos, Burnley, & Cross, 1993), and have positive expectations about hypnosis (Bates, 1994). In Western cultures, children between the ages of 8 and 12 are more susceptible to hypnosis than adults (Bates, 1994). In some non–Western cultures, this childhood susceptibility does not diminish in adulthood. It may be that achieving a trance state is more valued or widely accepted in these cultures (Ward, 1994). Hypnotic suggestibility does not appear to be related to such factors as intelligence, gender, sociability, or gullibility (Kirsch & Lynn, 1995).

Explaining Hypnosis: Is It an Altered State?

Currently, there are two theories explaining hypnosis: dissociation theory and the response set theory. Ernest Hilgard's (1977, 1992) **dissociation theory** suggests that hypnosis is truly an altered state of consciousness: a person feels, perceives, and behaves differently than in a conscious state. To dissociate means to split or break apart. Hilgard maintains that under hypnosis, your consciousness divides into two states. One level of your consciousness voluntarily agrees to behave according to the suggestions of the hypnotist. However, at the same time, a *hidden observer* state exists. This hidden observer is aware of all that is happening. Recall how David Pelzer engaged in dissociation from time to time to minimize the pain of his mother's brutal beatings and mental games.

You and I engage in dissociation at times as well. Have you ever driven to a familiar location, and realized when you arrived that you couldn't consciously remember driving there? Have you ever dissociated in a class—paying attention to the lesson while at the same time doodling, examining your fingernails, or mentally organizing the rest of your day? If you have experienced any of these behaviors, then you are familiar with the concept of dissociation. Hilgard believes that hypnosis works in much the same way, allowing the person to attend to the hypnotist's suggestions while still being aware of what is happening through the hidden observer.

dissociation theory Hilgard's proposal that hypnosis involves two simultaneous states: a hypnotic state and a hidden observer

Application >>

In a classic demonstration, Hilgard hypnotized participants and suggested that they would feel no pain. The participants then were instructed to submerge their arms in ice-cold water. When Hilgard asked them whether they felt pain, the participants replied, "No." However, when they were asked to press a key with their other hand if they felt pain, the participants did so. On one level, they agreed with the hypnotist that there was no pain, while at the same time a part of them indicated that there was pain (Hilgard, Morgan, & MacDonald, 1975). Nonhypnotized participants who put their arms in an ice-water bath typically feel pain within 25 seconds.

Another view, the **response set theory of hypnosis** (Kirsch, 2000; Kirsch & Lynn, 1997; Lynn, 1997), asserts that hypnosis is *not* an altered state of consciousness. Rather, hypnosis is merely a cognitive set to respond appropriately to suggestions. Highly hypnotizable people enter hypnosis with the intention of behaving as a "hypnotized person" and hold the expectation that they will succeed in following the hypnotist's suggestions. Their intentions and expectations become a response set that triggers the hypnotic response automatically, fulfilling their expectations of the hypnotic individual. Nonhypnotized participants also will show behaviors similar to hypnotized people such as behaving in strange ways or acting like they are at a younger age (Dasgupta, Juza, White, & Maloney, 1995; Kirsch, 1994).

Although researchers continue to debate whether hypnosis is truly an altered state (Holroyd, 2003; Rainville & Price, 2003), hypnosis does have proven benefits for pain relief and reducing anxiety. Unfortunately, hypnosis has acquired the reputation for doing some things that it cannot. Let's look at these myths and realities of hypnosis.

response set theory of hypnosis asserts that hypnosis is *not* an altered state of consciousness, but a cognitive set to respond appropriately to suggestions. The intent to behave as a "hypnotized person" and the expectation that one will succeed in following the hypnotist's suggestion becomes a response set that triggers the hypnotic response automatically

What Hypnosis Can and Cannot Do

Can hypnosis cure your smoking addiction? Can hypnosis help you recover lost memories from your childhood? A certain mystique surrounds hypnosis, leading some to believe that it is similar to a magic spell that can cure all ills and bestow special powers. Psychological research has investigated these issues in an attempt to separate fact from fiction. To date, research reveals the following:

- *Relieving Pain.* One of the most well-documented uses for hypnosis is pain relief (Clay, 1996). Under hypnosis, the client is given a posthypnotic suggestion, such as a suggestion that when the hypnosis is over, they will feel no pain. Hypnosis has been used to minimize pain in childbirth, to block pain during medical or dental treatments, and to relieve chronic pain from arthritis and from migraine headaches (Chaves, 1994; D'Eon, 1989; Nolan, Spanos, Hayward, & Scott, 1995). As you might guess, this pain relief is more pronounced for people who have a high susceptibility to hypnosis (Bates, 1994). Effective pain relief also can be achieved by other nonhypnotic treatments such as deep relaxation training or distraction techniques (Chaves, 1989). Research has shown that hypnosis does not reduce the sensation of pain, but rather the hypnotic suggestions help alleviate the feeling, or perception, of pain (Rainville, Duncan, Price, Carrier, & Bushnell, 1997). The pain is still there, but hypnosis changes one's subjective experience of pain. In all likelihood, David Pelzer's self-hypnosis minimized his physical and psychological pain.

- *Curing Addictions.* Posthypnotic suggestions have proven to be less successful for treating addictions or self-control behaviors, even for people with a high suggestibility to hypnosis (Bowers & LeBaron, 1986). Although hypnosis has been used as a treatment to stop smoking, nail biting, overeating, gambling, alcoholism, and other addictions, it has proven to be no more successful than other treatments at controlling these

WOMEN
And
CIGARETTES:

ARE YOU READY TO
QUIT
?

HYPNOSIS is safe, rapid,
and profoundly effective.

In three easy sessions, I
assist you in freeing yourself
from the smoking habit.

Day, evening, and weekend
Appointments available.

Fee: $275.00
Audio-cassette included

███████████**, B.A.**
Certified Clinical
Hypnotherapist

(510) ████████

© Rachel Epstein/PhotoEdit

Hypnosis is no more effective than other treatment approaches at curing addictions.

behaviors (Bates, 1994). Self-control behaviors such as smoking and alcoholism are some of the most difficult behaviors to change, and hypnosis doesn't appear to have an advantage over other types of treatment. But some form of treatment appears to be more effective in stopping these behaviors than no treatment at all (Rabkin, Boyko, Shane, & Kaufert, 1984).

- *Enhancing Physical Performance.* Hypnosis does not create superhuman capacities. However, being in a relaxed state such as hypnosis can enhance physical performance. This enhancement also can be achieved through other motivational techniques such as deep muscle relaxation and guided imagery (Druckman & Bjork, 1994).

- *Enhancing or Recovering Memory.* One of the most controversial applications of hypnosis has been in the area of memory enhancement. Research in this area has focused on two key main issues.

    Can hypnosis help an individual relive earlier childhood experiences? This is referred to as *age regression.* Numerous studies on age regression demonstrate that under hypnosis, adults act like the way they expect children to behave (Spanos, 1996). They may write, sing, or behave like a child, but it is more like an adult playing the role of a child. Their behavior is not different from nonhypnotized individuals who are asked to behave like a child (Nash, 1987).

    Can hypnosis help a person recall repressed events or information, such as from a crime scene or from one's childhood? This is referred to as *recovered memories.* Being in a relaxed state may facilitate recall under certain circumstances. However, research reveals that hypnotized people may also recall untrue events. For this reason, information gathered under hypnosis is not permissible in a court of law in the United States, Australia, or Great Britain. People are more suggestible under hypnosis, and consequently their memories are more likely to be influenced by the suggestions, tone, hints, questions, and remarks of the hypnotist. They may recall just as many events that did not occur as well as those that did, and they also may be more prone to distort information. For these reasons, the use of hypnosis in the area of memory enhancement should be viewed with skepticism (Gibson, 1995; McConkey, 1995; Perry, 1997).

- *Decreasing Anxiety.* Hypnosis has proven useful in decreasing fears and anxieties for people with a high suggestibility to hypnosis. David's self-hypnosis probably helped him deal with anxiety as well. However, there are numerous other equally effective anti-anxiety treatments that also promote relaxation and decrease anxiety (Bates, 1994).

- *Enhancing Psychotherapy.* Clinicians sometimes use hypnosis in therapy to help their clients solve problems, or cope with bodily symptoms such as headaches or stomach pains that appear to be related to psychological stress. Hypnosis has been helpful in reducing pain and tension. Again, it is most effective for clients who have a high susceptibility to hypnosis (Kirsch, Montgomery, & Sapirstein, 1995).

To summarize, hypnosis does not endow us with superhuman strength, allow us to reexperience childhood events, or improve the accuracy of our memories. However, hypnosis does appear to be of some benefit in decreasing pain, promoting relaxation, and perhaps enhancing therapy for *some* people. These benefits are not universal. The person must want to be hypnotized and have positive beliefs about hypnosis.

Drug Tolerance, Dependence, and Substance Abuse

Before discussing specific drugs and their effects, it is important to establish the scientific meaning of two specific drug terms: tolerance and dependence. Defining these terms will help you understand the effects of different psychoactive drugs.

Tolerance has to do with the amount of a drug required to produce its effect. After repeated use of a drug, it is usually the case that more and more of it is needed to achieve its initial effect (American Psychiatric Association, 2000). For example, when someone first drinks alcohol, he or she may have one beer or one glass of wine and get a buzz from it. However, after drinking alcohol frequently, this person will require more beers or glasses of wine to achieve the same high. This person has increased his or her tolerance to alcohol.

However, with the development of tolerance, the difference between a safe dose and a potentially harmful dose, called the *margin of safety*, narrows. Some drugs have a very narrow, or small, margin of safety. That is, their too-high, toxic dose differs only slightly from their too-low, ineffectual dose. In order to obtain the same level of intoxication, a user who has developed tolerance may raise his or her dose to a level that may result in coma or death—the too-high toxic dose.

Related to tolerance is the concept of dependence, which occurs when someone is either physically or psychologically reliant on a drug's effects. **Physical dependence** is a condition in which the body needs a drug in order to maintain normal functioning. Typically, physical dependence is operating when the person stops using the drug and experiences **withdrawal symptoms.** Withdrawal symptoms may include vomiting, shaking, sweating, physical pain, hallucinations, or headaches. Not all drugs produce the same withdrawal symptoms. In many cases, people may continue to use a drug just to ward off the unpleasantness of the withdrawal effects.

Psychological dependence, on the other hand, is when the person believes or feels that he or she needs the drug in order to emotionally and psychologically function properly. The body does not need the drug and will function normally without it. Thus, psychological dependence won't necessarily produce physical withdrawal symptoms when the person stops using the drug (Feldman & Meyer, 1996). However, do not underestimate the influence of psychological dependence. Believing you need a drug to function properly can be just as powerful as physical dependence.

It is possible to be both physically and psychologically dependent on a drug. Some researchers have essentially stopped distinguishing between the two types of dependence. They argue that in essence, psychological dependence involves the brain. Therefore, this dependence is really physical (Leshner, 1997). Consequently, the lines between physical and psychological dependence are becoming more blurred. Psychologists typically use the term *substance abuse* to indicate someone who has lost control over his or her drug use, for whatever reason.

How Drugs Work: Biology, Expectations, and Culture

Psychoactive drugs alter your state of functioning. They do this by interfering with the normal workings of the nervous system. Some drugs slow down normal brain activity whereas others speed it up. Typically, drugs achieve these effects by interfering with neurotransmitters in the brain. Recall from Chapter 2 how neurotransmitters are released into the synapse. Neurotransmitters influence the activity of the nervous system, the functioning of the brain, and thus a person's behavior. Some psychoactive drugs act by blocking the reuptake of the neurotransmitters as they are removed from the synapse. The neurotransmitters remain in the synapse longer, affecting functioning in a variety of ways. For example, the popular antidepressant drug Prozac inhibits the reuptake of the neurotransmitter substance serotonin, thereby affecting one's mood

tolerance   a condition in which after repeated use, more of a drug is needed to achieve the same effect

 Application

physical dependence   a condition in which a person's body needs a drug in order to maintain normal functioning

withdrawal symptoms   physical effects that occur after a person stops using a drug

psychological dependence   a condition in which a person believes that he or she needs a drug in order to function normally

and sleep. Other drugs mimic the properties of neurotransmitters by attaching to their receptor sites (Stahl, 1996). For example, drugs such as morphine and codeine relieve pain by mimicking the effects of the neurotransmitter endorphin.

The effects of drugs are also influenced by psychological factors such as your environment and expectations. Exposure to stress or trauma increases a person's vulnerability to drug dependence (Goeders, 2004). Environmental stimuli such as where a drug is taken or whether drug paraphernalia are present become associated with drug taking and later trigger the craving for the drug sensation (Crombag & Robinson, 2004). If you expect a drug to alter your behavior in a particular way, you are more likely to change your behavior to fit your expectations. For example, in several studies people who believed that they had consumed alcohol behaved as if they had been drinking alcohol (Leigh, 1989). Whether or not they had actually consumed it, their behavior was influenced by their expectations about the effects of alcohol. They reported strong sexual fantasies or drove more recklessly when they thought they had been drinking alcohol (Abrams & Wilson, 1983; McMillen, Smith, & Wells-Parker, 1989). Several studies have shown that people who believe that alcohol will help them handle stress better are more likely to develop drinking-related problems (Cooper, Russell, Skinner, Frone, & Mudor, 1992; Schuckit, 1998).

Expectations in turn are influenced by the culture in which you live. For example, there are very low rates of alcohol abuse in China, where traditional beliefs scorn alcohol use or behaving as if one is under the influence of alcohol. People in China are not only less likely to drink alcohol, they also would not advertise the fact that they have been drinking. In contrast, Korean men have a high rate of alcohol abuse. Their culture encourages drinking in social situations (Helzer & Canino, 1992).

How might North American attitudes toward alcohol influence your expectations about drinking alcohol and its effect? Drinking beer while you watch sports events such as football, baseball, and hockey is an accepted custom. Advertisers capitalize on this cultural "value" by depicting sports fans having a great time drinking beer at a game. Therefore, when you attend a football, baseball, or hockey game—or watch it on television— you may feel compelled to have a beer. You may be more likely to cheer, yell, and blow off steam because you believe that you are expected to behave this way. Culture and expectations, therefore, can influence the use and actual effects of drugs.

The variety of psychoactive drugs in use today can be classified into four main groups: depressants, opiates, stimulants, and hallucinogens. Table 4.1 ◆ on page 182 provides a summary comparing the effects of these drugs. We'll begin with depressants, continuing our discussion of alcohol.

© David Young-Wolff/PhotoEdit

Is the behavior of these fans due to alcohol or to their cultural expectations of alcohol?

Alcohol and Other Depressants

depressants drugs that inhibit or slow down normal neural functioning

Depressant drugs interfere with brain functioning by inhibiting or slowing normal neural functioning. In low doses, depressants often cause a feeling of well-being, or a "nice buzz." Anxiety is reduced when the nervous system slows down. This may be why many people mistakenly believe that alcohol is an "upper." In high dosages, depressants can cause blackouts, coma, or death. Marilyn Monroe and Kurt Cobain are just two examples of people whose deaths were attributed to overdoses of depressants. Depressants are usually grouped into alcohol, barbiturates, and sedatives.

Health Effects of Alcohol

After cancer and heart disease, alcoholism is the third leading health problem in the United States today. Alcohol abuse costs Americans over $100 billion per year due to its negative effects on health and the ability to work. Hundreds of thousands of lives are lost each year due to alcohol-related crimes or accidents (Rivers, 1994). David Pelzer experienced the devastating effects of alcohol on his parents and later his wife. Despite these statistics, alcohol remains one of the most popular drugs worldwide (Alvarez, Delrio, & Prado, 1995).

Alcohol's effects on the brain result in behavior changes. For example, alcohol affects the neurotransmitter GABA, which you may recall from Chapter 2 is related to anxiety levels. In low dosages, alcohol may make one feel more sociable and relaxed. Alcohol also depresses the functioning of the cerebral cortex. So, in addition to feeling calm and relaxed, we are more likely to shed our inhibitions in regard to our thoughts and behaviors (Koob & Bloom, 1988; Stahl, 1996). Consequently, when we drink alcohol, we are more willing to be silly or aggressive, share our emotions, or engage in behaviors that we would think twice about if we were sober.

《   Application

Alcohol also inhibits the functioning of the brain stem, impairing motor functioning and coordination. Reaction time and reflexes are slowed. When your tolerance is exceeded, your speech becomes slurred and your judgment is impaired. It is also harder for your brain to process information and to form new memories (Givens, 1995; Tsai, Gastfriend, & Coyle, 1995). Alcohol may cause *memory blackouts*—after a heavy night of drinking, you cannot remember the events of the night before. Alcohol also reduces the time spent in REM sleep, which as we have discussed plays a pivotal role in memory processing. Alcohol may make you drowsy, and you may even pass out, but the type of sleep that you are getting in this state is not the type of sleep you need. Chronic alcoholism can lead to *Korsakoff's syndrome*, a memory disorder caused by a deficiency of vitamin B (thiamine). The alcoholic often substitutes alcohol for more nutritious foods, which results in numerous vitamin deficiencies. Unfortunately, these memory deficits tend to be irreversible. David's mother experienced frequent memory lapses later in her life that might be attributed to her long-term abuse of alcohol.

Alcohol's effect on motor coordination can easily be seen in a police sobriety test.

© Corbis

Because drinking alcohol results in reduced inhibitions, people are more likely to engage in sexual activity. But alcohol impairs sexual performance. It makes it more difficult for a male to get and maintain an erection. The ability to achieve orgasm is also hampered by the effects of alcohol. We may think and feel that we are better lovers when under the influence of alcohol, but in reality we are not.

Women who drink alcohol heavily during pregnancy put their unborn child at risk for **Fetal Alcohol Syndrome (FAS).** Children born with FAS tend to have low birth weight, limb, head, and facial deformities, and suffer brain abnormalities. FAS is the leading cause of mental retardation (Ikonomidou et al., 2000; Young, 1997). Pregnant women who report alcohol use are more likely to be under 30 years of age, employed, and unmarried (Centers for Disease Control and Prevention, 2002).

The degree to which each of us experiences these effects depends on several individual factors. For example, alcohol has either more or less of an effect depending on your tolerance level: the higher your tolerance, the more alcohol you can consume before feeling its effects. Another factor is the rate of consumption. The faster you drink, the faster the alcohol is absorbed into the blood, increasing the alcohol's effect.

fetal alcohol syndrome (FAS)   a birth condition resulting from the mother's chronic use of alcohol during pregnancy that is characterized by facial and limb deformities, and mental retardation

◆ **Table 4.1**

Psychoactive Drugs and Their Effects

The four groups of substances most often leading to physical and psychological dependence are (1) depressants, (2) opiates, (3) stimulants, and (4) hallucinogens.

Psychoactive Drugs and their Effects

Substance	Trade Names Street Names	Medical Uses	Route of Administration	Main Effects	Potential for Physical/ Psychological Dependence
Depressants					
Alcohol	Beer, wine, liquor	Antidote for methanol poisoning, antiseptic	Oral, topical	Relaxation, lowered inhibitions, impaired reflexes, motor coordination and memory	High/High
Barbiturates	Nembutal, Seconal, Phenobarbital; **Barbs**	Anesthetic, anticonvulsant, sedative, relief of high blood pressure	Injected, oral	Anxiety relief, euphoria, severe withdrawal symptoms	High/High
Benzodiazepines	Librium, Rohypnol, Valium; Xanax, **roofies, tranks**	Antianxiety sedative	Injected, oral	Anxiety relief, irritability, confusion, depression, sleep problems	Moderate to High/High
Opiates					
Codeine	Tylenol with codeine, Fiorinal with codeine	Pain relief, antitussive	Injected, oral	Euphoria, constipation, loss of appetite	High/High
Heroin	**Horse, smack**	None	Injected, smoked, sniffed	Euphoria, pain control, constipation, loss of appetite	High/High
Methadone	Amidone, Methadose	Pain relief, treatment for opiate dependence	Injected, oral	Relief from withdrawal symptoms, constipation, loss of appetite	Moderate/High
Morphine	Roxanol	Pain relief	Injected, oral, smoked	Euphoria, pain control	High/High
Opium	Laudanum; **Dover's powder**	Pain relief, antidiarrheal	Oral, smoked	Euphoria	High/High
Stimulants					
Caffeine	Coffee, teas, sodas, chocolates	Treatment for migraine headaches	Oral	Alertness, insomnia, loss of appetite, high blood pressure	Low to Moderate/ Moderate
Nicotine	Nicorette gum, Nicotrol; **cigars, cigarettes, snuff**	Treatment for nicotine dependence	Smoked, sniffed, oral, transdermal	Alertness, calmness, loss of appetite	High/High

Psychoactive Drugs and their Effects

Substance	Trade Names Street Names	Medical Uses	Route of Administration	Main Effects	Potential for Physical/ Psychological Dependence
Stimulants, continued					
Cocaine	**coke, crack, rocks, snow, blow**	Local anesthetic	Injected, smoked, sniffed	Increased energy, excitation, insomnia, loss of appetite, mood swings, delusions, paranoia, heart problems	Moderate to High/High
MDMA	**Adam, Ecstasy, XTC**	None	Oral	Increased insight and emotion, muscle tension, sleep problems, anxiety, paranoia	Low/Moderate
Amphetamine	Dexedrine; **Black beauties; crosses**	ADHD, obesity, narcolepsy	Injected, oral, smoked, sniffed	Increased alertness and energy, insomnia, loss of appetite, delusions, paranoia	Moderate/High
Methamphetamine	**Crank, crystal, ice**	ADHD, obesity, narcolepsy	Injected, oral, smoked, sniffed	Mood elevation, alertness, insomnia, loss of appetite, anxiety, paranoia	High/High
Hallucinogens					
Marijuana	**Grass, herb, pot, reefer, weed, sinsemilla**	Glaucoma, nausea from chemotherapy	Oral, smoked	Relaxation, altered perceptions, sleep problems, paranoia, amotivation	Low/ Moderate to High
Phencyclidine	PCP; **Angel dust, hog**	Anesthetic (veterinary)	Injected, oral, smoked	Euphoria, unpredictable moods, hostility, violence	Low/High
LSD	**Acid, microdot**	None	Oral	Altered perceptions, distortion of senses, panic reactions, flashback effects	Low/Low

Gender influences alcohol's effect as well. Metabolic and weight differences between males and females make it easier for male bodies to tolerate higher levels of alcohol (York & Welte, 1994).

Alcohol and Genetics

Research suggests a possible genetic factor in alcohol's effect. Studies of twins show that if one identical twin is an alcoholic, the other twin has almost a 40% chance of developing a drinking problem. Rates for fraternal twins are much lower (Prescott et al., 1994). Research on sons of alcoholic fathers also suggests a possible genetic predisposition to alcohol dependence. The sons are likely to have an overall higher tolerance for the effects of alcohol, requiring more alcohol before feeling its effects, and therefore being more at risk for abusing alcohol (Schuckit & Smith, 1997).

Cultural studies also support a possible genetic link. For instance, in some ethnic groups such as the Japanese and Chinese, drinking alcohol can cause facial flushing. This sudden reddening of the face is a genetic trait that rarely occurs in Caucasians. The physical and social discomfort tends to reduce the rate of alcohol consumption and alcoholism in these groups. People in these groups who do not experience facial flushing are more likely to become alcoholics (Helzer & Canino, 1992).

Related to cultural differences is the role of ethnicity in alcohol use. Patterns of drinking also vary across ethnic groups in the United States as It's a Diverse World explains.

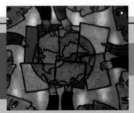

IT'S A DIVERSE WORLD

Alcohol and Ethnicity in the United States

National surveys and studies of adult community samples have generally found the highest drinking levels among European Americans and Native Americans, followed by Latino/Hispanic Americans and African Americans. The lowest drinking levels are for Asian Americans (Caetano, 1988; Chi, Lubben, & Kitano, 1989; Clark & Midanik, 1982; Gilbert & Cervantes, 1987; Herd, 1990, 1994; Substance Abuse and Mental Health Services Administration, 2002). These findings are consistent with drinking patterns among college and secondary school students as well (Skager, Frifth, & Maddahian, 1989; Welte & Barnes, 1987). Gender differences in drinking among most ethnic minorities parallel those found in the majority culture; males typically consume more alcohol and do so more often than females (Mooney, Fromme, Kivlahan, & Marlatt, 1987; Substance Abuse and Mental Health Services Administration, 2002, Welte & Barnes, 1987).

How might we interpret such differences? Could we assume that ethnicity is the cause of these differences in alcohol use?

The answer is No. These results are correlational, not causal, and causal conclusions cannot be drawn from correlational data (Chapter 1) because factors other than ethnicity may be operating. As such, these results should be interpreted with caution. Each ethnic group is highly diverse. Hispanic Americans include groups whose ancestors originated from such diverse regions as Central America, Puerto Rico, Cuba, Spain, Mexico, and South America. Drinking levels and frequency within each subgroup may differ. For example, some survey data (Caetano, 1988) has shown a higher incidence of alcohol-related problems among Mexican Americans than the other Hispanic groups. Moreover, attitudes toward alcohol may vary considerably within these Hispanic subcultures, influencing the level of drinking. Broad-based national surveys, however, fail to consider such diversity when compiling data on alcohol consumption (Jung, 2001).

Alcohol use also varies across social classes and among religious groups. These factors are not typically controlled for when studying rates of alcohol use among different ethnic groups (Jung, 2001). For example, African American men from lower socioeconomic levels report more drinking problems than White men from lower socioeconomic levels. The reverse appears to apply at higher socioeconomic levels—White males report more drinking problems than African American males do (Jones, Webb, Hsiao, & Hannan, 1995). Consequently, one cannot tell whether the differences in alcohol use are due to socioeconomic level, religious differences, or ethnicity.

Many other factors also may play a role in ethnic differences and alcohol use, including education level, urban–rural differences, and the impact of having minority status in a majority culture. Environmental factors such as learning also play a role. Children of alcoholics have an increased risk of developing alcoholism that cannot be solely attributed to genetics. As adults, they are more likely to cope with personal or work-related stress by imitating the behavior of their alcoholic parent (Blane, 1988; Rivers, 1994). In our case study, David Pelzer was able to overcome any possible genetic or environmental effects of having alcoholic parents. Clearly, the effects of alcohol and whether or not one becomes an abuser of alcohol depend on the interaction among genetic, cultural, individual, and environmental factors.

Social Costs of Alcohol Use

Alcohol dependence is devastating to individuals and families like the Pelzers. But its social effects reach beyond individuals and families. Nearly half of all highway deaths (Centers for Disease Control and Prevention, 1998) and 30% of all automobile fatalities (Yi, Stinson, Williams, & Dufour, 1999) in the United States involve alcohol. Over half of rapists report that they drank alcohol before committing their crime. In college campus surveys, alcohol plays a role in the majority of sexual assaults and rapes. Over half of spousal abuse incidents involve alcohol (Adler & Rosenberg, 1994; Camper, 1990; Seto & Barbaree, 1995). Millions of children who live with alcoholic parents also are seriously affected. High levels of conflict—as well as physical, emotional, and sexual abuse—are likely in these households, as the opening case study illustrates (Mathew, Wilson, Blazer, & George, 1993). There are economic costs associated with alcohol abuse. Several studies suggest that alcohol abuse is associated with excessive absenteeism, lost productivity at work, and higher rates of on-the-job injury. These costs also tend to be significantly higher for heavy drinkers (Fisher, Hoffman, Austin-Lane, & Kao, 2000; Gorsky, Schwartz, & Dennis, 1988; Jones, Casswell, & Zhang, 1995). Alcohol, contrary to the beer commercials, is indeed dangerous to our health and our society.

Barbiturates and Sedatives

Barbiturates, commonly called "downers," are a category of depressants that are typically prescribed to reduce anxiety or to induce sleep. Well-known barbiturate drugs include Nembutal and Seconal. Sedatives or tranquilizers are also prescribed to reduce anxiety. They include a class of drugs called the *benzodiazepines*, including Valium and Xanax. Both types of depressants have effects similar to alcohol. In small dosages, they slow the nervous system, promoting relaxation. In high dosages, though, they severely impair motor functioning, memory, and judgment. Like alcohol, these drugs influence the functioning of the neurotransmitter GABA (Barbee, 1993). When these drugs are taken in combination with alcohol, they are potentially lethal because they can cause suppression of those brain areas that control breathing and heart rate, which can lead to unconsciousness, coma, or death. You may have heard of the tranquilizer called Rohypnol ("roofies"), which is commonly used as a *date rape drug*. It is placed in a female's drink at a party or club without her knowledge or consent, and the combined effect of alcohol and Rohypnol renders her unconscious. In this state she is then sexually assaulted or raped. In the morning, because of the drugs' effects on memory, she may not recall the event (Navarro, 1995).

 Application

When used as prescribed, barbiturates and sedatives can be helpful in the short-term treatment of anxiety disorders and sleeping problems such as insomnia. However, over the long term, there is a risk of physical and psychological dependence. Long-term use of barbiturates actually alters sleep patterns, lessening time spent in REM sleep (Kales & Kales, 1973). Severe emotional depression also may set in, increasing the risk

Alcohol has devastating effects on families.

Never leave drinks unattended at a party. Drink coasters can be used to detect unwanted additives. When dipped into your drink, they change colors if something has been added to your drink.

opiates painkilling drugs that depress some brain areas and excite others

stimulants drugs that speed up normal brain functioning

of suicide. Long-term use of tranquilizers leads to memory loss and actually heightens anxiety. When the effect of the drug has worn off, the body goes into "overdrive" to overcome its depressing effects (McKim, 1997). Withdrawal from these drugs can be brutal and includes convulsions, hallucinations, and intense anxiety.

Opiates (Narcotics): Morphine, Codeine, Opium, and Heroin

The **opiates,** or narcotics, are another type of psychoactive drug. Opiates are used to treat pain by mimicking the effects of naturally occurring, pain-inhibiting neurotransmitters in the body such as endorphins. They include morphine, codeine, opium, and heroin, although heroin is not considered or prescribed as a medicine. While depressing some brain areas, these drugs also create excitation in other brain areas. In addition to blocking pain, they produce a feeling of pleasure that is almost like floating on a cloud or being in a dreamlike state (Bozarth & Wise, 1984). The opiates are extremely addictive, causing physical dependence within a few weeks. When you take opiates, your brain recognizes an abundance of pain inhibitors in the body, and decreases its own production of endorphins. So when the effect of the opiate wears off, you feel your earlier pain *and* the absence of pleasure, and will want another, larger dose (Hughes et. al., 1975; Zadina, Hackler, Ge, & Kastin, 1997). It is for this reason that narcotic administration is so closely monitored by health professionals.

Withdrawal symptoms related to opiate use include hot and cold flashes, cramps, sweating, and shaking. These symptoms typically last anywhere from 4 to 7 days and are not life-threatening. What *is* life-threatening is the risk of overdose. Street concentrations of narcotic drugs such as heroin and opium can vary widely. In addition, a person's sensitivity to opiates—either self-administered or medically given to prevent withdrawal symptoms—may fluctuate on a daily basis (Gallerani et al., 2001). The user never knows, therefore, if the concentration of drug he or she is taking will exceed the body's ability to handle it. There is an added risk of contracting HIV/AIDS from using contaminated needles because opiates are often injected into a vein.

Currently, many heroin addicts are treated with the chemical methadone which is chemically similar to heroin. It reduces the unpleasantness of the withdrawal symptoms yet does not produce the intense high of heroin. It is relatively effective in decreasing heroin use (Payte, 1997), however, it is also a drug that creates dependence. Methadone addicts are now increasing in number and medical researchers are looking for other, equally effective treatments.

Stimulants: Legal and Otherwise

The **stimulants** include drugs that interfere with brain functioning by speeding up normal brain activity. Five stimulant substances we will review are caffeine, nicotine, cocaine, amphetamines, and MDMA (Ecstasy).

Caffeine: Java Jitters

Because many of us wake up each morning reaching for that cup of coffee to get us going, we may not even consider caffeine a mind-altering drug. Caffeine is a psychoactive drug because of its effects on the brain. It is perhaps the most frequently used psychoactive drug in the world. Caffeine is an active ingredient in coffee, of course, but it is also found in teas, sodas, chocolate, and diet pills. It stimulates the brain by blocking neurotransmitters (primarily adenosine) that slow nerve activity and cause sleep (Julien, 1995). In small doses, caffeine gives us a physiological and psychological boost, keeping us more alert and helping us focus. It enhances problem solving and decreases reaction time (Warburton, 1995). However, in large doses, caffeine can "wire" you, causing insomnia, upset stomach, racing heartbeat, nervousness, and irritability.

Regular caffeine use can lead to physical and psychological dependence. If you stop drinking coffee suddenly or kick your cola habit, you will likely experience headaches, irritability, increased fatigue, and flu-like symptoms (Schuh & Griffiths, 1997). These withdrawal symptoms, even if they aren't severe, can last a week. Excessive caffeine use also can be potentially damaging to one's health. It increases the risk of high blood pressure and encourages the development of fibroid cysts in women's breasts. Pregnant women in particular should reduce or eliminate caffeine intake because caffeine is associated with an increased risk of miscarriage and has been linked with birth defects (Infante-Rivard, Fernandez, Gauthier, David, & Rivard, 1993). As you can see from these effects, caffeine is a potent psychoactive drug. An even more potent stimulant is nicotine.

Nicotine: A Really Bad Habit

Nicotine, the active ingredient in tobacco and the source of a smoker's craving for cigarettes, is a powerful stimulant. Tobacco use is the most preventable cause of death in the United States. More than 400,000 deaths result each year from tobacco use, at an annual price tag of more than $50 billion in direct medical costs (Centers for Disease Control and Prevention, 1996). As seen in Figure 4.7, smoking kills more people than AIDS, alcohol, motor vehicle accidents, drug overdoses, murders, and suicides combined!

Most adult smokers started smoking before the age of 18, and every day, nearly 3,000 more people under the age of 18 become regular smokers (Figure 4.8). The percentage of people in the United States who smoke has decreased considerably in the

Figure 4.7 Causes of Annual Deaths in the United States

Cigarette smoking causes more deaths in the United States than AIDS, alcohol, motor vehicle accidents, homicides, suicides, and other drug use combined.

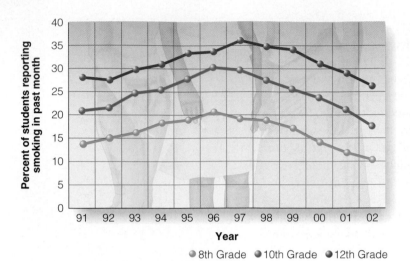

Figure 4.8 **Cigarette Smoking Among High School Students**

In the last decade, cigarette smoking has decreased among high school students. However, in 2002, approximately 1 out of every 4 high school seniors reported smoking cigarettes in the past month.

last 50 years, but in 2002, 28.7% of adult men and 23.4% of adult women continued to smoke regularly (Substance Abuse and Mental Health Services Administation, 2002). The percentages are slightly higher for college students (Rigotti, Lee, & Wechsler, 2000). Native Americans have the highest rates of tobacco use, and African American and Southeast Asian men also have high rates of smoking. Asian American and Hispanic women have the lowest rates (Substance Abuse and Mental Health Services Administration, 2002; U.S. Department of Health and Human Services, 1998).

Why is nicotine so powerful? Much of nicotine's allure comes from its effect on the brain. Nicotine affects several neurotransmitters. It first activates acetylcholine receptors, which affects the availability of the excitatory neurotransmitter, glutamate. In low doses, nicotine improves attention and memory (McGehee, Heath, Gelber, Devay, & Role, 1995). Nicotine, like heroin and cocaine, also elevates dopamine levels, leading to feelings of pleasure and reward (Pidoplichko, DeBiasi, Williams, & Dani, 1997). However, in high doses, nicotine causes vomiting, diarrhea, sweating, and dizziness. Most first-time users report nausea and dizziness from smoking cigarettes. Yet users quickly develop a tolerance to nicotine.

The U.S. Food and Drug Administration officially named nicotine an addictive substance in 1997 because users can become both physically and psychologically dependent, often in just a few days. Withdrawal from chronic nicotine use rivals withdrawal from other abused drugs such as cocaine, morphine, and alcohol (Epping-Jordan, Watkins, Koob, & Markou, 1998). Withdrawal symptoms last anywhere from 2 to 6 weeks. They include headaches, irritability, stomach upset, difficulty sleeping, and an intense craving for the drug. This helps explain why it is so hard for people to stop smoking. Although 3 out of every 4 smokers have tried to quit, only 2 out of 10 succeed. High relapse rates occur. On average, it takes smokers 4 to 5 attempts at quitting before they succeed (Jarvik, 1995). This indeed illustrates the power of dependence. Cigarette smokers and users of smokeless (chewing) tobacco also are endangering their health and the health of others. Tobacco use has been linked to lung cancer, throat cancer, emphysema, and heart disease (Noah, 1997). Women who smoke during pregnancy reduce the flow of oxygen to the fetus. Their babies tend to be irritable, have respiratory problems, and have lower birth weight (Rosenblith, 1992).

Cocaine and Crack

At the age of 23, actor River Phoenix exited a movie theater and started to shake and have convulsions. He subsequently died from an overdose of cocaine and heroin. Len Bias, a promising young basketball player bound for the Boston Celtics, died from cardiac arrest just hours after ingesting cocaine. Chris Farley, a comedian who starred on television's *Saturday Night Live* and in the movie *Tommy Boy*, died in 1997 at the age of 33. An autopsy revealed an overdose of morphine and cocaine. Actor Robert Downey, Jr.'s battle with cocaine addiction also has played itself

Nicotine is an addictive substance that makes it difficult for young people to quit smoking once they have started.

© Penny Tweddie/Getty Images

out in the media. Cocaine and its derivative, crack, are powerful and dangerous stimulant drugs. They can be quickly absorbed into the body and thus reach the brain quickly. Typically, the faster a drug reaches the brain, the more immediate the high and the more addictive it is (Kato, Wakasa, & Yanagita, 1987). Cocaine is smoked (in the case of crack), injected, or snorted into the nose. When snorted or injected, it reaches the brain in a minute; when smoked, it reaches the brain in seconds.

Overdoses and legal problems can occur from stimulant drug use.

Cocaine, like nicotine, stimulates dopamine activity (Balter, 1996). It also affects norepinephrine and serotonin levels (Ray & Ksir, 1990). This produces an instant surge of arousal, a feeling of pleasure and optimism. Appetite decreases but heart rate, blood pressure, and alertness increase. Used in low doses, the effect of cocaine is short-lived—lasting roughly 10 to 30 minutes. However, users typically repeat doses, making its effect last longer. When the effect of the cocaine wears off, the person "crashes," showing decreased energy and depressed mood. This low creates an intense craving for the drug that sets up a cycle of continued use and physical and psychological dependence (Gawin, 1991). High doses of cocaine (relative to one's tolerance) can also cause paranoia, sleeplessness, delusions, seizures, strokes, and potentially cardiac arrest (as in the case of Len Bias; Lacayo, 1995). Users who are dependent on cocaine may lose interest in their usual friends and activities, lose weight, have chronic sore throats and difficulty sleeping, and there may be a noticeable change in their finances.

Health effects of repeated use of cocaine also include chronic nosebleeds, damage to nasal cartilage (from snorting), and respiratory and heart problems. Spontaneous abortions and miscarriages are common for pregnant women who use cocaine. If the pregnancy continues, the infant is more likely to be born premature, and these "crack babies" have further obstacles to overcome. As newborns, they must be weaned from the effects of the drug. By school age, they are more likely to be hyperactive, and show delayed language learning and disorganized thinking (Konkol, Murphey, Ferriero, Dempsey, & Olsen, 1994; Lester et al., 1991; Mayes, Bornstein, Chawarska, & Haynes, 1996).

Amphetamines

Amphetamines, called "uppers" or "speed," are drugs that have effects similar to cocaine. However, the high produced from these drugs is less intense but generally lasts longer (a few hours). At one time amphetamines such as Dexedrine, Methedrine, and Benzedrine were widely prescribed for weight loss and depression. So many people became dependent on them that their use is now limited to treating people with narcolepsy and children who are diagnosed with attention deficit hyperactivity disorder (ADHD). They may be abused in these situations as well, and other medications are available for these conditions.

Currently, the most abused form of amphetamine is *methamphetamine*, commonly called crystal, ice, or crank. Methamphetamine use is the fastest growing drug problem in much of the Far West and Southwest United States. Over 2,400 deaths related to methamphetamine were reported between 1991 and 1995 (*San Jose Mercury News*, 1996). The Bureau of Narcotics Enforcement raids an average of more than three methamphetamine labs a day in California. In August of 2000, agents seized more than 10 tons of pseudoephedrine, the main chemical ingredient in methamphetamine (Schrader, 2000). Pseudoephedrine is a key component of over-the-counter cold remedies such as Sudafed. The pseudoephedrine is combined with other chemicals readily available in gasoline, rubbing alcohol, pool cleaning supplies, or drain cleaners to produce methamphetamine. Methamphetamine can be used in pill form or powder by snorting or injecting. Crystallized methamphetamine, known as ice, is smoked and is a more powerful form of the drug.

Methamphetamine, like cocaine, affects dopamine and norepinephrine levels in the brain. The result is enhanced mood and pleasure, energy, alertness, and reduced appetite. Heart rate and blood pressure also increase. Like cocaine, it also leads to a crash to low energy levels, paranoia, and depressed mood when the effects of the drug have subsided. Continued use results in insomnia, paranoia, agitation, confusion, violent behavior, and physical and psychological dependence. Methamphetamine use also can cause strokes, cardiovascular problems, and extreme anorexia. An overdose can cause coma and death. Users who inject the drug and share needles also are at risk for acquiring HIV/AIDS (Bezchlibnyk-Butler & Jeffries, 1998).

MDMA (Ecstasy)

MDMA, called "Ecstasy," "Adam," or "XTC," is a designer drug chemically similar to amphetamine. A "designer drug" is a substance that is produced by changing the chemical composition of an existing drug. Although it has been available as a street drug since the 1980s, MDMA's use dramatically increased in the 1990s, particularly among college students and young adults. In 1995, 2.3% of college students reported using Ecstasy at some point during the year. It also is being used at relatively high levels by eighth graders and high school students in the United States (Figure 4.9; National Institute on Drug Abuse, 2002).

Taken orally, usually in a tablet or a capsule, Ecstasy enhances mood and energy levels, and heightens users' sensory experiences. The effect begins very fast, within half an hour of consumption, and lasts approximately 3 to 6 hours. MDMA increases the activity of several neurotransmitters in the brain: serotonin, dopamine, and norepinephrine. Problems encountered with Ecstasy are very similar to those encountered with cocaine and amphetamines: insomnia, teeth-clenching, nausea, increases in heart rate and blood pressure, paranoia, confusion, depression, and drug craving. Overheating, cardiac complications, kidney failure, seizures, strokes, and/or psychoses may also occur (Bezchlibnyk-Butler & Jeffries, 1998). Animal studies show that MDMA selectively damages neurons that contain the neurotransmitter serotonin (Figure 4.10). Whether this also occurs in humans is unclear (Fischer, Hatzidimitriou, Wlos, Katz, & Ricaurte, 1995). It also is unclear whether Ecstasy has properties of the hallucinogens. Users regularly report hallucinations, but it is impossible to know whether they really have been using MDMA or have bought low doses of LSD instead. More about LSD will be revealed as we now turn our attention to the hallucinogens.

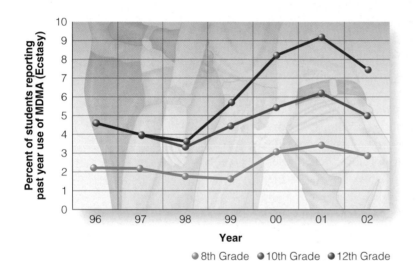

Figure 4.9

Ecstasy Use by High School Students

Since 1999, Ecstasy (MDMA) use by high school students has been slowly increasing. In 2002, roughly 3% of eighth graders, 5% of tenth graders, and 7% of high school seniors reported past year use of Ecstasy.

Hallucinogens: Distorting Reality

hallucinogens drugs that simultaneously excite and inhibit normal neural activity, thereby causing distortions in perception

Hallucinogens are drugs that interfere with brain functioning by simultaneously exciting and inhibiting normal neural activity. These contrasting effects often cause distortions in perception, or *hallucinations*. Hallucinogenic substances include marijuana, PCP, and LSD.

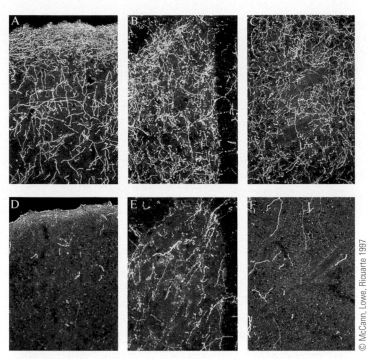

© McCann, Lowe, Ricuarte 1997

Figure 4.10
Brain Damage in Monkeys Given Ecstasy

Brain sections have been chemically stained to make neurons containing serotonin turn white.
Monkeys given MDMA (Ecstasy) a year earlier show neurons that have less serotonin (bottom row)
compared to monkeys that were not given MDMA (top row).

Marijuana

Marijuana, also called pot, reefer, or weed, is a mild hallucinogen. It rarely if ever leads
to overdoses that cause death (Zimmer & Morgan, 1997). Marijuana has been prescribed for medical conditions such as glaucoma, chronic pain, and nausea from cancer
chemotherapy (Grinspoon & Bakalar, 1995). It also is the most widely used illegal substance in the United States (Schlosser, 1994; Substance Abuse and Mental Health Services Administration). The effects of marijuana are very much dependent on the expectations and current mood of the user (Jones, 1971). If you expect to become mellow
under the influence of pot, you are more likely to act mellow when you're high. Similarly, if you are depressed before smoking pot, the drug is more likely to intensify this
mood. Of course, marijuana's effect will also depend on your tolerance level and the
amount of the drug consumed.

The active ingredient in marijuana is **THC (tetrahydrocannabinol).** THC is absorbed by the lungs and produces a high that lasts for several hours. A neurotransmitter
called anandamide influences learning, short-term memory, coordination, emotions,
and appetite stimulation—all behaviors that are all affected when people are high on
marijuana. THC is an anandamidelike chemical that easily influences these processes
(Matsuda, Lolait, Brownstein, Young, & Bonner, 1990). In low doses, THC binds to
anandamide receptors, causing users to feel good and experience vivid sensations. THC
also slows reaction time and impairs judgment and peripheral vision. For this reason,
marijuana users are just as dangerous driving a car or operating machinery as users of
other drugs. Marijuana use also interferes with memory, disrupting both the formation of memories and the recall of information (Pope & Yurgelun-Todd, 1996). Its stimulation of appetite and increased sensitivity to taste may result in an attack of the
"munchies." In high doses, THC may produce hallucinations, delusions, paranoia, and
distortions in time and body image (Hanson & Venturelli, 1998). Controversy still exists

tetrahydrocannabinol (THC)   the active
ingredient in marijuana that affects learning,
short-term memory, coordination, emotion,
and appetite

over whether marijuana use leads to physical dependence. Many people maintain that it does not, whereas others report mild withdrawal symptoms when marijuana use is stopped (de Fonseca, Carrera, Navarro, Koob, & Weiss, 1997; Grinspoon, Bakalar, Zimmer, & Morgan, 1997; Wickelgren, 1997). Psychological dependence on marijuana, however, is easily possible (Stephens, Roffman, & Simpson, 1994).

Studies on long-term users of marijuana have shown impaired attention, learning, and coordination (Pope & Yurgelun-Todd, 1996; Volkow, Gillespie, Mullani, & Tancredi, 1996). Marijuana also has serious long-term health effects. Because it is typically smoked, users may experience respiratory problems such as bronchitis and lung damage. A few marijuana cigarettes (or joints) contain more carcinogenic substances than a half a pack of cigarettes (Ferrell, 1996)!

PCP

In the 1950s, Parke, Davis and Company developed PCP (phencyclidine) as an anesthetic for surgery. However, following surgery, individuals showed worrisome side effects including hallucinations, delirium, and disorientation. Consequently, it was removed from the market (for humans) in 1965 and sold to veterinarians for use in animal surgery. Its use as a street drug spread significantly until 1978, when it was taken off the market completely (Rudgley, 1998). Today, PCP is manufactured illegally and sold on the street by such names as "angel dust" and "rocket fuel." "Sherm," "killer joints," or "KJs" are names that refer to PCP poured over cigarettes or marijuana joints. Although the use of PCP declined steadily since 1979, its use has recently increased again. According to surveys conducted by the National Institute on Drug Abuse, from 1991 to 1995, an average of 2.8% of high school seniors had tried PCP. In 1996 and 1997 that average rose to 4% (National Institute on Drug Abuse, 1997).

PCP has hallucinogenic properties as well as stimulant and depressant effects. As such, it has unpredictable effects that often lead to distress, disorientation, and violent behavior. PCP affects the neurotransmitter glutamate. In low doses, PCP acts like a stimulant, producing a sudden increase in blood pressure, pulse rate, and breathing. Flushing, profuse sweating, and numbness of the limbs also may occur. Out-of-body experiences and the sensation of walking on a spongy surface also are reported. In higher doses, PCP acts like a depressant, causing a drop in blood pressure, pulse rate, and respiration. This may be accompanied by nausea, vomiting, blurred vision, drooling, loss of balance, and dizziness. Hallucinations, disordered thinking, paranoia, and garbled speech also result. Users may become violent or suicidal, and therefore, are a danger to themselves or others. Seizures, coma, or death also may occur (Rudgley, 1998).

Using PCP can lead to psychological dependence. Users often crave the feelings of strength, power, invulnerability, and the escape from thinking that PCP brings. Long-term use of PCP is associated with memory loss, difficulty speaking and thinking, and may lead to permanent changes in fine motor abilities (Substance Abuse and Menta Health Services Administration, 1991). Like marijuana, PCP's effects are influenced by the users' personality, mood, and the setting at time of use.

LSD

LSD (lysergic acid diethylamide), more commonly referred to as acid, is a very powerful hallucinogen. Like PCP, LSD was popular in America during the 1960s and 1970s. But data indicate a new increase in its usage in the 1990s (Strassman, 1995). There were over 950,000 new users of LSD in 2000 (Substance Abuse and Mental Health Services Administration, 2002). Even at very low doses, LSD causes bizarre hallucinations, distortions in time and body image, and intense emotions that together are often referred to as "tripping." These "trips" may last anywhere from 8 to 10 hours.

The effects are due to LSD's resemblance to the neurotransmitter serotonin (Aghajanian, 1994). LSD stimulates serotonin receptors, influencing perceptions, emotions, and sleep. However, whether one's "trip" is pleasant or unpleasant is unpredictable and depends on the user's expectations and mood: if a person is tense and anxious about using LSD, it will be more likely to magnify these feelings, causing a "bad trip." Although physical dependence on LSD has not been documented, users quickly develop tolerance (Miller & Gold, 1994). LSD also can cause "flashbacks," or a reexperiencing of the drug episode hours, weeks, or even years after its initial use. Additional lasting side effects may include short-term memory loss, paranoia, nightmares, and panic attacks (Gold, 1994).

Despite the different effects of the drugs discussed, they all have one thing in common: they alter our state of consciousness—in sometimes unpredictable, and occasionally tragic, ways. Although much is still unknown about many of these drugs, it is clear that the long-term negative effects outweigh the short-term high and feelings of well-being that they produce. By understanding the physical and psychological effects and costs of drug use, you may well avoid or prevent their abuse in the future.

Let's Review!

This section has detailed the nature of psychoactive drugs—from caffeine to heroin—including how they work and their effects. As a quick check of your understanding, answer these questions.

1. Which category of drugs mainly has its effects by interfering with the neurotransmitter dopamine?

   a. stimulants   c. depressants

   b. hallucinogens   d. opiates

2. Rolanda takes a drug that raises her blood pressure and heart rate, makes her feel euphoric and excited, and suppresses her appetite. Rolanda in all likelihood has NOT taken _____.

   a. cocaine   c. methamphetamine

   b. alcohol   d. crack

3. Which of the following drugs is least likely to lead to physical addiction?

   a. marijuana   c. alcohol

   b. heroin   d. cocaine

4. The designer drug Ecstasy, or MDMA, produces effects similar to what two categories of drugs?

   a. stimulants and depressants   c. stimulants and hallucinogens

   b. hallucinogens and depressants   d. opiates and depressants

5. Which of the following categories of drugs produces the most intense withdrawal effects once the person stops using the drug?

   a. hallucinogens   c. stimulants

   b. barbiturates   d. a and c

ANSWERS:

1. a; 2. b; 3. a; 4. c; 5. b

Are You Getting the Big Picture?

This chapter highlighted three altered states of consciousness: sleep, hypnosis, and the effects of psychoactive drugs. We hope that as you read this chapter, you were able to see how seemingly simple states such as sleep, hypnosis, or the effects of drugs can powerfully influence behavior and the life of someone such as David Pelzer. As you study the material of this chapter, see how the information on these states applies to your own life. For instance, on average how much sleep do you get? Is this amount positively or negatively influencing your behavior and health? Consider your perspective on dreaming, or on the usefulness of hypnosis. How does your perspective compare to the theories outlined in this chapter? Examining such issues and your own responses will help you learn the material and will further your understanding of the behavior of those around you.

Once you feel that you understand these three states, relate this material to the biological, cognitive, and social frameworks of the big picture of psychology. For example, we saw how brain waves change during the sleep cycle and how drug substances alter neurotransmitters in the brain causing changes in behavior. We will look again at these drug categories when we discuss the biological therapies in Chapter 16. Your knowledge of these substances and their effects on the brain and behavior will further your understanding of why psychiatrists prescribe certain medications to treat specific mental health disorders.

Altered states also relate to cognitive dimensions of behavior such as perception and memory. Your knowledge of how sleep, hypnosis, and drugs influence memory will assist you in mastering this topic in Chapter 6. Also, consider how these states connect to your social relations with others. For example, it was suggested that hypnotized people act in accord with their expectations of the "hypnotized person." Consider the influence of peer pressure on drug use. Chapter 12 will expand on these issues when the topics of conformity and attitudes are discussed. Completing the Concept Check and answering the questions at the end of this chapter will also help you integrate the altered states into the big picture of psychology.

The information in this chapter also can be useful in future careers. If you are considering a career in the airline industry, the military, or the health or police fields, knowing the consequences of sleep loss and its effect on cognitive performance will directly affect your life. Counselors, teachers, and supervisors must all be aware of the warning signs of substance use and abuse.

David Pelzer's story, detailed in this chapter, gave us just a glimpse into how altered states may affect someone. His inspirational story is told in three memoirs—*A Child Called It* (1995), *The Lost Boy* (1997), and *A Man Named Dave* (1999). His case also powerfully highlights how people can change their circumstances to better themselves despite overwhelming odds.

Key Terms

consciousness (158)
microsleep (159)
circadian rhythm (163)
suprachiasmatic nucleus (SCN) (163)
melatonin (163)
non-REM sleep (165)
REM sleep (165)
REM behavior disorder (167)
REM rebound (167)
manifest content (168)
latent content (168)
activation-synthesis theory (169)

sleep disorder (169)
insomnia (169)
narcolepsy (170)
sleep apnea (171)
sleepwalking (171)
night terrors (171)
nightmare (172)
enuresis (172)
hypnosis (173)
dissociation theory (174)
response set theory of hypnosis (175)
psychoactive drugs (177)

tolerance (179)
physical dependence (179)
withdrawal symptoms (179)
psychological dependence (179)
depressants (180)
fetal alcohol syndrome (FAS) (181)
opiates (186)
stimulants (186)
hallucinogens (190)
THC (tetrahydrocannabinol) (191)

Test Yourself!

Concept Check

Test your knowledge of the chapter concepts by completing each of the following sentences with the correct term. For a more comprehensive review, visit the book Web site (http://psychology.wadsworth.com/pastorino1e) for online quizzes, flashcards, crosswords, and Internet links.

Sleep, hypnosis, and psychoactive drugs are three altered states of (1) _____. When we sleep, we alternate between two states; a relaxing phase called (2) _____ and an active state called (3) _____. Deep sleep occurs during (4) _____, and dreaming is most associated with (5) _____ sleep. There are several theories on dreaming. (6) _____ theory assumes that dreams represent hidden unconscious desires whereas (7) _____ theory assumes that dreams do not have symbolic meanings but are merely the byproduct of electrical signals being fired in the brain. Not everyone sleeps soundly at night. Some people stop breathing at night, a sleep disorder called (8) _____. Others experience (9) _____ and can't stay asleep. Because these sleep disorders disrupt our internal clock, or (10) _____, we may not get the benefits from sleep that we need.

Hypnosis is an altered state in which a person is more (11) _____ and shows increased (12) _____ brain waves. One of the most well known uses of hypnosis is (13) _____. However, it is less successful at treating (14) _____ and highly controversial in the area of (15) _____.

Psychoactive drugs have varying effects on consciousness. For example, (16) _____ speed up normal brain functioning whereas (17) _____ inhibit or slow normal neural functioning. In many cases drugs produce their effects by affecting neurotransmitters. For instance, alcohol affects the neurotransmitter (18) _____ and nicotine influences three neurotransmitters: (19) _____, (20) _____, and (21) _____. After repeated use, drug users develop (22) _____ and may become reliant on a drug. This may be evident by (23) _____, whereby the person exhibits negative side effects after discontinuing use of a drug. Such effects indicate that the user has become (24) _____ dependent.

Answers:

1. consciousness; 2. non-REM; 3. REM sleep; 4. stage IV; 5. REM; 6. Freudian; 7. activation synthesis; 8. sleep apnea; 9. insomnia; 10. circadian rhythm; 11. suggestible; 12. alpha; 13. pain relief; 14. addictive (self-control) behaviors; 15. recovered memories; 16. stimulants; 17. depressants; 18. GABA; 19. acetylcholine; 20. glutamate; 21. dopamine; 22. tolerance; 23. withdrawal symptoms; 24. physically.

Critical Thinking About the Chapter

1. How would you rate your hypnotic susceptibility? Under what circumstances would you consider using hypnosis as a therapy or treatment, and why?

2. Using the theories on hypnosis as a guide, explain how stage hypnotists alter the behavior of their audience volunteers.

3. How prevalent is drug use at your campus? Design a survey to assess this issue at your school. Administer the survey to student volunteers, and tabulate the results. What conclusions can be drawn from your results? What factors may have influenced your results?

Applying Psychology. Given the numerous factors that influence the amount of sleep you need such as age and lifestyle, detail how each of these factors influences the amount of sleep you get. How can you improve the quality of your sleep? What benefits might this change bring you?

Applying Psychology. Keep a dream log for a week. Using the different theories on dreaming, interpret what your dreams mean. Which of these interpretations seems the most plausible, and why?

Critical Thinking for Integration

1. Using the information from Chapter 1 on research methods, design a study that will confirm that sleep changes as we age.

2. Using Chapter 2 as a guide, draw a model of the brain and graphically represent where in the brain various psychoactive drugs have their effects. Also represent on this visual schemata the neurotransmitters that affect these areas of the brain.

3. Explain differences in hypnotic suggestibility as a result of variations in sensation, expectations, and perceptual errors. Use the information from Chapter 3 as a guide in formulating your answer.

Chapter Study Resources

Suggested Readings

1. Pelzer, D. (1995). *A child called "it."* Deerfield Beach, FL: Health Communications. David Pelzer's childhood account of dealing with abuse and neglect.

2. Knapp, C. (1996). *Drinking: A love story.* New York: The Dial Press. A case study on alcoholism in a professional young woman.

3. Maas, J. B. (1998). *The sleep advantage: Preparing your mind for peak performance.* New York: Villard. A leading researcher discusses how to reap the benefits of sleep.

4. For additional readings, explore InfoTrac College Edition, your online library of archived journal articles and periodicals. Go to http://www.infotrac-college.com/wadsworth and enter the passcode from the card that came with your book. For this chapter, search using these keywords:

stages of sleep

circadian rhythm

hypnosis

MDMA and Ecstasy

alcohol use and ethnicity

Web Links for Further Study

Additional information on chapter concepts can be found at these Web sites:

1. Sleepnet is an educational site that links all the information about sleep on the Internet.
www.sleepnet.com

2. The Dream Research site, created by Adam Schneider and G. William Domhoff from the University of California, Santa Cruz, provides access to relevant articles about dream research.
http://dreamresearch.net

3. The Web of Addictions site provides accurate information about alcohol and other drug addictions.
www.well.com/user/woa/

4. This site provides information on the self-help group Alcoholics Anonymous.
www.alcoholics-anonymous.org/

5. The Society for Clinical and Experimental Hypnosis site provides free access to a database on hypnosis-related research and information.
www.hypnosis-research.org/

Student Study Guide

To help organize your learning, work through Chapter 4 of the *What Is Psychology? Student Study Guide*. The study guide includes learning objectives, a chapter summary, fill-in review, key terms, a practice test, and other learning activities.

Psychology Now™

PsychologyNow is a Web-based, personalized study system that provides you with a pretest and a posttest for each chapter, quizzes you by chapter, and provides a personalized study plan, pointing you to elements in the text or in individual learning modules that will help you to achieve 80% mastery. Check out the learning modules that relate to this chapter: sleep; sleep stages, drugs–alcohol.

PsychNow CD ROM, Version 2.0

Go to the PsychNow CD-ROM for further study of the concepts in this chapter. The CD-ROM includes learning modules with videos, animations, and quizzes, as well as simulations of psychological phenomena. Each module follows a consistent Explore, Lesson, and Apply structure that allows you to experience the concept or principle, learn more about it, and then apply it. You and your friends can participate in a team-based Quiz Game that makes learning fun. Learning modules include: 3c. Sleep and Dreaming; 3d. Psychoactive Drugs.

Consciousness: Wide Awake, in a Daze, or Dreaming?

Consciousness includes the feelings, thoughts, and aroused states in which we are aware. Altered states of consciousness occur when we sleep, daydream, meditate, are hypnotized, or take any psychoactive drug.

SLEEP, DREAMING, AND CIRCADIAN RHYTHM

• Sleep serves several valuable functions. It restores body tissues, facilitates body growth, increases your immunity to disease, keeps your mind alert, helps you process memories, and enhances your mood.

• Teenagers and adults need at least 8 hours of sleep, although American adults average only 7 hours of sleep per night.

• Human biological clocks are set to a natural rhythm of sleep and waking that resembles a 25-hour day. This circadian rhythm is programmed by a group of brain cells in the hypothalamus called the suprachiasmatic nucleus.

• Sleep is divided into two major patterns: REM (rapid eye movement) sleep and non-REM sleep. Non-REM sleep is a progressively relaxing state of sleep, whereas REM sleep is very active.

• A typical night of sleep involves cycling through non-REM stages and shorter periods of REM sleep. Body-restoring deep sleep takes place during Stage IV of non-REM sleep.

• Freud considered dreams "the royal road to the unconscious," and believed that dreams allowed us to express fears and desires without the censorship of our conscious thought process.

• Freud distinguished between manifest content of dreams—what you recall when you awake—and latent content, which is the hidden meaning that could be uncovered through symbolic interpretation of dreams.

• Most psychologists and psychiatrists dispute Freud's emphasis on sex and aggression in interpreting dreams. A biologically based theory of dreams is the activation-synthesis theory, which suggests that dreaming is just a consequence of the highly aroused brain during REM sleep.

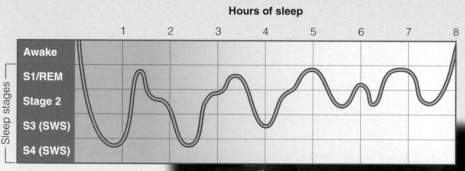

• Insomnia is the inability to get to sleep or to stay asleep, and it is the most common sleep disorder.

• Other sleep disorders include sleep apnea, in which a person stops breathing while asleep, and a rarer condition called narcolepsy, in which a person falls asleep during alert times of the day.

HYPNOSIS

• Hypnosis is a technique used to create a state of heightened suggestibility. Hypnosis usually involves being asked to close one's eyes and to mentally focus on an object, image, or the hypnotist's voice, thus creating a highly relaxed state.

• Hypnotic susceptibility varies greatly and does not seem to be related to intelligence, gender, or sociability. People who are easily hypnotized tend to be better able to focus their attention, have vivid imaginations, and have positive expectations about hypnosis.

• Hypnosis has been shown to be effective for some in providing pain relief, and decreasing anxiety. It has not been shown to be as effective in curing addictions or recovering accurate memories.

PSYCHOACTIVE DRUGS

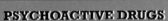

• Psychoactive drugs are substances that influence the brain and therefore the behavior of an individual.

• Drug tolerance refers to the amount of a drug required to produce its effects. After repeated use of a drug, more of it is usually needed to achieve its initial effect.

• Physical dependence is caused by the body needing a drug in order to maintain normal functioning.

• Psychological dependence refers to a person's feeling that she or he needs the drug in order to emotionally or psychologically function properly.

• Depressants such as alcohol, sedatives, and barbiturate drugs interfere with the brain functions by inhibiting or slowing normal neural function.

• Opiates such as morphine, codeine, and opium are used to treat pain by mimicking the effects of naturally occurring, pain-reducing neurotransmitters in the body such as endorphins.

• Stimulants are drugs such as caffeine, nicotine, cocaine, and amphetamines that interfere with brain functioning by speeding up normal brain activity.

• Hallucinogens, including marijuana and LSD, are drugs that interfere with brain functioning by simultaneously exciting and inhibiting normal neural activity. These contrasting effects often cause disruptions in perception or hallucinations.

I was the only child of my age in my village, but I managed to spend my time talking to adults who were around.

—FROM BENNETT SINGER (ED.), *42 UP: GIVE ME THE CHILD UNTIL HE IS SEVEN, AND I WILL SHOW YOU THE MAN* (*A book based on Michael Apted's award-winning documentary series*, p. 98)

Walter Hodges/Getty Images

CHAPTER 5

How Do We Learn?

CHAPTER PREVIEW

Lifetimes of Experience

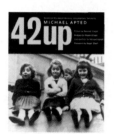

"I remember looking at various natural phenomena and being intrigued to try to understand what made them tick."

(Nick, quoted in Singer, 1998, p. 83)

Learning is a crucial part of life. It is through learning that we acquire many of the skills we need to survive in our world. It is also partly through learning that we grow from infants to adults. A remarkable British film project gave the world a unique window into the ways in which learning and other influences shape and change us over time.

In 1964, filmmaker Michael Apted gathered together a diverse group of 7-year-olds from Britain and filmed interviews with them. He asked the children a variety of questions about their lives. This documentary, entitled *7 Up,* was the first of what became a series. Every 7 years, Apted gathered the same 14 children together and reinterviewed them on film. Since 1964, there have been six *Up* films produced: *7 Up, 14 Up, 21 Up, 28 Up, 35 Up,* and *42 Up.* In 1998, some of the transcripts of the *Up* interviews were compiled in a book entitled *42 Up* (Singer, 1998). The book includes excerpts from each participant's interviews to give the reader a series of portraits of the person from age 7 to 42.*

Of the *42 Up* participants, one of the most interesting is Nick, a farmboy from the Yorkshire Dales area of northern England. At the time of the *7 Up* filming, times were difficult both financially and socially for Nick. The farmhouse he lived in had holes in walls that went clear through to the outside, and he and his 1-year-old brother were isolated because they were the only children in their village. His only contact with other children was at school in the one-room schoolhouse.

As a result of this environment, Nick spent most of his time in the company of adults, surrounded by nature, but with few other things to do. When asked what he wanted to be when he grew up, Nick said that he wanted to know more about the "moon and all that" (Singer, 1998, p. 79).

At 14, Nick won a scholarship to attend a boarding school in Yorkshire. He had no interest in farming. Instead, he wanted to study physics and chemistry. When questioned about girls, the shy Nick patently refused to answer any questions about his love life.

By 21, Nick was studying physics at Oxford University. When asked whether his isolated childhood had put him at a disadvantage at Oxford, Nick said that the harshness of farm life had given him a deep respect for life and a sense of what was really important. He had no regrets, but he still was not enjoying much of a social life.

By 28, Nick had received his doctorate and had come to the United States as an assistant professor at the University of Wisconsin. He had also married, and he was one of the most successful of the *7 Up* children. Not bad for a boy who once lived in a home with holes in the walls! So what accounted for all this "brain power" in a boy from an isolated and seemingly disadvantaged background? Nick attributed part of his success to his early life; with only adults to keep him company, Nick was forced to live in an adult world. He had little experience in dealing with his peers even after he attended boarding school and university. As a result, he profited intellectually, but he suffered socially.

Even as a child, Nick had begun to think like an adult. He learned to observe the abundant natural world of the farm and to question what made it "tick." In doing so, he became a scientist. But because he had little chance to interact with other children, he never learned how to deal with his peers on a social level. It wasn't until he went to Oxford in his 20s that he became better adjusted in terms of acquiring social skills. Once he was surrounded by his peers, Nick found himself learning to interact with them more effectively. At 28, he could see that his childhood isolation resulted in shyness and social awkwardness.

---

*Three of the original participants in the series declined to participate in *42 Up.*

Fourteen years later, the interview for *42 Up* found Nick on a visit back to Yorkshire Dales. His career was going extremely well. He had been promoted to full professor and was doing important research at the university. Looking out on the countryside of his youth, Nick summed up the influence his rural childhood had had on him: "Well, it's not an easy place to live, and people have to struggle quite a lot to just live their lives and do their work. And so Dales people, I think are very, very philosophical and they're quite profound, not trivial people. They just have a depth. A solidity" (Singer, 1998, p. 87).

Like Nick and the other *7 Up* children, we are all affected by our experiences. Every day, we learn from the events in our lives. In this chapter, we will examine some of the ways in which our experiences influence our behavior as we explore the different types of learning. Then, we will take a look at how the mind stores and processes the information we gather from our experiences when we look at memory in Chapter 6 and thinking in Chapter 7.

Before you continue reading any further, take a moment to consider this question: What have been the most important learning experiences of your life? Try to identify three or four life-changing events. Then, as you read this chapter, try to identify what type of learning took place in each of these experiences. By relating this information to your own life, you will have a much easier time remembering it on test day because of its personal relevance.

Defining Learning: >
In and Beyond the Classroom

LEARNING OBJECTIVE
Define learning.

When you hear the term *learning*, it probably brings to mind studying textbooks and lecture notes in preparation for exams. This isn't surprising because you are, after all, a college student. Much of your life now is spent in the pursuit of this particular type of learning. Although it is true that a lot of learning does occur in school, an extraordinary amount of learning occurs outside of the classroom.

Think about it—what have you learned outside of school? Here are just a very few of the possibilities. You learned to walk, to speak your native tongue, to have social skills, to have a sense of right and wrong, and possibly to play baseball. Now how did you learn these things? Perhaps you learned by watching others, by listening to others, by reading, or by doing. Learning occurs through a variety of means and in a variety of situations. As psychologists, we must define learning in terms broad enough to encompass all of these types of experiences.

Of all the possible definitions of learning, our favorite states that **learning** *is a relatively permanent change in behavior or the potential for behavior that results from experience.* We like this definition because it stresses some important aspects of learning. First, that learning is only a *relatively* permanent change. Once you have learned something, there are no guarantees that the learning will stick with you for a lifetime. For example, when one of the authors (Susann) was young, she spent hours playing Chinese jump rope in the street with her friends. Today, over 25 years later, she cannot recall how the game was played. If she were challenged to a game of Chinese jump rope today, she would be at a loss for what to do. It is obvious that this skill that she had once learned is no longer something she knows how to do.

Another reason we like this definition of learning is that it doesn't restrict learning solely to human beings. As we will see in this chapter, the principles of learning often hold true for many other species. Therefore, the information you learn in this chapter will be equally useful in understanding how you and your significant others

learning a relatively permanent change in behavior or behavior potential as a result of experience

 Application

© LWA-Sharie Kennedy/Corbis

© Mitch Tobias/Masterfile

© Ryan McVay/Getty Images

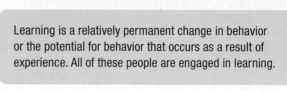

Learning is a relatively permanent change in behavior or the potential for behavior that occurs as a result of experience. All of these people are engaged in learning.

learn—as well as how your pets learn! Which, by the way, brings up a very important point. The principles of learning identified by psychologists have many practical applications to child rearing, the elimination of bad habits, learning good habits, and becoming a more successful student. So you may well be able to use the information in this chapter to improve the quality of your own life!

The third thing we like about this definition of learning is that it clearly relates learning to experience. As we mentioned before, many different types of experience can lead to learning. Sometimes we learn from direct experience, such as when we touch a hot stove and learn not to do *that* again. Other times learning experiences do not involve direct participation, such as when we learn how to cook a dish by watching a chef prepare it on a television show. In this chapter, we will examine four different types of experiences that can lead to learning. We will begin our discussion with habituation, a very simple type of learning. We'll move on to more complicated types of learning experiences: classical conditioning, operant conditioning, and social learning.

Let's Review!

In this section, we defined the process of learning. For a quick check of your understanding, answer these questions.

1. Renaldo, who is 7 years old, is learning to play the violin at school. Based on what you know about learning, what is your best prediction about Renaldo's future behavior?

   a. Renaldo may or may not be able to play the violin at age 50.

   b. Even if Renaldo stops playing the violin while he is still a child, if he picked up a violin at age 50, he would still be able to play it.

   c. Renaldo will definitely not be able to play the violin by the time he turns 50.

   d. Renaldo will still be playing the violin when he is 50 years old.

2. Which of the following is *not* an example of something that results from learning?

   a. Feeling sad when you see a rose because roses remind you of your deceased grandmother

   b. Not liking dogs because you were once bitten by a dog

   c. Being 5 feet 10 inches tall

   d. Being able to fix a flat tire on your car

3. Which of the following organisms does *not* have the capacity for learning?

   a. A human baby

   b. A human adult

   c. A cat

   d. All of the above have the capacity to learn

ANSWERS

1.a; 2.c; 3.d

Orienting and Habituation: Learning to Ignore

> > > > > > > > > > > >

LEARNING OBJECTIVE

Define and give examples of orienting reflexes, habituation, and dishabituation.

Suppose you are sitting in class, listening to your psychology professor and taking notes. All of a sudden there is a loud banging noise directly outside your classroom. What would your very *first* reaction to the unexpected noise be? If you are like most people, you would immediately stop listening to the lecture and turn your head in the direction of the noise. This very normal response is called an **orienting reflex** (Pavlov, 1927/1960). Orienting reflexes occur when we stop what we are doing to orient our sense organs in the direction of unexpected stimuli.

In our example, the stimulus was auditory, but this doesn't have to be the case. If you were standing in line at the cafeteria and someone poked you in the back, you would most likely turn to see what the person wanted. If you were having dinner in a restaurant and someone began to take pictures using a flash camera, you would likely look in the direction of the flashes of light. In short, we exhibit the orienting reflex to any type of novel stimulus.

Why do you think we exhibit orienting reflexes? What is the benefit to automatically paying attention to novel stimuli? If you said "self-protection," you would be correct. Orienting reflexes allow us to quickly gather information about stimuli that could potentially be threatening. For instance, that banging noise in the hallway could be a student dropping her books, or it could be a fight. In the case of a fight, you may want to take steps to ensure that the fight doesn't affect you in a negative way. By orienting your senses toward the event, you can quickly assess what, if any, action is needed to protect yourself.

The benefit of having orienting reflexes is limited though. Suppose that after looking up at the sound of the banging, you see that it is only a worker hammering as he

orienting reflex   the tendency of an organism to orient its sense toward unexpected stimuli

habituation the tendency of an organism to ignore repeated stimuli

installs a new bulletin board in the hallway. You would likely return your attention to the psychology lecture. If the banging noise continues, your tendency to look up at the noise in the hall would steadily decrease. In other words, your orienting reflex would diminish over time. This decrease in responding to a stimulus that occurs as the stimulus is repeated over and over is called **habituation.**

Despite its name, habituation does not refer to forming a habit (Figure 5.1). Instead, habituation ensures that we do not waste our energy and mental resources by responding to irrelevant stimuli. In our previous example, after you have established that the noise in the hallway is not threatening, there is no reason to keep looking up. If you did keep exhibiting the orienting reflex, you would needlessly miss part of your psychology lecture, as well as waste energy that could be spent more usefully.

Almost all creatures, including those with very simple nervous systems, seem to have the capacity for habituation (Harris, 1943). This universality of habituation implies that habituation is the simplest type of learning seen in organisms (Davis & Egger, 1992). Habituation can be seen in newborns, infants (Lavoie & Desrochers, 2002; Rose, 1980), and also in fetuses (Van Heteren, Boekkoi, Jongsma, & Nijhuis, 2000). This seems to indicate the primitive nature of habituation. Furthermore, because almost all species seem to have the ability to habituate, it seems likely that habituation evolved through the process of *natural selection*. Recall from Chapter 2 that due to natural selection, characteristics that promote reproductive success will be retained in a species. It is likely that habituation allowed our ancestors to deal more adaptively with their environment because it allowed them to ignore useless repetitive information.

Habituation as an Adaptive Asset

To get a better feel for the adaptive value of habituation, imagine what life would be like if you could *not* habituate. Without habituation, you would reflexively respond to every sight, sound, touch, and smell that you encountered every time you encountered them. You would not be able to ignore these stimuli. Think of how this would limit your ability to function. Every time the worker hammered the bulletin board in the hall, your attention would move away from the lecture and toward the hall. You sure

When you develop a habit, like smoking, there is an *increase* in your tendency to *engage in some behavior*. In this case, you are more likely to smoke cigarettes.

When you habituate, there is a *decrease* in your tendency to *respond to some stimulus*.

This person can't get enough smoke!

This person is ignoring the smoke!

Figure 5.1 The Difference Between Developing a Habit and Habituation

© Tom & Dee Ann McCarthy/Corbis

Habituation allows us to tune out unnecessary stimuli so that we can concentrate on the task at hand.

would not learn much psychology under these circumstances! With habituation, you get the best of both worlds. You can respond to new, novel stimuli that may pose a danger, and you can also ignore stimuli that have been checked out and deemed to be harmless. Habituation gives you flexibility in that you don't have to continue to respond to a stimulus. But once you have habituated to a stimulus, will you ignore the stimulus forever?

Dishabituation

Another aspect of this flexibility is the fact that you can also stop habituating when the circumstances warrant it. **Dishabituation** occurs when an organism begins to respond more intensely to a stimulus to which it had previously habituated. Let's return to our example of the worker in the hallway. Although you find the hammering distracting at first, you soon habituate to the sound. Then after several minutes of ignoring the steady hammering, you hear a new sound. The worker has turned on a radio at a rather high volume. Will you ignore this sound, too? No, you likely will not. Because the quality of the stimulus has changed dramatically, you will dishabituate. You will again find yourself orienting toward the hallway. This new sound is too dissimilar to the hammering, and you have to check it out. Once you recognize that it is the worker's radio (and that it poses no threat) you will likely habituate to this new sound as well as to the hammering.

A change in the quality of the stimulus is not the only thing that can cause dishabituation. So can the passage of time. For instance, if the worker took an hour-long lunch break, and then went back to hammering, you might briefly dishabituate to the hammering. This would not last long, however—after just a few bangs of the hammer, you would reenter habituation, and return your attention to the lecture. As you can see, adaptive functioning is a balance of responding, habituating, and dishabituating at the appropriate time. In addition to helping us function on a daily basis,

dishabituation   to begin reresponding to a stimulus to which one had been habituated

sometimes habituation principles can be applied to help people who suffer from certain physical problems.

Practical Applications of Habituation

Application

One practical application of habituation is the use of habituation training for people who suffer from chronic motion sickness, or vertigo. Motion sickness can be caused when the brain receives conflicting information from the visual and vestibular systems that you learned about in Chapter 3. These conflicts can be set off by certain movements or exposure to certain stimuli that give the illusion of movement, such as computer displays. For people who suffer from chronic motion sickness, simple tasks like working at a computer may be impossible. Physical therapists will often use habituation techniques to help people overcome chronic motion sickness. By repeatedly exposing the clients to the stimulation that produces motion sickness, the therapist can gradually train these clients to habituate, or stop responding, to some of the visual and vestibular signals that would normally cause them to feel sick (Rine, Schubert, & Balkany, 1999). Similar techniques have been used to train pilots and astronauts to do their jobs without experiencing motion sickness (e.g., Bagshaw, 1985).

Habituation is quite important to everyday life, but it is still a very simple type of learning. Habituation does not explain the bulk of the learning that we engage in during our lifetime, such as learning to play tennis or ride a bike. Nor does habituation explain how we come to associate certain emotions and physiological reactions with certain stimuli, such as learning to fear snakes or feeling happy when we smell grandma's perfume. For explanations of these more complex events, we will have to turn our attention to more sophisticated and complex types of learning.

Let's Review!

This section has given you an overview of the simplest type of learning, habituation, and the related concepts of orienting reflexes and dishabituation. For a quick check of your understanding, answer these questions.

1. Which of the following is an example of habituation?

   a. Juan was teasing the family dog when it bit him. Because of the pain of the bite, Juan learned not to tease the dog again.

   b. Teresa was trying to learn to knit. At first, Teresa had to consciously think about what she was doing, but after practicing for 3 hours, Teresa could knit without thinking about it.

   c. Janel just bought a new puppy. At first, the dog's barking was distracting to Janel as she tried to watch TV, but after a while Janel did not notice the puppy's barking.

   d. Kerry loved her boyfriend very much. Now that they have broken up, every time she hears his favorite song on the radio, Kerry starts to cry.

2. Habituation would *best* describe how one learns to:

   a. ski.

   b. play cards.

   c. study with the radio on.

   d. speak with an accent.

3. Which of the following organisms would likely have the capacity for habituation?

   a. a 3-month-old human baby

   b. an adult monkey

   c. an adult dog

   d. all of the above

ANSWERS
1.c 2.c 3.d

Classical Conditioning: Learning > > > > > > > Through the Association of Stimuli

LEARNING OBJECTIVES

- Describe Pavlov's paradigm of classical conditioning.
- Define classical conditioning and discuss the factors that affect it.
- Discuss classical conditioning in humans.
- Describe the process through which classically conditioned responses are removed.

The discovery of classical conditioning was something of an accident. In Russia around the turn of the 20th century, a young physiologist named Ivan Pavlov (1849–1936) was doing research on the digestive processes of dogs (for which he would eventually win a Nobel Prize). Pavlov was investigating the role that salivation plays in digestion. Pavlov had surgically implanted devices in the cheeks of dogs so that he could measure how much saliva they produced during salivation. Pavlov's experimental method was to place the dog in a harness, present the dog with some food, and then measure the amount of saliva the dog produced (see Figure 5.2).

While conducting these studies, Pavlov noticed that sometimes the dogs began to salivate *before* the food was presented to them. Sometimes the mere sight of the food dish or the sound of the approaching experimenter alone was enough to produce salivation. So what was going on here? Why would a dog start to salivate when it heard footsteps or saw an empty food bowl? Pavlov reasoned that the dog had learned to *associate* certain cues or stimuli with the presentation of food. To the dog, the approach of footsteps had come to mean that food was soon going to appear. Consequently, the dog had become *conditioned*, or taught, to respond to the footsteps the same way that it responded to the food—by salivating. Unwittingly, Pavlov had discovered a learning process, one that became extremely influential in psychology.

Pavlov began to investigate the learning process itself. He systematically paired different stimuli with food to see which could be conditioned to produce the reflexive response of salivation. In one of these investigations, Pavlov sounded a buzzer just before he gave the dog some food. He repeated these trials several times while measuring the amount of saliva the dog produced. After repeated pairing of the buzzer and the food, the dog soon began to salivate on hearing the buzzer—even on trials in which *the food was not presented after the buzzer sounded!* The dog had become conditioned to associate the buzzer with the presentation of food. As a result, the buzzer had taken on the same power as food to cause the dog to salivate.

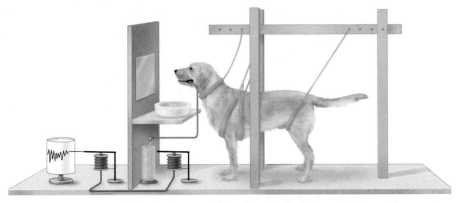

Figure 5.2 Pavlov's Original Experiment

The dog was held in the apparatus while food powder was placed before it. The presence of the food (unconditioned stimulus, or US) caused the dog to salivate (unconditioned response, or UR). After a while, cues in the laboratory situation (perhaps lights, sounds, or sights) became conditioned stimuli (CS) that also caused the dog to salivate (conditioned response, or CR).

From Basic Psychology, *5/e by Henry Gleitman, Alan J. Fridlund & Daniel Reisberg. Copyright © 2000, 1996, 1992, 1987, 1983 by W. W. Norton & Company, Inc. Used by permission of W. W. Norton & Company, Inc.*

The Elements of Classical Conditioning

This process of learning that Pavlov discovered is commonly referred to as *classical conditioning*, or *Pavlovian conditioning*. We will define it in a minute, but first let's look at the process that produces a conditioned response.

1. *The Unconditioned Stimulus and Response.* In order to classically condition an organism, you must first begin with a stimulus that naturally and reliably causes some response in the organism. Because this stimulus naturally causes the reflexive response, it is referred to as an **unconditioned stimulus (US),** and the response it evokes is called an **unconditioned response (UR).** The term *unconditioned* refers to the fact that the association between the stimulus and the response is unlearned. In Pavlov's case, the food was the US and

unconditioned stimulus (US)   a stimulus that naturally elicits a response in an organism

unconditioned response (UR)   the response that is elicited by an unconditioned stimulus

salivation was the UR. You do not need to teach a dog to salivate when food is presented. Instead, salivation occurs naturally when a dog sees food. Table 5.1 ◆ gives some more examples of US–UR pairs that could be used in classical conditioning.

neutral stimulus (NS) a stimulus that does not naturally elicit an unconditioned response in an organism

2. *The Neutral Stimulus.* The next step is the selection of a **neutral stimulus (NS)** that does *not* naturally elicit the UR. In Pavlov's case, the NS used was a buzzer. Prior to training or conditioning, a dog would not be likely to salivate when it heard a buzzer. Therefore the buzzer is said to be *neutral*. It has no power to naturally cause the UR.

3. *Pairing the Neutral and Unconditioned Stimuli.* The third step is to systematically pair the neutral stimulus and the unconditioned stimulus together. Pavlov accomplished this by repeatedly sounding the buzzer (NS) just prior to presenting the dog with the food (US). Through this repeated association of the US and the NS, the NS eventually loses its neutrality. In Pavlov's case, the dog began to salivate when the buzzer was presented without the food. At this point, classical conditioning had occurred because the buzzer was no longer neutral. The buzzer had become a **conditioned stimulus (CS)** that had the power to produce the **conditioned response (CR)** of salivation (Figure 5.3).

conditioned stimulus (CS) a stimulus that elicits a conditioned response in an organism

conditioned response (CR) the response elicited by a conditioned stimulus in an organism

Summing up classical conditioning in a nice, neat definition is a bit awkward but nonetheless extremely important. Once, when one of us asked a student to define classical conditioning, she replied, "What Pavlov did with his dogs." This isn't, of course, a definition of classical conditioning. It does reflect the student's difficulty in trying to understand the concept of classical conditioning apart from Pavlov's particular demonstration of it, however. Keep in mind that to truly understand a concept, you must be able to define it in abstract terms as well as give an example of it. So here goes.

classical conditioning learning that occurs when a neutral stimulus is repeatedly paired with an unconditioned stimulus; because of this pairing, the neutral stimulus becomes a conditioned stimulus with the same power as the unconditioned stimulus to elicit the response in the organism

We would define **classical conditioning** as *learning that occurs when a neutral stimulus is paired with an unconditioned stimulus that reliably causes an unconditioned response, and because of this association, the neutral stimulus loses its neutrality and takes on the same power as the unconditioned stimulus to cause the response.* This definition may seem a bit complex, but classical conditioning is actually a fairly simple process. The organism is merely learning to associate two stimuli, the unconditioned stimulus and the neutral stimulus. Through this association, the NS becomes a CS. In the next section, we will examine some of the factors that affect the strength of the association.

◆ **Table 5.1**

Some Examples of US-UR Pairs

Unconditioned Stimulus (US)	Unconditioned Response (UR)
A puff of air to the eye	The eye blinks
Ingestion of a toxin	Nausea
Being stuck with a pin	Flinching away from pin
Sour-flavor food placed on the tongue	Salivation
A light shown in the eye	The pupil contracts
A blow to the knee	Knee-jerk reflex

Source: Adapted from Flaherty, Hamilton, Gandelman, & Spear; 1977.

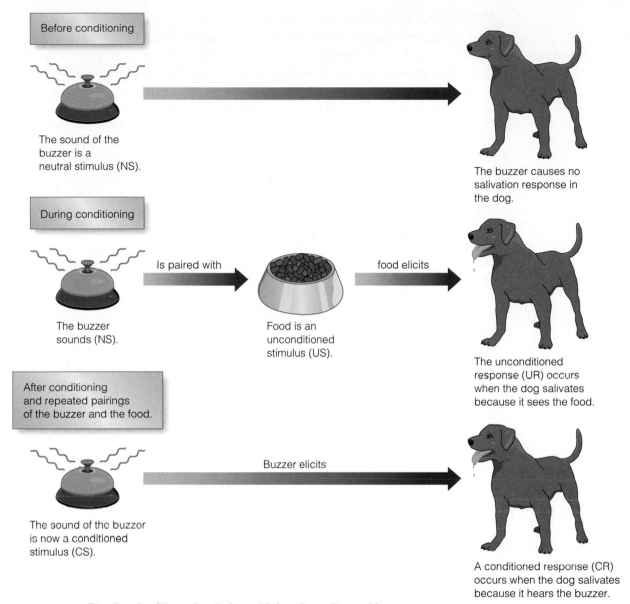

Figure 5.3 Pavlov's Classical Conditioning Paradigm

Before conditioning, the neutral stimulus has no power to cause the response. After repeated pairings of the neutral stimulus with an unconditioned stimulus, which naturally elicits an unconditioned response, the neutral stimulus becomes a conditioned stimulus with the power to elicit the response—now called the conditioned response.

Factors Affecting Classical Conditioning

What is it precisely that the organism learns in classical conditioning? Up to this point, we have sort of skirted around this issue. We said that the organism learns to associate the NS/CS with the US. This is true, but what is the nature of this association? Why does the organism associate these two particular stimuli? Why did Pavlov's dog associate the buzzer with the food instead of associating other stimuli from the situation with the food? Why didn't the dog begin to salivate when it heard the laboratory door open, or when the laboratory lights turned on? Why did it wait for the buzzer? To answer these questions, psychological researchers have experimentally examined different facets of the relationship between NS/CS and the US.

Relationship in Time: Contiguity

contiguity   the degree to which two stimuli follow one another in time

One variable that emerged from this research as an important factor in classical conditioning is contiguity. **Contiguity** refers to the degree to which the NS/CS and US occur close together in time. Generally speaking, for classical conditioning to occur, the NS/CS and the US must be separated by only a short period of time (Klein, 1987; Wasserman & Miller, 1997). If the interval between the presentation of the NS/CS and the US is too long, the two stimuli will not be associated, and conditioning will not occur. If Pavlov had sounded the buzzer and then 3 hours later given the dog some food, imagine what would have happened. It would have been very unlikely that the dog would have been conditioned to salivate when it heard the buzzer!

Studies have shown that in most cases, if the US lags behind the NS/CS for more than a few seconds, conditioning will not be as strong as it could have been (Church & Black, 1958; Noble & Harding, 1963; Smith, Coleman, & Gormezano, 1969). The exact length of the optimal time interval varies depending on what response is being conditioned. In the case of Pavlov's experiment, if he had waited more than 4 seconds after sounding the buzzer to give the dog the food, conditioning would have suffered (Gormezano, 1972).

Another aspect of contiguity is the actual placement of the NS/CS and the US in time—in other words, whether the NS/CS precedes the US or follows it. Imagine if Pavlov had first given the dog the food and *then* sounded the buzzer. In that case the dog would not have been as likely to associate the food with the buzzer. Figure 5.4 shows the five major ways to place the NS/CS and the US in classical conditioning. Of these placements, *delayed conditioning* produces the strongest conditioning, and *backward conditioning* produces the weakest conditioning (Klein, 1987).

contingency   the degree to which the presentation of one stimulus is contingent on the presentation of the other

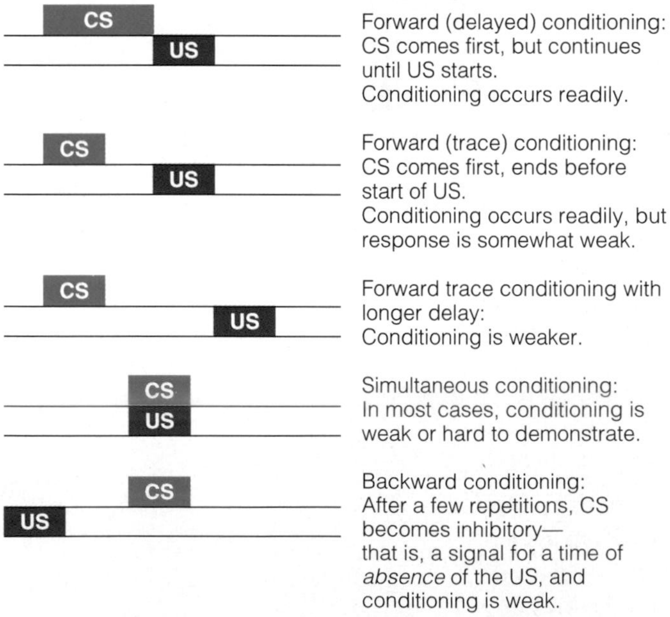

Consistency and Reliability: Contingency

Although contiguity is necessary for conditioning, it alone does not guarantee that conditioning will occur. Conditioning also requires **contingency,** which refers to the degree to which the NS/CS reliably signals to the organism that the US is going to be presented. If the NS/CS does not reliably predict the onset of the US, then conditioning will not occur (Bolles, 1972; Rescorla, 1967). For example, if Pavlov had sometimes fed the dog after sounding the buzzer and sometimes fed the dog without sounding the buzzer, conditioning would have been weakened. This inconsistency would not send the dog a clear message that the buzzer meant food was coming. Therefore, the dog would be less likely to salivate on hearing the buzzer. Given that both contiguity and contingency are necessary for strong classical conditioning, the best way to ensure strong conditioning is to consistently present only one NS/CS immediately before presenting the US.

The process of classical conditioning seems a bit complex, doesn't it? It also seems as if it could occur only in a laboratory (where USs and NSs could be systematically paired together)—but this is untrue. Classical conditioning occurs frequently in everyday life. In fact, each of us has probably felt the effects of classical conditioning many times. For example, we have been classically conditioned to have certain emotional reactions in our lives. You may feel happy when you smell a perfume that reminds you of your mother. You may feel fear when you see a snake. As we look at classical conditioning in the real world, keep in mind

Forward (delayed) conditioning: CS comes first, but continues until US starts.
Conditioning occurs readily.

Forward (trace) conditioning: CS comes first, ends before start of US.
Conditioning occurs readily, but response is somewhat weak.

Forward trace conditioning with longer delay:
Conditioning is weaker.

Simultaneous conditioning: In most cases, conditioning is weak or hard to demonstrate.

Backward conditioning: After a few repetitions, CS becomes inhibitory— that is, a signal for a time of *absence* of the US, and conditioning is weak.

Figure 5.4 Possible Placements of the CS and the US in Classical Conditioning

The positioning of the CS and US are shown for 5 different versions of classical conditioning: forward delayed, forward trace, forward trace with longer delay, simultaneous, and backward conditioning.

the general definition of classical conditioning, and try to generate your own examples of real-world classical conditioning. Table 5.2 ◆ gives some helpful tips for identifying classical conditioning situations and understanding the different components they involve.

Real-World Classical Conditioning: What Responses Can Be Classically Conditioned in Humans?

As you will recall, the starting point for classical conditioning is a pre-existing US-UR relationship. Because of the nature of most US-UR relationships (see Table 5.1), the types of responses that can be classically conditioned usually fall into two categories: *emotional responses* and *physiological responses.*

Classical Conditioning of Emotional Responses

The classical conditioning of emotional responses was clearly demonstrated in a famous—and now infamous—set of experiments conducted by John B. Watson and his student Rosalie Rayne in the early 1900s (Watson & Rayne, 1920). Watson set out to show that classical conditioning could be used to condition fear responses in a child. Because Watson used a 9 month-old boy named Albert, the experiments are now commonly referred to as the "Little Albert" experiments.

In the Little Albert experiments, Watson classically conditioned Albert to fear a white rat. To do this, Watson first gave Albert a white lab rat and allowed him to play with it. In the beginning, the rat was an NS for Albert because it did not cause him to be afraid. A few minutes after giving Albert the rat, Watson made a very loud noise by striking a piece of metal with a hammer. As with most 9-month-olds, a loud noise such as this was a US for Albert that reliably produced the UR of frightening Albert and making him cry. Over and over, Watson repeated this sequence of presenting the rat (NS), then making the noise (US), with the result that Albert would become afraid and cry (UR); (Figure 5.5).

◆ **Table 5.2**

Tips for Identifying and Analyzing Classical Conditioning Situations

1. Classical conditioning begins with a US-UR relationship. Because of this, most classical conditioning situations involve *the conditioning of emotional or physiological responses,* such as fear, nausea, happiness, anger, sweating, or salivation.

2. In a classical conditioning situation, *the UR and the CR are the same response.* The only difference is which stimulus elicits this response. For example, in Pavlov's experiment, salivation was the UR when it was caused by the food, but it also was the CR when it was caused by the buzzer.

3. In a classical conditioning situation, *the NS is the same stimulus as the CS.* The only difference is whether or not the stimulus has the power to elicit the response. In Pavlov's experiment, the buzzer began as a neutral stimulus with no power to cause salivation. But after conditioning, it became a CS with the power to cause salivation.

4. In a classical conditioning situation, *the NS/CS is* not *the same stimulus as the US.* For conditioning to occur, the CS must begin as a neutral stimulus. Because the US is never neutral (it always has the power to cause the response), the CS and the US have to be different stimuli.

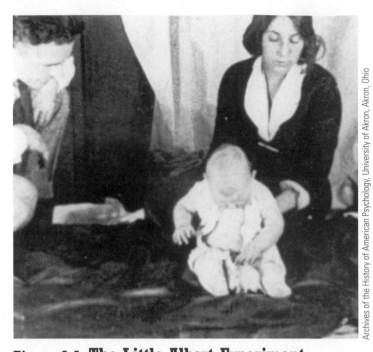

Archives of the History of American Psychology, University of Akron, Akron, Ohio

Figure 5.5 The Little Albert Experiment
Watson and his assistant, Rosalie Rayne, classically conditioned Albert to fear a white lab rat.

Phobias are classically conditioned responses. A fear-producing encounter with a stimulus can result in the stimulus—a needle—becoming a CS that can elicit fear in us.

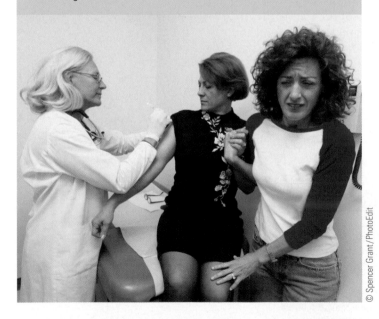

© Spencer Grant/PhotoEdit

stimulus generalization responding in a like fashion to similar stimuli

counterconditioning using classical conditioning to remove an undesired conditioned response in an organism

Can you see the parallels here between what Watson and Rayne were doing to Albert and what Pavlov did with his dogs? In the same way that Pavlov conditioned his dogs to salivate at the sound of the buzzer, Watson conditioned Albert to fear a white rat by associating the rat with a frightening noise. After several trials of pairing the noise and the rat, all Watson had to do to get Albert to cry was to show him the rat. Because the rat had been paired with the noise, the rat lost its neutrality and became a CS that was able to evoke the CR of fear in Albert.

Emotional reactions such as fear are also classically conditioned outside of the laboratory. For example, one of us once had a professor who had an intense fear of bees because earlier in his life, several bees had stung him after he accidentally disturbed a beehive. In this case of classical conditioning, the multiple bee stings were a US that elicited the UR of fear. The bees were initially an NS, but because they were paired with the bee stings, they became a CS that could produce the CR of fear. From that day onward, all the professor had to do was to see a bee to feel intense fear.

In fact, the professor's fear of bees was so great that it spread to other insects as well. Not only was he afraid of bees, he was also afraid of wasps, yellow jackets, and any other flying insect that could sting. In psychological terms, his fear had undergone **stimulus generalization,** which occurs when stimuli that are similar to the CS also have the same power to elicit the CR even though they have never been paired with the US. The professor had never been stung by a wasp, and yet he feared them because they are similar to bees.

Stimulus generalization also occurred in the Little Albert experiments. After being conditioned to fear the rat, Albert also exhibited fear when presented with a dog, a rabbit, a fur coat, and a fake white Santa Claus beard. His fear of white rats had generalized to several *furry* things (Watson & Rayne, 1920). This may leave you wondering what happened to Little Albert. Unfortunately, Albert's mother withdrew him from the program and moved away before Watson and colleagues could remove the fear they had conditioned in Albert.

A few years after the end of the Little Albert experiments, one of Watson's students, Mary Cover Jones, developed a technique for removing conditioned fears (Klein, 1987). Jones' technique involved gradually moving the fear-producing stimulus closer and closer to the participant while the participant was engaged in some task that made him or her have a positive emotional response, such as eating. By pairing the feared stimulus with positive emotion, Jones reduced the participant's phobia (Figure 5.6). This type of technique is called **counterconditioning** because the participant is slowly classically conditioned to have a positive rather than a negative reaction to the stimulus. Today, *systematic desensitization* is a modern technique for treating phobias that is based on Jones's procedure (Wolpe, 1958). We will explain systematic desensitization in more detail in Chapter 16 when we discuss psychotherapy.

Unfortunately, Albert was unable to benefit from any therapeutic intervention. Having possibly left Albert in a state of fearing furry things violates one of the most im-

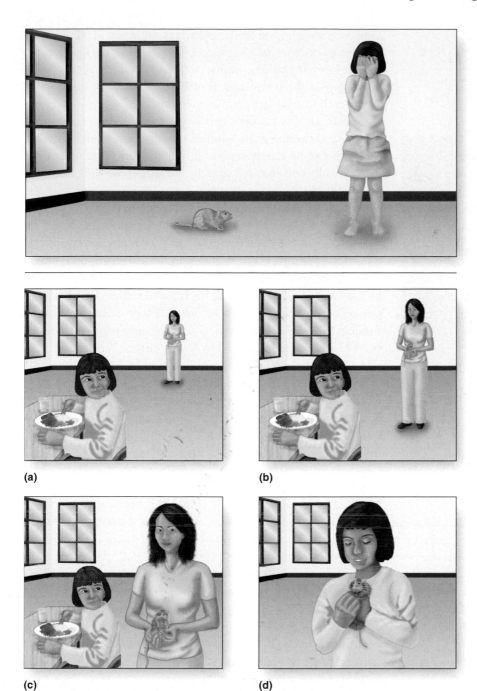

(a)

(b)

(c)

(d)

Figure 5.6 Mary Cover Jones's Counterconditioning Procedure for Removing Conditioned Phobias

portant ethical rules of psychology: that researchers should not do lasting harm to their participants. To be fair to Watson and Rayner, it is unknown if Albert suffered from a lasting phobia after leaving the experiment, or whether or not any conditioned fear generalized in the real world. However, the mere possibility that Albert may have been scarred by his experience warrants serious ethical consideration.

Not all classically conditioned responses will generalize. The opposite process, **stimulus discrimination,** often occurs. In stimulus discrimination, the CR occurs in response to a particular CS, but it does *not* occur in response to other stimuli that are similar to the CS. For instance, a woman who works in the reptile house at the zoo is probably not afraid of most snakes, but if she found herself face to face with a poisonous

stimulus discrimination   responding only to particular stimuli

For those who handle poisonous and nonpoisonous animals, being able to generalize and discriminate among them is an extremely important ability. Successful, experienced snake handlers, such as Steve Irwin, treat poisonous snakes with more caution than they treat nonpoisonous ones.

© Reuters/Corbis

Application

king cobra, she would likely feel afraid. In other words, she has learned to discriminate between poisonous and non-poisonous snakes. For her, this discrimination is very useful. It allows her to do her job without constant fear, but it also allows her to protect herself in truly dangerous situations.

Although conditioned fear may serve to protect us from harm by motivating us to avoid certain dangers, emotions other than fear can be classically conditioned. Positive emotions can be classically conditioned as well. For example, Nick, the man profiled in the *Up* series, likely had many positive emotional reactions upon revisiting his childhood home as an adult. Cues associated with his childhood home might act as CSs because they were associated with other stimuli that brought about positive emotional feelings. Consider a hypothetical example: seeing a farm tractor (NS/CS) makes Nick feel happy (UR/CR) because he has associated tractors with his beloved father (US). Many of our reactions are the result of our real-world classical conditioning. Given this, can classical conditioning be used to intentionally control our reactions to certain stimuli? In other words, is classical conditioning useful in everyday life?

Many advertisers use classical conditioning to get consumers to respond positively to their products. For example, television ads often use images of beautiful people, adorable animals, and beautiful scenery to sell products. The hope here is that the positive emotions (UR) elicited by these images (US) will become CRs that are elicited by the product (NS/CS). If you feel warm and fuzzy about the product, you may be more likely to buy it.

There is evidence to suggest that this application of classical conditioning does indeed work. In fact, classically conditioned positive emotions can have more impact on consumers' attitudes about the product than actual knowledge about the product. This is especially true when exposure to the product has been limited (Greenvale, Jeen-Su, & Mukesh, 1998). For example, even if you are not a beer drinker, you might feel happy when you see a store display for a particular brand of beer because you associate this brand with a cute, funny animal from the beer commercials on TV. With little firsthand knowledge of the product (you don't drink beer), this positive emotion might be just enough to get you to buy this brand for your next party. No wonder companies spend so much money developing ads that will make us feel good!

Classical Conditioning of Physiological Responses: The Special Case of Taste Aversion

Emotions are not the only things that can be classically conditioned. Pavlov's original demonstrations of classical conditioning show a physiological response, salivation. But what other kinds of physiological responses can be classically conditioned? Table 5.1 gives a list of some of the US-UR relationships that could form the basis of classical conditioning. Of these, one of the most important and common is the classical conditioning of nausea.

Have you ever eaten a food that you liked and soon after became sick to your stomach with the flu, food poisoning, motion sickness, or some other ailment? Then, after recovering from your sickness, did you find the sight, smell, or even the idea of that food nauseating? If you answered "yes" to both of these questions, you have experienced what psychologists call classically conditioned **taste aversion.**

taste aversion classical conditioning that occurs when an organism pairs the experience of nausea with a certain food and becomes conditioned to feel ill at the sight, smell, or idea of the food

One of the authors can vividly remember going through this type of conditioning as a child. After she ate a big dessert of peppermint ice cream, she came down with a severe case of tonsillitis that was accompanied by nausea and vomiting. After she recovered from the tonsillitis, it was *years* before she could even think about peppermint ice cream without feeling queasy. The same author regularly holds an informal contest in her classes to see who has had the longest running taste aversion. The current record stands at over 20 years!

It seems that taste aversion is something that we learn with particular ease (Garcia & Keolling, 1966). Taste aversion is unique in two ways. First, it often occurs with only one pairing of the NS/CS and the US. Unlike most cases of classical conditioning, in taste aversion a single pairing of the food (NS/CS) and the virus (US) is usually sufficient to cause strong conditioning. The second difference is that in taste aversion, the interval between the NS/CS and the US can be very long. Intervals as long as 24 hours can result in conditioning (Garcia, Ervin, & Koelling, 1966; Logue, 1979). Because taste aversion is an exception to some of the rules of conditioning, some psychologists believe that our genes biologically predispose or prepare us to learn taste aversion easily (Seligman, 1970).

By learning taste aversion easily, we are better able to avoid certain poisonous plants and substances. Once something has made us sick, we want no part of it in the future. No doubt the ability to learn taste aversion quickly and consequently avoid poisonous substances has survival value. Therefore, through natural selection, genes that enabled our ancestors to learn taste aversion quickly would have been retained in our species because those animals—human and non-human—would have lived whereas those with a sluggish response to taste aversion would likely die. Taste aversion may also have aided other species as well; it is widely seen in many species of animals (Garcia, 1992).

Application

In fact, because many other species are also susceptible to taste aversion, it can be used to help control the pesky nature of some animals. In the western United States, coyotes like to sneak into sheep pastures and kill sheep rather than hunt for food in the wild. In the past, frustrated sheep ranchers would be very tempted to either shoot the coyotes on sight or poison them. But thanks to psychologists, ranchers now have a more humane and ecologically sound alternative—using taste aversion to condition the coyotes to dislike sheep as a food source. They slaughter a few sheep and treat their carcasses with a chemical that causes nausea in coyotes. These tainted carcasses are then left out for the coyotes to eat. Because the coyotes can't pass up a free meal, they eat the sheep and get very sick to their stomachs. After they recover, they want nothing to do with sheep because of conditioned taste aversion (Gustavson & Garcia, 1974)!

This type of technique has also been used to keep black bears out of the military's supply of prepacked meals at the Camp Ripley Military Reservation in Minnesota. The bears had developed such a taste for military cooking that they were disrupting operations at the camp. So the military laced some meals with a chemical called thiabendazole that induces nausea and taste aversion in the bears. Now the bears and the military coexist more peacefully (Ternent & Garshelis, 1999).

A similar approach has been used to treat people with alcoholism. The idea behind this **aversion therapy** is to condition a taste aversion to alcohol. The person takes the drug Antabuse, and if he or she then drinks alcohol, the result is intense nausea and headache, which often leads to conditioned taste aversion. One of the author's fathers underwent such a treatment for his alcoholism. As a result of the treatment, he could not even stand the smell of perfume because of its alcohol base. Family members had to stop wearing cologne in his presence for fear of making him sick!

Aversion therapy has been shown to be modestly helpful in motivating alcoholics to remain abstinent (Smith, Frawley, & Polissar, 1997). However, it alone does not represent a "cure" for alcoholism. In one study, only 20% of the alcoholics tested remained abstinent for 1 year after being treated with aversion therapy alone (Landabaso et al.,

aversion therapy   a type of therapy that uses classical conditioning to condition people to avoid certain stimuli

Hangovers are nature's way of discouraging future intoxication. If you experience a hangover after getting drunk, alcohol may become a conditioned stimulus for nausea. This classically conditioned taste aversion may help ensure that you do not drink to excess again in the future.

extinction the removal of a conditioned response

acquisition the process of learning a conditioned response or behavior

spontaneous recovery during extinction, the tendency for a conditioned response to reappear and strengthen over a brief period of time before reextinguishing

1999). So although aversion therapy may be a useful part of a comprehensive treatment program, it should not be the only treatment used for alcoholism (Finn, 2003; Hunt, 2002).

The failure of aversion therapy to reliably produce long-term avoidance of alcohol indicates that although taste aversion is often an enduring type of learning, it doesn't necessarily last forever. What do you think causes the conditioned aversion to disappear? Or, more generally, what brings about the end of any classically conditioned response?

Extinction of Classically Conditioned Responses

Let's assume that you had the misfortune of developing a classically conditioned taste aversion to your favorite food because you ate this food just before you became ill with the flu. Furthermore, let's assume that you wanted to be able to eat your favorite food again without feeling sick to your stomach. How would you go about ridding yourself of your acquired taste aversion? One way would be to force yourself to eat the food over and over again. At first, you would feel nauseous due to the conditioning, but if you continued to eat the food, your conditioned nausea would eventually decrease, or undergo **extinction.**

In classical conditioning, extinction can be brought about by presenting the CS to the participant without also presenting the US. In our example, extinction would begin when you ate your favorite food (CS) and you did not have the flu (US). By presenting the CS alone, the CS no longer predicts the onset of the US, and the CR decreases. The author finally got over her taste aversion to peppermint ice cream after she took a job in a restaurant that sold a great deal of it. After scooping many scoops of peppermint ice cream, she found that the sight and smell of it no longer made her feel sick. It wasn't long before she was even able to eat peppermint ice cream without a problem.

Recently, some have argued that habituation may also play a role in extinction (McSweeney & Swindell, 2002). According to this argument, repeated exposure to the CS causes one to habituate to it. As long as you ignore the stimulus, it is less likely to elicit a response from you, and extinction ensues.

Pavlov's experiments with the dogs also included extinction trials with the dogs. Figure 5.7 shows the **acquisition,** or learning, curve for the CR and the extinction curve for the CR in Pavlov's experiment with the dogs. As you can see from this figure, the CR of salivation to the buzzer was acquired over several trials in which the CS and the US were paired. In the extinction trials, the buzzer was sounded but no food was presented, and there was a fairly steady decrease in the CR. In other words, the dog became less and less likely to salivate when it heard the buzzer. Does this mean, however, that once a response has been extinguished, it is gone forever?

The extinction curve in Figure 5.7 does not show a completely continuous pattern of decrease in the CR. Sometimes, after a response has been extinguished there will be a temporary increase in the CR. This phenomenon, called **spontaneous recovery,** can occur at any point during extinction (e.g., Troisi, 2003), or even after the response has been completely extinguished. For instance, let's go back to our example of taste aversion for peppermint ice cream. Today, although your author does not have an active, ongoing taste aversion for peppermint ice cream, every now and again when she thinks of peppermint ice cream, she will feel a bit sick. Thankfully, her spontaneous recovery doesn't last long. She soon reenters extinction, and she can think of peppermint ice cream and even eat it without a trace of nausea.

What do you suppose would happen if she happened to eat some peppermint ice cream on a hot day and suffered from a *small* amount of heat-induced nausea? Do you think her taste aversion to peppermint ice cream would return? It is likely that it would. In fact, responses that are extinguished are usually reacquired more easily than they were in the first place. Extinction does *not* mean that the organism forgets that there once was a connection between the CS and the US; it simply means that the CR is less likely to occur when the CS is presented.

So far, we have seen that learning can occur through habituation and classical conditioning. Habituation explains how we learn to ignore familiar stimuli, and classical conditioning explains how we come to have certain emotional and physiological responses to stimuli. Both of these types of learning occur frequently and are important to our ability to function, but together they do not explain all behaviors. For example, neither habituation nor classical conditioning can explain how we learn to drive a car or how a child learns to clean his room every day. To understand how we acquire these types of behavior, we will have to explore other types of learning.

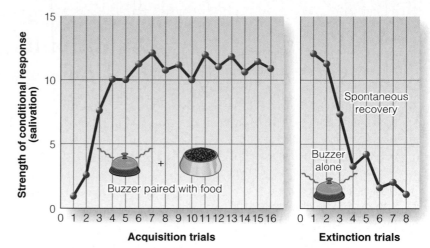

Figure 5.7 The Phases of Classical Conditioning

These plots show the number of conditioning trials on the *x* axis and the strength of the conditioned response on the *y* axis. During acquisition, the response increases in strength as a function of the number of times the CS and US have been paired together. During extinction, the CS is presented without the US, which leads to a decrease in the strength of the CR. Note that during extinction, sometimes there is a temporary, sharp increase in the strength of the CR despite the fact that the CS has not been recently presented with the US. This is called spontaneous recovery.

From Psychology in Action, *5/e, p. 185 by Huffman, et al. © 2000 John Wiley & Sons, Inc. Used by permission of John Wiley & Sons, Inc.*

Let's Review!

This section has given you a quick overview of some of the important issues in classical conditioning. As a quick check of your understanding, answer these questions.

1. Which of the following is an example of classical conditioning?
   a. Damon learns to ride a bike by watching his older brother.
   b. Sally dislikes the smell of rose perfume because her crabby third-grade teacher used to wear rose perfume.
   c. After 20 minutes in the day care center, Ralph barely notices the squealing of the children at play.
   d. Ted never speeds after receiving a $500 fine for speeding.

2. Which of the following is a US–UR pair?
   a. money–happiness
   b. an electric shock to the finger–jerking one's finger away
   c. receiving a paycheck–going to work
   d. seeing a spider–fear

3. Janna, a real-estate agent, desperately wants to sell a home. She tells the owner to place a pan of vanilla extract in the kitchen oven and heat it just before the prospective buyers arrive to look at the house. Janna knows that the smell of vanilla in the house will increase the chance that the buyers will like the house because they have been classically conditioned to respond favorably to the smell of vanilla. In this example, what is the CR?
   a. the pleasant emotions evoked by the smell of vanilla
   b. the smell of vanilla
   c. the memory of grandma baking cookies at Christmas
   d. the house

ANSWERS

1. b; 2. b; 3. a

instrumental conditioning   a type of learning in which the organism learns through the consequences of its behavior

Instrumental and Operant Conditioning: Learning from the Consequences of Our Actions

Suppose you are sitting in your psychology class, listening to a lecture, when your professor asks the class a question. For some reason, you raise your hand to answer the question even though you have never made a comment in this class before. The professor calls on you, and you give the correct answer. In response to your answer, the professor smiles widely and praises you for giving such an accurate and insightful answer.

How do you think this scenario would affect you? As a result of the professor's reaction, would you be more or less likely to raise your hand in the future when she asked a question? If you are like most people, this type of praise would indeed encourage you to raise your hand in the future. But what would happen if instead of praising you, she frowned and said that your answer was one of the stupidest that she had ever heard! How would this reaction affect your behavior? Obviously, after such a cruel response, many of us would be very unlikely to answer any more questions in that professor's class!

Both of these examples illustrate another type of learning, called **instrumental conditioning.** *In instrumental conditioning, we learn from the consequences of our behavior.* In our example, being praised for answering a question makes one more likely to answer questions in the future; being called "stupid" makes one less likely to answer future questions. We will see that instrumental conditioning is a powerful means of learning that explains how we learn many of the important lessons in our lives. But first, we will begin by looking at how instrumental conditioning was discovered.

E. L. Thorndike's Law of Effect

At about the same time that Ivan Pavlov was developing his theories about learning in Russia, American psychologist E. L. Thorndike (1874–1949) was busy conducting experiments on instrumental conditioning in New York. Thorndike was working with cats in specially constructed *puzzle boxes.* A puzzle box is a box with a lid or door that locks into place so that an animal can be locked inside of it. Once inside the box, the animal must activate some type of unlatching device to win its release. The device that unlatches the lid may be a rope pull, a pedal that needs to be pushed, or a switch that needs to be flipped. Figure 5.8 shows a typical puzzle box with a foot-pedal release.

Unlocking the Puzzle of Learning

In his research, E. L. Thorndike (1898) locked a hungry cat in one of these puzzle boxes and placed some food outside the box. Then he recorded how long it took the cat to figure out how to get out of the box. Once the cat activated the device and got out of the box, Thorndike would take the cat and place it back in the puzzle box. Over and over, Thorndike repeated this procedure of imprisoning the cat and measuring the time it took the cat to win its release.

Thorndike observed in these studies that when the cat was *first* placed in the puzzle box, it thrashed around *randomly* until, by *accident*, it tripped the mechanism and got out of the puzzle box. However, after several more trials with the cat in the box, the cat's behavior became *less random*, and the time it took to get out of the box declined. This decrease in the amount of time

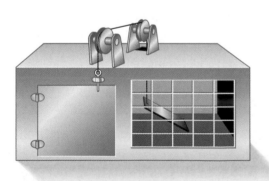

Figure 5.8 Puzzle Box

This is an example of a puzzle box like those used by Thorndike. To get out of the box, the cat would have to pull the string or step on the pedal.

From Basic Psychology, *5/e by Henry Gleitman, Alan J. Fridlund & Daniel Reisberg. Copyright © 2000, 1996, 1992, 1987, 1983 by W. W. Norton & Company, Inc. Used by permission of W. W. Norton & Company, Inc.*

it took the cat to get out of the box indicated to Thorndike that *learning* was taking place: The cat was learning to associate its behavior with the consequences that its behavior brought about.

Based on what he observed in his puzzle box studies, Thorndike developed a principle of learning that he called the **law of effect.** *The law of effect states that in a given situation, behaviors that lead to positive, satisfying consequences will be strengthened, such that the next time the situation occurs, the behavior is more likely to be emitted. In addition, the law of effect also states that in a given situation, behaviors that lead to negative, discomforting consequences will be weakened, such that the next time the situation occurs, the behavior will be less likely to be emitted* (Thorndike, 1905).

law of effect   a principle discovered by E. L. Thorndike, which states that random behaviors that lead to positive consequences will be strengthened and random behaviors that lead to negative consequences will be weakened

Random Actions and Reinforcement

Let's examine the law of effect in terms of a hungry cat in a puzzle box. When the cat is first trapped in the puzzle box, it will likely emit many random behaviors. For instance, it may claw, hiss, bite at the bars, roll over on its back, or meow. But none of these behaviors will open the puzzle box. The cat's early responses to being stuck in the box are emitted in a trial-and-error fashion. After some time, let's say that the cat happens to step on the foot pedal that opens the puzzle box and is able to get out to where the food is waiting. This particular random behavior has led to a consequence that is far more rewarding than any of the other random behaviors tried by the cat. The law of effect states that this particular response is strengthened, or *reinforced*, because it was *instrumental* in evoking reward. This process of **reinforcement** means that the rewarded behavior will become more likely in the future. The next time the cat is locked in the box, it will be more likely to step on the pedal than to try the other behaviors that did not lead to release on prior trials. Over many trials, the law of effect results in the cat becoming more and more likely to step on the pedal and less and less likely to use other behaviors that were not reinforced in the past. The behaviors that were not rewarded—and therefore not reinforced—are likely to die out (see Figure 5.9).

reinforcement   the strengthening of a response that occurs when the response is rewarded

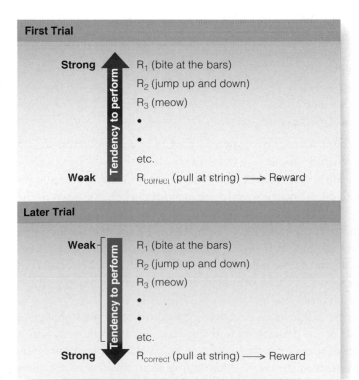

Figure 5.9
Reinforcement of a Successful Response in a Puzzle Box Experiment

The law of effect predicts that behaviors that lead to positive consequences will be strengthened whereas behaviors that fail to do so will weaken and be eliminated. Over the trials of Thorndike's study, the cats became successively less likely to engage in nonproductive behaviors—biting at the bars and jumping up and down—and more likely to engage in pulling the string.

From Basic Psychology, *5/e by Henry Gleitman, Alan J. Fridlund & Daniel Reisberg. Copyright © 2000, 1996, 1992, 1987, 1983 by W. W. Norton & Company, Inc. Used by permission of W. W. Norton & Company, Inc.*

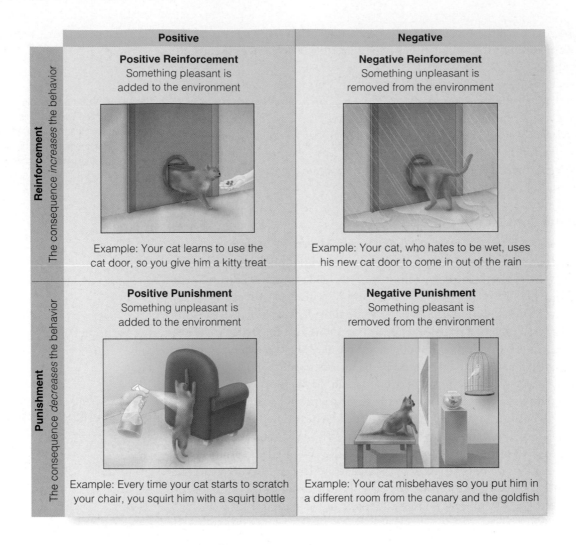

Figure 5.10 The Four Types of Consequences of Behavior
Reinforcement increases the likelihood of a behavior and punishment decreases it.

Positive and Negative Reinforcement

The two types of reinforcement are *positive reinforcement* and *negative reinforcement* (see Figure 5.10). In **positive reinforcement,** the behavior leads to the *addition* of something pleasant to the organism's environment. For instance, Thorndike positively reinforced the cat for stepping on the pedal by giving the cat food when it got out of the puzzle box.

In **negative reinforcement,** the behavior is rewarded by the *removal* of something unpleasant from the organism's environment. In Thorndike's case, the cat was negatively reinforced for stepping on the pedal because this behavior led to the removal of its imprisonment in the puzzle box. We are, of course, assuming that the hungry cat did *not* enjoy being trapped in the box.

The difference between *punishment* and negative reinforcement is a point that gives many students great trouble because they tend to think that negative reinforcement is a type of punishment. This is not true! The "negative" in negative reinforcement refers to the fact that negative reinforcement *removes* something from the organism's environment; it does not refer to a negative or unpleasant consequence of the behavior. When you see the term *reinforcement,* keep in mind that reinforcement leads to an

positive reinforcement   strengthening a behavior by adding something pleasant to the environment of the organism

negative reinforcement   reinforcing a behavior by removing something unpleasant from the environment of the organism

increase in behavior. **Punishment,** on the other hand, is an unpleasant consequence that leads to a *decrease* in behavior.

Positive and Negative Punishment

As you can see from Figure 5.10, punishment also comes in two varieties. **Positive punishment** occurs when a behavior results in the *addition* of something *unpleasant* to the organism's environment. For example, a puzzle box could be rigged to electrify the floor of the cage every time the cat stepped on the pedal. The cat would then be positively punished every time it stepped on the pedal because the resulting shock would add pain to the cat's environment.

In **negative punishment,** the behavior leads to the *removal* of something *pleasant* from the organism's environment. A puzzle box could be rigged so that when the cat presses the pedal, a drape falls over the cage, and the cat can no longer see outside the cage. If the cat enjoys seeing outside the cage, then stepping on the pedal would lead to negative punishment because it leads to the loss of a pleasant privilege for the cat. The effect of punishment is to decrease a behavior, regardless of whether the punishment is positive or negative.

In American psychology, we have traditionally looked to these four types of consequences to explain learning through the law of effect. However, some Japanese psychologists have taken a different approach to understanding the nature of the consequences that shape our behavior. This unique approach is outlined in It's a Diverse World.

punishment   the weakening of a response that occurs when a behavior leads to an unpleasant consequence

positive punishment   weakening a behavior by adding something unpleasant to the organism's environment

negative punishment   weakening a behavior by removing something pleasant from the organism's environment

---

IT'S A DIVERSE WORLD

A Japanese View of Reinforcement

Japanese culture differs from U.S. culture in many ways. We eat different foods, our predominant religions differ, and our expectations about how people should behave in social situations differ. The United States, like many Western cultures, is an *individualistic* society; people are judged on their individual accomplishments in life. To be successful in America, you must show that you have accomplished something of value—a prestigious job, an ability or talent that few others have, and so on. In Japan (and several other Asian cultures), accomplishments of the individual are not valued nearly as much as accomplishments of the *group*. For this reason, Japan is referred to as a *collectivistic* culture. To be successful in Japan, you must show that you have helped the group succeed. For example, a successful employee helps his company achieve prestige and financial gain; his success is not measured by how much he, as an individual, attains.

Given that psychologists are influenced by the cultures in which they live, we can reasonably expect to see our U.S. view of what is reinforcing and punishing reflects a bias toward individualistic rewards and punishments. If you look back to Figure 5.10, you will see that these four consequences of behavior all center on the person (or animal) being conditioned. So how might a Japanese psychologist view the concept of reinforcement in a collectivistic culture?

Researcher Yutaka Haruki has developed a theory of *human reinforcement* that describes additional consequences that are reinforcing. Haruki's reinforcements go beyond the Western notions of positive and negative reinforcement (Haruki, 2000; Haruki, Shigehisa, Nedate, Wajima, & Ogawa,, 1984), and his theory does not apply to nonhuman reinforcement because it reflects the values found in a collectivistic human society. According to Haruki's human reinforcement theory, there are four types of consequences that reinforce human behavior. These are: *External reinforcement (oshitsuke)*: You are rewarded by someone else with either positive or negative reinforcement. For example, a parent gives a child a new toy for earning a good grade on an exam. *Self-reinforcement (makase)*: You reward yourself—with either positive or negative reinforcement—for your own behavior. For example, you buy yourself a new CD or allow yourself to skip a day at the gym for doing well on an exam.

(continued)

A Japanese View of Reinforcement, *continued*

Internal reinforcement (uketome): You reward someone else for your own behavior. For example, you shake your professor's hand after earning an A in the professor's course.

Alien reinforcement (mitome): You reward yourself when someone else engages in a desired behavior. For example, you may be proud when your child scores a soccer goal. If your child accepts that you are proud of this behavior, the child is also rewarded.

The Japanese view of conditioning emphasizes the role that the opinions and actions of others play in reinforcing a person's behavior. This is what one would expect to see in a collectivistic culture, in which one's behavior is judged not on an individual basis, but rather on how that behavior affects the group. Numerous studies done by Yutaka Haruki and colleagues (for a review, see Haruki, 2000) have indicated that Japanese children can be conditioned by these types of reinforcement. However, these

studies have also shown that factors such as age, personality traits, and culture can affect the degree to which children find alien reinforcement rewarding. For example, Haruki and Shigehisa (cited in Triandis, 1994, p. 35) found that although Americans can be conditioned by both external and alien reinforcement, Americans learn *best* through external reinforcement. In contrast, Japanese participants learned *equally* well under conditions of external and alien reinforcement. The implication of these data is that the collectivistic or individualistic nature of cultures can influence what Japanese and Americans find reinforcing.

As you can see, although we may differ with respect to *what* we find rewarding and punishing, the principle of instrumental conditioning still predicts *how* the consequences of our behavior can work to change us. If we find that a behavior leads to a consequence that *we* find rewarding, we will be encouraged to repeat that behavior.

At this point, you might be tempted to say, "Isn't this obvious? So what?" Let's ask a more thoughtful question about instrumental conditioning. Why is instrumental conditioning a *useful* type of learning? To answer this, let's go back to the concept of *natural selection*, which we introduced in Chapter 2 (see p. 90). In a sense, Thorndike's law of effect is analogous to Darwin's theory of natural selection, which states that traits that are adaptive are selected, or kept, whereas traits that are not adaptive are weeded out of the species. Similarly, the law of effect says that behaviors that are adaptive and bring pleasant consequences are retained, but behaviors that lead to unpleasant consequences die out. Therefore, instrumental conditioning is very useful to an organism because it helps to ensure that the organism retains behaviors that lead to positive consequences and loses (or ceases) behaviors that lead to negative consequences.

Our opening story of Nick provides an example of this type of adaptation. As a child, Nick displayed both positive and negative behaviors. On the one hand, he was bright and inquisitive, but on the other hand, he was also very shy around girls. Nick may have found that his inquisitiveness was rewarded by his success as a student and scientist but that his shyness was punished by his failures in the social arena. The law of effect would work to retain Nick's adaptive behaviors and rid Nick of his maladaptive behaviors. As a result, over the years Nick retained his inquisitiveness, but he lost some of his shyness around females—at least to the extent that he married and has a family.

By now, we hope you have a fairly clear picture of instrumental conditioning and how it works. We also hope that you are beginning to wonder about how instrumental conditioning differs from classical conditioning because this is a very important distinction. There are a number of things that distinguish each of these types of learning.

How Classical and Instrumental Conditioning Differ

One way instrumental conditioning differs from classical conditioning is that in classical conditioning, the organism plays a rather passive role. A US naturally evokes a UR, and learning occurs because a CS is paired with the US. The organism doesn't have to actively do anything; it merely responds reflexively to the stimuli, just as Pavlov's dogs naturally salivated when food was presented.

In instrumental conditioning, however, the organism plays a more active role. The organism has to *first* engage in some nonreflexive behavior before learning can occur. In our example, the student had to first answer a question in class before any instrumental conditioning could occur (see p. 220). There is no US that will reliably cause a student to answer a question in class! The student must decide to answer on his own.

Another difference between classical and instrumental conditioning is that in classical conditioning, there is one clear response that is required of the organism. For example, in Pavlov's experiments the food would cause only salivation in the dog. Therefore, the only response that could be conditioned in this case would be salivation. In instrumental conditioning, the organism may emit any number of responses. For instance, while sitting in class, a student could answer the professor's question, not answer it, sleep, read a book, and so on. Any of these responses *could* be instrumentally conditioned to become stronger, but only if they evoke positive consequences from the environment.

A final difference between classical and instrumental conditioning is in the types of responses that tend to be conditioned through these processes. As you will recall, emotional and physiological responses tend to be classically conditioned. In instrumental conditioning, the responses that are conditioned tend to be more complex behaviors as opposed to simple emotional or physiological reactions. Therefore, instrumental conditioning can explain things as complex as how a student learns to freely answer questions in class or how a child learns to speak politely in public. Classical conditioning cannot account for these types of learning because there is simply no US that will evoke these types of responses, and without a preexisting US-UR relationship, there can be no classical conditioning.

As you study this material and prepare for your exams, keep in mind the important ways that classical and instrumental conditioning differ from each other. Keeping the points that distinguish these two types of learning foremost in your thoughts as you study and take exams can only help you succeed!

B. F. Skinner and Operant Responses

One psychologist who was concerned with clearly distinguishing instrumental conditioning from classical conditioning was a man named B. F. Skinner. Although E. L. Thorndike is generally credited with beginning the experimental study of instrumental conditioning, Skinner is more commonly associated with this type of learning. Skinner began to formally study instrumental conditioning in the late 1920s when he was a graduate student at Harvard University. During his long career—from the 1920s to the 1990s—Skinner made many significant contributions to our understanding of instrumental conditioning (Schultz & Schultz, 2000). Perhaps some of Skinner's most obvious contributions were to introduce new terminology and technology to the study of this type of learning.

Skinner introduced the term *operant* to the study of instrumental conditioning. Skinner felt that the term *operant* better distinguished this type of learning from classical conditioning than the term *instrumental* did. Skinner wanted to emphasize the fact that in classical conditioning, the organism does not actively choose to operate on the environment to produce some consequence, rather the response is forced from the

respondent behavior behavior that is emitted in response to some stimulus

operant behavior behavior that operates on the environment to cause some sort of consequence to occur

animal. Thus, Skinner referred to classically conditioned behavior as **respondent behavior.**

In contrast, Skinner wanted to emphasize that in instrumental conditioning, the animal makes a choice to respond to its environment in a certain way. Therefore, Skinner chose to refer to instrumental behavior as **operant behavior** or behavior that *operates* on an organism's environment to produce some consequence (Skinner, 1938). Today, psychologists use these terms, operant and instrumental conditioning, interchangeably. From this point on, we will refer to instrumental learning as operant conditioning.

© Zits Partnership. Reprinted with special permission of King Features Syndicate.

Operant conditioning at work!

Another of Skinner's contributions to the study of operant conditioning was the method he developed for studying animal behavior. Skinner felt that Thorndike's use of puzzle boxes required too much time for each trial. It took the animal a long time to figure out how to open the box and receive its reward, which limited the number of trials that could be run in a given experiment and caused problems for researchers because the animal might get tired before it had enough trials to be conditioned. To solve this problem, Skinner constructed an apparatus that allowed him to study the operant conditioning of a simpler response. This device, now called a **Skinner box,** is a chamber large enough to house a small animal, typically a rat (Figure 5.11). Inside the chamber, there would be a lever or a bar-press that the rat could press down. When the animal depressed the lever or the bar, it would receive reinforcement in the form of a pellet of food from an automatic feeding device attached to the chamber. Skinner boxes

Skinner box a device created by B. F. Skinner to study operant behavior in a compressed timeframe; in a Skinner box, an organism is automatically rewarded or punished for engaging in certain behaviors

Figure 5.11 Skinner Box

In these operant chambers the animals can be reinforced with food for pressing the bar or pecking the disk. Skinner boxes like these allow researchers to efficiently gather data on operant conditioning.

are also built for pigeons; the pigeon receives a reward by pecking at a disk on the side of the box.

To study operant behavior, Skinner would place a hungry rat in the Skinner box and wait for the rat to accidentally press the bar. Once the rat pressed the bar, a pellet would drop into the chamber to reinforce this operant behavior. The rat was free to press the bar as often as it wanted and whenever it wanted. By recording the number of bar presses and when they occurred, Skinner could get a good picture of the acquisition of the operant behavior. Using the Skinner box, researchers have been able to learn a great deal about the different aspects of operant conditioning. The advance in the methodology and apparatus for studying animal learning is one of B. F. Skinner's major contributions to psychology.

Acquisition and Extinction

Two areas Skinner explored were acquisition and extinction. You may recall from our discussion of classical conditioning (see p. 209), that acquisition refers to the conditioning of a response and extinction refers to the loss of a conditioned response. As in classical conditioning, it is possible to plot acquisition and extinction curves for operantly conditioned behaviors. In a Skinner box, the acquisition of the bar pressing response is, of course, brought about by the reinforcement of this response with the food pellets that drop down into the box when the bar is pressed. As the rat learns that pressing the bar leads to obtaining food, its tendency to press the bar increases. The intensity with which the rat will press the bar will continue to increase until it reaches some maximum strength. For example, the rat can eat the pellets only so fast. Therefore the number of times the rat will press the bar in a given time frame is limited by the speed at which it eats (Figure 5.12).

Extinction also occurs in operant conditioning, but it is caused by circumstances that are different from those that cause extinction in classical conditioning. In classical conditioning, extinction occurs because the CS is presented without the US. In operant conditioning, extinction occurs because the behavior is no longer reinforced (see Figure 5.12). Many of us hold jobs, and going to work is an example of an operantly

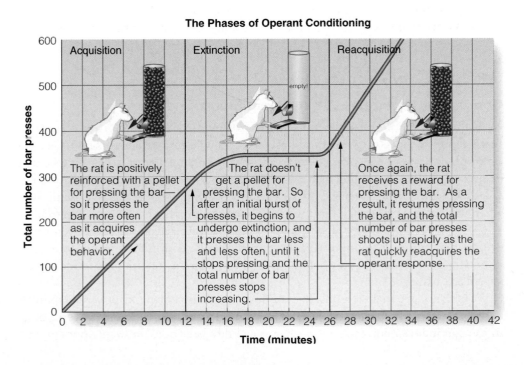

Figure 5.12 Acquisition and Extinction in Operant Conditioning

Just as we saw in classical conditioning, operant responses can also undergo acquisition, extinction, and reacquisition.

conditioned response. We go to work because we expect to be reinforced for this behavior on payday. What would it take to extinguish your going-to-work behavior? The answer is simple, isn't it? All it would take is the removal of your reinforcement. If your boss stopped paying you, you would likely stop going to work! In operant conditioning, withholding the reinforcement that maintains the behavior causes the extinction of that behavior.

extinction burst a temporary increase in a behavioral response that occurs immediately after extinction has begun

Like acquisition, extinction does not typically happen in one trial. Even if your boss failed to pay you on payday, you might very well return to work for a few days. In fact, you might even experience a temporary **extinction burst,** during which you might work *harder* in an attempt to obtain reward immediately after your boss withholds your pay (e.g., Galensky, Miltenberger, Stricker, & Garlinghouse, 2001). At the very least, you probably would not entirely abandon work until it became very clear that reinforcement would no longer be forthcoming. Extinction tends to occur over a number of trials. Each time the organism emits the operant response without being reinforced, its tendency to emit the response diminishes (see Figure 5.12).

Because extinction removes responses, it has many practical applications. One way to stop someone from engaging in an annoying behavior is to extinguish it by removing the reinforcement for that behavior. Take the example of a parent and child shopping together in a department store. The child sees a toy that he wants, but his parent refuses to buy it. At this refusal, the child begins to whine and cry, but instead of punishing the child for this behavior, the parent ignores the child. By not reinforcing the whining and crying, the parent begins to extinguish this annoying behavior. Once the child learns that crying and whining do not lead to reward, the child will stop using this behavioral strategy to get what he wants.

 Application

The trick to using extinction to reduce unwanted behaviors is in figuring out what is actually reinforcing the behavior in the first place, removing it, and then making sure that no other reinforcement of the unwanted behavior is occurring (Martin & Pear, 1983). If dad ignores the child's tantrums when he takes the child shopping, but mom gives in and buys the child toys when she is with the child, then the behavior will not be extinguished!

Acquisition and extinction of operant behavior seem simple enough, but numerous Skinner box studies have taught us that many factors can affect the rate at which an organism acquires or extinguishes a response. One extremely important factor is the **schedule of reinforcement**—the timing and the consistency of the reinforcement.

schedule of reinforcement the frequency and timing of the reinforcements that an organism receives

Schedules of Reinforcement

Continuous Schedules of Reinforcement

continuous reinforcement a schedule of reinforcement in which the organism is rewarded for every instance of the desired response

Conceptually, the simplest type of schedule of reinforcement is **continuous reinforcement,** in which each and every instance of the desired behavior is rewarded. In a Skinner box study, every time the rat presses the bar, a pellet of food would be delivered to the rat. In real life, many simple behaviors are reinforced on a continuous schedule. One example is when we reach for objects. The act of reaching is reinforced when we actually grasp the object we were trying to get. Except in unusual circumstances, such as reaching for an object on a shelf that is too high, reaching is rewarded every time we reach (Skinner, 1953). Unfortunately, continuous schedules of reinforcement are often not very helpful when using operant conditioning to modify an organism's behavior.

There are two main reasons that continuous reinforcement is not very helpful in modifying behavior. The first drawback is a practical one. Let's say that you were going to use continuous reinforcement to change a child's behavior. You want your child to be polite when speaking to others, so you decide to use a continuous schedule and reinforce your child with praise *every time* she is polite. Would this be feasible? We doubt it. A continuous schedule of reinforcement would mean that you would have to be around your child every time she was polite, and you would have to praise or otherwise reward her for this politeness. This just isn't practical or possible.

A second drawback of continuous schedules has to do with the fact that behaviors that are continuously reinforced are vulnerable to extinction. What happens when your children are not in your presence, and you are not there to continually reinforce their good behavior? As we have already seen, when reinforcement is withheld, behavior often starts to extinguish. The problem with using continuous schedules of reinforcement is that they lead to behaviors that extinguish very quickly once the reinforcement ceases.

Why would this be true? When a behavior has been continuously reinforced, there is a very clear *contingency* between the behavior and the reward. The organism learns that the behavior should *always* lead to a reward. When the reinforcement stops, a clear signal is sent that the contingency no longer holds true, and extinction occurs relatively rapidly. It is better to reinforce the behavior only some of the time so the child or animal is less likely to see the lack of reinforcement as a sign that the contingency is no longer operating. Schedules of reinforcement that reinforce a behavior only some of the times are called **partial reinforcement schedules.** *Ratio schedules* of partial reinforcement are based on the number of responses emitted, whereas *interval schedules* are based on the timing of responses.

By ignoring this child's tantrum, the parent is placing the child on an extinction schedule. If the parent does not reward the child for this behavior, the behavior should be less likely to occur in the future.

Ratio Schedules of Reinforcement

In a **fixed ratio schedule,** a set number of responses must be emitted before a reward is given. For example, suppose every third response is rewarded. A rat in a Skinner box would have to press the bar three times to get a food pellet. In the real world, some people are paid on fixed ratio schedules. A person who works in a manufacturing plant and is paid a bonus for every 100 parts assembled is being reinforced on a fixed ratio, as are agricultural workers who are paid per bushel of fruit picked, garment workers who are paid per piece sewn, and so on.

Aside from producing slower extinction than continuous reinforcement, fixed ratio schedules also have the benefit of leading to pretty high rates of responding (Figure 5.13). High rates of responding are especially likely if it takes many responses to get a reward (Collier, Hirsch & Hamlin, 1972; Stephens, Pear, Wray & Jackson, 1975). If your goal is to produce many instances of the behavior, such as many filled boxes of raspberries, in a short time frame, a fixed ratio schedule may just do the trick.

The second type of ratio schedule is the **variable ratio schedule,** in which the exact number of responses that are required to receive a reward varies around some average. For example, the rat may have to press the bar two times to receive the first reward, one time to receive the second reward, and then six times to receive the third reward.

Variable ratio schedules of reinforcement yield high rates of response (Figure 5.13) and even slower rates of extinction than fixed ratio schedules. A good example of this resistance to extinction comes from a real-world example of variable ratio reinforcement. Slot machines pay off on a variable ratio schedule of reinforcement. You never know how many pulls of the handle it will take to lead to the reward of a payoff. Consequently, people will play slot machines for long periods of time, even when they haven't hit the jackpot. One of us once knew a person who claimed to have lost $2,000 in slot machines during a weekend in Las Vegas. That type of resistance to extinction keeps many a casino owner very happy!

partial reinforcement schedule schedule of reinforcement in which the organism is rewarded for only some instances of the desired response

fixed ratio schedule schedule of reinforcement in which the organism is rewarded for every *x*th instance of the desired response

variable ratio schedule schedule of reinforcement in which the organism is rewarded on average for every *x*th instance of the desired response

 Application

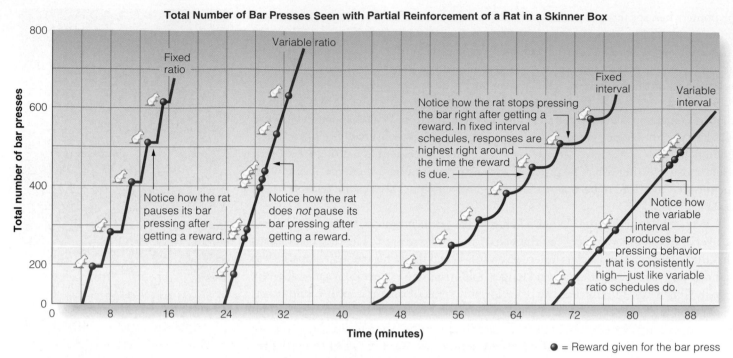

Total Number of Bar Presses Seen with Partial Reinforcement of a Rat in a Skinner Box

● = Reward given for the bar press

Figure 5.13 Partial Reinforcement of a Rat in a Skinner Box

This graph plots the rates of response for the different schedules of reinforcement and the points at which the rat is reinforced. Notice how the rat's bar pressing behavior changes before and after it receives a pellet on the different schedules of reinforcement. Which schedule would you use if you were going to use positive reinforcement to train your dog?

Interval Schedules of Reinforcement

Ratio schedules of reinforcement are based on the number of responses emitted by the organism. In interval schedules of reinforcement, the organism is rewarded only once per some interval of time. In a **fixed interval schedule,** the organism is rewarded for the first instance of the desired response, after which a set interval of time must pass before any other instances of the response will be rewarded. For example, if a rat in a Skinner box is reinforced on a fixed interval of 10 minutes, it will be rewarded for its first bar press, but not again until after 10 minutes had passed—no matter how many more times it pressed the bar. Then the first bar press after the 10-minute mark had passed would be rewarded (Figure 5.14).

The typical pattern of responding with a fixed interval schedule is to see most of the responding right around the time at which the reward is due. Then once the organism has received its reward for an interval, it usually stops responding for most of the remainder of the interval. One example of a fixed interval schedule is a yearly performance review at work. If an employee knows that she is going to be evaluated every January, she might be tempted to work her hardest in December. Immediately after being reviewed, the employee may be tempted to reduce her performance because she knows that she will not be reviewed again for another year. But as the end of the interval looms near and the next performance evaluation draws near, we could expect to see another increase in the employee's performance. This characteristic pause after reinforcement on a fixed interval schedule has been seen in rats (Innis, 1979) as well as humans (Shimoff, Cantania, & Matthews, 1981); (see Figure 5.13).

One way to avoid this pause in the behavior immediately after reinforcement is to make the interval *variable*. Similar to what we saw in the variable ratio schedule, in a **variable interval schedule,** the length of the interval varies. What if our employees

fixed interval schedule   schedule of reinforcement in which the organism is rewarded for the first desired response in an *x*th interval of time

Application ⏵⏵

variable interval schedules   schedule of reinforcement in which the organism is rewarded for the first desired response in an average *x*th interval of time

from the last example did not know when to expect their next evaluations? What if they could be evaluated during any month of the year? Under these circumstances, their only choice is to always perform well—assuming, of course, that they want to do well on their evaluation. As you can see from Figure 5.13, variable interval schedules produce steady rates of responding in rats. Another benefit of variable interval schedules is that they produce behaviors that are more resistant to extinction than those produced with fixed interval schedules.

In summary, when it comes to the effects that these different schedules have on operant conditioning:

1. Continuous reinforcement leads to high rates of responding but the quickest extinction.

2. Ratio schedules lead to higher rates of responding than do interval schedules.

3. Variable schedules lead to behaviors that are the most resistant to extinction.

Discrimination and Generalization

Discrimination

Just as classically conditioned responses undergo discrimination and generalization, so do operantly conditioned responses. In operant conditioning, discrimination occurs when the organism learns to distinguish among similar stimulus situations and to offer a particular response only in those specific situations in which reinforcement will be forthcoming. Discrimination occurs regularly in our lives. For instance,

Slot machines pay off on a variable ratio schedule of reinforcement. Because it is hard to predict when the next reward is due, people playing the machine are likely to show high rates of responding and very slow rates of extinction. This translates into big profits for the casinos!

© Bonnie Kamin / Photo Edit

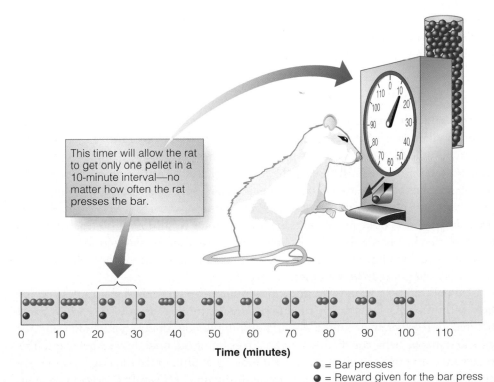

This timer will allow the rat to get only one pellet in a 10-minute interval—no matter how often the rat presses the bar.

0   10   20   30   40   50   60   70   80   90   100   110

Time (minutes)

● = Bar presses
● = Reward given for the bar press

Figure 5.14 Fixed Interval Schedule of Reinforcement

This is an example of an FI 10-minute schedule of reinforcement for a rat in a Skinner box. The "blue dots" indicate when the rat pressed the bar, and the orange "dots" indicate when the rat was rewarded for its bar-pressing behavior. On an FI of 10 minutes, the rat will receive a maximum of one reinforcement during any one 10-minute interval. Over time, the rat learns to press the bar only when a reward is due—right around the 10-minute interval mark. Yes, rats do have some sense of time!

when students learn that they will be rewarded for sitting quietly and attentively during a teacher's lecture, the reward may be the teacher's favor or being able to hear the lecture and learn from it. In this situation, sitting quietly is the "right" thing to do in that it will lead to reinforcement. But will being quiet always elicit reinforcement in the classroom? Of course not. When the teacher asks a student a question, remaining quiet and refusing to speak would not lead to reinforcement. In fact, silence could even lead to punishment if the teacher becomes frustrated with the student. Therefore, the student must learn to *discriminate* between situations in which remaining silent will and will not lead to reinforcement. As you can see, not only does the ability to discriminate lead us to reward, it also can keep us out of trouble!

Generalization

Equally important is our ability to generalize our operant responses. Generalization occurs when the organism emits the same operant behavior in response to different but similar stimuli. Let's say that you study very hard for your next psychology exam. You do your reading on time. You attend all lectures and take good notes. You study your psychology materials for at least 30 minutes each day, and you begin to study for the exam several days in advance. As a result of these good study habits, you earn an A on the exam. Receiving this A is a big reinforcement for your study habits. Given the success of your study methods in psychology, do you think that you might try these methods in your other courses? If so, your study behavior would generalize to your other courses. In this example, generalization is a good thing because it would lead to greater success in all of your courses.

In the previous examples, discrimination and generalization lead to positive outcomes. Unfortunately, this is not always the case. One example of the negative aspects of discrimination and generalization is found in prejudice and discrimination against certain groups of people. In prejudice, one's negative feelings about a few members of a group generalize to most or all members of that group. Similarly, one also learns to treat members of some groups in a kind manner and to treat all or most members of the disliked group in an unkind manner, thus discriminating against them. Here what we commonly refer to as discrimination in the social sense is also an example of what psychologists refer to as discrimination in learning. We will explore the downside of discrimination and generalization in Chapter 12 when we look at social psychology and the development of prejudices such as racism and gender bias.

Shaping New Behaviors

Before a behavior can be operantly conditioned, the organism must first emit the behavior spontaneously. Before Thorndike's cat learned to quickly receive its reward by stepping on the foot-release in the puzzle box, it first had to accidentally or spontaneously step on the pedal and open the box (see p. 220). Learning occurs only *after* the behavior has been emitted and the organism has been either punished or rewarded. Given this, how can operant conditioning explain the development of *novel* behaviors? For example, how could an animal trainer use operant conditioning to teach a dog to do a trick that involves walking on its hind legs? If you wait for a dog to spontaneously stand up on its hind legs and begin to walk so that you can reinforce this behavior with a treat, you are going to be waiting for a *long* time!

Animal trainers use an operant conditioning technique called **shaping**, in which the new, novel behavior is slowly conditioned by reinforcing *successive approximations* of the final desired behavior. In the case of training the dog, the trainer would reinforce *any* spontaneous behavior that was in the direction of the final desired behavior. The trainer may start by rewarding the dog for looking at him. Once the dog learns to pay attention, it may expand on this behavior by sitting up. This would also lead to a treat.

shaping   using operant conditioning to build a new behavior in an organism by rewarding successive approximations of the desired response

Then the dog must sit up to get the treat. Once the dog learns to sit up, it might go a bit further and rear up a bit on its hind legs. This would also earn the dog a treat. Now that the dog can rear up, it must do so to get a treat. After rearing up for a time, the dog may spontaneously go up all the way onto its hind legs. The trainer would respond with more treats. Soon the dog would progress to standing on its hind legs, and the trainer would reciprocate with more treats every time the dog stood up on its hind legs. The final step would come when the dog spontaneously took its first steps after being conditioned to stand on its hind legs. At this point, all the trainer has to do is reward the dog for walking on its hind legs.

Shaping has many useful purposes in the real world. A parent could use shaping to help a child become more successful in school. At first the parent could reward the child for any study-related behavior, such as doing reading assignments or homework. Then the parent could progress to rewarding the child for earning good grades on individual assignments, followed by a reward only for good grades on individual exams. Then the parent could reward the child for making good grades in individual courses. Finally, the parent could reward the child only for making good grades in *all* courses. By slowly rewarding closer and closer approximations of the final desired behavior, the parent can shape a behavior in the child that would, perhaps, have never occurred on its own.

These last examples point to the usefulness of operant conditioning in the real world. Can you think of a time in your own childhood when your parents consciously set out to classically condition you or habituate you? We bet you cannot. It is very likely that they did, but they probably conditioned you without even knowing it. With operant conditioning, it is another story.

If used correctly, operant conditioning can be very effective in modifying a child's behavior. This is not to say that operant conditioning can be used only with children. Operant conditioning can be used on any person or animal. However, the use of operant conditioning as a parental tool provides a nice backdrop for discussing some of the choices one must make before implementing an operant conditioning program of behavior modification with any organism.

《 Application

Animal trainers use shaping to get animals to perform behaviors that they would not typically perform in the wild.

© Lowell Georgia/Corbis

Decisions That Must Be Made When Using Operant Conditioning

Punishment or Reinforcement?

One of the first decisions that has to be made when using operant conditioning to change behavior is which type of consequence to use. Recall from Figure 5.10 that there are two basic types of consequences that follow behavior—reinforcement and punishment. When designing an operant conditioning program of behavior modification, one must first decide whether to punish or reinforce the behavior. Sometimes this choice will be a very clear one, but often it will not be.

At times, a parent will have a choice to either *reinforce* a child's *good* behavior or to *punish* her *bad* behavior. For example, suppose your child is not studying. You can punish the child for *not* studying or you can reward the child *for* studying. Which of these methods do you think will be more successful and cause fewer problems? If you guessed that reinforcement is the safer, more effective route, you guessed correctly. In fact, one of the most effective ways of controlling children's behavior is to show them how you want them to respond and then reward them for behaving that way (Kochanska, 1997; Zahn-Waxler & Robinson, 1995). So what makes punishment riskier and less effective?

- *Punishment doesn't teach the correct behavior.* Punishment has the disadvantage that by itself, it does not teach the child what the correct behavior is in a given situation. Think about it for a moment. Let's say you hear your

US ────► ────► ────► UR

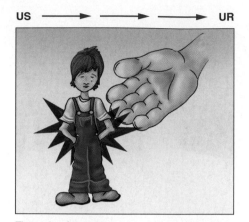

The pain of spanking   Fear

NS ────► ────► US ────► ────► UR

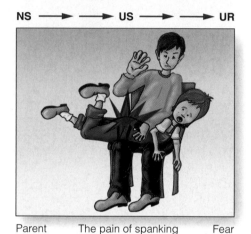

Parent   The pain of spanking   Fear

CS ────► ────► ────► CR

Parent   Fear

Figure 5.15 Classical Conditioning of Fear During a Spanking

Even though a parent may only intend to use operant conditioning when spanking a child, it is also possible that the child may also experience classical conditioning. Because a parent is the one delivering the punishment, a parent can become a conditioned stimulus that elicits fear in the child.

daughter getting frustrated with the family dog and cussing at the dog. As a result, you immediately yell at or spank her. What have you taught her? You have taught her not to use whatever cuss word she uttered at the dog. What you have *not* taught her, however, is how she *should have responded* in this situation. The next time she is frustrated with the dog, she will not know how to appropriately express her frustration. Because punishment does not teach the correct response, any use of punishment should include a discussion of appropriate behavior and reinforcement of that behavior (Martin & Pear, 1983).

■ *Harsh punishment teaches aggressive behavior.* Harsh punishment, especially physical punishment, has potential problems. One of the biggest is that harsh punishment provides an aggressive model for the child. When a parent spanks a child, the parent is teaching the child two things. First, that the child's behavior has had aversive consequences, and second, that being aggressive is a powerful means of controlling other people's behavior. In later sections of this chapter, we will see that children often imitate the behavior of others (Bandura, 1977). Therefore, while harsh punishment may stop an unwanted behavior, it may also teach the child to be aggressive. The next time the child feels frustrated or upset with another person, he or she may try using aggression to express those feelings. This is rarely the goal most parents have in mind!

■ *Harsh punishment is often ineffective at producing behavior change.* Harsh punishment is often ineffective in stopping the undesired behavior (Strassberg, Dodge, Pettit, & Bates, 1994). When punished, children often stop engaging in the undesired behavior, but only for as long as their parents are around. When the parents are out of sight—and the threat of immediate punishment is gone—the undesired behavior returns. Because the goal is usually to ensure that the child behaves even when the parents are not around, punishment is not always effective.

■ *Harsh punishment often leads to negative emotional reactions.* Another potential problem with harsh punishment is that it can lead to negative emotional reactions in the punished (Skinner, 1953). These negative reactions include emotions like anger, fear, and anxiety. If a child experiences fear and anxiety when a parent punishes him, he may come to fear the parent. Just as Little Albert came to associate the white rat with loud, frightening noises, a child could also come to associate a parent with pain and humiliation. Through classical conditioning, the parent could become a conditioned stimulus that evokes negative emotions in the child, and this conditioned fear could lead the child to want to avoid the parent (Figure 5.15).

    If the child perceives that the punishment is unpredictable and inescapable, an even more serious consequence could occur. Martin Seligman and S. F. Maier (1967) placed dogs in a cage and shocked them at random so that the dogs could neither escape the shock nor predict when it would occur. After a time, the dogs responded to this ill treatment by giving up all hope of escape. They merely sat down and took the shock. Later, even when they were given a means of escaping the shock, they didn't take it. According to Seligman and Maier, the dogs had acquired **learned help-lessness,** or a state of believing and acting as if they could not control what happened to them.

It appears that learned helplessness also occurs in humans (Seligman, 1974). If a child comes to believe that she cannot control when she will experience punishment, as in the case of an abusive alcoholic parent whose punishments are not closely tied to the child's behavior, she could develop learned helplessness that would adversely affect her future motivation and behavior (Elliott & Dweck, 1988; c.f., Ironsmith, Marva, Harju, & Eppler, 2003). Many researchers believe that learned helplessness is one cause of depression (Fredrickson, 2003; Seligman, 1974). We will discuss this and other theories of depression in Chapter 15.

> **learned helplessness**   a condition that occurs when an organism gives up as it learns that it can neither predict nor control punishing consequences associated with its behavior; learned helplessness may be a factor in depression

 **Application**

Harsh punishment, in particular, is riskier and less effective than reinforcement. If you do choose to use physical punishment on your children, how can you ensure its effectiveness? Before we begin, let us first state that physical punishment should be used only as a last resort. There are a number of alternatives to physical punishment, many of which are listed in Table 5.3 ◆. If none of these alternatives work, then perhaps you may wish to try physical punishment, but always be aware of the potential problems. Whether you choose to use physical or nonphysical punishment, here are a few tips for making punishment more effective in general:

1. Tell the child what the appropriate behavior is, and then reinforce.
2. Minimize situations that tempt the child to engage in bad behavior.
3. Use a punishment that really is punishing. If the child does not find the punishment aversive, it will fail to control the behavior.
4. Punishment must occur immediately after the bad behavior occurs.
5. Punishment must occur each and every time that the bad behavior occurs. Otherwise, the bad behavior is partially reinforced when the child escapes the punishment.
6. Remain calm while you are punishing a child. This will help ensure that you do not abuse the child.

As you can see, punishment, especially physical punishment, is riddled with possible dangers. Some countries, including England, are currently discussing whether or not to limit or even outlaw a parent's right to spank her child (O'Neill, 2004). When you have a choice, it is much safer and often more effective to use reinforcement of good behavior to control behavior. However, there are things to consider if you want to be sure your program of reinforcement has the desired effect on the behavior you are trying to change.

One theory of depression, learned helplessness, states that people learn to be depressed because they feel as if they cannot control or predict the consequences of their own behavior.

Choosing a Reinforcer That Is Reinforcing

It may seem like a trivial issue, but the first consideration in developing a program of reinforcement is to choose a reinforcer that is actually reinforcing for the person you are trying to condition. If the reinforcer is not something they like or value, it will not work. For example, if your significant other cleans the whole house, and you reward him by cooking a meal that he does *not* like, then he will not be more likely to clean the house again. Your attempt at operant conditioning will have failed.

◆ **Table 5.3**

Alternatives to Physical Punishment

Method	Examples
Time-out: A child is sent to sit in a quiet place where there are no toys, friends, or other reinforcements present.	Devon, 5 years old, is sent to sit in the laundry room for 5 minutes after hitting his sister.
Restitution: A child has to give up something.	Sabina broke her sister's toy on purpose. Now Sabina has to give one of her own toys to her sister.
Fines: The child has to pay a fine.	Every time a family member uses inappropriate language, he or she has to put 50 cents in the "swear jar."
Loss of privileges: Taking away privileges.	Giorgio is grounded for 2 weeks for breaking curfew and talking back to his parents.
Nonpunishment Method	
Empathy training: Teaching your child to empathize with others. If the child hurts another, she is encouraged to imagine what that person might have felt as a result of being hurt. The ability to empathize reduces the motivation to hurt others.	Suzy breaks her brother Jimmy's toy on purpose. To teach her empathy, her mother asks Suzy to think about how Suzy felt when Bobby broke her toy last week. Then Suzy is asked to think about whether Jimmy might be feeling the same way now that Suzy broke his toy. This should make Suzy feel bad about having hurt Jimmy.
Differential reinforcement of incompatible behavior (DRI): The child is rewarded for engaging in a desirable behavior that cannot be emitted at the same time as the undesirable behavior.	Marya's parents reward her for being quiet in church as opposed to punishing her for being loud in church.

On the surface, it may seem like choosing reinforcers that are reinforcing is a simple issue, but there are situations in which this task is not so simple, such as when you are trying to modify the behavior of people who are challenged by mental illnesses. One of the authors (Doyle-Portillo) once tried to reinforce a man who suffered from a mental illness, by giving him a new suit of clothes. To her dismay, he promptly traded these clothes to a fellow patient for a single pack of cigarettes! Obviously, cigarettes were more reinforcing for him than the new suit of clothes. The author made this mistake because she was thinking about what would reinforce her—not what would be reinforcing for him. As a result, her program of reinforcement was not very effective. When choosing a reinforcer, you must break out of your own way of thinking to think about what the other person is likely to find reinforcing.

Primary and Secondary Reinforcers

primary reinforcer reinforcer that is reinforcing in and of itself

secondary reinforcer reinforcer that is reinforcing only because it leads to a primary reinforcer

Reinforcers can be categorized as being either **primary** or **secondary reinforcers.** A primary reinforcer is a reinforcer that is directly reinforcing. Examples of primary reinforcers are food, water, a warm bed, sexual pleasure, and so forth. These reinforcers are primary because they, themselves, are pleasurable. If you are hungry, then food will reinforce you by removing your hunger.

In contrast, secondary reinforcers are rewarding only because they lead to primary reinforcers. A wonderful example of a secondary reinforcer in Western society is money. By itself, a dollar bill is not reinforcing. What makes a dollar reinforcing is what you can buy with it—food, water, shelter, and other primary reinforcers. When you get right down to it, you don't go to work for money per se. You go to work to ensure that you will be able to purchase an adequate supply of primary reinforcers!

token economy a system of operant conditioning in which participants are reinforced with tokens that can be later cashed in for primary reinforcers

One method of secondary reinforcement is to use a *token economy.* A **token economy** reinforces desired behavior with a token of some sort (e.g., a poker chip, gold star, and so on) that can later be cashed in for primary reinforcers (see Martin, England, Kaprowy; Kilgour, & Pilek, 1968). Token economies are often used to control the behavior of groups of people such as school children (Salend, 2001), mental hospital patients, or prisoners. Token economies can also be used in the context of a family (Kazdin, 1977).

« Application

To set up a token economy, the first step is to draw up a list of desired and undesired behaviors that you will try to control. The next step is to decide how many tokens to give (or take away) for each of the behaviors, and develop some sort of record-keeping system to keep track of each participant's tokens. One record-keeping approach is to draw a chart like the one shown in Figure 5.16 and hang it on the wall in a prominent place.

There are two main advantages to using token economies. One is that a token economy is effective when trying to simultaneously modify a number of behaviors in a group of people. For example, a token economy could be used on an entire class, which would be easier than trying to develop individual operant conditioning programs for each student.

The second major advantage is that token economies allow for immediate reinforcement with a token, even when it is not practical to immediately present the primary reinforcer. For example, it's disruptive for a teacher to stop the entire class to give a child a toy as a reinforcer. However, the teacher could immediately hand the child a token that could be used at week's end to purchase a toy. The use of tokens helps to bridge the gap between the behavior and the eventual primary reinforcement of the behavior.

A potential problem with token economies is that they often place the behavior on a continuous schedule of reinforcement. As we saw in previous sections, continuous reinforcement can lead to behavior that is vulnerable to extinction. It is possible that a token economy may lessen a person's desire to engage in a behavior when the behavior is not likely to lead to a token or some other reward. This potential problem may, however, be outweighed by the usefulness of the token economy in controlling the immediate behavior of the people in the program. For instance, in a prison you may be more worried about controlling the immediate, day-to-day behavior of the prison population. Facilitating the future motivation of the inmates to behave in a particular way once they are out of the token economy is likely to be less of a concern.

Mrs. Duncan's Class

Participants	Paying attention in class, +5 tokens	On time for class, +3 tokens	Homework completely done, +7 tokens	B or better on daily quiz, +10 tokens	Talking in class, −5 tokens	Fighting, −10 tokens	Calling people names −10 tokens
Johnny							
Mary							
Lou							
Billy							
George							
Eddie							
Lisa							

Token values
  25 tokens = 1 sticker, eraser, or pencil
  50 tokens = 1 small toy
  75 tokens = 1 medium-size toy
100 tokens = 1 coupon for free pizza
125 tokens = 1 videotape

Figure 5.16
A Sample Point System From a Token Economy

The Role of Cognition in Learning

So far in this chapter, we have discussed three major types of learning—habituation, classical conditioning, and operant conditioning—which have some important things in common. One common aspect is that all of these types of learning require that *the organism do something before learning can occur.* In habituation, the organism must emit an orienting reflex. In classical conditioning, the organism must emit an unconditioned response. In operant conditioning, the organism must first engage in some random behavior that is either reinforced or punished.

Another common facet of these learning theories is that they do not emphasize the role that mental or cognitive processes play in learning. Researchers like Ivan Pavlov, J. B. Watson, E. L. Thorndike, and B. F. Skinner did not discuss the thoughts and feelings of the organism and how these may affect the learning process. B. F. Skinner, in particular, felt that psychology should not seek to scientifically study the cognitive aspects of behavior because he felt that these things could not be studied scientifically and objectively. Skinner did not deny that organisms had thoughts and feelings. He simply felt they could not be studied adequately. Therefore, Skinner subscribed to a type of psychology called **behaviorism** (discussed in Chapter 1), which states that the *only* aspect of organisms that can and should be studied scientifically is behavior. As such, Skinner tried to explain behavior without discussing cognitive or mental processes (Skinner, 1953).

behaviorism a school of thought in psychology that emphasizes the study of observable behavior over the study of the mind

Because strict behaviorism totally ignores the influence of cognitive processes, it does not explain some of the learning we see in the real world, or in the lab. In the early 1900s, some researchers, including Wolfgang Köhler, became aware of the fact that cognitive processes must play a role in learning. Köhler observed that chimpanzees did not always attempt to solve problems in a trial-and-error fashion as predicted by the law of effect. Rather, they often seemed to study a problem for a long time—as if formulating a mental plan—before attempting to solve it. In one experiment, Köhler placed a banana just out of reach on the outside of a chimpanzee's cage, and he placed a stick inside the cage. The law of effect would predict that the chimpanzee would try many random behaviors—like shaking the bars and jumping up and down—before picking up the stick and using it to reach the banana. But this is not what Köhler observed. Instead, the chimpanzee studied the situation and then appeared to suddenly come up with the solution. After this flash of **insight** into how to solve its dilemma, the chimpanzee picked up the stick and used it to scoot the banana to a point where it could be reached (Köhler, 1925).

insight a sudden realization about how to solve a problem that occurs after an organism has studied the problem for a period of time

Köhler's work shows that learning can be a purely cognitive task. The chimpanzee did not have to wait for the consequences of its behavior to rule out behavioral strategies that would not accomplish the goal of obtaining the banana. Rather, the chimpanzee appeared to reason its way to a solution *before* acting.

In the 1930s, Edward Tolman found additional support for the idea that cognition plays a role in learning. Tolman discovered that rats would learn to run through a maze even when they were not rewarded for doing so (Tolman & Honzik, 1930). In Tolman's experiment, one group of rats was allowed to wander through the maze, and they were rewarded with food if they found their way to the end of the maze. Another group of rats was also allowed to explore the maze, but they were not rewarded even if they found their way to the end. As you might expect, after 10 days of training in the maze, the group that was rewarded could run through the maze more quickly than the unrewarded group could. On the 11th day, Tolman began to give rats in *both* groups a reward at the end of the maze. After just a few rewarded trials, the previously unrewarded rats could run through the maze just as fast as the rats that had been rewarded all along. This rapid learning in the previously unrewarded rats indicates that these rats had been learning even when they were not being rewarded!

Tolman's findings cannot be explained by operant conditioning alone because learning occurred *without* reinforcement. Tolman interpreted his results as being evidence that the rats had engaged in **latent learning,** or learning that cannot be directly observed in an organism's behavior. He proposed that while the unrewarded rats were

latent learning learning that cannot be directly observed in an organism's behavior

wandering through the maze, they were developing a **cognitive map,** or mental representation of the maze in their heads. Once the reward was presented, they used this map to help them get to the reward more quickly.

Although Tolman's experiments pointed to cognitive processes at work during learning, the impact of cognition on learning continued to be ignored by many psychologists because of the dominance of behaviorism in psychology at the time. It wasn't until the 1960s that learning researchers really began to look at the role of cognition in learning and behavior.

cognitive map   a mental representation of the environment that is formed through observation of one's environment

Let's Review!

This section has given you a quick overview of some of the important issues in instrumental, or operant, conditioning including the law of effect, the factors that affect instrumental/operant conditioning, the differences between instrumental/operant conditioning and classical conditioning, and B.F. Skinner's contributions to operant conditioning. As a quick check of your understanding, answer these questions.

1. Juan wants to increase his son Mario's tendency to mow the yard on Saturday mornings without having to repeatedly ask him. To do this, Juan tells Mario that he will pay Mario $5 when he mows the yard without first having been told to do so. Juan is using which schedule of reinforcement?
   a. fixed ratio
   b. variable interval
   c. variable ratio
   d. continuous

2. Which of the following is an example of operant conditioning?
   a. Byron doesn't go to the dentist because the last time he did, it was very painful.
   b. Byron is afraid of dentists because the last time he went to the dentist, it was very painful.
   c. Byron wants to go to the dentist because when his friend Gina went to the dentist, the dentist gave Gina a toy.
   d. All of the above are examples of operant conditioning.

3. Which of the following is a secondary reinforcer?
   a. good grades
   b. food, when you're hungry
   c. water, when you're thirsty
   d. None of the above are secondary reinforcers

ANSWERS
1. d; 2. a; 3. a

Social Learning or Modeling > > > > > > > > > > >

As we saw in the previous discussion, learning can occur without reinforcement, but even Tolman's unrewarded rats had at least engaged in the behavior of moving through the maze. Does all learning require that we actually engage in the behavior? As it turns out, we can learn by simply observing the behaviors of others. In this type of learning, called **social learning,** we *observe* others and imitate, or *model,* their behavior. For that reason, social learning is sometimes referred to as *observational learning* or *modeling.* Nick, from our opening story, is a good example of this type of learning. Because he spent all of his time in the company of adults, he had few models of childlike behavior. As a result, Nick came to act more like an adult even when he was still a child. This likely occurred because Nick imitated many of the behaviors that he saw in the adults. Even when Nick did not actually imitate the adults' behavior, he still probably learned something from watching their behavior.

LEARNING OBJECTIVES

≫ Describe Albert Bandura's Bobo doll experiments.
≫ Describe social learning theory.
≫ Describe the role that cognition plays in social learning.

social learning   learning through the observation and imitation of others' behavior

As you read the following sections, keep in mind that social learning departs from the behaviorism that Skinner so forcefully advocated on two major points. First, it acknowledges that learning can occur without an overt change in behavior; and, second, it takes into account the role of cognition in the learning process.

Albert Bandura and the Bobo Doll Experiments

In the 1960s, psychologist Albert Bandura (b. 1925) conducted several experiments on social learning that are now considered to be classic psychological experiments and contributed to his developing *social learning theory*. Collectively, these experiments are referred to as the *Bobo doll experiments* because the experimental procedure utilized a blow-up plastic "Bobo" doll, a popular child's toy.

In the Bobo doll experiments, children watched films in which a woman beat up the Bobo doll. She hit him with a mallet, sat on him, threw him in the air, and so on (Bandura, Ross, & Ross, 1961). After viewing the films, Bandura and his colleagues placed the children in a room alone with the Bobo doll and observed the children's behavior without their knowledge. If the children imitated the characteristic behaviors of the model, then Bandura knew that learning had occurred (Figure 5.17).

In one of the Bobo doll experiments (Bandura, 1965), three groups of children watched one of three films that were made of the model and Bobo. In the *reward* film condition, the model was rewarded after beating up on Bobo. In the *punishment* film condition, she was punished after beating up on Bobo. In the *no consequences* film condition, nothing happened to the model after she beat up on Bobo.

After viewing one of these films, the children were observed with Bobo, and their aggressive behaviors were recorded. As you might expect, the children who had seen the model rewarded for beating up Bobo were most likely to beat up on him themselves. However, an unexpected finding of the study was that the children who had seen the *no consequences* film were equally likely to beat up on Bobo! This means that seeing someone merely get away with aggressive behavior is just as likely to lead to modeling as seeing aggression rewarded. The only thing that deterred the children's aggression toward Bobo was having seen the punishment film in which the model was

A

B

© Albert Bandura

Figure 5.17 Bandura's Bobo Doll Experiments

These photos, taken from the Bobo doll experiments, clearly show the children (panel B) modeling what they saw the model (panel A) doing to Bobo.

punished for treating Bobo badly! Only these children were more hesitant to beat up on Bobo when they were left alone with him in the observation room.

By leaving the children alone with Bobo and recording their aggressive behavior, Bandura was able to assess how willing the children were to beat up on Bobo as a function of the consequences they expected would follow such aggression. But what about what they learned about how to be aggressive toward Bobo? Is it possible that some of the children who did *not* beat up Bobo had still learned *how* to beat up Bobo? To test the children's level of *learning*, Bandura (1965) asked the children to show him exactly what they had seen in the films. Here, the children were free to model the behavior without fear of any type of punishment. Under these conditions, Bandura found that there were no significant differences across the three groups. All of the groups exhibited equal levels of learning when it came to knowing how the model had beat up Bobo.

The Bobo doll experiments show us two things. First, you don't have to engage in a behavior or experience reinforcement for learning to occur. Second, just as Tolman discovered with his rats in the mazes, learning can be latent. The children who viewed the *punishment* film had learned how to beat up Bobo, but they were reluctant to beat him up because they feared there would be negative consequences for them if they did. We hope that the Bobo doll experiments make you think about the potential impact that violent movies, video games, and television may have on the children who view them because some very recent research seems to underscore the notion that kids do not merely watch TV—rather, they learn from TV.

Researchers Donna Mumme and Anne Fernald (2003) have found that children as young as 12 months old pay attention to how a televised model reacts to certain stimuli, and then they model their own reaction to the stimulus after the model's reaction. In this study, 12-month-old infants watched a televised actress interacting with certain toys. The actress responded either positively, neutrally, or negatively to certain toys. Later, the infants were allowed to play with the same toys.

The results showed that the infants were most likely to react favorably to the toys that the actress had either been neutral about or liked. Similarly, the infants were less likely to want to play with the toys to which the actress had reacted negatively. It seems that the infants disliked these toys simply because they had seen the actress reacting negatively toward them. Thus, the social learning that occurs when watching TV may have the power to influence the attitudes that even very young children hold about the objects in their world.

≪ **Application**

Think about the impact that this process may have on learning stereotypes and prejudices. If a child is subjected to models (in real life or on TV) who react negatively to specific groups of people, could this lead to modeling in which the child comes to react negatively to certain types of people simply because they have seen this reaction in others? It seems likely that it could, and perhaps even at a very young age! Later in this text, we will explore the causes of aggression and prejudice further in our discussions of social psychology in Chapter 12. But for now, let's take a closer look at this process of social learning and the variables that affect it.

Social Learning Theory and Cognition

The role of cognition in social learning can be clearly seen when you examine the conditions that are necessary for modeling to occur. According to Bandura (1986), modeling is a four-step process.

1. *Attention.* The observer must first pay attention to the model's behavior before he or she can model it. Research shows that children tend to model their behavior after people who are warm, nurturant, or powerful (Bandura,

What do we learn from watching TV?

© Jennie Woodcock; Reflections Photolibrary/Corbis

1977). For example, a child may pay attention to the behavior of loving parents, a nurturant teacher, or a popular and seemingly powerful classmate. As we have already seen, another type of model that is particularly good at grabbing our attention is televised models (Bandura, Grusec, & Menlove, 1966). As a result, it is quite common to see children on the playground modeling the behavior of their favorite TV cartoon character. As we age and mature, however, we tend to seek out models that seem similar to us in some way (Bandura, 1986). For example, we may model our behavior after people of the same sex, ethnicity, occupation, and so forth.

2. *Retention in memory.* The observer must retain a cognitive representation or memory of the model's behavior. For children on the playground to model the behavior of TV characters, they must have memories of what they have previously seen on TV.

3. *Reproduction of the behavior.* The observer must retrieve the mental representations of the behavior that they have stored in memory and then use them to reproduce the behavior. Of course, the person must have the physical abilities to actually reproduce the behavior if modeling is to occur. For instance, a child may remember seeing a cartoon superhero flying, and although he may be able to model an approximation of this behavior, he will not be able to model this behavior precisely.

4. *Motivation.* After retrieving the memory of the behavior and figuring out how to produce the behavior, the observer must be motivated to actually execute the behavior. As we saw in the Bobo doll experiments, the observer may sometimes not *want* to execute the behavior. This is especially true if the observer believes that execution of the behavior may lead to punishment.

Bandura's social learning theory brings an additional element to the study of learning, in that it addresses the role of cognition in the learning process. In the next two chapters, we will look more carefully at cognitive processes when we look at how memory works in Chapter 6 and the cognitive processes involved in solving problems and making decisions and judgments in Chapter 7.

Let's Review!

This section has given you a quick overview of some of the important aspects of social learning theory, including Bandura's Bobo doll experiments, the steps involved in modeling, and the role that cognition plays in social learning. As a quick check of your understanding, answer these questions.

1. Social learning differs from operant conditioning in that:
   a. in social learning, the organism is less aware that learning is taking place.
   b. in operant conditioning, the organism is less aware that learning is taking place.
   c. in social learning, the organism does not have to emit the response.
   d. in operant conditioning, the organism does not have to emit the response.

2. Which of the following is an example of social learning?
   a. Henri can cook because as a child, he spent a lot of time playing in the kitchen while his mother cooked dinner.

   b. Shalitha slaps another child for taking her toy away.
   c. Javier likes toy trains because they remind him of his childhood days.
   d. Billy is able to study with the neighbor's TV playing at full volume.

3. Tyrone watches a violent TV show, but he has never been seen to model any of the behaviors he saw on the show. Which of the following statements is true regarding Tyrone's learning?
   a. Tyrone has not learned anything from watching the show.
   b. Tyrone has definitely learned something from watching the show.
   c. Tyrone may have learned something from watching the show.
   d. At some point in time, Tyrone's behavior will definitely change as a result of watching the show.

ANSWERS

1. c; 2. a; 3. c

Are You Getting the Big Picture?

In this chapter, we looked at four different types of learning: habituation, classical conditioning, operant conditioning, and social learning. *Habituation* explains how we learn to ignore familiar stimuli. *Classical conditioning* explains how we come to have particular emotional and physiological reactions to certain stimuli. *Operant conditioning* explains how we learn from the consequences of our behavior, and *social learning* explains how we learn by watching other people. As you continue to study these different types of learning, keep in mind how what you have learned about these types of learning relates to everyday life.

All of us will experience habituation, classical conditioning, operant conditioning, and social learning in our lifetime. Likewise, we will use them to control the behavior of others. For example, law enforcement personnel use operant conditioning to deter people from breaking the law. Friends and lovers use operant conditioning to change each other—a simple smile or a frown

of disappointment can exert powerful influence on our behavior. Parents use social learning to model behaviors they want their children to acquire. Parents also use the rewards and punishments of operant conditioning to socialize their children. Similarly, managers use operant conditioning when they develop employee incentive and compensation plans. Advertisers use classical conditioning to get us to associate their products with positive emotions—thus increasing the odds that we will actually purchase them. And as we will see in Chapter 16, therapists use all of these types of learning to modify problematic behaviors in their clients.

Outside of understanding how learning impacts you in your everyday life, your understanding of learning is also going to help you understand the material we are about to embark on in chapters 6 and 7. In these chapters,

STUDYING THE **CHAPTER**

(continued)

Are You Getting the Big Picture? (continued)

we will be looking at learning from a more cognitive approach, covering topics such as memory, problem-solving skills, language, and intelligence. Although the cognitive approach to learning is a different perspective, what you have learned in this chapter will help you understand this new material. For example, when we examine how children learn to speak a language, we will see that language acquisition is due, in part, to modeling and operant conditioning. If a child has no one to model language for him, he will not acquire language. Luckily, most children acquire language easily because their parents model language for them and reinforce their attempts at speaking.

Learning also affects the quality of our social interactions. In Chapter 12, we will see that classical conditioning, operant conditioning, and social learning all play an integral role in the development of the beliefs and attitudes we hold about ourselves and others. For instance, if a person in Morocco is robbed by an American, the victim could develop a fear of Americans through classical conditioning. If that fear response undergoes generalization, the victim could develop a mistrust and fear of all people from the United States, and this fear could lead the victim to discriminate against all people from that country. If this happens, the victim has acquired a prejudice through learning.

We hope that the examples we have given here convince you of the importance of learning in everyday life. Learning goes far beyond what happens in the classroom. It affects our development, our social interactions, and the way we think.

Key Terms

learning (203)
orienting reflex (205)
habituation (206)
dishabituation (207)
unconditioned stimulus (US) (209)
unconditioned response (UR) (209)
neutral stimulus (NS) (210)
conditioned stimulus (CS) (210)
conditioned response (CR) (210)
classical conditioning (210)
contiguity (212)
contingency (212)
stimulus generalization (214)
counterconditioning (214)
stimulus discrimination (215)
taste aversion (216)
aversion therapy (217)

extinction (218)
acquisition (218)
spontaneous recovery (218)
instrumental conditioning (220)
law of effect (221)
reinforcement (221)
positive reinforcement (222)
negative reinforcement (222)
punishment (223)
positive punishment (223)
negative punishment (223)
respondent behavior (226)
operant behavior (226)
Skinner box (226)
extinction burst (228)
schedule of reinforcement (228)
continuous reinforcement (228)

partial reinforcement schedules (229)
fixed ratio schedule (229)
variable ratio schedule (229)
fixed interval schedule (230)
variable interval schedule (230)
shaping (232)
learned helplessness (235)
primary reinforcer (236)
secondary reinforcer (236)
token economy (236)
behaviorism (238)
insight (238)
latent learning (238)
cognitive map (239)
social learning (239)

Test Yourself!

Concept Check

Test your knowledge of the chapter concepts by completing each of the following sentences with the correct term. For a more comprehensive review, visit the book Web site (http://psychology.wadsworth.com/pastorinole/) for online quizzes, flashcards, crosswords, and Internet links.

(1) _____ is the simplest type of learning. Johnny jumped and looked toward the window when he heard a car backfire. Johnny's behavior is an example of a(n) (2) _____ _____. Haley the dog gets excited whenever she sees her owner pick up his coat because this indicates that he is about to take Haley outside for a walk. Haley's behavior is an example of (3) _____ conditioning. Patricia tells her son that he does not have to rake the lawn because he earned an A on his algebra test. Patricia is using (4) _____ reinforcement on her son. The fact that Miguel is afraid of *all* snakes is an example of

(5) _____ _____. Learning to be aggressive through (6) _____ _____ is a major concern for many parents whose children watch television. (7) _____ and _____ _____ can be classically conditioned in humans. (8) _____ _____ is the type of learning that *best* explains why many people go to work each day. Grades are an example of a(n) (9) _____ reinforcer. A mental representation of our environment is called a(n) (10) _____ _____.

Answers:

1. Habituation; 2. orienting reflex; 3. classical; 4. negative; 5. stimulus generalization; 6. social learning; 7. Emotional, physiological responses; 8. Operant conditioning; 9. secondary; 10. cognitive map

Critical Thinking About the Chapter

1. Identify a situation in which you were classically conditioned. Then identify the NS/CS, US, and UR/CR.

2. Could a species' ability to learn through instrumental conditioning be the result of natural selection? Why, or why not?

3. How do the types of learning in this chapter apply to parents and their children? In other words, how do parents use these types of learning in their roles as parents?

Applying Psychology. If you were an employer who wanted to maximize employee productivity, which schedule of reinforcement would you use when creating a timetable for performance reviews of your employees? Defend your choice.

Critical Thinking for Integration

1. Design an experiment to test the hypothesis that continuous reinforcement leads to behaviors that are less resistant to extinction than behaviors that are built with partial reinforcement.

2. What role might learning play in drug addiction?

3. What role might learning play in the treatment of drug addiction?

4. What role does sensation and perception play in learning?

Chapter Study Resources

Suggested Readings

1. Heyes, C. M., & Galef, B. G., Jr. (Eds.). (1996). *Social learning in animals: The roots of culture*. San Diego, CA: Academic Press.
   A text on how animals use social learning to transmit culture to their young.

2. Singer, B. (Ed.). (1998). *42 Up*. New York: The New Press.
   The book chronicling the lives of the *Up* participants at age 42.

3. Skinner, B. F. (1948). *Walden two*. New York: Macmillan.
   Skinner's famous novel in which he depicts a utopian community guided by positive reinforcement.

4. For additional readings, explore InfoTrac College Edition, your online library of archived journal articles and periodicals. Go to (http://www.infotrac-college .com/wadsworth) and enter the passcode from the card that came with your book. For this chapter, search using these keywords:

   operant conditioning

   shaping

   aversion therapy

   phobias and learning

   modeling

   habituation

Web Links for Further Study

1. *Whatever Happened to Little Albert?* A site containing a paper by author Ben Harris that discusses the Little Albert experiments and the fate of little Albert.
   http://faculty.concord.edu/rockc/articles/albert.html

2. The homepage of the B. F. Skinner Foundation, an organization devoted to educating the world about the work of B. F. Skinner.
   http://www.bfskinner.org/index.asp

3. A website containing a biographical sketch of Albert Bandura.
   http://www.emory.edu/EDUCATION/mfp/bandurabio.html

4. A SeaWorld Web site that discusses the use of behavior training on animals at SeaWorld.
   http://www.seaworld.org/infobooks/Training/home.html

Student Study Guide

To help organize your learning, go to Chapter 5 of the *What Is Psychology? Student Study Guide*. The study guide includes learning objectives, a chapter summary, fill-in review, key terms, a practice test, and activities.

Psychology Now™

PsychologyNow is a Web-based, personalized study system that provides you with a pretest and a posttest for each chapter, quizzes you by chapter, and provides a personalized study plan, pointing you to elements in the text or in individual learning modules that will help you to achieve 80% mastery. Check out the learning modules that relate to this chapter: classical conditioning; operant learning.

PsychNow CD-ROM, Version 2.0

Go to the PsychNow CD-ROM for further study of the concepts in this chapter. The CD-ROM includes learning modules with videos, animations, and quizzes, as well as simulations of psychological phenomena. Each module follows a consistent Explore, Lesson, and Apply structure that allows you to experience the concept or principle, learn more about it, and then apply it. You and your friends can participate in a team-based Quiz Game that makes learning fun. Learning modules include: 5a. Classical Conditioning; 5b. Operant Conditioning; 5c. Observational Learning.

How Do We Learn?

Learning is a relatively permanent change in behavior or the potential for behavior that results from experience.

ORIENTING AND HABITUATION

- Orienting reflexes occur when we stop what we are doing and orient our sense organs in the direction of the unexpected stimuli.

- Habituation involves a decrease in responding to a stimulus that occurs as the stimulus is repeated over and over.

- Dishabituation occurs when an organism begins to re-respond to a stimulus to which it had previously habituated.

CLASSICAL CONDITIONING

- The Russian physiologist Ivan Pavlov's surprising findings in his study of salivating dogs led to interest in how organisms become classically conditioned.

- Classical conditioning is learning that occurs when a neutral stimulus is paired with an unconditioned stimulus that reliably causes an unconditioned response, and because of this association, the neutral stimulus loses its neutrality and takes on the same power as the unconditioned stimulus to cause the response.

- Classical conditioning is most effective when the neutral or conditioned stimulus and the unconditioned stimulus, are separated by only a brief period of time (contiguity), and the pairing must reliably predict the response (contingency).

- In experiments such as the famous case of Little Albert and the white lab rat, John Watson and his assistant Rosalie Rayner studied how emotional responses could be classically conditioned.

- Stimulus generalization occurs when stimuli that are similar to the conditioned stimulus also have the same power to elicit the conditioned response.

- In stimulus discrimination, the conditioned response does not occur in response to other stimuli that are similar to the conditioned stimuli.

Pavlov's dog

- Taste aversion is a type of conditioning that occurs when we associate a particular food with some other ailment or condition that causes nausea.

- The elimination of a conditioned response is known as extinction.

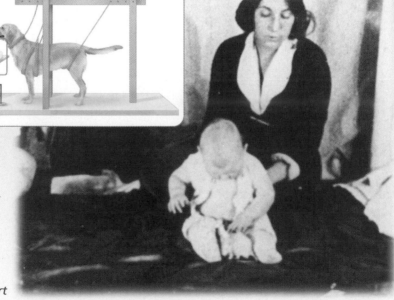

Little Albert

INSTRUMENTAL AND OPERANT CONDITIONING

- In instrumental conditioning, we learn from the consequences of our actions.

- American psychologist E. L. Thorndike developed the principle known as the law of effect, which emphasized the negative and positive consequences of behavior.

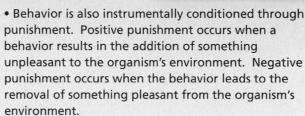

- In positive reinforcement, a behavior leads to the addition of something pleasant to an organism's environment. In negative reinforcement, the behavior is rewarded by the removal of something unpleasant from the environment.

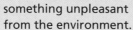

- Behavior is also instrumentally conditioned through punishment. Positive punishment occurs when a behavior results in the addition of something unpleasant to the organism's environment. Negative punishment occurs when the behavior leads to the removal of something pleasant from the organism's environment.

- American psychologist B. F. Skinner coined the term operant conditioning to refer to how certain behavior operates on the environment to produce some consequence. The Skinner box is a chamber used to study animal learning.

- Schedules of reinforcement state the timing and number of responses required to receive reinforcement.

- In shaping, a novel behavior is slowly conditioned by reinforcing successive approximations of the final desired behavior.

- A primary reinforcer is a reinforcer that reinforces directly. A secondary reinforcer is rewarding only because it leads to a primary reinforcer.

- Skinner was a strong adherent of a type of psychology called behaviorism, which proposes that the only aspect of an organism that can and should be studied scientifically is behavior.

- A token economy reinforces desired behavior with a token of some sort, such as a poker chip or a gold star, that can later be cashed in for primary reinforcers.

SOCIAL LEARNING OR MODELING

- Social learning is learning that occurs by observing others and modeling their behavior.

- In his Bobo doll experiments, Albert Bandura showed that you don't have to engage in a behavior or experience for learning to occur, and that learning can be latent.

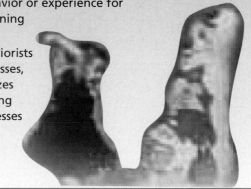

- Unlike Skinner and the behaviorists who downplayed mental processes, social learning theory emphasizes the role of cognition in modeling behavior. These cognitive processes include attention, retention in memory, reproduction of the behavior, and motivation.

At the trial Mr. Terry had testified that Ms. Gammill was the woman he surprised burglarizing his house and she fled . . .

FROM "WOMAN FREED AFTER LOOK-ALIKE IS NAMED AS SUSPECT," (*The New York Times,* April 17, 1995, p. B8.)

© David Turnley/Corbis

CHAPTER 6

How Does Memory Function?

CHAPTER PREVIEW

Memory's Imperfections

Using our memory, we can remember things that have happened in the past: our first date, the antics of childhood friends, the name of our second-grade teacher, lessons we have learned, and so on. It is our ability to remember that gives us our sense of self. Our memory connects us to the past and all the people, places, and experiences we have encountered in our lifetime. Our memory also allows us to learn from our experiences. For example, you probably know who B. F. Skinner was from reading the preceding chapter. As you read this chapter and listen to your professor's lectures, you will take in this information and store it in your memory for future use. If all goes well on test day, you will retrieve this information and use it to answer your professor's questions—at least that is the plan!

Our memory serves us well for the most part, and the mistakes we make are usually not of great importance. However, there are exceptions and errors in memory that can lead to devastating consequences as our case study illustrates.

In December 1993, Darron Terry surprised a woman in the act of burglarizing his Mississippi home. The startled burglar fled before the police arrived, but not before Terry got a look at her face. As is typical, the police had Terry look through their database of "mug shots" in the hopes that the woman who burglarized his home had been in trouble before and Terry would be able to pick her out. Terry was able to identify a suspect: 26-year-old Mellissa Gammill. The police had taken Gammill's photo in 1992 when she was booked on a misdemeanor charge. She was never convicted of the charge, but her photo remained on file. When Terry saw her mug shot, he recognized her as the young woman with long blond hair whom he had interrupted in the process of burglarizing his home!

On the strength of Terry's identification, the police decided to arrest Gammill. Three months had passed since the night of the burglary, and Gammill, a single mother, was working at a food court in a local mall. When the police questioned her about her whereabouts on the night of the burglary, Gammill could not recall where she had been that night. Because she had no alibi, Gammill was charged with the crime.

In court, Terry testified that Gammill was the woman who had robbed him, and without an alibi, she could not prove him wrong. She was convicted and sentenced to 10 years in prison. Gammill's attorney was convinced that Gammill was innocent and a victim of mistaken identity. After Gammill began her prison term, her attorney continued to pursue the theory that someone who looked like Gammill had actually robbed the Terry home. Gammill's attorney kept searching for the real burglar, and eventually the search paid off.

Another woman with a criminal record, Pauline Bailey, looked a great deal like Gammill. Both were White, in their mid-twenties, with long blond hair. After police were made aware of the look-alike woman, they realized that they might have made a mistake in prosecuting Gammill for the crime. Darron Terry, himself, testified before a judge that he felt he had made a mistake when he identified Mellissa Gammill as the woman who broke into his home. After Terry recanted his testimony, Gammill was released from prison after having served 10 months of her 10-year sentence for burglary ("Woman Freed," 1995; Figure 6.1).

What happened to Mellissa Gammill illustrates the imperfections of memory. Darron Terry's memory was less than accurate when he tried to recall what the woman he saw breaking into his home looked like. Mellissa Gammill's memory failed her when she could not remember where she was at the time of the burglary. These two failures of memory resulted in Mellissa Gammill being sentenced to jail for 10 years!

"It was certainly a case of mistaken identity."

(Deputy Police Chief Jimmy Houston, in "Woman Freed," 1995)

The Clarion-Ledger

Friday, April 14, 1995   Jackson, Mississippi

Probe shows wrong woman sent to prison

■ Investigation points to a look-alike as suspect in 1992 burglary.

By Jay Hughes
Clarion-Ledger Staff Writer

A Jackson woman's burglary conviction was overturned Thursday when the victim testified he mistakenly identified her instead of a suspect who looks almost exactly like her.

Mellissa Darlene Gammill h...

available late Thursday.

"It was certainly a case of m... identity. These people look... alike it's unbelievable," Hou... said. "This is a rare oppor... Police Department has to... wrong.

Bailey also is an inm... Central Mississippi C... Facility, serving a se... ery, Houston said.... could charge for... Hou... jail...

Figure 6.1
Burglar or Look-Alike?

Mellissa Gammill went to prison for 10 months in a case of mistaken identity.

Clarion-Ledger, with permission

The story of Mellissa Gammill's false conviction raises serious questions about memory. Why is memory sometimes inaccurate? Why do we sometimes forget things entirely? In this chapter, we will examine these issues by looking at how our memory works—or doesn't.

After learning this chapter's material, you will have a better understanding of the psychological processes that were at work when Mellissa Gammill was falsely identified. You will also learn how your own memory works. You can use this knowledge and understanding of memory to make yourself a more successful student. It is our hope that you will apply what you learn in this chapter to your own life. We will begin our journey toward an understanding of how memory works by looking at the basic functions of memory.

The Functions of Memory: >>>>>>>>>>>>>> Encoding, Storing, and Retrieving

LEARNING OBJECTIVE

Explain the functions of memory.
Tell the difference between implicit and explicit use of memory.

The computer provides a helpful model for thinking about the basic functions of memory. Like memory, a computer accepts input—the information you type into it—stores and processes the information, and allows you to go back and retrieve the same information. In essence, this is also what your mind does with information. As you read this chapter, you are inputting, or **encoding,** information into your memory in the form of **memory traces,** which are stored bits of information in memory. Your mind will process this information and put it into memory **storage,** and then on test day or some other day when an understanding of memory is needed, you will use **retrieval** processes to recall and output the information from memory as you answer questions on an exam.

encoding   the act of inputting information into memory

memory traces   the stored code that represents a piece of information that has been encoded into memory

storage   the place where information is retained in memory

retrieval   the process of accessing information in memory and pulling it into consciousness

The parallels between computers and the mind are hard to miss. After all, we built computers to mimic the mind's processing of information. We even speak of computers in human terms. We speak of computer *memory*, computer *languages*, and computers *talking* to other computers via modems and networks. Scientists have developed software programs that allow computers to solve complex problems, like making medical and psychological diagnoses (Patel & Ramoni, 1997; Weizenbaum, 1966), using what scientists call *artificial intelligence*. We humans built computers to take over some of our everyday processing of information, but does this mean that computers really function the same way as our minds do? No—even the fastest computers in the world cannot outthink the human mind!

«   Application

One of the greatest differences between computers and the human mind is the human capacity for **consciousness,** or an awareness of its own thoughts and the external world. When we focus our **attention** on something, we bring the stimulus into our consciousness and we become consciously aware of it. If we turn our attention inward, we become conscious of our own thoughts. If we focus our attention outward, we become conscious of the outside world. Computers do not have this ability because computers lack consciousness. A computer does not have an awareness of what it is doing in the manner that a human does.

consciousness   an organism's awareness of its own mental processes and/or its environment

attention   an organism's ability to focus its consciousness on some aspect of its own mental processes and/or its environment

Explicit Memory

Humans may have consciousness, but do we always know what's going on in our own memory? It appears that we do not. Human memory functions both in a conscious and a non-conscious fashion. Psychologists define the conscious use of memory as **explicit memory** (Bush & Greer, 2001; Graf & Schacter, 1985). We use explicit memory when we consciously search our memory for a previously stored bit of information. For ex-

explicit memory   the conscious use of memory

Is the mind just like a computer?

ample, try to answer the following question: "What part of the brain contains the cortex that processes visual information?" To answer, you must consciously search your memory for the information you learned in Chapter 2. We hope your search led you to the correct answer, the occipital lobe! While you were trying to answer this question, you were fully aware that you were searching your memory for the answer. In this respect, you were utilizing your memory explicitly.

We often use our memory in an explicit fashion—but not always. Sometimes we access and retrieve memories without having consciously tried to do so. For example, have you ever heard a song on the radio that caused you to spontaneously recall an old memory—perhaps a memory of an old friend you associate with the song or the exact place where you first heard the song? Or have you ever had some old memory pop into your head for no obvious reason? Most of us have had these experiences, in which previously stored memories were pulled into consciousness without our having consciously searched for them. These

implicit memory the unconscious use of memory

examples illustrate the phenomenon of **implicit memory,** which is the unconscious use of memory (Graf & Schacter, 1985; Squire, Knowlton, & Musen, 1993). For example, when we brush our teeth, tie our shoes, or make our bed, we usually do so without much conscious awareness of our body movements.

Implicit Memory and the Carrot Trick

Numerous studies on implicit memory have shown us that even when we are not consciously aware of it, our memory is still at work (for a review, see Richardson-Klavehn & Bjork, 1988). You can use the following demonstration to illustrate the function of implicit memory in your friends. This trick was first shown to one of the authors by a friend in graduate school. We do not know its origin, but give it a try anyway.

Demonstration

Get several of your friends to participate in this test, but conduct the test with only one participant at a time. Ahead of time, write the word "carrot" on a slip of paper and seal it in an envelope. Next, on a sheet of paper, write down 20 simple addition equations that add up to the number 14. For example: 8 + 6 = _____, 7 + 7 = _____, and so on. If you run out of combinations, it is OK to repeat the equations. Just be sure that all of them sum to 14. After you have done these things, you are ready to test your subjects.

Choose one of your friends and say, "I am going to try to read your mind, but first you must answer some questions." If he agrees, tell him that he should answer your questions as quickly as possible, without stopping to ponder his answers. Then quickly read the equations, one by one, pausing briefly for him to answer with the number 14. The object is to get the subject to say "14" over and over again. As soon as you have asked him to answer the last equation, quickly ask him to name the *first* vegetable that pops into his head. The chances are good that he will respond with "carrot"! You can then open the envelope with a flourish and tell him that you knew that he would say "carrot" because of your amazing ESP!

If you run this test on several of your friends, you should see that more people choose carrot over any other vegetable. How did we know that? As you might have guessed, we don't have ESP. Instead, our prediction that many subjects will say "carrot" is based on an understanding of how implicit memory works.

Have you guessed by now *why* people are likely to answer "carrot" when asked to think of a vegetable immediately after thinking and speaking the number 14? It has to do with the associations among concepts that we have stored in memory. Most of us associate the number 14 with the phrase "14 kt gold." So, while your participants said "14" over and over again, unconsciously the word "karat" was being activated in their memories. This activation, in turn, spread to the word "carrot" because the two words sound alike. When you asked your participants to name the first vegetable that popped into their heads, "carrot" was the most likely choice because it had already been activated, or *primed*, in memory. This demonstrates the function of implicit memory because the participants are not consciously aware that the word "carrot" is being activated. In fact, often participants are quite surprised that "carrot" is the first vegetable that pops into their head!

We have seen in this section that the function of memory involves three distinct processes: encoding, storage, and retrieval. We also saw that memory can be used in both a conscious, explicit fashion and an unconscious, implicit fashion. With this basic understanding of what memory does, we will move on to look at psychological theories of the structure and process of memory.

sensory memory   a system of memory that very briefly stores sensory impressions so that we can extract relevant information from them for further processing in memory

short-term memory   a system of memory that has both a limited capacity and duration; in the three stages model of memory, short-term memory is seen as the intermediate stage between sensory memory and long-term memory

Let's Review!

In this section, we discussed the functions of memory and described the difference between implicit and explicit use of memory. For a quick check of your understanding, answer these questions.

1. Putting money in the bank is analogous to which function of memory?

   a. encoding   c. retrieval

   b. storage   d. forgetting

2. Which of the following *best* illustrates the use of explicit memory?

   a. forgetting to get eggs at the grocery store

   b. trying to remember the name of a woman you once met at a party

   c. automatically thinking of a cat when you see a dog on TV

   d. guessing the correct answer on a multiple-choice test

3. Which of the following *best* illustrates the use of implicit memory?

   a. knowing the correct answer on a multiple-choice test

   b. trying to remember where you left your car keys

   c. forgetting where you left your car keys

   d. on a hunch, you guess the right answer on a multiple-choice test

ANSWERS

1. a; 2. b; 3. d

The Traditional Three Stages Model of Memory

> > > > > > > > > > >

The traditional view of memory conceptualizes it as being composed of three distinct stages of memory storage (Atkinson & Shiffrin, 1968). When information enters memory, its first stop is **sensory memory.** In sensory memory, information that comes in from our eyes, ears, and other senses is briefly stored in a sensory form, most often a sound or a visual image. If we pay attention to the information in our sensory memory, the information is sent on to the second stage, **short-term memory,** for further processing.

Short-term memory functions as a temporary holding tank for a limited amount of information. We can hold information in short-term memory for only a few seconds

LEARNING OBJECTIVES

≫ Describe the three stages model of memory.

≫ Describe the function and characteristics of sensory, short-term, and long-term memory.

≫ Describe the newer conception of working memory and how it relates to the three stage model of memory's concept of short-term memory.

before we must act to either send it further on in the memory system or to keep the information in short-term memory by refreshing it. If we do nothing, the information fades from short-term memory and is lost forever. For example, can you remember what you were thinking last night as you brushed your teeth? Probably not. Unless there was something important on your mind at the time, it is unlikely that you made note of it. If we decide to further process the information in short-term memory, we can move the information from temporary storage to the permanent storage system of **long-term memory.**

According to this model, we keep all of our permanent memories in our vast long-term memory storage system until we need to access them. Then we retrieve them from long-term memory back into short-term memory. Right now as you read this chapter, you store—very briefly—an image of these words in your sensory memory. From sensory memory, you move this information into short-term memory, where you hold it for a few seconds while you think about what you are reading. If you think hard enough about what you are reading, in a process known as *rehearsal*, and more commonly as *studying*, you will transfer this material to long-term memory. Then on test day, you will search your long-term memory for this information and pull it back into short-term memory when you need it to answer questions on your exam. Figure 6.2 gives a visual overview of the three stages model of memory. Forgetting can occur at any of the three stages of memory—but don't worry, when you have finished with this chapter, you will better understand how to prevent forgetting.

Sensory Memory: Where It All Begins

All of the information that enters our memory from the outside world must first pass through our senses. The information we receive from our sense organs lasts for a very brief period of time after the sensory stimulation has ended. This holding of the sensory information after the actual sensory stimulus ends is sensory memory. Perhaps you have noticed your sensory memory at work. Have you ever heard a fire engine's siren and then found that you could still hear the sound of the siren in your head for a short time after you could no longer actually hear the siren? If so, you caught your sensory memory at work!

Of all our senses, sight (iconic memory) and hearing (echoic memory), the two most studied by psychologists, are also the primary means through which we acquire information. But they are not the only useful senses. We also learn through our senses of taste, smell, and our sense of touch (haptic memory).

Visual Sensory Memory: Iconic Memory

Iconic memory is the sensory memory for visual stimuli. As we saw in Chapter 3, when you look at something, your eyes take in this information and *transduce* it into neural impulses (p. 100). These sensory impulses are then sent into the brain for further processing. To get information on what we have seen into our memory, our iconic memory takes a "snapshot" of our sensation and stores this image very briefly. This stored image is referred to as an *icon*.

Icons do not last very long. As soon as we see an object, an icon is formed (Coltheart, 1983), and it lasts for about only half a second before it decays (Sperling, 1960). Although icons do not last long, they last long enough for our minds to extract information about what we have seen and send it on to short-term memory. If the icon remained in our minds for a longer period of time, it is likely that it would overlap with icons for new visual stimuli, creating a confusing effect similar to that of superimposed photographs.

When you watch a movie, you experience this phenomenon of overlapping icons, but in this case the overlap leads to the illusion of movement. A movie is made up of

long-term memory   a system of memory that works to store memories in a long-term, or perhaps even a permanent fashion

iconic memory   sensory memory for visual information

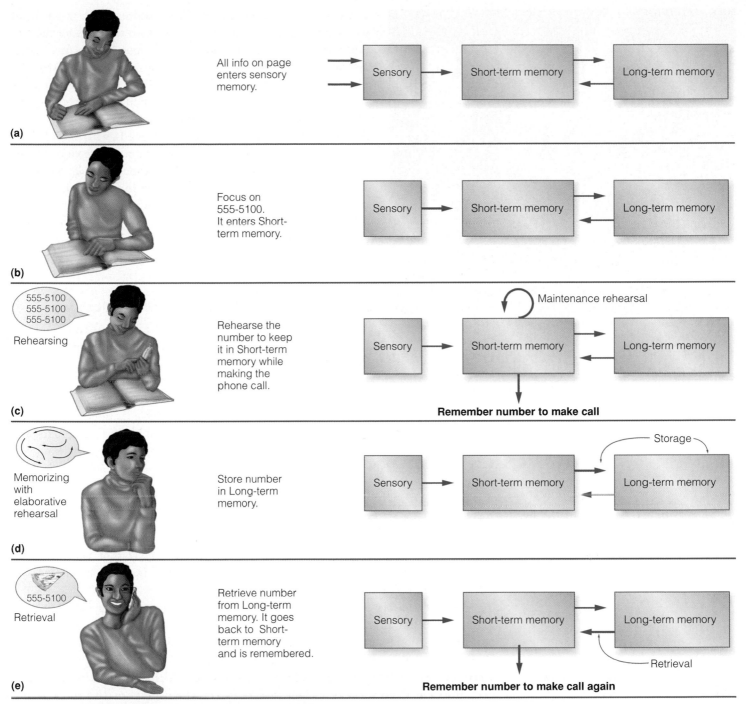

Figure 6.2 The Three Stages Model of Memory

(a). As Juanita looks up the phone number, the information enters into her visual sensory memory.
(b). As she focuses her attention on the phone number, the information now moves to her short-term memory. **(c).** To keep the number in mind while she goes to the phone and dials the pizza shop, Juanita uses maintenance rehearsal, repeating the number over and over to herself. **(d).** As Juanita continues to think about the number, she engages in elaborative rehearsal by associating the number to the idea of pizza in her mind—as a result the number is now stored in her long-term memory. **(e).** Later, Juanita retrieves the number from long-term memory when once again she wants to order a pizza.

frames, still shots all strung together, yet we perceive movement on the screen. How can we perceive movement when all we are seeing is a series of still pictures? The answer lies in the speed with which the frames of the movie are changed on the screen. The frames are projected on the screen at a speed faster than one frame per half second,

 Application

We perceive motion on the screen because the frames of film are projected at a speed that is faster than that at which our icons decay. The result is that when we see a frame of film on the screen and take an icon of it, we still have an icon of the previous frame in our mind. This overlap of icons gives us the perception of motion on the screen.

echoic memory sensory memory for auditory information

so the icon we make of an individual frame is still in our head when our eyes see the next frame. The icon we make for the second frame will be superimposed on the icon for the first frame, and we will perceive movement on the screen. To destroy the illusion of movement on the screen, all you would have to do is slow down the film. If you've ever watched old silent films, like Charlie Chaplin films, you probably noticed this effect. Silent films were shot and projected at slower speeds, with fewer frames per second. The result is less overlap of icons in the viewer's sensory memory, and so the movement in the film looks very jerky and halting. Our icons remain in effect long enough to allow us to perceive movement in movies, but not so long as to cause problems in our everyday perception of the world. We need to retain the icon only long enough for us to pay attention to it and transfer it to short-term memory. A similar process occurs when we hear something.

Auditory Sensory Memory: Echoic Memory

Auditory sensory memory is called **echoic memory.** When you hear something, your echoic memory makes an auditory image or recording of that sound and stores it briefly. This recording is called an *echo.* Echoes have a much longer duration than visual icons. Echoes last up to 2 seconds after your ears stop hearing the sound (Klatzky, 1980; Triesman, 1964). By holding the information you've just heard in echoic memory for 2 seconds, you have more time to process the information, which reduces the chance that you might miss something you hear. This is especially important for auditory information because once auditory information is lost, it is generally more difficult to retrieve than visual information.

For example, if your professor writes some important information on the board concerning an upcoming exam and you are not paying attention, all you have to do is look at the board again. If, instead, your professor gives the class the information verbally, and you do not hear the announcement the first time, you will be out of luck unless you can get someone to repeat the message for you. This is not as sure a bet as simply looking at the board again.

Because auditory information is easily lost, our echoic memory plays a crucial role in our processing of information. The echo you store of your professor's voice gives you a full 2 seconds after the message ends to process the information before it is lost. Perhaps you have reaped the benefits of echoic memory in the past. Have you ever asked someone to repeat herself, only to realize that you did, in fact, know what she had said? If so, you knew what she had said because your echoic memory gave you a second shot at processing her message. Think of how much you might have missed if it weren't for your echoic memory.

Transferring Information from Sensory to Short-Term Memory

As we have seen, the function of sensory memory is to hold sensory information long enough for us to process it and send it on to short-term memory for further processing. How do we transfer information from sensory memory to short-term memory? Does all sensory information reach short-term memory? Or do we lose some sensory information before it reaches short-term memory?

We receive an enormous amount of information everyday through our senses. Some of this information is important and needs to be processed more thoroughly in memory, but much of it does not need to be remembered or processed further. For

© Peter Turnley/Corbis

As you carry on a conversation, your echoic memory briefly stores a "recording" of the sounds you hear. This recording, called an echo, may help you avoid missing part of the conversation. If you didn't quite catch what your friend has just said, you have up to 2 seconds in which to reprocess the information still contained within the echo before this information is lost.

example, as you hold this book, do you need to be aware of the feel of the pages as you turn them? Tomorrow, will you have to recall and describe the ink color of these words, the exact texture of these pages, and the sounds the pages make as you turn them? What is important is the message of the text, and the rest is inconsequential. Because we receive so much useless sensory information each day, our memory system has mechanisms for getting rid of unneeded sensory information.

According to the three stages model, the transfer point between sensory memory provides one opportunity to eliminate unneeded information (Figure 6.2). For information to be transferred from sensory memory to short-term memory, we must first pay attention to the sensory information. We pay attention to something by focusing our consciousness on that stimulus. As you read this page, you pay attention to the words of this paragraph and you bring them into your consciousness. As you do this, you ensure that the sensory information held in the icons of these words will be transferred from iconic memory into short-term memory. Once the information is in short-term memory, it can be further processed into the permanent storage of long-term memory. At least, we hope that's what you're doing! If you are distracted or unmotivated, you could gaze at this page without paying attention to the words. In that case, the sensory information in the icons you store for the words on this page will be lost as the icons decay after a half second. As you can see, when you don't pay attention to what you are reading, you are wasting your time!

A lack of attention may have been one thing that caused Darron Terry to misidentify the woman who robbed his home. When Terry surprised the intruder, he was likely shocked and distracted, and he probably failed to pay close attention to many of the intruder's features and characteristics. He did remember that the intruder was female and had long blond hair, but much of the detailed information stored in the icon Terry took in of the intruder's face probably never made it to short-term memory! Later, when he tried to recall what she looked like, Terry probably had only a sketchy memory of the intruder's face. Under these circumstances, it is fairly easy to see how Terry could have incorrectly identified a suspect, especially one who resembled the intruder. Given the way memory works, many of us would have done the same thing under similar circumstances!

Attention is a necessary step in getting information into memory, but there is more to it than that. Once information makes it to your short-term memory, you have to take active steps to keep this information in memory.

Short-Term Memory: Where Memories Are Made (and Lost)

The three stages view of memory conceptualizes short-term memory as a temporary holding tank for information that has been transferred in from sensory memory (Figure 6.2). In sensory memory, information is encoded in its natural sensory form. Short-term memory uses a **dual-coding system** in which memories can be stored either visually or acoustically (Paivio, 1982).

dual-coding system a system of memory that encodes information in more than one type of code or format

Most verbal information appears to be encoded in short-term memory in an *acoustic* form. In other words, the information we store in short-term memory is primarily about the *sound* of the words that we are storing. This appears to be true even when the information we are storing came from our visual sensory memory. So, even if you initially read the material, you are still more likely to encode this information in an acoustic code (Conrad, 1964; Paivio, 1971).

When we see or hear a word, we draw out the sounds of the word from our sensory memory and temporarily store this information in our short-term memory. Try this example. Think about what you did yesterday. Can you "hear" your own voice describing the events in your mind? Most of us can. In this example, you are using the stored acoustic aspects of your memory as you recall yesterday's events. This type of acoustic information is what is most often stored in short-term memory.

We often store acoustic information in short-term memory, but we are also able to store visual information in short-term memory. When we are presented with information that is nonverbal, we may store it in a visual form in short-term memory. For example, if you see a picture of a house, you might store the memory of the house in the form of a visual image. The fact that information can be stored in either an acoustic or visual form in short-term memory gives us flexibility as we process information. You may recall the directions to a place of business in the next town visually or auditorally.

Although short-term memory serves us well, it is another point in the system where information can be lost. If you look again at Figure 6.2, you will see that from short-term memory, information either transfers to long-term memory or is lost. Because short-term memory is designed for temporary memory storage, both its capacity and duration are limited. If you've ever tried to hold a phone number in your head while you make it to the phone, then you know just how limited short-term memory is and how susceptible it is to forgetting!

The Capacity of Short-Term Memory: Seven (Plus or Minus Two)

In 1956, psychologist George Miller published a landmark paper on the capacity of short-term memory. In this research, Miller had participants try to remember as many items from a list as they could. Using this type of approach, Miller found that the average subject could hold about 7 ± 2 items in her short-term memory. This 7 ± 2 capacity applies to such items as numbers, words, and other small bits of information.

 **Demonstration**

To illustrate the capacity of short-term memory, read the following list of numbers to a friend and then immediately after, ask them to recall as many of the numbers as they can. We bet you'll find that they are able to remember only around 7 ± 2 of them.

1, 7, 3, 0, 6, 2, 4, 1, 8, 6, 7, 4, 0, 8, 1, 3, 5, 2, 8, 9, 1

Given this 7 ± 2 capacity, we can easily hold a phone number, short grocery list, or the name of a person we just met in our short-term memory. But what if we need to hold more information in our short-term memory? Can we fit more than seven items in this memory store? Maybe. One technique for extending the amount of information we can hold in short-term memory is called **chunking** (Simon, 1974). Chunking involves grouping information together into meaningful units, or *chunks*. Take the following string of digits as an example:

3127241257

You could view this as ten separate numbers:

3 1 2 7 2 4 1 2 5 7

Or, you could chunk this digit string into three numbers:

312 724 1257

Does this grouping look familiar to you? You probably cannot keep ten separate numbers in your short-term memory, but you can—and probably often do—keep three chunks in short-term memory with little difficulty. Many of the important numbers in our culture—social security numbers, phone numbers, license plates, credit card numbers, and so on—are usually presented to us in a prechunked style so as to facilitate our memory for them!

However, there is also a limit to how much information can be chunked. The number of chunks that we can store in short-term memory decreases as the size of the chunks gets larger. In other words, you can hold more 3-digit numbers in short-term memory than you can 8-digit numbers (Simon, 1974). Think of short-term memory as a bookshelf. You can fit only so many books on the shelf at one time. If the books are skinny, you can fit as many as 9. If the books are fat, you will be able to fit only 4 or 5. If you add more books to an already full shelf, some books will be pushed off. Like the bookshelf in our metaphor, the capacity of short-term memory is similarly limited. The magic number 7 holds, but only for relatively small chunks of information.

chunking the process of using one's limited short-term memory resources more efficiently by combining small bits of information to form larger bits of information, or chunks

《 | Application

The Duration of Short-Term Memory: It's Yours for 20 Seconds

Duration is the second major limitation on short-term memory. Once information passes into short-term memory, it can only be kept there for around 20 seconds without some type of rehearsal or refreshing of the material (Brown, 1958; Peterson & Peterson, 1959).

In a typical experiment to determine the duration of short-term memory, participants hear a 3-letter combination or syllable (such as HJL) and are asked to remember it. Immediately after, the participants are asked to start counting backward by threes from some starting number (for example, starting with 505: 502, 499, 496, . . .). Counting backward prevents the participants from studying or rehearsing the syllable they heard. To measure how well the participants retain the syllable in short-term memory, the researchers stop the counting at specific intervals and ask the participants to recall the syllable. Figure 6.3 shows the retention as a function of time. As you can see, retention drops off rapidly. After only 18 seconds, the participants failed to remember many of the words.

So what if you have to keep some information in short-term memory for more than 20 seconds? Suppose you look up a phone number and have to remember it while you take a 2-minute walk to the pay phone. If you can't write the phone number down, you need to find a way to keep it in your short-term memory for longer than 20 seconds. Off the top of your head, what do you think you would you do in this situation? One simple solution would be to repeat the phone number over and over out loud as you walk to the phone. This repetition of the material in short-term memory is called

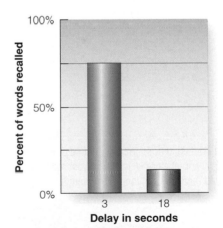

Figure 6.3 Short-Term Memory Duration

As you can see, the duration of short-term memory is very limited. Without rehearsal, information stored in short-term memory will be lost in a matter of seconds. Peterson and Peterson (1959) found that participants could remember most of a list of words 3 seconds after hearing it, but few of the words were recalled after 18 seconds.

maintenance rehearsal repeating information over and over again to keep it in short-term memory for an extended period of time

maintenance rehearsal, and is useful for extending the duration of short-term memory. When you repeat the information over and over again, you resupply it to short-term memory before it can decay. The information goes back through echoic memory, and it reenters short-term memory, where it can sit for another 20 seconds or so before you must repeat the number to yourself again. You can keep this up all day, as long as no one interrupts or distracts you!

How We Transfer Information From Short-Term to Long-Term Memory

Maintenance rehearsal may be useful for keeping information in short-term memory, but what if you want to move information from short-term memory into permanent, long-term memory storage? We know from Figure 6.2 that rehearsal moves information from short-term memory into long-term memory, but not just any type of rehearsal will do the trick. Maintenance rehearsal accomplishes only a *weak* transfer of information into long-term memory (Glenberg, Smith, & Green, 1977; Lockhart & Craik, 1990). You may have learned this lesson the hard way if repetition is your primary means of studying material for exams. If you simply repeat information over and over in your head, or repeatedly read over the information in your text and notes, your studying will not accomplish strong transfer of information into long-term memory, and you may find yourself in trouble on test day.

Elaborative Rehearsal

elaborative rehearsal forming associations or links between information one is trying to learn with information already stored in long-term memory so as to facilitate the transfer of this new information into long-term memory

Repetition of information is merely maintenance rehearsal. As we just saw, the main function of maintenance rehearsal is to keep information in short-term memory—and information in short-term memory is only temporary! To really get information into your long-term memory, you use another type of rehearsal, called **elaborative rehearsal** (Craik & Lockhart, 1972). Elaborative rehearsal involves forming *associations*, or mental connections, between the information in short-term memory that you want to store and information you already have stored in your permanent long-term memory. For example, we have been encouraging you to generate personally relevant examples of the material you are learning in this text. Every time you generate an example from your own life that demonstrates a psychological principle, you are engaging in elaborative rehearsal and you will have a better chance of recalling the material later.

Application

Levels of Processing

levels-of-processing model a model that predicts that information that is processed deeply and elaboratively will be best retained in and recalled from long-term memory

This notion that the more thoroughly or deeply you process information, the more strongly you transfer it to long-term memory is referred to as the **levels-of-processing model** of memory (Craik & Lockhart, 1972). When Fergus Craik and Robert Lockhart (1972) first proposed the levels-of-processing approach, it was assumed that the *only* way to get information into long-term memory was to use elaborative rehearsal. Subsequent research has shown that this isn't necessarily the case. Although maintenance rehearsal is a shallow form of processing that doesn't involve much elaboration of the material, it will allow for some transfer of information into long-term memory (Lockhart & Craik, 1990). For example, you may eventually remember your checking account number if you have to write it, and thus repeat it, frequently enough. However, the type of transfer to long-term memory that occurs with maintenance rehearsal doesn't really help students pass an exam in which they actually have to understand what they are talking or writing about! In one study, it was found that if you increase the amount of your maintenance rehearsal by 9 times (900%), you increase your recall of the information only by 1.5% (Glenberg, Smith, & Green, 1977). On the other hand, elaborative rehearsal involves a very deep level of processing, in that to elaborate material, you must access information stored in long-term memory and associate it to the information you are trying to learn. This requires much more effort and thought than merely mentally repeating the information over and over. The good news is that this effort pays off in terms of better memory for the information. Elaborative rehearsal is clearly your best bet if you want to successfully master the material in a course.

As an example, let's say that in zoology class you learn about a new species of animal, the *kiwi*. You learn that the kiwi is a flightless bird native to New Zealand, and that it is unique among birds because it has some features that are similar to those of mammals. Like a mammal, the kiwi has bone marrow, a higher body temperature, and a well-developed sense of smell. In contrast, most birds have hollow bones, lower body temperatures, and a poorly developed sense of smell. Kiwis are also notable because they lay very large eggs.

If you want to commit information about the kiwi to long-term memory, you must associate it with what you already know in your long-term memory. For example, you would want to think about how a kiwi is like other mammals that you know, like cats and dogs. Kiwis, cats, and dogs all share a well-developed sense of smell and have marrow in their bones. You may go on to think about what having bone marrow implies about the kiwi's immune system or how the kiwi may be able to use its sense of smell to find food the way a dog might.

You could also think about how a kiwi is like a bird. A kiwi lays an egg the size of an ostrich egg, yet a kiwi is the size of a chicken. A kiwi has wings, but does not fly. Chickens also have wings, but they cannot fly very well. Do you see what we're doing here? We are finding ways to *associate* and *link* the kiwi to concepts that you already have stored in long-term memory, like dogs, cats, and chickens. This is what elaborative rehearsal is all about. You go beyond simply repeating information to actually *think* about the information, and in doing so, you process the information deeply enough to efficiently transfer it to long-term memory.

A kiwi is a bird from New Zealand.

When you use elaborative rehearsal as you study, you will retain the information in the permanent storage system of long-term memory in a way that maximizes the chances that you will be able to retrieve it when you need it, like on test day!

Does Short-Term Memory Really Exist?

Recall that the three stages model proposes short-term memory as a separate, intermediate stage of memory that is limited in capacity and duration (Figure 6.2). As you learned in Chapter 1, any scientific theory must be backed up by the results of scientific experiments before we place much stock in it. As you will shortly see, not all of the available research supports the three stages model, particularly in its conception of short-term memory. Let's take a look at the evidence that supports and that calls into doubt the three stages model.

The Serial-Position Curve, Primacy, and Recency

In a serial-position experiment, participants listen to a list of around 20 words slowly read aloud by the experimenter. Immediately following the last word, the participants are asked to engage in *free recall* of the words, that is, to recall the words in any order that they can. The tendency for the participants to recall the words correctly is plotted against the position of the word in the original list. Figure 6.4 shows a typical serial-position curve. You will notice in Figure 6.4 that not all of the words in the list have an equal chance of being recalled by the participants. Rather, words at the beginning and the end of the list are better recalled than words in the center of the list.

Figure 6.4
Serial-Position Curve

In a serial-position experiment (Murdoch, 1962), participants are asked to remember a list of words that are read aloud to them. In such an experiment, words at the beginning of the list (primacy effect) and words at the end of the list (recency effect) are best remembered.

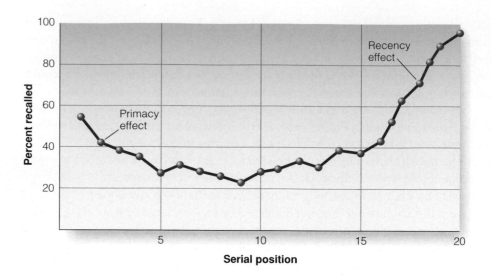

primacy effect the tendency for people to recall words from the beginning of a list better than words that appeared in the middle of the list

recency effect the tendency for people to recall words from the end of a list better than words that appeared in the middle of the list

The overall shape of the serial-position curve fits well with the three stages view of memory. In fact, the three stages model predicts that you will obtain a curve like that shown in Figure 6.4. The tendency for the words at the beginning of the list to be better recalled, the **primacy effect,** can be explained in terms of long-term memory. As the participants listen to the list of words, they spend considerable time rehearsing the words at the beginning of the list in their short-term memory. While they are doing this, they have no short-term memory capacity left to rehearse the words in the center of the list. Therefore, words in the center of the list are lost from short-term memory, but the words at the beginning of the list are moved to long-term memory and thus are remembered well at recall.

The words at the end of the list are also well remembered, in what is called the **recency effect.** The recency effect is thought to occur because participants still have these words in short-term memory at the time they are asked to recall the list. Therefore, all the participants have to do is dump these words from their short-term memory before going on to retrieve the other words (from the beginning of the list) from long-term memory. In the serial position experiment, participants should be able to recall the last two or three words they heard from the list (Glanzer & Cunitz, 1966). The recency effect does not extend to the full 7 ± 2 capacity of short-term memory because some of the capacity of short-term memory is taken up in rehearsing the words from the start of the list and continuing to hear new words.

Although numerous serial position experiments support the three stages model of memory, some scientists still express doubts about the model, especially its conception of short-term memory. One lingering question is whether short-term memory is one single storage system. Anecdotal evidence from case studies suggests that short-term memory may not be a single storage system. One case concerns a man named K.F., who suffered damage to his left parietal and occipital lobes in a motorcycle accident. After the accident, K.F. had no impairment of his long-term memory, but he did experience problems with his short-term memory. K.F.'s memory span was greatly reduced, and he had a very small recency effect during serial position experiments (Shallice & Warrington, 1970). These findings indicate that K.F. had lost some of his short-term memory functioning, but further research produced findings that are inconsistent with the three stages view of short-term memory. K.F. was found to have noticeable problems with his short-term memory for orally presented letters and digits, but fewer problems with visually presented stimuli (Warrington & Shallice, 1972). K.F. also had no short-term memory problems for sounds that were not words, such as sirens and car horns (Shallice & Warrington, 1974). These findings suggest that K.F.'s short-term memory was not a single storage system. If it were, he would have had problems with *all* types of short-term memory.

The case study of K.F. does not prove that short-term memory consists of multiple storage systems. As you learned in Chapter 1, cases studies are of limited value in helping us understand how the average person functions (p. 28). It is possible that K.F.'s brain and mind functioned differently from the rest of us even before his accident. However, the case of K.F. raises some interesting concerns about the three stages view of short-term memory.

Another potential problem with the three stages model has to do with how it proposes we process information in memory. The three stages model proposes that the only route for information to reach long-term memory is through short-term memory. There is some doubt as to whether this is true (Logie, 1999). If information must pass from sensory memory into short-term memory without having made contact with long-term memory, then long-term memory is activated only *after* information is processed in short-term memory. The problem is that this will not always be the case. If you are given a list of seven words to remember, you will likely use maintenance rehearsal (repeating the words over and over to yourself) to keep these words in short-term memory. To do so, you would have to know how to pronounce the words, which you could only know by accessing your knowledge (from long-term memory) of how to pronounce the words. You must access and retrieve information in long-term memory *before* you have processed the information into long-term memory (Logie, 1999).

These questions about whether or not short-term memory is a single storage system and whether or not short-term memory is wholly separate from long-term memory have cast doubt on the traditional three stages model of memory and led to the development of alternative views of memory. One of the most influential alternatives to the three stages model is the *working memory* view of memory (Baddeley, 1986; Baddeley & Hitch, 1974).

The Working Memory View: Master and Slaves

Today, many researchers reject the notion that information passes sequentially through the three stages of memory and instead propose a view of memory that suggests a new type of memory called **working memory** (for a review, see Richardson et al., 1996). The working memory model views the memory stages in more of a *parallel* fashion as opposed to a *serial* fashion. In this view, working memory and short-term memory are parts contained within long-term memory (Figure 6.5). Working memory moves information into and out of long-term memory, whereas, short-term memory operates as

working memory a multi-faceted component of long-term memory that contains short-term memory, a central executive, a phonological loop, and a visuospatial sketch pad; the function of working memory is to access, move, and process information that we are currently using

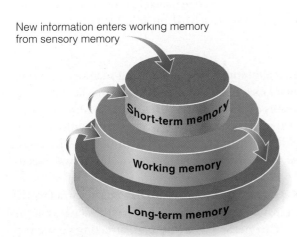

New information enters working memory from sensory memory

- Working memory retrieves information from Long-term memory to help process information in Short-term memory—for example, the meaning of words stored in short-term memory may be accessed from Long-term memory.

- Working memory also retrieves stored information when you need it—for an exam, your address, directions to your aunt's house—and sends it to Short-term memory.

- Working memory also moves information from Short-term memory into Long-term memory for storage—for example, when you are studying, working memory will move the information you want to remember in Long-term memory.

Figure 6.5 **The Working Memory View of Memory**

In the working memory view of memory, the stages of memory work in more of a parallel fashion rather than a sequential fashion. In this view, short-term memory and working memory are parts of memory that are contained within long-term memory. Working memory moves information in and out of both short-term and long-term memory as necessary.

the part of working memory that briefly stores the information that we are using at any one particular time.

Suppose a bee stings you. As your haptic sensory memory registers the pain of the sting and the sight of the bee and sends it on to short-term memory, your working memory may simultaneously activate a long-term memory of what you learned in first-aid class about allergic reactions to bee stings. Working memory pulls this information on allergic reactions into short-term memory, and you now consciously think about the signs of an allergic reaction as you check to see if you are having one. You conclude that you are not having an allergic reaction. So you cease to think about the possibility of an allergic reaction, and working memory transfers the new knowledge that you are not allergic to bee stings to long-term memory.

As you can see, in this view of memory, information does not flow sequentially from sensory to short-term to long-term memory. Rather, working memory plays several roles. The short-term memory part of working memory acts as a storage system for information that is currently being used. At the same time, other parts of working memory act to retrieve information, process new information, and send new and revised information on to long-term memory. The order in which the different memory stages are activated can vary depending on the circumstances.

One advantage of the working memory model is that it can explain why we sometimes seem to access long-term memory before we process information in short-term memory. Take, for instance, the phenomenon of *top down perceptual processing* that you learned about in Chapter 3 (p. 138). Top-down perceptual processing occurs when we use stored knowledge (from long-term memory) to interpret sensory information. As you read the words on this page, you must access information that you have stored in long-term memory about the English language so that you can pronounce and read these words. As the words on the page enter your short-term memory, you know what they mean and how they are pronounced. The working memory view of memory can explain this, but the three stages model cannot. Because the working memory view is more of a parallel-processing model, it allows for the possibility that you can access long-term memory as you are reading the words on the page. In this model, you can go to your long-term memories to help you process perceptual information in a top-down fashion (Logie, 1996).

Another advantage of the working memory view of memory is that it can explain some of the memory data found in people like K.F. who suffer from brain damage. As you will recall, the three stages model of memory didn't fit K.F.'s case because he had problems with some, but not all, aspects of his short-term memory. The selective nature of K.F.'s short-term memory problems argued against the three stages model of a single short-term memory store (Shallice & Warrington, 1974; Warrington & Shallice, 1972). In the working memory model, such selective problems could occur because working memory is not viewed as a single entity (Richardson et al., 1996).

The Central Executive

One of the more prominent theories of a multicomponent working memory proposes that working memory contains a **central executive** component and two slave systems: the **phonological loop,** which processes auditory information (e.g., the buzzing of a bee), and the **visuospatial sketch pad,** which processes visual and spatial information (e.g., the sight of a bumble bee); (Baddeley, 1992; Baddeley & Hitch, 1974). These systems are called slave systems because they fall under the control of the central executive (Figure 6.6).

The central executive functions as an attention-controlling mechanism within working memory. The central executive must coordinate the actions of the slave systems and integrate information that comes in from these systems (e.g., directing you to pay attention to how close a bee gets to your arm). This makes the central executive com-

central executive the attention-controlling component of working memory

phonological loop in the working memory model, the part of working memory that processes the phonological, or sound, qualities of information

visuospatial sketch pad in the working memory model, the part of working memory that processes the visual and spatial aspects of information

Figure 6.6
Baddeley's Central Executive Model of Working Memory

In Baddeley's model of working memory, the central executive part of working memory integrates visual information from the visuospatial sketch pad and auditory information from the phonological loop. The integration of information that the central executive provides is crucial when we are engaged in activities that require us to use both visual and auditory information—as in deciding how to react when you both see and hear nearby bumblebees.

ponent especially important when we are engaged in tasks that require attention and the coordination of visual and auditory information, such as when playing a video game (Baddeley, 1992). Recently, some researchers have proposed that faulty executive functioning—or an inability to direct one's attention while using working memory—may be one of the underlying mechanisms in attention deficit hyperactivity disorder (ADHD) in children (Sonuga-Barke, Dalen, & Remington, 2003).

Interestingly, there is also evidence to suggest that one of the results of Alzheimer's disease, which is characterized by an increasing loss of memory, is a loss of central executive functioning (Crowell, Luis, Vanderploeg, Schinka, & Mullan, 2002). The loss of central executive functioning in Alzheimer's patients can be seen when the patients are asked to do visual and auditory tasks at the same time. Because their central executive is not functioning properly, the Alzheimer's patients have trouble coordinating and integrating information from visual and auditory sources, and they experience more problems than a normal person does on the simultaneous tasks. However, when the Alzheimer's patients are tested on a single task that is scaled to their ability, the Alzheimer's patients do not perform more poorly than control participants on the single task (Baddeley, Logie, Bressi, Della Sala, & Spinnler, 1986). This pattern of results supports

 **Application**

the notion that the structure of working memory has multiple components, with at least one component that integrates information.

The central executive model of working memory also fits well with K.F.'s memory problems. As you will recall, K.F. had substantial problems holding most auditory information in short-term memory (p. 264). The pattern of K.F.'s problems seems to work with the idea of a central executive and its two slave systems, the phonological loop and the visuospatial sketch pad. If we assume that K.F.'s brain damage affected the phonological loop part of his working memory, but not the visuospatial sketch pad, we would expect him to have trouble processing auditory information, but not to have trouble processing visual information. This is exactly what we see in the case of K.F.!

The working memory view of memory offers a more complex model than the traditional three stages model, one that explains more of what researchers observe about memory. This does not mean, however, that psychologists have a complete understanding of how memory works. There is disagreement even among working memory theorists as to exactly what role working memory plays in the memory system (Richardson et al., 1996). Theorists also disagree as to whether working memory is separate from long-term memory. Not all researchers are convinced that working memory is composed of multiple components, and those who are convinced of its multiplicity do not agree on the number of components in working memory. Future research will have to sort out some of these issues before we have a full understanding of how memory is temporarily stored and processed as it passes to and from long-term memory.

Let's Review!

In this section, we described the three stages model of memory and its limitations. We also introduced the newer idea of working memory that deals with some of the limits of the three stages model. For a quick check of your understanding, answer these questions.

1. Which view of memory holds that information must pass through the memory storage systems in a specific sequence?
   a. the three stages model
   b. the working memory view of memory
   c. the parallel processing view of memory
   d. all of the above

2. When you are talking on the phone with your friend, which component of working memory are you *least* likely to be using?

   a. the phonological loop
   b. the central executive
   c. the visuospatial sketch pad
   d. short-term memory

3. Which of the following is the *best* example of elaborative rehearsal?
   a. reading and outlining a chapter in your text
   b. outlining the material from your text and your lecture notes
   c. using flashcards of key concepts in the chapter
   d. repeatedly reading over your lecture notes

ANSWERS
1. a; 2. c; 3. b

LEARNING OBJECTIVES

Explain how memory is organized in long-term memory.

Describe the different types of long-term memory and their characteristics.

Long-Term Memory: Permanent Storage

According to both of the two memory models we've explored—the three stages model and the working memory model—long-term memory is our largest and most permanent memory storage system (Figures 6.2 and 6.5). Long-term memory is where we store information that we wish to keep for a long period of time. Information there remains unconscious until we activate it and call it into working memory or short-term memory.

For example, in our case of Darron Terry and Mellissa Gammill, we can presume that some information about the intruder made it into Terry's long-term memory. If it hadn't, Terry would have had *no* idea what she looked like. The memory of the intruder's face was stored in Terry's long-term memory waiting to be retrieved when it was needed. When Terry recalled the incident for police, he would have retrieved from long-term memory any relevant information about the incident and the burglar. (He probably retrieved this information *whenever* he thought of the burglary.) Later in this chapter, we will see that repeated retrieval can actually *decrease* the accuracy of long-term memories, which may have further contributed to Darron Terry's mistaken identification of Mellissa Gammill. First, however, we must get a better feel for the nature of the long-term memory.

The Capacity of Long-Term Memory

For all practical purposes, long-term memory seems to have a limitless capacity. To date, psychologists have not found any reason to believe that long-term memory has a limited capacity in the manner that short-term memory and working memory do. We can safely say that you are unlikely to ever run out of room in your long-term memory. It may sometimes feel like your brain is full, but you still have the capacity to store more information in long-term memory. What you are feeling is more likely to be related to problems in focusing your attention or a lack of available capacity in short-term or working memory. If you can pay enough attention to move the information through sensory memory to short-term/working memory, and then rehearse the material enough to get it to long-term memory, you will find that you have ample storage space for the information!

Although you may sometimes feel as if your long-term memory is "full," you always have the capacity to store information—provided that you are not too tired, distracted, or unmotivated to rehearse and elaborate the material you wish to learn.

© David Butow/Corbis SABA

Encoding in Long-Term Memory

Information is encoded in long-term memory in several forms. As in the other parts of memory storage, information in long-term memory may be stored in both acoustic and visual forms (Paivo, 1986). However, we more often encode long-term memories semantically in terms of the meaning of the information. **Semantic encoding** stores the gist, or general meaning, of the stimulus rather than storing all of the sensory details (Anderson, 1974; Gernsbacher, 1985; Wanner, 1968).

semantic encoding encoding memory traces in terms of the meaning of the information being stored

Semantic encoding may offer some distinct advantages over acoustic and visual encoding in long-term memory even though it sacrifices a lot of the details. For example, if you read a description of a kiwi in a zoology textbook, you could store information about the sound of the word, *kiwi*, or the visual image of a kiwi in your long-term memory, but this won't do much for you on test day. What do you think is truly important in memory? Do you need to store an *exact* picture of a kiwi? If you have an *exact* picture of kiwi in your memory—but that's all the kiwi information you have—what would you still not know about kiwis? Would you know that a kiwi is from New Zealand and that it has marrow in its bones like a mammal does? The visual image of kiwi wouldn't help you here. You could know what every feather on a kiwi looks like, and still not know *what* a kiwi is. On the other hand, you could store the following semantic information about the kiwi:

A kiwi is a bird.

Like all birds, a kiwi has feathers.

A kiwi is as big as a chicken.

Like a mammal, kiwis have marrow in their bones.

With this information, you will be able to answer many more test questions about the kiwi.

Similarly, as you read this page, you do not need to store a visual image of the page or an acoustic recording of your voice reading these words. You need to store the gist of the information contained on this page and how the information relates to what you have already stored in long-term memory. You accomplish this by encoding this information—in a semantic code—and connecting this new information with the other information you have already stored in long-term memory.

Organization in Long-Term Memory

One aspect of encoding information in long-term memory is how we organize it. What would life be like if you did not organize the contents of your long-term memory? Think of your long-term memory as a library. Imagine going to the library to look for a specific book, only to find that the librarians had been tossing the books up on the shelf, in no particular order, for the last 10 years. How would you find the book you need? You would have to start on the first shelf of the first bookcase and search book by book until you found the book that you were seeking! This could take considerable time, and you could also make a mistake and overlook the book you were searching for.

The same thing would occur if your long-term memory had no organization. Every time you tried to retrieve a memory or a bit of knowledge, you might have to search through everything in your memory! To make matters worse, you have much more information in your long-term memory than there are books in a library (Landauer, 1986).

Over the years, psychologists have proposed various means by which we organize our knowledge categorically (for a review, see Anderson, 2000). One of these strategies involves the use of a generalized knowledge structure called a **schema** (Bartlett, 1932; Rumelhart, 1980). We have *schemata* (plural for schema) for people, places, concepts, events, groups of people, and just about everything else that we know.

schema an organized, generalized knowledge structure in long-term memory

Schemata can be thought of as filing systems we use for knowledge about particular concepts. Schemata contain general information on the characteristics of the concept's category, its function, and so on. For each of these general characteristics, the schema has slots for information specific to the concept. For example, let's look at a portion of a hypothetical schema for a kiwi. On the left are the names of the slots in the schema found for *birds*. On the right are the specific bits of information that would be placed in these slots for the kiwi.

Kiwi

Is a:	bird
Has:	feathers, beak, wings, legs, feet
Abilities:	flightless; has a great sense of smell; lays eggs
Size:	chicken-sized
Location:	New Zealand
Egg size:	very large, ostrich-sized

These slots can also have default values that are used when information is missing from our perception. For instance, if you did not read that the kiwi was flightless, you might assume that because the kiwi is a bird, it must be able to fly. One of the default values for the slot "abilities" may be "able to fly." We probably rely on these default values in schemata when we engage in *top-down perceptual processing* (p. XX). For instance, look at the picture of the kiwi in Figure 6.7. Even though you can see only the kiwi's head, do you have a good idea of what the rest of the kiwi looks like? Sure, because your schema for a bird tells you that most birds have two legs, feet, wings, and a feather-covered body!

Obviously, kiwis are not the only objects for which we have schemata. In fact, we have schemata for many different types of information. In addition to schemata for objects, we have schemata for abstract concepts, like psychology, love, and hate. We also have schemata to categorize our social world. We use *person schemata* for specific people, such as one's best friend, mother, or brother, *stereotypes* for groups of people, such as Blacks, Whites, Latinos, and so on, and *scripts* for events, like going to the doctor, eating at a fancy restaurant, or going on a date. In Chapter 12, we will take a closer look at how schemata affect our behavior in social situations.

© Bank of New Zealand Kiwi Recovery Trust

Figure 6.7
Schematic Assumptions
Schematic assumptions help us fill in missing details in our perceptions and memories. As you look at this picture, what assumptions do you make about this kiwi?

Types of Long-Term Memory

Most research on memory has concerned itself with a type of explicit memory called **declarative memory.** Declarative memory is memory for knowledge that can be easily verbalized: names, dates, events, concepts, and so on. Declarative memory can be divided into two subtypes: **semantic memory,** which is conceptual memory, and **episodic memory,** which is memory for the events in one's life.

Right now, as you read this chapter, you are adding to your semantic memory. As you read and study the chapter, you will add to the schemata you have stored in long-term memory for the concepts in the chapter. For example, you may think of semantic and episodic memories from your own life and tie your growing knowledge of psychology to the well-formed schemata you have for the world. By building and strengthening these schemata, you are helping to build a knowledge base for psychology that will later enable you to apply this information to problems that require some understanding of psychology, including the exam on test day!

As you attend school and go about the business of your everyday life, you are also adding to your episodic memory (Tulving, 1972; Wheeler, Stuss, & Tulving, 1997). Episodic memory, sometimes referred to as autobiographical memory, contains your

declarative memory   a type of long-term memory that encompasses memories that are easily verbalized including episodic and semantic memories

semantic memory   long-term, declarative memory for conceptual information

episodic memory   long-term, declarative memory for autobiographical events

Episodic memory gives us our past—such as these childhood memories.

memory of what has happened in your life. You store memories of your conversations with others, events you have attended, and your activities in your episodic, or autobiographical, memory. Episodic memories are associated with a unique sense of personal awareness (Wheeler et al., 1997). Later, when you remember reading this chapter, you will experience a sense of *self-knowing* as you recall this episodic memory. You'll think, *I* was there. *I* remember reading that chapter. This self-awareness makes episodic memory the most personal part of our long-term memory. It is because of episodic memory that we have cherished memories of childhood, our first date, or days spent with dear friends. In fact, if you think about it, our entire sense of history is largely based on the episodic memories that have been stored both in our mind and those of others who have gone before us (Cappelletto, 2003).

Take a moment now to recall some of your own episodic memories. What comes to mind when you think of your past? Is it easy to recall the events of your life, or is it a struggle? Interestingly, researchers have found that how easily you recall episodic memories may be a function of your gender (Colley, Ball, Kirby, Harvey, & Vingelen, 2002; Niedzwienska, 2003). Why would gender be related to recall of episodic memories? For the answer, check out It's a Diverse World.

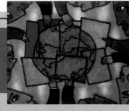

IT'S A DIVERSE WORLD

Gender and Autobiographical Memory

In 1999, researcher Penelope Davis decided to ask a question that hadn't received much attention to date: Do men and women differ with respect to their childhood memories? Davis hypothesized that when it came to recalling their childhood, women might be able to outperform men. Prior research had shown that when discussing past events, parents tend to *elaborate* more with their daughters than they do with their sons. In other words, parents tend to discuss past events in more detail with their daughters. For example, a parent is more likely to discuss with a daughter how a family trip to the zoo affects other family members. A parent is less likely to discuss such implications with a son. Indeed, parents are less likely to even discuss social events with their sons (Buckner & Fivush, 2002).

These different styles of communication between parents and their children may ultimately influence how children later recall childhood events. As we saw earlier in this chapter, the more elaboration that takes place at encoding, the more easily the information will be retrieved. If parents engage in conversations with their daughters that encourage elaboration of autobiographic information, then it stands to reason that females should have an easier time retrieving memories of childhood events from long-term memory.

To test this hypothesis, Davis (1999) conducted a series of five experiments in which she asked males and females to recall as many events from their childhood as they could in a given time frame. In one experiment, Davis asked her participants to retrieve memories under six different conditions. In the first condition, the participants were asked to free-recall as many childhood memories as they could in a 4-minute time frame. In the five other recall conditions, the participants were told by the experimenter: "I'm going to name a feeling and I want you to recall as many different times as you can when you felt this way." The experimenter then asked the participants to recall instances in which they felt happy, sad, angry, fearful/anxious, and self-conscious. For each of these emotions, the participants were allowed 4 minutes to name as many memories of times they had felt the emotion. As she predicted, Davis found that the females were able to consistently recall more memories than their male counterparts, and they were generally faster at this recall.

The story doesn't end here, however. Recall that in the first condition, participants were not guided in their recall. They simply had to recall any childhood memories, and these memories did not have to be associated with any particular emotion. It turns out that Davis's participants still recalled many emotion-laden memories in this condition because, in general, our autobiographical memories tend to be emotional. This brings up the question of whether or not females would recall more childhood memories if the memories were nonemotional. To address

Years from now, will these two people have different recollections of this date?

this question, Davis looked at the memories retrieved by the participants in the free-recall condition and categorized them as being emotional or nonemotional. She then reanalyzed her data to see if gender interacted with the emotional content of the participant's memories. What she found was that the female participants were only better at recalling emotional childhood memories!

Davis hypothesized that gender differences are evident only for emotional memories because females' greater tendency to elaborate is particular to emotional event memories. To test this notion, Davis first had all participants retrieve emotion-laden childhood memories. Then they were asked to sort their memories into categories of memories that seemed to go together. The participants were free to use as many or as few categories as they chose. As predicted, the females sorted their memories into significantly more categories than the males did. From these data, Davis concluded that females' enhanced autobiographical memory for emotional events is due to the fact that women tend to organize their autobiographical memories into more diverse categories. In other words, women have been socialized to do more elaborative processing of emotion-laden autobiographical memories, and this processing pays off in terms of better recall.

Just as we saw with semantic memory, elaboration also enhances episodic memory. Does this mean that our episodic and semantic memories are stored in the same fashion? In our next section, we take a look at research that addresses this question.

Currently in psychology, there is some debate over whether episodic memories are stored in the same manner as semantic memories. Although it is controversial, a number of recent studies suggest that episodic and semantic memory may indeed be separate memory systems (Graham, Simons, Pratt, Patterson, & Hodges, 2000; Wheeler et al., 1997). Some of the most persuasive research on this issue comes from studies that utilized the PET scan technology that you learned about in Chapter 2 (p. 81). PET scans allow researchers to see which parts of the brain are most active while the participant is engaged in certain activities. By taking PET scans of participants while they perform semantic and episodic memory tasks, researchers can get a feel for which parts of the brain are involved in these two types of memory.

The results of such PET scan studies suggest that the prefrontal cortex plays a much larger role in episodic memory than it does in semantic memory (Figure 2.15a, p. 73). Given that episodic memory and semantic memory seem to stem from activity in different parts of the brain, it is not a far leap to assume that they must be separate memory systems. However, as we pointed out, the interpretation of the PET scan findings in these studies is controversial. At present, all we can say is that the available data *suggest* that episodic and semantic memory are separate memory systems, but more research is needed to further examine the validity of this suggestion. Regardless of whether or not semantic and episodic memory are part of the same memory system, they share the characteristic of being easily verbalized. This is not true of all of our knowledge. **Procedural memory,** our memory for skills, is not readily declarative in nature. To illustrate the difference between declarative and procedural memories, take a moment to try the following demonstration.

First, think of a skill that you know very well, such as walking, riding a bike, or driving a car. Then attempt to tell someone else how to execute that skill without showing her how to do it. You can use only words to describe the skill. Now, choose something about which you have declarative memory—the directions to your favorite music store or the plot to your favorite movie—and try to communicate that using only words.

Which task did you find to be more difficult? We bet that you found the first task to be much harder than the second! The first task asked you to verbalize a *procedural* memory, whereas the second asked you to verbalize a *semantic* memory. As we said before, procedural memories are not easily verbalized, and we've demonstrated just how hard it can be to find words to describe even everyday skills.

Another defining characteristic of procedural memory is that it is often *implicit* memory (Cohen, 1984; Squire et al., 1993). Recall that implicit memory is memory that is used unconsciously (p. 254). We remember without being aware that we are remembering. For the most part, the skills we execute every day are done in an unconscious, implicit fashion. As you walk to your classes, are you consciously aware of what you need to do to get your body to walk? When you take notes in class, are you aware of what you need to do to get your hand to write? Of course not! We walk, write, drive a car, and so on without thinking about it. The fact that procedural memories are implicit also may help explain why we have a difficult time verbalizing them. How can you verbalize your execution of a behavior when you are not aware of how you do it? You can't.

A final aspect of procedural memory that separates it from declarative memory is its longevity. Procedural memories tend to last for a long time in long-term memory. You've probably heard the saying "It's like riding a bike. You never forget how to do it." There is a great deal of truth in this folk wisdom—once we have mastered a skill, it does stay with us for a long time. For example, one of the authors recently purchased a bike. She hadn't ridden one in almost 10 years, but when she tried it, it was as if she had ridden just yesterday. Declarative memory, on the other hand, does not enjoy the same longevity as procedural memory. If you put aside your studies of psychology and never thought about it, how much psychology do you think you would be able to recall

procedural memory long-term memory for skills and behaviors

Demonstration

Application >>

10 years from now? We bet you wouldn't be able to recall much—psychology is not like riding a bike!

As you can see, procedural memory seems to differ substantially from declarative memory. The degree of disparity between these two types of memory brings up the question of whether they are separate memory systems. Strong evidence to support the notion that procedural memory is a separate memory system comes from studies done with people suffering from *amnesia*.

Amnesia is a condition in which a person cannot recall certain declarative memories. Amnesia can be classified as **retrograde** or **anterograde amnesia.** Retrograde amnesia is an inability to recall previously stored declarative memories, and anterograde amnesia is an inability to encode new declarative memories in long-term memory. In short, retrograde amnesia is amnesia for one's past, and anterograde amnesia is amnesia for one's present and future.

There are several causes for amnesia, but of most interest to us here is amnesia that is caused by brain injury or illness. In particular, studies of brain-injured people with anterograde amnesia have taught us much about the distinction between declarative and procedural memory. One of the most famous cases of anterograde amnesia involved H.M. (Corkin, 1968), who suffered from severe epilepsy that was centered in the vicinity of his hippocampal regions in the temporal lobe (p. 73). H.M.'s epilepsy was severe and did not respond to medication. In an effort to curb H.M.'s seizures, doctors removed the hippocamal regions in both hemispheres of his brain (Squire, 1992). In this respect the surgery was a success—H.M.'s seizures were drastically reduced. However, in another sense, the operation was a serious failure. After he recovered from the surgery, it became apparent that he could no longer store new declarative memories. He had severe anterograde amnesia!

Interestingly, however, H.M. did not completely lose his ability to store new long-term memories. After the surgery, he could still store procedural memories. For instance, H.M. could learn to do certain perceptual-motor tasks, such as tracing a stimulus while looking at its image in a mirror. Furthermore, he was seen to improve on these tasks with time (Milner, 1962). Results similar to those found in H.M. have also been found in other amnesiac patients (for example, Cermak, Lewis, Butters, & Goodglass, 1973). The fact that H.M. and other amnesiacs can still learn new skills indicates that procedural memory is not stored in long-term memory in the same way as declarative memory.

For people with amnesia, the ability to learn new skills is very fortunate. They can still use their procedural memory to learn new skills that may allow them to perform certain jobs, although they will not remember where they acquired these new skills. If they also lost their ability to encode procedural memories, they would be even more impaired. They would not be able to add anything to their long-term memory!

Most of us will never face amnesia to the degree that H.M. did. However, amnesia may be more common than you think. One study reported that in the United States, some 50,000 to 300,000 athletes can be expected to suffer a concussion during a given sports season. Many of these injured athletes will suffer at least mild, temporary amnesia (Collins et al., 2003). If you add to these numbers the people who will suffer from other forms of brain injury—from car accidents, illnesses, drug overdoses, and falls—you can see how amnesia may be more common than you might think. This is why it is important to always follow safety procedures, such as wearing a helmet while bicycling.

Even without brain injury or amnesia, you may still encounter mild problems with your memory from time to time. Normal, everyday forgetting can be an annoyance. In the next sections, we will discuss how we retrieve information from long-term memory and theories of why we sometimes forget the information we have encoded in our memory.

retrograde amnesia   a type of amnesia in which one is unable to retrieve previously stored memories from long-term memory

anterograde amnesia   a type of amnesia in which one is unable to store new memories in long-term memory

Let's Review!

In this section, we described the characteristics of long-term memory including the types of long-term memory and the organization of long-term memory. For a quick check of your understanding, answer these questions.

1. Remembering the fun you had last week when you went to the movies with your friends would be an example of a(n) _____ memory.
   a. semantic
   b. procedural
   c. episodic
   d. sensory

2. You know how to behave when you go to a fast-food restaurant because you have a(n) _____ stored in long-term memory.
   a. episode
   b. icon
   c. script
   d. proposition

3. Which of the following is the *best* example of semantic encoding in long-term memory?
   a. remembering how to play the tune to your favorite song on a guitar
   b. remembering the name of the artist who sings your favorite song
   c. hearing the tune to your favorite song in your head
   d. seeing the face of the artist who sings your favorite song in your head

ANSWERS
1.c, 2.c, 3.b

LEARNING OBJECTIVE ‹ ‹ ‹ ‹ ‹ ‹ ‹

Explain retrieval processes in memory.

Describe and give examples of the various theories of forgetting in long-term memory.

Retrieval and Forgetting: Random Access Memory?

We store memories so that we can later retrieve them. *Retrieval* is the act of moving information from long-term memory back into working memory or consciousness. Retrieval occurs when we send a *probe* or *cue* into long-term memory in search of *memory traces* or encoded memories that we have stored there. A probe or cue can be many things, a test question, the sight of a playground, the sound of a roller coaster, or the smell of popcorn. For example, if you see an old friend on the street, the sight of her face may act as a cue that allows you to retrieve her name from your long-term memory. If you had not seen your friend on the street, her name would not have spontaneously popped into your consciousness. Rather, it would have remained tucked away in your long-term memory. Seeing her face was the cue that prompted your recall of her name. Similarly, on exams, your professor's test questions act as probes that prompt you to search your long-term memory for the answers.

Think for a moment about the types of exams you have had in the past—for example, multiple-choice, essay, fill-in-the-blank, and true/false. Which of these is your *least* favorite type of exam question? If you are like the typical college student, you probably dislike the dreaded essay test the most! Why would most of us much rather take a multiple-choice test than an essay test? Why are essay exams so much harder than multiple-choice exams? The answer lies in the type of retrieval task we engage in when we take these types of exams.

Recognition and Recall

recall a type of retrieval process in which the probe or cue does not contain much information

An essay question is an example of a **recall** task. In a recall task, the probe is relatively weak and does not contain a great deal of information to go on as you search your memory for the answer. You can't guess your way through an essay test. You must really

Jump Start © Reprinted by permission of United Feature Syndicate, Inc.

All types of things can act like probes or cues in the retrieval process.

know the information to answer the question. If you have not elaborated the material in long-term memory, you will likely find it difficult to recall.

A multiple-choice question, on the other hand, is an example of a **recognition** task. In recognition, the probe is stronger and contains much more information than does a recall cue. Several researchers have proposed theories to explain why recognition is typically easier than recall (for example, Gillund & Shiffrin, 1984; Tulving, 1983). One theory proposes that recognition is easier because of the overlap between the content of the probe and the content of the memory trace (Tulving, 1983). Think about it for a minute: in a multiple-choice question, the answer is actually part of the probe!

One word of caution: As you study for exams, keep in mind that recognition tasks are easier than recall tasks. If you quiz yourself using multiple-choice questions (such as those provided in this book), keep in mind that you are testing yourself in the easiest possible way because the probe itself provides much of the answer. Just because you can pass a multiple-choice test on the material doesn't mean that you could pass a recall test on the material! If you really want to test your knowledge, you would do better to test yourself using some form of recall test instead, with short answer or fill-in-the-blank questions. This strategy will help ensure your success and long-term retention of the material.

Unfortunately, no method of study is foolproof. Despite your best efforts at studying, there will always be times when retrieval is difficult. We've all known times when the probes and cues we sent into long-term memory were not successful in retrieving the desired information. For a memory to actually be retrieved from long-term memory, two conditions must be met: the memory must be both *available* and *accessible*. A memory is available when it has been encoded in long-term memory and the memory trace is still present in long-term memory. Obviously, if you never encoded the memory in long-term memory, you won't be able to retrieve it later! The memory must be available if retrieval is to occur.

However, availability is not enough by itself to ensure retrieval. Accessibility of the memory trace is also important. If the probe cannot reach the memory trace in long-term memory, the memory will not be retrieved, even if it is available. As we will see in the next section, there are a variety of circumstances in which the probe fails to retrieve an available, but inaccessible, memory.

When Retrieval Fails: Forgetting

What student hasn't asked herself this question: "I studied that material, so why did I forget it on the test?" Forgetting occurs when we cannot, for some reason, retrieve information from long-term memory. One theory of forgetting, **decay theory,** maintains that once a memory trace is stored in long-term memory, it must be routinely activated to keep it there (Ebbinghaus, 1885/1913). If we store a memory and then fail to

recognition   a type of retrieval process in which the probe or cue contains a great deal of information including the item that we are searching for in memory

   **Application**

On exam day, you really hope that your retrieval methods work!

© Jose Luis Pelaez, inc./Corbis

decay theory   a theory of forgetting that proposes that memory traces that are not routinely activated in long-term memory will decay

recall it periodically, the memory trace weakens and decays. If the decay is not stopped by recalling the memory, the memory trace will be lost forever from long-term memory.

Although decay theory seems to make sense, there are some good reasons to doubt that memory traces decay from disuse. One is that memories seem to last for very long periods of time, even when we do not routinely access these memories. For example, in one study, participants' recognition of English–Spanish vocabulary words was tested anywhere from 1 to 50 years after they had studied Spanish. The results showed that recognition memory for these vocabulary words declined little over the years (Bahrick, 1984).

Another reason to doubt decay theory comes from the methodology used in the experiments that have been done to support it. These experiments usually involve having participants learn a list of words or syllables and then testing the participants on their recall of the items at various intervals of time (for example, Jenkins & Dallenbach, 1924). These experiments usually show that memory for the items drops off as time passes, suggesting that memory traces do decay with time. However, interpreting the results of such experiments is tricky. The participants' tendency to forget the material could have been due to decay or it could have been due to another process called *interference*.

proactive interference a type of forgetting that occurs when older memory traces inhibit the retrieval of newer memory traces

Interference occurs when other information blocks the retrieval of a memory trace. In interference the memory trace is still available, but it is inaccessible. **Proactive interference** occurs when older information inhibits our ability to retrieve other, newer information from memory. For example, one of the authors (Doyle) spells her first name in an unusual way that often causes proactive interference in others. Her name is pronounced *Suzanne*, but it is spelled *Susann*. Because of its spelling, people often pronounce her name as *Susan* when they first see it in print. Then, no matter how many times she corrects them, they seem to always want to call her *Susan*! This example is one of proactive interference because the *older* pronunciation of her name inhibits the *newer* pronunciation in people's memory. It's also the reason she started going by *Sue* early in childhood!

retroactive interference a type of forgetting that occurs when newer memory traces inhibit the retrieval of older memory traces

We can also experience **retroactive interference,** in which *newer* information inhibits the retrieval of *older* information in memory. Suppose you move to a new home and work very hard to memorize your new address and phone number. Chances are, you will soon find it hard to recall your old address and phone number. This is an example of retroactive interference, when the newer phone number and address interfere with your ability to retrieve the old phone number and address from long-term memory.

cue-dependent forgetting a type of forgetting that occurs when one cannot recall information in a context other than the context in which it was encoded

Interference theory does seem to describe one way in which we forget information, but there is reason to suspect that interference may not occur as often in the real world as it does in laboratory experiments (Slameka, 1966). **Cue-dependent forgetting** may be a better explanation of forgetting in the real world. Cue-dependent forgetting (Tulving, 1974) asserts that the amount of information we can retrieve from long-term memory is a function of the type of cue or probe we use. If the memory cues we use are not the right ones, we might experience forgetting. For example, assume you have the following words to memorize,

Bread	*Sally*
Soda	*Pearl*
Bologna	*Laura*
Pear	*Mary*
Potato chips	*Candy*

and later you are asked to recall all of the foods on the list. You are likely to recall *Bread, Soda, Bologna, Pear, Potato chips,* but what about *Candy*? You are likely to forget about *Candy* because you encoded *Candy* as a name and not as a food. If the cue used at recall is stated "Recall all of the names you learned," you will surely recall the word *Candy!* Your forgetting was cue-dependent.

The cue-dependent forgetting theory is part of the *encoding specificity principle* that was developed by Endel Tulving (Wiseman & Tulving, 1976). According to this principle, we encode aspects of the context in which we learn information, later using these contextual aspects as cues to help us retrieve the information from long-term memory. If the encoding specificity principle is correct, then we should have better memory when we retrieve information in the same setting that we learned it. Does this mean that taking a test in the same room in which you had lectures improves your retrieval? Yes! If you take an exam in the room in which you heard lectures on the material, you should be able to retrieve somewhat more information than if you took the test in another room. In one distinctive study, researchers asked divers to learn a list of words while they were either on shore or 20 feet under the water (Godden & Baddeley, 1975). Later, researchers tested the divers' recall for the words in either the context in which they studied the words or the context in which they did not study the words. Consistent with the encoding-specificity principle, the researchers found that when the divers recalled the words in the same context in which they had learned the words, their recall was better.

Application

Encoding-specificity has also been shown to hold true for mood states and states of consciousness. People can recall information they learned while drinking alcohol better when they have been drinking (Eich, Weingartner, Stillman, & Gillin, 1975). Information learned while smoking marijuana is better recalled while smoking marijuana (Parker, Birnbaum, & Noble, 1976). And information learned while in a bad mood is better recalled in a negative mood state than when one is happy (Teasdale & Russell, 1983). These findings do not mean that it is better to learn while in these states. For example, alcohol can actually reduce one's ability to encode information in the first place (Parker, Birnbaum, & Noble, 1976)!

The final theory of forgetting we will discuss is Sigmund Freud's (1915, 1943) proposal that the emotional aspects of a memory can impact our ability to retrieve that memory. According to Freud, when we experience emotionally threatening events, we push or *repress* these memories into an inaccessible part of our mind called the *unconscious* (p. 10). This **repression** results in amnesia for this information.

repression a type of forgetting proposed by Sigmund Freud in which memories for events, desires, or impulses that we find threatening are pushed into an inaccessible part of the mind called the unconscious

Repression of memories has become a very controversial subject in the past 15 years because of its relationship to cases of childhood sexual abuse. Some people have claimed that they had suddenly "remembered" abuse that occurred many years before. After many years have passed, there is often no corroborating evidence to support such claims. Furthermore, some experiments indicate that the details of memories for past events can be incorrect, and that this may be especially true for children (Brainerd & Reyna, 2002; Howe, 2000). In one study, researchers found that preschool children could not distinguish memories for fictitious events from memories for real events after 10 weeks of thinking about the events. More alarming was the fact that the children were able to give detailed accounts of the fictitious events, and they seemed to *really* believe that the fictitious events had happened (Ceci, 1995).

The frequent lack of corroborating evidence for recovered memories and experimental evidence that questions the accuracy of memory has led some to charge that these memories are not true memories, but rather *false memories*. The debate is further fueled by the lack of experimental data to support the notion that repression can occur. To test the theory of repression, researchers would have to traumatize participants and then see whether they repressed their memories of the trauma. Obviously, this type of study cannot be done for ethical reasons! So, for now, psychologists cannot say for sure whether or not repression is one of the reasons we forget.

The debate over whether or not memories of abuse that are "de-repressed" by therapeutic suggestion are true memories is one aspect of a larger issue concerning memory—that of just how accurate our memory generally is.

Let's Review!

In this section, we discussed how information is retrieved from long-term memory and some theories of why we sometimes forget information that we have stored in long-term memory. As a quick check of your understanding, answer these questions.

1. You take a test in your history class in which the professor gives you a list of events and a list of dates. You must match each event with the date on which it occurred in history. This test is an example of which type of retrieval?

   a. recall
   b. recognition
   c. implicit retrieval
   d. retrieval based on encoding specificity

2. Decay theory states that forgetting is due to a lack of _____, whereas interference theory states that forgetting is due to a lack of _____.

   a. availability; accessibility
   b. accessibility; availability
   c. encoding; accessibility
   d. encoding; availability

3. Mary was married 6 months ago. Much to her dismay, her friends continue to call her by her maiden name even though she has legally taken her husband's name. Mary's friends are experiencing which memory phenomenon?

   a. encoding specificity
   b. repression
   c. proactive interference
   d. retroactive interference

ANSWERS

1. b; 2. a; 3. c

LEARNING OBJECTIVE < < < < < < < <

Discuss the accuracy of memory and its implications for eyewitness memory.

Is Memory Accurate?

Can you remember what you were doing when you heard that:

- John Lennon had been murdered?
- The *Challenger* space shuttle had exploded?
- The Federal Building in Oklahoma City had been bombed?
- Kurt Cobain had committed suicide?
- OJ Simpson was suspected of murder?
- Students had gone on a murderous rampage at Columbine High School?
- Terrorists had attacked the World Trade Center towers on September 11, 2001?

flashbulb memory an unusually detailed and seemingly accurate memory for an emotionally charged event

Can you recall the details of what you were doing when you heard of any of these events? If you can, then you have what psychologists call a **flashbulb memory,** or an unusually detailed memory for an emotionally charged event (Brown & Kulik, 1977). Often people claim that they can recall the exact details: where they were, what they were doing, what they were wearing, what the weather was like at the moment when they heard of emotional events like these. For example, one of the authors recalls that she was sitting on the couch in her parents' home, recovering from a serious car accident, and wearing a lavender sweat suit, when she first saw the news that the *Challenger* space shuttle had exploded. She cannot recall any details of the day before the explosion or the day after it, but the details of seeing the *Challenger* news story seem very clear to her.

There is good reason to expect that the author's flashbulb memory for the *Challenger* explosion may not be very accurate. Researchers studied participants' flashbulb memories for the *Challenger* explosion 1 week after the explosion and again 9 months after the tragedy. They found that the participants' so-called flashbulb memories were actually riddled with inaccuracies (McCloskey, Wible, & Cohen, 1988). Even though the participants felt that they could vividly recall their whereabouts at the time of the tragedy, their memories were often full of incorrect details for where they were and what they were doing at the time.

Try it yourself. Do you remember where you were on September 11, 2001, at the time of the attacks on the World Trade Center towers? Do you recall watching the live TV coverage as the tragedy was taking place? If so, answer this question: How long after the plane hit the first tower did it take for both towers to fall? Researchers interviewed 690 people 7 weeks after the attack and asked them this question. On average, the participants reported that it took 62 minutes for the towers to collapse—when in reality it took almost 2 hours. On the day of the attack, do you remember watching news coverage of the first plane hitting the towers? If so, you are not alone—despite the fact that this video footage did not air until the next day (Perina, 2002). So how did you do on this task? How accurate (or inaccurate) is your memory of that day?

Demonstration

Interestingly, some researchers now suspect that stress hormones that act on the amygdala (p. 69) may be responsible for certain aspects of flashbulb memories. A current theory is that when you experience an emotional event, such as watching a horrific terrorist attack, your body releases stress hormones that direct your brain's amygdala to initiate storage of a long-term memory of that event. However, these stress hormones also seem to block the formation of accurate memories for what was happening immediately before the emotional event. Therefore, you may end up with a memory for the emotional event that may not be entirely accurate because you have something of a "gap" in your memory (Bower, 2003).

Memory Is Not a Videotape

Doesn't it surprise you to know that memory is often inaccurate? But think about it: Even when we store memories of the everyday events in our lives, we do not store memory traces for every detail. Memory does not work like a video recorder! It's more of a construction project. We store the gist of the information in long-term memory with the help of schemata (p. 270), but we do not store all of the exact details of the event. This means that when we retrieve a memory from long-term memory, we do not merely recall all of the details of the event and then use them to *reconstruct* the event. Memory is more than just **reconstructive,** or based on actual events. It is also *constructive.*

reconstructive memory   memory that is based on the retrieval of memory traces that contain the actual details of the events that we have experienced

constructive memory   memory that utilizes knowledge and expectations to fill in the missing details in our retrieved memory traces

Memory is **constructive** in that we use the knowledge and expectations that we have stored in our schemata to help us fill in the missing details in our stored memories. It is very possible that you filled in the gaps in your memory of September 11, 2001. Likewise, the author may have filled in certain details of her memory of seeing the *Challenger* story on television. She may have recalled that she was wearing a lavender sweat suit simply because in her memory, she associates this sweat suit with her car accident. This sweat suit was a Christmas gift she received when she was in the hospital after the accident, and she often wore it while she was recovering. It is possible, however, that she was not wearing it when she heard about the *Challenger* explosion, but she has falsely remembered this detail because she knows the *Challenger* disaster occurred during the period of time in which she was recovering from the accident. In her head, she has a schema for the accident and her recovery. This schema may be filling in details that she failed to encode at the time of the *Challenger* explosion. In this manner, she may be *constructing* her memory of this event. Yet, these "filled-in" details feel very much as if they are true! Without some corroborating evidence, we cannot say for sure what she was wearing at the time she heard about the disaster.

Most of the time, it makes little difference whether or not we recall such details accurately. In reality, it does not matter what the author was wearing at the time of the

Do you remember what you were doing when you heard about the September 11 attacks?

Challenger explosion. But sometimes the details of our recollections can be extremely important, even a matter of life and death. As we saw in our chapter case of Mellissa Gammill, eyewitness testimony can put the wrong person in jail. It has even wrongfully condemned a defendant to death row.

Eyewitness Memory

If the error in Darron Terry's memory hadn't been discovered, Mellissa Gammill, an innocent woman, could have remained in jail for 10 years instead of 10 months. One problem with eyewitness memory, as with other memories, is that we do not store all the details of what we see in the world in our memory. Darron Terry could not have stored every feature of the burglar's appearance. Under the circumstances, Terry was likely caught off-guard, scared, and a bit confused. He probably processed only certain striking details of the burglar's appearance. For example, he likely stored the memory that the burglar was a *white woman with long, blond hair*. Later when he was shown pictures of suspects, he may have used these rather general characteristics to help him identify the suspect. Because Mellissa Gammill had these characteristics and her picture appeared in a book of police mug shots, Terry identified her. Then later, when Terry thought of the burglar's face, he may have filled in his memory of her face with the details he had seen in Mellissa Gammill's mug-shot. In his mind, the burglar now looked like Mellissa Gammill, and he probably had no idea that he was making a mistake! The available research on eyewitness memory shows that we can make serious errors without knowing it. So what kinds of situations make such errors in eyewitness memory more likely?

Psychologist Elizabeth Loftus has spent a good part of her career showing that eyewitness memory can be manipulated by the expectations we hold about the world. For example, in one experiment (Loftus & Palmer, 1974), Loftus showed participants a film of a car accident. After viewing the film, the participants were randomly divided into several groups and questioned about their memory of the film. In one group, the participants were asked, "About how fast were the cars going when they *smashed into* each other?" In another group, the participants were asked, "About how fast were the cars going when they *hit* each other?" In the control group, the participants were not asked to estimate the speed of the cars. The results showed that the verb used in the question affected the participants' estimates of the speed of the cars. Participants in the "smashed into" group estimated the speed of the cars at 41 mph. In contrast, the participants in the "hit" group estimated the speed as being 34 mph.

It seems that the words "smashed" and "hit" activated different expectations that were used to fill in the missing details in the participants' memories of the film, and the result was that they remembered the film differently. Imagine how a lawyer's choice of words might influence a witness's memory on the witness stand.

Even more dramatic is the fact that our memories can be permanently altered by things that happen *after* we encode the memories. In another study (Loftus & Zanni, 1975), Elizabeth Loftus showed participants a film of a car crash and then asked them a series of questions about the accident. The participants in one group were asked, "Did you see *a* broken headlight?" In a second group, the participants were asked," Did you see *the* broken headlight?" Although there had been no broken headlight in the film, some of the participants reported that they had seen one. Of those who were asked if they saw *a* broken headlight, only 7% reported that they saw a broken headlight in the film. On the other hand, of the participants who were asked if they had seen *the* broken headlight, 17% said they had seen it. By subtly suggesting to them that there *had* been a broken headlight, Loftus caused the participants to remember seeing something that they had not seen. She created a false memory in her participants.

These false memories do not seem to be motivated by a participant's desire to please the researcher. In another study Loftus offered participants $25 if they could accurately recall an event. Even with this motivation to be accurate, the participants could not prevent their memories from being distorted by the misleading information they heard *after* viewing the incident (Loftus, 1979). Although it is clear that eyewitness memory is susceptible to errors, there is some disagreement as to why these errors occur.

According to Elizabeth Loftus (2000), we accept subsequent misinformation as being correct, and this information becomes part of our memory for the original event. Others propose that eyewitness memory becomes faulty when we make errors in identifying the source of information we have stored in long-term memory (Johnson, Hashtroudi, & Lindsay, 1993). According to this view, when we retrieve a memory for a particular event from long-term memory, we also retrieve information from other sources relevant to the event. For instance, we might retrieve information from times when we discussed the event with others, from comments others made about the event, from things we read about the event in the newspaper, and so on. Because there is considerable overlap between our memory for the original event and our memories of information related to the event, it is easy for us to get confused about the source of these bits of information. We might misattribute the source of a particular detail to our memory of the original event, when we actually encoded it in another situation.

Regardless of which interpretation is correct, after we witness the original event, the more information we are faced with, the more likely it is that our memory will become faulty. The same problems that plague eyewitness memory also affect our memory for the everyday events in our lives. It may be unsettling to you to realize that your memory can be faulty. As we have seen, at times faulty memory can lead to tragic events like those experienced by Mellissa Gammill. But don't despair—we don't always make mistakes, and many times when we do, they are not of great consequence.

In the next section, we will explore ways you can improve your everyday memory. In this section, you will find ways to apply what you have learned in this chapter to make yourself a more successful student. First, though, take a moment to check your progress with the following quiz.

Let's Review!

In this section, we discussed the accuracy of memories we retrieve from long-term memory in particular eyewitness accounts of events. For a quick check of your understanding, answer these questions.

1. In recalling his date from last Saturday night, Juan assumes that his date was wearing shoes, even though he did not encode the details of what her shoes looked like. Juan's memory is an example of _____.

   a. constructive memory
   b. reconstructive memory
   c. procedural memory
   d. encoding specificity

2. Which of the following is true?

   a. All memory is reconstructive.
   b. All memory is constructive.

c. Memory is both constructive and reconstructive.
   d. Memory is like a video tape. We store an exact copy of what we experience.

3. Which of the following events is most likely to produce a flashbulb memory?

   a. taking a hard math test
   b. being in a serious car accident
   c. having a heated discussion with your best friend
   d. going to a very scary movie on a date

ANSWERS

1. a; 2. c; 3. b

LEARNING < < < < < < < < < <
OBJECTIVE

Discuss ways in which to improve your memory.

Application ≫

Improving Your Memory: Tips to Remember

So much of academic performance relies on our ability to remember information. Now that you have learned a bit about how your memory works, you can apply this knowledge to your own life. As you have seen in this chapter, memory involves three processes: encoding, storage, and retrieval. To be a successful student, you have to study in a way that works with these processes, not against them. We'll outline some strategies that will help maximize your memory.

Pay Attention

You can't learn well if you don't pay attention!

© LWA–Dann Tardif/Corbis

Attention is the first step to getting information into memory. If you are distracted while studying, you won't be able to devote your full attention to the information you are trying to learn, and your ability to later recall information may be affected (Iidaka, Anderson, Kapur, Cabeza, & Craik, 2000). Therefore, you should study when and where you can focus your full attention on your studies. Try studying in a quiet, distraction-free environment. Turn off the music and the TV, and focus on what you are doing. Don't try studying while lying on your bed because the next thing you know, you'll be asleep. Sitting upright at a desk in a quiet room is the best setting. Luckily, most college libraries offer just such a place. Try using the library if you can't find peace and quiet at home or in your dorm room.

Do Not Cram for Exams

Cramming is one of the worst ways to study for an exam! Unfortunately, many students procrastinate and then try to make up for it by pulling an all-nighter right before the exam. If this is the way that you approach your studies, you are begging for failure. Even if you manage to pull it off, and you actually pass the exam, the information you stored in long-term memory is likely to become inaccessible shortly after the exam. In short, you waste your time when you cram.

Studies have shown that **massed practice**—when you try to learn a great deal of information in one study session—results in poor recall of the information. Recall suffers because massed practice results in fatigue, which leads to a lack of attention, and the shortened time frame also does not give you time to adequately rehearse information. Without adequate attention and elaborative rehearsal, information will not be efficiently stored in long-term memory.

A better way to study is to use **distributed practice,** distributing your study time across several days rather than bunching it up on one day (or night). The beauty of distributed practice is that you don't necessarily have to study *longer,* you just need to space out the time you spend studying! For example, in one study (Krug, Davis, & Glover, 1990) participants who repeatedly read a passage over a series of sittings recalled more of the passage than those who repeatedly read the passage in a single sitting. So, it's not necessarily how *long* you study, but also how *often* you study that matters.

Use Elaborative Rehearsal

As we saw in the *levels-of-processing model* of memory (p. 262) , how you rehearse material affects how well you will be able to retrieve that material. Maintenance rehearsal does not aid retention and retrieval of information in long-term memory as well as elaborative rehearsal does. If you study by reading the material over and over, you use maintenance rehearsal, which is only meant to keep information in short-term memory.

To study efficiently, you must process the information at a deeper level, finding ways to elaborate on the *meaning* of the material in your memory. This means you must form connections or associations among the bits of information you are trying to learn and the information you already know. Outlining is one way to do this. Take all of the material you are trying to learn, and create an outline for the material. When you create an outline, you must elaborate the material because you have to think about the relationships that exist among the concepts that you are outlining. It also helps to come up with your own original examples of the concepts you are learning—a technique we've encouraged you to use throughout this text. By generating examples, you once again elaborate the material. If the examples are from your own life, this is even better because it ties the material to your *self*, and we remember information that relates to the self better than information that does not (Symons & Johnson, 1997).

Use Overlearning

Overlearning is a technique in which you learn the material until you feel that you have mastered it, and then you *continue* to study it some more. By doing this, you help ensure that you will be able to retrieve it at a later date because every time you activate information in long-term memory, you help to make it more available for retrieval. Overlearning can also make you feel more confident as you sit down to take an exam. Knowing that you really know the material, as opposed to "sort of" knowing it, can lessen the anxiety that you feel during an exam, which in turn can improve your performance.

Mnemonics Make Your Memory Mighty

If you find it difficult to elaborate the material, you might try using **mnemonic devices,** memory tricks that help you recall information. There are many different types of mnemonics. Here are a few that you might try.

massed practice   cramming or attempting to learn large amounts of information in a single session of study

distributed practice   spreading one's study time across a series of study sessions

overlearning   improving memory for material that is already known by continuing to rehearse it

mnemonic device   a cognitive procedure or mental trick that is designed to improve one's memory

Acronyms

To create an acronym, you take the first letter of each word you want to remember and use these first letters to form a word. For example, *USA* stands for *United States of America*. *ESR* could stand for the three memory processes of *encoding, storage,* and *retrieval*. Acronyms can also be useful in many practical situations. For example, they can be used to remind physicians to ask important questions of their patients when diagnosing them for certain illnesses (Sherman, 2001).

Acrostics

Using an acrostic, you create a rhyme or saying in which each word starts with the first letter of each of the to-be-remembered words. For example, *Ellen steals rabbits*, could

be an acrostic to help you remember the three memory processes of *encoding, storage,* and *retrieval*.

Pegword System

Using a pegword system, you associate each to-be-remembered word or concept with an easily remembered pegword. For example, a classic pegword system uses the old counting rhyme—"one is a bun," "two is a shoe," "three is a tree," "four is a door"—as

the basis for the pegs. Each to-be-remembered item is tied in memory to one of these phrases. If you wanted to remember *decay, interference, repression,* and *change in context* as forms of forgetting, you would associate each of these concepts with one of the pegs. You might think of *decaying buns, interfering shoes, repressed trees,* and *changing the context by opening the door.* Then by recalling the well-remembered rhyme, you will also be cueing your memory for the to-be-remembered concepts.

Method of Loci

Using the method of loci, you connect each to-be-remembered item to the visual image of a point along a path you are very familiar with. You might, for instance, use the visual image of the route you take to walk (or drive) to school. You would mentally place a bizarre visual image of each to-be-remembered item at a specific point along this route. To recall the items, you would visualize yourself taking this route and encountering the

concepts along the way. For example, to remember the types of forgetting, you might visualize a heap of *decaying* trash next to your front door; a TV with *interference* on the screen along the road you take to get to school; an image of a very *repressed*, uptight person sitting huddled by the door to your building at school; and an image of a clown that is out of *context* because it is in the middle of the hallway of your classroom building at school.

The SQ3R Method

SQ3R is an acronym mnemonic for: Survey, Question, Read, Recite, and Review. Using this method when studing a chapter, you first *survey* the whole chapter, noting the section headings. As you survey them, you formulate *questions* based on these headings. Then, as you *read* the chapter, you search for answers to your questions. After you read the chapter, you reread the material and *recite*, or summarize, the meaning of each section. Finally, you *review* what you have learned from reading and reciting the material. The SQ3R seems to foster memory because it encourages elaboration and integration of the material. Give it a try when you read the next chapter!

Let's Review!

In this section, we discussed some techniques for improving your own memory. For a quick check of your understanding, answer these questions.

1. Which of the following is an acronym for the *United States Marine Corps*?
   a. USMC
   b. Umberto stole more corn
   c. united is a bun; states are a shoe, marines are a tree, and corps is a door
   d. none of the above

2. Which of the following mnemonics would likely foster the *most* elaboration of the material one is trying to remember?
   a. an acronym
   b. an acrostic

   c. the method of loci
   d. all of the above would foster equal amounts of elaboration

3. Sally studies psychology for 12 hours on Saturday. Billy studies psychology for 1 hour each day for 12 days. All other factors being equal, who is most likely to do the best on the upcoming psychology exam?
   a. Sally
   b. Billy
   c. Both Sally and Billy have an equal chance of doing well on the exam.
   d. We don't have enough information to predict who will do better.

ANSWERS

1. a; 2. c; 3. b

The Biology of Memory > > > > > > > > > > > > > > > >

LEARNING OBJECTIVE
Discuss what is known about the biology of memory.

Much of what we know about the role that the brain plays in memory comes from studies of people with amnesia. People with amnesia often experience severe memory problems that can be traced to damage or disease in particular parts of the brain. Recall the case of H.M. that we introduced in Chapter 2 (p. 70). H.M.'s hippocampal regions were removed in an attempt to control his epilepsy, and he lost his ability to store new declarative memories as a result of the surgery (Figure 6.8). In addition to the case of H.M., other amnesic cases have supported the notion that the hippocampus plays a significant role in the storage of declarative memories (Parkin & Leng, 1993).

Mapping Memory in the Brain

Scientists also use brain-imaging technology, like the techniques we discussed in Chapter 2, to study the function of the brain during memory tasks (for example, see Finn, 2004). Similarly, these studies indicate that the hippocampus plays an important role in the declarative memory function of people without amnesia. For instance, PET scans show that blood flow in the normal brain is higher in the right hippocampal region during declarative memory tasks, but not during procedural memory tasks (Schacter, Alpert, Savage, Rauch, & Alpert, 1996; Squire et al., 1992).

Research suggests that people who use their memory a great deal may have structural differences in their hippocampal regions. Do you recall the study of the London taxi drivers from Chapter 2 (p. 71)? That study used MRI technology to show that London cab drivers have larger than average hippocampal regions. London's street system is old and complicated, and drivers must memorize it in order to be licensed. Is it possible that these drivers experienced greater hippocampal development because they relied on their memory so much in doing their job? No one can say for sure at this time,

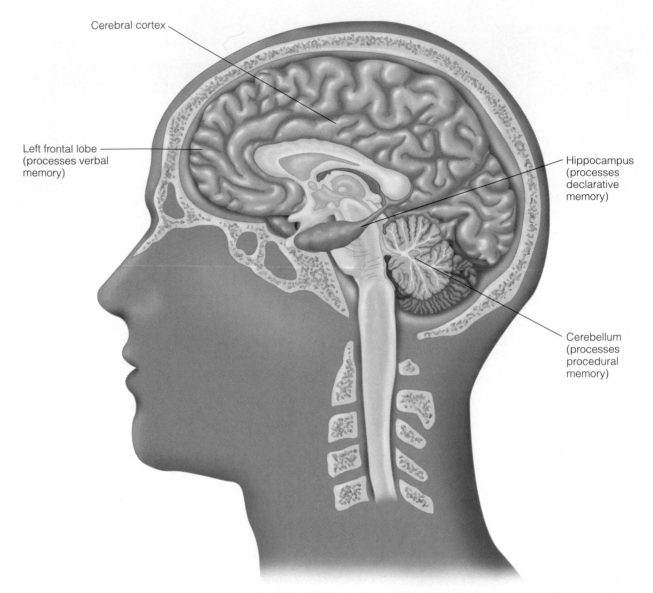

Cerebral cortex

Left frontal lobe
(processes verbal
memory)

Hippocampus
(processes
declarative
memory)

Cerebellum
(processes
procedural
memory)

Figure 6.8 Brain Structures That Are Important to Memory
The hippocampus processes declarative memories, the left frontal lobe processes verbal memories, and the cerebellum processes procedural memories.

but the researchers did find that the drivers who had been driving the longest tended to have the biggest hippocampal regions (Maguire et al., 2000).

Like the hippocampus, the frontal lobe also seems to play a significant role in the processing of declarative memory. Evoked response potential (ERP) recordings have revealed that the left frontal lobe is very active during the processing of verbal information. This makes sense because one of the language centers of the brain, Broca's area (recall Chapter 2, p. XXX), is in the left frontal lobe (Anderson, 2000). Similarly, PET scans of the brain in action have revealed that the amount of left frontal lobe activation seems to be related to the degree to which the participant is processing the material. Left frontal lobe activity is especially likely to occur when participants are *deeply* processing the material. In fact, the more activation there is in the participants' left frontal lobe, the better they tend to recall the information (Kapur et al., 1994). Findings like these seem to suggest that the levels-of-processing approach to memory may have some biological correlate.

It appears that the hippocampus and the frontal lobes play a crucial role in the processing of declarative memory, but what about procedural memory? How is it that a person with severe hippocampal damage, like H.M., can still learn new skills?

Declarative memory is usually explicit, but procedural memory is typically executed in an implicit, nonconscious manner. Therefore, we may gain some insight into how the brain processes procedural memory by examining the brain function that underlies implicit memory. To examine brain function during implicit memory processing, researchers took PET scans of participants while they completed implicit and explicit memory tasks. As expected, the explicit memory task was associated with increased blood flow in the hippocampal regions of the brain. However, when the participants used their implicit memory, all of the blood flow changes that occurred were *outside* of the hippocampal regions of the brain (Schacter et al., 1996). It appears that the hippocampus is not involved when memory is processed implicitly, or when we process procedural memories.

Other brain-imaging studies have shown that procedural memory is linked to brain structures outside the hippocampus. For instance, motor skill memory seems to rely, in part, on the cerebellum (Sanes, Dimitrov, & Hallett, 1990; Figure 6.8). But perceptual skills, like being able to read the mirror image of a word, seem to rely on certain parts of the cortex (Poldrack, Desmond, Glover, & Gabrieli, 1996). These studies indicate that people with amnesia, like H.M., are able to acquire new skills simply because procedural memories do not rely on the function of the hippocampus.

Let's Review!

In this section, we discussed the biological underpinnings of memory. Research indicates that the frontal lobes, the hippocampus and the cerebellum each play a role in certain aspects of memorial processing. For a quick check of your understanding, answer these questions.

1. Which of the following tasks would be most difficult for a person with amnesia like H.M.?
   a. learning to jump rope
   b. learning to embroider
   c. recalling his fifth birthday party
   d. learning psychology

2. Sarah is learning a list of new words. If you took a PET scan of Sarah's brain as she completed this task, where would you expect to see the greatest brain activity?

   a. the cerebellum
   b. the pons
   c. the hippocampus
   d. the septum

3. José was in a car accident and he damaged his cerebellum. Which of the following tasks would be most difficult for José after his accident?
   a. learning to play tennis
   b. learning psychology
   c. recalling his childhood
   d. forming new episodic memories

ANSWERS

1.d; 2.c; 3.a

Are You Getting the Big Picture?

Over the course of our evolution, humans have acquired an advanced brain that contains a very well developed cortex. One of the benefits of having a brain like ours is our complex system of *memory*, which can be used to store information. Psychologists have not yet determined exactly how the brain stores information, but it is abundantly evident that certain brain structures do play a role in memory.

We can think of memory as a personal library that each of us carries around in our heads. Our memory contains the information that we need to live our lives. In it, we store our past, our sense of self, and our knowledge of the world. Without memory, we could only live in the moment like those with amnesia who do not recall the people, places, and conversations that they experience each day. If we lost our memory, we could not make sense of the world around us, for we often perceive the world in a top-down fashion. We would also be unable to learn, solve problems, communicate, or perform routine tasks.

Understanding how memory works helps many professionals do their jobs better. For example, lawyers and law enforcement personnel must understand the strengths and weaknesses of eyewitness memory. Advertisers and marketers must understand memory so that they can create product ads that will produce memorable images of the product in consumers' minds. Educators use their knowledge of memory to help students learn better. And doctors must understand memory when diagnosing memory problems in people with brain injuries and diseases. These are just a few of the careers that require some understanding of how our memory functions.

In the next chapter, we further explore the workings of the mind when we look at *cognition* (thinking), *language*, and *intelligence*. What you have learned about memory will be invaluable to understanding these processes because memory is an essential element of our ability to think, speak a language, and have the intelligence needed to survive in our environment.

STUDYING THE CHAPTER

Key Terms

encoding (253)
memory traces (253)
storage (253)
retrieval (253)
consciousness (253)
attention (253)
explicit memory (253)
implicit memory (254)
sensory memory (255)
short-term memory (255)
long-term memory (256)
iconic memory (256)
echoic memory (258)
dual-coding system (260)
chunking (261)
maintenance rehearsal (262)

elaborative rehearsal (262)
levels-of-processing model (262)
primacy effect (264)
recency effect (264)
working memory (265)
central executive (266)
phonological loop (266)
visuospatial sketch pad (266)
semantic encoding (270)
schema (270)
declarative memory (271)
semantic memory (271)
episodic memory (271)
procedural memory (274)
retrograde amnesia (275)
anterograde amnesia (275)

recall (276)
recognition (277)
decay theory (277)
proactive interference (278)
retroactive interference (278)
cue-dependent forgetting (278)
repression (279)
flashbulb memory (280)
reconstructive memory (281)
constructive memory (281)
massed practice (285)
distributed practice (285)
overlearning (285)
mnemonic device (285)

Test Yourself!

Concept Check

Test your knowledge of the chapter concepts by completing each of the following sentences with the correct term. For a more comprehensive review, visit the book Web site (http:// psychology.wadsworth.com/pastorinole/) for online quizzes, flashcards, crosswords, and Internet links.

(1) Inputting information into a computer is analogous to the cognitive process of _____. (2) Maintenance rehearsal is to _____ as _____ rehearsal is to long-term memory. (3) _____ memory is the conscious use of memory. (4) After losing her grocery list, Janie's enhanced memory for the first items on the list is likely an example of the _____ effect. (5) A crystal clear memory of an emotionally charged event is called a _____ _____. (6) "The more you elaborate information in memory, the better you can recall it," is the basic idea behind the _____ theory of memory. (7) _____ amnesia is an inability to retrieve memories for events that occurred prior to a brain injury. (8) _____ interference occurs when older information in memory inhibits our ability to retrieve newer information in memory. (9) The _____ _____ is the part of working memory that processes the auditory characteristics of information. (10) A _____ is a generalized knowledge structure that organizes our knowledge about a particular concept. (11) _____ memories are memories that can be easily verbalized.

Answers:

1. encoding; 2. short-term memory, elaborative; 3. Explicit; 4. primacy; 5. flashbulb memory; 6. levels-of-processing; 7. Retrograde; 8. Proactive; 9. phonological loop; 10. schema; 11. Declarative

Critical Thinking About the Chapter

1. Compare and contrast the three stages model of memory and the working memory model of memory.

2. Your best friend tells you about a very detailed memory she has for her first day of kindergarten 16 years ago. She claims to recall all of the details of that special day—everything from what she had for breakfast to the color and design of the dress she wore. After telling you of her memory, your friend asks you how it is possible that she can remember that day in such detail. Given what you know about memory, what would you say to your friend about her childhood memory?

3. Assume that you are a psychologist who is called to testify in court. The defense attorney asks you to describe for the jury how humans store memories for everyday events. What would your testimony be?

Applying Psychology Your grandmother thinks she is having some problems with her memory. However, her doctor has assured her that her forgetting is normal and that she does *not* have Alzheimer's disease. How would you explain to her why she sometimes forgets things that she meant to buy at the store and the names of old friends that she hasn't seen in years?

Critical Thinking for Integration

1. Explain the evolutionary value of implicit memory.

2. Design an experiment to test the hypothesis that the use of mnemonics improves one's recall of information.

3. Draw a picture of the brain and label the parts that are known to play a role in the processing of memory.

4. Explain how memory influences top-down perceptual processing.

5. Use what you have learned about learning in Chapter 5 *and* what you have learned about memory in this chapter to design a plan to make yourself a more motivated, successful student.

Chapter Study Resources

Suggested Readings

1. Loftus, E. F. (1979). *Eyewitness testimony*. Cambridge, MA: Harvard University Press.
   A look at the weaknesses in eyewitness memory.

2. Schacter, D. L. (1996). *Searching for memory: The brain, the mind, and the past*. New York: Basic Books.
   A comprehensive text on memory written for the average reader.

3. Fara, P. & Patterson, K. (Eds). (1998). *Memory*. Cambridge, UK: Cambridge University Press.
   An interesting text that looks at memory from both a psychological and an anthropological perspective.

4. For additional readings, explore InfoTrac College Edition, your online library of archived journal articles and periodicals. Go to http://www.infotrac-college .com/wadsworth and enter the passcode from the card that came with your book. For this chapter, search using these keywords:

mnemonics

Alzheimer's disease

flashbulb memories

episodic memory

gender and memory

Web Links for Further Study

1. The Mind Tools site details various techniques for enhancing one's memory in different situations. http://www.mindtools.com/memory.html

2. A Web site containing some simple memory tests. These are designed for kids, but fun for adults too. http://faculty.washington.edu/chudler/chmemory.html

3. An interactive site with ELIZA, an artificial intelligence program, that simulates a Rogerian psychotherapist. http://www.manifestation.com/neurotoys/eliza.php3

4. The Wadsworth CogLab site that contains some demonstrations of memory and other aspects of cognition. http://coglab.wadsworth.com/

5. A site from MSNBC concerning amnesia, the brain, and memory. http://www.msnbc.com/onair/nbc/dateline/amnesia/default.asp

6. Amanda's Mnemonics Page is a privately maintained Web site with mnemonics for many fields of study. Be aware that some of these mnemonics may contain sexual references. http://www.frii.com/~geomanda/mnemonics.html

Student Study Guide

To help organize your learning, work through Chapter 6 of the *What Is Psychology? Student Study Guide*. The study guide includes learning objectives, a chapter summary, fill-in review, key terms, a practice test, and activities.

Psychology Now™

PsychologyNow is a Web-based, personalized study system that provides you with a pretest and a posttest for each chapter, quizzes you by chapter, and provides a personalized study plan, pointing you to elements in the text or in individual learning modules that will help you to achieve 80% mastery. Check out the learning modules that relate to this chapter: methods of studying memory; levels of processing—methods of studying.

PsychNow CD-ROM, Version 2.0

Go to the PsychNow CD-ROM for further study of the concepts in this chapter. The CD-ROM includes learning modules with videos, animations, and quizzes, as well as simulations of psychological phenomena. Each module follows a consistent Explore, Lesson, and Apply structure that allows you to experience the concept or principle, learn more about it, and then apply it. You and your friends can participate in a team-based Quiz Game that makes learning fun. You can also participate in experiments such as Brown-Peterson, False Memory, Memory span, and Serial position. Learning modules include: 5d. Memory Systems; 5e. Forgetting.

How Does Memory Function?

The human brain encodes memory in the form of memory traces, which are bits of information placed in storage and available for retrieval. The conscious use of memory is defined as explicit memory. Implicit memory is when we use memory without conscious effort.

THE TRADITIONAL THREE STAGES MODEL OF MEMORY

• According to the three-stages model of memory, information coming from our eyes, ears, and other senses is briefly stored in a sensory form called sensory memory. If we pay attention to the information in our sensory memory, it is sent to our short-term memory for further processing. If we choose to process further, we can move the information to long-term memory.

New information enters working memory from sensory memory

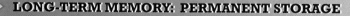

• Iconic memory is the sensory memory for visual stimuli, whereas echoic memory is an auditory image or recording of sound we hear.

• For information to be transferred from sensory memory to short-term memory, we must first pay attention to the sensory information.

• Short-term memory uses a dual coding system in which memories can be stored either visually or acoustically.

• Capacity limits the amount of information we can hold in short-term memory. Chunking of information, such as a series of numbers, words, or other items, can assist short-term memory.

• Information in short-term memory can be retained for only about 20 seconds. To keep information in short-term memory for a longer time requires repeating it in a process known as maintenance rehearsal.

• Transferring information into long-term memory involves elaborative rehearsal, which includes forming associations to what is already in long-term memory.

• The tendency to remember the words at the beginning of a list is known as the primacy effect, whereas the tendency to remember the words at the end of the list is called the recency effect.

• Many researchers today reject the rigid three-stages process of memory and suggest a different type of memory, called working memory, is important in moving information in and out of long-term memory.

• A prominent theory of multicomponent working memory proposes that working memory is a part of long-term memory that contains short-term memory and a central executive component and with two slave systems: the phonological loop, which processes auditory information, and the visuospatial sketch pad, which processes visual and spatial information.

LONG-TERM MEMORY: PERMANENT STORAGE

• Long-term memory is our largest and most permanent memory storage system. Unlike short-term memory, long-term memory seems to have a limitless capacity.

• Semantic encoding is important in long-term memory. It is the process of storing the gist, or general meaning, of a stimulus rather than storing all the sensory details.

• Schemata are generalized knowledge structures that we use to organize our knowledge by categories.

• Long-term memory includes declarative memory (for names, dates, and facts), semantic memory (conceptual memory), and episodic memory (memories of events in one's life).

• Procedural memory is often implicit and tends to last longer in long-term memory.

• Amnesia is a condition in which a person cannot recall certain declarative memories. Amnesia is classified as either retrograde (inability to recall previously stored declarative memories) or anteretrograde (inability to encode new declarative memories in long-term memory.

RETRIEVAL AND FORGETTING: RANDOM ACCESS MEMORY?

• Retrieval is the act of moving information from long-term memory back into working memory or consciousness. Retrieval occurs when we send a probe or cue into long-term memory in search of memory traces or encoded memories we have stored there.

• In a recall task, the probe is weak and does not contain much information as you search your memory. In recognition tasks, the probe is stronger and contains more information than a recall cue.

• Decay theory maintains that once a memory trace is stored in long-term memory, it must be routinely activated to keep it there.

• Proactive interference occurs when older information inhibits our ability to retrieve other, newer information from memory. Retroactive interference occurs when newer information inhibits the retrieval of older information in memory.

• The theory of cue-dependent forgetting asserts that the amount of information we can retrieve from memory is a function of the type of cue or probe we use.

• Freud proposed that memories that are emotionally threatening can be pushed or repressed into an inaccessible part of the mind called the unconscious.

IS MEMORY ACCURATE?

• Flashbulb memories are unusually detailed memories for emotionally charged events—memories that are quite powerful but not always accurate.

• Memory is not a video recorder, and it is not just reconstructive, or based on actual events. Memory is constructive, in that we use the knowledge and expectations that we have stored in our schemata to help us fill in missing details in our stored memory.

• Eyewitness memory can be subject to manipulation, even the planting of and false memories are even possible.

THE BIOLOGY OF MEMORY

• Brain-imaging research shows that people who use their memory a great deal may have structural differences in their hippocampal regions. The hippocampus and frontal lobe seem to play significant roles in processing declarative memory.

• Studies suggest that procedural memory is linked to brain structures outside the hippocampus.

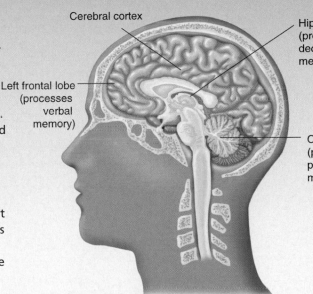

Cerebral cortex

Hippocampus (processes declarative memory)

Left frontal lobe (processes verbal memory)

Cerebellum (processes procedural memory)

IMPROVING YOUR MEMORY

• Pay attention to what you are trying to remember; avoid distractions.

• Do not cram for exams.

• Use elaborative rehearsal to reinforce retention of information.

• Use overlearning.

• Mnemonics Makes Your Memory Mighty.

• The SQ3R method for studying material encourages a process of Survey, Question, Read, Recite, Review.

"*The bridge was built, the connection made. Now we could cross the chasm and face each other, sharing our new gift of conversation.*"

(FROM SUSAN SCHALLER. *A MAN WITHOUT WORDS*,
(New York: Summit Books,1991)

© Helen King/Corbis

Cognition, Language, and Intelligence: How Do We Think?

CHAPTER

7

A Life Without Language?

There are a number of things that many of us tend to take for granted in our lives—our health, our friends, our freedom, and so on. Often, we do not realize the importance of certain things until we are faced with life without them. As the old saying goes, "You never miss the water until the well runs dry!" For instance, let's look at our ability to use language. If you are like most people, you probably have never stopped to think about a life without language. And because language touches so many aspects of our lives, it is virtually impossible for us to truly understand what life would be like if we knew *no* language at all! Just try to imagine it. What if you knew no words or gestures that symbolized the objects and concepts in your life? Even those with deafness or those who don't speak the dominant language in their culture still have ways of symbolizing the world. Without any language, how would you communicate? What would your thoughts be like without words? How would you view yourself if you didn't have a name? Can a person be intelligent without knowing a language? Most of us cannot truly answer these questions, but unfortunately there are a few people in the world who know exactly what it is to live without language. In *A Man Without Words,* author Susan Schaller (1995) captured the remarkable story of one languageless man.

Susan met Ildefonso when she was working as an American Sign Language interpreter in a Los Angeles program for deaf persons. Ildefonso was one of Susan's students. At the time, Ildefonso was a 27-year-old undocumented worker from Mexico who had come to the United States to work as a crop harvester. Prior to being enrolled in the deaf education program by his uncle, Ildefonso had worked all over the country picking crops, but he was unable to participate in many aspects of life because of his impairment.

Like most of the other students in Susan's class, Ildefonso had been born completely deaf. But unlike the other students in the class, Ildefonso had *no* understanding of any spoken or signed language. He knew no Spanish, English, American Sign Language, or Mexican Sign Language. In fact, Ildefonso did not even know that language existed. He communicated by pantomime; his world was completely devoid of words or gestures that functioned as symbols for things. He did not even know that he had a name!

Ildefonso was born in a rural area of Oaxaca in southern Mexico. When Ildefonso's parents realized that he was deaf, they labeled him as a "dummy" and refused to send him to school. By the time he was about 5, Ildefonso was working in the sugarcane fields and tending flocks of sheep and goats. When work was not available on the local farms, Ildefonso would beg for money and food. At age 10, Ildefonso's parents sent him to live with his grandfather in Mexico City, but there, too, he was deprived of any formal education. Without education or exposure to people who knew sign language, Ildefonso grew up without learning a language. Without words with which to communicate, Ildefonso pantomimed his thoughts and desires, just as you do when you play the game charades. Pantomime allowed Ildefonso to communicate with others in a crude fashion, but his lack of language isolated him from others and prevented him from understanding much of his world.

Eventually, Ildefonso wound up in Los Angeles, where he met Susan Schaller. Although Susan would be instrumental in dramatically changing Ildefonso's life for the better, at first she had little success in working with him. Susan began teaching sign language, or signing, to Ildefonso, but she found it impossible to teach him sign language using conventional methods of instruction. She would sign the sign for a word and then point to the thing it represented in the real world. For example, she would sign the word "tree" and then point to a tree in the yard. Ildefonso would

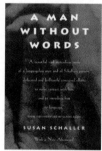

Susan Schaller's book *A Man Without Words* chronicles the time she spent teaching Ildefonso, who was unable to hear or speak, his first language.

"I was suddenly impatient to see Ildefonso. . . . That day he had grasped the rope I had been throwing him."

(Schaller, p. 46)

mimic her actions. He would sign the word "tree" and point to the tree, but he did not understand what she meant. He did not understand that things had labels. Even though Susan tried to stop Ildefonso from mimicking her gestures, no amount of signing and pointing to objects seemed to reach him. He continued mimicking Susan's signs without understanding the significance of his own actions.

Then Susan had in inspiration. Instead of repeatedly signing a word and pointing to its referent, she acted out a skit of a teacher teaching a student to sign words. In this skit, she played both the role of the teacher and the role of the student. She would pantomime a teacher signing the word "cat," and then she would write the word "cat" on the board and pantomime stroking the fur of an imaginary cat. Then she would play the role of the student, who sat and watched what the teacher was doing, studied the sign for the word, and then appeared to understand the significance of the word and its sign. The genius of this approach was that it freed Ildefonso to merely sit back and watch. During the skit, Susan completely ignored Ildefonso, so there was no need for him to concentrate on mimicking her actions. All he had to do was watch and try to understand the meaning of the skit. When Ildefonso was free to merely watch, with no pressure to mimic the signs he was seeing, he finally began to understand the message Susan was trying to convey. He finally understood that things, such as a "cat," had labels and these labels could be written words or gestured signs. He finally understood the concept of language.

Once Ildefonso recognized the existence of language in the world, he realized how much he had been deprived of as a child. His first reaction was one of sorrow, and he wept openly at the knowledge of all that he did not know. Then he got down to the business of learning his first language, American Sign Language (ASL), at age 27!

Eventually, Ildefonso learned enough ASL to function adequately in the deaf world, but he still relied heavily on pantomime to communicate with others. With his newfound abilities, Ildefonso became a legal resident and got a good job as a landscape artist. He continued to study ASL and to learn about the world that had excluded him for so long. He also went on to mentor other languageless people, including his own brother who had also been born deaf. In short, Ildefonso became an engaged and productive citizen of the world.

The story of Ildefonso is both a tragedy and a triumph of the human spirit. It also gives us a glimpse into a world that most of us can barely imagine. Ildefonso's lack of language touched nearly every aspect of his life, particularly his thinking. People with language—most of us—tend to think in terms of words. For us, much of our knowledge is stored in a verbal form, but for Ildefonso that was impossible. His knowledge of the world had to be stored in some other form, most likely in pictures. This no doubt affected the way that he thought, solved problems, and even the way that he viewed himself—Idelfonso wasn't aware that he had a name until he learned language. Despite his lack of language, Ildefonso was obviously an intelligent man, even though he would have scored low on many commonly used intelligence tests because they are verbally based.

By considering the case of Ildefonso, we see the interconnectedness of thought, language, and intelligence. This interdependence is also true for the vast majority of us who use language everyday. Language is related to just about every aspect of the way in which we store and use information, or what psychologists refer to as **cognition.** In this chapter, we will explore many aspects of cognition including *thinking, language,* and *intelligence.* As you read this chapter, reflect on your own use of language, and try to imagine what life must be like for those who've been deprived of language because of prejudice against the deaf or a lack of exposure to appropriate deaf education.

cognition   the way in which we use and store information in memory

LEARNING OBJECTIVE

‹ ‹ ‹ ‹ ‹ ‹ ‹ ‹

Describe the process of thinking and the manner in which we represent knowledge in our memory.

knowledge   information stored in our long-term memory about the world and how it works

thinking   the use of knowledge to accomplish some sort of goal

mental representation   memory traces that represent objects, events, people, and so on, that are not present at the time

Thinking: How We Use What We Know

Most people would agree that thinking is fundamental to our everyday lives. We engage in some sort of thinking every waking moment. We think about others, we think hard on exams, and we think about what we'll have for dinner. But most of us would have difficulty defining what it is that we actually *do* when we think. As we saw in Chapters 3 and 6, we are continually taking in information from the outside world, some of which we process and store in long-term memory. The information we store in long-term memory about the world and how it works constitutes our **knowledge** base. Psychologists define **thinking** as the use of knowledge to accomplish some sort of goal: to perceive and understand our world, to communicate with others, and to solve the problems we encounter in our lives (Mayer, 1983). Every time you retrieve some bit of knowledge from long-term memory to help answer a test question or remember the name of an old friend, you are *thinking.*

Thinking involves the use of all types of knowledge. In our long-term memory, we store our knowledge as **mental representations**—bits of memory—that represent objects, events, people, and so on, that are not actually present now. For instance, most of us can close our eyes and think about what our best friend looks like even though she isn't present. To do this, we call on the mental representations we have stored of our knowledge of what our friend looks like. Similarly, we can recall the name of our best friend, the smell of her perfume, and the color of her hair by recalling the various mental representations of her that we have stored in our knowledge base.

In general, thinking involves the use of two broad classes of mental representations—those based on *sensory* aspects of the object, like its visual appearance, smell, taste, and so forth; and those based on the *meaning* of the object, like the object's name, definition, and properties. We will now turn our attention to a discussion of the best-studied forms of these mental representations: *visual images* and *concepts.*

Visual Images: How Good Is the Mental Picture?

With no words to work with, Ildefonso probably encoded much of his knowledge of the world as visual images. Prior to learning his first language, Ildefonso's knowledge must have been primarily a conglomeration of pictures. Unlike Ildefonso, most of us have the ability to store information in a verbal form, but this does not mean that visual images are not important means of storing knowledge of the world. The ability to "see" a friend's face in our mind or to visualize a map of our hometown in our head can be very useful in everyday life. Over the years, psychologists have studied visual images by examining how people perform on certain tasks in which they must mentally manipulate visual images.

One task that is used to study visual images is *mental rotation.* In a mental-rotation task, participants are asked to mentally rotate, or turn, an image of some stimulus in their head. For example, in one such experiment participants were shown a series of letters that were oriented at different angles. In addition to being rotated, some of the letters were normal (right-reading), whereas others were reversed in mirror-image format (Figure 7.1). After viewing the letter, the participant had to determine whether or not the letter was normal or reversed. The results of the experiment showed that as the letter was rotated further from an upright position, it took the participant more time to judge whether the letter was normal or reversed (Cooper & Shepard, 1973). These results indicate that the task of judging the letter required that the participants mentally rotate a visual image of the letter from its rotated position back to an upright position before they made a judgment. The further rotated the stimulus letter was, the further they had to rotate their visual image and the longer it took them.

The results of this and numerous other mental-rotation experiments (see Shepard, 1978, for a review) suggest that visual images may have all of the spatial properties of the real stimulus. In other words, the visual image we store is essentially a *copy* of the stimulus we see in the world. Another line of evidence for this match between mental image and external reality comes from *image-scanning* studies that examine how we mentally scan images in our head (Denis & Cocude, 1999; Kosslyn, Ball, & Reiser, 1978).

In a typical image-scanning experiment, like the one done by Stephen Kosslyn and colleagues (Kosslyn et al., 1978), participants are asked to memorize a map of a fictitious island with several objects depicted on it (see Figure 7.2). After the participants have memorized the map, they are then asked to mentally scan the path that a black dot would take as it travels from one point on the map to another. Because the points exist at various distances from one another, researchers can then correlate the time it takes the participants to mentally scan the image with the distance between the points on the actual map. If the participants' visual images of the map are copies of the actual map, then the time it takes to scan longer distances should be longer than the time it takes to scan short distances on the map. This is exactly what Stephen Kosslyn found (see Figure 7.2). The time it took to scan distances increased proportionately with the increase in the actual distances on the map.

The Limits of the Mental Picture

As convincing as the mental-rotation and image-scanning experiments are in supporting the argument that visual images have spatial properties that mimic those of the actual stimulus, the question still remains: Do we actually store photographic images of the things that we see? As it turns out, there are reasons to suspect that this may not always be true. For one, several studies indicate that mental rotation does not always correlate with the physical properties of the stimulus (Boden, 1988; Hinton, 1979), and there is also evidence to suggest we cannot always manipulate our visual images in the same manner that we could manipulate the actual object (Chambers & Reisberg, 1985).

For example, participants in one study were shown an ambiguous figure, like that shown in Figure 3.1 (page 100), and asked to form a visual image of it in their heads. As we saw in Chapter 3, because this figure can be interpreted as a duck or a rabbit, some of the participants interpreted the image in their heads as a duck and others as a rabbit. While the participants were holding the image of the ambiguous figure in their heads, they were asked to reinterpret it as something else—to see it as a duck, if they had originally seen it as a rabbit, or vice versa. Astonishingly, none of them could do so. They could see the image in their heads only as being what they had originally interpreted it to be. However, the participants were able to draw a picture of the figure, and once they had drawn it, they could interpret the figure as being either a duck or a rabbit (Chambers & Reisberg, 1985). They could see the figure both ways on paper, but only one way in their heads! If the visual image in their heads had all of the same properties as the actual stimulus, then why were the participants unable to reinterpret their visual image? Apparently, although the visual images we have in our heads do retain some characteristics of the actual stimulus, they are also influenced by the verbal interpretation we place on them (Chambers & Reisberg, 1992).

The Map in Your Mind

The imprecision of visual images can be further seen in the following demonstration. Let's look at your ability to answer questions about a visual stimulus that you have seen many times, a map of North America. Answer these questions:

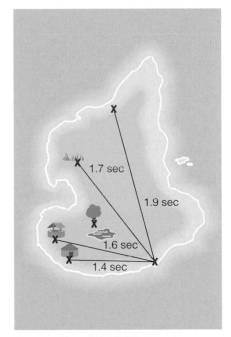

Normal		Mirror-image	
R 0°	R 300°	Я 0°	Я 300°
R 60°	R 240°	Я 60°	Я 240°
R 120°	R 180°	Я 120°	Я 180°

Figure 7.1 A Mental Rotation Task

In this task, participants were asked to determine whether the letter was right-reading or reversed. The greater the rotation, the longer it took.

From M. W. Eysenck and M. T. Keene, Cognitive Psychology, 4/e, p. 258. © Psychological Press.

Figure 7.2 An Image Scanning Task

In this task, participants were asked to imagine a black dot moving across the map to the points indicated by the Xs. The average amount of time to do this was proportionate with the distance between the starting point and the ending point on the map.

Source: © Stephen Kosslyn 1983.

 Demonstration

Which is farther east: Reno, NV, or San Diego, CA?

Which is farther north: Montreal, Canada, or Seattle, WA?

Which is farther west: the Atlantic or the Pacific entrance
to the Panama Canal?

The answers seem obvious, but researchers have found that most people tend to answer them incorrectly (Stevens & Coupe, 1978). The correct answers are *San Diego*, *Seattle*, and the *Atlantic entrance*. Do these answers surprise you? They do most people. In fact, one of the authors (Doyle-Portillo) had to convince herself by checking a map, and you may need to look at Figure 7.3, too.

Why so many of us answer these questions incorrectly has to do with how we have organized our knowledge about the geography of the world, in what are called **cognitive maps.** We introduced cognitive maps in Chapter 5 in our discussion of the role cognition plays in learning—remember Edward Tolman's work with rats learning the path through a maze (p. 238)? In this case, our cognitive maps are mental representations for geographical information. It appears that we do not store an exact visual image of a map of the world in our cognitive map. Rather, we store an approximate visual image of the map as well as some general knowledge about the geography of the area. Furthermore, when we try to visualize maps in our heads, we tend to think of geographical locations in terms of larger units (Stevens & Coupe, 1978), and we use this knowledge to help us deduce the needed geographical information (B. Tversky, 1981). In response to the first question, "Which is farther east?," we know that San Diego is in California, and we know that California is west of Nevada. Therefore, when we recall our cognitive map of the United States, we assume that Reno, Nevada, must be east of San Diego, and we visualize a map in which this is true. In fact, this is not true, as you can see in Figure 7.3.

So, where does all of this research leave us with respect to visual images? Isn't it a bit contradictory? Some studies suggest that visual images are precise mental copies of the actual stimuli, but other studies show that visual images may deviate significantly from the actual stimuli. According to Stephen Kosslyn (1994), our mental representation of visual stimuli relies on *both* visual images and verbal knowledge. In other words, we use both types of mental representations—sensory (pictures) and meaning (words)—to fully represent visual stimuli. The pictures represent parts of the stimulus, and the words describe the stimulus and tell us how the pieces of the picture fit together. For example, when you look at a flower, you might store, among other things, a visual image of the shape of a petal, the stem, and the center along with verbal instructions that the petals are placed around the center and the stem descends from the bottom of the flower.

In Kosslyn's view, we do not store a carbon copy of the flower. Instead, we use this mixture of verbal and pictorial pieces to *construct* our visual image of the flower. This should ring some bells in your head. As we learned in Chapter 6 (p. XXX), memory is *constructive*, and unfortunately, the constructive nature of memory does sometimes lead to inaccuracies. So, don't feel bad if you thought Reno was east of San Diego!

It appears that language plays an important role in our representation of knowledge even when we are dealing with visual information. It would be interesting to know how Ildefonso stored visual images without the use of any verbal instructions. We will never know how Ildefonso's mind was able to cope with this lack of language. Psychologists have not had much opportunity to study people like Ildefonso, but we have had the chance to study those of us who do use language as part of our mental representation of the world. Later in this chapter, we will take a closer look at how we use language to represent the *meaning* of our world.

cognitive map   a mental representation of the environment that is formed through observation of one's environment

Concepts: How We Organize What We Know

As we saw in Chapter 6, we have a tendency to organize our knowledge in long-term memory. We store mental representations for related objects together in the same mental category. For example, we would store our knowledge of cats, dogs, and elephants together in the category for *animals*, and pineapple, oranges, and grapes together in the category for *fruits*. This tendency to organize information based on similarity shows the *conceptual* nature of human cognition. **Concepts,** the mental categories that contain related bits of knowledge, are organized around the *meaning* of the information they represent. For instance, *animal* is a concept. In our mind we know what it means to be an animal. Animals must be animate, but we also distinguish animals from humans, and so on.

We store conceptual information in a verbal, or *prepositional*, form (recall Chapter 6, p. 270), and we use this information to perceive, think about, and deal with our world. Conceptually organizing our knowledge helps us use our knowledge more efficiently. Concepts can be viewed as a type of mental shorthand that both organizes and saves space in our cognitive system. Let's look at an example of a well-known concept: oranges. Close your eyes and picture an orange in your mind's eye. Can you see it clearly? Can you describe it in detail? Most of us can do this easily for something as familiar as an orange. Now look carefully at your mental orange. Is this concept that you have stored in your mind an *actual* orange that you have seen? In other words, is this orange number 123,675 that you saw one Sunday morning at the local market? Not likely! Instead, your concept of an orange is an abstraction, or a general idea, of what an orange is. You don't have to store mental representations for each and every orange you have seen. Rather, you only need to store a generalized concept of what an orange is and what it looks like. This is a great cognitive space-saver when you think about all of the oranges you'll see in your lifetime!

concept mental category that contains related bits of knowledge

Organizing Concepts Into Categories

Another benefit of mental concepts is that we can organize them into hierarchical categories. Psychologists have found that we tend to organize our knowledge into three levels of categorization (Rosch, Mervis, Gray, Johnson, & Boyes-Braem, 1976). The highest, most general level is called the **supcrordinate category.** The superordinate level contains concepts that are broad and general in their description. For example, fruit would be considered to be a superordinate category. The intermediate level of categorization is the **basic level category.** The basic level seems to be the level that we use most often to think about our world. For example, when we write out a shopping list, we probably list basic level concepts, such as oranges rather than fruit.

The third level in the hierarchy is the **subordinate category.** Concepts at the subordinate level are less general and more specific than those at the basic level. When speaking of oranges, the subordinate category would contain items like Valencia oranges, navel oranges, and blood oranges. Although the subordinate level is the most specific, it is not the first level that springs to mind when we think about our world. You would be much more likely to place the basic level concept—oranges—on your shopping list than you would be to place Valencia oranges. Interestingly, the basic level is also the first level of knowledge young children acquire (Rosch et al., 1976).

superordinate category the highest, most general level of a concept

basic level category the intermediate level of categorization that seems to be the level that we use most to think about our world

subordinate category the lowest level of categorization, which contains concepts that are less general and more specific than those at the basic level

Formal and Natural Categories

So, how do we acquire concepts in the first place? Simply put, we acquire concepts from an early age as we observe and learn from our world. We acquire **formal concepts** as we learn the rigid rules that define certain categories of things. For example, for an

formal concept concept that is based on the rigid rules we learn that define certain categories of things

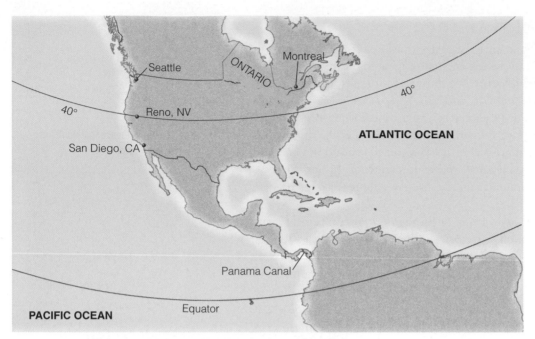

ATLANTIC OCEAN

PACIFIC OCEAN

Equator

Figure 7.3 A Map of North and South America

Most people incorrectly answer many questions about this map even though they have seen it many times before. It is highly unlikely that we have an exact visual image of this map stored in our long-term memory.

The basic level category of *apples* falls under the superordinate category of *fruit*. The label *Granny Smith* is a subordinate category to the basic level concept of *apples*.

natural concept   concept that develops naturally as we live our lives and experience the world

Demonstration

animal to be considered to be a member of the category *female*, it must possess certain attributes or characteristics. All females are genetically designed to produce either offspring or eggs. If an animal does not have this attribute, it cannot be a female.

The lines that define formal categories are very clear-cut. Unfortunately, life is not always so neat and tidy as to provide us with formal rules for everything, and much of our knowledge of the world does not fit cleanly into only one category. For example, do you consider a tomato to be a fruit or a vegetable? How do you categorize cucumbers? Many people consider tomatoes and cucumbers to be vegetables, whereas others—including botanists—categorize them as fruits. Why the confusion? Perhaps because we associate fruits with sweetness, we tend not to classify cucumbers and tomatoes as fruit even though they do contain seeds, which is a defining attribute of fruit. Most of us are aware of the rules for membership as a female, but not aware of the botanical definition of a fruit. We have organized our fruit and vegetable concepts in a less distinct and orderly fashion based on our own experiences with them.

Concepts that develop naturally as we live our lives and experience the world are referred to as **natural concepts.** We do not learn formal rules for these concepts; rather, we intuit and create the rules as we learn about our world. As such, the boundaries defining natural concept categories are often blurry, or "fuzzy" (Rosch, 1973a). Our example of the tomato is a good illustration of this. You can classify the tomato as a vegetable, a fruit, or both depending on your experience. How do you see it?

Because natural concept categories have fuzzy boundaries, the task of deciding which concepts to include and which to exclude from the category varies in difficulty. Sometimes it's an easy task, and other times it's not. Take a look at Figure 7.4, and answer the questions as quickly as you can. Which of the questions are you able to answer quickly? Which ones take longer? Why do you think some of them are easier than others?

	Is a bat a mammal?	Yes ☐	No ☐
	Is a dolphin a mammal?	Yes ☐	No ☐
	Is a penguin a bird?	Yes ☐	No ☐
	Is a cat a mammal?	Yes ☐	No ☐
	Is a robin a bird?	Yes ☐	No ☐
	Is a whale a mammal?	Yes ☐	No ☐
	Is an eagle a bird?	Yes ☐	No ☐

All answers are "Yes".

Figure 7.4 Natural Concept Categories

Answer these as fast as you can.

Most people find it easier to decide that a robin is a bird than that a penguin is a bird. This is because a robin is a more typical example of the category "bird" than a penguin is. We form what are called **prototypes** for natural concept categories, much like the mental image of the orange we examined on page 303. A prototype is our concept of the most typical member of the category—in essence, a summary of all the members of the category (Medin, 1989). When we judge whether or not something belongs in a natural concept category, we compare it to the prototype of the category. Otherwise, we would have to examine the specific attributes of the stimulus—the robin or the penguin—and compare these to the defining attributes of the concept category, bird (Rosch, 1973b). So, even though robins and penguins both have defining attributes of birds—wings and the ability to lay eggs—a robin is more birdlike. Therefore, we are quicker to decide that a robin belongs in the category of birds.

Recall that *thinking* is defined as our ability to use the knowledge that we have stored in our long-term memory to accomplish some goal (p. 300). In our next section, we will see just what we can accomplish with all of our thinking. But first, take a moment to test your *knowledge* of this last section on the following quiz!

prototype   our concept of the most typical member of the category

Let's Review!

In this section, we discussed thinking and how we represent information in memory. We discussed not only the format of stored knowledge, but also its organizational structure. For a quick check of your understanding, answer these questions.

1. One piece of evidence that indicates our visual images contain all the properties of the actual stimulus is:
   a. memory for images is near perfect in children.
   b. the time it takes to mentally scan an image of an object is related to the actual size of the object.
   c. most people can visualize familiar objects in great detail.
   d. our mental maps of the world are perfect in their detail.

2. Which of the following would be a superordinate concept for the category of "hammers"?
   a. ball-peen hammers   c. tools
   b. saws   d. screwdrivers

3. In an experiment, Dr. Kelly asks participants to name the first example of a "vehicle" that comes to mind. Based on what you know about concepts, which of the following vehicles would the average participant be *most* likely to name?
   a. a tractor   c. an airplane
   b. a train   d. a truck

ANSWERS

1.b; 2. c; 3.d

LEARNING OBJECTIVES

Describe the different types of problems we are faced with and the ways in which we may attempt to solve them.

Discuss common obstacles to problem solving.

Problem Solving: Where Does Our Thinking Get Us?

Imagine that you get into your car one morning, only to find that it won't start. It's 7:30 and you have an 8:00 class. Today of all days, you don't need this because you have a final exam in your psychology class. You have a problem! As you can see from this example, we never know when a problem will arise. What would you do in this situation? Call a friend for a ride? Walk to school? Call your professor and arrange to take a makeup final? Or fix your own car? In general, when we solve problems, we go through a series of six stages (Hayes, 1989), as outlined in Figure 7.5.

Although the prospect of missing a final exam is frightening, there are a variety of obvious solutions to this problem. This is not the case for all problems, however. If it were, we would have ended hunger, war, and pollution long ago. Why do some problems seem to have obvious possible solutions whereas others do not? The answer lies in the type of problem we are facing.

Well-Structured Problems: The Answer Is Out There

Well-structured problems are problems for which there is a clear pathway to the solution. For example, what if your best friend asks you to make him *crème brulée* (pronounced *KREM-bru-LAY*), a French dessert, for his birthday? Even if you don't know how to make crème brulée, you know that you can find a recipe and follow the instructions to produce the desired result. Making crème brulée may not be simple, but you can get the information you need to accomplish your goal.

We face well-structured problems every day. Programming your VCR, calculating your income taxes, and finding the cheapest hotel at your vacation destination are all examples of well-structured problems. When we solve well-structured problems, we tend to go about it in one of two ways. We use either an algorithm or a heuristic to bring about a solution.

well-structured problem problem for which there is a clear pathway to the solution

Application

Problem-Solving Step	Example
Identify the Problem.	The car won't start, and I have a final exam.
Represent the Problem.	If I miss this exam without permission, I'll fail the course.
Plan a Solution.	I will call a taxi.
Execute the Plan.	Call the taxi.
Evaluate the Plan.	The taxi will get me to school, but I will be late. Maybe I should also have called my professor?
Evaluate the Solution.	I did make it to school, and I took the exam. My professor was a bit angry that I didn't call to say I'd be late, but I did pass the exam. I handled this situation adequately, but next time I'll call my professor.

Figure 7.5 The Steps to Problem Solving

Source: Hayes, 1989.

Algorithms and Heuristics:
The Long and Short of Problem Solving

An **algorithm** is a method of solving a particular problem that always leads to the correct solution, and a **heuristic** is a shortcut or rule-of-thumb that may or may not lead to a correct solution. Imagine that you're going to paint your bedroom, but you don't know how much paint to buy. The algorithmic solution to this problem is to measure the height and width of all your walls, calculate the square area, and look up how many gallons of paint are required to cover this area. This algorithm will lead to the correct answer, and as a result, you will buy just the right amount of paint. However, this strategy also takes considerable time. You must measure the walls, find the formula for paint coverage, and calculate the required figures. If you are in a hurry or impatient, this strategy may not be your first choice!

So how can you solve your problem more quickly? You could use a heuristic, such as simply guessing how much paint you will need to do the job. Guessing is quick, but you do run the risk of not buying the right amount of paint. You might have to go back to the store for more paint, or you might have a lot of paint left over. *Guessing* and repeated guessing, or *trial and error*, are two very common heuristics.

As you look at this example, you may feel that is seems foolish to guess at the amount of paint to buy when a clear algorithm exists for this problem. Why would anyone approach a problem in this seemingly haphazard fashion? There are several reasons why one would choose a heuristic over an algorithm. First, heuristics can save time. Heuristics are mental shortcuts that can quickly lead us to quick solutions. You might correctly guess that you need 2 gallons of paint to cover your room, especially if you have experience painting rooms. In this case, measuring the room would be an unnecessary waste of time. Second, we do not always know the correct algorithm for the problem we are facing. What if you lack the mathematical knowledge to calculate the surface area of your bedroom walls? Even though there is a formula for calculating the surface area and paint coverage, if you don't know what it is, you cannot implement the algorithm, and you would have to use a heuristic.

Ill-structured problems are problems for which there is no known algorithm. For example, do you know an algorithm for bringing about world peace? Unfortunately, neither do we. In the case of an ill-structured problem, we have no choice but

« | Application

algorithm   a method of solving a particular problem that always leads to the correct solution

heuristic   a shortcut or rule-of-thumb that may or may not lead to a correct solution to the problem

Successfully balancing your checkbook is best accomplished using an algorithm. By systematically adding up your deposits and subtracting your withdrawals, you will arrive at the correct balance.

ill-structured problem   a problem for which an algorithm is not known

to use a heuristic, but this does not mean that there is no chance the problem will be solved.

Ill-Structured Problems: The Answer May Be Out There

As we said, ill-structured problems are those that do not have clear algorithms, but they sometimes can be solved. Try this problem, which is like the one used by researcher James Adams (1976).

Demonstration Assume that you are one of six people in a room. In the center of the room is a pipe that is embedded in the concrete floor (Figure 7.6). The pipe extends for 4 inches above the surface of the floor. In the pipe is a ping-pong ball. The ping-pong ball has a diameter of 1.5 inches, and the inside diameter of the pipe is 2.1 inches. Among the six people in the room, you have the following items: a file, 100 feet of clothesline, a hammer, a chisel, a box of cornflakes, a wire coat hanger, a monkey wrench, and a lightbulb. Your task is to remove the ping-pong ball from the pipe *without* damaging the pipe, the floor, or the ball.

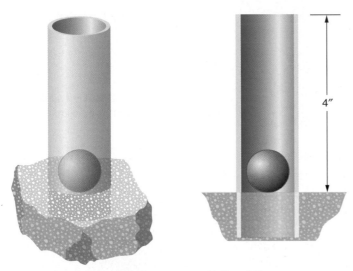

Figure 7.6 An Ill-Structured Problem

How would you get the ball out of the pipe?

From Robert L. Solso, Cognitive Psychology, 3/e. *Published by Allyn & Bacon, Boston, MA. Copyright © 1991 by Pearson Education. Reprinted by permission of the publisher.*

With no clear algorithm for this problem, how would you proceed? Most people would probably try some form of the trial-and-error heuristic to get the ball out. You might try to hit the pipe with the hammer in hopes of vibrating the ball upward. You might try using the wire from the coat hanger to lift the ball out. Or you might try sucking the ball out of the pipe with your mouth because ping-pong balls are so light. But these techniques are unlikely to achieve the desired result. Many of us would be stumped by this problem, especially if we are from a Western culture. That's a hint! Why would your culture make a difference in this case?

One interesting thing about culture is that it influences the approach we take to solving problems. In the United States, we have learned to approach problems like this one with tools, so our first instinct is to make or use some sort of tool to mechanically remove the ball from the pipe. Our culture also dictates what is and is not appropriate public behavior. There is a way to get the ball out of the pipe, but to do it, you have to break one of our Western cultural taboos. Have you guessed the solution yet? *Have one of the people in the room pee into the pipe.* The ball will float to the surface on the urine. By now, you're probably saying, "Yuck! I don't want to get the ball out of the pipe that badly!" Your disgust for this solution is part of the point. In many Western cultures, urinating in public is considered to be socially unacceptable behavior. Therefore, many Westerners would not attempt to solve this problem in this fashion. However, in a culture in which public urination is not so taboo, people would have no qualms about using this effective strategy.

Aside from an unwillingness to use socially undesirable methods of solving problems, we may not even *think* of certain possible solutions. This is often the case with ill-structured problems. Often we get stuck in particular ways of trying to solve problems, and we lack the required **insight** needed to find a true solution. Insight occurs when we find a new way of looking at the problem that leads to a sudden understanding of how to solve it (Dominowski & Dallob, 1995). Because of its perceived suddenness, insight is often referred to as the "Aha!" experience. Insight often feels as if a "lightbulb" has

insight   when we find a new way of looking at the problem that leads to a sudden understanding of how to solve it turned on, illuminating the answer for us. But current research indicates that insight isn't such a sudden process. Insight often occurs only after we have thought about the problem for awhile (Kaplan & Simon, 1990). Furthermore, truly understanding a problem and how to solve it often occurs only as the result of much thought and gradual acquisition of knowledge about the problem (Hamel & Elshout, 2000).

Creativity: Overcoming Obstacles to Problem Solving

We do not need to tell you that some problems in life are more difficult to face than others are. At times, all of us may encounter problems that challenge even our best problem-solving skills. For example, Susan Schaller's early attempts to teach language to Ildefonso failed. To solve the difficult problem of getting Ildefonso to grasp the concept of language, Schaller had to use what we commonly refer to as *creativity*. To reach Ildefonso, Schaller came up with the unconventional idea of ignoring him while she pantomimed a scene of a teacher teaching language to an imaginary student. She had to abandon the typical approaches to teaching sign language that had worked for her in the past in favor of this novel, creative approach.

For over 50 years, psychologists have been trying to define exactly what creativity is and what abilities or traits creative people possess (Mumford, 2003). To date, the major agreement among researchers has been that **creativity** involves the ability to combine mental elements in new and useful ways (e.g., Sternberg, 1999; Vartanian, Martindale, & Kwiatkowski, 2003). As such, creativity may mean finding a novel solution to a problem, like Schaller did, or coming up with a unique approach to creating some new product   a piece of music, a painting, or a scientific theory that is widely recognized by society as being creative (Gelade, 2002).

Certainly all of us can think of people whom we feel are creative. But what makes one person more creative than another? Are there special traits or abilities that creative people possess? Over the years, psychologists have proposed several variables that may underlie creativity, but the one that has received the most attention is a skill called *divergent thinking* (Vartanian et al., 2003). Divergent thinking is the ability to generate many ideas quickly in response to a single prompt (Eysenck, 1995). For example, a divergent thinker can quickly come up with many different ways to tie a scarf or many different uses for an ink pen.

Divergent thinking aids creativity because it allows you to come up with many different ideas about how to solve a problem. As we will see, when you can think quickly to generate many different ideas, you are less likely to be blocked by some of the common obstacles to problem solving including *functional fixedness* and *mental sets*.

Functional Fixedness

When we attempt to solve problems, we often rely on well-used strategies. We look at the tools that we have at our disposal, and we evaluate them in terms of their common, everyday uses. We think of a hammer as a tool for pounding and a box as an object for holding other objects. We often cannot conceive of using these tools in new, novel ways. This limitation of being able to see objects only in their familiar roles is called **functional fixedness.** Functional fixedness can prevent us from solving problems that otherwise could be solved. But as the following story illustrates, sometimes we must break out of functional fixedness and find creative ways to solve our problems.

When one of us (Susann Doyle-Portillo) was a child, she and her family experienced car trouble on the way home from a visit at her grandmother's home in Chicago. It was midnight, and the car's fuel pump failed (this was back when cars had carburetors!). Susann's father had only a few tools available to fix the car—a long piece of plastic tubing, a bicycle tire pump, and a hand drill. He drilled a hole in the car's gas cap

creativity the ability to combine mental elements in new and useful ways

functional fixedness being able to see objects only in their familiar roles

 Application

and attached the tube to it so that the tube entered the gas tank through the gas cap. He threaded the other end of the tube into the backseat of the car and attached it to the tire pump. This way, Susann's mother could pump the tire pump, which would pressurize the gas tank, and force the gasoline through the fuel line to the engine. They drove 30 miles this way! Without this creativity, the family would have been stranded on the highway until morning. To keep the car working, Susann's father had to break out of functional fixedness, think divergently, and realize that a bicycle pump was good for more than pumping bicycle tires. You can exercise your own ability to break out of functional fixedness by trying the exercise in Figure 7.7.

Mental Sets

mental set the tendency to habitually use methods of problem solving that have worked for you in the past

incubation a period of not thinking about the problem that helps one solve the problem

Another obstacle to problem solving is a **mental set.** A mental set is a tendency to habitually use the methods of problem solving that have worked for you in the past. Mental sets become an obstacle when we persist in trying solutions that may have worked in the past but are *not* working in the current situation. Take a look at the problem in Figure 7.8. It is a "connect-the-dots" problem, but there is a twist. You must connect all the dots without picking up your pencil, and you can use only four straight lines. Is it impossible? No, it is just difficult because of our mental sets. When we do a "connect-the-dot" puzzle, we are used to drawing lines that go directly from dot to dot. In this case, that strategy will not work. You must draw lines that extend *beyond* the dots (Figure 7.9, page 312). Mental sets can keep us stuck in a rut of trying solutions over and over again that just aren't working.

If you find yourself having little success in solving a problem, stop working on the problem for a while and let it *incubate*. **Incubation,** or a period of not thinking about the problem, sometimes helps us solve a problem (Ohlsson, 1992). When we incubate, the unproductive strategies recede from memory, and we are better able to attack the problem from a fresh, more productive perspective when we return to it. If we are locked in a mental set, incubation may be just what is needed to solve the problem.

As we've seen in this section, problem solving is a matter of generating possible solutions and then selecting from them the solution that will ultimately solve the problem. If your car

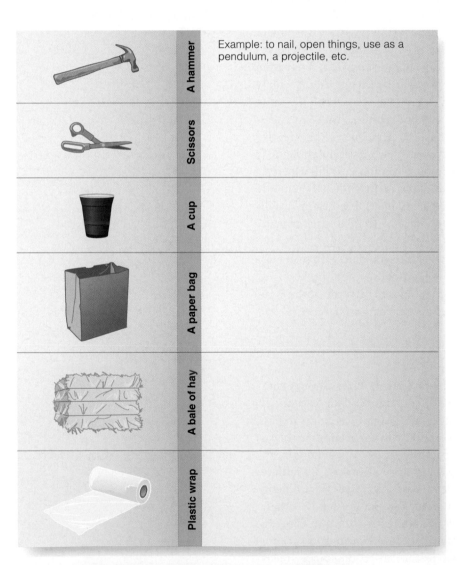

		Example: to nail, open things, use as a pendulum, a projectile, etc.
	A hammer	
	Scissors	
	A cup	
	A paper bag	
	A bale of hay	
	Plastic wrap	

Figure 7.7 Breaking Out of Functional Fixedness
Name as many uses as you can for the objects above.

Figure 7.8
The Nine-Dot Problem
Connect the dots with four straight lines without lifting your pencil. Can you do it?

broke down tomorrow, how would you decide which course of action to take? Would you call in absent to school? Call a mechanic? Call a taxi? Walk to school? Go back to bed and forget it? Many times, choosing the *best* solution from among all the possibilities is the real task. In our next section, we will look a bit closer at the cognitive processes that we engage in when we reason, make decisions, and make judgments.

Let's Review!

In this section, we discussed the process of problem solving, including the types of problems we might be faced with, the manner in which we tend to solve such problems, and common obstacles to problem solving. For a quick check of your understanding, answer these questions.

1. Which of the following is the *best* example of an ill-structured problem?
   a. balancing your monthly checking account statement
   b. losing weight
   c. reducing crime in your neighborhood
   d. solving a crossword puzzle
2. Incubation sometimes aids problem solving because it:
   a. reduces fatigue.
   b. allows insight.

c. allows us to forget unproductive strategies.
d. allows us to work out a solution subconsciously.

3. Sue used a chair with wheels to carry a load of books to her car. She piled the books in the seat of the chair and pushed it to her car. Trina, on the other hand, carried her books by hand, even though she also had a chair with wheels in her office. Trina was most likely suffering the effects of:
   a. functional fixedness.   c. insight.
   b. an ill-structured problem.   d. stupidity.

ANSWERS
1.c 2.c 3.a

Reasoning, Decision Making, and Judgment

Reasoning, decision making, and judgments are cognitive processes that use some of the same strategies as problem solving. We engage in *reasoning* when we draw conclusions based on certain assumptions about the world. For example, you might reason your friend Jamal is a nice person because he has many friends. *Decision making* is choosing among several options, as in our example of what you might do if your car breaks down. *Judgments* are also related to solving problems, often using two particular heuristics that we'll discuss.

Deductive and Inductive Reasoning

We engage in **reasoning** when we draw conclusions that are based on certain assumptions about the world. For example, you might reason that your friend Rick has money because he drives a nice car. Or, based on your experiences, you might reason that studying leads to better grades. Psychologists who study reasoning have traditionally looked at two types of reasoning processes: *deductive reasoning* and *inductive reasoning*. **Deductive reasoning** involves reasoning from the *general* to the *specific*. In other words, you start with a general rule and apply it to particular cases. For example, you

LEARNING OBJECTIVES

Describe the processes of making decisions and judgments.

Discuss the availability and representativeness heuristics and how they may bias our decisions and judgments.

reasoning   drawing conclusions about the world based on certain assumptions

deductive reasoning   reasoning from the general to the specific

inductive reasoning reasoning from the specific to the general

might *deduce* that because studying leads to good grades your friend Melissa, who makes good grades, must also study hard.

Inductive reasoning, on the other hand, is the opposite. When using inductive reasoning, one reasons from the *specific* to the *general.* Here the object is to begin with specific instances and to discover what general rule fits for all of these instances. For example, as children, we may have noticed time and time again that our classmates who did well were also those who seemed to study the most, so we induced that studying hard leads to good grades. We used these specific instances to help us *induce* the rule that studying hard leads to good grades.

We hope you see the parallels between inductive reasoning and the *scientific method* that psychologists use to conduct research (see p. 4). When testing theories with their studies, psychologists try to induce the general rules that explain mental processes and behavior. Then once these rules have been induced, they can be applied to individual situations to help deduce, or predict, how people and animals are likely to behave. This, of course, does not mean that reasoning is just for scientists. Deductive and inductive reasoning are equally important to everyday life. Effective reasoning can be a very important aspect of making good decisions in our lives.

Decision Making: Outcomes and Probabilities

decision making making a choice from among a series of alternatives

Decision making involves choosing from among several alternatives. As such, decision making is often a part of the problem-solving process. We must first choose a course of action before we can implement a solution to our problem. As part of the problem-solving process, the decisions we make can have serious implications for our lives. Decisions about what subject to major in, whom to marry, and where to invest your money are just some of the life-altering decisions you might have to make in your lifetime. Given the importance of the decision-making process, researchers have been looking at *how* we make decisions.

Application

Two factors that influence our decisions are the perceived *outcomes* of our decisions and the *probability* of achieving these outcomes. For example, when you choose a major, you weigh the expected outcomes of the major. How interesting is the subject area to you? What kind of job will it lead to? How difficult will the course work be? What is the pay like in this field? You also temper these judgments with your perception of whether these outcomes will actually occur. There may be high-salaried jobs in your major area, but if you see little chance of actually getting one of them, then you are likely to decide against that major.

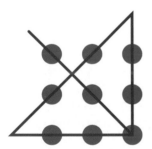

Figure 7.9 The Solution to the Nine-Dot Problem

As you can see, to solve this problem you have to try a solution that is different from the ones that you would normally use. You have to break out of your mental set.

Logically, we would seek to make decisions that we feel have a good chance of leading to favorable outcomes. However, our decision-making processes are a bit more complex than this. Another factor that affects our decisions is how the possible courses of action are presented, or *framed* (Kahneman & Tversky, 1984). For example, which of the following options would you choose? Would you choose to take a class in which you had a 60% chance of passing? Or one in which you had a 40% chance of failing? Many people would choose the first option because it is positively framed, even though the chance of succeeding in the course is the same in both cases. Whether you prefer a positively framed option or a negatively framed one depends on your orientation. Sometimes we exhibit *loss aversion,* or a tendency to focus on what a certain decision could cost us in terms of potential gain. Other times, we exhibit *risk aversion,* or concern over losing what we already have.

In general, when we focus on our potential losses, we are more likely to gamble in hopes of avoiding a loss. But if we focus on the potential risk of losing what we already have, we will make choices that avoid gambling at all costs. Financial planners have to consider how their clients view loss and risk when they set up investment

Application

strategies for their clients. Different investments carry different earning potentials as well as different levels of risk of losing money. In general, you can earn more return on money placed in the stock market than in some other investments, but you also have a greater risk of losing your money. Placing your money in bonds is safe, but it doesn't usually return as much profit as the stock market does (Figure 7.10). Which option would you choose when investing *your* money? People with an aversion to *loss* would likely gamble on the stock market. In contrast, people with an aversion to *risk* would likely choose the safer avenues of the bond market.

You can see that several factors affect the decisions we make. The expected outcomes of a decision, the probability of certain outcomes, the way a choice is framed, and our tolerance for loss and risk all affect the decisions that we make in life. But, what if you were missing some of this information? How would you decide among your options if you didn't know how probable certain outcomes were? Sometimes we know the exact probability of certain outcomes, as in the case of knowing the exact odds of winning a contest, but more often we do not.

Uncertainty complicates our decision making. In our earlier example, how would you decide between the stock market and bonds if you were uncertain about the probability of a stock market rally (or crash) in the near future? Investors face just this situation every day. When we do not know the probability of a certain event, we must use our **judgment** to estimate the probability—which, as we will see in the next section, is sometimes faulty.

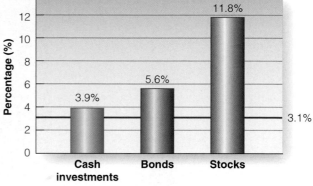

The rewards of investing: Comparing the three primary asset classes with inflation
Average annual returns: 1926–2000

Figure 7.10 Stock Market and Bond Market Returns
Where would you put your money?
Source: Vanguard Investment Manual p. 8, Fig. 1.

judgment   the act of estimating the probability of an event

Judgments: Estimating the Likelihood of Events

Judgment can be seen as a type of problem solving. If you don't know what the probability of a certain event is, and you need to have this probability to make a decision, what will you do? Well, as with all problems you can solve this one using either an algorithm or a heuristic. An algorithm would involve somehow looking up or calculating the exact probability of the event occurring, but this is often neither possible nor practical, as in the case of trying to figure out what the stock market will do in the coming months. So, as we saw before, we tend to rely on heuristics when we make our judgments.

The Availability Heuristic

Many people are afraid to fly, even though air travel is statistically safer than traveling by automobile ("Air Travel Remains Safe," 1999). Why would people be afraid to choose a *safer* form of travel? The answer lies in the manner in which we make judgments about the frequency of events. When we estimate the frequency of events, we heuristically base our judgments on the ease with which we can recall instances of the event in memory. The more easily we can recall a memory for an event, the more frequent we estimate the event to be. This heuristic is called the **availability heuristic** (Tversky & Kahneman, 1974).

The availability heuristic explains the previous example of choosing air travel over driving. Although fatal car accidents occur every day, they are not as widely covered by the media as plane crashes are. A fatal car crash is likely to produce a few deaths, but a plane crash usually involves larger numbers of fatalities. Therefore, when a plane goes down, the news coverage is graphic, horrifying, and prolonged. This leaves us with a strong, easily accessible memory for the plane crash. The result is that when we think of ways to travel, we more readily recall memories of plane crashes, and we may mistakenly overestimate the risk associated with air travel. The upshot of this is that many people fear flying, when they really ought to be more afraid of traveling by car.

   Application

availability heuristic   a heuristic in which we use the ease with which we can recall instances of an event in memory to help us estimate the frequency of the event

According to the availability heuristic, the ease with which we can retrieve memories of events from long-term memory biases our judgments of how frequently the event occurs in real life. Seeing news coverage of air disasters like this one leaves us with vivid memories of plane crashes that cause us to overestimate the probability of a plane crash occurring in the future. As a result, air traffic often falls off immediately following a crash, although in general flying is still safer than driving to your destination.

representativeness heuristic   a heuristic in which we rely on the degree to which something is representative of a category to help us judge whether or not it belongs in the category

The Representativeness Heuristic

We also make heuristic judgments when deciding whether or not an object, event, or person belongs in a particular category by relying on the degree to which the person or thing in question is representative of the category. This tendency, called the **representativeness heuristic,** explains some of the mistakes we make in judgment (Tversky & Kahneman, 1974). For instance, let's assume that at a party you meet a man named Mark, who is about 35, tall, muscular, confident, brave, and rugged. As you speak with him, you learn that his favorite hobbies are rock climbing and scuba diving. Based on this description, do you think Mark is a firefighter, an accountant, or a manager?

If you are like most people, you guessed that Mark is a firefighter. Because of the representativeness heuristic, most of us would make this judgment based on the fact that Mark is very *representative* of our concept of a firefighter, but he is not very representative of our concepts for an accountant or manager. Ironically, we would jump to this conclusion, even though there are more accountants and managers than firefighters in the world!

Availability and representativeness are powerful heuristics. In fact, we use them so often that we tend to ignore the true probability, or *base rate*, of events in favor of our heuristic judgments. In one experiment, participants were told that a group of 100 people contained 70 engineers and 30 lawyers. They were also given a description of one of the group members—a man—that included the traits: conservative, ambitious, nonpolitical, likes carpentry, and enjoys solving mathematical puzzles. Then they were asked to judge the probability that he was an engineer or a lawyer. If we were to approach this question logically, we would always say that there is a 70% chance that the man is an engineer and a 30% chance that he is a lawyer, but the participants did not approach this task logically. Instead, they based their judgments on the representativeness of the description that they were given and ignored the base rate information. As a result, the particpants judged that there was a 90% chance that the man was an engineer (Kahneman & Tversky, 1973). Clearly, we often irrationally place more confidence in judgments based on heuristics than those based on more factual probabilities (Tversky & Kahneman, 1980)!

If all of this sounds like humans are incapable of making good judgments, don't despair. This is not the case. Often heuristics do lead to correct judgments. In addition, we do not always behave in a heuristic way. Sometimes, we do pay attention to probabilities (Cosmides & Tooby, 1996). Whether or not we make judgments algorithmically or heuristically is a product of both the situation (c.f. Cosmides & Tooby, 1996) and the characteristic way that we as individuals tend to think (Stanovich & West, 1998). When the conditions are right, we do make good and logical judgments. This is especially true when we are making judgments in everyday, real-life situations (Anderson, 2000). Take a moment to test your knowledge of this section before moving on to learn about language and its relationship to thought.

Let's Review!

This section described how people make decisions and judgments, and some of the shortcomings of using heuristics. For a quick check of your understanding, answer these questions.

1. Yesterday it rained. Today, when you are asked to estimate the number of days it rains each year in your area, you are likely to _____ this figure because of the _____.
   a. underestimate; availability heuristic
   b. overestimate; availability heuristic
   c. underestimate; representativeness heuristic
   d. overestimate; representativeness heuristic

2. When we make decisions, we base our decisions in part on:
   a. the likely outcomes of the decision.
   b. the probability of obtaining certain outcomes.
   c. our aversion to risk and loss.
   d. all of the above.

3. Of the 100 people in Harry's psychology class, 60 are education majors and 40 are psychology majors. Yet when Harry first met a classmate named Sally, he guessed that there was a 90% chance that she was a psychology major because she had a poster of Sigmund Freud on her dorm room wall. Harry likely based his judgment on:
   a. the base rate.
   b. an algorithm.
   c. representativeness.
   d. availability.

ANSWERS
1. b; 2. d; 3. c

Language: Essential to Thought and Action > > > > > > > > > >

Our capacity for **language** is one of our most spectacular human abilities. No other species has such a well developed, syntactical verbal system for representing its world. We use words in just about every aspect of our lives. As we have seen, much of our knowledge is represented in memory using words. Without words, our ability to mentally represent our world, solve problems, and make decisions would be drastically altered. Imagine trying to learn psychology without using any language! When you think about it, it is truly remarkable that Ildefonso was able to do as well as he did in the world before he was introduced to language. Luckily, most of us are introduced to language at a much younger age than Ildefonso was.

How Humans Acquire Language

Some researchers have proposed that humans are born with an innate tendency to acquire language (Bohannon & Bovillian, 1997; Chomsky, 1957). According to this view, we are born with a *language acquisition device*, or a biological makeup that gives

LEARNING OBJECTIVES

≫ Describe how children acquire language.

≫ Discuss the usefulness of language.

≫ Discuss current research on the issue of nonhuman language.

language   a well-developed, syntactical verbal system for representing the world

us an innate knowledge of the syntax of a language (Chomsky, 1965). Some disagree with this idea of innate language, believing instead that children are natural problem solvers, and language is a means of solving one of their greatest problems—the need to communicate with others (see Helmuth, 2001).

Deciding which perspective is correct has challenged psychologists for decades. A complicating factor in settling this debate is that it is practically impossible to isolate the effects that *nature* and *nurture* have on language development. How can we determine if children are born with innate knowledge of language (nature), when nearly all children in the world are immediately exposed to language after birth (nurture)? When children begin speaking (at about 1 year), it could be due to some innate, biological mechanism, or it could be that they learned to speak from interacting with others who use language. In normal children, it is impossible to tell exactly why language develops, but what if we could find children who were never exposed to language? What if we could find more children like Ildefonso to study—children who had never heard spoken language and who also had never been taught sign language? What could these children teach us about the development of human language? In It's A Diverse World, we describe such a group of children and what they have taught psychologists about how language develops.

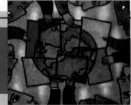

IT'S A DIVERSE WORLD

The Spontaneous Development of a Language in Nicaragua

Like many developing countries, at times the Central American nation of Nicaragua has struggled to provide citizens with social services. For many years, Nicaragua had no formal education for the deaf. As a result, deaf children were often isolated from other deaf children and had no access to schools that taught sign language.

In the late 1970s, the situation began to improve. In 1977, a school for the deaf was opened in the capital city of Managua, but none of the teachers knew sign language. Instead of teaching signing, the hearing teachers attempted to teach the children Spanish. During class time, the students were required to focus on learning Spanish, but during recesses, they were free to communicate in any way they wished. On the playground, something truly amazing began to happen with these children. When they were alone, the children began creating gestures that they then used to communicate with each other. At first they had just a few gestures or signs, but soon this system of communication began to develop into a *true* sign language. As more and more children enrolled at the school over the years, the language grew and developed. Not only did the number of signs grow, but grammatical rules of syntax also evolved. This language, now officially called Nicaraguan Sign Language (NSL), is so well developed that it is actively taught to deaf children in Nicaragua.

Because NSL developed in children who had never been exposed to a formal sign language, psychologists were excited at this opportunity to test whether we are innately prepared to use language. Researchers Ann Senghas and Marie Coppola (2001) conducted a series of studies that compared the relative fluency and characteristic usage of the language in deaf speakers of NSL aged 7 to 32 years. These NSL speakers were also classified based on how old they were when they were first exposed to the deaf community that spoke NSL (early exposure < 6½ yrs.; middle exposure 6½ to 10 yrs.; and late exposure 10+ yrs.). Senghas and Coppola found that NSL developed over a period of years in the deaf community and that by the mid-1980s, NSL was still changing. What was really interesting, however, was what prompted the changes in NSL. It was not the older children who seemed to be shaping the language, but rather the *younger* ones. Even though they had fewer years of experience with NSL, the younger children were most responsible for making NSL more syntactically structured and systematic.

The idea that the ways children use language often differ from the language to which they have been exposed by family and teachers is underscored in another study that examined U.S. and Chinese deaf children's usage of spontaneous gestural language (Goldin-Meadow & Mylander, 1998). These were deaf children with hearing mothers, and they had not been exposed to conventional sign language. Thus, when the mother and child needed to communicate, they often used spontaneous gestures. In analyzing these gestures, the researchers found that certain grammatical features of the Chinese and U.S. children's gestures were identical. This was of particular interest because the grammatical rules that the children seemed to be following did not resemble the grammatical rules of English or Chinese. Furthermore, the U.S. children's gestural language differed significantly from their mother's gestural language, so the U.S. children were apparently not simply modeling their mothers' language. Curiously, the Chinese children's gestural language was closely related to their mothers'. The significance of this is unclear—it could be that the Chinese children did model their linguistic rules after their mothers', or possibly the mothers were modeling their language after their children's. Overall, the study indicated once again that children do not merely model language, they develop it. These studies seem to suggest that there are some innate aspects to language—at least in deaf children.

So what about spoken language? Is there any evidence that hearing children also have an innate capacity for language? Well, yes there is. Evidence for the innate nature of language also comes from cross-cultural studies on language development in hearing children. These studies show that regardless of the culture, language seems to develop in children at about the same age and in the same sequence of stages. This similarity in the developmental process, which occurs despite cultural differences, argues for some biological mechanism that underlies language.

Cooing and Babbling: Baby Steps to Speech

Most of us acquire our first language beginning in the first couple of years of our lives. Research indicates that newborns from birth to 1 month are capable of categorizing vowel sounds in an adultlike manner (Alderidge, Stillman, & Bower, 2001), and by about 2 months, infants begin **cooing.** Cooing involves making vowel sounds, like "ooo" and "ah." By 4 months, infants begin to engage in **babbling,** which adds consonant sounds to the vowel sounds they emitted during cooing. For example, an infant might repeat the sound "ka, ka, ka" over and over. Infants' first babbles are very similar across cultures, but soon this changes (Stoel-Gammon & Otomo, 1986). By 7 months, infants begin to emit babbles that contain sounds that are part of the language that they have been exposed to in their environment. In this fashion, the infant's language system apparently tunes itself to the language or languages that the infant hears on a regular basis. By 1 year, children's babbling contains the sounds and intonations of their native languages (Levitt & Utmann, 1992).

But what if the child is not exposed to any language, as was the case with Ildefonso? With no exposure to spoken language (because they are unable to hear), deaf infants fail to emit languagelike babbling (Eilers & Oiler, 1994). Therefore, deaf infants do not progress to learn a spoken language the way hearing children do. What about learning written language or sign language? How do deaf children fare here? Unfortunately, many deaf children are developmentally delayed when it comes to learning any form of language because most have hearing parents. If parents do not already know and use sign language, they will not provide the necessary stimulation for their deaf infant to naturally acquire sign language in the same way the infant would have acquired a spoken language. We saw this in Ildefonso's case, in which his parents did not know a sign language and worse, considered him to be a "dummy." Even when deaf children are later taught to sign, they may not catch up developmentally and often struggle in school and in social relationships. Interestingly, these developmental delays are not seen in deaf children of deaf parents (Bornstein, Selmi, Haynes, Painter, & Marx, 1999). It appears that when deaf children are exposed to sign language from infancy, they tend to acquire sign language in a manner that is analogous to language development in hearing children.

cooing   the vowel sounds made by infants beginning at 2 months

babbling   the combination of vowel and consonant sounds uttered by infants beginning around 4 months

phoneme the smallest unit of sound in a language

Once a child achieves the stage of babbling the basic sounds, or **phonemes,** of her native tongue, the next step in language development is learning to communicate. At around 12 months, children begin trying to communicate with others. This communication is often initially based on gestures before it is based on words. For example, a child may point at a toy that he wants. When parents learn to interpret these *preverbal gestures*, communication is accomplished. As they catch on to their child's preverbal gestures, parents often verbalize the meaning of the gesture for the child. Parents say things like, "Oh, do you want this toy?" This verbalization of the child's intention allows the child to begin to learn **morphemes,** or the smallest sounds in a language that have meaning. As a result, by the end of the first year or so, children begin to speak their first words.

morpheme the smallest unit of sound in a language that has meaning

From "Mama" and "Dada" to Sentences

A child's first words are usually the names of familiar objects, people, actions, or situations, ones with which they have had a great deal of contact. Typically, these words are *Dada, Mama, hi, hot,* and the like. During the first 6 months or so of speech, children utter only one word at a time, and often they convey tremendous meaning with these one-word sentences. For example, the utterance, "Milk!" may stand for "I want some milk please!" Interestingly, as Ildefonso began to learn his first language, there were some similarities between his early sign language and the speech of a child who is just learning to speak. Just as in young children, the first words Ildefonso learned tended to be concrete nouns, like "cat" and "table," and these words would often convey whole sentences of meaning. One example of this was the word "green." For Ildefonso, "green" stood for anything that had to do with the U.S. Border Patrol because U.S. Border Patrol uniforms and trucks are green. So Ildefonso attached a great deal of meaning to the word "green" when he finally learned it (Schaller, 1995, pp. 64, 93). Similar overuse of a word is also seen in young children.

overextension when a child uses one word to symbolize all manners of similar instances (e.g., calling all birds *parakeet*)

Young children may exhibit **overextension** in their language, in that one word will be used to symbolize all manners of similar instances. For instance, the word "dog" may be used to symbolize *any* animal. During this period, the opposite problem may also occur when children exhibit **underextension** of language. In this situation, children inappropriately restrict their use of a word to a particular case, such as when a child uses the word "dog" to refer *only* to the family pet.

underextension when a child inappropriately restricts her use of a word to a particular case (e.g., using the word *cat* to describe only the family pet)

By the time children reach 20–26 months, they begin to combine words into two-word sentences in what is called **telegraphic speech.** Telegraphic speech is often ungrammatical, but it does convey meaning, such as "Doggie bad," meaning "The dog was bad." From here, children rapidly acquire vocabulary and the grammatical rules of the language, such as word order in a sentence and tense. By age 6, the average child has an impressive vocabulary of around 10,000 words and a fairly competent mastery of grammar (Tager-Flusberg, 1997). These hard-earned linguistic abilities will be very valuable to the child as they are to us all. Let's take a closer look at what, exactly, language does for us.

telegraphic speech two-word sentences that begin to be uttered by children at 20–26 months

The Function of Language in Culture and Perception

It is not difficult to see that language impacts us in many ways. Obviously, one of language's main functions is to facilitate communication. We use language to describe our world, our thoughts, and our experiences to others. Without language, we would lead lives of isolation just like Ildefonso did before he learned sign language.

Language and the Development of Culture

Because language brings us together and allows us to share ideas and experiences, language also plays a role in the development of our *culture*. Russian psychologist Lev

Vygotsky (1896–1934) noted the influence of language in the development of culture in his *sociocultural theory* (Vygotsky, 1934/1987) (p. 410). According to sociocultural theory, older and more knowledgeable members of a society pass on the values, beliefs, and customs of their culture to children by telling the children stories and by engaging in conversations with them. The children store these dialogues in their memory and then later use this knowledge to guide their behavior.

Perhaps you can identify how your own elders used language to pass along the elements of your particular culture. Have you ever found yourself saying things that you have heard your parents say before? Do you still celebrate holidays with the traditions your parents and grandparents shared with you as a child? If you have children of your own, do you ever tell them stories from your childhood? Most of us can relate to these examples of Vygotsky's ideas on language and culture. Although we can readily see how language facilitates the transmission of culture from generation to generation, how language affects our cognitive processes is the subject of much more debate. Does the language we speak affect the way we view the world? In our next section, we'll take a look at this interesting issue.

Linguistic Relativity: Language Directs Our Thoughts

One of the most intriguing theories about language came from an unlikely source. Benjamin Whorf was a Connecticut fire insurance inspector whose unusual hobby was *linguistics*, or the study of language. After intensive studies of the languages of Native Americans, Whorf became convinced that one's language could directly determine or influence one's thoughts (Whorf, 1956). This notion has since come to be called the **Whorfian hypothesis** or the **linguistic relativity hypothesis.**

In its strongest form, the linguistic relativity hypothesis states that one's language actually determines one's thoughts and one's perception of the world. According to this view, people who have different native languages think differently and perceive the world in a different light. Whorf claimed that differences among languages make it impossible to express all thoughts equally in all languages. Therefore, you could think and see the world only in terms of the language that you know. Your language would determine what you think and how you perceive the world. For example, Whorf claimed that Eskimos have many different words for *snow*, but in English, we have only the word *snow*. Because of this vocabulary difference, Whorf argued that Eskimos would perceive snow and think about snow in ways that English speakers cannot.

The strong form of Whorf's linguistic relativity hypothesis has not withstood the tests of science. Careful examination of both Eskimo languages and English offer little reason to believe that Eskimos and English speakers would necessarily perceive and think about snow differently. As it turns out, Eskimos do not have a tremendous number of words for *snow* (Martin, 1986; Pullman, 1989), and English speakers have multiple words to describe snow (e.g., slush, sleet, flurries, and so on; Figure 7.11). Furthermore, researchers have found that despite significant differences in language, cognitive processing of information is often very similar across cultures.

In one study, English speakers were compared to members of the Dani culture, a nonindustrialized culture from New Guinea. The Dani have only two words to describe different colors, *mili* for cool dark colors and *mola* for bright warm colors, whereas English speakers have many color names. Despite this difference, the Dani performed similarly to English speakers when they were asked to memorize a list of madeup names for different colors. Both the Dani and the English speakers found it easier to remember the madeup names that were associated with basic colors, like red and blue, as opposed to remembering the madeup names associated with unusual colors, such as saffron and magenta (Rosch, 1973b). This is not what the linguistic relativity hypothesis would predict. If the strong form of the linguistic relativity hypothesis were true, the Dani should

Whorfian hypothesis/linguistic relativity hypothesis   the theory that one's language could directly determine or influence one's thoughts

Eskimo	English
qanuk: "snowflake"	snowflake
qanir: "to snow"	snow
kanevvluk: "fine snow/rain particles"	snowfall
muruaneq: "soft deep snow"	powder
pirta: "blizzard, snowstorm"	blizzard, snowstorm
nutaryuk: "fresh snow"	powder
qengaruk: "snow bank"	snowbank
qetrar: "for snow to crust"	hardpack

Figure 7.11 Different Words for Snow

Contrary to Whorf's hypothesis, like the Eskimo, English speakers do have several words for snow.

have performed differently from the English speakers on this memory task because their limited vocabulary for colors would have affected the way they perceived and thought about the colors in the experiment.

The Modern View: Language Influences Our Thoughts

To date, the bulk of the evidence does not support the strong form of Whorf's linguistic relativity hypothesis. However, there is reason to think that a modified, or weaker, interpretation of the Whorfian hypothesis may hold true. The weaker version states that instead of language *determining* thought processes, language merely *influences* them. For example, when Spanish speakers were compared to Mayan speakers, differences were seen in their ability to remember colors. Furthermore, these memory differences were related to how easy it is to verbally label colors in Spanish and Mayan (Stefflre, Castillo-Vales, & Morley, 1966). It appears that how easily you can label a color in your language does affect your memory for that color.

However, it is also true that putting a verbal label on a color may also lessen your memory for that color. In another study, participants were shown color swatches. Participants were asked to verbally label some of the color swatches, but not asked to label others. Later, the participants' memory for the color swatches was tested. Participants were best able to recognize the color swatches that they had *not* verbally labeled (Schooler & Engstler-Schooler, 1990). It appears that sometimes language, in the form of verbal labels, can distort memory.

It is also likely that language can influence our perception of the world. In one study involving the sorting of color samples, participants who spoke Setswana were more likely to group blues and greens together than were those who spoke English or Russian. This finding was attributed to the fact that in Setswana, one word describes both blue and green colors (Davies, 1998).

Verbal labels can also affect how we perceive people and situations. For instance, if you hear the phrase "bleached blond," what image comes to mind? Now contrast that image with the one that comes to mind when you hear the phrase "blond woman." Do you see the difference that a few words can make? In Chapter 12, we will look specifically at labels we place on groups of people in the form of prejudices and the manner in which they affect our perception of others.

To sum up, language does not seem to have the strong deterministic effect on cognitive processes that Benjamin Whorf first proposed. There appear to be far more similarities in the cognitive processes of people with different languages than there are differences. On the other hand, there are many differences in the languages of the world, and these may exert some influence on cognitive processes such as perception and memory. So although the strong form of the linguistic relativity hypothesis must be rejected, we have some reason to hang on to the weaker version of it.

Language in Other Species: Are We the Only Speakers?

Are humans the only animals to use language? For centuries, humans believed that they alone had the ability to use language. It was assumed that only the advanced human mind was capable of dealing with the complexities of a language. Remarkably, this assumption has been called into question. Although it is very controversial, today some researchers believe that some animals may possess linguistic abilities (e.g., Shanker, Savage-Rumbaugh, & Taylor, 1999).

Rose is Rose © reprinted by permission of United Features Syndicate, Inc.

Language is a means of communicating.

In looking at the linguistic abilities of other species, we first have to make a distinction between *language* and *communication*. Language is a system of communication that has a set vocabulary and a set structure, or grammar. For instance, English sentences generally follow a subject, verb, object pattern:

Billy (subject) threw (verb) the ball (object).

Although many languages reverse the order of the verb and the object, most of the world's languages place the subject at the beginning of the sentence (Ultan, 1969).

Languages also differ with respect to the placement of adjectives and adverbs. In Spanish and French, adjectives usually follow the noun they modify, but in English adjectives precede the noun. The Spanish phrase "caballo blanco" translates to "horse white" in English. As you can see, each language has its own set of grammatical and syntactical rules. In contrast to the structure and order of language, communication can be very unstructured. All that is required in a communication system is that your meaning be conveyed to others. By this definition, Ildefonso could communicate via pantomime before he even knew that language existed in the world!

There is little argument that animals can communicate. For example, a rooster will emit an alarm cry to warn other chickens of danger (Marler, Duffy, & Pickert, 1986). Young chimpanzees use physical gestures to communicate with other chimpanzees (Tomasello, Call, Nagell, Olguin, & Carpenter, 1994). King penguins use vocalizations to find their mates when they are in a large group or colony (Lengagne, Jouventin, & Aubin, 1999). And domestic dogs respond to specific play signals of their masters (Rooney, Bradshaw, & Robinson, 2001). It appears that many species have evolved specific means of communicating with other species members, but does this ability of some animals to communicate equate with the capacity for language?

Bonobos: Matata and Kanzi

Some of the best evidence for animal language comes from studies done on Bonobo chimpanzees. Bonobos, also known as pygmy chimpanzees, are perhaps our closest genetic relatives, even more closely related to us than the common chimpanzee. During the 1980s, researcher Sue Savage-Rumbaugh and others attempted to teach English to a Bonobo named Matata. Because Bonobos do not have vocal cords that produce humanlike speech, they cannot actually speak. To get around this problem, the researchers used a special computer keyboard during the language training. On the surface of the keyboard were pictures, and when a picture was pressed, a computer-generated voice spoke the name of the object in the picture. Using this keyboard, Savage-Rumbaugh tried to teach Matata the meaning of certain words, but Matata did not catch on well. After 2 years of training and over 30,000 research trials, Matata learned to use only six of the pictures on the keyboard (Wise, 2000, p. 223).

Although the experiments with Matata failed to show that Bonobos could learn English, there was a remarkable and unexpected outcome of the research. While

Figure 7.12 Kanzi and His Keyboard
As an infant, Kanzi learned to use the language keyboard to communicate just by watching researchers who were working with his mother, Matata.

Matata was being trained to use the keyboard, her infant stepson, Kanzi, was observing what was going on (Figure 7.12). Although Savage-Rumbaugh and her colleagues never attempted to teach Kanzi to use the keyboard, he picked up this skill on his own (Savage-Rumbaugh, McDonald, Sevcik, Hopkins, & Rupert, 1986). By age 2 1/2, Kanzi had begun to use some of the symbols his mother was trying to learn on the keyboard. When experimenters gave up trying to teach Matata to use the keyboard, they separated her from Kanzi. The day Matata left, Kanzi approached the keyboard and began to use it to make requests and express himself. In fact, he used it a total of 120 times on that first day (Wise, 2000).

Much like a young child, Kanzi appeared to have learned some vocabulary just by observing language being used around him. Kanzi's acquisition of language seemed to occur quite naturally (Shanker, Savage-Rumbaugh, & Taylor, 1999). For example, a patch of wild strawberries grew outside of Kanzi's laboratory, and when he discovered them, Kanzi began to eat them. He overheard researchers referring to them by the word *strawberries* and soon appeared to understand what the word *strawberries* means. After apparently learning the meaning of the word *strawberries*, Kanzi would head for the berry patch whenever he heard someone speak the word (Savage-Rumbaugh, 1987).

Overall, Kanzi's use of language is quite impressive. He uses the keyboard to make requests, such as to visit another chimpanzee named Austin. If he is told that he cannot visit because it's too cold to go outside, Kanzi modifies his request to ask to see a picture of Austin on TV (Savage-Rumbaugh, 1987). Furthermore, Kanzi seems to be able to respond to very unusual and novel requests such as "put the pine needles in the refrigerator" or "put the soap on the ball."

Talking Parrots and Dolphins

Language abilities have been shown in species other than the Bonobos, as well. Researcher Irene Pepperberg (1993, 1999) has had some success in training an African gray parrot named Alex to speak some English. Unlike the Bonobo, a parrot has the physical ability to produce speech, as well as comprehend it. After years of training, Alex is able to speak some words in English, and he can identify the shape, color, and material of many objects (Pepperberg, 1991).

Dolphins have also shown some linguistic promise. Researcher Louis Herman and his colleagues have had some success in training dolphins to understand a language that the researchers created. This created language is based on gestures, but it has a set vocabulary in which certain gestures stand for certain words, and a specific set of grammatical rules that dictate how gestures can be combined into phrases. One of the dolphins, named Phoenix, was shown to follow a complex sequence of instructions delivered in this gestured language (Herman & Uyeyma, 1999). Furthermore, another dolphin, Ake, seemed to notice when the grammatical laws of the language had been violated (Herman, Kuczaj, & Holder, 1993).

Can Other Animals Really Use Language?

As impressive as the linguistic abilities of Kanzi, Alex, Ake, and Phoenix are, not everyone is convinced that animals truly have the capacity for language. Some argue that these animals are merely highly trained (Pinker, 1994). Skeptics propose that rather than actually using language, the animals are engaging in trained behaviors that they hope will lead to some reward. Certainly, Alex, Ake, and Phoenix were trained to use language, but what about Kanzi, who was never trained to use language? He learned it on his own during his early years, just as children learn language (Shanker, Savage-Rumbaugh, & Taylor, 1999).

Another criticism of animal language research directly questions the linguistic abilities of animals. Some argue that animal language researchers have not adequately demonstrated that animals can follow all of the grammatical and syntactical rules of human language (Kako, 1999). Animal language researchers counter that their critics have unfairly focused on the linguistic abilities that animals lack and have largely ignored the linguistic abilities that animals *do* have (Shanker, Savage-Rumbaugh, & Taylor, 1999). Some have even argued that critics of animal language keep changing the very definition of what language is—redefining language to include the linguistic abilities that animals do not have (Fouts, 1973).

You can see that this is a very passionate debate. As well it should be, for there is a great deal at stake here. If we ultimately determine that animals do have linguistic capacities, then we may have to reconsider what separates humans from the rest of the animal kingdom! This possibility brings up a whole host of questions concerning animals and the manner in which we treat animals in human society (Wise, 2000). For example, if some animals have linguistic capacities, what does that say about their intelligence in comparison to ours? And do we have the ethical right to perform experiments on animals that are so similar to ourselves? These are questions that we may have to tackle in the near future. For the moment, the jury is still out on the issue of language in animals.

© Rick Friedman / Corbis

Although controversial, studies of animals like Alex, the African gray parrot, challenge the presumption that language is a solely human attribute.

Let's Review!

In this section, we covered many aspects of language including how we acquire language, what it does for us, and the debate over language as a purely human attribute. For a quick check of your understanding, answer these questions.

1. Babies begin _____ when they begin to make_____ sounds.
   a. cooing; consonant
   b. babbling; vowel
   c. cooing; vowel and consonant
   d. babbling; vowel and consonant

2. Which of the following people would be the *most* likely to agree with the statement, "Language facilitates the development of culture?"

   a. Lev Vygotsky
   b. Benjamin Whorf
   c. Sue Savage-Rumbaugh
   d. Eleanor Rosch

3. One's language can influence one's _____.
   a. speech
   b. memory
   c. perception
   d. all of the above

ANSWERS

1. d; 2. a; 3. d

LEARNING OBJECTIVES < < < < < < < <

Discuss historical and modern attempts to measure intelligence, and some of the advantages and disadvantages of these methods.

Discuss the various ways that researchers have conceptualized intelligence.

Discuss the nature versus nurture debate as it applies to intelligence.

intelligence having abilities that allow you to adapt to your environment and behave in a goal-directed way

Defining and Measuring Intelligence

What makes a person intelligent? Is it earning good grades? Knowing how to survive in the wilderness? Knowing how to make large amounts of money in the stock market? Having social skills? What do you think? How do *you* define intelligence? Today, many psychologists broadly view **intelligence** as having abilities that allow you to adapt to your environment and behave in a goal-directed way. But over the years, psychologists have found that precise definition of intelligence is not as easy as it may seem, and our conception of intelligence has undergone several revisions in the history of psychology. Equally challenging has been finding ways of measuring intelligence.

Measuring Intelligence by Abilities and IQs

Francis Galton: Measuring Intelligence by Measuring Sensory Abilities

One of the first people to study the measurement of intelligence was British psychologist Sir Francis Galton (1822–1911). In the mid-1800s, Galton wrote a book entitled *Hereditary Intelligence* (1869), in which he claimed that intelligence is an inherited trait. He based this claim on his perception that high levels of intelligence seemed to run in families (including his own—he was a cousin to Charles Darwin). Furthermore, Galton (1883/1907) believed that high levels of intelligence were associated with high levels of sensory acuity and physical abilities, such as having a quick reaction time. In other words, if you possess exceptional physical agility and have good eyesight, hearing, and so on, you are also likely to be intelligent. To further his hypothesis, Galton set up a booth at the 1884 International Health Exhibition in London, where for a small fee he would measure volunteers on 13 physical and sensory characteristics, including things like color discrimination, hearing, and lung capacity (Forest, 1974).

Galton's work inspired American psychologist James McKeen Cattell (1860–1944), to collect large amounts of sensory and physical data on his students, which he then tried to correlate with their academic performance. Unfortunately for Cattell, he found that sensory and physical measures did *not* predict how well students did in college (Schultz & Schultz, 2000). After this failure, Cattell abandoned the idea that intelligence was related to sensory and physical abilities, and this notion of Galton's soon fell out of favor with many psychologists.

Recently, one study tested Galton's ideas of inherited intelligence by testing the hypothesis that literary genius was inherited from one's parents. The researchers examined 236 award-winning authors to see whether they had parents who were also gifted writers. They found no support for Galton's ideas of inherited intelligence (Rothenberg & Wyshak, 2004). As we will see in a later section, many modern psychologists tend to see intelligence as a result of the interaction between the nature and nurture influences we discussed in Chapter 2 (p. 88).

Alfred Binet: Measuring Intelligence by Measuring Cognitive Abilities

Although Francis Galton was influential in starting psychologists thinking about ways to measure intelligence, the modern intelligence test is credited to Alfred Binet (1857–1911). In 1904, the French government appointed Alfred Binet and psychiatrist Théodore Simon to a commission charged with developing a means of measuring the intelligence of French schoolchildren. The ultimate goal of this project was to give the government a process for identifying children who were mentally deficient so that these children could be placed in special education programs. Binet was chosen for this project because he had already conducted research on human abilities

(Binet, 1890), but despite this experience, Binet and Simon had little past research to guide them. Researchers had failed to show that physical characteristics were good measures of intelligence (Wissler, 1901), so it was up to Binet and Simon to redefine intelligence as a set of *cognitive* abilities.

Specifically, Binet saw intelligence as our capacity to *find and maintain a purpose, adapt our strategy to reach that purpose,* and *evaluate the strategy so it can be adjusted as necessary* (Terman, 1916). Binet's definition should sound somewhat familiar to you because, in essence, he suggested that having intelligence makes one a good problem solver! As such, Binet aimed to develop an intelligence test that focused on the assessment of general cognitive abilities—specifically, the individual's attention, judgment, and reasoning (Binet & Simon, 1905).

Binet prepared a set of 30 tasks that measured these skills and arranged them in order of difficulty. He placed the easiest questions first and the hardest questions last, and then he administered the test to the schoolchildren. Not surprisingly, the brighter students could answer more of the questions than the not-so-bright students could. Also, not surprisingly, the older children tended to answer more questions correctly than the younger children. In fact, Binet noticed that the brighter, younger children could sometimes correctly answer as many questions as the average child of an older age. For example, a very smart 6-year-old might be able to answer as many questions as the average 10-year-old child could. So Binet began to quantify children's intelligence in terms of **mental age,** or the age that reflects a child's mental abilities in comparison to the "average" child. In Binet's scheme, a mental age that exceeds one's chronological age indicates above-average intelligence, and a mental age that is below a child's actual age indicates a below-average level of intelligence.

mental age   the age that reflects the child's mental abilities in comparison to the average child of the same age

Recall that at the government's request, Binet's test was created to identify those who were mentally deficient. Therefore, Binet defined cutoff points on his test for these children. Unfortunately, they were categorized as "idiots," "imbeciles," and "morons" (Kaplan & Saccuzzo, 1989). Imagine being told by your teacher that you scored as an imbecile on an intelligence test! By today's standards Binet's approach seems very insensitive. Nonetheless, Binet's concept of mental age became the foundation for the very familiar IQ score, and his test became the basis for modern intelligence tests.

Lewis Terman: The Intelligence Quotient and the Stanford-Binet

In 1916, Stanford psychologist Lewis Terman completed an American revision of the intelligence test that Binet and Simon had developed. Terman translated the test into English and refined and added some test items. He named his version of the test the Stanford Revision of the Binet-Simon Scale, which became known as the Stanford-Binet. Perhaps his most significant contribution to the test was to introduce an **intelligence quotient,** or **IQ score,** as the measure of an individual's intelligence. An IQ score is calculated as:

intelligence quotient (IQ score)   one's mental age divided by one's chronological age times 100

$$IQ = (MA/CA) \times 100$$

where

$$MA = \text{mental age}$$

and

$$CA = \text{chronological, or actual, age}$$

Using the concept of an IQ, a person of average abilities has, by definition, an IQ of 100 or, in other words, a mental age equal to her or his actual age. IQs over 100 indicate above-average intelligence and IQs below 100 indicate below-average intelligence.

The Stanford-Binet has undergone four major revisions since 1916 and is still in wide use today. The most recent edition, The Stanford-Binet Intelligence Scales, Fifth Edition (SB5) was released in 2003. However, a modern IQ test developed by psychologist David Wechsler (1896–1981) and first released in 1939 has challenged the popularity of the Stanford-Binet.

David Wechsler's Intelligence Scales

Wechsler (1939) developed an intelligence test in response to shortcomings he saw in the Stanford-Binet. Wechsler objected to the fact that the Stanford-Binet test tried to sum up intelligence in a single score. He felt that one number could not adequately express something as complex as intelligence. Furthermore, Wechsler objected to the use of the mental age concept for adults (Kaplan & Saccuzzo, 1989). After all, would you necessarily expect a 40-year-old to correctly answer more questions than a 35-year-old? The concept of mental age doesn't apply as well to adults as it does to children because adults do not change as much from year to year as children do. Therefore, mental age has little significance in adulthood.

To correct these problems, Wechsler developed an intelligence test that yields scores on individual *subscales* that measure different mental abilities. Furthermore, instead of using mental age to determine IQ, Wechsler's tests compare a participant's performance to the average person's performance to determine IQ. The Wechsler tests are devised so that an average person's performance on the test results in an IQ of 100. Using this number as a benchmark, people who score above average on the test are given IQ scores above 100, and people who perform below average are given IQ scores below 100. Most people can expect to score near this average IQ, somewhere in the range of 85–115 (Figure 7.13).

Today there are three separate Wechsler intelligence tests. The Wechsler Preschool and Primary Scale of Intelligence (WPPSI) is administered to children aged 3–6. The Wechsler Intelligence Scale for Children, 3rd edition (WISC-III) is used on children aged 5–15. And the Wechsler Adult Intelligence Scale, 3rd edition (WAIS-III) is used on people over age 15.

The WAIS-III yields three separate scores, a *verbal* score, a *performance* score, and an *overall* score. The verbal score is based on the individual's performance on six types of verbal ability: comprehension, vocabulary, information, similarities, arithmetic, and digit span. The performance score is based on five types of performance ability: object assembly, block design, picture comprehension, picture arrangement, and digit symbol. The third score, the overall score, is a combination of the verbal and performance scores. The design of the WAIS-III makes it flexible. Testers can administer the verbal scale, the performance scale, or both. Figure 7.14 further describes these scales.

Testing the Test: What Makes a Good Intelligence Test?

So far, we have looked at two widely accepted tests that psychologists and educators use to measure intelligence. These are but two of a great many tests that have been devised to measure intelligence and other psychological traits in people. When choosing which test to administer or when interpreting the scores yielded by these tests, we have to ask, "Is this a good test?" If psychologists never worried about the quality of our measurements, we could well find ourselves making many faulty judgments about the people that we measure. Think about it—how would

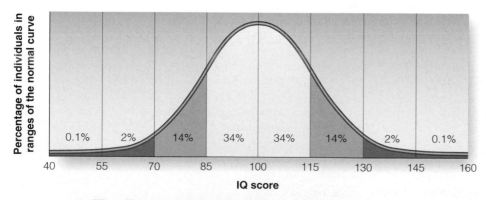

Figure 7.13 **The Normal Distribution of IQ Scores**

IQs tend to be normally distributed across the population. This means that when a frequency distribution of IQ scores is plotted, it has a bell-shaped curve, with most people scoring an average of 100 on the IQ test and very few scoring extremely high or low.

Content area	Explanation of tasks/questions	Examples of a possible task/question
Verbal Scale		
Comprehension	Answer questions of social knowledge	What does it mean when people say, "A stitch in time saves nine"? Why are convicted criminals put into prison?
Vocabulary	Define the meaning of the word	What does **persistent** mean? What does **archaeology** mean?
Information	Supply generally known information	Who is Chelsea Clinton? What are six New England states?
Similarities	Explain how two things or concepts are similar	In what ways are an ostrich and a penguin alike? In what ways are a lamp and a heater alike?
Arithmetic	Solve simple arithmetical-word problems	If Paul has $14.43, and he buys two sandwiches, which cost $5.23 each, how much change will he receive?
Digit span	Listen to a series of digits (numbers), then repeat the numbers either forward, backward, or both	Repeat these numbers backward: "9, 1, 8, 3, 6."
Performance Scale		
Object assembly	Put together a puzzle by combining pieces to form a particular common object	Put together these pieces to make something. 
Block design	Use patterned blocks to form a design that looks identical to a design shown by the examiner	Assemble the blocks on the left to make the design on the right. 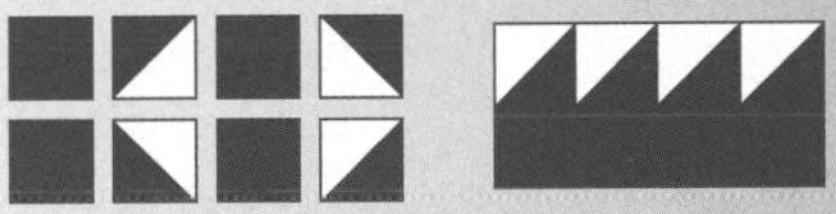
Picture completion	Tell what is missing from each picture	What is missing from this picture? 
Picture arrangement	Put a set of cartoonlike pictures into chronological order, so they tell a coherent story	Arrange these pictures in an order that tells a story, and then tell what is happening in the story. 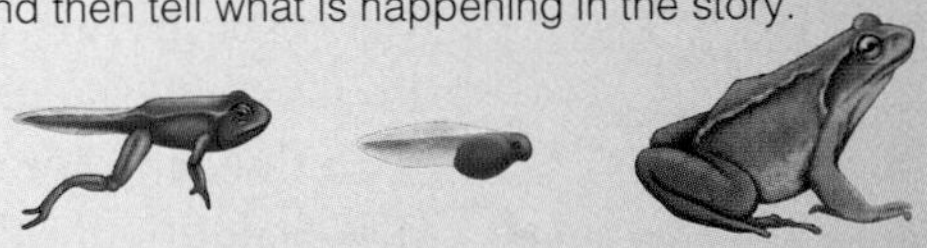
Digit symbol	When given a key matching particular symbols to particular numerals, copy a sequence of symbols, transcribing from symbols to numerals, using the key	Look carefully at the key. In the blanks, write the correct numeral for the symbol below each symbol. 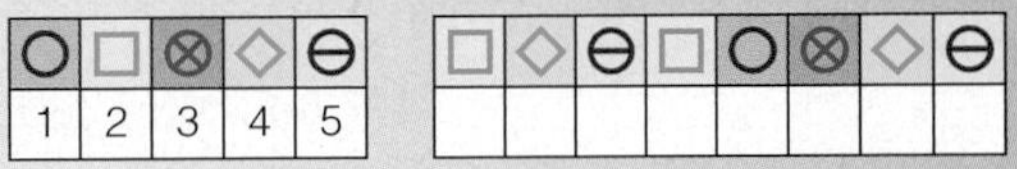

Figure 7.14 The Wechsler Adult Intelligence Scale (WAIS-III) and Its Subscales

The test items shown are examples—they do not appear in the actual test.

The WISC and WAIS use different types of tasks to assess IQ.

reliability the degree to which a test yields consistent measurements of a trait

validity the degree to which a test measures the trait that it was designed to measure

cultural bias the degree to which a test puts people from other cultures at an unfair disadvantage due to the culturally specific nature of the test items

Demonstration

you feel if someone gave you an IQ test, and then told you that your score on the test would determine whether or not you got a job? Wouldn't you want some assurance that the test would actually reflect your true intellectual ability? Most of us would. So how do psychologists ensure that their tests are good measures of people's abilities?

Before a test is used to make decisions about anyone's life, the test itself must be tested and evaluated (in Chapter 14, p. 643, we will see that this is also true of personality tests). Psychologists must be assured that the test is both *reliable* and *valid* before it can be put into widespread use. The **reliability** of a test refers to the degree to which the test yields consistent measurements over time. Although intelligence can change over time, it usually does so very slowly. On average, if you are intelligent today, you will be intelligent 6 months from now. So, if we use a test to measure your IQ today and then again in 6 months, the scores should be comparable. This doesn't mean that the test has to yield *exactly* the same score, but the scores should be close.

The simplest way to assess the reliability of a test is to look at the *test–retest reliability* of the test in an experimental setting. To do this, the test is administered to a large group of people, and their scores are computed. Then later, after 6 months or a year, the test is readministered to the same people, and their new scores are computed. If the test is reliable, the two sets of scores should correlate. If they do not correlate, the test should not be used because measuring IQ with an unreliable test is a lot like trying to measure distance with an elastic ruler. The scores will keep changing, and you will not be able to determine which, if any, of the scores are correct.

Establishing the reliability of an intelligence test is very important, but the **validity** of the test is an equally important characteristic. Validity is the degree to which the test measures what it was designed to measure. In the case of an intelligence test, one must show that the test actually measures intelligence!

Psychologists often assess the validity of their tests by assessing *predictive validity*. To establish predictive validity, we must show that scores on the test reliably predict future behavior. For example, if we expect that intelligence is related to doing well in school, then scores on a *valid* IQ test should predict who does well in school—and who does not. To assess for our test's validity, we would test a large number of students and then correlate their IQ scores with their high school GPA. If our test is valid, IQ and GPA should correlate. If they do not, the IQ test is not a valid predictor of academic success, and it should not be used as such!

You might be thinking that validity seems like a trivial issue. After all, if you create an IQ test that asks people questions that *seem* to require intelligence to answer, won't the test tell you who is smart and who is not? As it turns out, it is quite easy to devise tests that are invalid. For example, questions on a test that require specific cultural knowledge may not actually assess the intelligence of people who are unfamiliar with the culture being referenced—even though the people may be very intelligent. This validity problem is referred to as a **cultural bias,** and some people have argued that intelligence tests are often biased and invalid for cultural minority members (Reynolds & Brown, 1984). To illustrate this point, take a look at the following sample IQ test question:

Choose the term that best completes this analogy:
Chayote is to soup as scissors are to _____.
a. a drawer
b. paper
c. eggs
d. a bird

If you are from a culture that is not familiar with the word *chayote,* which is a type of squash eaten in some Latin American cultures, you might not realize that you put scissors *into* a drawer the way you put chayote *into* soup. Does this mean you are un-intelligent? Of course not—but an incorrect answer would count against you if it were on an IQ test! Some people contend that IQ tests can't help but reflect the cultural values, language, and knowledge of the people who develop them, and as such, all IQ tests carry with them some form of cultural bias (Greenfield, 1997). We should always keep in mind that IQ tests do not measure all human abilities, and our cultural environment can affect our performance on these tests (Sternberg, 1997a).

The Nature of Intelligence: The Search Continues

Back in the early 1900s, when psychologists were busily trying to measure intelligence, psychological historian E. G. Boring noted that "intelligence is what the tests test" (Boring, quoted in Gardner, 1999, p. 13). By this, Boring meant that psychologists had placed a great deal of emphasis on developing tests to measure intelligence, but they had not spent adequate time exploring what intelligence actually is. Rather than developing theories about the nature of intelligence, researchers had focused in on devising tests; the tests would yield scores; and the scores could then be used to predict how well a person would function in a given situation. In many respects, Boring was correct in his appraisal of the situation. However, in the intervening decades psychologists have not completely ignored the question of the nature of intelligence.

Intelligence as a Single Factor

In the last century, British statistician Charles Spearman argued that because test scores of separate mental abilities (e.g., verbal skills, mathematical ability, deductive reasoning skills) tend to correlate, there must be one general level of intelligence that underlies these separate mental abilities (Spearman, 1904). Spearman referred to this **generalized intelligence** as *g*. In Spearman's view, one's level of *g* would determine how well he or she functioned on any number of cognitive tasks. This idea of intelligence as a single, unitary factor helped lead to the rapid expansion of intelligence testing in schools, the workplace, and the military. But Spearman's notion that intelligence is a single factor would soon be challenged.

generalized intelligence (*g*) Charles Spearman's notion that there is a general level of intelligence that underlies our separate abilities

Intelligence as a Collection of Abilities

Is intelligence really one single factor? Can't a person be smart in some areas, but not in others? By the 1930s, some theorists were beginning to challenge the idea of a single intelligence. The notion of *g* fell from favor as psychologists proposed theories that described intelligence as a set of abilities rather than a single trait. One of the earliest of these theories came from psychologist L. L. Thurstone (1938), who argued that intelligence was made up of seven distinct mental abilities. These were reasoning, associative memory, spatial visualization, numerical fluency, verbal comprehension, perceptual speed, and word fluency. Others would eventually propose as many as 120 different factors underlying intelligence (Guilford, 1967).

However, not everyone was convinced that intelligence was made up of many different factors. In the 1960s, Raymond Cattell (1963) revived the idea of *g* when he argued that Thurstone had been wrong in his interpretation of his data. Raymond Cattell proposed that *g* does exist, but in two different forms, which he called **crystallized intelligence** and **fluid intelligence.** Crystallized intelligence refers to our accumulation of knowledge. For example, your knowledge of psychology is part of your crystallized intelligence. Fluid intelligence refers to the speed and efficiency with which we learn new information and solve problems. For instance, the higher your fluid intelligence, the more quickly you will learn the material in this chapter.

crystallized intelligence our accumulation of knowledge

fluid intelligence the speed and efficiency with which we learn new information and solve problems

There is both good and bad news when it comes to our levels of fluid and crystallized intelligence over a lifetime. The evidence shows that crystallized intelligence can continue to grow well into late adulthood (Horn, Donaldson, & Engstrom, 1981), but our fluid intelligence tends to decrease across adulthood (Schaie, 1994). The degree to which we retain these abilities throughout life is affected by our environment and our physical well-being, although environment is much more important in the case of crystallized intelligence (Horn, 1982). We'll discuss this in more detail when we describe cognitive changes in adolescence and adulthood in Chapter 10 (p. 449).

As you can see, there has been much disagreement as to exactly what intelligence is, and this debate is likely to continue for some time. Today, many psychologists still favor the idea of a generalized intelligence, especially among those psychologists who focus on the need to measure intelligence (Gardner, 1999, p. 14). However, other psychologists have gone on to develop newer theories that conceptualize intelligence as a multifaceted set of abilities or *intelligences*. In the next section we will take a look at two of the most popular and influential of these modern theories.

A New Spin: Howard Gardner's Multiple Intelligences

In the early 1980s, Harvard psychologist Howard Gardner proposed a theory of intelligence that views humans as possessing many different intelligences (Gardner, 1983). According to Gardner, an intelligence is "a biopsychological potential to process information that can be activated in a cultural setting to solve problems or create products that are of value in a culture" (Gardner, 1999, pp. 33–34). This definition emphasizes the fact that intelligence allows us to function efficiently in our own environment, and it also highlights the fact that different cultures and environments place different demands on our intelligence.

For example, in the United States today, we might consider the ability to understand and predict fluctuations in the stock market as a sign of intelligence. In an unindustrialized, nomadic culture, however, the ability to seek out a source of water may be a more highly valued intelligence. After carefully considering the different human abilities that allow us to function in our environment, Gardner developed a strict set of criteria for identifying an intelligence (Gardner, 1999). Using these criteria, Gardner has identified nine different intelligences and allowed for the possibility that more may someday be identified (Gardner, 2004). Gardner's theory of **multiple intelligences** is summarized in Figure 7.15.

multiple intelligences the idea that we possess different types of intelligence rather than a single, overall level of intelligence

As you look at Figure 7.15, can you see that you have more of some types of intelligence and less of others? Most of us do not possess equal levels of all types of intelligence. Rather, we each have our own strengths and weaknesses. Therefore, Gardner doesn't have much use for measures of intelligence that seek to measure one's generalized intelligence. For Gardner, it is far more important to look at a person's intelligence *profile*—his or her level of ability across the different types of intelligence.

Robert Sternberg's Triarchic Theory of Intelligence

Yale psychologist Robert Sternberg has taken an approach somewhat similar to Howard Gardner's. Like Gardner, Sternberg rejects the usefulness of trying to measure a single, generalized intelligence. However, Sternberg doesn't subscribe to the idea that we possess many separate intelligences. Sternberg considers some of Gardner's intelligences as *talents* that some people possess. For example, it's hard to see why musical intelligence would be important in many cultures. Even if you have little or no musical ability, you could still function very well in many cultures, including American society. However, in the United States and many other cultures, the ability to think logically would be very important to your survival and well-being.

Intelligence	Description	Examples
Linguistic	The ability to learn and use languages	An author has good command of language and can express ideas well in written form.
Spatial	The ability to recognize and manipulate patterns of space	A surveyor is very good at judging distances. A seamstress designs a pattern for a jacket.
Logical-mathematical	The ability to attack problems in a logical manner, solve mathematical problems, and in general exhibit scientific thought	A psychologist can develop and test theories in a scientific manner. A physician examines a patient and makes a diagnosis.
Musical	The ability to perform, compose, and appreciate music	A songwriter can create unique melodies and perform them.
Bodily-kinesthetic	The ability to use one's body to solve problems and create products	A gymnast can perform intricate maneuvers on the balance beam.
Interpersonal	The ability to understand the intentions, motivations, and desires of others	A manager is good at working with others, and can inspire others to perform at their optimal level of performance.
Intrapersonal	The ability to understand oneself	A student knows what she wants in terms of her career and future life, and she uses this information to choose an appropriate major.
Naturalistic	Paying attention to nature and understanding environmental issues	A homemaker recycles her trash and avoids using household cleaners that are harmful to the environment.
Existential	Being concerned with "ultimate" issues; seeking higher truths	A philosophy student ponders the meaning of life.

Figure 7.15 Gardner's Multiple Intelligences
Source: Gardner, 1999, 2004.

Sternberg suggests that *successful intelligence*, or intelligence that helps us function in our world, is composed of three types of cognitive abilities. Accordingly, Sternberg calls his theory of intelligence the **triarchic theory of intelligence** (Sternberg, 1985, 1997b). According to the triarchic theory, intelligence is composed of analytical, practical, and creative abilities that help us successfully adapt to our environment.

Analytical intelligence is seen in our ability to use logic to reason our way through problems. Going back to our earlier example, if your car breaks down on exam day, you would use your analytical powers to generate possible solutions to this dilemma. Analytical intelligence is also important as we implement and evaluate problem-solving strategies. For example, analytical intelligence allows us to evaluate whether or not a particular problem-solving strategy is working well.

Practical intelligence is our ability to adapt to our environment. This is the type of intelligence that we see in people who have a great deal of common sense. People who are high in practical intelligence exhibit savvy. They know how to function efficiently within their environment. For example, a Central American farmer may be able to predict the weather by noticing changes in the environment. Or a woman who lives in New York City may be very good at finding the quickest way across town during rush hour. Both of these people, although they possess very different skills, exhibit practical intelligence.

triarchic theory of intelligence a theory of intelligence that proposes that intelligence is composed of *analytical, practical,* and *creative* abilities that help us successfully adapt to our environment

Keep in mind that behaviors and skills may be intelligent in some environments, but not in others. The skills that Ildefonso used to survive in his world may be very different from the skills you or I use, but nonetheless, Ildefonso exhibited practical intelligence in the way in which he survived languageless in a language-rich world!

Application »

Creative intelligence is our ability to use our knowledge of the world in novel situations. For example, suppose you found yourself in a foreign culture where you did not know the language or the customs. Would you be able to function? People who are high in creative intelligence can adapt what they know about the world to meet the unique demands of new situations. For instance, you might use the pantomime skills you learned while playing charades to help you communicate with those whose language you do not speak or understand. Creative intelligence is also seen when people break out of *mental sets* (see p. 310) to solve problems in unique ways. For example, in the earlier story of the author's father using the tire pump as a fuel pump on his car, we saw an example of creative intelligence.

Daniel Goleman's Theory of Emotional Intelligence

Yet another way of conceptualizing intelligence comes from psychologist Daniel Goleman. In his best-selling book *Emotional Intelligence*, Goleman (1995) argues that a concept of intelligence that is based solely on cognitive abilities is too limiting. He notes that even people with relatively high IQs can fail to succeed in life and sometimes do things that appear to be downright unintelligent. For example, a gifted student with a perfect score of 1,600 on the SAT may turn out to be a poor college student who takes 10 years to earn a degree (Goleman, 1995). According to Goleman, the reason for this is that many times our actions are guided not by our intellectual abilities, but rather by our emotions. Goleman contends that just as some of us are intellectually gifted, some of us are also endowed with emotional prowess—an ability he calls *emotional intelligence*.

In Goleman's view, emotional intelligence includes awareness of your own emotional states, accurate assessment of your own abilities, self-confidence, self-control, trustworthiness, conscientiousness, the ability to adapt to changes, innovation or creativity, achievement motivation, commitment to completing goals, initiative or self-motivation, and a sense of optimism (Goleman, 1998; Petrides, Furnham, & Martin, 2004). In other words, an emotionally intelligent person is a confident self-starter, who is ethical and adaptable—the kind of person who sets a goal and works toward it without letting minor obstacles derail his or her progress. With this sort of determination, confidence, and ability to adapt, a person with only an average IQ might be able to go far. Likewise, a bright person with low emotional intelligence might become overwhelmed with self-doubt or lack of motivation and as a result, fail to perform well in life.

Today, the concept of emotional intelligence is sparking interest among researchers and in the workplace (Yunker & Yunker, 2002). For instance, Goleman and his colleagues have suggested that one way to increase effective leadership in the corporate world is to teach personnel to acquire higher levels of emotional intelligence (Goleman, Boyatzis, & McKee, 2002). Toward such an application of their ideas, Goleman and his colleagues have also developed a test to measure one's emotional intelligence, called the Emotional Competence Inventory (Boyatzis, Goleman, & Rhee, 2000).

So, What Is Intelligence After All?

As you can see from our discussions, there has always been a great deal of controversy over the nature of intelligence. Over the years, people have argued for viewing intelligence as a single factor (Spearman, 1904), as a combination of various multiple mental abilities (e.g., R. Cattell, 1963; Sternberg, 1985), or as a variety of independent multiple intelligences (Gardner, 1999). So who is correct? Well, at this time, we cannot say for sure, and the controversy is likely to continue. We will all have to wait and see what researchers will uncover about intelligence in the years to come. The issue of *what* intelligence is has certainly stimulated a great deal of debate among researchers, but another issue has captured the attention of the public even more. Where does intelligence come from—our genes or our environment (Gardner, 1999)?

Nature, Nurture, and IQ: Are We Born Intelligent, or Do We Learn to Be?

The *nature–nurture debate* that you learned about in Chapter 2 is never more contentious than it is when it's applied to the issue of intelligence. The argument over whether intelligence is primarily due to genetic factors (the nature side of the debate) or to environmental influences (the nurture side) has at times been a very heated and emotional debate in our society. Most recently, this debate was brought into the public eye with the publication of the book *The Bell Curve* (Herrnstein & Murray, 1994). The title of this book refers to the fact that IQ scores tend to follow a normal distribution, which is shaped like a bell (see Figure 7.13, p. 326). In *The Bell Curve*, the authors argued that intelligence is primarily encoded in our genes and that environmental influences do little to change our intelligence. This extreme position was largely denounced by scholars (Gardner, 1999), but the public became engaged in heated discussions about the merits of this position, as well as the implications of the authors' claims. Of particular concern was the implication that some minority groups may be genetically inferior with respect to intelligence. While the authors never stated that minorities were genetically inferior, this conclusion was clearly to be drawn from their argument and the data that has been collected on IQ differences across racial groups.

Generally speaking, studies have shown that *average* IQ scores tend to vary across racial groups in America. As a group, African Americans tend to score about 10 points lower on IQ tests than Whites do (Nisbett, 1995). On the other hand, as a group, Asians sometimes outscore Whites on intelligence tests (e.g., Stevenson & Lee, 1990). If we are to believe the message of *The Bell Curve*, then, the inference would be that these differences exist because of genetic tendencies and not because of environmental differences. Furthermore, we would then assume that any attempt to improve children's environment to raise their IQ scores would be an utter waste of time and money.

As unpleasant as they were to many, the arguments made in *The Bell Curve* were not new. Others had made similar claims before (Jensen, 1969). Psychologists have been grappling with the issue of genetics, intelligence, and racial differences in IQ for some time. Overall, the conclusions most psychologists have come to about nature, nurture, and intelligence have been very different from those seen in *The Bell Curve*.

Twin Studies: Nature *and* Nurture

As we discussed in Chapter 2, *twin studies* are the best way to study the relative contributions of genetics and environmental influences. Recall that in twin studies identical twins and fraternal twins are compared with respect to their characteristics and abilities. Because only identical twins share 100% of their genes, identical twins should be more alike than fraternal twins if the characteristic in question has a genetic basis. Overall, the results of twin studies (and other studies) on the inheritance of traits in families have not supported the strong nature claims made in *The Bell Curve*. Rather, these studies support an *interactionist* perspective on intelligence—in other words, intelligence seems to stem almost equally from our genes and our environment (Chipuer, Rovine, & Polmin, 1990; Polmin, 1994). Therefore, it is just as likely that racial differences in IQ are due to environmental differences.

An impoverished environment may contribute to lesser performance on IQ tests for a number of reasons. Poorer parents cannot afford educational toys, good schools, computers, and so on for their children. Poorer parents may themselves not be highly educated and therefore may be less able to stimulate their children in the ways that highly educated parents can. Poverty-stricken children may not receive adequate nutrition and medical care, and this may affect neural development. We could go on listing the possibilities for pages, but a stronger argument can be made by looking at what happens when poorer minority children are placed in a different environment. One study (Moore, 1986) showed that African American children who were placed in affluent White families as infants had average IQs that were above average for *White* children by the time they had reached middle school.

It is also worth noting that there is more variability in intelligence within racial groups than there is between racial groups. In other words, the range of IQ scores among Whites, African Americans, and other races is wider than the average differences between these groups.

Interpreting Intelligence Studies

Data like these seriously question the notion that intelligence is primarily an inherited characteristic. Furthermore, we all would do well to keep in mind that *group* characteristics do not predict individual characteristics. For instance, let's say that through some magic we could tell you with 100% accuracy that the class average on your next psychology exam will be a 71. Does this mean that you are going to earn a 71? Not at all—you could earn *any* grade on the exam! You might earn a 95. There is no way to predict your performance based on the class average. The same is true of IQ scores. Even if, for whatever reason, the average IQ for a minority group is higher or lower than the average IQ in the majority group, we cannot predict what an individual minority member's IQ will be. It is a mistake to assume that an individual minority member has a lower IQ based on data that was obtained from a group of people. It would be equally wrong to assume that a majority member would necessarily have a comparatively high IQ. When we make assumptions about individuals based on group characteristics, and we ignore individual characteristics, we are engaging in a *prejudice*. We will have more to say about prejudice in Chapter 12 when we look at social psychology. For now, let's take a look at another controversial area of intelligence research—the question of whether men and women differ in intelligence.

Gender and Intellectual Abilities: Are We Really All That Different?

Just as we saw in our discussion on race and IQ, data are at times open to different interpretations. One area in which the interpretation of data has been varied and sometimes contentious is in the study of how gender relates to intellectual abilities. Beliefs or stereotypes about male and female intellectual abilities abound. For example, in the United States (and many other cultures), people tend to believe that men are better at math and women are better at verbal tasks. Another common stereotype is that men are more intelligent than women and women are more emotional than men. But stereotypes are just our perceptions or beliefs. Are there truly gender differences in intelligence levels?

The answer to this question has proved to be somewhat complicated. Over the last several decades, many researchers have investigated the issue of gender differences in intelligence, and often their results have been difficult to interpret (Galliano, 2003). In part, the confusion has had to do with how individual researchers have defined specific abilities. For example, in evaluating a person's mathematical ability, you could look at his or her ability to solve equations, the speed with which he or she can solve word problems, whether he or she succeeds in math classes, and so on. Another problem is that studies that fail to find predicted gender differences are often not published. Therefore, if we look only at studies that do show gender differences in intelligence, we may falsely assume that gender differences are more prevalent than they actually are (Galliano, 2003).

After examining the available research, many psychologists have concluded that men and women do not differ in general intelligence, or *g* (Halpern & LeMay, 2000). On the other hand, some gender differences have been indicated with respect to specific multiple intelligences. We have summarized some of these suspected differences in Table 7.1 ◆. Keep a few things in mind as you read Table 7.1. First, many gender differences are small (e.g., Galliano, 2003; Hyde, Fennema, & Lamon, 1990). Second, finding such differences often depends on how they were measured. For example, females tend to earn better grades in math classes, but males tend to do better on standardized tests of mathematical ability (Hyde & McKinley, 1997). Third, gender differences can vary by culture, age, and race. For instance, in Thailand girls outperform boys in math, but in France boys do better than girls (Galliano, 2003). And in the United States, male superiority on math SAT scores occurs only among White students (Robinson, Abbott, Berninger, & Busse, 1996). Finally, gender differences are at times a product of bias in the tests used to measure different abilities. For example, David Share and Phil Silva (2003) found that in a sample of New Zealand students, boys were more likely to be labeled as having reading disabilities due to a statistical bias in the way that reading disability scores were calculated.

Given these types of idiosyncrasies in the data, it is difficult to conclude that there are broad-based, global differences between men and women when it comes to intelligence. Despite the lack of clarity concerning the differences, it is fairly clear that we tend to believe the stereotypes we have about men and women's abilities. Belief in these stereotypes has been well-documented in studies that ask men and women to assess their own intellectual abilities. For example, in one study Adrian Furnham and colleagues found that parents tended to estimate their sons' IQs as being higher than their daughters', indicating that they had more confidence in their sons' overall intelligence, or *g*. When asked to rate their children on specific multiple intelligences, the parents tended to rate their sons higher on mathematical and spatial intelligence and their daughters higher on verbal and musical intelligences (Furnham, Reeves, & Budhani, 2002).

Compared to women, men also rate themselves as having higher IQs, lower levels of emotional intelligence (Petrides, Furnham, & Martin, 2004), better general knowledge, and more skill on tasks of visual perception (Pallier, 2003). Studies like these

◆ **Table 7.1**

Gender Differences on Some Cognitive Tasks

Tasks on Which Women Often Have Higher Average Scores	Tasks on Which Men Often Have Higher Average Scores
Verbal Tasks	**Visual Memory Tasks**
• verbal fluency • synonym generation • spelling • anagrams • reading comprehension • writing • foreign languages • tongue twisters • knowledge about literature	• mental-rotation tasks
Perceptual Tasks	**Spatial Tasks**
• searching for letters within lines of text • detecting touch, taste, odor, and sound stimuli at low levels of intensity	• making judgments about moving objects—for example judging how far away a moving object is
Motor Skill Tasks	**Motor Skill Tasks**
• fine motor skill tasks like tracing the mirror image of a stimulus on a piece of paper	• motor skills that involve aiming, such as throwing a baseball or darts
Academic Performance	**Knowledge Areas**
• most subject areas at school	• general knowledge • knowledge about math, geography, and science
	Fluid Reasoning Tasks
	• mechanical reasoning • quantitative reasoning • verbal analogies • scientific reasoning • proportional reasoning

Source: Adapted from Halpern, 1996.

seem to suggest that both men and women have (perhaps misguidedly) bought into the commonly held stereotypes about their respective abilities. Just as with race, stereotypes like these can be the basis for prejudice and discrimination—topics that we will discuss more in Chapter 12.

Let's Review!

In this section, we discussed intelligence. We looked at ways psychologists attempt to test, measure, and define intelligence, and the controversy concerning influences that affect an individual's level of intelligence. As a quick check of your understanding, answer these questions.

1. Which psychologist would be *most* likely to agree with the following statements: "Intelligence is not a single ability. We do not possess intelligence. We possess many intelligences."

   a. Robert Sternberg   c. Howard Gardner

   b. Francis Galton   d. James McKeen Cattel

2. Gilbert recently developed a new intelligence test that he plans to administer to second-grade children, but when Gilbert wrote the questions, he used an adult-level vocabulary. Based on your understanding of intelligence tests, what would you predict the test to be?

   a. valid and reliable   c. invalid

   b. unreliable   d. valid, but not reliable

3. One day, Sabrina's front door started squeaking at the hinges. She was out of the spray-lubricant that she normally would use for this purpose, so she went to her kitchen and got a bottle of cooking oil. After dabbing a bit of the corn oil on the hinge, the squeak went away. Sabrina *best* exhibits a high level of _____ intelligence.

   a. analytical   c. practical

   b. existential   d. creative

ANSWERS

1. c; 2. c; 3. d

Are You Getting the Big Picture?

In this chapter, we explored the cognitive processes of *thinking*, *language*, and *intelligence*. These abilities are essential to our everyday functioning because they allow us to perceive and understand our world, solve problems, and communicate with others. To a large extent these processes are interdependent. The efficiency and accuracy of our thought is partly due to the conceptual nature of our knowledge. We don't just throw bits of information into our minds; rather, we store knowledge in highly organized conceptual categories. These categories allow us to efficiently find information in memory, as well as to efficiently store new information in memory.

For most of us, conceptual knowledge is heavily intertwined with language. We use words to label the contents of our world, and so the mental representations of the world that we store in memory are often verbal. Language also allows us to communicate our thoughts to others. We use language to communicate the values, customs, and beliefs of our culture to our children. As such, language plays a critical role in the transmission of culture from generation to generation. Language also may influence our perception of the world and the people in it. For instance, the verbal labels we use to describe groups of people can color our perception of people who belong to those groups. In Chapter 12, we will take a closer look at our perception of others and the prejudices that can affect perception.

STUDYING **THE CHAPTER**

The conceptual knowledge we have stored about the world also helps us to solve problems. Some problems have clear paths to their solutions, whereas others do not. Whether we solve problems using algorithms or heuristics, we must call on our conceptual knowledge of the world when solving problems. We use knowledge to help us generate possible solutions to problems, to decide which solutions to implement, and to make judgments when we are uncertain about the world.

How well we use what we know about the world to solve problems is a fundamental aspect of intelligence. Historically, psychologists have focused on measuring intelligence using intelligence tests. These tests are, by and large, verbal tests. Because intelligence tests are created within a specific culture and use the language of that culture, they may be biased against people who are not of that culture. Furthermore, intelligence tests do not measure all human abilities, and there is considerable debate as to what, exactly, constitutes intelligence.

Another debate concerns the source of intelligence. The nature-nurture debate has been hotly fought in the area of intelligence. Despite the extremity of a few people's stances on this issue, most psychologists agree that nature and nurture jointly influence our level of intelligence. Our genes may set some parameters on our cognitive development, but the influence of the environment is also important. This can be seen clearly in the development of language. Without exposure to language during early development, children do not develop language. Despite his deafness, Ildefonso would likely have learned sign language much like hearing children learn to speak their native tongue—if only his environment had exposed him to sign language during early childhood.

Despite the interdependence of thinking, language, and intelligence, the case of Ildefonso does illustrate that cognition does not necessarily require language. Ildefonso was obviously a man of some intelligence, who could think and solve problems without the use of language. How he managed to do this is not clear. We have no good research data on the cognitive processes of languageless people. Nonetheless, it is interesting to ponder what Ildefonso's life must have been like before he learned a language.

An understanding of thinking, language, and intelligence also has application to many professions. Teachers use their understanding of these processes to help students learn better. Computer programmers in the field of artificial intelligence use their understanding of thinking in writing computer programs that solve problems like we do. People in the business world use their knowledge of thinking, intelligence, and language as well. For example, salespeople benefit from understanding how consumers reason and make decisions about products and services. Personnel managers sometimes use intelligence tests to evaluate prospective employees. And recently, Howard Gardner (2004) has even argued that understanding and cultivating certain intelligences can help make some people more persuasive—a talent that has numerous applications in the work world.

Key Terms

cognition (299)
knowledge (300)
thinking (300)
mental representation (300)
cognitive map (302)
concept (303)
superordinate category (303)
basic level category (303)
subordinate category (303)
formal concept (303)
natural concept (304)
prototype (305)
well-structured problem (306)
algorithm (307)
heuristic (307)
ill-structured problem (307)
insight (308)

creativity (309)
functional fixedness (309)
mental set (310)
incubation (310)
reasoning (311)
deductive reasoning (311)
inductive reasoning (312)
decision making (312)
judgment (313)
availability heuristic (313)
representativeness heuristic (314)
language (315)
cooing (317)
babbling (317)
phoneme (318)
morpheme (318)
overextension (318)

underextension (318)
telegraphic speech (318)
Whorfian hypothesis/linguistic
    relativity hypothesis (319)
intelligence (324)
mental age (325)
intelligence quotient (325)
reliability (328)
validity (328)
cultural bias (328)
generalized intelligence (329)
crystallized intelligence (329)
fluid intelligence (329)
multiple intelligences (330)
triarchic theory of intelligence (331)

Test Yourself!

Concept Check

Test your knowledge of the chapter concepts by completing each of the following sentences with the correct term. For a more comprehensive review, visit the book Web site (http://psychology.wadsworth.com/pastorino1e/) for online quizzes, flashcards, crosswords, and Internet links.

_____ **1.** A concept that develops through the course of leading one's life.

_____ **2.** The smallest unit of sound in a language.

_____ **3.** The process of making choices.

_____ **4.** A period of rest during problem solving that helps one find a solution.

_____ **5.** Judging an event's frequency based on how easily one can recall instances of the event in memory.

_____ **6.** The most typical member of a category.

_____ **7.** This refers to the speed at which one can process information.

_____ **8.** Drawing conclusions about the world based on certain assumptions.

_____ **9.** Making vowel-based sounds.

_____ **10.** A problem solving strategy that always leads to a solution.

_____ **11.** Reasoning from the general to the specific.

_____ **12.** Measuring what you intend to measure with a test.

_____ **13.** Mental category that contains related bits of information.

_____ **14.** The highest, most general level of a concept.

A. inductive reasoning

B. prototype

C. algorithm

D. phoneme

E. fluid intelligence

F. superordinate category

G. concept

H. reasoning

I. validity

J. natural concept

K. decision making

L. availability heuristic

M. cooing

N. incubation

Answers

1. J; 2. D; 3. K; 4. N; 5. L; 6. B; 7. E; 8. H; 9. M; 10. C; 11. A; 12. I; 13. G; 14. F

Critical Thinking About the Chapter

1. What abilities define our concept of an intelligent person in the United States? What abilities do you think would define the concept of an intelligent person in rural Africa?

2. Make a case for why one would *want* to use heuristics for solving problems and making decisions and judgments.

3. Give an original example of an ill-structured and a well-structured problem.

4. Describe the stages that children go through as they develop language. If you wanted to raise a bilingual child, how do you think you could best accomplish this?

Applying Psychology. Create your own intelligence test, and then describe how you would test its reliability and validity.

Critical Thinking for Integration

1. How would you suppose B. F. Skinner would explain the development of language in human beings?

2. Presume that someday we finally do provide conclusive evidence that animals have linguistic abilities. How do you think this would change psychology and other sciences?

3. Given what you have learned about language, intelligence, and psychology in general, what advice would you

give a first-time parent who is concerned about raising the best child he or she can?

4. Design a study to test the hypothesis that IQ remains stable across the life span.

5. How could cultural bias in intelligence testing facilitate the development or maintenance of racial prejudices?

Chapter Study Resources

Suggested Readings

1. Pepperberg, I. M. (2002). *The Alex studies.* Cambridge, MA: Harvard University Press.
   Pepperberg presents a thorough overview of studies that investigate the cognitive and linguistic abilities of African gray parrots.

2. Goleman, D. (1995). *Emotional intelligence.* New York: Bantam.
   Goleman's best-selling book deals with the concept of emotional intelligence and its application to every-day life.

3. Gardner, H. (2004). *Changing minds: The art and science of changing our own and others' minds.* Boston: Harvard Business School Press.
   In this book, Gardner discusses the psychology of being persuasive and includes his work on multiple intelligences and how they relate to our ability to influence other's minds.

4. Wise, S. M. (2000). *Rattling the cage.* Cambridge, MA: Perseus.
   Wise presents a fascinating look at the cognitive abilities of animals while examining the question of what separates humans from the rest of the animal kingdom.

5. For additional readings, explore InfoTrac College Edition, your online library of archived journal articles and periodicals. Go to http://www.infotrac-college.com/wadsworth enter the passcode from the card that came with your book. For this chapter, search using these keywords:

   animal cognition

   deductive reasoning

   divergent thinking

   intelligence

Web Links for Further Study

1. A site from an organization called Mathcounts that outlines problem-solving steps involved in doing mathematics.
   http://mathcounts.org

2. A Web site for the Journal of Artificial Intelligence Research.
   http://www.cs.washington.edu/research/jair/home.html

3. A site that has many different IQ, personality, and aptitude tests. Some of these tests are just for fun, but others are claimed by the Web site to be serious psychological tests. Try it just for fun.
   http://www.queendom.com/index.html

4. AltaVista's version of Babelfish. You can use this site to translate text to and from several different languages.
   http://world.altavista.com/

Student Study Guide

To help organize your learning, work through Chapter 7 of the *What Is Psychology? Student Study Guide.* The study guide includes learning objectives, a chapter summary, fill-in review, key terms, a practice test, and activities.

Psychology Now™

PsychologyNow is a Web-based, personalized study system that provides you with a pretest and a post-test for each chapter, quizzes you by chapter, and provides a personalized study plan, pointing you to elements in the text or in individual learning modules that will help you to achieve 80% mastery. Check out the learning module that relates to this chapter: cultural biases in intelligence testing.

PsychNow CD-ROM, Version 2.0

Go to the PsychNow CD-ROM for further study of the concepts in this chapter. The CD-ROM includes learning modules with videos, animations, and quizzes, as well as simulations of psychological phenomena. Each module follows a consistent Explore, Lesson, and Apply structure that allows you to experience the concept or principle, learn more about it, and then apply it. You and your friends can participate in a team-based Quiz Game that makes learning fun. You can also participate in experiments such as Prototypes and Mental Rotation. Learning modules include: 5f. Cognition and Language; 5g. Problem Solving and Creativity; 7e. Assessment.

Cognition, Language, and Intelligence

THINKING

• Cognition can be defined as the way in which we store and use information.

• The information we store in long-term memory about the world and how it works constitutes our knowledge base.

• Psychologists define thinking as the use of knowledge to accomplish a goal: to perceive and understand our world, to communicate with others, or to solve the problems we encounter in our lives.

• In our long-term memory, we store our knowledge of the world as mental representations—bits of memory—that represent objects, events, people, and so on that are not actually present now.

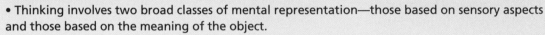

• Thinking involves two broad classes of mental representation—those based on sensory aspects and those based on the meaning of the object.

• Visual images are powerful mental representations that allow us to remember a person's face or a map of one's town. One way in which visual images are studied is by the mental rotation task.

• Concepts are mental categories that contain related bits of knowledge and are organized around the meaning of the information they represent.

• Cognitive maps are mental representations for geographical information.

• Psychologists have found that we tend to organize our knowledge into three levels of categorization: the general, broad, superordinate category; the basic-level category; and the subordinate category, which is the most specific.

• We acquire formal concepts as we learn the rigid rules that define certain categories of things. Concepts that develop naturally as we live our lives and experience the world are known as natural concepts.

• A prototype is our concept of the most typical member of a category—in essence, a summary of all members of that category.

PROBLEM SOLVING

• An algorithm is a method of solving a particular problem that always leads to the correct solution. A heuristic is a shortcut, or rule of thumb, that may or may not lead to the solution of a problem.

• Insight occurs when we find a new way of looking at a problem that leads to a sudden understanding of how to solve it.

• Creativity involves the ability to combine mental elements in new and useful ways.

• The limitation of being able to see objects only in their familiar roles is called functional fixedness.

• A mental set is a tendency to habitually use the methods of problem solving that have worked for you in the past.

• Incubation, or a period of not thinking about a problem, sometimes helps us to solve a problem.

REASONING, DECISION MAKING, AND JUDGMENT

• We engage in reasoning when we draw conclusions that are based on certain assumptions about the world. Deductive reasoning involves reasoning from the general to the specific, whereas inductive reasoning involves reasoning from the specific to the general.

• Decision making involves choosing among several alternatives and is often part of the problem-solving process.

• How possible courses of action are presented—or framed—can affect our decisions.

• Two mental shortcuts that can be useful but that can also lead to mistakes are the availability and representative heuristics. The availability heuristic refers to the idea that the more easily we can recall a memory for an event, the more frequent we estimate the event to be. The representativeness heuristic is in use when we rely on the degree to which the person or thing in question is representative of some category in judging its category membership.

LANGUAGE: ESSENTIAL TO THOUGHT AND ACTION

• Human language is unique among animals in its well-developed, syntactical, verbal system for representing the world.

• Scientists debate the idea that humans are born with an innate "language acquisition device"—a programmed capacity for language.

• Research indicates that infants generally proceed from cooing to babbling to morphemes on their road to language skills. By the time a child is approximately 2 years old, he or she begins to combine words into two-word sentences, in what is called telegraphic speech.

• One theory, known as the Whorfian hypothesis or the linguistic relativity hypothesis, suggests that one's language actually determines thoughts and perceptions of the world. A more widely held view is that language influences, rather than determines, our thoughts.

• Although animals communicate, it is hotly debated whether they have the capacity for language.

DEFINING AND MEASURING INTELLIGENCE

• Defining intelligence is not easy, and the widely accepted definition has undergone serious revisions over the years. Today, many psychologists broadly view intelligence as having abilities that allow you to adapt to your environment and behave in a goal-oriented way.

• Early intelligence testing by Alfred Binet in France in the early 20th century led to the establishment of a measurement of mental age that reflected an individual's mental abilities compared to the "average" child.

• Stanford psychologist Lewis Terman translated into English and revised Binet's testing procedures, and introduced the intelligence quotient, or IQ score, which divided one's mental age by one's chronological age. The Stanford-Binet test is still in use today.

• An alternative measurement of intelligence was conceived by David Wechsler in the late 1930s. Believing that the Stanford-Binet test was too limited, Wechsler introduced subscales to measure different mental abilities and abandoned the idea of mental age.

• The current version of the adult version of Wechsler's test (WAIS-III) yields three separate scores: a verbal score, a performance score, and an overall score.

• Intelligence tests are frequently criticized for having a cultural bias, the charge being that such tests reflect the cultural values, language, and knowledge of the people who develop them.

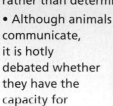

• The idea of mental ability as a single unitary factor is known as generalized intelligence, or "g."

• Crystallized intelligence refers to our accumulation of knowledge, whereas fluid intelligence refers to the speed and efficiency with which we learn new information and solve problems.

• Some theorists argue that we have multiple intelligences. Psychologist Robert Sternberg, in his triarchic theory, offers that there are three types of intelligence—analytical, practical, and creative abilities. Another theorist, Daniel Goleman, argues that measuring only cognitive abilities is too limiting, and proposes that emotional intelligence is an important component in successful living.

• Although a heated debate continues over whether intelligence is "inherited," most research suggests that an interaction of heredity and environment contribute to our intellectual capabilities.

How will I throw up without offending?
How will I do my calisthenics at night
while reading a book?

FROM MARYA HORNBACHER, *WASTED: A MEMOIR OF ANOREXIA
AND BULIMIA,* (New York, Harper Flamingo, 1998, p. 101)

© Wally McNamee /Corbis

CHAPTER 8

Motivation and Emotion: What Guides Behavior?

CHAPTER PREVIEW

Why We Do What We Do

You have obviously started to read this chapter in your psychology text—good for you! Because we teach psychology and we wrote this book, we think that this is worthwhile. But what are *your* reasons for reading this chapter? What has *motivated* you to read this chapter at this moment? Do you want to earn a good grade on an upcoming exam? Do you want to learn more about motivation, the subject of this chapter? Do you want to feel good about yourself as a student? What is it that is driving you right now?

When we are *motivated,* we are *driven* to engage in some form of behavior. Just as something motivated you to start to read this chapter, every day we are motivated to do many different things. For example, we are motivated to eat, to drink, attend school, go to work, interact with family and friends, and so on. In psychological terms, a **motive** is our tendency to desire and seek out positive incentives or rewards and to avoid negative outcomes (Atkinson, 1958/1983; McClelland, 1987). This means that we are motivated to avoid aversive states and to seek more pleasant states. When we experience the motive of hunger, we eat to avoid this aversive feeling. We are motivated to study because we want the feelings of pride and the opportunities for advancement that accompany academic success. We drink to quench our thirst, and so on.

Because we are generally motivated to avoid pain and other aversive states, our motives often serve to protect us. Without the motivation to eat, we could suffer from malnutrition or even starvation. Without thirst, we would face dehydration, and so on. Our motives tend to direct our behavior in ways that benefit us—but there are exceptions to this rule. Sometimes our motivations are in conflict, and we can end up being motivated to engage in behaviors that are detrimental to our well-being. For example, we may overeat to the point of gaining excess weight. Some of us may take illegal drugs that compromise our health and safety. Sometimes we ignore our studies even though this may result in academic failure. In short, we are not always motivated to do the "right" thing. Our case study for this chapter is the tale of a young woman named Marya whose motives were at odds with one another. Marya was motivated to eat and to live, but she was also motivated to starve herself and to die. Marya's struggle began when she was a child. Before she was out of grade school, her struggle blossomed into a full-blown eating disorder. Marya chronicles her lifelong struggle with eating disorders in *Wasted,* her beautifully written autobiography (Hornbacher, 1998).

Marya was born into a chaotic family. Her parents were part of the theatrical community. They were caring parents, but they were also very self-absorbed, fought constantly, and often burdened Marya with their marital problems. Her mother was cold and distant, and her father was overly intrusive and gave Marya little room for privacy. Marya often found herself in the middle of her parents' battles.

Both of her parents had unusual relationships with food. Marya's mother ate very little, rigidly controlling her diet to maintain her weight. Her father was prone to overeating, and alternated between overindulging himself and dieting. Despite the chaos at home, Marya was a very bright and talented child. Although the trouble at home did not appear to detract from her intellectual development, it did take a serious toll on her psychological well-being. Marya was driven to succeed in life, but she was also plagued by fears of inadequacy. At only 9 years old, she already felt as if she had no control over much of her life. The one area where Marya did feel she had control was over her own body and what she put into it. At this young age, Marya was already obsessed with her body, which she hated. She had felt that she was both fat and ugly from the age of 4 or 5. Her feelings about her body and her

motive a tendency to desire and seek out positive incentives or rewards and to avoid negative outcomes

> *"I distinctly did not want to be seen as bulimic. I wanted to be an anorexic . . . a person whose passions were ascetic rather than hedonistic. . . ."*
>
> (Hornbacher, 1998, p. 107)

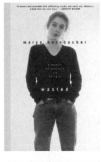

Marya Hornbacher has struggled with eating disorders for much of her life. She chronicles her struggle in this well-written and moving memoir, *Wasted.*

life led Marya to experience negative *emotions,* such as anxiety and fear in many situations. For example, she feared being alone at her home after school; being home alone made her feel very anxious. In response to her anxieties and fears, Marya's behavior began to change.

When Marya was 9, she began to experiment with **bulimia nervosa.** Bulimia nervosa is an eating disorder in which people *binge* on large quantities of food and then *purge* the food from their systems by vomiting or abusing laxatives that move the food quickly through the digestive tract. Marya would come home from school and eat anything she could get her hands on. It was as if the eating could somehow calm the almost constant anxiety that she felt about life. She began to gain some weight, although she was never fat. Already convinced that her normal body was horribly fat, Marya did not welcome any weight gain. One day, without any prodding from anyone, she walked down the hall to the bathroom, stuck her fingers down her throat, and vomited the bag of corn chips she had just eaten. At first, the purging was infrequent, but soon it became a constant obsession. Bingeing was the only way Marya knew to fill the emotional void in her life. Purging was the only way to avoid the intense anxiety she felt after stuffing herself with food. Anxiety, emptiness, and self-loathing were daily emotional states that drove Marya further and further into bulimia nervosa.

By age 9, Marya was bingeing and purging daily. She would first eat a brightly colored *marker* food, such as orange-colored cheese tortilla chips. Then she would eat large quantities of other foods and vomit until she saw the color orange. About the time Marya entered junior high school at age 12, she began to suffer physical damage from her bulimic behavior. The strain of vomiting ruptured the blood vessels in her eyes, and she began to suffer severe headaches. Later, she would develop a hole in her esophagus from regurgitating stomach acid while vomiting.

During junior high school, Marya began developing other dangerous habits. By age 13, she was sexually active, drinking, and abusing illegal substances including cocaine and intravenous drugs. It was also at this time that Marya began moving toward **anorexia nervosa,** an eating disorder in which people starve themselves. Anorectics eat very little food and often exercise intensely. This combination of starvation and intense exercise produces extreme weight loss that can easily lead to death.

In the 10th grade, Marya began attending an exclusive private high school for artists in Michigan, and during this time at boarding school, she became mostly anorectic. In fact, abandoning her bulimia in favor of becoming anorectic was one of Marya's major goals in life. She admired the self-control and the thinness of anorectics. Although she was strongly motivated toward anorexia, Marya's desire to eat was so strong at times that she would slip back into bulimic bingeing and purging. By the end of that year, Marya's behavior landed her in the hospital.

Within a year of her first hospitalization, Marya had to be hospitalized two more times, and there would be more hospitalizations to follow. At age 18, Marya was near death when she was hospitalized at the astounding weight of 52 pounds. At this point, Marya had a choice to make. She could die, or she could find a way to fight her way back from bulimia and anorexia. She decided to fight.

Marya slowly worked her way to some level of normal life. Her issues with food have not gone away and she is still underweight, but Marya is able to maintain a healthier lifestyle. She is married and has become a successful writer and author. Her intense desire to succeed is still there, only now, instead of being driven to be anorectic, she channels her motivation to achieve into healthier pursuits. Marya's life is still no picnic and she still periodically battles with her illnesses and the damage they inflicted on her body.

Marya can never erase the damage that years of starvation and bingeing and purging brought on her body. As a result of her disorders, she cannot have children.

bulimia nervosa   a mental disorder in which a person alternately binges on food and then purges it

anorexia nervosa   a mental disorder in which one drastically reduces their caloric intake and often increases their physical activity to effect dramatic, unhealthy weight loss

She has a heart murmur, and she has lost 25% of her heart muscle. She also has ulcers in her esophagus, and she has lost a significant amount of her bone mass. In short, Marya's *past* behavior is still a threat to her life. In her condition, getting the flu could be fatal.

Marya's story illustrates the devastating effects of having one's motives go astray. What would motivate anyone to deliberately starve herself? Why would anyone behave this way? To answer these questions, we will first look at the roles that motivation and emotion play in our everyday lives. By understanding the forces that drive normal behaviors such as eating and drinking, we may gain some understanding of what goes wrong in cases like Marya's. Let's begin by taking a look at some of the ways psychologists have conceptualized the process of motivation over the years.

Theories About Motivation

LEARNING OBJECTIVES

- Define motivation.
- Describe the different theoretical ways of conceptualizing motivation.
- Describe Maslow's hierarchy of needs.

Over the years, psychologists have viewed motivation in several different ways—as *instincts* that direct our behavior, as uncomfortable biological states called *drives* that motivate us to find ways to feel better, as the desire to maintain an optimal level of *arousal* in our body, or as *incentives* that guide us to seek reward from the world. However, none of these theories seems to fully explain all aspects of motivation. Instincts prove too difficult to define and limit. Drives explain some biological motives pretty well, but fail to fully explain our need for arousal and social incentives. Today psychologists do not expect any single theory to explain all our motivations. Instead, we recognize that each of these theories has its own strengths and weaknesses. Let's take a closer look at these different theories of motivation.

Motivation as an Instinct

One of the earliest views on motivation was one that was heavily influenced by the work of Charles Darwin and the theory of natural selection (Darwin, 1859/1939). As you may recall from Chapter 2, the theory of natural selection states that genes for characteristics that help a species survive will continue in the species, and genes for characteristics that make it more difficult for the species to survive will tend to die out. The theory of natural selection has been very influential in many areas of psychology, including the study of motivation.

Back in the 1800s, American psychologist William James proposed that motives are, in fact, genetically determined **instincts** (James, 1890/1950). According to William James, instincts are impulses from within a person that direct or *motivate* that person's behavior. For example, James believed that *sucking* and *carrying to the mouth* are instincts that give rise to the eating of food. A newborn infant is born with the instinct of sucking, which allows the child to take in nutrients through nursing. Nursing is later replaced by the act of consuming food that one instinctively *carries to the mouth*. In James's view, our innate instincts allow us to form habits that allow us to fulfill our daily needs.

Over time, the idea that motives are inborn instincts gradually fell out of favor with psychologists. One problem with James's view was that the list of proposed instincts kept getting longer and longer (see Figure 8.1 for some of James's proposed instincts). Taken to its logical extreme, instinct theory could be used to argue that all behavior was due to instinct. Furthermore, it became apparent that it is impossible to determine whether or not many of the proposed instincts are truly inborn. Many of our so-called instincts may result from learning. For instance, an infant could learn to put

instinct   innate impulse from within a person that directs or motivates one's behavior

Figure 8.1 **William James's Proposed Human Instincts**

William James proposed that we are motivated by many different instincts. Here is a partial list of these instincts.
Source: Data from James (1890/1950).

Acquisitiveness	Love
Anger	Modesty
Biting	Parental love
Carrying to the mouth	Play
Clasping	Pugnacity
Cleanliness	Resentment
Constructiveness	Secretiveness
Crying	Shame
Curiosity	Shyness
Emulation	Sitting up
Fear of dark places	Smiling
Fear of noise	Sociability
Fear of strange animals	Standing
Fear of strange men	Sucking
Holding the head erect	Sympathy
Hunting	Turning the head to one side
Imitation	Vocalization
Jealousy	Walking
Locomotion	

things in her mouth by watching others. As a result of these questions, instinct theory became less popular, and newer approaches to motivation were proposed.

Motivation as a Drive

Instinct theory was followed by **drive-reduction theories** of motivation. According to the drive-reduction approach, motivation stems from the desire to reduce an uncomfortable, internal state, called a **drive,** that results when our needs are not fulfilled (Hull, 1943). For instance, when we do not have enough food in our system, we feel the uncomfortable state of *hunger*, which *drives* us to eat until we have taken in the food that our bodies require. Then, when we have taken in enough food, the hunger drive dissipates, and we stop eating. Similarly, when we are dehydrated, we feel thirsty, and our thirst drives us to drink fluids. In this fashion, our drives can help us survive by creating what psychologists call a drive-state, which ensures that we will be motivated to meet our biological needs.

Primary drives, such as needing food, water, and warmth, motivate us to maintain certain bodily processes at an internal state of equilibrium, or **homeostasis.** Obviously, it would be desirable for us to take in just the right amount of food and water, to sleep just enough, and to maintain our body temperature at 98.6 degrees. Without the motivation from drives, we would not keep our bodies at homeostasis because we would not know when to eat, sleep, drink, and so on. But what causes a drive-state in the first place?

Primary drives begin in the body when the brain recognizes that we are lacking in some biological need. The brain recognizes need based on the *feedback* that it receives from the body's systems and organs. One type of feedback system is called a **negative feedback loop** (Figure 8.2). Negative feedback loops are information systems in the body that monitor the level of a bodily process—such as thirst—and adjust it up and down accordingly. A good analogy for a negative feedback loop is that of a thermostat. In your home, you set the thermostat at a desired level, and the thermostat monitors the air temperature and compares it to that set level. If the room gets too cold, the heater turns on. If the room gets too warm, the heater turns off. Many primary drives in the body work in the same fashion. Take hunger, for example. When our body is lacking nutrients, various organs and systems in the body send feedback to the brain, which

drive-reduction theory theory of motivation that proposes that motivation seeks to reduce internal levels of drive

drive an uncomfortable internal state that motivates us to reduce this discomfort through our behavior

primary drive a drive that motivates us to maintain homeostasis in certain biological processes within our body

homeostasis an internal state of equilibrium in the body

negative feedback loop a system of feedback in the body that monitors and adjusts our motivation level so as to maintain homeostasis in the body

According to drive-reduction theory, we are motivated to eat when our body sends feedback to the brain indicating that our energy supplies are running low. This need for fuel sets up a primary drive-state, which motivates us to eat so that we can reduce our hunger.

© Ashley Cooper/Corbis

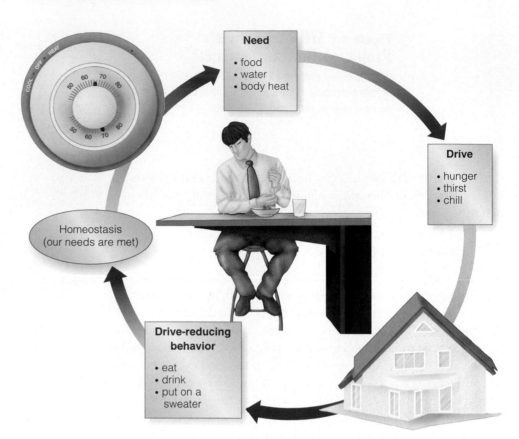

Figure 8.2 Negative Feedback Loops

Negative feedback loops maintain homeostasis in our bodies by monitoring certain physiological conditions in our body (e.g., glucose levels and fluid levels). When levels drop too low, feedback from the body tells that brain to increase motivation levels (i.e., hunger or thirst). When levels are too high, feedback from the body tells the brain to decrease those motivation levels.

secondary drive learned drive that is not directly related to biological needs

then initiates the hunger drive. When we have taken in enough food at a meal, these organs and systems send feedback to the brain, which shuts off the hunger drive, and we should stop eating. Later in this chapter, we will take a closer look at some of the systems in the body that provide this negative feedback to the brain.

The idea that motivation in the form of primary drives serves to maintain homeostasis makes a great deal of sense. Without primary drives, our biological needs would likely not be met and we might not survive. However, how well does the idea of drive explain some of our other motivations? For example, does drive-reduction theory explain academic achievement motivation, or motivation to be loved? To help explain what motivates those behaviors not directly related to survival, drive-reduction theorists developed the notion of **secondary drives,** or drives that motivate us to perform behaviors that are not directly related to biological needs.

Secondary drives are presumed to have developed through learning and experience. For example, a child's drive to do well in school may have resulted from a parent who used food to reward and reinforce the child for good scholastic performance. Because the child experienced the primary drive of hunger, he may also have learned to be *driven* to achieve high marks in school. According to some psychologists, the *need* to fulfill certain secondary drives differs from person to person, like any other personality characteristic. For example, some people may be more or less motivated to achieve than others. Figure 8.3 shows a list of secondary needs that were identified by psychologist Henry Murray back in the 1930s (Murray, 1938). As you can see, there are many different secondary needs that could motivate our behavior.

There's no doubt that at times we are motivated by the things listed in Figure 8.3. But do things like achievement and the desire for love really represent "needs" that are ultimately related to our biological needs? If we did learn to desire love or achievement because somewhere in our past love and achievement were associated with our more biological motives or primary drives, then we should be able to identify specific physi-

Achievement
(the need to achieve success in life)
Counteraction (the need to overcome one's fears and failures)
Abasement
(the need to admit inferiority)
Narcissism
(the need to be self-absorbed)
Autonomy (the need to be independent)
Understanding
(the need to understand one's world)
Play (the need to have fun)
Sentience (the need to seek out experiences that are pleasing to the senses)
Order (the need to be neat and organized)
Harmavoidance (the need to avoid pain and harm to oneself)
Infavoidance (the need to avoid humiliation and embarrassment)

Affiliation
(the need to be close to others)
Rejection
(the need to reject those you do not like)
Defendance
(the need to defend oneself against others)
Nurturance
(the need to be nurturing and care for others)
Succorance
(the need to have others care for you)
Sex (the need to engage in sexual relations)
Blamavoidance (the need to avoid being blamed or rejected by others)
Aggression
(the need to be aggressive and to fight)
Dominance (the need to control your environment and the people in it)
Exhibition (the need to have others notice you)
Deference (the need to defer to others)

Figure 8.3 **Murray's Needs**

Psychologist Henry Murray developed a list of secondary needs, or drives, that motivate us beyond our primary drives of hunger, thirst, and so on.
Source: Murray, 1938.

ological changes that occur in us when we are motivated by these so-called secondary needs or drives. So far, attempts to do this have not been too successful (Deckers, 2001).

The concept of motivation as a means of reducing drives seems to make more sense when we look at primary drives, but even here, it is not without its faults. There are times when drive-reduction theory cannot explain certain aspects of our more biological motives. For example, what about overeating? Think about a typical holiday meal in your family. At holiday dinners, do you eat *only enough* food to satisfy your primary drive of hunger? We bet not. How many times have you eaten until you felt ill because it was a special occasion? If our sole motivation for eating was drive reduction, we would not "pig out" in instances like these. Likewise, Marya's story goes against the predictions of drive-reduction theory, which cannot easily explain why she refused to eat even though her body was screaming for her to satisfy its primary biological needs.

 Application

Drive-reduction theories also fail to account for times when we seem to be motivated to *increase* the tension or arousal levels in our bodies. For instance, when you decide to ride a roller coaster at an amusement park or to try skydiving, what possible drive could these behaviors lower? Activities such as these do not appear to reduce any of our primary drives. Rather, the sole purpose of these activities seems to be to *arouse* us physiologically. Clearly, we will have to conceptualize motivation in some other way to account for these types of behavior.

Arousal Theories of Motivation

Arousal theories of motivation state that each of us has a level of physiological arousal at which we operate best, an *optimal* level of arousal. In general, we perform best on tasks when we are moderately aroused (Figure 8.4). Too much or too little arousal generally weakens our performance on tasks (Berlyne, 1967; Hebb, 1955; Sonstroem & Bernardo, 1982). Therefore, each of us is motivated to seek out arousal when we find ourselves underaroused, and we are motivated to reduce our arousal level when we are overaroused.

Figure 8.4 **Performance as a Function of Arousal**

Our best performance often occurs at moderate levels of arousal. You would likely do your best on an exam if you were neither too sleepy nor too anxious.

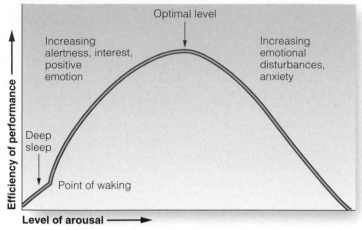

General relationship between performance and arousal level

Application >>

sensation seeker   person who by trait tends to seek out arousing activities

According to psychologist Marvin Zuckerman, some people are sensation seekers, who are motivated to engage in highly energizing and stimulating activities like skydiving and extreme sports. Sensation seekers may have lower levels of MAO in their brains, which causes them to ultimately have higher levels of some neurotransmitters like dopamine that motivate them to seek out higher levels of arousal and reward.

David Madison/Getty Images

Although most of us perform best at moderate levels of arousal, some people seem to crave arousal, seeking out higher levels of arousal than the rest of us. In fact, sometimes they seek out levels of arousal that the rest of us would find *aversive*. For example, think of Evel Knievel, who tried to jump the Snake River in a rocket-powered motorcycle (but failed when his parachute opened too soon); or extreme sports enthusiasts who try to ski off dangerous mountainsides, climb skyscrapers without protective gear, or bungee jump off bridges. Many of us wouldn't try these activities even if we were *paid* to! So what motivates some people to habitually seek out such arousing activities? Some people are what psychologists call **sensation seekers,** those who habitually tend to seek out high levels of physiological arousal by engaging in intensely stimulating experiences (Zuckerman, 1978, 1994). Some sensation seekers pursue daring activities such as mountain climbing, skydiving, and fast driving, whereas others may be stimulated by travel to new places, taking drugs, having multiple sexual experiences, and gambling.

One theory that seeks to explain the causes of sensation seeking looks at biological differences in the brains of sensation seekers. Psychologist Marvin Zuckerman found that sensation seekers tend to have low levels of a substance called *monoamine oxidase (MAO)* (Zuckerman, 1994). MAO is an enzyme that breaks down neurotransmitters like serotonin, dopamine, and norepinephrine (see p. 59). One of these neurotransmitters, dopamine, seems to be responsible for motivating us to obtain rewards. The low level of MAO in the brains of sensation seekers may mean that the sensation seekers experience more dopamine activity than that found in nonsensation seekers' brains. This increased dopamine activity may be related to the sensation seeker's motivation to experience intense arousal. Without MAO to break it down, the dopamine would remain in the synapse longer, continuing to stimulate the neuron. This increased dopamine action may motivate sensation seekers to look for more and more reward in the form of arousal. But sometimes the pursuit of arousal can have negative effects: Evel Knievel broke many of the bones of his body in his pursuit of arousal!

Are you a sensation seeker? To get a feel for your level of sensation seeking, take the questionnaire in Figure 8.5. Just keep in mind that this questionnaire is a brief version of the full Zuckerman Sensation Seeking Scale (Zuckerman, 1994). Therefore, your true level of sensation seeking may differ from your test results.

 **Demonstration**

Incentive Theories of Motivation

Perhaps jumping out of airplanes and skiing off mountainsides is not your cup of tea. Take a moment to think about what does motivate you. What gets you out of bed in the morning? Is it money, material goods, or approval from others? These things are motivating for many of us. As we saw before, drive theory states that nonbiological motives like these are the result of prior learning—that somewhere along the way we learned to associate approval, money, and material goods with our primary drives. But researchers have had trouble finding support for this idea, and today many psychologists no longer think of these nonbiological motives in terms of drives. Instead they tend to see things like money, praise, and material goods as **incentives** that can motivate many of us into action (Atkinson, 1958/1983). You can think of incentives as goals or desires that you wish to satisfy or fulfill. For example, someone who desires money will be motivated to engage in behaviors that will likely lead to her obtaining money, such as taking a job or buying lottery tickets.

We have discussed instincts, drives, and arousal, which are always *intrinsic* parts of who we are. Incentives, however, can be either *intrinsic* or *extrinsic*. Drives, instincts, and physiological arousal originate from inside of our bodies and motivate us to behave in certain ways. In contrast, extrinsic incentives have the power to motivate us in ways that can be unrelated to our internal states. For instance, someone might be motivated

incentive   a goal or desire that we are motivated to fulfill

---

Measuring sensation seeking

Answer "true" or "false" to each item listed below by circling "T" or "F." A "true" means that the item expresses your preference most of the time. A "false" means that you do not agree that the item is generally true for you. After completing the test, score your responses according to the instructions that follow the test items.

T F   1. I would really enjoy skydiving.
T F   2. I can imagine myself driving a sports car in a race and loving it.
T F   3. My life is very secure and comfortable—the way I like it.
T F   4. I usually like emotionally expressive or artistic people, even if they are sort of wild.
T F   5. I like the idea of seeing many of the same warm, supportive faces in everyday life.
T F   6. I like doing adventurous things and would have enjoyed being a pioneer in the early days of this country.
T F   7. A good photograph should express peacefulness creatively.
T F   8. The most important thing in living is fully experiencing all emotions.
T F   9. I like creature comforts when I go on a trip or vacation.
T F 10. Doing the same things each day really gets to me.
T F 11. I love snuggling in front of a fire on a wintry day.
T F 12. I would like to try several types of drugs as long as they didn't harm me permanently.
T F 13. Drinking and being rowdy really appeals to me on weekends.
T F 14. Rational people try to avoid dangerous situations.
T F 15. I prefer figure A to figure B.

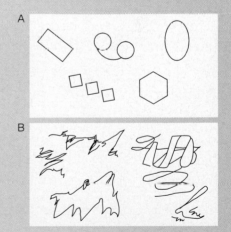

Give yourself 1 point for answering "true" to the following items: 1, 2, 4, 6, 8, 10, 12, and 13. Also give yourself 1 point for answering "false" to the following items: 3, 5, 7, 9, 11, 14, and 15. Add up your points, and compare your total to the following norms: 11–15, high sensation seeker; 6–10, moderate sensation seeker; 1–5, low sensation seeker. Bear in mind that this is a shortened version of the Sensation Seeking Scale and that it provides only a rough approximation of your status on this personality trait.

Figure 8.5 **Brief Sensation-Seeking Questionnaire**

Are you a sensation seeker? This questionnaire will give you some insight into your sensation seeking tendencies, but please recognize that this test gives you only a rough idea of where you fall on this dimension.

Source: A. F. Grasha & D. S. Kirschenbaum (1986). Adjustment and competence: Concepts and applications. St. Paul, MN: West Publishing. Reprinted by permission of Anthony F. Grasha.

to have a drink at a party, not due to thirst but because he wants to seek the approval of others who are drinking. Although this person is *not pushed* to have a drink by some internal drive, he is *pulled* toward drinking because of the surrounding social circumstances. Because this behavior is motivated from outside of the person, he is experiencing what psychologists call **extrinsic motivation** (Deci & Ryan, 1985).

extrinsic motivation   motivation that comes from outside of the person

Extrinsic incentives can also interact with drives to motivate our behavior (Petri, 1996). For example, if the man at the party is thirsty and also wants to fit in with others, he might drink even more. In this situation, the man is both *pushed* by an internal drive and *pulled* by the social circumstances to drink. The interaction of drives and incentives can also be seen when we go grocery shopping. Experts always advise us not to go grocery shopping when we are hungry because both the internal drive of hunger and the extrinsic incentives provided by the advertisements and displays conspire to make us spend lots of money on lots of food. A hungry shopper may well spend much more money than she intends, and on foods that she might not ordinarily buy.

Application

Sometimes the goal we wish to accomplish leads to some sort of internal reward. For instance, you may wish to do well on an exam, not because it will lead to a good grade or a better job, but rather because earning a good grade will make you feel good about yourself. The internal feeling of pride can be a powerful incentive in motivating behavior! When we are motivated by *intrinsic* incentives, we are said to be experiencing **intrinsic motivation** (Deci & Ryan, 1985).

intrinsic motivation   motivation that comes from within the person

Assume that you are the parent of a 10-year-old child who is not doing well in school, and you want to take steps to motivate your child to do better. Which do you think would work better to motivate your child to perform—extrinsic or intrinsic incentives? In other words, would you favor using external rewards like money, toys, and privileges to motivate your child? Or would you favor making your child *want* to do better just for the sake of feeling proud or happy about his or her performance?

If you instinctively chose intrinsic motivation as the better choice, there is good reason to believe you chose well. Intrinsic motivation has several advantages over extrinsic motivation. First, intrinsic motivation does not require outside rewards or incentives to maintain the behavior. For example, the parents of an intrinsically motivated child do not have to spend money on toys, food, or prizes to keep their child motivated. In fact, they don't have to do anything to keep the child motivated, because the motivation comes from within the child.

overjustification effect   the idea that the more extrinsic motivation we have for an activity, the less intrinsic motivation we will have for engaging in that activity

Second, evidence suggests that adding extrinsic incentives to entice a person to engage in a behavior may actually lower a person's intrinsic motivation to engage in the task. This is sometimes called the **overjustification effect** (Deci, Koestner, & Ryan, 1999). For instance, if children are paid to do their schoolwork, they may be extrinsically motivated to study as long as the money keeps coming. But when the money stops, the students will actually be *less* motivated to study than if they had never been paid to study! Because no parent can keep paying her child for making good grades forever, it may be wiser to never begin a program of regularly re-

The incentive theory of motivation states that many of us are motivated by extrinsic rewards like money, material goods, and praise from others.

© Bill Aron/PhotoEdit

warding the child with money! Instead, parents can use encouragement and praise to reward their children. These *intangible reinforcers* can become internalized because praise and encouragement can make a child feel pride in his performance. Wanting to feel proud of yourself is an intrinsic incentive that can motivate you to do well even without any extrinsic incentive.

This does not mean that extrinsic motivation is inherently bad. We are motivated by extrinsic incentives every day of our lives. We work for money, we are nice to others so that they will be nice to us, and we work hard for good grades. Even parents can find extrinsic incentives valuable when trying to mold the behavior of their children. Extrinsic incentives are especially helpful for motivating a behavior that the person is not intrinsically motivated to perform. For example, if a child hates studying his math, one way to initially motivate him is to offer an extrinsic incentive, such as money or an extra privilege for studying. This extrinsic incentive could motivate the child to do something that he is not doing on his own—and might never do. There is nothing wrong with an occasional extrinsic incentive, but keep in mind that the *environment* must maintain extrinsic motivation (e.g., the parent has to keep paying for grades). Therefore, once the behavior has been established through extrinsic motivation, the parent may wish to switch over to using a program of encouraging intrinsic motivation in the child.

Maslow's Hierarchy of Needs

Imagine that you have to miss lunch because you don't have time to stop and eat. On this particular day, you have a paper to write, an exam to study for, and a long list of algebra problems to finish. As you sit down to study, you find that several different motives are all trying to motivate your behavior at the same time. You need to study, you are very hungry, you are quite sleepy because you did not sleep well last night, and you really want to go to the movies with your friends. Which of these motives will win? What will your *first* course of action be in this situation? Will you eat, study, go to the movies, or fall asleep? We often find ourselves pulled in different directions by our motives. Are some types of motives inherently stronger than others? Perhaps.

hierarchy of needs   Maslow's theory that humans are motivated by different motives, some of which take precedence over others

Psychologist Abraham Maslow (1908–1970), recognized that in certain circumstances, some motives yield greater influence over our behavior than others do. Maslow conceptualized both our physiological and psychological motives as different classes of *needs* to which we assign different levels of priority. These different classes form a **hierarchy of needs,** in which the lower-level needs have the first priority (Maslow, 1970). Maslow's hierarchy of needs is usually presented as a pyramid, as shown in Figure 8.6.

The lowest level of Maslow's hierarchy—the base of the pyramid—is our physiological needs. Maslow theorized that we will seek to satisfy our *physiological needs*—hunger, thirst, and need for warmth—before we are motivated to satisfy any of our other needs. If our physiological needs are met, then our next level of concern would be satisfying our

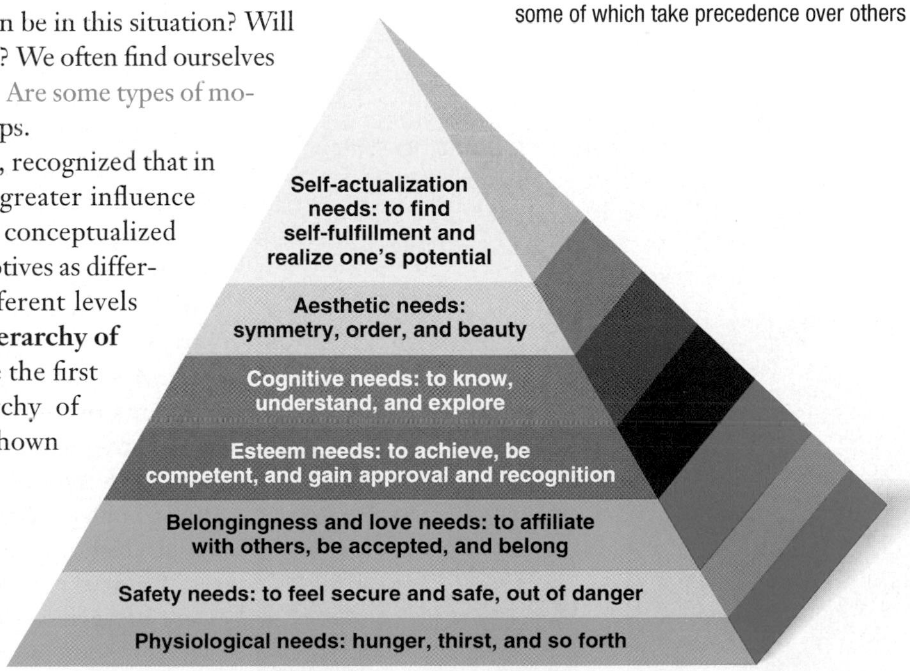

Self-actualization needs: to find self-fulfillment and realize one's potential

Aesthetic needs: symmetry, order, and beauty

Cognitive needs: to know, understand, and explore

Esteem needs: to achieve, be competent, and gain approval and recognition

Belongingness and love needs: to affiliate with others, be accepted, and belong

Safety needs: to feel secure and safe, out of danger

Physiological needs: hunger, thirst, and so forth

Figure 8.6 Maslow's Hierarchy of Needs

Source: Maslow, "Hierarchy of Needs," from Motivation and Personality. *Copyright © 1954 by Harper and Row Publishers, Inc. Reprinted by permission of Pearson Education, Inc., Upper Saddle River, NJ.*

safety and *security needs*, such as having a safe place to live. Maslow grouped these needs together as *basic human needs*, those that concern us day to day and ensure our survival and safety.

At the next level, Maslow identified two levels of *psychological needs*, belongingness and love, and esteem. *Belongingness and love needs* are our motivation to be loved by others, be with others, and be appreciated by others. At the next level we would seek to satisfy our *esteem needs, cognitive needs, and aesthetic needs.*

If we meet our aesthetic needs, we may seek to move to the next tier, the *self-fulfillment needs.* These include the level most associated with Maslow, *self-actualization needs,* or our motivation to reach all of our potentials, and the *need for transcendence.* Achieving transcendence would mean reaching our full spiritual fulfillment in life.

Abraham Maslow had little hope that the average person would actually reach the self-fulfillment level. He felt that most of us are unable to adequately fulfill enough of the needs at the lower and middle levels of the pyramid, although some of us satisfy enough of our lower-level needs to at least try for self-actualization and transcendence.

At first glance, Maslow's hierarchy seems to make sense. If you are starving, you will probably be less concerned with whether or not people love you, and more concerned with finding food. Unfortunately, there is not much evidence to support Maslow's hierarchy of needs (Soper, Milford, & Rosenthal, 1995). In fact, often we seem to behave in ways that contradict Maslow's notion that we must fulfill lower needs before we can be concerned with higher-order needs. For instance, Marya's behavior did not fit Maslow's theory very well. She denied herself food, a physiological need, even as she pursued higher-level needs, of belongingness and love. Even if you argue that Marya's behavior was abnormal, and therefore should be expected to deviate from Maslow's hierarchy, there are many cases of "normal" people pursuing higher-level needs even though they have not yet met lower-level needs. Have you ever gone without lunch to pursue some other activity, such as studying for an exam? In that case, you were motivated by esteem needs even though your physiological needs had not been met! Likewise, the research also indicates that when we have satisfied our needs at a certain level of the hierarchy, we do not always move up to the next level and attempt to satisfy those needs (Hall & Nougaim, 1968).

Despite the fact that Maslow's hierarchy does not have much empirical support behind it, the theory is still used widely in the field of business—especially in the area of marketing (Soper et al., 1995). Although the data do not fully support Maslow's theory, some have found ways to apply certain elements of Malsow's theory to the business world. For example, the idea that people are motivated by different needs may affect the way a manager deals with employees (Antonioni, 2003; Buhler, 2003), or the way that a firm markets a particular product.

In marketing, advertisers often try to relate the current state of society to certain levels of Maslow's hierarchy. At present, some advertisers have proposed that the attacks of September 11, 2001, and lingering fears of additional terrorism have left many people afraid and insecure—placing them back at the safety and security needs level of Maslow's hierarchy. With this assumption in mind, some advertisers advocate marketing

According to Abraham Maslow, few of us will ever fulfill enough of our lower-level needs to actually reach the level of self-actualization. During her lifetime, Mother Teresa appeared to have reached the levels of self-actualization and need for transcendence. Similarly, singer Bono of the group U2 appears to be striving for self-actualization, in that he spends much of his time engaged in humanitarian causes.

products by billing them as being *dependable* and *consistent*—on the theory that this sense of dependability and security is just what many of us are seeking at the moment (DeJoseph, 2003).

So far, we have seen that there are many different ways to look at motivation. However, whether you view motivation as an instinct, a drive, a need, or an incentive, one thing is certain: Motivation is what catalyzes our behavior and moves us into action. In the coming sections, we will explore some specific motivations in more depth, but before we do that, take a moment to test your mastery of the preceding material.

Let's Review!

In this section, we defined motivation and discussed some of the theoretical perspectives on motivation—as an instinct, a drive, the maintenance of arousal, or our desire to achieve certain incentives. We also discussed Maslow's hierarchy of needs and the notion that we are motivated to fulfill basic needs before higher-order needs in life. For a quick check of your understanding, answer these questions.

1. Which of the following approaches to motivation is most closely aligned with Darwin's theory of evolution?
   a. drive theory
   b. instinct theory
   c. incentive approaches
   d. Maslow's hierarchy of needs
2. Which of the following approaches to motivation assumes that motivation can come from outside the person?
   a. instinct theory
   b. drive theory
   c. incentive theory
   d. none of the above
3. Which of the following is an example of intrinsic motivation?
   a. studying hard to earn an A on an exam
   b. staying late at work to earn overtime
   c. cleaning your house because you enjoy a tidy home
   d. dressing up for a job interview because you want to make a good impression

ANSWERS
1.b; 2.c; 3.c

Hunger and Thirst: What Makes Us Eat and Drink? > > > > > >

Eating is one of our most fundamental motivations, basic to survival. To protect us from starvation, the motivation to eat remains strong even when we have competing or conflicting motivations. At the height of her anorexia, Marya Hornbacher still had motivation to eat. As hard as she tried to stamp out her desire to eat, she was unable to completely eliminate eating from her daily routine. No matter what she did, the hunger was always there, and despite her strong will, she had to give in to its powerful motivation at times (Hornbacher, 1998). Because of her persistent motivation to eat, Marya survived, albeit just barely, despite her disorder. Marya's case shows us the primal strength of our motivation to eat. But what is it in our bodies that initiates the hunger that motivates us to eat?

LEARNING OBJECTIVES

≫ Describe positive and negative feedback in the body.

≫ Discuss the feedback our bodies use to regulate hunger.

≫ Explain what is known about why some people become obese.

≫ Describe anorexia and bulimia, and discuss their possible causes.

≫ Explain the feedback in the body that leads to thirst.

Hunger and Feedback in the Body

Hunger is a motive that helps us maintain homeostasis in the body, as we explained in the section on primary drives (see p. 347). The goal of hunger is to motivate us to eat when our bodies need fuel. As such, we should feel hungry when we are lacking fuel and nutrients, but we should also *not* feel the motivation to eat when we have enough fuel and nutrients in our bodies. Recall that hunger works on a *negative feedback* loop system (see Figure 8.2). Like a thermostat, our brain turns our hunger on and off in order to maintain homeostasis in our bodies. To maintain homeostasis, our brain must receive accurate and reliable feedback from the rest of our body. But where in the body does this feedback about the current status of our body's fuel supply originate?

Hunger Feedback From the Stomach

If you ask the average person on the street why he feels hunger, he will probably say something about feeling hungry when his stomach is empty. One of the first places psychologists looked for clues to hunger was the stomach, and there is some evidence to suggest that one part of the feedback that initiates hunger is an empty stomach.

When our stomachs become empty, the walls of the stomach contract, and these contractions appear to stimulate hunger. In one early study, a researcher swallowed a balloon that was then inflated in his stomach. The balloon was also attached to a device that could measure the contractions of the stomach walls around the balloon. With the balloon in his stomach, the researcher could then correlate his feelings of hunger with the number of stomach contractions. The results showed that stomach contractions occurred just prior to increased feelings of hunger (Cannon & Washburn, 1912).

Similarly, the stomach may also play a role in telling our brains when it is time to stop eating. When we eat, our stomach's walls must distend to expand the volume of the stomach and allow room for the food we eat. When we have eaten enough, and our stomachs are full, this distention of the stomach is one source of feedback that signals to our brains that it is time to stop eating (Deutsch, 1990). Anyone who has ever overindulged at mealtime can attest to the fact that a feeling of fullness in the stomach shuts off hunger!

Stomach contractions and distention may not be the only bits of feedback from the stomach that are related to hunger, however. There is evidence to suggest that receptors in the walls of the stomach may actually be able to measure the nutritive value of the food we eat, and that this feedback may play a role in regulating hunger. For instance, researchers have shown that the degree to which we feel hungry is directly correlated with the number of calories that we have in our stomachs (deCastro & Elmore, 1988). And animal studies indicate that when an animal eats a highly nutritious food, it may stop eating well before its stomach is full (Deutsch, Puerto, & Wang, 1978). Findings like these indicate that both the *quality* and the *quantity* of food in the stomach are important in regulating hunger.

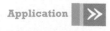

The importance of the quality of the food we eat is also demonstrated by the fact that the rate at which food leaves the stomach during the digestive process is related to the caloric content of the food. Low-calorie foods will exit the stomach faster than high-calorie foods. In part, this explains why a salad usually won't hold hunger at bay as long as a nice steak dinner will! When we eat low-calorie foods, we tend to feel hungry sooner and we eat more than we would if we were eating foods with more calories (Fomon, Filer, Thomas, Rogers, & Proksch, 1969). No wonder dieting is so hard!

Although the stomach is an important source of feedback in the hunger process, it is not the only source. Surprisingly, even people who don't experience stomach contractions and distention feel hunger! People who have had their stomachs completely *removed* due to cancer usually still feel hunger (Janowitz & Grossman, 1950). If the stomach is not essential to our sensation of hunger, then what are the body's other sources of hunger feedback?

Hunger Feedback From the Liver

The liver is another source of feedback for hunger. Our liver has the capacity to help regulate hunger by monitoring the levels of **glucose** and **glycogen** in our body. Glucose is the form of sugar that our bodies burn for energy, and glycogen is the form of starch that we store along with fatty acids. When we have excess glucose in our body, we convert it into glycogen and then we store it for future use. The liver determines what our energy requirements are by monitoring our levels of glucose and glycogen. If the liver detects that we are converting glucose into glycogen, indicating that we have too much fuel in our bodies, it will send signals to the brain to shut off hunger. On the other hand, if the liver notices that glycogen is being turned back into glucose, indicating that we are dipping into our energy reserves, it will send signals to the brain to initiate hunger.

Our bodies are able to dip into our reserves at the same time that the liver is signaling us to begin eating so we have a sufficient supply of glucose on hand. If we had to wait for our bodies to metabolize glucose from the new food we take in to feel hunger, we'd run out of glucose before we could digest our food.

Hunger Feedback From Hormones

Our endocrine system also plays a role in regulating our hunger. The hormone *insulin* can increase feelings of hunger (c.f. Grossman & Stein, 1948). Made in the pancreas, insulin facilitates the movement of glucose from our blood into our cells, where it is metabolized. When glucose moves into our cells, our blood levels of glucose drop, so we begin to dip into our glycogen reserves, and hunger is initiated. In this indirect way, insulin can produce feelings of hunger.

Other hormones affect our hunger even more directly. When we eat food, our small intestines release the hormone **cholecystokinin (CCK)** into our bloodstream. CCK appears to shut off eating. A rat that is injected with CCK will drink less milk than a rat that has not been injected with CCK (Canova & Geary, 1991). Likewise, the presence of CCK in the bloodstream decreases human hunger (Holt, Brand, Soveny, & Hansky, 1992). However, the level of hunger that we experience is due to more than just the amount of CCK in our bloodstream. How much food we have recently eaten also seems to influence our hunger. In one experiment, participants ate either 100 or 500 grams of soup and were then given either CCK or a placebo substance. Afterward, they were allowed to eat a meal. The dependent variable in the study was how much the participants ate of the meal that followed the soup. The results showed that the amount eaten was a function of both the amount of soup the participants had eaten and whether or not they had received the CCK. Participants who had eaten the larger amount of soup (500 grams) and also received the CCK tended to eat less at the meal. But for participants who had eaten only 100 grams of soup, the CCK did not reduce the amount of food eaten at the meal. It appears that if we have not taken in enough food, CCK by itself may not be enough to stop our hunger and our eating (Muurahainen, Kisileff, Lechaussee, & Pi-Sunyer, 1991).

Hunger Feedback From Fat Cells

Our fat cells may provide yet another source of feedback for hunger regulation. Fat cells store our fuel reserves, swelling up as the liver converts excess glucose into glycogen and fatty acids. When we need to utilize our reserves, the fatty acids are mobilized out of the fat cells and converted back into glucose, which our bodies then burn

glucose   the form of sugar that our body burns as a fuel

glycogen   a starchy molecule that is produced from excess glucose in the body, it can be thought of as our body's stored energy reserves

cholecystokinin (CCK)   a hormone released by the small intestines that plays a role in hunger regulation

as fuel. We need to have some reserves of energy stored in our fat cells, but we do not want to have too much fat in reserve. So how does the body maintain just enough fat, without becoming obese?

One possible answer lies in the fat cells themselves. Fat cells make and secrete a chemical called **leptin.** When fat cells release leptin into the bloodstream, it travels to the brain, where it is picked up by receptors near the brain's *ventricles* (the fluid-filled cavities in the brain) and in the *hypothalamus* (McGregor et al., 1996). Leptin is thought to inform the brain about the level of fat reserves available in our bodies. For example, when the brain senses high leptin levels, this may indicate a large number of fat cells that are full of fat reserves. Therefore, we do not need to take in more fuel, and our hunger may be reduced. In support of this hypothesis, researchers have found that mice that are bred to be genetically fat will lose weight if they are given injections of leptin (Pelleymounter et al., 1995). Unfortunately, we are a long way from understanding the exact role of leptin in motivating human eating. At the moment, we have no body of evidence to support the notion that losing weight is as simple as taking a few leptin injections!

Hunger Regulation in the Brain

The brain, of course, plays a significant role in our eating behavior. It receives and processes signals from the stomach about contractions and distention, from the liver about the glucose-glycogen balance, and from leptin. The brain may also directly monitor our energy supplies. There is evidence to suggest that the brain, like the liver, monitors the level of glucose in our blood. There appear to be specialized *glucoreceptors* in the hypothalamus that measure the glucose levels in the bloodstream. Glucoreceptors are thought to exist in the hypothalamus because if an animal is given a substance that makes its hypothalamus unresponsive to glucose, the animal goes on an eating binge (Miselis & Epstein, 1970). Disabling the hypothalamus's glucoreceptors tricks the brain into thinking that the body is critically low on fuel. The brain in turn signals extreme hunger to quickly replenish the body's glucose.

Further clues about the role of the hypothalamus in hunger regulation come from animal studies in which surgical lesions are made in the brain. By destroying part of the hypothalamus and observing the effect that this destruction has on behavior, psychologists have uncovered some clues about the role that the different parts of the hypothalamus play in both initiating and stopping eating.

One part of the hypothalamus, the **lateral hypothalamus,** or **LH,** seems to function as an "on switch" for hunger. When the LH is destroyed in a rat, the rat stops eating. As a result, the rat loses a great deal of weight and eventually will die. Without the LH, the rat simply starves to death (Teitelbaum & Stellar, 1954), which seems to indicate that the LH turns *on* hunger. However, further investigation has shown that the LH is not the only "on switch" for hunger. Curiously, if a rat is force-fed for long enough after having had its LH destroyed, the rat will eventually get some of its appetite back. Its appetite will not be as great as it was prior to losing its LH, but the rat will eat, particularly very tasty foods (Teitelbaum & Epstein, 1962).

Another bit of evidence that suggests an "on switch" for hunger outside of the LH comes from studies using **neuropeptide Y,** the most powerful hunger stimulant that is known (Gibbs, 1996). When an animal is injected with neuropeptide Y, its strongest effect occurs outside of the LH (Leibowitz, 1991). It stands to reason that if the LH were the *primary* "on switch" for hunger, then this powerful stimulant would have its strongest effect in the LH, but this does not appear to be the case, suggesting that there is an even more important "on switch" for hunger elsewhere in the brain.

The hypothalamus is also thought to play a role in shutting off hunger. Some evidence suggests that a part of the hypothalamus, the **ventromedial hypothalamus,**

leptin a hormone released by adipose cells in the body that plays a role in hunger regulation

lateral hypothalamus (LH) a region of the hypothalamus once thought to be the hunger center in the brain

neuropeptide Y the most powerful hunger stimulant known

ventromedial hypothalamus (VMH) a region of the hypothalamus that plays an indirect role in creating a feeling of satiety

or **VMH,** plays a role in creating a feeling of *satiety* in us. When we are sated, we feel full and do not wish to eat more. Rats who have had their VMH destroyed will begin to eat ravenously and will gain enormous amounts of weight (Figure 8.7). If the VMH were the rat's only satiety center, or hunger "off switch," then destroying its VMH should make the rat eat continuously until it dies. But this doesn't happen! A rat without a VMH will eat a great deal of food and gain a great deal of weight, but after a certain amount of weight gain, its appetite will level off and the rat will then eat only enough food to maintain its new, higher weight. It's as if losing the VMH changes the rat's **set point.** In other words, the weight that the rat's body tries to maintain through homeostatic regulation has been shifted upward to a new, higher weight.

set point   the theory that our body has a particular weight or set point that it is designed to maintain

These and other studies indicate that the VMH is not the only "off switch" for hunger in the brain. In fact, it is now believed that the VMH may only indirectly impact satiety. When the VMH is destroyed, the endocrine system's control over insulin release is disturbed. The result is an increased release of insulin into the bloodstream, which produces great hunger and subsequent increases in eating. Loss of the VMH doesn't remove our satiety center, but rather causes disturbances in our endocrine system that result in increased eating.

What we have learned from studies of the hunger centers in the brain is that many mechanisms create and shut off feelings of hunger in our bodies. There does not appear to be a single "on" or "off" switch for hunger. Rather, it seems to be regulated by a complex network of feedback to the brain from various sources in the body, as well as direct signaling in the brain. We have presented some of the abundant evidence for physiological controls on our eating, but is hunger solely the product of physiological mechanisms? And is eating motivated entirely by our drive to maintain homeostasis of our energy supplies? If the answer to these questions was a simple "Yes," then we would not see some of the behavior we see in the real world. For instance, Marya's bulimic and anorectic behaviors, hunger strikes for political reasons, and rampant obesity defy explanations of hunger as a simple physiological process of homeostatic regulation. Our eating behavior can apparently be modified by other sources of feedback that have little to do with maintaining homeostasis.

© Richard Howard

Figure 8.7 A Rat With a Lesion in the Ventromedial Hypothalamus (VMH)
This rat had its ventromedial hypothalamus damaged. As a result, the rat has eaten more than normal and gained a great deal of weight. But this rat will not eat itself to death. Rather, it will now eat just enough to maintain this new, higher set-point weight.

External Cues That Influence Eating: Culture and Consumerism

Have you ever eaten until you felt as if you were going to burst? Have you ever eaten a big bag of popcorn at the movies just minutes after you finished a very large meal? Have you ever gone all day without eating because you were busy at school or work? If so, your behavior has shown that eating is often more than just satisfying biological needs. Hunger and eating can be influenced by external sources of feedback that have little connection to our energy requirements. For example, the smell of popping popcorn at a theater can make you want to eat popcorn, even shortly after you've had a full meal. The sight of a piping hot pizza on TV may send you reaching for the phone to order a pizza, even when you know you're not hungry.

We have many external cues for hunger. The sight or smell of a delicious food can spark hunger, but so can the context in which we find ourselves. Food and feasting are an integral part of many cultural customs. This is especially true in the United States, where our holiday celebrations—including Christmas, Thanksgiving, Halloween, Hanukkah, Passover, Kwanzaa, and New Year's—are all associated with special foods in large quantities. The same holds true for more personal celebrations—

birthdays, weddings, reunions, and even funerals. Americans and many other peoples around the world use food and eating to celebrate. This connection between joy and food can lead to eating when we do not really need to.

What Causes Obesity: Nature and Nurture, Again

We Americans are obsessed with weight. Collectively we spend millions and millions of dollars each year on diets, exercise equipment, diet pills, and gym memberships, yet roughly two-thirds of all Americans are considered to be *overweight* and almost a third are **obese** (Figure 8.8). One way to define overweight and obesity is to look at the *body mass index* (*BMI*; Figure 8.9). A BMI of 25 or higher indicates overweight, and a BMI of 30 or more indicates obesity (National Institutes of Health, 2000). BMIs over 30 are correlated with higher incidences of many diseases, including type II diabetes, heart disease, and some cancers (Kopelman, 2000). In light of these problems, the government-funded Medicare program recently began considering obesity a disease (CBS News, 2004). Why then, despite our great concern over the issues of weight and health, are so many of us losing the battle of the bulge?

obese   having a body mass index of 30 or over

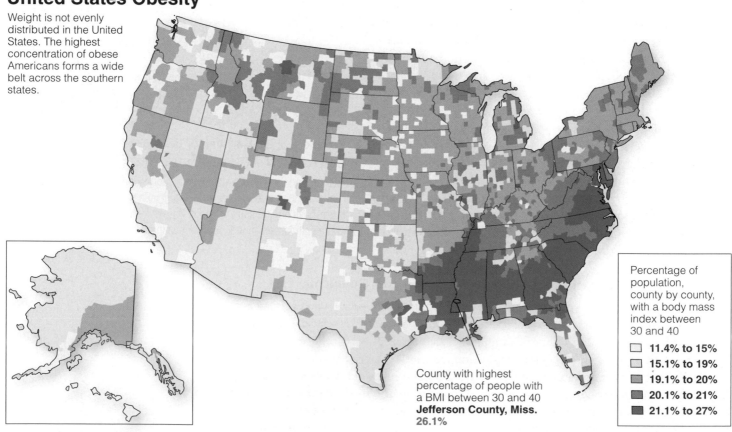

United States Obesity

Weight is not evenly distributed in the United States. The highest concentration of obese Americans forms a wide belt across the southern states.

County with highest percentage of people with a BMI between 30 and 40
Jefferson County, Miss.
26.1%

Percentage of population, county by county, with a body mass index between 30 and 40

☐ **11.4% to 15%**
☐ **15.1% to 19%**
☐ **19.1% to 20%**
■ **20.1% to 21%**
■ **21.1% to 27%**

Source: Medstat, part of the Thomson Corp.

Figure 8.8 **The Obesity Epidemic in the United States**

In the United States, almost one-third of all adults are obese. This map shows the percentage of obese people county by county throughout the United States. The highest concentrations of obese people (shown in red) seem to be in the southern states. The reasons for this epidemic are the subject of much debate, but it is likely that several causes are at work—including genetic, lifestyle, and diet factors.

From TIME, 6/7/2004. Reprinted with permission.

Behavioral Factors in Obesity

Poor diet is one reason that some people gain weight. Simply put, consuming more calories than you can burn leads to weight gain. But given the negative feedback loop systems we've described, why would one eat too much? One culprit is the high-fat diet common in many Western cultures. A typical fast-food lunch can contain a whole day's worth of fat and calories. Coupled with a lack of exercise, this diet leads to weight gain in many. Another factor comes from the way our society views food. As we mentioned earlier, we tend to eat food for reasons that have little to do with maintaining homeostasis. Many of us use food as a means of dealing with our emotions, such as eating when we are lonely, sad, or nervous (Edelman, 1981). This *emotional eating* may be one of the factors involved in weight gain for some, but emotional distress has not been shown to be a general cause of obesity. In general, overweight people are *not* more likely to suffer from anxiety or depression (Wadden & Stunkard, 1987). However, the prejudices that overweight people experience can lead some of them to suffer low self-esteem (Friedman & Brownell, 1996).

Body mass index (BMI) = (weight in pounds × 703) ÷ (height in inches)²	
Multiply your weight in pounds by 703 _____ × 703 = _____	Example 155 lbs × 703 = 108,965
Multiply your height in inches by itself (squared) _____² = _____	68 × 68 [inches] = 4,624
Divide the first number by the second: $\dfrac{\text{_____}}{\text{Weight} \times 703} \div \dfrac{\text{_____}}{\text{Height squared}} = \dfrac{\text{_____}}{\text{BMI}}$	$\dfrac{108{,}965}{4{,}624} = 23.6$ BMI

BMI	Weight status
below 18.5	Underweight
18.5–24.9	Normal
25.0–29.9	Overweight
30.0 and above	Obese

Figure 8.9 Calculating Your BMI

This chart shows how to calculate your own body mass index (BMI). To do so, you will need a calculator, your weight in pounds, and your height measured in inches.

Curiously, prejudice toward obese people is a cultural phenomenon. Americans abhor fat. Overweight Americans are often ridiculed, socially isolated, and even discriminated against in the workplace. This negative attitude about obesity is not worldwide, however. One of the authors (Doyle-Portillo) once had an overweight friend from a North Atlantic country. After living in the United States for a few years, she observed that although there were fewer obese people in her native country, she was treated more normally there than she was in the United States, where so many people are overweight. Keep this in mind when you read about stereotypes and prejudices in Chapter 12. Although some prejudices may be tolerated in a culture, they still exact a human toll on their victims. Furthermore, a little later in this chapter, we will see that our cultural fear of fat may also play a role in the development of certain eating disorders.

 Application

Because of health concerns and social pressure, many people spend a good deal of their time dieting. When following a weight-loss diet, the idea is to decrease your caloric intake so that the body will burn up its reserves of fat. Diets restrict the dieter's eating to varying degrees. Unfortunately, depriving yourself of food is also one reason that most diets fail. When we reduce our caloric intake to the point that we begin to lose weight, our bodies try to counteract the diet. Recall that our motivation to eat is designed to keep us from starving. When we begin to draw on our fat reserves while dieting, our body takes steps to avoid "starvation." At first, we may feel increased hunger as our body tries to avoid burning up fat reserves by urging us to eat. Later, our metabolic rate—the rate at which we burn energy in our bodies—may drop as the body tries to conserve energy, again in order to avoid burning up its fat reserves. The drop in metabolic rate may offset the reduction in calories on the diet, with the end result being little or no weight loss. Even more discouraging is the fact that our metabolism may drop even lower with each successive diet we go on (Brownell, 1988). This means that the more you diet, the harder it may become to lose weight! Our bodies appear inclined to fight against weight loss and to maintain our typical, or *set-point*, weight.

There are psychological factors in dieting, too. Depriving yourself of food often leads to bingeing on food. It appears that when a dieter strays from his diet program, he feels as if he might as well *really* go off the diet. In one study that illustrated this reaction, dieters and nondieters were given a liquid drink. Half of each group was told that the drink was very high in calories. The other half of each group was told that the drink was very low in calories. In reality, all the drinks were the same in caloric and nutritional content. After the drink, all participants were allowed to eat as much ice cream as they wanted. The nondieters ate the same amount of ice cream regardless of whether they thought they had just consumed a high- or low-calorie drink. This was not true, however, for the dieters. The dieters who thought they had had a high-calorie drink were more likely to eat more ice cream than the dieters who thought their drink had been low-calorie. It appears that the dieters felt that having already "ruined" their diet with the high-calorie drink, there was little point in restraining themselves when it came to the ice cream (Spencer & Fremouw, 1979).

People who restrain their eating are most at risk for this bingeing when they are emotionally aroused. Emotional distress can make a dieter slip off her diet (Ruderman, 1985), but so can positive emotions (Cools, Schotte, & McNally, 1992). Whether one is happy or sad, it seems that dieting makes eating binges more likely.

So how does one succeed in losing weight? The recipe for dieting success involves two factors. First, you have to make permanent changes in your eating behavior. "Dieting" is forever, and it is probably a mistake to think of losing weight as dieting. It's generally better to focus on eating healthy, balanced meals that are lower in calories, and not to focus on how many pounds you can lose in a week. The best way to lose weight is to do it *slowly*. People don't typically gain 15 pounds in a week, so why should we expect to lose weight that fast?

The second aspect of successful weight-loss is exercise. Any weight-loss plan that does not include exercise is likely to fail. Exercise not only burns extra calories and causes weight loss, it also increases your metabolism. Recall that when we diet, our body adjusts its metabolic rate downward to prevent starvation. You can help keep your metabolism higher by exercising, which will lead to a more permanent weight loss as our set point moves to a lower weight. So next time you see an advertisement for some miracle diet that allows you to eat all you want without exercising and still promises to safely take off 10 pounds a week, save your money and possibly your health! There are no quick fixes when it comes to shedding pounds.

Biological Factors in Obesity

Given that so many people have a difficult time achieving permanent weight loss, some scientists have questioned whether obesity is always a simple matter of eating too much and exercising too little. Are some people actually predisposed to being overweight? Yes, indeed. Some obese people suffer from biological conditions that predispose them to gaining extra weight. One biological reason for obesity is having a *low metabolic rate*. People differ with respect to how much energy is required to run their bodies. Some people have high metabolic rates so that they require large amounts of fuel to power their bodies. Others have low metabolic rates and require relatively little energy to survive. A person with a very low metabolic rate who eats the same number of calories and exercises just as much as a person with a normal metabolic rate will still gain more weight than the normal person will. Over time, this weight gain could lead to obesity (Friedman, 1990).

Research indicates that it is possible to change your set point. It takes time, and it takes work, but exercise combined with a well-balanced, sensible diet can help you achieve permanent weight loss. Exercise is essential to weight loss because building lean muscle mass helps increase your metabolic rate and lower your set point.

© T. Garcha/Masterfile

Genetics play a role in obesity for some overweight people. So called "thrifty genes" that lead to low metabolic rates or efficient digestive systems may cause some overweight people to gain weight even though they eat and exercise at the same levels as their thin counterparts.

Ironically, having a low metabolic rate isn't always a disadvantage. In fact, across our evolutionary history, a low metabolic rate was probably a decided advantage at times. For instance, our ancestors had to hunt and forage for enough food to eat. Those early humans who required less energy to survive probably had an easier time finding enough food to meet their needs. Therefore, those with low metabolic rates probably survived better and procreated more than their counterparts with high metabolic rates. This advantage could have led to some members of our modern society having "thrifty genes" that conserve energy, but it may have also led to obesity in a world in which hunting and gathering high-calorie foods is as simple as a trip to the grocery store or fast-food drive-through. The typical American diet is far different from that of our ancestors. Today, we Americans consume large amounts of red meat, fat, eggs, and dairy products, but few fruits and vegetables.

By examining cultural groups that have more recently adapted to the American high-fat diet, we can see more clearly the impact of that diet on health. For example, ethnic Hawaiians have the shortest life span of any ethnic group on the Hawaiian Islands. As a group, ethnic Hawaiians show high rates of high blood pressure, diabetes, obesity, and high cholesterol. One major culprit in these health problems appears to be the fat-heavy American diet they have taken on. When ethnic Hawaiians return to their native diet of sweet potatoes, taro root, breadfruit, fish, chicken, and vegetables, their health significantly improves. In one study, after only 21 days of eating their native diet instead of the typical American diet, the Hawaiians had significant drops in blood pressure, weight, and cholesterol (Shintani, Hughes, Beckham, & O'Connor, 1991). Perhaps many native Hawaiians are biologically unsuited to eat the American diet, and the same may be true of many other obese Americans.

Another biological factor is how our body extracts nutrients from food. When we eat, we lose some of the nutritive content of our food due to the inefficiency of our digestive systems. Therefore some of the nutrients of the food will be expelled as waste from our bodies. Some obese people may have *more efficient* digestive systems that can

Application

extract and use more of the nutritive content in the food they eat. Because of this increased efficiency, an obese person can gain weight by eating the exact same diet as someone who is not obese (Friedman, 1990).

Another possibility is that obese people may automatically convert some of the nutrients they eat into fat (Friedman, 1990). This would leave fewer calories immediately available to be burned as fuel, and the person would be motivated to eat more food. In addition, a portion of any extra food eaten would *also* be automatically converted into fat. This vicious cycle would ensure that the person continues to eat more than necessary and that too much of that food would be stored as fat! As you can see, for some people, gaining excess weight is not a simple matter of self-control or poor habits.

Obesity is a problem for many people, exposing them to social ridicule and discrimination as well as health risks. Yet despite our awareness of these problems, obesity is on the rise in America—especially among our children. Although all racial and ethnic groups are affected by obesity, African American girls seem to be particularly vulnerable to this condition, as we discuss in It's a Diverse World!

IT'S A DIVERSE WORLD

Obesity in White and Black American Adolescent Females

Researcher Sue Kimm has spent a great deal of time trying to determine why obesity rates are skyrocketing among young women in the United States. Using data gathered in the National Heart, Lung, and Blood Institute Growth and Health Study (NGHS), Kimm has uncovered some potential explanations for the frightening increase in childhood obesity in the United States over the last several decades. The NGHS tracked 1,213 African American and 1,166 White girls from age 9 or 10 to age 18 or 19, repeatedly measuring them on variables such as weight, body-fat distribution, activity level, self-esteem, and eating habits. The results are sobering.

By age 9, Black girls were 37% more likely to be overweight than White girls (30.6% vs. 22.4%), and these numbers nearly doubled over the next 10 years for all the girls in the study. By age 19, 56.9% of the Black girls and 41.3% of the White girls were overweight. Over 33% of the Black girls were obese versus almost 20% of the White girls. As you can see, extra weight was a significant problem for *both* groups, although even more so for the Black girls (Kimm, Barton, Obarzanek, et al., 2002). What may account for these numbers?

Lifestyle and Demographic Factors: For White girls, watching more TV, eating more, having a less educated mother, and living in a lower-income family were correlated with being obese. For Black girls, however, watching more TV was the only predictor of obesity. For Black girls, their caloric intake, parental income level, and education did not seem to predict obesity levels (Kimm, Obarzanek, et al., 1996). So why is TV so important? Well, watching TV doesn't expend many calories, so children who watch a lot of TV may tend to gain weight because they do not burn off the calories they eat. Unfortunately, the NGHS study showed that as all of the girls approached adolescence, they became successively *less* physically active! By age 16 or 17, 56% of the Black girls and 31% of the White girls reported that they did not routinely engage in physical activity during their leisure time. Furthermore, for both races, being overweight and/or having a less educated mother predicted that they would engage in less physical activity (Kimm, Glynn, Kriska, et al., 2002). Some possible explanations are that educated mothers may promote exercise to their children, and already being overweight may make exercise less appealing and more difficult.

Social Factors: The NGHS study also showed racial differences in attitudes toward the girls' bodies and obesity. White girls in the study seemed to be more concerned about weight gain than the Black girls did. Overweight White girls felt less socially accepted, whereas social acceptance did not change with weight for Black girls. For both Black and White girls, self-perceived physical appearance and self-worth declined as weight increased, but the trend was much stronger for the White girls (Kimm, Barton, Berhane, et al., 1997). These data suggest that there is more cultural acceptance of heavier and overweight women among African Americans. Therefore, it is possible that Black girls do not feel as pressured to maintain a lower body weight.

Genetic Factors: One particularly interesting finding of the NGHS study was the suggestion that Black girls tend more toward obesity because of genetically thrifty metabolisms. In a sample of approximately 150 girls from the NGHS study, Black girls were found to have a resting metabolism that on average burned 71 fewer calories per day (adjusted for body weight) (Kimm, Glynn, Aston, Poehlman, et al., 2001). Furthermore, there is some suggestion that this metabolic difference may be due to a gene that some African American women inherit (Kimm, Glynn, Aston, Damcott, et al., 2002; Kimm & Obarzanek, 2002).

As you can see, the battle of the bulge must be fought on many different fronts. Childhood obesity is a significant problem for both White and Black girls, and it is likely to be due to a combination of physical, behavioral, sociocultural, and psychological factors. One of the most curious things about the NGHS study was that caloric intake was not shown to be a good predictor of obesity across all the participants. This could be due to problems in having teenage participants self-report how much they eat, but at this stage researchers do not yet know the degree to which a simple calorie count will predict eventual weight gain (Kimm & Obarzanek, 2002). For now, parents should definitely educate themselves and their children about the need to exercise regularly—and turn off the TV!

Obesity is not, however, the only problematic condition that involves eating. Our chapter case study of Maya Hornbacher illustrates the devastating toll that *eating disorders*, or mental illnesses that are associated with eating, can take on a person's health and life. Why would anyone be *motivated* to binge and purge or to starve themselves the way that Marya did? We'll examine the answer to this question as we take a closer look at these two eating disorders.

Eating Disorders: Bulimia Nervosa and Anorexia Nervosa

Marya's eating disorder formally began while she was still in grade school, but the seeds of Marya's problems were there long before her disorder emerged. From early childhood on, Marya had an unhealthy preoccupation with her body, its size, and its shape, as well as an unhealthy feeling of not having any control over her troubled home life. These factors are part of the unhealthy mix that seems to give rise to eating disorders.

Bulimia Nervosa

Marya's eating disorders began with the onset of *bulimia*. As we described at the start of this chapter, bulimia is an eating disorder that is characterized by alternating bouts of *bingeing* and *self-starvation* that often includes *purging* (see p. 345). People who are bulimic will gorge on large quantities of food, sometimes as much as 20,000 calories at a time, and then they will either go on a very rigid starvation diet or they will purge the food from their systems (Schiesler-Stropp, 1984). Purging is achieved by self-induced vomiting or the abuse of laxatives to help move food quickly through the digestive tract before the body can absorb its nutrients.

Application

One of the authors (Doyle-Portillo) once met a bulimic girl who spent an entire semester's tuition on a 2-week cycle of bingeing and purging. She would go out at night and travel from one drive-through restaurant to another buying large quantities of tacos, hamburgers, and other fast food. She would take the food back to her dorm room, where she would quickly eat all of it and then purge it through vomiting. Luckily, this 2-week binge probably saved her life. When she was unable to explain the missing tuition money, her parents insisted she enter a treatment program. After intense treatment, she regained some measure of normalcy in her eating behavior.

© AP Photo/The Grand Island Independent, Barnett Stinson

Anorexia nervosa is a devastating disorder in which people are motivated to drastically restrict their eating while simultaneously increasing their level of exercise. The result is extreme weight loss, but this weight loss is never enough to please the anorectic. Anorectics like this woman still look in the mirror and feel like they need to lose more weight.

Application

Like this woman, the typical victim of bulimia is a young female who is of average to slightly-above-average weight. Approximately 1–2% of American women suffer from bulimia (Vogeltanz-Holm et al., 2000), and the disorder is especially likely among female college students (Thelen, Farmer, Mann, & Pruitt, 1990). Bulimia can be a socially isolating disorder. A college student who spends her evenings gathering up large quantities of food and bingeing and purging usually does so alone. In Marya's memoir *Wasted*, she speaks frequently of the steps she took to hide her disorders and of how isolated she felt from everyone around her (Hornbacher, 1998). Aside from its social toll, bulimia can also be fatal. The frequent purging of food can lead to dehydration and electrolyte imbalances, which can lead to serious cardiac problems and other problems like the hole in Marya's esophagus.

Given the devastating toll that bulimia can take on one's life, what would motivate anyone to engage in bulimic behavior? At this time, no one can say for sure why people become bulimic. However, many bulimic people are troubled by low self-esteem and depression (Perez, Joiner, & Lewinsohn, 2004). Bulimics tend to be perfectionists who have negative views of their bodies. They tend to have grown up in families that were troubled somehow (Bardone, Vohs, Abramson, Heatherton, & Joiner, 2000). All of these things were true of Marya. In her case, it appeared that her bulimic behavior was in some way a response to the chaos of her home life. By rigidly controlling her body, she felt a tiny bit more in control of her life. Unfortunately, Marya could never quite control her body well enough to feel actually happy, and her bulimic behavior turned into full-blown *anorexia nervosa*.

Anorexia Nervosa

As we discussed in the opening case study, *anorexia nervosa* is an eating disorder that is characterized by self-starvation, intense exercise, and a distorted body image. Unlike people suffering from bulimia, anorectics can be easily spotted by their very low body weight. An anorectic can weigh *less* than the 52 pounds that Marya got down to during the height of her illness. The most bizarre aspect of anorexia is that even at such a low weight, an anorectic can look in the mirror and *see* herself as being fat (Grant & Phillips, 2004). Even when others easily recognized Marya's obvious anorexia, she was convinced that she still looked as "fat" as she always did—even though she had never been what most people would call fat (Hornbacher, 1998).

Most anorectics are females from middle- and upper-class families in industrialized countries. Anorexia is rarely found in men, and it is rarely found in cultures that hold a fuller-figured woman up as the standard of beauty. It appears that one of the contributing factors in the development of anorexia is societal pressure placed on young women to be very thin—unrealistically thin. If you pick up just about any American fashion magazine or watch just about any American television show, you will find that most of the females depicted are thin—very thin. Sometimes they actually look anorectic (Figure 8.10). Many television stars and models wear size 2 or 3 clothes, whereas many American women wear size 10 or 12 (or larger)! If you do the math, you'll see that many American women fall short of the standard of beauty that is depicted in the media. What do you do if you are a young girl who aspires to look like the actors you see on TV, and a healthy diet and exercise does not allow you to meet your goals? Some girls take drastic steps to reach their "ideal" body image, and anorexia may be the result.

Researchers have found wide cultural variations in women's perceptions of their ideal body image. For example, in one study that compared U.S., Israeli, Spanish, and Brazilian women, the American women were found to be the least satisfied with their bodies. The American women reported that they felt the most pressure to be thin (e.g., Joliot, 2001). This is significant because in cultures that portray beautiful women as being somewhat plumper—for example in Jamaica (Smith & Cogswell, 1994) or even in American culture prior to the 1970s—anorexia is uncommon. Pre-1970s, women who were considered beautiful were considerably heavier than those who are considered beautiful today. For example, Marilyn Monroe was considered to be the standard of beauty in the 1950s and early 1960s, and before her, Mae West—these two women were not the ultrathin models of today (Figure 8.11)!

Obviously, every American girl does *not* become an anorectic despite being bombarded with images of very thin women. Why then do some become anorectic whereas others do not? No one knows for sure, but there are some clues. Some characteristics that seem to be *correlated* with anorexia include perfectionism and faulty thinking about food (Steinhausen & Vollrath, 1993), as well as certain biochemical abnormalities (Ferguson & Pigott, 2000). Additionally, many people suffering from eating disorders also suffer from *personality disorders*—characteristic, maladaptive ways of dealing with the world (see Chapter 15, p. 693; Marañon, Echeburúa, & Grijalvo, 2004). We do not yet know if these are *causal* factors or merely factors that *correlate* with eating disorders. Another piece of the puzzle seems to be genetics. If one identical twin is anorectic, the other twin's chances of becoming anorectic are drastically increased. However, having a fraternal twin who is anorectic only modestly increases one's chances of becoming anorectic (Holland, Sicotte, & Treasure, 1988). This pattern of results indicates that there may be some genetic influence that predisposes one to anorexia. At present, it appears that both bulimia and anorexia may result from a complex mix of cultural factors, personality characteristics, environmental issues, and biological factors.

Kevin Winter/Getty Images

Figure 8.10 Too Thin?

Many models and actresses are *very* thin. The steady parade of these women in the media may have contributed to the increase in eating disorders seen in the 1980s and 1990s.

Figure 8.11 How the American Standard of Female Beauty Has Changed Over Time

Standards of beauty in the United States have changed over time, and they also differ across cultures. In the 1930s, Mae West was considered to be an icon of feminine beauty. In the 1950s and early 1960s, it was Marilyn Monroe. Today, women like Jennifer Aniston are the standard of beauty.

Hulton Archive/Stringer/Getty Images

© Bettmann/Corbis

Getty Images

© jackhollingsworth.com/Alamy

© Buddy Mays/Corbis

Greer & Associates, Inc./Alamy

In cultures like Jamaica, Fiji, and Mexico the standard of beauty leans toward heavier women. Cultures such as these have far lower rates of eating disorders than the United States.

Thirst

As we have seen, the hunger motive drives us to take in food to meet our nutritional requirements. Yet for most of us a typical meal will include both food and a beverage. Does this mean that hunger motivates us to eat *and* drink? It appears not. Maintaining homeostasis of our fluid level is made possible by another motive—thirst, which is in some ways a more important motivation than hunger. If deprived of food and water, we would die from dehydration *before* we starved to death.

To function well, our bodies must have enough fluid. Fluid is critical because it allows for the ions in our body to travel into and out of our cells. As we saw in Chapter 2, ions like potassium and sodium are absolutely essential to the functioning of our nervous system. If we were to become dehydrated, these ions would not be able to flow across the cell membranes during the firing of neural impulses, which could mean nervous system collapse and death! In fact, you can live for quite some time without food, but you would not be able to live 1 week without water. Even anorectics like Marya, who would go for days without eating, must take in fluids regularly.

Given that water is so crucial to survival, how do you know when you are thirsty? Many people would say that thirst is a feeling of having a parched throat or a dry mouth. Certainly, these characteristics are indicative of thirst, but just as the stomach plays only a partial role in the sensation of hunger, the mouth and throat play only a partial role in thirst. Even people who have had their larynx (part of the throat containing the vocal cords) removed still feel thirst and still drink (Miyaoka, Sawada, Sakaguchi, & Shingai, 1987).

To understand thirst, you must first understand where the body stores fluids. Fluid that is stored inside our cells is called **intracellular fluid.** Fluid that is stored outside our cells, in the spaces that exist *between* our cells, is called **extracellular fluid.** To maintain optimum fluid levels, our brain's hypothalamus monitors the levels of both intracellular and extracellular fluid of its neurons. If we eat a salty meal, the sodium concentration in our extracellular fluid increases, which causes intracellular fluid from inside our hypothalamic neurons to cross the cell membrane into the extracelluar space. This dilutes, or lowers, the sodium content of the extracellular fluid, but it also decreases the pressure inside our hypothalamic neurons. When this transition begins, and the hypothalamic neurons begin to lose their intracellular fluids, the hypothalamus signals thirst to motivate fluid intake (Memmler, Cohen, & Wood, 1992).

Another mechanism of thirst comes from cells that monitor the body's extracellular fluid levels outside of the brain. As we sweat, exhale, and urinate, we lose fluid from our extracellular fluid. As we become dehydrated, this loss of fluid causes a drop in our blood volume and a corresponding drop in our blood pressure. Specialized *pressure receptors* in our heart, kidneys, and blood vessels detect this slight drop in blood pressure, and they send signals to the brain that will eventually initiate thirst. These pressure receptors also signal the start of measures to conserve the water that is already inside our body (Pinel, 1997).

intracellular fluid   the fluid found inside the cells of the body, which is used to regulate thirst

extracellular fluid   the fluid found in the spaces outside the cells of the body, which is used to regulate thirst

Dehydration results in the loss of extracellular fluid in our bodies. This loss of fluid causes a drop in blood pressure that signals our brain to initiate thirst. This athlete will likely feel tremendous thirst, which will motivate her to replace the fluids she has lost through sweating.

© Neal Preston/Corbis

Let's Review!

In this section, we discussed our motivation to eat and drink. We described the systems of feedback in the body that inform our brain when we need food and water, and therefore play a role in regulating our thirst and hunger. We also looked at what happens when our motivation to eat goes awry and problems such as obesity, anorexia, and bulimia result. As a quick check of your understanding, answer these questions.

1. A friend of yours was recently in a car accident and suffered damage to his ventromedial hypothalamus. What effect would you expect this damage to have on your friend's behavior?
   a. He will likely stop eating.
   b. He will likely die.
   c. He will likely gain a great deal of weight.
   d. He will likely gain a great deal of weight, but then he will lose the pounds and return to his normal weight.

2. Which of the following is the hormone that the small intestines release to shut off hunger?
   a. insulin
   b. CCK
   c. leptin
   d. serotonin

3. You just ran a 10-mile marathon, and you are now very thirsty. Which of the following is the *most* likely reason for your excessive thirst?
   a. loss of intracellular fluid
   b. loss of extracellular fluid
   c. loss of sodium in the body
   d. loss of potassium in the body

ANSWERS

1.c; 2.b; 3.b

The Puzzle of Destructive Motivation › › › ›

LEARNING OBJECTIVE

Explain the role that motivation may play in drug-taking behavior.

For the most part, our motives help us survive. Motives like hunger and thirst are essential to life because they help maintain homeostasis in our bodies. But not all motives are helpful. Obviously, in the case of anorexia and bulimia the motivation to stop eating or to purge what you have eaten is detrimental to the body's health and well-being. But there are other disorders in which our motives are destructive—self-injury, suicide, and substance abuse are some others. For instance, in addition to having eating disorders, Marya also had problems with drugs. Although she was not motivated to eat food, she was motivated to take all types of drugs—everything from huge quantities of nicotine and caffeine to cocaine and alcohol and any type of pill she could get her hands on. Marya had a substance abuse problem.

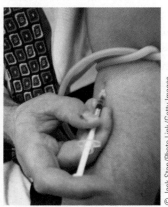

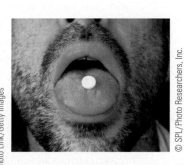

Substance abuse is a form of destructive motivation that causes problems in many people's lives. Understanding people's motivation to begin abusing substances is a complicated matter, but it is clear that tolerance and physical dependence can motivate them to continue abusing substances once they have started.

Why Do Some People Abuse Drugs?

You may recall from Chapter 4 (see p. 178) that caffeine, nicotine, and alcohol are the three most widely used psychoactive substances. Many people struggle with substance abuse problems such as drug addiction, alcoholism, smoking, inhalant use, and even caffeine addiction. In fact, substance abuse disorders are some of the most common mental disorders in the general population. Males have close to a 35% chance of being diagnosed with a substance disorder in their lifetime, and females have nearly a 20% chance (Kessler et al., 1994). These are *high* numbers!

What makes substance abuse such a common problem? It is hard to say what motivates people to abuse substances in the first place, but many sociological and psychological factors have been shown to correlate with drug use. These include exposure to drugs, low self-esteem, boredom, and depression. One perspective on drug-taking is that of *operant conditioning* (remember Chapter 5?—see p. 225). In operant conditioning terms, drugs can be seen as both *positive* and *negative reinforcers*. Drugs can be positive reinforcers by producing feelings of pleasure and euphoria. You'll recall from Chapter 4 that users often report pleasurable feelings as part of a drug-induced altered state of consciousness. So the drugs may have initial appeal for some because they produce these pleasurable feelings, however temporary.

On the flip side, some people take drugs so that they don't feel bad. For people who are in physical or psychological pain, drugs can act as negative reinforcers, removing their discomfort. When you think about it, this is the purpose behind many *legal* drugs. We take aspirin to stop the pain of a headache. Some substance abusers take drugs to lessen or stop the pain of low self-esteem, bad relationships, or depression. Perhaps Marya was trying to self-medicate her eating disorder and her unhappiness with alcohol, caffeine, and illegal drugs.

Although it is difficult to come up with a theoretical explanation for taking drugs in the first place, it is easier to explain why someone would continue to take them. In fact, one theory of motivation, called **opponent-process theory,** provides an elegant explanation of continued drug use (Solomon, 1980). (Note that this theory is not the same opponent-process theory we covered in Chapter 3 when we were discussing color vision.) Opponent-process theory proposes that when a person takes a drug repeatedly, the body attempts to counteract the effects of the drug by engaging in an *opponent process.* For example, with a stimulant drug, the opponent process will *decrease* the user's physiological arousal to counteract the drug's arousal effects. If the drug is a depressant, then the opponent process will *increase* the user's physiological arousal to counteract the drug's effects. The problem is that the body's opponent process is slow to start and the effect lasts longer than the drug does. As you can see in Figure 8.12, the opponent process is still going strong after the effects of the drug have worn off. Without the drug to balance out the opponent process, the user starts to feel unpleasant **withdrawal** symptoms that are opposite to the drug's effects. In other words, coming down from depressants will make the person feel anxious, and coming down from stimulants will make people feel depressed.

Because withdrawal symptoms are uncomfortable and aversive, the user will be *motivated* to continue taking the drug because it has become a negative reinforcer that can remove the withdrawal symptoms. Removal of the withdrawal symptoms is reinforcing—so operant conditioning ensures that the user will be more likely to take drugs the next time withdrawal symptoms occur—which will be shortly after the drug begins to wear off. Do you recognize the vicious circle of **physical dependence** here? The opponent-process mechanism in the body ensures that withdrawing from the drug will produce aversive symptoms, which is just another way of saying that the opponent process creates a physical dependence.

opponent-process theory a theory of motivation that states that the body will counteract the effects of ingested drugs by adjusting its arousal level in a direction opposite that of the drug's effect on the body

withdrawal an unpleasant physiological state that results when one stops taking a drug to which he or she has built up a tolerance

physical dependence a condition that occurs when a person is motivated to continue taking a drug because to stop taking the drug would result in painful withdrawal symptoms

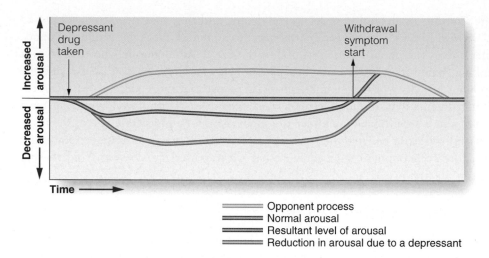

Figure 8.12 An Opponent-Process View of Drug Taking

Notice how the body tries to counteract the effects of the depressant by increasing its baseline level of arousal.

To make matters worse, opponent processes also cause drug **tolerance,** or the phenomenon of needing more and more of a drug to get the same "high" after repeated drug use. Tolerance develops as the user continues to take the drug in order to avoid withdrawal. The opponent process keeps adjusting the body's state to offset the drug, and as time goes on, the opponent process gets stronger and stronger. In other words, the body tries more intently to counteract the drug. The net effect is that it takes larger and larger doses of the drug to achieve the effect that the user once got from the initial dose. Figure 8.13 shows the strengthening of the opponent process as the user develops a tolerance to a depressant. If this user were to stop taking the depressant, the jitters would set in!

Not everyone develops physical dependence and tolerance at exactly the same rate, however. For instance, human and animal studies suggest that females may develop physical dependence for certain drugs—including alcohol and cocaine—more quickly than males (Carroll, Morgan, Lynch, Campbell, & Dess, 2002; Lynch, Roth, & Carroll, 2002). And recent research has suggested that people with a family history of alcoholism may be at higher risk for developing alcoholism because they easily develop a tolerance to alcohol (see p. 184). In fact, they begin to develop tolerance to alcohol within a few hours of starting to drink (Morzorati, Ramchandani, Flury, Li, & O'Connor, 2002)! This early tolerance may encourage them to drink larger and larger amounts of alcohol, resulting in physical dependence.

When people become severely alcoholic, tolerance can be so severe that withdrawal from alcohol is physically dangerous. Longtime alcoholics may have to drink

tolerance a condition that results after repeated drug use in which more and more of the drug is required to produce the same results

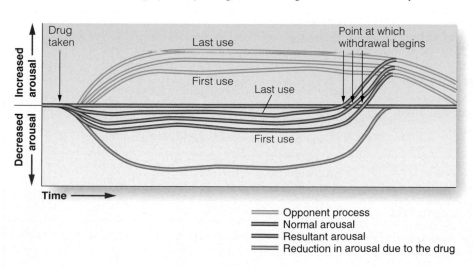

Figure 8.13 An Opponent-Process View of Physical Dependence to a Drug

Notice how successive doses of the depressant force the body to successively increase its baseline level of arousal? This is how physical dependence on a drug develops.

large amounts of alcohol in order to feel drunk, and they may need to drink just to feel *normal*. Because alcohol is a central nervous system (CNS) depressant, the opponent process for alcohol causes arousal of the CNS. An alcoholic who tries to quit drinking "cold turkey" risks being in a state of having a *hyperaroused* CNS because the opponent process will still be in effect—with or without more alcohol. This can result in hallucinations, tremors, seizures—and even death. Withdrawal from long-term alcohol abuse should be done under the supervision of a physician who can control the withdrawal so as to avoid these problems. Given the dangers of substance abuse and the vicious cycle of physical dependence that can trap users, it is best to avoid abusing drugs in the first place.

Other Destructive Behaviors

Self-injurious behavior is another example of destructive motivation. For reasons that are not completely clear, some people are motivated to cut, burn, scratch, beat, mutilate, and otherwise do harm to themselves. Often the desire to engage in self-injurious behavior is seen in individuals who are suffering from some form of psychological disorder, such as *borderline personality disorder*. People with borderline personality disorder do not have a well-developed understanding of themselves, and often suffer from instability in their emotions and in their relationships with others. Frequently, they are also found to engage in self-destructive behaviors like drug abuse or self-mutilation, including burning themselves with cigarettes or cutting themselves with knives or razors (see Chapter 15, p. 695).

Suicide is the ultimate form of self-destructive behavior. The motivation to commit suicide goes against all of our survival instincts and is almost always considered to be abnormal behavior. As we will see in Chapter 15, the majority of people who commit suicide also suffer from some diagnosable mental disorder—often depression. We don't fully understand why a person might be motivated to take his or her own life. It is likely that people have many different individual motives for taking such a drastic step. We will discuss what we do know about suicide in Chapter 15 when we look at psychological disorders.

Let's Review!

In this section, we discussed the destructive side of motivation in looking at why some people are motivated to abuse drugs and other substances. As a quick check of your understanding, answer these questions.

1. Craig is trying to stop drinking coffee. For the last year, Craig has consumed a full pot of strong coffee on a daily basis, but today he has not had any coffee at all. How would you expect Craig to be feeling?

   a. anxious and jittery

   b. sluggish and tired

   c. alert and refreshed

   d. none of the above

2. _____ ensure(s) that drug users will need to take higher and higher doses of their preferred drug to experience the feeling of their first high.

   a. Withdrawal

   b. Tolerance

   c. Opponent processes

   d. b and c

3. Opponent process theory does *not* explain why _____.

   a. people begin taking drugs

   b. people continue to take drugs

   c. drug addictions are hard to kick

   d. drug addictions form

ANSWERS

1. b; 2. d; 3. a

Theories and Expression of Emotion › › › › ›

⌄⌄ **LEARNING**
⌄⌄ **OBJECTIVES**
⌄ Discuss the various theoretical perspectives on emotion.
⌄ Discuss how we express our emotional states through facial expressions.
⌄

What is an emotion? If you ask people that question, you will get a variety of answers. Most will probably say that emotions are *feelings*. Some will give examples, like *happiness, sadness,* or *anger,* but few will be able to produce a good definition of what an emotion actually is. Even psychologists have had trouble defining what is meant by an emotion. One definition is that an **emotion** is a complex reaction to some internal or external event that involves physiological reactions, behavioral reactions, facial expressions, cognition, and affective responses (cf. Lazarus, 1991). For example, let's imagine that you are walking through the woods and you hear some rustling up ahead. You look up to see a large black bear in your path. This event would likely cause an emotional reaction of *fear.* Your experience of fear would have several aspects to it:

≪ Application

emotion   a complex reaction to some internal or external event that involves physiological reactions, behavioral reactions, facial expressions, cognition, and affective responses

Physiological reactions: Your heart rate would increase, your respiration would increase, your pupils would dilate, and your muscles would tense.

Behavioral reactions: You might freeze in your tracks. You might run (an unwise choice in this situation). You might yell at the bear.

Facial expressions: Fear would show on your face. If someone were to observe you at this moment, they would likely recognize that you were afraid.

Cognition: You might think about the TV show you saw on bears last week and what the experts said that you should do in this situation. You might wonder if this is a female bear with cubs just out of sight in the brush. You might think about the danger that faces you should the bear charge.

Affective responses: You would have some subjective reaction to this situation. For example, "I am scared," "I am terrified," or—if you are an animal lover—"I'm thrilled!"

As you can see, emotions are complex. Perhaps that is why psychologists have had a difficult time defining just exactly what an emotion is. Another confusing aspect of emotion is that emotion is very similar to motivation. In fact, emotions can produce motivation (e.g., Zaalberg, Manstead, & Fischer, 2004). In our previous example, your fear of the bear might motivate you to run or to yell at the bear. So what separates emotions from motivation? What makes *fear* different from *hunger*? One unique element is the **affective component of emotion,** the subjective experience of what you are *feeling* that fills your consciousness during the emotion. When you are scared you *know* that you are scared because you *feel* the affective state of fear. This affective quality of emotion allows us to clearly know when we are feeling an emotion.

affective component of emotion the subjective experience of what you are *feeling* during the emotion

Emotions can also be distinguished from motivation in that they are usually (but not always) sparked by things outside of our bodies. For instance, when we see a tragic movie, we may feel sad. Or when we see a baby, we may feel happy. Motivation, on the other hand, often comes from some internal source—hunger may be initiated by low blood sugar or thirst by low blood pressure. And motives tend to be sparked by a specific need or goal, but emotions can be elicited by many stimuli. For instance, many things can make us happy, but only a few conditions will lead to hunger.

Although psychologists have struggled with the concept of emotion, several notable theories of emotion have been set out over the years. Let's take a look at some of them now.

The James-Lange Theory of Emotion

American psychologist William James and Danish physiologist Carl Lange each proposed one of the earliest theories of emotion at approximately the same point in history (James, 1884). Their theory, now called the **James-Lange theory** of emotion, states

James-Lange theory   a theory of emotion that defines an emotion as a unique pattern of physiological arousal

According to the James-Lange theory of emotion, this woman is experiencing anger because her body has reacted with a characteristic pattern of physiological changes in response to this event.

© LA Daily News/David Crane/Corbis Sygma

that emotion *is equal to* the pattern of physiological arousal that the person experiences during an emotion. In short, emotion is a physiological response to some stimulus. In our example of meeting up with the bear in the woods, from the James-Lange point of view, the emotion you feel is the pattern of physical and physiological reactions you have as you see the bear. The increased heart rate, the increased respiration, the running—these constitute the emotion of fear that you would experience in this situation.

Walter Cannon's Criticisms of the James-Lange Theory

The James-Lange view of emotion has had many critics. One important critic was Walter Cannon, who noted that for the James-Lange theory to adequately explain emotion there would have to be a different bodily response for *each* emotion we experience. Because emotion equals a physiological and bodily response in the James-Lange view, the only way to discriminate among emotions would be if there were different physical reactions for each emotion. Walter Cannon doubted that this was true, and in fact, offered three good reasons to doubt the James-Lange view of emotion (Cannon, 1927). His first criticism, which we just mentioned, is that the physiological experience of emotion does not appear to vary from emotion to emotion to the degree that would be necessary to distinguish one emotion from another based purely on our physiological reaction. For example, anger doesn't feel very different from terror—both involve increased heart rate, muscle tension, and so forth.

Second, Cannon argued that the physiological, bodily aspect of emotion sometimes follows our subjective experience of the emotion. For example, we may know that we are afraid *before* we feel our heart pounding and our muscles tensing. In the James-Lange view, there can be no emotion before there is a physiological response.

Cannon's third criticism was that artificially created physiological responses do not give rise to emotions. For example, drinking a lot of coffee may increase one's physiological arousal, but it does not cause you to experience fear, excitement, love, or any other emotion. If emotion were nothing more than a physiological response, it would stand to reason that artificially caused physiological responses would also cause emotional responses.

In light of these criticisms, Cannon proposed that emotion does not originate in the body; rather, it originates in the brain. According to Cannon, when you see a bear in the woods, your fear is not due to the increased heart rate and rapid breathing you experience. Instead, when you see the bear your brain causes you to feel fear. You may even be aware that you are afraid *before* you become aware of your rapidly beating heart and your panting breath. Cannon's explanation of emotion was later extended by a man named Philip Bard, so today this theory is called the **Cannon-Bard theory** of emotion.

Cannon-Bard theory a theory of emotion that states that emotions originate in the brain, not the body

Some Validation of the James-Lange Theory

Of Cannon's three criticisms, by far the most problematic criticism was the first one—that physiological responses are too similar to allow us to adequately discriminate among the many emotions we feel. For many years this criticism was seen as a fatal blow to the James-Lange theory. Things change, however, and in the 1990s, some new evidence gave the James-Lange theory new life. By the 1990s, psychologists had new tools for studying bodily reactions. In addition to precisely measuring heart rate, researchers could now measure minute changes in skin temperature and in the electrical conductivity of the skin that indicate small changes in the moisture of the skin. With these measurement techniques, it was now possible to examine the physiological response that accompanies emotions in greater detail than was possible in Walter Cannon's time.

Using measures such as these, researchers have been able to show that some emotions do indeed involve different bodily reactions. In one particularly clever study (Levenson, Ekman, & Friesen, 1990), participants were asked to make facial expressions for the emotions of fear, anger, happiness, disgust, sadness, and surprise and to hold these expressions for 10 seconds. While the participants held these expressions, their physiological reactions were measured very precisely. Just as the James-Lange theory predicts, there were slight but noticeable differences in heart rate, skin temperature, and other physiological reactions for the different emotions. Although all of the emotions caused changes in heart rate and skin temperature, it was the *degree* of change that separated the emotions from one another (Figure 8.14).

These results indicate that there may be some merit to the James-Lange approach, but they do not necessarily support the entire theory. These results do not address Walter Cannon's other two criticisms—that physiological reactions sometimes follow our awareness of emotions and that artificially created arousal does not seem to directly cause the experience of emotion. Even if patterns of physiological arousal do help us

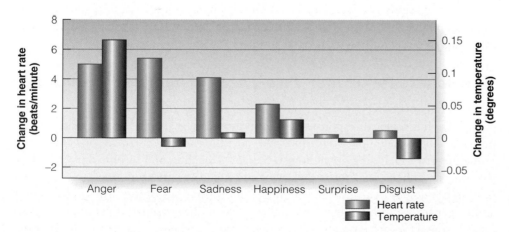

Figure 8.14 Physiological Changes for Six Different Emotions

Note the varying degrees of change among these emotions.

Source: Levenson, Ekman, & Friesen, 1990.

discriminate among our emotions, there still may be other factors involved in the experience of emotion. One of these factors could be feedback from our faces.

The Facial-Feedback Hypothesis

You may have noticed that in the experiment we just described, the researchers induced the different emotions in an unusual way (Levensen et al., 1990): having the participants make and hold facial expressions of the desired emotion for 10 seconds. In other words, they induced the emotional state through the facial expression of the emotion. How does this work? Doesn't the emotion come *before* the facial expression? Well, maybe not entirely, according to the **facial feedback hypothesis** (McIntosh, 1996). This theory proposes that our experience of an emotion is affected by the feedback our brain gets from our facial muscles. Thus smiling can influence us to feel happy, and frowning can influence us to feel bad. There is evidence to suggest some merit to the facial feedback hypothesis. In one study, participants were asked to smell and rate a series of odors while either smiling or frowning. Consistent with the facial feedback hypothesis, they rated the smells more positively when they were smiling and less positively when they were frowning (Kraut, 1982). Based on this and other studies, it appears as if the configuration of your facial muscles does influence your mood. But why would this be true?

One possibility is that the configuration of your facial muscles affects the blood flow to your brain, which in turn affects the temperature of your brain. Certain configurations, like frowns, may change blood flow to the brain, increasing the temperature of one's brain. Other facial configurations, like smiles, may result in blood flow changes that decrease the brain's temperature. Brain temperature, in turn, may affect the release of certain neurotransmitters that affect mood. As wild as this sounds, there is some evidence to suggest that it might be true. In one study, one group of participants was asked to read a story that contained words that forced them to repeatedly hold their mouths in a position that was similar to smiling (Zajonc, Murphy, & Inglehart, 1989). The other group of participants was asked to read a story that did *not* contain such words. Both stories were of similar emotional tone. As the participants read the stories, the temperature of their foreheads was measured as a crude measure of their brain's internal temperature.

After they had read the stories, the participants were asked to rate the stories for pleasantness. As the facial feedback hypothesis would predict, those who read the story that forced them to use their facial muscles in a manner consistent with a smile rated their story more positively than the other participants rated theirs. Furthermore, when researchers looked at the participants' forehead temperatures, those who read the story that forced them to approximate a smile had lower forehead temperatures! It appears that when we smile, we hold our facial muscles in such a way as to promote blood flow that reduces our brain's temperature, which somehow improves our mood. There may after all be something to being a "hothead" or keeping a "cool head"!

The Schachter-Singer Two-Factor Theory of Emotion

So far, the theories of emotion we have looked at see emotion in physiological terms. Certainly physiological responses and facial expressions are part of an emotional experience—but what about cognition? Do our thoughts play a role in our emotions? Some theorists, including psychologists Stanley Schachter and Jerome Singer, believe that they do. Their **two-factor theory** of emotion states that emotions are a product of both physiological arousal and cognitive interpretations of this arousal. Schachter and Singer agreed with Walter Cannon that we do not have a separate pattern of physiological arousal for each emotion we experience; rather, when we experience an emotion,

---

facial feedback hypothesis   a theory that states that our emotional state is affected by the feedback our brain gets from facial muscles

two-factor theory   a theory that states that emotions result when we cognitively interpret our physiological reactions in light of the situation

we experience a diffuse and general physiological arousal. We then use the situational context to help us cognitively interpret the meaning of this arousal. This cognitive interpretation leads to the experience of an emotion. Going back to our example of the bear in the woods, when we see the bear, we become aroused and our heart begins to beat faster. Next, we interpret why we are reacting this way, given the context of the situation. Because we are faced with a potentially dangerous wild animal, our arousal is likely to be interpreted as stemming from fear. Therefore, we label our emotional experience as one of fear.

In one of their studies, Schachter and Singer (1962) gave participants an injection of epinephrine, a stimulant that causes increased heart rate, respiration, and nervousness. Some of the participants were accurately informed about what to expect from the injection. Others were not. Instead, they were told that the injection was a harmless shot that would produce no symptoms. After receiving the injection, all of the participants were asked to wait in a waiting room with another participant. But the "participants" they were sent to wait with were *confederates*, or actors playing a part in the experiment. In one condition, the confederate acted angry. He complained, stomped his feet, and eventually left the waiting room in a huff. In the other condition, the confederate acted happy. He appeared joyful, tossed paper airplanes, and generally acted a bit silly.

The dependent variable in the experiment was the mood of the participants *after* their time in the waiting room with the confederate. Schachter and Singer reasoned that the mood of the informed participants would not be influenced by the mood of the confederate. Because the informed participants would interpret their arousal as being due to the drug and not due to some emotional state, there was no reason for their mood to be influenced by the confederate. On the other hand, Schachter and Singer predicted that the mood of the uninformed participants would indeed be influenced by the mood of the confederate. Because they did not have a ready (cognitive) explanation for their arousal, the uninformed participants would look to the situation to help them interpret their reactions. If the confederate was happy, the participants would interpret their arousal as part of a positive emotional state. If the confederate was angry, then the participants would interpret their arousal as part of a negative emotional state.

The results confirmed Schacter and Singer's predictions. The mood of the informed participants was not influenced by the confederate's mood, but the confederate did influence the mood of the uninformed participants. The uninformed participants who waited with the angry confederate reported feeling angrier than did the informed participants. The uninformed participants who waited with the happy confederate reported feeling happier than did the informed participants. It appears that the uninformed participants used the situation to help them figure out their own emotions.

Although Schachter and Singer produced experimental evidence to support their theory, the two-factor theory has not stood the test of time well. Decades of research on the two-factor theory show that there is little reason to believe that emotions require physiological arousal or that emotions can come from labeling unexplained physiological arousal (Reisenzein, 1983). Despite doubts about the two-factor theory, Schachter and Singer's contribution to the study of emotion is significant. They introduced the idea that cognition plays an important role in emotion, and many theorists recognize that thoughts are part of the emotional experience.

Lazarus's Cognitive-Mediational Theory of Emotion

According to Richard Lazarus (1995), cognition is the most important part of emotion. Lazarus's **cognitive-mediational theory** of emotion states that our *cognitive appraisal* of a situation determines what emotion we will feel in the situation. Going back to the bear example, if you see a bear in the woods one day after having seen a show on TV about some hikers who were killed by a bear, you would likely feel a lot of fear! On

cognitive-mediational theory   a theory of emotion that states that our cognitive appraisal of a situation determines what emotion we will feel in the situation

the other hand, you might feel less fear on encountering the bear if your only knowledge of bears came from a TV show about a boy and his pet bear. According to cognitive-mediational theory, your appraisal of the situation determines your specific emotion. All the other components of emotions—the physiological reactions, the behavioral reactions, and so on—come after the cognitive appraisal of the situation. Your thoughts are the first and primary determinants of your emotions.

Cognitive-mediational theory explains why different people react with different emotions in the same situation. For instance, have you ever known someone who gets angry at the drop of a hat? Someone who blows up in situations that you simply blow off? The roots of their aggressiveness may be in how they see the situation. Aggressive people tend to negatively appraise situations. If someone bumps into them, they perceive it as a deliberate attack and react with anger. A calmer person will usually perceive the bump as an accident and not get mad. Sometimes the best way to control our emotions is by controlling how we perceive situations in life. We will address the role that cognition plays in emotion again later in the text when we look at aggression (Chapter 12) and psychotherapy (Chapter 16).

Although it is clear that cognitive appraisals do impact our emotional states (e.g., vanReekum, Johnstone, Etter, Wehrle, & Scherer, 2004), not everyone agrees that cognition is an essential part of emotion. Robert Zajonc has argued that we can have an emotional reaction to something that is completely independent of our thoughts. In one study, Zajonc (1980) showed English-speaking participants Japanese ideographs (the symbols of the Japanese language). These ideographs were presented to the participants either frequently or infrequently. Later, the participants were asked to rate their preference for ideographs. Despite having no knowledge about the meaning of the ideographs, the participants showed a clear preference for some of them. They preferred the ideographs that they had seen more frequently to the ones they had seen infrequently. Zajonc called this phenomenon of preferring things with which we have the most exposure the **mere exposure effect.** He reasoned that because the participants did not know the meaning of the ideographs, their emotional reactions to them could not have been influenced by cognition. Rather, their emotions were purely physiological. We will examine the mere exposure effect again in Chapter 12 when we look at its implications for romantic attraction.

mere exposure effect   the idea that the more one is exposed to something, the more they grow to like it

Communicating Emotions: Culture, Gender, and Facial Expressions

Imagine that you have traveled to a place where you do not speak the local language at all. You do not recognize any of the words being spoken all around you. In fact, you can't even tell how many words are being spoken in each sentence, because they all seem to run together as the people speak. You are all alone in this place, and you have to somehow survive. How will you communicate with these people? Perhaps you will try to use pantomime to communicate with someone, but how will you choose *which* person? How will you tell if a particular person is likely to react kindly to your attempts at communication? One way would be to read the emotional expression on the person's face. Does she look happy? Does he look angry? This could be a crucial source of information for you. But what about the cultural differences in this situation? Can we read the emotional expressions of someone from an unfamiliar culture? This is another question psychologists have tried to answer.

Before you read any further, look at the pictures in Figure 8.15. Can you identify the emotions that these people are feeling? These pictures represent the facial expressions of what psychologists call **basic emotions.** Basic emotions are defined as emotions that all humans are thought to have, regardless of cultural background. The idea

basic emotion   a proposed set of innate emotions that are common to all humans and from which other higher-order emotions may stem

behind basic emotions is that the capacity for these emotions is genetically programmed in us as a result of evolution. Many psychologists believe that anger, happiness, fear, and sadness are basic emotions, but there is disagreement about what other emotions might be basic. Some add disgust, shame, interest, surprise, and anxiety to the list (Turner & Ortony, 1992). But others do not. Furthermore, some believe that basic emotions can blend together to give us more complex emotions like guilt, pride, and disappointment (Plutchik, 1984).

Paul Ekman (1973) showed pictures like these to people from Argentina, Brazil, Chile, Japan, and the United States, and then he asked participants to identify the emotions being expressed. He found that people were pretty much able to identify the emotions regardless of their culture, although some emotions appeared to be more universal than others. Happiness appeared to be the easiest emotion to identify. People from the different cultures disagreed the most when identifying fear and anger. Other studies have shown that fear and surprise are also easily confused, but curiously women are better at discriminating between these emotions. This may be due to women's concern for relating to others and an increased tendency for women to look at other people's faces (McAndrew, 1986).

Does the fact that some emotions translate well across cultures guarantee that these emotions are basic emotions? Perhaps not. Some cultures list "basic" emotions that may be recognizable to people from other cultures but would not be considered by

Figure 8.15 **Can You Identify These Emotions?**

Source: Ekman & Friesen, 1984.

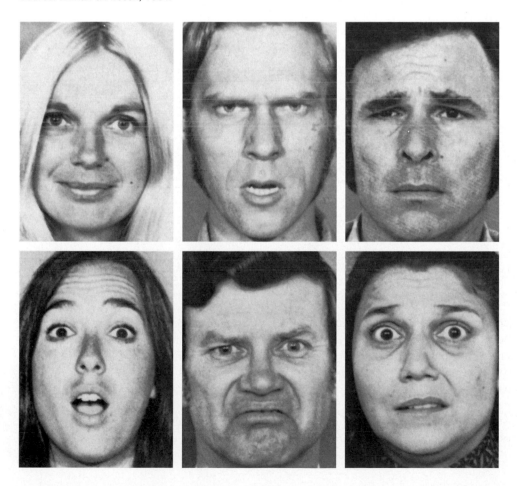

those people to be basic emotions in their culture. Hindus list *peace, wonder, amusement,* and *heroism* as basic emotions (Hejmadi, Davidson, & Rozin, 2000). Americans may be able to feel these emotions and recognize them in others, but they may not be what we would consider to be basic emotions. For reasons like these, some people have begun to question whether basic emotions truly exist (Ortony & Turner, 1990).

Whether or not we humans have basic emotions is an open question. An even more open question is: if we do have basic emotions, what are they? Regardless of whether basic emotions exist, emotions are powerful tools of communication. A smile can signal friendliness to many people—regardless of background or culture.

Let's Review!

In this section, we defined emotion and discussed some theories of emotion. We also looked at how humans tend to show emotions through facial expressions. For a quick check of your understanding, answer these questions.

1. Which of the following is not typically thought of as a basic emotion?
   a. fear
   c. pride
   b. sadness
   d. happiness

2. Derrick and Monique each went out on blind dates. Derrick took his date to dinner. Monique took her date to a football game. According to the two-factor theory of emotion, who is most likely to go out on a second date with their partner?
   a. Derrick
   b. Monique
   c. Monique and Derrick are equally likely to go out on a second date.

   d. Two-factor theory makes no predictions about this situation.

3. Mohammed and Betty are each stuck in a traffic jam. Mohammed remains calm, but Betty begins to get very angry. Which theory of emotion best explains Mohammed's and Betty's different emotions in this situation?
   a. cognitive-mediational theory
   b. two-factor theory
   c. facial feedback theory
   d. James-Lange theory

ANSWERS

1. c; 2. b; 3. a

Are You Getting the Big Picture?

Motivation and emotion are intertwined processes. Both have the power to direct our behavior, and both play an important role in our survival. Motivation usually occurs in response to some specific, internal state, like the need for energy or water. Emotions, on the other hand, are often sparked by external stimuli. We may feel happy or sad in response to a wide range of situations. Both motivation and emotion are influenced by physiological states. Hunger and thirst are governed by physiological feedback from various parts of the body. As part of the limbic system, the hypothalamus plays a crucial role in regulating motivations like these.

Physiological reactions are also an important part of emotions. Few

STUDYING THE **CHAPTER**

theorists go so far as to equate emotions with physiological reactions, but all theories of emotion recognize that physiological reactions are an essential component of an emotional state. This is not to imply that motivation and emotion are purely physiological processes. Cognition plays a significant role in both motivation and emotion. As we saw in Marya's case, sometimes our thoughts can change the course of our motivation. Sometimes, we eat, drink, and take drugs more for psychological reasons than physiological. Cognition also plays a crucial role in emotional states. How we appraise a situation can actually determine our emotional reaction to the situation.

Social factors also play a role in motivation and emotion. Some motives, like the need for love, are essentially social motives that tend to drive us toward other people. Even primary drives like hunger and thirst are influenced by social factors. Cultural values we all place on food affect our motivation to eat or not to eat. Marya's case is a dramatic example of how social pressure can impact motivation. Like Marya, many young women are motivated toward an unattainable standard of beauty that is culturally defined. Others battle obesity in a culture where food is often associated with celebrations and emotional states more than with meeting our physiological needs.

Emotions can be evoked by social situations, and they can also influence our social interactions. In social interactions, we read others' facial expressions for their emotional states, and we use this information to guide our own behavior. Even when we do not share a common culture or language, we can often tell whether another person is happy, sad, or angry. Perhaps facial expression of emotion is as close to a universal language as it gets.

In a sense, motivation and emotion are somewhat primal forces that allow us to function in a variety of situations. Although both are influenced by social factors, cognition, and past experience, it is the physiological aspects of motivation and emotion that seem to unite all people in a form of common experience. A smile indicates a positive emotional state in all parts of the world. When we see someone smiling, we can empathize with what they are feeling. Similarly, hunger is painful no matter who you are. Regardless of our culture or language, we all experience basic motivations that direct our behavior and emotions that punctuate our lives.

The study of motivation and emotion also applies to the world of work. Understanding our motives and emotions is an important part of some professions. Psychotherapists must understand their clients' feelings and know how to motivate them to change their lives. Physicians need to understand what motivates patients to engage in healthy and unhealthy behaviors. Teachers strive to find ways to motivate their students to succeed academically. And successful managers must motivate employees to perform their jobs well.

Key Terms

motive (344)

bulimia nervosa (345)

anorexia nervosa (345)

instinct (346)

drive-reduction theory (347)

drive (347)

primary drive (347)

homeostasis (347)

negative feedback loop (347)

secondary drive (348)

sensation seeker (350)

incentive (351)

extrinsic motivation (352)

intrinsic motivation (352)

overjustification effect (352)

hierarchy of needs (353)

glucose (357)

glycogen (357)

cholecystokinin (CCK) (357)

leptin (358)

lateral hypothalamus (358)

neuropeptide Y (358)

ventromedial hypothalamus
    (VMH) (358)

set point (359)

obese (360)

intracellular fluid (368)

extracellular fluid (368)

opponent-process theory (370)

withdrawal (370)

physical dependence (370)

tolerance (371)

emotion (373)

affective component of emotion (373)

James-Lange theory (373)

Cannon-Bard theory (375)

facial feedback hypothesis (376)

two-factor theory (376)

cognitive-mediational theory (377)

mere exposure effect (378)

basic emotion (379)

Test Yourself!

Concept Check

Test your knowledge of the chapter concepts by completing each of the following sentences with the correct term. For a more comprehensive review, visit the book Web site (http://psychology.wadsworth.com/pastorino1e/) for online quizzes, flashcards, crosswords, and Internet links.

_____ **1.** The idea that emotions are patterns of physiological responses in the body.

_____ **2.** The form of fuel that we store in our body.

_____ **3.** Plays a role in regulating thirst.

_____ **4.** Considered to be a basic emotion.

_____ **5.** Money would be an example of this.

_____ **6.** Believed that motives were innate instincts.

_____ **7.** This best explains your motivation to put on a coat when you are cold.

_____ **8.** A hormone released by the small intestines.

_____ **9.** One of Maslow's needs.

_____ **10.** Not considered to be a basic emotion.

_____ **11.** Criticized the idea that emotions are merely physiological reactions.

_____ **12.** The form of fuel that our body burns for energy.

_____ **13.** An eating disorder involving bingeing and purging of food.

A. safety

B. William James

C. glucose

D. cholecystokinin

E. bulimia nervosa

F. extrinsic motivation

G. intracellular fluid levels

H. the James-Lange Theory

I. negative feedback loop

J. happiness

K. glycogen

L. guilt

M. Walter Cannon

Answers

1.H; 2.K; 3.G; 4.J; 5.F; 6.B; 7.I; 8.D; 9.A; 10.L; 11.M; 12.C; 13.E

Critical Thinking About the Chapter

1. Compare and contrast instinct theories, drive reduction theories, and incentive theories of motivation.

2. Assume that you are a scientist who is trying to develop a new appetite suppressant pill for weight loss. Given your understanding of hunger, what kind of an effect would you want your pill to have on a person's body?

3. What would life be like if humans did not have the capacity for emotion?

4. How are emotion and motivation alike? How are they different?

5. Sabina was cut off in traffic on the way home from work—nearly causing her to have a serious accident. Immediately on arriving home, Sabina finds that her husband has left a dirty towel on the bathroom floor, something Sabina dislikes. What predictions would Schacter and Singer make about Sabina's emotional reaction to finding the dirty towel? Explain.

Applying Psychology. Pretend that you are in charge of developing a campaign to prevent eating disorders in teenage girls. What type of campaign would you develop?

Critical Thinking for Integration

1. How can the theory of natural selection explain destructive behaviors like eating disorders, drug abuse, and self-injury?

2. Given your understanding of physiology, what impact do you think emotion has on our health?

3. Design an experiment to test the validity of the over-justification effect.

4. What role do you think learning plays in drug abuse? Explain.

5. How might theories of motivation and emotion help explain romantic attraction?

Chapter Study Resources

Suggested Readings

1. Slater, L. (2004). *Opening Skinner's box.* New York: Norton.
   Slater discusses some of the most important psychological experiments of the 20th century, including a chapter on Bruce Alexander's addiction research.

2. Pert, C. B. (1997). *Why you feel the way you feel: Molecules of emotion.* New York: Scribner.
   Pert discusses the biological underpinnings of emotion with a special emphasis on biochemicals and emotion.

3. Brand-Miller, J., Wolever, T. M. S., Colagiuri, S., & Foster-Powell, K. (1999). *The glucose revolution.* New York: Marlowe.
   A scientifically based diet book that discusses the glycemic index, a measure of how quickly certain foods can increase blood sugar levels. The message of this book is that all carbohydrates are not created equal.

4. For additional readings, explore InfoTrac College Edition, your online library of archived journal articles and periodicals. Go to http://www.infotrac-college.com/wadsworth and enter the passcode from the card that came with your book. For this chapter, search using these keywords:

   diet

   leptin

   bulimia

   anorexia

   facial feedback

Web Links for Further Study

Additional information on chapter concepts can be found at these Web sites:

1. A Web site for the general public that includes information on how to increase the level of motivation in your personal life.
   http://www.motivation123.com/

2. This Web site contains an article on motivation in the workplace that covers some of the pertinent theories of how managers can motivate employees.
   http://www.accel-team.com/motivation/

3. The National Eating Disorders Association site contains all kinds of valuable information on bulimia nervosa and anorexia nervosa.
   www.nationaleatingdisorders.org/

4. This site has an interactive feature that allows you to select specific facial features and create a face that you feel indicates a particular emotional state.
   http://www.dushkin.com/connectext/psy/ch10/facex.mhtml

Student Study Guide

To help organize your learning, work through Chapter 8 of the *What Is Psychology? Student Study Guide.* The study guide includes learning objectives, a chapter summary, fill-in review, key terms, a practice test, and activities.

Psychology Now™

PsychologyNow is a Web-based, personalized study system that provides you with a pretest and a posttest for each chapter, quizzes you by chapter, and provides a personalized study plan, pointing you to elements in the text or in individual learning modules that will help you to achieve 80% mastery. Learning modules include: 6a. Motivation, 6b. Emotion, 6c. Coping with Emotion.

PsychNow CD-ROM, Version 2.0

Go to the PsychNow CD-ROM for further study of the concepts in this chapter. The CD-ROM includes learning modules with videos, animations, and quizzes, as well as simulations of psychological phenomena. Each module follows a consistent Explore, Lesson, and Apply structure that allows you to experience the concept or principle, learn more about it, and then apply it. You and your friends can participate in a team-based Quiz Game that makes learning fun. Learning modules include: 6a. Motivation; 6b. Emotion; 6c. Coping with Emotion.

Motivation and Emotion: What Guides Our Behavior

In psychological terms, a motive is our tendency to desire and seek out positive incentives and rewards and to avoid negative outcomes.

THEORIES ABOUT MOTIVATION

• The early American psychologist William James believed that motives are, for the most part, genetically programmed instincts.

• According to the drive-reduction theory, motivation stems from needs. Primary drives maintain homeostasis, and secondary motives are learned.

• Arousal theories of motivation suggest that each of us has a level of psychological arousal at which we operate best—an optimal level of arousal.

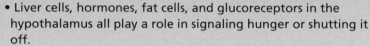

Self-actualization needs: to find self-fulfillment and realize one's potential

Aesthetic needs: symmetry, order, and beauty

Cognitive needs: to know, understand, and explore

Esteem needs: to achieve, be competent, and gain approval and recognition

Belongingness and love needs: to affiliate with others, be accepted, and belong

Safety needs: to feel secure and safe, out of danger

Physiological needs: hunger, thirst, and so forth

• According to incentive theories of motivation, motivation is directed at attaining certain incentives. Extrinsic motivation comes from outside of us, whereas intrinsic motivation comes from within.

• The psychologist Abraham Maslow proposed a hierarchy of needs, best thought of as a pyramid, with basic physiological needs at the base, and self-fulfillment and self-actualization at the top.

HUNGER AND THIRST

• Receptors in the stomach monitor the intake of food and contractions of the stomach, and signal the brain when to make us hungry or to shut off hunger.

• Liver cells, hormones, fat cells, and glucoreceptors in the hypothalamus all play a role in signaling hunger or shutting it off.

• External cues such as advertisements and the sight or smell of delicious food can also trigger hunger.

• Obesity can be caused by biological factors such as a slow metabolism, as well a number of behavioral factors, including a poor diet, excessive food intake, and emotional eating.

• Anorexia nervosa is a serious eating disorder that involves extreme reduction in caloric intake and/or excessive exercise that leads to a drastic weight loss.

• Bulimia nervosa involves bingeing on food followed by purging or drastic reduction in caloric intake to rid the body of the extra calories.

• The body uses two mechanisms to regulate and signal thirst: a drop in intracellular fluid pressure, and a drop in extracellular fluid pressure (which leads to drop in blood pressure).

DESTRUCTIVE MOTIVATION

• Many factors correlate with substance abuse: exposure to drugs, low self-esteem, boredom, and depression.

• Opponent-process theory of motivation holds that the body counteracts the effects of a drug with an opposite physiological reaction, resulting in withdrawal symptoms, growing tolerance for the drug, and physical dependence.

• Suicide is the ultimate form of self-destructive behavior and is an abnormal behavior that runs counter to our strong survival instinct.

EMOTION

• Components of emotion include physiological reactions, behavioral reactions, facial expressions, cognition, and affective response.

• The James-Lange theory of emotion proposes that emotion can be understood as a physiological response to some stimulus.

• The Cannon-Bard theory of emotion holds that emotion is the brain responding to some stimulus or situation, then prompting an emotional reaction.

• In the facial feedback hypothesis, our experience of an emotion is affected by the feedback our brain receives from the muscles in our faces. Thus smiling can influence us to feel happy, and frowning can influence us to feel bad.

• Schachter-Singer's two-factor theory of emotion states that emotions are a product of both physiological arousal and cognitive interpretations of this arousal.

• Cognitive meditational theory states that our cognitive appraisal of a situation determines what emotion we well feel in the situation, thus different people react with different emotions in the same situation.

• Basic emotions include happiness, sadness, anger, and fear, and have been found to be present across cultures.

When I look back on my childhood
I wonder how I survived at all.

FROM FRANK MCCOURT, *ANGELA'S ASHES: A MEMOIR.*

(New York: Scribner, 1996, p. 11)

© Andy Cox / Getty Images

How Do Children Grow, Change, and Develop?

CHAPTER PREVIEW

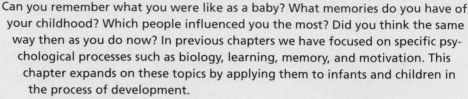

What Is Childhood All About?

Can you remember what you were like as a baby? What memories do you have of your childhood? Which people influenced you the most? Did you think the same way then as you do now? In previous chapters we have focused on specific psychological processes such as biology, learning, memory, and motivation. This chapter expands on these topics by applying them to infants and children in the process of development.

Development consists of changes in behavior and abilities. In this chapter, we will see that human development is complicated. Physical growth is occurring along with emotional, social, and mental (or cognitive) development. At the same time, social forces (such as people around us) and our environment also impact these processes. Our chapter case study powerfully illustrates these mutually influential forces. It is the story of a boy's growth and development in childhood. As you read about Frankie McCourt, think about your own childhood. How was your development similar to and different from Frankie's?

Frank McCourt was the firstborn child of recent Irish immigrants in Brooklyn, New York, during the Great Depression of the 1930s. During Frankie's childhood, his father, Malachy, is continually in the process of finding a job. When his father does find work, the family may be happy and may enjoy at least one meal a day. But more often than not, Frankie's father spends his wages on alcohol. His mother, Angela, makes do with what little they have, and poverty is a constant presence in Frankie's life.

At the age of 4 in Frankie's environment, the babies wear rags for diapers and are fed sugar water in their bottles rather than milk or formula. A meal, when available, might be stale bread soaked in sour milk. Frankie is increasingly responsible for taking care of his younger siblings: his brother Malachy, the twins, Eugene and Oliver, and his baby sister, Margaret. On one occasion, he steals a bunch of bananas from the local grocer so that his twin brothers will stop crying with hunger. When his sister dies, Frankie struggles to understand the concept of death. His father copes by drinking, while his mother gives in to depression. Living conditions for the family worsen. Malachy and Angela decide to return to their homeland, searching for a new start with the help of Angela's family.

In Ireland, Frankie and his brother are initially puzzled by their new environment. They bombard their parents with questions, trying to make sense of the new creatures that they have never seen before (cows, goats, and sheep), and trying to understand the differences in dialect (the word "boxty" to refer to potato pancakes). They must modify their everyday behaviors, learning to use a chamber pot and an outhouse to go to the bathroom. Conditions in Ireland are no better than in Brooklyn, and in some cases they prove even more distressing.

The family of six moves into a furnished one-room house and goes "on the dole," the equivalent of welfare in the United States. They frequently rely on charity for food and clothing. When money or charity is not available, the family falls back on their own initiative and creativity. For example, Frankie and his brothers pick small bits of coal off the road so the family can light a fire to lessen the bone-chilling cold. When the dole money comes in, Frankie's father often spends it drinking, furthering the destitution of his family. Within a year of arriving in Ireland, the 2-year-old twin boys get sick and die.

The family moves to another slum house that has two rooms on a top floor and two on the bottom, and where one lavatory is shared by six households. The McCourt family lives at the end of the lane, near the lavatory. When it rains, the

development changes in behavior and/or abilities

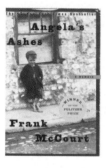

"It was, of course, a miserable childhood: the happy childhood is hardly worth your while."

(McCourt, 1996 p. 11)

Angela's Ashes summary: Summarized with permission of Scribner, an imprint of Simon & Schuster Adult Publishing Group, from *Angela's Ashes* by Frank McCourt. Copyright © 1996 by Frank McCourt.

bottom floor of the house floods with water and the overflow of sewage from the lavatory. The family adapts by living in the upstairs rooms during the winter and going downstairs in the spring when the walls are dry. The family refers to the upstairs rooms as Italy and the bottom floor as Ireland with the River Shannon.

Despite the McCourts' ability to use humor to lighten the burden of their poverty, the winters continue to bring hardship to the family. Frankie accompanies his mother to a local charity to get a coupon for food for a Christmas dinner. The coupon gets them a pig's head from the local butcher. Frankie's peers laugh at him as he carries the pig's head home for Christmas dinner. School also brings embarrassment and ridicule; his peers and teachers call him the "stupid Yank." The teachers hit Frankie for being late, for talking, or for giving a wrong answer. Crying from the punishment brings on more ridicule and teasing from the other boys.

Soon two more sons are added to the family. When the first is born, Frankie's father tells him that the Angel on the seventh step brought baby Michael. Frankie now gets up at night and confides in the Angel on the seventh step, talking to it about school, the events around him that he cannot understand, and his problems—issues he feels he cannot discuss with his parents for fear of getting hit over the head. Gradually, Frankie's social networks widen. He establishes friendships with other boys in the neighborhood. His mother sends him to dance lessons, but after a few, Frankie skips them and sneaks into the local cinema instead. Frankie takes on his first job when he is 9 years old, to help his family survive. However, within a year, Frankie contracts typhoid fever.

Frankie stays at the Fever Hospital for fourteen weeks, where he receives the best physical care of his life. He sleeps on clean sheets, eats three meals a day, and has the use of his own bathroom. But he is socially isolated. His mother can visit him 1 day a week, but interacting with the other children on the ward is prohibited. Frankie and Patricia, a young girl with diptheria, disobey this rule, whispering stories and poems to each other across the walls. However, their communications are soon discovered, and he is moved to a ward with no other children. He is no longer allowed visitors and later learns that Patricia has died. Frankie is sure he is to blame because he broke the rules. Books and his imagination become Frankie's only companions.

Frankie survives what most children then did not. He returns home and to school, physically weak from the fever but strong in spirit. Frankie reconnects with his family and enjoys the special time he spends with his father in the morning. At age 11, he conceptualizes his father as similar to the Holy Trinity, with three people in him: ". . . the one in the morning with the paper, the one at night with the stories and the prayers, and then the one who does the bad thing and comes home with the smell of whiskey and wants us to die for Ireland" (p. 210).

During Frankie's teenage years, his father leaves Ireland to join the English military as World War II approaches. Frankie spends most of his time working to help his now working mother and brothers survive. At the same time, Frankie saves as much money as he can to fulfill his dream of returning to America. At 19, Frankie's dream is realized. Before he leaves, he wanders the streets of Limerick trying to memorize all the places and people, in case he never comes back. He spends time with his mother and brothers by the fire, holding back tears of sorrow. Standing on the deck of the Irish Oak, bound for New York, Frank McCourt has a chance at a new beginning.

Despite a childhood blighted by poverty, death, and disease, Frank McCourt emerges as an adaptable young man capable of expressing his experiences with humor and love. His memoir, entitled *Angela's Ashes* (1996) to honor his mother's continued fight against the fires of poverty and suffering, won him the National Book Critic's Circle Award, a Pulitzer Prize, and other awards. After reading his story, you may feel that Frankie's experiences are far removed from those of children today. Yet his experience growing up in an immigrant ghetto has much in common with children growing up today in the South Bronx in New York or a child born and raised in poverty in Somalia. You may or may not see any similarity between your childhood and young Frankie's. We believe, however, that his experiences are relevant to understanding the nature of development. As we saw with Frankie, a multitude of forces help or hinder our development: poverty and hunger, the love or ridicule of others, our ability to overcome illness, just to name a few. Frankie's experiences also shed light on the way children process information and distinguish right from wrong. And his behavior shows how he believed he should behave based on his gender. Perhaps all of these factors contributed to Frankie's ability to look at life with humor and humility, and motivated him to learn more about the world through books and literature, and ultimately to move back to America for a better life.

As we will see, the material in this chapter can be of practical value to you, especially when you interact with infants and children. After you have completed this chapter, you should have a better understanding of the physical, mental, and social developments of infants and children. We hope this understanding will lead to more productive and enjoyable interactions with them.

≫ **LEARNING** < < < < < < < <
≫ **OBJECTIVE**
≫ Explain the nature–nurture issue,
≫ and describe the research designs
≫ that psychologists use to isolate these
≫ influences and to measure age-
≫ related changes in development.
≫

Why Study Development?

Why do psychologists study development? Psychologists study development in order to understand the changes that humans experience from conception to the end of life. Because this period covers such a large time span, developmental psychologists typically further specialize by limiting their investigations to a particular age group such as infancy, childhood, adolescence, or adulthood. Within any one of these age stages, psychologists may focus on different aspects of development: physical, mental, social, or personality development. One developmental psychologist may study how language develops in infants while another may research how peer pressure affects drug use in adolescents.

Recall from Chapter 1 that psychology seeks to describe, predict, and explain behavior. If psychologists can accomplish these goals, then we can promote healthy development and prevent or alter maladaptive patterns of development. For example, if we can explain how children think, we can then create appropriate educational environments, thus maximizing each child's potential. Understanding the dynamics of peer pressure during adolescence may suggest strategies to reduce drug use, delinquency, and teenage pregnancy. Stories like Frankie's illustrate the importance of understanding more fully how poverty and parental alcoholism affect developing children. Knowing about developmental processes, therefore, has numerous real-world applications.

The Nature–Nurture Issue: Biology and Culture

Although psychologists' ultimate goal is to explain developmental changes, this by no means is easy to do. Think about all the variables that can potentially influence how a person grows and changes. What factors may have played a role in Frankie's development? In addition to a unique biological foundation (our genetics), every individual is also influenced by a multitude of environments: family, school, friends, neighborhoods, religion, and culture. The potential contribution of these factors to a child's development has become a central issue to developmental psychologists. Referred to as the **nature–nurture controversy**, psychologists are interested in how much one's biology, or nature, contributes to a person's development versus how much one's environment and culture, or nurture, impacts this process. Think about the members of your family. Sisters and brothers are endowed with a similar gene pool and raised in a similar environment, yet they often turn out quite differently. How can psychologists explain this difference?

nature–nurture controversy the degree to which biology (nature) or the environment (nurture) contributes to one's development

Nature refers to your heredity, the genetic transmission of information from your parents. Heredity influences such traits as eye color and hair color. It influences your body size and athletic ability. Today, psychologists recognize that genetics influence almost every aspect of development, from personality and gender-role development to cognitive processes such as language development and intelligence (Bouchard, 2004; Gottlieb, Wahlsten, & Lickliter, 1998; Rose, 1995). We explained the dynamics of heredity and how it operates in Chapter 2. *Nurture* is the total effect of all the external environmental events that influence your development. It includes your family, friends, how others perceive and behave toward you, events that happen to you, television programs that you watch, music that you listen to, the customs and rituals of your ethnic background, your culture, your schooling, and so on.

Today, psychologists recognize that it is not really a case of nature *or* nurture. Rather, it is the *interaction* of these two forces that play a role in behavior. For example, depression or anxiety may have a genetic component, but this tendency may not be expressed unless your circumstances or environment are such that your weakness is tested. On the nature side, scientists have selectively bred animals and plants to investigate the role genetics plays in development. More recently, scientists have mapped the human genetic code and cloned organisms including early-stage human embryos (Cibelli, Lanza, & West, 2002). Such activities have raised concerns that we may be able to directly alter the role genetics plays in human development (Wilmut, Schnieke, McWhir, Kind, & Campbell, 1997). On the nurture side, psychologists investigate how environments can be structured to enhance each person's development. As we will see, this focus on environment has led to an abundance of research into issues ranging from the importance of a positive prenatal environment to ways to reduce cognitive decline in the elderly.

Both nature and nurture influence every aspect of development.

© Tom Stewart/Corbis

Developmental Research Designs: Isolating Nature, Nurture, and Changes Over Time

How are the developmental forces of nature and nurture studied? Psychologists use a variety of developmental research techniques to attempt to isolate nature from nurture influences on human development. Some of the more important techniques include twin studies, adoption studies, and kinship studies (Segal, 1993). These studies are correlational, so keep in mind that cause-and-effect conclusions cannot be made.

Twin Studies

We cannot ethically selectively breed or clone humans, so genetic studies of humans rely on a natural population of genetically similar individuals: twins. Identical (*monozygotic*) twins develop from the same fertilized egg and as such are genetically the same. They are "natural" clones. In twin studies, researchers look at whether identical twins are more similar in behavior when compared to nonidentical (fraternal or *dizygotic*) twins. These similarities may indicate which behaviors are primarily influenced by heredity. Such studies suggest that intelligence, some mental disorders, and certain complex behaviors such as personality, abilities, and interests reflect genetic influences (Loehlin & Nichols, 1976; Rose, 1995). For example, if one identical twin has schizophrenia, the other twin has about a 46% chance of also having this disorder. This probability is far higher than the 2% incidence rate of schizophrenia in the general population (National Institute on Mental Health Genetics Workgroup, 1998). But schizophrenia doesn't always occur in both identical twins, so it isn't purely genetic. Environmental or situational factors also play a role. Identical twins often share the same environment and are treated more similarly than nonidentical twins.

Identical twins are not always reared in the same environment, however. Researchers at the University of Minnesota have studied identical twins who were separated sometime after birth. In this study, the twins were located and reunited. They then completed numerous tests and inventories of personality, cognitive abilities, family and social relationships, medical histories, and interests. These assessments revealed that the identical twins were still remarkably similar even when they were raised in very different environments (Bouchard, Lykken, McGrue, Segal, & Tellegen, 1990; Lykken, McGue, Tellegen, & Bouchard, 1992). Separated twins tended to show similar facial gestures and hand movements. If one twin had a particular talent for art, music, or poetry, the other twin was likely to share the same ability. One of the more famous separated pairs is the "Jim twins." James Lewis and James Springer had both married and later divorced women named Linda. Both of their second wives were named Betty. Both had named their sons James Allan. Both drove Chevrolets and chain-smoked Salem cigarettes. Each worked as a sheriff's deputy and listed stock-car racing, carpentry, and mechanical drawing as interests and hobbies. Most amazing though, is that both Jims had built circular white benches around the trees in their yards (Holden, 1980).

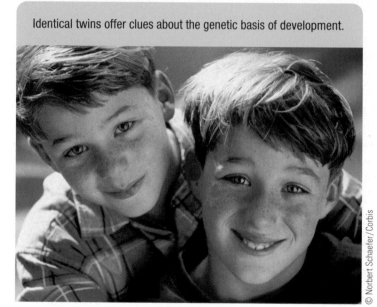

Identical twins offer clues about the genetic basis of development.

© Norbert Schaefer/Corbis

We must be cautious, however, when interpreting these results. Adoption agencies typically place separated twins in similar environments, which means that these shared characteristics could still be due to the environment. A twin study asks participants hundreds of questions. In asking so many questions, there is the likelihood of getting "matches" just by coincidence or chance. You are just as likely to share similarities with someone who is not related to you. For example, one study found that pairs of unrelated students were almost as similar to twins when compared on job histories, political beliefs, musical tastes, favorite foods, and so on (Wyatt, Posey, Welker, & Seamonds, 1984). Given that people of the same age also share the same historical and cultural backgrounds, the similarities between the Jim twins are not without some environmental influences. Overall, though, twin studies reinforce the profound effect of genetics on development.

Adoption Studies

Adoption studies are another way scientists can explore the relative contributions of nature and nurture to development. In these studies, researchers compare the behavior and traits of adopted individuals to their biological parents and to their adoptive parents. Suppose, for example, that the child of two concert pianists is adopted. The adopted parents show no interest or aptitude for music. Will the child's musical ability be more like the biological parents, or more like the adoptive parents? It is assumed that if the adopted child is more similar to his or her biological parents for a given behavior, then nature plays a larger role in determining that trait. In contrast, if the child is more similar to the adoptive parents on a particular characteristic, then nurture, or the environment, must play a larger role in that aspect of development.

Studies suggest that individuals who grow up in the same home are not particularly similar in terms of their personality, whether they are adopted or not (Rowe, 1990). However, adopted children do tend to share similar values and beliefs with their adoptive parents. Adopted children also tend to score higher than their biological parents on intelligence tests given a positive family environment (Benson, Sharma, &

Roehlkepartain, 1994). Again, the influences of nature and nurture seem to interact in a complex fashion.

Kinship Studies

The relative roles of nature and nurture in development are also studied in the patterns of behaviors within families from generation to generation, in what are called kinship studies. For example, a researcher may investigate how many individuals from one family—from children to parents to grandparents to great-grandparents—had a learning disability. If genetically more similar family members (such as siblings) share certain characteristics when compared to genetically less similar family members (such as first cousins), then a possible role of genetics is inferred. Data from kinship studies suggest a genetic role for schizophrenia and manic-depressive disorder (Gottesman, 1991; Winokur, Coryell, Keller, Endicott, & Leon, 1995). However, close family members also are more likely to come from shared environments, so these results are not clear-cut.

Studying Development Over Time

Developmental psychologists do not focus solely on the nature–nurture issue. They also are interested in when and in what manner we develop. To do this, researchers must rely on other experimental methods, which include cross-sectional designs, longitudinal designs, and cross-sequential designs.

Cross-sectional designs study groups of people of different ages on some aspect of development at one point in time. For example, a researcher who is interested in cognitive changes randomly selects three age groups: 10-year-olds, 20-year-olds, and 30-year-olds. All participants are given the same memory test and are treated identically during the research investigation. The advantages of such a design are that it is quick and easy to do at relatively little cost. However, the cross-sectional design also has disadvantages.

Suppose that the researcher finds that the 30-year-olds perform significantly more poorly than the other two age groups. Can we conclude that age is the reason for this finding? Possibly, but other confounding, or uncontrolled, variables may explain the difference in scores. Can you think of any? The younger participants are more likely to be enrolled in a learning institution, and therefore exercising their memory more. Or perhaps the memory tests were timed. Given the natural increase in reaction time as we age, maybe the difference in performance reflects a change in reaction time. A third possibility is that the difference in memory performance is due to different historical influences that each age group has experienced. The 30-year-old group probably was exposed to less technology when they were young compared to the other two age groups.

These generational differences, or what is referred to as **cohort effects,** are the main disadvantage of a cross-sectional design. Every *cohort*, or group of people of relatively the same age, experiences different historical, economic, and political events in their lives. The McCourts experienced the Great Depression of the 1930s and World War II. These historical events are unique to their generation and affected their development. Reflect on historical events that are unique to your age group. They may include the technology boom, the AIDS epidemic, civil unrest, and the September 11 terrorist attacks. When groups of different ages are measured only once, it is impossible to control for such influences, and therefore these cohort differences may account for the research findings. For this reason, some researchers study development using longitudinal designs.

A **longitudinal design** follows one cohort group over a longer period of time and measures the group several times on some aspect of development. Using our previous example, a longitudinal design would randomly select a group of 10-year-olds and measure their memory several times over a period of 10 or 20 years. Because they are all from the same cohort, using this design minimizes the influence of cohort effects.

cross-sectional design a research design in which several age groups are tested at one time on a dependent variable

cohort effect generational differences in historic, economic, or political events among age groups that may cause a difference in the dependent variable rather than their age

 Application

longitudinal design a research design that follows one age group over a long period of time to assess changes in development

cross-sequential design a research design in which different age groups are followed over a short period of time to assess developmental changes

However, longitudinal designs also have disadvantages. They are much more costly and time-consuming, and participants may drop out over the course of the study. For this reason, psychologists sometimes use cross-sequential designs.

A **cross-sequential design** combines features from the cross-sectional and longitudinal designs. In this design, participants from different age groups are measured on some aspect of development over a shorter period of time. For example, a researcher may randomly select a group of 10-year-olds, 15-year-olds, and 20-year-olds, and test their memory several times over the course of a 2- or a 5-year period. Although the groups represent different cohorts, repeating measurements over time allows for a more detailed picture of changes in memory to emerge. Also, given that the study is not overly long, it is less costly and time-consuming, and fewer participants are likely to drop out of the study. Figure 9.1 summarizes the three different designs.

As you can see, psychologists have devised numerous ways to investigate changes across the life span and to assess the relative roles of nature and nurture in producing these changes. Perhaps nowhere are these changes more dramatic than during the prenatal stage—our next topic of discussion.

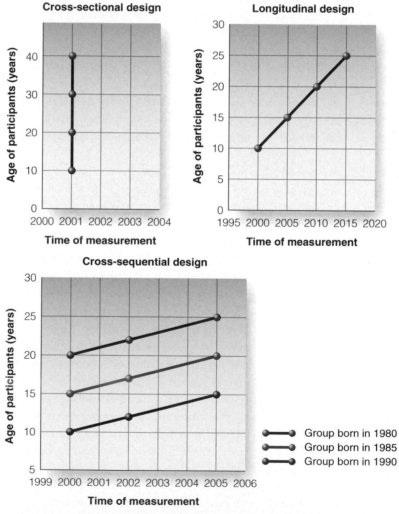

Figure 9.1 **Developmental Research Designs**

In a cross-sectional study, participants of different ages are measured at one point in time. In a longitudinal design, same-aged participants are measured at several different times. In a cross-sequential study, participants of different ages are measured at several different times.

Let's Review!

In this section we outlined the nature–nurture issue and described the research methods psychologists use to study development. As a quick check of your understanding, answer these questions.

1. A researcher studies a group of 9-year-olds for 10 years to measure changes in self-esteem. This is an example of what type of developmental design?

   a. cross-sectional   c. longitudinal

   b. cross-sequential   d. latitudinal

2. Studying identical twins to assess the degree to which they are similar focuses on the _____ side of a key developmental issue.

   a. nature   c. development

   b. nurture   d. learning

3. Current thinking on the nature–nurture issue suggests that:

   a. nature is more important than nurture in determining development.

   b. nurture is more important than nature in determining development.

   c. neither nature nor nurture is important in determining development.

   d. nature and nurture interact in determining development.

ANSWERS

1. c; 2. a; 3. d

Prenatal Development: Conception to Birth > > > > > > > > > > > > > > >

LEARNING OBJECTIVE

Identify and describe the three stages of prenatal development—germinal, embryonic, and fetal—and explain the importance of a positive prenatal environment.

What happens during prenatal development? From the outside, all we see is a woman with a swollen belly who walks with a waddle. We may even have the opportunity to see or feel movement occurring inside her belly. Any woman who has been pregnant has experienced having some people want to touch her stomach or to treat her more delicately because of her "condition." Both tendencies speak to our fascination with the developments going on inside.

As we saw in Chapter 2, all the genetic material for development is inherited from your biological parents at the time of conception (see p. 89). The male sperm cell, containing 23 single chromosomes, fertilizes the female ova, also containing 23 single chromosomes, to create a fertilized egg, called a **zygote,** that contains 23 pairs of chromosomes. Over the next 38 to 40 weeks, the average gestation period for a human, the zygote will experience dramatic changes as it evolves into a baby. So many changes occur during this time that scientists divide the prenatal period into three stages: the germinal or zygotic stage, the embryonic stage, and the fetal stage. Let's detail the major changes that occur during each of these stages.

zygote a fertilized egg

Germinal Stage

The first 14 days after conception are the **germinal stage** of development. The major characteristic of this stage is cell division. Following conception, the zygote starts to replicate itself and divide. This ensures that all the cells of the organism contain the same genetic material. It divides into two cells, which then replicate and divide again, creating a 4-cell organism. The cells continue replicating and dividing, and around the 5th day after conception the zygote has become a 100-cell organism, called a *blastocyst*. In addition to cell division, this mass of cells also travels down the fallopian tubes to the uterus. On approximately the 9th day after conception, the blastocyst implants itself on the lining of the uterine wall. Cell division continues through the 2nd week.

germinal stage the first stage of prenatal development from conception to 14 days

Embryonic Stage

embryonic stage the second stage of prenatal development lasting from the 2nd through the 8th week

The **embryonic stage** covers development of the organism, now called an *embryo,* from the 2nd through the 8th week. After the blastocyst attaches to the uterine wall, its outside cells develop into the support structures: the placenta, umbilical cord, and amniotic sac. The inner cells become the embryo. The major characteristic of the embryonic period is the development and formation of the major organs and systems. Cells start to specialize into bone, muscle, and body organs. All the major biological systems—the cardiovascular system, the digestive system, the skeletal system, the excretory system, the respiratory system, and the nervous system—are forming. Given the importance of these systems for survival and well-being, the embryonic stage is perhaps the most precarious stage of prenatal development. Most miscarriages and genetic defects occur during this stage. The embryo's development may also be harmed by outside environmental factors, producing devastating effects. We will return to these topics in a moment.

By the end of the embryonic stage, all basic bodily structures and systems have formed. About 3 weeks after conception, the heart is beating. The spinal cord has formed. The liver is producing red blood cells. Ovaries or testes have formed (but gender is not apparent by ultrasound until between 12 and 18 weeks). Although only an inch long, the embryo already looks human. Facial features, such as the eyes, lips, nose, and jaw, have taken shape. Short stubs represent arms and legs, and the beginnings of fingers and toes are apparent.

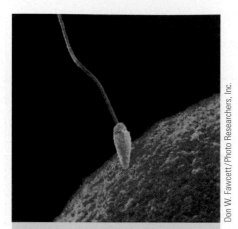

Human sperm and egg at the moment of penetration. The sperm cell fertilizes the female ova to create a zygote.

Don W. Fawcett/Photo Researchers, Inc.

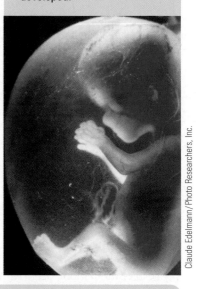

At 14 weeks, the fetus's lungs and external sex organs have developed.

Claude Edelmann/Photo Researchers, Inc.

Fetal Stage

The third prenatal development period, the **fetal stage,** begins the 9th week after conception. From now until birth, the organism is referred to as a *fetus.* The major characteristic of the fetal stage is continued growth and maturation. The fetus grows larger and starts to move. By 14 weeks, the fetus can kick, open its mouth, swallow, and turn its head. Its lungs begin to function and the external sex organs have developed. By the end of the 6th month (24 weeks), the organs are sufficiently formed such that the fetus has reached *viability*—the possibility of surviving outside the womb (but only in a neonatal intensive care unit). During the last 3 months, the fetus is responsive to sound, light, and touch.

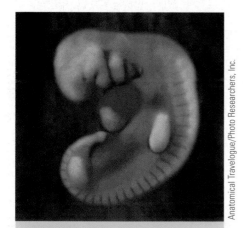

Micro-MRI, reconstructed with 3D imagery, actual size of embryo = 4.0 mm. The image depicts a human embryo during its 4th week of development. Age is calculated from the day of fertilization. In this image, the fusing tubes of the heart are highlighted in red. Early growth of the cardiovascular system begins during the 3rd week, when blood vessels form, and continue into the following weeks of development. Image from the book *From Conception to Birth: A Life Unfolds.*

Anatomical Travelogue/Photo Researchers, Inc.

View of a 5-month-old male fetus (20-week) holding his hand over his mouth. By this time the fetus appears completely human, with fully developed lips, eyelids, eyebrows, external ears, fingers and toes. There is not much subcutaneous fat on the limbs or face, and the weight of the fetus by the end of the 5th month is still less than 500 grams. Fetal movements can now usually be felt by the mother.

Neil Bromhall/Photo Researchers, Inc.

From the union of a single sperm cell and egg, the fetus has undergone significant and complex changes over the course of 40 weeks. However, not all zygotes experience these changes. About half of all fertilized eggs die and are miscarried, usually before the woman knows she is pregnant. Of pregnancies that the mother knows about (because of a missed menstrual cycle), approximately 10 to 20% end in miscarriage, making miscarriage and its emotional effects very common (Mortenson, Sever, & Oakley, 1991), as It's a Diverse World highlights.

fetal stage   the stage of prenatal development from the 9th week through the 9th month

---

IT'S A DIVERSE WORLD

The Emotional Effects of Miscarriage on Women and Men

A miscarriage, or spontaneous abortion, is a pregnancy that ends by itself within the first 20 weeks, usually because the pregnancy is not developing normally. "Stillbirth" refers to the same condition when it occurs after the first 20 weeks. The experience of loss that follows a miscarriage or stillbirth tends not to be recognized by many key people in a couple's life. Health professionals, families, and friends may avoid discussing these losses because the grief that follows a miscarriage is frequently considered minor.

Over the last decade, research has revealed significant psychological effects for women who experience miscarriage and stillbirth. Surveys of patient satisfaction following miscarriage indicate a high degree of anger and dissatisfaction with the medical care received. The complaints focus on insensitivity from the physician and lack of opportunity to discuss the personal significance of the loss (Brier, 1999). After a miscarriage, many women experience a relatively brief period of loss that is characterized by grief, sadness, and anxiety. Women whose grief is unrecognized are likely to experience more intense grief, for a longer time (Van, 2001). Increased grief after a miscarriage also is more likely when the woman is younger, has high levels of self-blame, when the loss occurs later in the pregnancy, or when a woman has a history of prior miscarriages (Brier, 1999; Franche, 2001; Goldbach, Dunn, Toedter, & Lasker, 1991; Neugebauer, 2003). However, when physicians can identify a cause for the miscarriage (such as a chromosomal abnormality), the woman's feelings of self-blame and hence grief are reduced (Nikcevic, Tunkel, Kuczmierczyk, & Nicolaides, 1999). A longer time between a miscarriage and a new pregnancy is also likely to result in increased grief for women (Franche, 2001). African American women are especially vulnerable as they experience pregnancy and infant losses at rates twice those of Caucasian American women and women of other ethnic groups (Van, 2001).

The psychological impact of miscarriage on women's male partners has been largely overlooked. The few studies that have been conducted on male partners' grief reactions following miscarriage suggest that fathers grieve differently from mothers. Males experience less guilt, meaninglessness, and fear, and they cry less than their wives. Men's grief is less intense, and men feel less need to talk about it. They are more likely to experience grief mixed with frustration and anger (Beutel, Willner, Deckhardt, Von Rad, & Weiner, 1996; Goldbach et al., 1991; Lang, Gottlieb, & Amsel, 1996; McGreal, Evans, & Burrows, 1997).

However, other studies contradict these findings. For example, in one study, partners' scores on a grief scale were significantly higher than the mothers' scores (Conway & Russell, 2000). Other studies found that males' and females' emotional reactions to miscarriage are similar. Giving up their expectations, hopes, and fantasies about the unborn child is a major source of grieving for both parents (Beutel et al., 1996). Husbands and wives who reported low levels of marital adjustment and intimacy soon after the loss experienced more intense grief (Franche, 2001). For both men and women, grief reactions following the loss of a pregnancy typically decrease 1 to 2 years after the loss, although couples continue to be vulnerable to renewed grief even years later (Goldbach et al., 1991; Lang et al., 1996).

What causes miscarriages? There are numerous risk factors—the woman's age, certain health conditions, and a history of previous miscarriages or stillbirth—factors that neither a woman nor her doctor may be able to control. A miscarriage often ends a pregnancy that would not have developed into a healthy baby due to chromosomal abnormalities or environmental factors. As we'll see next, miscarriages underscore the significant roles that nature and nurture play even before we are born.

The Importance of a Positive Prenatal Environment

The support structures of the intrauterine environment are designed to protect the developing organism. However, internal and external forces can still interfere with this natural defense system and cause birth defects. When internal chromosomal abnormalities occur, they typically arise during the embryonic stage. For example, **Down syndrome** results from an extra 21st chromosome. Babies with Down syndrome are characterized by distinct facial features and are more likely to experience heart defects and varying degrees of mental retardation. We now have medical tests that can identify the presence of Down syndrome and more than 450 inherited genetic disorders (Painter, 1997). This highlights the importance of regular prenatal consultations with one's physician.

Birth defects may also be caused by outside environmental forces. Any environmental agent that has the potential to harm the embryo is referred to as a **teratogen.** It may be a drug such as cocaine or alcohol, a disease such as German measles (rubella), or a chemical such as cleaning fluids. All of these substances have the potential to cause birth defects. The critical factor seems to be *when* the mother is exposed to these agents. These **critical periods** emphasize the complex interplay of nature and nurture on development. Certain organs and systems are more vulnerable to the effects of teratogens during different stages of prenatal development (Figure 9.2). Notice how the most severe effects are more likely to occur during the embryonic stage of devel-

Down syndrome a genetic birth disorder resulting from an extra 21st chromosome, characterized by distinct facial features and a greater likelihood of heart defects and mental retardation

teratogen an environmental substance that has the potential to harm the developing organism

critical period in prenatal development, a time when genetic and environmental agents are most likely to cause birth defects

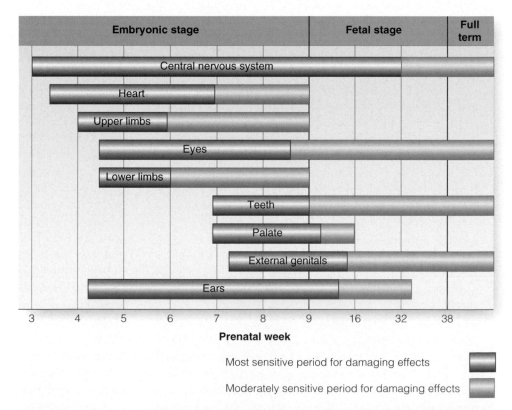

Figure 9.2 Critical Periods and Effect on Prenatal Development
The darker bars indicate the most sensitive period for certain organs and structures, and the lighter bars indicate lessened vulnerability. Sensitivity is greatest during the embryonic period, although some structures remain vulnerable throughout the prenatal period.

Adapted from K. L. Moore and T. V. N. Persaud, Before We Are Born: Essentials of Embryology and Birth Defects. *Philadelphia: Saunders. Copyright © 1998 Elsevier Science (USA). All rights reserved. Reprinted by permission.*

opment. Because a woman usually does not discover that she is pregnant until the embryo is already formed and developing, she may inadvertently expose her developing baby to harm.

Women who use any type of drug during pregnancy can potentially affect their babies. Women who smoke during pregnancy reduce the flow of oxygen to the fetus, and their babies tend to be irritable, have respiratory problems, and have lower birth weight (Rosenblith, 1992). Women who drink alcohol heavily during pregnancy put their unborn children at risk for **fetal alcohol syndrome (FAS).** Children suffering from FAS tend to have low birth weight, limb, head, and facial deformities, and suffer brain abnormalities. FAS is the leading cause of mental retardation (Ikonomidou et al., 2000; Niccols, 1994; Young, 1997). Even moderate drinking can affect the embryo's brain development, resulting in lowered levels of intellectual functioning later (Kraft, 1996). Pregnant women who report alcohol use are more likely to be under 30, employed, and unmarried (Centers for Disease Control, 2002). Illegal drugs also produce damaging effects. If the mother is a heroin addict, the baby will also be born addicted and have to undergo withdrawal. Crack or cocaine babies are often born premature, underweight, and irritable, and tend to have poor feeding habits (Inciardi, Surratt, & Saum, 1997; Richardson & Day, 1994).

Prenatal exposure to teratogens also may have long-term effects. Children exposed to drugs during pregnancy tend to be more impulsive, less adaptable, and evidence more behavioral problems later in life compared to children whose mothers had not used drugs during pregnancy (Espy, Riese, & Francis, 1997). In southern Japan, adults exposed during pregnancy to high levels of methylmercury (found in fish) have shown accelerated rates of aging (Newland & Rasmussen, 2003).

Prescription and over-the-counter medicines may also influence fetal development. For example, physicians once prescribed the drug Thalidomide to reduce morning sickness and related discomforts of pregnancy, with disastrous consequences. Many of these women gave birth to brain-damaged babies who were blind, deaf, and had deformed or missing limbs. Similarly, between 1938 and 1971, an estimated 5 to 10 million pregnant women were prescribed DES (diethylstilbestrol) to prevent miscarriages or premature delivery. In 1972, the U.S. Food and Drug Administration advised physicians to stop prescribing it to pregnant women, citing its connection to a rare vaginal and cervical cancer in DES daughters. Follow-up studies found additional risks to DES children, including pregnancy complications and a higher risk of miscarriage, infertility, breast cancer, and testicular growths (Kaufman et al., 2000; Palmer et al., 2001; Palmer et al., 2002). A recent study (Li, Liu, & Odouli, 2003) indicates that using nonsteroidal anti-inflammatory drugs (NSAIDs) during pregnancy also may contribute to miscarriage. Read the warning labels on any over-the-counter medication, and you will see that pregnant women are cautioned to seek a doctor's advice before using any medicine. Even aspirin use during pregnancy has been linked with lowered infant IQs (Streissguth et al., 1987). Whatever the mother takes in, so does the fetus.

Think about Frankie's mom, Angela, for a moment. Although not optimal, Angela's nutrition and diet while she was pregnant with Frankie and her second child was much more substantial and healthy than it was with her daughter and the twins. Their severe poverty made it difficult for Angela to provide a positive prenatal environment. These differences may be one factor in the children's developmental differences and ultimately in the deaths of Frankie's sister and brothers. Proper nutrition and a healthy lifestyle are paramount for a pregnant woman. They increase the chances of producing a healthy newborn who is better prepared to face the developmental and life challenges ahead. These challenges, which we will outline in this chapter and the next, include the enormous physical changes that occur throughout infancy, childhood, and adolescence.

fetal alcohol syndrome (FAS)   a birth condition resulting from the mother's chronic use of alcohol during pregnancy; it is characterized by facial and limb deformities, and mental retardation

 Application

Let's Review!

In this section we described the three stages of prenatal development and emphasized the importance of a positive prenatal environment. For a quick check of your understanding, answer these questions.

1. Loretta is in her 5th month of pregnancy. What stage of development is her unborn child in?
   a. germinal
   c. embryonic
   b. zygote
   d. fetal
2. Which of the following is *most* characteristic of the germinal stage of prenatal development?

a. cell division
c. birth defects
b. organogenesis
d. formation of major body systems

3. Environmental substances that can do harm to the developing organism are called:
   a. organogenesis.
   c. critical periods.
   b. teratogens.
   d. prehension.

ANSWERS

1. d; 2. a; 3. b

LEARNING OBJECTIVE

Describe major physical changes that infants and children experience as their brains and bodies develop.

neonate a newborn during the first 28 days of life

Physical Development: Growing, Moving, and Exploring

What physical changes do infants and children experience? The average **neonate,** or newborn up to 28 days old, enters the world 21 inches long, weighing 7 pounds. One year later, the infant will have doubled in height and tripled in weight, emphasizing how rapidly babies grow during infancy. Physical growth and developmental changes result from the complex interaction of the forces of nature and nurture. Our genetic program lays the foundation for how tall we grow or how our body fat is distributed. The environmental factors of nutrition, health care, and lifestyle also impact our height and build. For example, Frankie's battle with typhoid fever affected his height and weight. When he returned to school after his stay in the hospital, he was significantly shorter than his peers. A similar interplay of nature and nurture is seen in brain and motor development.

Brain Development

What is your very first childhood memory? How old were you then? Most people do not recall events in infancy or before 3 years old. Frank McCourt's childhood memories start sometime between his 3rd and 4th birthday. This lack of memory may be related to the development of our nervous systems (Chapter 2). At birth, an infant's brain has billions of neurons, but the connections between the neurons is very limited, and myelin (see p. 49) is incomplete. Experience and learning, however, mix with our heredity to shape brain development. Neural pathways grow rapidly, and by the time a child is 3 years old, 1,000 trillion connections have formed (Garlick, 2003). This reflects again the interplay of nature and nurture. A 2-month-old has very few neural connections compared to the billions a 2-year-old has. More experience and increased activity equals more neural connections.

During childhood and early adolescence, the brain prunes and discards unnecessary connections, reducing the total number of synapses (Cook & Cook, 2005; Seeman, 1999; Thompson et al., 2000). Those connections that are used repeatedly become permanent, whereas those that are used infrequently or not at all are unlikely to survive (Greenough et al., 1993). This discovery has altered researchers' thinking on infant care and early education. Providing stimulating age-appropriate activities fosters and strengthens brain development. Impoverished environments weaken neural connections—fewer connections are made, and unexercised connections are likely to be discarded.

 Application

A young child's brain is highly plastic, or changeable, and very dense with neurons when compared to adults' brains. If a certain area of the brain is damaged in infancy, other areas of the brain can compensate by reorganizing neural connections (Kolb, 1989; Rakic, 1991). However, there are individual inherited differences in this process such that some brains may be better able to adapt than others (Garlick, 2002). As children age, the brain is less able to change and adapt because neural connections have already been formed and in some cases discarded. Yet sufficient plasticity remains throughout adulthood (Huttenlocher, 2002). For example, children who are rarely spoken to or read to in their early years are more likely to have difficulty mastering language skills. Similarly, young children have an easier time learning a second language compared to adolescents and adults, whose brains are less malleable (Johnson & Newport, 1991). The plasticity and density of the brain ensures a child's best chance of adapting to his or her environment. This adaptation also is evident in the development of children's motor skills.

 Application

Reflexes and Motor Development

Infants are born relatively helpless creatures. They cannot feed themselves, are unable to walk, and can't push, or run. Infants do have certain sensory abilities, a good set of lungs that enable them to cry, and a set of reflexes, all of which biologically prepare them to get the help they need to survive. A **reflex** is an *automatic* response to a particular stimulus. Reflexes enable infants to learn about their environment, thus establishing important neural connections for *voluntary* motor behaviors. Hence, reflexes serve as the foundation for behaviors such as walking, eating, crying, smiling, and grasping. For example, infants are born with a sucking reflex**.** They will automatically suck on any object that touches their lips. Infants also have a rooting reflex. When you touch the side of infants' cheeks, they will turn in that direction and open their mouth. These two reflexes teach infants how to use their mouths to get food. Infants are also born with a grasping reflex. When an object is placed on their palm, they will automatically grasp it. From this reflex, infants learn to handle items with their hands, an ability referred to as *prehension*. Their brains and bodies learn, through grasping, the necessary skills that will later be used to write with a pen, play a musical instrument, tie their shoes, or give a parent a hug.

reflex   an automatic response to a specific environmental stimulus

Infants also are biologically prepared to communicate, despite lacking formal language skills. A crying reflex—automatically crying when distressed—alerts the caretaker to the infant's needs. In a matter of weeks, the baby learns to use crying to get the caretaker's attention. Luckily, infants are also born with a smiling reflex to use when they are pleased. This reflex evolves into a *social smile* at about 8 to 12 weeks of age, when the infant smiles at everybody. Their smiles then become more discriminating by 6 months of age, when infants reserve their smiles for familiar voices and faces. Imagine taking care of a baby that seldom smiled. Parents would receive very little positive reinforcement for all their caretaking.

Reflexes also initiate locomotive ability, or the ability to move around. Crawling and stepping reflexes prepare the brain and body for motions involved in pulling oneself up, crawling, and walking. These abilities develop in much the same sequence for all infants around the world, evidence of our genetic heritage. However, experience may partly speed up this process and lack of opportunities may slow it down (Thelen, 1995).

Synaptic connections proliferate during infancy and early childhood. The brain then selectively prunes and discards unused connections during childhood and early adolescence.

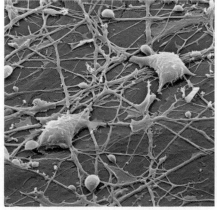

Juergen Berger, Max-planck Institute/Photo Researchers, Inc.

gross motor skills motor behaviors involving the large muscles of the body

fine motor skills motor behaviors involving the small muscles of the body

By age 2, infants are walking, running, and getting into everything. However, motor development, the changes in a child's body activities, does not end there. As children age, gross motor skills become more proficient. **Gross motor skills** refer to behaviors that involve large muscle groups such as the biceps or quadriceps. These include running, walking, jumping, and hopping. This proficiency is apparent when you watch a toddler, a preschooler, and an 8-year-old run. The toddler waddles and is unsteady on her feet. The preschooler is more coordinated compared to the toddler, but less fluid and not as fast as the 8-year-old.

Similar changes occur in **fine motor skills,** which involve small muscle groups. Fine motor skills include such activities as writing, using utensils, or playing a musical instrument. Toddlers and preschoolers are less adept at tasks involving fine motor skills, but as the school years approach, children become much more proficient. Table 9.1 ◆ details average age ranges for specific gross and fine motor skills achieved in infancy and in childhood. Notice that the achievement of a particular task lays the foundation for attaining the subsequent, more difficult, task. In other words, babies must be able to sit up before they can crawl. Children must walk before they learn to jump rope.

As you can see, enormous changes occur in physical development all through the infant and childhood years. A rapid growth spurt combined with the establishment of neural connections and motor skills has transformed our helpless being into an active one. The same magnitude of change characterizes cognitive development, or how children think, which we'll turn to next.

◆ **Table 9.1**
Motor Milestones in Infancy and Childhood

3 mos.	6 mos.	1 yr.	18 mos.	2 yrs.	3 yrs.	4 yrs.	5 yrs.	6–8 yrs.	9–11 yrs
Lifts head and chest when lying on stomach	Reaches for and grasps objects	Sits alone	Pulls and pushes objects	Drinks from a straw	Puts on shoes	Runs, jumps, hops, and skips	Rides a bicycle with training wheels	Ties shoelaces	Body strength increases
Grasps rattle	Helps hold a bottle	Crawls	Turns pages in a book	Tosses a ball	Dresses self with help	Jumps over objects	Balances on one foot	Good sense of balance	Increased hand dexterity
Waves arms	Shakes a rattle	Pulls self up	Scribbles	Opens drawers	Kicks a ball	Brushes teeth	Cuts with scissors	Prints name	Faster reaction time
Kicks legs	Sits with little support	Uses finger to point	Stacks a few blocks	Feeds self with a spoon	Hops on one foot	Catches, bounces, and throws a ball	Jump-ropes	Catches small balls	Better coordination
	Rolls over	Grasps objects with thumb and index finger	Walks	Bends over without falling	Pedals		Capable of swimming and skating	Copies designs and shapes	
			Runs stiffly	Takes backward steps	Climbs		Copies simple designs		

Note: The motor milestones listed here represent average age of attainment. Children's achievement of these motor milestones is highly variable.

Let's Review!

This section dealt with the major physical changes that infants and children undergo as their brains and motor skills develop. For a quick check of your understanding, answer these questions.

1. Which of the following infants is *most* likely to have the fewest neural connections?
   a. a 1-month-old   c. a 3-month-old
   b. a 2-month-old   d. a 4-month-old
2. Which of the following skills illustrates a fine motor skill?

a. hopping   c. writing
b. running   d. jumping
3. The grasping reflex lays the foundation for which one of the following motor abilities?
   a. walking   c. eating
   b. prehension   d. crawling

ANSWERS
1. a; 2. c; 3. b

Cognitive Development: Perception and Thinking

LEARNING OBJECTIVES

Describe the perceptual abilities of infants and how these abilities develop in the first weeks and months of life.

Compare and contrast Piaget's and Vygotsky's theories of cognitive development.

How do infants and children think? Television shows, motion pictures, and comic strips capitalize on the unique way in which children develop mentally. What is it about children's thinking that makes adults laugh? How has your thinking changed over the years? Did you ever believe in monsters, Santa Claus, or the tooth fairy? Did you have an imaginary friend, or speak to the Angel on the seventh step like Frankie McCourt did? This section reviews psychological research into how infants first learn to conceptualize the world and how this thinking changes as they proceed through childhood. We will start with perceptual development.

Perceptual Development

Infants are hard to study. They sleep most of the time, and they can't talk. We can't remember what it's like to be an infant. Researchers must therefore study infants when they are awake and active, and devise clever ways to measure what infants know. The best way to gather information about what infants can and can't perceive seems to be to measure certain behaviors and see how those behaviors may change under particular conditions. For example, researchers may measure how long an infant spends looking at a stimulus or how long an infant sucks when exposed to different sounds. Not surprisingly, as researchers create more precise ways of measuring infant behavior, we are discovering that infants know a lot more than we once believed.

Vision

Babies are very nearsighted at birth. Objects need to be close in order for babies to see them, and even then, these objects look blurry. In addition, a baby's eyes lack *convergence*, or the ability to focus both eyes on an object. This may be why newborns typically look cross-eyed in snapshots. However, as the structure of the eyes and the neural connections in the brain mature, babies attain visual convergence. Newborns also show a preference for looking at complex stimuli. If given a choice of various complex visual stimuli, infants will spend most of their time looking at faces (Turati, 2004; Turati & Simion, 2002; Valenza, Simion, Cassia, & Umilta, 1996). This preference is adaptive, as it will help foster a social bond with the major caretaker. What if your baby didn't seem

Application

Eleanor Gibson and Richard Walk's visual-cliff apparatus tests depth perception in infants.

interested in looking at you? It would be much less rewarding to nurture and care for that baby. By 3 months old, babies can tell the difference between their mothers' faces and that of a stranger, another ability that promotes a social relationship (Burnham, 1993).

During their first year, infants develop depth perception. In a classic experiment conducted in 1960, researchers Eleanor Gibson and Richard Walk created an apparatus called a "visual cliff" (see photo). They then observed at what age infants would or would not cross over the surface where it appeared to drop off. Infants as young as 6 months of age hesitated when approaching this perceived cliff. Again, we see that biology prepares us for developmental challenges. Babies acquire depth perception at about the same time they become mobile. Because depth perception and body coordination may not yet be developed in some infants, it is extremely important to never leave a baby unattended on a bed, a changing table, or any other elevated surface. Immature depth perception, as well as inadequate body control, makes it more likely that infants will fall and hurt themselves.

 Application

Hearing

Unborn babies react to sounds in the intrauterine environment at around the 20th week. A mother's voice is one of those sounds, which may explain why babies are likely to recognize their mothers' voice soon after birth (DeCasper & Fifer, 1980). Infants can locate the direction of sounds. They readily learn the difference between similar consonant sounds, such as /d/ and /p/, and appear to remember simple speech sounds a day after hearing them (Swain, Zelazo, & Clifton, 1993). Current research also suggests that these abilities to discriminate sounds and familiar voices from unfamiliar ones may be present in fetuses (Kisilevsky et al., 2003; Lecanuet, Manera, & Jacquet, 2002).

Babies also show preferences for sounds. They enjoy soft and rhythmic sounds, which explain why babies enjoy lullabies so much. They prefer most to listen to voices, specifically the rising tones used by women and children (Sullivan & Horowitz, 1983), and the exaggerated, high-pitched sounds typically used in baby talk. These preferences are an advantage to social interactions with caretakers. Infants do not like loud noises, which may explain why some children become classically conditioned to fear thunderstorms or the vacuum cleaner.

Taste, Touch, and Smell

Taste, touch, and smell are other ways that infants gather meaning from their environment. Infants' taste buds are functional at birth, and infants prefer sweet tastes.

This too is advantageous because breast milk is sweet. Think about that! You come into the world preferring the food that you're going to be given. Many times, glucose or sugar water is used to assist nursing mothers in breast-feeding. Given the newborn's innate sucking reflex and preference for sweet tastes, placing sugar water on the mother's nipple will help the infant latch on to it.

Infants also are born with an acute sense of smell. As soon as 3 days after birth, breastfed infants can discriminate the odor of their own mother from that of other mothers (Cernoch & Porter, 1985). Infants also are very responsive to touch, and touching and caressing infants stimulates their growth and brain development. In one study, two groups of premature infants were given the same neonatal care with one exception—half the infants were routinely massaged, and the other half were not. Those receiving the massages gained weight faster, developed faster neurologically, and therefore were able to leave the hospital sooner when compared to the control group (Field et al., 1986). Today, it is standard practice to encourage parents of preterm babies to hold them often. Holding and touching infants also fosters their social development. Perhaps the McCourt family environment provided warmth and touch. This atmosphere, combined with the right genes, may account for the McCourt children's more or less normal growth despite inadequate nourishment.

As we have seen, infants' senses and rudimentary perceptual abilities allow them to gather much needed information from the environment—how their caretakers look, sound, and smell, where the food is, and what sounds contribute to language. From these beginnings, infants develop the abilities to know, think, and remember, a process called **cognition.** Perhaps no one has advanced our understanding more about children's thinking than Jean Piaget, whose ideas and research are presented next.

 **‹‹** Application

cognition the ability to know, think, and remember

Piaget's Theory of Cognitive Development

While developing an intelligence test for the French government, Swiss psychologist Jean Piaget noticed error patterns in children of the same age. He wondered why children routinely got certain answers wrong and what it was about children's thinking that led them to reach the same kinds of erroneous conclusions. To satisfy his curiosity, Piaget interviewed and observed infants and children, including his own, to discover and describe the changes in thinking that occur in childhood. Piaget gave children certain tasks to perform, observed their problem-solving strategies, and then asked them how they came to their conclusions.

From these observations and interviews, Piaget (1929, 1952) developed a theory about how children acquire their mental abilities. His theory traces the shifts in thinking from infants' reflexes to a teenager's reasoning abilities. He believed that cognition advances in a series of distinct stages, and that how a preschooler thinks differs dramatically from how an elementary school student thinks. Three concepts central to his theory are schema, assimilation, and accommodation.

Schemas

To Piaget, any mental idea, concept, or thought is a **schema.** We form these schemas based on our experiences of the world. For example, a baby may have a sucking schema, "Is this object suckable?" or a mother schema, "Does this person fit with my cognitive framework of mother?" A preschooler may have the schema "the sun follows me wherever I go." Adults' schemas may be very simple—"a key will start a car"— or more complex, such as individual ideas of justice, morality, or love.

schema a mental idea, concept, or thought

Piaget believed that our brains were biologically programmed to seek understanding of our world. So we form schemas to fit with our perceptions of the world. When we achieve this fit, we have mental equilibrium, and our cognitions are congruent with the environment. However, when there is not a fit between our schemas

Piaget observed children's problem-solving strategies to describe the changes in thinking that they experience.

© Bill Anderson/Photo Researchers, Inc.

assimilation   the process by which an already existing scheme is used to understand something new in the environment

accommodation   the process by which a scheme is changed, modified, or created anew in order to understand something new in the environment

sensorimotor stage   Piaget's first stage of cognitive development in which infants learn schemes through their senses and motor abilities

and the world, we experience mental disequilibrium, an uncomfortable state that we are motivated to get rid of so our mental harmony can be restored. The processes of assimilation and accommodation explain how we use existing schemas and create new ones to fit our experiences and, therefore, maintain mental equilibrium.

Assimilation and Accommodation

Assimilation is the process by which we apply an already existing schema to our understanding of the environment. For example, a young child is traveling in a car with her parents. As they pass by an open field the child sees some cows. The only schema that the child has for a four-legged animal is dog. So the child says, "Look at the doggies!" The parents may correct the child—"No, those are called cows"—but she may persist in calling them "doggies" because that is her framework for understanding four-legged animals. Notice how the child has assimilated her experience of "cow" into her existing schema of "dog." However, many times our existing schemas will not fit our new experiences. At times like these, the process of accommodation takes center stage.

Accommodation is the process we use to change or modify our existing schemas—or even create new ones—to adapt to some change in the environment. For example, suppose the child in the previous example sees a dog and a cow side by side. The differences in the animals can't be ignored and will create disequilibrium in the child's mental state. In this situation, she may now come to call the new animal a cow. Her existing schema for four-legged animals has now been modified. The child will go through the same process when she sees a horse, a cat, or a hippopotamus. Recall Frankie's accommodation on arriving in Ireland. He had no experience of goats or sheep and had to modify his existing schema to accommodate them.

Piaget's Stages of Cognitive Development

For Piaget, assimilation and accommodation create shifts in mental thinking that allow the child to progress through four stages of cognition: sensorimotor, preoperational, concrete operational, and formal operations (1952; summarized in Table 9.2 ◆). Each stage has characteristics that permit the child to conceptualize the world in a unique fashion. Let's look at each stage.

During the first cognitive stage, the **sensorimotor stage,** from birth to 2 years, Piaget suggested that infants acquire knowledge through their senses and through their motor abilities, hence the name *sensorimotor*. We already have seen how infants use their senses to understand the world. For example, we saw how infants quickly recognize and prefer to look at their mothers' faces. Similarly, infants use their hearing to form schemas of what certain utterances mean, establishing the foundation for language. Taste, touch, and smell also are used to gather information and to form schemas as infants explore objects with their hands, mouth, and feet. We also saw that infant reflexes establish schemas for grasping, sitting, crawling, and walking.

◆ **Table 9.2**

Piaget's Stages of Cognitive Development			
Sensorimotor	**Preoperational**	**Concrete Operations**	**Formal Operations**
(birth–2 yrs.)	(2–6/7 yrs.)	(6/7 yrs.–11/12 yrs.)	(12 yrs.–adult)
• reflexes	• egocentrism	• conservation	• abstract reasoning
• object permanence	• illogical thinking	• logical thinking	
	• centration	• decentration	
	• no conservation		

Piaget believed that during this stage infants could form schemas only of objects and actions that are in their immediate perception; in other words, what they currently see, hear, or touch. They learn by doing and by acting on objects. They lack the ability to represent an object when it is not present. For infants, it is truly "out of sight, out of mind," according to Piaget. The baby thinks of his pacifier when it is present by manipulating it with his mouth or hands. An infant can think about her "blankie" only when it is present. If these objects are not present, they no longer exist for the infant. However, as the infant grows and the brain matures, babies begin to have mental representations. One sign of this milestone is object permanence.

Object permanence is the understanding that an object continues to exist even when it is not present. We can see this in infants' behavior when they start to search for hidden objects. For example, Piaget would show a baby an interesting toy and then cover it. Before the age of 6 months, infants would not search for the toy, lacking the understanding that the toy still existed. The infant could not keep a mental representation of the object and its location in mind. However, by 8 months, infants will begin to search for the toy, suggesting the beginnings of object permanence. This ability steadily improves through 24 months, when infants will search long and hard for hidden objects, indicating that they have fully achieved object permanence.

> **object permanence**   the understanding that an object continues to exist even when it is not present

Although Piaget accurately described the process of object permanence in infancy, he may have underestimated infants' abilities. Current research suggests that infants as young as 1 month old (Kaye & Bower, 1994) and 3 months old (Bailargeon & DeVos, 1992; Johnson & Nanez, 1995) have a rudimentary understanding of object permanence. Moreover, infant abilities that Piaget observed at 18 months of age are now being seen as early as 6 to 8 months of age, as researchers use newer, more sensitive devices for measuring infants' abilities (Hayne & Rovee-Collier, 1995; Mareschal, 2000).

Once they understand that objects continue to exist even when not present, infants are on their way to **symbolic thinking.** This is the understanding that an object can be represented with symbols such as gestures or language. This ability to use symbols propels the child to the second stage of cognitive development: the preoperational stage.

> **symbolic thinking**   the understanding that an object can be represented with a symbol such as bodily gestures or language

> **preoperational stage**   Piaget's second stage of cognitive development, which is characterized by the use of symbols and illogical thought

During the **preoperational stage**, from about age 2 to age 6 or 7, preschoolers are actively acquiring and using symbols (DeLoache, 2001). Being able to use symbols opens up a new world to the preschooler. It is the foundation of a child's language development. A word symbolizes or stands for an object that may or may not be present. A child's vocabulary and understanding of language dramatically increases during these years. For example, when a mother asks, "Do you want some juice?," the preoperational child knows what juice is and may even go to the refrigerator to get it. Young children's pretend play also demonstrates their use of symbols, such as a stick to represent a sword or children taking on family roles when they play "house." However, the child's new ability to symbolize objects is still illogical and does not always make sense to adults. For example, a child may believe that a switch turns on ocean waves, or that there are monsters hiding under the bed despite parents' repeated search-and-destroy missions.

 Application

The illogical thinking of preschoolers is due to cognitive limitations that include centration and egocentrism. **Centration** occurs when one focuses on only one feature or aspect of an object. For instance, a child who sees a man with long hair or an earring may conclude that the man is a girl. She focuses on one feature, the man's hair length, and this man's hair length fits with her schema for females. For preschoolers, if it looks like a duck, it is a duck. They cannot distinguish between appearance and reality. Centration so dominates children's thinking at this stage that they do not realize that something is the same if its appearance changes, an ability called **conservation.**

> **centration** the act of focusing on only one aspect or feature of an object

> **conservation**   the understanding that an object retains its original properties even though it may look different

In classic experiments, Piaget tested preschoolers and school-age children's conservation abilities (Figure 9.3 on p. 409). Children were shown two equal-sized glasses containing the same amount of water. In front of the child, Piaget poured the water from one

Lacking the ability of conservation, young children are likely to believe that the amount of liquid has changed when it is poured into the thinner, taller glass. They believe the taller, thinner glass has more liquid.

© Laura Dwight / Photo Edit

egocentrism the belief that everyone thinks like you do

concrete operations Piaget's third stage of cognitive development, which is characterized by logical thought

of the glasses into a taller, thinner glass. Children were then asked whether the glasses had equal amounts of water or whether one glass had more water than the other. Children in the preoperational stage were most likely to reply that the tall, thin glass had more. Centering on the height of the liquid in the glass, it looked like it had more, so it must have more. For preschoolers at a party, then, adults should be aware that it must look like the children all have the same amount of cake or punch, otherwise the preschoolers will think they are receiving different amounts—which can create havoc.

An additional limitation to the preschooler's thinking is **egocentrism,** or the belief that everyone else thinks like you do. For example, when one of the authors was playing hide-and-seek with her 3-year-old son, he hid in his room in the corner. His face was turned into the wall, much like a child who is sent to stand in a corner for misbehaving. On entering the room, the author said, "I see you." Her son replied, "No, you don't." From the child's perspective, he could not see his mother, so therefore she could not see him. Egocentrism can also be seen in the way preschoolers use language. Often, children at this age will all talk at the same time, sometimes referred to as a *collective monologue.* They don't yet understand that communication requires listening and taking turns. It is not that these children are selfish; their behavior simply reflects a cognitive limitation. They believe that others see things as they do and therefore think like they do, a finding that has been repeatedly replicated using a range of different methods (Wellman, Cross, & Watson, 2001). A child may give a doll for a Mother's Day gift because that is what the child believes girls play with, or that the doll is a gift that anyone would like to receive.

Although adults may find it frustrating, the illogical thinking of a preschooler lends an almost magical quality to their thought processes. For example, they believe in monsters, bad-dream catchers over their beds to prevent nightmares, the tooth fairy, and fantasy. It is no wonder that Frankie spoke to and believed in the Angel on the seventh step. Imaginary friends are not uncommon during this age period. However, current research suggests that here, too, Piaget's ideas probably underestimate children's thinking abilities. Egocentrism, centration, and the inability to tell the difference between appearance and reality do not *always* characterize preschoolers' thoughts (Jenkins & Astington, 1996; Siegel & Hodkin, 1982). Rather, these limitations are sometimes present in children's thinking and gradually fade as the child matures. Fortunately and unfortunately, this way of thinking soon disappears and is replaced with more logical thought processes.

During Piaget's third cognitive stage, **concrete operations,** from about age 6 or 7 through age 12, schoolchildren become logical thinkers. They no longer center on one feature or facet of an object as the preschooler did, and their conservation abilities improve. Children realize that although the tall, thin glass looks like it has more water, in reality the glasses have

Rose is Rose © reprinted by permission of United Feature Syndicate, Inc.

Typical tasks used to measure conservation		Typical age of mastery
	Conservation of number Two equivalent rows of objects are shown to the child, who agrees that they have the same number of objects.	6–7
	One row is lengthened, and the child is asked whether one row has more objects.	
	Conservation of mass The child acknowledges that two clay balls have equal amounts of clay.	7–8
	The experimenter changes the shape of one of the balls and asks the child whether they still contain equal amounts of clay.	
	Conservation of length The child agrees that two sticks aligned with each other are the same length.	7–8
	After moving one of the sticks to the left or right, the experimenter asks the child whether the sticks are of equal length.	
	Conservation of area Two identical sheets of cardboard have wooden blocks placed on them in identical positions; the child confirms that the same amount of space is left on each piece of cardboard.	8–9
	The experimenter scatters the blocks on one piece of cardboard and again asks the child whether the two blocks have the same amount of unoccupied space.	

Figure 9.3 **Piaget's Conservation Experiment**

Mastery of conservation tasks begins gradually during the concrete operations stage. Children typically master conservation of number by age 6 or 7. Conservation of area may not be grasped until age 8 or 9.

equivalent volume. Changes in these abilities force the child to recognize that previous beliefs may be mistaken, so accommodation occurs. It also brings about a reduction in egocentrism as the child now can consider the perspectives of others. This enables empathy, persuasion, and a sense of humor to grow. For example, school-age children can now consider that a word may have more than one meaning. This play on words is evident in their use of knock-knock jokes:

> Knock knock.
> Who's there?
> Dwayne.
> Dwayne who?
> Dwayne the bathtub, I'm drowning!

At this age, children who believed in the existence of Santa Claus may begin to question that belief as certain facts just don't add up. For example, if it takes the family 8 hours to travel to a different state for a vacation, how can Santa Claus travel

 Application

around the world in 1 night? Given Santa Claus's plump physique, how can he fit down a chimney half his size? What if you don't have a chimney? Children may hold onto their belief in Santa Claus because of parents' logical answers to their questions. For example, if a child asks how Santa can deliver toys when they don't have a chimney, a parent may reply that he uses the door. It is the child's questioning, not his or her conclusions, that reflect this stage of cognitive development.

Although the concrete operational child thinks more logically, as the name of this stage implies, these schemas are limited to actual experience or concrete objects and situations. School-age children cannot reason abstractly about what may be or what could be without being able to test their ideas in an observable way. This is why class demonstrations and hands-on activities of abstract ideas for school subjects like geometry and science are necessary in elementary and middle school. Recall how Frankie thought about his father in logical but concrete terms. He is the man with the newspaper in the morning, the man who tells stories at night, and the man who comes home drunk. Frankie does not understand his father in terms of personality, motives, or intentions. These are abstract concepts that are difficult for a boy his age to comprehend. Being able to think about situations that are not present occurs in the final stage of Piaget's theory, formal operations.

According to Piaget, as children approach their teenage years, they may achieve the final cognitive stage, **formal operations.** They are no longer limited to the concrete; they can now engage in abstract reasoning. Teenagers can imagine and hypothesize what *may* be. This ability expands teenagers' horizons. They are able to understand more abstract, scientific, and mathematical concepts. They can imagine potential careers and envision future consequences for current behavior. We will expand on this ability further in the next chapter when we describe adolescent cognitive development.

Piaget's theory revolutionized our understanding of children's thinking abilities and stimulated much research in cognition. But we now recognize that the changes in thinking that Piaget proposed do not always proceed according to the precise stages and timetable he originally proposed (Haith & Benson, 1998). Children's mental abilities develop at different ages. Nurture, culture, or experience can facilitate growth and change in these abilities. However, Piaget very accurately described the *sequence* in which these changes occur, even in diverse societies (Dasen, 1994; Lourenco & Machado, 1996). His ideas also inspired other psychologists to question how children think, including his student, Lawrence Kohlberg, whose theory on moral reasoning is discussed later in this chapter. One final criticism of Piaget's theory is that it overlooks the important effects of culture on cognitive development. The ideas of Lev Vygotsky explore this connection between culture and cognition.

Vygotsky's Theory of Cognitive Development: Culture and Thinking

Lev Vygotsky (1896–1934) was a Russian psychologist whose work was banned in communist Russia for referencing Western psychologists. Although he died more than 50 years ago, over the past 25 years Vygotsky has been rediscovered. His ideas have influenced how psychologists and educators think about children's cog-

© 2000 Baldo Partnership/Dist. By Universal Press Syndicate. Reprinted with permission. All rights reserved.

formal operations   Piaget's final stage of cognitive development, which is characterized by the ability to engage in abstract thought

Vygotsky emphasized the importance of culture and social interactions in his theory of cognitive development.

nitive development and has provided an alternative to Piaget's theory (John-Steiner & Mahn, 1996).

In contrast to Piaget's emphasis on the internal origin of schemas, Vygotsky (1978, 1986) emphasized that mental processes begin externally with our social interactions with others. For example, children initially use language to regulate the behavior of others ("I want juice," "Pick me up"). A child internalizes these mental processes to create a cognitive framework for understanding the world. Young children often talk to themselves as they play, a behavior Vygotsky called **private speech.** For Vygotsky, private speech represented an internal monitor that guided the child's actions. Private speech, or self-talk, as it is sometimes called, is common among preschoolers, and peaks around 5 to 7 years of age. Around 9 years of age these spoken words are further internalized into silent lip movements. Eventually, children just think the thoughts rather than saying them. However, private speech can return at any age when we are confused or having difficulties in problem solving. Such inner speech cues and guides our thinking. Much research supports Vygotsky's ideas on private speech (Berk & Spuhl, 1995; Bivens & Berk, 1990; Diaz & Berk, 1992). It makes sense, therefore, to allow and even encourage children to use private speech to talk themselves through a problem.

According to Vygotsky, because cognition is so intimately tied to our social interactions, culture has a profound influence on our mental processing. The language, numerical system, rituals, beliefs, and technology of a culture both limits and supports certain ways of thinking (Tomasello, 2000). For instance, if your language does not have a word to capture an idea or expression, it is difficult to imagine or understand that concept. Similarly, children who have the opportunity to read books, use the Internet, travel, and attend cultural events would be more capable of conceptualizing ideas than children without such tools. According to Vygostsky, cognitive development does not occur in fixed stages as Piaget theorized. Rather, cognitive development may proceed in any number of directions, depending on our culture, social interactions with others, and the environment we live in.

Representing concepts is not achieved by simply having these tools. Conceptual thinking is taught to children by parents, teachers, siblings, coaches, and other important people in their lives. This instruction is most helpful when it is within a child's **zone of proximal development (ZPD)**—that is, the gap between what a child can already do and what he or she is not yet capable of doing. Through collaborative interaction, the adult initially guides and supports the child's efforts to master a task. The less able a child is to do a task, the more direction and guidance an adult must give. The adult then gradually minimizes their guidance and support until the child can do it alone in a process called **scaffolding.** For example, when learning to ride a bicycle, an adult first supports the child on the bicycle and walks or runs alongside as the child pedals. When the child seems ready, less support is given until the child is riding on his or her own. It is through these interactions with others that children internalize strategies, reasoning skills, and problem-solving abilities, according to Vygotsky. This is why Vygotsky believed that children's cognitive development benefits most when they interact with people who are more capable or advanced in their thinking than they are.

private speech   Vygotsky's term to describe when young children talk to themselves to guide their actions during play

 Application

zone of proximal development (ZPD) according to Vygotsky, the gap between what a child is already able to do and what he or she is not yet capable of doing

scaffolding   a process by which initially adults offer much guidance and support in helping a child reason, problem solve, or master a task; as the child becomes more proficient and capable, the adult helps less and less until the child can master it on his or her own

Let's Review!

We have described how infants and children develop perceptual abilities, and outlined two major theories on cognitive development. Piaget's theory outlines shifts in internal schemas as the child moves through four stages of cognition. Vygotsky's theory emphasizes how social interactions influence children's mental processes. As a quick check of your understanding, answer these questions.

1. Which of the following substances would an infant most prefer to taste?
   a. a lollipop   c. pizza
   b. french fries   d. mashed potatoes

2. Simone sees a military tank on the highway and calls it a "truck." According to Piaget, Simone is engaging in _____.
   a. disequilibrium   c. assimilation
   b. private speech   d. accommodation

3. Which of the following is a true statement regarding the cognitive theories of Piaget and Vygotsky?
   a. Piaget and Vygotsky both believed that cognitive processes begin internally.

b. Piaget believed that cognitive processes begin externally from our social interactions, whereas Vygotsky believed that cognitive processes begin internally.

c. Piaget believed that cognitive processes begin internally, whereas Vygotsky believed that cognitive processes begin externally from our social interactions.

d. Piaget and Vygotsky both believed that cognitive processes begin externally from our social interactions with others.

4. Which of the following cognitive abilities *most* characterizes a child in Piaget's preoperational stage of development?
   a. logical thought   c. object permanence
   b. conservation   d. egocentrism

ANSWERS
1. a; 2. c; 3. c; 4. d

LEARNING OBJECTIVE < < < < < < < < <

Compare and contrast Kohlberg's and Gilligan's theories of moral reasoning.

moral reasoning how you decide what is right and what is wrong

Moral Reasoning: How We Think About Right and Wrong

How do children distinguish right from wrong, and how does their thinking about right and wrong change as they grow? Consider the following situation. An automatic teller machine dispenses $10,000 to you and there is no way that this error ever would be discovered. You keep the money, but you donate half of it to the soup kitchen in your town. Should you have kept the money? How did you decide what to do? Your answer to this situation would provide clues to psychologists about your level of **moral reasoning**, or how you distinguish right from wrong.

Lawrence Kohlberg, a student of Piaget's, became intrigued by this notion. So he developed moral dilemmas, situations like the one we posed to you. At the end of the situation, Kohlberg would ask participants to detail what the main character should do and why. Kohlberg was interested not so much in whether the participant believed the person's action to be right or wrong, but *why* the participant judged the person's actions as right or wrong. After analyzing data from thousands of subjects, Kohlberg created a theory of how children morally reason and the changes in this reasoning that they experience as they develop (Kohlberg, 1969; Kohlberg, Levine, & Hewer, 1983).

Kohlberg's Stages of Moral Reasoning

Like Piaget, Kohlberg proposed that our ability to think about issues of right and wrong develops in six stages, which he arranged in three levels: preconventional, conventional, and postconventional (Table 9.3 ◆). As you read through the description of Kohlberg's theory, consider Frankie McCourt's moral reasoning. How could he steal

◆ **Table 9.3**

Kohlberg's Stages of Moral Reasoning

Preconventional Level (most children)

Stage 1: Obedience and Punishment Orientation. Children obey rules to avoid punishment. "Frankie stole the bananas to avoid his mother's punishment."

Stage 2: Naively Egoistic Orientation. Children view morally right action as that which increases their personal rewards and needs. "You scratch my back, and I will scratch yours."

Conventional Level (most adolescents and adults)

Stage 3: Good Boy/Good Girl Orientation. Moral rightness is based on maintaining the approval and/or avoiding the disapproval of others such as family and friends. "I will return the rest of the money so my parents won't be disappointed in me."

Stage 4: Law and Order Orientation. Moral rightness is based on following the rules or laws of the society. Exceptions to the rules are not allowed. "Stealing is wrong because it is against the law."

Postconventional Level (some but not all adults)

Stage 5: Contractual/Legalistic Orientation. Exceptions to rules can now be considered, as the protection of individual rights is emphasized over societal laws. "I confessed to the crime, but I was not read my rights, so the confession does not stand."

Stage 6: Universal Principles Orientation. Individuals develop their own set of universal principles that guide their judgments of right and wrong across all situations and all societies.

bananas and have no remorse? Why would he disobey the hospital's rules and talk with Patricia? Why does he refer to his father's drinking as "the bad thing"?

Preconventional Level

At the *preconventional level* of reasoning, children make decisions about right or wrong based on their ability to avoid punishment or to gain rewards. For example, it is wrong to take a cookie without asking because a parent may then scold you. It is right to share with your sister because then you may get a smile or a reassuring pat from your parent. Recall that at this age, children are egocentric and have difficulty understanding the nature of rules. Consequently, children are centered on the immediate consequences of their actions. Frankie steals bananas; the immediate consequence is that the twins stop crying, and he avoids his mother's anger.

 Application

Conventional Level

With the ability to think logically and to understand another person's perspective, children at the *conventional level* of reasoning can now understand rules and expectations that others may have for them. Therefore, their moral reasoning is based on the standards of the group or society. They believe behaviors are right or wrong because they gain the approval or avoid the disapproval of parents, teachers, or peers. Do you remember pleading with your parent(s) to let you participate in an activity with a friend? If your friend's parent(s) let him or her participate, you probably asked why you couldn't, too. At this level, children also come to appreciate society's rules or laws for moral behavior. However, because they lack the ability to reason abstractly, children apply these laws to every situation and every person very rigidly. Exceptions based on circumstances are not considered. Frankie believes that he is to blame for Patricia's death because he broke the hospital rules. Frankie refers to his father's drinking as "the bad thing" because his mother, her friends, and all the relatives get mad at him when he drinks.

 Application

Postconventional Level

At the *postconventional level* of moral reasoning, people base their judgments of right or wrong on contractual or universal principles of morality. The person can appreciate

Dr. Martin Luther King, Jr.'s level of moral reasoning was extraordinary; few others have reached Kohlberg's highest level of moral reasoning.

© Bettman/Corbis

extenuating circumstances and realizes that external standards handed down from society cannot always be applied to all the situations in the same manner. Therefore, the individual develops internal standards of right and wrong.

At the postconventional level, we choose certain principles to guide our moral behavior. These abstract principles may include the Golden Rule (Do unto others as you would have them do unto you) or values such as respecting the dignity of all persons regardless of race, creed, or culture. Consider the moral values evidenced by Martin Luther King, Jr. Dr. King lived in a society in which "separate but equal" was the law of the land. It was mandated that Blacks and Whites use separate restrooms, attend different schools, sit in different locations on public transport, and eat in different sections of a restaurant. Yet Dr. King believed that this segregation was immoral, that regardless of a person's skin color, all people should be treated the same and have equal access to public facilities—a universal principle (Stage 6 in Table 9.3) that was self-chosen.

Kohlberg's theory has stimulated much research—as well as much criticism and controversy. Kohlberg-like studies in 27 cultures support Kohlberg's stage sequence of moral reasoning. People typically move through these stages in the way that Kohlberg proposed (Damon, 1999; Helwig, 1997; Walker, 1989; Walker & Taylor, 1991). By adulthood, most people have progressed to conventional moral reasoning, but few people move on to postconventional reasoning, especially the highest stage. This suggests that postconventional reasoning may apply more to people from Western culture and industrialized societies than to individuals from non-Western, nonindustrial societies. (Snarey, 1995). Another area in which Kohlberg's theory has been criticized is that of gender, a controversy initiated by a student of Kohlberg's, Carol Gilligan.

Gilligan's Theory: Gender and Moral Reasoning

Are there gender differences in moral reasoning? Carol Gilligan was assigned to code participants' responses according to the three levels theorized by Kohlberg. While she was involved in this task, Gilligan believed she noticed differences between male and female responses. To her, it seemed that male responses consistently received rankings of higher stages than did the females. Were males more morally developed, or were the differences due to the criteria of moral reasoning that were being used? Gilligan hypothesized that males and females do not judge right and wrong in the same manner. She believed that Kohlberg's model emphasized the male perspective on moral reasoning more than the female view.

In her book *A Different Voice* (1982), Gilligan speculates that males and females focus on different principles for deciding what is right and wrong. Males tend to be more focused on concepts of fairness and justice. Females are more likely to emphasize their concern, care, and relations with others in making judgments about right and wrong. Gilligan asserts that women's ethic of care is a different, but not a less valid, basis for moral reasoning.

Research evaluating gender differences in moral reasoning has not strongly supported Gilligan's claims. On hypothetical dilemmas, both males and females emphasize themes of justice and caring in their responses (Jadack, Hyde, Moore, & Keller, 1995; Jaffee & Hyde, 2000; Walker, 1995). Therefore, rather than concluding that one theory is right and the other is wrong, we can see that moral reasoning may not occur in one set pattern, but rather can take many forms. Although males and females may tend to use different standards when making moral decisions, these differences appear more often in response to real life rather than to hypothetical moral dilemmas. Consequently, any gender differences in moral reasoning may be more the result of how we expect males and females to behave, an area of social development that we turn to next.

Let's Review!

In this section we outlined Kohlberg's theory of how we develop our moral reasoning, along with Gilligan's further theory about gender differences. For a quick check of your understanding, answer these questions.

1. Making moral judgments based on social and societal rules is characteristic of which level of Kohlberg's theory?

   a. preconventional
   b. preoperational
   c. conventional
   d. postconventional

2. Gilligan asserted that males and females reason differently in regard to moral issues. She believes that females are more likely to base moral judgments on what principles?

   a. justice
   b. fairness
   c. equity
   d. relations with others

3. Kayla, a 4-year-old, shares her toys with June so that June will also share her toys. Kayla is operating at what level of Kohlberg's theory?

   a. preconventional
   b. preoperational
   c. conventional
   d. postconventional

ANSWERS
1.c;2.d;3.a

Social Development

> > > > > > > > > > > > > > > > > > > >

LEARNING OBJECTIVES

- Explain gender-schema theory and describe how nature and nurture influence gender-role behavior.
- Describe behaviors that indicate that an attachment has been formed, distinguish between different attachment patterns, and describe the three parenting styles that Baumrind documented.

How do our social relationships influence our development? Gender and parents are two major influences on infants' and children's personal and social development. Whether it is your parents and their style of parenting and the quality of your relationship to them, or society's attitudes regarding your gender, the social relationships that you establish during your infancy and childhood have a profound effect on your development. We recognize that there are other social or environmental variables that influence development, such as peer relations, teachers, and childhood trauma, but such topics are beyond the scope of this chapter.

Gender and Gender-Role Development

Our biological sex and our feelings about it are key aspects of our social development. *Sex* refers to our biological makeup, starting with our chromosomes (XX for female, XY for male) and proceeding to our internal and external genitalia. *Gender* refers to our feelings about our biological makeup or assigned sex. How do boys and girls understand gender, and what do they learn about appropriate behavior for males and females? Is this in some way determined by differences in our biological makeup (nature) or are gender differences the result of society (nurture)? These are just some of the issues we explore as we take a look at the influence of gender on development. Chapter 11 investigates further the impact of gender and sexuality on our development.

Gender Roles

How does our society expect males and females to behave? At around 2 years old, toddlers are able to label their gender and the gender of others. These labels then provide a framework for understanding what clothes, toys, colors, jobs, and behaviors are appropriate for each sex. Thus, children at a very early age are processing and developing schemas about **gender roles,** or society's expectations for how a female and a male should behave. For example, one day one of the authors was driving in her car with her then-4-year-old son. She asked him what he wanted to do when he got older.

gender roles   societal expectations of how a male and a female should behave

Young children lack gender permanence, the knowledge that our assigned gender does not change. Playing dress-up allows them to explore the gender roles of the opposite sex.

gender permanence the understanding that one's gender will not change

gender-schema theory the idea that gender roles are acquired through modeling and reinforcement processes that work together with a child's mental abilities

He replied, "I want to be a firefighter and drive a fire truck." Her son then asked her what she wanted to be when she was older and suggested that she may also want to consider being a firefighter like him. His mother stated, "It would be cool to drive a fire truck." He replied, "Oh, no Mommy, you can't drive the fire truck. Only boys can drive fire trucks because only boys can drive." His mother replied, "Well, who is driving this car?" "You are, Mommy," the young boy replied. "And am I a boy or a girl?" his mother questioned. "You're a girl," he replied. "But it doesn't matter, you still can't drive the fire truck." For him, males had received the label of drivers and flexibility in this rule was not allowed.

This gender rigidity in preschoolers is an extension of the rigidity of their thinking in general. Recall how black and white their moral judgments are. It is a very common consequence of their cognitive development. **Gender permanence** or constancy is the knowledge that our assigned gender will not change. Typically, children under the age of 6 years do not yet understand that their gender is permanent (De Lisi & Gallagher, 1991; Szkrybalo & Ruble, 1999). Recall that at this age children center in on only one aspect of a situation or an object (see p. 407). If one of your features or behaviors looks like a male, then you are a male. If the feature fits with the child's concept of a female, then you are a female. Consequently, if a little boy puts on his mother's dress, he may believe that he is now a girl. Children extend their rules on gender indiscriminately. Their perspective on gender applies to everyone equally, without exception. So they may state that boys can't play with dolls or that girls can't climb trees. However, with logical reasoning comes gender permanence. It is almost as if the child has learned to conserve gender. In the same way they become aware that the liquid in the glass has not changed even though its appearance has, children come to understand that a person's gender has not changed even though their appearance might have.

How do children learn gender roles? The process by which a child develops gender roles and comes to label specific behaviors and activities as either male or female is not completely understood. Psychologists currently endorse a perspective that combines elements of social learning theory and cognitive development, called gender-schema theory.

Gender-schema theory suggests that the social-learning processes of modeling and reinforcement work together with a child's developing mental abilities to facilitate the child's understanding of gender (Martin & Halverson, 1981, 1987). From a very early age, children are keen observers of their environment. They see which behaviors men and women engage in, and which of those behaviors are reinforced or punished. With these observations, children actively construct schemas on gender behaviors. These schemas then guide children's decisions about how they and others should behave (Martin & Ruble, 2004). Recall Frank McCourt's observation that if he cried when the teacher punished him, he suffered the further ridicule of the other boys. This observation contributed to his developing a gender schema that boys don't cry. The developed schema then guided his behavior with his family as we see him hold back his tears when he departs for America.

Nature and Nurture Influences on Gender-Role Behavior

Psychologists have explored the extent to which gender-role behavior is due to nature and/or nurture, and evidence for both exists. For example, research suggests that many gender differences appear across cultures and in other species, such as the preference to develop same-sex friendships and the higher level of activity and aggressiveness in males (Beatty, 1992). These findings suggest that gender differences may in part be influenced by hormonal or genetic differences between males and females. On the other hand, the child's environment is filled with messages about gender. These messages come from parents, teachers, peers, and the larger society as a whole and illustrate the power and impact of nurture on gender behavior (Bussey & Bandura, 1999).

Moms and Dads are the first source of information for babies on gender. Very early in infancy, babies learn to respond differently to their mothers and fathers, suggesting that schemas for gender roles are already developing. For example, on seeing the mother approach, babies are more likely to relax their bodies, showing lowered heart and respiration rates. When the father approaches, babies' heart and respiration rates increase, and they open their eyes wide, almost expecting the fun and games to begin. Do the babies' behaviors reflect actual differences in parental behaviors?

An extensive analysis of over 150 studies on parenting suggest that in many ways, sons and daughters are treated similarly (Lytton & Romney, 1991). Mothers and fathers encourage both their sons and daughters to be independent. Parents are equally warm to their children regardless of gender. However, it is in the area of gender roles that parents are most likely to respond differently to their daughters and sons. For example, parents hold different expectations for their children depending on their gender. Parents expect their children to play with gender-appropriate toys. Boys play with guns, cars, blocks, and balls. Girls are expected to play with dolls and tea sets, and enjoy activities such as dress-up, house, and school. Parents assign different household chores to their sons and daughters. Girls wash the dishes and do chores inside the house such as vacuuming and dusting. Boys take out the trash and do outdoor chores such as mowing the lawn, washing cars, and cleaning out the garage. Fathers are much more likely to hold to these gender stereotypes and tend to be less accepting of cross-gender behaviors, especially in their sons (Lytton & Romney, 1991).

Parents who are less likely to hold these gender expectations tend to have children who are less gender-typed (Weisner & Wilson-Mitchell, 1990). Moreover, children who *see* their parents behave in a less stereotypical fashion—moms taking out the trash or dads performing household tasks—also tend to be less gender-typed (Turner & Gervai, 1995). Parents, however, are not the only ones who influence children's gender roles. Once children begin school, teachers and peers influence gender schemas as well.

« **Application**

Are boys and girls treated differently in the classroom? Research suggests that gender bias exists in most classrooms. Gender bias is the favoring of one gender over the other because of different views of male and female roles. Teachers are more likely to reward girls for remaining close to the teacher. Boys are rewarded for behaviors away from the teacher, on the periphery of the classroom. Boys tend to receive both more positive and negative attention from teachers, and are called on more often (Beal, 1994; Hamilton, Blumenfeld, Akoh, & Miura, 1991). Teachers even respond differently to boys' and girls' schoolwork. Girls are praised when their work is orderly and neat. Boys are praised for their problem-solving ability (Sadker & Sadker, 1986). Teachers also may be more likely to accept wrong answers from girls but encourage boys to try harder when they make errors (Horgan, 1995).

After these differences were documented 10 to 20 years ago, many scholars and educators, believing that girls were being shortchanged in the classroom, argued for more same-sex education. Early studies suggested some benefits to all-girl schooling (Lee & Byrk, 1986), but more recent and more carefully controlled longitudinal studies indicate that students in single-sex schools generally do not perform any better than students from coed schools (LePore & Warren, 1997). Some researchers even argue that such concern over females has actually resulted in *reverse discrimination*, in which boys, rather than girls, are discriminated against in classrooms today (Sommers, 2000). For example, did you know that females, on average, earn higher grades than males in all subjects from elementary school through college (Halpern, 2000)?

Children's notions about gender also are reinforced within their peer groups, starting as early as 3 years old. Same-sex peers praise the child for engaging in gender-appropriate behaviors. Children who engage in gender-inappropriate behavior may be teased, laughed at, and even isolated from the group. Boys are particularly critical of same-sex peers who engage in "girlish" behavior resulting in even more harsh punishment for their activities (Levy, Taylor, & Gelman, 1995.)

Although sexism in general has decreased in the United States over the past 50 years, gender stereotypes have remained relatively stable over the last 25 years (Spence & Buckner, 2000). Society in many ways still contributes to children's gender stereotypes. Fast-food chains offer boy and girl toys with their children's meals. Some toy stores still have aisles marked "Boys" and "Girls." Many television shows still hold to traditional gender stereotypes. Males appear more frequently and tend to be the dominant characters. Only one-third of all television roles are for women. Male characters are more likely than female characters to engage in active tasks such as climbing or riding a bike. Females are more often depicted as passive, dependent, and emotional. Many of the female characters on television are not employed. When they do have jobs, they are often stereotypical ones such as teachers, nurses, and secretaries (Huston & Wright, 1998; Signorielli & Bacue, 1999). Not surprisingly, children—especially children who watch television frequently—adopt these gender-role stereotypes (Kimball, 1986; Signorielli & Lears, 1992).

Children's textbooks and picture books show similar stereotypes despite publishing guidelines to prevent them (Turner-Bowker, 1996). For example, Purcell and Stewart (1990) analyzed 62 elementary readers and found that although the number of male and female characters was about equal, and females were shown in a variety of activities, they were still portrayed as more helpless and dependent than males.

Daily interactions with others in society also reinforce traditional gender stereotypes. For example, the authors know a woman who ordered a suitcase for her daughter from a catalog. The suitcase was available in two color schemes: pastels and primary colors. The woman ordered the one in the bright primary colors. When the salesperson heard that it was for her daughter, the salesperson insisted that the woman order the pastel suitcase because that was meant for girls. The salesperson persisted for over 5 minutes in trying to get the woman to change her mind.

Parenting Styles and Attachment

Although most psychologists agree that parents are a major influence on a child's development, not all agree on the degree to which parents fit into this equation. Some suggest that parents' major influence is during the early years. Others argue that parents are but one influence of nurture that increasingly competes with nature and other environmental forces, such as a child's peers. Research on these issues has focused predominately in two areas: the attachment process and parenting styles.

Attachment

How does a bond form between an infant and a caretaker? **Attachment,** the emotional tie between the infant and the major caretaker, is usually firmly established by 8 to 9 months. Initially, psychologists believed that feeding provided the basis for building the attachment relationship: the baby feels connected to the major caretaker because the parent fulfills the infant's hunger. However, animal research by Harry Harlow in the 1950s changed the way we view the attachment process today.

attachment the emotional bond between the caretaker and infant that is established by 8 or 9 months

Harlow and Zimmerman (1959) wanted to investigate the nature of attachment. They used infant rhesus monkeys as subjects because ethical principles would prohibit such a study with human infants. They designed two artificial monkeys to act as surrogate mothers for the babies. One of the "surrogate mothers" was covered with a soft terry cloth fabric. The other "surrogate mother" was made of wire and had a feeding tube attached. The researchers wanted to see which "surrogate mother" the infants preferred. The infant monkeys went to the wire "surrogate mother" for food, but they clung to and spent most of their time with the cloth-covered "surrogate mother." This showed that feeding was not the reason the monkeys attached; rather, it was the close, warm contact that facilitated this bond. Establishing close warm contact through holding and caressing facilitates attachment. Human infants can easily attach to multiple people and objects, including fathers, grandparents, siblings, and teddy bears.

≪ Application

How can we tell whether an infant has formed an attachment? The attachment bond is readily seen in specific infant behaviors by the end of the first year. For example, most babies reserve certain behaviors for their parents. The infants smile when the parent approaches them, raise their hands toward the parent to be picked up, and nestle closer when the parent holds them.

Two additional signs of attachment include separation anxiety and stranger anxiety. **Separation anxiety** is a fear the infant expresses when separated from the major caretaker. This normally appears at about 6 or 7 months of age, and peaks at about 14 to 18 months of age. Separation anxiety gradually becomes less frequent and less intense throughout the toddler and preschool years. However, it is not uncommon for even older children to become anxious and fearful when separated from their parents for a long period of time (Thurber, 1995). In **stranger anxiety,** the infant becomes distressed when approached by unfamiliar people. Stranger anxiety typically appears between 8 and 10 months of age. It may intensify through the end of the first year, but usually subsides over the second year. Therefore, it is not unusual for a 1- or 2-year-old to cry or cling to a parent when she is approached by a doctor, an unfamiliar relative, or a new babysitter.

separation anxiety   the fear an infant expresses when separated from the major caretaker

stranger anxiety   the distress an infant expresses when faced with unfamiliar people

≪ Application

Close, warm contact facilitates the attachment bond.

Courtesy of Harlow Primate Lab, U. Of Wisconsin (both)

Although most infants will establish an attachment with a caregiver by the end of the first year, the quality of these attachments is not necessarily the same from infant to infant. Mary Ainsworth and her colleagues (Ainsworth, Blehar, Waters, & Wall, 1978) designed a research tool called the *strange situation procedure* to try to measure qualitative differences in infant attachments. In the strange situation procedure, infants and their parents are placed in an unfamiliar playroom. The infant's behavior is observed and measured as certain events occur. For example, does the infant explore the new situation and the toys when left in the playroom with the parent? How does the infant behave when a stranger enters the room? What is the baby's response when the parent leaves the room? What is the infant's reaction when the parent returns?

Observations of infants under these circumstances uncovered several patterns, or styles of attachment. Ainsworth described a secure attachment style and two patterns of insecure attachment: avoidant, and resistant.

- *Secure attachment.* Infants characterized as securely attached used the parent as a supportive base from which to operate and explore. They explore the toys while in the new situation, paying attention to any new strangers that may enter the room. They may or may not cry when the parent leaves, but this emotional upset quickly subsides once the parent returns.

- *Avoidant attachment.* Infants showing an avoidant attachment pattern appear to ignore the parent. They pay the parent little attention. They do not appear to be distressed when the parent leaves and they show little emotional response when the parent reappears.

- *Resistant attachment.* Infants who display this pattern of attachment very much resemble a "clinging" baby. They remain close to the parent and do not actively explore the new situation. They show extreme distress when the parent leaves and appear to be angry when the parent returns. They may hit and push at the parent and are less easily consoled.

Although the secure attachment is the most common pattern in the United States and in other industrialized cultures such as Germany and Japan (van Ijzendoorn & Kroonenberg, 1988), we must be cautious in interpreting the "insecure" patterns of attachment. Different child-rearing practices and cultural attitudes influence how we interact with our children, and these interactions as well as the larger social context appear to influence attachment. In some countries, children's independence is encouraged; in other countries, a closeness with the caretaker is emphasized. However, these same styles of attachment have generally emerged when infants are observed in natural, nonexperimental surroundings (Vaughn et al., 1992), suggesting that these styles of attachment are observed worldwide.

How does attachment influence development? Many psychologists endorse the notion that the quality of this first attachment relationship lays the foundation for the quality of all other relationships with friends and lovers. Research supports this reasoning to a certain degree. Securely attached infants are more likely to become curious, resilient, and self-controlled preschoolers. Such children also are more likely to persist in problem-solving tasks, do well in school, and interact more skillfully with their peers during the school years (Elicker, Englund, & Sroufe, 1992; Jacobsen & Hofmann, 1997; Kerns, Klepac, & Cole, 1996).

However, being securely attached at an early age does not guarantee an absence of problems later. Moreover, research has not been able to consistently document a negative or unfavorable picture of development for insecurely attached infants. Some studies suggest that insecurely attached infants are more prone to behavioral and adjustment problems in their social relations with others, whereas other studies do not

(Fagot & Kavanaugh, 1990; Hamilton, 2000; Rothbaum, Schneider Rosen, Pott, & Beatty, 1995). Bonds with individuals other than the caretaker can compensate for insecure attachments at home. Moreover, given the number of variables that can influence attachment, an early pattern of insecure attachment does not guarantee a lifelong pattern of insecure attachment. As family circumstances improve, so too may the quality of the attachment. Similarly, social relationships *after* infancy must also be considered when we evaluate children's psychological adjustment.

Recognizing that insecure attachments might be detrimental to development has led psychologists to investigate additional questions. For example, what happens if an infant is deprived of an attachment relationship? What if an infant is separated from the caretaker after establishing a relationship? Will these children suffer disastrous consequences? These questions are extremely important when we consider several modern-day scenarios.

- In the last decade, many court cases have had to consider the rights of biological parents compared with the rights of adoptive parents. For example, in March 1991, Jane and John Doe adopted a 4-day-old baby named Richard. Richard's biological mother gave up her son for adoption while her ex-boyfriend (the biological father) was out of the country. She told him that the baby had died after birth. In May 1991, the biological father returned to the country and the couple reconciled. When he was told that his son survived, the biological father challenged the adoption. Three and a half years later, a judge ruled in favor of the biological father, and Richard had to leave the two people he knew as parents for 4 years to live with a new family. Would Richard be able to make this adjustment?

  « Application

- Family and child service agencies across the nation must frequently make judgments concerning whether children living in negative environments should remain in their homes or be put in foster care. How does foster care influence the social development of the child?

  « Application

- Consider the plight of numerous Romanian babies left in orphanages who received only basic care during the totalitarian regime of Ceausescu. They were bathed, changed, and fed, but few had crib toys, were talked to, or were held. One caretaker was responsible for tending 10 to 20 babies at a time. Given these conditions, very few of the orphans had an opportunity to develop an attachment during their infancy. After the downfall of the Romanian government in 1990, many of these orphans were adopted by North American families. What impact may this lack of attachment have on their development?

  « Application

All of these real-world situations speak to the importance and consequences of attachment. Research on the institutionalized Romanian babies was not initially encouraging. It appeared that many infants who spent 8 months or more in the orphanages had problems in socialization. Many were withdrawn and had a difficult time relating to peers and family members (Fisher, Ames, Chisholm, & Savoie, 1997). However, a more recent investigation (Rutter & O'Connor, 2004) assessing attachment of these children to their adoptive parents when they were 4 and 6 years old, suggests that such negative effects were more likely in Romanian babies adopted between 24 and 42 months. It is difficult to know whether these negative effects will continue long term, given that these children are now in more positive environments. Yet most research supports the assertion that early severe deprivation of an attachment figure is likely to affect the quality of a relationship with an adoptive caregiver (O'Connor, Marvin, Rutter, Olrick, & Britner, 2003; Rutter & O'Connor, 2004).

Research on babies who are separated from their caregivers is somewhat more promising. For example, Bowlby (1960, 1980) studied infants who were separated from their caretakers due to the parent's illness or death. For infants who had already formed an attachment, certain patterns of grief emerged:

1. a protest stage, characterized by intense crying and searching for the caregiver

2. a despair stage, in which the infants became increasingly withdrawn and sad

3. a detachment stage, in which infants displayed a renewed interest in their usual activities; if the caregiver returned during this phase, she typically was ignored by the infant

In *Good Will Hunting,* Matt Damon plays the role of a man who lacked appropriate attachment figures in infancy, which then affects his ability to connect with others in adulthood.

For those situations in which the caregiver returned, many infants, although initially anxious, were able to reattach. However, babies who experienced repeated separations from caregivers entered a fourth phase of grieving in which they totally withdrew from relationships (Bowlby, 1980; Colin, 1996). Yet these patterns of grief, their intensity, and their duration, were highly variable. They were influenced by a large number of variables, including the new quality of care compared to the old quality of care, the level of security the infant exhibited toward the caregiver, and the personal qualities of the infant such as how readily he or she adapted to new situations (Rutter, 1981). In addition, family circumstances, such as a depressed mother, unemployment, or high levels of marital conflict, have the potential to influence the attachment relationship (Murray, Fiori-Cowley, Hooper, & Cooper, 1996; Touris, Kromelow, & Harding, 1995).

Parenting Styles

A parent's influence does not stop once the child reaches preschool age. At this time parents usually begin to employ what they feel are appropriate child-rearing practices to influence their children's behaviors and attitudes. Diana Baumrind (1967, 1971) investigated such practices by observing parents' interactions with their children. From her observations, three styles of parenting emerged.

Authoritarian parents tend to exert a high level of control and a low level of affection toward their children. They set high expectations for their children but without communicating to the children the reasons behind their expectations. "It's my way or the highway," would be a characteristic attitude of authoritarian parents. The children are not included in discussions of family issues, rules, or roles. They are to do what they are told. If they do not obey, force and physical punishment are used to get the child to comply. Baumrind found that children from these authoritarian households tended to be more withdrawn, anxious, and conforming compared to other children.

authoritarian parent a parenting style characterized by high levels of control and low levels of affection

Authoritative parents tend to exert moderate levels of control and affection toward their children. Authoritative parents are least likely to spank or hit their children. Rules—and the consequences for the rules—are established in a democratic manner, and children are included in family discussions. Reasonable expectations and demands are made of the children, and the children respond accordingly. Baumrind found that parents who use this style of parenting tended to have competent, happy, and self-confident children. It appeared to be the most effective approach to parenting. While Baumrind's sample was predominantly restricted to Caucasian Americans, these benefits to authoritative parenting also have been found to apply to several U.S. ethnic groups including African Americans, Asian Americans, and Hispanic Americans (Querido, Warner, & Eyberg, 2002; Steinberg, Lamborn, Dornbusch, & Darling, 1992). However, some research suggests that authoritative parenting does not have as beneficial effects for first-generation Chinese Americans (Chao, 2001).

authoritative parent   a parenting style characterized by moderate levels of control and affection

Permissive parents tend to show warmth and affection to their children, but have very little control over them. Discipline is lax. Children make their own decisions even when they may not be capable of doing so. Very few demands are made of the children in terms of rules or chores. In a way, permissive parents are kind but neglectful. Baumrind found that children of permissive parents tended to be the most immature. They were disobedient, lacked impulse control, and were most likely to be rebellious.

permissive parent   a parenting style characterized by moderate levels of affection but low levels of control

Now reflect on Frankie's parents for a moment. Did they *cause* him to act a certain way? Certainly not! Recall that these are correlations. As we discussed in Chapter 1, causal connections cannot be made from correlational data. A parent–child relationship is not a one-way street. Children influence the way parents treat them, beginning at birth. Children's different dispositions, gender, or birth order may influence how parents act. As the eldest, Frankie was often given the responsibility to care for his younger siblings, and as a male, he was encouraged at an early age to work and help support the family. The parent–child bond is a reciprocal relationship. Parents and children influence each other's behavior in a multitude of ways (Parke & Buriel, 1998).

Let's Review!

This section has described how infants and children socially develop—how nature and nurture influence gender role behavior and the attachment process—and described three different types of parenting. For a quick check of your understanding, answer these questions.

1. Ted is 12 months old and cries bitterly when his mother leaves him to go to work. Ted is most likely experiencing _____.

   a. an anxiety attack
   b. stranger anxiety
   c. separation anxiety
   d. assimilation

2. In the strange situation procedure, a baby who clings to the mother while she is present and who shows extreme distress when the mother leaves would be exhibiting which style of attachment?

   a. secure
   b. avoidant
   c. confused
   d. resistant

3. Parents who are extremely high in control and show little warmth to their children are characteristic of which parenting style?

   a. authoritarian
   b. authoritative
   c. permissive
   d. dependent

4. Which of the following statements about gender-role development is *false*?

   a. At 2 years old, toddlers can label their gender.
   b. At 4 years old, preschoolers have gender permanence.
   c. At 6 years old, children have gender roles.
   d. At 8 years old, children have gender permanence.

ANSWERS
1. c; 2. d; 3. a; 4. b

LEARNING OBJECTIVES < < < < < < < < <

Define temperament, and distinguish between the three temperamental styles of infants.

Describe Erikson's theory of psychosocial development as it applies to infants and children.

Personality Development

How does your personality develop? In the previous section we detailed how gender and your interactions with others influence your development. An equally powerful influence on development is your individual personality. Frankie McCourt's childhood was very much influenced by his personality. He was able to interpret events using humor, and he showed a consistent curiosity and continued quest to understand the world around him. In many cases, he took the initiative to help himself and his family survive. We do not develop solely in response to things happening to us. Part of our development is in fact influenced by what we bring to the situation. Two such ingredients include temperament and personality.

Temperament: Biology's Influence on Personality

Babies come into the world showing a general disposition to behave in certain ways in response to their surroundings. These differences are believed to be due more to the child's biological makeup than to his or her environment, especially because the child has not yet been exposed to any environment other than the womb. These differences at birth in behavioral style are referred to as **temperament.** In pioneering research, Stella Chess and Alexander Thomas (Chess & Thomas, 1984; Thomas & Chess, 1977, 1986) gathered information on numerous infant behaviors such as:

temperament a person's general pattern of attention, arousal, and mood that is evident at birth

- general activity level
- general mood
- ability to establish a regular pattern of eating and sleeping
- likelihood of approaching or withdrawing from new people and new situations
- ability to adapt to changes from their normal routine

From observing babies' tendencies on such variables, three temperamental styles of behavior emerged: easy infants, difficult infants, and slow-to-warm-up infants.

As the label implies, *easy infants* are generally in a good mood, establish a regular pattern of eating and sleeping, readily approach new objects and people, and adapt readily to changes in their routines. *Difficult infants*, in contrast, show more intense negative emotions such as crying. They have a more irregular pattern of eating and sleeping and are not as likely to approach new people and situations. Parents may even call such babies "colicky." *Slow-to-warm-up infants* are in between these two extremes. They are not as negative in response as difficult infants, and it takes them some time to adapt to new situations.

How does an infant's temperament influence parenting? Imagine that you have just become a parent and that your baby's temperament is easy. How would you feel about yourself as a parent? Your self-esteem would probably be very high and positive. Now consider the opposite situation—your baby has a difficult temperament. How would you feel as a parent? You would probably feel less capable. When we discussed the attachment process and parenting styles, we emphasized how children influence the parent–child relationship because of their individual unique qualities. One of these qualities is temperament. Does this mean that difficult infants are destined to become maladjusted adults? No. Although Thomas and Chess's longitudinal research (1986; Chess & Thomas, 1984) does suggest some stability in temperament from infancy to adulthood, other research has highlighted how weak these relationships are. For example, in one study, only 39% of the sample fell in the same temperamental category as adults that they had been placed in as preschoolers (Korn, 1984).

The persistence of these qualities into childhood and adulthood appears to depend on the *goodness of fit* between the child's temperament and his or her surrounding social relationships, like those with parents (Chess & Thomas, 1984; Kochanska, 1995). Consider a difficult infant with a permissive parent. Emotional outbursts may be met with attempts to "bribe" the baby into calming down, with little effort made to help the infant begin to handle being upset. The result may be immaturity and defiance that are likely to persist into childhood, causing additional problems in the family, school environment, and then the work world. Adolescents who have serious behavior problems are more likely to have had parents who could not manage their behavior (Maziade et al., 1990). Consider a difficult infant with an authoritarian parent. The parent will in all likelihood become increasingly frustrated with the difficult child's propensity to test the limits. Physical punishment or other consequences may continually escalate, leading to even further withdrawal or depression in a child or rebellion in an adolescent. The bad fit under these circumstances may result in the persistence of the difficult temperament.

In most cases, a difficult child needs a firm but loving hand, a parent who will adapt to the child's temperament, an authoritative parent. This parenting style will provide a good fit between the child and his or her environment. The difficult child will receive patience and reasonable limits within an atmosphere of love and caring. In such an environment, the difficult temperament may not be as evident in childhood or adulthood. The good fit between the child's temperament and the parent's style will result in a healthy parent–child relationship. Positive "nurturing" can modify the "nature" portion of a difficult temperament. Fortunately for Frankie, his easy temperament made a good fit with his parents' authoritarian and permissive styles.

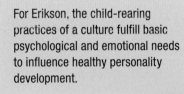

≪   Application

Erikson's Stages of Psychosocial Development: Culture's Influence on Personality

Not only does one's temperament influence the parent–child relationship, but so too does one's personality. Personality is the collection of one's enduring qualities that appear to be due to the influence of nature and nurture. In Chapter 14 we will discuss the major psychological theories of personality. For our purposes here, we will describe a well-known theory that emphasizes how children's personalities grow and develop as they are influenced by those around them: Erik Erikson's (1902–1994) stages of psychosocial development.

After studying child-rearing practices in several cultures, Erikson came to believe that all children have the same basic psychological and emotional needs that must be provided by their cultures or social environments, hence the name *psychosocial*. Erikson (1963, 1968, 1980) believed that children and adults progress through eight stages, or developmental crises. At each stage, the environment and the person's responses to the environment influence the development of either a healthy or an unhealthy personality characteristic. At each stage, the person incorporates a new quality into his or her personality. Resolving earlier stages with healthy outcomes makes it easier to resolve later stages with positive outcomes. An unhealthy resolution of a stage can have potential negative effects throughout life, although damage can sometimes be repaired at later stages. Four of Erikson's eight stages pertain to the childhood years and are discussed here. The other four stages focus on the adolescent and adult years and are discussed in the next chapter. Table 9.4 ◆ briefly describes all eight stages.

For Erikson, the child-rearing practices of a culture fulfill basic psychological and emotional needs to influence healthy personality development.

Archives of the History of American Psychology, University of Akron, Akron, Ohio

◆ **Table 9.4**

Erikson's Stages of Psychosocial Development

AGE	STAGE	DEVELOPMENTAL CHALLENGE
birth–1 year	Trust versus mistrust	Sense of security
1–3 years	Autonomy versus shame and doubt	Independence
3–6 years	Initiative versus guilt	Trying new things
6–12 years	Industry versus inferiority	Sense of mastery and competence
Adolescence	Identity versus role confusion	Sense of self, personal values, and beliefs
Young adulthood	Intimacy versus isolation	Commit to a mutually loving relationship
Middle adulthood	Generativity versus stagnation	Contributing to society through one's work, family, or community services
Late adulthood	Ego integrity versus despair	Viewing one's life as satisfactory and worthwhile

1. *Trust versus mistrust.* This stage occurs during the first year of life, when infants are totally dependent on others in their environment to meet their needs. An infant whose needs are met is more likely to develop trust in others than one whose needs are not met. Developing a sense of trust also fosters the development of a secure attachment.

2. *Autonomy versus shame and doubt.* From 1 to 3 years of age—the "terrible two's" as they are fondly referred to—toddlers struggle with separating from the major caretaker. They must negotiate an appropriate balance between autonomy, or independence, and dependence. If people in the toddler's environment belittle the child's efforts at independence or encourage dependence by being overly protective, then Erikson believed the child would be more likely to develop shame and doubt.

3. *Initiative versus guilt.* During the preschool years, Erikson believed that children's environments encourage the development of either initiative or guilt. When children develop initiative, they are motivated to take the first step, to start something on their own, and to be ambitious. Preschoolers are actively exploring their environments through trial and error. At the same time, they start to understand that others have expectations for their behavior, and they learn to read people's reactions to their explorations. From these explorations and observations, they begin to develop schemas of what they "ought to do." If these schemas conflict with what others in their environment expect from them, guilt may develop.

 Application »

4. *Industry versus inferiority.* During the elementary school years, children receive a great amount of feedback on their performance. They are in school 6 hours a day, where they receive a steady stream of information on their abilities. Their papers may have stars, red marks, or numbers on them. They may be grouped according to ability. Even though the groups may have neutral names such as the hawks, the blue jays, or the crows, children this age easily figure out the ability level of the group. Recall that children this age can reason logically, which enables them to compare their performance on a task with that of their peers. Consequently, they form opinions about which activities make them feel industrious, masterful, or competent, as well as ideas about activities or tasks that make them feel inferior or less capable of performing.

According to Erikson, by the time children approach adolescence, their personality has been shaped by the resolution of each of these developmental challenges. How the child resolves these issues has encouraged the development of either a healthy or a not so healthy personality. Erikson's other stages will be described in the next chapter.

Let's Review!

This section outlined personality development by defining temperament, describing three temperament styles, and describing the first stages of Erikson's theory of psychosocial development. For a quick check of your understanding, answer these questions.

1. Differences in behavioral style at birth are called

   _____.

   a. temperament   c. attachment patterns
   b. personality   d. goodness of fit

2. Jose is a very active toddler who prefers to do things by himself. According to Erikson, Jose appears to be successfully resolving which developmental crisis?

   a. trust versus mistrust   c. initiative versus guilt
   b. autonomy versus   d. industry versus inferiority
      shame and doubt

3. Because Lucinda feels competent and productive at school, Erikson would say she has successfully resolved which developmental crisis?

   a. trust versus mistrust   c. initiative versus guilt
   b. autonomy versus   d. industry versus inferiority
      shame and doubt

ANSWERS

1. a; 2. b; 3. d

Are You Getting the Big Picture?

In this chapter, we examined the many different ways in which infants and children develop. We hope that as you read this chapter, you were able to see how physical, cognitive, and social aspects of development influenced the life of Frankie McCourt. As you study the material of this chapter, see if you can apply the same developmental factors to your own life. For instance, how have nature and nurture influenced your development? Can you remember when you may have thought differently or had difficulty understanding a concept without observing it firsthand? (You may need to ask parents or older siblings to recall some of these instances.) How do you reason about moral issues, and has this changed over the years? Consider too how social and personal forces such as your temperament, your parents, your relationship with your parents, and your gender have influenced your life story.

As you look through the summary and key terms that follow, relate the material to your own life by generating personal examples that illustrate these concepts.

For example, identify children you know who are at different stages of cognitive development, moral reasoning, or psychosocial development. Try to identify different parenting styles in adults or temperaments in infants. Generating such examples will help you learn the material as well as provide you with more understanding of those around you. This understanding will be helpful in many careers: education, nursing, social services, emergency and safety personnel, and businesses that market toward children and/or parents.

Once you understand the major aspects of development, relate this material to the other areas of psychology that you have studied. For example, our description of infant motor and brain development reinforces many of the biological processes discussed in Chapter 2. Piaget's, Vygotsky's, and Kohlberg's theories are different perspectives on cognition and moral reasoning. We

(continued)

presented other perspectives on how we view the world and why we behave the way we do in three previous chapters on learning, memory, and problem solving. This chapter also has highlighted social and personal themes: gender, parents, temperament, and Erikson's aspects of psychosocial development. Many of these themes will be reinforced in later chapters as we explore gender and sexuality, social psychology, and personality. Work through the questions at the end of this chapter. They will help you integrate specific developmental terms and concepts into a big picture while enhancing your critical thinking skills.

After you have mastered the contents of this chapter, you will be ready to tackle the second chapter on development. Frankie McCourt's life story does not end on a ship bound for New York. Frank McCourt's second memoir, *Tis* (1999), describes his adolescent and young adulthood years. The saga for all of us continues in much the same way. We say goodbye to our childhood and enter the turbulent years of adolescence before saying hello to adulthood—where we spend the majority of our life. What do these years bring in the form of development? The next chapter addresses these issues.

Key Terms

development (388)
nature–nurture controversy (390)
cross-sectional design (393)
cohort effects (393)
longitudinal design (393)
cross-sequential design (394)
zygote (395)
germinal stage (395)
embryonic stage (396)
fetal stage (396)
Down syndrome (398)
teratogen (398)
critical periods (398)
fetal alcohol syndrome (FAS) (399)
neonate (400)
reflex (401)

gross motor skills (402)
fine motor skills (402)
cognition (405)
schema (405)
assimilation (406)
accommodation (406)
sensorimotor stage (406)
object permanence (407)
symbolic thinking (407)
preoperational stage (407)
centration (407)
conservation (407)
egocentrism (408)
concrete operations (408)
formal operations (410)
private speech (411)

zone of proximal development (ZPD) (411)
scaffolding (411)
moral reasoning (412)
gender roles (415)
gender permanence (416)
gender-schema theory (416)
attachment (418)
separation anxiety (419)
stranger anxiety (419)
authoritarian parent (422)
authoritative parent (423)
permissive parent (423)
temperament (424)

Test Yourself!

Concept Check

Test your knowledge of the chapter concepts by completing each of the following sentences with the correct term. For a more comprehensive review, visit the book Web site (http://psychology.wadsworth.com/pastorino1e/) for on-line quizzes, flashcards, crosswords, and Internet links.

(1) Pablo sees a porpoise for the first time and exclaims, "Look at the fishy, dad." Pablo is engaging in the cognitive process of _____. (2) Suzanne thinks it is wrong to take a cookie without asking because she knows she will get punished. Suzanne is at Kohlberg's _____ level of moral reasoning. (3) A basic unit of thought or idea is

called a(n) _____. (4) Ms. Lucy, the kindergarten teacher, tries her best to coach her students by making each task somewhat more difficult than the last and modeling how best to approach each task. Ms. Lucy's practice is consistent with _____ theory of cognitive development. (5) Baby Marissa seems to put everything in her mouth in order to learn about these objects. Piaget would say that baby Marissa is at the _____ stage of cognitive development. (6) Some students think it is wrong to cheat because it violates the student's code of conduct. Such students are operating at the _____ level of moral reasoning. (7) Jamal sees two differently shaped glasses filled with fluid. He recognizes that even though they look different, the glasses hold the same amount of fluid. Piaget would say that Jamal is operating at the _____ stage of cognitive development. (8) Teresa believed that all nurses were females until her recent hospital visit when two male nurses attended to her. Her change in attitude is probably due to the cognitive process of _____. (9) According to _____ theory of cognitive development, children are biologically programmed to seek to understand the world. (10) Honlei believes that there is a switch that turns the ocean's tide on and off. Honlei is most likely at Piaget's _____ stage of cognitive development.

accommodation

assimilation

concrete operations

conventional

Piaget's

preconventional

preoperational

schema

sensorimotor

Vygotsky's

Answers:

1. assimilation; 2. preconventional; 3. schema; 4. Vygotsky's; 5. sensorimotor; 6. conventional; 7. concrete operations; 8. accommodation; 9. Piaget's; 10. preoperational

Critical Thinking About the Chapter

1. At what age would you introduce your child to the following games and toys, and why?

a. a board game

b. building blocks

c. constructing a model spaceship

d. hide-and-seek

e. a chemistry set

2. Spend an hour watching television shows aimed at children, playing children's video games, or using computer programs developed for children. What messages, schemes, or concepts will children acquire from these sources? How might these messages influence their moral reasoning or gender attitudes? In your opinion, are these messages appropriate for children?

3. Analyze your parent(s)' style of discipline during your childhood. How would Baumrind classify their parenting style? How well did their style complement your temperament? What impact do you think your parent's style of discipline had on your development? Be specific, and cite examples to support your answer.

4. For each of Erikson's psychosocial stages of childhood, detail what specific behaviors may suggest that an individual is having difficulty resolving that particular stage.

Applying Psychology. Imagine that you have just been told that you are going to have a baby. Using your knowledge about infant development, design a nursery for your baby. Create a list of items you'd like to include such as furniture, toys, and bedding, and describe how you would decorate the walls.

Critical Thinking for Integration

1. How may operant conditioning (Chapter 5) influence children's understanding of gender? In your opinion, are males and females reinforced for the same behaviors? Do they receive the same reinforcers? Similarly, are males and females punished for the same behaviors? How do their punishments differ? How may differences in reinforcers and punishers influence gender typing in males and females?

2. Review the information on memory processing (Chapter 6) and problem solving (Chapter 7). What strategies and activities would Piaget and Vygotsky suggest are best for improving children's memory and problem-solving skills? Would they suggest the same techniques or different ones?

3. What variables could be used in a twin study that would suggest the degree to which intelligence (Chapter 7) is due to nature and nurture?

Chapter Study Resources

Suggested Readings

1. McCourt, F. (1996). *Angela's ashes.* New York: Scribner. Frank McCourt's childhood memoir of poverty and despair in Ireland.

2. Honig, A. S. (2000). Raising happy achieving children in the new millennium. *Early Child Development and Care, 163,* 79–106.
   This article brings together research on biology and socialization in discussing how to raise a happy, well-adjusted child.

3. Sommers, C. H. (2000). *The war against boys: How misguided feminism is harming our young men.* New York: Simon & Schuster.
   This book details recent educational findings on how boys and girls are treated in the classroom and how such treatment may influence their achievement and development.

4. For additional readings, explore InfoTrac College Edition, your online library of archived journal articles and periodicals. Go to http://www.infotrac-college .com/wadsworth and enter the passcode from the card that came with your book. For this chapter, search using these keywords:

   infant motor skills

   Piaget and concrete operations

   gender schema theory

   attachment style

   parenting style

Web Links for Further Study

Additional information on chapter concepts can be found at these Web sites:

1. Parent Soup is a useful site that links to relevant information on infant and children's health and behavior.
   http://www.parentsoup.com/

2. Baby Bag provides numerous links to developmental information including pregnancy and childbirth, parenting, health and safety, feeding and nutrition, and childcare.
   http://www.babybag.com/

3. The Jean Piaget Archives provides a list of Piaget's writings and access to publications inspired by Piaget's writings in the field of developmental psychology.
   http://www.unige.ch/piaget

4. The American Association of University Women (AAUW) provides links to research, issues, and community programs that promote education and equity for women and girls.
   http://www.aauw.org

5. Students will find detailed information, key facts, critiques, and other links on Erikson's stages of psychosocial development at this site.
   http://facultyweb.cortland.edu/~ANDERSMD/ERIK/welcome.HTML

Student Study Guide

To help organize your learning, work through Chapter 9 of the *What Is Psychology? Student Study Guide*. The study guide includes learning objectives, a chapter summary, fill-in review, key terms, a practice test, and other learning activities.

Psychology Now™

PsychologyNow is a Web-based, personalized study system that provides you with a pretest and a posttest for each chapter, quizzes you by chapter, and provides a personalized study plan, pointing you to elements in the text or in individual learning modules that will help you to achieve 80% mastery. Check out the learning modules that relate to this chapter: Piaget—the conservation of volume; moral development—Kohlberg.

PsychNow CD-ROM, Version 2.0

Go to the PsychNow CD-ROM for further study of the concepts in this chapter. The CD-ROM includes the learning modules with videos, animations, and quizzes, as well as simulations of psychological phenomena. Each module follows a consistent Explore, Lesson, and Apply structure that allows you to experience the concept or principle, learn more about it, and then apply it. You and your friends can participate in a team-based Quiz Game that makes learning fun. Learning modules include:
2a. Infant Development; 2b. Child Development.

How Do Children Grow, Change, and Develop?

Child development includes changes in physical, emotional, social, and cognitive behavior and abilities over time.

WHY STUDY DEVELOPMENT?

• Most psychologists today recognize that an interaction of nature (one's biology) and nurture (one's environment and culture) shape a person's development. Twin studies, adoption studies, and kinship studies are used to study the effects of nature and nurture.

• To study age changes in development, psychologists use cross-sectional designs (studying people of different ages on some aspect of development at one time), longitudinal designs (following one cohort group over a lengthy period of time), and cross-sequential designs (which combines features of the cross-sectional and longitudinal designs).

PRENATAL DEVELOPMENT: CONCEPTION TO BIRTH

• During the first 14 days after conception, known as the germinal state, the fertilized egg—or zygote—undergoes rapid cell division and duplication.

• During the embryonic stage, from 2 weeks after conception through the 8th week, major organs and organ systems form.

• During the fetal stage, from the 9th week of pregnancy until birth, body organs and systems more fully develop.

• Any environmental agent that poses harm during prenatal development is considered a teratogen. One of the most prevalent teratogens is alcohol.

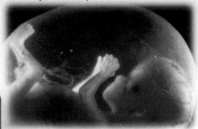

PHYSICAL DEVELOPMENT: GROWING, MOVING, EXPLORING

• A young child's brain is highly plastic, or changeable, and very dense compared to the adult brain. This ensures the child's best chance of adapting to the environment.

• An infant is born with a set of reflexes, such as sucking, rooting, and grasping, that help the infant survive.

• Motor development refers to the changes in a child's physical capabilities.

• Gross motor skills refer to behaviors that involve large muscle groups and allow the child to run, walk, jump, and hop.

• Fine motor skills involving small muscle groups develop later, and include such activities as writing, using utensils, or playing a musical instrument.

COGNITIVE DEVELOPMENT

• Jean Piaget suggested that children's mental abilities are biologically programmed and predictable, and his theory of cognitive development is still widely appreciated today.

• Piaget found that a child forms a schema (a mental idea or concept) that helps the child organize his or her world. In assimilation, children apply an already existing schema to understand their environment. In accommodation, existing schemas are changed or modified, or new ones are created in order to adapt to some change in the environment.

• Piaget explained the following states of cognitive development:
  • Sensorimotor stage (from birth to 2 years)
    • Preoperational stage (from age 2 to age 6 or 7)
    • Concrete operational stage (from age 6 or 7 through age 12)
    • Formal operational stage (from the teenage years)
    • Unlike Piaget, Lev Vygotsky emphasized that mental processes begin externally and stressed the importance of culture and social interactions in a child's cognitive development.
      • Vygotsky argued that a child's private speech represented an internal monitor that guided the child's actions.
      • According to Vygotsky, a child's zone of proximal development was the gap between what a child can already do and what he or she is not yet capable of doing. Scaffolding provides children with enough assistance until they are able to accomplish something on their own.

MORAL REASONING

• Lawrence Kohlberg suggested that moral reasoning in children develops in stages.

• At the preconventional level, children make decisions about right or wrong based on their ability to avoid punishment or gain rewards.

• At the conventional level, children understand rules and expectations of others, so their moral reasoning is based on the standards of the group or society.

• At the postconventional level, the individual understands contractual and universal principles of morality, realizes extenuating circumstances, and develops internal standards of right and wrong.

• Carol Gilligan criticized Kohlberg's theory for not noting how male and female responses differ. Gilligan proposed that males tend to be more focused on concepts of fairness and justice, whereas females are more likely to emphasize their concern, care, and relations with others. Research evaluating gender differences in moral reasoning has not strongly supported Gilligan's claims.

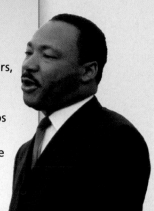

SOCIAL DEVELOPMENT

• From a very early age children process and develop schemas about gender roles—society's expectations for how a female or a male should behave.

• Gender-schema theory suggests that the social learning process of modeling and reinforcement work together with a child's developing mental abilities to facilitate the child's understanding of gender.

• Attachment is the emotional tie between the infant and the primary caregiver that is usually firmly established by 8 or 9 months. Mary Ainsworth's research identified three major patterns of attachment: secure, avoidant, and resistant.

• Children's first relationships in life are very important to their cognitive, emotional, and social growth. A secure attachment during infancy provides the child with a positive model of the dynamics of relationships with others.

• Diana Baumrind identified three major styles of parenting: authoritarian, authoritative, and permissive. Research shows that the most effective is authoritative parenting, in which parents exert moderate control over their children while also exhibiting warmth and affection.

PERSONALITY DEVELOPMENT

• A general disposition, evident from birth, to behave in certain ways in response to one's surroundings is known as temperament. Three temperamental styles include easy infants, difficult infants, and slow-to-warm-up infants.

• Temperamental qualities appear to persist into childhood and adulthood and depend on the goodness of fit between the child's temperament and his or her surrounding social relationships.

• Psychologist Erik Erikson argued that children and adults progress through eight stages of psychosocial development, or developmental crises. At each stage, the environment and the child's responses to the environment influence the development of either a healthy or an unhealthy personality characteristic.

"At thirty-nine, I became the master of my own destiny, but I did not have the freedom to choose freedom. It was thrust upon me."

FROM HELIE LEE, *STILL LIFE WITH RICE: A YOUNG AMERICAN WOMAN DISCOVERS THE LIFE AND LEGACY OF HER KOREAN GRANDMOTHER.* (New York: Simon and © Schuster, 1996, p. 278.)

Wilfried Krecichwost/Getty Images

How Do Adolescents and Adults Change and Develop?

CHAPTER PREVIEW

The Changes and Challenges of Life

In the previous chapter we discussed the developmental changes that occur from infancy through childhood. This chapter tracks the changes that occur as a child develops into an adolescent, and the changes that take the adolescent into adulthood. Development continues during the adult years, too. In adulthood we experience physical, cognitive, and social changes, but these changes can be much more variable than the stages of childhood and adolescence. For example, some of us may face enormous challenges or go through many changes in establishing a career. Others may readily find their life's work and maintain a relatively smooth career path. For some people adulthood may be marked by abrupt changes due to divorce, illness, or death. Others may coast through adulthood experiencing few such disruptions.

This chapter's case study is the life story of Hongyong Baek, as told by her granddaughter Helie Lee in *Still Life with Rice* (1996). As you read about the challenges that she faced, think about those changes that have already affected your development. At the same time, consider and imagine what challenges may still lie ahead of you. Is the person you are today capable of surviving the journey of adulthood?

Hongyong Baek was born in Korea in 1912, the second of four children and the first daughter. Her parents were wealthy, and Hongyong was her father's favorite. As was the custom for Korean girls, at the age of 9 Hongyong began daily lessons in virtue, womanhood, and managing a household, but her headstrong temperament made it hard for her to accept this teaching. Some of these messages were confusing too. For example, her mother told her that menstruation was a woman's curse. Yet she also was told that her body should remain untouched—"As long as you are untouched, you are worth something. Protect it with your life." Her younger sister became crippled by disease and was renamed Crippled Sister. Hongyong was given the responsibility of carrying Crippled Sister everywhere. In addition, Crippled Sister became their father's favorite, a change that made Hongyong feel as if *her* life was crippled.

Unwed at 22, Hongyong feared she was too plain and clumsy to marry. She prayed to Buddha for a husband; without one she was considered a burden on her family. A marriage was arranged, to 19-year-old Dukpil Lee. Hongyong now belonged to another man's family: "My position as first daughter . . . was over. . . . From this day forward I would never be called by my childhood name. 'Lee's wife' was my new title" (p. 65). To her surprise, Hongyong's husband encouraged her to share her ideas and opinions, and her affection for him grew. She gave birth to a boy, Yongwoon, fulfilling her most important wifely duty by giving her husband a son. Over the next 15 years, Hongyong was pregnant seven times and bore four more children, two daughters and two sons.

In 1939, as Hongyong gloried in the role of wife and mother, civil unrest in her country, long occupied by the Japanese, grew. Korean culture was being forcibly replaced by Japanese customs. Schoolchildren were forbidden to speak Korean and were taught to read and write only in Japanese. Children were given Japanese names, retaining their Korean given and family names in secret. Not wanting to lose their Korean heritage, Hongyong and Dukpil and two of their children left behind all that was familiar and went to China.

At Hongyong's suggestion, they started a sesame-oil business. The business prospered, yet Hongyong grew bored. Against her husband's wishes, she began to smuggle opium. Soon they had more money than they could spend. However, her husband spent more and more time away from her and had affairs with other women.

With permission of Simon & Schuster Adult Publishing Group

"Gradually freedom transformed me into a totally daring woman."

(Lee, 1996 p. 278)

Summary of *Still Life with Rice: A Young American Woman Discovers the Life and Legacy of Her Korean Grandmother* by Helie Lee. Copyright © 1996 by Helie Lee. Used by permission of Scribner, an imprint of Simon & Schuster Adult Publishing Group. Used with permission

Hongyong's insecurities about her appearance resurfaced. In an effort to keep her husband's attention, they opened a restaurant to entertain the most prominent and powerful people in China, including Japanese and Chinese officials.

In her 30s, health problems plagued Hongyong. She discovered the ancient art of *ch'iryo,* a healing technique in which the flesh is pinched and slapped in order to improve blood circulation. Hongyong used *ch'iryo* to improve her health. She felt as if she had discovered the fountain of youth. She treated herself and her children daily.

When she was 32 years old, Hongyong received news of her father's and older brother's deaths. A year later, in 1945, Americans dropped the atomic bomb on Japan, and the Japanese surrendered Korea. Thousands of Koreans boarded trains to head to their homeland, the Lee family among them. The family returned to North Korea, which was quickly occupied by Korean communists. Most of their land and money were confiscated. As her husband turned to alcohol, Hongyong converted to Christianity and developed a thirst for knowledge. She questioned her reason for living, learned how to read and write, and gave away what little riches they had left.

In 1950, the Korean War erupted at the 38th parallel. North Koreans and South Koreans fought over differing political and religious ideologies. The sounds of air-raid sirens and bombing attacks filled the air. All men were being forced into the Red Army, and the police came looking for Dukpil and their oldest son. Because of her religion, Hongyong was imprisoned for "treasonous" activities. She spent 30 days in an overcrowded prison cell, secretly praying at night. Her daughter Dukwah dodged bombs and gunfire to bring her baby sister Dukhae to be breast-fed by Hongyong every day. Once she was released, Hongyong knew the men would not be safe unless they went to South Korea.

Hongyong watched her husband leave, and then bid farewell to her eldest son. Unable to bear the waiting, Hongyong packed up her four remaining children to cross the Taedong River. Of course, thousands of other refugees had the same idea. During the crossing, Hongyong and her baby were trampled. They eventually made it across and Hongyong prepared to bury her baby. Miraculously, Dukhae was still breathing, although barely. With frozen feet, empty bellies, and little energy, the family continued to walk, hoping to find shelter and peace. At one point, Hongyong was so tired and exhausted that she wanted to leave Dukhae under a tree to die. Because the baby was practically dead, Hongyong thought to sacrifice her in hopes that the rest of the family would survive. But Dukwah refused to leave her sister and the two women took turns carrying her.

Amidst exploding bombs, throngs of people, and piles of wreckage, the Lee family made it to Seoul, 2 weeks before the South Korean borders closed. Hongyong found her husband in a refugee camp, but her eldest son, Yongwoon, never appeared. The agony was too much for Hongyong. For 8 months, she was a living ghost, ignoring her husband and children, forgetting to pray. She sat on a crate all day, staring into space, barely eating or sleeping. Her husband took care of the children and made ends meet by peddling gum and cigarettes. Finally, Hongyong's two sisters found her and took in the entire family.

Just as their lives were returning to some sort of normalcy, Hongyong's husband contracted diphtheria. She watched him die and vowed to find her way back to God. Just shy of 40 years old, she was a widow. She again questioned her purpose in life and turned back to her *ch'iryo.* As her patients' health improved, more clients— prestigious clients who repaid her in goods—came looking for her services. Her hands could not keep up with the demand, so she developed an internship program to train other women in the art of *ch'iryo.*

As Hongyong's practice expanded, her children grew. Her youngest was in high school and her two sons were attending college. Dukwah had graduated from college, married, and had given Hongyong two granddaughters. She enjoyed being a grandmother and doted on them with affection. Yet fear of war encouraged her to use her connections to get immigrant papers processed for Dukwah and her family to go first to Canada and then to the United States. As her 60th birthday approached, Hongyong waved goodbye to her daughter and granddaughters.

Eight years later, Hongyong bid farewell to Korea and immigrated to America herself, but she never stopped searching for her eldest son. After 40 years, she finally received news. He was alive! He had been caught behind the lines in North Korea. At 80 years of age, Hongyong finally achieved peace of mind.

Hongyong's story illustrates the sometimes dramatic kinds of turning points that shape adolescent and adult development. You can see the complex interplay of Hongyong's own physical, cognitive, social, and emotional development with circumstance and culture. From puberty to pregnancy to old age, physical processes influenced how Hongyong thought of herself and her abilities. Such thinking also influenced her values and goals in terms of what she wanted to be. At first, she worried over who her husband would be. She then wanted power, money, and a family. During and after the war she searched for personal meaning in her life and questioned her purpose on earth.

Hongyong's relations with others also influenced her development. She went from being a child in her father's household to being a wife and mother in her husband's family home. She went off to China, traveled back to Korea, fled South during the war, and eventually went to the United States. She bore five children and later became a grandmother. She adopted several work roles: businesswoman, opium madam, restaurateur, and *ch'iryo* therapist.

She experienced numerous losses in her life, including three miscarriages. She watched her husband die, and bore the loss of her brother and parents when she was far from them. She went years before knowing that her eldest son had survived the war. She was raised a Buddhist and became a Christian; she grew up a Korean and became a U.S. citizen on her 80th birthday.

We hope that by understanding the physical, cognitive, and social aspects of adult development, you will be able to appreciate the many forces that make you, your parents, your grandparents, and your spouses unique, just as Hongyong Baek's adulthood journey makes her tale one of a kind. We'll begin with the physical changes that characterize adolescence and adulthood. Then we'll review cognitive changes and psychological transitions, including more of the developmental stages outlined by Erik Erikson, which we discussed in the previous chapter. We'll also look at social relationships, work and careers, and the end of life.

LEARNING OBJECTIVE < < < < < < < <

Describe the physical changes that occur in adolescence and adulthood.

Physical Changes in Adolescence and Adulthood

During adolescence and adulthood we both peak and decline in terms of our physical development. How much and how rapidly we decline are very much influenced by both nature and nurture. Genes affect how we age, but so does the degree to which we exercise mind and body, and the experiences we have as we age. What we think of as aging is an incremental and gradual process, but growing into our sexual maturation can be abrupt and actually quite dramatic. We are referring of course to the onset of puberty.

Puberty: Big Changes, Rapid Growth

puberty   the period and process of sexual maturation

Puberty is the process of sexual maturation. These developmental changes involve overall body growth and maturation of sex characteristics that enable people to sexually reproduce. Puberty generally occurs 2 years earlier in girls than boys, but the timing of puberty from one person to another and from one culture to another varies greatly (Rice, 1992). Over the last 100 years, the age when puberty begins dropped in the United States, Western Europe, and Japan. Even within the United States, African American girls tend to enter puberty a year earlier on average than white girls (Kaplowitz et al., 1999).

Physical Changes That Puberty Brings

What physical changes do adolescents experience? A growth spurt shortly after age 10 for girls and after age 12 for boys adds almost 10 inches in height and about 40 pounds in weight to the average adolescent's body. This growth spurt and the overall body changes in adolescents are the result of an increase in growth hormone released from the pituitary gland (see Chapter 2). Girls' hips broaden relative to their shoulders, and boys' shoulders widen relative to their hips. Both sexes gain muscle and fat during puberty; however, girls gain more fat and boys gain more muscle. Because these changes are abrupt and uneven at times, early adolescence is especially regarded as an awkward phase of development (Malina, 1990).

In addition to overall growth, puberty also includes maturation of the primary sex organs and secondary sexual characteristics, caused by the release of sex hormones. **Primary sexual characteristics** refer to the internal and external reproductive organs. **Secondary sexual characteristics** are external signs of sexual maturity such as the development of facial or pubic hair. In girls, sex hormones cause the breasts, ovaries, uterus, and vagina to mature, and initiate the start of their first menstrual cycle, or **menarche.** Pubic hair and underarm hair also develop. In boys, sex hormones cause the penis, scrotum, and testes to mature. These changes are accompanied by the growth of body hair and a deepening of the voice as the larynx enlarges. On average, males and females complete the process of puberty within 4 to 5 years (Wheeler, 1991). Figure 10.1 summarizes the physical changes that boys and girls experience during puberty.

primary sexual characteristics   organs directly related to reproduction that develop during puberty

secondary sexual characteristics physical signs of sexual maturation during puberty that do not involve the sex organs such as breast development in females and voice changes in males

menarche   a girl's first menstruation

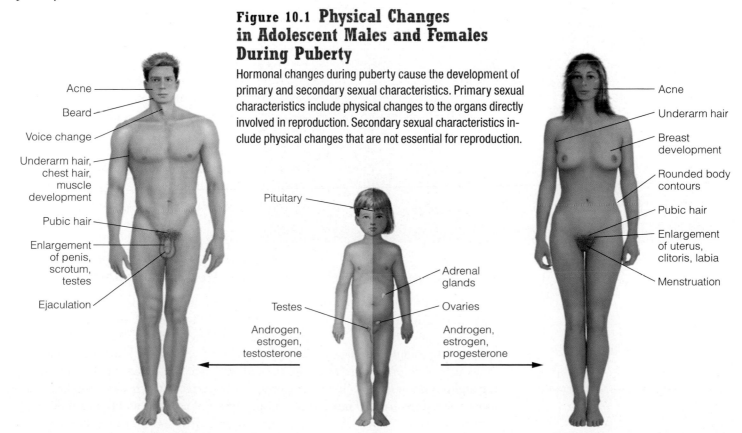

Figure 10.1 Physical Changes in Adolescent Males and Females During Puberty
Hormonal changes during puberty cause the development of primary and secondary sexual characteristics. Primary sexual characteristics include physical changes to the organs directly involved in reproduction. Secondary sexual characteristics include physical changes that are not essential for reproduction.

Acne
Beard
Voice change
Underarm hair, chest hair, muscle development
Pubic hair
Enlargement of penis, scrotum, testes
Ejaculation

Pituitary
Adrenal glands
Testes
Ovaries
Androgen, estrogen, testosterone
Androgen, estrogen, progesterone

Acne
Underarm hair
Breast development
Rounded body contours
Pubic hair
Enlargement of uterus, clitoris, labia
Menstruation

Psychological Changes of Puberty

How do adolescents react to the physical changes of puberty? Puberty has a definite emotional and psychological impact, particularly on the adolescent's self-image and mood. Typically, adolescents' reactions to these physical changes are mixed, but if they are prepared for the upcoming changes and have a supportive family, psychological adjustment to puberty is better (Koff & Rierdan, 1995; Moore, 1995; Stein & Reiser, 1994). As we saw in the opening case study, Hongyong's lack of knowledge and understanding of these changes made puberty confusing for her. Many adults attribute teenagers' moodiness to "raging hormones." Yet the link between higher hormone levels and moodiness is not strong (Nottelmann, Inoff-Germain, Susman, & Chrousos, 1990). Mood swings are very much influenced by adolescents' changing social environments as they frequently move from one activity to another.

The timing of puberty also has a psychological impact on the self-image of an adolescent, one that is different for boys and girls. For boys who mature early, the growth in stature and muscle brings with it a better self-image than for boys who mature later. In contrast, it is the early-maturing females who experience more adjustment difficulties during adolescence (Alsaker, 1995; Ge, Conger, & Elder, 1996). Girls whose breasts develop early may find the attention they receive hard to cope with and fraught with pressures to become sexually active when they may not be ready cognitively and emotionally to do so. Girls who develop later are better adjusted to these changes because the pressure to become sexually active occurs at an older age, when their cognitive abilities are better able to handle such pressures. We saw in Chapter 8 how females' eating disorders may be intimately tied to their body image in adolescence. For boys, developing facial hair, larger shoulders, and a deepening voice is less problematic. However, long-term studies suggest that the effects of early versus late maturation in puberty may be short-lived. In addition, some studies suggest a benefit to the turmoil caused by puberty. Many early-maturing females and late-maturing males who experienced difficulties during their teenage years exhibited more effective coping skills in adulthood (Livson & Peskin, 1980; Peskin, 1973).

The physical changes of puberty and the cognitive ability to think abstractly often make teenagers self-conscious about their appearance.

Greg Ceo/Getty Images

Brain Changes in Adolescence and Adulthood

In addition to pubertal changes, a tremendous amount of brain development takes place during adolescence and into early adulthood. Medical technology such as magnetic resonance imaging (MRI and fMRI; see Chapter 2, p. 81) has allowed researchers to examine teenage brains by repeatedly scanning the same individual over the course of several years. These studies indicate dynamic changes in brain anatomy throughout adolescence. Such changes appear to start at the back of the brain and move toward the front (Figure 10.2). The number of neurons and the complexity of

Figure 10.2 Changes in the Adolescent Brain

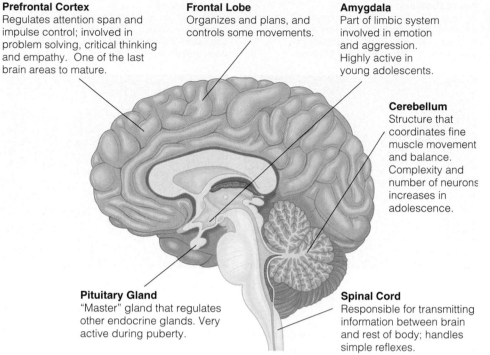

Prefrontal Cortex
Regulates attention span and impulse control; involved in problem solving, critical thinking and empathy. One of the last brain areas to mature.

Frontal Lobe
Organizes and plans, and controls some movements.

Amygdala
Part of limbic system involved in emotion and aggression. Highly active in young adolescents.

Cerebellum
Structure that coordinates fine muscle movement and balance. Complexity and number of neurons increases in adolescence.

Pituitary Gland
"Master" gland that regulates other endocrine glands. Very active during puberty.

Spinal Cord
Responsible for transmitting information between brain and rest of body; handles simple reflexes.

Figure 10.2 Changes in the Adolescent Brain

Changes in the adolescent brain generally start at the back of the brain and move toward the front. Hence the areas of the brain that are most involved in problem solving, planning, and critical thinking are the last areas to mature.

their connections increase in the cerebellum. Recall that the cerebellum is necessary for balance of the body, muscle tone, and performance of motor skills (p. 68). Compared to adults, the amygdala is more active in teens and larger in males (Baird et al., 1999; Durston et al., 2001). As we saw in Chapter 2 (p. 69) the amygdala regulates our emotional reactions. Nerve fibers in the corpus callosum—the band of nerves that connects the two cerebral hemispheres—also thickens before and during puberty (Thompson et al., 2000).

Just prior to puberty there appears to be a second wave of overproduction of cortical gray matter—the tissue that covers the outside of the cerebral hemispheres that appears gray due to the absence of myelin on the axons (Durston et al., 2001; Giedd et al., 1999; Sowell, Thompson, Tessner, & Toga, 2001). The brain then prunes these connections as it did earlier in life—keeping the connections that are used whereas those that are not used wither away (Figure 10.3). This gray matter growth spurt predominates in the prefrontal cortex—the area that plays a major role in cognitive processes like problem solving, judgment, reasoning, impulse control, and the planning and execution of behavior. This is among the latest brain area to mature, not reaching adult dimensions until the early 20s (Casey, Giedd, & Thomas, 2000; Giedd, 2004).

Do these brain changes cause teenagers' behavior? We may infer that these brain changes are responsible for adolescent behavior. For instance, the changes in the cerebellum may explain why young teens tend to be more physically uncoordinated and awkward than older teens and adults. The immaturity of the prefrontal cortex may explain why teenagers' judgment and reasoning may not always be sound. However, correlation does not mean causation (Chapter 1, pg. 30). Structural changes in the brain correlate with teenage behavior, but that does not mean that they cause their behavior. It is still too early to understand how brain development influences what teens do and why they do it. Brain-scanning techniques are a crude level of analysis. Many brain-cell responses are too fast for an MRI to track. Brain data also does not take into account environmental and cultural factors that contribute to brain processing and behavior. Adolescents all over the world experience roughly the same process

Figure 10.3 **Neural Growth and Pruning**

During early adolescence, new neural connections are formed. In a process called pruning, those that are used will be strengthened, whereas those that are not wither away. Hence engaging in stimulating and interesting activities during adolescence is good for our brains.

From TIME, 5/10/2004. Reprinted with permission.

Nerve Proliferation...
By age 11 for girls and 12 for boys, the neurons in the front of the brain have formed thousands of new connections. Over the next few years most of these links will be pruned.

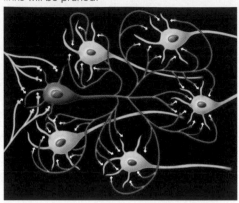

...and Pruning
Those that are used and reinforced—the pathways involved in language, for example—will be strengthened, while the ones that aren't used will die out.

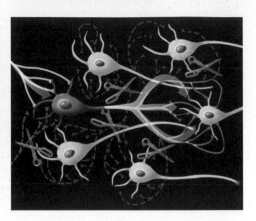

Application

of brain development, yet teenagers in different cultures and environments do not all behave the same way. However, we do know that teenagers and young adults have continued opportunity to develop their brain through activities in which they participate. Exercising their minds by reading, doing mathematics, and playing sports or music will strengthen neural connections. Research on changes in the adolescent brain also may help us understand why teenagers think differently than adults—a topic we will discuss shortly.

Is the brain completely developed at adolescence? No. The adult brain continues to grow and develop throughout our entire lives. Neural stem cells in various regions of the brain continuously generate neurons throughout life (Schmidt-Hieber, Jonas, & Bischofberger, 2004). The brain remains highly plastic—able to adapt in response to new experiences such as new jobs, marriage, divorce, children, new friends, and financial responsibilities.

Physical Changes From Early to Later Adulthood

What physical changes do we experience in adulthood? We hit our biological prime during early adulthood when all major biological systems reach full maturation. Both women and men peak during their late 20s and early 30s in terms of physical strength, stamina, coordination, dexterity, and endurance (Whitbourne, 1996). These abilities gradually and slowly decline in middle and late adulthood.

A similar process occurs in our sensory abilities. Visual acuity, or the ability to focus vision, peaks in our early 20s and remains fairly high until middle adulthood. As we age we become progressively farsighted, such that reading glasses or bifocals may become necessary in middle or late adulthood (see Chapter 3). Hearing also declines somewhat by the late 20s, especially for high-pitched tones such as a distant telephone or a doorbell. However, people's senses of taste, smell, and touch remain fairly stable until late adulthood.

We see additional signs of the aging process in people's physical appearance as they approach their 40s and 50s. The skin starts to show wrinkles and the hair may thin and turn gray. Weight gain is likely as metabolism slows, causing noticeable "love handles" or a "pot-belly." Then, as people approach their 60s, they typically begin to lose weight and muscle, which may result in a sagging of the skin (Haber, 1994). The compression of vertebrae combined with a loss of bone tissue result in a loss of height as people age.

Aging: The Influence of Lifestyle and Culture

Although many physical abilities decline over the adult years, it is not clear that these declines are inevitable. As we discuss in more detail in Chapter 13, lifestyle factors such as a poor diet, smoking, drinking alcohol, and lack of exercise contribute to the decline in physical functioning for some people. Moreover, culture markedly influences the way we think about aging and our expectations of our physical abilities in middle and later adulthood. In Western cultures such as the United States, becoming old is associated with being frail, useless, and ill, so that many people attempt to push back the aging process. Yet in countries such as Brazil, China, Japan, and Russia, where older people are more valued, aging is viewed more positively and is perceived as a time to look forward to rather than to dread (Gardiner, Mutter, & Kosmitzki, 1998). In addition, across the world many older people, despite changes in physical functioning, still lead an active lifestyle (Baltes, 1997). As people age, they can usually continue their daily activities by making some adjustments and allowing themselves more time.

<< Application

Gender and Reproductive Capacity

Our reproductive capacity also changes during the adulthood years. Women's fertility steadily decreases from age 15 to age 50 (McFalls, 1990). Sometime around age 50, on average, women undergo changes associated with the process of **menopause.** Menopause signals the end of a woman's childbearing years. Her body produces less and less estrogen, affecting the number of eggs that are released from the ovaries. Eventually ovulation and menstruation stop all together. Decreasing levels of estrogen also cause the breasts and the uterus to shrink. The vaginal walls produce less lubrication, which may make sexual intercourse somewhat more painful.

menopause   the period when a female stops menstruating and is no longer fertile

Although men do not experience a "male menopause," they too undergo hormonal changes after age 60 termed *andropause* (Finch, 2001; Whitbourne, 2001). They gradually produce fewer male hormones as they age, which lowers the concentration of sperm in the semen and results in hair loss on the legs and face. However, men are still capable of producing offspring into their 70s, 80s, and 90s.

Despite these reproductive changes, older adults can continue to have active and satisfying sex lives (Michael, Gagnon, Lauman, & Kolata, 1994). Women may feel renewed sexual energy after menopause because they are freed from the concerns of contraception and childcare. Moreover, older adults report high levels of satisfaction in intimacy in their sexual relations even into their 80s!

Because many cultures equate "looking old" with being unattractive, especially for women, middle age and later life may not seem very appealing. Look at how many American television commercials and print advertisements aimed at middle-aged people focus on staying thin and looking young and vibrant. Many times Hongyong Baek reflected on how her physical changes—wrinkled skin, gray hair, and drooping body parts—and appearance made her less desirable to her husband, and therefore less worthy of his love. Many of her physical changes undoubtedly were accelerated by her wartime experiences and by giving birth to five children. However, despite the effects of aging, almost 70% of people over 65 report being in excellent to good health (Hobbs, 1996). Although older adults may not be pleased with aspects of physical aging, they are no less content with their lives. Happiness and contentment perhaps have more to do with people's ability to adjust to these changes than the actual changes themselves. One important ingredient of adapting to change is how a person thinks and processes information, our next topic of discussion.

<< Application

Tony Randall fathered two children in his 70s.

Myrna Suarez/Getty Images

Let's Review!

This section detailed the physical changes of adolescence and adulthood. As a quick check of your understanding, answer these questions.

1. Which of the following is *not* a physical change associated with puberty in males?
   a. growth of the testes
   b. voice change
   c. widening hips
   d. broadening shoulders

2. Andre, a 50-year-old man, is likely to experience all of the following as the result of aging *except*:
   a. weight loss
   b. thinning of the hair
   c. loss in visual acuity
   d. loss of smell

3. Which one of the following adolescents is most likely to have a positive self-image?
   a. an early maturing female
   b. an early maturing male
   c. a late maturing female
   d. a late maturing male

ANSWERS

1.c.2.a.3.b

LEARNING OBJECTIVE
< < < < < < < <
Describe cognitive changes in reasoning, memory, and other mental abilities in adolescence and adulthood.

Cognitive Changes in Adolescence and Adulthood

Adolescence and adulthood are also marked by changes in the way that we think. Children on the threshold of adolescence are beginning to separate from their parents and to think of themselves as separate, independent beings in the world, apart from family. Consider how Hongyong Baek's thoughts and focus changed over time. Initially, as a young adolescent, her concerns and thoughts predominantly centered around herself. With her marriage, her focus expanded to include her husband and her family's views on herself. However, as she grew older, she became more accepting of others and realized how a multitude of forces influenced the direction of her life. This section examines these changes in the areas of reasoning, memory, and mental abilities.

Changes in How We Reason

As we saw in Chapter 9, children think and reason in ways that are qualitatively different from adolescents and adults. Similarly, teenagers do not necessarily think like adults, but they are beginning to practice the reasoning skills and the ability to think outside themselves that characterize later cognitive development. Consequently, research has examined the similarities and differences between adolescents and adults when it comes to reasoning about the world.

Formal Operations in Adolescence

How do teenagers think? Piaget's stages of cognitive development, discussed in the previous chapter, continue into adolescence. Piaget (1952) proposed that teenagers begin to be able to think abstractly during the **formal operations** stage. This ability to reason abstractly allows them to now imagine what could be and to hypothesize about future events and future outcomes. As a result, adolescents experience what they believe are—and often are—tremendous insights into how things could be rather than how they are. This phenomenon is often labeled the idealism of youth (Elkind, 1984, 1998). Adolescents believe that they have the answers to problems such as world hunger or conflicts. This mental ability also helps adolescents in discovering who they are as individuals—a topic that will be detailed later in this chapter.

formal operations Piaget's last stage of cognitive development characterized by abstract reasoning

Formal operational thinking also allows teenagers to tackle more challenging academic subjects (science, geometry, calculus) that rely on abstract visualization and reasoning powers. It also enables adolescents to argue more effectively, a power that may not be seen positively by their parents! They are more capable of suggesting hypothetical scenarios ("What if . . .") to justify their position, making them more effective debaters (Elkind, 1984, 1998). However, along with this ability to think abstractly comes the return of egocentrism.

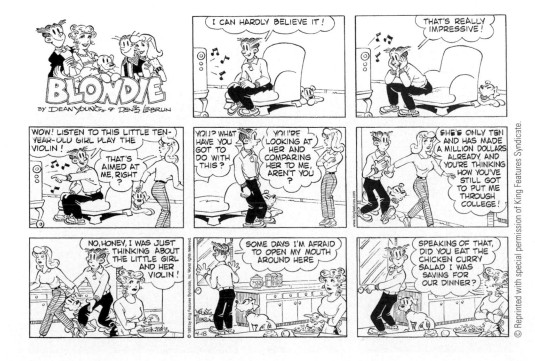

© Reprinted with special permission of King Features Syndicate.

egocentrism a characteristic of thought in which adolescents believe that everyone is thinking about the same things that they are

Application >>

imaginary audience the belief that adolescents hold that everyone is watching what they do

personal fable the belief held by adolescents that they are unique and special

Application >>

Application >>

Egocentrism in adolescence involves teenagers' imagining what others must be thinking. However, teens believe that other people are concerned with the same things they are. Because adolescents' ideas mainly focus on themselves, they believe that others are equally concerned about them (Elkind & Bowen, 1979). For example, a teen with a pimple on his face may imagine that his peers and teachers are thinking only about the pimple on his face. Recall how Hongyong believed her life was crippled because she had to take care of Crippled Sister. She felt as if her life was over because she was no longer the favored daughter. Considering the enormous physical changes that teens experience during puberty, they may think that others are just as concerned and aware of these changes as they are. A female teen may believe that everyone knows when she is menstruating, or a male teen may refuse to go to the blackboard in class because he thinks that everyone will notice that he has a spontaneous erection. Teenagers may not ask or answer questions in class because they are so sure that everyone is talking about them and thinking about them. They are newly and acutely aware of their own being. Because teens believe that others are focused on them, they behave as if they are on stage—playing to an audience—a phenomenon referred to as the **imaginary audience** (Elkind, 1984, 1998). They may laugh especially loud or behave dramatically because of their belief that they are being constantly watched.

Another feature of adolescents' thought that relates to egocentrism is the **personal fable** (Elkind, 1984, 1998). Teenagers develop the "personal fable" that they are special and unique, that their thoughts and feelings cannot be adequately understood by others (Elkind, 1994). Reflect back on your first love. When that relationship broke up, you may have felt as if no one in the world could identify with what you were feeling. You may have hated hearing your peers and parents try to cheer you up with phrases such as, "there are other fish in the sea" or "this too shall pass." You thought they were insensitive, or at least totally useless and beside the point. How could they understand what you were going through? The story you tell yourself is that this person, who is the only person in the world for you, has now gone away, and your life will never be happy again. This is one personal fable of adolescence.

Personal fables may contribute to adolescent risk taking. Because teenagers feel that they are special and unique, they often feel invincible and immune to the consequences that occur in life. For example, they may engage in unprotected sexual intercourse, feeling that they won't be the ones to contract a sexually transmitted disease

Teenagers' egocentrism leads them to believe that they are constantly being watched by others.

© Corbis

or conceive a child. They may experiment with different drugs, feeling that they will not become addicted. In their minds, addiction happens to other people. They are different, special. They may drink and drive, speed excessively, or engage in other risky behaviors because they believe that the typical consequences of these behaviors do not apply to them.

Although formal operational thinking is often perceived as the hallmark of adolescent thinking, this does not mean that *all* adolescents think abstractly in this way. Cross-cultural research (Hollos & Richards, 1993; Rogoff & Chavajay, 1995) suggests that the development of formal operational thinking is very much influenced by experience and culture. If abstract thought is necessary to "get by" in one's society or for a particular task then humans may learn it. This thinking is more likely to be found in youths who are formally educated and in societies with more specialized and technical occupations (Flieller, 1999). In addition to Piaget's stage of formal operations, research has documented that adolescents think in other ways that are qualitatively different from adults. One such discovery is from research studies on postformal thought.

Postformal Thought

Suppose you were in the same situation as Hongyong Baek. You are traveling in the middle of a war with a baby strapped to your back and three young children. Your baby's survival is questionable because she had been crushed by the crowds, and all of you are tired, hungry, and cold. Her added weight makes it difficult for you to walk, especially because you have been travelling for days with little food or water. What do you do? Would you, like Hongyong Baek, consider leaving the baby under a tree in the hopes of ensuring the survival of the rest of your family? Or would you, like Dukwah, insist that the baby continue to be carried? Is there a right or a wrong answer?

How do adolescents and adults think differently? When situations like this are presented to adolescents and older adults, differences emerge in their thinking. Adolescents may be capable of imagining such a dilemma because of their abstract reasoning abilities, but often this reasoning is in terms of black or white—what is called **dualistic thinking.** Teens divide information into right and wrong, good and bad (Perry, 1981). They may tend to believe that there is only one right answer or single solution to this situation. However, as people enter adulthood, they are more capable of what is called **relativistic thinking,** the idea that in many situations there is not necessarily one right or wrong answer. As adults we become aware that sometimes solutions and answers are relative to the situation or to the people in the situation. They are reluctant to settle a question or draw conclusions without first considering the context of the situation. In Hongyong's dilemma, for example, adults typically would consider additional situational aspects such as how much farther the family has to travel, whether the younger children can help carry the baby, and the likelihood of the mother surviving if she continues to carry the baby. Such relativistic thinking recognizes that other people's actions and experiences may be quite different from their own. The adolescent, thinking dualistically, may still feel the adult can do everything—carry the baby, lead the family, and reach safety.

Numerous research investigations support the notion that relativistic thinking represents a qualitative change beyond formal operations (King & Kitchener, 1994; Sinnott, 1998). In this context it has been termed **postformal thought.** It is characterized by the appreciation that a correct solution or answer may vary from situation to situation and that there may be multiple solutions, each equally viable, to a given problem. Postformal thought enables adults to navigate everyday life as they encounter problems in work, intimate relationships, and child rearing, issues we'll discuss later in this chapter. For now, we will turn our attention to memory, which is another area of cognition that changes as we age.

dualistic thinking   reasoning that divides situations and issues into right and wrong categories

relativistic thinking   the idea that in many situations there is not necessarily one right or wrong answer

postformal thought   the idea that a correct solution (or solutions) may vary, depending on the circumstances

How Our Memory Changes Over Time

Does memory get worse as we age? Are we all destined to become forgetful and feeble-minded simply as a function of age? No, not really, but changes in memory do occur as we age. Although some of these changes are influenced by age-related declines in neurological functioning, the majority of memory changes in adulthood can be attributed to factors other than aging.

Recall from Chapter 6 that one theoretical framework for understanding memory is the information-processing approach. This theory focuses on the ways people encode, store, and retrieve information. This approach also has been useful to researchers in investigating age-related changes in memory. Specific processes that have been investigated include attention, reaction time, working memory, and the retrieval of information.

Research on attention has focused on how capable young and old people are at performing several tasks at one time. If the two tasks are relatively easy or familiar to the person, both young people and older adults perform equally well. However, if the difficulty of the tasks increases or the tasks become less familiar to the individual, younger adults usually perform better (Stine-Morrow & Soederberg Miller, 1999). This may explain why it is relatively easy for an older adult in your family to still be able to prepare a holiday meal for a large gathering of people. The multiple tasks involved in such an endeavor are familiar and automatic to the person. However, the same individual may experience confusion or difficulty when faced with the numerous tasks involved in playing a new board game.

 Application

In the area of reaction time, or the speed with which a person can respond, similar results have emerged. We know from hundreds of studies that there appears to be age-related slowing in reaction time starting at age 25. However, the rate at which one's reaction time slows is very much influenced by the nature of the task. If older adults are experienced in the task or given the opportunity to practice, the differences are less noticeable. For an ambiguous or unfamiliar task, slower reaction time with increased age seems to be a universal finding (Kail & Salthouse, 1994). However, this increase in reaction time also is influenced by changes in working memory, or short-term memory.

Recall that our working memory has a limited capacity. To keep the information active and then transfer it to long-term memory requires continued encoding. Young adults excel at encoding and storing vast amounts of details. They can rapidly encode and store lists of information into long-term memory, and rapidly retrieve specific information. After age 60, adults perform less well at these tasks (Salthouse, 1994). When younger and older adults are asked to remember stories (rather than lists), again younger adults do exceedingly well at remembering the details, yet they may not be able to analyze the meaning of the story. Adults over age 50 do very well at remembering the meaning of the story, but forget most of the details (Schacter, 1996).

Such research suggests that as we get older, working memory declines (A. D. Smith, 1996). The exact reason for this decline is unclear. Some research suggests that the answer may lie in the slower functioning of the nervous system, specifically, age-related changes in the frontal lobe of the brain (Johnson, Mitchell, Raye, & Greene, 2004). Other research suggests that older adults use less effective memory strategies to keep information active in working memory (A. D. Smith & Earles, 1996). We must also consider such factors as motivational, educational, and lifestyle differences between younger and older adults who participate in such research. Older adults on average lead less active lives and are less involved in cognitively demanding activities on a day-to-day basis when compared to younger adults. The younger adults may be in school or performing varied tasks in a demanding job (Luszcz, Bryan, & Kent, 1997). Differences such as these could account for differences in memory performance.

Research into differences in memory retrieval is also difficult to interpret. Many investigations differentiate between processes of recognition and recall. As we saw in Chapter 6, *recognition* involves identifying the correct answer from a list of correct and incorrect choices. *Recall* involves generating the correct answer on your own from the information that you remember. Over the adulthood years, recognition abilities remain strong. Researchers find minimal differences between younger and older participants on recognition tests. However, recall abilities decrease as we age, and these differences become quite large from early to late adulthood (Figure 10.4; Balota, Dolan, & Duchek, 2000; Grady, 2000; Verhaeghen, Marcoen, & Goosens, 1993). Again, though, researchers do not understand why such differences occur. Are these differences in recall predominantly due to the slower reaction times of older adults, since recall tests are usually timed? Perhaps the differences in performance are due to motivational or lifestyle differences between younger and older participants, as discussed earlier.

In summary, the research on age-related changes in memory suggests that older adults, when faced with unfamiliar tasks or information, are more likely to respond slower and have more difficulty remembering what they have learned. However, it is extremely important to keep in mind that these changes may be due to factors other than age. In addition, these declines do not typically become noticeable until people are in their late 60s or 70s, and not all older people experience these difficulties. The ability to perform familiar tasks and remember everyday information tends to improve through middle to late adulthood. By remaining involved in cognitively challenging activities, using one's expertise, and practicing memory strategies, adults do not experience steep declines in memory as they grow older. A similar message appears as we examine age-related changes in mental abilities.

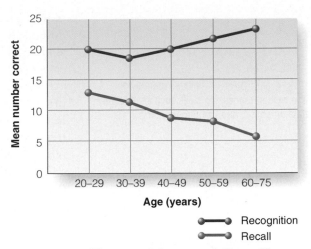

Figure 10.4 Recognition and Recall Changes as a Function of Age

Over the adulthood years, recognition abilities remain strong. However, recall abilities decrease as we age, probably due to the influence of both nature and nurture.

《 Application

Changes in Our Mental Abilities

What happens to other mental abilities in adulthood? For many years, psychologists believed that intellectual functioning peaked in young adulthood around age 20, and then steadily declined. This belief was derived from cross-sectional studies that showed IQ-type test scores slowly decreasing from groups of 20-year-olds to groups of 50- and 60-year-olds (Yerkes, 1921). However, you may recall from the previous chapter that one of the major limitations of cross-sectional research is potential cohort or generational differences between the age groups. The 20-year-olds in the study probably had different educational expectations and opportunities than the 50- and 60-year-olds. This variable could have contributed to the difference in test performance. Follow-up studies using longitudinal designs painted a different picture of intellectual functioning across the life span. When a group of adults were tested at different intervals over their adulthood, test scores steadily *improved* on nearly every measure of intelligence (Owens, 1953). These contradictory findings prompted decades of research into how intellectual abilities change with age.

The most comprehensive such research to date was undertaken by Schaie (1983, 1994, 1996; Schaie & Willis, 2000). Using

Although recall abilities may decrease as we age, remaining cognitively active will minimize such memory changes.

Nick Dolding/Getty Images

fluid intelligence abilities that rely on information processing skills such as reaction time, attention, and working memory

crystallized intelligence abilities that rely on knowledge, expertise, and judgment

Application

sequential studies that combine features of both cross-sectional and longitudinal designs, Schaie's research revealed that patterns of aging differ for different mental abilities. These differing mental abilities could be better understood within two broad categories of skills, called *fluid* intelligence and *crystallized* intelligence.

Fluid intelligence is those abilities that rely heavily on basic information-processing skills such as reaction time, attention, and working memory (just discussed in the section on memory). Fluid intelligence develops early during childhood and tends to decline earlier in one's life. It is presumed to be primarily based on nature or biology, peaking when brain maturity has been reached (Li et al., 2004). There is variation within the category of fluid intelligence—some mental abilities remain stronger than others. For example, perceptual speed and numeric ability tend to decline in one's late 20s and early 30s. Yet fluid skills such as spatial orientation and inductive reasoning remain strong and steady through one's 50s, and then decline (Salthouse, 2004).

In contrast, **crystallized intelligence** is abilities involving the use of knowledge, expertise, and good judgment. It depends more on nurture or experience such as educational background and occupational expertise. These abilities increase with age into late adulthood and then decline somewhat after one's 70s or 80s, perhaps due to the constraining influence of deficits in fluid intelligence (Li et al., 2004; Salthouse, 2004; Willis & Schaie, 1999). Crystallized skills include vocabulary, verbal memory, and responses to social situations. These age-related trends in mental abilities are summarized in Figure 10.5.

As was the case with memory, many factors other than age shape how well we function mentally. Poor health, diseases, and prescription medications contribute to a rapid decline in mental abilities. Older adults can benefit cognitively from regular physical exercise (Colcombe & Kramer, 2003). A mentally inactive lifestyle also is a potential factor in cognitive decline and Alzheimer's disease (Schaie, 1996; Wilson & Bennett, 2003). The motto "Use it or lose it!" seems most appropriate in this context. Doing crossword puzzles, watching *Jeopardy*, and continuing to read, travel, or participate in educational pursuits are all activities that help sustain cognitive functioning.

In conclusion, memory loss and declines in mental abilities are *not* inevitable in adulthood. Many of us will continue to perform well in cognitive functioning through our 50s and 60s. When we do show declines, it is more likely to be in late adulthood and on skills that require speed or on unfamiliar tasks. Good health, an active lifestyle, and continuing education are key factors for maintaining those cognitive skills most relevant to our daily activities.

Wisdom: Life Expertise

Do we get wiser as we get older? No discussion on cognitive change in adulthood would be complete without examining the worldwide stereotype that with old age comes wisdom. Think about the term *wise*. It is not a term we typically use to describe teenagers or children. Rather, we often reserve it to describe older adults. Let's examine the exact nature of wisdom and whether it truly is exclusive to old age.

Wisdom has not been studied to the same degree as other cognitive processes in adulthood, making our information incomplete. From those studies that have investigated this ability (Ardelt, 1997; Baltes & Staudinger, 1993; Staudinger, Smith, & Baltes, 1992), it appears that wisdom includes these aspects:

- the ability to solve problems from multiple perspectives
- superior practical knowledge or insight into what life is about
- good judgment and advice
- genuine care, empathy, and concern for others.

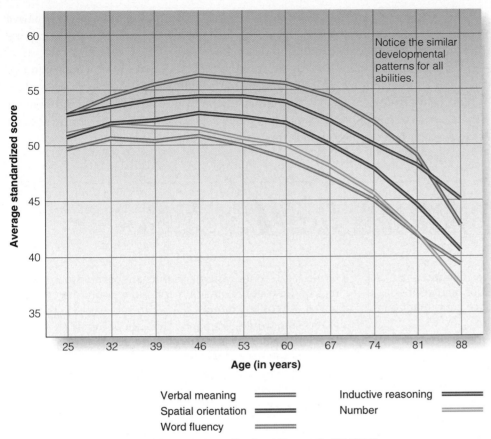

Notice the similar developmental patterns for all abilities.

Verbal meaning ══════   Inductive reasoning ══════

Spatial orientation ══════   Number ══════

Word fluency ══════

Figure 10.5 **Longitudinal Trends in Mental Abilities**

In his ongoing longitudinal study of mental abilities, Schaie (1983, 1994, 1996) has documented that most mental abilities remain strong through early and middle adulthood. Eighty percent showed no declines by age 60, and almost two-thirds were still stable through age 80.

From "The Course of Adult Intellectual Development," by K. W. Schaie, 1994, American Psychologists, 49, 304–313. Copyright © by the American Psychological Association. Reprinted by permission of the author.

In essence, wise people are life experts. They know a great deal about life and the human condition. They know how to analyze and interpret life's problems. Think about Hongyong for a moment. Do you think she meets these criteria? Now that we have some idea of what wisdom entails, we can explore the issue of whether this characteristic is unique to old age.

In a series of studies throughout the 1990s, Baltes and his colleagues have investigated this issue using in-depth interviews. Young, middle-aged, and older adults were asked to respond to situations in which people faced both normal and unusual problems. For example, participants were asked to consider the situation of a 15-year-old girl who wants to get married right away. What should she do? Should she wait until finishing high school or college? Should she "follow her heart"? Answers were then analyzed as to whether they met the criteria for wisdom that we outlined previously. Their findings do not support the common stereotype that old age has a monopoly on wisdom. Expertise proved a better predictor of wisdom than age did. Older and younger adults with greater depth and breadth of experience were more likely to display wisdom (Staudinger et al., 1992). The type of experience also makes a difference (J. Smith & Baltes, 1990). Individuals from social service occupations such as teachers, social workers, and health-care professionals are more likely to meet the criteria for wisdom (J. Smith, Staudinger, & Baltes, 1994). These people are more likely to have experience in dealing with human problems. Age itself does not guarantee

« Application

wisdom. Older and younger adults are more likely to be considered wise if they have a lot of life experience. However, age does afford people the time to gain the experience and expertise that contributes to wisdom.

We have seen in the preceding sections the progression of physical and cognitive changes that characterize adolescence and adulthood. A similar process takes place within the individual. As each of us journeys through adolescence and adulthood, we may face transitions in our personal adjustment. The nature of these transitions and what characterizes them is our next topic of discussion.

Let's Review!

In this section we described the cognitive changes in reasoning, memory, and other mental abilities, and defined the nature of wisdom. For a quick check of your understanding, answer these questions.

1. Maria says to her mother, "I can't wear that dress. Everyone will think I'm a dork!" Maria's statement is an example of:
   a. egocentrism.
   c. dualistic thinking.
   b. wisdom.
   d. relativistic thinking.

2. Which of the following is a true statement regarding research on memory changes in adulthood?
   a. In recalling lists of information, younger and older adults perform equally well.
   b. In recalling lists of information, older adults perform better than younger adults.
   c. In recalling stories, younger adults are better at recalling the story's meaning and older adults are better at recalling details.
   d. In recalling stories, younger adults are better at recalling details and older adults are better at recalling the story's meaning.

3. Which of the following gets better as we get older?
   a. fluid intelligence
   c. crystallized intelligence
   b. working memory
   d. reaction time

ANSWERS
1. a; 2. d; 3. c

LEARNING OBJECTIVE

Compare Erikson's and Levinson's psychological transitions in adolescence and adulthood.

Psychological Transitions in Adolescence and Adulthood

How peoples' individuality and character develop and change in adolescence and adulthood, and how people navigate their social environment is a challenging research area in contemporary psychology. Two prominent theorists in this research area, Erik Erikson and Daniel Levinson, see adolescence and adulthood as a process of building, modifying, and sustaining a personal identity. As we review their theories, keep in mind Hongyong Baek's story. Which of these psychological transitions did she experience?

Erikson's Psychosocial Stages of Adolescence and Adulthood

Recall Erikson's psychosocial stages of development from Chapter 9 (see p. 425 and Table 9.4). Erikson believed that children, adolescents, and adults face developmental events that establish their individuality. Successfully mastering each stage strengthens the individual's capacity to confront and negotiate the next stages. In fact, not all people fully realize their development in the later stages of Erikson's model. If a particular developmental crisis is not resolved adequately, the person is more likely to have trouble in resolving subsequent stages. In this section, we will examine the four stages Erikson attributed to the adolescent and adult years.

Identity Versus Role Confusion: Know Who You Are!

How does an adolescent figure out who he or she is? For Erikson (1956, 1958, 1959), adolescence represents the integration and summation of the previous crises of childhood into an appropriate **identity.** It is a time when teenagers must figure out who they are and what they believe in, what their values are, and how they may be similar to or different from peers and parents. This search for personal identity is thought to be very much influenced by both the biological changes of puberty and the newly acquired cognitive ability of abstract reasoning. Teenagers begin to imagine what they want to be and experiment with new roles and responsibilities as they figure out their personal identity. For example, teenagers may try out different styles of clothing or listen to many types of music. They may join different peer groups or try out different college courses to explore various career options. Sometimes adolescents and young adults become so involved in constantly trying out new roles that they fail to form a stable identity. Erikson referred to this condition as **role confusion.**

Building on this aspect of Erikson's work, James Marcia (1966, 1968) chose two variables that he believed accurately reflected the process of attaining an identity: exploration and commitment. Exploration involves activities geared toward discovering and testing out the range of roles an adolescent is considering. Commitment involves actions that reflect a loyalty to a particular role choice. From these two variables, Marcia developed a typology of possible "normal" conditions or states of identity formation, referred to as *identity statuses*. The four statuses (Figure 10.6) are diffusion, moratorium, foreclosure, and achievement.

Initially, the teen identity seekers have minimally confronted and explored identity issues. They have not yet committed to any personal values. Marcia called this **diffusion.** For example, middle school and high school youth may not yet be focused on what they will do for a living or even whether they will go to college. The state of diffusion ends when the youth begins to recognize his or her uncertainty about identity and begins to cope with this uncertainty and explore his or her options.

identity   one's unique qualities, beliefs, and values

 **Application**

role confusion   continually testing new roles such that a stable identity is not formed

diffusion   according to Marcia, an identity status in which the individual has not explored or committed to any personal values

---

Exploration

		Present	Absent
Commitment	**Present**	**Identity achievement** (successful achievement of a sense of identity)	**Identity foreclosure** (unquestioning adoption of parental or societal values)
	Absent	**Identity moratorium** (active struggling for a sense of identity)	**Identity diffusion** (absence of struggle for identity, with no obvious concern about it)

Figure 10.6 **Marcia's Four Identity Statuses**

According to Marcia (1966, 1968) the presence or absence of exploration and commitment define four conditions of identity formation.

Adapted from "Identity in Adolescence," by J. E. Marcia, 1980.
In J. Adelson (Ed.), Handbook of Adolescent Psychology, *pp. 159–210.*
Copyright © 1980 by John Wiley & Sons, Inc. Adapted by permission of John Wiley & Sons, Inc.

Participating in career fairs allows students to explore identity options.

moratorium   according to Marcia, an identity status in which the individual actively explores personal values

foreclosure   according to Marcia, an identity status in which the individual prematurely commits to personal values before exploration is complete

achievement   according to Marcia and Erikson, an identity state in which a commitment to personal values that have been adequately explored is attained

The second state in the identity search, and the one most characteristic of adolescence, is called **moratorium.** The teenager begins exploring and experimenting with different roles. However, the teen does not make a commitment to a personal identity. This moratorium phase may be brief in simpler societies or for individuals who have handled previous developmental crises well. In other cases, the adolescent may feel overwhelmed by all the options. For example, in our experience as college professors, we often find students quite anxious about making a career choice. There are so many options, courses, and activities to explore that students often feel overwhelmed and agitated. Students may feel that by taking one career path, they automatically cut off other possibilities.

Sometimes the uncertainty or anxiety of establishing an identity is too great, and the person makes a decision prematurely, before exploration is complete. When this occurs, the individual has entered the state Marcia called **foreclosure.** The person has made a choice or commitment to an identity that may not be secure and stable over the rest of his or her life. According to Marcia, not all of us enter foreclosure. It is a way to avoid or reduce the anxiety that characterizes the moratorium phase. Foreclosure is thought most likely to occur when parents, teachers, or peers offer little support for the teenager's indecision. These influential people also may pressure the teenager to make a specific decision, so he or she commits to a choice that has not been fully explored. For example, a student may choose to pursue a medical career because this is what his or her parents expect. Foreclosure in and of itself is not bad, but it makes the person more likely to become disenchanted with his or her choice at some future point. This may result in a dramatic personal change years later, as the person questions why he or she is pursuing a particular path.

The final state in the adolescent passage, as conceptualized by Erikson and Marcia, is **achievement.** Achievement occurs when adolescents have explored enough to be confident and comfortable with their identity decisions. They have developed a coherent personal position and a commitment based on adequate exploration of who and what they are. For example, after taking a variety of college courses such as accounting, creative writing, and biology, a young man may decide that what interests him most is the field of nursing. He enjoys working with people, and feels capable of and enjoys the scientific and mathematical reasoning involved in such a choice. He declares nursing as his major despite the tough competition he will face to get into a nursing program. Across cultures, people who have achieved identity tend to be more mature and more competent in relationships than people in the other three identity statuses (Marcia, 1993).

Even when the achievement status is realized, the teen's identity is not permanently etched in stone. Rather, adolescence represents a time when the core of our identity is established. We continue to refine and modify our identity as adults (Marcia, 2002). We encounter and resolve additional developmental crises such as intimacy, work productivity, and facing our own death. Think back to Hongyong's identity. Although headstrong, she adopted the values specified for her as a Korean female. Yet given an unusual husband who valued her opinions, she was able to explore her potential as a businessperson. She had initially foreclosed on religion, accepting her parents' values, but then achieved her own understanding of faith and forgiveness.

Intimacy Versus Isolation: Connect With Others

intimacy versus isolation   according to Erikson, a period during young adulthood that focuses on forming close relationships

In Erikson's model, successful resolution of the identity crisis of adolescence prepares the young adult for the next developmental crisis: **intimacy versus isolation.** Having formed a stable identity, the person is now prepared to make a permanent commitment to a partner. Intimacy requires that people refine and modify their identity to accommodate the values and interests of another. In successfully meeting this challenge, neither partner's identity would be sacrificed. For Erikson, *intimacy* is characterized by cooperation, tolerance, and an acceptance of others' different views and values. This secure sense of intimacy may be expressed through marriage, close friendships, or through work relationships, topics that we'll explore later in this chapter. Some people may lose their sense of identity—or fear losing it—and therefore they are reluctant to connect with others. Erikson referred to this state as *isolation*. Isolated individuals are easily threatened by close relations with others and hesitate to establish close ties. They are more defensive in the relationships they do form and they have less tolerance for the varying views and opinions of others.

Consider Hongyong and Dukpil's relationship. They met for the first time when they were joined in marriage, but were fortunate to build an intimate relationship. They confided in one another and valued each other's opinions. They each deferred to the other when the other had more interest or expertise on the subject. Hongyong forgave Dukpil and accepted him despite his infidelities and drinking. He accepted her despite her willfulness and conversion to Christianity. They were tolerant of one another.

Generativity Versus Stagnation: Make the World a Better Place!

According to Erikson, resolving the intimacy versus isolation stage prepares adults for the developmental crisis of the middle adulthood years: **generativity versus stagnation.** This stage of development has to do with our feeling that we have made significant and meaningful contributions to our society. Middle adulthood is often the time when people become aware of their mortality. They recognize that their time here on earth is limited. As a result, they then begin to think about their accomplishments and effect on society. Erikson believed that if a middle-aged adult feels that he or she has contributed something worthwhile to society, then a sense of *generativity* has been achieved. Marriage, child rearing, career accomplishments, and service to the community may all contribute to this sense of having lived a productive life. On the other hand, those middle-aged adults who conclude that they have contributed very little to improve society will experience *stagnation*, a sense of failure, and an absence of meaningful purpose in life.

generativity versus stagnation
according to Erikson, a period during middle adulthood that focuses on how productive one's life has been

For many, having a family and raising children provides a sense of having lived a productive life.

© Ed Bock/Corbis

People cope with these feelings of stagnation in a variety of ways. Some remain disenchanted and bitter with their lives. Others attempt to change their lives in order to regain a sense of generativity and identity. Such attempts are often perceived by society as a *midlife crisis*. Is a midlife crisis inevitable? No. The number of individuals who actually experience such dramatic shifts in their life structure are actually quite small (Wrightsman, 1988, 1994). For example, in a 12-year study of people over age 40, Sadler (2000) found that a significant number of middle-aged adults are productive, enjoy their close relationships, and have begun to take risks. They experience what Sadler calls a "second growth" in midlife, characterized by enjoyment of life.

In our case study, Hongyong went through changes in how she felt productive. At first, having children made her ecstatic, as she believed that her offspring reflected her worth. She then sought achievement by earning money, power, and influence—all of which vanished with the coming of the war. After her husband's death she searched again for her purpose and found it in the healing art of *ch'iryo*.

Integrity Versus Despair: No Regrets

integrity versus despair according to Erikson, a period during late adulthood when individuals evaluate the life that they have led

At the end of the life span, adults begin to review their lives and judge their satisfaction with the choices they have made and the direction that their lives have taken. Erikson believed that the issue facing people in their 60s and beyond was one of **integrity versus despair.** When this evaluation is generally positive and satisfying, the individual has achieved a sense of *integrity*, which allows them to face their eventual deaths without fear or regret. However, if this life review results in dissatisfaction and a sense of regret over roads not taken, the person is more likely to experience *despair* or hopelessness stemming from the knowledge that one cannot relive one's life. In such a case, the person may become fearful of death.

After reading about Erikson's stages, you may be wondering how the turmoil of adolescence and adulthood can be fully understood within only these four issues: identity, intimacy, generativity, and integrity. Erikson's model represents only a general or broad sketch of the issues and challenges we all face. Other researchers have attempted to more specifically explain and describe adolescent and adult transitions. One such researcher is Daniel Levinson.

For older adults, reminiscing about their experiences provides a sense of integrity and life satisfaction.

© John Henley/Corbis

Levinson's Seasons of Adulthood

Daniel Levinson (1978, 1996) attempted to uncover psychological transitions that characterize the adolescent and adulthood years. Levinson interviewed male and female adults from a variety of occupations. He, too, saw changes, or seasons, in adolescence and adulthood as marked by distinct critical challenges.

life structure in Levinson's theory, the pattern of a person's life, comprised of those aspects that the person finds most important at a given time

Each decade begins with a transition in which previous issues and challenges are synthesized. This prepares the person for the subsequent stable periods. It is during the stable periods that people build their **life structures,** or the design of what they want their values, goals, and lifestyle to be. This may include a focus on marriage, children, careers, or service to the community. As each new component of a life structure is added, the adult is then thrust back into a transition stage, to accommodate the old life structure into the new one. Therefore, people alternate between transition stages and life-building stages as they progress through adolescence and adulthood. Table 10.1 ◆ summarizes these stages.

◆ **Table 10.1**

A Comparison of Erikson's and Levinson's Psychosocial Transitions in Adolescence and Adulthood

Age	Erikson's Stage	Erikson's Challenge	Levinson's Stage (ages)	Levinson's Challenge
Adolescence	Identity versus role confusion	Discover and formulate one's personal goals and values	Early adult transition (17–22)	Construct a dream of self
Early adulthood	Intimacy versus isolation	Commit to a mutually loving relationship	Entry early adult life structure (22–28) Age 30 transition (28–33) Ending early adult life structure (33–40)	Modify dream to establish a stable place in society
Middle adulthood	Generativity versus stagnation	Contribute to society through work, family, or community service	Midlife transition (40–45) Entry middle adult life structure (45–50) Age 50 transition (50–55) Ending middle adult life structure (55–60)	Reflect on successfulness of meeting dream of early adulthood; reassess relation of self to world and modify marriage, family, and/or occupational components of life structure
Late adulthood	Integrity versus despair	View one's life as satisfactory and worthwhile	Late adult transition (60–65) Late adulthood life structure (65–death)	Modifying and questioning of life structure continues

Notice how Levinson's stages emphasize many of the same issues and tasks as Erikson's stages. For example, early adulthood is depicted as constructing a dream or an image of the self, much like Erikson's notion of adolescent identity. Hongyong had a dream of domestic bliss with her husband and children, which then incorporated the wealth and prestige of their businesses. The dream, however, then must be modified during one's 30s to establish a stable place in society. It is during this settling down phase that people may decide to emphasize some goals or commitments over secondary ones to establish a firmer footing within society. Hongyong's dream crumbled during the war and she had to rebuild a life structure as a widow, mother, and therapist. In the middle adulthood years, according to Levinson, individuals reflect on how successful they have been in meeting the dreams of their early adulthood years. A similar assessment was suggested in Erikson's generativity versus stagnation stage. For Levinson, the degree of satisfaction we feel about fulfilling earlier dreams determines the degree of turmoil we may experience in middle age. Consequently, a midlife crisis would represent our attempts to modify and change our existing life structure, a conceptualization very much similar to Erikson's.

We have attempted to outline in this section two views on the psychological transitions that people face during adolescence and adulthood. Both views detail similar issues and challenges during these years: identity, relationships, a period of questioning during midlife, and an assessment of the life one has lived. Not all individuals may experience these issues at exactly the same time or in exactly the same manner as Erikson and Levinson proposed, but the broad themes and trends that they describe are supported by research. This research is highlighted in the next two sections, as we examine the impact of social relationships and careers on adolescent and adult development.

Let's Review!

In this section, we presented two views on psychological change in adolescence and adulthood: Erikson's theory of psychosocial developmental changes and Levinson's theory on adult transitions. As a quick check of your understanding, try answering these questions.

1. Tess is a college freshman taking pre-med courses because her parents have always wanted her to be a doctor. She has never considered any other career choice. Marcia would characterize Tess's career identity as _____.

   a. foreclosed   c. diffused

   b. achieved   d. moratorium

2. According to Erikson, feeling that you have made important contributions to society will lead to a sense of _____.

   a. integrity   c. industry

   b. generativity   d. identity

3. Levinson uses the term _____ to refer to the design of what you want your values, goals, and lifestyle to be.

   a. identity   c. life structure

   b. transition   d. critical dream

ANSWERS

1. a; 2. b; 3. c

LEARNING OBJECTIVES

- Describe the varieties of social relations in adolescence and adulthood.
- Describe the new roles and responsibilities of being a parent or grandparent.

Social Relations in Adolescence and Adulthood

Hongyong Baek followed the prescribed social roles for her time and for her culture. She did not socialize with boys or date, and her parents arranged her marriage. Despite her husband's infidelities, she never considered divorce. She and her husband expected to have children. If they did not, they would have been viewed as abnormal. Although in many cultures such prescribed social roles may still be the norm, in Western societies, today's adolescents and adults express intimacy in relationships in a wide range of lifestyles including dating, marriage, cohabitation, divorce, and parenthood.

Dating and Singlehood

In adolescence, the same-sex peer groups of childhood ultimately evolve into small groups of males and females going out together as a group. They may hang out together at the mall, see a movie, or meet at parties and dances. These groups eventually give rise to well-defined couples. The dating game has begun. On average, American boys and girls begin to date at age 15 (Feiring, 1996; Miller, Hemesath, & Nelson, 1997). However, this is not true for all cultural subgroups. Asian American and Hispanic American teenagers tend to begin dating at a later age (Xiaohe & Whyte, 1990).

Dating serves several functions for teenagers. Besides being an outlet for fun and recreation, dating gives teenagers a chance to learn how to cooperate and compromise with people in a variety of situations (Lambeth & Hallett, 2002). For example, choosing a movie or a restaurant entails listening to the other person's wishes and then resolving any differences. Teens can discover more about themselves and how others' needs may differ from their own. Sexual experimentation also may be involved

Application

(Sanderson & Cantor, 1995; Zani, 1993). Although early dating relationships tend to be short-lived, they pave the way for establishing adult intimate relationships.

What do adult lifestyles look like? It is typical to start one's adulthood as unmarried—and the number of young single adults is growing. In 2000, about 45% of 25- to 29-year-olds and 15% of 35- to 44-year-olds had never married (Fields & Casper, 2001). Among African American women, 35% remain unmarried into their late 30s (Teachman, Tedrow, & Crowder, 2000). Young adults are delaying marriage. In the United States, the average age for first marriages is 26.8 for men and 25 for women (Fields & Casper, 2001; Kreider & Fields, 2002; U.S. Census Bureau, 1998). Being single allows young adults a chance to explore different types of friendships and relationships as well as to continue refining and defining their identities. Young single adults also may be moving or traveling as part of building careers, which can make it harder to start or maintain a relationship.

People of any age can be single due to divorce, the death of a spouse, or because they have never married. The image of these older singles tends to be more negative. They are seen as somehow flawed, socially inept, and characterized as losers (De-Frain & Olson, 1999). This is more a cultural interpretation than the truth. In fact, single people continue to form close bonds with others and do not describe themselves as lonely (Rubinstein, Alexander, Goodman, & Luborsky, 1991; Stull & Scarisbrick-Hauser, 1989). However, there are exceptions. Divorced singles do report feelings of loneliness and dissatisfaction (Peters & Liefbroer, 1997) and interestingly, being single has more negative health effects on males than females (Murphy, Glaser, & Grundy, 1997; Whitbourne, 1996).

Dating gives teenagers a chance to learn how to cooperate and compromise with people in a variety of situations.

Being single allows young adults a chance to explore different types of friendships and relationships.

Figure 10.7 **Cohabitation in the United States**

According to U.S. Census data, the number of unmarried couples living together has been steadily increasing since 1970.

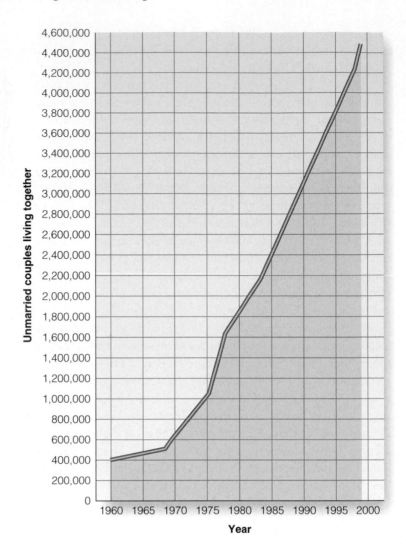

Cohabitation

Some adults choose to live together, or *cohabit* with an intimate partner, one with whom they enjoy a sexual relationship. Cohabitation rates have been steadily increasing over the past 20 years in the United States, as depicted in Figure 10.7 (U.S. Census Bureau, 2000). Yet these unions tend to be short-lived; about half of cohabiting couples either get married or break up within a year (Bumpass & Lu, 2000). Moreover, the increased rate of cohabiting couples is not unique to the United States—an even higher level exists in many other countries such as Sweden and Denmark (Seltzer, 2001). However, cohabitation is rarer in more traditional societies. It is frowned on in Asian societies and severely discouraged in Islamic societies.

Couples cohabit for various reasons. Many couples feel that cohabiting before marriage will give them the opportunity to see whether they are truly compatible before approaching the serious commitment of marriage. Some couples cohabit after divorce as an alternative to remarriage (Coleman, Ganong, & Fine, 2000). However, couples who marry after cohabitation tend to be less satisfied with their marriages and are more likely to get a divorce (Berrington & Diamond, 1999; Bramlett & Mosher, 2002; Bumpass & Lu, 2000; DeMaris & Rao, 1992; Hall & Zhao, 1995; Thomson & Colella, 1992). Before we jump to causal conclusions from this correlation, let's examine this finding more closely. People who choose to live together tend to be less conventional, less religious, tend to come from lower income levels, and are more open to the idea of divorce compared to couples who do not live together before marriage (Axinn & Barber, 1997; Cohan & Kleinbaum, 2002; DeMaris & MacDonald, 1993; Smock, 2000). These factors, rather than cohabitation itself, may put a couple more at risk for divorce. Moreover, much of the research on cohabiting couples was gathered during a time when cohabitation was viewed more negatively than today. As more and more couples cohabit, it is becoming more acceptable in society. A more recent study has found that premarital cohabitation is not associated with an elevated risk for divorce (Teachman, 2003), and hence this correlation may weaken (McCrae, 1997).

Marriage

Over 95% of Americans choose to get married at some point in their lives (U.S. Census Bureau, 2000). Survey research indicates that married couples in the United States are as happy today as they were 20 years ago (Amato, Johnson, Booth, & Rogers, 2003). Yet 60% of marriages worldwide are arranged (Mackay, 2000). In Japan, 25 to 30 percent of marriages still are arranged (Applbaum, 1995). Parents, relatives, and friends choose marriage partners based on their finances, family values, social status, and perceived compatibility with the potential bride or groom (Batabyal, 2001).

Over 95% of people in the United States choose to get married at some point in their lives.

Marriage, like any other lifestyle choice, involves adaptation. A new role as husband or wife has been added, and people must adjust to living as a couple rather than as an individual. Researchers have found that many aspects of the marital relationship change after the first year. The "I love you's" become less frequent, sexual activity becomes less frequent, and couples spend more time performing daily chores and tasks together rather than talking and having fun (Huston & Vangelisti, 1991). Despite these changes, many couples continue to report satisfaction in their marital relationships.

What distinguishes satisfying marital relationships from dissatisfying ones? Research has discovered many factors that are related to marital satisfaction. For example, when both people are from similar family backgrounds, social class, education, and religion, couples report more satisfying relationships. Couples who wait to marry until after age 20 also are more likely to report happier marriages compared to those who marry before age 20. Warm and positive extended family relationships as well as secure financial circumstances also increase the chances of a satisfying marital relationship (Bramlett & Mosher, 2002; Rank, 2000). Supportive spouse behavior also is associated with greater marital satisfaction. Even support obtained outside the marriage can positively influence how the spouse behaves within the marriage (Fincham, 2003). Perhaps the biggest detriment to a healthy, happy, and long-lasting relationship is negative comments, contempt, defensiveness, and criticism (Gottman, 1999a, 1999b; Levenson, Carstensen, & Gottman, 1993; Russell & Wells, 1994). Hongyong and Dukpil had many qualities that are related to marital satisfaction.

Research also shows some interesting gender differences in marital satisfaction. Although women report being as happy in marriage as men (Myers, 2000), marriage is associated with better mental and physical health for men. In contrast, single women are emotionally and physically healthier than married women (Levenson et al., 1993; Kaslow, Hansson, & Lundblad, 1994). As gender roles have become more flexible for females, more demands tend to be made on the married woman. More married women are employed, but they still perform the majority of household tasks and have more responsibility for child rearing than married men (Bianchi, Kilkie, Sayer, & Robinson, 2000). In dual-earner couples, wives average almost three times as many hours per week on household tasks compared to their husbands (Coltrane, 2001; Starrels, 1994).

Given these circumstances, it is not surprising that when divorce does occur it is more likely to be initiated by the female (Amato & Rogers, 1997).

Divorce

What changes does divorce bring? Although it takes two people to consent to marry, in many U.S. states it only takes one person to decide to divorce. About 43% of first marriages currently end in separation or divorce within 15 years (Bramlett & Mosher, 2002; U.S. Census Bureau, 1998). One-fifth of first marriages end within 5 years, and one-third end within 10 years (Centers for Disease Control and Prevention, 2001). Divorce rates are higher among couples who do not have children, who marry at a young age, or whose parents divorced (Amato & DeBoer, 2001; Faust & McKibben, 1999; Kurdek, 1993; Shulman, Scharf, Lumer, & Maurer, 2001). Divorce rates also are higher among African Americans compared to European and Hispanic Americans, and among lower-income couples (Faust & McKibben, 1999; Rank, 2000).

Like other lifestyle changes, divorce brings with it stresses and adaptations that the couple and the family must negotiate. Typically, divorce is preceded by a period of conflict and dissatisfaction. Emotional, economic, legal, and practical difficulties follow. What was once one household must now be divided into two. If there are children involved, custody arrangements must be made. Identities are reshaped and redefined as the couple mentally shifts from thinking in terms of "we" to "me." Friendships with other couples may fade. Simultaneously, each member of the couple is resolving feelings of anger, rejection, disappointment, or loneliness (Amato, 2000). Given these changes, it is not surprising that divorced people are more likely to be depressed or experience physical health problems (Lillard & Panis, 1996; Lorenz et al., 1997). Perhaps for these reasons, many divorced adults, especially young people, choose to marry again. This is more common for males than for females (Buckle, Gallup, & Rodd, 1996).

Divorce also has negative effects on the family. Previous styles of parenting are affected, as the custodial parent must assume the most responsibility for disciplining children. The noncustodial parent may become more permissive due to less time spent with the children. Children experience many of the same emotions as their parents, such as loss, grieving for the family that was, and anger that their parents were not able to make the marriage work. As a result, they are more likely to misbehave. Children of divorce may act more aggressive, disrespectful, disobedient, withdrawn, or moody. School performance may deteriorate. Their misbehavior makes it even more difficult for parents to be effective. Studies suggest that it is this breakdown in parenting and children's exposure to marital conflict that are most detrimental to a child's development (Amato, 1993; Amato & Booth, 1996; Erel & Burman, 1995). Hence, a two-parent household filled with strife and discord is as difficult for a child as the experience of divorce (Booth & Amato, 2001; Davies & Cummings, 1998; Harold, Fincham, Osborne, & Conger, 1997).

Within 2 years following a divorce, many families experience less stress and are recovering from their difficulties. Children and adults adjust to these life transitions. Yet one long-term consequence is that children from divorced families are themselves more likely to divorce in adulthood (Amato, 1996; Shulman et al., 2001).

Parenting

At one time marriage was synonymous with becoming a parent, but that is not necessarily the case today. With increasing numbers of birth control options available, parenthood is more of a choice today than it used to be. In 1996, 28% of couples chose not to become parents for a variety of reasons (U.S. Census Bureau, 1996). On the other hand, more single women and cohabitating couples are having or adopting children (Teachman et al., 2000). For those who choose to have children, parenthood becomes another life transition, which includes adaptation to new roles and responsibilities.

Adapting to Parenting and Marital Satisfaction

How does parenthood change one's life? Although most prospective parents look forward to the birth of their child, childbirth radically changes people's lives. With the joy and elation of a newborn baby comes less sleep, leisure time, and time spent together as a couple. Financial planning is a must: it will cost a middle class family about $160,000 ($237,000 when adjusted for inflation) to raise one child from 1999 over the next 17 years—and that's not including college expenses (Lino, 2000). Life becomes a juggling act as the couple tries to keep an eye on all the responsibilities of work and family at one time! Although fathers today are more involved in childcare and housework than ever before (Coley, 2001), mothers, even working mothers, are more likely to become the primary caregiver of the child as the man intensifies his role as provider (Cowan & Cowan, 2000; Deutsch, 2001; Emery & Tuer, 1993; Haas, 1999). Typically, the greater the change in marital roles that results from having children, the higher the reported marital dissatisfaction, especially for women (Levy-Shiff, 1994). For example, prior to having children a couple may have cooked dinner together or shared the responsibilities of yard care and laundry. With children, the woman may now be responsible for all the laundry and the cooking, a change that she may not find satisfying. If she perceives this new division of labor as unfair, she is more likely to report lower satisfaction with the marriage (Haas, 1999).

>> **Application**

However, other variables also influence the degree of marital dissatisfaction following the birth of a baby. For example, the baby's temperament (see p. 424) may create less or more stress on a new mother. Difficult babies who cry all the time are more of a challenge than are babies who are quiet or who are generally cheerful. The parent makes a difference too. Generally, older parents who have waited longer after marrying to have children are better able to adjust to parenthood (Belsky & Rovine, 1990). Younger couples who have children right away are adjusting to marriage at the same time that they are coping with being new parents. Resources such as money, spousal support, and support from extended family and friends must also be added to the equation as these factors can increase or decrease the amount of stress that comes with parenting (Levy-Shiff, 1994). In Hongyong's cultural tradition, the mother and baby stay at her parents' house for the first 100 days following the child's birth. This allowed the mother to bond with her baby and at the same time ensured the health of the baby. Such a tradition was advantageous for Hongyong and her children.

As the child grows older, the demands of parenting do not ease up. Parents continually need to adjust their styles of discipline (as discussed in Chapter 9) to meet the new challenges their children pose as they grow older and become established. There are new routines to adjust to when the child enters school, and in suburban areas, chauffeuring becomes a second full-time job! If additional children join the family, the parents' workload increases considerably (O'Brien, 1996).

As the child enters adolescence, parenthood may become even more stressful, and marital satisfaction tends to hit an

Parenting may bring changes in gender roles and the division of labor in the home. Such changes may increase or decrease marital satisfaction.

Barbara Peacock/Getty Images

Figure 10.8 **Marital Satisfaction and Stages of Parenting**

First documented by Rollins and Feldman (1975) and later replicated in many studies, the graph shows the percentage of husbands and wives who say their marriage was going well "all the time" at various stages while raising children.

Adapted from Boyd C. Rollins and Harold Feldman, "Marital Satisfaction Over the Family Cycle," Journal of Marriage and the Family, 32 (February), 25. Copyrighted 1975 by the National Council on Family Relations, 3989 Central Ave., N.E., Suite 550, Minneapolis, MN 55421. Reprinted by permission.

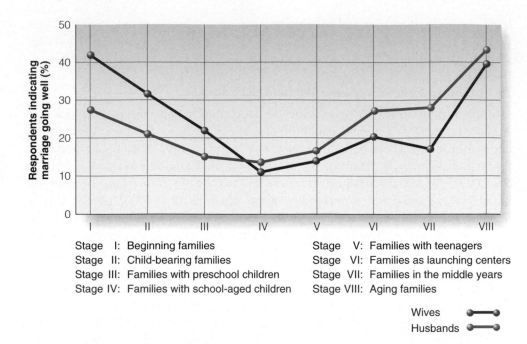

Stage I: Beginning families
Stage II: Child-bearing families
Stage III: Families with preschool children
Stage IV: Families with school-aged children

Stage V: Families with teenagers
Stage VI: Families as launching centers
Stage VII: Families in the middle years
Stage VIII: Aging families

Wives
Husbands

all-time low (Figure 10.8; Kurdek, 1999; Waldron-Hennessey & Sabatelli, 1997). Parent-child conflicts increase, as adolescents achieve formal operational abilities and begin defining their own identity (Steinberg & Morris, 2001). At the same time, parents, who are typically middle-aged at this time, may also be evaluating and questioning the direction of their own lives (see pp. 455). As a result of this conflict and tension, parents may relinquish some controls. Parent-child relationships are renegotiated with both parents and adolescents moving toward more shared decision making. Fortunately, most parents survive their children's teenage years and look forward to unleashing their offspring on society!

The Empty Nest and Boomerangs

Once the last child has departed, parents are left with what is referred to as the *empty nest*. Parents may be lonely at times and feel that a major chapter in their family life is over. The parents are also aware of their own aging. Yet this stage represents lots of opportunity, too. Most parents enjoy the changes brought about by the empty nest, especially women. Marital satisfaction tends to increase, and women generally feel better about themselves as the stress and responsibilities of parenthood decrease (White & Edwards, 1990).

So what happens to parents if their children don't leave—or if they come back due to divorce, limited finances, or extended schooling? This is more common today, when almost 25% of young adults between the ages of 22 and 25 live with their parents (Ward, Logan, & Spitze, 1992). This phenomenon is referred to as the *full nest*, or *boomerang generation*. If these young adults act responsibly, by going to school or by working, parents appear to adjust well. However, some parents do find living with their young adult children stressful (Treas & Lawton, 1999; White & Rogers, 1997).

We see, then, that children complicate the lives of young and middle-aged adults. Parenthood tends to correlate with lower rates of marital satisfaction and higher levels of stress. Yet despite these negative effects, most parents don't regret the experience. Children also bring many joys, highs, and experiences that strengthen and enrich their parents' lives. Historically, most of the research on parenting has emphasized and explored the mother's role. It's a Diverse World examines the role of fatherhood and how it has changed.

IT'S A DIVERSE WORLD

The Culture of Fatherhood

Over the past 2 decades, the culture of fatherhood—the *beliefs* about how men should parent— has been more in the spotlight. Yet the ideals of fatherhood portrayed in our culture do not adequately reflect the *conduct* of fathers or the immense diversity in fathering styles. Traditionally, the father's role has been seen as that of provider, or breadwinner. During the 1990s, this role supposedly changed to that of "co-parent," a caring and nurturing man sharing parenting responsibilities with the mother (Pleck & Pleck, 1997). At the same time, other more negative images emerged, such as the "deadbeat dad" or the "absent father." This father was absent from child involvement either due to work obligations or due to the parents' divorce (Mackey, 1996). The research indicates that the behaviors of fathers are more likely to fall somewhere within this spectrum rather than at one end or the other.

Undoubtedly, fathers are still the main breadwinners, earning on average two-thirds of family incomes (Lewis, 2000). The male breadwinner model is not only a reality, but is evident in young men's expectations about their future roles as fathers (Edley & Wetherell, 1999). Many teenagers equate being a man with "having a job" and "defending the family" rather than with being a good father (Lewis, 2000). We already have seen that even in dual-earner couples, women generally carry the major share of household duties and childcare responsibilities especially on weekdays and when children are in infancy (Deutsch, 2001; Laflamme, Pomerlau, & Malcult, 2002). Fathers are more likely to share equal responsibility for childcare and domestic chores on the weekends (Auster & Ohm, 2000). Fathers spend more time with children than with mothers in television viewing, outdoor play, and teaching sports (Yeung, Sandberg, Davis-Kean, & Hofferth, 2001).

Does this mean that men do not care about or want to be involved with their children? Absolutely not! The cultural stereotype of men as breadwinners is very powerful. Moreover, our society tends to see men as workers first and as fathers second. Fathers work more hours, have fewer days off, and are less likely to take off for family tasks or activities than mothers (Levine & Pittinsky, 1997). Fathers also are less likely to choose part-time work or use parental leave options (Kitterod & Kjeldstad, 2002). When fathers are involved with their children in ways that affect their work role, they experience more stress, role conflict, and report being more dissatisfied with their work lives (Berry & Rao, 1997). Hence, there is a high level of stress associated with being an involved father. Yet the most involved fathers report being more satisfied with their lives (Eggebeen & Knoester, 2001). Fathers today also report that they don't have role models as coparents because their fathers were not actively involved in their own child upbringing (Daly, 1993; McBride & Darragh, 1995).

Marital status and income level also may influence a father's role. Research findings support the view that a father's role changes following divorce. Fathers tend to see themselves as less competent at child-rearing tasks than mothers. Consequently, divorced fathers may feel less competent and therefore may find fathering less satisfying (Milton & Pasley, 1996). Even in inner city and urban areas, the role of father takes various forms. Some of these fathers exhibit little or no involvement whereas others are significantly involved with their children (Coley & Chase-Lansdale, 1999). For example, in one study in a low-income neighborhood of Chicago, in 75% of the families, the father had frequent contact with the mother and child, and in more than half of these families, the father was involved in the rearing of his children (Hans, Ray, Bernstein, & Halpern, 1995). Such findings defy widely held perceptions of low-income families and highlight the diversity and complexity of the role of the father in American society today. Parenthood also is the entry-level position for another life role: grandparenting.

Grandparenting

Picture a grandparent. What does this person look like? Most people tend to see a white-haired, elderly person with wrinkles, sitting in a rocking chair or walking stiffly with a cane. Nowadays, this image is becoming more the exception than the rule. Most people become grandparents in their middle-adult years, 10 to 20 years before the external effects of aging are as advanced as our mental image of grandparents. Adults in the United States become grandparents at an average age of 48 (C. Davies & Williams, 2002). These people are still highly active in their careers and communi-

Grandparents provide an additional loving bond that nurtures and promotes children's development.

ties. Hongyong had a flourishing *ch'iryo* practice, attended church daily, and was putting two sons through college and a daughter through high school when she became a grandparent! Some people become grandparents as early as their late 20s or early 30s as their teenagers become parents. These people certainly do not fit our stereotypical image of grandparents. Just as our image of grandparents does not fit a particular mold, neither do their styles or roles in young people's lives.

Grandparents take many shapes and forms. In the United States, it is more common for grandparents to live geographically far from their grandchildren, which makes emotional closeness difficult. In developing countries such as Latin America and Asia, the extended-family household is more common. Grandparents are more involved in child raising and family decisions. They may adopt the role of substitute parent, seeing their grandchildren often and frequently helping out with child care responsibilities (C. Davies & Williams, 2002; Kinsella & Velkoff, 2001). The majority of grandparents, like Hongyong, however, fall somewhere in between. They interact with their grandchildren often, sharing activities and assuming the role of a companion rather than a parent (Cherlin & Furstenberg, 1986). Many people see this as the major benefit of being a grandparent—enjoying loving and spoiling the child, but then giving him or her back to the parent at the end of the day! Typically, relationships are closer between grandparents and grandchildren of the same gender (Smith, 1991). This may explain Helie Lee's desire to understand and then write about her grandmother's life. Grandparental relationships may suffer when the parents and grandparents do not get along. However, if the parent–grandparent relationship is positive, youngsters establish an additional loving bond that nurtures and promotes their development.

We have illustrated in this section the potential impact that lovers and children can have on our development in adolescence and adulthood. Whether it is a marital relationship, being a parent, or deciding to remain single, people traverse these roles and responsibilities in a variety of ways. Consequently, each individual develops in different ways. Another significant environment that influences adult development is the work world.

Let's Review!

This section detailed the various social relations in adolescence and adulthood and the role changes of becoming a parent and grandparent. For a quick check of your understanding, answer these questions.

1. Which of the following is *false* in regard to social relations in adulthood?

   a. Cohabitation rates have increased over the past decade.

   b. More males than females report being happily married.

   c. Singlehood is associated with better mental and physical health for males.

   d. Divorced people are more likely to experience physical health problems.

2. Marital satisfaction tends to be lowest for parents:

   a. following the birth of a baby.

   b. after children leave home.

   c. when the children are in preschool.

   d. when the children are in adolescence.

ANSWERS

1. c 2. a

Adult Development and the World of Work

> > > > > > > > > > > > > > > > > >

LEARNING OBJECTIVE

Explain the stages of career choice, the predictable changes people experience in occupational development, and the factors that determine how satisfied people are with their jobs.

Finding satisfying work and holding a job is part of adult development. It involves creating an economic stake in the universe for oneself, and then later one's family. Most often, people enter the work world during their adolescence, getting part-time jobs so that they have spending money. In fact, nearly half of American high school students work part time during the school year. Unfortunately, these jobs are more often low-level, service jobs that have little to do with future career choices. Yet even these jobs offer adolescents financial independence that is a part of personal independence and the shift from adolescence to adulthood. Teens also learn the value of showing up on time. How, then, do young adults make a career choice? What predictable changes (if any) do people experience in their occupational development? What factors determine how satisfied people are with their jobs? The following sections address these issues as we examine the influence of the work world on our development.

Career Choices in Adolescence and Young Adulthood

What do you want to be when you grow up? Thousands of times this question has been posed to you as a child with the expectation that you will answer it with some type of career choice. What we do for a living, or what we hope to do for a living, becomes an integral part of our identity. It also may determine who we socialize with and where we live. How, then, do people decide on a career?

According to one model (Ginzberg, 1972, 1984), the seeds for career choice are actually sown in childhood and steadily grow as we develop through young adulthood. Children enter a first stage of career choice, referred to as the *fantasy stage*. At this stage, children dream about what they want to be. When youngsters state that they want to be teachers, race-car drivers, nurses, or dump truck operators, they are already narrowing their field of future career selections. These wishes are often consistent with the child's developing self-image and gender roles (Gottfredson, 1996). For Hongyong, this image was basically prescribed by her culture. She was to be a good wife and mother.

Teenagers then enter a second stage of career choice, called the *tentative stage*. Adolescents consider such factors as interests (what they like to do), capacities (what they are good at), and values (what they believe to be important, like money, power, or prestige). However, because adolescents aren't involved in the actual work world, these decisions may not be based on the realities of the job market.

After teens graduate from high school and enter the work force or enroll in college, these considerations are weighed during the third and final stage of career choice, the *realistic stage*. Young adults narrow their career selections as they learn about the job opportunities in a specific field, the educational requirements, and the outlook for their profession. Hongyong suggested she and her husband start a sesame oil business because she felt that in both good times and bad the Chinese people would need oil to cook their food.

Notice how your progression in career choice mirrors other developmental changes that we have discussed. Recall the cognitive changes that take place from childhood to adulthood. We begin as illogical thinkers and steadily progress to more logical and abstract thinking during adolescence and young adulthood. Our career choices follow a similar path. They start out rooted in fantasy, but narrow and become more realistic as we approach adulthood. We achieve a firmer occupational identity in much the same manner that we achieve a clearer definition of our self-concepts and identities as we progress from childhood to adulthood.

Career Development Through the Adult Years

What developmental changes do people experience in their careers? With a clear vision of what we want to do, how do we carry out this dream, and what modifications do we make along the way? For the past 5 decades, Donald Super (1957, 1976, 1980, 1991) has addressed such issues, outlining a progression through seven stages of career development: crystallization, specification, implementation, establishment, maintenance, deceleration, and retirement.

In early adolescence, as teenagers begin to form their identities, they envision and experiment with how various career options fit with their ideas of who they are and what they want to be. During this *crystallization phase*, potential career options that fit with this image begin to crystallize into a few choices. For example, a teenager who views himself as outgoing, quick thinking, and motivated, may imagine himself in a marketing or law career. Notice how this phase is consistent with the tentative stage of career choice discussed previously.

During the *specification phase*, teenagers and young adults further explore career options by testing out prospective career choices. For example, a young woman who is considering becoming a doctor may volunteer at a hospital or take a part-time job in a physician's office to determine whether medicine is congruent with her interests and abilities. College freshmen may investigate different majors, exploring the educational requirements associated with different career tracks. Although somewhat older, Hongyong explored her talents as an entrepreneur through the sesame oil business, as an opium madam, and as a restaurant owner.

Young people enter the workforce and begin to learn about jobs firsthand in what Super calls the *implementation phase*. The young adult learns both the actual tasks of the job and job-related skills such as getting along with coworkers, getting to work on time, and responding to authority figures. The actual reality of the work may not meet the person's initial expectations. For example, a college student who dreams of becoming a dentist may realize during an internship that people skills are just as necessary to the job as dental skills. A teacher's aide may discover that working with children for 6 hours a day is not what he expected it to be. Everyone experiences this sort of *reality shock* in some form. However, it is the degree of reality shock that typically determines our willingness to stay on a particular career path. For this reason, the implementation phase can be quite unsettling and unstable. Young adults may find themselves changing positions frequently as they attempt to adjust their expectations to the realities of a particular career.

Application

When a young adult decides on a specific occupation, he or she enters the *establishment phase*. Career expectations continue to be refined and adjusted as the person settles into an occupation and advances in his or her career. Today, however, it is unlikely that this establishment will be with one company or on one career path (Cascio, 1995). In their 20s, young adults change jobs every 2 years on average (Seligman, 1994). The establishment phase also may be more characteristic of men's career pathways. Women's careers may be interrupted during these years for childbearing and child rearing (Betz, 1993; Ornstein & Isabella, 1990). For Hongyong, the establishment phase came with her *ch'iryo* practice. She knew this was what she wanted to do.

During middle adulthood, career development is characterized by a *maintenance phase*. Although some individuals may question their career choices and opt for a career change, most middle-aged adults strengthen their commitment to their careers and are more likely to find personal meaning from their work. This personal meaning more often focuses on internal factors such as job satisfaction and contentment rather than with external factors such as salary and benefits (Warr, 1994). At this point in Hongyong's life, she was willing to treat people free of charge, accepting whatever her clients

During the establishment phase, young adults settle into an occupation or a career.

© Peter Beck/Corbis

could give. Her contentment and satisfaction came from seeing their improved health.

Contrary to stereotypes, middle-aged workers have some advantages over younger workers. They have lower rates of absenteeism, job turnover, and on-the-job accidents. Moreover, they are just as productive as younger workers even in physically demanding jobs. They generally have a more positive attitude toward work than younger people (Hansson, DeKockkoek, Neece, & Patterson, 1997; Warr, 1992). Corporate America is realizing these assets of middle-aged workers. For example, in 1996, the average time spent job hunting was 15.5 weeks for workers 55 years and older compared with 7.9 weeks for those 35 to 44. Today, on average, it takes older workers only 7.9 weeks to find a new job compared with the 8.2 weeks for younger workers ("In Demand Again," 2000).

Workers enter the *deceleration phase* when they begin planning for their upcoming retirement. Older adults consider such things as finances, where they want to live, and how they want to spend their retirement years. They

Older adults generally adapt well to the new role of retiree.

must evaluate their options and plan for the financial and emotional changes ahead. Today, many companies offer retirement planning seminars and workshops to facilitate this adjustment.

When people stop working full time, the *retirement phase* begins. Most Americans choose to retire sometime in their 60s and look forward to retirement living. The average retirement age for both men and women is about 63 (Gendell & Siegel, 1996). This means that people will spend 10 to 15 years of their life as retirees. As with other developmental processes that we have discussed, retirement is a process of adjustment. Research suggests that many factors influence one's adjustment to retirement (Kim & Moen, 2001, 2002):

- *Health.* Ill health often causes retirement rather than the other way around. As such, people may have difficulty adjusting to retirement because they were forced to retire or because they did not imagine living their retirement years with health problems.

- *High work involvement.* Older adults may adjust less positively to retirement if their career represented a significant part of their identity. Others may find it difficult to give up the predictable pattern of their jobs for a less structured way of life.

- *Control over the decision to retire.* People who voluntarily decide to retire are more likely to report positive adjustment to retirement than people who are forced to retire because of ill health or mandatory retirement age.

- *Finances.* Those who have the financial resources to live comfortably following retirement perceive less stress than do those of more limited means.

- *Social support.* Retirees who are married or who have other social support networks report more positive adjustment to retirement than those with fewer social ties.

Older adults generally adapt well to retirement. The size of their social networks and frequency of social contacts remain stable. Life satisfaction and mental health are not reduced, and retirees' activity patterns don't change much either (Bosse, Spiro, & Kressin,

1996; Gall, Evans, & Howard, 1997; Hansson et al., 1997; Palmore, Burchett, Fillenbaum, George, & Wallman, 1985). After immigrating to America, Hongyong gave up her *ch'iryo* practice but still remained active. She continued to rise early and attend church, and she became a U.S. citizen on her 80th birthday!

Job Satisfaction: If You Enjoy It, Is It Work?

What determines how satisfied people are with their jobs? Many factors determine not only how well people adjust to retirement, but also how satisfied they are with their careers. **Job satisfaction** refers to positive feelings about one's work performance. Several variables contribute to job satisfaction:

job satisfaction   positive feelings about one's work performance

- *Involvement in decision making.* Workers who feel that they are included in the communication process and whose input is valued tend to be more satisfied with their jobs (Roth, 1991).

- *Good working conditions.* A physically appealing work setting as well as job flexibility improve job satisfaction.

- *Realistic expectations.* When workers set practical guidelines for how much work they can accomplish within a constrained time limit, job satisfaction is enhanced. Unrealistic expectations, especially within highly stressful jobs, can lead to a condition called burnout. **Burnout** is a psychological state characterized by emotional exhaustion, frustration, and negative feelings about the significance of one's contributions (Cordes & Dougherty, 1993).

burnout   a psychological condition characterized by emotional exhaustion and negative feelings about one's job

- *Support from coworkers.* Social support from coworkers enhances job satisfaction. Feeling that you are a part of a team, and working cooperatively with others reduces alienation and burnout (Corrigan, Holmes, Luchins, Buichan, & Basit, 1994).

In general, job satisfaction increases with age, but this relationship is weaker for women than for men (Stagner, 1985). This gender difference may be linked to several issues. First, although the gap between men's and women's earnings has narrowed, on average women still earn less than men do even with similar education and training. In 1995, a woman could expect to earn 70 cents for every dollar earned by a man (Bernhardt, Morris, & Handcock, 1995). Second, women are more likely to experience role conflict and role overload due to their dual roles as primary child caretaker and employee (Parasuraman & Greenhaus, 1997). A woman's career is more likely to be interrupted or even suspended for some time to bear and raise children. She is more likely than a man to juggle getting herself and the children ready for school or daycare in the morning, put in a full day's work, and then shift once again to child care and household duties once she returns home.

Women tend to experience more sex discrimination and sexual harassment in the workforce. At major firms in the United States, only 9% of senior executives are female, and this percentage falls to less than 1% for minority women (Barr, 1996). Women are much more likely to face a *glass ceiling*, or barrier to advancement in the work world, and are less likely to receive promotions. Women receive fewer career opportunities than their male counterparts, even though several surveys have rated female managers as more effective and satisfying to work for than male managers (Bass & Avolio, 1994). As a result, it's not surprising that in the United States today, women are six times more likely than men to start their own businesses (Mergenhagen, 1996). Being one's own employer allows for more flexibility, involvement, and opportunity—conditions that increase job satisfaction.

© Reprinted with special permission of King Features Syndicate.

Let's Review!

This section dealt with the process of career choice, career development, and what influences job satisfaction. For a quick check of your understanding, answer these questions.

1. Jerome is considering what his interests are, what he likes to do, and what he is good at in trying to arrive at a career choice. Which stage of career choice would Jerome fit best?
   a. fantasy stage
   b. tentative stage
   c. realistic stage
   d. maintenance stage
2. "Reality shock" is most likely to happen during which phase of career development?
   a. specification phase
   b. establishment phase
   c. implementation phase
   d. deceleration phase
3. Job satisfaction is related to all of the following *except*:
   a. competition among coworkers.
   b. a physically appealing work setting.
   c. realistic expectations.
   d. involvement in decision making.

ANSWERS
1.b; 2.c; 3.a

Death and Dying >

Hongyong Baek witnessed many people's deaths due to war, disease, and starvation. She also personally grieved for the lives of her unborn children, her father, her brother, and her husband. She grappled with the knowledge that her eldest son might be dead and had difficulty coping with this news. What do people experience psychologically when they know they will die? How do they cope with such news? What do survivors experience? How may others help survivors navigate the storm of grief? Psychologists also are interested in these issues of the last life stage.

Death is a process rather than a point in time. Decades ago it was a process that took place at home, with family members present. Today, it is more likely to occur in a hospital or medical facility, surrounded by doctors, nurses, and machines. In our society, death is more removed from our everyday experiences. Consequently, our society has come to view death as somehow unnatural. This insulation from death increases our uneasiness about talking about or dealing with death. As a result, when we face death, we and our families are often unprepared for it. Nevertheless, loss is an inevitable part of our development. Knowing what happens when a loved one is dying and how people respond to the death of a loved one may better prepare us for this final journey.

LEARNING OBJECTIVE

Describe how people cope psychologically with their own impending death and the death of their loved ones.

Reactions to Death: Kübler-Ross's Stages

How do people face death? If you were told today that you only had 6 months to live, how would you react? Elisabeth Kübler-Ross (1969, 1974), a pioneer researcher on death and dying, interviewed over 200 terminally ill people to address this question. She wanted to investigate any predictable emotional and psychological changes that people might experience as they confront their own death. From her research, she noted five reactions that may characterize dying people: denial, anger, bargaining, depression, and acceptance.

When people first learn that they have a terminal illness, a typical reaction is *denial*. They behave as if they have not just been told that they are going to die. For example, they may insist on a second or third medical opinion. Others may continue in their normal activities, behaving as if they had never received this news. People may make extensive plans for the future. Denial is an effective coping strategy that allows the person time to come to terms with impending death.

As denial dwindles, it is replaced by the emotional reaction of *anger*. People lash out at loved ones and medical personnel over the unfairness of death. "Why me?" may be a common statement during this stage. Looking for others to blame may also be an expression of this anger. One of the authors watched her father, diagnosed with a terminal illness, turn away from his devout faith in God. He refused to attend church. He believed that it was unfair for his life to be cut short after trying so hard to be a good person and live a good life.

Hospice settings provide comfort care to the dying to facilitate their acceptance of death.

Photodisc Collection/Getty Images

Following denial and anger, some dying people may also express emotions indicative of *bargaining*. They attempt to strike a deal for more time with the doctors, God, or the universe. For example, a man may want to live just long enough to see his daughter get married. Another person may bargain to make it through a particular holiday. These bargains may be unrealistic and impossible to fulfill.

People who are dying may become *depressed*, or extremely sad, when denial, anger, and bargaining fail to delay the progress of their illness. They may lose interest in their usual activities or refuse to participate. The author's father stopped playing golf or even watching it on television. For hours, he would just sit in his chair staring at the wall with a morose expression on his face. This depression may be one way for those who are near the end of life to mourn their own death.

The final emotional state detailed by Kübler-Ross is *acceptance*. A peace and calm characterizes the dying as they face the end of life. They may separate themselves from all but a few of their loved ones as they prepare for life's ending.

Much research confirms the legitimacy of Kübler-Ross's reaction stages (Kalish, 1985; Samarel, 1995; D. C. Smith, 1993). However, not every dying person experiences all these reactions. Moreover, not all dying persons go through these reactions in the same order. Death, like many other developmental processes, is influenced by a variety of individual circumstances. These include one's personality and coping style, the type of support received from family members and health professionals, and the nature of the terminal illness. Yet Kübler-Ross's model is useful for understanding the emotions of dying people and for supporting anyone suffering from loss. People may also experience similar reactions when they face a divorce, unemployment, or the impending death of a loved one.

Application ≫

Hongyong experienced many of these emotions as she wondered over the fate of her son and watched her husband die. At first, she denied the possibility that her son was dead or that her husband's illness was fatal. She turned away in anger from her religion when her son did not appear at the refugee camp. Her depression was so intense that she ignored her living children. But as time went by, she slowly accepted her husband's death as well as not knowing the fate of her son.

Bereavement and Grief: How We Respond to Death

How do we cope with the death of a loved one? When someone's death is anticipated, his or her family and close friends already have been experiencing an assortment of emotions. When the person dies, bereavement and grief follow. **Bereavement** is the experience of losing a loved one; **grief** is our emotional reaction to that loss. Just as death is a highly individualized experience, so too is grief. However, research on bereaved people has identified common themes and emotional reactions within three phases: impact/shock, confrontation, and accommodation/acceptance (Bowlby, 1980; Parkes, 1986, 1991; Rando, 1995).

Typically, most people's first reaction to the loss of a loved one is shock during the *impact phase*. This may include disbelief on hearing that a loved one has died. It may feel as if a numbness has settled within one's body or mind. This numbness is adaptive, dulling the painful emotions of loss. People in this stage may perform such actions as picking out a casket, making arrangements for a funeral or a burial, and even calling friends and relatives to inform them of the death, as if in a dream. This shock is particularly intense if the person's death was sudden. Do you recall your own shock on September 11, 2001, when two planes hit the twin towers of the World Trade Center and another plane hit the Pentagon? Think about the numbness and body aches that Hongyong experienced when she thought that her son was dead. She operated as if she was in a fog, a living ghost.

Deep despair and agony may soon follow the numbness and shock in the *confrontation phase*. Uncontrollable weeping, anxiety, and feelings of guilt and anger are

bereavement the experience of losing a loved one

grief one's emotional reaction to the death of a loved one

 Application

© Mark Richards/Photo Edit

Shock, disbelief, and numbness are common emotional reactions to the loss of a loved one.

not uncommon as the grieving person yearns for the loved one to return. The survivor must confront the reality of the loss, and this can be especially painful. The person may have difficulty concentrating, sleeping, and eating. By confronting each wave of despair, the person moves closer to realizing that the loved one is gone.

As the pain of the confrontation phase subsides, the survivors begin to accept the death of the loved one in the *accommodation phase.* The survivors reengage with life, and the memories of the deceased are internalized. People are now able to refocus their emotional energies on normal daily events and relationships with the living. At milestones such as birthdays, anniversaries, or special occasions, the grief may resurface. However, these grief episodes are less intense and less painful than they were during the confrontation phase. Hongyong grieved at each death, but then she moved forward, refocusing her energies on her children, grandchildren, and *ch'iryo* practice.

How long does this grieving process take? A definitive answer is not possible. The course and intensity of these phases differs from person to person. Personality traits, cultural background, and the circumstances surrounding the death of the loved one are all factors that influence one's grief responses. Some people function considerably better after a year or two whereas others may take several years. Some may never recover, especially from the death of one's child (Klass, 1993; Rubin, 1993; Stroebe & Stroebe, 1993). This may explain Hongyong's 40-year search for her son. Research also suggests that women may be better able to handle grief, as they are more likely than men to seek social support and express their feelings more openly (Rando, 1995; Stroebe & Stroebe, 1987).

Let's Review!

In this section we discussed how people cope with their own impending death and the death of loved ones. For a quick check of your understanding, answer these questions.

1. Caryn has just been diagnosed with cancer and has been given 6 months to live. The next week she signs a 2-year lease on a car. Which stage of dying is Caryn most likely in?
   a. acceptance   c. anger
   b. bargaining   d. denial

2. Our emotional reaction to the loss of a loved one is called _____.
   a. bereavement   c. bargaining
   b. grief   d. reality shock

3. The most intense emotional reactions to the loss of a loved one typically occur during which grief phase?
   a. impact   c. confrontation
   b. shock   d. accommodation

ANSWERS
1. d; 2. b; 3. c

Are You Getting the Big Picture?

In this chapter, we continued the examination of development that we began in Chapter 9, How Do Children Grow, Change, and Develop? We discussed the many ways in which adolescents and adults change and develop. We hope that as you read this chapter you were able to see how Hongyong Baek's life was influenced by physical, cognitive, social, and emotional aspects of development. As you study the chapter, review the visual summary and key terms that follow. See if you can apply these same themes to your own life or to the lives of your family members, coworkers, and friends. Apply the biological, psychological, and social themes emphasized throughout this text. For example, how did puberty impact your behavior during your early teenage years? What aspects of aging have you observed in yourself and in your parents or grandparents? These are biological factors that impact our development. Did you exhibit egocentrism or experience personal fables during your teenage years? Are you more a dualistic or relativistic thinker? How would you characterize older adults in your life, and have you noticed any memory changes as they have aged? Examining such issues helps highlight the influence of cognitive factors on development. How would you characterize your own identity or career development? What dreams did your parents have for their lives, and how have they adjusted those dreams? What types of lifestyles do your friends have? What future predictions would you make for them given the research we've presented on marriage, divorce, and parenting? Analyzing these issues will illustrate the nature of psychological and social development as well as provide you with more understanding of those around you.

Understanding adolescent and adult development is also relevant to many career choices. If you plan to work in any field that deals with teenagers or adults, this information will prove useful. In order to fulfill their job roles, it is important for teachers, health-care professionals, counselors, and police officers to understand the physical, cognitive, and social changes that adolescents and adults experience. Business professionals in marketing, finance, insurance, and tourism also need to understand the concerns of young adults, middle-aged adults, and older adults. The products they make or sell will be profitable only if they meet people's developmental needs.

Once you feel that you have mastered this chapter, relate this material to the other areas of psychology that you have studied. For example, cognitive development reviews many of the same concepts introduced in the chapters on memory (Chapter 6) and thinking (Chapter 7). Physical development includes sensory changes that relate to information presented in Chapter 3. The questions at the end of this chapter will help you with this integration and enhance your critical thinking skills. The next chapter explores how gender and sexuality influence our behavior. It will extend your understanding of the developmental processes presented in this chapter.

STUDYING THE **CHAPTER**

Key Terms

puberty (438)
primary sexual characteristics (439)
secondary sexual characteristics (439)
menarche (439)
menopause (443)
formal operations (445)
egocentrism (446)
imaginary audience (446)
personal fable (446)
dualistic thinking (447)

relativistic thinking (447)
postformal thought (447)
fluid intelligence (450)
crystallized intelligence (450)
identity (453)
role confusion (453)
diffusion (453)
moratorium (454)
foreclosure (454)
achievement (454)

intimacy versus isolation (454)
generativity versus stagnation (455)
integrity versus despair (456)
life structure (456)
job satisfaction (470)
burnout (470)
bereavement (473)
grief (473)

Test Yourself!

Concept Check

Test your knowledge of the chapter concepts by completing each of the following sentences with the correct term. For a more comprehensive review, visit the book Web site (http://psychology.wadsworth.com/pastorinole/) for online quizzes, flashcards, crosswords, Internet links.

During adolescence and adulthood we both peak and decline in terms of our physical development. Adolescent changes include the process of (1) _____ , in which sexual maturation is attained. Changes associated with the middle-aged female occur during (2)_____, when fertility steadily decreases.

Adolescence and adulthood also are marked by changes in the way that we think. According to Piaget, adolescents reach the (3) _____ stage, characterized by abstract reasoning. Unfortunately, such reasoning also is accompanied by (4) _____, in which they believe that others are just as concerned about them as they are. Their thoughts also are characterized by (5) _____, the tendency to believe that there is only one right answer or single solution to a situation. In adulthood, reasoning is more characterized by (6) _____, or the appreciation that a correct answer may vary from situation to situation. Other differences in cognitive abilities between adolescents and adults are found in the area of memory. Specifically in regard to memory retrieval, (7)_____ abilities remain strong over the adulthood years, whereas (8) _____ abilities decrease as we age.

The development of one's personal values and character, referred to as (9) _____, has also been an area of investigation in developmental psychology. According to Erikson, adolescents confront the psychosocial challenge of (10) _____, whereas young adults face the crisis of (11) _____. Middle-aged adults must evaluate how productive their lives have been in the psychosocial crisis of (12) _____, whereas older adults evaluate their lives during the (13) _____ stage.

Finding satisfying work also is a large part of adult development. Typically, teenagers test out prospective career choices during the (14)_____ phase before deciding on a specific occupation in the (15)_____ phase of career development.

Answers:

1. puberty; 2. menopause; 3. formal operations; 4. egocentrism; 5. dualistic thinking; 6. relativistic thinking; 7. recognition; 8. recall; 9. identity; 10. identity versus role confusion; 11. intimacy versus isolation; 12. generativity versus stagnation; 13. integrity versus despair; 14. specification; 15. establishment.

Critical Thinking About the Chapter

1. Explain teenage pregnancy or juvenile delinquency in terms of the physical, cognitive, and social developmental forces experienced in adolescence.

2. Describe what you feel are benefits to aging, and give examples to support your arguments.

3. Use the information in this chapter to analyze your current identity. How have peers and parents influenced how you see yourself? What modifications in your identity do you expect in the coming years?

4. Detail how others in your life such as friends, parents, and grandparents have influenced your development. In what ways do you think that you have influenced their development?

Applying Psychology. Explain how you arrived at your current career choice. How does your selection of a career compare and contrast with the research presented in this chapter?

Critical Thinking for Integration

1. Use operant conditioning (Chapter 5) to explain why it might be difficult for older adults to acquire new abilities.

2. Given children's cognitive abilities (Chapter 9), how might they conceptualize or understand their parent's divorce or the death of a loved one?

3. Use each of the different psychological perspectives introduced in Chapter 1 to explain career choice in adulthood.

4. How do the aging trends described in this chapter relate to the information on sensation and perception discussed in Chapter 3?

5. How does the information on memory presented in Chapter 6 integrate with the information on cognitive change presented in this chapter?

Chapter Study Resources

Suggested Readings

1. Lee, H. (1996). *Still life with rice*. New York: Touchstone.
   Helie Lee's riveting account of the developmental challenges faced by her grandmother Hongyong Baek.

2. Kübler-Ross, E. (1969). *On death and dying*. New York: Macmillan.
   Elisabeth Kübler-Ross's pioneer work on the psychological reactions to dying.

3. Whitehead, B. D. (2003). *Why there are no good men left: The romantic plight of the new single woman*. New York: Broadway Books.
   Explores the changes in social conditions and culture that have resulted in women staying single longer.

4. For additional readings, explore InfoTrac College Edition, your online library of archived journal articles and periodicals. Go to http://www.infotrac-college.com/wadsworth and enter the passcode from the card that came with your book. For this chapter, search using these keywords:

   egocentrism

   careers and women

   identity development

   fluid intelligence

   long-term marriages

Web Links for Further Study

Additional information on some of the chapter's concepts can be found at these Web sites:

1. The Menopause Online site provides current information about women's health issues and menopause.
   http://www.menopause-online.com

2. The UCLA Memory and Aging Research Center site offers many links to resources dealing with age-related memory losses and neuroscience.
   http://www.memory.ucla.edu

3. The United States Census Bureau provides a wealth of statistical information on various lifestyles in adulthood such as marriage, divorce and cohabitation rates.
   http://www.census.gov

4. The Career Development eManual guides students through six steps as they analyze their career decisions and progress. The site includes self-assessments of personality, values, and interests and the formulation of career and lifelong learning goals.
   http://cdm.uwaterloo.ca

5. The Funerals and Grief Support site is a free consumer information and education resource on funeral planning and grief support and counseling.
   http://www.funeralplan.com

Student Study Guide

To help you organize your learning, work through Chapter 10 of the *What Is Psychology? Student Study Guide*. The study guide includes learning objectives, a chapter summary, fill-in review, key terms, a practice test, and other learning activities.

Psychology Now™

PsychologyNow is a Web-based, personalized study system that provides you with a pretest and a posttest for each chapter, quizzes you by chapter, and provides a personalized study plan, pointing you to elements in the text or in individual learning modules that will help you to achieve 80% mastery. Learning modules include: 2c. Adolescent Development, 2d. Adult Development, Aging, and Death.

PsychNow CD-ROM, Version 2.0

Go to the PsychNow CD-ROM for further study of the concepts in this chapter. The CD-ROM includes learning modules with videos, animations, and quizzes, as well as simulations of psychological phenomena. Each module follows a consistent Explore, Lesson, and Apply structure that allows you to experience the concept or principle, learn more about it, and then apply it. You and your friends can participate in a team-based Quiz Game that makes learning fun. Learning modules include: 2c. Adolescent Development, 2d. Adult Development, Aging, and Death.

How Do Adolescents and Adults Develop?

PHYSICAL CHANGES IN ADOLESCENCE AND ADULTHOOD

- During adolescence and adulthood, we both peak and decline in terms of our physical development.
- Genes affect how we age, but so does the degree to which we exercise our minds and our bodies, and the experiences we have.
- Puberty involves body growth and maturation of sex characteristics that enable us to sexually reproduce.
- During adolescence, the brain continues to grow and develop. Throughout life, the brain remains highly plastic, allowing us to adapt to changing conditions.
- The ability to reproduce changes during adulthood. At around age 50, women experience menopause and hormonal changes that eventually bring an end to reproductive capacity.

COGNITIVE CHANGES IN ADOLESCENCE AND ADULTHOOD

- Teenagers tend to be egocentric, believing that others are concerned with the same things that they are.
- Adolescents often behave as though they are onstage, playing to an imaginary audience and embracing a personal fable that they are unique and that they can't be understood fully by others.
- Postformal thought is characterized by an appreciation that the correct solution or answer may vary from situation to situation and that there may be multiple solutions, each equally viable, to a given problem.
- By remaining involved in cognitively challenging activities, using one's expertise, and practicing memory strategies, adults may avoid steep declines in memory as they grow older.
- With old age often comes wisdom, which includes the ability to solve problems from multiple perspectives, superior practical knowledge about life, and good judgment.
- Age itself does not guarantee wisdom; however, age does afford people the time to gain the experience and expertise that contribute to wisdom.

PSYCHOLOGICAL TRANSITIONS IN ADOLESCENCE AND ADULTHOOD

- Erik Erikson considered adolescence the key stage for developing one's identity.
- Erikson believed that adults continued to develop in psychosocial stages and that successful development would include intimacy over isolation in young adulthood, generativity over stagnation in middle adulthood, and integrity over despair in later adulthood.
- Similar to Erikson, Daniel Levinson saw changes, or seasons, in adolescence and adulthood as marked by distinct critical challenges.
- Levinson suggested that every decade begins with a transition in which previous issues and challenges are synthesized. Levinson felt this synthesis prepared people for stable periods during which they built their life structures.

SOCIAL RELATIONS IN ADOLESCENCE AND ADULTHOOD

• Dating in adolescence serves as an outlet for recreation, gives teenagers a chance to learn how to cooperate and compromise with people in a variety of situations, and may involve sexual experimentation.

• Over 95% of Americans marry at some point in their lives. Research shows that marital satisfaction is higher in couples with similar backgrounds, those who wait until after age 20 to marry, those with warm and positive extended family relationships, and those with secure financial circumstances.

• Approximately 43% of first marriages in the United States end in divorce or separation within 15 years. Divorce affects all members of the family negatively, but research shows that within 2 years, adults and children usually adjust to these life transitions.

• Although a significant number of married couples don't have children, most married couples do become parents, and a significant number of single women and cohabiting couples also choose to adopt or have children.

• In the United States, it is common for grandparents to live geographically far from their grandchildren, which makes close emotional relationships rarer than such bonds among families in developing countries.

THE WORLD OF WORK

• Finding satisfying work and holding a job is part of adult development. It involves creating an economic stake for oneself in society.

• According to one model, deciding on a career choice proceeds through three major steps: the fantasy stage, the tentative stage, and the realistic stage.

• Several factors contribute to job satisfaction, or positive feelings about one's work: involvement in decision making, good working conditions, realistic expectations, and support from coworkers.

DEATH AND DYING

• Death is a process rather than a point in time. Although modern society often treats death as unnatural, it is an inevitable part of our development.

• Elizabeth Kübler-Ross, a researcher on death and dying, identified five reactions that may characterize people who know they are dying: denial, anger, bargaining, depression, and acceptance. Not all people experience all of these stages or follow them in order.

• Bereavement is the experience of losing a loved one, whereas grief is our emotional reaction to that loss.

• Although grief varies greatly among individuals, three typical stages of grief are the initial impact phase (shock), the confrontation phase (often including anxiety, guilt, anger, and weeping), and the accommodation phase (acceptance of the death and reengagement with life).

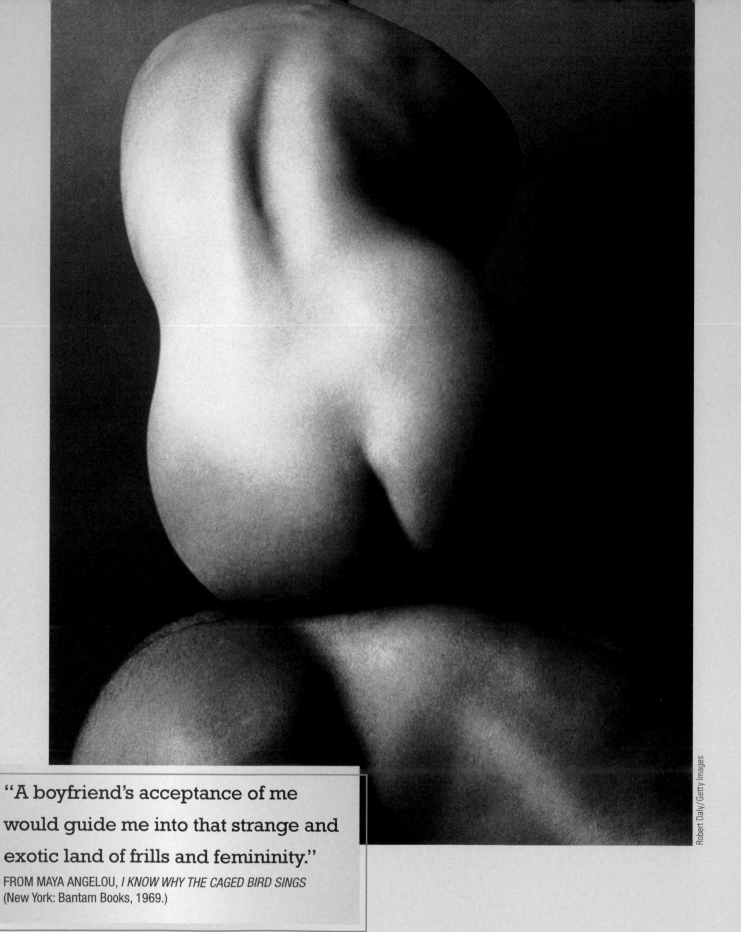

"A boyfriend's acceptance of me would guide me into that strange and exotic land of frills and femininity."

FROM MAYA ANGELOU, *I KNOW WHY THE CAGED BIRD SINGS*
(New York: Bantam Books, 1969.)

Robert Daly/Getty Images

How Do Gender and Sexuality Impact Our Behavior?

CHAPTER PREVIEW

Developing a Gender and Sexual Identity

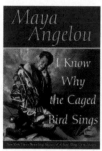

"*What I needed was a boyfriend. A boyfriend would clarify my position to the world and even more importantly, to myself.*"
(Angelou, 1969, p. 280)

gender   the experience of being male or female

gender identity   one's personal experience of being male or female

sexuality   the ways we express ourselves as sexual beings

The two previous chapters outlined the developmental changes that we experience as we progress from infants to elder adults. This chapter extends that discussion on development by looking more specifically at the influence of gender and sexuality on our behavior. Recall from Chapter 9 that **gender** refers to the experience of being male or female. It represents how we think and feel about ourselves in terms of our anatomical sex. By age 2, most toddlers can identify whether they are a male or a female. This is one of the first steps in establishing our **gender identity,** or personal experience of being male or female. **Sexuality** includes the ways we experience and express ourselves as sexual beings. This includes our sexual behaviors and experiences as well as our sexual attitudes, feelings, and beliefs. Often, gender and sexuality become intertwined within the social and cultural context of the particular time and place, as the following case study illustrates.

In 1993, award-winning poet Maya Angelou read her poem "On the Pulse of the Morning" at President Bill Clinton's inauguration. This honor brought Maya and her work to national prominence. Although she had been publishing her work since the early 1970s, with the inaugural address, Maya Angelou became a household name. By the late 1990s, Maya Angelou was one of America's most famous African American women. This fame was well-deserved for the accomplishments of Maya Angelou are quite impressive. She has published 10 best-selling books, in addition to having a successful career as a mother, college professor, poet, singer, actor, playwright, magazine editor, and civil rights activist.

Born Marguerite Johnson in 1928 in St. Louis, Missouri, Maya spent much of her childhood living with her brother, Bailey, and her grandmother after her parents separated. They lived in the small rural town of Stamps, Arkansas, where the family ran a small general store. Her grandmother's loving care provided Maya with an exceptional female role model. Although life with her grandmother was stable and loving, Maya's mother would periodically send for her children. During one of these stays, Maya was raped at age 8 by her mother's boyfriend. The man was later found dead, and Maya blamed herself for his death. Without access to professional counseling, Maya was pretty much left on her own to deal with and recover from such a tragedy. Maya coped by not speaking. She was voluntarily mute until she was almost 13 years old, but amazingly she did recover.

Even without such a tragedy, Maya's life was not destined to be an easy one. As she entered adolescence, she was continually confronted with the limitations that society attempted to place on a Black woman. She felt physically plain and self-conscious about her 6-foot frame. Yet her brother Bailey reminded her that size had nothing to do with being female. Like many adolescents, Maya felt the desire to explore the romantic side of life. In doubt about her sexual orientation, Maya gave her virginity to a young man whom she scarcely knew in order to find out whether she was a lesbian. She simply asked the most popular boy in town if he wanted to have sex with her. She found the experience awkward and unromantic. And, as for many young people, these explorations led to some very grown-up problems. At 16 and unmarried, Maya became pregnant, giving birth 3 weeks after graduating from high school. Her son, Guy, became the focus of her life.

For an unwed African American woman, raising a child in the 1940s was no easy feat. Poverty, racism, and sexism were constant obstacles, and the attitudes that many held about Black women led to discrimination in the workplace. Back then, a Black woman could look forward to a career as a maid or a cook, but she would not normally be permitted to hold more prestigious positions. On one occasion, Maya was denied a job as a telephone operator even though she passed the operator's exam with flying colors. The company did, however, offer her a job that they deemed to be more appropriate for a Black woman, that of busgirl in the company cafeteria (Angelou, 1997). Maya also danced in a strip joint. She didn't have to strip though because she barely wore anything to begin with. Her costume consisted of two sequins and a feather.

During young adulthood, Maya went through a series of relationships with men. Unfortunately for Maya, however, these relationships often did not fulfill her conception of what a romantic relationship was all about. She wrote of her dreams as a young woman, "Like most young women, I wanted a man, any man to give me a June Allyson screen-role life with sunken living room, cashmere-sweater sets, and I, for one, obviously would have done anything to get that life" (Angelou, 1997; p. 192).

Maya grew up with the idea that the female had to be the weak person in a relationship. She believed it would be heaven to find a husband who told her what to think and how to act. But for Maya, such an experience was sheer hell. Maya's desire for a fairy-tale romance was not very realistic in the 1940s, and it is still unrealistic today. But nonetheless it drove Maya to enter into several doomed relationships with married and/or abusive men. She was tricked by one lover into becoming a prostitute and managed a house of prostitution in order to earn him money. She married an African diplomat and moved to Egypt for 2 years, where she observed that "a woman is less important than the water buffalo." She wanted to work while she was there, but her husband said it would be impossible in Egypt because nice women did not work. Maya got a job anyway, writing for an English newsweekly. All the other journalists were male, and the idea of having a woman work there, let alone a woman boss, was ridiculous.

Maya's life experiences beautifully illustrate the powerful connection between gender, sexuality, and behavior. Her feelings about her femininity and sexuality influenced her sexual behavior, resulting in an unplanned pregnancy. Her ideas and attitudes about appropriate male and female gender roles influenced the jobs she took as well as the success of her romantic relationships. Being abused at such a young age also probably influenced her ideas about herself, men, and sexuality.

As you read this chapter, keep in mind Maya's story and the complex relationship between gender and sexuality, and attempt to understand how each has made you who you are today. You may not have thought that so many different types of experiences related to gender and sexuality could lie beneath Maya's many accomplishments and achievements. Yet gender and sexuality greatly influence who we are, what we do, the decisions we make, and how we interact with others. It's only by examining such topics more closely that we see their subtle yet enormous influence on our behavior. We will begin the chapter by taking a closer look at gender identity and gender differences and how both may impact our behavior.

Despite a history of sexual abuse and gender discrimination, Maya Angelou is an accomplished actress, author, poet, and civil rights activist.

© Gary Hershorn/Reuters/Corbis

≫ **LEARNING** < < < < < < < <
≫ **OBJECTIVE**
≫ Explain the development of gender
≫ identity and its influence on gender
≫ differences in cognitive abilities and
≫ in personality.
≫

Gender Identity and Gender Differences

This section details the biological, psychological, and social components of gender. We will discuss the biological process of sexual differentiation or the process by which males and females develop their sexual anatomy. We will then turn our attention to how nature and nurture impact our gender identity. We will examine how the genders differ in cognitive abilities and personality. Understanding gender identity will then allow us later in this chapter to explore their influence on sexual behavior.

Sexual Differentiation: How Do We Develop Our Sexual Anatomy?

sexual differentiation the process by which males and females develop their sexual anatomy

Sexual differentiation is the process by which males and females develop their sexual anatomy. This process begins in the womb during the embryonic stage of prenatal development. Recall from our discussion of prenatal development in Chapter 9 (see p. 395) that the first determination of gender begins at conception with sex chromosomes. All female eggs, or ova, carry an X chromosome. Sperm carry either an X chromosome or a Y chromosome. If the ovum is fertilized by a sperm carrying an X chromosome, then the resulting embryo will typically develop into a female (XX sex chromosomes). If the ovum is fertilized by a sperm carrying a Y chromosome, then the embryo will normally develop into a male (XY sex chromosomes).

During the first 6 weeks of prenatal development, the embryos of both genders develop along similar lines (Figure 11.1). Both resemble female structures. Embryos have two internal structures to support the sexual development of both a male and a female. Embryos also possess external tissue that is undifferentiated—that is, it could develop either into a male or a female. In the seventh week, if the Y chromosome is present, it produces a chemical called *H-Y antigen*. H-Y antigen causes the testes, part of the male genitalia, to develop. Once the testes develop in the male, they start to produce male sex hormones such as testosterone to further develop the internal and external genitalia. These hormones also suppress the development of the female internal system.

In the absence of the Y chromosome, no H-Y antigen is produced, which causes ovaries to develop. The relative absence of male sex hormones also prompts the development of female internal and external sexual organs and suppresses the development of the internal male system. Consequently, if something were to go wrong such that a genetic male (XY) embryo did not secrete H-Y antigen or male sex hormones, female internal and external sexual organs would develop (Federman, 1994).

Can a person develop both male and female sexual anatomy? Yes. Hormonal errors make it possible for a person to develop both fully formed testicular and ovarian tissue, referred to as **hermaphroditism.** However, true hermaphroditism is quite rare (Krstic, Smoljanic, Vukanic, Varinac, & Janiic, 2000). More common than hermaphroditism is pseudohermaphroditism. A **pseudohermaphrodite** develops ambiguous internal or external sexual anatomy because of prenatal hormonal errors. For example, a genetic female may have developed ovaries along with an enlarged clitoris that resembles a small penis. Conversely, a genetic male may be born with undescended testes and feminized genitals including a vagina. Hermaphrodites and pseudohermaphrodites are a unique and rare population that allows psychologists to take a closer look at gender identity, our next topic of discussion.

hermaphrodite a person who develops both fully formed testicular and ovarian tissue

pseudohermaphrodite a person who develops ambiguous internal or external sexual anatomy

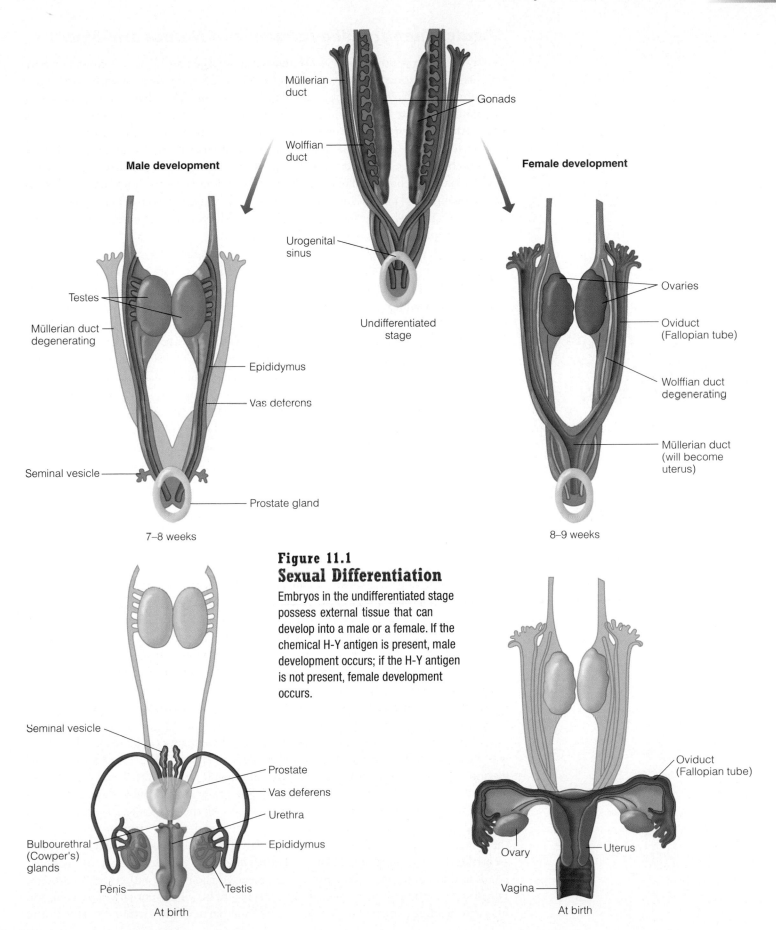

Male development

Müllerian duct

Gonads

Wolffian duct

Female development

Urogenital sinus

Testes

Müllerian duct degenerating

Epididymus

Vas deferens

Undifferentiated stage

Ovaries

Oviduct (Fallopian tube)

Wolffian duct degenerating

Seminal vesicle

Prostate gland

Müllerian duct (will become uterus)

7–8 weeks

8–9 weeks

Seminal vesicle

Prostate

Vas deferens

Urethra

Bulbourethral (Cowper's) glands

Epididymus

Penis

Testis

At birth

Oviduct (Fallopian tube)

Ovary

Uterus

Vagina

At birth

Figure 11.1
Sexual Differentiation

Embryos in the undifferentiated stage possess external tissue that can develop into a male or a female. If the chemical H-Y antigen is present, male development occurs; if the H-Y antigen is not present, female development occurs.

Gender Identity: The Influence of Nature and Nurture

What causes our gender identity? For most of us, our gender identity is consistent with our sex chromosomes and sexual anatomy. Most XX individuals with female sexual anatomy tend to have a female gender identity, and most XY individuals with male sexual anatomy tend to have a male gender identity. We saw in the opening case study how Maya Angelou, born as a chromosomal female, identified herself as having a female gender identity. Many would conclude from such consistencies that gender identity must be biological. However, most people born with the XX sex chromosomes and female sexual anatomy tend to be raised as girls, and most people born with the XY sex chromosomes and male sexual anatomy tend to be raised as boys. Consequently, it is difficult to know whether biology or the way in which we were reared and treated by society is responsible for our gender identity.

Research examining the gender identity of hermaphrodites and pseudohermaphrodites has helped psychologists examine this issue further. Sometimes these people are reared as the opposite gender of their chromosomal sex. Such a situation allows psychologists to examine whether their gender identities match their chromosomal sex or the gender assignment that they are given at birth. For example, in one case, two children, born genetically female, both had masculinized external sex organs. One was surgically treated to resemble a girl, was reared as a girl, and received hormone injections at puberty to bring about female development. This child acquired a female gender identity, an identity consistent with her chromosomal sex. The other child's masculinized external sex organs were surgically enhanced to resemble a male. He was reared as a boy and given hormone injections at puberty to foster male development. He acquired a male gender identity, an identity consistent with his gender assignment but not his chromosomal sex (Money & Ehrhardt, 1972). Studies on genetic males who are born with feminized genitals and reared as females also suggest a large environmental role in shaping gender identity. These males develop a female gender identity indistinguishable from genetic females (Brooks-Gunn & Matthews, 1979; Money & Ehrhardt, 1972). However, in most of these cases, the individuals are treated with sex hormones appropriate to their assigned gender. Therefore, it is possible that biology (in the form of the sex hormones) is still playing a role in their gender identity.

Another famous case illustrates the potential power of biology in shaping our gender identity. Detailed in the book *As Nature Made Him: The Boy Who Was Raised as a Girl* (Colapinto, 2000), Bruce and Brian Reimer were identical male twins at birth. At 7 months old, Bruce's circumcision went wrong, and his penis was severed. On the advice of John Money, a famous psychologist at John Hopkins University, Bruce's parents decided to raise him as a girl. Notice that Money is the referenced author whose gender identity research we just discussed. His research on pseudohermaphrodites suggested that gender identity was strongly influenced by environmental factors rather than biology.

Bruce's testicles were removed and an artificial vagina was constructed. His name was changed to Brenda. He was dressed in girl's clothing and received hormone injections at adolescence to bring about female development. Yet Brenda never felt, acted, or looked like a girl during childhood. She preferred playing with guns and cars despite ridicule from her peers. When Brenda was told the truth at age 14, she adopted a male gender identity and a new name, David. He took hormone treatments to reverse the effects of puberty, underwent a double mastectomy to remove his breasts, and had an artificial penis constructed. David eventually married, establishing his role as a husband, and adopted three daughters as he assumed the role of father. Sadly though, David's life continued to bring hardships. David and his wife eventually separated, and his twin brother committed suicide. He became particularly distraught after losing

Most people have a gender identity that matches their assigned sex.

© Corbis

thousands of dollars in an investment that flopped. David committed suicide on May 4, 2004. He was 38 years old. David's case suggests that gender identity is largely influenced by biology.

So where does that leave us in understanding the origins of gender identity? Some research suggests that it is environmentally constructed, whereas other research suggests that it is biologically determined. The answer in all likelihood lies in both our biology and our environment. Yet the debate over the relative contribution of each is likely to continue.

Gender Differences: Do Males and Females Think and Act Differently?

Do men's and women's behavior differ? Given that males and females arise from similar tissue, you may not be surprised to learn that males and females are more similar than they are different. Just as one particular female may differ from one specific male, there are also wide differences among females and there are wide differences among males. This section details consistent gender differences that have been found between men and women in the areas of cognitive abilities and personality.

Cognitive Abilities

Society tends to endorse the notion that males do better at some tasks whereas females excel at others. Such attitudes may foster in people expectations about what a particular male or female can or cannot do. For example, we saw that Maya Angelou was denied a job as a telephone operator and told not to work at all in Egypt because of sexist stereotypes concerning what a female can do. Are there differences in males' and females' cognitive abilities? Let's look at what the research suggests.

Studies in the 1970s found that females were somewhat superior to males in verbal abilities (Maccoby & Jacklin, 1974). However, since then studies have shown that these differences are quite small and getting smaller (Hyde & Linn, 1988; Hyde & Plant, 1995). On average, girls speak earlier than boys, yet boys eventually catch up. However, boys are more often diagnosed with learning disabilities such as dyslexia and attention deficit disorder with hyperactivity (P. Cohen et al., 1993). Boys also tend to lag behind girls on tests in reading comprehension and writing (Halpern, 2004; Hedge & Nowell, 1995; Hoff-Sommers, 2000).

The research detailing gender differences in math abilities also is quite complex. Again, the stereotype is that males do better in math than females. So it might surprise you to learn that females tend to excel in mathematical ability in elementary school. By fifth grade, no significant gender differences are noticeable (C. W. Hall, Davis, Bolen, & Chia, 1999). Males do not outperform females in math until adolescence (Hyde, Fenneman, & Lamon, 1990). Such a change could easily be attributed to both nature and nurture. The hormonal changes of puberty may have brain effects. Yet gender typing females as poorer at math may also play a role as females enter the high school years.

At the end of high school, males tend to outperform females on the math portion of the SAT (Byrnes & Takahira, 1993). Specifically, males do better on math items requiring spatial skills or multiple solutions (Gallagher et al., 2000). Females do better than males on algebra problems in which the cognitive strategy to solve the problem is similar to language-processing strategies (Gallagher, Levin, & Cahalan, 2002). Yet these findings may be misleading because more "at risk" females than "at risk" males take the SAT. Being "at risk" means you are more likely to come from a low-income home or have parents who never graduated from high school or attended college, hence "at-risk" students are more likely to score lower on the SAT. Because fewer

Despite being raised as a girl, Bruce/David Reimer identified more strongly with a male gender identity.

© Reuters/Corbis

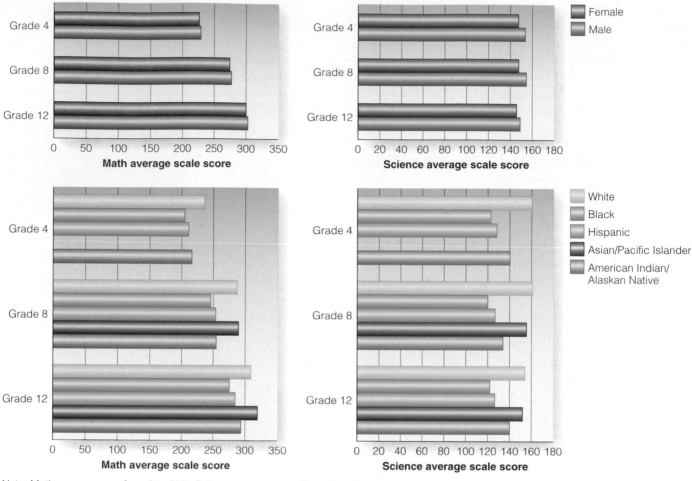

Note: Math scores range from 0 to 500. Science scores range from 0 to 300.

Figure 11.2 Average Math and Science Scores in Grades 4, 8, and 12 by Sex and Ethnicity

Males and females do not differ significantly in their performance on national math and science scores. Ethnic differences are more significant.

"at-risk" males show up to take the SAT (Hoff-Sommers, 2000), the males who do take the test are more likely to be better students and may not fairly represent all males.

In the area of visuospatial skills, it appears that males have the advantage (Halpern, 2004; Voyer, Voyer, & Bryden, 1995). By the age of 4, males excel at tasks that require visuospatial processing. Visuospatial tasks would include the ability to follow a map, construct a puzzle, build a piece of equipment, or make a judgment about a moving object.

When we examine national average math and science scores for males and females in grades 4, 8, and 12 for the year 2000, we can see that the gender differences are small and insignificant (Figure 11.2). More readily apparent are the wide ethnic differences in national math and science scores. Whites and Asian/Pacific Islanders perform significantly better than African Americans, Hispanics, and American Indian/Alaskan Native groups. These ethnic differences in math and science performance are more striking than male/female differences.

A similar picture emerges when looking at college completion rates (Figure 11.3; U.S. Dept. of Education, 2001). From 1990 through 2000, we can see that men and women have similar rates of completion. Although in one year males may have a higher rate, we see that in the next year females may have a higher completion rate. More notable are the ethnic differences in college completion rates. Whites have signifi-

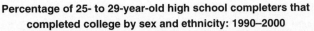

Percentage of 25- to 29-year-old high school completers that completed college by sex and ethnicity: 1990–2000

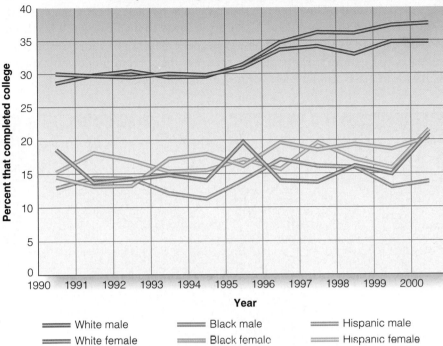

White male   Black male   Hispanic male
White female   Black female   Hispanic female

Figure 11.3 College Completion Rates by Sex and Ethnicity

In the Hispanic population, females have a significantly higher college completion rate than males. African American and White males and females do not show these gender differences in college completion rates.

cantly higher completion rates compared to African Americans and Hispanics. The only significant gender difference is within the Hispanic population. Hispanic females have much higher rates of completion than do Hispanic males. Looking at total male and female numbers may obscure such significant ethnic differences.

The shrinking differences in cognitive abilities between males and females may reflect changing gender stereotypes toward men and women. As discussed in Chapter 9, **gender roles,** or society's expectations for how males and females should behave, are readily learned by young children. If a society has a gender stereotype that males should be better at math and females should be better at reading, we are more likely to urge and promote these differences among the sexes. The fact that we are less likely to find these differences today than 25 years ago suggests perhaps a loosening of such rigid gender stereotypes.

gender roles   society's expectations for how males and females should behave

 Application

Personality Factors

Psychologists also have examined the influence of gender on personality. Such research suggests that females are more extraverted, anxious, trusting, and nurturing than males. Males tend to be more assertive, tough-minded, and have more self-esteem than females (Feingold, 1994). Although females tend to be more talkative during the preschool years, males tend to dominate classroom conversations starting in the elementary school years and spend more time talking than females (Sadker & Sadker, 1994). Men also are more likely to interrupt others and to introduce new topics (Deaux, 1985; C. S. Hall, 1984). However, females are more likely to disclose or reveal personal information about themselves to others (Dindia & Allen, 1992). These gender differences are present in Western populations and therefore may not apply to men and women in other cultures (e.g., Watkins et al., 2003).

Interesting gender differences also have been found in the area of aggression, or the intention to hurt or harm someone. Aggression can be overt and physical, such as physically injuring another person, or it may be verbal or relational, such as in spreading a rumor or making someone a social outcast through gossip or exclusion from a group. Males tend to engage in more overt aggression than females (Whiting & Edwards, 1988), and females tend to engage in more relational aggression than males (Crick, Casas & Ku, 1999). Consequently, both males and females behave aggressively, but the form in which the aggression is expressed tends to be different. This difference also conforms to gender stereotypes. We expect males to be more physical and expect females to be more verbal. Gender roles also have an influence on expected sexual behavior in males and females, our next topic of discussion.

© Reuters/Corbis

From the age of 2, males are more physically aggressive than females.

Let's Review!

For a quick check of your understanding of sexual differentiation, gender differences, and factors that influence one's gender identity, answer these questions.

1. Which chemical is most responsible for the prenatal sexual differentiation of males and females?

   a. estrogen
   b. testosterone
   c. H-Y antigen
   d. anti-testosterone

2. Consuelo dresses and acts like a girl. She feels that she is a female. This describes Consuelo's:

   a. gender role.
   b. gender identity.
   c. sexuality.
   d. gender typing.

3. Which of the following has been found in regard to males' and females' cognitive abilities?

   a. Males outperform females on verbal tasks.
   b. Females outperform males on spatial tasks.
   c. Males outperform females on math tests through the elementary school years.
   d. Females outperform males on math tests through the elementary school years.

4. Which of the following statements is true?

   a. Males are physically and relationally more aggressive than females.
   b. Females are physically and relationally more aggressive than males.
   c. Females are relationally more aggressive than males.
   d. Males are relationally more aggressive than females.

ANSWERS

1. c; 2. b; 3. d; 4. c

Sexual Behavior and Attitudes: > > > > > > > > > >
And the Survey Says . . .

LEARNING OBJECTIVE

Detail changes in sexual attitudes and behaviors gathered through the survey method over the past 50 years.

Gender roles govern many aspects of male and female behavior. They direct how we expect males and females to dress, the toys they select, how or what they should play, and what tasks they should excel at or not perform as well on. These expectations also influence our ideas about appropriate sexual behavior in males and females. Recall Maya's conception of what a romantic relationship was all about and how her expectations led to many doomed relationships. Such cultural and societal norms, together with biology, produce some interesting gender differences in the sexual behavior and attitudes of men and women.

What sexual behaviors do people report engaging in? In the 1930s and 1940s, Indiana psychologist, Alfred Kinsey, and his team (1948, 1953) began a mammoth project of interviewing more than 10,000 Americans about their sexual behavior. This survey research represented the first comprehensive picture of sexual behavior and attitudes in the United States. Kinsey's work has been continued by other major surveys such as the Playboy Foundation (Hunt, 1974), the University of Chicago group (Laumann, Gagnon, Michael, & Michaels, 1994) and others. In 2002, Pfizer Pharmaceuticals completed the most comprehensive global study of sexuality to assess behaviors, attitudes, and beliefs in 28 countries (Pfizer, 2002). Because not everyone is willing to disclose what they consider to be the most intimate aspects of their life, namely sexual behavior, none of these surveys are truly representative of the entire population. However, they do offer our best approximation of the sexual attitudes, behaviors, and beliefs of men and women, married and single, and young and old people in the world today. Such an approximation hopefully will further our understanding of human sexuality.

Alfred Kinsey was a pioneer in surveying Americans' sexual attitudes and behaviors.

© Bettmann/Corbis

Masturbation and Sexual Fantasy

Masturbation, or sexual self-stimulation, is a sexual behavior that historically has been condemned as physically, mentally, and morally harmful. Despite such negative attitudes, most surveys indicate that most people masturbate at some time. Generally, men masturbate more frequently than women. For example, in Kinsey's samples (1948, 1953), nearly all of the adult men and two-thirds of the adult women reported that they had masturbated at some time. Laumann and his colleagues (1994) found that 63% of the men and 42% of the women sampled reported that they had masturbated during the previous 12 months. For adolescent males, masturbation is a very common sexual behavior. Research also has found a large gender difference in masturbation among college students—college men masturbate three times more frequently than college women do during the same period (Hyde & Oliver, 2000; Schwartz, 1999).

Married people and some ethnic groups report lower rates of masturbation. For example, Laumann et al. found that 57% of the married men and 37% of the married women sampled reported that they had masturbated in the preceding year. Only 40% of the African American males and 32% of the African American females in the

masturbation   sexual self-stimulation

sample reported masturbating in the previous 12 months. Gail Wyatt (1997), a sex therapist who has been researching Black sexuality for over 15 years, has found that 83% of African American women reported not masturbating during childhood. Asian American women have been found to masturbate significantly less than non-Asian women (Meston, Trapnell, & Gorzalka, 1996). Laumann et al. (1994) also found that education appears to influence rates of masturbation. In both genders, people with more education reported more frequent masturbation.

sexual fantasy a mental thought or image that is sexually arousing to a person

Survey research also has investigated the sexual fantasies of adults. A **sexual fantasy** is a mental thought or image that is arousing to a person. Sexual fantasy may be used during or outside of sexual activity. Many people believe that those who engage in sexual fantasy have deficient sex lives, yet survey research suggests that this is not the case. Such research shows that the majority of adults and college students engage in sexual fantasies from time to time (Reinisch, 1991; Strassberg & Lockerd, 1998) and that men tend to have more frequent sexual fantasies than women (Hsu, 1994). For example, in one national survey, 54% of men and 19% of women said that they thought about sex at least once a day (Laumann et al., 1994). Men's fantasies tend to involve different partners and more varied activities than women's. They generally include visualizing more body parts and specific sexual acts (Leitenberg & Henning, 1995). Engaging in different sexual positions, having an aggressive sexual partner, and getting oral sex are common sexual fantasies for men (Maltz & Boss, 2001). Women's sexual fantasies tend to be more romantic than men's. Women report using sexual fantasies to increase sexual arousal and interest. Common sexual fantasies among women include sex with a current partner, reliving a past sexual experience, and engaging in different sexual positions (Maltz & Boss, 2001).

Sex With Others

Sex survey research also has asked adult men and women about their attitudes and behaviors in regard to sexual intercourse, oral sex, premarital sex, extramarital sex, and number of sexual partners. Many of these findings are consistent with stereotypical gender roles. That is, we expect women to suppress their sexuality more so than men. We expect females to be responsible for limiting, restricting, and controlling sexual activity, and expect men to pursue sex. Much of the research supports these expectations. For example, men want sex more than women. They think about sex more often, have more frequent sexual fantasies, and desire more sex partners than women (Laumann et al., 1994; Leitenberg & Henning, 1995; Miller & Fishkin, 1997; Peplau, 2003). Men are more likely to engage in extramarital sex, and when they do stray they tend to seek out more partners than women (Lawson, 1988).

Men tend to be more favorable toward casual sex than women (Knox, Sturdivant, & Zusman, 2001; Oliver & Hyde, 1993). Males are typically ready for sex earlier in a relationship than females (McCabe, 1987). Women expect more time spent together before starting to have sex and are less likely to consent to sex after having known someone for only a short time (L. L. Cohen & Shotland, 1996). Women are more likely to endorse the attitude of a *double standard,* or the notion that certain sexual acts are okay for a man but not for a woman. Women also report more negative feelings such as anxiety and guilt about sex than men do (Oliver & Hyde, 1993). Yet about a third of today's adolescents express positive attitudes toward premarital sex, and a majority indicates that they would engage in sexual intercourse before marriage (Martin, Specter, Martin, & Martin, 2003).

Such findings suggest that men have a stronger desire for sex and a larger sex drive than women (Baumeister, Catanese, & Vohs, 2001). However, such a conclusion must be qualified by the profound influence of socialization experiences and social pressure on women's sexuality. In the United States, as well as in many other societies (see Broude & Greene, 1976), males are allowed greater sexual freedom than females. Although some of these attitudes have changed in the past 20 years, female sexuality is still not as liberated as male sexuality. Highly sexual American women are often ignored or stigmatized and experience challenges in their lives because of their sexuality (Blumberg, 2003). Moreover, males and females may just be more likely to report these attitudes and behaviors to be consistent with gender stereotypes. For example, in a recent study, Alexander and Fischer (2003) found no gender differences in self-reported sexual behavior when the participants believed that lying could be detected. However, when the participants believed that the researcher could not view their responses, gender differences were greatest.

How often do adults engage in sexual intercourse? In Pfizer's global study on sexual behavior (2002), more than half of adults in 29 countries report engaging in sexual intercourse over the past 12 months (Figure 11.4). These rates tend to be higher for males than for females (Figure 11.5). The U.S. national average for frequency of sexual activity is about once a week (Robinson & Godbey, 1998). Pfizer (2002) reports a similar trend worldwide (Figure 11.6).

Research also has investigated the frequency of other forms of sexual expression, including oral and anal sex. Survey research suggests that oral sex has increased in acceptance among young people, and that many people may engage in oral sex prior to their first experience with sexual intercourse (Schwartz, 1999). Although men are more likely to engage in oral sex, it appears that level of education and ethnicity may be more likely to influence this behavior. For example, in Kinsey's surveys (1948, 1953) it was found that 60% of married, college-educated couples had experienced oral sex, whereas only 20% of couples with a high school education and 10% of couples with a grade school education had engaged in oral sex. In the 1990s, 80% of the married men and 71% of the married women had performed oral sex (Laumann et al., 1994). In a study of White college-aged students, Schwartz (1999) found that 70% of males and 57% of females reported having given oral sex to their partners before they first had sexual intercourse. So for today's young and educated married couples, a majority of men and women report engaging in oral sex. However, African American men and women were less likely to have engaged in oral sex than people from other ethnic backgrounds (Laumann et al., 1994). For example, Wyatt (1997) found that 93% of White women and

Application

Which person do you perceive more negatively? Society tends to view highly sexualized men more positively than highly sexualized women.

© Michael Keller/Corbis

Figure 11.4 Adult Sexual Intercourse Over the Last 12 Months in 29 Countries

Across 29 countries, the majority of adults report having had sexual intercourse in the last 12 months.

Copyright © 2002 Pfizer, Inc. All rights reserved.

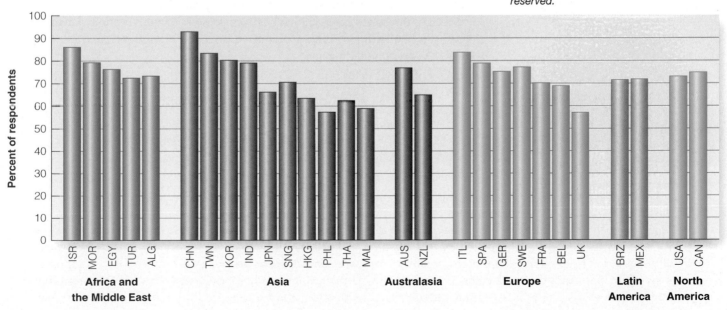

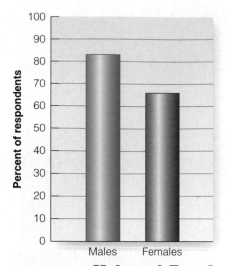

Figure 11.5 Male and Female Sexual Intercourse Over the Last 12 Months

Across 29 countries, males are more likely to report that they have had sexual intercourse over the last 12 months.

Copyright © 2002 Pfizer, Inc. All rights reserved.

Figure 11.6 Frequency of Sexual Intercourse

Worldwide, among those who have had sex in the last 12 months, adult males and females report similar levels of sexual activity.

Copyright © 2002 Pfizer, Inc. All rights reserved.

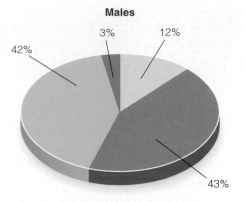

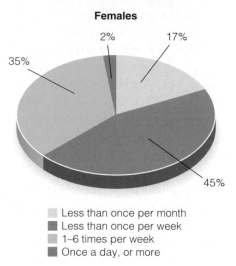

- Less than once per month
- Less than once per week
- 1–6 times per week
- Once a day, or more

55% of African American women have experienced oral sex, whereas 93% of White women and 65% of African American women have performed oral sex on a man.

Anal sex also is becoming more common and is practiced by heterosexual, gay, lesbian, and bisexual men and women. Between 15 and 18% of college men and women report at least one experience with anal sex (Gladue, 1990). Approximately 25% of adults have engaged in anal sex at least once (Seidman & Rieder, 1994).

Much of the survey research that has been presented in this section concerns males and females in adulthood. Yet sexual behavior occurs throughout the life span, as It's a Diverse World highlights.

IT'S A DIVERSE WORLD

Sexuality Across the Life Span

Even before you were born, you were a sexual being with the capacity for sexual pleasure and response. Male fetuses have erections, and boys are often born with erections or experience them during the first few weeks of life. Baby girls can have vaginal lubrication and clitoral erections within the first 24 hours after birth (Langfeldt, 1982). However, do not interpret a capacity for sexual response as an "interest" in sex like adults experience. Typically, infants and young children engage in sexual activity for the pleasure of it. It feels good, and they are naturally curious about their own bodies and those of others. Babies explore their bodies and quickly learn that self-stimulation is pleasurable. Infants are capable of having orgasms, although deliberate masturbation to orgasm rarely occurs before age 1 or 2 (Reinisch, 1991).

During the preschool years, self-stimulatory behavior may continue. Young children also are likely to be interested in seeing adults and other children nude or undressing. They may hug, cuddle, or kiss other children and are curious about other children's genitals such that instances of "I'll show you mine if you'll show me yours" may occur (Friedrich, Fisher, Broughton, Houston, & Shafran, 1998). By the time children start school, sexual behaviors decrease as children become more modest and develop better self-control. Yet it is still normal sexual behavior for children between the ages of 6 and 9 to touch their own genitals and try to see others nude or undressing. Touching others' genitals, buttocks, or breast area, or "playing doctor" also might take place (Kaeser, DiSalvo, & Moglia, 2001).

Preadolescents grow increasingly self-conscious about their bodies. Mutual display of the genitals or mutual masturbation is quite common. These sexual behaviors are often within their genders and are simply exploration (Leitenberg, Greenwald, & Tarran, 1989). Heterosexuals' interest in the other gender gradually increases as they approach puberty. As we saw in Chapter 10, puberty is accompanied by surges in sex hormones that heighten sex drive.

Among adolescents, the frequency of masturbation increases, especially among males (Smith, Rosenthal, & Reichler, 1996). Sexual experimentation is common among both virgins and nonvirgins (Woody, Russel, D'Souza, & Woody, 2000). Many adolescents engage in kissing and petting. Since Kinsey's surveys, higher rates of oral sex among high school students also have been reported (Coles & Stokes, 1985; Schwartz, 1999). Half of the high school students in the United States report being sexually active (Kolbe, 1998). By the age of 12, 12% of males and 3% of females report that they have engaged in sexual intercourse (Meschke, Bartholomae, & Zentall, 2000). Sixty-three percent of teens have had sexual intercourse by age 18 (Boonstra, 2002). Only one in five adolescents has not had intercourse by age 19 (Singh & Darroch, 1999). African American and Hispanic boys have higher rates of sexual activity than White boys, and Hispanic girls have lower rates than White girls (Upchurch, Aneshensel, Sucoff, & Levy-Storm, 1999). Yet the age at which teenagers become sexually active is similar across Canada, France, Great Britain, Sweden, and the United States (Alan Guttmacher Institute, 2001).

Intercourse among adolescents is very episodic, perhaps because teenagers do not consistently have an available venue for sexual activity. It should not be surprising, therefore, that youths who are unsupervised for 30 or more hours per week have higher rates of sexual activity than youths who are unsupervised for 5 hours a week or less (D. A. Cohen, Farley, Taylor, Martin, & Schuster, 2002). Moreover, teenagers who view more sexual content on television are more likely to engage in sexual activities such as "making-out," petting, and oral sex, and are also more likely to engage in sexual intercourse earlier than teenagers who view less sexual content on television (Collins et al., 2004).

Society tends to equate sexuality with young adults and see older adults as sexless. Yet the needs for intimacy and pleasure continue throughout life. Although sexual activity may decline as we progress through adulthood, a significant proportion of older people remain sexually active. In Kinsey's samples (1948, 1953), 94% of the men and 84% of the women remained sexually active at age 60. A Roper Starch poll of adults over the age of 60 in the United States found that 74% of the men and 70% of the women who had remained sexually active reported being as satisfied or more satisfied with sex than they were in their 40s (Leary, 1998). Many older people engage in intercourse, oral sex, and masturbation. Although the physical changes that accompany aging may produce less energy and desire for sex, the biggest obstacle to enjoying sexual pleasure in later adulthood appears to be social, rather than physical. The availability of sex partners diminishes as partners or spouses may die. Women still tend to live longer than men, creating a shortage of male partners for women such that many women simply give up and stop having sex as they grow older (Laumann et al., 1994). Most nursing homes segregate men and women and may discourage sexual relationships. Yet with Americans now living longer, there is no reason to forgo satisfying and pleasurable sexual relationships into one's 80s and beyond.

POOCH CAFÉ © 2004 Paul Gilligan. Dist. by Universal Press syndicate. Reprinted with permission. All rights reserved.

Let's Review!

For a quick check of your understanding of the survey research detailing the sexual attitudes and behaviors of males and females, answer these questions.

1. Masturbation is:
   a. more common among women than among men.
   b. more common among married people than single people.
   c. more common among Whites than among African Americans.
   d. more common among older people than younger people.

2. Which of the following statements is *true*?
   a. Infants are capable of having orgasms.
   b. Mutual masturbation among children is common.
   c. A significant proportion of older adults remain sexually active.
   d. All of the above statements are true.

3. Which of the following is a consistent finding among sex survey research?
   a. Men desire more sex partners than women.
   b. Women have more frequent sexual fantasies than men.
   c. Women want sex more than men.
   d. Women are more likely to engage in extramarital sex than men.

ANSWERS

1.c; 2.d; 3.a

LEARNING OBJECTIVE < < < < < < < < <

Distinguish between sexual orientation and sexual behavior, and analyze the research investigating the causes of sexual orientation.

sexual orientation one's sexual attraction for members of the same and/or other sex

heterosexual one who is sexually attracted only to members of the other sex

homosexual one who is sexually attracted only to members of the same sex

bisexual one who is sexually attracted to members of both sexes

Application

Sexual Orientation

A more controversial topic in sexuality is **sexual orientation,** or one's sexual attraction for members of the same and/or other sex. Many people never question their sexual orientation, whereas others may be in doubt as they grapple with the developmental task of establishing their identity in adolescence (see Chapter 10, pg. 453). Recall how such confusion led Maya to engage in sexual intercourse resulting in a teenage pregnancy. There are three types of sexual orientation. **Heterosexuals** are attracted to members of the other sex, **homosexuals** are attracted to members of the same sex, and **bisexuals** are attracted to members of both sexes. Because the word "homosexual" tends to bear a negative social stigma and therefore perpetuate negative stereotypes, we will more often use the term *gay males* to refer to homosexual men and *lesbians* to refer to homosexual women. Let's take a look at aspects of sexual orientation, what causes it, and current attitudes toward gay males and lesbians.

Sexual Orientation and Sexual Behavior

Do people's sexual orientations predict their sexual behavior? When speaking of sexual orientation, one must be careful to distinguish between attraction and behavior. Sexual orientation is not simply a matter of with whom you have sex. A man could be married to a woman, never had sex with a man, but still be gay because he is truly attracted only to men. A woman could have sex with other women but still consider herself to be heterosexual.

Kinsey's studies (1948, 1953) revealed that 37% of men and 13% of women had had at least one same-sex sexual encounter, but not all of these people considered themselves to be gay males or lesbians. If this sounds confusing, it is. When trying to determine just how many people are homosexual, bisexual, or heterosexual, researchers have had some problems. Kinsey and his colleagues (1948) estimated the incidence of homosexuality at roughly 3% of the general population. More modern figures, however, indicate that the rate of homosexuality could be more like 4–6% for males and 2–4% for females (LeVay, 1996). The negative attitudes that many hold about homosexuality make it difficult to get accurate data. It could well be that some people are reluctant to admit their true sexual feelings because they fear reprisals or they themselves feel stigmatized by their sexuality.

Attitudes Toward Gay Males and Lesbians: Differing Views Across the World

American attitudes toward gays and lesbians have become somewhat less negative over the last few decades. Television shows such as *Will and Grace* and *Queer Eye for the Straight Guy* suggest that the public is becoming more comfortable with homosexuality. Some corporations now extend employee benefits to same-sex couples. In 1973 the American Psychological Association eliminated homosexuality from its list of mental illnesses and, in 1980, dropped it from its *Diagnostic and Statistical Manual (DSM)* (discussed in Chapter 15).

But **homophobia,** or negative prejudice against homosexuals, has not disappeared. Many states do not recognize same-sex marriages. Gay males and lesbians do not have the same legal protection against discrimination as other minority members in the United States, and gay males and lesbians continue to be the victims of hate crimes. Approximately 80% of gay, lesbian, and bisexual youth are verbally abused, and 17% are physically abused (Meyer, 1999). As of 2004, 29 states and the District of Columbia have enacted laws against hate crimes motivated by sexual orientation (National Gay and Lesbian Task Force, 2004). Yet many religions in the Judeo-Christian tradition condemn homosexual behavior as an immoral act. It is quite possible to turn on the television to see a preacher warning of the dangers of homosexual sin. Another negative viewpoint on homosexuality is to see it as a mental illness that should be cured. However, there is little evidence to support the view that homosexuality is a mental health problem. Gay males and lesbians are no less well adjusted than their heterosexual counterparts (Weinrich, 1994).

Curiously, the negative attitudes that many Americans hold toward gays and lesbians are not shared by all cultures. In fact, many cultures openly accept homosexuality as a natural part of life. One study of 190 societies across the world found that approximately two-thirds of the world's societies accepted homosexuality (Ford & Beach, 1951). A historical study of 225 Native American tribes found that over half of them accepted male homosexuality and 17% accepted female homosexuality (Pomeroy, 1965). Why do some people abhor homosexuality or see it as a mental illness, whereas others see it as a normal variation of human sexuality? Perhaps these differing points of view stem from beliefs about what causes sexual orientation.

Sexual orientation doesn't always correspond to sexual behavior.

homophobia   prejudicial attitudes held against homosexuals and homosexuality

Gays and lesbians face many prejudices in today's society.

What Causes One's Sexual Orientation? The Influence of Biology and the Environment

What causes one's sexual orientation? One common mistake that people make when trying to answer this question is to confuse sexual orientation with gender. Recall that gender is the collection of personality traits that you possess, which your society typically associates with either males or females. Gender is not the same thing as sexual orientation. For instance, a gay male might be very masculine or very feminine. Likewise, a heterosexual woman might be either masculine or feminine. In other words, all feminine men are not gay, and all masculine women are not lesbians.

Having said that, there is some indication in the research that early gender-related behavior may be a predictor of later sexual orientation *for some*. A few studies have shown that some boys who later become gay preferred traditionally feminine activities to male ones during childhood (Bell, Weinberg, & Hammersmith, 1981; Green, 1987). Be careful about how you interpret these findings though. Not all boys who preferred feminine activities became gay. In fact, approximately half of the adult gay males in one study had preferences for traditionally masculine activities in childhood (Bell et al., 1981). Also, even if some gay males showed a preference for feminine activities in childhood, this does not necessarily indicate that the activities made them gay. It is just as likely that their homosexuality stemmed from other causes. In fact, in less stereotyped cultures in which children are not pressured to be masculine or feminine, there was less of a tendency for gay males to have exhibited feminine behavior in childhood (Ross, 1980).

Another environmental theory of homosexuality comes from observations of gay males who were involved in psychoanalytic therapy. Researchers noticed that many, but not all, of the gay males in their sample came from families in which there was a strong, domineering mother and a detached, rejecting, or hostile father. Therefore, they proposed that such a family environment could cause a son to grow up to be gay (Bieber, Dain, & Dince, 1962). Unfortunately, one serious limitation of this approach to understanding homosexuality was that all of the participants were in therapy. When we take a broader look at gay males who are not in therapy, there is no support for the idea that these family dynamics cause homosexuality (Siegelman, 1987). Given the relatively weak evidence for a universal, environmental cause of homosexuality, another reasonable question is to ask whether homosexuality could be encoded in our genes.

There is no evidence that cross-gender toy selection causes a homosexual orientation.

© Monika Graff/ The Image Works

A genetic link for homosexuality has been investigated in the traditional way—by examining pairs of identical and fraternal twins who are gay. Based on one study, if a man has an identical twin who is gay, he has a 52% chance of being gay himself. But if a man has a fraternal twin brother who is gay, he has a 22% chance of being gay himself (Bailey & Pillard, 1991). A similar pattern was found for females (Bailey, Pillard, Neale, & Agyei, 1993). Other investigations have found that gay men have a greater number of older brothers than heterosexual men (Blanchard, Zucker, Siegelman, Dickey, & Klassen, 1998; Ridley, 2003), suggesting that some mothers may become more immune to prenatal male hormones. In other words, their bodies produce more antibodies to such male hormones, creating a different prenatal hormonal environment that may affect succeeding male fetuses. These data indicate that biological factors are at least related to homosexuality, but they also indicate that some environmental factors must play a role in our sexual orientation.

As of this moment, no one can say for sure just what does cause our sexual orientation. The causes of sexual orientation are likely to remain a controversial and emotional issue for some time to come.

Let's Review!

For a quick check of your understanding of sexual orientation and sexual behavior, answer these questions.

1. Which is true about homosexuality?
   a. Some cultures fully accept homosexual behavior.
   b. Homosexuality is condemned in many Judeo-Christian religions.
   c. Homosexuality is likely influenced both by genetics and environment.
   d. All of the above are true.

2. Which of the following is true about gender and sexual orientation?
   a. They are the same thing.
   b. They are unrelated.
   c. They may be related for some people.
   d. Sexual orientation causes gender.

3. Paul has been married for 5 years to Lisa. However, Paul is primarily sexually attracted to men and not to women. What is Paul's sexual orientation?
   a. heterosexual   c. bisexual
   b. homosexual   d. both a and b

ANSWERS

1.d; 2.c; 3.b

Sexual Arousal and Response > > > > > > > > > >

LEARNING OBJECTIVE

Explain the biological and psychological components of sexual desire, and outline the phases of the sexual response cycle in men and women.

What is sexual arousal, and what factors contribute to sexual arousal in humans? **Sexual arousal** is a heightened state of sexual interest and excitement. Like many other behaviors that we have discussed, it is influenced by our biology as well as our learning experiences and cultural expectations. This section details the factors that influence our desire to engage in sexual activity and describes the cycle of physical processes and events that occur during sexual activity.

Sexual Desire: A Mixture of Chemicals, Thoughts, and Culture

Sexual desire is our motivation and interest in engaging in sexual activity. It is the first step in being sexually aroused. Biological and psychological processes influence sexual desire. Our physical desire to have sex, or our **libido,** is affected by both the hypothalamus and certain hormones of the endocrine system. As discussed in Chapter 2 (see p. 86), the brain's hypothalamus communicates with the master gland of the body, the pituitary gland, which in turn communicates with other glands in the body and instructs them to release hormones into the bloodstream. These hormones travel throughout the bloodstream and influence the functioning of many of the cells in our bodies. In just this fashion, our hypothalamus plays a key role in regulating our sexual behavior. The hypothalamus continually monitors the level of sex hormones in our bloodstream and directs the endocrine system to either increase or decrease the release of these hormones as required.

In mammals, **estrogens** are female hormones that regulate the female animal's desire to mate. Female animals' estrogen levels increase dramatically during a period

sexual arousal   a heightened state of sexual interest and excitement

sexual desire   one's motivation and interest in engaging in sexual activity

libido   one's physical desire, or drive, to have sex

estrogens   a class of female hormones that regulate many aspects of sexuality

Some female mammals show visible signs when they are receptive to mating.

ovaries   the organs in a female's body that produce eggs, or ova

Application

testosterone   a male hormone that plays a role in many aspects of sexuality, including sexual desire

testes   the organs in a male's body that produce both sperm and testosterone

Application

erogenous zones   areas of the skin that are sensitive to touch

called *estrus* ("being in heat"), in which the female is receptive to males' attempts to mate with her. Estrus coincides with ovulation in the female. During ovulation, the female's egg (or eggs) matures, so that it can be fertilized by the male sperm during mating. If fertilization does not occur, the female will pass out of estrus, and she will shed the egg along with the lining of her uterus during *menstruation*. If a pregnancy is going to occur, estrus is when it will happen. Therefore, it is in both the male and female animals' best interest to mate during estrus. To ensure that mating will occur, estrus is usually marked by some physical change in the female that signals to males of the species that she is in estrus and ready to mate. For example, many female chimpanzees have sexual swelling, or engorgement, of the external female genitals that indicate to male chimpanzees that it is time to mate.

Humans are a bit different from the rest of the animal kingdom in that for a human, there is no defined period of estrus. Human females can mate at any time in the menstrual cycle, and although female estrogen levels do fluctuate during the menstrual cycle, estrogen is not closely related to human female libido. Evidence for the limited role of estrogen in sexual desire comes from cases of women who have had hysterectomies that involved removal of their ovaries. **Ovaries** are organs that produce eggs and estrogen in a woman's body. Without ovaries, a woman's estrogen levels plummet. Despite the drastic loss of estrogen, many women do not experience a loss of sexual desire after a hysterectomy (Sherwin & Gelfand, 1987).

In humans, the hormone that seems to govern libido is **testosterone.** Testosterone is part of a class of male hormones called androgens. Although testosterone is a male hormone, it is also found in females (likewise, males have estrogen). In males, the **testes** produce testosterone (in addition to sperm). In women it is produced by the adrenal glands that sit above the kidneys. Adequate testosterone levels seem to be important in maintaining sexual desire. If testosterone levels fall too low, both males and females experience disinterest in sex. Testosterone may not be the only hormone that drives our desire, however. Another hormone, called *gonadotropin-releasing hormone (GnRH)*, may also play some role. GnRH has been shown to increase libido in men who lack testosterone (Dornan & Malsbury, 1989).

Are hormones the sole cause of our sexual desire? No. Although hormones play a significant role in our libido, sexual desire is not merely a function of chemicals in our bodies. Our senses, our thoughts, and our culture also impact human sexual desire. Visual cues can increase or decrease sexual desire. Erotic photographs or movies may be a sexual turn-on to some, but not to others. Seeing a lover nude or in sexy lingerie may for some be stimulating. Such visual stimulation seems to have more of an effect on men than on women (Reinisch, 1991). Sounds, such as a lover's voice or romantic music, may be appealing to some. Research also suggests that our sense of smell may play a role in sexual arousal, although again people vary greatly in the types of smells that they find arousing (Stern & McClintock, 1998). For some it may be the scent of a particular cologne or perfume, whereas for others it may be natural body scents such as sweat. For example, one study found that the aromas of pumpkin pie and lavender evoked the greatest sexual response in males, whereas the smell of candy-coated licorice, cucumbers, and baby powder elicited the greatest sexual response in females (Hirsch et al., 1998). Our sense of touch plays more of a direct role in sexual desire. Because nerve endings are unevenly distributed throughout the body, some areas of the skin are more sensitive to touch than others. These areas, called **erogenous zones,** include the genitals, buttocks, breasts, armpits, ears, navel, mouth, and the inner

Human sexuality is more than just a matter of hormones.

surfaces of the thighs. However, areas that may be highly stimulating to one person may produce a negative reaction in another. Hence, our preferences in reaction to touch differ.

Many of the differences in our reactions to sensory cues exist because we all think differently about what should be or should not be sexually stimulating. Such expectations may be learned or reflect the larger influence of gender roles and culture on our behavior. For instance, in the United States we emphasize cleanliness and the masking of natural body odors with perfumes and deodorants. Americans may learn to associate such odors as more sexually appealing than body sweat. Similarly, one age group may find jazz music or hard rock sexually stimulating because such sounds are associated with dating. In contrast, funeral music or the sound of a baby crying may dampen sexual desire. These learned experiences and our culture, along with our biology, shape our sexual desire. Once we are willing to engage in sexual activity, a predictable cycle of physical responses occurs, which we detail in the next section.

≪ Application

The Sexual Response Cycle

What physical changes do we experience during sexual activity? In the 1960s, William Masters, a gynecologist, and Virginia Johnson, a nurse, were the first researchers to directly observe and measure the sexual responses of men and women engaged in a variety of activities. Electronic sensors were placed on the bodies of the participants to directly measure physical responses. The participants also were interviewed in detail about their experiences. The information gathered in this study, and subsequently published in Masters and Johnson's *Human Sexual Response* (1966), described the common physical changes that we experience in our sexual encounters. The model includes four successive phases: excitement, plateau, orgasm, and resolution (Figure 11.7). Men and women were remarkably similar in their physical responses.

Masters and Johnson established pioneer field research on the sexual response of males and females.

During the **excitement phase,** men and women experience an increase in heart rate and blood pressure. The nipples may become erect and blood flow is increased to the genital area. Males experience penile erection, and the scrotal sac thickens. Females produce

excitement phase   the first stage of the sexual response cycle in which males get erections and females produce vaginal lubrication

Female Sexual Response

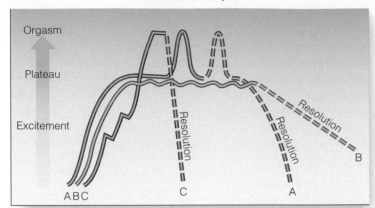

Male Sexual Response

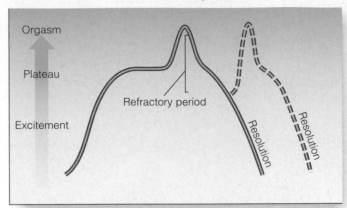

Figure 11.7 **The Sexual Response Cycle**

Masters and Johnson identified three basic patterns of response in females. A female may experience one or more orgasms (A); an extended plateau with no orgasm (B); or a rapid rise to orgasm with a quick resolution (C). Males show less variability in their sexual responses due to the refractory period.

From Human Sexual Response *by W. H. Masters and V. E. Johnson. Copyright © 1966 Little, Brown & Co. Reprinted by permission of Lippincott, Williams & Wilkins.*

plateau phase   the second stage of the sexual response cycle in which excitement peaks

orgasm phase   the third stage of the sexual response cycle in which the pelvic and anal muscles contract

resolution phase   the final stage of the sexual response cycle in which the body returns to homeostasis

refractory period   a time during the resolution phase in which males are incapable of experiencing another orgasm or ejaculation

vaginal lubrication, and the inner two-thirds of the vagina expand. The clitoris, the female sex organ that is extremely sensitive to sensation, swells. During the **plateau phase,** excitement peaks and remains somewhat constant. Breathing becomes rapid and blood pressure and heart rate continue to rise. Men experience a full penile erection and the testes are fully elevated. A few droplets of fluid that can contain sperm may appear at the tip of the penis. In women, the inner part of the vagina expands fully and the uterus becomes elevated. The clitoris shortens and withdraws.

During the **orgasm phase,** breathing, blood pressure, and heart rate peak. Contractions of the pelvic muscles and the anal sphincter produce the sensation of orgasm. Muscles throughout the body may spasm. In the male, the internal bodily contractions propel seminal fluid through the penis, causing ejaculation. Hence, in the male, the orgasm phase consists of two processes: orgasm and ejaculation. However, males' and females' subjective experience of orgasm is actually quite similar (Proctor, Wagner, & Butler, 1974; Vance & Wagner, 1976; Wiest, 1977). Men and women describe the experience in much the same way.

The sexual response cycle concludes with the **resolution phase,** in which the body returns to its prearoused state. Breathing, heart rate, and blood pressure return to normal. The male loses his erection, and in the female the vagina, clitoris, and uterus return to their normal size and position. Yet a distinct gender difference occurs in sexual response during the resolution phase. Unlike women, men experience a **refractory period,** or a time during which they are physically incapable of experiencing another orgasm or ejaculation. This measure of time increases as men age. For an adolescent male, the refractory period may last only a few minutes, whereas for men over age 50, it may last from several minutes to a day. Because women do not undergo a refractory period, they can more easily be rearoused to the point of multiple, or repeated, orgasms. Consequently, there is greater variability in the female response pattern (Figure 11.7; Masters, Johnson, & Kolodny, 1993).

Masters and Johnson's research was pivotal in describing the successive physical changes that occur during sexual response. This knowledge along with our understanding of sexual desire has been extremely important in helping people who experience sexual problems, our next topic of discussion.

Let's Review!

For a quick check of your understanding of the factors that influence sexual desire and the phases of the sexual response cycle, answer these questions.

1. Which is true of animals, but *not* of humans?
   a. testosterone regulates sex drive
   b. menstruation follows ovulation
   c. mating occurs only during estrus
   d. hormones influence sexual behavior

2. While dancing with his girlfriend, Malik notices that he has an erection. Malik is in which stage of the sexual response cycle?

   a. excitement   c. orgasm
   b. plateau   d. resolution

3. Males and females differ most strongly in their sexual response during which phase?
   a. excitement   c. orgasm
   b. plateau   d. resolution

ANSWERS

1.c; 2.a; 3.d

Sexual Disorders >>>>>>>>>>>>>>>>>>>>>>>>>>>

LEARNING OBJECTIVE

Discriminate between the various sexual dysfunctions and paraphilias, and explain nature and nurture's role in causing these disorders.

What is a sexual disorder, and how do I know if I have one? Many people experience sexual problems from time to time. A recent study reported that 43% of U.S. women and 31% of men ages 18 to 59 said they suffered from one or more sexual problems (Laumann, Paik, & Rosen, 1999). The Pfizer Global Study of Sexual Behavior (2002) reported that 42% of men and 47% of women in 29 countries experienced sexual difficulties over the past year (Figure 11.8). However, when these problems become persistent, cause a person a great deal of distress, and interfere with an individual's ability to function, it is called a **sexual disorder.** This section describes two broad categories of sexual disorders: sexual dysfunctions and paraphilias.

sexual disorder   a persistent sexual problem that causes a person a great deal of distress and interferes with an individual's ability to function sexually

Sexual Dysfunctions: Problems in Sexual Desire or Response

The previous section outlined aspects of sexual desire and detailed the phases of the sexual response cycle. **Sexual dysfunction** is a disorder characterized by a problem with sexual desire, arousal, or satisfaction. Sexual dysfunctions are grouped into four categories related to desire and the stage of sexual response that is being affected. They include disorders of sexual desire and arousal, orgasmic disorders, and sexual pain disorders. In general, women's sexual problems have been researched less than men's (Bartlik & Goldstein, 2001).

sexual dysfunction   a disorder characterized by a problem with sexual desire, arousal, or satisfaction

Disorders of Sexual Desire

Disorders of sexual desire involve a lack of interest in or an aversion to sexual activity. Again, it is normal to have occasional disinterest in sexual activity. For instance, you may want to watch television or sleep instead of having sex. Sexual desire in the same person varies from day to day, month to month, and from year to year. However, when such disinterest is persistent and causes personal unhappiness, it may represent a disorder of sexual desire. Two main sexual desire disorders include hypoactive sexual desire disorder and sexual aversion disorder.

Hypoactive sexual desire disorder is characterized by a persistent disinterest in sex and sexual activities (American Psychiatric Association, 2000). It is one of the most

 Application

hypoactive sexual desire disorder a disorder characterized by a persistent disinterest in sex and sexual activities

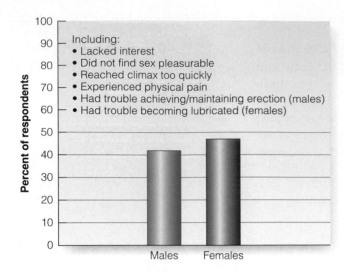

Carol Ford / Getty Images

Figure 11.8 Sexual Difficulties Lasting More Than 2 Months in the Last Year

Men and women across the world experience sexual problems from time to time. If the problem persists, causes distress, and interferes with a person's ability to function, it is called a sexual disorder.

Copyright © 2002 Pfizer, Inc. All rights reserved.

One of the most commonly reported sexual dysfunctions is low sexual desire.

commonly diagnosed sexual dysfunctions and is more common among women than men (Bach, Wincze, & Barlow, 2001; Laumann et al., 1999; Letourneau & O'Donohue, 1993; Reinisch, 1991). As we have seen, sexual desire is affected by biological and psychological processes. Hypoactive sexual desire disorder may result from hormone deficiencies, anxiety involving fears of pleasure or of a lack of control, or from previous negative sexual experiences and trauma such as rape or childhood sexual abuse (DiLillo, 2001). Additional conditions that may inhibit desire include stress and depression. Medications that are used to control anxiety, depression, or high blood pressure also may dampen sexual desire.

sexual aversion disorder is characterized by a persistent disgust and aversion toward sexual activity (American Psychiatric Association, 2000). Such individuals may avoid genital contact. Sexual aversion disorder is less common than lack of desire (Spark, 2000). Its cause appears to be more influenced by psychological factors such as a history of sexual trauma, especially for women. A history of erectile problems in men can cause sexual aversion.

sexual aversion disorder a disorder characterized by a persistent disgust and aversion toward sexual activity

Disorders of Sexual Arousal

During excitement, the first stage of the sexual response cycle, males get erections and females produce vaginal lubrication. Such excitement is necessary to facilitate sexual activity. People with sexual arousal disorders experience persistent difficulty in these responses or they lack the feelings of sexual excitement that normally accompany sexual arousal (American Psychiatric Association, 2000). Disorders of sexual arousal include male erectile disorder and female sexual arousal disorder.

In his commercials for Viagra, Bob Dole has made erectile dysfunction, or male erectile disorder, a household name. **Male erectile disorder** is characterized by the persistent inability to attain or sustain an erection sufficient to complete sexual activity

male erectile disorder a disorder in males characterized by the persistent inability to attain or sustain an erection sufficient to complete sexual activity

(American Psychiatric Association, 2000). More than 50% of U.S. men between the ages of 40 and 70 experience some degree of erectile dysfunction (Goldstein et al., 1998). Similar numbers are reported among men in Egypt, suggesting that occasional erectile failure occurs worldwide in older men (Seyam et al., 2003). Erectile disorder tends to increase with age, yet all healthy males experience difficulty in getting or sustaining an erection from time to time. Such occasional problems may be due to fatigue, stress, alcohol use, or a short-term illness. If the man begins to fear that such occurrences will continue, he is more likely to suffer from *performance anxiety,* or the fear that he will not be able to perform sexually. Such performance anxiety might cause further instances of erectile failure leading to erectile disorder. Other psychological factors might also contribute to erectile dysfunction such as poor self-esteem, depression, or problems in a relationship (Bach et al., 2001). However, chronic problems of erectile disorder typically stem from physical causes such as diabetes, prostate surgery, and multiple sclerosis. These physical problems impair blood flow to the penis that results in an erection (Goldstein, 1998; Kedia, 1983; Leland, 1997). Prescription drugs such as anti-anxiety medication, antidepressants, and heart medication also may impair erectile functioning (Morales, 2003). The regular use of psychoactive drugs such as alcohol, heroin, morphine, marijuana, or cocaine can lead to erectile failure as well (Nelson, 1988; Segraves, 1988; Spark, 2000; Weiss & Mirin, 1987).

Female sexual arousal disorder is characterized by persistent difficulty in becoming sexually excited or sufficiently lubricated in response to sexual stimulation (American Psychiatric Association, 2000). About 20% of women report difficulties with lubrication or arousal during sexual activity (Laumann et al., 1999). Like erectile disorder, female sexual arousal disorder can have physical causes related to a lack of blood flow to the genital area (Graber, 1993). Any neurological or hormonal problem that interferes with vaginal lubrication can lead to diminished sexual excitement. For example, during menopause it is common for women to experience vaginal dryness at times due to the decreased levels of estrogen in their bodies. Prescription medications and illicit drug use also may dampen sexual excitement. However, in many cases female sexual arousal disorder may stem from psychological factors such as feelings of guilt, anger, helplessness, or anxiety, a history of sexual trauma, or ineffective sexual stimulation (Morokoff, 1993).

female sexual arousal disorder a disorder in females characterized by persistent difficulty in becoming sexually excited or sufficiently lubricated in response to stimulation

Orgasmic Disorders

Three sexual disorders relate to the orgasm phase of the sexual response cycle: female orgasmic disorder, male orgasmic disorder, and premature ejaculation. **Orgasmic disorder,** which can occur in males and females, is characterized by a lack of orgasm or a persistent delay in reaching orgasm despite adequate stimulation. Approximately 4 to 9% of men report an inability to ejaculate during sexual intercourse (Laumann et al., 1999). Some may be able to ejaculate by masturbating or through oral sex, but cannot climax during sexual intercourse. About 25% of women report difficulty in reaching orgasm, whereas 5 to 10% of women report suffering from orgasmic dysfunction (Laumann et al., 1999; Spector & Carey, 1990). Laumann and his colleagues (1994) found that African American men and women reported higher rates of orgasmic difficulty than White men and women. Physical causes of orgasmic disorder are evident and may include any disease, condition, or drug that interferes with neural control of ejaculation or that causes damage to the pelvic muscles. Orgasmic disorders also may be related to psychological causes such as feelings of guilt, anger, or resentment, previous negative sexual experiences, or ineffective sexual stimulation. Many women still report a fear of "letting go" that may interfere with orgasm (Tugrul & Kabakci, 1997).

orgasmic disorder a disorder characterized by a lack of orgasm or a persistent delay in reaching orgasm despite adequate stimulation

premature ejaculation   a disorder in males characterized by persistent or recurrent ejaculation with minimal sexual stimulation before he wishes it

Premature ejaculation is characterized by persistent or recurrent ejaculation with minimal sexual stimulation before the person wishes it (American Psychiatric Association, 2000). It can occur in men of all ages and backgrounds. Roughly 28% of White males and 34% of African American males reported reaching climax too soon during the past year (Laumann et al., 1994). In contrast to the other sexual dysfunctions, less is known about definitive causes of premature ejaculation. In the past, premature ejaculation has been attributed to the inability of the male to employ self-control strategies when he is reaching the threshold of ejaculation (Kaplan, 1974). However, current research fails to show that men who experience premature ejaculation are less accurate than other men in gauging their sexual arousal (Kinder & Curtiss, 1988; Strassberg, Mahoney, Schaugaard, & Hale, 1990). For some men, performance anxiety may result in reaching orgasm too fast. They are so anxious about performing that they fail to pay attention to their level of sexual arousal (McCarthy, 2001). Future research may unravel a more definitive explanation of premature ejaculation.

Sexual Pain Disorders

dyspareunia   a disorder characterized by painful sexual intercourse

The last category of sexual dysfunctions includes the sexual pain disorders of dyspareunia and vaginismus. **Dyspareunia,** or painful sexual intercourse, can affect both men and women, although women more frequently report it. For example, Laumann and his colleagues (1994) found that roughly 3% of White and African American men reported pain during sex within the past year. In contrast, 15% of White women and 12.5% of African American women reported experiencing pain during sex in the past year. Dyspareunia may result from physical causes such as genital and vaginal infections, pelvic inflammatory disease (PID), or allergic reactions to spermicides, condoms, or diaphragms. The most common cause of pain in women is inadequate vaginal lubrication. Psychological factors such as feelings of guilt or anxiety about sex also may be involved in sexual pain in women. Such feelings inhibit vaginal lubrication and tighten the vaginal muscles making penile penetration uncomfortable.

vaginismus   a disorder in females characterized by involuntary contractions of the vaginal muscles making penetration painful or impossible

In women, dyspareunia can sometimes lead to vaginismus. **Vaginismus** involves involuntary contractions of the vaginal muscles, making penetration painful and sometimes impossible. Approximately 5 to 17% of women experience vaginismus (Reissing, Binik, & Khalife, 1999). It may develop in response to sexual trauma or a medical condition such that they come to fear vaginal penetration (Beck, 1993; Lagana, McGarvey, Classen, & Koopman, 2001; LoPiccolo & Stock, 1986).

Paraphilias: Sexually Aroused by an Object or Situation

paraphilia   a disorder that involves sexual arousal in response to an unusual object, situation, or unconsenting person

Another broad category of sexual disorders is the **paraphilias.** They involve sexual arousal in response to an unusual object, situation, or nonconsenting person. Such disorders include voyeurism, exhibitionism, fetishism, transvestism, pedophilia, sexual sadism, and sexual masochism.

fetishism   a paraphilia characterized by sexual arousal to inanimate objects

Fetishism and transvestism are noncoercive paraphilias. That is, they do not exploit others in order to achieve sexual gratification. Being sexually aroused by inanimate objects characterizes **fetishism.** Clothing, such as women's lingerie and high-heeled shoes, and certain materials such as leather or silk, are common fetish objects. The fetishist may compulsively fantasize about such objects in order to become sexually aroused, or he may act on such fantasies by stroking such an object during masturbation. In **transvestism,** a person is sexually aroused by wearing clothing of the opposite gender. The typical transvestite is a heterosexual, married male (Talamini, 1982;

transvestism   a paraphilia in which a person is sexually aroused by wearing clothing of the opposite gender

Wise & Meyer, 1980). Transvestites are more likely than other people to be the oldest

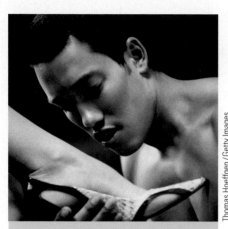

A person with a fetish is sexually aroused by an inanimate object.

or only child and report closer relationships with their mothers than with their fathers (Schott, 1995). Is a female impersonator a transvestite? Not necessarily. The distinguishing feature is whether the person cross-dresses in order to achieve sexual arousal. Many female impersonators cross-dress for entertainment purposes and thereby would not be considered transvestites.

Voyeurism, exhibitionism, and pedophilia are coercive paraphilias. That is, they involve achieving sexual arousal and gratification at the expense of another without his or her permission. **Voyeurism** involves repeated urges to observe unsuspecting strangers who are naked, disrobing, or engaged in sexual activity (American Psychiatric Association, 2000). It is normal for people to get aroused while watching erotic materials or their lovers disrobe. Such people know that they are being observed. In contrast, the voyeur watches people who do not know that they are being observed. Voyeurs may risk physical injury by hiding in a tree or on a rooftop. They generally put themselves in risky situations in which they may be discovered. Such risk appears to increase their sexual arousal (Tollison & Adams, 1979).

In **exhibitionism,** a person is sexually aroused by fantasies involving exposing his genitals to some unsuspecting individual. He may or may not act on these fantasies yet feel a compulsion to do so. Are strippers or exotic dancers exhibitionists? No. Strippers remove their clothing to excite others sexually in order to earn a living, as Maya Angelou did as a single mother. They do not remove their clothing in front of unsuspecting people to arouse themselves.

Pedophilia involves a person who is sexually aroused by fantasies of or engaging in sexual activity with a prepubescent child. Most pedophiles are heterosexual men abusing young girls (Cole, 1992). However, all sex offenders are not pedophiles, and not all pedophiles sexually molest children. A pedophile may have fantasies about engaging in sexual activity with children but never act on those desires. A larger proportion of pedophiles and other sex offenders report being sexually abused in childhood compared to men who have not committed a sexual offense (Freund & Kuban, 1994). However, this does not mean that all adults who were abused as children go on to molest children. If they do act on their compulsions, pedophiles may victimize children of the same gender, opposite gender, or both. Sexual abuse is extremely damaging to children. Its effects are discussed in more detail later in this chapter.

In sexual sadism and sexual masochism, pain becomes connected with sexual pleasure. **Sexual sadism** refers to a situation in which a person achieves sexual satisfaction by inflicting pain or humiliation on a sex partner. **Sexual masochism** involves the desire to be humiliated or receive pain in order to attain sexual pleasure. Sexual sadists and sexual masochists often form consenting sexual relationships based on *sadomasochism (S & M)*. S & M participants may be heterosexual, bisexual, or gay (Breslow, Evans, & Langley, 1986). They may engage in elaborate rituals involving dominant and submissive roles such as master and slave. Of all the paraphilias, women are most likely to engage in sexual masochism yet male masochists still outnumber female masochists (American Psychiatric Association, 2000).

voyeurism   a paraphilia in which one is sexually aroused by observing unsuspecting strangers who are undressing or engaged in sexual activity

 Application

exhibitionism   a paraphilia in which one is sexually aroused by the fantasies or the behavior of exposing his or her genitals to some unsuspecting individual

pedophilia   a paraphilia in which one is sexually aroused by fantasies of or engaging in sexual activity with a pre-pubescent child

sexual sadism   a paraphilia in which a person achieves sexual satisfaction by inflicting pain or humiliation on a sex partner

sexual masochism   a paraphilia in which a person desires to be humiliated or receive pain in order to attain sexual pleasure

Let's Review!

For a quick check of your understanding of the sexual dysfunctions and paraphilias that some people experience, answer these questions.

1. Andrew persistently gets sexually aroused by cross-dressing. Andrew would be considered a(n)

   a. transsexual.
   b. female impersonator.
   c. exhibitionist.
   d. transvestite.

2. Since Mona's rape, she has been repulsed by the thought of engaging in sexual activity. Most likely Mona is suffering from:

   a. hypoactive sexual desire.
   b. sexual aversion disorder.
   c. orgasmic disorder.
   d. inhibited excitement.

3. Which of the following paraphilias does *not* involve achieving sexual arousal and gratification at the expense of another without his or her consent?

   a. pedophilia
   b. exhibitionism
   c. fetishism
   d. voyeurism

ANSWERS

1. d; 2. b; 3. c

LEARNING OBJECTIVE ‹ ‹ ‹ ‹ ‹ ‹ ‹ ‹

Define the various forms of sexual coercion, and describe how they might be prevented.

sexual coercion sexual behaviors that are nonconsenting, abusive, or forcible

sexual harassment the repeated use of unwanted verbal comments, gestures, or physical contact of a sexual nature against another person in a subordinate position

Sexual Coercion

We saw in the previous section that a few of the paraphilias are coercive because the sexual behavior was directed at nonconsenting persons. This section expands that discussion by looking at other sexual behaviors that are coercive. **Sexual coercion** involves behaviors that are nonconsenting, abusive, or forcible such as sexual harassment, sexual abuse, and rape.

Sexual Harassment: Unwelcome Comments, Gestures, or Contact

In 1991, law professor Anita Hill alleged that Supreme Court nominee Clarence Thomas sexually harassed her when she worked in his office. Hill's testimony at Thomas's Supreme Court confirmation hearing threw the subject of sexual harassment into the national limelight. It was quickly followed by the 1991 Tailhook scandal in which 26 women accused Navy personnel of sexual assault during a Las Vegas convention. Since then, high-profile cases such as allegations of sexual harassment against Senator Robert Packwood and Paula Jones's charges of sexual harassment against President Clinton have brought continued attention to this topic. So what is sexual harassment?

Sexual harassment includes the repeated use of unwanted verbal comments, gestures, or physical contact of a sexual nature against another person in a subordinate position. The victim of sexual harassment may be made to feel that tolerating such behavior is a condition of employment, promotion, or satisfactory evaluation. In 1986, the U.S. Supreme Court recognized sexual harassment as a form of sex discrimination under Title VII of the Civil Rights Act of 1964. Although both men and women can commit sexual harassment, a recent report by the Equal Employment Opportunity Commission (2003) finds that fewer complaints are filed by men, and the majority of these involve same sex harassment. For example, of all the sexual harassment complaints filed in 2002 only 14.9% were filed by men, and only 1% of these complaints involved a woman harassing a man. Similar results have been found when investigating sexual harassment complaints in the military (Magley, Hulin, Fitzgerald, & DeNardo, 1999).

Obvious forms of sexual harassment may include demands for sexual favors in order to maintain a job. However, many forms of sexual harassment are subtle, such as unwanted sexual comments, jokes, or gestures. Sexual harassment is further complicated by the fact that the recipient must find such behavior unwelcome. One person may be offended by such behavior whereas another may not. For example, in a recent study by Woodzicka and LaFrance (2001), women participants were described a situation in which a male interviewer asked a female job applicant several questions that involved mild sexual harassment such as, "Do you have a boyfriend?" The women were asked how they would respond in such a situation. Many women reported that they would object to such behavior in a clear and overt way. However, when the researchers staged an actual interview by advertising for an actual job and employed a male confederate to conduct the interviews, the women's behaviors were quite different. They did not object or leave the interview, but more frequently avoided the questions. Moreover, the researchers had to hire a second male confederate because some of the women found the first confederate to be charming. They did not perceive his behavior as sexual harassment. Clearly, sexually harassing behaviors are highly dependent on the reaction and perceptions of the recipient.

Despite our increased awareness about sexual harassment, such behavior continues to go unreported. Many who experience sexual harassment choose to ignore the behavior or to avoid the person (Barringer, 1993b; Magley, 2002; Maypole, 1987). However, if you are being sexually harassed, a direct, businesslike response to communicate that the behavior is offensive or unwanted is appropriate. People differ in their perceptions of what constitutes sexually offensive behavior, but if a person is told that his or her behavior is offensive and he or she continues to harass someone, that person can no longer claim that he or she did not know that his or her behavior was objectionable. For repeated instances of sexual harassment, file a complaint. Organizations and companies are required by law to respond to such a complaint. It is best to have written documentation of sexually harassing behavior, including when and where it occurred, as well as any witnesses that were present to substantiate the complaint.

 Application

Child Molestation and Sexual Abuse: Short- and Long-Term Effects

What is child sexual abuse? Sexual abuse is any sexual activity between an adult and a child. Even if children cooperate in sexual activity with an adult, they are legally incapable of consenting to such activity. Maya's rape at the age of 8 constitutes child sexual abuse. Sexual abuse may include fondling, kissing, oral sex, and anal or vaginal intercourse. The prevalence of child sexual abuse is difficult to determine because many cases go unreported. Only about 1 in 10 cases is reported to the authorities (Maletzky, 1998). However, researchers estimate that 4–16% of boys and roughly 20–25% of girls experience sexual abuse as a child (Fieldman & Crespi, 2002; Gorey & Leslie, 1997; Janus & Janus, 1993; Laumann et al., 1994). Sexual abuse occurs across all racial, ethnic, and economic categories (Alter-Reid, Gibbs, Lachenmeyer, Sigal, & Massoth, 1986). However, in one study (Wyatt, Loeb, Solis, Carmona, & Romero, 1999), the incidence of sexual abuse reported by Whites was higher than that reported by African Americans. The average age of sexual abuse in girls ranges from 6 to 12 years, and from 7 to 10 years for boys (Knudsen, 1991).

Who sexually abuses children? Although children are often educated during the preschool years about "stranger danger," in roughly 75–80% of cases, the child knows the molester. It is estimated that family members perpetrate abuse in 10–50% of sexual abuse cases (Waterman & Lusk, 1986). Initially, the child may trust the abuser and give compliance. Although many sexually abused children are molested only once like

Sexual abuse can have devastating effects on a child's self-image.

Maya, repeated acts of abuse are more common when a family member is the abuser (Dube & Hebert, 1988). In such instances of repeated abuse, affectionate fondling and kissing may progress to genital touching or oral sex, and then to penetration (anal or vaginal) over the course of the person's childhood (Waterman & Lusk, 1986). Children may fear retaliation by the molester if they tell, or they may believe that they are to blame for the sexual abuse. The overwhelming majority of child sexual abusers are male (Thomlison, Stephens, Cunes, & Grinnell, 1991).

What are the effects of being sexually abused? They include both short- and long-term physical and psychological effects (Finkelhor, 1990). Physically, children may suffer genital injuries, sleep disturbances, contract sexually transmitted infections, or develop stomachaches and headaches in an attempt to cope with the abuse. Psychologically, sexually abused children often externalize or internalize their distress. External behavioral changes include "acting out," such as tantrums, aggressive behavior, or drug use. Other children may respond by becoming withdrawn or depressed, internal behaviors of distress. Maya Angelou internalized her distress by not speaking for 5 years. Although the effects of sexual abuse on males and females are quite similar, boys tend to engage in more external behavior, whereas girls are more likely to internalize their distress. In adolescence, child sexual abuse survivors may become prematurely sexually active or promiscuous.

The long-term effects of sexual abuse may continue into adulthood in the form of depression, eating disorders, suicide attempts, drug abuse, and self-destructive behavior (Beitchman et al., 1992; Cheasty, Clare, & Collins, 2002; Jones & Emerson, 1994). Negative attitudes about sex and sexual dysfunctions in adulthood also are commonly reported by adult survivors of sexual abuse (Courtois, 2000; DiLillo, 2002; Maltz, 2002). However, in a comprehensive review of the research on the effects of child sexual abuse, Rind and his colleagues (Rind, Tromovitch, & Bauseman, 1998) found that adult survivors of child sexual abuse were only 1% more likely to be less well-adjusted in adulthood than nonvictims. Moreover, in this study, it appeared that problem-filled family environments were more likely to account for these differences than the sexual abuse. This in no way minimizes the pain of experiencing child sexual abuse. However, it does offer hope in that many of these people go on to establish healthy lives and loving adult relationships. Maya's many accomplishments, achievements, and experiences are a rich illustration of such resilience.

Application

Rape: Forcing Sex on Someone

Another type of sexual pressure or coercion is rape. What is rape? Although the legal definition of rape varies from state to state, generally **rape** involves the threat or use of force to obtain sex. Surveys suggest that between 15% and 23% of women and 2% of men in the United States are raped at some time in their lives (Michael, Gagnon, Laumann, Kolata, 1994; Tjaden & Thoennes, 1998). Across college campuses, approximately 3% of women experience an attempted and/or completed rape during a typical college year (Fisher, Cullen, & Turner, 2000). However, like child sexual abuse, these numbers may seriously underestimate the number of rapes that occur. Women may fear rejection from their families or fear revenge from the offender. Men and women may feel that they will be humiliated by the criminal justice system or assume that they will not be believed and the offender will go free. Many women may not even

rape the threat or use of force to obtain sex

define the incident as a rape especially if it took place within a marriage or a dating relationship. Yet women are more likely to be raped, injured, or killed by their current or former partner than by other types of assailants (Nevid, Rathus, & Greene, 2000).

Men can be raped, too, although the majority of rape victims are women (Houry, Feldman, & Abbott, 2000). Women of all ages, races, and social classes are raped. Yet women between the ages of 16 and 24 are three times more likely to be raped than older women (National Crime Victimization Survey, 1995). The prevalence of rape in the United States is eight times greater than that in Europe and more than 20 times greater than that in Japan (Mann, 1991). Many social scientists attribute such cultural differences to U.S. attitudes and beliefs about rape.

Attitudes and Beliefs About Rape

Do you believe that a prostitute cannot be raped? Do you believe that men see sex as an achievement, or a notch on their belts? Endorsing such attitudes helps create a climate that justifies rape and blames the victim (Table 11.1 ◆). Among college students, males tend to show greater agreement with statements that are supportive of rape (Holcomb, Holcomb, Sondag, & Williams, 1991). Other studies find that those holding more traditional gender roles also are more likely to be tolerant of rape and less tolerant of rape victims (Check & Malamuth, 1983; Simonson & Subich, 1999). Their belief that "real" men are sexual aggressors who need to overcome a woman's resistance may make them more accepting of violence against women.

≪ Application

Many people also believe a number of myths about rape such as "the way women dress, they are just asking to be raped," or that deep down inside, women want to be raped (Powell, 1996). Believing such myths further condones rape. Although both men and women are susceptible to rape myths, studies find that college men show a greater acceptance of these myths than do women even after receiving rape education classes that are designed to challenge such views (Brady, Chrisler, Hosdale, Osowiecki, & Veal, 1991; Lenihan, Rawlins, Eberly, Buckley, & Masters, 1992). Where do such attitudes and beliefs stem from? Many believe that reinforcing aggression and competition in males from a very early age socializes males into a sexually dominant role such

◆ **Table 11.1**

Attitudes That Support Rape

Do you agree with any of the following statements?

- A man sees sex as an achievement, or notch on his belt.
- Rape really only occurs when a man has a weapon.
- Deep down, a woman likes to be whistled at on the street.
- If a woman is heavily intoxicated, it is okay to have sex with her.
- Women frequently cry false rape.
- In a woman, submissiveness equals femininity.
- In a man, aggressiveness equals masculinity.
- A prostitute cannot be raped.
- Some women ask to be raped and may enjoy it.
- Any woman could prevent rape if she wanted to.
- The victim often provokes rape.
- If a woman says "no" to having sex, she means "maybe" or even "yes."

Note: People who agree with these statements tend to be more supportive of rape.

that they see interpersonal relationships and sex as adversarial (Stock, 1991). Such socialization experiences are evident when we examine date rape.

Date Rape

One commonly held belief about rape is that strangers commit it. However, most women are raped by men they know, not strangers. This particular type of rape is referred to as *acquaintance rape.* For example, 80% of the rapes reported in the National Crime Victimization Survey (U.S. Bureau of Justice Statistics, 1995) were perpetrated by an acquaintance of the victim. Among college women who experience a rape or an attempted rape, the majority of these women knew the person who assaulted them. Nine out of ten of the perpetrators were ex-boyfriends, classmates, friends, and/or coworkers (Fisher et al., 2000). Moreover, Laumann and his colleagues (1994) found that strangers committed only 4% of the sexual assaults reported in their study. Acquaintance rapes are much less likely than stranger rapes to be reported (Schafran, 1995), and even when they are reported, they are more often treated as "misunderstandings" than as violent crimes. Such interpretations are especially likely in the case of **date rape,** one form of acquaintance rape.

Often date rape charges boil down to a case of "he said, she said," as we have seen in Kobe Bryant's recent legal problems.

Unlike stranger rape, date rape occurs within a context in which sexual relations could occur. The woman has voluntarily agreed to spend time with this man. Moreover, she may have consented to some sexual activity, such as kissing or fondling, but did not consent to sexual intercourse. In such instances, a charge of date rape often comes down to a case of her word against his. If she has consented to a series of acts such as sharing dinner, accompanying him to his hotel room or apartment, and perhaps even to kissing, her word is less likely to be persuasive to a jury. However, if a woman says no, a man should take no for an answer.

Studies of U.S. college women show that 10–20% of women report being forced into sexual intercourse by dates (Tang, Critelli, & Porter, 1995). Men who commit date rape tend to believe that acceptance of a date indicates a willingness to engage in sexual intercourse. If she is willing to return home with him, he may interpret this as a signal of sexual interest (Muehlenhard & McCoy, 1991). Date rapists are also more likely to interpret resistance as "playing hard to get" or not wanting to appear "too easy." Date rape is most likely to occur in the earlier stages of dating rather than on the first date, and it is more likely to occur when the couple has drunk too much alcohol (Coperhaver & Grauerholz, 1991; Hensley, 2002). To deter unwanted sexual advances, it is important for women to be very clear and direct about their sexual wishes. Even more important is for men to examine their attitudes toward sexual activity within a dating relationship.

date rape   a form of acquaintance rape in which an individual is forced or threatened to engage in sexual activity with a social escort

Application

Application

Let's Review!

For a quick check of your understanding of sexual co-ercion, including child molestation, sexual abuse, and rape, answer these questions.

1. Which of the following individuals is less likely to blame a victim of rape?

   a. a male holding less traditional gender-role stereotypes

   b. a male holding more traditional gender-role stereotypes

   c. a male who believes that men are expected to be sexually aggressive

   d. a female who believes that women frequently cry false rape

2. Which of the following statements about childhood sexual abuse is true?

   a. Males are sexually abused at a higher rate than females.

   b. In the majority of child sexual abuse cases, the perpetrator is unknown to the child.

   c. Sexual abuse occurs across all racial, ethnic, and economic categories.

   d. Male sexual abuse victims are more likely to internalize their distress, whereas female sexual abuse victims are more likely to engage in external behavior.

3. The repeated use of unwanted verbal comments, gestures, or physical contact of a sexual nature against another person in a subordinate position is called:

   a. sexual abuse.   c. date rape.

   b. sexual assault.   d. sexual harassment.

ANSWERS

1. a; 2. c; 3. d

Sexually Transmitted Infections > > > > > > > >

LEARNING OBJECTIVE

Discriminate among the various sexually transmitted infections, their causes, modes of transmission and treatment options.

What are sexually transmitted infections? **Sexually transmitted infections (STIs)** are infections that are passed from one person to another, usually through sexual contact. However, some STIs may be spread by nonsexual contact as well as from a mother to her unborn child. Every day we hear news accounts of the spread of AIDS and the HIV virus. Yet AIDS and the HIV virus are not the only types of STIs, and these other STIs are more widespread, especially in the United States.

Prevalence of STIs: Will I Get an STI?

The World Health Organization estimates that there are over 333 million new adult cases of curable STIs across the world each year (World Health Organization, 1998). The Centers for Disease Control and Prevention (2001) estimates that over 65 million people in the United States are currently living with an STI. An additional 15 million become infected each year. The United States has the highest rates of STIs in the industrialized world. The U.S. rate of infection is 50 to 100 times higher than that of other industrialized nations (Eng & Butler, 1997). At least one in three sexually active men and women in the United States is likely to contract an STI by age 24 (Boyer et al., 1999). At least one in four Americans will contract an STI at some time in their lives (Barringer, 1993a).

Why are STIs so widespread? One reason is that younger people today are more likely to engage in sexual intercourse. At least 25% of new cases of STIs occur among teenagers (Kaiser Family Foundation, 1998), who may not use condoms or use them infrequently (Kamb et al., 1998), or the woman may be "on the pill" or using oral contraceptives, which does not prevent STIs. A second reason is that many STIs often have no symptoms, so they are unknowingly passed from one person to the next (Bowie,

sexually transmitted infections infections that are passed from one person to another primarily through sexual contact

Is this couple at risk for an STI?

Stuart McClymont/Getty Images

Application

Hammerschlag, & Martin, 1994). A third reason is the social stigma attached to those infected with an STI. Such negative perceptions may prevent people from openly discussing their conditions with medical personnel, partners, and other loved ones.

Risk Factors: Age, Gender, Ethnicity, and Behavior

Who is most at risk for getting an STI? Anyone who is sexually active risks contracting an STI. However, women, teenagers and some ethnic groups are more likely to have an STI in the United States. Men and women between the ages of 15 and 25 are most at risk for contracting an STI (Gilson & Mindel, 2001). Young people are at increased risk because they engage in many high-risk sexual behaviors such as having multiple partners and engaging in unprotected sexual intercourse. Women also are at higher risk for contracting an STI than men because the warm, moist environment of the vagina renders women more susceptible to infection. It is twice as easy for a male to transmit an STI to a female as it is for a female to transmit one to a male (Laumann et al., 1994). Younger women are especially vulnerable as viruses and bacteria can more easily invade immature cervical cells than mature ones (Farley et al., 1997; Parker-Pope, 2002). Some STIs are more common among African Americans and Hispanics than among Whites. For example, from 1996 to 1997, the rate of gonorrhea among African Americans was 30 times higher than among Whites. In the same year, the rate for Hispanics was two-thirds higher than among Whites. Similarly, syphilis rates in 1998 were higher in African Americans and Hispanics than among Whites (Centers for Disease Control and Prevention, 2001).

Engaging in certain sexual behaviors also puts one at a higher risk for contracting an STI. High-risk sexual behaviors include oral–genital sex without a condom or dental dam, semen in the mouth, and vaginal or anal intercourse without a condom (Hatcher et al., 1994). Sex with multiple partners also increases one's chances of contracting an STI. Moreover, some STIs are contracted through nonsexual means. Certain forms of drug use increase your risk, as sharing contaminated needles can directly transmit organisms like HIV. An infected pregnant woman also risks transmitting the infection to her unborn child and causing serious birth defects.

STIs can cause irreparable damage. The financial cost to our health-care system is enormous. Left untreated, STIs can cause pelvic inflammatory disease (PID), chronic pelvic pain, and infertility in women (Eng & Butler, 1997; Howell, Kassler, & Haddix, 1997). They can also result in arthritis, heart problems, brain damage, and even death. Yet the human cost to partners, families, and infected persons is incalculable. It's a cost that does not necessarily have to be paid, as many STIs are easily treated.

Types of STIs: Bacterial, Viral, and Parasitic

Table 11.2 ◆ shows the main types of sexually transmitted infections, modes of transmission, symptoms, and treatment. There are three basic categories of STIs: bacterial infections, viral infections, and parasitic infections.

Bacterial infections include chlamydia, gonorrhea, and syphilis. Bacteria are microorganisms or germs that can quickly reproduce and cause disease in the body. Chlamydia, gonorrhea, and syphilis are primarily transmitted by vaginal, anal, or oral sexual activity. If present in the vagina, these infections also can be transmitted from a mother to a newborn during delivery. An unusual discharge, sore, or painful urination are common symptoms of these infections. However, many men and women show no symptoms during the early stages and therefore do not seek treatment until symptoms that are more serious develop. Antibiotics are typically used to treat bacterial infections (Cates, 1998).

◆ **Table 11.2**

Sexually Transmitted Infections

STI	Transmission Modes	Symptoms	Treatments
BACTERIAL			
Chlamydia	Vaginal, oral, or anal sexual activity, or from an infected mother to her newborn during a vaginal birth	In females: frequent and painful urination, lower abdominal pain, and vaginal discharge. In males: burning or painful urination, and slight penile discharge. However, many people show no symptoms.	Antibiotics
Gonorrhea	Vaginal, oral, or anal sexual activity, or from an infected mother to her newborn during a vaginal birth	In females: increased vaginal discharge, burning urination, or irregular menstrual bleeding (many women show no early symptoms). In males: yellowish, thick penile discharge, or burning urination.	Antibiotics
Syphilis	Vaginal, oral, or anal sexual activity, or by touching an infected chancre or sore	A hard, round painless chancre or sore appears at site of infection within 2 to 4 weeks.	Penicillin or other antibiotics for penicillin-allergic patients
VIRAL			
Genital Herpes	Vaginal, oral, or anal sexual activity	Painful, reddish bumps around the genitals, thighs or buttocks, and for females on the vagina or cervix. Other symptoms may include burning urination, flu-like symptoms, or vaginal discharge in females.	There is no cure, although certain drugs can provide relief and help sores heal
Genital Warts	Sexual contact or contact with infected towels or clothing	Painless warts appear in the genital area.	Cryotherapy (freezing), acid burning, or surgical removal
HIV/AIDS	Sexual contact, infusion with contaminated blood, or from mother to child during pregnancy, childbirth, or breast-feeding	May develop mild flu-like symptoms that may disappear for many years before developing full-blown AIDS. AIDS symptoms include fever, weight loss, fatigue, diarrhea, and susceptibility to infection.	There is no cure; treatment includes a combination of antiviral drugs
PARASITES			
Pubic Lice	Sexual contact or contact with infested linens or toilet seats	Intense itching in hairy regions of the body, especially the pubic area.	Prescription shampoos or nonprescription medications
Scabies	Sexual contact or contact with infested linens or toilet seats	Intense itching, reddish lines on skin, welts, and pus-filled blisters in affected area.	Prescription shampoos

Viral infections include genital herpes, genital warts, and HIV/AIDS. Viruses are incapable of reproducing on their own. They invade a normal cell and direct that cell to make new viral copies. These copies then invade other healthy cells, causing infection. Many of the symptoms of these infections can be treated, but the virus remains in the body and is yours for life. In genital herpes and genital warts, noticeable sores or warts appear. In HIV/AIDS, the HIV attacks the immune system, resulting in mild flu-like symptoms that may then disappear for years before developing into a full-blown case of AIDS. Although symptoms may not be present, you still carry the virus and therefore are capable of transmitting it to a partner during sexual activity. HIV/AIDS can also be contracted through the exchange of contaminated blood, to a fetus during pregnancy, or to an infant during breast-feeding.

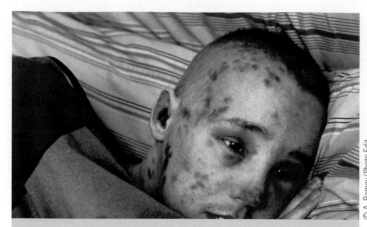

AIDS is a fatal sexually transmitted infection.

Parasitic infections include pubic lice and scabies. A parasite lives off of another organism or host to survive. Pubic lice, or "crabs," survive by feeding on human blood. Scabies are tiny mites that burrow under the skin and lay eggs. Both infections can be spread through sexual contact or by contact with infested towels, linens, or clothing. The most common symptom is intense itching in the genital area. Parasitic infections typically are treated with a solution that kills the lice or mites and their eggs. It is important to carefully reexamine the body 4 to 7 days after treatment to ensure that all the eggs were killed. Similarly, towels, linens, and clothing also need to be treated to prevent reinfection (Reinisch, 1991).

Application

Pubic lice are often called "crabs" because of the organism's resemblance to a crab.

Let's Review!

For a quick check of your understanding of sexually transmitted infections, answer these questions.

1. Which of the following STIs can be transmitted in the *absence* of sexual contact?
   a. gonorrhea   c. genital warts
   b. genital herpes   d. syphilis

2. Pedro has experienced an intense, burning sensation during urination and a thick, yellowish penile discharge. Pedro most likely has which STI?
   a. gonorrhea   c. genital warts
   b. genital herpes   d. syphilis

3. Which of the following is a low-risk sexual behavior for contracting a STI?
   a. Semen in the mouth
   b. Vaginal intercourse while the woman is "on the pill"
   c. Sex with multiple partners
   d. Oral sex with a dental dam

ANSWERS

1.c; 2.a; 3.d

Are You Getting the Big Picture?

In this chapter we have examined the influence of gender and sexuality on our behavior. Just as we saw in the chapters on development (9 and 10), gender and sexuality also are influenced by the interaction between nature and nurture. Our biology, in the form of anatomy, hormones, and infections, plays a role in our sexual behaviors and expressions. However, this biology is strongly influenced by our attitudes, learning experiences, and cultural expectations.

Understanding the influence of gender and sexuality on our behavior is not only important to our personal relationships, but in many ways may influence our careers and work environments. For example, health professionals must be knowledgeable about sexually trans-mitted infections. People in the helping professions need to be aware of the effects of sexual abuse and what constitutes normal and dysfunctional sexual behavior. Understanding gender and sexuality is even important in business environments where policies on sex discrimination and sexual harassment exist.

Gender and sexuality illustrate how others may perceive us and thereby treat us in a specific way. In the next chapter, we will take a broader look at this topic by examining social psychology and the influence that others have on our behavior.

STUDYING THE CHAPTER

Key Terms

gender (482)
gender identity (482)
sexuality (482)
sexual differentiation (484)
hermaphroditism (484)
pseudohermaphrodites (484)
gender roles (489)
masturbation (491)
sexual fantasy (492)
sexual orientation (496)
heterosexual (496)
homosexual (496)
bisexual (496)
homophobia (497)
sexual arousal (499)
sexual desire (499)
libido (499)

estrogens (499)
ovaries (500)
testosterone (500)
testes (500)
erogenous zones (500)
excitement phase (501)
plateau phase (502)
orgasm phase (502)
resolution phase (502)
refractory period (502)
sexual disorder (503)
sexual dysfunctions (503)
hypoactive sexual desire disorder (503)
sexual aversion disorder (504)
male erectile disorder (504)
female sexual arousal disorder (505)
orgasmic disorder (505)

premature ejaculation (506)
dyspareunia (506)
vaginismus (506)
paraphilias (506)
fetishism (506)
transvestism (506)
voyeurism (507)
exhibitionism (507)
pedophilia (507)
sexual sadism (507)
sexual masochism (507)
sexual coercion (508)
sexual harassment (508)
rape (510)
date rape (512)
sexually transmitted infection (STI) (513)

Test Yourself!

Concept Check

Test your knowledge of the chapter concepts by completing each of the following sentences with the correct term. For a more comprehensive review, visit the book Web site (http://psychology.wadsworth.com/pastorino1e/) for online quizzes, flashcards, crosswords, and Internet links.

One's sense of being a male or female is called (1) _____, whereas the way one expresses him or herself sexually is called (2) _____. If the Y chromosome is present, it produces a chemical called (3) _____ that causes the testes or male genitalia to develop. In elementary school,

(4) _____ tend to excel in mathematical ability. Most of our knowledge on the sexual behavior and attitudes of people in the United States has been gathered by (5) _____ research. Women are more likely to endorse the attitude of a (6) _____, or the notion that certain sexual acts are okay for a man but not for a woman. One's sexual attraction for members of the same and/or opposite sex is called (7) _____. A heightened state of sexual interest and excitement is called (8) _____. Our motivation and interest to engage in sexual activity is (9) _____. In humans, the hormone that seems to govern libido is (10) _____. Areas of the skin that are sensitive to touch are called (11) _____. Male erections and female lubrication occur during the (12) _____ phase of the sexual response cycle. Males and females most strongly differ during the (13) _____ phase of the sexual response cycle as males experience a (14) _____ and females do not. A group of disorders characterized by problems in sexual desire, arousal, or satisfaction are called (15) _____, whereas (16) _____ are disorders that involve sexual arousal in response to an unusual object, situation, or nonconsenting person. A persistent difficulty in becoming sexually aroused or suffi-

ciently lubricated in response to sexual stimulation is called (17) _____. (18) _____, or painful sexual intercourse, can affect both men and women. Being sexually aroused by inanimate objects is (19) _____, and being sexually aroused by fantasies or behavior involving exposing one's genitals to an unsuspecting individual is called (20) _____. The repeated use of unwanted verbal comments, gestures, or physical contact of a sexual nature against another person in a subordinate position constitutes (21) _____. Viral sexually transmitted infections include (22) _____, (23) _____, and (24) _____.

Answers:

1. gender identity; 2. sexuality; 3. H-Y antigen; 4. females; 5. survey; 6. double standard; 7. sexual orientation; 8. sexual arousal; 9. sexual desire; 10. testosterone; 11. erogenous zones; 12. excitement; 13. resolution; 14. refractory period; 15. sexual dysfunctions; 16. paraphilias; 17. female sexual arousal disorder; 18. Dyspareunia; 19. fetishism; 20. exhibitionism; 21. sexual harassment; 22. genital herpes; 23. genital warts; 24. HIV/AIDS.

Critical Thinking About the Chapter

1. Explain how your gender identity has influenced your sexual attitudes and behaviors.

2. Examine the gender differences in the prevalence of sexual dysfunctions and paraphilias, and develop a gender theory to account for these differences.

3. Research your state's laws on same-sex marriages and adoptions. What companies in your area recognize same-sex partnerships in their benefit packages? Do you agree or disagree with these policies and/or laws? Defend your position.

4. How does one's gender identity impact one's definition of sexual harassment or rape? What general attitudes about males and females facilitate harassment and rape? Which attitudes would decrease sexual coercion?

Applying Psychology. If one of your children were born as a hermaphrodite, would you raise your child as a boy or as a girl? Why did you choose that specific gender?

Critical Thinking for Integration

1. Explain the development of fetishism in classical conditioning terms (Chapter 5).

2. Review the milestones of adolescent development presented in Chapter 10. How might these characteristics explain why teenagers may be more likely to develop a sexually transmitted infection? Develop several strategies for reducing STIs in the teenage population.

3. Create a chart or graph that details how the brain (Chapter 2) integrates sensory (Chapter 3), hormonal (Chapter 2), and learning information (Chapter 5) to produce human sexual desire.

Chapter Study Resources
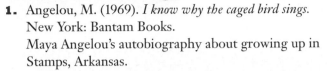

Suggested Readings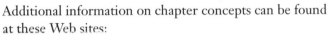

1. Angelou, M. (1969). *I know why the caged bird sings.* New York: Bantam Books.
   Maya Angelou's autobiography about growing up in Stamps, Arkansas.

2. Colapinto, J. (2000). *As nature made him: The boy who was raised as a girl.* New York: HarperCollins.
   Details Bruce Reimer's struggles with gender identity after a botched circumcision destroyed his penis.

3. Brannigan, G. G., Allgeier, E. R., & Allgeier, G. (Eds.). (1997). *The sex scientists.* Reading, MA: Addison-Wesley.
   Leading researchers in human sexuality tell their stories.

4. For additional readings, explore InfoTrac College Edition, your online library of archived journal articles and periodicals. You can access InfoTrac by going to http://www.infotrac-college.com/wadsworth and using the passcode from the InfoTrac card that came with your book. For this chapter, try these keyword search terms:

   sexual orientation

   sexual excitement

   sexual intercourse

   sexual fantasies

   teenage sexual behavior

Web Links for Further Study

Additional information on chapter concepts can be found at these Web sites:

1. The Kinsey Institute's Sexuality Information Service for Students is a tool for students to use to gather information on sexual matters. Students can ask questions about sexuality or read from the archives of past questions and answers.
   http://www.indiana.edu/~kisiss/

2. An online journal devoted to safer sexuality provides readings, topics and links to sexual issues.
   http://www.safersex.org

3. The Parents, Families, and Friends of Lesbian and Gays (PFLAG) site is a national organization support-ing gay, lesbian, bisexual, and transgendered persons, and their families and friends, and provides opportunity for dialogue about sexual orientation and gender identity.
   http://www.pflag.org

4. The International Foundation for Gender Education site provides announcements, news, opinions, and reports related to gender and sexual orientation.
   http://www.ifge.org

5. The original sexpert, Dr. Ruth Westheimer offers advice on many sexual issues at this site.
   http://love.ivillage.com/author/bio/0,,prtr,00.html

Student Study Guide

To help you organize your learning, work through Chapter 11 of the *What Is Psychology? Student Study Guide.* The study guide includes learning objectives, a chapter summary, fill-in review, key terms, a practice test, and other learning activities.

Psychology Now™

PsychologyNow is a Web-based, personalized study system that provides you with a pretest and a posttest for each chapter, quizzes you by chapter, and provides a personalized study plan, pointing you to elements in the text or in individual learning modules that will help you to achieve 80% mastery. Learning modules include: 2c. Adolescent Development, 2d. Adult Development, Aging, and Death.

PsychNow CD-ROM, Version 2.0

Go to the PsychNow CD-ROM for further study of the concepts in this chapter. The CD-ROM includes learning modules with videos, animations, and quizzes, as well as simulations of psychological phenomena. Each module follows a consistent Explore, Lesson, and Apply structure that allows you to experience the concept or principle, learn more about it, and then apply it. You and your friends can participate in a team-based Quiz Game that makes learning fun. Learning modules include: 6e. Human Sexuality; 8g. Gender and Stereotyping.

How Do Gender and Sexuality Impact Our Behavior?

Gender refers to the state of being male or female. Our gender identity represents our personal experience of being male or female. Sexuality includes the ways we experience and express ourselves as sexual beings.

GENDER IDENTITY AND GENDER DIFFERENCES

• Gender is first determined by the sex chromosomes we receive at conception, then by hormonal influences on prenatal development of internal and external genitalia.

• Typically, our gender identity is consistent with our sex chromosomes and sexual anatomy.

• Consistent gender differences have been found in certain cognitive abilities. Differences in verbal abilities are quite small. Females tend to excel in mathematical ability in elementary school and males outperform females in math starting in adolescence. Males also have the advantage in the area of visuospatial skills.

• Men and women also tend to differ in personality. Females tend to be more extraverted, anxious, trusting, and nurturing than males. Males tend to be more assertive, tough-minded, and have more self-esteem than females. Males tend to engage in more physical or overt aggression and females tend to engage in more relational aggression.

SEXUAL BEHAVIOR AND ATTITUDES

• Alfred Kinsey's comprehensive survey on sexuality in the United States in the 1930s and 1940s has been followed by numerous scholarly surveys that have helped us approximate sexual attitudes, behaviors, and beliefs.

• Despite negative attitudes toward masturbation, most surveys indicate that most people masturbate at some time. Generally, men masturbate more frequently than women.

• The majority of adults engage in sexual fantasies from time to time, with men tending to have more frequent sexual fantasies than women.

• Men report wanting sex more often and thinking about sex more often than women. Men also tend to be more favorable toward casual sex and are more likely to engage in extramarital sex than women.

• The national average for frequency of sexual activity is about once a week and cross-cultural research reports a similar trend worldwide.

• Oral sex has increased in acceptance among young people. Although men are more likely to engage in oral sex, it also is more common among married people and college-educated people.

SEXUAL ORIENTATION

• Heterosexuals are attracted to members of the other sex. Homosexuals are attracted to members of the same sex. Bisexuals are attracted to members of both sexes.

• Sexual orientation is not simply a matter of with whom you have sex. Survey research reveals that some people may have same-sex sexual encounters, but not consider themselves to be gay or lesbian.

• Homophobia or negative prejudice against homosexuals has not disappeared. In the United States, many gay, lesbian, and bisexual youth are verbally or physically abused, yet not all cultures hold negative attitudes toward gays and lesbians.

• Research suggests that biological and environmental factors both play a role in our sexual orientation.

SEXUAL AROUSAL AND RESPONSE

• Sexual desire, our motivation and interest in engaging in sexual activity, is influenced by hormones, sensory cues, and cultural attitudes about what is sexually appealing.

• Masters and Johnson directly measured and observed men and women engaged in a variety of sexual activities to detail the physical changes experienced during sexual activity. These common physical changes occur in four phases: excitement, plateau, orgasm, and resolution.

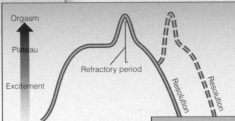

Male Sexual Response

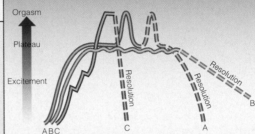

Female Sexual Response

SEXUAL DISORDERS

• Many people experience sexual problems from time to time. When these problems persist, cause distress, and interfere with one's ability to function, it is called a sexual disorder.

• A sexual dysfunction is characterized by a problem with sexual desire, arousal, or satisfaction.

• Paraphilias involve sexual arousal in response to an unusual object (fetishism), situation (such as sexual sadism), or nonconsenting person (such as voyeurism).

SEXUAL COERCION

• Sexual coercion involves behaviors that are nonconsenting, abusive, or forcible in nature.

• Sexual harassment includes the repeated use of unwelcome verbal comments, gestures, or physical contact of a sexual nature against another person.

• Any sexual activity between an adult and a child is sexual abuse, even if the child cooperates in the sexual activity. Sexual abuse occurs across all racial, ethnic, and economic categories. In many cases, the child knows the molester.

• Rape generally involves the threat or use of force to obtain sex. The majority of rape victims are women of all ages, races, and social classes. Yet, women between the ages of 16 and 24 are more likely to be raped than older women.

• Most women are raped by men they know, not by strangers. Date rape, a form of acquaintance rape, is often underreported since it occurs in a context in which sexual relations could have occurred.

SEXUALLY TRANSMITTED INFECTIONS

• Sexually transmitted infections are passed from one person to another, primarily through sexual contact. At least 1 in 4 Americans will contract an STI at some time in their lives.

• Young people are at greater risk for contracting STIs because they engage in many high-risk sexual behaviors such as having multiple partners and sex without a condom.

• Bacterial infections include chlamydia, gonorrhea, and syphilis. An unusual discharge, sore, or painful urination are common symptoms of these infections.

• Viral infections include genital herpes, genital warts, and HIV/AIDS. Many of the symptoms of these infections can be treated, but the virus remains in the body and is yours for life.

• Parasitic infections such as pubic lice and scabies can be spread through sexual contact or by contact with infested clothing. The most common symptom of these infections is intense genital itching.

If you come from the Hills, you were labeled from the start. . . . Already a thug. It was harder to defy this expectation than just accept it and fall into the trappings.

FROM LUIS J. RODRIGUEZ, *ALWAYS RUNNING: LA VIDA LOCA, GANG DAYS IN L.A.,* (New York: 1994. Simon & Schuster)

© Chuck Savage/Corbis.

How Do We Understand and Relate to Others?

CHAPTER PREVIEW

What Does It Mean to Be a Social Animal?

Psychology is often a very practical science that seeks to make our world a better place. Nowhere is this more the case than in an area of psychology known as **social psychology.** Broadly defined, social psychology is the study of how we think and behave in social situations. Because humans are social animals who spend much of their time in the company of others, the study of social psychology encompasses many different topic areas. One subarea, **social cognition,** investigates the ways in which we think (cognition) about ourselves and others—for example, how do we form prejudices about people, make judgments about others, or become attracted to others? Another area of social psychology, called **social influence,** deals with the ways in which other people influence our behavior—for example, can others make us change our attitudes or do things that we know we shouldn't be doing? As we go through this chapter, we will be looking at these types of questions. We hope that you will see that understanding how we think and behave in social situations has great practical significance to all our lives— a fact that is well-illustrated in the following case study.

The story of Luis Rodriguez shows us that at times the power others have to change our thoughts and behavior can be very dramatic. Luis's life was greatly influenced by two opposing forces: one, the street gangs of Los Angeles that threatened to destroy him, and the other, the antiviolence activist groups that ultimately saved him.

Luis Rodriguez immigrated to the United States from Mexico at the age of 2. His father had been a high school principal in Ciudad Juarez until he lost his position during a period of political turmoil within the local school system. With no employment prospects in Mexico, the Rodriguez family came to America in hope of a better life. However, the "American dream" is elusive for many, especially those who face language and cultural barriers, and the Rodriguez family found life in the United States to be challenging. In Los Angeles, Luis's father was able to find only temporary work as a laborer, while Luis's mother worked as a housekeeper to make ends meet. Like so many immigrant families, poverty was a constant presence in the Rodriguez home.

When Luis started school, he felt isolated and embarrassed by his inability to speak English fluently. Speaking Spanish was not allowed at school, so students who were not proficient in English often found themselves unable to understand their teachers. Just as frustrating for the Spanish-speaking students was getting others to understand the broken English they spoke. Although Luis eventually mastered English, he grew up—like many minority members—with the persistent feeling that he didn't really belong in the community or his school.

By the time Luis was 11, he had joined his first *clica,* or "club." These clubs began as social groups that provided members with a sense of belonging and some protection against the growing violence of the streets. But the clubs were quickly transformed. Many of these *clicas* became part of the local gangs of East Los Angeles. Luis became a regular participant in the gang lifestyle. Drugs, stabbings and gunfights, armed robbery, arrests, and beatings became a way of life for Luis.

One night, as Luis and his gang brothers drove up in front of a rival gang member's home, several of the gang members began to pull the makings of Molotov cocktails from under the seats of the car. Their intentions were clear—they were going to firebomb the rival gang member's home, a fact unknown to Luis when he got into the car that night. Years later, Luis described how it felt that night to be caught in such a desperate situation. "I didn't want to do it, but I couldn't stop. I felt trapped. I knew the only thing for me was to go through with it, and get out of there as fast as possible. I felt excitement. And an ache of grief" (Rodriguez, 1994, p. 119). The home Luis and his fellow gang members attacked that night was destroyed, but luckily no one was killed.

social psychology the branch of psychology that studies how we think and behave in social situations

social cognition the area of social psychology that deals with the ways in which we think about other people and ourselves

social influence pressures placed on us by others to change our behavior and/or our beliefs

"It [the stereotype] was a jacket I could try to take off, but they kept putting it back on."
(Rodriguez, 1994, p. 84)

Unfortunately, the violence did not end with the firebombing, and eventually Luis lost 25 friends to violent deaths. On more than one occasion, Luis found life so bleak that he contemplated suicide. Luis seemed destined to become another gang-related statistic when his life began to take a different turn.

While in high school, Luis got to know some student and faculty activists who were interested in improving race relations and educational standards for minority students in the school system. They also sought ways to stop gang violence, an idea that struck a chord in Luis. Luis joined several student-activist groups and began to take an active leadership role in these groups. But people do not change overnight, and for several years, Luis walked in both worlds. While working as an activist for Latino and Latina rights within the schools, Luis still felt strong ties to his fellow gang members, and he continued to participate in gang activities. Slowly, Luis's eyes were opening to the realization that life does not have to be ruled by violence and death, but his fellow gang members did not share Luis's newfound optimism.

One night as Luis stood on a street corner with some other young men, a car approached. Luis knew all the passengers in the car. They were friends, or at least they had been. The man in the front passenger seat was the one who had initiated Luis to life in the "hood," but tonight he was not a friend. Instead, the man leveled a gun at Luis and began to fire. The message was clear. Luis was no longer one of them. The next time, they would not miss with their bullets. Luis had to leave.

Luis left Los Angeles soon after the drive-by shooting. He worked at several jobs and traveled to several different cities before settling in Chicago. Eventually, he achieved recognition and success as an activist and author. Among other things, Luis now works to reach out to young people who feel the same pressures he felt as a teenager on the streets of Los Angeles. He is involved in several youth outreach and antiviolence programs in Chicago. He has published several books of poetry and prose, and his writings have won many awards, including the 15th Carl Sandburg Book Award for his moving account of surviving gang life, *Always Running: Mi Vida Loca, Gang Days in L.A.* (Rodriguez, 1994).

Luis Rodriguez survived what many do not. Luckily, Luis found refuge with groups that saw life very differently from the gangs he joined while still a child. The expectations these activist groups had of him and their support gave Luis the courage to say "No" to the violence of the gangs. Luis was strong, and today in his work with at-risk youth, Luis is demonstrating his courage by fighting for change.

After reading this case study, you may or may not feel as if you have much in common with Luis Rodriguez, but we believe that this story has relevance for all of us. Whether or not you have ever been in a gang or experienced life as a minority member, you have felt some type of social influence pressure. Like Luis, have you ever done something that you really didn't want to do just because your friends wanted to do it? Have you ever failed to answer a question in class because you were afraid of being wrong in front of your classmates? In situations like these, your behavior is indeed influenced by those around you, but it is also influenced by your own cognition. The thoughts and beliefs that you hold about the world also impact how you behave. Just as Luis's dislike for gang violence finally led him to resist the social influence of the gang and find a better way of life, perhaps you can think of instances in which you were true to your own values and resisted pressure from others.

Attitudes and beliefs affect many of the daily choices you make—which products you buy, whom you choose as friends, and whom you choose to avoid. Furthermore, social cognition also affects how other people will perceive and treat *you*. By understanding the processes of social cognition, you will be better able to understand the social world in which you live. So let's get started by looking at a fundamental aspect of social cognition—our *attitudes.*

Explain attitudes, how they develop, and how they affect behavior.

Describe dissonance theory, and explain the role of dissonance in attitude change.

Discuss the major theories of persuasion and how the communicator, the message, and the audience affect persuasion.

attitude an evaluative belief that we hold about something

Application

Attitudes and Attitude Change

Attitudes are evaluative, sometimes emotionally charged, beliefs about people, places, or things. We all have attitudes for a multitude of things. Our attitudes represent the ways in which we have sized up the contents of our world. So where do our attitudes come from? Like all of our beliefs, we acquire attitudes through *learning*. We learn to like certain things, and we learn to dislike others as a result of the same processes you learned about in Chapter 5: *classical conditioning*, *operant conditioning*, and *social learning*.

Classical Conditioning of Attitudes

Recall that classical conditioning is often responsible for the development of certain learned *emotional* and *physiological* responses in humans (Figure 12.1). Because classical conditioning has the power to change the way we *feel* about certain stimuli, it also has the power to influence our attitude toward these stimuli. For example, if man is robbed by a gang member, he may be classically conditioned to fear (CR) people who wear gang colors and clothes (CS).

Classical conditioning can explain some emotional and physiological reactions we have to certain stimuli (Grossman & Till, 1998), but it does not explain how all aspects of attitudes are formed. For example, it does not explain the thoughts we have about certain stimuli. Nor does classical conditioning explain how we learn to behave positively or negatively toward certain people or things. To understand the more complicated aspects of attitudes, we examine some more complicated forms of learning, starting with operant conditioning.

Operant Conditioning of Attitudes

Recall that in operant conditioning an initial, random behavior is strengthened if it results in reward and weakened if it results in punishment. Operant conditioning can affect the development of attitudes in at least two ways. First, if you are rewarded for having certain attitudes, the attitude will be strengthened. But if you are punished for having certain attitudes, the attitude will be weakened.

A second way that operant conditioning can influence the development of attitudes is through the consequences of our direct interaction with the objects of our attitude. For example, suppose a friend convinces you try a new dish with lots of very hot habanero peppers. When you taste the dish, it burns your mouth so badly that your eyes water. As a result of this experience, you would be less likely to want to eat habanero peppers again because you found doing so to be punishing! Your attitude toward habanero peppers would probably be "Stay away from them!"

As you can see in this example, for an attitude to be operantly conditioned, you must first *do something* to interact with the attitude object. Or you must make an evaluative comment. Only after you are rewarded or punished for your behavior does operant conditioning occur. As you will recall from Chapter 5 (p. 225), this is always the case with operant conditioning. Before any operant conditioning can occur, you must first emit a behavior. However, we have attitudes about things that we have never encountered. For example, you may believe you wouldn't like to live in the city, even though you never have. How can operant conditioning account for your dislike of living in the city if you haven't experienced it? The answer is that it can't. To examine how attitudes can develop in the absence of direct experience, we will look at a third type of learning, social learning, or modeling.

Social Learning, or Modeling of Attitudes

Recall from Chapter 5 that in social learning we learn by watching the actions of others. We pay attention to how a model behaves and store a mental representation of that behavior. Later, we may retrieve that mental representation from long-term memory. At that point, we may or may not choose to actually execute that behavior.

Take a minute to think about your attitudes and the attitudes of those who are closest to you. How do your attitudes compare to theirs? If you are like most people, you will find that overall, your attitudes are quite similar to those of your parents (Rohan & Zanna, 1996) and those around you (Kowalski, 2003). There will, of course, be some notable differences, but overall we tend to be more like those we love when it comes to attitudes. In fact, such similarity in attitudes is a factor in attraction, which we'll discuss later in this chapter (p. 545).

We learn attitudes the way that we learn everything in life—through experience. Can you see how Luis may have come to hold both positive and negative attitudes about gangs at different times in his life? Once we form our attitudes about the world, they then have the power to affect what we know, how we feel, and how we behave toward just about everything we encounter in our lives. But is this always the case—do our attitudes always predict our behavior?

The Link Between Attitudes and Behavior

Do you ever find yourself behaving in a manner that contradicts your attitudes? For example, have you ever gone to see a movie that you weren't all that interested in seeing? Do you engage in bad habits that you know are harmful to you? If so, your behavior is not unusual. We often behave in ways that go against our attitudes. This lack of *attitude-behavior consistency* has intrigued researchers because it seems so counterintuitive and illogical.

If social pressures can make it difficult for us to behave consistently with our attitudes, what factors will make it *more* likely that we will behave in ways that are consistent

Whether we like it or not, we often take on the attitudes of our parents through social learning.

© Mark Richards/Photo Edit

US ⟶ ⟶ ⟶ UR

Mom shows fear.   Child is afraid.

NS ⟶ ⟶ US ⟶ ⟶ UR

Dog+Mom shows fear.   Child is afraid.

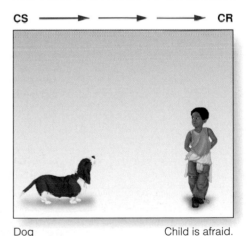

CS ⟶ ⟶ ⟶ CR

Dog   Child is afraid.

Figure 12.1 Classical Conditioning a Negative Attitude Toward Dogs

For a young child, a fear response in her mother (US) will naturally cause fear in the child (UR). On the other hand, the sight of a dog will not reliably elicit fear in a small child. Therefore, the dog is initially a neutral stimulus (NS). When the sight of the dog (NS) is repeatedly paired with a fear response in the mother (US), the child can easily acquire a conditioned fear of dogs (CR) that is elicited by the mere sight of a dog (CS).

with our attitudes? Answers to this question have great practical value in society. For instance, under what circumstances might people's positive attitudes toward safer sex actually lead them to engage in protected sex? When might political attitudes accurately predict voting behavior? And in which situations can a company assume that consumer attitudes toward their products will actually translate into sales? Researchers have been diligently trying to answer such questions. Table 12.1 ◆ describes variables that have been shown to influence attitude-behavior consistency.

Application Given that our attitudes develop through experience and because once in place they influence our behavior at least part of the time, many psychologists are interested in how attitudes can be changed. This information also has great practical value. If we knew how to change attitudes, we might be able to reverse social problems like prejudice and alcoholism. Beyond social change, knowing how attitudes change has immediate applications in certain fields. Political strategists want to know how to change voters' attitudes toward certain candidates and issues. Marketing advertisers want to know how to increase favorable attitudes toward their products. Parents want to influence the attitudes of their children. These and other pragmatic concerns have fueled a great deal of research on attitude change.

◆ **Table 12.1**

Factors That Affect Attitude-Behavior Consistency

Variable	Description	Example
The match between the specificity of the attitude and the specificity of the behavior (Ajzen & Fishbein, 1977; Sherman, Beike, & Ryalls, 1999)	Specific attitudes best predict specific behaviors.	Sally claims to be afraid of *poodles.* Jill claims to be afraid of *dogs.* Sally is less likely to own a *poodle* than Jill.
Thought–feeling consistency (Chaiken & Baldwin, 1981)	When the cognitive and affective components of the attitude are in the same direction (both positive or both negative), the attitude-behavior consistency will be higher.	Sally *feels* afraid of dogs. Sally also *believes* that dogs are vicious animals. Jill *feels* afraid of dogs, but she *does not believe* that they are particularly vicious. Sally will be less likely to own a dog than Jill.
Automaticity of attitudes (Schuette & Fazio, 1995)	Attitudes that spring to mind easily and automatically are more likely to be expressed in one's behavior.	When Sally sees a dog, she *automatically* thinks it is dangerous. When Jill sees a dog, she *does not automatically* assume it is dangerous. Sally is less likely to approach a dog than Jill.
Subjective norms (Ajzen & Fishbein, 1980)	When people perceive that the norms of the situation call for them to behave in a manner that is contradictory to their attitudes, they are more likely to do so.	Sally's neighbor just bought a new puppy. She brings the dog over to Sally's party for a visit. It is clear to Sally that the neighbor expects her to pet the dog. All of Sally's friends are petting the dog, so Sally *feels obliged* to pet the dog, too, even though Sally is afraid of dogs.
Direct experience (Chaiken & Baldwin, 1981)	Attitudes that are developed through direct experience with the attitude object are more likely to predict behavior toward the attitude object than attitudes developed without direct experience.	Sally fears dogs because *she* was bitten by a dog as a child. Jill fears dogs because *her mother* was bitten by a dog. Sally is less likely to own a dog than Jill.
Introspection about one's feeling toward the attitude object (Millar & Tessar, 1986)	If one has recently thought about the *affective* part of his attitude toward the object, he is more likely to behave in a manner consistent with his attitude.	While talking to a friend, Sally recently discussed the *fear* she experiences when she sees a dog. As a result, Sally is now even less likely to get a dog.

Cognitive Consistency and Attitude Change

Throughout our lifetime, our attitudes will change as we acquire new knowledge and have different experiences. For example, a favorable attitude toward a particular restaurant may change if you read in the paper that the restaurant failed its last health inspection. In light of this new information, the old attitude may be discarded in favor of a less favorable one. In this example, the attitude change was motivated from *within* the attitude holder. The change was not the result of a concerted effort on the part of others. It was motivated more by your desire to maintain what psychologists refer to as **cognitive consistency,** or the desire to avoid contradictions among our attitudes and behaviors (Festinger, 1957). Cognitive consistency theories (Festinger, 1957; Heider, 1946) propose that humans find it uncomfortable when there is an inconsistency among their attitudes or between their attitudes and their behavior. Most of us believe that we are intelligent, logical beings. The attitude of being intelligent and logical would be inconsistent with an attitude that an unhealthy restaurant is a good place to eat! So you adjust one of your attitudes (the one concerning the restaurant) to avoid such an inconsistency. But why does inconsistency make us uncomfortable and therefore motivate attitude change?

One explanation of how cognitive inconsistency motivates attitude change is **dissonance theory** (Festinger, 1957). According to dissonance theory, inconsistencies among attitudes or between attitudes and behavior cause an unpleasant physical state called *dissonance*. Think of dissonance as a state of unease much like being hungry or being anxious. It stems from the realization that we have behaved in a way that is contrary to our self-concept (Aronson, 1998). Because dissonance makes us feel bad, we are motivated to stop this unpleasant feeling, which can lead to attitude and/or behavior change (Wood, 2000). For example, a health-conscious person who smokes is likely to experience dissonance because smoking is inconsistent with being health conscious. Once the person experiences dissonance, she will be motivated to stop the dissonance by removing the inconsistency.

In general, there are three ways to remove the inconsistencies that cause dissonance. First, she can change her behavior (stop smoking). Second, she can change her attitudes (decide that she is not health conscious after all). Or third, she can remove the inconsistency by bringing new beliefs and attitudes to bear on the situation (convince herself that smoking has never really been *proven* to cause health problems). Any of these three methods will reduce the dissonance felt by the person and restore a state of *consonance*, in which there is no inconsistency among attitudes and behavior.

In this fashion, dissonance theory can explain certain aspects of how we change and grow as human beings. Recall the story of Luis Rodriguez. As Luis began to confront the fact that whiling away his life on drugs and violence was inconsistent with being an intelligent person who wanted to make a positive contribution to the world, he likely began to experience an increasing level of dissonance. For a time, he walked with feet in two worlds—he was a loyal gang member and a student activist. Dissonance theory would predict that eventually something would have to change for Luis. Either he had to stop seeing himself as a gang member engaging in gang activities or he had to give up on the idea of being a community-minded activist. To his credit, he chose the more positive route back to consonance and left the gang life.

Dissonance theory can also potentially explain some of our odder behaviors. For example, when you pay a high price for goods, it tends to make you like them more. You figure that only an idiot would pay top dollar for junk, and being an idiot is dissonant with seeing yourself as an intelligent person, so you convince yourself that the goods are worth the price you paid. Dissonance theory also predicts that going through painful, embarrassing initiations to join certain groups, such as fraternities and sororities, actually makes you like these groups more (Aronson & Mills, 1959). It appears that during

cognitive consistency the idea that we strive to have attitudes and behaviors that do not contradict one another

dissonance theory a theory that predicts that we will be motivated to change our attitudes and/or our behaviors to the extent that they cause us to feel dissonance, or uncomfortable physical state.

Because smoking is inconsistent with being health conscious, this person is likely to experience dissonance that may lead to attitude or behavior change.

the painful ritual, dissonance is aroused because smart, independent people do not allow others to abuse them for no good reason. Further, it appears that the only way to reduce the dissonance you feel following the abuse is to convince yourself that the pain of the ritual was justified because it allowed you to gain entry into an especially attractive group. Even a smart, independent person may be willing to suffer for a good cause!

Although dissonance theory certainly predicts that severe initiations will lead to increased attraction to the group, some recent studies have questioned whether this actually happens in the real world. In one study, researchers found that all initiations to student organizations increased attraction for the group—regardless of the severity of the initiation. The researchers attributed this increase in attraction to the group to the interaction, or *affiliation* the group members had with other group members during the initiation (Lodewijkx & Syroit, 2001). Whether the attraction we feel is a result of dissonance or affiliations, belonging to groups is important to many of us. We will talk more about the power of groups when we discuss social influence.

Keep in mind that attitude change through dissonance does not involve attempts on the part of others to cause attitude change. Attitude change through dissonance is motivated from *within* the individual experiencing the attitude change. When another person or persons attempt to change our attitudes, we are facing the powers of **persuasion.**

persuasion   a type of social influence in which someone tries to change our attitudes

Persuasion and Attitude Change

 Application

In addition to changing our own attitudes, we all encounter situations in which others directly attempt to change the way we think and feel about an attitude object. Every day we face persuasive attempts from friends, family members, politicians, the media, and advertisers. By some estimates, the average American encounters a whopping 3,000 advertisements per day (Stanton, 2004)! With all of these persuasive attempts being hurled at us on a daily basis, an understanding of how persuasion occurs becomes almost a necessity.

Obviously, not all of the persuasive attempts we are subjected to actually produce attitude change. We do not become loyal to every product we see advertised on TV. We do not vote for every political candidate we hear speak. So just what makes persuasion successful—or what makes it fail? One very important factor in the effectiveness of persuasion is the type of *cognitive processes* that we engage in during the persuasive attempt. The degree to which we analyze persuasive arguments can influence whether or not those arguments are effective in changing our attitudes.

elaboration likelihood model (ELM)
a theory of persuasion which states that the more people are able to critically evaluate the logic of persuasive arguments, and the more able they are to generate counterarguments to these persuasive attempts, the less likely it is that they will be persuaded

Routes to Persuasion

The **elaboration likelihood model (ELM**; Petty & Cacioppo, 1986; Stephenson, Benoit, & Tschida, 2001) states that the more a person is able to critically evaluate the logic of persuasive arguments, and the more able he is to generate counterarguments, the less likely he will be persuaded. Furthermore, the elaboration likelihood model states that a person's ability to evaluate and generate counterarguments is a function of the type of thinking he is engaged in when the persuasive arguments are presented to him.

central route to persuasion   a style of thinking in which the person carefully and critically evaluates persuasive arguments and generates counterarguments; the central route requires motivation and available cognitive resources

In ELM terminology, we process on the **central route to persuasion** when we have the motivation and the time to think critically about the logic of the arguments presented to us. For example, you might process on the central route if you were carefully watching the presidential debates in an attempt to decide how to vote. We don't always process centrally, however. Sometimes we are either unmotivated or do not have the time to critically evaluate the arguments presented to us—which might happen if you tried to watch the presidential debates and do your calculus homework at the same time. Under these conditions, you would be on the **peripheral route to persuasion,** and you would not critically evaluate the logic of the arguments you heard. Accord-

peripheral route to persuasion   a style of thinking in which the person does not carefully and critically evaluate persuasive arguments or generate counterarguments; the peripheral route ensues when one lacks motivation and/or available cognitive resources

ing to the ELM, on the peripheral route, we do not generate effective counterarguments and are therefore more susceptible to persuasion. As a result, you might simply accept what the candidates said as being true.

The **heuristic-systematic persuasion model** (Chaiken, 1987) predicts a similar outcome in our example. This model states that when people are processing on the peripheral route, they often use *heuristics* as a substitute for systematic critical and logical thought (Darke et al., 1998). As we saw in Chapter 7 (p. 307), heuristics are shortcuts to problem solving that don't always lead to the correct answer. In persuasion, heuristics can lead people to be persuaded by aspects of the argument that are superficial and unrelated to the logic of the argument. For example, when processing peripherally, you might be persuaded by the candidate because he is handsome and not because of the validity or quality of his arguments (Petty, Wegener, & Fabrigar, 1997).

This means that when we are processing peripherally, we make it easier for others to persuade us. They do not have to give us good reasons to change our minds because we're not going to actually evaluate the reasons! All they have to do is give us some superficial reasons to change our attitudes. Think of the television commercials you have recently seen—many are designed for people who are processing peripherally. They are glitzy, catchy, humorous, and so on, but they do not present good, logical arguments for the products that they advertise.

Although it may be easier to persuade an audience that is processing peripherally, one drawback is that attitudes that are formed through peripheral processing are not as enduring. (Chaiken, 1987). Furthermore, attitudes formed peripherally do not predict behavior as well as attitudes formed centrally (Fazio, 1990). Advertisers who really want to sell a product and develop a faithful consumer base may be well advised to court consumers who process advertisements on the central route, as outlined in Table 12.2 ◆.

Other Factors That Affect Persuasion

There are other variables that affect the success of persuasion. These variables fall into three categories: variables associated with the *communicator* of the message, variables associated with the persuasive *message* itself, and variables associated with the *audience* that receives the persuasive message.

Communicator Variables. We tend to be most persuaded when the person communicating the message to us is attractive (Eagly & Chaiken, 1975), appears to be credible (Hovland & Weiss, 1951; Petty, Wegener, & Fabrigar, 1997), and appears to be expert (Petty, Cacioppo, & Goldman, 1981). This is one reason that advertisers hire well-respected, attractive actors and actresses to sell their products. They know that we will be more likely to be persuaded because we place our trust in such people. This effect is enhanced if we are processing on the peripheral route because we are not likely to look beyond the superficial qualities of the communicator to actually evaluate the quality of the arguments (Petty, Cacioppo, & Goldman, 1981). When we're watching a television ad, we are often not thinking on the central route, and we don't think about the fact that the communicators are paid to say favorable things about the products they advertise. Therefore, we simply tend to believe what they tell us about the products.

Message Variables. When the arguments given by the communicator do not seem like attempts to persuade us, we are more easily persuaded (Petty & Cacioppo, 1986). Similarly, we are more likely to be persuaded if the communicator effectively presents both the pros (why we should accept the arguments) and cons (why we might not accept the arguments) of the proposal. Of course, for a two-sided argument to be effective, the communicator must be able to effectively argue against the reasons for not accepting the proposal (Crowley & Hoyer, 1994). This superiority of two-sided arguments over one-sided arguments (only the pros) occurs in part because we tend to trust a communicator who is willing to openly discuss the drawbacks to the proposal.

heuristic-systematic persuasion model a model of persuasion that states that when people are processing on the peripheral route, they often use *heuristics* as a substitute for *systematic* critical and logical thought

 Application

◆ **Table 12.2**

Characteristics of Central Route Processors

Characteristic	Description	Example
Personal relevance of the issue being argued (Petty, Cacioppo, & Goldman, 1981)	If the topic of the persuasive arguments has personal relevance for the person being persuaded, then she or he will be more motivated to carefully evaluate the arguments on the central route.	Juanita hears a speech advocating a tuition increase at *her school.* Joel hears a speech advocating a tuition increase at *a school he has no intention of ever attending.* Juanita is more likely to process the speech on the central route.
Need for cognition (Cacioppo, Petty, Feinstein, & Jarvis, 1996)	People who are high in the personality variable need for cognition are more motivated to process on the central route because these people in general like to think more deeply about things than those low in need for cognition.	Juanita is high in *need for cognition,* whereas Joel is low in *need for cognition.* Both attend a speech advocating a tuition increase at their school. Juanita is more likely to process the speech on the central route.
Ability to pay attention to the arguments being presented (Petty & Brock, 1981)	If the person being persuaded is free of distraction and has the cognitive resources to critically evaluate the arguments presented, central route processing is more likely.	Juanita has the afternoon free, so she attends a speech on a tuition increase at her school. Joel attends the same speech, but he is preoccupied with trying to remember mathematical formulas he will need on a math exam that is scheduled to occur immediately following the speech. Juanita is more likely to process the speech on the central route.

Audience Variables. Effective persuasion is heavily dependent on who is being persuaded. Some people are more persuadable than are others. People who are processing peripherally are easier to persuade than people who process centrally (Petty, Cacioppo, & Goldman, 1981). As we stated before, this occurs because peripheral processors do not effectively generate counterarguments to the communicator's claims, nor do they critically evaluate the goodness of the arguments presented to them.

Another reason that people may fail to effectively evaluate a persuasive message is that they lack an ability to do so. People who are low in IQ have sometimes been shown to be more easily persuaded than those who have moderate and high IQ levels (Rhodes & Wood, 1992). Presumably this finding is based on the fact that those low in IQ do not have the cognitive ability to critically evaluate a persuasive message and generate effective counterarguments. Therefore, they are more easily persuaded to accept the persuasive message.

Attractiveness of a communicator can be one factor that makes you more likely to accept his arguments. This is especially true when you are processing on the peripheral or heuristic routes to persuasion.

However, under certain conditions, people high in IQ are more easily persuaded than those who are low in IQ. For instance, research has shown that when the arguments given are complex and valid, high IQ people are more likely to be persuaded than people of lesser IQ (Eagly & Warren, 1976). This relationship is believed to reflect the fact that if complex, valid arguments are to work, they have to be appreciated by the audience. People of higher intelligence have the ability to understand and appreciate the logic of such arguments, so they are more easily persuaded.

The self-esteem of the audience can also affect persuasion. People of moderate self-esteem have been found to be more easily persuaded than those with either high or low self-esteem (Rhodes & Wood, 1992). This finding is explained in terms that are similar to those used to explain the relationship between IQ and persuasion. People who are low in self-esteem tend to be distracted and unable to concentrate on the arguments given to them, so they do not process the arguments well. If the arguments are complex, they will not be likely to appreciate the arguments, and persuasion is less likely to occur. On the other hand, people who are high in self-esteem are able to comprehend the arguments, but they also have a lot of confidence in their own opinions and are therefore less likely to yield to persuasive arguments.

Confidence in one's own attitudes also comes with age. Adolescence is a crucial time in people's lives—they are trying to develop the attitudes they will hold as adults (Erikson, 1968; Marcia, 1980). Young people in this process of developing their own attitudes are more vulnerable to persuasive attempts. Perhaps youth is one of the many reasons Luis was persuaded to follow the direction of his gang throughout most of his childhood and adolescence. By the time we reach young adulthood, we are less vulnerable to persuasive attempts than we once were (Krosnick & Alwin, 1989).

The last characteristic of the audience that we will discuss is mood. When people are in a good mood, they seem to be unwilling to do anything that will potentially disrupt their good mood. This apparently includes thinking hard because people in a good mood have been shown to be more likely to process persuasive arguments on the peripheral route as opposed to the central route. Because peripheral processors are more susceptible to superficial qualities of persuasive arguments such as communicator attractiveness, they are often more easily persuaded (Bless, Bohner, Schwarz, & Strack, 1990). When people are in a neutral or negative mood, they do not seem to have reservations about engaging in careful evaluation of the persuasive arguments delivered by the communicator. As such, they tend to process more centrally and will be persuaded only if the arguments are based on sound logic.

So far, we have looked at the nature of attitudes, their development, and how they change over time. Our attitudes describe how we feel about the things we encounter in life. We have attitudes about everything from spinach to specific groups of people. Because our attitudes can potentially influence the way that we behave, certain attitudes have great impact on our society and on our relationships with others. For instance, some of our most important attitudes are the ones that we hold about other people. Whom we choose to associate with, love, hire, help, and so on depends in part on the attitudes we hold about people.

Let's Review!

In this section we covered ways in which our attitudes can change. For a quick check of your understanding, answer these questions.

1. Because he is trying to decide how to vote in the upcoming election, Delbert is closely watching the presidential debates on television. Under these circumstances, which route to persuasion will Delbert *most* likely use to process the candidates' arguments?
   a. the central route
   b. the peripheral route
   c. the algorithmic route
   d. the shortest route

2. A politician is attempting to persuade people to vote for her in an upcoming election. All other things being equal, with which group of voters would you expect her to have the most success?
   a. middle-aged health-care workers
   b. senior citizens
   c. housewives 25–45 years old
   d. young voters 18–21 years old

3. Ted recently discovered that his favorite actress supports a radical political group that Ted despises. According to dissonance theory, what is *most* likely to happen in this situation?
   a. Ted will begin to like the actress more.
   b. Ted will begin to like the actress less.
   c. Ted will begin to dislike the political group more.
   d. Ted's attitudes toward the actress and the group will not change.

ANSWERS
1. a; 2. d; 3. b

LEARNING < < < < < < < <
OBJECTIVE

Describe how we form impressions about ourselves and others, and explain the attribution process.

impression formation the way that we understand and make judgments about others

How We Form Impressions of Others

One of the most important aspects of social cognition is **impression formation,** or how we understand and make judgments about others. When we meet someone for the first time, we usually attempt to determine what type of person he is. Is this person kind, smart, aggressive, or untrustworthy? We want to know. Why do we want to know what other people are like? In short, if we have a good understanding of other people's traits and abilities, we can predict how they will behave in certain situations. This will allow us to guide our own behavior in social situations. If you find that a particular coworker has a bad temper, you may go out of your way to not provoke her. On the other hand, if you know that another coworker is particularly kind, you behave in a more relaxed fashion around him. Without some understanding of others, social interactions would be much more awkward and uncertain.

The Attribution Process

It appears that one of our basic social cognitive tendencies is to try to explain the behavior of ourselves and others, but just how do we make such judgments? How do you determine the traits and characteristics of someone you just met? If you're thinking that we pay attention to what the person says and does, you're correct. When we judge a person, we observe his behavior, and then we attempt to determine the cause of this behavior (Heider, 1958). This process of assigning cause to behavior is called **attribution.** For example, imagine that you enter a local café and see a man yelling at a woman in the corner booth. Witnessing his outburst, you would likely try to determine why the man was yelling. Is it because he is an aggressive person? Or did the woman somehow provoke this type of outburst in an otherwise kind man? Questions like these may pass through your mind as you watch the scene unfold.

attribution the act of assigning cause to behavior

In this example, we can attribute the cause of someone's behavior to one of two things. We can attribute the behavior to his/her traits, abilities, or characteristics, in which case we are making a **trait attribution.** Or we may attribute the behavior to something in the environment, in which case we are making a **situational attribution.** If we make a trait attribution about the yelling man, we would assume that the man yelled because he was an aggressive person. If we make a situational attribution, we would assume that something happened in the environment to cause the man to yell. Perhaps his female companion just told him that she has been unfaithful. Maybe she just spilled hot coffee in his lap. Note that when we make a situational attribution, we do *not* attribute the man's behavior to his personality.

trait attribution an attribution that assigns the cause of the behavior to the traits and characteristics of the person being judged

situational attribution an attribution that assigns the cause of the behavior to some characteristic of the situation or environment in which a behavior occurs

Ideally, we would weigh all the available evidence before making either a trait attribution or a situational attribution. Unfortunately, the realities of the world do not always allow us to make careful, analytic attributions. Humans are *cognitive misers,* meaning we try to conserve our cognitive resources whenever we can (Fiske & Taylor, 1991). We have seen evidence of our miserliness in earlier discussions. As we saw in Chapter 7 (p. 307), when we have a problem to solve and we don't have much time, we often use shortcuts, or *heuristics,* in an attempt to find a quick solution. Heuristics may lead to quick answers, but they do not always lead to accurate answers. People have been shown to employ several time-saving heuristics while making attributions, and these shortcuts often lead to errors and biases in the attribution process.

Heuristics and Biases in Attribution

Fundamental Attribution Error

When we first mentioned the example of the man in the café who was yelling at the woman, did you first assume that his behavior was a result of one of his personality characteristics? Or did you first assume that the situation somehow caused his behavior? For many people, a trait attribution would have been their first tendency. Many would have automatically attributed the man's yelling to the fact that he was an aggressive or mean person without taking much time to analyze the possible situational causes of his behavior. This tendency to rely more on trait attributions and to discount situational explanations of behavior is called the **fundamental attribution error** because it is so commonly seen in people.

Why we tend to engage in the fundamental attribution error is not entirely clear. Perhaps it reflects our preference to know more about a person's traits than to know about a person's environment. After all, the goal of forming attributions is to understand the person, not the environment (Jones, 1979). Another explanation is that when we view another person in a social setting, we tend to focus our attention on that person and her behavior, paying less attention to the situation. If we don't pay enough attention to the situation, we are unlikely to give situational factors much weight when making our attributions.

Engaging in the fundamental attribution error varies with the degree to which our culture emphasizes individual behavior over group behavior. Some cultures, like those in North America and Western Europe, are **individualistic cultures,** emphasizing individual behavior and success over that of groups. Some other cultures, like those in India and Japan, are **collectivistic cultures,** emphasizing group behavior and success over that of the individual (Triandis, 1990). Research on the fundamental attribution error has shown that people from individualistic cultures are more likely to engage in the fundamental attribution error (Choi & Nesbitt, 1998). Presumably, our Western focus on the individual accounts for this difference in attribution, but more research needs to be done to pinpoint the difference between individualistic and collectivistic cultures.

Actor-Observer Bias

What kind of attributions do we make when we are examining our own behavior? What if you found yourself yelling at a companion in a café? How would you attribute your behavior? Would you be *as likely* to label yourself as a mean person as you would the man in the previous example? Probably not. When we observe our own behavior, we tend to take situational factors more into account than we do for others. This bias has been called the **actor-observer bias** because we make different attributions as *actors* than we make as *observers* of others (Choi & Nesbitt, 1998; Jones & Nesbitt, 1971). The actor-observer bias predicts that you may attribute your yelling to some situational factor. Perhaps your companion unduly angered you, or perhaps you had a bad day at work. However, the explanation you would likely use for others, that you are a mean person, would be low on your list of attributions.

The actor-observer bias may seem self-serving, but this is not always the case. You would also be more likely to attribute a classmate's unexpected A on an exam to his traits than you would your own unexpected A. In this case, the actor-observer bias predicts that you would consider situational causes, such as an easy exam, more for yourself than for others. So why do we treat ourselves differently from others when it comes to attribution?

One potential reason for the actor-observer bias stems from the way we perceive our own behavior versus the behavior of others. When we are the actor, we cannot literally see our own behavior, and our attention is generally focused outward on the environment. But when we are the observer, our attention is generally focused on the other person's behavior. Therefore, because we are relatively unaware of our own behavior and very aware of the environment, we are more likely to consider situational factors in making attributions for ourselves (Storms, 1973).

The actor-observer bias may also stem from the different knowledge we have about ourselves and other people (Eisen, 1979). When we are making attributions

fundamental attribution error our tendency to overuse trait information when making attributions about others

individualistic culture a culture, like many Western cultures, in which individual accomplishments are valued over group accomplishments

collectivistic culture a culture, like many Asian cultures, in which group accomplishments are valued over individual accomplishments

actor-observer bias our tendency to make the fundamental attribution error when judging others, while being less likely to commit the fundamental attribution error when making attributions about ourselves

about our own behavior, we are usually very aware of the way in which the environment influences our behavior. Because we do not typically know other people's thoughts, we usually do not know how other people perceive the situation and whether it indeed influences their behavior.

In our example of the man in the café, unless you had seen the woman provoke the man, you may not have had any reason to attribute the yelling behavior to the situation. If you had been the one yelling, you would have clearly known whether or not your companion was at all responsible for your behavior. In part, the actor-observer effect seems to occur because we are more *able* to examine the potential situational causes of our own behavior.

Self-Serving Bias

Application

self-serving bias   our tendency to make attributions that preserve our own self-esteem; for example, making trait attributions for our success and situational attributions for our failures

As we just stated, the actor-observer bias does not stem from a desire to enhance one's self-esteem. This does not mean that we never seek to make ourselves look better, however. Often we do just that when making attributions. The **self-serving bias** refers to our tendency to make trait attributions for our successes and situational attributions for our failures (Miller & Ross, 1975). If you were to earn an A on your next psychology exam, you would likely attribute this A to your ability or your study habits. However, if you were to fail your next psychology exam (and we hope that you do not!), you would be more likely to attribute this grade to some situational factor, such as an unfair exam or the fact that your roommate interfered with your studying.

The major reason for the self-serving bias appears to be our desire to feel good about ourselves (Brown & Rogers, 1991; Trafimow, Armendariz, & Madseon, 2004). This bias helps protect our self-esteem, although it can also cause problems if we become too self-serving. For instance, not taking credit for our failures can lead others to like us less (Carlston & Shovar, 1983).

As we have seen in this section, we often take shortcuts, or heuristics, when making attributions about others. Heuristics may save us time, but often they lead to incorrect attributions and judgments about others. As we will see in our next section, our tendency to use mental shortcuts can also lead to bigger problems, such as prejudice and discrimination.

Let's Review!

In this section, we discussed how we form impressions of ourselves and others. For a quick check of your understanding, answer these questions.

1. Our tendency to overuse trait attributions and to ignore the situational influences on behavior is known as the:
   a. fundamental attribution error.
   b. self-serving bias.
   c. social desirability bias.
   d. actor-observer bias.

2. Which of the following people would be *least* likely to exhibit the fundamental attribution error?
   a. Henri from Canada
   b. Kiko from Japan
   c. Lamont from the United States
   d. Greta from Germany

3. Jasper was quick to assume that Susan was intelligent when he saw that she earned an A on her last psychology exam. However, when Jasper earned an A on his history test, he was not so quick to assume that he was intelligent. Which of the following biases in social cognition *best* explains Jasper's behavior?
   a. the fundamental attribution error
   b. the self-serving bias
   c. the social desirability bias
   d. the actor-observer bias

ANSWERS
1. a; 2. b; 3. d

Prejudice: How It Occurs, and How to Reduce It

> > > > > > > > > > > > > > >

⩔ **LEARNING**
⩔ **OBJECTIVE**
⩔ Define and distinguish among preju-
⩔ dice, stereotypes, and discrimination,
⩔ and explain how prejudice develops.
⩔

Prejudices based on race, gender, sexual orientation, age, religion, country of origin, and other perceived differences still hamper many people's ability to live a productive and happy life. People have been harassed, belittled, lost jobs, and even been killed because of prejudice. In 2002, the FBI reported a total of 7,459 hate crimes. Most of these incidents were motivated by racial prejudice with religious prejudice and prejudice based on sexual orientation being the next most frequent motives for hate crimes (Federal Bureau of Investigation, 2002).

Aside from violent crimes and crimes against property, there are subtler forms of discrimination. One study found that African American loan applicants in Columbus, Ohio, were more likely to have their loan applications denied when they were trying to buy homes in White neighborhoods versus when they attempted to secure financing for homes in Black neighborhoods (Holloway, 1998). And despite gains in equal rights over the last several decades, women have still not achieved equal status in the workforce, academia, or the government (Fischer, 1992; Smith, 2002). Prejudice remains a serious social problem. Because prejudice poses a threat to all of us, understanding where prejudice comes from is essential.

≪ Application

We can view prejudice as an extension of normal cognitive processes, in that prejudices are attitudes that develop like all other attitudes. On the other hand, prejudices are unique because they are especially problematic and divisive attitudes that can cause upheaval in a society. As we look at the development of prejudice, we will examine the similarities between normal cognition and prejudiced thought.

Prejudice and Stereotypes

You will recall from Chapters 6 and 7 that as we acquire knowledge about our world, we store that information in generalized knowledge structures, called *schemata*. Schemata reside in our long-term memory and allow us to more efficiently encode, store, and retrieve information (Fiske & Taylor, 1991). When we form a schema for a particular group of people, that schema is referred to as a **stereotype.** All of us have stereotypes for the various groups of people we encounter in life. Our stereotypes allow us to make assumptions about others and to have certain expectations about how others will behave. For example, when you walk into your local library, you have some idea of what to expect from the people working there because you have a stereotype for librarians stored in your long-term memory. Without stereotypes, we would be unable to predict the behavior of others, and every social interaction would be a completely new experience for us. Every time you walked into a library, you would have to re-learn what a librarian is like. In the terminology of developmental psychology (Chapter 9), without stereotypes we would not be able to *assimilate* in social situations. If you were to find yourself in a situation in which you had no stereotypes to guide your behavior, such as in meeting someone from a culture that you knew nothing about, you would likely feel unsure of yourself and not know what to do.

stereotype   a schema for a particular group of people

So if stereotypes are generally helpful to us, how do they become the prejudices that cause problems in a society, such as the racism and other forms of bias that many must endure? One way to conceptualize a **prejudice** is as a stereotype that has gone awry. A stereotype can be thought of as the *cognitive* component of an attitude (Aronson, Wilson, & Akert, 2005). In other words, a stereotype is the knowledge you have stored in memory about some group of people. Stereotypes become problematic when we generically apply them to all members of a group without regard to those individuals' unique characteristics. Furthermore, when a stereotype contains biased and

prejudice   a largely negative stereotype that is unfairly applied to all members of a group regardless of their individual characteristics negative information about a particular group of people, the stereotype begins to look like a prejudice (e.g., Chory-Assad & Tamborini, 2003). And, finally, when a biased, negative stereotype becomes coupled with a negative *affective* or emotional reaction toward all (or most) people belonging to that group, a prejudice results. In the mind of the prejudiced person, all members of a particular group are disliked and labeled as having negative characteristics, regardless of the individual qualities that they might possess. These prejudiced beliefs in turn affect how the prejudiced person *behaves* toward all or most members of a particular group.

All too often, prejudice motivates people to treat others poorly. **Discrimination** is the behavioral expression of a prejudice. In Luis's case, he saw his father, who was a high school principal in Mexico, offered only jobs as a laborer in the United States, because that's how many people stereotyped Mexican immigrants—as laborers and housekeepers.

Knowing that prejudice and discrimination exist makes life difficult for people who are the objects of negative stereotypes. How would you be affected if you knew that many people in the world held negative stereotypes about you? Unfortunately, many people live their entire lives with this knowledge. As we will see in It's a Diverse World, knowing that others might view you in a prejudiced manner can affect a person in a decidedly negative fashion.

discrimination the behavioral expression of a prejudice

IT'S A DIVERSE WORLD

Stereotype Threat: How Prejudice Affects Female Performance

Psychologist Claude Steele proposes that some victims of prejudice end up reinforcing certain aspects of the prejudices held against them due to a phenomenon called *stereotype threat.* Stereotype threat exists when a person fears that others will judge her not on her own qualities, but rather on prejudicial stereotypes held about the group(s) to which she belongs (C. M. Steele, 1997). Understandably, this fear can lead to considerable anxiety in minorities due to the negative nature of the prejudices that exist for many minority groups. For example, women often suffer stereotype threat in the workplace. Due to widespread, negative stereotyping of women in the workplace, females expect their coworkers to give them less credit for successes and more blame for failures (e.g., Heilman & Kram, 1983).

Studies have shown that stereotype threat can actually inhibit one's performance on a task. For example, normally high achieving females tend to score less well on mathematics problems, but not on verbal tasks, when they are asked to perform these tasks in an environment where they are outnumbered by men (Inzlicht & Ben-Zeev, 2000). In this situation, females presumably become aware of the negative stereotypes that many people hold—that men are better at math—and the fear of being perceived to be

mathematically inept (stereotype threat) then impairs their math performance. Females are not stereotyped as being poor at verbal tasks, so there is no stereotype threat for verbal tasks, and females exhibit no impairment in performance even when they are outnumbered by males. Stereotype threat can become a self-fulfilling prophecy, in which a woman behaves in a manner that actually reinforces negative stereotypes about females. But why would this be true?

Stereotype threat may cause a woman to feel aversive emotions that then hinder her task performance. In a recent study, researchers found that female high school students performed more poorly on a math test when they believed that the test had a history of showing gender differences in math performance (stereotype threat condition) than they did when they felt that the test did not have such a history (nonstereotype threat condition). The reduced performance under stereotype threat is even more notable because the girls took the math test under conditions of complete anonymity, and the situation was constructed to motivate the girls to attempt as many problems as they could. After completing the test, the girls in the stereotype threat condition reported feeling more dejected. Their dejection seemed to stem from the stereotype threat and not from their poor performance. This could mean that being aware of a negative stereotype about women's math performance causes females to feel dejected, which negatively affects their math performance. However, exactly how dejection leads to poor performance has not yet been established (Keller & Dauenheimer, 2003). Under certain circumstances, it is also possible that stereotype threat elicits anxiety, which affects performance. However, a definite causal role of anxiety in stereotype threat impairment for women has not yet been firmly established (e.g., Osborne, 2001).

Although psychologists do not yet fully understand how stereotype threat affects female performance, a growing number of studies show that it is does (e.g., Davies, Spencer, Quinn, & Gerhardstein, 2002; Quinn & Spencer, 2001; J. Steele, James, & Barnett, 2002). Furthermore, stereotype threat has also been shown to impair African Americans' academic performance (e.g., Steele & Aronson, 1995). As long as negative stereotypes persist, it's a safe bet that many people will suffer as a result.

It is easy to see that prejudice and discrimination are harmful. But why do we form negative, prejudicial stereotypes about others in the first place?

Social Transmission of Prejudice

Like other attitudes, prejudices can develop through the processes of classical conditioning, operant conditioning, and social learning (Duckitt, 1992). As you can see in Table 12.3 ◆, these types of learning allow for prejudices to develop and also be passed from person to person within a culture. The experiences we have with other groups of people, the models we are exposed to (Kowalski, 2003), and the rewards and punishment we receive in life all have the power to mold our stereotypes and prejudices about others.

How easily prejudices can be learned was dramatically demonstrated in one of the most famous classroom exercises ever done on prejudice. In the 1970s, grade school teacher Jane Elliot decided to teach her third-grade class an important lesson in prejudice. She decided that her students, who were all rural White children, could benefit from learning about prejudice from both sides of the fence.

One day in class, Elliot told her students that she had recently heard that scientists had determined that brown-eyed people were inferior to blue-eyed people. She told the class that the brown-eyed were less intelligent, trustworthy, and nice than the "superior" blue-eyed people were. To make the group differences very salient, Elliot had all the brown-eyed children wear brown-cloth collars over their clothing so they could be immediately identified as being members of the "inferior" group of students.

Within hours of her announcement concerning eye color, Elliot had created a strong prejudice in her classroom. The blue-eyed children made fun of the brown-eyed children. The blue-eyes called the brown-eyes names, ostracized them, and in general treated them cruelly. A fight even occurred on the playground as a result of the prejudice. In less than a day, Elliot turned a once peaceful, egalitarian classroom into a hotbed of prejudice and discrimination (Monteith & Winters, 2002).

Elliot's demonstration showed us how quickly prejudice can be learned. Admittedly, the environment Elliot created in her classroom was directly designed to create prejudice. What other types of environments may contribute to the development of prejudices? Can prejudice be developed within a family, for instance? There is some evidence to suggest that we do adopt the prejudices of our parents, but having prejudiced parents does not guarantee that we will become prejudiced. In one study that examined the match between parental values and those held by the children, it was found that children are most likely to have attitudes similar to their parents when their parents hold egalitarian beliefs. When parents hold prejudicial attitudes, on the other

 Application

This child is likely to adopt the prejudices of her parents due to modeling.

© Mark Peterson/Corbis

◆ **Table 12.3**

Learning to Be Prejudiced

Type of Learning	Situation	Outcome
Classical conditioning	Marlita is robbed at knifepoint (US) by a White man (CS). During the attack, she feels terror and anger (CR/UR).	After the attack, Marlita feels anger and terror when she sees White men. She has been classically conditioned to feel negative emotions in response to White men.
Operant conditioning	Bobby makes fun of some girls at his school. He calls them "stupid crybabies" (behavior). All of Bobby's friends laugh when they see him behaving this way (reward).	Bobby is more likely to make fun of girls in the future because in the past he has been rewarded for doing so. His friends have operantly conditioned his prejudiced, discriminatory behavior.
Social learning	From a young age, Jackie hears her mother frequently say that men are sloppy, stubborn, insensitive creatures.	Jackie is likely to model her mother's prejudices, and adopt her mother's belief that men are sloppy, stubborn, and insensitive.

hand, the match between their values and their children's values is less strong (Rohan & Zanna, 1996).

It appears that when parents hold strong prejudices, the children may pick up these prejudices but later find that their peers do not reinforce them for holding such negative views. Because they are not reinforced and may even be punished by their peers for holding prejudices, they experience a decline in their prejudice that distances them from their parent's values. But when parents hold egalitarian values, their children may pick up these values and be reinforced by their peers for having them. Their values then remain more like those of their parents when they are egalitarian (Aronson, Wilson & Akert, 2005). This line of research makes a powerful argument for teaching tolerance in our schools and in our society because if tolerance becomes prevalent in a culture, it *may* have the power to override what happens in the home.

Intergroup Dynamics and Prejudice

Group Membership and Prejudice

We all belong to certain groups: families, schools, clubs, states, countries, religions, and races. These groups and the roles we play in them help define who we are as individuals (e.g., Gergen & Gergen, 1988). Because we tend to identify with the groups to which we belong, we also tend to prefer the groups of which we are members. We tend to like the people in our group a little bit more than we like the people who are not members. In other words, we exhibit an **in-group bias** (Hewstone, Rubin, & Willis, 2002). We tend to like our family members a little more than strangers. We like those that attend our school more than those who do not. We have a bias toward liking our country's citizens a little more than foreigners.

in-group bias our tendency to favor people who belong to the same groups that we do

Think of the groups of spectators at a sporting event. Each group sits on their team's side, and at times the rivalry between the two sides erupts into name-calling and even violence. If these same people had met under other conditions in which their team affiliations were not made obvious, such as at the grocery store or library, do you think that they would be as likely to call each other names and fight? They probably would not. Why do we sometimes allow our group affiliations to bias how we feel about and treat others? It appears to boil down to self-esteem.

Application

We apparently derive some of our self-esteem from the groups in which we are members. One way to enhance self-esteem is by belonging to a group we perceive as good and desirable. For example, if you perceive your religion as being the *best* religion, then belonging to this religious group increases your self-esteem. Unfortunately, one way to perceive your particular group as being good is to believe that other groups are not as good (Tajfel, 1982). When our group succeeds at something, we tend to be especially proud (Cialdini et al., 1976). In the absence of meaningful victory, we still tend to view our in-group members as superior to **out-group** members (Brewer, 1979; Molero, Navas, Gonzalez, Aleman, & Cuadrado, 2003; Tajfel, 1982).

The in-group bias tends to make us prejudiced against those who are not part of our social groups. Further, the in-group bias also tends to affect the way we actually *perceive* out-group members, causing us to perceive members of an out-group as being pretty much all alike. Researchers call this tendency the **out-group homogeneity bias** (Linville, Fischer, & Salovey, 1989). The old phrase "they all look alike" in reference to a minority group is a clear expression of the out-group homogeneity bias. Individual characteristics are perceived not to differ much from the stereotype that defines the group. So once we have knowledge about one member of an out-group, we tend to apply it to all people in that out-group (Quattrone & Jones, 1980).

Intergroup Conflict and Prejudice

Realistic-conflict theory (Levine & Campbell, 1972) proposes that conflict among groups for resources motivates the development of prejudice. In the United States, immigrants are often the targets of prejudice because they are perceived as coming to here "to steal jobs away from hard-working Americans" (Esses, Dovidio, Jackson, & Armstrong, 2001). One of the authors lives in a predominantly White town that has recently experienced large influxes of Latino immigrants from Mexico, and Central and South America. At times, she has heard comments reflecting anti-Latino sentiments in her community. Typically these comments speak of the loss of jobs to immigrants, even though unemployment is low in her community, and most of the immigrants hold low-paying jobs in poultry-processing plants that many community members do not want. Minority out-group members often play the role of *scapegoat* when times are hard (Allport, 1954/1979). In modern America, as you might expect, racial prejudice most often exists when groups are in direct competition for the same jobs (Simpson & Yinger, 1985).

Possibly the most famous study ever conducted on conflict and prejudice is Muzafer Sherif's Robber's Cave experiment (Sherif, Harvey, White, Hood, & Sherif, 1961). Sherif and his colleagues conducted this experiment in a naturalistic setting, a summer boys' camp at Robber's Cave State Park in Oklahoma (hence the experiment's nickname). The participants were normal, healthy, middle-class, White, Protestant, 11- to 12-year-old boys who attended Boy Scout camp at the park. Prior to participation in the camp, the boys were all strangers to one another.

As they arrived at the camp, the boys were randomly assigned to one of two cabins, Eagles' cabin or Rattlers' cabin. The cabins were situated fairly far apart to ensure that the two groups would not have much contact with each other. The boys in each group lived together, ate together, and spent much of their time together. Under these conditions of isolation from each other, the Eagles and the Rattlers became separate, tight-knit in-groups. Once each group bonded, the experimenters placed the Eagles and Rattlers together under conditions of conflict.

In this next phase, the experimenters had the Eagles and Rattlers compete with each other in sporting events. The winning group would get prizes that 12-year-old boys find quite attractive, such as pocketknives. The losers got nothing for their efforts except defeat. As a result of this competition, the Eagles and the Rattlers began to call each other names, sabotage each other's cabins and belongings, and even engage in physical violence against one another. In short, the Eagles hated the Rattlers, and the

out-group   a group that is distinct from one's own and so usually an object of more hostility or dislike than one's in-group

out-group homogeneity bias   our tendency to see out-group members as being pretty much all alike

realistic-conflict theory   the theory that prejudice stems from competition for scarce resources

 Application

Rattlers hated the Eagles. A prejudice based on the relatively meaningless distinctions of being Eagles or Rattlers was fully developed in the boys. When the prejudice between the Eagles and Rattlers reached the point of physical violence, the experimenters stopped the competition between the boys and sought ways to reduce the prejudice that had developed. But how do you remove a prejudice once it has formed?

Does Social Contact Reduce Prejudice?

One of Sherif's strategies to reduce prejudice was to increase the noncompetitive contact (e.g., watching movies together) between the Eagles and the Rattlers. In fact, the idea that contact between groups is enough to reduce prejudice, the so-called **contact hypothesis,** has been around for quite some time (Lee & Humphrey, 1943, cited in Allport, 1954/1979). If people from different in-groups see a lot of each other, won't they realize that the prejudices they hold about one another are unfounded and abandon them?

As Sherif found out, mere contact often does little to reduce prejudice (e.g., Poore et al., 2002). One reason contact doesn't work is that when people from different groups are thrown together, they tend to self-segregate. A drive through any big city illustrates this point. Neighborhoods are often well defined on the basis of ethnicity and race—even though people are legally free to live where they choose. If contact is to reduce prejudice, it has to be of a certain kind—it has to be *cooperative contact.*

After experimenting with increased contact between the Eagles and the Rattlers, Sherif and his colleagues (1961) did find a way to reduce the prejudice between the two groups of boys. The key was a special type of contact. Sherif and his colleagues created superordinate goals for the Eagles and the Rattlers. A **superordinate goal** is a goal that both groups want to accomplish but cannot without the help of the other group. For instance, the researchers disrupted the water supply that both groups used by tampering with the water pipes. To reestablish water to the camp, the Eagles and Rattlers had to work together to find the source of the trouble. While they were trying to solve their mutual problem, the Eagles and Rattlers did not seem to have much time to hate one another. In another instance, a food supply truck broke down, and the two groups had to work together to push-start the truck. Without their combined efforts, both groups would have gone hungry. After a series of such contacts, the prejudice between the groups began to dissolve, perhaps because the Eagles and Rattlers now saw themselves as part of the same group—the group that was trying to find food and water. Without clear lines between the boys, there was no basis for in-group or out-group bias or prejudice. The researchers noted that friendships began to form between individual Eagles and Rattlers, and as a whole, the Rattlers and Eagles began to cooperate, spend time together, and even to share their money. The prejudice that was once so virulent was dramatically reduced (Sherif, 1966).

Based in part on the results of the Robber's Cave study, researchers have attempted to outline the characteristics of the type of contact between groups that reduces prejudice. Figure 12.2 summarizes the conditions that seem to best foster the reduction of prejudices. One practical application of these conditions is something called a *jigsaw classroom* (Aronson, 2000). A jigsaw classroom is one in which students from diverse ethnic groups are asked to work together on a project in a cooperative way. Each child is responsible for a different piece of the project, which forces the children to be interdependent. Because they must rely on each other, the children begin to focus more on the tasks at hand and less on their differences. According to psychologist Elliot Aronson (2000), research on the outcomes of jigsaw classrooms over the last 25 years consistently indicate that as participants begin to identify as members of the same in-group, prejudice and hostility among the children are reduced, and self-esteem and

contact hypothesis a theory that states that contact among groups is an effective means of reducing prejudice among the groups

superordinate goal a goal that is shared by different groups of people

Application ≫

Figure 12.2 **Contact That Works**

These conditions make it more likely that contact will work to reduce prejudice.
We explained superordinate goals in our discussions of the Robber's Cave study.

Condition	Description	Example 1	Example 2
Mutual Interdependence (Amir, 1976)	The different groups must need each other.	A manufacturing plant is troubled by strong gender prejudice within its male and female managers. Survival of the plant is threatened by the loss of its business to foreign competitors who are taking over their market.	A multi-racial community is threatened by rising crime rates and racial tensions. The criminals target all community members. To protect oneself, one needs the help of all one's neighbors to start a community watch program.
Superordinate Goals (Amir, 1976)	The different groups must have a common goal, and achievement of this goal must require the effort of both groups.	All the middle management employees have the goal of finding a way to stop the loss of revenue to foreign competitors.	Everyone's goal is to stop crime in the neighborhood.
Equal Status Partnership (Allport, 1954; Sherif 1961, 1966)	The different groups must work shoulder to shoulder on an equal playing field to accomplish their mutual goal.	The company creates a taskforce to find a way to stop the revenue losses. The taskforce is composed of equal numbers of male and females from middle management.	To accomplish this goal, all the races will have to work together to start an effective community watch program. No one race will have a higher position of authority in the watch program. All participants will be on an equal level.
Friendly, Informal Contact Between Groups (Wilder, 1986)	The contact must be hospitable and free from negative emotional interaction and rigid structure.	The taskforce meets weekly to find a solution to its problem. After each meeting, the taskforce members lunch together and have time to talk informally.	During the organizational meetings for the program, all participants meet over donuts and coffee to discuss their plans. Aside from business, small talk occurs between participants.
Groups Members Must Have Enough Friendly Contact With Out-Group Members to Realize that Their Prejudices Are Unfounded (Wilder, 1984).	There has to be enough contact with many individuals of one's out-group before one will begin to realize the inaccuracy of one's prejudicial stereotypes.	During the weekly meetings and lunches, the male and female co-workers come to see each other as being pretty much the same. They share many of the same values and challenges in life.	During the weekly meetings, people begin to realize that they are more alike than they are different. They find that they share many of the same attitudes and challenges in life.
Social Norms That Promote Equality Are Operating During the Inter-Group Contact (Wilder, 1984).	The situation in which the contact occurs should be one in which the overall agreement among participants is that equality and tolerance are expected for all. The situation cannot be one in which participants feel free to behave in a discriminatory fashion.	The norms of the company do not support sexist attitudes. There is little tolerance for infighting within the taskforce that may distract the group from solving the problem of lost revenue.	During the meetings, the norms do not support discriminatory behavior. For instance, if anyone starts blaming a particular race for the crime problems or name-calling, the group immediately censures them. All participants feel respected during the meetings.
END RESULT	Prejudices begin to break down.	People begin to focus less on the gender of the other people in the group and more on their individual strengths and weaknesses. Tensions ease between the genders.	People begin to focus less on the race of the other people in the group and more on their individual strengths and weaknesses. Tensions ease between the races.

academic performance are increased. These findings further underscore the message of the Robber's Cave experiment—that cooperation rather than competition can best work to lower prejudice in the world.

We have seen that prejudices can affect the judgments we make about other people. When we attribute negative characteristics to someone simply because they belong to a certain social group, we are behaving prejudicially. Our prejudices can, in turn, affect the way we treat other people.

Regardless of whether we base our impressions on a prejudice or on actual behavior, we tend to want to spend more time with people we *like*. We may decide to enter into a friendship or a romantic relationship with someone for whom we have formed a positive impression. The relationship may turn out to be wonderful, or it may fail.

In the aftermath of the breakup of a relationship, we often ask ourselves, "What did I ever see in this person?" This is the question that we will tackle next as we look what attracts us to others.

Tim Boyles/Getty Images

Superordinate goals are an effective means of reducing prejudice. These people are likely to see themselves as members of the same in-group as they work together to survive this challenge, and as a result, they are likely to experience less prejudice for one another.

Let's Review!

In this section, we discussed prejudice and ways to reduce it. As a quick check of your understanding, answer these questions.

1. Kelly is a manager at a firm that has been troubled by considerable prejudice between its male and female employees. Kelly wants to institute a program that will reduce the level of prejudice that exists between the sexes. Which of the following plans has the best chance of working?

   a. Appointing opposite-sex managers to supervise workers.

   b. Have a "battle of the sexes" to see which sex can outperform the other on the job.

   c. Form work teams to solve company problems, and make sure that the teams contain both male and female members.

   d. Threaten to fire anyone who says or does anything prejudicial, and post this message around the workplace to ensure that everyone knows about the policy.

2. Relative to in-group members, we tend to view out-group members as being _____.

   a. less like us   c. less favorable

   b. more homogeneous   d. all of the above

3. Which of the following is the best example of cooperative contact?

   a. teachers supervising students taking a math test

   b. a manager meeting with employees to discuss sales figures

   c. a police officer lecturing to an elementary school class about the dangers of drugs

   d. a citizen's group meeting to find ways to reduce crime in their neighborhood

   ANSWERS

   1. c; 2. d; 3. d

The Nature of Attraction › › › › › › › › › › › › › › ›

LEARNING OBJECTIVE

Discuss the factors affecting attraction—exposure, proximity, similarity, balance, and physical attractiveness.

The attitudes that we form about a person determine whether or not we will be attracted to them as a friend or as a lover. The affective component of the attitudes we hold about someone is particularly important. If a person produces positive emotional reactions in us, we are much more likely to find them attractive. Think about those people closest to you. How do you *feel* about your best friend and your significant others? We are betting that most of you generally feel positive emotions about those you love. Most of us do. When it comes to attraction, the most important question is: What makes us feel good about another person?

Proximity

One of the most intriguing findings in the area of attraction concerns how much exposure we have to certain people and how the exposure affects our feelings of attraction for them. It appears that the more often we have seen a person or an object, the more we tend to like it. This trend, called the **mere exposure effect** (Lee, 2001; Zajonc, 1968), appears to be true for a variety of stimuli. One study found that participants liked Japanese ideographs (written characters) more if they had been repeatedly exposed to them (Moreland & Zajonc, 1977). Another study found that participants preferred tones that they had heard repeatedly over those they had heard only a few times (W. R. Wilson, 1979).

mere exposure effect   the theory that the more we are exposed to something, the more we grow to like it

Mere exposure also seems to play a role in interpersonal attraction. Many studies have shown that we tend to be friends and lovers with those who live and work close to us (Clarke, 1952; Festinger, 1951; Festinger, Schachter, & Back, 1950; Ineichen, 1979; Segal, 1974). The more **proximity,** or physical closeness, we have to someone in our daily lives, the more exposure we have to them, and the more we tend to like them. For example, within an apartment building, the closer a person's apartment is to yours, the higher the probability that you will be friends with that person (Festinger, 1951). This is true even when apartments are assigned on a random basis, as you might find in university housing (Festinger, Schachter, & Back, 1950). Attraction to those who live and work close seems to hold across cultures as well. Studies have found evidence supporting a relationship between proximity and liking in both Africa (Brewer & Campbell, 1976) and France (Maisonneuve, Palmade, & Fourment, 1952).

proximity   the physical closeness of people to one another

Think about the people you sit close to in your classes. You may have not realized it, but your seat in a classroom may have an impact on your social relationships. The closer you sit to someone in a classroom, the more likely you are to be friends (and perhaps more) with that person (Segal, 1974). The effects of proximity also indicate that the architecture of apartment buildings and office buildings may impact the social relationships we form. If, for example, you live or work on a busy hallway, you may have more relationships than someone who is on a less-traveled hallway. So a smart person would choose his or her classroom seat, apartment, or office wisely!

 Application

Similarity

There are two old adages about the people we tend to choose as friends or lovers. One says, "Birds of a feather flock together" and the other says, "Opposites attract." You probably know some couples who demonstrate both views of attraction. But what does the average person look for? Do we want someone who is similar to us, or are we looking for someone who is different to complement our personality?

Research on this issue indicates that indeed, "Birds of a feather flock together." When choosing a romantic partner, we tend to gravitate to people who are of similar

Students who sit in close proximity to each other in the classroom are more likely to be friends and lovers.

age, socioeconomic status, education, intelligence, race, religion, attitudes, power, and physical attractiveness (Brehm, 1992; Browning, Kessler, Hatfield, & Choo, 1999; Hendrick & Hendrick, 1983). Furthermore, similarity seems to predict attraction across a variety of cultures, including Mexico, India, and Japan (Byrne et al., 1971). Similarity also seems to be a factor in the friends we choose (Kandel, 1978; Newcomb, 1961; Rubin, Lynch, Coplan, Rose-Krasnor, & Booth, 1994).

One possible explanation for the influence of similarity on attraction is an application of dissonance theory called **balance theory** (Heider, 1958). Balance theory states that when we like someone who does not like the things we like, we experience an *imbalance* that causes dissonance. As we saw earlier, dissonance motivates change that restores consonance. To restore consonance in this case, we would have to either change the other person's attitudes or change our own attitudes (Figure 12.3). Because it is easier to change our own opinions, we may stop liking that person in order to restore consonance. Therefore, we tend to like most those who are similar to us, and liking leads to attraction.

balance theory a theory that states that when we are attracted to people who do not share our attitudes, we feel dissonance, which motivates us to change in some way to reduce this dissonance

Physical Attractiveness

One of the first things we notice about a potential romantic partner is his or her physical attractiveness. In a classic study that examined physical attractiveness and attraction in a blind-date type scenario, physical attractiveness was the *only* factor found to predict whether a person wanted to go out on a second date (Walster, Aronson, Abrahams, & Rottman, 1966).

When it comes to choosing potential partners, physical attractiveness seems to be important both to men and women, but men seem to place particular emphasis on how attractive their potential romantic partners are (Green, Buchanan, & Heuer, 1984; Woll, 1986). This special emphasis that men place on physical attractiveness seems to hold for both homosexual and heterosexual men. Heterosexual and homosexual

Imbalanced (dissonant)

Mary

John loves Mary. **(+)**   Mary hates football. **(−)**

John   Football

John loves football. **(+)**

Balanced (consonant)

Mary

John loves Mary. **(+)**   Mary loves football. **(+)**

John   Football

John loves football. **(+)**

Mary

John doesn't love Mary. **(−)**   Mary hates football. **(−)**

John   Football

John loves football. **(+)**

Figure 12.3 **Balance Theory and Attraction: Two Ways of Restoring Consonance**

John and Mary are attracted to each other. Unfortunately, John loves football, and Mary hates it. If John can convince Mary to love football, he is back in balance. If John can't convince Mary, he may decide he doesn't love her after all.

women, on the other hand, place more importance on the psychological traits of their potential partners. So it seems that although physical attractiveness is important to women, it is not the *most* important aspect of a partner (Deaux & Hanna, 1984).

Female or male, we tend to be romantically involved with people whose level of physical attractiveness is comparable to our own. This tendency, called the **matching hypothesis,** seems to be true of both dating and married couples (Zajonc, Adelmann, Murphy, & Neidenthal, 1987).

Interestingly, the influence of physical attractiveness on romantic relationships seems to be mirrored in our same-sex friendships. The matching hypothesis predicts that our same-sex friends will be, on average, about as attractive as we are (McKillip & Reidel, 1983). And although both men and women seem to choose their friends on the basis of their physical attractiveness, again men place more emphasis on this characteristic than do women (Berscheid, Dion, Walster, & Walster, 1971; Feingold, 1988; Perlini, Bertolissi, & Lind, 1999). The importance of physical attractiveness in social relationships isn't surprising in light of findings that we tend to perceive attractive people differently from the unattractive. For example, attractive people are perceived to be more interesting, sociable, kind, sensitive, and nurturing than unattractive people (Dion, Berscheid, & Walster, 1972). With all these *perceived* qualities, no wonder we want to be friends and lovers with the attractive!

However, there may also be another reason why we prefer attractive people. In an interesting study, researchers found that babies as young as 2 months old looked longer at attractive faces than they did at unattractive ones (Langlois et al., 1987),

matching hypothesis the theory that we are attracted to people whose level of physical attractiveness is similar to our own

According to the matching hypothesis, we tend to have romantic partners who are close to our level of physical attractiveness.

We tend to ascribe positive traits to those that we find attractive.

indicating that they preferred the attractive faces. Because it is hard to imagine that 2-month-old babies have had time to *learn* to be biased toward attractive people, these findings suggest that we are born with an instinctive preference for the good-looking. Perhaps this instinct has evolved in humans because certain features that are found in attractive people (i.e., having symmetrical facial features) indicate good health. In terms of natural selection and evolution (see Chapter 2, p. 90), it makes sense for us to be sexually attracted to people who are healthy and therefore able to facilitate our ability to produce offspring.

Pure attraction is not the only reason that we are drawn to others, however. Sometimes our desire to be with others serves a purpose other than sex and reproduction. In our next section, we will further explore our social nature by examining some of the reasons we are driven to be with others in the form of social groups.

Let's Review!

In this section, we discussed what attracts us to others. For a quick assessment of your understanding, answer these questions.

1. Based on the available psychological research, you are *most* likely to end up in a romantic relationship with:
   a. a neighbor who shares your same values.
   b. a person from another state who shares your same values.
   c. a fellow student who does not share your values.
   d. a coworker who has opposite views.

2. Attractive people are assumed to be all of the following things, *except* which one?
   a. interesting
   b. sociable
   c. nurturant
   d. egotistical

3. Which of the following statements is true?
   a. Women are unconcerned with physical attractiveness when choosing a romantic partner.
   b. Women and men are equally interested in physical attractiveness when choosing a romantic partner.
   c. Neither men nor women pay that much attention to physical attractiveness when choosing a romantic partner.
   d. Men pay more attention to physical attractiveness when choosing a romantic partner.

ANSWERS
1. a; 2. d; 3. d

Groups and Group Influence ⟩ ⟩ ⟩ ⟩ ⟩ ⟩ ⟩ ⟩ ⟩ ⟩ ⟩

Think about the groups to which you belong. Can you identify those that you freely chose to join and those that you were forced into by circumstance? Think about Luis. He joined some groups that many of us will never join. Why would *anyone* join organizations like gangs or activist groups? Although we have no way of knowing why Luis in particular joined the groups he did, we can discuss the general reasons that a person might have for joining a group.

Psychologists who study the formation of groups suggest several potential explanations (Baumeister & Leary, 1995; Paulus, 1989). One is that group membership can fulfill *social needs*, such as the need for companionship and a sense of belonging. Being a group member can also provide a sense of *security*. For example, gang members often feel as though the gang provides them with protection against aggressive attacks from others (c.f. Rodriguez, 1994). Furthermore, groups can serve to give members a sense of *social identity*. We often define ourselves in part by the groups to which we belong—for example, as members of a baseball team. A final reason people may join groups is to gain *information* and to ensure the *achievement of goals*. For example, your authors are both psychologists, and we belong to several organizations for psychologists. We joined these groups to learn more about psychology and to achieve our goals of becoming better teachers of psychology. As students, perhaps you have already joined groups for the same reasons. Study groups, clubs, and preprofessional organizations all help students learn more and achieve career-related goals.

 **Application**

Regardless of why we join a group, once we do join, the group and its collective members then have the power to influence our behavior. What gives groups the power to change the way we behave?

Social Forces Within Groups: Norms and Cohesiveness

Groups are characterized by the expectations and attitudes of their members. One way that the expectations of group members manifest themselves is through the formation of group **norms**. Norms are the laws that guide the behavior of group members. Norms can be explicitly stated rules or unwritten expectations that members have for behavior within the group. Virtually every group that we belong to has its own set of norms. For example, think of the group of students in your psychology class. What expectations do your classmates have for your behavior? What expectations do you have of them? Do you expect your classmates to dress casually? Or do you expect them to dress in formal business attire? Do you expect your classmates to sit *at* their desks instead of *on* their desks during lectures? These and your other expectations are the norms that operate in your particular class.

norm unwritten rule or expectation for how group members should behave

How you would feel if you had to break some of the norms in your class—for example, going to class in your bathing suit after someone robbed your gym locker? Would you be comfortable as you sat in class in this attire? Most of us would find this type of situation stressful, but why?

In general, we do not like to break the norms of the groups to which we belong. When we do, we may face several unpleasant consequences. Group members may ridicule us or try to persuade us to change our behavior, or—perhaps most threatening—we might be thrown out or ostracized from the group.

Recall that groups often fulfill our social needs and give us a sense of security and identity. Because of these benefits, we often value our group memberships and wish to protect them. The degree to which members wish to maintain membership in the group is referred to as **cohesiveness.** In groups in which members tend to have very

cohesiveness the degree to which members of a group value their group membership; cohesive groups are tight-knit groups

We are likely to conform to the norms of groups because we do not wish to be ostracized or ridiculed.

positive attitudes about their membership in the group, cohesiveness is high, and the group tends to be close-knit. When cohesiveness is high, the pressure we feel to meet group norms is also high. This means that as our attraction for certain groups increases, so does the influence these groups have over us. The more we value our membership in a group, the less willing we are to risk losing that membership. Therefore, group cohesiveness helps ensure **conformity** within a group as group members modify their behavior to avoid breaking the group's norms (Crandall, 1988; Latané & L'Herrou, 1996; Schachter, 1951).

conformity behaving in accordance with group norms

Conformity Within a Group

One of the most influential psychologists to formally study the process of conformity was Solomon Asch. During the 1950s Asch conducted a series of classic experiments on conformity and the factors that make us more or less likely to conform in a given situation. Asch (1951) had male participants engage in a perceptual task with eight other men. The participants were unaware that the eight other men in the experiment were *confederates*, or actors posing as participants. Each participant, along with the eight confederates, was shown a series of lines and asked to match the length of a test line to one of three other comparison lines (Figure 12.4). The experiment was set up so that the confederates made their judgments first. The participants heard all of the confederates in turn choose—aloud—the wrong line (in this case, the 6¼″ line). By the time the true participants' turn came, they had heard every single other person choose what was clearly the wrong line. A norm had formed in the group, the norm of choosing the wrong line. The *dependent variable* in Asch's study was whether the participants would conform to the norm or whether they would go with their own perception and choose the correct comparison line.

What do you think Asch found? What would you have done in this situation? Well, Asch found that 74% of his participants conformed at least once during the experiment. Apparently, many people can be easily made to conform. Only 26% of the participants firmly stood by their convictions and refused to conform.

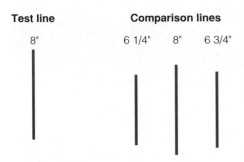

Test line **Comparison lines**

8" 6 1/4" 8" 6 3/4"

Figure 12.4 The Asch Procedure for Testing Conformity (after Asch, 1951)

In Asch's study, 74% of the subjects conformed and chose the 6¼" line as the match for the comparison line after hearing the confederates make this obviously incorrect choice.

Resisting Conformity

Asch's next step was to ask whether certain situations made it easier or harder to resist the pressure to conform. In a variation of the first experiment, Asch had one of the confederates choose the correct line, whereas the other seven were instructed to choose the incorrect line. In this situation, the participant had one ally, or partner, and the *unanimity* of the confederates was destroyed. Did this make the participants less likely to conform? Under these conditions, Asch found that conformity dropped significantly. Having at least one person to back you up against the majority seems to give us more courage to break the norms of a group. It seems there truly is strength in numbers! If having one person on our side gives us strength, how many people must oppose us before we yield? This was the next question Asch tackled.

Asch varied the number of confederates in the procedure to test the effect that the size of the *majority group* (the members who conform to the norm) has on the conformity of the *minority* (those members opposed to the norm—in this case, the participant). In this variation, Asch tested participants in groups with 1, 2, 3, 4, 8, and 16 confederates who all chose the wrong comparison line. By manipulating the *independent variable* of majority group size or number of confederates, Asch was able to examine its effects on the *dependent variable* of conformity. Asch's results for this variation are rather surprising. He found that 3 majority members were enough to produce maximum conformity in a participant. A majority of 16 produced no more conformity than a majority of 3. More recent research, however, has questioned these findings. Newer evidence suggests that conformity may continue to increase up to a majority group size of 8 and perhaps more (Bond & Smith, 1996). How many friends would it take to get you to see that movie you don't really want to see?

A final variable examined in Asch's study was the effect of *anonymity* on conformity. If the participant was allowed to make his judgments of the lines in private, rather than in public, would this affect conformity? Asch tested this by running experimental conditions that allowed participants to record their judgments on paper rather than choosing a comparison line out loud (they still had knowledge of how the majority had voted, however). Under these conditions, conformity dropped to nearly zero. It appears that anonymity provides us the security we need to not conform to group norms.

Since Asch's original experiments, others have studied the factors that affect conformity in groups. Table 12.4 ◆ summarizes the particular influence of some of these factors. Overall, the picture that emerges from the research on conformity is that we are most likely to conform if:

- we do not feel confident of our abilities
- cohesiveness is high in the group
- our responses are made public (we are not anonymous)
- the group has at least three members who are unanimous in their dedication to the norm
- the idea that one *should* conform is itself a norm in our culture.

◆ **Table 12.4**

Factors That Affect Conformity

Factor	Effect on Conformity	Relevant Study
Majority group size	As majority group size increases to three members, so does conformity.	Asch, 1951
Unanimity of the group	Unanimity increases conformity. One dissenter can dramatically reduce conformity.	Asch, 1951
Anonymity	When we are anonymous, we are much less likely to conform.	Asch, 1951
Cohesiveness of the group	As cohesiveness increases, so does conformity in the group.	Crandall, 1988
Self-esteem	Those high in self-esteem are less likely to conform.	Kurosawa, 1993; Maslach, Stapp, & Santee, 1985
Gender	Males and females conform at *equal* rates but in different situations. It appears that gender-based knowledge differences account for this discrepancy.	Cacioppo & Petty, 1980; Karabenick, 1983; Sistrunk & McDavid, 1971
Knowledge/confidence about the issue or task at hand (i.e., judging lengths in Asch's experiment)	The more expert we are about the issue or task at hand, the less likely we are to conform with regard to this issue or task.	Cacioppo & Petty, 1980
Tendency to feel anxious in social situations	People who tend to feel anxious in social situations are more likely to conform.	Maslach et al., 1985
The need to be *individuated*, or individualistic and nonconforming	Those who tend to feel the need to not conform are less likely to actually conform.	Maslach et al., 1985

These appear to be some of the many factors that predict *when* we are likely to conform in particular situations, but *why* do we conform in the first place?

Explaining Conformity

After conducting his experiments, Asch *debriefed* the participants—he told them about the deception that took place in the experiment. As part of this debriefing, Asch asked his participants why they had conformed and chosen the wrong line. In general, Asch received two types of answers to this question.

Some participants indicated that they chose the wrong line even though they knew it was wrong. This type of conformity involves a change of behavior to fit a norm, but it does not involve actual attitude change or persuasion; it is called **normative conformity.** The primary motive for normative conformity seems to be a desire to fit in with the group and to be liked by others. This is one reason that cohesiveness tends to increase conformity. When we like being in the group, we want others to like us as well (Sakari, 1975). Research has shown that people in cultures that value individualism (for example, in the United States) are less likely to conform than are people from cultures that place more value on being part of a group (such as Japan; Bond & Smith, 1996; Hamilton & Sanders, 1995; Killen, Crystal, & Wantanbe, 2002). In cultures in which nonconformists are admired, you can expect to see less conformity!

Some of Asch's participants indicated motives for conforming other than wanting to be liked. Some reported that they chose the wrong line because they became convinced that it was the correct choice. These participants were actually persuaded by the

normative conformity   conformity that occurs when group members change their behavior to meet group norms but fail to be persuaded to change their beliefs and attitudes

majority group. Recall that persuasion leads to attitude change. The way these participants perceived the lines and what they believed to be true about the lines changed as a function of the majority opinion. The majority opinion *informed* these participants of what the correct choice was. For this reason, conformity that results in actual attitude change is referred to as **informational conformity.** Informational conformity is heightened when people are unsure of their opinions and insecure about their abilities (Cacioppo & Petty, 1980).

Most of us will belong to many different groups in our lifetime, and these groups will have the power to influence our behavior through conformity. It is worthwhile to look at how groups make the decisions that set up an agenda for the group.

Decision Making in Groups

Based on the old saying, "Two heads are better than one," we often seek out others when we have important decisions to make. We form committees to set policy for organizations. We choose juries to try court cases. The assumption is that important decisions are best placed in the hands of many. Ironically, psychological research indicates that in some instances our faith in the wisdom of groups may be misplaced. Group decisions are not necessarily better, more effective, or more logical than decisions made by individuals.

One factor that can contribute to poor group decisions is a condition known as **groupthink.** Groupthink occurs when a group fixates on one decision and members assume that they must be correct in their decision, without carefully examining other alternatives (Janis, 1982). When groupthink occurs, the group does not weigh all of the options, often resulting in disastrous decisions. There are a number of unfortunate historical examples of groupthink that have had dire consequences (Figure 12.5).

Nonconformists seem to enjoy breaking the norms of the majority group.

informational conformity   conformity that occurs when conformity pressures actually persuade group members to adopt new beliefs and/or attitudes

groupthink   a situation in which a group fixates on one decision, and members blindly assume that it is the correct decision

World War II
In September 1938, Adolph Hitler demanded that parts of Czechoslovakia be given to Germany. In a hastily organized conference held at Munich in October 1938, European leaders, including Germans, British, French, and Italians, decided to give in to Hitler even though it was apparent that Hitler was gaining the strength needed to formidably fight a world war (Dukier & Spielvolgel, 2004; Janus, 1982).

The Bay of Pigs
In 1961. President John F. Kennedy commited the United States to the Bay of Pigs invasion of Cuba in an attempt to overthrow Fidel Castro's regime. It was an utter failure. In fact, it *almost* led to the placement of Soviet nuclear missiles in Cuba and an escalation of the Cold War (Dukier & Spielvolgel, 2004; Janus, 1982).

The Vietnam War
In the mid-1960's, President Lyndon B. Johnson and his advisors decided to escalate U.S. involvement in Vietnam despite the growing lack of public support and intelligence reports that advised against it. Although the Johnson administration increased U.S. involvement in the war, it never fully committed U.S. forces to full-blown war with Vietnam. The result was a disasterous, unwinnable conflict (Dukier & Spielvolgel, 2004; Janus, 1982).

The *Challenger* Disaster
In 1986, NASA decided to launch the *Challenger* space shuttle despite troubling data from engineers that indicated O-rings on the rocket booster could fail. The result was the *Challenger* explosion that claimed the lives of all aboard and brought intense public and governmental scrutiny on NASA.

Figure 12.5 Some Historical Examples of Groupthink

Factors such as group isolation, group cohesiveness, strong dictatorial leadership, and stress may have contributed to these examples of groupthink.

What factors increase the likelihood of groupthink? *Group isolation, group cohesiveness, strong dictatorial leadership,* and *stress within the group* have all been implicated as factors that promote groupthink (Janis, 1985). Sometimes groups must work in isolation because the issues they are dealing with are secret or confidential. This was likely the case in most of the historical examples of groupthink given in Figure 12.5. An isolated group is unable to get information from or call on outside sources. Therefore, they are able to consider only solutions that are generated within the group. Because the group cannot consider all possible solutions, some potentially good solutions may be overlooked, and groupthink is more likely.

Group cohesiveness also contributes to groupthink. As we have seen, when a group is very cohesive, members highly value their membership in the group. When this is the case, the group's norms become powerful influences on the members' behavior. In a cohesive group, members may be hesitant to voice their objections to the prevailing group attitude because they do not want to "rock the boat." When members hesitate to voice objections, groupthink becomes more likely because potentially poor decisions are not adequately critiqued and rejected (Esser, 1998).

For the same reason, a dictatorial group leader would also facilitate groupthink. When members are afraid to disagree with a leader, they tend to go along with the leader's position, and groupthink is more likely (Shafer & Crichlow, 1996). Cohesiveness and strong, authoritarian leadership are two of the reasons gangs, such as the one Luis belonged to, tend to make poor decisions that often lead to dire consequences for individual group members. Recall that even though Luis really didn't want to go through with the firebombing of the rival gang member's home, he went along with the decision anyway and did not voice his concerns.

A final reason for groupthink is stress. When a group is making decisions under some form of duress, they may not behave in as logical a manner as they would if they were not stressed. Time pressure is one such stressor that can contribute to groupthink. When a group has a very short time in which to generate a solution to some problem, they are less likely to be able to examine all possible options, and groupthink is made more likely. Take a minute to think about the historical examples of groupthink in Figure 12.5. Which of these factors do you think contributed to groupthink in these cases?

Let's Review!

In this section, we explored groups and how they influence us. For a quick check of your understanding, answer these questions.

1. Which of the following would *not* typically increase conformity in a group?
   a. high cohesiveness among the group members
   b. unanimity of the majority
   c. anonymity of group members
   d. all of the above would increase conformity

2. Which of the following is an example of conformity?
   a. donating to a charity after receiving a request for funding in the mail
   b. driving 55 mph in a 45 mph zone
   c. wearing fashionable clothes
   d. cleaning your room because your parents ask you to clean it

3. Which of the following is probably *not* a benefit that Luis derived from being in a gang?
   a. The gang gave Luis a sense of security.
   b. The gang gave Luis a sense of social identity.
   c. The gang helped Luis gather needed information.
   d. The gang fulfilled Luis's social needs.

ANSWERS
1. c; 2. c; 3. c

Requests and Demands: >>>>>>>>>>>>>>>> Compliance and Obedience

Imagine that you answer the phone one evening and hear a telemarketer on the other end. After she identifies herself as a telemarketer, she asks you to contribute to the local police organization. How would you respond to her request? Would you agree to contribute, or would you refuse? Would you be polite, or would you hang up on her? Now compare this situation with a similar one. This time, you answer the phone and hear a police officer on the other end. After identifying herself as a local officer, she asks you to contribute to the police organization. Would you be *more* inclined to agree to the officer's request? Many people would, but why? What makes these two situations different?

One difference is the source of the request. A police officer represents an authority figure to many people. Many of us would perceive a request coming from an authority figure to be more of a demand. On the other hand, we are less likely to be intimidated by a telemarketer, and therefore we would likely perceive her request as just that, a *simple request.* Although the differences may appear to be subtle, they have great implications for how we respond to these situations. Although it's true that we often give in to simple requests, we are even more likely to give in to demands that come from perceived authority figures. Because we respond differently to requests and demands, psychologists have traditionally made a distinction between situations involving these different types of social influence. In psychological terminology, yielding to a simple request is called **compliance,** and giving in to a demand is called **obedience.** Let's begin by taking a closer look at some of the situations in which we are pressured to comply.

compliance   yielding to someone's simple request

obedience   yielding to someone's demand

Compliance Techniques

Compliance situations are very common in life. For instance, salespeople try to get us to agree to buy their products. Doctors ask us to follow their instructions. Spouses ask their partners to do household chores. Given that pressures to comply are inescapable, psychologists are interested in identifying compliance techniques that seem to work well. They also seek to understand why these techniques produce high rates of compliance. Psychologists are not the only people interested in understanding compliance. Marketers and other professionals also want to understand compliance so that they can create more effective campaigns for changing public behavior. For example, research on direct-mail (e.g., catalog) marketing, often centers on effective use of compliance techniques (e.g., Weyant, 1996). It's a good idea for us to become familiar with compliance techniques because others will be using them on us.

 Application

Foot-in-the-Door Compliance

Suppose a friend asks to borrow a dollar and you comply. Later, if that same friend asks you to lend them $5, would it be harder to refuse the request because you had previously lent him or her the dollar? Research on compliance suggests that it would. Once a person gets a foot in the door, so to speak, by getting us to comply with a small request, it seems to open that door to getting us to comply with another, larger, request. In a classic experiment on **foot-in-the door compliance,** researchers approached some homes and asked the person answering the door to sign a petition to promote safe driving. Other homes in the neighborhood were also selected by the researchers to participate in the study, but they were not approached at this time. Two weeks later, the researchers returned to the neighborhood and approached the homes they had previously visited as well as the homes that were not visited on the first day. This time, the

foot-in-the-door compliance   increasing compliance by first asking the person to give in to a smaller request that paves the way for further compliance

Compliance techniques, like foot-in-the-door, door-in-the-face, and reciprocity, can be used to increase charitable donations.

door-in-the-face compliance increasing compliance by first asking the person to give in to a very larger request and after their refusal, asking them to give in to a smaller request

reciprocity a strong norm that states that we should treat others as they treat us

researchers asked if they could put up a huge billboard that said "Drive Carefully" in the front yard. The data showed that those people who had complied with the first request to sign the petition were most likely to comply with the request for the billboard (Freedman & Fraser, 1966). Similarly, researchers in Israel found that people who had previously signed a petition for a specific charity were more likely to agree to donate money to the charity at a later date (Schwarzwald, Bizman, & Raz, 1983). It appears that giving in to a small request paves the way for us to give in to a larger request.

Why does foot-in-the-door compliance work? One explanation for this technique's effectiveness is that our general desire to behave in a consistent fashion makes it hard for us to refuse subsequent requests. When you give in to the initial small request, your self-image changes ever so slightly. Having already complied, you are now the type of person who complies with requests made by this person or group. Because your self-image has changed, you now feel compelled to behave consistently with this new self-image. Recall that to not act in accordance with one's attitudes would likely produce *dissonance*. So when the person or group makes a subsequent request, to deny it would mean going against one's self-image and perhaps feeling dissonance. Therefore, compliance is more likely. When a clever manipulator does get a person to give in on a small matter, it does indeed seem to lead to future compliance (Cialdini, 2001; Girandola, 2002).

Door-in-the-Face Compliance

The opposite of the foot-in-the-door approach also seems to lead to high rates of compliance. In this technique, called **door-in-the-face compliance,** a very large request is made followed by a smaller target request. For example, researchers asked college students whether they would agree to commit to volunteering 2 hours a week for the next 2 years in a program to help juvenile delinquents. As you might guess, all the students declined. Then the researchers asked if the students would be willing to volunteer to take the juveniles to the zoo for a couple of hours. A full 50% of the students agreed to take the trip to the zoo *after* they had refused to volunteer weekly. This number was significantly higher than the 17% of students in a control group who agreed after being asked only whether they would take the trip to the zoo (Cialdini, Vincent, Catalan, Wheeler, & Darby, 1975). It appears that if we figuratively "slam the door" in the face of a person's request, we are more likely to comply if she makes a more reasonable request later. Why should this be the case?

There are several explanations for door-in-the-face compliance. One centers on the *perceptual contrast* between the two requests. After the extremity of the first request, the second, smaller, request may seem more reasonable to you than if it had been the only request you had faced. Research shows that perceptual contrast explains part, but not all, of door-in-the-face compliance (Cialdini et al., 1975).

Another explanation for door-in-the-face compliance centers on **reciprocity,** a very strong norm in many cultures (Mowen & Cialdini, 1980). Reciprocity is a norm in which we expect others to reciprocate our behaviors. For example, if you do something nice for someone else, you expect that the person will, in turn, do something nice for you. If you are cruel to another, then you do not expect the person to be especially kind toward you. This notion of reciprocity explains in part why we feel more obligated to comply in a door-in-the-face situation than to a single request. In a door-in-the-face situation, after you refuse the initial request, the requester then concedes the initial position and makes a more reasonable request. Because the requester has made a concession, we feel as though we must reciprocate and also make a concession. The easiest way to do this is to comply with the second request. If we don't make this concession, then we may feel as if we are breaking an important social norm!

A third explanation of door-in-the-face compliance is emotional. Some researchers (e.g., O'Keefe & Figge, 1997) propose that when we turn down the initial large request, we feel negative emotions, such as guilt. Because we do not enjoy feeling bad, we look for a way to reduce these negative emotions. With the opportunity to comply when a second, more reasonable, request is presented, we are more likely to comply to relieve our guilt and make ourselves feel better (Millar, 2002).

The research on compliance shows that we are fairly likely to give in to simple requests from others. What happens when others do more than make a simple request—how do we respond to demands for obedience?

Obedience

Application

In the aftermath of the Holocaust, the people of the world were astounded and horrified as the details of the Nazis' destruction became public. By most estimates, the Nazis' "Final Solution," as they called it, took the lives of 5 to 6 million Jews, as well as the lives of approximately 9 to 10 million other Europeans whom Adolph Hitler and the Nazis deemed unworthy of life (Duiker & Spielvogel, 2004). Many people found these numbers and the extremely grisly details of the death camps incomprehensible. What kind of person would carry out orders to send thousands of defenseless men, women, and children to die in gas chambers? Were the Nazis successful in their attempt to commit genocide because they recruited legions of sadistic, criminally insane people to do their bidding in the death camps? Or could it be that some of the people working in the camps were fairly normal, everyday people who gave in to extreme forms of social influence? In other words, is it possible that the *average* person could be influenced to hurt others if an authority figure gave orders to do so? This is the question Stanley Milgram at Yale University set out to answer in a series of famous experiments he conducted on obedience during the 1960s.

To test his ideas about obedience and the average person, Stanley Milgram ran an ad in a New Haven, Connecticut, newspaper that solicited participants for an experiment that would investigate the role of punishment in learning. In actuality, the experiment would measure the participants' willingness to obey an order to administer a very painful electric shock to another person. The participants weren't told this until *after* the experiment was over. As far as the participants knew, they were participating in a study on learning, not obedience.

In all, 40 men participated in Milgram's first study (Milgram, 1963). These men ranged from 20 to 50 years of age, and they represented a variety of professions, including teachers, engineers, and postal clerks. All of the men were paid $4.50 (approximately $30 in today's money) for their participation *before* the experiment began.

When they arrived at the lab, the participants were told that they would be playing the role of a teacher in the experiment. As the teacher, their job would be to administer electric shocks, using an apparatus that delivered shocks from 15 volts to 450 volts, to a participant playing the role of the learner (Figure 12.6). The learner was supposed to learn a list of words, and the teachers were told that the purpose of the experiment was to see whether the shocks would improve the learner's rate of learning. In actuality the learner was a confederate, an actor who only pretended to be shocked, but the participants did not know this until after the experiment ended.

During the procedure, the experimenter, a 31-year-old high school biology teacher dressed in a lab coat, stood slightly behind the seated teacher. Throughout the experiment, the teacher and learner communicated via an intercom system, but they did not have visual contact. The teacher was

Figure 12.6 The Apparatus Used by Milgram in His Famous Obedience Studies How far would you go before you refused to obey?

instructed to read a list of words to the learner via the intercom, and then to listen as the learner recalled the words from memory. Every time the learner made a mistake, the teacher was told to deliver a shock to the learner by flipping one of the switches on the apparatus. The procedure began with the 15-volt switch, and the teacher was instructed to move progressively up the scale toward the 450-volt switch as the learner made more and more mistakes.

Stanley Milgram was primarily interested in seeing how far up the scale the teachers would go before they refused to obey orders to shock the learner further. At the 300-volt mark, the learner began to pound on the wall as if in great pain, protesting the continued shocking. At this point, most participants began to question the experimenter as to whether they should continue to shock the learner, who was obviously in pain. The teachers began to show clear signs of distress, including shaking, stuttering, sweating, nervous laughter, and biting their lips and fingernails. The teachers often protested verbally and indicated that they didn't feel good about continuing to shock the learner.

In response to such displays and protests, the experimenter merely calmly prodded the participants to continue with the procedure. The experimenter never yelled. He never made verbal or physical threats. He never threatened to take away their $4.50. The experimenter merely requested that the participants continue following orders. The strongest statement by the experimenter was, "You have no other choice, you must go on" (Milgram, 1963, p. 374).

After the 315-volt mark, the learner fell completely silent and unresponsive, as if he had lost consciousness or was injured. Because the learner missed all the words on the trial by not responding, the experimenter instructed the teacher to continue delivering the shocks. At this point, it is likely that the teacher believed that he was being asked to shock an injured—or even unconscious—man! What would you do in this situation? What do you think the teachers did? Did they confirm Milgram's hypothesis that the average person is willing to follow orders even when it means hurting others? Or do you think they rebelled and refused to obey?

The results of Milgram's study were nothing short of shocking. A full 65% of the teachers continued to shock the learner all the way up to the 450-volt mark. Despite believing the learner to be ill or worse, most of the teachers continued to follow the experimenter's orders. Even Stanley Milgram was somewhat surprised by his findings. Prior to the experiment, Milgram had surveyed psychology students and behavioral science professionals to get a feel for how many participants they thought would go all the way to 450 volts (Milgram, 1963, 1974). Most people believed that only 1–3% would. The results showed, of course, a very different picture. Over half did go all the way to 450 volts, and no participant refused to obey before the 300-volt mark had been reached! Figure 12.7 shows the distribution of maximum shock intensities delivered by the teachers (Milgram, 1963).

Are these results for real? Would the *average* person really go all the way to 450 volts? As you might imagine, a great deal of skepticism was generated by Milgram's findings. Some questioned whether the participants in Milgram's (1963) study were abnormal in some way. To answer such skepticism and to further investigate the variables that affect the rate of obedience, Milgram repeated his procedure on different participants. He replicated the study in another town (Bridgeport, CT) and found similar results (Milgram, 1965). Milgram also conducted the study using female participants and found high rates of obedience (Milgram, 1974).

Other researchers have since replicated Milgram's findings. High school students were found to be even *more* willing to obey orders (Rosenhan, 1969). Cross-cultural research in other Western cultures has also yielded high rates of obedience using Milgram's procedure (Triandis, 1994). Unfortunately, it seems as though Milgram's

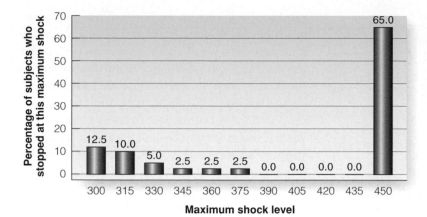

Figure 12.7 Maximum Shocks Delivered to the Learner by Milgram's Participants

Twenty-six out of the forty participants went all the way to the 450-volt level!

Based on Table 2, p. 376 "Behavioral Study of Obedience" by Stanley Milgram in Journal of Abnormal and Social Psychology, *67, p. 371–378, © 1963. Used by permission.*

results were not flukes. So what accounts for our tendency to obey such orders to hurt another?

Factors That Affect Obedience

One factor that contributed to the high rate of obedience in the Milgram studies was the presence of a perceived *authority figure*. During the procedure, the experimenter, dressed in a lab coat and looking official, stood close by the participant and issued orders to deliver the shocks. Authority figures work in two ways to ensure obedience. First, the fact that the authority figure is ultimately in charge may seem to relieve the person following orders from responsibility for his actions. A person can always tell himself that he was only following orders. Second, the presence of official-looking authority figures tends to intimidate us, and we are therefore more likely to obey their orders (Bushman, 1988). Sometimes it makes sense to be intimidated by authority figures. Recall what happened to Luis after he refused to give his complete allegiance to the gang. The leaders of the gang sent him a very clear message (with bullets!) that there would be serious consequences for those who disobeyed. If you perceive that authority figures can observe your behavior and that you may suffer negative consequences for disobeying, you might obey out of fear alone.

In later experiments, Milgram found that he could reduce obedience in his participants by increasing the physical distance between the experimenter and the teacher. If the experimenter was not physically present to watch the teacher's behavior, the teachers were much less likely to obey the orders to shock the participant. Table 12.5 ◆ summarizes some of the later experimental manipulations that Milgram (1965) used to test variables that affect rates of obedience. From Table 12.5, you can see that when the experimenter telephoned his orders to the teachers, obedience dropped to a mere 27.5%.

Another reason for the high rates of obedience in Milgram's studies is the *timing of the requests* made by the experimenter. When the participants arrived at the lab, they very quickly found themselves faced with orders from an authority figure to shock another human being. Because the orders began almost immediately after the participants arrived, they did not have much time to think about their actions. As we saw earlier, when we do not have time to think things through, we are more susceptible to persuasive attempts.

Another factor that contributed to high rates of obedience was the fact that the shock levels were increased incrementally. In essence, Milgram's procedure was a textbook example of foot-in-the-door compliance in action. The first orders were for the teachers to deliver a 15-volt shock, a mere tingle compared to the final shock level of 450 volts! Few people would have qualms about following an order to deliver an almost

◆ **Table 12.5**

Some Experimental Conditions in Milgram's Experiments and Their Resultant Rates of Obedience

Experimental Manipulation	Percentage of Subjects Who Obeyed All the Way to the 450-Volt Level
The learner was seated in the same room with the teacher.	40%
The teacher had to hold the learner's hand down on the shock plate.	30%
The experimenter delivered his orders via telephone instead of in person	27.5%
The teacher was tested with two *confederates* who pretended to be subjects also playing the role of teacher. Halfway through the experiment, the two confederate "teachers" refuse to shock the learner any further.	10% of the participants continued to obey after the confederates refused to further shock the learner.
The teacher was tested with two *confederates* who pretended to be participants also playing the role of teacher. One of the confederate teachers was the one who actually flipped the switch to shock the learner. The real participant merely played an auxiliary role in the shocking of the learner.	92.5%
Female participants played the role of the teacher.	65%

From Milgram, 1965.

slippery slope the use of foot-in-the-door compliance in an obedience situation to get people to obey increasing demands

psychological distance the degree to which one can disassociate oneself from the consequences of his/her actions

destructive obedience obedience to immoral, unethical demands that cause harm to others

painless shock, so why not obey? What the participants did not know was that by obeying the order to deliver the 15-volt shock, they were paving the way for their own obedience to further orders to shock the learner! Every time the participants obeyed an order to shock, it became harder for them to refuse to continue. Some have likened this type of incremental obedience to standing on a **slippery slope.** Once you begin to obey, it's like beginning to slide down the slope. The farther you go, the more momentum you gain, and the harder it is to stop obeying. If Milgram's procedure had begun with an order to deliver the potentially dangerous shock of 450 volts, it is unlikely that he would have obtained such high rates of obedience. Similarly, if Luis had been asked to participate in a firebombing immediately after he joined the gang, it's likely that he would have refused. However, after years of giving in to many smaller requests from the gang, he was more likely to be obedient—so despite his better judgment, he went along with the bombing.

A final factor that affects obedience is the **psychological distance** we feel between our actions and the results of those actions. In Milgram's first experiment (Milgram, 1963), the teacher could not see the learner during the procedure. In this type of condition, psychological distance is large, meaning that it was relatively easy for the teachers to not think about the consequences of their actions. If you don't think about the consequences of your actions, then you don't have to consciously come to terms with and take responsibility for those actions. This allows you to obey even in situations in which your actions may harm others.

In one dramatic experiment, Milgram had the teacher and learner sit side by side during the procedure. In this variation of the experiment, the teacher had to reach over and hold the learner's hand down on the shock plate! As you might guess, this procedure dramatically reduced the psychological distance for the teacher. It's hard to dissociate yourself from the consequences of your actions when you're actually touching your victim! Under these conditions, only 30% of the participants delivered the maximum 450-volt shock. Note, however, that although obedience was more than cut in half by reducing the psychological distance, obedience was *not* eliminated. Almost one-third of the participants still continued to obey the experimenter despite these conditions.

As you read about Stanley Milgram's research, you may have found yourself troubled by what you read. Certainly Milgram provided the world with disturbing evidence of our willingness to obey authority figures. Based on Milgram's findings, it would appear that the average person has the capacity to obey orders even when doing so hurts others. Some researchers have termed this type of obedience **destructive obedience** to distinguish it from obedience that does not lead to harming others. Certainly there are many instances in which obedience is a good thing. For instance, we want people to obey the laws of our society, or else chaos would ensue. Therefore, you should not conclude from Milgram's studies that all obedience is bad.

Another aspect of Milgram's work that may have bothered you is the obvious discomfort Milgram inflicted on his research participants. As we mentioned earlier, during the procedure, his participants did exhibit many forms of stress-related behaviors. Their obvious discomfort indicated that they did, in fact, believe that they were hurting the learner. The fact that Milgram used *deception* to convince his participants that they were hurting another person has been heavily criticized by other psychologists (e.g., Baumrind, 1964).

Milgram did **debrief** his participants afterward, explaining that they had never actually hurt the learner and that the purpose of the experiment was to study obedience and not learning. Recall our discussion of ethics in psychological research from Chapter 1 (p. 35) and the ethical mandate that all human participants in psychological experiments should leave the experiment in *at least as good a condition as they were prior to the experiment*. Critics maintain that the participants left the Milgram studies knowing that they were capable of hurting another human being simply because they were told to do so. This is not a very positive thing to learn about oneself. Additionally, critics have asserted that exposing participants to the trauma of the procedure itself was an ethical violation of their rights (Baumrind, 1964). Today, at most universities in the United States, it would be virtually impossible to get approval to do an experiment such as Milgram's because of the possible ethical problems associated with it. Modern psychologists are extremely protective of the rights of research participants.

Despite the criticisms, Milgram's work remains one of the most powerful statements ever made about human behavior. Aside from demonstrating our obedience to authority, Milgram's work also brings up some important and perhaps frightening questions about basic human nature. For instance, how can psychologists explain the tendency of some people to behave aggressively? We will look at this issue next when we ask, "What causes aggression?" Don't get too depressed, though. Humans also have great capacity for goodness. Before this chapter is finished, we will also look at the positive side of human nature.

debrief   a procedure in which experiment participants are told the true purpose of an experiment, informed of any deception in the experiment, and given the chance to ask questions

Let's Review!

In this section we examined the social influence that occurs in compliance and obedience. As a quick check of your understanding, answer these questions.

1. You want your friend to lend you $50. If you want to use the door-in-the-face compliance technique to ensure that your friend will comply with your request, what should you do?
   a. First ask for $1,000 before asking for the $50.
   b. First ask for $10 before asking for the $50.
   c. Wash your friend's car before you ask for the $50.
   d. Tell your friend that you will pay the money back in 1 week.

2. In Milgram's original experiment, what percentage of participants went all the way to 450 volts when "shocking" the learner?
   a. 35%   c. 65%
   b. 55%   d. 75%

3. Which of the following compliance techniques best explains Milgram's findings in his study on obedience?
   a. foot-in-the-door   c. reciprocity
   b. door-in-the-face   d. low-balling

ANSWERS
1. a; 2. c; 3. a

LEARNING OBJECTIVE < < < < < < < <

Discuss the factors that affect our tendency to behave aggressively.

instrumental aggression aggression used to facilitate the attainment of one's goals

hostile aggression aggression that is meant to cause harm to others

Application >>

Instrumental aggression is aimed at satisfying some goal. This child is being aggressive to obtain a toy.

Aggression

Psychologists define aggression as an action that is intended to somehow cause harm to another person who does not want to be harmed (Baron & Richardson, 1992; Brehm, Kassin, & Fein, 2002; Huesmann, 1994). Aggressive acts can be classified as being *instrumental* or *hostile*. **Instrumental aggression** is aimed at satisfying some goal. For example, a child might hit a playmate to distract her while the child takes away her toy. **Hostile aggression,** on the other hand, is motivated solely by the desire to hurt others. For example, a bully may punch another child on the playground just to see the child cry.

Although both types of aggression are widespread in many cultures, the overall prevalence of aggression varies across cultures. Among developed countries, the United States is considered to be an aggressive society (c.f. Osterman et al., 1994). Pick up a major American metropolitan newspaper on any given day of the week, and you will see abundant evidence of this trend in the daily crime reports. In the first 6 months of 2003, New York City, Los Angeles, Chicago, and Dallas reported a combined total of 973 murders and many more rapes, assaults, and robberies (Federal Bureau of Investigation, 2003).

Aside from the almost daily reports of violent crime in the United States, it appears that even noncriminals have aggression on their minds. Researchers surveyed 312 college students at a U.S. university about whether they had ever thought about killing someone. Seventy-three percent of male students and 66% of female students reported that they had (Kenrick & Sheets, 1993)! What could account for such numbers? Could aggressive feelings be more natural than we like to think?

Biological Theories of Aggression: The Role of Sex-Hormones, Neurotransmitters, and Brain Damage

It has been widely documented that among many species, including humans, males tend to be more aggressive than females (e.g., Eagly & Steffen, 1986). In 2002, males accounted for 82.6% of those arrested for murder, and they were also almost four times more likely to be the victim of a murder (Federal Bureau of Investigation, 2002). Because males have more of the hormone testosterone in their bodies, researchers have long suspected that testosterone and aggressive behavior are related. But the research on the relationship between aggression and testosterone has yielded a somewhat confusing picture. Sometimes higher levels of testosterone are associated with higher levels of aggression in animals (Wagner, Bueving, & Hutchinson, 1980), and sometimes they are not (Eaton & Resko, 1974). Likewise, human studies sometimes show a correlation between high testosterone levels and aggression (Dabbs & Morris, 1990; Van Goozen, Frijda, & de Poll, 1994), and sometimes they fail to find a clear relationship (Archer, Birring, & Wu, 1998; Tremblay, et al., 1998).

Even if the correlation between testosterone and aggressive behavior were more consistent in the literature, it would still be difficult to determine the actual cause(s) of aggressive behavior. Recall that *correlation does not imply causation*. Higher levels of testosterone are associated with muscularity and strength, which may simply give one the ability to be a bully. Some researchers have found that in adolescent boys, aggression is correlated with physical size, but *not* correlated with levels of testosterone (Tremblay et al., 1998).

A Possible Role for Serotonin

Research has also suggested that another chemical, serotonin, may also play a role in regulation of aggressive behavior (Liberstat & Pflueger, 2004). Researchers measured levels of the neurotransmitter *serotonin* in the bloodstream of three groups of people:

survivors of suicide attempts, people institutionalized since childhood for aggressive behavior, and a normal control group (Marazzitti, et al., 1993). They found that the suicide survivors and the aggressive patients had *lower* levels of serotonin when compared to the normal control group.

Low levels of serotonin are associated with diseases like *obsessive-compulsive disorder*, in which the person has difficulty controlling his or her behavior and feels compelled to repeat certain actions (Chapter 15, p. 669). If we extend this thinking to the relationship between serotonin and aggression, we can speculate that people with lowered levels of serotonin may have difficulty in controlling their aggressive impulses toward themselves (as in suicide) and toward others (as in the institutionalized patients). However, more research will be needed before any firm conclusions can be drawn about the role of serotonin in aggression.

Childhood Abuse and Aggression

Another connection between biology and aggression comes from research into the backgrounds of incarcerated criminals. During the 1980s and 1990s, psychiatrist Dorothy Otnow Lewis interviewed over 100 murderers in attempt to discover whether they had experienced physical abuse as children (Lewis, 1992). During these interviews, Lewis discovered that an overwhelming majority of these murderers had suffered extreme abuse during childhood. In particular, many had suffered severe head injuries as a result of the abuse, which led Lewis and her colleagues to hypothesize that the murderers' aggressive tendencies may have resulted from brain damage (Lewis, Picus, Feldman, Jackson, & Bard, 1986).

More recent research seems to reinforce Lewis's notions. It is now thought that childhood abuse and neglect are related to the development of several brain abnormalities. Using some of the techniques for studying the brain that we discussed in Chapter 2 (such as, EEG, MRI, and fMRI), researchers have found that childhood abuse and neglect correlate with having structural abnormalities in the amygdala, hippocampus, corpus callosum, left frontal lobe, left temporal lobe, and cerebellum (Teicher, 2002).

Virtually no one would disagree that an end to child abuse would be great for society. Aside from a possible link between aggression and the physical damage caused by child abuse and later aggression, psychologists have other reasons to fear the destructive influence of child abuse. An aggressive model, such as an aggressive, punitive parent, or a violent TV character, can teach a child to be aggressive.

Learning Theories of Aggression

In Chapter 5, we described Albert Bandura's *Bobo doll* experiments, in which children who watched an adult model beat up a plastic Bobo doll were likely to mimic the model's aggression when later left alone with the doll (Bandura, Ross, & Ross, 1963). After being exposed to an *aggressive model*, the children acquired new and aggressive behaviors. Many psychologists believe that aggression is often learned through this type of *social learning*. For a child like Luis, growing up in a neighborhood dominated by gangs and violence, becoming a gang member may seem to the child to be the natural thing to do. Gang life may be perceived as "normal" for a child who has been exposed to only that sort of model.

However, exposure to violence and aggression may promote more than mere modeling of aggressive behavior. Such exposure may actually influence the cognitive, emotional, and behavioral responses we have to events in our daily lives. One model of aggression, the *cognitive neoassociation theory*, proposes that cues present during an aggressive event can become associated in memory with the thoughts and emotions you experience during that event (Anderson & Bushman, 2002; Berkowitz, 1990). For example, if you see many instances (real or televised) in which people use guns to shoot and hurt those who have humiliated them, you may begin to associate concepts from these events in your memory. You may begin to associate guns with *anger, hurt, fear,* and *humiliation*—or conflict with *shooting.* Because these concepts become tightly linked in memory, activation of one of them can *prime* (Chapter 6, p. 255) other related concepts and cause them to become active. In other words, merely seeing a gun may cause you to have aggressive thoughts and being humiliated may tend to activate feelings of anger and the desire to use a gun to retaliate against those who hurt you. Indeed, research participants have been shown to have aggressive thoughts after simply being shown pictures of weapons (Anderson, Benjamin, & Bartholow, 1998).

If our behavior is heavily influenced by the cues we perceive to be associated with aggression and violence in our world, then the nature of such perceptions is very important. Given that many of our ideas about the world are influenced by the media, it is worthwhile to ask the question, Does television portray violence and its consequences accurately?

Violence and Television

Application

TV has been shown to portray many aspects of life unrealistically, including marriage (Segrin & Nabi, 2002), the medical profession (Chory-Assad & Tamborini, 2001), and violence. One study reported a total of 2,126 antisocial acts in 65.5 hours of so-called reality television programming, or shows that are supposed to document real life, like *Cops* and *Rescue 911.* The problem is that these "reality shows" do not give an accurate picture of real life. They portray acts of aggression at rates that are far above the actual rates at which they occur in U.S. society (Potter et al., 1997).

Even more disturbing is that many televised acts of aggression are ones in which the aggressor experiences no negative repercussions for his or her actions. Criminals and other aggressors often go unpunished on TV, and victims are typically not shown to suffer realistic consequences as a result of their victimization. Movies and television shows often do not accurately show the physical pain, mental anguish, and economic costs victims suffer. In 1996, a report sponsored by the National Cable Television Association indicated that perpetrators go unpunished in 73% of all violent scenes on TV and that only 16% of all violent acts on TV portrayed long-term negative consequences of violence for the victim. Worse yet, the genre that was least likely to portray the long-term consequences of aggression was children's programming (Mediascope, Inc., 1996)! These figures indicate that not only is television programming violent, it may also leave children with the false impression that aggression often goes unpunished and that victims do not really suffer painful consequences. These false impressions may increase the likelihood that children will actually model the behavior they see on TV (Bandura, 1965; Hogben, 1998).

Are these children learning to be aggressive as they watch television?

© PHOTICK/IndexStock

Situations That Promote Aggressive Behavior

When are you most likely to behave aggressively? Are there circumstances in which you might behave in a physically aggressive manner toward another? What would it take? One key factor in aggression appears to be frustration. According to the **frustration-aggression hypothesis** (Dollard, Doob, Miller, Mowrer, & Sears, 1939), when we become frustrated, we activate a motive to harm other people or objects. These motives are likely to be directed at those people or objects that we perceive to be the source of our frustration. For example, most abusive parents never *intend* to threaten or harm their children. But in the heat of the moment some parents take out their frustration on their children. Parents in high-stress situations—such as extreme

frustration-aggression hypothesis the idea that frustration causes aggressive behavior

poverty—who do not have good coping skills are most at risk for becoming abusive (Garbarino, 1997). Recall from Chapter 8 that motives drive and catalyze behavior. Consequently, when we are frustrated, our chances of behaving aggressively increase. Therefore, during stressful, frustrating situations, we have to be on guard for possible aggressive behavior in ourselves and in others.

Let's Review!

In this section, we explored the nature of aggression. As a quick check of your understanding, answer these questions.

1. Which neurotransmitter has been implicated as possibly playing a role in aggressive behavior?

   a. testosterone   c. dopamine

   b. serotonin   d. estrogen

2. Road rage incidents are more likely to occur in heavy traffic. This fact can *best* be explained due to the increase in _____ that occurs among drivers in heavy traffic.

   a. frustration   c. fear

   b. fatigue   d. anxiety

3. Little Sabina wants to play with her sister's doll, but her sister will not let Sabina have the doll. So Sabina hits her sister and takes the doll away while her sister cries. Sabina's behavior is *best* characterized as an example of _____.

   a. hostile aggression   c. biological aggression

   b. instrumental aggression   d. learned aggression

ANSWERS

1. b; 2. a; 3. b

Helping Behavior: >>>>>>>>>>>>>>>>>>>>>>>> Will You, or Won't You?

LEARNING OBJECTIVE

Discuss helping behavior, and the factors that influence helping, including the bystander effect.

By now you might be thinking that humans are pretty rotten creatures. We seem to be easily biased against others, easily influenced by others, aggressive, and even easily convinced to do real harm to others. In fact, humans are often very generous as well. Sometimes we even demonstrate **altruism**, or a willingness to help others without considering any possible benefit for ourselves. Just as we have the capacity for violence, we also have the capacity for kindness and compassion.

altruism   helping another without being motivated by self-gain

The Murder of Kitty Genovese

As was the case with the study of obedience, the psychological study of altruism, or **helping behavior,** was prompted by a tragedy, the murder of Kitty Genovese in New York City on March 13, 1964. Kitty Genovese, age 28, was returning to her apartment in Queens at 3:20 A.M. when she was approached and murdered by a man in a prolonged assault that lasted 30 minutes. During the attack, Kitty's screams and pleas for help awakened 38 of her neighbors. But, remarkably, not *one* of these people called the police while Kitty was being attacked. Only after the attack, when Kitty was dead, did one man finally phone the police.

People reacted with shock and outrage when they learned that so many people had heard the attack on Kitty Genovese and failed to call the police. When many of the 38 witnesses were interviewed, they explained their inaction by saying, "I didn't want to get involved." Even the man who finally called the police first called a friend for

Application

helping behavior   another term for altruism

Humans do often come to the aid of others.

© Tom Stewart/Corbis

advice because he was so afraid of getting involved (Mohr, 1964). What explains the behavior of these witnesses? Are most people so callous and unconcerned that they would let someone die right before their eyes without lifting a finger to help?

Researchers who have studied helping behavior (Latané & Darley, 1969) find that apathy or lack of concern is not the reason that people fail to help in situations like the Genovese murder. Research indicates that deciding whether or not to help someone is not necessarily a single decision, nor is it a simple decision to make. You must first *notice* that something out of the ordinary is occurring. Second, you must correctly *interpret* the situation as one that requires your aid. It is very possible that some of those who heard Kitty Genovese's cries did not realize that they were anything other than the normal sounds of a New York City street at night. Third, you must feel that you have a *responsibility* to intervene in the situation. Some of the 38 witnesses may have believed that someone else was coming to Kitty Genovese's aid. Fourth, you must decide *how to help* the person in distress. If you don't know what to do, you cannot offer help to someone in need. And, finally, you must *implement* your helping strategy, and actually help the person in need.

The Bystander Effect

Because deciding to help is a multistep process, failure can occur at any of the five steps. Early studies of helping behavior focused on responsibility and the thought processes that might contribute to one person feeling responsibile to help another in need. Researchers Bibb Latané and John Darley hypothesized what they called the **bystander effect.** As the number of bystanders *increases* in an emergency situation, the probability that any one of the bystanders will actually intervene *decreases*. To test their theory, Latané and Darley conducted a number of experiments (Latané & Darley, 1969). In one study, participants worked on a questionnaire either alone or in the presence of two other people. Halfway through the questionnaire, smoke began to filter into the room through a wall vent, as if there was a fire nearby. The dependent variable in the study was whether or not the participant got up to investigate the source of the smoke and how quickly he or she did so. The results of this experiment supported the idea of the bystander effect. When participants were in the room alone, 75% of them got up to investigate the source of the smoke. When there were two other people in the room, only 10% of the participants got up to investigate. It appears that even when you may be helping yourself, the presence of other bystanders can reduce your tendency to help! Why would this be the case?

Explaining the Bystander Effect

One explanation for the bystander effect is **diffusion of responsibility,** or the idea that all bystanders *equally* share the responsibility for helping in an emergency. To put this into perspective, each of the 38 witnesses would have borne $\frac{1}{38}$ of the responsibility for helping Kitty Genovese. Therefore as the number of bystanders *decreases*, the amount of responsibility any one bystander bears *increases*. When you are the only witness, you bear all of the responsibility for helping. So what can you do if you need help and there are several bystanders present? You can reduce the bystander effect by clearly identifying one bystander and requesting his or her help. By singling out one person,

bystander effect the idea that the more witnesses there are to an emergency, the less likely any one of them is to offer help

diffusion of responsibility the idea that the responsibility for taking action is diffused across all people witnessing an event

you eliminate the diffusion of responsibility, placing all of the responsibility on that one person. Remembering this could save your life someday!

Diffusion of responsibility is not the only factor that prevents people from helping others. Another possible explanation for a bystander's failure to help is **pluralistic ignorance,** or the failure of a group of witnesses to perceive there is a problem that requires their help (Latané & Darley, 1969). When the 38 witnesses saw each other doing nothing to help Kitty, this lack of action and excitement on the part of the other witnesses may have caused the individual witnesses to inaccurately perceive that Kitty did not need help (Sexton, 1995). In other words, when we see that others are not interpreting a situation as an emergency, we are less likely to interpret the situation as an emergency, and therefore we are less likely to help.

pluralistic ignorance   the idea that we use the behavior of other witnesses to help us determine whether a situation is really an emergency that requires our help; if no one else is helping, we may conclude that help isn't needed

A New Twist on the Bystander Effect: Taking Care of Our Own

Researchers now believe that the number of witnesses to an emergency is only one factor that influences helping. There are several other variables that have been shown to impact helping behavior. Table 12.6 ◆ summarizes these variables and some of the relevant studies that have been done on these variables. As you read through Table 12.6, you'll notice that unfortunately all people are not equally likely to receive help.

Interestingly, whether or not a victim receives help may be influenced by the degree to which the bystander sees the victim as belonging to the bystander's in-group (see p. 540). In a very recent study, Mark Levine and Kirstien Thompson (2004) tested a *social categorization theory* of helping behavior, which predicts that you are most likely to help another when you *perceive* that they belong to the same in-group as you do. To test this, Levine and Thompson used British research participants who belong to two major in-groups—being British and being part of the European Union (EU). The participants were randomly divided into two groups: a British identity group and a European identity group. In the British group, participants were reminded of their British identity when the researchers placed a color copy of the British flag on the cover of their research questionnaire. In the European identity group, participants were reminded of their European identity with a picture of the European Union flag on the cover of their questionnaire. These flags served to make the participants focus on particular aspects of their own in-group membership (i.e., being British or European). The questionnaires that were attached to the cover sheets contained two scenarios that described natural disasters (floods and earthquakes) in Europe and in South America. After reading about the disasters in these places, the participants were asked to rate their willingness to give financial support to the victims of the disasters.

Consistent with the social categorization theory, Levine and Thompson found that the British identity group did not differ with respect to its willingness to help Europeans or South Americans, presumably because both types of victims were perceived as out-group members. The European identity group, however, was found to be more willing to help victims of the European disaster (in-group members) and less willing to aid the South Americans (out-group members). And most interestingly, the European identity group was more willing than the British identity group to help victims of a European disaster. Although Britain is part of the EU, when one is focused on her "Britishness," Europeans from the other countries in Europe are less likely to be perceived as in-group members—therefore the British identity participants were less willing to help European victims.

What's important in this study is that the same place and people (Europeans in Europe) can be defined as an in-group or an out-group simply by manipulating which aspect of the bystander's identity (British or European) is activated in memory. Britain is a part of the EU, and as such the British belong to the same in-group as Europeans—

◆ **Table 12.6**

Variables That Affect Helping Behavior and Some Relevant Research

Variable	Description	Some Relevant Studies
Level of bystander's hurry	Bystanders who are in a hurry are less likely to stop and help someone in distress.	Darley & Batson, 1973
Bystander's relationship to other bystanders	When bystanders are friends, they are more likely to help a stranger in need.	Latané & Darley, 1969; Rutkowski, Gruder, & Romer, 1983
Relationship between the victim and the bystander	A bystander who knows the victim is more likely to help.	Latané & Darley, 1969
Bystander's perceived ambiguity	If the situation is ambiguous, bystanders will tend to see it as a nonemergency and therefore be less likely to help.	Macrae & Milne, 1992; Wilson & Petruska, 1984
Bystander's fear for his or her own safety	If bystanders are afraid they will be harmed, they are less likely to help.	McGuire, 1994
Bystander's prejudice against the victim or belief that the victim is an out-group member	Bystanders who are prejudiced against the victim or see the victim as an out-group member will be less likely to help.	Shaw, Borough, & Fink, 1994; Levine & Thompson, 2004
Victim's level of dependency	Bystanders are more likely to help victims they perceive to be dependent—for example, a child.	Bornstein, 1994
Responsibility of the victim for his or her plight	Bystanders are less likely to offer help if they perceive the emergency to be the victim's own fault.	Weiner, 1980

but when it comes to helping, it appears that actual group membership is not as important as *perceived* group membership. We are most likely to help victims from our ingroup when we have reason to focus on the fact that we are indeed members of the same group. In other words, we do tend to take care of our own, but who we perceive to be "our own" can vary across situations.

The results of this experiment may have implications for all of us. If we are more willing to help people who belong to our own in-groups, then one way to facilitate helping might be to encourage people to see others as belonging to their in-group. For example, during times of racial unrest like the L.A. riots following the Rodney King verdict, if leaders urged people to see themselves not as members of any particular racial in-group, but rather as members of the in-group containing all citizens of their community, then perhaps people would be less motivated to wreak havoc on out-group members and be more willing to help people of all kinds. Ultimately, if we all perceived ourselves to be members of the "human" in-group, we might see a lot less war and a great deal more cooperation in the world.

When People Choose to Help

Although help did not come for Kitty Genovese, there are many examples of situations in which people have come forward to help total strangers. Figure 12.8 lists several dramatic examples in which people put their lives in danger to help total strangers. As

April 1, 2003, in Nasiriyah, Iraq. At great danger to himself, an Iraqi lawyer named Mohammed hiked 6 miles through the middle of a war to inform American Marines that POW Jessica Lynch was being held in an Iraqi hospital (Rose, 2003).

February 26, 1999, in Norton, Massachusetts. Hundreds of people turn out to help look for a boy who was lost in a snowstorm (Howland, 1999).

January 10, 1999, in Sacramento, California. A woman runs into a burning building three separate times to help save victims of a house fire (Wiley, 1999).

November 18, 1998, in Tampa, Florida. A man dives into Tampa Bay to help rescue a motorist whose car plunged into the bay after he suffered a diabetic reaction (Wilson, 1998).

September 3, 1998, in Kansas City, Missouri. Bystanders rush to save an 11-year-old girl whose foot was sucked into a swimming pool drain. Bystanders had to gulp mouthfuls of air and deliver them to the child, whose head was underwater (Vendel, 1998).

November 1, 1998, in Buffalo, New York. A man chases and helps apprehend a suspect accused of stabbing another man (Haarlander, 1998).

November 18, 1997, in Denver, Colorado. A woman intervenes to help a man who was being attacked by skinheads in a racially motivated hate crime. The woman is shot and paralyzed (Pankratz, 1999).

Figure 12.8 **Some Examples of Human Altruism**

Despite tragedies like the murder of Kitty Genovese, humans are not typically cold, uncaring and apathetic. In fact, we often do come to the aid of others in distress—even when it means placing ourselves at risk.

these examples indicate, we do not always think of ourselves first, and we frequently are motivated to help others in need. But must we behave like superheroes, running into burning buildings to exhibit altruism? Of course not.

Altruism takes many forms. For example, Luis Rodriguez has dedicated much of his time to working with at-risk youth in an attempt to prevent them from making the same mistakes he made as a young man. One of the authors (Doyle-Portillo) works with two women who regularly grow their hair long so that they can cut it off and send it to a charity that makes wigs for women undergoing chemotherapy. And millions of people across the world contribute time and money to innumerable charities and prosocial organizations. Many of us find simple, everyday means of helping others lead better lives.

In a recent *New York Times* article, reporter Susan Orr Braudy (2003) examined the ways that New Yorkers exhibit altruism on a daily basis. Her analysis of what she calls "urban altruism" is especially uplifting because she easily found numerous examples of human kindness in the same city that failed to aid Kitty Genovese over 35 years ago. These include a doctor who helps homeless people get access to social services, an antique dealer who spontaneously helps a woman who was short on cash buy a gift for her friend, an apartment dweller who spends days watching over a fellow tenant whom she fears may become suicidal, passersby who immediately stop to help a woman after she falls on a icy sidewalk, an office worker who quickly steps in to stop a coworker's diabetic reaction, and an artist who volunteers once a month at a homeless shelter. In their own way, each of these people exhibited concern for the well-being and comfort of others with little concern for their own interests—in other words, *altruism*. Despite tragedies like the Kitty Genovese murder, it does appear that humans are generally concerned with the welfare of others. When we do fail to help it is usually not out of a sense of apathy or cruelty, but rather out of misunderstanding, confusion, or fear (Latané & Darley, 1969).

Let's Review!

In this section, we discussed altruism, or helping behavior. As a quick check of your understanding, answer these questions.

1. What did Darley and Latané conclude about the witnesses in the Kitty Genovese murder case?

   a. Many of the witnesses were uncaring people, and that is why they failed to help.

   b. The witnesses were not really witnesses. They did not actually see or hear Kitty being attacked.

   c. Many of the witnesses did not help because they felt that someone else would help.

   d. Fear was the best explanation for why the witnesses did not help Kitty Genovese.

2. Recently, one of the authors was sitting in her office when the fire alarms in her building went off. To her amazement, everyone seemed to ignore the sirens, and no one evacuated the building until security forced them to leave. Which of the following best explains their reluctance to leave the building?

   a. diffusion of responsibility   c. apathy

   b. pluralistic ignorance   d. a lack of conformity

3. If you are ever the victim of an accident, and there are many witnesses, what should you do to help ensure that one of the witnesses helps you?

   a. Scream for help.

   b. Remain quiet so as not to scare the witnesses.

   c. Single out one of the witnesses, and request that he or she help you.

   d. Yell "Fire!"

ANSWERS

1.c; 2.b; 3.c

Are You Getting the Big Picture?

In this chapter, we examined how we think and behave in social situations. Because we are social animals who spend most of our time in the company of others, this is a very important topic in psychology. The social cognitive processes of forming attitudes about the world, impressions of others, and stereotypes or prejudices have great implications for how we treat others and how others treat us. Many decisions—whom we choose as friends and lovers, whom we choose to help or hurt, and even whom we hire—all depend on our social judgments.

Our thoughts and values are only part of the forces that control our behavior in social situations. Others also have the power to change our attitudes and behavior. Social influence comes in the form of group processes like conformity, decision making, compliance, and obedience.

Understanding social cognition and social influence is important to many different professions. Lawyers must understand how persuasion affects juries. Law enforcement officials must understand the factors that make someone likely to obey laws. Salespeople and telemarketers use compliance techniques to help sell their products. Charities use compliance techniques to solicit donations. People in the helping professions must understand the factors that influence our tendency to help others in doing their jobs. Politicians and lobbyists use social influence to win votes. Managers use social influence to increase performance and compliance in employees. The list goes on and on. No matter what your profession, understanding social psychology is important to anyone who plans to interact with others—and that includes just about all of us.

STUDYING THE CHAPTER

Key Terms

social psychology (524)
social cognition (524)
social influence (524)
attitude (526)
cognitive consistency (529)
dissonance theory (529)
persuasion (530)
elaboration likelihood model
    (ELM) (530)
central route to persuasion (530)
peripheral route to persuasion (530)
heuristic-systematic persuasion
    model (531)
impression formation (534)
attribution (534)
trait attribution (534)
situational attribution (534)
fundamental attribution error (535)
individualistic culture (535)
collectivistic culture (535)

actor-observer bias (535)
self-serving bias (536)
stereotype (537)
prejudice (537)
discrimination (538)
in-group bias (540)
out-group (541)
out-group homogeneity bias (541)
realistic-conflict theory (541)
contact hypothesis (542)
superordinate goals (542)
mere exposure effect (545)
proximity (545)
balance theory (546)
matching hypothesis (547)
norm (549)
cohesiveness (549)
conformity (550)
normative conformity (552)
informational conformity (553)

groupthink (553)
compliance (555)
obedience (555)
foot-in-the-door compliance (555)
door-in-the-face compliance (556)
reciprocity (556)
slippery slope (560)
psychological distance (560)
destructive obedience (560)
debrief (561)
instrumental aggression (562)
hostile aggression (562)
frustration-aggression hypothesis
    (564)
altruism (565)
helping behavior (565)
bystander effect (566)
diffusion of responsibility (566)
pluralistic ignorance (567)

▶ *Test Yourself!*

Concept Check

Test your knowledge of the chapter concepts by completing each of the following sentences with the correct term. For a more comprehensive review, visit the book Web site (http://psychology.wadsworth.com/pastorinole/) for online quizzes, flashcards, crosswords, Internet links, and interactive versions of the Visual Summary, Concept Check, and Let's Review! text features.

The (1) _____ is making trait attributions for your successes and situational attributions for your failures. (2) _____ is an uncomfortable internal state that motivates change. (3) _____ states that prejudices arise out of competition for scarce resources. (4) _____ are schemata that apply to a particular group or type of people. A (5) _____ is an unwritten expectation for how group members should behave. (6) _____ occurs when we change our behavior to meet the expectations of a group to which we belong. (7) _____ occurs when one increases the chances of compliance by first requesting

something small from a potential target and then requesting something bigger. (8) _____ is a type of social influence that occurs when we give in to a simple request. (9) _____ is a type of social influence that occurs when we give in to a perceived demand. (10) _____ is a neurotransmitter that may be related to aggression. (11) _____ is another name for helping behavior. The (12) _____ occurs when a crowd of witnesses are individually less likely to help the victim because they feel as if the responsibility for helping is dispersed across all the members of the crowd. (13) _____ aggression is goal-directed aggression.

Answers:

1. self-serving bias; 2. Dissonance; 3. Realistic-conflict theory; 4. Stereotypes; 5. norm; 6. Conformity; 7. Foot-in-the-door compliance; 8. Compliance; 9. Obedience; 10. Serotonin; 11. Altruism; 12. bystander effect; 13. Instrumental.

Critical Thinking About the Chapter

1. Given what you have learned about obedience and compliance, what precautions would you urge people to take if they wanted to make themselves less vulnerable to requests and demands from others?

2. Pretend you have just been appointed to a committee at your place of work, and your mission is to develop a strategic plan that will take your company beyond the 21st century. What precautions would you take to ensure that your group does not develop groupthink?

3. Pretend you are an advertising account executive working for a new client. Using your knowledge of persuasion, design a television ad campaign to sell a new type of dishwashing detergent called Squeeky Clean Suds. Then justify *why* your plan should be successful to your client.

4. Pretend you are a community leader in a racially divided community. Design a program to reduce racial tensions among your community's citizens. Then explain why your plan should work.

5. Watch two television shows that feature male and female characters, one modern show and one older show from the 1950s, 1960s, or 1970s. What gender stereotypes are portrayed in these two shows? How do the shows differ in their depiction of male and female roles? Do these differences reflect changes in our culture over the past 50 years?

6. Keep a log of the attributions you make in a single day. How often did you use the heuristics discussed in this chapter? How often did you engage in careful attributions?

Applying Psychology. Find an article from a major metropolitan newspaper that discusses an instance in which someone committed an act of altruism. Then find an article that describes an emergency in which no one came to the aid of the victim. Compare and contrast the two situations in terms of the variables that affect helping behavior. Do these situations fit with what you have learned about helping behavior? If not, how do they differ?

Critical Thinking for Integration

1. Generate specific, original examples of how classical conditioning, operant conditioning, and social learning can contribute to the development of a prejudice.

2. Given what you have learned about developmental psychology, when would you expect to see prejudice develop in children? Explain your answer.

3. Design an experiment to test the matching hypothesis.

4. Design an experiment to test the hypothesis that bystanders will be less likely to help a victim whom they perceive to be responsible for his own plight.

Chapter Study Resources

Suggested Readings

1. Allport, G. W. (1979). *The nature of prejudice.* Reading, MA: Addison-Wesley.
A classic text on prejudice from Gordon Allport.

2. Gallagher, W. (1993). *The power of place: How our surroundings shape our thoughts, emotions, and actions.* New York: Harper-Perennial.
A thorough discussion of how the environment affects our social behavior.

3. Cialdini, R. B. (2001). *Influence: Science and practice* (4th ed.). Needham Heights, MA: Allyn & Bacon.
A text on social influence from one of its foremost researchers.

4. For additional readings, explore InfoTrac College Edition, your online library of archived journal articles and periodicals. Go to http://www.infotrac-college .com/wadsworth and enter the passcode from the card that came with your book. For this chapter, search using these keywords:

prejudice

compliance

altruism

groupthink

stereotype threat

Web Links for Further Study

Additional information on chapter concepts can be found at these Web sites:

1. The official Web site of Luis J. Rodriguez outlines his literary achievements and work.
    http://www.luisjrodriguez.com

2. A Web site describing persuasion tactics commonly used by con artists.
    http://www.crimes-of-persuasion.com/

3. The Anti-Defamation League's Web site entitled "101 Ways to Combat Prejudice" outlines practical ways to reduce prejudice in our world.
    http://www.adl.org/prejudice/default.asp

4. A page from the Jacksonville State University Encyclopedia of Psychology Web site that deals with information on attraction.

http://www.psychology.org/links/Environment _Behavior_Relationships/Attraction/

5. A Web site from Crime TV that discusses the Kitty Genovese murder.
    http://www.crimelibrary.com/serial_killers/predators/ kitty_genovese/

6. A site called Classics in the History of Psychology that contains a transcript of Bandura's article on modeled aggression in children.
    http://psychclassics.yorku.ca/Bandura/bobo.htm

7. A Web site dedicated to Stanley Milgram and his research.
    http://www.stanleymilgram.com/

Student Study Guide

To help organize your learning, work through Chapter 12 of the *What Is Psychology? Student Study Guide.* The study guide includes learning objectives, a chapter summary, fill-in review, key terms, a practice test, and activities.

Psychology Now™

PsychologyNow is a Web-based, personalized study system that provides you with a pretest and a posttest for each chapter, quizzes you by chapter, and provides a personalized study plan, pointing you to elements in the text or in individual learning modules that will help you to achieve 80% mastery. Check out the learning module that relates to this chapter: social influence

PsychNow CD-ROM, Version 2.0

Go to the PsychNow CD-ROM for further study of the concepts in this chapter. The CD-ROM includes learning modules with videos, animations, and quizzes, as well as simulations of psychological phenomena. Each module follows a consistent Explore, Lesson, and Apply structure that allows you to experience the concept or principle, learn more about it, and then apply it. You and your friends can participate in a team-based Quiz Game that makes learning fun. Learning modules include: 8a. Helping Others; 8b. Attribution; 8c. Social Influence; 8d. Attitudes and Prejudice; 8e. Aggression.

How Do We Understand and Relate to Others?

Social Psychology is the study of how we think and behave in social situations. Two subfields of social psychology are social cognition (the ways in which we think about ourselves and others) and social influence (the ways in which people affect our behavior).

ATTITUDES AND ATTITUDE CHANGE

• Attitudes are evaluative beliefs that contain affective, behavioral, and cognitive components.

• Attitudes develop through learning processes like classical conditioning, operant conditioning, and social learning or modeling.

• Attitudes best predict behavior when they:
— are learned through direct experience;
— are automatically activated in memory;
— are consistent with subjective norms;
— are consistent with respect to their cognitive and affective components;
— are specific; and
— have been recently thought about.

• Dissonance is an unpleasant state that motivates us to change either our attitudes or our behavior. Dissonance occurs when we discover an inconsistency among our attitudes and/or our behavior.

• Persuasion occurs when someone makes a direct attempt to change our attitudes.

• We tend to be most persuaded by people who appear to be attractive, credible, and expert.

• Typically, people are easier to persuade when they are processing on the peripheral route rather than the central route.

FORMING IMPRESSIONS OF OTHERS

• In forming impressions of others, we make attributions in which we assign cause to their behavior. Trait attributions assume the cause of the behavior comes from the person, whereas situational attributions assume the cause is external to the person.

• The fundamental attribution error is the tendency to overuse trait attributions when evaluating the behavior of others, while discounting situational explanations.

• The actor/observer bias and the self-serving bias are two other sources of mistaken or biased attributions.

PREJUDICE

• Prejudices are negatively biased stereotypes that are applied to all members of a social group regardless of the members' individual characteristics.

• Prejudices develop through classical conditioning, operant conditioning, and social learning.

• Inter-group dynamics such as in-group bias, out-group homogeneity bias, and scapegoating often play a role in prejudice.

• The contact hypothesis states that mere contact between in-group and out-group members can reduce prejudice. Cooperative contact and superordinate goals have been shown to be more effective in reducing prejudice.

ATTRACTION

• Some of the factors that affect our attraction to others include proximity, similarity of their attitudes and characteristics to ours, and physical attractiveness.

GROUPS AND GROUP INFLUENCES

• Conformity is our tendency to behave in ways that are consistent with the norms or expectations of a group.

• In normative conformity, we conform just to avoid breaking norms. In informational conformity, we conform because we are persuaded by conformity pressure to believe the group's stance is correct.

• Conformity is influenced by such factors as majority group size, unanimity of the majority group, anonymity, group cohesion, and self-esteem.

• Groupthink occurs when groups working under conditions of isolation, high cohesiveness, stress, and dictatorial leadership make very poor decisions after failing to examine all possible solutions to a problem.

COMPLIANCE AND DEMANDS

• Compliance is giving in to a simple request.
— In foot-in-the-door compliance, one is more likely to yield to a second larger request after having already complied with a first, smaller request.
— In door-in-the-face compliance, one is more likely to yield to a second smaller request after having refused an earlier large request.

— Reciprocity, or feeling obligated to return others' favors, is a major reason why we comply.

• Obedience is giving in to a demand. Factors that make us more likely to obey orders, even when they direct us to behave destructively, include:
— the presence of an authority figure,
— the foot-in-the door compliance of the slippery slope, and
— psychological distance.

AGGRESSION

• Aggression is causing harm or injury to someone who does not wish to be harmed.

• Instrumental aggression is goal-directed aggression, while hostile aggression is aimed solely at hurting others.

• Potential causes of aggression include high levels of testosterone, a lack of serotonin, brain damage caused by child abuse, social learning or modeling the aggression of others, cognitive neoassociation theory, and the frustration-aggression hypothesis.

HELPING BEHAVIOR

• Helping behavior, or altruism, is the tendency to help others in need with little concern for our own gain.

• One of the factors affecting helping behavior is the bystander effect, in which diffusion of responsibility reduces your chance of obtaining help when there are many witnesses.

• We are more likely to help in-group members than out-group members, and are least likely to help out-group members about whom we hold prejudices.

Perhaps due to advances in medical knowledge, or perhaps due to differences in their personalities or coping styles, Joan fared much better than Edward.

FROM ELLEN PASTORINO'S ACCOUNT OF HER FATHER EDWARD, AND MOTHER, JOAN.

© Ellen Pastorino

CHAPTER 13

Health, Stress, and Coping: How Can You Create a Healthy Life?

CHAPTER PREVIEW

What Can Psychology Tell Us About Health?

Previous chapters have shown you how your physiology and your environment (your family, economic situation, and culture) can influence how you grow, develop, and interact with others. In this chapter we'll explore the field of **health psychology.** Health psychologists study how peoples' behavior influences their health for better and for worse. In this regard, health is seen as a result of the interaction among biological, psychological, and social forces (Brannon & Feist, 2004; S. E. Taylor, 2003). We present the topics of stress, coping, and health. Because all of us cope with stress on a daily basis, this chapter offers much psychological research that will be relevant to your day-to-day living. It will help you realize how some of your personal habits, thoughts, or daily actions may be unhealthy, and hopefully will encourage you to live a healthier, longer life! Consider the following case.

Ellen, a 19-year-old college student, was looking forward to her spring break. She had decided to travel home to Florida to enjoy the beach, sunshine, and her family, a welcome diversion from midterm exams and the hassles of college life. On the third day of her vacation, her father, Edward, arrived home at his usual time and excitedly announced that he had great news—he had just found out that he was going to live!

Ellen was confused. What did he mean by this statement? Edward explained that over the past 4 months he had seen some medical specialists because he had been experiencing abdominal pain and weight loss. The doctors had discovered that he had cancer, specifically, a blood cancer called leukemia. Luckily, though, it was a treatable form of leukemia. Ellen was shocked by the news. Her father was only 53 years old. His parents had lived into their 80s, and his brother and sisters were in their 60s. None of them had experienced any significant health problems, let alone a cancer diagnosis. He had no family history of any form of cancer. Ellen reflected on all she knew about her father. Perhaps the clues to his illness could be found there.

Edward was born in 1930 in the Bronx, New York. His childhood was unremarkable, and he experienced no major medical illnesses or injuries other than frequent sinus difficulties. At 18, he received an appointment to the U.S. Naval Academy. After graduation, Edward entered the Marine Corps, was sent to Korea, and became involved in negotiating the trading of POWs.

Out of the Marine Corps and back in the United States, Edward started working for an electronics company. About the same time, he met Joan Cantelmo on a blind date. She was a recent graduate of Duquesne University and now a fifth-grade teacher. The couple fell in love and after 6 months got engaged. Once married, Edward climbed the corporate ladder, eventually becoming president of the company. In the meantime, he and Joan had five children—four girls and a boy, all healthy and sound. Edward was driven, ambitious, and determined to succeed. He was hot-tempered and had a strong desire to be in control. He was also affable and well liked, as evidenced by his large network of friends.

A year after he became head of the company, its parent company filed for bankruptcy, and Edward decided to leave. He soon bought a plastic manufacturing company that he ran well, achieving much success.

Edward lived by two maxims: "Don't put off until tomorrow what you can do today," and "Take the bull by the horns." In other words, he attacked problems. At times, he talked vociferously to his loved ones about his problems. At other times, he did not talk at all. He was a smoker for most of his life but quit in his 40s. He loved sports, but never established a regular exercise program. He had a sweet tooth, but was never overweight. Aside from the occasional cold, he had been a healthy man.

health psychology the subfield of psychology that investigates the relationship between people's behaviors and their health

© Ellen Pastorino

"Eventually, he gave up hope of beating the cancer."

(Ellen Pastorino)

Following his diagnosis of leukemia, Edward received radiation therapy. At first, it was successful. He enjoyed a 3-year remission period. Then the disease changed in form to non-Hodgkin's lymphoma, a cancerous growth of white blood cells in the lymph system. Edward received chemotherapy, but this time the therapy did not help. Ellen watched her father resume smoking and lose all his usual drive and ambition. Eventually, he gave up hope of beating the cancer. Not surprisingly, within months, at 56 years of age, Edward died. It was a devastating blow to Ellen and her family. All of them had relied on his guidance, tutelage, and strength. After a period of grieving, Ellen's family learned to cope with his passing. Sadly, Ellen and her family received a second blow 10 years later. Joan, Ellen's mother, was diagnosed with the same form of cancer! She was given 5 years to live. Joan also was a smoker, but she was an avid bowler and was optimistic that she could beat the cancer. For the next 8 years, she led a high quality life, mostly unimpeded by the disease. She died quietly in her sleep just 2 months shy of her 71st birthday. Perhaps due to advances in medical knowledge, or perhaps due to differences in their personalities or coping styles, Joan fared much better than Edward. Their daughter Ellen is one of the authors of this textbook.

At this point, you too may be wondering why a person whose life included so many opportunities and blessings could become ill. Edward's illness serves as a prime example of the complex relationship between behavior and health. Health psychologists examine how a person's behavior, thoughts, personality, and attitudes influence his or her health for better and for worse. They try to understand the nature of stress and how one's perception of stress and coping styles may influence the effect of stress on the body. This knowledge can help us understand Edward's illness. It also helps us recognize the complex interplay between our behavior and our health.

Stress and Stressors

LEARNING OBJECTIVE
Define stress, and identify stressors and conflict situations.

You are running late for school and your car breaks down—today of all days, when you have a major project due in one class and a midterm in another. Or maybe you're a working parent, trying to get the kids off to school in the morning, when your youngest can't find her shoes and the dog just got into the garbage. Perhaps you have just fallen in love and are contemplating getting married. Or maybe you have been married and have grown dissatisfied with your relationship and are contemplating divorce. Or consider the plight of one of your authors. In 1 week, the transmission went out on her car, the refrigerator compressor died, and her mother was involved in an automobile accident! All of these situations have one thing in common. They all include stress, an inevitable and unavoidable fact of life.

Stress can be defined as any event or environmental stimulus that we respond to because we perceive it as challenging or threatening. A closer look at this definition infers three aspects to stress. First, there are stressors, stimuli in our lives that we perceive as challenges or threats such as traffic, an approaching midterm exam, or a hurricane. Second, our reactions to these stressors include bodily reactions. Third, by perceiving and then reacting, we cope with the challenges or threats (successfully or not, as we will see). This section explores these three aspects to stress.

stress any event or environmental stimulus that we respond to because we perceive it as challenging or threatening

What are stressors? Let's first look at different types of stressors. Briefly reflect on an ordinary day in your life. There are probably many events or stimuli that you perceive as provoking or annoying: a long line at the fast-food drive-thru, a confrontation with your boss, or having several errands to run in a limited amount of time. There probably also have been events in your life that you found to be particularly

 Application

Ralph Dunagin & Dana Summers. © 1999 Tribune Media Services, Inc. Reprinted with permission.

trying or traumatic, such as the death of a loved one, hearing that you will soon be a parent, or being fired from your job. Stressors come in all shapes and sizes. Psychological research classifies these stressors into four types:

- major life events
- catastrophes
- daily hassles
- conflict.

Let's take a look at how each of these stressors is defined and what comprises each category.

Life Events: Change Is Stressful

How do we know which events in our life qualify as major, rather than minor, stressors when they all *feel* stressful? Believe it or not, psychologists have tried to measure this difference. Pioneering research by Thomas Holmes and Richard Rahe in 1967 set out to measure the impact of particular stressors on peoples' health. They asked a large sample group to rate **life events,** or changes in one's living, both good and bad, that require us to adjust to them. In other words, which life events did the respondents perceive as more stressful? From these ratings, Holmes and Rahe developed the Social Readjustment Rating Scale (SRRS), reprinted in Table 13.1 ◆.

life event a change in one's living, both good and bad, that requires readjustment

Life events, both good and bad, can be perceived as stressful and require us to adjust to them.

© Streetstock Images/Corbis

Holmes and Rahe assigned each major life event a numerical value, referred to as a *life change unit*. The higher the number, the more stressful this life event was rated by Holmes and Rahe's sample. Notice that Edward and his family experienced several stressors that fall at the top of this list. Being diagnosed with cancer, a personal illness, was a major stressor for Edward. Experiencing the death of a loved one was a major stressor for Ellen and her family. Notice too that the life events on the scale also include positive as well as negative changes—for example, marriage, a new family member, and outstanding personal achievement. However, it is not just experiencing one of these events that is at issue. Rather, it is reacting to several of these events within a year that Holmes and Rahe found may influence one's health.

Take a moment to look at the scale (Table 13.1). Add up the life change units for all those events you have experienced in the last year. Compare your total to the standards devised by Holmes and Rahe:

≪ ▐ **Demonstration**

0–150:	No significant problems
150–199:	Mild life crisis
200–299:	Moderate life crisis
300–or more:	Major life crisis

◆ **Table 13.1**

Holmes & Rahe's Social Readjustment Scale

Rank	Life Event	Life Change Units	Rank	Life Event	Life Change Units
1	Death of spouse	100	23	Son or daughter leaving home	29
2	Divorce	73	24	Trouble with in-laws	29
3	Marital separation	65	25	Outstanding personal achievement	28
4	Jail term	63	26	Spouse begins or stops work	26
5	Death of a close family member	63	27	Begin or end school	26
6	Personal injury or illness	53	28	Change in living conditions	25
7	Marriage	50	29	Revision of personal habits	24
8	Fired at work	47	30	Trouble with boss	23
9	Marital reconciliation	45	31	Change in work hours or conditions	20
10	Retirement	45	32	Change in residence	20
11	Change in health of family member	44	33	Change in school	20
12	Pregnancy	40	34	Change in recreation	19
13	Sex difficulties	39	35	Change in church activities	19
14	Gain of new family member	39	36	Change in social activities	18
15	Business readjustment	39	37	Take out loan less than $20,000	17
16	Change in financial state	38	38	Change in sleeping habits	16
17	Death of a close friend	37	39	Change in number of family get-togethers	15
18	Change to different line of work	36	40	Change in eating habits	15
19	Change in number of arguments with spouse	35	41	Vacation	13
20	Take out mortgage or loan for major purchase	31	42	Christmas	12
21	Foreclosure of mortgage or loan	30	43	Minor violation of the law	11
22	Change in responsibilities at work	29			

Reprinted with permission from T. H. Holmes & R. H. Rahe (1967) "The Social Readjustment Rating Scale," in the Journal of Psychosomatic Research, *Vol. 11, No. 2, p. 213–218. Copyright © 1967 Elsevier Science.*

Note: In Holmes and Rahe's Social Readjustment Rating Scale, each major life event is assigned a numerical value. The higher the numerical value, the more stressful the life event is perceived to be. Add up the life change units for all those events you have experienced in the past year. Then compare your total to the standards indicated in the text.

Holmes and Rahe (1967) found that the higher people scored on the SRRS, the more prone they were to illness. Of those who scored within the mild life crisis range, 37% had experienced deteriorated health. This figure rose to 51% for those whose scores indicated they were experiencing a moderate life crisis, and 79% for those in the major life crisis range. Follow-up studies have supported Holmes and Rahe's findings (Gruen, 1993; Scully, Tosi, & Banning, 2000). However, keep in mind that these are correlations, and as we discussed in Chapter 1, correlation does not mean causation. Life events do not directly cause illness, but they may make a person more vulnerable to illness and disease.

Subsequent research (Pearlin, 1993) evaluating Holmes and Rahe's scale indicates that it's not simply how many of these life changes one experiences. We need to take several other variables into account when we assess the impact of these life changes. Three such factors include:

- the voluntary or involuntary nature of the life change
- how desirable or undesirable the life change is perceived to be
- whether the life change is scheduled or unscheduled.

For example, Edward's cancer diagnosis can be considered involuntary because he did not choose to get cancer (although he did choose to smoke) and undesirable as a threat to his life. It was unscheduled because he did not foresee (even in his family's history) his susceptibility to a cancer. Consider as another example a couple about to divorce. Typically, the partner who asks for a divorce feels less stress after she has informed her mate of her decision. In this context, the divorce is seen as voluntary, desirable, and scheduled. At the same time, her husband may then experience increased stress, as the divorce for him may be involuntary (not of his choosing), undesirable, and unscheduled. As these examples illustrate, the amount of stress one experiences when faced with life changes may vary across individuals. We can consider Holmes and Rahe's scale as a rough index of how susceptible some may be to illness, given the number of major stressors the person encounters. If you scored significantly high on the scale, you may want to consider adjusting your lifestyle in ways that reduce your chances of becoming ill.

Application ≫

You also may have noticed that the scale has very few life events that may apply to college students and younger people. The SRRS has been criticized for not adequately defining stress events among younger age groups. Yet research supports the notion that major changes, such as the breakup of a relationship, academic pressure, or even college itself, may also influence the health of college students (Crandall, Preisler, & Aussprung, 1992). This is important because perceived stress also seems to predict how well students perform academically in college. High levels of perceived stress in college students correlate with lower grade point averages (Lloyd, Alexander, Rice, & Greenfield, 1980). You may find that the Undergraduate Stress Questionnaire (Table 13.2 ◆) includes more of the typical stressors that you face, compared with Holmes and Rahe's SRRS. It may therefore be a more accurate assessment of your stress level and hence your susceptibility to illness.

Application ≫

Catastrophes: Natural Disasters and Wars

Unexpected traumatic events or catastrophes that almost all people perceive as threats also qualify as stressors. Catastrophes may affect one's physical and psychological health. After catastrophic events such as floods, earthquakes, hurricanes, tornadoes, or fires, people are generally more likely to experience depression or anxiety (Brende, 2000; Davidson, 2000; Rubonis & Bickman, 1991). We have for a long time recognized

◆ **Table 13.2**

Undergraduate Stress Questionnaire

Have any of the following stressful events happened to you at any time during the last 2 weeks? If any has, please check the space next to it. If an item has not occurred, then please leave it blank.

___ Death (family member or friend)

___ Death of a pet

___ Working while in school

___ Parents getting a divorce

___ Registration for classes

___ Trying to decide on major

___ Talked with a professor

___ Trying to get into your college

___ Had a class presentation

___ Had projects, research papers due

___ Had a lot of tests

___ It's finals week

___ Applying to graduate school

___ You have a hard upcoming week

___ Lots of deadlines to meet

___ Missed your menstrual period and waiting

___ Had an interview

___ Applying for a job

___ Sat through a boring class

___ Can't understand your professor

___ Did badly on a test

___ Went into a test unprepared

___ Crammed for a test

___ Used a fake I.D.

___ Breaking up with boy/girlfriend

___ Holiday

___ Bad haircut today

___ Victim of a crime

___ Can't concentrate

___ Coping with addictions

___ Found out boy/girlfriend cheated on you

___ Did worse than expected on test

___ Stayed up late writing a paper

___ Problems with your computer

___ Favorite sports team lost

___ Ran out of typewriter ribbon while typing

___ Change of environment (new doctor, dentist, etc.)

___ Bothered by not having family's social support

___ Arguments, conflict of values with friends

___ Had a visit from a relative and entertained him/her

___ Noise disturbed you while trying to study

___ Maintaining a long distance boy/girlfriend

___ Assignments in all classes due the same day

___ Dealt with incompetence at the registrar's office

___ Someone borrowed something without your permission

___ Exposed to upsetting TV show, book, or movie

___ Problem getting home when drunk

___ Had confrontation with an authority figure

___ Got to class late

___ Parents controlling with money

___ Feel isolated

___ Decision to have sex on your mind

___ No sex in a while

___ Living with boy/girlfriend

___ Felt some peer pressure

___ Felt need for transportation

___ Couldn't find a parking space

___ Property stolen

___ Car/bike broke down, flat tire, etc.

___ Got a traffic ticket

___ No time to eat

___ Having roommate conflicts

___ Had to ask for money

___ Lack money

___ Checkbook didn't balance

___ You have a hangover

___ Someone you expected to call did not

___ Lost something (especially, wallet)

___ Erratic schedule

___ Thoughts about future

___ Dependent on other people

___ No sleep

___ Sick, injury

___ Fought with boy/girlfriend

___ Performed poorly at a task

___ Heard bad news

___ Thought about unfinished work

___ Feel unorganized

___ Someone cut ahead of you in line

___ Job requirements changed

___ Someone broke a promise

___ Someone did a "pet peeve" of yours

___ Can't finish everything you need to do

From C. S. Crandall, et al., "Measuring Life Event Stress in the Lives of College Students: The Undergraduate Stress Questionnaire (USQ)," in Journal of Behavioral Medicine, *15(6), p. 627–662, © 1992. Reprinted with kind permission of Springer Science and Business Media.*

Unexpected traumatic events also cause stress and can affect one's physical and psychological health.

the stress of war on soldiers, as evidenced by the various names we have given to the pattern of symptoms that soldiers experience when they return. We called it shell shock in World War I, battle fatigue in World War II, and posttraumatic stress disorder (PTSD) following the Vietnam War and Operation Desert Storm. Soldiers experienced nightmares, flashbacks, and vivid memories as they relived their war experiences. They evidenced intense startle responses to loud noises and had difficulty concentrating and getting along with others. Rape victims report similar physical and psychological symptoms that may meet the criteria for what is referred to as *rape trauma syndrome*, more evidence that unexpected events may take their toll on one's health. Given that these events are often involuntary, undesirable, and somewhat unscheduled in that we typically don't have a lot of time to prepare for them, it is relatively easy to see how they may influence our health and well being. We'll discuss PTSD in more detail in Chapter 15.

Terrorism has become a stressor for many in the 21st century. The Oklahoma City bombing or the September 11 terrorist attacks on New York City and Washington D.C. were extraordinary forms of stress experienced during peacetime in the United States. For example, several studies (Galea et al., 2002; Schlenger et al., 2002) found that New York City residents, particularly those living closer to the World Trade Center had higher rates of stress disorders than those from other major cities. Even in one country such as the United States, we find differences in the stressors experienced by particular groups, as It's a Diverse World feature highlights.

IT'S A DIVERSE WORLD

The Stress of Discrimination

As we learned in Chapter 12, prejudicial stereotypes are an unfortunate by-product of our tendency to categorize people as a way to understand our social world. Often such prejudicial attitudes motivate people to discriminate or treat others poorly. There is a growing body of literature suggesting that such discrimination is a unique source of stress to minority groups (Clark, Anderson, Clark, & Williams, 1999; Thompson, 1996). For example, in a study by Klonoff & Landrine (1999), 95% of the 520 African American respondents reported experiencing some form of racial discrimination in the past year that they perceived as stressful. Other research indicates that Hispanics and Asian Americans also experience discrimination and perceive it as stressful (Jackson, Williams, & Torres, 1997). Mays and Cochran (2001) found that homosexuals and bisexuals more frequently

reported both lifetime and day-to-day experiences with discrimination than heterosexuals.

You would think that in a nation in which overt discrimination in housing, educational access, and employment is against the law that such a stressor would not be as evident. However, recall from the previous chapter how easy it is for people to acquire negative stereotypes of a group. Such schemes may be expressed overtly or subtly toward members of other groups through derogatory insults, avoidance, threats, or denial of service or treatment. For example, in 1993, on the very day that Denny's Restaurants settled a federal suit over racial discrimination, six African American Secret Service agents at a Denny's restaurant in Maryland waited nearly an hour for breakfast while their white colleagues sitting at a nearby table were served promptly. Consider the events of the 1999 Black College Reunion in Daytona Beach,

Florida. African American students complained that the Adam's Mark Hotel required that Blacks wear bright orange wrist bands that identified them as guests of the resort, a requirement not made of Whites also staying there. In addition, African American patrons were charged higher room rates than Whites and were required to pay the entire cost of their rooms in cash at the time of reservation. Women are not exempt from discrimination either. In November 2002, Augusta National Golf Club chairman Hootie Johnson stated that a woman would not be among the 300 members for the 2003 Masters Golf tournament as the club refuses to admit female members ("Woods Plays Down Augusta Row," 2002).

The anticipation of being discriminated against may also be a source of stress for members of minority groups.

In addition, minority individuals may worry that their behavior will be interpreted in a way that confirms negative stereotypes (Steele, 1997). If they try to behave in a way that does not conform to these stereotypes, they may then be ridiculed by members of their own group for "selling out" or "acting White" (Contrada et al., 2000). All of these situations are potentially stressful. Researchers are just beginning to evaluate the potential ill effects of such stress on the physical and mental health of minorities (e.g., Rich-Edwards, Krieger, Majzoub, Zierler, Liberman, & Gillman, 2001; Williams, Yu, Jackson, & Anderson, 1997). Such research illustrates the impact that our interactions with others can have on our physical and mental well being. Our interactions with others also may lead to another source of stress—daily hassles, our next topic of discussion.

Daily Hassles: Little Things Add Up!

When psychologists evaluate the relationship between stress and health, they not only measure life changes and analyze the influence of catastrophes, they also evaluate the impact of everyday irritations and frustrations that we face. These **daily hassles** also appear to play a role in our health. At times these irritants add to the stress of major life changes and catastrophic events, such as the daily planning for a wedding or getting stuck in traffic during an evacuation due to a natural disaster. But for most of us, the routine annoyances and frustrations we experience on a daily basis are themselves stressful. Can you think of any examples of daily hassles? Waiting in lines, lack of money, losing your keys, or fights with loved ones may be a few that come to mind. The daily hassles may in fact be the most significant source of stress and as such, place a great burden on our immediate health and well-being (Kohn & Macdonald, 1992; Lazarus, 1990; Roberts, 1995; Ruffin, 1993). As daily hassles increase, our physical and mental health decreases (Chamberlain & Zika, 1990; Sim, 2000). However, whether we perceive these frustrations as stressful is of prime importance in determining our susceptibility to illness. Some of us may easily shrug off these annoyances, whereas they may particularly perturb others of us.

In a 2002 Harris Poll (H. Taylor, 2002), the most frequently reported daily hassles were rising prices and having too many things to do. Yet gender, race, age, socioeconomic status, and education seem to influence our perception of stress from daily hassles. Women are more likely than men to perceive stress from concerns about money, having too many things to do, health concerns, and having trouble relaxing. In general, younger people report having more hassles in their lives than older people. Those with more money and more education also report lower levels of perceived stress from daily hassles than those with lower income and less education. Although people who make more money and have more education may lead full

daily hassles   the everyday irritations and frustrations that individuals face

Everyday irritations and frustrations increase our stress level and can influence our health.

© Michael Newman/Photo Edit

and hectic lives, they generally perceive that they have more control over their lives and report having more fun. They are less likely to experience hassles concerning health, illness of a family member, trouble relaxing, problems at work, and exposure to excessive noise than people with less education and lower incomes. Race differences also appear in reports on daily hassles. African Americans are more likely than Whites and Hispanics to report economic hassles, exposure to noise, feeling lonely, and abuse of personal privacy as frequent day-to-day hassles. Hispanics are more likely than Whites and African Americans to report problems with aging parents as a hassle of daily living.

Conflict: Approach and Avoidance

conflict having to choose between two or more needs, desires, or demands

Conflict, or having to choose between two or more needs, desires, or demands, can also place stress on us. Should you take the required science course or the required math course? Should you wear the blue or the gray suit to the job interview? Considering whether you perceive these options as positive or negative results in four basic forms of conflict (Figure 13.1).

1. *Approach-approach conflicts.* The easiest conflict to resolve and therefore the conflict that is accompanied by the least amount of perceived stress is the **approach-approach conflict,** in which a person must choose between two likeable, or positive, events. Choosing between seeing an old friend who is passing through town or going out on a date with someone you've been hoping would ask you out is an example of an approach-approach conflict.

approach-approach conflict a situation in which a person must choose between two likeable events

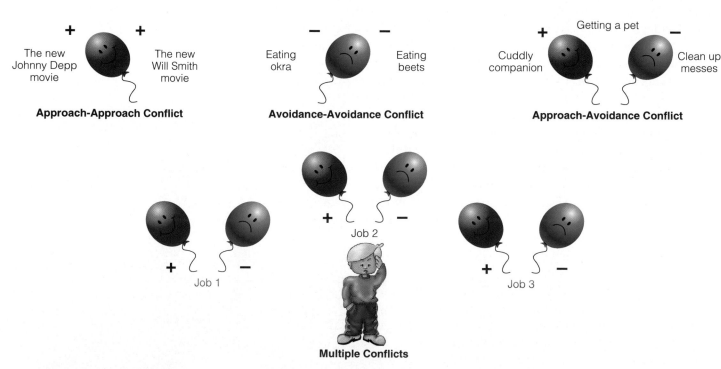

Figure 13.1 Four Common Conflict Situations
In an approach-approach conflict, a person must choose between two appealing choices—in this example, two movies one would like to see. In an avoidance-avoidance conflict, a person must choose between two undesirable choices—in this example, two disliked vegetables to eat. In an approach-avoidance conflict, a person faces a decision that has both positive and negative features—in this example, owning a pet that cuddles yet also makes messes. Multiple conflicts involve several choices that have both positive and negative qualities—in this example, choosing from among three jobs.

A more stressful approach-approach example could be liking and being challenged in your job and being offered another attractive and challenging position in the same company. In this type of conflict you really can't lose because both options are favorable.

2. *Avoidance-avoidance conflicts.* The opposite of the approach-approach conflict is the **avoidance-avoidance conflict,** in which a person has to choose between two undesirable, or negative, events. You can think of this type of conflict as a "Catch-22" or a "damned if you do, damned if you don't" situation. For example, do you spend the morning in line to register your car, or do you get your car towed because the registration has expired? On a more serious note, think of the plight of many of the passengers of the *Titanic.* You are on a sinking ship, and there are no more lifeboats available. Do you stay on the ship, or do you jump into the icy waters? Both choices will almost surely result in your death. What do you do? Because both options in an avoidance-avoidance conflict are unappealing, many people remain undecided and inactive, or "frozen." They don't do anything. Consequently, avoidance-avoidance conflicts are accompanied by a greater degree of perceived stress than are approach-approach conflicts.

avoidance-avoidance conflict   a situation in which a person must choose between two undesirable events

3. *Approach-avoidance conflicts.* Another stressful conflict to resolve is the **approach-avoidance conflict,** in which a person is faced with a desire or need that has both positive and negative qualities. Consequently, he or she is drawn to the situation because of its positive features (approach), but is also repelled and would rather not experience the negative aspects of the situation (avoidance). Edward's decision to receive radiation treatment, followed 3 years later by chemotherapy treatment had elements of an approach-avoidance conflict. The positive qualities of such treatments are the increased chance of survival. The major side effects, which most of us would like to avoid, include extreme fatigue, nausea, hair loss, loss of taste, and a high susceptibility to viruses and bacteria, which means avoiding situations in which there may be a lot of people. These side effects may lessen one's quality of life, a consideration particularly for the terminally ill. Or think of being in a home fire in which your dog is trapped in the burning flames. You don't want to lose your lifelong friend and therefore would want to save the dog, but doing so may also be very risky and result in compromising your own safety. As with avoidance-avoidance conflicts, these situations may immobilize the person so that they cannot make a decision or resolve the conflict, which leads to the experience of stress.

approach-avoidance conflict   a situation in which a person is faced with a need that has both positive and negative aspects

4. *Multiple conflicts.* In real life, many of our conflicts consist of several alternatives that we may choose from, each with both positive and negative features. These **multiple approach-avoidance conflicts** can contribute to the amount of stress we feel. In deciding which college to attend, you may have been faced with several choices. Each school may have had its good points and bad points (how far away from home they were, the tuition costs, the programs of studies, the social life of the campus). Deciding on a major or a career, choosing between two job offers, or deciding on which house or car to buy also illustrate multiple conflicts. This may account for buyer's remorse, which some people experience after making a major purchase. They bought, or approached, an item because of its attractive features but afterward felt regret as they contemplated the purchased item's negative features or the alternative brands that they might have considered more seriously.

multiple approach-avoidance conflicts a situation that poses several alternatives that each have positive and negative features

 Application

Let's Review!

In this section we defined stress and described four types of stressors: major life events, catastrophes, daily hassles, and conflict situations. For a quick check of your understanding, answer these questions.

1. You go to the dentist and find out that you have to get a tooth extracted. The only time the dentist can schedule your appointment is at the same time as a traffic court appointment. This situation is an example of an:

   a. approach-approach conflict.

   b. approach-avoidance conflict.

   c. avoidance-avoidance conflict.

   d. seek-and-destroy conflict.

2. Which of the following is considered to be the most stressful major life event by the Social Readjustment Scale?

   a. a jail term   c. divorce

   b. death of a spouse   d. pregnancy

3. Getting stuck in traffic on your way to a job interview is an example of a:

   a. daily hassle.   c. catastrophe.

   b. major life event.   d. stress response.

ANSWERS

1.c, 2.b, 3.a

LEARNING OBJECTIVES ‹ ‹ ‹ ‹ ‹ ‹ ‹ ‹ ‹

Discuss the concept of appraisal in the stress response.

Explain how the body responds to stress and how that response influences our immunity to disease.

The Stress Response: Is This Stress? How Do I React?

Now that we have looked at the types of stressors that may influence our health, we will examine the second feature of stress: the reactions that accompany stress. This analysis will further your understanding of the relationship between stress and health.

Appraisal: Assessing Stress

How does stress start? We all experience many of the stressors discussed in the previous section, especially daily hassles. We all wait in lines, sit in traffic, and pay bills. Yet not all of us interpret these events as equally stressful. Some people view giving blood as less stressful than others. You may feel excited about giving a speech, whereas others cringe at the same prospect. Therefore, the first step in experiencing stress is how you think about or interpret an event or situation. Our initial interpretation of an event is called **primary appraisal** (Lazarus, 1991, 1993). Primary appraisal can be irrelevant, positive, or stressful.

If your primary appraisal of an event is *irrelevant*, you interpret the situation as immaterial or unrelated to your happiness or safety. For example, the number of students in a particular course of yours may not make a difference to you one way or another. Class size may be appraised as not relevant to your performance in the class, and therefore viewed as not stressful. Primary appraisals also can be *positive*. For example, you may take a class in which there are a small number of students and view this situation as something good. Again, we typically don't feel much stress in situations such as these. However, when we appraise a situation as *stressful*, we believe it will require much of our emotional and psychological resources. For example, you may view a small class size as stressful if you fear speaking in front of a group and there is the expectation that class discussion will occur frequently.

Our primary appraisal of an event as stressful can lead to positive or negative emotions that either increase or decrease our perceived stress levels (Barlow, 2002). How much stress we experience will depend on whether we see the situation as a threat, harm, or challenge. If we appraise a stressful event as a *threat*, we believe that the

primary appraisal   our initial interpretation of an event as either irrelevant, positive, or stressful

situation will cause us some harm in the future. When we interpret an event in this manner we typically feel fear, anxiety, or anger—negative emotions that increase our stress levels. For example, having to give an oral presentation on a project later in the term may be perceived as threatening by a student. He may fear negative evaluations by the professor or other students or be anxious that his voice will crack or that he will stammer. If we appraise an event as *harmful*, we believe it will do us some damage or injury. For example, one of the authors of your textbook appraised putting holiday lights up on her house as stressful because she believed that getting on the roof of her house would lead to injury. Again, such appraisals typically lead to feelings of fear and anxiety that increase our feelings of stress. However, situations also can be appraised as *challenging*, or as a means for personal growth or personal gain. For example, taking a new job may be appraised as an opportunity for career growth or getting married may be appraised as an opportunity to deepen and expand the nature of an intimate relationship. Challenge appraisals typically elicit positive emotions such as excitement and are therefore perceived as less stressful.

        《 Application

Not all primary appraisals easily break down into the categories of threat, harm, or challenge. A situation or event may involve a combination of appraisals. For example, getting married, finding a job, or having a baby are complex situations that may involve appraisals of threat and challenge. Also, the appraisal process is an individual one. Not everyone appraises the same situation in the same manner. For example, some students may perceive course exams as threats, whereas other students may see them as challenges. Yet for everyone, primary appraisal is the first step in experiencing stress. Once you appraise a situation or event as stressful, your body changes to deal with the stressor.

Selye's General Adaptation Syndrome

How does our body respond to stress? Many of us recognize stressful situations because of the bodily reactions that accompany them. For example, if you perceive giving a speech as a stressor, when faced with doing so, you may feel shaky, perspire more, feel your heart race, or even experience difficulty breathing. You may experience these same reactions on the day of your wedding or before an important job interview. These reactions are a part of a general bodily pattern termed the **general adaptation syndrome** (**GAS**; Selye, 1976). Figure 13.2 shows the GAS as three phases that we all experience when we face a stressor in the environment: an initial alarm reaction, resistance, and exhaustion.

        《 Application

general adaptation syndrome the general physical responses we experience when faced with a stressor

Alarm Reaction

The **alarm reaction** consists of those bodily responses that are immediately triggered when we initially appraise an event as stressful. It is much like the car alarm that goes

alarm reaction the first phase of the general adaptation syndrome, characterized by the immediate activation of the nervous and endocrine systems

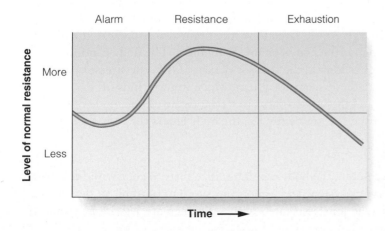

Figure 13.2 **General Adaptation Syndrome**
According to Hans Selye, the biological stress response consists of three phases. In the alarm reaction, the nervous system and hormonal system release chemicals to deal with the stressor. In the resistance stage, the body continues its efforts to cope with the stressor. If the stressor persists, the body enters the exhaustion stage in which bodily resources dwindle, and wear and tear on the body begin.

Figure 13.3 Biological Pathway of the Stress Response

When we perceive an event as stressful, the hypothalamus in the brain activates two systems: the sympathetic branch of the nervous system and the pituitary gland of the hormonal system. The nervous system sends neural messages to the major glands and muscles to prepare for fight or flight. At the same time, neural messages activate the adrenal gland to secrete the stress hormone adrenaline. The pituitary gland sends hormonal messages to the adrenal gland to secrete the stress hormones corticosteroids. The combined effects of these stress hormones prepare our bodies to face stressors.

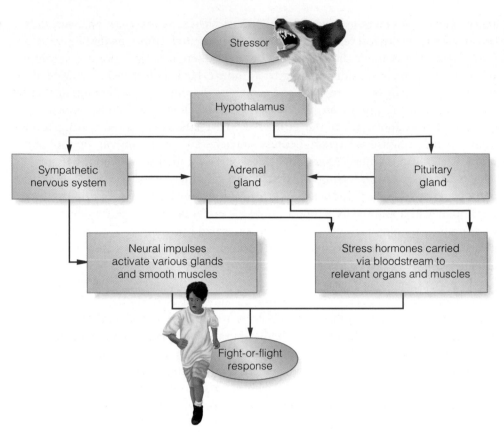

off the moment an intruder tries to open the car door. In the body, this consists of the activation of the nervous system and the endocrine system (Figure 13.3).

Recall from Chapter 2 that your nervous system has two branches: the central nervous system, consisting of the brain and the spinal cord, and the peripheral nervous system, including the somatic and autonomic divisions (see p. 63). The autonomic division includes two systems: the parasympathetic branch, which operates when we are calm and relaxed, and the sympathetic nervous system, our fight-or-flight mechanism that prepares us to face a threat in the environment. This sympathetic branch of the nervous system is at the heart of the stress response.

When a person perceives a threat in the environment—or what we have now referred to as a stressor—the sympathetic nervous system is activated. In order to prepare the body to deal with the stressor, the sympathetic nervous system works in conjunction with the endocrine (or hormonal) system. It stimulates the adrenal gland to secrete two hormones: adrenaline and corticosteroids. These hormones travel to the major organs (liver, heart, lungs) to prepare the body for fight or flight. Our heart rate and blood pressure increase, our lungs expand, and our liver releases stored sugars that can be used for energy. At the same time, the brain also stimulates the pituitary gland to release endorphins, the body's natural painkillers. The body continues to expend these resources for as long as the stressor persists. Once the stressor passes, the brain turns off the sympathetic nervous system, which in turn shuts off the release of these stress hormones and the body returns to its parasympathetic mode of calm and relaxation. However, if the stressor continues, the body enters the resistance stage.

Resistance Stage

resistance stage the second phase of the general adaptation syndrome, in which the nervous and endocrine systems continue to be activated

During the **resistance stage,** the body continues its efforts to cope with the stressor. The sympathetic nervous system and endocrine system continue to be activated. However, the bodily reactions associated with resistance are less intense than the alarm reaction, as the body's resources begin to dwindle. When the body has drained its resources such that energy is no longer available, we enter the exhaustion stage.

Exhaustion Stage

It is during the **exhaustion stage** that wear and tear on the body begins. High levels of adrenaline and corticosteroids in the body over a prolonged period of time damage the heart and lessen the effectiveness of the immune system. The result is that you become more vulnerable at this time to heart disease, ulcers, high blood pressure, and colds and flus (Cohen, 1996; Doctor & Doctor, 1994; Kiecolt-Glaser, McGuire, Robles, & Glaser, 2002; Rice, 2000). Excessive and prolonged exposure to stress hormones also may produce headaches, backaches, indigestion, constipation, diarrhea, fatigue, insomnia, mood swings, and muscle tension (B. Brown, 1980; De Benedittis, Lorenzetti, & Pieri, 1990).

exhaustion stage   the third and final phase of the general adaptation syndrome, in which bodily resources are drained, and wear and tear on the body begins

Stress and the Immune System: Resistance to Disease

As we have seen, our body's reaction to stress, particularly during the exhaustion phase, can influence the effectiveness of our immune system. The immune system is our body's best defense against illness because it destroys and fights bacteria, viruses, and other foreign substances that may invade our bodies. If this system is impaired, as in the case of prolonged stress, we are more prone to illness and disease.

How does stress affect our immune system? The corticosteroids and endorphins that are released into our body during the stress response actually reduce and dampen the activity of our immune system. This is referred to as **immunosuppression.** Consequently, turning on our stress response, which ensures our ability to survive immediate danger, is at the expense of our immune system, our long-term survival mechanism.

immunosuppression   the reduction in activity of the immune system

Much research supports the notion that stress suppresses the functioning of the immune system, which then increases one's chances of developing infections such as the common cold (Anderson, 2003; Cohen, Tyrrell, & Smith, 1991; Kiecolt-Glaser et al., 2002; Rice, 2000). During final exam time and other periods of academic pressure, students show a weakened immune system (D. G. Gilbert, Stunkard, Jensen, & Detwiler, 1996; Jemmott, Borysenko, McClelland, Chapman, & Benson, 1985). This may explain why you catch a cold or are more likely to experience allergies and sinus infections during finals week or when you have several projects or papers due at one time! Immunosuppression also occurs in men and women following the death of their spouses (Schleifer, Keller, Camerino, Thornton, & Stein, 1983) and in people going through separation and divorce (Kiecolt-Glaser & Glaser, 1992). There also is evidence that when people experience high levels of stress as the result of caring for a relative or friend with a terminal disease or dementia, they also experience immunosuppression (Kiecolt-Glaser, Marucha, Malarkey, Mercado, & Glaser, 1995; Vitaliano et al., 1998; Vitaliano, Young, & Zhang, 2004).

More serious, though, is the correlation between stress, the immune system, and cancer. For example, cancer occurs more often than usual in people who are divorced, separated, or widowed (Schleifer, Keller, McKegney, & Stein, 1979). Moreover, our response and attitude toward having cancer may influence the eventual spread and fatality of the disease. Most people's initial reaction to a cancer diagnosis is panic, anger, or depression—emotions that activate the stress response and momentarily retard immune system functioning (Ader, 2001).

But what about our long-term attitude toward a disease? Research suggests that here, too, our perception and handling of an extended illness influence our health. For example, emotional distress in breast cancer patients is associated with a shorter survival rate (Luecken & Compas, 2002; Osborne et al., 2004). Expressing our emotions about the disease—both positive and negative—is associated with a higher chance of survival when compared to patients who hold in their emotions (O'Leary, 1990; Temoshok, 1992). Similarly, cancer patients with an optimistic attitude who are determined to beat the disease often outlive patients with a less positive attitude (Carver et al., 2000; Gilbert, 1998; Shen, McCreary & Myers, 2004). Notice that this research does not say that stress causes cancer but, rather, that stress may influence the rate at which cancer cells grow. If your immune system is functioning at reduced levels during times of stress, it is less available to fight these life-threatening cells.

To illustrate, let's use these research findings to analyze the opening case study. The initial diagnosis of cancer may have made Edward's body even more susceptible to the growth of cancer cells. His attitude and inability to express his feelings about the illness may have hampered his body's defense against the cancer. Consequently, Edward's steady decline over a 3-year period may be related to his reactions to the cancer diagnosis, which in turn impaired the functioning of his immune system. These research findings also may account for Joan's eventual cancer diagnosis. Being widowed at a relatively young age may have increased her susceptibility to cancer. However, Joan's reaction to the illness was much different from her husband's. She was more optimistic and hopeful about beating the cancer than he was. This may account for why she developed a milder form of cancer and survived longer with generally the same type of illness.

We are by no means saying that surviving or not surviving cancer is totally up to the individual. The onset, course, and magnitude of cancer in patients is influenced by variables that include the type of cancer, when it was detected, social support, and treatments available. Our response and attitude about developing cancer and receiving cancer treatment is only one factor of many to consider when examining the connection between stress and health. Moreover, there is virtually no scientific evidence that our mental state *causes* cancer or that our mental state *cures* cancer.

We don't yet understand the exact relationship between stress, cancer, and immune system functioning. There is also research that suggests that low to moderate stress can *enhance* immune system functioning (Bosch et al., 2001; Dhabhar, Miller, McEwen, & Spencer, 1995). The exact nature of our physical response to stress is dependent on the specific stressor and our cognitive appraisals of those stressors (Kemeny, 2003). We look to future research to fill in the blanks so that our knowledge will be more complete. We have seen throughout our discussion on stress that our

---

Let's Review!

This section detailed how we appraise an event as stressful or not stressful and explained the bodily response to stress that we term the general adaptation syndrome. We also discussed the relationship between stress and the functioning of our immune systems. As a quick check of your understanding, answer these questions.

1. You are more vulnerable to illness during which stage of Selye's stress response model?
   a. alarm reaction
   c. rejuvenation
   b. resistance
   d. exhaustion

2. Immunosuppression refers to:
   a. the activation of the immune system when we are faced with a stressor.
   b. the reduction in the activity of our immune system.
   c. the immune system's ability to survive immediate danger.
   d. the activation of the release of endorphins and corticosteroids to help the immune system function.

3. The first step in experiencing stress is:
   a. the alarm reaction.
   c. primary appraisal.
   b. resistance.
   d. exhaustion.

ANSWERS
1.d; 2.b; 3.a

perception and response to an event definitely influences the eventual outcome. Stress ultimately impacts our health. With that in mind, we now turn our attention to the many ways all of us cope with and handle stress.

Coping With Stress ›

How do we cope with stress? Think of the exam or exams you will take for this course. Does your body evidence the telltale signs of the stress response when thinking about your exam? What do you do when faced with stress like this? Are you likely to react emotionally and become very anxious, worrying about what the test will be like? Are you likely to tackle the stressor directly and put all your energy toward studying and preparing for the exam? Do you just ignore your stress completely, hoping for some miracle like the postponement or cancellation of the exam? Maybe you experience some or all of these reactions.

Whatever you do to manage an event or stimulus that you perceive as threatening is part of **coping.** How we cope with stress influences the way stress affects us. We will discuss two broad categories, or strategies for coping: problem-focused coping and emotion-focused coping (Folkman & Lazarus, 1988). You may use one or both types of coping when you're faced with a stressor. Each has its benefits and costs (Lazarus & Folkman, 1984; Roth & Cohen, 1986).

Problem-Focused Coping: Change the Situation

Problem-focused coping is aimed at controlling or altering the environment that caused the stress. Let's say for example that you are working while going to school and your boss just increased your work hours. You now feel that you don't have enough time for school or your social life. A problem-focused approach to coping with this increased workload may include finding another job without as many required hours, or reducing the number of credit hours you are taking in school. Both of these strategies are aimed at changing the situation to reduce the amount of perceived stress. One benefit of either of these problem-focused coping strategies would be eliminating the perceived stressor. At the same time you benefit by experiencing more control over your environment, which also may enhance your self-esteem. However, it also is possible that you have misdiagnosed the problem, which is a cost of problem-focused coping. Maybe the number of work hours isn't affecting your college work so much as your motivation or your social schedule. You may actually increase your long-term level of stress by choosing an inappropriate course of action, another possible cost of problem-focused coping. Reducing your college hours increases the time it will take to complete your college education. Changing jobs may result in lower wages, making it more difficult to pay for your education.

Generally, problem-focused coping tends to be most useful when we feel that we actually can do something about a situation (Folkman & Moskowitz, 2000). Under these circumstances, problem-focused coping is more likely to lead to a more positive health outcome (Penley, Tomaka, & Wiebe, 2002). However, when we do not feel that a situation is controllable, we often rely more on emotion-focused coping strategies (Lazarus, 1993).

Emotion-Focused Coping: Change Your Reaction

Emotion-focused coping is aimed at controlling your internal, subjective, emotional reactions to stress. You alter the way you feel or think in order to reduce stress. Stressors activate a variety of emotions including anxiety, worry, guilt, shame, jealousy, envy, and anger. Because these emotions are usually experienced as unpleasant, we are

⋙ LEARNING
⋙ OBJECTIVES
⋙ Distinguish between problem-focused
⋙ and emotion-focused coping styles.
⋙ Indicate adaptive ways to manage
⋙ stress.

coping   the behaviors that we engage in to manage stressors

problem-focused coping   behaviors that aim to control or alter the environment that is causing stress

emotion-focused coping   behaviors aimed at controlling the internal emotional reactions to a stressor

Taking your anger out on someone to relieve stress illustrates emotion-focused coping.

motivated to reduce or avoid them. For example, suppose that a young woman is anticipating the arrival of her boyfriend at a party where they planned to meet up, and he already is an hour late. The stress of this situation not only activates the physical sensations that we have discussed previously but also triggers emotional reactions. She may be angry with him because she feels that he is purposely ignoring her wants and desires. She may take her anger out on a friend, or she may turn all of her emotional energy into being the life of the party. Conversely, she may experience anxiety and worry, fearing that something harmful has occurred to him. When he arrives, she may express her anger by complaining about his lateness or ignoring him all together, or she may be especially loving and attentive. Either way, her coping behavior is directed at reducing the emotions that she is experiencing.

We attempt to lessen the effects of these emotions in primarily two ways: cognitive reappraisal and by engaging in psychological defense mechanisms. **Cognitive reappraisal** is an active and conscious process in which we alter our interpretation of the stressful event. In the previous example, the young woman has appraised her boyfriend's lateness in a negative manner (he's ignoring her or something bad happened to him). These appraisals have led to feelings of anger and anxiety. She can reappraise or reinterpret his lateness in a more realistic manner—he got caught in traffic or he had to work late. These reappraisals are less likely to lead to emotional distress. Consequently, cognitive reappraisal can be an emotionally constructive way of coping with a stressful event.

A more automatic and unconscious way in which we lessen the effects of our emotions is by engaging in defense mechanisms. Sigmund Freud was one of the first theorists to identify psychological **defense mechanisms.** You will learn more about Freud's ideas on personality and coping in the next chapter. For now, what is relevant is that Freud suggested that coping strategies are employed unconsciously to allow us to reduce our anxiety and maintain a positive self-image and self-esteem. Because of these features, we now consider these defense mechanisms as emotion-focused coping strategies. We use them to avoid or reduce the emotions associated with a stressor, but they do not necessarily eliminate the source of stress. For example, you might

cognitive reappraisal an active and conscious process in which we alter our interpretation of the stressful event

defense mechanisms unconscious, emotional strategies that are engaged in to reduce anxiety and maintain a positive self-image

use the defense mechanism of *displacement* to deal with your anger toward a boss, parent, or a significant other. You take your anger out on a friend by yelling at her, or on an object by throwing it against the wall. Afterward, you may *feel* better, but it does not resolve the issue that made you angry in the first place. The stressor is still present and may resurface again in the future.

Everyone uses defense mechanisms from time to time. Typically, we rely on those defense mechanisms that have worked for us in the past. That is, we are more likely to use in the future those methods that have been effective in sufficiently reducing our emotional reactions to a stressor. Some of these defense mechanisms are adaptive. Putting your anger into a more constructive activity such as cleaning your house or washing your car is more productive than hurting yourself or someone else (see sublimation in Table 13.3 ◆). Other defense mechanisms, especially when we use them to excess, can prevent us from developing effective ways of coping or learning how we can avoid creating the stressful situations. For example, the student who fails to study for a test may decide that his roommate who watches television is at fault. Such a defense on the part of the student does not promote an adaptive way of coping with failure. The more common of these defense mechanisms are displayed in Table 13.3. See if you can identify the defense mechanisms that you tend to use.

The use of defense mechanisms also involves costs and benefits. The main reason we use them is to restore our self-image. Yet, we also benefit because defense mechanisms reduce the intensity of the physical stress response as our anxiety decreases. We may also give ourselves the confidence to handle additional stressors. These benefits, however, are typically outweighed by the costs. Defense mechanisms often inhibit our ability to act to resolve the problem. Using our emotions to cope with stressors may impede our functioning in other daily activities—yelling at our friends too often may drive them away. Most importantly, using defense mechanisms keeps us in a state of unawareness as to the true source of any stress-related symptoms. Given these disadvantages, why do we continue to use defense mechanisms? Basically, they are easier and produce quicker results in reducing our feelings of anxiety. Unfortunately, this is often at the expense of our physical health.

Managing Stress

What are truly effective ways to manage stress? A discussion of stress would by no means be complete without detailing effective means by which to handle or manage stress. Because stress affects our health, considerable research has addressed what techniques or strategies may reduce our risk of illness and disease. For all their varied names, these techniques all focus on changing one or more aspects of the stress response: your physical, bodily reactions, your emotional reactions, your thoughts or appraisal of events (cognitive), and your responses (behavioral). Many of these methods address both problem-focused and emotion-focused coping.

Physical Methods of Stress Management

Physical methods of stress management focus on managing the body's fight-or-flight mechanism. As we have seen, the stress response entails the activation of the sympathetic nervous system, which makes our bodies tense and prepared to respond to a threatening situation. In the face of chronic stress, we reach exhaustion, having depleted the body's resources. This exhaustion can lead to immunosuppression and increased risk of illness. However, when we are able to release this tension, we allow the body to replenish its resources, so these ill effects are less likely to occur. Releasing physical tension can be achieved in several ways.

◆ Table 13-3

Some of the More Common Defense Mechanisms

Defense Mechanism	Definition	Examples
Denial	Refusing to accept or acknowledge the reality of a situation or idea.	Going out partying the night before an exam denies how this behavior will affect your exam performance. Engaging in unprotected sexual activities denies the possibility of an unwanted pregnancy or contracting a STI.
Rationalization	Devising a plausible reason or motive to explain one's behavior.	Rationalizing one's excessive consumption of alcohol by saying that it makes one more sociable or improves one's personality.
Reaction formation	Engaging in a behavior or attitude that is the opposite extreme of the true motive or impulse.	A young boy who pulls the ponytail of the girl sitting in front of him is behaving aggressively to cover up the opposite emotion—liking her. Bumping into someone at the mall whom you dislike, but whom you approach and say warmly, "Hi. How have you been? You look great!"
Regression	Returning to an earlier stage of development in one's behavior, thinking, or attitudes.	Adults who throw tantrums, pout, or whine are engaging in childlike behaviors. An older child who reacts to the birth of a sibling by wetting the bed or sucking her thumb again.
Sublimation	Directing emotions into an activity that is more constructive and socially acceptable.	Exercising or cleaning your room when you are angry or upset. Directing your emotions into writing, sculpting, music, or painting.
Repression	Excluding wishes, impulses, ideas, or memories from consciousness, and putting them in one's subconscious.	Forgetting the details of an accident or crime or other situations associated with trauma or harm.
Projection	Attributing one's own ideas, feelings, or attitudes to other people.	Accusing another student of brown-nosing the professor when it is you who engages in this behavior. A person in a relationship may accuse his partner of wanting to date other people when this is his own desire.
Displacement	Directing emotions toward a less threatening source.	Yelling at your spouse after an argument with your boss. Athletes who throw objects or kick the bench after a missed play.

 Application

- *Physical exercise.* Some form of regular aerobic exercise, such as swimming, walking, running, or dancing, can be an effective strategy for reducing physical stress reactions (Anshel, 1995; Langreth, 2000; Stear, 2003). Many studies also confirm that exercise reduces the negative emotions such as depression and anxiety that we often feel in response to stress (Brugman & Ferguson, 2002; Long & van Stavel, 1995). Exercise raises energy levels, strengthens the heart, and lowers muscle tension. We sleep more soundly after exercise and also feel better as the body increases its production of natural mood elevators like serotonin and endorphins.

- *Biofeedback training.* Up until the 1960s, most scientists believed that the bodily reactions involved in the stress response were totally involuntary— not under our control. In the past 40 years, several electronic devices have been created that can measure and record these bodily changes. Referred to as **biofeedback,** training on these devices can increase your awareness of bodily reactions and may teach you to increase control over them. Biofeedback training has been somewhat successful for people experiencing migraine and tension headaches (Landy, 2004; McGrady, Bush, & Grubb, 1997; Rokicki et al., 1997), asthma (Lehrer, Feldman, Giardino, Song, & Schmaling, 2002), incontinence (Ozturk, Niazi, Stessman, & Rao, 2004), and chronic pain (Turk, Meichenbaum, & Nerman, 1979). Biofeedback is not the only way to decrease tension. There are other, less expensive methods for achieving the same results. In one way or another, they all focus on increasing your state of relaxation.

- *Relaxation techniques.* One of the most successful nonchemical ways to treat people with stress disorders is the application of relaxation techniques. This may include **progressive relaxation training** in which you learn to alternately tense and then relax each muscle group of the body in a systematic fashion. This gives you an awareness of when and where you feel tension when you're under stress. You then learn to manage and control the tension that you feel by relaxing on command. Other relaxation techniques may include regular massages, meditation, or yoga. For others, relaxation may be achieved by deep breathing exercises, engaging in a hobby, or by listening to music.

    Regardless of the specific technique, taking the time to relax the whole body breaks up the stress response, moderates its intensity, and assists the body in returning to homeostasis (Stoyva & Budzynski, 1974). Consider-

 Application

biofeedback   an electronic device that measures and records bodily changes so that an individual can monitor and control these changes more effectively

progressive relaxation training   a stress management technique in which a person learns how to systematically tense and relax the muscle groups of the body

Application

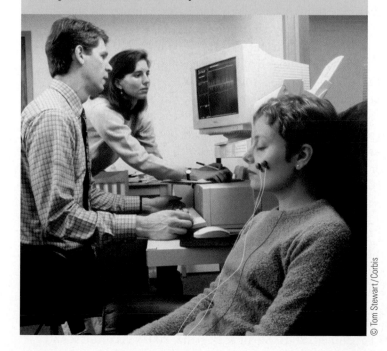

Biofeedback training helps you manage stress by making you aware of your bodily reactions to perceived stressors and then using this awareness to control your stress reactions.

© Tom Stewart / Corbis

able evidence has accumulated showing that daily use of relaxation procedures, regardless of the form, are effective in lessening symptoms of asthma, insomnia, tension headaches, migraine headaches, high blood pressure, intestinal problems, and chronic anxiety (Astin, 2004; Benson, 1996; Meissner, Blanchard, & Malamood, 1997; Smyth, Litcher, Hurewitz, & Stone, 2001).

Emotional Methods of Stress Management

- *Social support.* Remember the telephone company slogan "Reach out and touch someone"? Little did they know how appropriate this slogan is for reducing stress and promoting well-being. Having friends, a shoulder to cry on, or someone to discuss an issue or trying event with are all examples of **social support**—having close and positive relationships with others. Scores of studies suggest that social support buffers the effects of stress (Cohen, Doyle, Turner, Alper, & Skoner, 2003; Diener & Seligman, 2004; Ornish, 1998; Shields, 2004; Wills & Fegan, 2001).

  Social support helps us weather stress. Family stability, spousal support, or simply having friends to confide in is related to a longer life span, as well as a longer survival rate for those with cancer or heart disease (Case, Moss, Case, McDermott, & Eberly, 1992; Colon et al., 1991; Krantz & McCeney, 2002; Schwartz et al., 1995; Shen, McCreary, & Myers, 2004). Even giving social support to others appears to buffer the effects of stress (S. L. Brown, Nesse, Vinokur, & Smith, 2003). Social support also may act to decrease the release of stress hormones (Uchino, Cacioppo, & Kiecolt-Glaser, 1996).

  How does social support reduce stress? We don't yet understand exact causal mechanisms for the relationship between social support and health. Perhaps a social network promotes more self-disclosure and expression of our feelings, which makes us feel better (Kowalski, 1996; Lepore, Ragan, & Jones, 2000). Perhaps being loved and liked enhances self-esteem and encourages a sense of purpose and optimism toward life. Social support may provide a combination of these effects. Only future research will tell.

- *Religion and spirituality.* Numerous research studies have shown the importance of spiritual faith, prayer, church membership, and strong value systems in promoting physical health and well-being (Hawks, Hull, Thalman, & Richins, 1995; W. R. Miller & Thoresen, 2003; Powell, Shahabi, & Thoresen, 2003). In this research, spirituality often means having a purpose in life, self-awareness, and connectedness with self, others, and a larger community. Religiousness is typically defined as participation in an institutionalized doctrine. For example, in several studies it has been found that prayer and spirituality are associated with reduced symptoms of distress in cancer patients (Laubmeier, Zakowski, & Bair, 2004; E. J. Taylor & Outlaw, 2002). Religiousness and spirituality also have been shown to be significantly associated with reduced symptoms in people with serious mental illness (Corrigan, McCorkle, Schell, & Kidder, 2003).

  How do religion and spirituality promote health? We don't yet know the reason for these associations. Religion, spirituality, and health are correlated. We cannot conclude that religiousness or spirituality causes better health. Which specific religious or spiritual factors enhance health and well-being remains unclear. Many of the studies have significant methodological flaws and define religion and spirituality in an assortment of ways (Hill & Pargament, 2003; Sloan & Bagiella, 2002). As more sound

social support having close and positive relationships with others

research is conducted, psychologists will be able to uncover the distinct contribution of religion and spirituality to health and well-being.

Cognitive Methods of Stress Management

Another group of stress management techniques focuses on changing how we think about or appraise our situations. We can reduce the effects of stress by using our cognitions to either promote relaxation or to change the way we view the world. Here are three such examples.

- *Guided imagery.* This procedure is a cognitive equivalent of progressive relaxation. Rather than systematically relaxing each muscle group, you learn to use your mind to achieve a state of relaxation. You imagine that you are in a safe, pleasant, calming environment, perhaps walking along a beach or in a forest. You maintain your focus on this image as you feel the tensions associated with stress leave your body. Similar to progressive relaxation, you become trained to automatically summon up this image when you feel stressed. For some people, guided imagery is just as effective as the relaxation techniques discussed previously (Astin, 2004). Can you think of your own image, scene, or memory that would provide these benefits for you? How does your body feel as you think about it?

- *Meditation.* **Meditation** in the form of yoga, Zen, or transcendental meditation also may reduce tension and anxiety caused by stress (Andresen, 2000). They are mental exercises in which people consciously focus their attention to heighten awareness and bring their mental processes under more control. The person sits in a comfortable position with her eyes closed and silently focuses her attention on a specially assigned word that creates a resonant sound. Meditation appears to decrease heart rate, respiration, and oxygen consumption, bodily changes that are also achieved through progressive muscle relaxation techniques (Carrington, 1993; D. S. Holmes, 1987). Some studies also have found that meditation can improve mood, lessen tiredness, and enhance immune system responses (Solberg, Halvorsen, & Holen, 2000), although such evidence has been too inconsistent to make solid conclusions (Lehrer & Woolfork, 1993).

meditation   mental exercises in which people consciously focus their attention to heighten awareness and bring their mental processes under more control

- *Optimistic attitude.* Simply expecting good things to happen may influence your health. We already have seen how an optimistic attitude influences the survival rate of cancer patients. This same effect occurs in healthy participants. For example, in a study on first-year law students, those students who endorsed optimistic beliefs, such as believing they could succeed and having confidence about their abilities, had better immune system functioning at midsemester than students with a more pessimistic outlook (Segerstrom, Taylor, Kemeny, & Fahey, 1998). Optimists report lower stress levels and have fewer stress-related physical complaints (Peterson, 2000; Peterson & Bossio, 2001; Wiebe & Smith, 1997). Cancer and heart disease patients with an optimistic attitude often show a better response to treatment than patients with a less positive attitude (Carver et al., 2000; Shen, McCreary & Myers, 2004). Focusing on the half of the glass that is full is better for your health than focusing on the half that is empty.

Behavioral Methods of Stress Management

In addition to changing one's thoughts, physical reactions, and emotional responses, you can engage in several behaviors that will reduce the influence of stress on your health. Two such methods include laughing and managing your time more effectively.

Application

- *Laughter.* He who laughs, lasts! Psychological research supports this idiom (Lefcourt, 2001). Laughter promotes relaxation, which may explain why good-humored people perceive less stress when faced with life's challenges (Lefcourt & Davidson-Katz, 1991). This information is not news in India, where in March of 1995, the first laughing club was founded. This number has since grown to over 80! Members meet in a parking lot or a park and simply practice laughing. They claim that this behavior helps them combat stress by reducing blood pressure, boosting the immune system, and raising energy levels. We might add that these clubs also offer companionship and exercise, and members engage in deep breathing exercises as a prelude to laughing (Roach, 1996). Any one or all of these factors may be responsible for the positive health effects.

Application

- *Time management.* Many of us experience stress because we feel that there is not enough time to accomplish all the tasks, errands, and work that we have established for ourselves. One way to minimize the stress resulting from such pressures is to organize your time better. Keeping a daily planner or formal time schedule to record your obligations, commitments, and deadlines for study, work, and leisure activities can ease tension. Remembering to schedule time with loved ones (social support), time for exercise, and time to simply relax will further your ammunition against stress. Writing out a formal time schedule also allows you to evaluate the number and importance of your commitments. Prioritizing your activities and possibly reducing their number illustrates problem-focused coping strategies. Be sure to schedule *enough* time for activities, factoring in travel time (and traffic). One of the most common time management mistakes that college students make is not allowing enough time to study all of the assigned material (Bueler, Griffen, & Ross, 1994). The key to effective time management is to treat each responsibility—whether it is work, studying, or play—as a serious commitment.

Laughter promotes relaxation, which helps manage our stress level.

© Picturequest

These are just a few techniques that can be used to reduce the effects of stress. How many do you use? Could you use more of them? By using these methods, you have the opportunity to reduce the ill effects of stress on your health right now, as well as the cumulative effect of stress on your body in the future. However, if you sometimes feel that you cannot manage the stress in your life, or you aren't coping well with your stressors, then it may be time to seek professional help. Chapter 16 describes the different types of mental health professionals who can help us cope more effectively.

As you have seen, psychological research into the influence of stress on health has resulted in the development of various techniques to increase our ability to cope with stress. However, one area of behavior that is more difficult to change is one's personality. Some people are just naturally more optimistic than others. Health psychologists also deal with this issue, which we'll look at next.

Let's Review!

This section distinguished between problem-focused and emotion-focused coping styles and described some stress-management techniques. For a quick check of your understanding, answer these questions.

1. Organizing your time better would be best classified as a(n) _____ coping skill.
   - a. problem-focused
   - c. avoidance-focused
   - b. emotion-focused
   - d. encounter-focused

2. It is common for young children to react to the birth of a sibling by regressing to earlier behaviors such as sucking their thumb again or wanting to feed from a bottle. Such behaviors exemplify _____ coping skills.

   - a. problem-focused
   - c. avoidance-focused
   - b. emotion-focused
   - d. encounter-focused

3. Which of the following is the *least* effective stress management technique?
   - a. guided imagery
   - c. defense mechanisms
   - b. physical exercise
   - d. relaxation techniques

ANSWERS

1. a; 2. b; 3. c

Personality and Health > > > > > > > > > > > > > > > > > >

LEARNING OBJECTIVE

Discuss the relationship between personality and health.

Does your personality influence your health? Think about Edward from the opening case study. Is it possible that his personality made him more susceptible to disease? If so, which particular features of his personality do you think might be critical? Health psychologists also have been interested in how personality influences our health. A number of personality dimensions have been related to health, specifically to the functioning of the immune system (Segerstrom, 2000). We consider three such avenues of research here: the Type A personality, learned helplessness, and the hardy personality.

Type A Personality: Ambition, Drive, and Competitiveness

Take a moment to look at Table 13.4 ◆. Which of these descriptions more accurately reflects your personality? Would you consider yourself more of a **Type A personality,** a person who is aggressive, competitive, and driven to achieve? Or do you characterize yourself as more of a **Type B personality,** a person who is more relaxed, easygoing,

Type A personality   a person who is aggressive, ambitious, and competitive

Type B personality   a person who is characterized by patience, flexibility, and an easygoing manner

◆ Table 13.4

Type A and Type B Personalities—Which Type Are You?

Type A	Type B
competitive	easygoing
verbally aggressive	calm
overcommitted to achieving	relaxed
impatient	patient
hostile attitude when frustrated	trusting
sense of time urgency	good-natured
workaholic	lower need for achievement
easily angered	

patient, and flexible? Edward probably fit the Type A description more than the Type B. Could this be a possible factor in his illness?

At one time, having a Type A personality was considered a risk factor for heart disease. You already may have been aware of this information; this particular psychological issue has received considerable public attention. Because heart disease is one of the leading causes of death in the United States, there has been a lot of research devoted to its causes. Let's look at this research more closely because the results are not clear cut, and we can see the complexity of studying behavior and how psychological research evolves over time.

Cardiologists Meyer Friedman and Ray Rosenman (1974) were the first to examine the connection between personality and heart disease. They suspected that personality or behavior patterns may play a role in the lives of men who were more likely to develop heart disease, and in men more likely to die from a heart attack. To test their idea, the researchers gathered a sample of 3,000 men between the ages of 35 and 59 with no known health problems. Each man was interviewed, and based on the man's behavior during the interview, each was designated as a Type A personality, a Type B personality, or somewhere in between. A label of Type A or Type B was given to those men who very much exemplified those traits listed in Table 13.4. The majority of the sample fell somewhere in between, but in comparing the two types over the next decade, Friedman and Rosenman found that Type A personalities were two to three times more likely to have suffered a heart attack. Keep in mind that the majority of the sample could not easily be categorized as either Type A or Type B.

Friedman and Rosenman's landmark study stimulated additional research on how personality factors may place people at risk for disease. However, subsequent research on the connection between Type A personality and the risk of heart disease has not been able to replicate these results (Booth-Kewley & Friedman, 1987; T. Q. Miller, Turner, Tindale, Posavac, & Dugoni, 1991). Given the broad definitions of Type A and Type B personalities, this should not be surprising, especially when Friedman and Rosenman themselves had difficulty in classifying their sample. In later research, psychologists attempted to isolate which specific behaviors of the Type A personality may predispose a person to heart problems.

Further research suggests that specific features of Type A behavior seem to be more related to coronary heart disease. The key features included anger, mistrust, and hostility. People who are frequently angry, suspicious, bitter, antagonistic, and distrustful of others seem more likely to experience heart-related health problems (Denollet, 1993; Krantz, & McCeney, 2002; T. Q. Miller, Smith, Turner, Guijarro, & Hallet, 1996; J. E. Williams et al., 2000; R. Williams, 1993). People with a Type A personality who do not show these specific behaviors appear to be no more at risk for heart disease than their Type B counterparts. Thus, it is not the entire Type A personality that leads to heart disease, but the negative emotions, especially anger and hostility, that do the most damage.

Research continues to investigate the precise relationship between hostility, anger, and heart disease. For example, perhaps the culprit is the increased stress level and lack of social support that goes along with being a hostile person (Helmers et al., 1995). Efforts to modify Type A behavior as a means of reducing repeat heart attacks have achieved modest success (Friedman, Thoresen, Gill, & Powell, 1984; Nakano, 1996). Yet in one study of a follow-up of patients who had already experienced heart attacks, Type A behavior was associated with a greater probability of a second heart attack, whereas Type B behavior was associated with a greater probability of death (Catipovic-Veselica, Glavas, Kristek, & Sram, 2001). Such a finding argues against modifying Type A behavior following a heart attack. Because our American culture highly values achievement and competition, this behavior pattern may prove difficult to change before people develop heart disease.

Learned Helplessness: I Can't Do It

Do you believe that you have no control over stressful life events? Do you believe that even your best efforts will result in failure? When you blame yourself for any failure you experience, are you more likely to attribute your failure to a specific factor—you're just not good at soccer—or to a more global feature—you're just too uncoordinated to do any athletic activity? These questions illustrate the key features of a personality factor called **learned helplessness,** in which people develop a passive response to stressors based on their exposure to previously uncontrolled, negative events.

learned helplessness   a passive response to stressors based on the exposure to previously uncontrolled, negative events

Learned helplessness was first demonstrated on dogs in a psychological laboratory (Seligman & Maier, 1967). The dogs were placed in a cage that was equipped with an electrified grid. When the dogs received shock they could not escape from, after repeated trials, the dogs' escape responses slowly decreased. Recall from Chapter 5 that this decrease in responding is called extinction (see p. 218). Even when they were later given the opportunity to escape the shock, the dogs remained in the cage. The dogs had learned to be helpless. Experiments using human participants (not using shock) have produced similar results (Hiroto, 1974; W. R. Miller & Seligman, 1975). Consequently, when previous experiences lead you to believe that you cannot "fix" the problems facing you, you may approach new situations with this perceived lack of control and passively endure what ever comes your way (Dweck, Chiu, & Hong, 1995; Peterson, Maier, & Seligman, 1993). You are likely to view stressors as threats rather than as challenges. As a result, your levels of stress increase, and you are more likely to develop stress-related physical illnesses (Stern, McCants, & Pettine, 1982).

Application

Research supports the notion that college students who feel helpless are less likely to persist, more likely to give up easily, and as a result earn poor grades and report unhappiness (McKean, 1994). Adults and adolescents who react to stress by feeling at a loss to do anything about the situation are more prone to depression and other stress problems (Haack, Dykman, Metalsky, & Abramson, 1996; Waschbusch, Sellers, LeBlanc, & Kelley, 2003). Learned helplessness also has been documented in children with a history of reading failure (Fowler & Peterson, 1981). It can develop in elderly people in nursing homes who are not given choices about their daily activities and routines (Seligman, 1989). In all of these situations, the *expectation* of failure and lack of control are what influence one's perceived level of stress, one's subsequent response to stress, and ultimately, one's mental and physical health. In analyzing the opening case study, it is possible that once Edward was told that his disease was no longer manageable, he adopted an attitude of learned helplessness. This attitude may have contributed to the continued spread of the disease.

The Hardy Personality: Control, Commitment, and Challenge

Do you view stressors as challenges rather than as threats? For example, if you try out for the soccer team one year and do not make it, do you try out again the next year or do you simply give up? Do you stay committed to the pursuit of your goals and values? If you fail an exam, do you go and get help, or do you just assume that you'll never understand the material and withdraw from the class—possibly spoiling your chance at a college degree? Do you believe that your actions influence the outcome of a situation? Your answers to these questions outline three factors that appear to be related to health: challenge, commitment, and control.

- The tendency to see life as a series of *challenges*.
- A sense of personal *commitment* to self, work, family, and other values.
- A perception of *control* over life and work.

hardy personality a person who is high in the traits of commitment, control, and challenge that appear to be associated with strong stress resistance

The "three Cs" taken together were labeled by psychologists Salvatore Maddi and Suzanne Kobasa (1984) as the **hardy personality.**

This term resulted from Kobasa's (1982) research on upper-level executives and attorneys who had experienced considerable stress over a 3-year period. Those who exemplified hardy traits were less likely to get ill during this time of stress. Even Type A people who scored high on measures of hardiness were less likely to get ill compared to Type A people who scored low on hardiness. This led Kobasa to conclude that hardiness traits may decrease stress levels, thereby decreasing one's chances of developing illness.

Psychological research confirms that hardy people seem to be unusually resistant to stress. They endorse a positive worldview in which stressors are appraised as challenges rather than threats, so they feel less potential harm from them (Wiebe, 1991). Notice how these qualities are in direct contrast to people with learned helplessness. This positive attitude appears to promote more problem-focused coping, such that they handle conflict better and are willing to rely on the help of others when weathering stress (Scheir & Carver, 1992). Hardy people also report higher levels of personal satisfaction with their work (Rush, Schoel, & Barnard, 1995) and show greater immune system responses to bacteria (Dolbier et al., 2001).

Taken together, what does all this research on personality tell us? First, we can recognize that negative emotions such as anger and hostility do not promote good health. Similarly, negative cognitions such as expecting failure or a lack of control do not appear to be good for our health. In contrast, it is the "three Cs" of hardiness—a sense of control, being comfortable with challenge, and maintaining commitment—that appear to be most beneficial to our ability to deal with stress and therefore most advantageous to our health. Are there other personal factors that

Despite her physical limitations, Helen Keller perceived life as a challenge, was committed to learning, and believed she had control over such learning. She exemplifies the three traits of a hardy personality.

© Bradley Smith/Corbis

must be considered in addressing the issue of health? Yes, there are. Lifestyle behaviors such as diet, exercise, and use of alcohol or tobacco also must be factored into the equation of stress and health. We turn our attention to these lifestyle issues in the last section of this chapter.

Let's Review!

This section detailed research investigating the relationship between personality and health. As a quick check of your understanding, answer these questions.

1. Donald is described by his friends as easygoing, calm, and patient. Donald would most likely be classified as a:

   a. Type A personality.
   b. Type B personality.
   c. hardy personality.
   d. learned helpless personality.

2. Which of the following personality factors has been strongly linked to depression and other stress problems?

   a. Type A traits
   b. Type B traits
   c. hardiness
   d. learned helplessness

3. After working on a project for more than 3 years, Zilmarie is told by her boss to redesign the project in a new way. Zilmarie considers such a task a challenge and commits herself to the new project with gusto. Zilmarie is probably high on which personality dimension?

   a. Type A personality
   b. Type B personality
   c. hardiness
   d. learned helplessness

ANSWERS
1.b; 2.d; 3.c

Lifestyle and Health ≫ ＞ ＞ ＞ ＞ ＞ ＞ ＞ ＞ ＞ ＞ ＞ ＞ ＞ ＞ ＞ ＞ ＞

> **≫ LEARNING**
> **≫ OBJECTIVE**
> ≫ Identify health-defeating and
> ≫ health-promoting behaviors.
> ≫

Health psychologists also examine lifestyle and environmental factors that may play a role in our susceptibility to illness and disease. These behaviors are not a part of our personality or genetic constitution, so it follows that they should be easier to change or to prevent. As such, considerable research has examined those behaviors that have been found to put us at more risk for illness and disease and those behaviors or lifestyle choices that have been linked to healthier living. You may want to keep these questions in mind as we explore these issues: How can we get people to stop engaging in the unhealthy behaviors? How can we get them to develop healthier lifestyle habits? These are the questions that always interest health psychologists.

Health-Defeating Behaviors

We already have seen that high levels of stress may increase our chances of illness. Some of these events may or may not be under your control. Health psychologists define **health-defeating behaviors** as those that increase the chance of illness, disease, or death. This includes risky behaviors such as driving at excessive speeds, carrying a weapon, or being a passenger in a car with a driver who is under the influence of drugs or alcohol. Risky behaviors endanger your health, as you place yourself in a situation in which you have a higher risk of physical injury. Many of the leading causes of death are related to unsafe health practices (Figure 13.4). Over 45% of all deaths are in some way related to personal habits that damage our health (McGinnis & Foege, 1993). This is our focus in this section. We will examine behavior patterns, usually engaged in over a long period of time, that *are* controllable and seriously put your health at risk. These behaviors include alcohol consumption, smoking, and engaging in unsafe sex practices.

health-defeating behaviors behaviors that increase the chance of illness, disease, or death

Figure 13.4 **Leading Causes of Death in the United States**

In 2001, heart disease, cancer, strokes, respiratory diseases, and accidents were the top five causes of deaths in the United States. Many of these deaths could have been prevented by engaging in better health practices.

Top 3 causes of death are the same for males and females.

Top 2 causes of death are the same for the four major race groups.

National Vital Statistics Report, Vol 52, No 3, September 18, 2003.

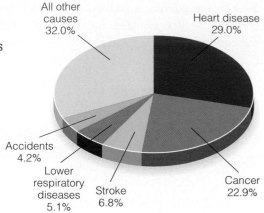

All other causes 32.0%

Heart disease 29.0%

Accidents 4.2%

Lower respiratory diseases 5.1%

Stroke 6.8%

Cancer 22.9%

Alcohol

Recall from Chapter 4 the specific effects that alcohol has on the body and brain. These effects can be seen within a larger context by detailing the social and physical ramifications of alcohol abuse on peoples' health and well-being. Consider that the majority of manslaughter convictions, assaults, and spousal abuse incidents involve alcohol. Nearly half of all of our highway deaths involve alcohol. Fetal alcohol syndrome (FAS), caused by a mother's excessive ingestion of alcohol during pregnancy, is the leading cause of mental retardation (Adler & Rosenberg, 1994). In one psychological survey (Kolbe, Collins, & Cortese, 1997) 30% of high school students reported having five or more drinks on one occasion in the past month. The students reported this behavior despite being underage! For college men and women, the rate is even higher.

Alcohol abuse not only leads to social problems, but also is associated with major health problems including heart disease, stroke, cancer, liver disease, memory blackouts, and erectile dysfunction in males. These statistics signify the drastic impact that alcohol abuse has on our nation's health and would suggest that alcohol be used only in moderation, if at all.

In the United States, drinking alcohol is often marketed as a fun-loving activity. Yet the majority of manslaughter convictions, assaults, and spousal abuse incidents involve alcohol use.

© Bill Aron / Photo Edit

Smoking

Another easily preventable behavior is cigarette smoking. In 1997, the U.S. Food and Drug Administration officially labeled the main drug in cigarettes, nicotine, as an addictive substance (Raloff, 1997). In developing countries, smoking is the norm, whereas in the United States smoking has declined over the past 30 thirty years. Still, one in five adults over the age of 18 smoke (National Center for Health Statistics, 2003), and 29% of high school students have smoked cigarettes in the past 30 days (National Center for Health Statistics, 2001). These smokers are more likely to be poorer, less educated, and of minority status.

In 2000, an estimated 70% of smokers said they wanted to quit, and 41% had tried to quit during the preceding year (Trosclair, Husten, Pederson, & Dhillon, 2002). Numerous treatments and therapies have been developed to help people stop smoking. They include the use of nicotine patches or gum, psychotherapy, hypnosis, antidepressant medication, and support groups. Unfortunately, these treatments are not very effective over the long term. Only one-third of smokers are able to break the habit, although three in four smokers have attempted to quit (Niemi, Mueller, & Smith, 1989). It typically may take three to four tries before the person is successful at quitting. For this reason, many antismoking programs aim to prevent smoking in the first place. Many of these programs are aimed at teenagers because this seems to be the prime age when smoking begins. Health officials have determined that the cost of treating the health problems associated with smoking far outweighs the cost of prevention programs.

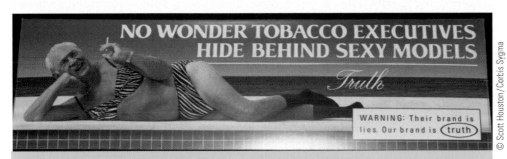

Today, antismoking ads aimed at young people attempt to prevent teenagers from smoking.

Additional attempts have been made on the governmental level to reduce smoking. In 1997 the state of Florida sued a tobacco company to recover damages for smoking-related illnesses. In a landmark court decision, the state won. The tobacco companies eventually negotiated an agreement to pay billions of dollars to all states to compensate them for the costs related to smoking-related illnesses. In addition, federal taxes on cigarettes continue to rise. Typically, as taxes rise, consumption decreases (Brown, Kane, & Ayers, 1993). Perhaps, if cigarettes become too expensive, teenagers will be less likely to start smoking.

Although numerous efforts are being made here in the United States to reduce smoking, this is not the case worldwide. Tobacco companies have taken their products to other, less developed (and less regulated) countries and marketed them there (Shenon, 1994). Until prevention programs operate worldwide, the ill effects of smoking will continue to be a concern for health psychologists. Just think back to the opening case study. Could Edward's smoking habit have contributed to his cancer diagnosis (even though it was not lung cancer)? His smoking may have played a negative role in his body's ability to fight this disease.

Unsafe Sex

Several years ago, Christine, a young White woman in her early 20s, had just experienced an intense breakup of a long-term relationship. The next time she saw her ex-boyfriend, he was on a talk show describing how he was coping with an illness. As it turned out, he was HIV-positive. This was news to Christine! She was devastated, but had the personal strength and wisdom to get tested. Sadly, the news was not good. Christine had contracted the AIDS virus. This is a true story. The woman referred to as Christine is a childhood friend of one of your authors.

Since the discovery of the AIDS (acquired immune deficiency syndrome) virus in the late 1970s, health psychologists have been concerned with the number of people who engage in unsafe sex. Sexually active people who have multiple partners, engage in oral sex, or have sexual intercourse without using a condom, increase their risk of becoming HIV-positive. HIV-positive means that a person has been infected with the human immunodeficiency virus (HIV). Communicable through blood, semen, or vaginal fluids, this virus steadily destroys your immune system. Engaging in unprotected sex even within a monogamous relationship also can be risky. If either partner is an intravenous drug user, or has had multiple sexual partners in the past in which unsafe sex has occurred, the risk of being HIV-positive also is increased. But note that you cannot contract AIDS through casual contact.

Although most adults and adolescents are aware of what constitutes safe sex practices, they continue to engage in unprotected sexual relations (Morrill, Ickovics, Golubchikov, Beren, & Rodin, 1996). There are an estimated 800,000 to 900,000 people currently living with HIV in the United States, with approximately 40,000 new HIV infections occurring in the United States every year. (Centers for Disease Control, 2001). Seventy percent of the new HIV infections each year occur among men. People with HIV tend to come from lower socioeconomic groups, are more likely to be uneducated, and are more likely to belong to minority groups (Centers for Disease Control, 2001). However, anyone—regardless of age, wealth, or race—can contract this potentially deadly disease.

Today, treatment to suppress or halt HIV typically consists of a steady regime of 20 or more pills a day. This treatment offers AIDS patients the *chance* of a longer life (Katz et al., 2002; Rabkin & Ferrando, 1997). Unfortunately, the drugs are costly, and not everyone responds to these drugs. For this reason, health psychologists try to prevent the spread of HIV and AIDS mainly through educational prevention programs (Carey et al., 1997). Success in these efforts with adolescents, however, is hampered by the tendency of adolescents to believe it can't happen to them (a cognitive fallacy we highlighted in Chapter 10—see p. 446).

AIDS/HIV does not discriminate. Anyone—regardless of age, gender, wealth, race, or sexual orientation—can contract this potentially deadly disease. Former NBA player Magic Johnson contracted HIV through sexual relations.

© Rufus F. Folkks/Corbis

Health-Promoting Behaviors

It is only fitting to end this chapter by exploring health-promoting behaviors. Health psychologists define **health-promoting behaviors** as those that decrease the chance of illness, disease, or death. Throughout this chapter we have indicated behaviors that you can engage in that appear to be related to better physical and psychological functioning. Take a moment to reflect on all that you have learned from our discussion on behavior and health.

health-promoting behaviors behaviors that decrease the chance of illness, disease, or death

What behaviors would you suggest promote health and well-being? Now read the
following list to see how many behaviors you were able to correctly identify.

- commit yourself to a value and belief system
- view stressors as challenges rather than threats
- perceive events as controllable
- do not rely exclusively on one or two defense mechanisms for coping
- engage in problem-focused coping
- cultivate an optimistic, positive attitude
- develop a social support network
- don't expect failure
- be patient and flexible
- laugh
- manage your time wisely
- engage in relaxing activities
- get regular physical exercise
- avoid being hostile, bitter, and resentful
- avoid the use of cigarettes
- use alcohol in moderation
- engage in safe sex

In addition to these behaviors, health research also suggests additional behaviors
that we can engage in that promote healthier living (Glik, Kronenfeld, & Jackson,
1996). These behaviors include:

- sleeping 7 to 8 hours a night
- maintaining your ideal body weight
- avoiding a high-fat diet
- receiving regular medical check-ups

This checklist will undoubtedly grow as we discover more about the intimate connection between our bodies and minds. This knowledge will enable health psychologists
to continue their efforts at understanding stress, preventing illnesses, and promoting
lifelong well-being.

Let's Review!

This section examined those behaviors that have been
found to put us at more risk for illness and disease, and
those behaviors or lifestyle choices that have been linked
to healthier living. For a quick check of your understanding,
answer these questions:

1. Which of the following is *not* a health-promoting behavior?
   a. viewing stressors as challenges rather than as threats
   b. perceiving events as controllable
   c. relying exclusively on one defense mechanism for coping
   d. engaging in problem-focused coping

2. Which of the following would be considered a safe sex
   practice?
   a. engaging only in oral sex
   b. using a condom when having sexual intercourse
   c. having multiple sexual partners
   d. having unprotected sex only within a monogamous
      relationship

ANSWERS

1. c; 2. b

Are You Getting the Big Picture?

This chapter explored the topics of stress, coping, and health—topics that are bound to be relevant to you. Try to integrate the material into your existing knowledge and current circumstances. Notice how the information in this chapter emphasizes biological, psychological, and social factors discussed throughout this textbook. The physical aspect of the stress response and the functioning of our immune systems constitute biological elements that influence our health. What we perceive as stressors and how we cope with stress, as well as dimensions of our personality illustrate psychological factors involved in our general health. How we deal with different social or environmental types of stressors such as major life events, daily hassles, and catastrophes also influence our health. You may find it useful while reading this section to refer to the visual summary at the end of the chapter. In this way, your recall of the material will be enhanced.

Think about people in your life whom you believe exemplify the behaviors, thoughts, and actions, of a healthy individual. What specific behaviors do they engage in that bring you to this conclusion? How do these behaviors correspond with the material discussed in this chapter? For example, how do they approach stressful situations? What is their outlook on life? How would you describe their personality? What is their lifestyle like? What predictions would you make about their health in the future?

Next, think about people in your life whom, in your opinion, would be characterized as living in an unhealthy manner. Now, examine the reasons why you believe their lives are unhealthy. What may be some of the cognitive, behavioral, or personal traits influencing their health? Again, tie this information to the concepts outlined in this chapter.

Now for the real test! How might the information in this chapter apply to you? For a moment, reflect on what your life is like. How do you look for your age, what activities comprise your daily routine, and what is your health like? Examine the ways in which you handle stress. Do you spend a significant amount of your time watching television, drinking alcohol, smoking, exercising, or using drugs? Are these methods adaptive or maladaptive? Why do you manage stress in these ways? Detail any stress-related symptoms such as headaches, backaches, muscle tension, anxiety, or upset stomach that you have experienced over the past year. How might your coping style be influencing your health? What stress management techniques do you currently use? Could you adopt the use of others? Analyze your personality and lifestyle behaviors. Are there any improvements that you could make in these areas that would enhance your health, and how might you begin to make these changes? Now reflect on what your life will be like 30 to 40 years from now. What will you look like then, what activities will you be engaged in, what career will you be in, and what will your health be like? In this futuristic look at your life, what specific health ailments do you think you will be experiencing? How might your behavior today be related to what you predicted for the future? Are you ignoring the effect of health-defeating behaviors on your future health? Addressing issues such as these in this manner will help you master the material. It is our hope that it will also cause you to pause for a moment to contemplate how your health may be improved for today and for the future.

Key Terms

health psychology (578)
stress (579)
life events (580)
daily hassles (585)
conflict (586)
approach-approach conflict (586)
avoidance-avoidance
    conflict (587)
approach-avoidance conflict (587)
multiple approach-avoidance
    conflicts (587)

primary appraisal (588)
general adaptation syndrome
    (GAS) (589)
alarm reaction (589)
resistance stage (590)
exhaustion stage (591)
immunosuppression (591)
coping (593)
problem-focused coping (593)
emotion-focused coping (593)
cognitive reappraisal (594)

defense mechanisms (594)
biofeedback (597)
progressive relaxation training (597)
social support (598)
meditation (599)
Type A personality (601)
Type B personality (601)
learned helplessness (603)
hardy personality (604)
health-defeating behaviors (605)
health-promoting behaviors (608)

Test Yourself!

Concept Check

Test your knowledge of the chapter concepts by completing each of the following sentences with the correct term. For a more comprehensive review, visit the book Web site (http://psychology.wadsworth.com/pastorinole/) for online quizzes, flashcards, crosswords, and Internet links.

(1) _____ is any environmental event that we respond to because we perceive it as threatening or challenging. It comes in many forms, including major life events, catastrophes, and (2) _____. It also may include conflict, which is defined as (3) _____. There are four basic types of conflict situations. One in which we must choose between two alternatives that both have negative consequences is a(n) (4) _____ conflict situation. However, most conflicts we experience can be categorized as (5) _____ because they include several alternative choices that each have positive and negative features.

Our initial interpretation of an event is called (6) _____. Once we interpret an event as stressful, our body changes in three stages, termed the (7) _____. The first stage, alarm reaction, is characterized by the activation of the (8) _____ nervous system and the (9) _____ system. During the (10) _____ stage, our bodies continue to cope with the stressor. When bodily resources that are available to deal with a stressor are depleted, we then enter the (11) _____ stage.

Whatever we do to manage a stressful event is part of (12) _____. It includes two broad categories: problem-focused coping and emotion-focused coping. Controlling or altering the environment that caused the stress is called (13) _____, whereas actions aimed at controlling the internal reactions we feel when faced with a stressor are called (14) _____. There are many effective stress management techniques. An example of a physical method of stress management is (15) _____. An emotional method of stress management is to increase (16) _____, or positive relationships with others. You can also use your mind to achieve relaxation through the process of (17) _____.

A number of personality dimensions also may relate to stress and health. For example, research suggests that dimensions of (18) _____ personality are related to heart disease. Similarly, the expectation of failure and lack of control, called (19) _____, also may be related to health problems. However, a (20) _____ personality, characterized by commitment, challenge, and control, appears to be positively related to our health.

Answers:

1. Stress; 2. daily hassles; 3. having to choose between two or more needs, desires, or demands; 4. avoidance-avoidance; 5. multiple approach-avoidance conflicts; 6. primary appraisal; 7. general adaptation syndrome; 8. sympathetic; 9. endocrine (hormone); 10. resistance; 11. exhaustion; 12. coping; 13. problem-focused coping; 14. emotion-focused coping; 15. physical exercise, biofeedback, or relaxation techniques; 16. social support; 17. guided imagery; 18. Type A; 19. learned helplessness; 20. hardy.

Critical Thinking About the Chapter

1. What defense mechanisms do you think are more often employed by people who engage in health-defeating behaviors? Provide examples to illustrate and support your answer.

2. Look once again at the opening case study. Given that Edward did not have a family history of cancer, what specific behaviors and stressors do you think contributed to the development of his illness?

3. Using your own behavior, give an example of each of the following defense mechanisms: projection, denial, reaction formation, displacement, and sublimation.

4. Using your own behavior, give an example of each of the conflict situations discussed in this chapter. How did you respond to each of these situations? Indicate whether your response reflected a problem-focused coping strategy or an emotion-focused coping strategy.

Applying Psychology. Develop a formal time schedule to better manage your time. First create a chart showing all the hours in a day and all the days of the week. Block out all those times that already are committed, such as sleeping, class time, work, daily chores, and so on. Now allocate a specific amount of time to studying for your classes and physical exercise. Follow this plan for a week to see whether any modifications need to be made.

Critical Thinking for Integration

1. Review the three types of learning detailed in Chapter 5. How can these theories be used to explain why people smoke or engage in unsafe sex practices?

2. After reviewing the processes of memory in Chapter 6, suggest how learned helplessness may be a process of memory.

3. What obstacles or aids to problem solving (Chapter 7) may be connected to maladaptive and adaptive forms of coping?

4. Combining information from Chapters 4, 8, and 13, develop an antialcohol campaign program addressing the effects of alcohol (Chapter 4), the motivating forces behind using alcohol (Chapter 8), and the effects that alcohol has on one's health (Chapter 13).

5. Given that pregnancy is a stressor, how might women best cope with the immediate changes associated with pregnancy and childbirth (Chapter 9), as well as the transition to parenthood (Chapter 10)? What might be indicators of maladaptive coping patterns during pregnancy?

6. Review the cognitive changes that take place in adolescence (Chapter 10). How might adolescent cognitive development account for teenagers' willingness to engage in health-defeating behaviors?

Chapter Study Resources

Suggested Readings

1. Sapolsky, R. M. (2004). *Why zebras don't get ulcers* (3rd ed.). New York: Owl Books.
Neuroscientist Sapolsky discusses the nature and effects of stress in a humorous manner. The third edition features new chapters on how stress affects sleep and addiction, new insights into anxiety, and the impact of spirituality on managing stress.

2. Seligman, M. (2002). *Authentic happiness: Using the new positive psychology to realize your potential for lasting fulfillment.* New York: Free Press.
Psychologist Martin Seligman explains the merits of happiness, presents brief tests, and even directs readers to an interactive Web site to help readers increase the happiness quotient in their own lives.

3. Weil, M. M., & Rosen, L. D. (1997). *Technostress: Coping with technology @ work @ home @ play.* New York: Wiley.
The authors explain how technology is a stressor, directly and indirectly negatively affecting our attitudes, thoughts, behaviors, and physical reactions.

4. For additional readings, explore InfoTrac College Edition, your online library of archived journal articles and periodicals. Go to http://www.infotrac-college .com/wadsworth and enter the passcode from the card that came with your book. For this chapter, search using these keywords:

> problem-focused coping
>
> daily hassles
>
> hardy personality
>
> stress and cancer
>
> cognitive appraisal

Web Links for Further Study

Additional information on some of the chapter's concepts can be found at the following Web sites:

1. The Drug Info Net provides information and links to healthcare issues. Includes a healthcare e-encyclopedia and up-to-date health news.
http://www.druginfonet.com

2. The Physician-Patient Communications Network provides information about numerous diseases, therapies and self-care regimens. It also includes special sections on specific health issues of men, women, children, and seniors.
http://www.medem.com

3. The Health Psychology and Rehabilitation Web site addresses research and viewpoints about the practice of health psychology.
http://www.healthpsych.com

4. This site provides numerous links to psychoneuro-immunology sites.
http://www.psychnet-uk.com/pni/pni.htm

5. The Health Journeys Web site provides numerous links to stress-related health disorders, health-promoting behaviors, and stress management techniques.
http://www.healthjourneys.com

Student Study Guide

To help you organize your learning, work through Chapter 13 of the *What Is Psychology? Student Study Guide*. The study guide includes learning objectives, a chapter summary, fill-in review, key terms, a practice test, and other learning activities.

Psychology Now™

PsychologyNow is a Web-based, personalized study system that provides you with a pretest and a posttest for each chapter, quizzes you by chapter, and provides a personalized study plan, pointing you to elements in the text or in individual learning modules that will help you to achieve 80% mastery. Check out the learning module that relates to this chapter: Type A versus Type B personality test.

PsychNow CD-ROM, Version 2.0

Go to the PsychNow CD-ROM for further study of the concepts in this chapter. The CD-ROM includes the learning modules with videos, animations, and quizzes, as well as simulations of psychological phenomena. Each module follows a consistent Explore, Lesson, and Apply structure that allows you to experience the concept or principle, learn more about it, and then apply it. You and your friends can participate in a team-based Quiz Game that makes learning fun. Learning modules include: 6d. Stress and Health.

Health, Stress, and Coping

Health psychology is the study of how people's behavior influences their health for better and for worse.

STRESS AND STRESSORS

• Stress can be defined as any event or environmental stimulus (stressor) that we respond to because we perceive it as challenging or threatening.

• Significant changes in one's living such as the death of a loved one, marriage, or a new job—called life events—are major stressors. Everyday frustrations—called daily hassles—are less serious stressors, but can have a negative effect on health.

• Conflict also produces stress of varying degrees. Four examples include:
— Approach-approach conflicts, in which a person must choose between two likable or positive events.

— Avoidance-avoidance conflicts, in which a person has to choose between two undesirable or negative events.
— Approach-avoidance conflicts, in which a person is faced with a desire or need that has both positive and negative qualities.
— Multiple approach-avoidance conflicts are those in which we have several alternatives to choose from, each with positive and negative features.

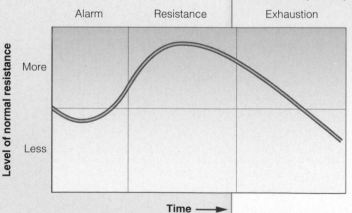

THE STRESS RESPONSE

• Our initial interpretation of an event is called primary appraisal. If our primary appraisal of an event is that it is stressful, we may view it as a threat, as harmful, or as merely a challenge.

• According to Selye's general adaptation syndrome, our body responds to stress in a three-phase process: an initial alarm reaction, resistance, and exhaustion.
— An alarm reaction consists of those bodily responses, including the nervous system and endocrine system, which are immediately triggered when we initially appraise an event as stressful.
— During the resistance stage, the body continues to cope with the stressor, but the bodily reactions are less intense than during the alarm reaction.
— In the exhaustion phase, the wear and tear on the body begins, which can cause serious damage if stress continues over an extended period of time.

• The corticosteroids and endorphins that are released into our body during the stress response actually reduce and dampen the activity of our immune system. This is known as immunosuppression, and makes us more vulnerable to both minor and major health problems.

Alarm   Resistance   Exhaustion

Level of normal resistance

More

Less

Time ⟶

COPING WITH STRESS

• Coping is how we manage an event or stimulus that is perceived as threatening.

• Problem-focused coping is aimed at controlling or altering the environment that caused the stress. It tends to be most useful when we feel that we can actually do something about the stressor.

• Emotion-focused coping is aimed at controlling your internal, subjective, emotional responses to stress. Rather than trying to change your environment, you alter the way you feel or think in order to reduce stress.

• Defense mechanisms are unconscious coping strategies that allow us to reduce our anxiety and maintain a positive self-image and self-esteem.

• A number of strategies can be used to reduce stress in one's life, including physical techniques (such as exercise), emotional methods (such as having strong social support), cognitive methods (such as guided imagery and meditation), and behavioral methods (such as laughter and time management).

PERSONALITY AND HEALTH

• A Type A personality is a person who is aggressive, competitive, and driven to achieve, while a Type B personality is a person who is relaxed, easygoing, patient, and flexible. The Type A personality trait of hostility is related to a higher incidence of heart disease.

• Learned helplessness is a condition in which we believe we have no control over stressful life events.

• The hardy personality is one that is resistant to stress, and includes characteristics such as:
— The tendency to see life as a series of challenges.
— A sense of personal commitment to self, work, family, and other values.
— A perception of control over life and work.

LIFESTYLE AND HEALTH

• Health-defeating behaviors are those that increase the chance of illness, disease, or death. Alcohol and substance abuse, smoking, driving recklessly, and unsafe sex are examples of such behaviors.

• Health-promoting behaviors are those that decrease the chance of illness, disease, or death.

• Regular exercise, adequate sleep, an appropriate body weight, a healthy diet, good time management, a strong social support network, an optimistic outlook, and avoiding health-defeating behaviors promote good health.

As a boy, he believed he was neither black nor white, but rather green like the comic book character the Incredible Hulk.

FROM JAMES MCBRIDE, *THE COLOR OF WATER: A BLACK MAN'S TRIBUTE TO HIS WHITE MOTHER.* (New York: Riverhead Books, 1996)

© David Young-Wolff/ Photo Edit

What Is Personality, and How Do We Measure It?

CHAPTER PREVIEW

Understanding Personality

This chapter and the following two cover what you probably originally thought psychology was all about: the unique and sometimes strange qualities of our behavior. This chapter's topic is **personality,** or the unique collection of attitudes, emotions, thoughts, habits, impulses, and behaviors that define how a person typically behaves across situations. As we have seen from previous topics, psychologists have more than one explanation for our individual differences. The nature of personality and how it develops has been a hot debate in psychology for over 100 years. As new research is conducted, psychologists construct alternate views of personality. Each theory is in part a response to those theories that preceded it.

The material in this chapter will remind you of theories we have covered throughout this textbook, and the four perspectives on personality introduced in this chapter will be revisited in the next two chapters as well. Understanding how different perspectives explain the formation of personality will help you understand psychologists' explanations of why some people respond to difficulty by becoming depressed or anxious—material addressed in the next chapter. Similarly, the four personality perspectives presented here are the basis for many of the treatment methods discussed in Chapter 16.

personality   the unique collection of attitudes, emotions, thoughts, habits, impulses, and behaviors that define how a person typically behaves across situations

In his memoir *The Color of Water: A Black Man's Tribute to His White Mother* (1996), James McBride describes the different personalities in his large family. His remarkable mother, Rachel, grew up an Orthodox Jew in Virginia during the Great Depression. Rachel's father owned a general store that served mainly poor, rural African Americans, yet he was blatantly racist. At 21 years old, despite her parents' protests, Rachel married Andrew McBride, an African American from New York. Andrew and Rachel settled in Harlem and established their own family. Andrew died before their eighth child, James, was born in 1957. Rachel then married Hunter Jordan, also an African American, and they added four more children to the family. These twelve African American Jewish children grew up in cramped quarters in Brooklyn and Queens, yet all went to college; they became doctors, teachers, and scientists.

Riverhead Books, an imprint of Penguin Group (USA) Inc.

This family stood out at a time when interracial marriage was rare. It also contained a lively mix of personalities. Rachel was intensely private, and mistrustful and suspicious of all authority figures. She had a strict, no-nonsense approach to parenting and to life in general. She was hard working and religious, and she insisted that all of her children work hard in school. Hunter Jordan, the only father James ever knew, had quite the opposite personality. He was easygoing, quiet, and tough, yet open-minded. He was a methodical worker with abundant patience. He was a suave and handsome man who worked hard and drank hard. He was rarely angry and he never worried about anything.

"Mommy's house was orchestrated chaos and as the eighth of twelve children, I was lost in the sauce, so to speak."

(McBride, 1996, p. 49)

Rachel's 12 children made for a hectic household of interesting and diverse personalities. For example, Dennis, the eldest son was an artist and a straight-A student in his childhood. In college, he became an active civil rights proponent. Richie was a tenor sax player, creative yet absent-minded, and considered more of a free spirit by his siblings. He went on to become a chemist. Rosetta, the eldest daughter, was intelligent and bossy and went to Howard University on a full scholarship. Helen, another sister, was pretty, talkative, and obstinate. Helen played the piano and was accepted to and briefly attended several music and art schools before eventually obtaining a nursing degree.

Like his siblings, James was cute, smart, and musically talented. In other ways, James was quite different from them. As a child, he recalls being "shy, passive, and quiet." He spent a lot of time reading or talking to imaginary friends. By 10 years old, James became secretive, angry, and very fearful—fearful in particular that his friends would discover that his mother was white. His stepfather died when James was 14, and his personality appeared to completely change. He failed all his subjects at school and became a truant. He joined a soul band, smoked marijuana, and began drinking heavily. He and his friends broke into cars, shoplifted, and even mugged older women. Fortunately, at age 16 James realized that his behavior needed to change. The family moved to Delaware, and James made a fresh start. He gave up pot smoking and drinking but remained interested in music. He graduated from Oberlin College and received a master's degree in journalism from Columbia University. He currently describes himself as a black man with something of a Jewish soul.

Within every family is a complex and rich array of personalities.

We can see just within this one family a complex and rich array of personalities. There were similarities and differences. All the children were creative and artistic either in music, writing, or the arts. They were all excellent students. Some were more outgoing and independent, whereas others were more quiet and unassuming. Perhaps your family is similarly varied, seeming like a cast of actors put together for an off-Broadway play! How can we understand these similarities and differences in personality? That is the focus of this chapter as we explore the critical question: How do we get our personalities, and how stable—or changeable—are they?

As we stated at the beginning of this chapter, personality is the unique collection of attitudes, emotions, thoughts, habits, impulses, and behaviors that define how a person typically behaves across situations. Some of us are slow to anger, whereas others become angry quickly. Some people look for opportunities to be the star, whereas others shrink from the limelight. Where does this unique way of responding come from? Psychologists do not agree on a single, specific answer to this question—personality is difficult to define, difficult to measure, and is influenced by many factors (Schultz & Schultz, 2005).

Four dominant perspectives have emerged to explain our personalities: the psychoanalytic approach, the trait approach, the social cognitive approach, and the humanistic approach. Each attempts to provide answers to different questions about personality. For example, some approaches focus more on the factors that influence our personalities. Others concentrate more on explaining the causes or problems of personality development, or how we can reach our fullest potential. No single theoretical approach can explain all facets of personality development in all people. Each perspective on personality has its advantages and disadvantages. The disadvantages prompted development of other perspectives to explain personality, whereas the advantages demonstrate the contributions to the field of psychology and, specifically, to our understanding of personality.

As we describe each major perspective, consider your own ideas about personality and how different or similar they are to each approach. Do you think that you inherit your personality, or that it is formed from your experiences? Do you think that your behavior is influenced by your unconscious? Do you think that people strive to be all that they can be? Examining such ideas will allow you to connect the material to your values, experiences, and current way of thinking.

LEARNING OBJECTIVES < < < < < < < < <

▼ Discuss Freud's perspective on personality, detailing how the levels of consciousness, resolution of psychosexual stages, and component parts of the personality interact to generate behavior.

▼ Detail neo-Freudian perspectives on personality, indicating their differences and similarities with Freud's theory.

psychoanalytic perspective a personality approach developed by Sigmund Freud that saw personality as the product of driving forces within a person that were often conflicting and sometimes unconscious

conscious level the level of consciousness that holds all the thoughts, perceptions, and impulses of which we are aware

The Psychoanalytic Approach: Sigmund Freud and the Neo-Freudians

The **psychoanalytic perspective** on personality originated with Sigmund Freud. We introduced his approach to understanding behavior in Chapter 1 (see p. 10). Recall that Freud was not a psychologist. He practiced medicine, specializing in nervous diseases. However, soon after beginning private practice, Freud moved away from physical explanations of nervous disorders and focused more on investigating psychological causes of these disorders. His ideas about personality were based on case studies of his patients, his reading of literature, and his own self-analysis. Freud saw personality as the product of driving forces within a person that were often conflicting and sometimes unconscious. As we saw in Chapter 4 (see p. 168), Freud believed that dreams were one of the ways these unconscious forces expressed themselves. Freud's theory is unique from all the other approaches in that it strongly emphasizes unconscious aspects of personality. How does Freud explain personality?

The Levels of Awareness

Freud (1940/1964) proposed that human personality operates at three different levels of awareness. A person's awareness at each level of consciousness differs, and Freud believed that each level of awareness influences behavior. Freud viewed consciousness like an iceberg (Figure 14.1). For Freud, when we look at behavior, all we usually see is the tip of the iceberg, or the **conscious level:** the thoughts, perceptions, and explanations of behavior of which the person is aware. The major portion of the iceberg is below the surface of the water. The impulses, memories, and thoughts below are unseen but have a huge impact on personality. Freud believed that because so large a portion of one's personality lies below the surface of consciousness, or awareness, *any* explanation of personality and behavior must focus on these unconscious forces. We must look at not only what is showing above the surface but, more importantly, all that goes on beneath the surface of consciousness.

The psychoanalytic perspective on personality originated with Sigmund Freud. His ideas about personality were based on case studies of his patients, his reading of literature, and his own self-analysis. Freud saw personality as the product of driving forces within a person that were often conflicting and sometimes unconscious.

Getty Images

Below the surface of the conscious level are the preconscious and unconscious levels. The preconscious level comes right before your conscious level. Your conscious level, as previously stated, includes any memories, thoughts, or urges of which you are currently aware. You know you want the new Usher CD, or you know that it is important to read this chapter and study for the test next week. But the things that you could potentially be aware of at any one time are infinite, and you cannot hold more than a couple of thoughts, urges, and memories in consciousness at any one time. So according to Freud, it is necessary to have a holding place for easily accessible memories, thoughts, or impulses of which you could potentially be aware. This is the role of the **preconscious level.** Think about what you had for breakfast this morning. Were you thinking about breakfast prior to being asked this question? Probably not, yet it probably wasn't too difficult or traumatic for you to remember. This information was stored in your preconscious. You readily became aware of it—it was in your conscious level—when you answered the question.

The **unconscious level** contains all those thoughts, impulses, memories, and behaviors of which you are unaware. However, although you are unaware of them, they always influence your behavior. Consider the 4-year-old boy who stops his parents from hugging or inserts himself between them to prevent them from kissing. He is not aware that this behavior stems from a need or wish to bond with his mother, yet it is still influencing his behavior.

In summary, Freud saw consciousness as having three levels: the conscious, preconscious, and unconscious levels. As Freud saw it, these unconscious and conscious forces do exist and are the energy behind one's personality.

The Structure of Personality

How did Freud believe that the energy of one's personality is distributed? To Freud (1933/1964), human personality is an energy system that is comprised of three major personality structures: the id, the ego, and the superego. At birth, all of the energy of the personality is contained within a structure called the **id.** The id is an unconscious

« Application

preconscious level the level of consciousness that holds thoughts, perceptions, and impulses of which we could potentially be aware

unconscious level the level of awareness that contains all the thoughts, perceptions, and impulses of which we are unaware

id the unconscious part of the personality that seeks pleasure and gratification

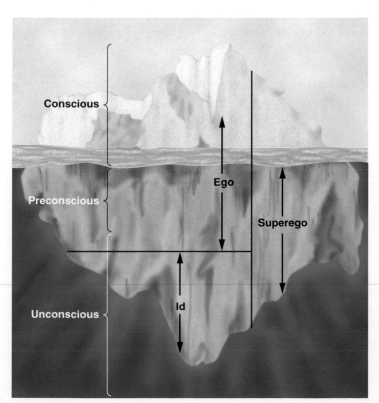

Figure 14.1 **Iceberg Analogy of Freud's Levels of Awareness**

In Freud's "iceberg" analogy of the mind, the id and parts of the ego and superego are submerged below the water in the unconscious. Parts of the ego and superego show in the conscious and preconscious.

pleasure principle   the basis by which the id operates; to feel good and maximize gratification

ego   the conscious part of the personality that attempts to meet the demands of the id in a socially appropriate way

reality principle   the basis by which the ego operates; finding socially appropriate means to fulfill id demands

superego   the part of the personality that represents your moral conscience

energy force that seeks pleasure and gratification. Hungry infants cry for food or because they are wet or tired. The id operates according to the **pleasure principle;** it drives people to feel good and to maximize pleasure and gratification. Freud saw the impulses driving the id as sexual and aggressive in nature. In this way, he viewed humans as very similar to animals—unconsciously and selfishly motivated by basic sexual and aggressive instincts. Such basic instincts ensure and promote the survival of the individual, and therefore, the survival of the species as a whole. When we grow and begin to interact with our environment, we realize that our demands cannot always be immediately fulfilled. For example, when a baby's cry for food is not met every time, the baby has encountered reality. As such, part of the energy of the id becomes directed to the ego.

The **ego,** the second personality structure, acts as a negotiator between the instinctual needs of the id and the demands of membership in human society. Children learn that their id demands can be fulfilled only in a socially appropriate manner. The ego operates according to the **reality principle.** It realizes that the desires of the id can be met only by successfully dealing with the environment, by finding appropriate or attainable means by which to fulfill id impulses. Suppose a 4-year-old wants something to eat. Does he immediately cry like a baby? Not typically. The 4-year-old with a functioning ego knows that there are more appropriate and acceptable ways of getting something to eat. He will probably ask for something to eat and be willing to wait (at least for a little while) for his caregiver to prepare it for him. We see the ego functioning in the child's ability to delay his desire for food, for example. But the ego's job is still to fulfill the instinctual demands of the id—the unseen force beneath the tip of the iceberg (see Figure 14.1).

As the child continues to grow, parents and other important people impart their values and standards of behavior to the child. Parents convey the right and wrong ways to feel, think, and behave. The child incorporates these standards as the energy of the personality further divides into a third personality structure. The **superego** typically emerges during the resolution of the phallic stage (discussed shortly) and represents your moral conscience. Your superego judges the rightness or wrongness of your actions. When you have the sense that you did something wrong, your superego is talking. The moral directives of the superego must also be taken into account by the ego. Just like id demands, superego demands must be met realistically by the ego after it has considered what the environment offers.

The energy that these three personality components use cannot be cut apart. For Freud, personality is a dynamic, or active, process. The id, ego, and superego are not fixed entities but rather parts of our personality that serve different functions. A healthy personality will have developed a strong ego that appropriately releases and controls instinctual energy. However, problems may arise in personality functioning if id energy or superego energy overwhelm the functioning of the ego.

All adult behaviors then, to Freud, are a reflection of the interplay between these three structures. When examining behavior, we see only the functioning of the ego, but this ego is simultaneously being influenced by the unconscious demands of the id and superego. *Freudian slips* help explain this interaction. Freudian slips refer to an unconscious impulse from the id that is expressed before the ego controls the impulse. The ego then may state that it did not mean to say something and corrects the slip to conform to socially approved behavior. For example, one may say to a rival businessperson at a meeting, "Would you like to hit in this chair?" instead of "Would you like to sit in this chair?" and then quickly correct the error. Freud would state that what "slipped out" was meant. It just hadn't yet been socially screened by the ego. An older sibling may hit a younger sibling and claim that she did not mean to do it. Freud would state that the aggressive impulse was meant indeed, yet just not caught in time by the functioning ego.

To Freud, every behavior you engage in—including supposed errors or mistakes—has meaning or can be analyzed within the context of these three interacting personality structures. Let's work through another example. Suppose that you are attracted to someone. What is your id telling you to do? It would urge you to go for it! Just do it, seek that which pleasures you. Meanwhile, what will the demands of your superego be? What moral precepts do we carry around with us? We learn that we must respect the rights and bodies of others. Your ego must now balance these opposing demands in a socially appropriate way. So what might your ego do? It might prompt you to strike up a conversation or ask the person out on a date. These are just two ways a healthy ego may resolve the demands of the id and superego in this situation.

You can see that the demands from the id and superego are often in direct opposition to one another. This internal conflict sometimes overwhelms the ego, creating anxiety. The ego, however, handles this anxiety by using **defense mechanisms** (Freud, 1936). Defense mechanisms, discussed in Chapter 13 (see p. 594), protect the ego by reducing the anxiety it feels when faced with the conflicting demands of the id and superego. We all engage in these *coping mechanisms*, as they are now familiarly called. We tend to use those defense mechanisms that have been previously reinforced or that successfully reduce anxiety. For example, if you rationalized behavior as a child, you probably continue to use this defense mechanism as an adult.

Consider our chapter case story. From a psychoanalytic perspective, James McBride's truancy and delinquency would be related to his efforts to cope with his stepfather's death. Emotionally, James would feel anger at this loss. It is normal to feel anger when a loved one dies, to be mad at them for leaving and abandoning us. We cannot direct our anger toward its true source because that person is dead. We may also feel it is wrong to be angry with someone we love. So James's superego would attempt to squelch his anger, but the energy of those feelings would still need an outlet. James's ego satisfies both the id and the superego by taking his anger out on others, using the defense mechanism of displacement (see p. 596).

Differences in personality, then, arise from internal energy conflicts among the id, ego, and superego (called intrapsychic conflicts). Freud further believed that personality is shaped by differences in how we resolve psychosexual stages of development that we all experience from infancy through puberty.

Psychosexual Development

What are psychosexual stages, and how do they influence personality development? According to Freud (1940/1964), personality develops through a series of five psychosexual stages. These stages represent a complex interaction between natural shifts of pleasure from one part of the body to another and the environmental factors that influence how we handle these sexual desires. From birth through adolescence, children must resolve numerous unconscious conflicts that arise from sexual pleasure associated with stimulation of certain body parts, or what Freud called *erogenous zones*. For example, the infant nursing (from the mother's breast or from a bottle) derives a great deal of sensual pleasure from the feel of the nipple on his or her lips, and the satisfaction of hunger the milk brings. The child must balance his or her need for sexual pleasure with the parental restrictions or permissiveness placed on his or her behavior. This creates an internal struggle, or "conflict," that significantly influences the resulting personality. Freud uses the term *psychosexual* to refer to how these sexual drives have psychological significance in the formation of a healthy personality. Because we all have varying environmental circumstances in terms of how we are parented or how we respond to these socialization experiences, it results in individual differences in personality. Let's take a brief look at each of Freud's psychosexual stages.

Application

defense mechanism a process used to protect the ego by reducing the anxiety it feels when faced with the conflicting demands of the id and superego

oral stage   Freud's first psychosexual stage of development, which occurs during the first year of life, in which the handling of the child's feeding experiences affects personality development

anal stage   Freud's second psychosexual stage, which occurs from approximately 18 months to 3 years, in which the parents' regulation of the child's biological urge to expel or retain feces affects personality development

phallic stage   Freud's third psychosexual stage of development, which occurs between 3 and 6 years of age, in which little boys experience the Oedipus complex and little girls the Electra complex

Oedipus complex   in the male, an unconscious sexual urge for the mother that develops during the phallic psychosexual stage

Electra complex   in the female, an unconscious sexual urge for the father that develops during the phallic psychosexual stage

latency stage   Freud's fourth psychosexual stage of development, which occurs from around age 6 to puberty, in which the child's sexuality is suppressed due to widening social contacts with school, peers, and family

genital stage   Freud's final psychosexual stage of development, which occurs during puberty, in which sexual energy is transferred toward peers of the other sex (heterosexual orientation) or same sex (homosexual orientation)

- *Oral stage:* As Freud saw it, the **oral stage** lasts from birth until approximately 18 months of age. The mouth, tongue, and lips are the erogenous zones, or focus of pleasure. Babies receive pleasure from sucking, licking, biting, and chewing.

- *Anal stage:* The **anal stage** lasts from approximately 18 months to 3 years. The anus and rectum are the erogenous zones. Freud viewed production of feces in particular as a creative act. The toddler typically feels quite proud of them, either holding them in or spreading them around. How the parent then responds to this or how the parent attempts to control this production through toilet-training practices is the key to adequately resolving this stage.

Parents' toilet-training practices influence a toddler's attempt to resolve the anal psychosexual stage, according to Freud.

© Ryan McVay/Getty Images

- *Phallic stage:* During the **phallic stage,** from 3 to 6 years of age, the genitals are the primary erogenous zones, and children receive pleasure from self-stimulation. This stage is particularly important for personality development as it represents the time when the **Oedipus complex** and the **Electra complex** occur. Freud believed that at this age, young children develop unconscious sexual urges for the parent of the other sex. The child wants to bond with the parent of the other sex as the child sees the parents bonding. Using the terms *Oedipus* and *Electra* from two ancient Greek tragedies, Freud believed that at this psychosexual stage little boys unconsciously fall in love with their mothers and experience hostile feelings toward their fathers much like Oedipus (unknowingly) married his mother and killed his father. Like Electra, little girls unconsciously fall in love with their fathers and feel jealousy toward their mothers.

  For example, children at this age may prevent their parents from hugging or be jealous of the parents spending time alone together. Children then resolve these complexes by identifying with and behaving more like the same-sex parent. The child incorporates the values and standards of the same-sex parent, thus ending the rivalry. The child's psychic energy is then redirected to the growth of the superego (discussed earlier). A young boy may start to imitate the way his father eats or a young girl may mimic the way her mother brushes her hair.

- *Latency stage:* The **latency stage** occurs from 6 years of age until puberty. During the latency stage, sexual impulses are pushed into the background. The child's energy focuses on other demands of the environment, most noticeably school and peer relations. Sexuality reappears at puberty as reflected in the final psychosexual stage, the genital stage.

- *Genital stage:* The **genital stage** occurs during puberty. The genitals again become the source of pleasure, as the adolescent must revisit the sexual urges that first appeared during the phallic stage. Recall that during the phallic stage, children developed unconscious attractions to the other-sex parent. Recognizing now that the love for the parent cannot be fulfilled, adequate resolution of the genital stage entails the transference of this love on to an other-sex mate. Consequently, for Freud, adult heterosexual intimate relations reflect the unconscious desire to choose a mate in the image of one's other-sex parent. If during the phallic stage the child develops unconscious attractions to the same-sex parent, then during the genital stage, homosexual intimate relations arise from the transference of love onto a same-sex partner.

A daughter's imitation of her mother reflects the youngster's attempt to resolve the negative emotions of the Electra complex, according to Freud.

As Freud saw it, children develop through these predictable stages that are primarily sexual but psychologically significant in forming a healthy personality. Successfully resolving these stages entails receiving an optimal amount of gratification at each stage—not too much and not too little. A child who receives too much satisfaction at one stage may be reluctant to move on to the next stage. Too little satisfaction may result in frustration for the child, who may continue to seek gratification instead of moving on. These examples of inadequate resolution of a stage result in what Freud called a *fixation*. Those who fixate at one stage remain stuck and so their personalities, too, remain immature or underdeveloped in these ways. Part of the psychic energy of the personality remains focused on these concerns.

For Freud, problems in adult personality reflect these unresolved issues or fixations from childhood. For example, a baby who did not adequately satisfy oral urges in infancy would develop an *oral fixation*. An oral fixation might be expressed in the adult behaviors of overeating, nail biting, constantly chewing on pens or pencils, or boasting. More serious behaviors reflecting oral fixations include smoking, alcoholism, or binge eating. Fixation at the anal stage may express itself in a person's personality as *anal-retentiveness* or *anal-expulsiveness*. Being overly neat, stingy, or orderly (anal-retentive), or being excessively sloppy, generous, or carefree (anal-expulsive) both result from inadequate resolution of the anal stage. Think for a moment about the general condition of your car's interior as a reflection of your anal tendencies. Is it spotless, with all your CDs and maps stored in alphabetical order? Or is it crammed with papers, clothes, and old fast-food wrappers? The former reflects a tendency toward anal-retentiveness, whereas the latter represents more anal-expulsiveness. These are just two examples of how fixations might manifest themselves into an adult personality.

Application

Neo-Freudians: Alfred Adler, Karen Horney, and Carl Jung

Freud's work created much controversy among professionals in the developing field of psychology. Many physicians and psychologists were initially intrigued by Freud's ideas but had their differences with aspects of his theory and eventually separated from Freud. These *neo-Freudians* agreed with Freud that unconscious conflicts were important to understanding the personality of the individual, but they placed less emphasis on the role of the instinctual impulses of sex and aggression in motivating behavior. We already introduced one neo-Freudian, Erik Erikson, whose theory of psychosocial development we discussed in Chapters 9 and 10 (see pp. 425 and 452). His eight stages detailed the influence of the environment on the developing ego over the life span. Three other examples of neo-Freudian theories are presented here, in the ideas of Alfred Adler, Karen Horney, and Carl Jung.

Carl Jung and The Collective Unconscious

Carl Jung was a student of Freud's who came to reject his ideas about personality, particularly the sexual aspects of Freud's theory. Like Freud, Jung maintained that personality was a function of the interplay between conscious and unconscious processes. However, Jung (1917/1966) divided the unconscious into the personal unconscious and the collective unconscious. The **personal unconscious,** much like Freud's unconscious, consisted of forgotten memories and repressed experiences. The **collective unconscious** is unique to Jung and not endorsed by Freud. According to Jung (1967), the contents of the collective unconscious are universal to all people of all time periods and cultures. The collective unconscious represents the collected images and ideas from the earliest development of the human psyche. In particular, the collective unconscious includes **archetypes,** mental representations or symbols of themes and predispositions to respond to the world in a certain way. According to Jung, two of the major archetypes of the personality are the *anima* and the *animus,* the female and male aspects of each person, respectively. Among the other archetypes Jung identified are the *persona* and the *shadow.* The persona is the appearance we present to the world, the role or character we assume when relating to others, such as the martyr, the rebel, or the teacher. The *shadow* includes those negative tendencies or qualities of the self that the individual tries to deny or hide from the world. Jung's emphasis on the collective unconscious and his belief that spiritual and religious drives are just as important as sexual ones continues to draw attention. He also stressed the importance of enduring personality traits such as introversion and extraversion.

personal unconscious according to Jung, the part of the unconscious that consists of forgotten memories and repressed experiences from one's past

collective unconscious according to Jung, the part of the unconscious that contains images and material universal to people of all time periods and cultures

archetypes according to Jung, mental representations or symbols of themes and predispositions to respond to the world in a certain way that are contained in the collective unconscious

© Bettmann/Corbis

Like Freud, Jung believed that personality was influenced by conscious and unconscious processes. However, Jung (1917) divided the unconscious into the personal unconscious (forgotten memories and repressed experiences) and the collective unconscious (the collected images and ideas from the earliest development of the human psyche).

Alfred Adler and the Inferiority Complex

Alfred Adler also began as a student of Freud's but disagreed with Freud's emphasis on aggressive and sexual urges as the major force in personality development. Adler (1928) believed that it is the child's desire to overcome feelings of helplessness and to master the environment that directs behavior. In the world of adults, children are small and helpless and feel inadequate and weak. Children have to be bathed by their parents or hold their parent's hand when crossing a street. These feelings of inferiority motivate the child—and later the adult—toward achievement. Consequently, to Adler, personality develops from our attempts to compensate for inferiority feelings. Moderate feelings of inferiority will result in constructive achievement and creative growth, but deep feelings of inferiority will impede positive growth and development and result in an *inferiority complex.*

Adler also emphasized the importance of birth order as a factor in personality development. He argued that firstborns, middle-borns, and youngest children grow up in differing family environments and are not necessarily treated the same by parents. These different experiences are likely to affect personality development. Adler's

Adler believed that it is the child's desire to overcome feelings of helplessness and to master the environment that directs behavior.

© Bettmann/Corbis

notions of birth order have resulted in hundreds of studies on the effects of birth order. However, they have generally not found any reliable relationships between birth order and personality (Harris, 2000). Yet people generally believe that birth order affects personality, which may then actually encourage the various birth ranks to differ in their personalities (Herrera, Zajonc, Wieczorkowska, & Cichomski, 2003).

Karen Horney and Basic Anxiety

Although Karen Horney agreed with Freud on the significance of early childhood in personality development, she rejected his belief that this development arose from instinctual conflicts. Instead, Horney (1937, 1939) suggested that family environments and disturbances in early relationships lead to **basic anxiety,** or a feeling of helplessness in children. Children cope with this basic anxiety by pursuing love, power, prestige, or detachment. Horney further argued, in contrast to Freud, that culture plays a larger role in personality development than biology and instinct. Consequently, our personalities are not merely the result of our psychosexual conflicts, as Freud would argue, but rather are influenced by all the events and people in the culture that make a child feel unsafe and unloved that give rise to basic anxiety.

basic anxiety according to Horney, the feeling of helplessness that develops in children from early relationships

Criticisms and Contributions of the Psychoanalytic Approach

Freud's contributions to psychology have been immense (Erwin, 2002). He is regarded as one of the most influential thinkers of the 20th century (Gedo, 2002). His presence is still felt among the general public through literature, arts, and the movies. For example, in 1993, 54 years after his death, Freud appeared on the cover of *Time* magazine. His theory on dreams stimulated much research on the nature of sleep. His notion of defense mechanisms extensively elaborated on by his daughter, Anna Freud, and his focus on coping and well-being sparked interest and research on health psychology. His ideas are evident in tests designed to measure personality (discussed later in this chapter), and therapy approaches to help people with psychological problems (Chapter 16). Freud's basic notion of the unconscious influencing our behavior also has merit (Gedo, 2002; Greenwald & Draine, 1997; Kihlstrom, 1993). How many of us can say that we know why we have engaged in every single behavior that we have ever committed? Isn't it possible that there are unconscious forces influencing our behavior?

Furthermore, Freud was one of the first to see the importance of early development on later adult behavior (Gedo, 2002). In the early 1900s, children were seen as mini-adults. People did not believe as strongly as we do now that how infants and children are treated impacts their adult behavior. Although we know that infancy and childhood experiences do not *determine* adult behavior, as Freud asserted, his emphasis on the importance of these early years was a critical departure from accepted beliefs at that time. Through his psychosexual stages, Freud placed much emphasis on explaining the developmental nature of personality, probably more so than any other theoretical approach.

Freud's perspective has been criticized on several counts. First, many believe that Freud placed too much emphasis on sexual and aggressive instincts. His perspective shines very little light on environmental and social conditions that may affect personality functioning. We have just seen that many neo-Freudians diverged from Freud on this point, creating alternate views of the ego and personality that take our interactions with others into account (Horgan, 1996). His ideas and themes also have been attacked for his focus on male development and perpetuating the idea of male superiority (Person, 1990).

© Bettmann/Corbis

Horney suggested that family environments and disturbances in early relationships lead to basic anxiety, or a feeling of helplessness in children. Children cope with this basic anxiety by pursuing love, power, prestige, or detachment. Horney argued that culture plays a larger role in personality development than biology and instinct.

Much more problematic is Freud's method of data collection and that his theories cannot readily be scientifically tested (Crews, 1996). His theories are based almost entirely on case study research and his own self-analysis. His observations may not have been objective, and his case studies were on patients who were suffering from nervous disorders. What his patients told him may not have been accurate, and their statements were not corroborated by other sources. These issues make it difficult to generalize Freud's observations to all people. Scientifically testing Freud's theoretical concepts also is quite challenging. Measuring the unconscious is impossible if participants are unaware of these impulses. It is equally difficult to measure psychosexual stages of development. For this reason, we cannot prove that Freud's theory is true, but we also cannot disprove it. As such, it remains a possible explanation of personality functioning, though not as popular as it was in the past. Freud's ideas have not been supported by data from other cultures possibly because his theories reflect the Western cultural value of individualism. They may not apply in collectivist cultures that emphasize the importance of the group (Matsumoto, 1994).

Let's Review!

This section outlined psychoanalytic perspectives on personality, including Freud's levels of consciousness, psychosexual stages of development, and the structure of personality, as well as the neo-Freudian perspectives of Alfred Adler, Carl Jung, and Karen Horney. For a quick check of your understanding, answer these questions.

1. The psychoanalytic perspective emphasizes the influence of _____ on personality.
   a. unconscious desires
   c. self-actualization
   b. traits
   d. environmental factors

2. Maria often feels guilty when she engages in even the slightest offensive behavior. Freud would say that Maria has a strong:

   a. id.
   c. superego.
   b. ego.
   d. collective unconscious.

3. One of the major criticisms of Freud's theory is its:
   a. overemphasis on environmental and cognitive factors in explaining behavior.
   b. difficulty in being experimentally tested and validated.
   c. emphasis on the unconscious.
   d. assumption that all people are good.

ANSWERS
1. a; 2. c; 3. b

LEARNING < < < < < < < < <
OBJECTIVES

Define traits and compare the various trait approaches to understanding personality (Allport, Cattell, Eysenck, the "big five" theory).

Discuss genetic contributions to personality, and address whether personality is consistent and stable over time.

The Trait Approach: Describing Personality

A second major perspective on personality is called the **trait approach.** Recall the four goals of psychology we introduced in Chapter 1 (see p. 23): describe, predict, control, and explain behavior. The trait approach, like the psychoanalytic approach, focuses on internal aspects of personality. The psychoanalytic approach attempts to explain personality by focusing on unconscious forces and their influence on the functioning of the ego. The trait perspective attempts to describe personality. It also emphasizes the more biological aspects of personality. Trait theory assumes that we all have internal **traits,** or tendencies we have across most situations to behave in a certain way. These traits remain relatively stable as we age and explain why people generally behave the same way across a variety of situations. Yet because people differ in the degree to which

© 2000 by King Features Syndicate. Reprinted with permission.

trait approach   a personality perspective that attempts to describe personality by emphasizing internal, biological aspects of personality called traits

trait   tendency we have across most situations to behave in a certain way

they possess a particular trait, we develop unique personalities. We will describe four major approaches to understanding these personality traits in the theories of Gordon Allport, Raymond Cattell, Hans Eysenck, and the five-factor theory.

Gordon Allport's Trait Theory

Psychologist Gordon Allport (1961) believed there are three types of traits: central traits, secondary traits, and cardinal traits. **Central traits** include those tendencies we have across most situations; they are the core qualities your friends would state if they were asked to describe you. For example, if you are friendly in most situations, then friendly would be considered a central trait. Similarly, if your sister is generally shy most of the time, then shyness would be considered a central trait for your sister. We all have central traits, yet the actual qualities that are considered a central trait may differ from person to person. In the McBride family, we saw examples of different central traits: Dennis, Rosetta, and Helen were generally outgoing, whereas James was generally quiet.

central traits   according to Allport, those tendencies we have to behave in a certain way across most situations

Secondary traits describe how we behave in certain situations; they are tendencies that are less consistent and more situation-specific. Many of us behave aggressively in certain situations, such as when we are frustrated or when we see others behave aggressively. For us, aggression is an example of a secondary trait. However, for someone who is aggressive across most situations, aggression would be an example of a central trait. Again, we all have secondary traits, but whether a specific quality is considered a secondary trait may differ from person to person.

secondary traits   according to Allport, the tendencies that we have that are less consistent and describe how we behave in certain situations

Cardinal traits describe how we behave across all situations. Allport considered these a very basic and dominant element of our personalities—but he had difficulty in finding cardinal traits in all people that he studied. Consequently, the validity of cardinal traits became suspect. Recall from Chapter 5 on learning and Chapter 12 on social psychology the powerful effect the environment can have on our behavior. This effect often makes us behave differently across situations. However, Allport's subjective classification of traits did set the stage for Raymond Cattell's statistical analysis of personality traits.

cardinal traits   according to Allport, those dominant elements of our personalities that drive all of our behaviors

Raymond Cattell's Factor Analytic Trait Theory

Raymond Cattell (1943) attempted to document relationships among traits using a sophisticated statistical technique called *factor analysis.* In contemporary factor analysis, data is entered into a computer. The computer is then asked to find shared qualities among the data and to group these shared relationships into factors. For example, suppose we perform a factor analysis on soups. All the ingredients for all soups are entered into the computer database. The computer is then instructed to generate a list of any shared ingredients among all the soups. If it finds a shared "quality" among them— perhaps salt or water was in every soup—then these items would be called soup factors. Psychologists can do the same thing with personality traits. All traits that are used to

© Courtesy of Cattell Family

Using factor analysis, Cattell reduced the number of personality traits that could be used to describe all people to 16 basic traits, referred to as source traits.

source traits basic, broad, and somewhat universal tendencies at the core of personalities that could be measured in everyone, according to Cattell

introversion personality traits that involve energy directed inward, such as being calm or peaceful

extraversion personality traits that involve energy directed outward, such as being easygoing, lively, or excitable

describe people are entered into a computer, then the computer is instructed to find any shared qualities or factors. In this way, Cattell reduced the number of personality traits that could be used to describe all people.

Cattell's research (1965) originally yielded 35 basic traits that could describe differences in personality. He subsequently reduced this number to 16 basic traits. Cattell referred to these qualities or dimensions that could be measured in everyone as **source traits.** Source traits are basic, broad, and somewhat universal tendencies at the core of our personalities. We may differ in the amount or quality of these traits but they are present in everyone's personality to some degree. However, even Cattell's reduced number of basic traits did not easily lend itself to research. Research led by British psychologist Hans Eysenck would further reduce the number.

Hans Eysenck Narrows Down the Traits

Building on Cattell's factor analytic studies, Eysenck and Rachman (1965) found two factors that they believed measured people's key characteristics: introversion/extraversion and emotional stability/instability (Figure 14.2). Introversion and extraversion define where a person's energy is directed. **Introversion** means that the person's energy is directed inward. This could include being rigid, reliable, sober, or controlled. In all of these traits, energy is directed inward. **Extraversion** means that the person's energy is directed outward. This could include being easygoing, lively, or excitable, all traits in which energy is directed outward. *Emotional stability* and *emotional instability* refer to the control directed over emotions. Being even-tempered, calm, or a leader are traits that include more control over emotions, whereas moody and touchy describe traits that represent emotional instability. We all are somewhere on the introversion/extraversion scale and somewhere on the emotional stability/instability continuum, we just differ in the degree to which we express the two factors. Eysenck (1967, 1982, 1991) proposed that variations in these personality characteristics were partly due to genetics. Specifically, Eysenck proposed that introverts inherit the tendency toward higher levels of physical arousal than extraverts. Introverts are more likely to avoid social situations because such experiences will elevate their arousal and lead to overstimulation and discomfort. Hence, they are more likely than extraverts to turn inward and become introverted.

Research investigating Eysenck's ideas on introversion have been mixed. Some studies confirm that introverts tend to show higher levels of physical arousal than extraverts (e.g., Bullock & Gilliland, 1993; LeBlanc, Ducharme, & Thompson, 2004), but other studies have failed to find this difference (e.g., Koelega, 1992). However, as we will soon see, personality traits that are closely linked to introversion, such as temperament, may also be linked to our biology.

Figure 14.2 **Eysenck's Trait Theory**

British psychologist Hans Eysenck arrived at two universal traits using factor analysis. The stable–unstable axis defines one's emotionality; the introversion–extraversion axis defines the degree to which a person's energy is directed inward or outward. The traits in each quadrant indicate where they are placed with respect to these two factors.

Source: From H. J. Eysenck and S. Rachman (1965), The Causes and Curses of Neurosis. *Copyright © 1965 by J. J. Eysenck and R. Rachman. Reprinted by permission of EdiTS.*

The Five-Factor Trait Theory: The "Big Five"

Currently, the most widely accepted trait theory derived from factor analysis is Paul Costa and Robert McCrae's (1992) "big five" theory. This theory proposes five core traits that can be measured in all individuals:

- extraversion: the degree to which energy is directed inward or outward
- neuroticism: the degree to which one is emotionally stable or unstable
- openness: the degree to which one is thoughtful and rational in considering new ideas
- agreeableness: the degree to which one gets along well with others
- conscientiousness: the degree to which one is aware of and attentive to others around him/her and/or the details of a task

These five traits appear in all cultures, suggesting that these five factors may represent universal personality components (Katigbak, Church, Guanzon-Lapena, Carlota, & del, 2002; McCrae & Costa, 1998). An easy way to remember the five factors is with the acronym OCEAN. Each letter in OCEAN stands for one of the five factors: O = openness, C = conscientiousness, E = extraversion, A = agreeableness, and N = neuroticism.

 Application

Table 14.1 ◆ compares the four trait theories. Notice that the main difference in these theories is the number of basic traits that are proposed. Allport's theory proposes 3, Eysenck's theory proposes 2, Cattell's theory proposes 16, and the "big five" theory proposes 5. A question that follows from these theories is: Where do these traits come from?

Genetic Contributions to Personality

The trait perspective assumes that people have internal dispositions to behave consistently across situations. As such, some researchers have speculated that we inherit some aspects of our personalities. Recall that newborn infants do show differences in behavior that we refer to as temperament (see p. 424), and that these temperamental differences appear to be strongly related to our genes (Braungart, Plomin, DeFries, & Fulker, 1992) and are quite stable over time (McCrae et al., 2000; Rothbart, Ahadi, & Evans, 2000). In one study, children's temperament type at age 3 was strongly correlated with their behavioral style at age 26 (Caspi et al., 2003). It seems possible that other characteristics or personality dispositions are also inherited, as Eysenck proposed.

◆ **Table 14.1**
Summary of Trait Theories

Theorist/Theory	Method of Collection	Results
Allport	Subjectively collected traits	3 traits: central, secondary, and cardinal
Cattell	Factor analysis	16 source traits
Eysenck	Factor analysis	2 basic dimensions that underlie all traits: introversion/extraversion and emotional stability/instability
Costa and McCrae's five-factor theory	Factor analysis	5 basic traits that form the acronym OCEAN: openness, conscientiousness, extraversion, agreeableness, and neuroticism

Some studies have found that children's personality test scores do moderately correlate with those of their parents and siblings (Davis, Luce & Kraus, 1994). But what does this finding mean? It could be that you are hot-tempered because you have inherited your quick temper from your mother or father. However, your temper might also be due to being exposed to your parent's temper. It may upset you and make you temperamental in response, or you may be modeling your parents' behavior—or both. It is not possible to tell exactly where environmental influences end and genetic ones begin when children share genes and a family environment. To unravel such a puzzle, adoption and twin studies are used.

Recall from Chapter 9 (see p. 392) that one way to study genetic contributions—the nature side of personality—is to look at children who are adopted. Because adopted children have no genes in common with their adoptive family members, any similarities in personality characteristics found between these children and their adoptive parents must be due to learning or modeling. On the other hand, because these children have genes in common with their biological parents but do not share a family environment, any similarities in personality must be due to genetics. These research studies have found more personality similarities between adoptive children and their biological parents (Carey & DiLalla, 1994). This suggests a strong genetic component to personality.

Another method we described in Chapter 9 (see p. 391) for investigating the contribution of genes—or nature—is to study identical twins. Research on identical twins provides even more compelling evidence that at least some personality tendencies may be inherited (Bouchard, 2004). Recall the Minnesota Twin studies that were discussed in Chapter 9 on development: identical twins reared in separate environments appeared to show remarkable similarities in behavior years later when they were reunited (Bouchard, Lykken, McGue, Segal, & Tellegen, 1990; Holden, 1980; Lykken, McGue, Tellegen, & Bouchard, 1992). Studies have found more similarities between the personalities of identical twins' than between nonidentical twins' personalities (Buss, 1995; Plomin, DeFries, McClearn, & McGuffin, 2001; Saudino, McQuire, Reiss, Heatherington, & Plomin, 1995). Such evidence indicates a significant genetic role in the personalities that we exhibit. Perhaps such research can explain why all of Rachel McBride's children were creative in some way and academically successful—maybe their intelligence and creativity were inherited.

Other research on the heritability of personality traits has focused on gene markers that direct our neurotransmitter functioning and how the gene markers influence behavior. For example, as we saw in Chapter 2, the neurotransmitter serotonin, is associated with regulating our behavior, moods, and thought processes. Low serotonin activity has been linked to traits such as aggression and impulsivity. Low serotonin activity can be caused by a multitude of factors, including how we think about our environments or ourselves. However, increasing evidence indicates that serotonin responsivity may be partly genetically determined (Lesch & Merschdorf, 2000; Manuck, Flory, Ferrell, Mann, & Muldoon, 2000; Twitchell et al., 1998). Several studies have found an association between the serotonin transporter gene and anxiety-related personality traits (Greenberg et al., 2000; Jang et al., 2001; Melke et al., 2001; Osher, Hamer, & Benjamin, 2000; Sen, Burmeister, & Ghosh, 2004; Sen, Villafuerte, et al., 2004). This gene influences the levels of serotonin in the brain and may account for differences in anxiety levels from person to person.

Studies have found more similarities between identical twins' personalities than between nonidentical twins' personalities, indicating a significant genetic role in the personalities that we exhibit.

Mel Yates/Getty Images

Other studies have investigated the relationship between a dopamine receptor gene and the personality trait of novelty-seeking (Jonsson, Burgert, Crocq et al., 2003; Jonsson et al., 2002; Katsuragi et al., 2001; Schinka, Letsch, & Crawford, 2002). No significant relationships emerged from those studies. There has also been little success in attempting to link neurotransmitter gene regions with infant temperaments (Garpenstrand et al., 2002; Lakatos et al., 2003). Such results suggest a complex interaction between biology, environment, and personality. Human behavior is the product of many genes working simultaneously, together with multiple environmental and developmental events (Ebstein, Zohar, Benjamin & Belmaker, 2002; Hamer, 2002). Unraveling these connections and influences will keep scientists very busy in the years ahead.

If personality is engineered by our biology, then we might assume that it would remain stable and consistent over our lifetime. Would this stability and consistency also be evident in other cultures? We turn to this topic next.

Stability and Change in Personality

Has your personality changed over time, or do you still show the same tendencies that you did when you were a child? The trait approach not only assumes that traits are inherited, it also assumes that these internal tendencies are consistent and stable over time. What does the research indicate? Longitudinal research does support the stability of *some* personality traits over the course of adulthood. After the age of 30 changes in personality traits are very small (Costa & McCrae, 1997). A more recent analysis of 150 studies (Roberts & DelVecchio, 2000) also supports the notion that some personality traits are stable. This study analyzed results from nearly 50,000 participants and concluded that personality in early adulthood was a good predictor of personality in late adulthood. However, other research suggests that age, culture, and gender are important when considering stability and change in personality, as It's a Diverse World highlights.

IT'S A DIVERSE WORLD

How Age, Culture, and Gender Influence Personality

Evidence on the stability of traits prior to age 30 is quite complex. As a part of the developmental process, children, adolescents, and young adults experiment with new identities and ways of behaving. They may adopt new values and attitudes or revise existing ones. Changes in personality, therefore, are more frequent during these periods. Some studies suggest that at least for some traits, there is a consistency from childhood to adulthood.

For example, McCrae and colleagues (2002) found stability in the traits of extraversion, agreeableness, and conscientiousness from age 12 to age 18. Shiner, Masten, and Roberts (2003) found modest continuity in the traits of motivation, academic conscientiousness, and agreeableness from childhood to adulthood. Another longitudinal study (Robins, Fraley, Roberts, & Trzesniewski, 2001) found consistency in the "big five" personality traits when following the same people from the beginning to the end of their college years. A longitudinal study on young adults also found consistency in some personality traits, yet also found that the adolescents became more confident and controlled and less angry and alienated as they got older (Roberts, Caspi, & Moffitt, 2001). Other longitudinal research has supported a consistency in the trait of ill-temperedness from childhood to adulthood (Caspi, Bem, & Elder, 1989). In adulthood, these same individuals were rated by family, friends, and spouses as ill-tempered.

Age differences in personality have also been investigated in other cultures, with a similar picture emerging. Data from Germany, Britain, Spain, Italy, Portugal, Croatia, Turkey, South Korea, and the Czech Republic are consistent

How Age, Culture, and Gender Influence Personality, *continued*

with findings on the "big five" personality factors in U.S. samples (McCrae et al., 1999, 2000). Older men and women in these cultures also tended to be lower in extraversion and openness to experience and higher in agreeableness and conscientiousness. Such findings appear to support the universality of some personality traits. These societies differ from each other dramatically in language, culture, and historical experiences and from the experiences of most people in the United States. Yet the cultural differences seemed to have little impact on age differences in personality traits.

Cultures also differ markedly in how they define themselves and in which traits they find most admirable. Recall from Chapter 12 (see p. 535) that individualistic cultures like the United States and Canada, Western Europe, and Australia emphasize individual behavior, whereas collectivistic cultures like India and Japan emphasize group behavior. Such cultural orientations also influence how we see ourselves. People from individualistic cultures are more likely to use personal traits to describe themselves. Individuals from collectivistic cultures are more likely to describe themselves in a social context such as their group memberships and social activities (Gardiner, Mutter, & Kosmitzki, 1998). This cultural difference makes it difficult to assess similarities in traits across cultures.

Although some research has indicated a consistency in personality traits in adulthood and across cultures, other research suggests substantial changes in personality even during the course of adulthood (Ravenna, Jones, & Kwan, 2002; Whitbourne, Zuschlag, Elliot, & Waterman, 1992). For example, in a 30- or 40-year time span, Jones and Meredith (1996) found changes in the personality traits of self-confidence, cognitive commitment, outgoingness, and dependability. The 211 participants in this study also

showed differences in the degree and direction of these changes. That is, they did not exhibit a consistent pattern of change as they aged. People generally become more introspective, cautious, and conforming as they approach late adulthood (Reedy, 1983). In one study, conscientiousness and agreeableness showed *increases* throughout early and middle adulthood (Srivastava, John, Gosling, & Potter, 2003). Many people also became more androgynous, or exhibiting both male and female traits, as they aged (Fiske, 1980). Even McCrae and colleagues' (1999, 2000) cross-cultural research did not find consistency across all of the "big five" traits. Only two cultures looked similar to U.S. samples on the neuroticism trait.

Gender differences in personality traits also show evidence of both stability and change. Across cultures and for both college-age and adult samples, women report themselves to be higher in neuroticism, agreeableness, and openness to feelings, whereas men report themselves higher in assertiveness and openness to ideas (Costa, Terracciano, & McCrae, 2001). Yet in the same study, it was found that the participants within each gender varied more in personality traits than they did between the genders. Neuroticism also tends to decrease in women as they age but stays the same for men (Srivastava et al., 2003). Helson and Wink (1992) found that women in their early 40s and 50s increased in confidence and decisiveness and decreased in dependence and self-criticism. Similarly, personality changes have also been found to be influenced by parenting roles (Wink & Helson, 1993) and the impact of the women's movement (Duncan & Agronick, 1995). Such findings suggest that our societies, cultures, gender, and historical events are important considerations when examining the stability of personality traits.

---

person-situation interaction the influence of the situation on the stability of traits; when in the same situation, we display similar behavior, but when the situation is different, behavior may change

Situational factors also influence the stability and consistency of traits. Many of us will display the same trait (behave the same way) when faced with similar circumstances—that is, when the environmental cues are the same. However, when the situation is different, our behavior may change. This is referred to as the **person-situation interaction** (Mischel & Shoda, 1995). For example, the students of one of the authors of this textbook are always surprised to hear that she has a fear of public speaking. They see her speak every week in class with enthusiasm, humor, and little anxiety. They know that she has been teaching for over 15 years. From such knowledge, they predict that she would not fear public speaking in other situations, such as at a research conference or at a community function. But in these different situations, she is extremely anxious, panicked, and nauseated at the thought of speaking in front of a group. The cues of the two different situations evoke different behaviors and reactions. Consequently, our traits do not always predict how we will behave across different situations.

How do psychologists reconcile these seemingly contradictory findings? By recognizing that personality is both stable *and* changeable. Some traits are probably more consistent across our life span and from culture to culture, whereas others are more easily influenced by our societies, gender, environments, and daily situations (Fleeson, 2004).

Criticisms and Contributions of the Trait Approach

The trait perspective has contributed to our understanding of personality by providing psychologists with a common language and vocabulary to describe people's personalities. Because this common language facilitates communication within the field, the trait approach has been useful particularly in the area of personality assessment, a topic we will turn to shortly. Knowing a person's tendencies or traits also helps psychologists predict future behavior. These predictions, however, will be influenced by the nature of the situation (Johnson, 1997). The assumptions of the trait perspective—that traits are internal and stable—have also fueled research investigating the biological aspects of personality and the consistency and stability of personality traits across the life span.

However, the objective of personality research is to uncover how we are all different and unique from one another. Although the trait perspective does a good job of *describing* people's personalities, it is criticized for not *explaining why* we behave in a particular way (Digman, 1997; Funder, 1993). Critics further argue that it portrays personality too simplistically and fails to reflect its complexity and depth (Block, 1995; Epstein, 1994; Gladwell, 2004). Can everyone really be reduced to 2, 5, or 16 dimensions? Can we cleanly slice the pie of personality into biological and environmental components without taking into account the complex interactions among them? We have also seen its shortcomings in predicting people's behavior across different situations (Wiggins, 1997). This should not be surprising, though, given the power of situational forces on behavior.

Let's Review!

This section presented the trait approach to personality, including the theories of Allport, Cattell, Eysenck, and the five-factor model. It also discussed genetic aspects of personality and its stability over time. For a quick check of your understanding, answer these questions.

1. The trait perspective emphasizes the influence of _____ on personality.
   a. unconscious impulses
   c. self-actualization
   b. internal tendencies
   d. environmental factors

2. Terrence is outgoing in most situations. Allport would describe this tendency in Terrence as a:
   a. source trait.
   c. cardinal trait.
   b. secondary trait.
   d. central trait.

3. Which of the following is *not* considered one of the "big five" traits of personality?
   a. achievement
   c. conscientiousness
   b. extraversion
   d. agreeableness

ANSWERS
1.b; 2.d; 3.a

LEARNING
OBJECTIVE < < < < < < < <
Describe social-cognitive approaches
to personality such as Bandura's
reciprocal determinism and Rotter's
locus of control.

The Social Cognitive Approach: The Environment and Patterns of Thought

How might the environment and your thoughts influence your personality? From a **social cognitive approach,** personality is seen as a construct that is influenced by both the environment and one's thoughts. Consequently, whereas Freud focused on how unconscious forces influence behavior and the trait perspective investigates internal dispositions, the social cognitive approach looks at the characteristic ways a person perceives and interprets events in the environment. Patterns of thought that we regularly engage in influence our behavior. For example, the person who generally assumes that others are unlikely to treat her fairly is more likely to have a quarrelsome personality than a person who tends to generally assume that things happen for the best. These patterns of thoughts are established through our interactions with and observations of other people. Two examples of this approach include Albert Bandura's reciprocal determinism and Julian Rotter's locus of control theory.

social cognitive approach a personality perspective that emphasizes the influence of one's thoughts and social experiences in formulating personality

Reciprocal Determinism: Albert Bandura's Interacting Forces

Albert Bandura (1986) speculates that personality is the product of the mutual forces of the environment, one's behavior, and one's thoughts. Bandura called the constant interaction among these three factors **reciprocal determinism** (Figure 14.3). We choose to place ourselves in certain environments, and these environments then impact our behavior and the way we think. However, the way we think—our attributions, goals, values, and perceptions—also may guide which environments we choose to be in as well as the behavior we exhibit. Our behavior may change the environment as well as the way we think. All three variables influence each other in a reciprocal manner.

reciprocal determinism according to Bandura, the constant interaction among one's behavior, thoughts, and environment determines personality

Bandura speculates that personality is the product of reciprocal determinism, or the mutual interaction between one's environment, behavior, and thoughts.

Archives of the History of American Psychology, University of Akron, Akron, Ohio

Application

For example, when we were children, we were placed in a family environment that modeled specific child-rearing techniques. We tend to think that everything that we experienced in our home was normal, and that these same experiences occurred everywhere else, too. We tend to think everyone else grew up with the parental discipline style we had. When we ourselves have children, if we have not learned anything different, we tend to behave in the same way toward our children. The family environment and our understanding of the way we were raised have now influenced our own parenting behavior.

A critical cognitive element in this interplay is what Bandura (1997) termed **self-efficacy,** or the expectation one has for success in a given situation. Self-efficacy can differ among different domains in one's life. People with high self-efficacy in a certain domain believe that they will be successful in that domain. Approaching a situation with this belief is more likely to result in actual success. On the other hand, people with low self-efficacy in a particular domain are more likely to approach a task believing that they won't succeed in it. This mind-set then decreases their chance of succeeding by causing them to give up too easily or not even really try in the first place.

self-efficacy the expectation that one has for success in a given situation

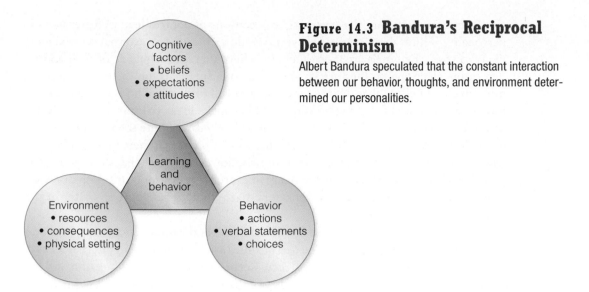

Figure 14.3 **Bandura's Reciprocal Determinism**
Albert Bandura speculated that the constant interaction between our behavior, thoughts, and environment determined our personalities.

 Application

Returning to our previous example, if you believe that you will be a successful parent by using the same discipline techniques that your parents used on you, you would be more likely to use such measures. If such practices are successful—in other words, your children behave as you would like—you feel even better as a parent. However, if you do not believe that you will be a successful parent, you may constantly equivocate or change the methods that you use to discipline your children. Such inconsistency will make it even more likely that your children will not behave in the manner that you want, which only reinforces your lack of confidence in your parenting ability.

Julian Rotter's Locus of Control: Internal and External Expectations

Julian Rotter provides another example of a social cognitive approach to personality. His theory (Rotter, 1982) is referred to as **locus of control,** or *location of control.* Rotter believes that we all have expectations for how much we can control the outcome of an event. These expectations fall on a continuum from internal to external. For example, you probably enter the testing room on exam day already expecting to do well, average, or poorly on the exam. This is your expectation of the event. Some of us attribute the outcome of an event to internal forces such as hard work. If you expect to do well on an exam because you studied hard, then that is more of an *internal locus of control.* You are attributing the outcome of the event to factors within your control. However, others of us attribute the outcome of an event to external forces such as good luck, fate, or environmental factors. If you believe you will do well on the exam because the course or test is easy or because the professor likes you, these expectations demonstrate more of an *external locus of control.* You attribute the outcome to factors outside of your control.

In an analysis of 97 samples of college students and 41 samples of children collected between 1960 and 2002, Twenge, Zhang, and Im (2004) found that young people in the United States increasingly believe that their lives are controlled by external forces. Locus of control became substantially more external from 1960 to 2002. Not surprisingly, internals demonstrate higher academic achievement compared to externals. Externals also tend to believe that only fate or the luck of a sympathetic teacher will get them a good grade, and so they do not study as much as internals (Schultz & Schultz, 2005). Similarly, externals also are more likely to endorse paranormal beliefs (Newby & Davis, 2004).

locus of control   the expectation of control we have over the outcome of an event; an internal locus expects some degree of control over an outcome, whereas an external locus expects little control over an outcome

 Application

Rotter suggests that these varying expectations of control lead to differences in personality. Think about voting behavior. Would an internal or external type be more likely to vote? Externals are more likely to believe that forces outside of their control determine elections, so they are less likely to vote. Internals, on the other hand, are more likely to believe that their votes count and will influence who is elected. Therefore, they are more likely to vote. Who would be more likely to exercise regularly and maintain a healthy lifestyle? Externals are more likely to attribute their weight, health, or medical condition to fate. "What will be, will be" could be their motto. They feel when their time is up, their time is up. Internals, however, believe that they can control their health and are therefore more likely to exercise, follow doctor's directions, get regular checkups, and eat wisely, behaviors that actually contribute to better health (Phares, 1991; Strickland, 1989).

In examining the opening case study, Bandura's and Rotter's social cognitive perspectives would explain the McBride personalities as expressions of an internal locus of control and a strong sense of self-efficacy. Rachel's insistence on education and her pursuit of the best schools and scholarships influenced her children's subsequent academic achievement. Her determination to be treated fairly modeled to her children high self-efficacy and an internal locus of control. The children adopted these attitudes, leading to their own successes and fights for equality.

Criticisms and Contributions of the Social Cognitive Approach

The social cognitive approach has made major contributions to the field of psychology. By detailing the influence of cognitive processes such as thinking, expectations, and other mental events on behavior, it has expanded our conceptualization and understanding of personality. This in turn has stimulated an enormous amount of research focusing on how environmental and cognitive factors influence behavior. Our knowledge of memory, attributions, and problem solving stem directly from this perspective, which easily lends itself to research, specifically experimental testing. Objectively measuring social and cognitive processes is easier than measuring unconscious forces or biological tendencies. Despite these contributions, the social cognitive approach has been criticized for not addressing biological, unconscious, and emotional factors that influence personality (Liebert & Spiegler, 1998). It also has been criticized for not detailing the exact nature of personality development.

Let's Review!

This section described social cognitive approaches to personality, including Albert Bandura's reciprocal determinism and Julian Rotter's locus of control. For a quick check of your understanding, answer these questions.

1. The social cognitive perspective emphasizes the influence of _____ on personality.
   a. unconscious impulses   c. self-actualization
   b. internal tendencies   d. patterns of thoughts

2. Dylan is sure he will do poorly on his next psychology exam. Dylan often thinks this way in regard to his academic studies. Bandura would say that Dylan has:
   a. low self-esteem.   c. an internal locus of control.
   b. low self-efficacy.   d. reciprocal determinism.

3. Juanita believes that finding a job is a matter of being in the right place at the right time. Rotter would classify Juanita as having:
   a. low self-efficacy.   c. an internal locus of control.
   b. low determinism.   d. an external locus of control.

ANSWERS

1.d; 2.b; 3.d

The Humanistic Approach: > > > > > > > > > > > > > Free Will and Self-Actualization

The fourth and final personality perspective we will discuss is the humanistic approach. Humanistic psychology viewed itself as a "third force" in American psychology, following behavioral (the first force) and psychoanalytic (the second force) views. The **humanistic approach** emphasizes the individual, personal choice, and free will in shaping personality, as opposed to internal or external forces. The humanists view the individual as an active participant in his or her growth as a person. The humanistic view further assumes that humans have a built-in drive toward fulfilling their own natural potentials. The attainment of this potential is referred to as **self-actualization.** Two well-known humanistic theorists charted somewhat different paths to achieving self-actualization. One was Abraham Maslow, whose hierarchy of needs theory was introduced in Chapter 8. The other is Carl Rogers and self-theory.

Abraham Maslow and the Hierarchy of Needs Theory

Recall from Chapter 8 that Maslow (1968, 1970) believed that the pathway to achieving self-actualization was in the form of a hierarchy, with physical or biological needs at the bottom and more psychological or social needs at the top. According to Maslow, a person must satisfy lower-level needs before higher-level needs can be attained. At the bottom of the hierarchy are basic physiological needs, such as the need for food and water. Without food and water, we cannot proceed to the next rung of the ladder. At this next level, safety becomes the concern: the need to be free from harm and to feel secure. Once this safety need is met, the person focuses on psychological needs, such as feeling a sense of belongingness (the need to fit in) and feeling esteem or respect from others. Once these needs have been satisfied, self-actualization can be attained.

How do self-actualized people differ from people at other need levels? Maslow estimated that only 1 person in 10 operates from self-actualized needs. Research on individuals who Maslow believed were self-actualized, such as Eleanor Roosevelt, Walt Whitman, and Albert Einstein, has revealed certain personal qualities or attributes (Maslow, 1971), listed in Table 14.2 ◆. Read through this list of qualities. What general impression do you get about self-actualized people? Although it may seem attractive to be self-actualized, many people perceive self-actualized individuals as proud and stubborn. Fortunately, these evaluations would not affect the well-being of a truly actualized personality.

Unfortunately, Maslow's hierarchy does not explain why some people would deprive themselves of lower food and safety needs in favor of higher needs, such as esteem or self-actualization. For example, Mohandas Gandhi voluntarily fasted in protest of English rule over India. He fasted again in protest of the civil wars following independence from

People who meet the criteria for self-actualization such as Mother Teresa might actually deprive themselves of lower base needs, such as food or shelter.

© Corbis Sygma

LEARNING OBJECTIVES

⌄ Define self-actualization, and describe how the humanistic views of Maslow and Rogers propose that it can be achieved.

⌄ Compare and contrast the four perspectives on personality, indicating the strengths and weaknesses of each approach.

humanistic approach   a personality perspective that emphasizes the individual, personal choice, and free will in shaping personality, as opposed to internal or external forces; assumes that humans have a built-in drive toward fulfilling their own natural potentials

self-actualization   the fulfillment of one's natural potential

◆ **Table 14.2**

Characteristics of a Self-Actualized Person

- Perceives reality accurately
- Accepts self, others, and nature
- Tends to be autonomous
- Is more concerned with problem solving than with themselves
- Is spontaneous, engaged, and alive
- Deeply cares and identifies with all people
- Possesses a nonhostile sense of humor
- Values solitude and feels at ease when by him- or herself
- Shares deep loving bonds with only a few people
- Renews appreciation of life's basic elements
- Accepts democratic values
- Has a strong ethical sense
- Tends to be creative
- Frequently has peak experiences or feels ecstatic, harmonious, and one with the world; is filled with beauty and good.

Source: Adapted from Maslow, 1970.

actualizing tendency according to Rogers, the natural drive in humans to strive for fulfillment and enhancement

self-concept one's perception or image of his/her abilities and uniqueness

English rule and was assassinated shortly thereafter. Nelson Mandela preferred to remain imprisoned in South Africa for many years over losing his right to criticize the apartheid government. Salman Rushdie was forced into exile under threat from an Islamic *fatwah* and other death threats he received for publishing *The Satanic Verses*, a critique on life in Islamic countries. Many argue that Maslow's hierarchy is too simple a view of personality (Neher, 1991). Another view of self-actualization is in Carl Rogers' self theory.

Carl Rogers and Self Theory

Carl Rogers received his undergraduate degree in history in 1924. He began his graduate studies at the Union Theological Seminary in New York but transferred to Teachers College, Columbia University, to receive his Ph.D. in clinical and educational psychology. Rogers (1942, 1951, 1961, 1970, 1980) believed that understanding human personality required an understanding of how people view themselves and how they interpret events around them. He believed that human beings naturally strive for fulfillment and enhancement, a basic motive that he referred to as the **actualizing tendency.**

Rogers' proposed actualizing tendency is set at birth and moves the infant to recognize that she is separate from the mother and an independent being. The infant begins to experience the self as "I" or "me." This self gradually evolves into the person's self-concept. **Self-concept** is our perception or image of our abilities and our uniqueness. At first one's self-concept is very general and changeable, like the 4-year-old who describes herself as a girl with brown hair or the 3-year-old who states in one moment that he is happy, yet 5 minutes later says that he is sad. As we grow older these self-perceptions and viewpoints become much more organized, detailed, and specific. For example, a 15-year-old is more likely to describe himself in terms of his academic abilities, athletic abilities, social abilities, and talents. For example, he may say, "I'm a decent second baseman, a B student, and I have a lot of friends."

Underlying Rogers' actualizing tendency is an *organismic valuing process.* Experiences and sensations that maintain or enhance the individual are valued, and therefore preferred and liked. Experiences that do not maintain or enhance the person are not valued, and therefore are rejected (Sheldon, Arndt, & Houser-Marko, 2003). An infant's valuing process is quite direct and simple. We know as infants what we like and what we dislike. We value food because it reduces the sensation of hunger. We value being held in a parent's arms because it makes us feel secure.

Rogers believed that understanding human personality required an understanding of how people view themselves and how they interpret events around them.

© Roger Ressmeyer/Corbis

However, such an internal evaluation of our values is soon influenced by our interactions with others and our basic need for love and acceptance.

Application

As children, we come to realize that other important people in our lives (such as parents, teachers, siblings, or other relatives) also place value on our experiences. They communicate to us what is "right" and "wrong" to think, feel, or behave. Because we desire their love and affection, we incorporate these messages into our valuing process. Experiences that meet these imposed values tend to be incorporated into our self-concepts. For example, if a parent has communicated to a child that good grades are valued, and the child makes good grades, he may describe himself as a good student. A child may come home every day from school reporting his test scores or give other indications of how well he did in school. This gives a child the opportunity to gain acceptance and love from the parent. On the other hand, suppose the child does not make good grades at school. This child may hide test scores from parents for fear of being rejected and unloved. This example illustrates the enormous influence of others' standards and values on our self-concepts. We may no longer listen to our own internal valuing system but pay more attention to the views and values of loved ones. Our worth and regard is now judged on the basis of the imposed opinions, judgments, and values of others, rather than our own internal organismic valuing process. We have come to see ourselves as others see us.

What determines the degree to which we "listen" to, or incorporate, these parental and other outside norms and standards? For Rogers, it is the degree of **unconditional positive regard,** or acceptance and love with no strings attached that we receive from others. Our good points as well as bad points are accepted. People accept us and love us for who we are. This does not mean that a person's *actions* always receive approval. For example, suppose a youngster kicks the dog because the dog chewed a cherished toy. A parent can express displeasure at the child's actions, yet still let the child know that the angry behavior is understood and that the child is still loved by the parent despite the behavior. However, if the parent attacks the child's self, calling the child "bad," the parent has now communicated *conditional* positive regard. The child will believe that feeling angry is wrong because feeling angry will lose his parent's love and acceptance. In other words, unconditional positive regard communicates respect for a person's thoughts and feelings.

unconditional positive regard
acceptance and love of another's thoughts and feelings without expecting anything in return

It isn't easy to be always accepting of a person's thoughts and feelings, and it is impossible to experience complete unconditional positive regard. Parents naturally have expectations about how their children will think and behave. However, if a child, especially during the early years of life, experiences unconditional positive regard, he or she is less likely to lose contact with the organismic valuing process established at birth. In this way, the child grows into an adult who chooses to act, feel, or think on the basis of his or her inner evaluations, taking into consideration the effect of his or her behavior on others. For Rogers, this represented a healthy personality. On the other hand, if a child experiences primarily conditional positive regard during these years, he or she is more likely to develop a self-concept that is based on how others see him or her and disregard the inner guiding voice of his or her behavior. Such people think, act, or behave in a certain way in hope of ensuring the continued love and acceptance of others. They believe that if they don't meet certain self-imposed expectations, then their parents will not love them any more. For example, many students perceive that if they do not receive good grades, their parents will love them less. These perceptions, whether accurate or not, impede our ability to fulfill our potential, according to Rogers. In such situations, healthy development of the personality is hindered, and psychological discomfort may occur (Assor, Roth, & Deci, 2004).

Application

Let's take one more look at the McBride family from a humanistic perspective. What factors might Maslow and Rogers consider in evaluating their personalities?

Growing up Black with a White mother during a time of racial discrimination, the civil rights movement, and integration potentially influenced the McBride children's perception of reality and their evaluations of their self-concepts. For example, James expresses his struggle with reconciling his Black identity with his mother's Whiteness and Jewish background. Others' opinions and judgments affected his view of himself. Moreover, the McBrides' everyday struggle to fulfill basic biological and security needs may have influenced the attainment of higher psychological needs.

Criticisms and Contributions of the Humanistic Approach

Many humanistic ideas have been incorporated into individual, family, and group therapy approaches, as we will see in Chapter 16. The humanistic approach has encouraged many people to become more aware of themselves and their interactions with others. However, the humanistic perspective has been criticized for its seemingly naïve and optimistic view of behavior: it assumes that all people are good and are motivated toward good in attaining self-actualization. Critics argue that all people are not necessarily good and pure in their intentions. They believe that humanists underestimate the capacity for evil in some individuals (Coffer & Appley, 1964; Ellis, 1959). Equally problematic is the difficulty in validating through experiments many of the humanistic concepts such as actualizing tendency, organismic valuing process, and unconditional positive regard (Burger, 2004). The major source of data for Rogers' self-theory has been under scrutiny as well, as it was derived from clients' self-statements. How reliable and valid are such statements? It's possible that clients did not always present their "true" selves to Rogers, and that as a listener Rogers was biased. As such, humanistic psychology has not become as major a force in psychology as Maslow once hoped.

Let's Review!

This section presented the humanistic view of personality, specifically Maslow's and Roger's theories on self-actualization. For a quick check of your understanding, answer these questions.

1. The humanistic perspective emphasizes the influence of _____ on personality.
   a. unconscious impulses
   b. internal tendencies
   c. self-actualization
   d. environmental and cognitive factors

2. Which of the following elements does Rogers believe promotes self-actualization?
   a. unconditional positive regard
   b. esteem
   c. sympathy
   d. adaptability

3. SuLing was recently mugged. Since the mugging, she has been suspicious and paranoid of others. She locks her doors at night and suffers from nightmares. Maslow would attribute SuLing's behavior to:
   a. esteem needs.
   c. belongingness needs.
   b. safety needs.
   d. biological needs.

ANSWERS
1. c; 2. a; 3. b

Measuring Personality >>>>>>>>>>>>>>>>>>>>

LEARNING OBJECTIVE

Detail the various methods psychologists use to measure personality and the theoretical perspective that gave rise to each method. Compare the advantages and disadvantages of each measure.

How do psychologists measure your personality? We have detailed four approaches on personality. Each perspective tends to employ certain tools to measure or assess personality. As with any tool or measuring device, it is important that the test be reliable and valid. **Reliability** refers to the consistency of a measurement tool. If we were to assess your height as an adult with a tape measure, we would want to get a consistent "reading" every time we measured your height. Personality tests also need to be reliable, or yield similar results over time. This reliability will not be perfect as we are not consistent in our behavior at all times. However, personality tests should report similar trends if they are reliable.

Measurement tools like personality tests also need to be valid. **Validity** refers to the ability of a test to measure what it says it is measuring. If a test states that it is measuring your intelligence and it does so by measuring your foot size, this test would not be valid. There is no relationship between foot size and intelligence. Notice that this test would be reliable (that is, yield a consistent measure from time to time), but it does not measure what we think of as intelligence. Therefore, personality tests should measure what we believe personality to be.

Each of the four major perspectives, or ideas, on the nature of personality has developed its own way of measuring personality. They include personality inventories, projective tests, rating scales, and clinical interviews. See if you can identify the psychological perspective that correlates with each type of test. Also, see if you can evaluate each method of assessment in terms of reliability and validity. Would such instruments yield similar results from one time to the next, and is each instrument truly measuring what is meant by personality?

Personality Inventories: Mark Which One Best Describes You

Personality inventories are objective paper-and-pencil self-report forms. You are typically asked to indicate how well a statement describes you or to answer true or false to a specific statement. For example, in college settings many students have completed the *Myers-Briggs Personality Inventory*. This test details an individual's personality on four different dimensions. In clinical settings, the most frequently used personality inventory is the **Minnesota Multiphasic Personality Inventory (MMPI-2).**

The MMPI-2 is a 567-item true-false questionnaire that takes about 1 hour to complete. The questions describe a wide range of behaviors (Table 14.3 ◆). Its purpose is to identify problem areas of functioning in a person's personality. The MMPI-2 is organized into 10 groups of items, called *clinical scales*. These scales measure patterns of responses associated with specific psychological disorders such as depression, paranoia, and schizophrenia. A person's response patterns are reviewed to see whether they resemble the pattern of responses from groups of people who have specific mental health disorders. Interpreting the MMPI-2 involves comparing the test-taker's responses to those of the norming population.

As part of its construction, the MMPI-2 was given to thousands of people, called a *norming group*. Individuals in the norming group represented people who had no psychological disorders and people who had particular disorders. In this way the test-constructors could see how frequently someone without the disorder would respond "yes" to these items and how frequently someone with the psychological disorder would respond "yes." The first group established the average, or "normal," number of items for each of these clinical scales, whereas the latter group gave an indication

reliability the consistency of a test's measurements over time

validity the ability of a test to measure what it says it is measuring

personality inventory objective paper-and-pencil self-report form that measures personality on several dimensions

Minnesota Multiphasic Personality Inventory (MMPI-2) a personality inventory that is designed to identify problem areas of functioning in a person's personality

◆ **Table 14.3**

Sample MMPI-2 Items

I have trouble with my bowel movements.	T	F
I do not sleep well.	T	F
At parties, I sit by myself or with one other person.	T	F
A lot of people have it in for me.	T	F
In school, I was frequently in trouble for acting up.	T	F
I am anxious most of the time.	T	F
I hear strange things that others do not hear.	T	F
I am a very important person.	T	F

of what would be considered problematic functioning. A psychologist is interested in detailing any areas of your personality that fall outside the normal range. These areas would be considered problem areas of your personality and may suggest issues for therapy.

One of the main problems with self-report measures such as the MMPI-2 is the test-taker's honesty or truthfulness. For this reason, the MMPI-2 also contains four *validity scales* to assess the truthfulness of the individual's responses. Given the nature and description of personality inventories such as the MMPI-2, which personality approach do you think is most closely connected to it? The correct answer is the trait approach. Notice how the MMPI-2 measures 10 different traits in individuals. Figure 14.4 provides an example of a MMPI-2 personality profile.

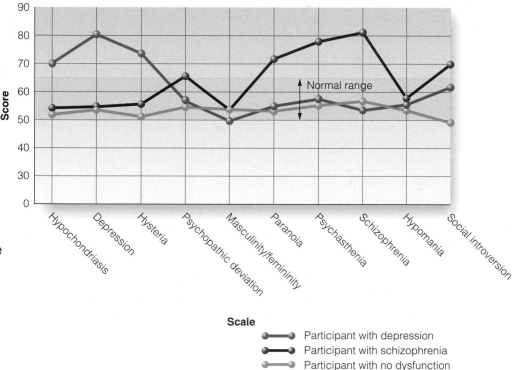

Figure 14.4 MMPI-2 Personality Profiles

Scores on the 10 clinical scales of the MMPI-2 are plotted to show a client where his or her behavior is in the normal range and where it is abnormal. Presented here are three participants: one that shows elevated scores on hypochondriasis, depression, and hysteria; one that shows elevated scores on paranoia, psychasthenia, schizophrenia, and social introversion; and one that shows scores within the normal range on all 10 scales.

projective test unstructured and subjective personality test in which an individual is shown an ambiguous stimulus and then asked to describe what he or she sees

Rorschach inkblot test a projective personality test consisting of ten ambiguous inkblots in which a person is asked to describe what he or she sees; the person's responses are then coded for consistent themes and issues

Projective Tests: Tell Me What You See

Another type of tool to measure personality, the **projective test,** is unstructured and subjective compared to the personality inventory. When taking this test, you are shown an ambiguous image and then asked to describe what you see or to tell a story about the picture. Children may be asked to draw pictures and describe what they have drawn. Such tests rely on the idea that whatever stories, motives, or explanations are offered by the person reflect his or her own issues and concerns, projected onto the image.

One of the most famous projective tests is the **Rorschach inkblot test.** The Rorschach inkblot test consists of ten inkblots on cards. As each card is presented, you indicate what images you see on the cards. The person's responses are then coded according to specific guidelines. A sample card is shown in Figure 14.5. (A television commercial in 2002 showed the same card and asked, "Do you see two sheep driving a car?")

Another widely used projective test is the **Thematic Apperception Test (TAT)**. In the TAT, you are shown images that are not as ambiguous as inkblots yet still allow for a variety of interpretations. You are then asked to tell a story about the image, and your responses are then coded for any consistent themes, emotions, or issues. A sample TAT image is depicted in Figure 14.6. After being shown this image, a client may relate the following story. "It's a picture of a young man who has been waiting several hours at a park for his girlfriend to arrive. He is tired, anxious, and angry. He is hoping that nothing bad has happened to his girlfriend. He is also hoping that she didn't just stand him up."

The purpose of projective tests is similar to that of personality inventories. Psychologists want to detail healthy and unhealthy areas of functioning in the individual. However, unlike personality inventories, projective tests are derived from the psychoanalytic perspective. Consequently, the images and stories described are purported to

Thematic Apperception Test (TAT)
a projective personality test consisting of a series of pictures in which the respondent is asked to tell a story about each scene; the responses are then coded for consistent themes and issues

reflect underlying unconscious urges and desires. The images also may symbolically represent the core issues and concerns of the individual. For example, suppose a person may see a rabbit in one of the Rorschach inkblots. It is probably not that rabbits are an issue for the individual, but rather what rabbits symbolically represent, such as fertility, or anxiety and fear about pregnancy or childbearing. Notice that projective tests are much more subject to the interpretation of the clinician than are personality inventories. As such, they are a less reliable and valid tool for measuring personality compared to objective tests (Aiken, 1996; Lilienfeld, Wood, & Garb, 2000, T. B. Rogers, 1995). Projective tests are most useful for identifying themes in a person's life or for delineating an individual's problem-solving style.

Figure 14.5 Sample Rorschach Inkblot

After being shown an inkblot like this one, the person indicates what he or she sees on the card.

Figure 14.6 Sample Thematic Apperception (TAT) Card

In taking the TAT, a person is asked to tell a story about a scene such as this one.

Direct Observation and Rating Scales

A third type of tool used by psychologists to measure personality is observation and rating scales. Rating scales are formatted similarly to checklists. You check off the statements or behaviors that most apply to you. A child behavior rating scale is depicted in Table 14.4 ◆. Because the person being evaluated may not answer the statements truthfully, teachers, parents, spouses, and clinicians also can complete rating scales on the person being evaluated. These alternate perspectives minimize the self-distortions that are associated with self-report instruments.

Psychologists also might rely on directly observing a client's behavior and interactions with others to assess personality. Closely watching how you behave in particular situations can be helpful in determining what happens before and after your responses. Such information is particularly important to clinicians from a social cognitive approach who want to understand the social or environmental factors that may be influencing problem behavior. Humanists also find rating scales on self-esteem and

◆ **Table 14.4**

Sample Rating Scale

Child Behavior Checklist

Below is a list of items that describe children and youth. For each item that describes your child now or within the past 6 months, please circle the 2 if the item is very true or often true of your child. Circle the 1 if the item is somewhat or sometimes true of your child. If the item is not true of your child, circle the 0. Please answer all items as well as you can, even if some do not seem to apply to your child.

0 = NOT TRUE (AS FAR AS YOU KNOW)	1 = SOMEWHAT OR SOMETIMES TRUE	2 = VERY TRUE OR OFTEN TRUE

0 1 2   1. Acts too young for his/her age

0 1 2   2. Drinks alcohol without parents' approval (describe): _____ _____

0 1 2   3. Argues a lot

0 1 2   4. Fails to finsh things he/she starts

0 1 2   5. There is very little he/she enjoys

0 1 2   6. Bowel movements outside toilet

0 1 2   7. Bragging, boasting

0 1 2   8. Can't concentrate, can't pay attention for long

0 1 2   9. Can't get his/her mind off certain thoughts; obsessions (describe): _____ _____

0 1 2 10. Can't sit still, restless, or hyperactive

0 1 2 11. Clings to adults or too dependent

0 1 2 12. Complains of loneliness

0 1 2 13. Confused or seems to be in a fog

0 1 2 14. Cries a lot

0 1 2 15. Cruel to animals

0 1 2 16. Cruelty, bullying, or meanness to others

0 1 2 17. Daydreams or gets lost in his/her thoughts

0 1 2 18. Deliberately harms self or attempts suicide

0 1 2 19. Demands a lot of attention

0 1 2 20. Destroys his/her own things

0 1 2 21. Destroys things belonging to his/her family or others

0 1 2 22. Disobedient at home

0 1 2 23. Disobedient at school

0 1 2 24. Doesn't eat well

0 1 2 25. Doesn't get along with other kids

0 1 2 26. Doesn't seem to feel guilty after misbehaving

0 1 2 27. Easily jealous

0 1 2 28. Breaks rules at home, school, or elsewhere

0 1 2 29. Fears certain animals, situations, or places, other than school (describe): _____ _____

0 1 2 30. Fears going to school

0 1 2 31. Fears he/she might think or do something bad

0 1 2 32. Feels he/she has to be perfect

0 1 2 33. Feels or complains that no one loves him/her

0 1 2 34. Feels others are out to get him/her

0 1 2 35. Feels worthless or inferior

0 1 2 36. Gets hurt a lot, accident-prone

0 1 2 37. Gets in many fights

0 1 2 38. Gets teased a lot

0 1 2 39. Hangs around with others who get in trouble

0 1 2 40. Hears sounds or voices that aren't there (describe): _____ _____

0 1 2 41. Impulsive or acts without thinking

0 1 2 42. Would rather be alone than with others

0 1 2 43. Lying or cheating

0 1 2 44. Bites fingernails

0 1 2 45. Nervous, highstrung, or tense

0 1 2 46. Nervous movements or twitching (describe): _____ _____

0 1 2 47. Nightmares

0 1 2 48. Not liked by other kids

0 1 2 49. Constipated, doesn't move bowels

0 1 2 50. Too fearful or anxious

0 1 2 51. Feels dizzy or lightheaded

0 1 2 52. Feels too guilty

0 1 2 53. Overeating

0 1 2 54. Overtired without good reason

0 1 2 55. Overweight

0 1 2 56. Physical problems without known medical cause:

0 1 2   a. Aches or pains (*not* stomach or headaches)

0 1 2   b. Headaches

0 1 2   c. Nausea, feels sick

0 1 2   d. Problems with eyes (*not* if corrected by glasses) (describe): _____ _____

0 1 2   e. Rashes or other skin problems

0 1 2   f. Stomachaches

0 1 2   g. Vomiting, throwing up

0 1 2   h. Other (describe): _____ _____

Copyright by T. M. Achenbach. Reproduced by permission.

self-concept useful to understanding how a person perceives reality and the degree to which one's real self is congruent with one's ideal self.

Clinical Interviews

One tool used by all clinical psychologists is the **clinical interview.** This interview typically takes place during the first meeting between the client and the clinician and involves the clinician asking the client questions to identify the client's difficulty in functioning. The format and length of the interview as well as the questions that are asked during the interview may differ from clinician to clinician. These differences again relate to the alternate views on personality that were discussed in this chapter. For example, a clinician who works primarily from the psychoanalytic approach is more likely to ask questions about your childhood, your dreams, and your relationship with your mother. In contrast, a clinician who favors the social cognitive approach is more likely to ask specific questions about social situations and patterns of thoughts. This clinician may want to know what you were thinking about prior to, during, and after a particular behavior occurred. A humanist is more likely to focus on the client's interpretation and perception of reality. The focus of any clinical interview, however, is to identify as clearly as possible the difficulty in functioning that the person is experiencing. This difficulty is often given a name, or diagnosis. The exact nature of these diagnoses is the subject of the next chapter.

Zigy Kaluzny/Getty Images

A clinical interview typically takes place during the first meeting between the client and the clinician. Although the format and length of the interview as well as the questions that are asked during the interview may differ from clinician to clinician, the focus is to identify as clearly as possible the difficulty in functioning that the person is experiencing.

clinical interview the initial meeting between a client and a clinician in which the clinician asks questions to identify the difficulty in functioning that the person is experiencing

Let's Review!

This section detailed the various methods psychologists use to measure personality. For a quick check of your understanding, answer these questions.

1. Tamara goes to see a clinical psychologist. The psychologist asks Tamara to look at some vague pictures and report what she sees. Most likely Tamara is taking a:
   a. personality inventory.   c. rating scale.
   b. projective test.   d. clinical interview.
2. The major disadvantage of self-report instruments, such as the MMPI-2, is:
   a. the subjective interpretation of the results by the clinician.

   b. the respondents may not tell the truth.
   c. the scoring criteria are very vague and unreliable.
   d. there are no norms to compare one's responses against.
3. When going to a clinical psychologist, the first session is most likely to involve:
   a. personality testing.   c. hypnosis.
   b. a physical examination.   d. a clinical interview.

ANSWERS

1. b; 2. b; 3. d

Are You Getting the Big Picture?

This chapter presented four different views of personality: the psychoanalytic perspective, the trait approach, the social cognitive perspective, and the humanistic approach. Rather than debating which of these perspectives is "right," many psychologists prefer instead to see these viewpoints as complementary. Just as a photographer may take the same picture from many different angles, psychologists, too, like to understand personality from varying viewpoints. When taken together as a whole, these theories provide a much more complex and richer view of the forces that make us unique than any one alone could.

Reconsider all the potential forces that we have outlined as influencing the personalities of the McBride family. Unconscious motives in the form of anger help us to understand some of the siblings' difficulty in functioning. Add to this their varying inherited dispositions. All were creative and intelligent, yet they differed in their degree of extraversion and agreeableness, and had different temperaments. Throw into this mix the influence of education, growing up in the projects, and their expectations of control. Their difficulty in meeting basic needs as well as the added task of establishing a biracial self-concept furthers our understanding of their personalities. It is all of these forces rather than just one that constitutes our personality.

As you study the material in this chapter, try viewing your own personality through the lens of each perspective. What traits do you seem to have inherited? How might your patterns of thoughts, self-efficacy, or locus of control influence the way you typically behave? Has peer pressure or the need to feel secure and safe motivated

your behavior in any way? Applying the material in this way will help you learn the material and perhaps make you more self-aware of your patterns and tendencies.

The material in this chapter provides a helpful framework for reviewing the biological, cognitive, social, and developmental themes that we have emphasized throughout this textbook. We have seen that some perspectives, most notably the trait approach, highlight the biological role of genes and neurotransmitters in personality. Some explanations of personality are more developmental. For example, Freud and Rogers both examine the beginnings of personality in the infant and describe how an adult's personality may be healthy or maladjusted because of these developmental experiences. We then also must consider environmental and cognitive forces that affect personality—expectations, locus of control, self-efficacy, self-perceptions, and our interactions with others. Although no theoretical framework can explain all facets of personality, we can appreciate how considering all of these forces in their totality helps us understand the nature and complexity of personality.

Understanding the nature of personality is also useful to your future career choice. You will be more successful in your interactions with coworkers, bosses, subordinates, or customers if you understand their motives, traits, patterns of thoughts, and environmental circumstances. Understanding these theoretical approaches will also help you grasp the concepts in our next chapter as we move on to consider abnormal behavior.

Key Terms

personality (618)
psychoanalytic perspective (620)
conscious level (620)
preconscious level (621)
unconscious level (621)
id (621)
pleasure principle (622)
ego (622)
reality principle (622)
superego (622)
defense mechanism (623)
oral stage (624)
anal stage (624)

phallic stage (624)
Oedipus complex (624)
Electra complex (624)
latency stage (624)
genital stage (624)
personal unconscious (626)
collective unconscious (626)
archetypes (626)
basic anxiety (627)
trait approach (628)
trait (628)
central traits (629)
secondary traits (629)

cardinal traits (629)
source traits (630)
introversion (630)
extraversion (630)
person-situation interaction (634)
social cognitive approach (636)
reciprocal determinism (636)
self-efficacy (636)
locus of control (637)
humanistic approach (639)
self-actualization (639)
actualizing tendency (640)
self-concept (640)

unconditional positive regard (641)
reliability (643)
validity (643)
personality inventory (643)
Minnesota Multiphasic Personality Inventory
   (MMPI-2) (643)

projective test (644)
Rorschach Inkblot test (644)
Thematic Apperception Test (TAT) (645)
clinical interview (647)

Test Yourself!

Concept Check

Test your knowledge of the chapter concepts by completing each of the following sentences with the correct term. For a more comprehensive review, visit the book Web site (http://psychology.wadsworth.com/pastorino1e/) for online quizzes, flashcards, crosswords, and Internet links.

_____ **1.** psychosexual stages of development

_____ **2.** internal and external locus of control

_____ **3.** human beings naturally strive for fulfillment and enhancement

_____ **4.** universal tendencies that we have across most situations govern our personalities and behavior

_____ **5.** looks at the genetic contributions to personality

_____ **6.** driving forces within a person that are often conflictual and unconscious

_____ **7.** hierarchy of needs

_____ **8.** self-efficacy influences our behavior

_____ **9.** id, ego, and superego are the three personality structures

_____ **10.** unconditional positive regard fosters healthy personality development

_____ **11.** the five-factor theory

_____ **12.** defense mechanisms are used to handle intrapsychic conflict

_____ **13.** the environment, one's behaviors, and one's thoughts influence personality

_____ **14.** self-concept

_____ **15.** Oedipus and Electra complexes

a. psychoanalytic perspective

b. trait perspective

c. humanistic perspective

d. social cognitive perspective

Answers:

1. a; 2. d; 3. c; 4. b; 5. b; 6. a; 7. c; 8. d; 9. a; 10. c; 11. b; 12. a; 13. d; 14. c; 15. a

Critical Thinking About the Chapter

1. Which theory on personality do you find most compelling, and why?

2. Using one of the personality perspectives discussed in this chapter, analyze the personality of a favorite television or movie character.

3. How has your personality changed over the years? How has it remained the same? What theory or theories can best explain these changes and consistencies?

4. How would you go about constructing a personality test? How does this construction relate to your perspective on personality?

Applying Psychology. Try to detail your personality from each of the perspectives discussed in this chapter.

Critical Thinking for Integration

1. Review the theories of motivation discussed in Chapter 8. How do they correlate with the views on personality discussed in this chapter?

2. In Chapter 12, we discussed behaviors such as conformity, aggression, and helpfulness in relation to the effect that others have on our behavior. How would the psycho-

analytic perspective explain such behaviors? How would they be explained from the humanistic perspective?

3. Discuss how memory (Chapter 6), problem solving (Chapter 7), and intelligence (Chapter 7) relate to personality.

Chapter Study Resources

Suggested Readings

1. McBride, J. (1996). *The color of water: A black man's tribute to his white mother.* New York: Riverhead Books. James McBride's inspiring account of his family's challenges.

2. Nye, R. D. (2000). *Three psychologies: Perspectives from Freud, Skinner, and Rogers.* Belmont, CA: Wadsworth. A highly readable book that provides a simple introduction to the influential ideas of Sigmund Freud, B. F. Skinner and Carl Rogers.

3. Diener, E., Oishi, S., & Lucas, R. E. (2003). Personality, culture, and subjective well being: Emotional and cognitive evaluations of life. *Annual Reviews of Psychology, 54,* 403-425.
Reviews research showing how both culture and personality are influenced by biology, learning, and their interactions, and how they significantly influence life happiness and life satisfaction.

4. For additional readings, explore InfoTrac College Edition, your online library of archived journal articles and periodicals. Go to http://www.infotrac-college .com/wadsworth and enter the passcode from the card that came with your book. For this chapter, search using these keywords:

five-factor personality theory

locus of control

unconditional positive regard

MMPI personality test

archetypes

Web Links for Further Study

Additional information on chapter concepts can be found at these Web sites:

1. The Association for Humanistic Psychology, formed in 1962 by Abraham Maslow, Carl Rogers, Charlotte Buhler, Rollo May, Virginia Satir, and others, now provides online access to Web resources on humanism and the personal growth movement.
http://www.ahpweb.org

2. PsychTests provides online psychological assessments in the areas of personality, career, health, intelligence, and relationships.
http://www.psychtests.com

3. The Personality Project guides users to current personality research literature. It also provides links to examples of personality and ability tests that are similar to standard testing instruments.
http://www.personality-project.org

4. The Freud Archives is a collection of links that point to Internet resources related to Sigmund Freud and his works.
http://users.rcn.com/brill/freudarc.html

5. Great Ideas in Personality offers links to scientific research programs on personality. Personality papers and tests are also included.
http://www.personalityresearch.org

Student Study Guide

To help organize your learning, work through Chapter 14 of the *What Is Psychology? Student Study Guide*. The study guide includes learning objectives, a chapter summary, fill-in review, key terms, a practice test, and other learning activities.

Psychology Now™

Psychology NOW is a Web-based, personalized study system that provides you with a pretest and a posttest for each chapter, quizzes you by chapter, and provides a personalized study plan, pointing you to elements in the text or in individual learning modules that will help you to achieve 80% mastery. Check out the learning modules that relate to this chapter: the Big Five; the MMPI.

PsychNow CD-ROM, Version 2.0

Go to the PsychNow CD-ROM for further study of the concepts in this chapter. The CD-ROM includes learning modules with videos, animations, and quizzes, as well as simulations of psychological phenomena. Each module follows a consistent Explore, Lesson, and Apply structure that allows you to experience the concept or principle, learn more about it, and then apply it. You and your friends can participate in a team-based Quiz Game that makes learning fun. Learning modules include:
7a. Theories of Personality.

What Is Personality, and How Do We Measure It?

Personality is the unique collection of attitudes, emotions, thoughts, habits, impulses, and behaviors that defines how a person typically behaves across situations.

THE PSYCHOANALYTIC APPROACH

• Sigmund Freud's psychoanalytic perspective emphasizes unconscious aspects of personality. It proposes that personality operates at three levels of awareness: the conscious, the preconscious, and the unconscious.

• According to Freud, personality is comprised of three major structures: the unconscious id that operates according to the pleasure principle, the conscious ego that operates according to the reality principle, and the moral directives of the superego.

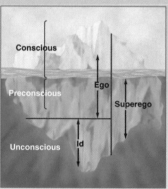

• The ego uses defense mechanisms to cope with the anxiety that is produced by the internal conflicts of the id and superego.

• For Freud, personality develops through a series of five psychosexual stages (oral, anal, phallic, latency, and genital) that represent a complex interaction between natural sexual urges and our socialization experiences.

• Neo-Freudians also emphasized the importance of unconscious conflicts, but placed less emphasis on the role of the instinctual impulses in motivating behavior.
— Carl Jung divided the unconscious into the personal conscious and collective unconscious.
— Alfred Adler emphasized the child's desire to overcome feelings of inferiority.
— Karen Horney suggested that family environments and disturbances in early relationships lead to basic anxiety, or a feeling of helplessness in children.

• Freud's ideas on dreaming, defense mechanisms, and coping sparked research in several fields. His ideas are evident in personality testing and therapy approaches. His notion of the unconscious and his emphasis on the importance of early childhood on later adult behavior also have merit.

• Freud's ideas are not supported by cross-cultural data and his theory does not easily lend itself to scientific testing. Critics assert that he placed too much emphasis on basic instincts and perpetuates the idea of male superiority.

THE TRAIT APPROACH

• The trait approach attempts to describe personality by identifying the internal traits, or tendencies that we have across most situations.

• Gordon Allport subjectively classified traits into three types: central, cardinal, and secondary traits.

• Raymond Cattell's factor analysis of traits yielded 16 source traits that could be measured in everyone. Hans Eysenck narrowed down these universal traits to two: extraversion/introversion and emotional stability/instability.

• Costa and McCrae's Five Factor theory proposes five core universal traits: openness, conscientiousness, extraversion, agreeableness, and neuroticism (OCEAN).

• Research suggests a complex interaction between genes and the environment in producing personality. Some traits remain stable over the course of adulthood, but situational factors also influence the consistency of traits.

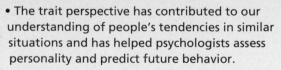

• The trait perspective has contributed to our understanding of people's tendencies in similar situations and has helped psychologists assess personality and predict future behavior.

• Critics argue that the trait perspective provides a simplistic picture of personality, does not explain why we behave the way we do, and does not always predict how we will behave in different situations.

THE HUMANISTIC APPROACH

• The humanistic approach emphasizes one's strive toward uniqueness and self-actualization.

• Abraham Maslow believed that the pathway to self-actualization was in fulfilling a hierarchy of needs with physical or biological needs at the bottom and more psychological or social needs at the top.

• Carl Rogers's self theory emphasizes how one's self-concept or perception of self is influenced by the standards and values of others, most notably the degree to which we perceive and receive unconditional positive regard from others.

• The humanistic approach promotes self-awareness and positive interactions with others, and its ideas have been incorporated into several therapy approaches.

• Critics argue that the humanistic approach provides a naïve and optimistic view of behavior. It is difficult to experimentally test and validate its concepts. It describes but does not explain personality.

THE SOCIAL COGNITIVE APPROACH

• The social cognitive approach evaluates environmental and cognitive factors that influence personality.

• Albert Bandura's reciprocal determinism speculates that personality is due to the constant interaction between the environment, one's behavior, and one's thoughts. A critical cognitive element in this interplay is self-efficacy or the expectation one has for success in a given situation.

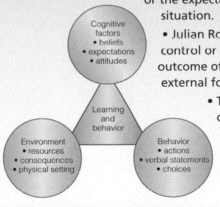

• Julian Rotter believes that one's locus of control or one's expectations of whether the outcome of an event is due to internal or external forces, influences personality.

• The social cognitive approach is comprehensive, has many applications and is easily tested experimentally. However, it does not detail the biological, unconscious, and emotional factors that influence personality.

MEASURING PERSONALITY

• Tools that assess personality should be reliable or consistent, and valid, that is measure the construct of personality.

• Personality inventories such as the MMPI-2 are objective paper and pencil self-report forms that can reliably detail an individual's personality traits if answered honestly.

• Projective tests such as the Rorschach Inkblot Test and the Thematic Apperception Test are unstructured and subjective tests in which an individual is shown an ambiguous image and asked to describe it. A person's responses purportedly reflect underlying unconscious concerns according to the psychoanalytic perspective.

• Direct observation and rating scales also may be used by psychologists to measure behaviors and interactions with others.

• The focus of the clinical interview is to identify the difficulty in functioning that a person is experiencing.

Nash's behavior had become more and more peculiar. He was irritable and hypersensitive one minute, eerily withdrawn the next.

FROM SYLVIA NASAR, *A BEAUTIFUL MIND*, (New York: Simon & Schuster, p. 248)

Jean-Noel Reichel / Getty Images

What Are Psychological Disorders, and How Can We Understand Them?

CHAPTER PREVIEW

When a Beautiful Mind Goes Awry

THE BIG PICTURE

The previous chapter on personality detailed four main perspectives for understanding how we each develop our own unique way of behaving and operating in our environments. This chapter extends that discussion by examining how at times our behavior may make it difficult for us to function.

This chapter outlines several major categories of mental health disorders. For each type of disorder, we will consider the possible reasons why a person behaves this way. Although the research presented may seem overwhelming at times, keep in mind that these explanations are closely tied to topics with which you are already familiar. For example, many of the symptoms of mental health disorders are physical in nature. Hence, many of the explanations of these disorders focus on brain functioning, neurotransmitters, hormones, and genetics—biological factors that were introduced in Chapter 2. Many of the symptoms also focus on psychological concepts such as learning, cognitions, personality, and emotions—again, topics that have been addressed in previous chapters. Furthermore, we will see that certain disorders are more common among certain segments of the population. Your familiarity with previous discussions on gender, race, and culture will assist you in understanding the influence of these social factors on mental health.

Consider the following stories.

Amy Tan, author of *The Joy Luck Club* and *The Bonesetter's Daughter,* first attempted suicide at the age of 6. She was deeply unhappy and tried to drag a butter knife across her wrists. The daughter of Chinese immigrants, Tan can recall in her childhood her mother's dramatic outbursts and suicide threats. When she was 15 years old, her father and brother both died of brain tumors within 6 months of each other. She was angry about losing them, and started to believe that she too would die soon. She saw a counselor, but discontinued the treatment when he molested her. Her deep unhappiness continued throughout her childhood and young adulthood. She was often lethargic, angry, and couldn't eat or sleep at times. There were other suicide attempts along the way and a profound sense of meaninglessness (Tan, 2003). What was wrong with her?

© Universal Studios. All rights reserved.

Author Amy Tan has experienced bouts of severe unhappiness throughout her childhood and young adulthood.

John Nash is an extraordinary mathematician. He received his doctorate in mathematics at Princeton and was a young professor at the Massachusetts Institute of Technology (MIT). Nash had always been a bit eccentric and aloof, yet at age 30 his behavior became more bizarre. He wrote letters to government agencies complaining of conspiracies to take over the world. He believed that alien powers were communicating with him through the *New York Times.* Over the next 10 years, Nash was frequently hospitalized for his behavior. He would hide his beliefs and ideas while medicated, and then on release from the hospital would act in an unpredictable and bizarre manner. Yet, at sane times he continued to publish mathematical papers in scientific journals, and in 1994 he received the Nobel Prize in

G. P. Putnam's Sons, a division of Penguin Group (USA) Inc.

AMY TAN
The OPPOSITE of *Fate*
A BOOK OF MUSINGS

"He complained that he 'knew something was going on' and that he was being 'bugged.'"
(Nasar, 1998)

Simon & Schuster Adult Publishing Group

SYLVIA NASAR
A BEAUTIFUL MIND

Economics. Recently his life has been highlighted in the book (Nasar, 1998) and the film *A Beautiful Mind.* How can we understand such a man?

Howard Hughes (1905–1976), founder of Hughes Aircraft and Hughes Electronics, was a billionaire, aviator, and motion-picture producer. His friends and acquaintances viewed him as a man of bizarre and strange habits. Hughes had an obsession with germs and cleanliness. He would seal the doors and windows in his house to keep it germproof. He insisted that any item handed to him be covered with a tissue. He made his assistants wash their hands frequently and at times wear white gloves before handling any documents he might touch later. He was so fearful of germs that he walked around in tissue boxes instead of shoes. He repeated sentences a certain number of times and would practice aircraft takeoffs and landings thousands of times. In his later years, he became a recluse, shutting himself off from the world. Why would anyone, especially a powerful and wealthy person like Howard Hughes, behave this way?

These are all real people and real stories. These three cases exemplify people having difficulty functioning. Each of them suffered from a mental health disorder. This chapter examines what qualifies as a mental health disorder and explains the symptoms necessary to be diagnosed with a particular disorder. An estimated 18.5% of Americans 18 and older will suffer from a diagnosable mental disorder in a given year (Narrow, Rae, Robins, & Regier, 2002). In addition, 4 of the top 10 leading causes of disability in the United States and other developed countries are mental disorders: major depression, bipolar disorder, schizophrenia, and obsessive-compulsive disorder (Murray & Lopez, 1996). Consequently, it is likely that you or someone close to you will at some time experience a mental health disorder. Recognizing abnormal behavior and knowing psychology's current understanding of such behavior may assist you in managing such a situation. We will begin by defining the nature of abnormal behavior.

What Makes Behavior Abnormal? ❯ ❯ ❯ ❯ ❯ ❯

LEARNING OBJECTIVE

Identify the criteria that psychologists use for determining abnormal behavior.

What is abnormal behavior? Psychologists use several criteria when distinguishing normal from abnormal behavior. If we judge normal as what most people do, then one criterion that may be used to gauge abnormality is engaging in a behavior a lot less than others. This criterion is referred to as *statistical infrequency.* For example, it is considered crucial for survival to ingest a minimum amount of food per day. People who engage in this behavior a lot less than everyone else—as in the case of anorexics—would qualify as abnormal. Autistic people engage in social communication far less than everyone else does. As such, their behavior may be considered abnormal. Statistical infrequency can also include engaging in a behavior that most people do not. For example, believing that you are from another planet or galaxy is a thought that most people do not have. As such it represents an unusual, or statistically infrequent, thought and therefore may be judged as abnormal. However, there are problems with using the criteria of statistical infrequency—only one person holds the record for running a mile the fastest, a person who certainly is atypical but not necessarily abnormal.

Another measure of abnormality is to assess whether the behavior *violates social norms* of how people are supposed to behave. However, it is extremely important to emphasize that social norms vary widely across cultures, within cultures, and across historical times. What is considered socially acceptable in San Francisco may be considered unacceptable in KeoKuk, Iowa. Similarly, what was deemed unacceptable in the 1950s may be considered acceptable today. Changing views on homosexuality in part influenced the American Psychiatric Association to remove homosexuality from its list of psychological disorders in 1973. Because social norms vary so widely, judging the abnormality of behavior on this criterion alone is especially problematic.

A third criterion for assessing the abnormality of a behavior is whether it causes great *personal distress* to the individual. Oftentimes people seek treatment when a behavior causes such suffering. Amy Tan sought help after feeling so grieved by her family members'

Autism is a childhood disorder that is marked by disordered communication.

deaths. Problems can also arise from judging a behavior by this criterion alone. A person may murder one or more people and not be distressed by such behavior, although it causes great harm to others.

Because each of these criteria by itself is not adequate in defining abnormality, many psychologists find that combining them and assessing whether a behavior *interferes with a person's ability to function and/or causes distress to oneself or others* may best explain abnormality (Wakefield, 1992). By using this broader criterion, we can see that all three of the people in the opening section clearly were engaging in abnormal behavior.

Let's Review!

In this section, we looked at the criteria that psychologists use to distinguish abnormal from normal behavior. For a quick check of your understanding, answer these questions.

1. Susann enjoys eating garbage when she is hungry. By which criteria can Susann's behavior be considered abnormal?

   a. danger to others
   b. violates social norms
   c. personal distress
   d. all of the above

2. Which of the following is the *best* criterion by which to judge the abnormality of behavior?

   a. violation of social norms
   b. statistical infrequency
   c. personal distress
   d. impairs ability to function

3. Judging abnormality by social norms is especially problematic because social norms:

   a. may be atypical or rare, but not abnormal.
   b. cause great distress to the individual.
   c. interfere with a person's ability to function.
   d. vary widely across and within cultures.

ANSWERS

1. b; 2. d; 3. d

Four Perspectives to Explain > > > > > > > > > > > > Abnormal Behavior

LEARNING OBJECTIVE

Compare and contrast the varying perspectives on explaining abnormal behavior and formulate an integrated perspective to explain a particular behavior.

Why do people behave abnormally? Since the beginning of time, doctors and philosophers have tried to understand *why* people behave abnormally. We classify these explanations into four main models or approaches for understanding abnormal behavior: supernatural theories, biological or natural theories, psychological theories, and social or cultural theories.

Supernatural Theories: Gods and Demons

Supernatural theories assume that abnormal behavior results from evil forces, demonic possession, or from some intervention by a god or other supreme being. Consequently, curing someone who behaves abnormally involves religious ritual or exorcism. For example, during the Stone Age, abnormal behavior was attributed to possession by evil spirits. Treating someone who was possessed might entail drilling holes in the person's skull, a process called *trephining*, in order to allow the evil spirits to escape (Selling, 1940). Similarly, during the late Middle Ages (around A.D. 1000–1400), bizarre behavior was seen as a result of witchcraft or supernatural spirits. Thousands of people, typically older, unmarried, poor women, were sentenced to death or were brutally tortured to confess their satanic beliefs. Although some cultures today continue to emphasize spiritual causes of abnormality, Western cultures predominantly lean toward more biological, psychological, or social causes of abnormality. Today, the Roman Catholic Church still occasionally agrees to exorcisms, but only after all other therapeutic measures have failed (Barlow & Durand, 2005).

Biological Theories: From Yin-Yang to the Medical Model

Biological theories attribute abnormal behavior to some physical process: genetics, an imbalance in hormones or neurotransmitters, or some brain or bodily dysfunction. The biological perspective can be traced back to ancient China, Egypt, and Greece. For example, ancient Chinese texts on medicine (around 2674 B.C.) suggest that one's health is the result of two opposing forces in the body: *yin* and *yang*. When these forces are out of balance, illness, including abnormal behavior, will result (Tseng, 1973). Ancient Egyptian writings (around 1900 B.C.) similarly explained abnormal behavior by physical dysfunction. For instance, unknown pains or extreme sadness in women were attributed to a "wandering uterus." Perhaps the best-known ancient to support a biological or natural theory of abnormality was the Greek physician Hippocrates (460–377 B.C.), the father of medicine. Hippocrates argued that abnormal behavior results from an imbalance of four bodily fluids called *humors* (phlegm, blood, yellow bile, black bile). Treatments aimed at curing abnormal behavior focused on restoring balance among these four body fluids.

Because these early philosophies saw psychological disorders as similar to physical diseases, this perspective became known as the **medical model** and the concept of mental illness was born. It became more firmly embedded in Western culture during the Renaissance (A.D. 1400–1700s). Special treatment centers, called asylums, were established for the care of the mentally ill. Often such centers offered medical procedures to treat the mentally ill such as bleeding the patient, cold baths, physical restraints, electrical shocks, or starvation (Bennett, 1947). Unfortunately, many of these asylums became "warehouses" for the mentally ill, where deplorable living conditions

medical model   this perspective views psychological disorders as similar to physical diseases; they result from biological disturbances and can be diagnosed, treated, and cured like other physical illnesses

and inhumane treatment were standard. One of the most famous—or infamous—of these asylums was London's Hospital of Saint Mary of Bethlehem, nicknamed Bedlam, where mental patients were put on exhibit to the public for a fee, much like animals at the zoo.

The medical model and the notion of mental illness persist today. Physicians and psychiatrists generally believe that psychological disorders are the result of biological disturbances. As such, they can be diagnosed, treated, and cured in much the same way as other physical illnesses. Fortunately, treatment approaches from the medical model have advanced from the days of bloodletting, most notably through the development of medications to treat some mental disorders. For example, antidepressant medications are used to treat eating disorders, substance abuse disorders, as well as depression. Other biological treatments (covered in more detail in the next chapter) include electroconvulsive therapy and neurosurgery (psychosurgery).

Psychological Theories: Humane Treatment and Psychological Processes

Psychological theories attribute abnormal behavior to internal or external stressors facing the individual. Beginning in the 1700s, dissatisfaction with the treatment of the mentally ill led many to believe that dignity, tranquility, rest, and relaxation would restore normal functioning to the mentally ill. Such moral therapy was championed by Phillipe Pinel in France and later by Dorothea Dix in the United States and Canada. *Moral* in this case referred to "emotional" or "psychological" rather than a code of conduct. As a physician in charge of the La Bicetre asylum in Paris, Pinel ordered that patients be released from their chains and be provided humane treatment in the form of clean rooms, fresh air, adequate food, and planned social activities. Dorothea Dix, a teacher and social reformer in the mid-19th century, lobbied legislators and communities to reform the conditions in mental hospitals in the United States. Such efforts led to more humane treatment of the mentally ill and opened the doors to the exploration of psychological processes that underlie mental illness. You will recall from the previous chapter on personality that four predominant perspectives resulted, which we briefly review here.

Dorothea Dix's lobbying efforts to reform the conditions in mental hospitals in the United States led to more humane treatment of the mentally ill.

© Bettmann/Corbis

Psychoanalytic Perspective

The psychoanalytic perspective attributes abnormal behavior to unresolved unconscious conflicts. This view is most closely connected with the theories and ideas of Sigmund Freud (1856–1939). According to Freud, psychological disorders result from the conflict between the unconscious sexual and aggressive instinctual desires of the id and the outward demands of society. Recall that Freud was a psychiatrist, educated within the medical model. However, for Freud, the physical symptoms that accompanied mental illness were not the cause of the illness, and simply treating the physical problems would not cure the illness. Rather, Freud suggested that underlying internal psychological conflicts were at the root of mental disorders. Analyzing these issues was necessary to treat psychological disorders. Newer theories, referred to as psycho-dynamic theories, developed by Freud's followers such as Alfred Adler and Karen Horney, downplayed the role of sexual and aggressive instincts and instead emphasized the role of the ego and interpersonal relationships in maintaining or restoring psychological health.

Social Learning Perspective

Learning or behavior theorists (particularly B. F. Skinner and his successors) explain abnormal behavior as a result of the same learning processes as normal behavior—through classical conditioning, operant conditioning, and observational learning. The individual's responses to stimuli in the environment and the consequences of these behaviors are what lead to abnormal behavior. For example, Howard Hughes learned to respond with fear to germs in his environment. Avoiding the germs by wearing tissue boxes as shoes reinforced his fear because this behavior reduced his anxiety about germs—a positive consequence. Consequently, a person's past learning, observing, and current experiences can explain psychological disorders.

Cognitive Perspective

The cognitive perspective emphasizes the role of thinking, expectations, mental assumptions, and other mental processes in abnormal behavior. For example, anxiety results from irrational assumptions or from believing that negative outcomes will occur despite one's best efforts. Think about the little voice inside of you that comments on your behavior. Does it encourage you to do well, or does it berate you for your stupidity? Is it possible that such internal messages influence your behavior? The cognitive perspective maintains that they do. Such "self-talk" demonstrates the influence our thoughts have on our behavior and those thought processes are the focus of this perspective.

 Application

Humanistic Perspective

Humanists like Carl Rogers see abnormal behavior as resulting from a distorted perception of the self and reality. When people lose touch with their personal values and their sense of self, or when they fail to fulfill their basic biological and psychological needs, they cannot attain self-actualization. Instead, they experience personal distress and maladaptive behavior.

Sociocultural Theories: The Individual in Context

Sociocultural theories emphasize social or cultural factors that may play a role in psychological disorders. Such a perspective argues that internal biological and psychological processes cannot by themselves explain abnormality. These individual, internal processes can be understood only in the context of the larger society and culture that shape and influence people's behavior. Abnormal behavior, therefore, can be fully understood only when social factors are taken into account. These factors might include age, race, gender, social roles, and cultural values, expectations, and traditions. In addition, social conditions such as poverty, discrimination, and environmental stressors must be included when evaluating abnormal behavior.

Consider the increasing prevalence of eating disorders in the United States, Europe, and Japan over the past few decades (Stunkard, 1997). In other cultures, eating disorders are uncommon. This difference may stem in part from the cultural differences

Female celebrities such as Halle Berry illustrate cultural values that associate attractiveness and beauty with extreme thinness.

© Frank Trapper/Corbis

in ideal body images. The ideal shape, especially for women, has become progressively thinner over the last few decades in the United States, Europe, and Japan. In other, less developed countries, heavier bodies are seen as more beautiful (Wiseman, Gray, Mosimann, & Ahrens, 1992). Even within the United States and Europe, ethnic and socioeconomic differences in the rates of eating disorders are apparent. Eating disorders are more prevalent among those in the upper and middle socioeconomic classes than among people from the lower classes. In addition, White females have a higher incidence of eating disorders than do African American or Hispanic females (Pate, Pumariega, Hester, & Garner, 1992). Again, such differences may be related to differences in cultural values concerning attractiveness and beauty. African American and Hispanic cultures tend to hold a more voluptuous and rounded ideal of feminine beauty than does the White culture. Hence, White women may be more susceptible to starving themselves to attain the thinner ideal image of attractiveness (Osvold & Sodowsky, 1993). But with the high visibility of Hispanic and African American celebrities like Penelope Cruz, Salma Hayek, Jennifer Lopez, Halle Berry, and Tyra Banks, these cultural trends at least in the United States are changing. Weight-related concerns and behaviors are prevalent among adolescents in the United States, regardless of their ethnic/racial background (McKnight Investigators, 2003; Neumark-Sztainer et al., 2002). These results highlight how social factors such as gender and class as well as cultural ideals and expectations may influence behavior.

Integrating Perspectives: Putting the Puzzle Together

Which viewpoint really explains abnormal behavior? Despite decades of research, no single theory or perspective is correct. In the upcoming sections we'll explore several theories that have been helpful in understanding the causes of specific psychological disorders. However, it is only by integrating all the perspectives that our explanations of abnormality become comprehensive. We often hear in the popular press and in television commercials that a psychological disorder such as depression or anxiety is caused by "a specific gene" or "a chemical imbalance." But such reports are too simplistic to encompass the complexity of factors that contribute to mental health or mental illness. Most psychological disorders result from a combination of biological, psychological, and social factors; they do not have just one cause.

For example, as we will soon see, people diagnosed with major depression often show changes in brain chemistry—a biological cause. They also are likely to engage in a negative pattern of thinking, which is a cognitive symptom that we would characterize as a psychological factor. In addition, major depression is more likely to be diagnosed in women—a sociocultural factor. Current research in clinical psychology focuses on understanding how these forces operate together, much like the way pieces of a jigsaw puzzle fit together. Although our understanding of the *causes* of abnormality may be in its infancy, we can *describe* fairly well the specific behaviors that accompany certain mental health disorders. Such descriptors allow us to diagnosis a mental health disorder in a person who is having difficulty functioning.

Let's Review!

We've given you some of the historical and modern perspectives on explaining abnormal behavior in this section, and explained how an integrated perspective provides a more comprehensive explanation of any behavior. For a quick check of your understanding, answer these questions.

1. Dr. Kwan believes that Ken's abnormal behavior has resulted from a distorted sense of self and a loss of personal values. Dr. Kwan is adopting which perspective?
   a. humanistic
   c. learning
   b. psychoanalytic
   d. cognitive

2. Environmental conditions such as poverty, discrimination, and violent crime are most likely to be considered important causes of abnormal behavior by which perspective?
   a. psychoanalytic
   c. learning
   b. sociocultural
   d. supernatural

3. The medical model is also known as the _____ perspective.
   a. psychoanalytic
   c. biological
   b. supernatural
   d. cognitive

4. Lorena gets very nervous in social situations. Her therapist believes this anxiety represents an unconscious defense mechanism to repress her sexuality. Lorena's therapist has adopted which perspective?
   a. psychoanalytic
   c. learning
   b. humanistic
   d. cognitive

5. The saying "The devil made me do it" would fit with which perspective on abnormal behavior?
   a. biological
   c. psychoanalytic
   b. supernatural
   d. cognitive

ANSWERS

1.a; 2.b; 3.c; 4.a; 5.b

The *DSM* Model for Classifying Abnormal Behavior

> > > > > > > > >

LEARNING OBJECTIVE
Describe the nature of the DSM model, and identify its strengths and weaknesses.

How do psychologists diagnose people's abnormal behaviors? In 1952 the American Psychiatric Association published a book listing the criteria, or symptoms, a person must show to be diagnosed with a specific mental health disorder. Fifty years later this guide, the *Diagnostic and Statistical Manual of Mental Disorders (DSM)*, is in its fourth edition, published in 1994. In 2000, the American Psychiatric Association revised the text (but not the criteria) to clarify the diagnosis of some psychological disorders (*DSM-IV-TR*). With each new edition of the *DSM*, the APA has attempted to be more specific and precise when describing disorders. Therefore, the *DSM-IV-TR* lists specific and concrete criteria for diagnosing nearly 400 disorders in children, adolescents, and adults.

The *DSM-IV-TR* describes the conditions or symptoms that must be present in order for someone to be diagnosed with a specific mental health disorder. It also indicates the length of time that a person must show these symptoms to qualify for a diagnosis. These criteria require that the symptoms interfere with the person's ability to function, adopting the maladaptive criteria we discussed at the start of this chapter and that is accepted by many professionals today. However, the current version of the *DSM* does not speculate as to the causes of the individual's behavior—it is *atheoretical*. This atheoretical position underscores the complex nature of the causes of mental illness.

Diagnostic and Statistical Manual of Mental Disorders (DSM) a book published by the APA that lists the criteria for close to 400 mental health disorders

A Multidimensional Evaluation

With the third edition of the *DSM*, published in 1980, clinicians began to evaluate patients along five dimensions or *axes*, listed in Table 15.1 ◆. Axis I represents conditions that impair a person's ability to function. It includes 15 major categories of

◆ **Table 15.1**

DSM-IV-TR **Diagnostic Axes**

Axis I Clinical disorders	Major categories of mental disorders, including depression, anxiety disorders, phobias, amnesia, substance abuse, and schizophrenia. (See Table 15.2.)
Axis II Personality disorders; mental retardation	Lifelong conditions that negatively affect a person's ability to function. Divided into two major classes, mental retardation and the personality disorders. (See Table 15.7.)
Axis III General medical conditions	Physical problems or conditions—such as cancer diagnosis and treatment, diabetes, and arthritis—that may influence the person's mental health and that must also be considered when medication is prescribed.
Axis IV Psychosocial and environmental problems	*Psychosocial* problems might include problems holding a job or staying in school, or lack of social support. *Environmental* problems might include physical or sexual abuse, or experiencing a traumatic event.
Axis V Global assessment of functioning	A numerical scale for evaluating the person's level of functioning. *A rating of 90* indicates a person who is functioning very well in all areas of life and has minimal symptoms, if any, and is experiencing only everyday problems. At *a rating of 50,* a person shows serious symptoms or one or more problems with relationships, work, or school, including possible suicidal thoughts and obsessional behavior.

Reprinted with permission from the Diagnostic and Statistical Manual of Mental Disorders, *Fourth Edition, Text revision, Copyright 2000. American Psychiatric Association.*

mental disorders, such as anxiety and eating disorders. These disorders are the focus of this chapter and are listed in Table 15.2 ◆. Axis II represents any lifelong conditions that interfere with the person's ability to function, including any personality disorder or mental retardation. Axis III indicates any medical or physical conditions that the person is experiencing. It is important for the clinician to be aware of medical issues because they may be related to the individual's mental health. For example, a woman might be depressed because of recent diagnosis and treatment for breast cancer. Knowledge of medical conditions is also important when considering appropriate treatment options, especially if medication will be prescribed. Axis IV indicates any psychosocial or environmental stressors facing the person. These may include education problems, occupational problems, housing problems, economic problems, physical or sexual abuse, legal problems, or lack of adequate social support. For instance, a person may be anxious over losing a job and concerned about paying the bills. Again, such information will assist the clinician in understanding the client's behavior, as well as feasible treatment options. Axis V rates (on a scale of 1 to 100) the person's current level of functioning on a global level, taking into account all the previously mentioned psychological, social, and medical conditions. This number communicates to others the degree of impairment in the person's overall functioning. The multiaxial system of the *DSM* attempts to provide as comprehensive a picture as possible of a person's behavior.

How Good Is the DSM Model?

How well does the *DSM-IV* do its job? How *reliable* and *valid* is the *DSM* model? Recall from our discussion in Chapter 14 on personality assessment (see p. 643) that *reliability* refers to the consistency of a measurement system. We would expect two different clinicians to give a similar judgment or a consistent rating when presented with the same symptoms. Different clinicians should make a similar diagnosis when presented with the same individual, and similar diagnoses should be made when different people exhibit the same symptoms.

Validity refers to how well a rating system does what it was intended to do and refers to the accuracy of the test. We would expect that the *DSM* model should be accurate in diagnosing people who are having difficulty functioning. In addition, it should be accurate in the label it applies to an individual's condition. Depressed people should be diagnosed as depressed and drug addicts should be diagnosed as having a substance abuse problem. The numerous revisions of the *DSM* have attempted to improve its reliability and validity. As such, the reliability and validity for many of the Axis I clinical disorders are very high (Brown, DiNardo, Lehman, & Campbell, 2001; Foa & Kozak, 1995). However, the reliability of Axis II personality disorders is considered extremely low, calling into question the validity of diagnosing the personality disorders

◆ **Table 15.2**

DSM-IV-TR Axis I Major Categories of Mental Disorders

Axis I Major Category	Some Included Disorders	Examples
Disorders usually first diagnosed in infancy, childhood, or adolescence	• Learning disorders • Pervasive developmental disorders • Disruptive behavior and attention-deficit disorders • Tic disorders • Communication disorders	Attention-deficit disorder, autism, enuresis (bedwetting), stuttering, and academic skills disorders
Delirium, dementia, amnesia, and other cognitive disorders	• Deliria • Dementias • Amnestic disorders	Delirium (due to a general medical condition or substance induced), dementia (Alzheimer's), amnesia (due to a general medical condition or substance induced)
Substance-related disorders (see Chapter 4)	• Alcohol use disorders • Cocaine use disorders • Inhalant use disorders • Polysubstance use disorders	Alcoholism, cocaine or crack addiction, use of inhalants (sniffing glue or paint)
Schizophrenia and other psychotic disorders (see Table 15.4)	• Schizophrenia • Delusional disorder • Brief psychotic disorder • Psychotic disorder due to a general medical condition	Paranoid type, catatonic type
Mood disorders	• Depressive disorders • Bipolar disorders • Substance-induced mood disorder	Major depressive disorder, dysthymic disorder, bipolar I disorder, cyclothymic disorder
Anxiety disorders	• Panic disorder • Agoraphobia without history of panic disorder • Specific phobia (simple phobia) • Obsessive-compulsive disorder • Posttraumatic stress disorder	Panic disorder without agoraphobia, acrophobia
Somatoform disorders (see Table 15.6)	• Conversion disorder • Hypochondriasis • Body dysmorphic disorder • Pain disorder	
Dissociative disorders (see Table 15.5)	• Dissociative amnesia • Dissociative fugue • Dissociative identity disorder (multiple personality disorder)	
Sexual and gender identity disorders (see Chapter 11)	• Sexual dysfunction • Paraphilias • Gender identity disorder	Sexual aversion disorder, male erectile disorder, fetishism, pedophilia
Eating disorders (see Chapter 8)	• Anorexia nervosa • Bulimia nervosa	
Sleep disorders (see Chapter 4)	• Primary sleep disorders • Dyssomnia not otherwise specified	Sleepwalking disorder, narcolepsy, primary insomnia
Factitious disorders	• Factitious disorder	
Impulse control disorders not elsewhere classified	• Kleptomania • Pyromania • Pathological gambling	
Adjustment disorder	• Adjustment disorder with anxiety • Adjustment disorder with disturbance of conduct	
Other conditions that may be a focus of clinical attention	• Medication-induced movement disorders • Relational problems • Problems related to abuse or neglect	Parent-child relational problem, occupational problem, borderline intellectual functioning

Reprinted with permission from the Diagnostic and Statistical Manual of Mental Disorders, *Fourth Edition, Text revision, Copyright 2000. American Psychiatric Association.*

(Jablensky, 2002; Livesley, Jang, & Vernon, 1998; Livesley, Schroeder, Jackson, & Jang, 1994; Widiger, 2003; Zanarini et al., 2000). Future revisions of the *DSM* model will need to address such inadequacies. The preparatory work for the next edition of the *DSM* (*DSM-V*) has begun and is due to be published around 2011 or later.

Having a standard system does not guarantee an accurate diagnosis. Making diagnostic judgments will always involve some subjectivity and personal bias by the clinician, as people's symptoms often do not neatly fit into one category. Biases having to do with gender, race, or culture—whether conscious or unconscious—also can skew a diagnosis. For example, females are more likely to be diagnosed with personality disorders that are characterized by emotionality and dependence on others—behaviors that conform to negative stereotypes of the female gender role. Similarly, males are more likely to be diagnosed with personality disorders that are characterized by hostility and control of others—behaviors that conform to negative stereotypes of the male gender role. It has been argued that these gender differences in the frequency of personality disorders result from gender biases in diagnosis (Hartung & Widiger, 1998; Widiger, 1998; Widiger & Chaynes, 2003).

Critics of the *DSM* model also point out the possible negative effects of labeling someone with a mental health disorder. Diagnostic labels may serve as a self-fulfilling prophecy, encouraging a person to behave in a way consistent with the disorder. Others in the person's environment might also treat this person in a way that encourages the symptoms of the disorder as well. We as a society also tend to treat people with any diagnostic label negatively, perhaps increasing their maladaptive functioning through prejudice and discrimination. Such negative treatment may persist even after the person's behavior returns to normal (Rosenhan, 1973; Szasz, 1987).

 Application

The *DSM* model is not perfect, and can provide only a general description of the problem a person is experiencing. It does not take into account the uniqueness of each individual, nor can it tell us how this person will behave in the future. The effects of labeling a person's disorder should also be kept in mind as we review some of the more prevalent and more interesting mental health disorders, starting with the anxiety disorders.

Let's Review!

This section detailed the general structure of the *DSM* model and reviewed its major strengths and weaknesses. For a quick check of your understanding, answer these questions.

1. The purpose of the *DSM* is to:
   a. explain the causes of mental disorders.
   b. describe the symptoms of mental disorders.
   c. indicate the frequency of mental disorders.
   d. prescribe treatment methods for mental disorders.

2. The *DSM* model relies mainly on which criteria of abnormality?
   a. statistical infrequency
   b. violation of social norms
   c. inability to function
   d. mentally insane

3. Which of the following is *not* information gained by using the multiaxial system of the current *DSM*?
   a. existence of mental retardation
   b. degree of social support
   c. medical conditions
   d. future behavior

ANSWERS
1.b; 2.c; 3.d

Anxiety Disorders: > It's Not Just "Nerves"

≫ LEARNING
≫ OBJECTIVE
≫ Distinguish the symptoms among the
≫ five anxiety disorders, and discuss
≫ our current understanding of the
≫ causes of anxiety disorders.
≫

What is abnormal anxiety? We all experience some anxiety from time to time. Many students are anxious when they have to make an oral presentation. Other people are nervous when they have to meet new people or fly in an airplane. In these examples, however, the anxiety tends to decrease once the situation is over. People with **anxiety disorders** are different in that they experience chronic anxiety that seriously interferes with their ability to function. Howard Hughes, whom we introduced at the beginning of this chapter, is a prime example of a person with an anxiety disorder.

anxiety disorder   a disorder marked by excessive apprehension that seriously interferes with a person's ability to function

Components of the Anxiety Disorders

Typically, anxiety disorders in general can be characterized by four components: physical, cognitive, emotional, and behavioral. These components interact powerfully, creating an unpleasant experience of fear or dread, although there may not be a specific fear-producing stimulus present.

Physical Anxiety: Fight or Flight

The physical components of anxiety include dizziness, elevated heart rate and blood pressure, muscle tension, sweating palms, and dry mouth. These physical symptoms stem from the activation of the sympathetic nervous system, which we discussed in Chapter 2. The hormonal system is also activated as adrenaline is released into the bloodstream. You will recall that this is referred to as the fight-or-flight response (see p.65). This fight-or-flight response occurs every time we perceive a threat in our environment, which brings us to the cognitive and emotional components of anxiety.

Cognitive and Emotional Anxiety

Typically, the body reacts to realistic threats in our environment, but for people with anxiety disorders, their concerns are unrealistic and out of proportion to the amount of harm that could occur. The cognitive component of anxiety, therefore, may include worrying, fear of losing control, exaggerating (in one's mind) the danger of a situation, paranoia, or being extremely wary and watchful of people and events. These thoughts then may lead to specific emotional reactions such as a sense of dread, terror, panic, irritability, or restlessness. Finally, these thoughts and emotions then propel the person to behave in ways meant to cope with the anxiety.

Approximately 13% of American adults between the ages of 18 and 54 are diagnosed with an anxiety disorder in a given year.

© Creatas/Picturequest

Behavioral Anxiety

Coping with abnormal anxiety may include escaping, or fleeing, from the situation, behaving aggressively, "freezing," or avoiding the situation in the future. Again, these symptoms are so intense that they interfere with people's ability to function and as such disrupt the quality of their lives. In Howard Hughes's case, he became a recluse, obsessed with avoiding contamination.

Types of Anxiety Disorders

Approximately 13% of American adults between the ages of 18 and 54 are diagnosed with an anxiety disorder in a given year (Narrow, Rae, & Regier, 1998). We will discuss five of the most prevalent anxiety disorders: panic disorder, phobic disorder, obsessive-compulsive disorder, posttraumatic stress disorder, and generalized anxiety disorder.

Panic Disorder

 Application

panic disorder   an anxiety disorder characterized by intense fear and anxiety in the absence of danger that is accompanied by strong physical symptoms

Imagine that you are attending a party given by a good friend. When you arrive at the party, a feeling of panic suddenly overwhelms you. Your heart begins to pound, you hear ringing in your ears, your skin feels tingly and numb, and it becomes harder and harder to breathe. These are common symptoms that occur during a *panic attack*, a short but intense episode of severe anxiety. As many as 30–40% of young adults in the United States report occasional panic attacks that do not interfere with their daily functioning (Ehlers, 1995; King, Gullone, Tonge, & Ollendick, 1993). However, when panic attacks are more common and a person begins to fear having panic attacks, to the extent that it interferes with the ability to function, a diagnosis of **panic disorder** may be given (American Psychiatric Association, 2000).

It is estimated that between 1.5% and 4% of people will develop panic disorder at some time in their lives (American Psychiatric Association, 2000). It typically develops in late adolescence or early adulthood, and is twice as common in women as in men (Craske & Barlow, 2001; Robins & Regier, 1991). People with panic disorder often feel so overwhelmed by the feelings of panic that they think they are having a heart attack or a seizure. They may believe that they are "going crazy" or going to die, and many seek medical attention to find out what is wrong with them. The panic attacks may occur frequently or only sporadically. Most people with panic disorder cannot identify any specific thing that they were doing or thinking at the time that might have triggered the panic attack. However, with each panic attack that occurs, that situation may then become a future trigger of a panic attack. The person may then become so fearful of having another panic attack in that particular situation that the person begins to experience **agoraphobia,** or a fear of being in places from which escape might be difficult or where help may not be available if one were to experience panic. People affected with agoraphobia avoid any place—the mall, the grocery store, or the theater—in which they believe a panic attack may occur. They may also fear that no one will help them, or that they may embarrass themselves. Such fears can leave people housebound for years. Seventy-five percent or more of those who suffer from agoraphobia are women (Barlow, 2002). Note that people without panic disorder can experience agoraphobia (Eaton & Keyl, 1990). When agoraphobia occurs in the absence of panic disorder, it is characterized as a phobic disorder, our next topic of discussion.

agoraphobia   an excessive fear of being in places from which escape might be difficult or where help may not be available if one were to experience panic

Phobic Disorders

 Application

phobic disorder   an anxiety disorder characterized by an intense fear of a specific object or situation

specific phobia   a persistent fear and avoidance of a specific object or situation

All of us have fears. Some of us get anxious when we think of or see a snake or spider. Others may fear public speaking or eating in public. As children, we may have been afraid of the dark or the dentist. These are normal fears. However, when our fears become so intense that they cause severe anxiety, possibly even full blown panic attacks that interfere with our ability to function, then a diagnosis of **phobic disorder** is made (American Psychiatric Association, 2000). We have already mentioned one type of phobic disorder, *agoraphobia*. Two other types of phobic disorders classified by the *DSM-IV-TR* are *specific phobias* and *social phobias*.

Specific phobias involve a persistent fear and avoidance of a specific object or situation—animals, heights, bridges—or other specific stimuli. These are the most common phobias, affecting as many as 1 in 10 people at some time in their lives (Kessler et al., 1994). Celebrity Whoopie Goldberg and sportscaster John Madden so fear air travel that they avoid flying altogether and travel in private buses. Table 15.3 ◆ describes a few of the hundreds of specific phobias that have been identified.

Social phobias include an irrational, persistent fear of being negatively evaluated by others in a social situation. The socially phobic person may have an extreme fear of embarrassment or humiliation. This may include fear of public speaking, fear of eating or undressing in front of others, or fear of using public restrooms. Barbra Streisand is just one of many celebrities who has experienced extreme "stage fright," a social phobia. Although she continued to produce albums and release films, Streisand didn't perform publicly for more than 20 years. Social phobias tend to develop in the early preschool years and in adolescence, and are somewhat more likely to develop in women than in men (Lang & Stein, 2001; Turk, Heimberg, & Hope, 2001).

People with phobic disorders typically recognize that their fears are irrational, but they cannot stop the overwhelming anxiety that they feel when faced with the feared object or situation. Most phobic disorders develop during childhood and adolescence. Agoraphobics are more likely to seek treatment than people with specific or social phobias are, perhaps because agoraphobia is more likely to severely impair normal functioning (Kessler, Stein, & Berglund, 1998).

social phobia   an irrational, persistent fear of being negatively evaluated by others in a social situation

◆ **Table 15.3**
Common Specific Phobias

Phobia Name	Fear
Acrophobia	Heights
Aerophobia	Flying
Astraphobia	Storms, thunder, lightning
Arachnophobia	Spiders
Aviophobia	Airplanes
Claustrophobia	Closed spaces
Cynophobia	Dogs
Gephyrophobia	Crossing bridges
Hematophobia	Blood
Microphobia	Germs or contamination
Nyctophobia	Darkness
Ophidophobia	Snakes
Pathophobia	Disease
Phonophobia	Public speaking
Pyrophobia	Fire
Thanatophobia	Death
Xenophobia	Strangers
Zoophobia	Animals

For many college students, giving a speech or presentation is an anxiety-producing event.

© Barbara Stizer/Photo Edit

Obsessive-Compulsive Disorder (OCD)

Obsessions are recurrent thoughts or images that intrude on a person's consciousness or awareness. **Compulsions** are repetitive behaviors that a person feels a strong urge to perform. All of us experience obsessions and compulsions. For example, you leave your house in the morning to go to school or work. On the way, the thought pops into your head that you left the coffeepot or iron on, or that you forgot to shut the garage door or lock the front door. Immediately, thoughts of the house on fire or ransacked by thieves follow. What do you do when faced with these obsessive thoughts? Many of us feel compelled to turn the car around to check that everything is okay. However, what if this scenario occurred each and every time you got in the car, and you spent hours going back and forth to make sure that everything was fine? In such a case, you might be diagnosed with **obsessive-compulsive disorder (OCD)**.

According to the *DSM-IV-TR*, obsessive-compulsive disorder is an anxiety disorder in which a person experiences recurrent obsessions or compulsions that he or she feels cannot be controlled (American Psychiatric Association, 2000). The person

obsession   a recurrent thought or image that intrudes on a person's awareness

 Application

compulsion   repetitive behavior that a person feels a strong urge to perform

obsessive-compulsive disorder (OCD)
an anxiety disorder involving a pattern of unwanted intrusive thoughts and the urge to engage in repetitive actions

For Better or For Worse ©1998 Lynn Johnston Productions. Dist. by Universal Press Syndicate. Reprinted with permission. All rights reserved.

recognizes that these thoughts or behaviors are irrational, yet cannot seem to control them. Obsessions often center on dirt and contamination, doing harm to oneself or others, sexual thoughts, or repeated doubts (such as not having locked the house). Common compulsions include cleaning, checking, counting things, or arranging and straightening things in a particular fashion. The compulsions often are performed with the hope of preventing the obsessive thoughts or making them go away. However, performing these "rituals" provides only temporary relief. Not performing the rituals increases the person's anxiety. Howard Hughes's constant obsessions with cleanliness and order made him compulsively seal up the windows and doors, handle items only with a tissue, and repeat airplane landings over and over again.

The recurrent obsessions cause great personal distress and the compulsions can be time-consuming and in some cases harmful—as when a person washes his or her hands so frequently that they bleed. It is estimated that between 1% and 3% of individuals will develop OCD at some time in their lives, and in the United States, the rates among Whites are higher compared to Hispanics and African Americans (Hewlett, 2000). Males and females are equally affected by this disorder (Karno & Golding, 1991).

Posttraumatic Stress Disorder (PTSD)

posttraumatic stress disorder (PTSD)
an anxiety disorder, characterized by distressing memories, emotional numbness, and hypervigilance, that develops after exposure to a traumatic event

Another type of anxiety disorder is **posttraumatic stress disorder (PTSD).** Although panic disorder appears to occur without any identifiable trigger, PTSD arises in the wake of a clear trigger—a traumatic event. PTSD develops after exposure to a terrifying event or ordeal in which grave physical harm occurred or was threatened. Traumatic events may include:

- violent personal assaults such as rape, physical abuse, or sexual abuse
- natural or human-caused disasters such as an earthquake, hurricane, terrorist attack, bombing, or an outbreak of an infectious disease
- military combat
- events that anyone might experience—the sudden, unexpected death of a loved one or witnessing a violent crime or a deadly traffic accident.

A diagnosis of PTSD requires that the person repeatedly reexperience the ordeal in the form of distressing memories, nightmares, frightening thoughts, or flashback episodes, especially when exposed to situations that are similar to the original trauma. For example, a car backfire might trigger a flashback to a combat trauma or being the victim of an armed robbery. Anniversaries of the event also can trigger symptoms. In addition, people diagnosed with PTSD may experience emotional numbness or withdrawal from themselves or others such that they lose interest in usual activities or are regarded as distant and emotionally unavailable. Lastly, PTSD sufferers are always on guard—showing hypervigilance, having difficulty concentrating, or having difficulty sleeping (American Psychiatric Association, 2000). They may experience depression, anxiety, irritability, or outbursts of anger; physical symptoms such as headaches, dizziness, or chest pain; or feelings of intense guilt. For some people, such symptoms can seriously disrupt the ability to work or to meet social and family obligations.

An estimated 3.6% of U.S. adults between the ages of 18 and 54 are diagnosed with PTSD in a given year (Narrow et al., 1998). More than twice as many females as males experience PTSD following exposure to a trauma (Davidson, 2000). Approximately 30% of Vietnam veterans developed PTSD at some point after the war (Kulka et al., 1988). The disorder also has been reported among Persian Gulf war veterans, with estimates running as high as 8% (Wolfe, Erickson, Sharkansky, King, & King, 1999). After 2 decades of conflict in Afghanistan, 42% of participants in a national population-based survey reported PTSD symptoms (Cardozo ct al., 2004). Roughly 15% of a sample of U.S. military in Iraq indicated problems in mental health, most notably PTSD (Hoge et al., 2004).

Research on the effects of the September 11 attacks on mental health has revealed a remarkable degree of PTSD. New Yorkers who viewed more television images in the days after September 11 had more probable PTSD (Ahern, Galea, Resnick, & Vlahov, 2004). In June 2002, over 18% of American Airlines flight attendants reported symptoms consistent with PTSD (Lating, Sherman, Everly, Lowry, & Peragine, 2004). In a sample of Pentagon staff, 23% had probable PTSD (Grieger, Fullerton, & Ursano, 2004). A comprehensive mental health screening of over 11,000 rescue and recovery workers and volunteers of the World Trade Center revealed that over 20% of the participants experienced symptoms of PTSD and 13% met the diagnostic criteria for PTSD (Centers for Disease Control, 2004).

Exposure to a trauma can lead to the development of PTSD.

© Najlah Feanny/Corbis Saba

Generalized Anxiety Disorder (GAD)

generalized anxiety disorder (GAD)
an anxiety disorder characterized by chronic, constant worry in almost all situations

Although phobic disorder and panic disorder are linked to specific situations that cause anxiety, some people are anxious all the time in almost all situations. These individuals may be diagnosed with **generalized anxiety disorder (GAD).** Symptoms of GAD include excessive anxiety, worry, and difficulty in controlling such worries. The person may be easily fatigued, restless, irritable, and experience difficulty concentrating or sleeping (American Psychiatric Association, 2000). The person's worrying and anxiety seem to be chronic, and many report having felt this way their entire lives. They worry not only about major issues, such as which car or house to buy, their children's health, or their job performance, but also about minor issues such as being late, wearing the right outfit, or what to make for dinner. It is estimated that about 4% of the U.S. population experience GAD in any 6-month period (Kessler et al., 1994).

Explaining Anxiety Disorders

What causes anxiety disorders? Research on people with anxiety disorders suggests biological, psychological, and sociocultural factors that may contribute to such behavior.

Biology and the Brain

From a biological perspective, the functioning of several neurotransmitters has been linked to anxiety disorders. For example, some research suggests that abnormal activity of norepinephrine, serotonin, and/or GABA is involved in panic attacks (Bell & Nutt, 1998; Bourin, Baker, & Bradwejn, 1998; Charney et al., 2000; Levy, Kimhi, Barak, Demmer, Harel, & Elizur, 1996). Abnormal activity of GABA also has been linked to people with generalized anxiety disorder (GAD). Problems in serotonin regulation have been suggested as a cause for obsessive-compulsive disorder (OCD; Sanders & Shekhar, 1995; Saxena, Brody, Schwartz, & Baxter, 1998). Moreover, twin and family studies have found that panic disorder and OCD appear to run in families, suggesting a genetic link (Biederman et al., 2001; Crowe, 1990; Grados, Walkup, & Walford, 2003; Hettema, Neale, & Kendler, 2001; Samuels & Nestadt, 1997; Scherrer et al., 2000).

Studies in animals and humans have focused on specific brain areas that are involved in anxiety and fear. Our fear response is coordinated by the *amygdala*, a small structure deep inside the brain (see p. 69). Research done in the last decade on panic disorder and posttraumatic stress disorder (PTSD) suggests that these anxiety disorders may be linked to the malfunctioning of this brain structure (LeDoux, 1998; Rosen, 2004). Research on OCD suggests abnormal functioning of a part of the forebrain called the *striatum*. For example, in one study (Rauch et al., 1997) PET scans of individuals with OCD showed different brain circuitry in the striatum when performing a cognitive task than the PET scans of individuals without OCD. Other research suggests that an overactive monitoring system in the brain is related to the symptoms of OCD (Gehring, Himle, & Nisenson, 2000; Ursu, Stenger, Shear, Jones, & Carter, 2003). Such evidence suggests that biological factors may play a role in anxiety disorders.

This biological research can help us understand Howard Hughes's OCD. His mother appeared to have suffered from the same disorder, suggesting a genetic link. He had experienced several airplane crashes and had contracted syphilis, two circumstances that could have resulted in abnormal brain functioning. Moreover, the pain from his crash injuries led to a dependence on codeine, a habit that could have altered his brain chemistry.

Psychological Perspectives

Psychological factors also help in explaining anxiety disorders. The psychoanalytic perspective suggests that anxiety is linked to unresolved unconscious conflicts. For example, Freud would attribute GAD to a weak ego. Recall that it is the ego's job to handle anxiety that stems from the natural conflict between the id and superego. Typically, the ego does this by using defense mechanisms. Consequently, if a person feels anxious all the time, the ego—with its defense mechanisms—must not be doing its job. Freud (1909) also suggested that phobias result when unconscious anxiety is displaced onto a symbolic object or situation. Fear of being abandoned may express itself as a fear of the dark. Similarly, Freud attributed the obsessions and compulsions of OCD to symbolic manifestations of unconscious conflicts. Although the psychoanalytic perspective offers interesting explanations of anxiety disorders, psychoanalysis (therapy that addresses such issues) has not been very effective in treating anxiety disorders (Bachrach, Galatzer-Levy, Skolnikoff, & Waldron, 1991; Wolitzky, 1995).

Social learning research suggests that anxieties are learned. Recall from Chapter 5 how Watson and Raynor were able to condition Little Albert to fear a white rat (see p. 213). Learning theorists suggest that phobias develop in much the same fashion. A neutral stimulus (the phobia) gets paired with a stimulus that naturally elicits fear. So when a thunderstorm gets paired with a loud noise (thunder) that naturally evokes fear, we learn to be fearful of thunderstorms. Direct experience is not always necessary to develop a phobia. We may acquire fears simply by observing or hearing about others' negative experiences (Kleinknecht, 1991). How many of us have come face to face with a shark? But after seeing the *Jaws* movies, we may be more cautious and fearful when swimming in the ocean. In either case, our behavior toward the feared object is then often reinforced. We avoid or run away from objects or situations that cause fear. If we fear a shark attack in the ocean, we avoid swimming in the sea. Avoiding or running away reduces our anxiety and thereby helps maintain our fear of the object or situation. Reinforcement also helps explain compulsions. If you engage in a certain behavior following an anxiety-provoking obsession, your anxiety is often reduced. The next time the obsession occurs, you feel more compelled to engage in the behavior so that you can reduce your anxiety (Barlow, 2002). Learning and conditioning theories have also been useful in understanding PTSD. Sights, sounds, or images of the trauma all become conditioned stimuli that trigger the fear reaction.

 Application

Cognitive research suggests that our thinking processes play a role in the development of anxiety disorders. For example, studies show that people with panic disorder sometimes misinterpret their bodily sensations, thinking they are beginning a panic attack. Their negative and catastrophic thinking then heightens their anxiety (Barlow, 2000; Craske & Barlow, 2001; Ehlers & Breuer, 1992). Research on generalized anxiety disorder (GAD) also suggests the role of cognitive factors. People diagnosed with GAD tend to make maladaptive assumptions. They anticipate something bad happening to them, especially that they will feel out of control. While driving in a car, they may worry that they will get lost or in an accident. In an airplane, they may worry that it will crash. These worries become constant and almost automatic in their thought process (Beck, 1997; Riskind, Williams, Gessner, Chrosniak, & Cortina., 2000). Research has found that the shattering of certain basic assumptions of life may bring on PTSD. An unpredictable trauma—such as rape, an earthquake, or an automobile accident—may make us question our assumptions that the world is safe, and just, and that events happen for a reason. It dispels our illusion of control and invincibility, and our assumption that bad things only happen to bad people (Janoff-Bulman, 1992; Terr, 1983). Some research suggests that people who suffer from OCD are less able to turn off the intrusive, negative obsessions that we all experience from time to time (Salkovskis, Westbrook, Davis, Jeavons, & Gledhill, 1997).

Carl Rogers and other humanists attribute anxiety to an unrealistic self-image (Rogers, 1959), although this idea has not been extensively researched. An unrealistic self-image results in being overly critical of oneself and setting unrealistic standards for acceptance by others. Because neither the standards nor the self-image can ever be attained, anxiety results.

Sociocultural Factors

Sociocultural factors also must be considered when explaining anxiety disorders. For example, in cultures where there is rapid social change or war, people are more likely to exhibit anxiety symptoms compared to more stable countries (Compton et al., 1991). Similarly, people who have been abused as children or who have had other previous traumatic or stressful experiences are more likely to develop anxiety disorders (Hyman & Rudorfer, 2000; Widom, 1999). In the United States, people from lower socioeconomic groups and with lower levels of education are more at risk for developing an anxiety disorder (Manson et al., 1996). Women also are more likely to be diagnosed with an anxiety disorder than men are (Kessler et al., 1994). This gender difference has been attributed to women's relative lack of power in society, differences in gender-role socialization in which it is acceptable for women to report fear (Arrindell et al., 2003), differences in coping styles, and the greater likelihood that women will be victims of violence, crime, or abuse. More research will have to examine the role of gender and culture in anxiety disorders before we fully understand their influence.

Let's Review!

This section outlined the five main anxiety disorders and detailed our current understanding of the biological, psychological, and sociocultural factors that may play a role in causing anxiety disorders. For a quick check of your understanding, answer these questions.

1. Marilu is anxious and nervous all the time. She constantly worries over her family, her job, and her schoolwork. Which anxiety disorder *best* describes Marilu's behavior?

   a. panic disorder
   b. generalized anxiety disorder
   c. phobic disorder
   d. obsessive-compulsive disorder

2. Learning theories suggest that obsessive-compulsive disorder is the result of:

   a. reinforcement.
   b. faulty cognitions.
   c. low self-esteem.
   d. unconscious impulses.

3. Abdul was involved in a four-car pile-up on the interstate 8 months ago. Since then, he has been having nightmares and flashback episodes of the accident.

He has difficulty concentrating and has withdrawn from his family and friends. Abdul is most likely suffering from which anxiety disorder?

   a. panic disorder
   b. posttraumatic stress disorder
   c. phobic disorder
   d. generalized anxiety disorder

4. Which of the following neurotransmitters has *not* been linked to anxiety disorders?

   a. GABA
   b. norepinephrine
   c. serotonin
   d. acetylcholine

5. Denise has an intense fear of driving over bridges. She will go hours out of her way to avoid driving over a bridge. Denise's fear can best be characterized as:

   a. a social phobia.
   b. a specific phobia.
   c. panic disorder.
   d. agoraphobia.

ANSWERS
1. b; 2. a; 3. b; 4. d; 5. b

Mood Disorders: Beyond the Blues > > > > >

LEARNING OBJECTIVES

❯ Distinguish the symptoms between unipolar and bipolar depressive disorders, and discuss our current understanding of the causes of mood disorders.

❯ Detail common misconceptions that individuals hold about suicide.

❯

A second major category of disorders described in the *DSM-IV-TR* is mood disorders. **Mood disorders** involve a significant change in a person's emotional state. This may include feeling depressed or extremely elated for an extended time. But don't we all get blue from time to time?

How does clinical depression differ from normal periods of sadness? As we will see, the main distinctions are in (1) the length of time a person experiences the mood change and (2) whether the conditions and events around the person are consistent with the mood change. For example, many of us experience sadness, but typically this period of sadness lasts only a few days. In clinical depression, the mood change is persistent and interferes significantly with a person's ability to function. Also, normal periods of sadness are usually brought on by environmental events—the loss of a loved one, a break up of a relationship, or a disappointment in one's life. People with clinical depression are sad over a longer period, in the absence of such external events or long after most people would have adjusted to such changes. Mood disorders can be devastating to personal relationships and to the ability to work or go to school. Many people think that the symptoms are not "real" and that the person should be able to "snap out of it." But these inaccurate beliefs may cause shame, which discourages people from seeking appropriate treatment. Recall Amy Tan's periods of deep sadness that indicate a mood disorder. We will discuss two basic types of mood disorders: unipolar depression and bipolar depression.

≪ Application

mood disorder   a disorder marked by a significant change in one's emotional state that seriously interferes with a person's ability to function

Unipolar Depressive Disorders: A Change to Sadness

Unipolar depressive disorders involve a variety of physical, cognitive, emotional, and behavioral symptoms. The *DSM-IV-TR* indicates two categories of unipolar depressive disorder: major depression and dysthymic disorder.

A diagnosis of **major depression** requires that a person experience either extreme sadness—referred to as **dysphoria**—or extreme apathy (loss of interest in usual activities), plus at least four other symptoms of depression for a period of at least 2 weeks. These symptoms must be severe enough that they interfere with the person's ability to function (American Psychiatric Association, 2000). In addition to the emotional symptoms of dysphoria and apathy, people diagnosed with major depression show four or more of the following symptoms nearly every day during the two-week period:

major depression   a mood disorder involving dysphoria, feelings of worthlessness, loss of interest in one's usual activities, and changes in bodily activities such as sleep and appetite that persists for at least 2 weeks

dysphoria   an extreme state of sadness

Physical and Behavioral Symptoms

- Change in sleep patterns—either sleeping too much (hypersomnia) or too little (insomnia)
- Change in appetite—either eating too much (resulting in weight gain) or too little (resulting in weight loss)
- Change in motor functioning—either moving slowly and sluggishly or appearing agitated in movement
- Fatigue, or loss of energy

Cognitive Symptoms

- Inability to concentrate or pay attention
- Difficulty in making decisions
- Low self-esteem

- Exaggerated feelings of worthlessness or guilt
- Thoughts of suicide
- Delusions (believing something that is not true) and hallucinations (seeing, hearing, or feeling things that are not there) with depressing themes

Major depression is marked by physical, behavioral, and cognitive symptoms, in addition to depressed mood.

dysthymic disorder a mood disorder that is a less severe but more chronic form of major depression

Major depression may occur as a single episode or as repeated episodes over the course of years. Some episodes may be so severe that the person requires hospitalization, especially in the presence of frequent suicide attempts or delusional thinking. Looking back on Tan's behavior, we see that she had many of the symptoms of major depression. She felt deeply sad, had difficulty sleeping and eating, felt worthless, and had suicidal thoughts.

Dysthymic disorder is a less severe but more chronic, or long-lasting, form of major depression. The person seems sad and downcast over a longer time. A diagnosis of dysthymic disorder requires the symptom of depressed mood plus at least two other symptoms of depression for a period of at least 2 years. Dysthymic disorder generally begins in childhood, adolescence, or early adulthood (American Psychiatric Association, 2000). Typically, the symptoms of dysthymic disorder are not severe enough to require hospitalization. However, most people with dysthymic disorder eventually experience a major depressive episode (Klein, Lewinsohn, & Seeley, 2001; Regier et al., 1993).

Major depression is the leading cause of disability in the United States and worldwide (Murray & Lopez, 1996). Following anxiety disorders, depression is one of the more common psychological disorders, affecting approximately 9.5% of adult Americans in a given year (Regier et al., 1993). In the United States, 17% of individuals will experience an acute episode of depression at some time in their lives, and 6% will experience more chronic depression (Kessler et al., 1994). Depression also appears to be related to age and gender. Although major depression can develop at any age, the average age of onset is the mid-20s. People between 15 and 24 years of age are most at risk for experiencing a major depressive episode, whereas 45- to 54-year-olds experience the lowest rates of depressive episodes (Blazer, Kessler, McGonagle, & Swartz, 1994; Kessler et al., 2003). Most studies have also found gender differences in adult depression rates. Women are twice as likely as men to experience both mild and more severe depression, a difference found in many different countries, ethnic groups, and across adult age groups (Culbertson, 1997; Nolen-Hoeksema, 2002; Weissman & Olfson, 1995).

Bipolar Depressive Disorders: The Presence of Mania

A second major group of mood disorders is the bipolar depressive disorders. The *DSM-IV-TR* indicates two categories of bipolar depressive disorders: bipolar disorder and cyclothymic disorder.

bipolar disorder a mood disorder characterized by both depression and mania

Bipolar disorder involves a shift in mood between two states, or *poles*. One of these shifts is to a depressed state, with symptoms similar to major depression. The person feels sad, lacks self-worth, and may show changes in sleeping and eating over a 2-week period. The second mood change is to the opposite extreme—to a "high," or euphoric state, called **mania.** During a manic state people feel elated and have high self-esteem, a decreased need for sleep, are more talkative than usual, and are highly distractible. Much energy is directed at achieving goals, although many projects may

mania a period of abnormally excessive energy and elation

be started and few finished. They have an inflated sense of self, feeling confident and able to accomplish anything. This may result in delusional thinking or hallucinations. Also, their boundless energy often results in more impulsive and risk-taking behaviors. When such symptoms of mania and depression interfere with the person's ability to function, a diagnosis of bipolar disorder is appropriate (American Psychiatric Association, 2000).

Cyclothymic disorder is a less severe but more chronic form of bipolar disorder, just as dysthymic disorder is a less severe but more chronic form of major depression. In cyclothymic disorder, a person alternates between milder periods of mania and more moderate depression over a 2-year period (American Psychiatric Association, 2000). The individual functions reasonably well during the mild mania, but is likely to be more impaired during the depressive phase.

Bipolar disorders are less common than unipolar disorders. It is estimated that only 1 to 2% of Americans will experience an episode of bipolar disorder at some time in their lives (Kessler et al., 1994; Lewinsohn, Klein, & Seeley, 2000). Research has not found any gender or ethnic differences in the incidence of bipolar disorders. Men are just as likely as women to be diagnosed with bipolar disorder. The typical age of onset for bipolar disorder is late adolescence and early adulthood (Angst & Sellaro, 2000; Burke, Burke, Regier, & Rae, 1990).

cyclothymic disorder   a mood disorder that is a less severe but more chronic form of bipolar disorder

Suicide Facts and Misconceptions

Our descriptions of depressive disorders include suicidal thoughts as one symptom of depression. Amy Tan had frequent suicidal thoughts and made several suicide attempts. Research suggests that nearly 90% of all people who commit suicide have some diagnosable mental disorder, commonly a depressive disorder or a substance abuse disorder (Conwell & Brent, 1995; National Institute of Mental Health, 2002; Wulsin, Vaillat, & Wells, 1999). In 2001, suicide was the 11th leading cause of death in the United States (higher than homicide; Arias, Anderson, Kung, Murphy, & Kockanek, 2003). Among 25- to 44-year-olds, it was the 4th leading cause of death. Among 15- to 24-year-olds, it was the 3rd leading cause of death, although both these rates are probably grossly underestimated given the negative stigma attached to suicide in this country (Anderson & Smith, 2003). Although young people have lower rates of suicide than adults do, these rates have been rising in recent decades, especially among 15- to 19-year-olds. Elderly men are at an especially high risk for suicide (Hoyert, Kochanek, & Murphy, 1999). Women are two to three times more likely than men to *attempt* suicide, but four times as many men actually kill themselves, in part due to the means of attempting suicide (Crosby, Cheltenham, & Sacks, 1999; Denning, Conwell, King, & Coz, 2000). Men tend to choose more lethal means of suicide, such as shooting, hanging, or stabbing themselves. Women are more likely than men to choose less lethal means, such as drug overdoses. This gender difference appears in many countries across the world (Weissman et al., 1999; Welch, 2001) except China, where more women commit suicide than men (Phillips, Li, & Zhang, 2002). Within the United States, Whites have higher rates of suicide than any other ethnic group with the exception of Native Americans (Hoyert et al., 1999). These statistics, depicted in Figure 15.1, highlight the importance of understanding and preventing suicide. So let's take a moment to dispel some of the more common misconceptions concerning suicide.

Misconception: People who talk of suicide will not kill themselves.

Although most people who talk of suicide do not go on to attempt suicide, people who commit suicide typically have expressed their intentions at some time to family

Figure 15.1 **U.S. Suicide Rates**

Although women attempt suicide more often, men of all ages are more likely to commit suicide. Elderly white men and young black men are specifically vulnerable to suicide.

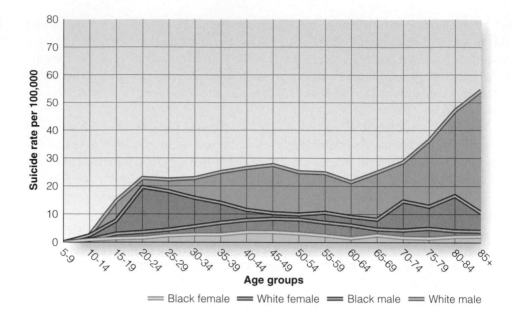

Black female — White female — Black male — White male

Application ≫

members or friends before their attempt (Shneidman, 1987). Therefore, any talk of suicide should be taken seriously. A suicidal person should not be left alone. You may need to contact a mental health professional, call 911, or call a suicide crisis hotline in your area.

Misconception: If you ask someone who is depressed whether he or she has thoughts of suicide, it will only plant the idea of suicide in his or her head.

Application ≫

Asking direct questions about a person's plan for suicide is the only way to assess the person's risk for committing suicide. Bringing up the subject can also give the person an opportunity to talk about his or her problem. People who have a concrete plan in mind for when or how they will end their life are more likely to attempt suicide than those whose plans are less specific (Clark, Gibbons, Fawcett, & Scheftner, 1989).

Misconception: People who have unsuccessfully attempted suicide will not try again.

Only 10% of people who unsuccessfully attempt suicide try again and succeed (Clark & Fawcett, 1992). Yet among adolescents, a previous history of suicide attempts is the single best predictor of future suicide attempts and completions (Lewinsohn, Rohde & Seeley, 1994). Therefore, a previous suicide attempt puts adolescents in particular at a higher risk for future suicide attempts.

Misconception: A better mood means the risk of suicide is gone.

Suicide does not typically happen when a person is in the depths of a deep depression. Rather, suicide attempts are more likely to occur when people with depression have energy and can think more clearly and make decisions. This energy and clearer thinking also make it appear to family members and friends that the depressed person is getting better and is therefore at a lower risk of suicide. However, this energy and decision-making ability allows the individual to make and carry out plans for suicide. So a better mood does not always mean a decreased risk of suicide, and sometimes actually indicates an increased risk of suicide.

Misconception: Only depressed people attempt suicide.

Although suicidal thoughts are a symptom of depression, those with other serious psychological disorders, including bipolar disorder, substance abuse disorder, and schizophrenia, are also at risk for suicide (Statham et al., 1998; Tsuang, Fleming, & Simpson, 1999). A number of events and situations besides depression also increase one's risk of suicide, including economic hardship, serious illness, drug abuse, loss of a relationship, childhood sexual or physical abuse, and the presence of a firearm in the home (Brent et al., 1991; Crosby, Cheltenham, & Sacks, 1999; Fergusson, Horwood, & Lynskey, 1996; Kaplan, Pelcovitz, Salzinger, Mandel, & Weiner, 1997; Lester, 1992; Welch, 2001). Suicide occurs among people who have psychological disorders as well as among people who face environmental stressors. The majority of suicide attempts are expressions of extreme distress and helplessness, and not just "harmless" bids for attention.

Explaining Mood Disorders

What causes mood disorders? Not surprisingly, research has identified biological, psychological, and sociocultural factors that may contribute to mood disorders.

Biological Factors: Genes, Neurotransmitters, and Stress Hormones

One biological factor indicated as a cause in mood disorders is our genes. The evidence from family history studies, twin studies, and adoption studies suggests that mood disorders may be genetically transmitted, especially in the case of bipolar disorder. For example, first-degree relatives (i.e., parent, child, or sibling) of persons with bipolar disorder are much more likely to develop the disorder than are relatives of people without the disorder. Similarly, if an identical twin is diagnosed as having bipolar disorder, the other identical twin has a higher probability of developing the disorder than if they were fraternal twins (MacKinnon, Jamison, & DePaulo, 1997; Wallace, Schneider, & McGuffin, 2002; Winokur, Coryell, Keller, Endicott, & Leon, 1995). It has even been found that adoptees who had relatives with bipolar disorder were much more likely to develop the disorder than adoptees who had relatives with no mood disorders (Wender et al., 1986).

The evidence for genetic factors in major depression is less consistent and clear. The trend toward genetic transmission is present, particularly in women, but it is not as strong as the evidence in bipolar disorders (Abkevich et al., 2003; Bierut et al., 1999; Kendler, Neale, Kessler, Heath, & Eaves, 1992; Nurnberger, 1993; Sullivan, Neale, & Kendler, 2000). In Amy Tan's case, her mother also suffered from depression. Her grandmother and three other relatives had committed suicide, suggesting possible depression in them as well.

The malfunctioning of certain brain neurotransmitters also has been linked to mood disorders. For example, some research suggests that abnormal sensitivity of receptors for serotonin and norepinephrine contributes to depression (Malone & Mann, 1993; Soares & Mann, 1997; Thase, Jindal, & Howland, 2002). Antidepressant drugs that act on serotonin and norepinephrine to relieve the symptoms of depression seem to offer evidence for the role of neurotransmitters in depression. The role of the neurotransmitters norepinephrine, serotonin, dopamine, and glutamate in bipolar disorder has been investigated, although their contribution to the bipolar disorders is less clear (Dixon & Hokin, 1998; Goodwin & Jamison, 1990).

The connection between depression and hormones also has been actively researched. Hormones regulate functions such as sleep, appetite, sexual desire, and pleasure. Symptoms of depression relate to these bodily functions and behaviors. Depressed people tend to show higher than usual levels of stress hormones (Young & Korzun, 1998). These stress hormones tend to inhibit the activity of brain neurotransmitters that are related to mood. Hence, repeated overactivation of the hormonal stress system may lay the groundwork for depression (Arborelius, Owens, Plotsky, & Nemeroff, 1999). Excessive levels of stress hormones has been linked to the shrinkage of certain brain areas that also may be related to depression (Sapolsky, 2000; Sheline, 2000). Recent research is also investigating how changes in the brain (specifically in the hippocampus) may be associated with depressive symptoms (Jacobs, 2004; Jacobs, van Praag, & Gage, 2000). We look to future technologies to assist us in sorting out the precise relationship between genes, brain neurotransmitters, the hormonal system, and mood disorders.

Psychological Factors: Abandonment, Learned Helplessness, and Negative Thinking

Psychological factors also help in explaining mood disorders, especially depression. Psychology tends to focus on depression, because the connection between biology and bipolar disorders appears to be quite strong. Psychoanalytic theory suggests that depression is linked to unresolved childhood issues of abandonment, rejection, and loss. For example, Freud (1917) believed that depression was merely a symbolic expression of anger. A child who perceives that he or she has been abandoned or rejected by loved ones is afraid to express such anger outward. Instead, the child redirects this anger onto the self, resulting in self-blame, self-hatred, and other symptoms of depression. As the child enters adolescence and adulthood and forms new relationships, these feelings of abandonment and separation may resurface. When they do, the person falls into another depression.

Some research is consistent with this view. A history of early adverse experiences such as insecure attachments, separations, and losses can lead to depression (Heim, Plotsky, & Nemeroff, 2004; Weissman, Markowitz, & Klerman, 2000). Depressed people do show low self-esteem, and some do have difficulty expressing anger (Bromberger & Matthews, 1996; Klein, Durbin, Shankman, & Santiago, 2002; Riley, Trieber, & Woods, 1989). So it is possible that early feelings of abandonment and rejection may play a role in depression, but this idea has not been thoroughly investigated. Moreover, therapy centering on resolving unconscious childhood issues of abandonment has not been very effective in treating depression (Robinson, Berman, & Neimeyer, 1990). But unresolved anger and childhood loss could be a possible factor in Amy Tan's depression. Recall that her brother and father died within 6 months of each other in Tan's early teenage years.

Behavioral or learning theories suggest that mood disorders are related to levels of positive reinforcement, learned helplessness, and ruminative coping styles. Peter Lewinsohn's (1974) behavioral theory of depression links depression to a reduction in the number of positive reinforcers we receive from others. This reduction is more likely in people with poor social skills. Imagine for a moment that you pass an acquaintance on your campus, someone who is in one of your courses. As you pass by, what do you do? Most people nod, say hello, or express some other indicator of acknowledgment; this is a social skill. Imagine further that the classmate fails to respond, continues walking, and does not reciprocate your casual greeting. What happens the next time that you walk by this person? In all likelihood, you will ignore the person, giving her or him no positive reinforcement. As this example illustrates, people with poor social skills or those who tend to withdraw receive less positive reinforcement from others. Lewinsohn suggests that such a pattern may result in depression.

learned helplessness the belief that one cannot control the outcome of events

Another behavioral explanation of depression is **learned helplessness.** Recall from Chapter 13 that learned helplessness involves the belief that you cannot control the outcome of events or what is going to happen (see p. 603). Therefore, you do not respond even when your response could lead to success. Initial evidence for learned helplessness came from studies in which dogs were administered controllable shock, uncontrollable shock, or no shock (Overmier & Seligman, 1967; Seligman & Maier, 1967). The dogs in the controllable shock situation had to learn to jump a barrier in order to turn off the shock. They quickly learned this behavior. The dogs in the uncontrollable shock situation could not turn off the shock. However, later when the dogs in the uncontrollable shock situation were given the same opportunity—jump the barrier to avoid the shock—they failed to respond. They had learned to be helpless and just sat there taking the shock *even when they could escape it.* Such research argues that depressed people respond similarly—failing to respond because they believe that life is uncontrollable.

Research by Susan Nolen-Hoeksema and her colleagues (Nolen-Hoeksema, 2001, 2002; Nolen-Hoeksema, Larson, & Grayson, 1999; Nolen-Hoeksema, Parker, & Larson, 1994) indicates that coping styles play a role in depression. Depressed people are more likely to engage in what is called a **ruminative coping style.** Rumination means to focus on your thoughts. Some depressed people spend a lot of time thinking about their depression and why they are depressed. They do not do anything about their depression or its causes, but rather remain focused on repetitively analyzing their feelings and concerns. This focus makes it more likely that they will become more severely depressed and also stay depressed longer.

ruminative coping style the tendency to persistently focus on how one feels without attempting to do anything about one's feelings

Cognitive research highlights the role of negative thinking patterns and pessimistic attributions in the development of mood disorders. If you have ever been around someone who is "down," or depressed, you realize that his or her thoughts tend to be pessimistic and negative. Depressed people are more likely to engage in negative thinking errors, called **cognitive distortions,** according to research by Aaron Beck (1967, 1976). For example, depressed people tend to reject positive experiences and focus only on the negative aspects of a situation. This negative worldview applies to their perceptions of themselves, the world, and the future. Beck believes that these people engage in such a negative view so automatically that they may not even realize their errors in thinking. Amy Tan believed that she would die, that she was worthless, that life was meaningless, and that the world could betray her at any time. Such a negative worldview probably contributed to her bouts of depression.

 **Application**

cognitive distortion a thought that tends to be pessimistic and negative

Research on the *attributions* that depressed people make further support's Beck's model. Recall from Chapter 12 that an attribution is an explanation of why an event happened (see p. 534). Depressed people tend to attribute negative environmental events to stable and global factors within themselves (Alloy, Abramson, & Francis, 1999; Peterson & Seligman, 1984). For instance, failing an exam would be attributed to the fact that a student believes that she is stupid and will always be stupid, and future failed exams should be expected. A relationship breakup is attributed to the fact that the person is not lovable and will always be unlovable. These pessimistic attributions and cognitive distortions appear to be related to depressed mood (Abramson et al., 2002; Gibb, Alloy, Abramson, Beevers, & Miller, 2004). However, it is still unclear whether these negative thinking patterns are the cause of depression or the consequence of it.

Sociocultural Factors

Sociocultural factors also must be considered when explaining mood disorders. Depression is more likely among people from lower social statuses (Blazer et al., 1994) as well as people from industrialized countries (Cross-National Collaborative Group, 1992). Explaining such differences is further complicated by the worldwide gender differences in depression. As we have noted, women are more likely to be diagnosed with depression than men. This gender difference has been attributed to a number of interrelated issues, as discussed in It's a Diverse World.

IT'S A DIVERSE WORLD

Women and Depression

Biological, psychological, and social forces that are unique to women may explain their higher vulnerability to depressive disorders when compared to men (Mazure, Keita, & Blehar, 2002). In the biological arena, we have already seen that the genetic risk of depression appears to be stronger in women than in men. Research has also investigated—over many years and many studies—the relationship between the female ovarian hormones, estrogen and progesterone, and mood in an effort to understand pathways to depression. Gender differences in depressive disorders first appear during adolescence (Compas et al., 1997) when dramatic changes in ovarian hormones occur. Pregnancy and childbirth also produce significant ovarian hormone changes that have long been suspected as links to mood changes in women. However, it is not as simple as saying ovarian hormones cause depression. Symptoms of depression do not appear to correspond to changes in levels of estrogen and progesterone across the menstrual cycle (Steiner & Born, 2000). Research has not linked depression solely to an imbalance in female hormones.

How these ovarian hormones act on neurotransmitter sensitivity and functioning may be one key to understanding depression in women. Recent research (Lu, Eshleman, Janowsky, & Bethea, 2003; Parker & Brotchie, 2004; Steiner, Dunn, & Born, 2003) has been investigating how levels of estrogen and progesterone may influence the functioning of the neurotransmitter serotonin, which plays a central role in mood. However, researchers don't yet understand the precise actions by which estrogen and progesterone influence serotonin functioning.

Psychological forces unique to women also must be considered when examining gender differences in depression. For example, women are more likely to engage in a ruminative coping style than are men (Nolen-Hoeksema, 2001; Nolen-Hoeksema et al., 1999). That is, women focus on how they feel and fret about their feelings. In contrast, men are more likely to engage in some activity to take their minds off their feelings, withdraw, or abuse drugs. As Nolen-Hoeksema et al. (1999) put it, "Women think and men drink." This adds to women's predisposition to depression. Women also are more likely to have an interpersonal orientation that puts them at risk for depression (Mazure, Keita, & Blehar, 2002). Relationships are more important to a woman's sense of self-worth than they are to a man's. As a result, women are more likely to silence their own demands in order to maintain a positive relationship and are more likely to place their needs secondary to those of others. This relational style may also predispose women to depression.

Tied to these biological and psychological factors are the social circumstances that women face. Women are at a disadvantage in society: they earn less and have less power than men. They report less satisfaction with work and family and are more likely to be victims of violence, discrimination, abuse, and poverty than are men (Klonoff, Landrine, & Campbell, 2000; Koss & Kilpatrick, 2001). Serious adverse life events such as these put women more at risk for depression. Experiencing such negative events is also more likely to foster feelings of uncontrollability and helplessness, perceptions that are intimately connected to mood disorders (Browne, 1993; Fitzgerald, 1993). These perceptions also relate to female gender-role socialization. Gender-role socialization encourages women to base their self-worth and self-esteem on the quality of relationships and discourages women from expressing anger (Helgeson, 1994; Jack, 1991). Gender roles also discourage women from being masterful, independent, and assertive and encourage them to be dependent and passive. These prescribed roles may increase their feelings of uncontrollability and helplessness (Barlow, 2002).

Understanding depression in light of these many issues becomes increasingly difficult. As a result, understanding and explaining the causes of depression for any one person requires an analysis and integration of that individual's unique biological, psychological, and sociocultural circumstances.

 Application

For both men and women, depression is a complex behavior affected by biological, psychological, and sociocultural variables. Each of us probably has some genetic vulnerability to mood disorders. For those of us with no family history of depression, this risk may be small. For others of us with a family history of mood disorders, the risk may be high. However, social and psychological factors may act to protect us from such vulnerability, or alternatively make us more likely to express this vulnerability. For Amy Tan, all the right ingredients seemed to combine to contribute to her depression. She had a family history of the disorder, she had numerous stressful life events including the death of her brother and father, she was female, and she engaged in cognitive distortions. Such a unique combination of factors may determine for each one of us whether we will become depressed. Research continues to explore the exact role these factors play. People's lives depend on it.

Let's Review!

This section outlined the major types of mood disorders—unipolar and bipolar depressive disorders. It has also reviewed common misconceptions about suicide and described our current understanding of the biological, psychological, and sociocultural factors that may underlie mood disorders. For a quick check of your understanding, answer these questions.

1. Maria has been sad for 3 weeks. She can't sleep, eat, or concentrate, and is constantly crying. She also has lost interest in her usual interests and activities. Maria's symptoms suggest she is suffering from which disorder?
   a. bipolar depression
   b. manic depression
   c. major depression
   d. cyclothymic disorder

2. Last week, Tyrone had little sleep but felt confident, exhilarated, and excessively happy. He talked fast and felt that he could accomplish anything. Now his energy has evaporated. He sleeps most of the time, feels worthless, and lacks his usual vitality. Tyrone's behavior suggests that he is suffering from which disorder?
   a. major depression
   b. bipolar depression
   c. dysthymic disorder
   d. unipolar depressive disorder

3. Research on depression has found that depressed people are more likely to:
   a. engage in negative thinking.
   b. engage in rumination.
   c. believe they have little control over events.
   d. all of the above

4. Dysthymic disorder is a less severe but more chronic form of _____.
   a. major depression
   b. bipolar disorder
   c. dysphoria
   d. apathy

5. Which of the following statements about suicide is true?
   a. People who talk of suicide will not kill themselves.
   b. Among adolescents, previous suicide attempts are a predictor of future attempts.
   c. A better mood means the risk of suicide is gone.
   d. Only depressed people commit suicide.

ANSWERS

1. c; 2. b; 3. d; 4. a; 5. b

Schizophrenic Disorders: Disintegration

> > > > > > > > > > > > > >

Schizophrenia is a chronic, disabling mental health disorder that affects roughly 1–2% of the general population worldwide (Ho, Black, & Andreasen, 2003). It involves the disintegration of one's personality.

Is schizophrenia the same thing as multiple personalities? No. Multiple personalities involve the existence of several *intact* personalities within one individual. In schizophrenia, the one personality is no longer intact, or held together and connected. If we think of an individual's personality as a related set of cognitive, emotional, perceptual, and motor behaviors, then in schizophrenia we see the disconnection between these personality elements. As these elements lose their connections with one another, the person loses his or her connection with reality. This results in impaired functioning. John Nash, whose story appeared in the beginning of the chapter, is an example of someone with schizophrenia.

LEARNING OBJECTIVE

Identify and describe the symptoms of schizophrenia, discriminate between the types of schizophrenia, and discuss our current understanding of the causes of schizophrenia.

schizophrenia   a severe disorder characterized by disturbances in thought, perceptions, emotions, and behavior

Onset, Gender, Ethnicity, and Prognosis

Symptoms of schizophrenia typically appear in adolescence or young adulthood. The later the symptoms appear, the better one's prognosis (McGlashan, 1988). For some, the symptoms come on gradually, whereas for others the symptoms appear more abruptly. Schizophrenia affects men and women with equal frequency, although it typically appears earlier in men than in women. Men tend to develop the disorder in their late teens or early 20s, and women are generally affected in their 20s or early 30s (Robins & Regier, 1991). Perhaps due to the earlier onset, men with schizophrenia tend to be more chronically impaired (Doering et al., 1998; Goldstein, 1997; Goldstein & Lewine, 2000; Ho et al., 2003). Although schizophrenia appears with equal frequency among various ethnic groups in the United States, it is more prevalent in lower socioeconomic groups (Escobar, 1993).

Symptoms of schizophrenia are often shocking and confusing to family members and friends. Most people with schizophrenia suffer throughout their adult lives, losing opportunities for careers and relationships (Harrow, Sands, Silverstein, & Goldberg, 1997). Several factors contribute to this suffering: the negative stigma that a schizophrenia diagnosis brings, the lack of public understanding, and inaccurate media portrayals of people with schizophrenia as criminally violent. Most people with schizophrenia are not violent toward others but are withdrawn and prefer to be left alone (Steadman et al., 1998). Although there currently is no cure, a diagnosis of schizophrenia does not necessarily mean progressive deterioration in functioning, as most people believe. Rather, for reasons we don't yet understand, schizophrenic symptoms and episodes tend to decline as a person ages, with 20–30% of people with schizophrenia showing only minor impairment 20 or 30 years later (Breier, Schreiber, Dyer, & Pickar, 1991; Eaton, Thara, Federman, & Tien, 1998; Jablensky, 2000). However, recovery is very much related to social factors such as economic and social support. Most people with schizophrenia continue to experience difficulties throughout their lives. John Nash's schizophrenia slowly went into remission 10 years after his initial episode, and he continues to work on mathematical theories today. His son Johnny also received a doctorate in mathematics and has been diagnosed with schizophrenia.

Symptoms of Schizophrenia

Schizophrenia may express itself in many forms depending on which domains of personality are impaired. We will review the various symptoms of schizophrenia that may be present, then describe the five subtypes of schizophrenia outlined in the *DSM-IV-TR*.

Disordered Thoughts: Loose Associations and Delusions

Thought disorder and delusions are two examples of symptoms that characterize the disorganized thinking that many people with schizophrenia experience (American Psychiatric Association, 2000). **Thought disorder** involves a lack of associations between ideas and events. Have you ever been around someone who seems to take forever to get to the point? The person may jump from one topic to the next or repeatedly go off on tangents. Magnify this behavior and you have approached the thought disorder of a person with schizophrenia. Because the ideas of people with schizophrenia lack connection, we refer to this as *loose associations*. *Poverty of content* describes their communications: their ideas seem unrelated to one another, and their speech is often characterized as a *word salad* (words seem tossed together without any apparent syntax or organization). They may be saying a lot, but what they say is not communicating anything to the sender. On several occasions, John Nash's classroom lectures were totally incoherent, suggesting the presence of thought disorder.

Application

thought disorder a symptom of schizophrenia that involves a lack of associations between one's ideas and the events that he or she is experiencing

© Jean-Michel Girand/Photo Researchers, Inc.

Schizophrenia is a severe mental disorder marked by disordered thoughts, perceptions, emotions, and/or motor behavior as depicted in this drawing by someone with schizophrenia.

Delusions are thoughts and beliefs that the thinker believes to be true but that have no basis in truth. We all carry some false beliefs, but the delusions of schizophrenia are typically less believable and more unusual. For example, *persecutory delusions* involve beliefs about being followed or watched, usually by agents of authorities such as the FBI or the government. John Nash's delusions about world conspiracies are a classic example of persecutory delusions. *Grandiose delusions* involve beliefs about being a famous or special person. For instance, a person with schizophrenia may believe that he is Julius Caesar or the president of France. People with schizophrenia may also hold *delusions of reference* (believing that others are talking about them) or *delusions of thought control* (believing that their thoughts are controlled by another person or force).

delusion   a thought or belief that a person believes to be true but in reality is not

Disordered Perceptions: Hallucinations

People who are diagnosed with schizophrenia also may experience hallucinations. **Hallucinations** represent a disorder in perception because the person sees, hears, tastes, smells, or feels something that others do not sense or perceive. In schizophrenia, hearing voices or other sounds (called *auditory hallucinations*) is the most common altered perception, followed by *visual hallucinations* (seeing things that aren't there). The hallucinations may tell the person to perform certain acts or may be frightening in nature.

hallucination   a disorder of perception in which a person senses something that does not exist in reality

Disordered Affect, or Emotion: Laughing at All the Wrong Things

Disordered emotional expression is another symptom of schizophrenia. **Affect,** in psychological terms, refers to expressing emotions. Some people with schizophrenia show *blunted affect*, or a lack of emotional expression. They appear passive and immobile. They do not respond to events in their environment with any emotion. Their speech lacks the inflection that usually communicates our mood. Others with schizophrenia may show *inappropriate affect*. They laugh at sad things, like when they are told that someone has died, or they may react with anger when they are given a gift. They do not show the emotion that we consider typical and appropriate to the event. They may laugh and giggle all the time or they may switch from one emotional extreme to another for no apparent reason.

affect   one's expressed emotion toward an action at a given time

Disordered Motor Behavior: Agitation and Stupor

Disordered behavior also may characterize some people with schizophrenia. This may take the form of unusual, odd, or repetitive behaviors and gestures. Head banging, finger flapping, or tracing a pattern over and over again are examples. Some people with schizophrenia may show an absence of all motor behaviors, remaining totally motionless and rigid for hours on end. Such behavior is referred to as a **catatonic stupor.** Alternatively, other people with schizophrenia may show **catatonic excitement** in which they are suddenly agitated, fidgety, shouting, swearing, or moving rapidly around.

catatonic stupor a disorder in motor behavior involving immobility

catatonic excitement a disorder in motor behavior involving excited agitation

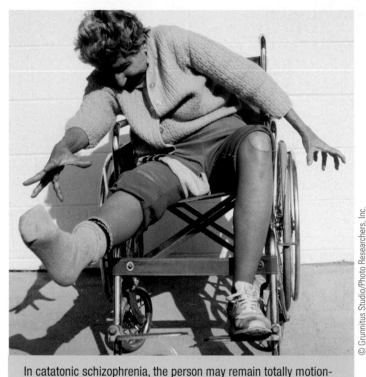

In catatonic schizophrenia, the person may remain totally motionless and rigid for hours on end in a catatonic stupor.

Types of Schizophrenia: Positive and Negative Symptoms

The *DSM-IV-TR* recognizes five subtypes of schizophrenia, classified according to which symptoms are most prevalent. The five types are paranoid, disorganized, catatonic, undifferentiated, and residual schizophrenia, described in Table 15.4 ◆.

However, more recently researchers have moved toward understanding schizophrenia in terms of *positive* and *negative symptoms* (Andreasen, Arndt, Alliger, Miller, & Flaum, 1995; Nicholson & Neufield, 1993). Imagine for a moment that behavior is represented on a number line in which zero indicates normal behavior (Figure 15.2). If we move to the negative side on this number line, there is a lessening or absence of the normal behavior. Therefore, *negative symptoms* of schizophrenia include those that represent losses in a domain of behavior. This would include the flattened affect, social withdrawal, and catatonic stupor described previously. Using the same analogy, if we move to the positive side on the same number line, we would see an increase, or addition, in a domain of behavior. Therefore, *positive symptoms* of schizophrenia include those that represent unusual perceptions, thoughts, or behaviors, including the symptoms of hallucinations and delusions discussed previously.

◆ **Table 15.4**

DSM-IV-TR **Types of Schizophrenia**

Type	Major Features
Catatonic schizophrenia	Disordered movement: total unresponsiveness to the environment (stupor) or agitated excitement
Disorganized schizophrenia	Delusions, hallucinations, incoherent thought and speech, flat or inappropriate emotions
Paranoid schizophrenia	Delusions of grandeur or persecution, hallucinations
Undifferentiated schizophrenia	Schizophrenic symptoms present but does not meet criteria for other subtypes
Residual schizophrenia	Prior schizophrenic episodes but does not currently display symptoms

Reprinted with permission from the Diagnostic and Statistical Manual of Mental Disorders, *Fourth Edition, Text Revision, Copyright 2000. American Psychiatric Association.*

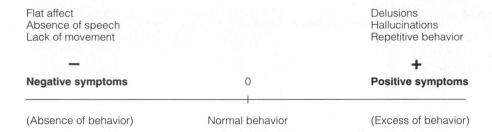

Figure 15.2 **Positive and Negative Symptoms of Schizophrenia**
Schizophrenia may express itself in positive and negative symptoms. Negative symptoms include those that represent less of a behavior than is normal, such as flat affect, absence of speech, or lack of movement. Positive symptoms represent an excess of behavior, such as delusions or hallucinations.

Although many people with schizophrenia exhibit both positive and negative symptoms, those who show predominantly positive symptoms tend to have a less severe course of schizophrenia and respond better to medication. For instance, positive symptoms predominate in *paranoid schizophrenia*, which may partly explain why people with paranoid schizophrenia tend to have a more favorable prognosis and better future functioning compared to those with other types of schizophrenia (Fenton, & McGlashan, 1994; Kendler, McGuire, Gruenberg, & Walsh, 1994). John Nash's schizophrenia unfolded in precisely this manner. Diagnosed with paranoid schizophrenia, he showed mostly positive symptoms, responded well to medication, and although not the same man he once was, has returned to a level of normal functioning. Such findings have led researchers to believe that positive symptoms of schizophrenia may have a different cause than negative symptoms. So let's look at our current understanding of the development of schizophrenia.

Explaining Schizophrenia: Genetics, the Brain, and the Environment

What causes schizophrenia? To date, biological factors account for the strongest evidence in the development of schizophrenia, although environmental factors must also be considered. It is likely that environmental conditions interact with biological factors to make a person either more or less susceptible to the illness. Biological research has focused on three main areas: genetics, brain abnormalities, and the malfunctioning of specific neurotransmitters in the brain. Environmental research has focused on prenatal and development factors, as well as the role of family and the environment.

A Strong Genetic Factor

Family, twin, and adoption studies have routinely demonstrated a high heritability of schizophrenia (NIMH Genetics Workgroup, 1998; Parnas et al., 1993). As Figure 15.3 shows, although the incidence of schizophrenia in the general population is 1–2%, the more genetically similar a person is to someone with schizophrenia, the more likely he or she will also develop the disorder. In identical-twin pairs, if one identical twin develops schizophrenia, the other twin has about a 48% chance of developing the disorder. However, in fraternal twins (who are not genetically identical), the probability is only 14%. Adoption studies show a similar trend (Heston, 1966; Kety et al., 1994; Tienari et al., 2003). Adopted children who have biological parents with schizophrenia are 10 times more likely to develop the disorder than are adopted children whose biological parents are not diagnosed with schizophrenia.

Figure 15.3 **Risk of Schizophrenia and Genetic Relatedness**

The incidence of schizophrenia in the general population is 1–2%. However, the more closely one is genetically related to a person with schizophrenia, the higher the risk of developing the disorder. *Reprinted by permission of Irving I. Gottesman.*

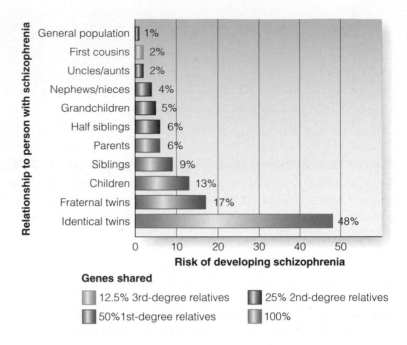

Yet despite these results, it is unlikely that a single gene is responsible for the illness, otherwise the rates would be higher. Research has therefore moved toward exploring several genes that may work together to increase a person's vulnerability to schizophrenia. Preliminary research suggests a strong connection between a location on Chromosome 1 and schizophrenia, and a weaker connection also has been found with a location on Chromosome 13 (Berry, Jobanputra, & Pal, 2003; Brzustowicz, Hodgkinson, Chow, Honer, & Bassett, 2000; McDonald & Murphy, 2003). Other research has focused on uncovering the genes that may be related to specific symptoms of schizophrenia such as hallucinations or delusions (Tsuang, Stone, & Faraone, 2001). These relatively recent results will need to be replicated to confirm their validity.

The Brain: Neurotransmitters and Structural Abnormalities

A second area of research on the development of schizophrenia looks at neurotransmitters. It was originally believed that schizophrenia was caused by excess activity of the neurotransmitter dopamine in the brain. The drugs that are prescribed for schizophrenia, called *phenothiazines*, reduce dopamine activity in the brain and are typically more effective in reducing the positive symptoms of schizophrenia. However, many people with schizophrenia do not respond to treatment with phenothiazines. One of the newest drugs to be used to treat schizophrenia, called *clozapine*, does not block the same dopamine receptors as the phenothiazines, clearly indicating that dopamine is involved, but in a more complex way (Conklin & Iacono, 2002). Other research suggests that excess dopamine activity in a certain area of the brain is responsible for the positive symptoms of schizophrenia. Low levels of dopamine, particularly in the frontal lobe, are linked to the negative symptoms of schizophrenia (Cohen & Servan-Schreiber, 1992; Davis, Kahn, Ko, & Davidson, 1991). Furthermore, recent research suggests neurotransmitters other than dopamine are linked to schizophrenia, namely serotonin and glutamate (Bondolfi et al., 1998; Faustman, Bardgett, Faull, Pfefferbaum, & Csernansky, 1999; Tsai & Coyle, 2002). Obviously, the relationship between neurotransmitters and schizophrenia remains a complex one.

Abnormalities in certain brain structures have also been investigated for their links to schizophrenia. The most consistent abnormality that has been found in patients with schizophrenia is enlarged ventricles (Andreasen, Swayze, Flaum, & Alliger, 1990; Lieberman et al., 2001; Suddath, Christison, Torrey, & Casanova, 1990; Zorrilla et al., 1997). A ventricle is a fluid-filled cavity in the brain. Enlarged ventricles reduce the overall size of the brain, which in turn may contribute to the development of schizophrenia (Wright et al., 2000). In people with schizophrenia who predominantly show negative symptoms, researchers speculate that an unusually small or inactive frontal lobe is responsible (Andreasen, 2001; Crespo-Facorro et al., 2001; Kim et al., 2000). You will recall from Chapter 2 that the frontal area is responsible for language, emotions, and social behavior (see p. 77). People who exhibit negative symptoms of schizophrenia (flat affect, social withdrawal, and catatonic stupor) show a reduction in these behaviors. For those people with positive symptoms of schizophrenia, the temporal lobe and limbic system have been implicated as dysfunctional brain areas. Recall that both the temporal lobe and the limbic system play an important role in memory. This may account for the thought disorder, delusions, and hallucinations that people with schizophrenia with positive symptoms exhibit (Andreasen, Rezai, Alliger, & Swayze, 1992; Cannon, 1996; Gur, Cowell, Turetsky et al., 1998; Lawrie & Abukmeil, 1998).

Prenatal and Developmental Factors

How do people with schizophrenia develop these brain abnormalities? These brain abnormalities have been linked to birth complications and the mother's exposure to prenatal viruses (Cannon, 1998; Goldstein et al., 2000; Jones & Cannon, 1998; Mednick, Machon, Huttunen, & Bonett, 1988; Mednick et al., 1998), although many other causes could exist. Some researchers propose that schizophrenia may be a developmental disorder resulting from abnormal neural development during the prenatal period (Murray, O'Callaghan, Castle, & Lewis, 1992). A genetic predisposition to schizophrenia interacts with prenatal environmental agents such as a maternal virus or poor nutrition, causing changes in normal brain development. Then, as the brain reaches maturation (during adolescence), a natural trimming away of brain synapses occurs. It is hypothesized that in people with schizophrenia, the brain trims away too many synapses, resulting in the expression of the disorder in the teenage years. Schizophrenic symptoms are particularly likely to appear if the person has a strong genetic disposition, or if environmental circumstances have encouraged the expression of the disorder in those with even a mild genetic link (McGlashan & Hoffman, 2000).

The Role of Family and Environment

What environmental and psychological factors appear to contribute to the onset and course of schizophrenia? Two critical factors appear to be family support and exposure to stressful living conditions. Studies on the families of people with schizophrenia have found that the quality of family communications and interactions may either encourage or discourage the onset of schizophrenia in people who are genetically at high risk. The quality of family interactions may also influence whether future psychotic episodes are triggered. Families that are critical, harsh, hostile, intrusive, and poor communicators may make a high-risk person more susceptible to the disorder (Butzlaff & Hooley, 1998; Hooley & Hiller, 1998). Chronic stress from living a high-risk or low-income lifestyle also appears to influence future relapses (Dohrenwend et al., 1987; Norman & Malla, 1993). Although it appears that our family and lifestyle does not cause schizophrenia, they are especially critical factors in people's susceptibility to the disorder, factors that must be taken into account when designing prevention or treatment programs for those with schizophrenia.

Let's Review!

In this section we described the symptoms and different types of schizophrenia, and outlined our current understanding of the biological, psychological, and sociocultural factors that play a role in its development. For a quick check of your understanding, answer these questions.

1. Schizophrenia has been linked most strongly to which neurotransmitter?
   a. dopamine
   b. GABA
   c. serotonin
   d. acetylcholine

2. People with _____ schizophrenia show predominantly positive symptoms, such as delusions and hallucinations.
   a. disorganized
   b. catatonic
   c. paranoid
   d. undifferentiated

3. The most consistent brain abnormality found among people with schizophrenia is _____.

a. a small frontal lobe
b. a small temporal lobe
c. enlarged ventricles
d. an enlarged frontal lobe

4. If you claim that you *see* George Washington it is a _____; if you believe that you *are* George Washington it is a _____.
   a. delusion; hallucination
   b. hallucination; delusion
   c. thought disorder; delusion
   d. delusion; thought disorder

5. Loose associations, poverty of content, and word salad characterize which symptom of schizophrenia?
   a. thought disorder
   b. catatonic stupor
   c. delusions
   d. flat affect

ANSWERS

1. a; 2. c; 3. c; 4. b; 5. a

LEARNING OBJECTIVE < < < < < < < <

Describe the nature of dissociative and somatoform disorders.

Application >>

dissociative disorder a disorder marked by a loss of awareness of some part of one's self or one's surroundings that seriously interferes with the person's ability to function

dissociative identity disorder (DID) a disorder in which two or more personalities coexist within the same individual; formerly called multiple personality disorder

Dissociative and Somatoform Disorders: Personalities and Illnesses

Dissociative and somatoform disorders are quite rare in the general population, but often are of the most interest to students. To *dissociate* means to break or pull apart. Consequently, the **dissociative disorders** involve a splitting off of our conscious state. We lose awareness of some part of our self, our surroundings, or what is going on around us. Mild dissociative experiences are common (Aderibigbe, Bloch, & Walker, 2001; Ross, 1997). For instance, have you ever driven somewhere and on arrival did not remember driving there? Have you ever missed a part of a conversation but can tell from the speaker's demeanor that you appeared to have been listening the whole time? Have you ever appeared attentive in class while you were daydreaming about your plans for the weekend? All of these are common everyday dissociative experiences.

However, when loss of awareness becomes more extreme, a diagnosis of a dissociative disorder may apply. It is believed that such extreme dissociation results from repressing, or excluding from consciousness, emotional pain or trauma. Table 15.5 ◆ provides a brief description of the dissociative disorders listed in the *DSM-IV-TR*. We will describe one of the more controversial dissociative disorders, called dissociative identity disorder, formerly known as multiple personality disorder, in detail in this section.

Dissociative Identity Disorder: Multiple Personalities

Dissociative identity disorder (DID), formerly called multiple personality disorder (MPD), involves the existence of two or more separate personalities in the same individual (American Psychiatric Association, 2000). Although the prevalence of dissocia-

◆ **Table 15.5**

Types of Dissociative Disorders

Disorder	Major Features
Dissociative identity disorder	Separate multiple personalities in the same individual.
Dissociative fugue	Person assumes a new identity with amnesia of previous identity.
Dissociative amnesia	Memory loss of important personal information. Not due to organic problems or brain injury.
Depersonalization disorder	Frequent episodes in which the person feels detached from own mental state or body.
Dissociative trance disorder	Temporary alterations in one's state of consciousness or loss of personal identity that causes significant distress and is not accepted as a normal part of a cultural or religious practice.

tive identity disorder is rare, it has become well known through the media. Two famous movies, *The Three Faces of Eve* and *Sybil*, and more recently a book, *When Rabbit Howls*, detail the experiences of three women suffering from DID. Such accounts attest to the public's fascination with this disorder.

The separate personalities—referred to as *alters* (for alternate personalities)—may or may not be known to the "core," or "host," personality—the person who asks for treatment. Each personality has its own perceptions, thoughts, mannerisms, speech characteristics, and gestures. Each alter appears to have a specific function. For example, one alter may arise to deal with romantic relationships, whereas another alter deals with academic work. The alter personalities may be of different ages, gender, or ethnicities. Some alters may even be animals or mythical creatures such as dragons. The majority of people diagnosed with DID are women (American Psychiatric Association, 2000).

Frequent blackouts or episodes of amnesia are common in people with dissociative identity disorder. They may notice money missing from their bank accounts that they don't remember spending or find objects in their home that they do not recognize. Self-mutilating behavior is also common in people with this disorder. They may repeatedly burn or cut themselves, and have a history of suicide attempts (Ross, 1997). Oftentimes they have previously been diagnosed with other disorders such as depression, posttraumatic stress disorder, substance abuse disorder, or schizophrenia, especially if they have reported hearing voices (Ellason, Ross, & Fuchs, 1996). One striking similarity among people with dissociative identity disorders is their backgrounds. Almost all have experienced chronic, horrific childhood physical or sexual abuse at the hands of family members (Coons, 1994; Ellason et al., 1996; Putnam, Guroff, Silberman, & Barban, 1986). Many clinicians feel that in an attempt to deal with such trauma, these people defensively dissociate, or repress, their true selves. They develop alter personalities that can protect them from experiencing such events in life or in memory. Research has found that people with dissociative identity disorder have a high level of hypnotic susceptibility (Kihlstrom, Glisky, & Angiulo, 1994). Thus, the ability to dissociate may have become an effective coping mechanism early in life (see p. 174 and Table 13.3).

Some researchers and clinicians question the validity of the dissociative identity disorder. There has been a great increase in the number of reported cases since 1980 (American Psychiatric Association, 2000). Only one third of a sample of U.S. psychiatrists believed it should have been included in the *DSM-IV* (Pope, Oliva, Hudson,

Bodkin, & Gruber, 1999). Verifying the claims of amnesia and blackouts are difficult, and people with dissociative identity disorder have already often been diagnosed with other psychological disorders (Ellason & Ross, 1997; Kluft, 1999). Some believe that dissociative identity disorder may represent an extreme form of posttraumatic stress disorder (Butler, Duran, Jasiukaitis, Koopman, & Spiegel, 1996). Future research may help us better understand the nature of this disorder.

Somatoform Disorders: Hypochondriasis, or Doctor, I'm Sure I'm Sick

somatoform disorder a disorder marked by physical complaints for which there is no physical cause

Somatic means related to the body. The **somatoform disorders** involve physical complaints for which there is no physical cause. The physical symptoms are real to the person, but physicians can find no medical reason why they are experiencing such symptoms. For example, a person may complain of constant hip pain. Numerous medical tests are completed, but there is no apparent physical cause for the hip ache. Because no physical cause can be found, it is assumed that psychological distress underlies the physical problem. Table 15.6 ◆ describes the somatoform disorders listed in the *DSM-IV-TR*. Our discussion in this section will focus on one of them, hypochondriasis.

hypochondriasis a somatoform disorder in which the person believes he or she has a disease, without any evident physical basis

In the somatoform disorder **hypochondriasis,** a person believes that he or she has a serious medical disease despite evidence to the contrary (American Psychiatric Association, 2000). Many of us tend to think that someone in our family is a hypochondriac because that person frequently complains about physical ailments. However, people with hypochondriasis are convinced that they have a disease, not just one or two specific symptoms. Yet the hypochondriac does not always report experiencing the physical symptoms of the disease. People with hypochondriasis may undergo extensive medical testing by several doctors to confirm the existence of their disease. When their doctors suggest that they may have a psychological problem, hypochondriacs are likely to seek out another physician rather than seek psychological treatment. People with hypochondriasis often also have a family history of depression or anxiety (Escobar et al., 1998).

◆ **Table 15.6**

Types of Somatoform Disorders

Disorder	Major Features
Conversion disorder	Loss of functioning in some part of the body, but no physical cause can be found.
Somatization disorder	Long history of physical complaints affecting several areas of the body. The person has sought medical attention, but no physical cause can be found.
Pain disorder	Long history of pain complaints. The person has sought medical attention, but no physical cause can be found.
Hypochondriasis	Persistent worry over having a physical disease. The person frequently seeks medical attention, but no physical disease can be found.
Body dysmorphic disorder	Extreme preoccupation and obsession with a part of the body that is believed to be defective. The person makes elaborate attempts to conceal or change the body part.

Let's Review!

This section described the nature of the dissociative and somatoform disorders. For a quick check of your understanding, answer these questions.

1. Dissociative disorders involve:
   a. the disintegration of one's personality.
   b. physical symptoms without any physical cause.
   c. a splitting off of one's conscious mind.
   d. a numbness or paralysis in some part of the body.

2. Alphonsia has recurrent abdominal pain. Her doctors have conducted numerous medical tests and can find no physical cause for her symptom. Alphonsia appears to have a _____.

   a. personality disorder   c. dissociative disorder
   b. somatoform disorder   d. depressive disorder

3. Dissociative disorders are believed to be the result of:
   a. repressed psychological distress.
   b. faulty cognitions.
   c. hormonal deficits.
   d. all of the above

ANSWERS:
1. c; 2. b; 3. a

Personality Disorders: Maladaptive Patterns of Behavior

Recall from our earlier discussion on the DSM model that the **personality disorders** are represented on Axis II (see Table 15.1). They consist of lifelong or long-standing patterns of malfunctioning. All of us have personality "quirks." Some people may be excessively neat. Others may be somewhat suspicious and mistrustful of others. Still others may appear to be conceited or selfish. However, these traits do not necessarily qualify someone for a personality disorder. In personality disorders, the person's behavior (1) is maladaptive to oneself or others and (2) has been stable across a long period of time and across many situations, typically evident in childhood or adolescence. Individuals with personality disorders also can be diagnosed with any of the clinical disorders previously discussed, and they typically seek treatment for these clinical disorders or because someone else has a problem with their behavior and encourages them to undergo therapy. Individuals with a personality disorder often don't see a problem with their behavior and, therefore, seldom seek treatment on their own. The list of personality disorders is long, and space considerations prohibit a discussion of all of them, but we give a brief description of the *DSM* personality disorders in Table 15.7 ◆. Here we will confine our discussion to two: antisocial personality disorder and borderline personality disorder.

Antisocial Personality Disorder: Charming and Dangerous

People who are impulsive and disregard the rights of others without showing any remorse or guilt are diagnosed with **antisocial personality disorder** (American Psychiatric Association, 2000). A person with this disorder is commonly referred to as a psychopath, or sociopath. People who have antisocial personalities are callous, malicious, blame others for their problems, and frequently have difficulty maintaining social relationships. They are also able to be superficially charming and sociable, typically

LEARNING OBJECTIVE

Describe the nature of personality disorders.

≪ Application

personality disorder a disorder marked by maladaptive behavior that has been stable across a long period of time and across many situations

antisocial personality disorder a personality disorder marked by a pattern of disregard for and violation of the rights of others with no remorse or guilt for one's actions

◆ **Table 15.7**

Types of Personality Disorders

Disorder	Major Feature
Paranoid personality disorder	Excessive suspicion and mistrust of others.
Schizoid personality disorder	Lack of desire to form close relationships with others. Emotional detachment and coldness toward others.
Schizotypal personality disorder	Considered a mild version of schizophrenia because the individual shows inappropriate social and emotional behavior, and unusual thoughts and speech.
Antisocial personality disorder	Chronic pattern of impulsive behavior; violates rights of others and does not show remorse or guilt for actions.
Borderline personality disorder	Instability in mood, self-concept, and interpersonal relationships.
Histrionic personality disorder	Intense need for attention. Always wants to be the center of attention. Excessively dramatic behavior. Rapidly changing moods.
Narcissistic personality disorder	Preoccupation with own sense of importance and view of self as above others. Typically ignores the needs and wants of others.
Avoidant personality disorder	Intense and chronic anxiety over being negatively evaluated by others so avoids social interactions.
Dependent personality disorder	Excessive need to be cared for by others. Denies own thoughts and feelings and clings to others.
Obsessive-compulsive personality disorder	Pattern of rigid and perfectionistic behavior. High self-control and emotionally restricted. Maintains an orderly routine and experiences anxiety when routine is disrupted.

in order to manipulate others to do what they want. Such antisocial behavior has often been present since childhood or adolescence. Serial murderers such as Charles Manson, Gary Gilmore, Andrew Cunanan, and Ted Bundy come to mind when thinking about the antisocial personality disorder. It is one of the most common personality disorders, and men are five times more likely than women to be diagnosed with this disorder (Cloninger, Bayon, & Przybeck, 1997).

People with antisocial personality disorder are more often sent to prison than to treatment. Does this mean that all criminals have antisocial personality disorder? No. Although antisocial behavior is highly correlated with criminal behavior, not all criminals are antisocial. One of the key features distinguishing the two is the lack of remorse and guilt for one's actions. Some thieves can commit armed robbery yet afterward regret their actions. The antisocial person does not experience such regret or remorse. People with antisocial personality disorder may not be violent. They may be "con artists," and more of them may live outside of prison than in it. They may function successfully in business, politics, or entertainment fields.

What causes antisocial personality disorder? Some research suggests biological factors. Twin studies, adoption studies, and family studies support a genetic influence

(Carey & Goldman, 1997; Cloninger & Gottesman, 1987). For example, family members of people with antisocial personality disorder have higher rates of the disorder than the general population. Other research suggests low levels of the neurotransmitter serotonin (Moffitt et al., 1998), deficits in brain areas that control impulsivity and decision making (Henry & Moffitt, 1997), and low arousal of the peripheral and central nervous systems (Raine, 1997; Raine, Lencz, Bihrle, LaCasse, & Colletti, 2000). However, psychological and social variables cannot be ruled out. People with antisocial personality disorder often experienced conflict-filled childhoods. Their parents may be neglectful, inconsistent in discipline, harsh, or hostile. As a result, they often learned to expect such treatment from others and adopted a mistrustful and aggressive stance toward others (Crick & Dodge, 1994; Dishion & Patterson, 1997; Tremblay, Pihl, Vitaro, & Dobkin, 1994).

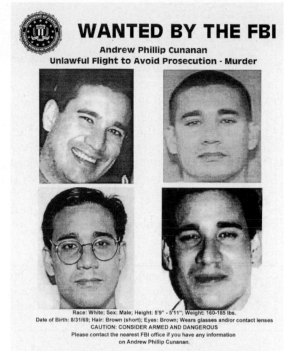

Andrew Cunanan murdered famous clothes designer Gianni Versace after killing several others. He was described by many as a charming and bright young man.

Borderline Personality Disorder: Living on Your Fault Line

Borderline personality disorder (BPD) is characterized by instability in moods, interpersonal relationships, self-image, and behavior (American Psychiatric Association, 2000). This key feature of instability often disrupts their relationships, career, and identity. Their unstable emotions result in intense bouts of anger, depression, or anxiety that may occur for hours or for a day. Their unstable self-concepts are reflected in extreme insecurity at some times and by exaggerated feelings of importance at other times. This instability may prompt frequent changes in goals, jobs, friendships, and values because people with borderline personalities lack a clear definition of themselves. They have little idea of who they are. Their interpersonal relationships also are characterized by instability. They may admire, idealize, and cling to loved ones at first, but when conflict occurs, feelings of abandonment and rejection surface, and their feelings quickly turn toward anger and dislike. They then seek out new friends or loved ones, and the cycle repeats itself. People with this disorder often feel unworthy, bad, or empty inside. At times of extreme insecurity and depression, self-injury and suicide attempts are common (Black, Blum, Pfohl, & Hale, 2004; Soloff, Lis, Kelly, Cornelius, & Ulrich, 1994). People with borderline personality disorder are often diagnosed with other clinical disorders such as depression, substance abuse, or anxiety (Weissman, 1993). It is estimated that approximately 2% of the population will develop BPD at some point in their lives, and it is diagnosed more often in young women than in men (Swartz, Blazer, George, & Winfield, 1990). Extensive mental health services are often needed to treat people with BPD.

borderline personality disorder (BPD) a personality disorder marked by a pattern of instability in mood, relationships, self-image, and behavior

As we saw with antisocial personality disorder, research on borderline personality disorder has focused on biological, psychological, and social factors. Low levels of serotonin are related to impulsive behaviors (Siever & Koenigsberg, 2000; Weston & Siever, 1993). Difficulty in regulating emotions may be related to abnormal brain functioning (Davidson, Jackson, & Kalin, 2000; Davidson, Putnam, & Larson, 2000). However, many people with borderline personality disorder report a history of abuse, neglect, or separation as young children, making environment a probable factor (Zanarini & Frankenburg, 1997). For example, in one recent study (Zanarini, 2000), 40–71% of borderline patients had reported being sexually abused. They are also more likely to be victims of rape and other violent crimes. Such social stressors may impede normal attachment patterns, identity development, and the ability to express appropriate emotions.

Let's Review!

This section described the nature of personality disorders, in particular antisocial and borderline personality disorders. As a quick check of your understanding, answer these questions.

1. Felicia is extremely insecure and lacks a clear sense of identity. She often clings to new friends and then hates them 2 weeks later. She has an intense fear of abandonment and rejection. Felicia's behavior best fits which personality disorder?

   a. narcissistic   c. borderline

   b. antisocial   d. paranoid

2. Marco seems charming and intelligent, but he always blames others for his problems. He frequently disregards the rights of others without showing any guilt or remorse. Marco's behavior best fits which personality disorder?

   a. narcissistic   c. borderline

   b. antisocial   d. paranoid

3. Personality disorders:

   a. do not coexist with clinical disorders such as depression or anxiety.

   b. generally appear in early or middle adulthood.

   c. are stable patterns of malfunctioning.

   d. do not pose any threats to others.

ANSWERS:

1. c; 2. b; 3. c

Are You Getting the Big Picture?

This chapter outlined 6 of the 13 major categories of mental health disorders listed in the *DSM-IV-TR.* Each disorder meets the criteria of abnormality endorsed at the beginning of the chapter—inability to function. Although research continues into the exact origins of each disorder, we have seen that in many cases, a person's biological vulnerability appears to combine with psychological and sociocultural factors—learning experiences, thinking patterns, family interactions, cultural attitudes, gender roles—to trigger the onset of the disorder. Such an interaction of variables is helpful in understanding why people like Howard Hughes, John Nash, and Amy Tan behaved the way they did.

Studying mental health is quite complex. We are looking at a continuum of behavior representing both normal and abnormal behavior. We all feel blue from time to time or may have a certain trait of OCD such as straightening our clothes or our rooms frequently. However, this does not necessarily indicate that we have a mental health disorder. These are normal dimensions of emotional expression. However, when a person's behavior crosses a subjective threshold such that the behavior now interferes with his or her ability to function, then a diagnosis of a mental health disorder may be appropriate.

If you plan on a career in any of the helping professions, this information will be especially helpful to your job performance. Physicians, nurses, teachers, social workers, police officers, counselors, as well as clinicians often rely on their knowledge of mental health when dealing with people in their jobs. The information in this chapter will also assist you in mastering the material of the next chapter, as we explore the different therapies psychologists and psychiatrists use to treat mental health disorders.

STUDYING THE CHAPTER

Key Terms

medical model (659)

Diagnostic and Statistical Manual of Mental Disorders (DSM) (663)

anxiety disorder (667)

panic disorder (668)

agoraphobia (668)

phobic disorder (668)

specific phobia (668)

social phobia (669)

obsession (669)

compulsion (669)

obsessive-compulsive disorder (669)

posttraumatic stress disorder (670)

generalized anxiety disorder (672)

mood disorder (675)

major depression (675)

dysphoria (675)

dysthymic disorder (676)

bipolar disorder (676)

mania (676)

cyclothymic disorder (677)

learned helplessness (680)

ruminative coping style (681)

cognitive distortion (681)

schizophrenia (683)

thought disorder (684)

delusion (685)

hallucination (685)

affect (685)

catatonic stupor (686)

catatonic excitement (686)

dissociative disorder (690)

dissociative identity disorder (690)

somatoform disorder (692)

hypochondriasis (692)

personality disorder (693)

antisocial personality disorder (693)

borderline personality disorder (695)

Test Yourself!

Concept Check

Test your knowledge of the chapter concepts by completing each of the following sentences with the correct term. For a more comprehensive review, visit the book Web site (http://psychology.wadsworth.com/pastorinole/) for online quizzes, flashcards, crosswords, and Internet links.

_D___ **1.** A disorder characterized by a persistent fear and avoidance of a specific object or situation.

_____ **2.** A disorder characterized by physical complaints for which there are no physical causes.

_I___ **3.** A disorder characterized by excessive anxiety, worry, and difficulty in controlling such worries.

_C___ **4.** A disorder in which a person experiences dysphoria, sleeplessness, weight loss, low self-esteem, and inability to concentrate for at least 3 weeks.

_____ **5.** A disorder characterized by delusions, hallucinations, incoherent thought and speech, and inappropriate emotions.

_____ **6.** A disorder characterized by an extreme splitting off of one's conscious state.

_____ **7.** A disorder characterized by an irrational fear of being negatively evaluated by others in a social situation.

_____ **8.** A disorder characterized by impulsivity and disregard for the rights of others without showing any remorse or guilt.

_____ **9.** A less severe but more chronic form of bipolar disorder.

_____ **10.** A disorder characterized by instability in moods, interpersonal relationships, self-image, and behavior.

a. cyclothymic disorder

b. dissociative disorder

c. borderline personality disorder

d. specific phobic disorder

e. major depressive disorder

f. social phobic disorder

g. somatoform disorder

h. antisocial personality disorder

i. generalized anxiety disorder

j. schizophrenia

Answers:

1. d; 2. g; 3. i; 4. e; 5. j; 6. b; 7. f; 8. h; 9. a; 10. c

Critical Thinking About the Chapter

1. Create a facility that would best address the treatment and care of individuals with schizophrenia.

2. What behaviors do you believe would be considered abnormal in every culture and society (present and past) and in all situations? Are these behaviors symptoms of any of the disorders discussed in this chapter? How does this help or hinder psychologists' understanding of abnormality?

3. Which disorders do you believe people would be least likely to seek treatment for, and why? Which disorders do you believe people would be most likely to seek treatment for, and why? Would the answers change for different ethnicities? Different age groups? Men or women? Why, or why not?

4. After reading this chapter, what factors appear to be most linked to mental illness? Is there anything that can be done to remove such factors from our society?

Applying Psychology. Which mental health disorders do you think you are most at risk for, and why? Be sure to consider biological, psychological, and sociocultural factors in formulating your response.

Critical Thinking for Integration

1. How may memory processes (Chapter 6) be linked to the development of anxiety disorders?

2. How may gender (discussed in Chapters 9 and 11) explain the gender differences in the prevalence of anxiety and depressive disorders? Describe what might be the attributional process (Chapter 12) for individual success and failure of a person with an anxiety or depressive disorder.

How might these individuals judge the behavior of others? Provide examples to support your ideas.

3. Refer to the section on research methods in Chapter 1. How might various types of schizophrenia in one sample complicate the conclusions of the study? How could more valid research on the origin of schizophrenia be obtained? What might make your solution difficult?

Chapter Study Resources

Suggested Readings

1. Tan, A. (2003). *The opposite of fate: A book of musings.* New York: Putnam.
A collection of nonfiction writings centered on Amy Tan's life experiences that have deeply affected her psychologically and physically.

2. Barlow, D. H. (2002). *Anxiety and its disorders: The nature and treatment of anxiety and panic* (2nd ed.). New York: Guilford Press.
David Barlow, Professor of Psychology and Director of Clinical Training Programs and Director of the Center for Anxiety and Related Disorders at Boston University, examines the origins of anxiety and panic and the roles that each plays in normal and abnormal functioning.

3. Marsh, D. T. & Dickens, R. M. (1997). *How to cope with mental illness in your family: A self-care guide for offspring and parents.* New York: Putnam Books.
This book discusses the effects that mental illness can have on a patient's family and how to deal with them.

4. For additional readings, explore InfoTrac College Edition, your online library of archived journal articles and periodicals. Go to http://www.infotrac-college .com/wadsworth and enter the passcode from the card that came with your book. For this chapter, search using these keywords:

posttraumatic stress disorder

gender and depression

ruminative coping

schizophrenia

borderline personality disorder

Web Links for Further Study

Additional information on some of the chapter's contents can be found at the following Web sites:

1. The National Institute of Mental Health site provides information and resources on many of the mental health disorders discussed in the chapter.
http://www.nimh.nih.gov/

2. The Mental Health Net allows users to search for a mental health specialist in their area and for their needs.
http://www.mentalhealth.net

3. The Mental Health Infosource site provides education, resources, and links on mental health. It also includes an A-to-Z disorders index.
http://www.mhsource.com/

4. The Center for Mental Health Services sponsored by the Substance Abuse and Mental Health Services Administration features information on children's mental health, suicide prevention, managing anxiety, and more.
http://www.mentalhealth.org

5. Suicide Awareness: Voices of Education seeks to educate the general public about clinical depression and suicide prevention.
http://www.save.org

Student Study Guide

To help organize your learning, work through Chapter 15 of the *What Is Psychology? Student Study Guide*. The study guide includes learning objectives, a chapter summary, fill-in review, key terms, a practice test, and other learning activities.

Psychology Now™

PsychologyNow is a Web-based, personalized study system that provides you with a pretest and a posttest for each chapter, quizzes you by chapter, and provides a personalized study plan, pointing you to elements in the text or in individual learning modules that will help you to achieve 80% mastery. Check out the learning module that relates to this chapter: disorder symptoms.

PsychNow CD-ROM, Version 2.0

Go to the PsychNow CD-ROM for further study of the concepts in this chapter. The CD-ROM includes learning modules with videos, animations, and quizzes, as well as simulations of psychological phenomena. Each module follows a consistent Explore, Lesson, and Apply structure that allows you to experience the concept or principle, learn more about it, and then apply it. You and your friends can participate in a team-based Quiz Game that makes learning fun. Learning modules include: 7c. Abnormality and Psychopathology; 7d. Nonpsychotic, Psychotic, and Affective Disorders.

What Are Psychological Disorders and How Can We Understand Them?

Psychologists use several criteria to define abnormal behavior such as statistical infrequency, violation of social norms, and personal distress. However, abnormality is best explained when a behavior interferes with a person's ability to function.

PERSPECTIVES TO EXPLAIN ABNORMAL BEHAVIOR

• Supernatural theories suggest that evil forces and demons cause abnormal behavior.

• Biological theories suggest that mental illness is a disease resulting from organic causes.

• Psychological theories propose that underlying psychological factors lead to abnormal behavior.
— Psychoanalytic theory emphasizes unconscious conflicts.
— Social learning theories look at conditioning processes, observational learning, or direct experience to explain abnormal behavior.
— Cognitive theories suggest that mental processes cause abnormal behavior.
— Humanistic theories examine how a distorted sense of self and reality leads to abnormal behavior.

• Sociocultural theories suggest that environmental stressors and social factors such as age, race, gender, and culture influence abnormal behavior.

• Psychological disorders result from a combination of biological, psychological, and social factors. They do not have just one cause.

THE *DSM* MODEL

• *The Diagnostic and Statistical Manual of Mental Disorders*, currently in its fourth edition, is an atheoretical, multiaxial system that details specific criteria for a diagnosis of a mental health disorder.

• The reliability and validity of Axis I clinical disorders are very high, but the reliability of Axis II personality disorders is low, calling into question their validity.

• There are negative effects of labeling someone with a mental health disorder as it may encourage a person to behave in a way that is consistent with the disorder.

ANXIETY DISORDERS

• Anxiety disorders include physical, cognitive, emotional, and behavioral components.

• Panic disorder is characterized by recurrent panic attacks or the persistent fear of having a panic attack.

• A persistent fear of a specific object or of being negatively evaluated by others comprises phobic disorder.

• In obsessive-compulsive disorder a person experiences recurrent obsessions or compulsions that cannot be controlled.

• Posttraumatic stress disorder develops after exposure to a terrifying event. The person experiences distressing memories, nightmares, thoughts, or flashback episodes of the event that interferes with his or her ability to function.

• Generalized anxiety disorder is characterized by excessive anxiety, worry, and difficulty in controlling such worries.

• Potential causes of anxiety disorders include:
— Biological factors such as genetics, neurotransmitter imbalances, and abnormal brain functioning
— Psychological factors such as conditioning, reinforcement, unconscious conflicts, maladaptive assumptions and cognitions, and an unrealistic self-image
— Social factors such as rapid social change, previous trauma or stress, low social status, and gender.

MOOD DISORDERS

• Mood disorders are characterized by a significant change in one's emotional state over an extended period of time.

• In unipolar depressive disorders such as Major Depressive disorder and Dysthymic disorder, the person experiences extreme or chronic sadness or apathy.

• The bipolar depressive disorders such as Bipolar Depression and Cyclothymic Disorder, involve a shift in mood between two states: sadness and mania.

• Potential causes of mood disorders include
— Biological factors such as genetics, neurotransmitter imbalances, and hormones
— Psychological factors such as unresolved issues of loss and rejection, low positive reinforcement, learned helplessness, ruminative coping style, cognitive distortions, and pessimistic attributions
— Social factors such as lower social status, stressful life events, and gender.

SCHIZOPHRENIC DISORDERS

• Schizophrenia is a chronic, disabling mental health disorder characterized by disordered thoughts (delusions, thought disorder), perception (hallucinations), emotion, and/or motor behavior (catatonic stupor and catatonic excitement).

• Types of schizophrenia include paranoid, disorganized, catatonic, undifferentiated, and residual.

• Positive symptoms of schizophrenia include excesses of a behavior whereas negative symptoms include those that represent losses in a domain of behavior.

• Potential causes of schizophrenia emphasize biological factors such as genetics, dopamine activity, and abnormal brain functioning. However, psychological factors in the form of family support and interactions, and social factors such as stressful living conditions may influence the course of the disorder.

DISSOCIATIVE AND SOMATOFORM DISORDERS

• Dissociative disorders are characterized by the splitting off of one's conscious mind.

• Dissociative Identity Disorder is believed to be related to the repression of psychological pain or trauma.

• Somatoform disorders are characterized by physical complaints or symptoms with no apparent physical cause as in hypochondriasis.

• Psychological distress appears to underlie the physical complaints of the somatoform disorders.

PERSONALITY DISORDERS

• The personality disorders consist of life-long or long-standing patterns of malfunctioning typically evident in childhood or adolescence.

WANTED BY THE FBI
Andrew Phillip Cunanan
Unlawful Flight to Avoid Prosecution - Murder

• People who are impulsive and disregard the rights of others without showing any remorse or guilt are diagnosed with antisocial personality disorder.

• Borderline personality disorder is characterized by instability in moods, interpersonal relationships, self-image, and behavior.

• Personality disorders are related to biological factors (genetics, neurotransmitters, abnormal brain functioning), inconsistent parenting practices, gender, and conflict-filled childhoods.

But in Dr. Farber's office, the world flowed in freely and surrounded us as we sat in those twin red leather chairs.

FROM EMILY FOX GORDON, *MOCKINGBIRD YEARS: A LIFE IN AND OUT OF THERAPY.* (New York: Basic Books, 2000.)

© Jose Luis Pelaez, Inc. /Corbis

CHAPTER 16

What Therapies Are Used to Treat Psychological Problems?

CHAPTER PREVIEW

The Ups and Downs of Life

The previous chapter outlined major psychological disorders such as depression, anxiety, and schizophrenia. It included the main symptoms of these disorders as well as our current understanding of what causes such problems. This chapter extends that discussion by examining the ways in which we treat those disorders. As such, this chapter nicely represents the big picture of psychology as we review many of the concepts and issues we have introduced throughout this textbook.

This chapter explores the principal approaches to therapy common today. **Therapy** consists of techniques that are used to help people with psychological or interpersonal problems. Each therapy approach stems from the main theoretical perspectives on behavior—themes introduced in the first chapter and explained in more detail in subsequent chapters. All therapies attempt to change a person's behavior. However, those who subscribe to the approaches differ in what they believe is the source of the problem. Consequently, the methods that are used to treat mental health disorders are directly tied to what is believed to be at the root of behavior.

For example, we will look at the techniques used by therapists who believe that unresolved childhood issues or unconscious desires are at the source of mental health problems. You know this more familiarly as the psychoanalytic perspective, an approach discussed in relation to other topics such as dreaming, coping, and personality. We will explore how altering a person's feelings and perceptions about themselves or those around them may improve psychological health—issues we discussed in the chapters on social and cognitive psychology. We also will describe the ways in which psychologists use behavioral techniques to reshape or recondition behavior—processes initially outlined in the chapter on learning. We also revisit the biology of behavior, introduced in Chapter 2, as we describe the medications that are used to treat psychological disorders.

What is the experience of therapy like? It varies considerably from person to person, from approach to approach, and from therapist to therapist. To illustrate, consider for a moment the following story:

At 18 years old, Emily should have been carefree and excited about life. She should have been going to college and discovering or nurturing her talents and ambitions. But that is not Emily's story. Before the age of 17, Emily had been to at least five therapists, and her world centered around mental health institutions. In Emily's words, "I was formed by therapy, absorbing its influence in ways that would require most of my life to raise to consciousness" (p. 29).

Dr. V. was her first therapist when Emily was in the eighth grade. Emily was sent to Dr. V. following an incident at school in which she angrily chased another student with what school administrators described as her intention to inflict physical harm on the student. In these therapy sessions, Emily would lie down on a couch while Dr. V. remained silent in a chair. Not knowing what to do, Emily remained silent as well, listening to Dr. V. steadily scribbling on a notepad. After a year, Emily's family moved, and she was sent to see Dr. H. There, Emily sat on a couch, and Dr. H. remained silent in a nearby chair, knitting a sweater. After a year of listening to the click clacking of knitting needles, therapy with Dr. H. was terminated. Given the amount of money involved and Emily's lack of progress, this should not be surprising.

Needless to say, Emily's problems continued. She was kicked out of several private schools for misbehavior and truancy. At 16, against her parents' orders, Emily attended an unchaperoned party. Her father found her there with a boy in a dark room kissing and groping one another. Her father dragged her out of the party to

therapy techniques that are used to help people with psychological or interpersonal problems

My sessions with Farber were utterly unlike my earlier experience of therapy."
(Gordon, 2000)

the car and drove her home. Furious with her parents, Emily broke an aspirin jar, and took a piece of the glass and scratched her wrists in a half-hearted suicide attempt. Her parents sent her to see another therapist, Dr. G.

Therapy with Dr. G. was different from what Emily had experienced before. She sat facing him and was encouraged to talk freely about her dreams and problems while Dr. G. looked for themes threaded through her discussions. She saw Dr. G. on and off through her high school years. Then, following another suicide attempt at age 18, Dr. G. recommended an inpatient facility for Emily. She was placed in the highly regarded Austen Riggs sanitarium in Massachusetts. She was diagnosed as having an anxiety problem with borderline personality trends. She stayed at Riggs for 3 years, 1 as an inpatient and 2 as an outpatient in residential apartments.

As an inpatient, she was told when to eat and sleep, and she attended group meetings. If she did not get her work-jobs done or go to bed at the appropriate time, she lost hospital privileges. She received medication at regular intervals. Her first therapist in the hospital was considerably different from her previous therapists. He took walks with Emily, drank wine with her and her roommate, and on one occasion put his arm around her waist. Emily knew he was becoming inappropriately attached to her, and so she searched for a new therapist. She was fortunate enough to find Dr. Leslie Farber.

Dr. Farber's approach seemed radically different. He emphasized the presence of will in human behavior. As such, he communicated to Emily that he believed in her and her value. He shared with Emily anecdotes about his own life that were similar to her own experiences and feelings. He treated her with warmth and understanding rather than aloofness or pity. He challenged her personal beliefs and highlighted her negative self-remarks. Through many years and many therapy sessions, Dr. Farber helped Emily "recover" her life.

As you can see, Emily experienced various forms of therapy and interacted with many different types of therapists. Her "therapeutic journey," detailed in her book *Mockingbird Years: A Life In and Out of Therapy* (2000), highlights the various forms of therapies and how therapists are a crucial variable in determining the effectiveness of therapy.

This chapter examines the nature of these varying types of therapy, explaining the techniques used in each approach, how they are conducted, and analyzing their effectiveness in treating people with mental health disorders. We will begin by defining therapy, examining who is qualified to give it, and addressing when it is appropriate for a person to seek therapy.

Providing Psychological Assistance ﹥﹥﹥﹥﹥

Today, mental health professionals use two broad forms of therapy to help individuals who are having difficulty functioning: psychotherapy and biological therapy. As we have seen, Emily received both. **Psychotherapy** is the use of psychological principles and techniques to treat the symptoms of mental health disorders, such as depression, or to treat interpersonal problems, such as troubled relationships. Psychotherapy is a general term that encompasses hundreds of different forms of therapy. However, all psychotherapies are based on the main assumption that underlying psychological factors such as emotions, cognitions, behavior, or relationships are at the root of interpersonal problems and mental health disorders.

In contrast, **biological therapy** uses medications or other medical interventions to treat the symptoms of mental health problems. Biological therapy assumes that biological factors, such as abnormal brain functioning or chemistry, are at the root of mental health problems. As we saw in the previous chapter on psychological disorders, both

LEARNING OBJECTIVE

Identify when a person should consider seeking therapy and who is qualified to give therapy, and describe the ethical standards that psychotherapists must follow when giving therapy.

psychotherapy the use of psychological principles and techniques to treat mental health disorders

biological therapy the use of medications or other medical interventions to treat mental health disorders

assumptions are supported by substantial research. Consequently, today many people receive therapy that combines both psychological and biological approaches.

Who Is Qualified to Give Therapy?

Trained professionals administer psychotherapy and biological therapy. A variety of educational and experiential backgrounds characterize psychotherapists (Table 16.1 ◆). These include clinical psychologists, psychoanalysts, licensed counselors or social workers, and marital or family therapists. Many of these professionals were highlighted when we discussed careers in psychology in Chapter 1 (p. 21). Recall that a master's degree is the minimum educational requirement for any of these professions. Many receive training in specialty areas or in specific forms of psychotherapy. For example, a psychoanalyst is trained in Freud's methods of treatments. Often their backgrounds include internships or practicums in which they have been supervised in administering treatment. In addition, most states require licensing and/or certification of mental health professionals.

In contrast, only licensed psychiatrists or other medical doctors can legally administer the biological therapies. A degree in psychiatry requires the completion of medical school before specializing in psychiatry. For the most part, a psychiatrist is the only mental health professional who can prescribe medication. However, the right of clinical psychologists to administer medications is currently the subject of a hot debate. For example, the state of New Mexico recently passed legislation allowing prescription privileges for clinical psychologists who completed additional training.

Ethical Standards for Psychotherapists

Are there any rules that mental health professionals must follow when administering therapy? Yes. In addition to being adequately trained and educated, mental health professionals are required to behave ethically and according to certain professional standards when conducting treatment. These are not legal statutes but rather standards established by the American Psychological Association (2002) indicating how psychotherapists should behave toward their clients. Violations of these standards should be reported to professional review boards that oversee the licensing of psychotherapists. Four essential ethical principles are competent treatment, informed consent, confidentiality, and appropriate interactions.

Competent Treatment and Informed Consent

The primary responsibility of the clinician toward a client is to provide *appropriate and adequate treatment*. Such a guideline prevents clinicians from merely warehousing clients in a treatment facility, a practice that we noted in Chapter 15 (p. 659) was quite common in previous decades and centuries. When providing treatment, psychotherapists must get *informed consent* from their clients. This involves fully informing clients of the nature of treatment and the details of their participation, including any potential side effects or consequences of treatment. These requirements are especially critical if any experimental types of treatment will be used.

Confidentiality

Psychotherapists also must respect the *confidentiality* of their communications with clients. They do not repeat to family members or friends any client discussions that occurred within the context of therapy. Consultations with other professionals are permitted only when the client has agreed to such a process. Using client stories or experiences in a published work also is not permitted without the expressed permission of the client. This ensures trust within the therapist–client relationship. However,

◆ **Table 16.1**

Types of Mental Health Professionals

Profession	Education	Training
Clinical psychologist	• College degree • Graduate school in clinical psychology to earn a doctorate (Ph.D. or Psy.D.; requires 5–8 years after college degree)	Supervised research and/or training in psychotherapy techniques, psychological testing, and the diagnosis of mental health disorders.
Counseling psychologist	• College degree • Graduate school in counseling psychology or education to earn a doctorate (Ph.D. or Ed.D.;.requires 4–6 years after college degree)	Supervised training in assessment, counseling, and therapy techniques.
Licensed professional counselor	• College degree • Graduate school to earn a master's degree in counseling (requires 3–5 years after college degree)	Supervised training in assessment, counseling, and therapy techniques.
Licensed social worker	• College degree • Graduate school in social work to receive a master's degree (M.S.W.; requires 3–5 years after college degree)	Supervised training in a social service agency or a mental health center. May or may not include training in psychotherapy.
Couple or family therapist	• College degree • Graduate school to receive a master's degree in counseling, psychology, or social work (requires 3–5 years after college degree)	Supervised training in family and couple therapy. May also include training in individual psychotherapy methods.
Psychiatrist	• College degree • Medical school to receive a medical degree (M.D.), and then specialize in psychiatry (requires 5–10 years after college degree)	Training in the diagnosis and prevention of mental health disorders with a focus on pharmaceutical treatment approaches. May include training in psychotherapy methods.

there are exceptions to this guideline. One exception is when the therapist believes that the client should be committed to a treatment facility. In this circumstance, the therapist will have to break confidentiality to convince a court that the client is a danger to him or herself or to others. Another exception to maintaining confidentiality is when others might be in danger. For example, if during therapy a client expresses violent intent toward another person, therapists are legally required to inform the potential victim of this potential harm. In addition, if a therapist suspects child abuse or elderly abuse, he or she is legally required to report such cases to the appropriate authorities.

Appropriate Interactions

Therapists must also *interact appropriately* with clients for successful therapy to occur. For example, psychotherapists are forbidden from becoming sexually involved with any client, and are not to date their clients either. Psychotherapists do not drink alcohol with their clients or engage in intimate demonstrations of affection such as an arm around the waist. The behavior of Emily's first therapist in the hospital was inappropriate and therefore unethical. Psychotherapists are not to go into business with clients or establish any other form of social relationship that would impede the course of therapy. Unfortunately, when therapists are depicted in movies and on television, they often do not maintain these ethical standards. Such media portrayals confuse the public as to the appropriate behavior of therapists.

When Does One Need to Consider Psychotherapy?

Why do people want psychotherapy? People seek psychotherapy for a variety of reasons. Many come to therapy because they are suffering from one of the many mental health disorders discussed in the previous chapter. Their behavior is maladaptive or they are experiencing difficulty in functioning in everyday life. They may be suffering from depression, extreme anxiety, or schizophrenia. Others who seek treatment have a history of mental illness or exhibit significant symptoms of a disorder. Some people are legally mandated to receive therapy by the court system. Yet, only about half of the people receiving therapy in a given year can be diagnosed with a psychological disorder (Narrow, Regier, Rae, Manderscheid, & Locke, 1993).

You do not have to be suffering from a psychological disorder in order to benefit from psychotherapy. Millions of people seek professional help to cope with other life problems. For example, couples and families in conflict may consider counseling to deal with their troubled relationships. People who have experienced major life transitions such as divorce, unemployment, retirement, or the death of a loved one may seek therapy to help them adjust to these changes.

When should therapy be considered? Consider therapy if you feel helpless, sad, blue, or nervous for a prolonged period or if such feelings do not improve despite several efforts to change them. You also may want to consider therapy if you are having difficulty carrying out your everyday activities. Therapy also may be useful if you want to make decisions differently, improve the functioning of important relationships, or change your life to feel more satisfied.

How do you find a therapist? Talk to family and friends, consult your local or state psychological association, or inquire at your community mental health center. Your church, synagogue, mosque, physician, or local college also may prove to be useful resources in finding a therapist. Given the hundreds of psychotherapy approaches that exist, which one should you choose? The next five sections of this chapter detail the main psychotherapy approaches. After reading about them, you may find that you are more comfortable with the philosophy, goals, and techniques of some over others. This information will assist you in understanding the nature of therapy, and in choosing a therapist if such a need ever arises.

Let's Review!

This section detailed who is qualified to give therapy, the ethical standards that psychotherapists must follow when giving therapy, and addresses under what conditions one should consider psychotherapy. As a quick check of your understanding, answer these questions.

1. Psychotherapy should be considered when:
   a. you get in trouble with your boss.
   b. you are having difficulty functioning in some aspect of your life.
   c. you have physical problems.
   d. all of the above

2. Michael is seeing a social worker to help him with his interpersonal problems. Michael is undergoing:
   a. psychiatric counseling.   c. psychotherapy.
   b. medical treatment.   d. biological therapy.

3. Which of the following professionals is most likely to administer medication as a form of therapy?
   a. clinical psychologist   c. biological psychologist
   b. social worker   d. psychiatrist

ANSWERS:
1.b; 2.c; 3.d

Psychoanalytic Therapies: Uncovering Reasons for Psychological Problems

> > >
LEARNING OBJECTIVE

Describe the aim of psychoanalytic therapies, and distinguish between traditional and modern psychoanalysis.

As we have seen from previous chapters, Sigmund Freud originally developed the psychoanalytic approach based on his ideas about different levels of consciousness and personality formation. Recall that Freud theorized that each of us has an unconscious level that contains desires, urges, thoughts, and memories of which we are unaware. In addition, our subconscious contains ideas, memories, and desires that have been repressed or hidden. These unconscious and subconscious parts remain deep down because they psychologically threaten the functioning of the ego by causing us distress and anxiety. Over the years, we continue to protect our ego by erecting more barriers to keep these conflicts hidden.

Freud assumed that symptoms of mental health disorders stem from these unresolved unconscious issues. Consequently, the goal of psychoanalytic therapies is to change maladaptive behavior by uncovering unconscious conflicts so that clients can gain *insight* into the real source of their problems (Wolitzky, 1995). Freud named this approach **psychoanalysis.** Professionals who administer this type of therapy are called *psychoanalysts.* Here we will detail two forms of psychoanalysis: traditional psychoanalysis and the more modern approach.

psychoanalysis   a method of therapy formulated by Freud that focuses on uncovering unconscious conflicts that drive maladaptive behavior

Traditional Psychoanalysis

What do psychoanalysts do? In traditional psychoanalysis as developed by Freud, the client lies down on a couch and is directed by the psychoanalyst what to discuss or talk about. It is the psychoanalyst's job to listen carefully and attentively to the client's discussion and discover what unconscious conflicts, themes, or concerns may be affecting the person. We saw that the first two therapists that Emily went to adopted such an approach. Uncovering unconscious conflicts is not an easy task. Therefore, the psychoanalyst uses several methods to help clients gain insight and uncover critical issues from their pasts (Freud, 1949). These include free association, dream analysis, interpretation, resistance, and transference.

In psychoanalysis, the patient lies down on a couch away from the therapist so that he or she may freely associate and express whatever comes to mind.

Free Association: Tell Me What's on Your Mind

Free association involves freely talking about a subject without censoring any thoughts. The client is fully awake and is asked to talk about a specific topic. Any and all thoughts are stated. The client says whatever comes to his or her mind. According to Freud (1949), we routinely censor or hide unpleasant or socially inappropriate desires and thoughts. Through free association, these unconscious urges are revealed. The psychoanalyst makes very few comments during free association, instead focusing on important themes or issues that may be revealed.

free association   a technique in psychoanalysis in which the client says whatever comes to mind

Dream Analysis: Revealing the Unconscious

As we saw in Chapter 4 (p. 168), Freud (1911) believed that dreams represented a pathway to the unconscious mind. Therefore, **dream analysis** is a tool used by some psychoanalysts to reveal unconscious conflicts (Pesant & Zadra, 2004). Recall as well that dreams do not directly represent unconscious conflicts but rather are comprised of symbols that reflect these underlying unconscious impulses. It is the psychoanalyst's job

dream analysis   a technique in psychoanalysis in which the therapist examines the hidden symbols in a client's dreams to decipher the true meaning or latent content of these dreams and thereby reveal important unconscious issues. Recall that one of Emily's therapists was very much interested in the content of her dreams and would attempt to find the themes embedded within them.

Interpretation: "I Believe That Means . . ."

Free association and dream content provide the psychoanalyst with a lot of information on the unconscious workings of the client's mind. The psychoanalyst takes this information and makes interpretations to the client. **Interpretations** are the psychoanalyst's views on the themes and issues that may be influencing the client's behavior. These interpretations may help the client gain insight into his or her problems. On the other hand, if the client is not psychologically ready to deal with these issues, he or she may resist these interpretations.

Resistance: Denying the Issues

Resistance occurs when a client behaves in such a way as to deny or avoid certain topics or issues. A client may resist a psychoanalyst's interpretation because it is too close to the truth and therefore creates anxiety in the client. Clients may express resistance in other ways as well. For example, clients may miss appointments or arrive late as a way of resisting the revealing nature of the therapy session. Clients may laugh or joke about certain topics that are actually quite painful for them. These resistant behaviors provide an additional clue to the psychoanalyst as to the unconscious conflicts affecting the client. A psychoanalyst may have interpreted Emily's continued silence in her initial therapy sessions as a form of resistance.

Transference: Emotional Reactions to the Therapist

The process of transference also is a clue to a client's unconscious conflicts. Freud (1949) believed that at some point during therapy, clients would unconsciously react to the therapist as if the therapist was his or her parent, friend, sibling, or lover. Freud termed this unconscious reaction **transference** because the client was unknowingly transferring feelings and emotions toward a loved one onto the therapist. Transference is a form of projection. Recall that projection is an ego defense mechanism in which a person attributes feelings and emotions to one person that they really feel toward another. The psychoanalyst can explore such instances of transference to reveal how the dynamics of clients' relationships may be influencing their behavior.

Traditional psychoanalysis was a dominant treatment approach through the 1950s. However, several factors contributed to its decline in popularity (Henry, Strupp, Schacht, & Gaston, 1994). Uncovering unconscious conflicts through these processes often took years and called for as many as five sessions per week. The client had to delve deeply into his or her past as well as establish trust with the psychoanalyst. This long-term nature of traditional psychoanalysis made it increasingly impractical and expensive for the average person and for the growing involvement of the health insurance industry. The development of other psychotherapies as well as the advent of drug therapy (discussed later) also led to its decrease in popularity. These new treatment approaches were just as effective as psychoanalysis and had the advantage of being shorter and, therefore, less costly. Questions about the effectiveness of traditional psychoanalysis also have arisen as few controlled studies have been conducted to test its success. Hence, psychoanalysis was forced to move in a new direction.

Modern Psychoanalysis

Modern psychoanalysis, often referred to as **psychodynamic therapy,** or *short-term dynamic therapy,* is evident in many different forms. Such therapies are consistent with

interpretation   the psychoanalyst's view on the themes and issues that may be influencing the client's behavior

resistance   a process in psychoanalysis whereby the client behaves in such a way as to deny or avoid sensitive issues

transference   a process in psychoanalysis in which the client unconsciously reacts to the therapist as if the therapist were a parent, friend, sibling, or lover

psychodynamic therapy   modern psychoanalysis delivered in a shorter time that focuses less on the client's past emphasizing instead current problems and the nature of interpersonal relationships

the views of Freud and the psychoanalytic approach. These newer therapy approaches continue to rely on the therapist's interpretations of the client's feelings and behavior, and identifying instances of transference and resistance. However, these therapies tend to focus less on the client's past than traditional psychoanalysis does. Current problems and the nature of interpersonal relationships are seen as more important in improving the client's behavior. The therapist also plays a more direct role, rapidly interviewing and questioning the client to uncover unconscious issues and themes in a shorter time. Then the therapist and client agree to focus on a limited set of problems that are seen as causing the client the most trouble. Hence, modern forms of psychoanalysis tend to be more short term, lasting no more than a few months, and appear to be effective in improving clients' symptoms (Blagys & Hilsenroth, 2000; Blatt & Shahar, 2004; Crits-Christoph, 1992; Reynolds, Stiles, Barkham, & Shapiro, 1996).

Let's Review!

This section detailed the aim of psychoanalytic therapies and has described traditional and modern psychoanalysis. As a quick check of your understanding, answer these questions.

1. The goal of psychoanalysis is to change behavior by:
   a. uncovering unconscious conflicts such that the client can gain insight into the source of his or her problems.
   b. uncovering negative cognitive patterns that impede the client's ability to function.
   c. examining environmental conditions and how they influence the client's responses.
   d. providing the client with unconditional support and love so that he or she makes adaptive and healthy behavioral choices.

2. Song often arrives late for her psychoanalysis appointment and sometimes forgets her appointments all together. Her psychoanalyst might interpret Song's behavior as a sign of:
   a. transference.   c. resistance.
   b. interpretation.   d. free association.

3. Modern psychoanalysis differs from traditional psychoanalysis in that:
   a. it is shorter in duration.
   b. it is focused less on the client's past and more on present relationships and issues.
   c. the therapist is more direct.
   d. all of the above

ANSWERS
1. a; 2. c; 3. d

Humanistic Therapy: Empathizing to Empower

> > > > > > > > > > > > > > > > > > >

⊗ **LEARNING**
⊗ **OBJECTIVE**
⊗ Describe humanistic therapy
⊗ approaches.

As we have just seen, problems with psychoanalysis forced it to move in a new direction that resulted in briefer psychodynamic therapies that were still connected to the ideas of Freud. However, some psychoanalysts radically departed from such views and developed newer forms of therapy. One example of this is humanistic therapy.

Recall from earlier discussions that the *humanistic approach* differs substantially from the psychoanalytic perspective in the assumptions that it makes about behavior and change. The humanistic approach focuses less on unconscious forces and more on the conscious actions that we take in controlling our behavior. Even though Dr. Farber was a trained psychoanalyst, his belief in Emily's value and his emphasis on her free will exemplifies this humanistic perspective. In Emily's words:

. . . Dr. Farber was both far humbler than his more conventional colleagues and far bolder. He was humbler because he approached his patients as a whole human being. . . . He was bolder because . . . he committed himself to a risky, open-ended friendship and to all the claims of responsibility that friendship entails." (p. 125).

Humanists believe that behavior is driven not by id impulses, but rather from how we interpret the world and our awareness of our feelings. The only way to understand a person's behavior, therefore, is to connect with and understand this view. Humanism further assumes that people will naturally strive toward personal growth and achieving their full potential when raised in a positive and accepting environment. When people hold distorted perceptions or lack self-awareness, mental health problems arise, preventing a person from becoming self-actualized. Yet the person is capable of healing himself, if only the right environment is provided. The therapist's role is to create this safe environment for self-exploration and facilitate the journey toward self-fulfillment (Greenberg & Rice, 1997). One of the most influential and best known of the humanistic therapies is client-centered therapy.

Client-Centered Therapy

Disillusioned with the goals, methods, and assumptions of psychoanalysis, Carl Rogers (1902–1987) developed a different therapy approach that exemplifies the humanistic perspective. Whereas Freud saw the analyst as all knowing, directive, and responsible for client change, Rogers believed that the therapist should serve more as a facilitator or coach to help move the client in the direction of change. Such a viewpoint resulted in **client-centered therapy,** or *person-centered therapy.* As the names imply, in client-centered therapy, the focus and direction of therapy comes from the person, or client. The client decides what to talk about without direction, interpretation, or judgment from the therapist.

What does a client-centered therapist do? According to Rogers (1951, 1980, 1986), the therapist creates a positive and accepting environment to facilitate self-awareness and personal growth by providing three key characteristics: empathy, genuineness, and unconditional positive regard.

In humanistic therapy, therapist and client sit face to face as they work together in solving the client's problems.

© Tom Stewart/Corbis

client-centered therapy   a humanistic psychotherapy approach formulated by Rogers that emphasizes the use of empathy, genuineness, and unconditional positive regard to help the client reach his/her potential

Application

empathy   the ability of a therapist to understand a client's feelings and thoughts without being judgmental

Empathy: Understanding the Client

Are you a good listener? Do friends and family frequently confide in you? If so, then maybe you possess empathy. According to Rogers, **empathy** is the ability to understand a client's feelings and thoughts without being judgmental. The therapist does not express disapproval toward the client but rather indicates understanding of the client's feelings. Conveying empathy involves actively listening to the client—making eye contact with the client, nodding as the client speaks, and assuming an interested and attentive pose. Empathy also involves *reflection.* The therapist restates, repeats, or summarizes the thoughts and feelings that he or she hears the client express. Reflected statements communicate to the client the active attention of the therapist and mirror the client's perceptions and views of reality.

Consider this example of empathy and reflection from Irvin Yalom's work, *Love's Executioner and Other Tales of Psychotherapy* (1989).

Client:	I believe he is intentionally trying to drive me to suicide. Does that sound like a crazy thought?
Therapist:	I don't know if its crazy, but it sounds like a desperate and terribly painful thought. (p. 29)

Notice in this example that the therapist does not judge the client's thoughts as crazy and reflects the emotions underlying the statement of suicide. Ideally, empathy and reflection will help clients see themselves and their problems more clearly, promoting a realistic self-image and greater self-acceptance.

Genuineness: Sharing Thoughts, Feelings, and Experiences

A second key therapist quality in client-centered therapy is genuineness. **Genuineness** is the ability to openly share one's thoughts and feelings with others. The therapist expresses his or her true feelings and thoughts to the client and does not hide behind the mask of being the "professional," "doctor," or authority figure. Establishing genuineness allows the client to see the therapist as a real, living person. It also creates an open environment that promotes trust and an honest expression of thoughts and feelings. Rogers believed that such an environment would model to the client how relationships can be built on a foundation of trust and honesty. Emily learned such a lesson from Dr. Farber. His genuineness made her believe he was a friend as well as a therapist.

genuineness the ability of a therapist to openly share his or her thoughts and feelings with a client

Unconditional Positive Regard: Valuing the Client

The third key quality in client-centered therapy, unconditional positive regard, was introduced in the chapter on personality (Chapter 14). Recall that Rogers defined **unconditional positive regard** as the ability to accept and value a person for who he or she is, regardless of his or her faults or problems. Also remember that Rogers believed that receiving unconditional positive regard in one's childhood was a key factor for healthy personality adjustment. A therapist who offers unconditional positive regard to a client does not indicate shock, dismay, or disapproval to any client statements. Instead, the therapist communicates caring and respect toward the client regardless of what the client says. This does not mean that the therapist has to personally *agree* with everything the client states. Rather, the therapist's job is to reflect the client's feelings and thoughts to further the client's self-knowledge and enable the client to solve problems in his or her own way. By offering unconditional positive regard, the client comes to believe that he or she has value and is competent at making decisions. Such attitudes foster self-confidence and self-acceptance that lead to healthier growth choices.

unconditional positive regard the ability of a therapist to accept and value a client for who he or she is, regardless of his or her faults or problems

For Rogers, when a therapist demonstrates all three qualities—empathy, genuineness, and unconditional positive regard—it creates a positive and nurturing environment. A person feels accepted, understood, and valued. These feelings help the client self-explore a more realistic self-image and perception of the world. This in turn removes the obstacles toward personal growth such that self-actualization can be realized.

Do these therapist qualities actually have an effect on changing people's behavior? Each quality by itself does not appear to help clients change (Beutler, Machado, & Neufeldt, 1994). Yet when used together, the results are more promising, emphasizing the importance of a positive client-therapist relationship. Compared to no-treatment control groups, client-centered therapy changes people's behavior (Greenberg & Rice, 1997; Hill & Nakayama, 2000). Compared to more structured therapy approaches, client-centered therapy is equally effective (Borkovec & Mathews, 1988; Greenberg, Elliot, & Lietaer, 1994). However, it may not be appropriate for people who are seriously distressed (Bohart, 1990).

Let's Review!

This section described humanistic approaches to therapy. As a quick check of your understanding, answer these questions.

1. The goal of humanistic therapy is to change behavior by:
   a. uncovering unconscious conflicts such that the client can gain insight into the source of his or her problems.
   b. uncovering negative cognitive patterns that impede the client's ability to function.
   c. examining environmental conditions and how they influence the client's responses.
   d. providing the client with a safe environment for self-exploration and facilitating the journey toward self-fulfillment.

2. Which of the following is *not* one of the elements used in client-centered therapy to help the client achieve self-fulfillment?
   a. genuineness   c. unconditional positive regard
   b. obedience   d. empathy

3. Marcos is receiving client-centered therapy. His therapist openly shares his thoughts and feelings with Marcos, relating his own experiences that are similar to Marcos'. Marcos' therapist is exhibiting which quality of client-centered therapy?
   a. genuineness   c. unconditional positive regard
   b. reflection   d. empathy

ANSWERS

1.d; 2.b; 3.a

LEARNING OBJECTIVE

Describe the aim of behavior therapy approaches, and explain how they operate by classical or operant conditioning processes.

behavior therapy therapy that applies the principles of classical and operant conditioning to help people change maladaptive behaviors

Behavior Therapies: Learning Healthier Behaviors

As we have seen, psychoanalytic and humanistic therapies focus more on internal reflection by the client. Self-understanding through self-exploration is assumed to be key for psychological health. In psychoanalysis, the client analyzes unconscious conflicts. In humanistic therapy, the perception of the self is explored. In contrast, **behavior therapy** directly focuses on changing current problem behaviors rather than delving into the client's past.

What do behavior therapists do? Behavior therapies, also called *behavior modification*, consist of techniques and methods that use learning principles to change problem behavior. Chapter 5 described the learning processes of classical conditioning and operant conditioning. The behavioral perspective relies on these principles to modify behavior. Recall that the *behavioral perspective* assumes that behavior is a result of environmental variables such as stimuli and consequences in the environment. It further assumes that people learn maladaptive behavior in the same way that they learn adaptive behavior. Hence, changing behavior involves changing the environmental circumstances that seem to elicit negative behavior. Learning principles that focus on extinction are used to stop disruptive behaviors. Similarly, learning principles that focus on shaping or acquiring behaviors are used to replace undesirable behaviors with more adaptive ones. Behavior therapy can take many forms. Here we discuss two broad categories of treatment: classical conditioning techniques and operant conditioning techniques.

Classical Conditioning Techniques

Some behavior therapies rely on the principles of classical conditioning outlined in Chapter 5. Briefly, classical conditioning is when stimuli in the environment become associated and thereby both produce the same response. For example, as a child, one of the authors was bitten by a dog twice within a 2-year period. In both instances, the dog was a German shepherd. Following those incidents, she developed an intense fear of large dogs despite having being raised with dogs her whole life. Her dog-biting experiences became associated with pain such that now she feared pain from all large dogs and avoided them routinely. Her fear was a learned behavior. Behavior therapy would focus on having her unlearn her response to dogs. Two behavior therapy techniques that rely on principles of classical conditioning to change behavior include systematic desensitization and aversion therapy.

Systematic Desensitization: Relax and Have No Fear

One effective tool for treating phobias and anxiety is systematic desensitization (Wolpe, 1958). **Systematic desensitization** involves replacing a fear or anxiety response with an incompatible response of relaxation. Anxiety and relaxation are *competing responses.* You cannot feel both at the same time; you can only feel one or the other. So the aim of systematic desensitization is to have a client learn how to relax and then slowly and systematically introduce the feared object, situation, or thought while the client maintains this state of relaxation.

Systematic desensitization is accomplished in three basic steps. First, the client is trained in *progressive muscle relaxation.* This method involves alternately tensing and relaxing different muscle groups, beginning with the toes and working up to the head, so that the client learns to distinguish when muscles are tense and when they are relaxed. Once the client has learned progressive relaxation, the client and therapist develop an anxiety hierarchy. An **anxiety hierarchy** (Figure 16.1) outlines, according to the degree of fear, the threatening images that the client experiences when faced with the feared object or situation. The hierarchy starts with the least frightening images and progresses to the most distressing. Progressive relaxation and the anxiety hierarchy are then combined in the final step. Relaxation is paired with each item in the hierarchy. As the client can imagine a feared situation and remain relaxed, the next item in the hierarchy is addressed. Over several therapy sessions, this systematic process is continued until the client has become desensitized to all items in the hierarchy.

You may be skeptical at this point, unconvinced that thinking about a feared stimulus is much different from actually encountering the object or situation. For that reason, behavior therapists can extend systematic desensitization to a simulated or actual environment once the client has mastered the mental images. For many fears, this is when systematic desensitization is most effective (Antony & Barlow, 2002; Menzies & Clark, 1993). For example, flight simulators can be used to help desensitize individuals to a fear of flying. Combining systematic desensitization with the actual situation, called *in vivo exposure*, also is a very effective tool in treating a variety of anxiety disorders (Follette & Hayes, 2000; Gould, Otto, Pollack, & Yap, 1997).

Recently, virtual reality computer technology has been added to this arsenal of weapons. Virtual reality bridges the gap between imagining feared stimuli in a therapist's office and in vivo exposure in the field by simulating a feared situation. Clients wear a head-mounted display with small video monitors and stereo earphones that integrate visual and auditory cues to immerse the client in a computer-generated

Virtual reality exposure therapy allows clients to experience their fears in a simulated, nonthreatening environment.

© Will Burgess/Reuters/Corbis

systematic desensitization   a behavior therapy technique in which a client is desensitized to a fear in a gradual, step-by-step process

anxiety hierarchy   outlines, according to the degree of fear, the threatening images that a person experiences when faced with a feared object or situation; the outline starts with the least frightening images and progresses to the most distressing

An Anxiety Hierarchy for Systematic Desensitization

Degree of fear	
5	I'm standing on the balcony of the top floor of an apartment tower.
10	I'm standing on a stepladder in the kitchen to change a light bulb.
15	I'm walking on a ridge. The edge is hidden by shrubs and treetops.
20	I'm sitting on the slope of a mountain, looking out over the horizon.
25	I'm crossing a bridge 6 feet above a creek. The bridge consists of an 18-inch-wide board with a handrail on one side.
30	I'm riding a ski lift 8 feet above the ground.
35	I'm crossing a shallow, wide creek on an 18-inch-wide board, 3 feet above water level.
40	I'm climbing a ladder outside the house to reach a second-story window.
45	I'm pulling myself up a 30-degree wet, slippery slope on a steel cable.
50	I'm scrambling up a rock, 8 feet high.
55	I'm walking 10 feet on a resilient, 18-inch-wide board which spans an 8-foot-deep gulch.
60	I'm walking on a wide plateau, 2 feet from the edge of a cliff.
65	I'm skiing an intermediate hill. The snow is packed.
70	I'm walking over a railway trestle.
75	I'm walking on the side of an embankment. The path slopes to the outside.
80	I'm riding a chair lift 15 feet above the ground.
85	I'm walking up a long, steep slope.
90	I'm walking up (or down) a 15-degree slope on a 3-foot-wide trail. On one side of the trail the terrain drops down sharply; on the other side is a steep upward slope.
95	I'm walking on a 3-foot-wide ridge. The slopes on both sides are long and more than 25 degrees steep.
100	I'm walking on a 3-foot-wide ridge. The trail slopes on one side. The drop on either side of the trail is more than 25 degrees.

Figure 16.1 Sample Anxiety Hierarchy

An anxiety hierarchy like the one shown here is used during systematic desensitization.
This hierarchy was developed for a woman who had a fear of heights.

From K. E. Rudestam, Methods of Self Change: An ABC Primer, © 1980 Wadsworth. Reprinted with permission of the author.

virtual environment. For example, a person with a fear of flying may be exposed to stimuli that simulate sitting in a plane with the plane's engines roaring beneath him. A person with a fear of public speaking may experience simulation of standing at a podium. Therapists can control the images the clients receive while monitoring the clients' heart rates, respiration, and skin temperature so that they can effectively grade the clients' fear responses during the sessions (Bender, 2004).

Evidence suggests that virtual reality technology is an effective treatment for people who have a fear of heights and of flying (Krijn, Emmelkamp, Olafsson, & Biemond, 2004; Rothbaum, Hodges, Kooper, Opdyke, & Williford, 1995; Rothbaum, Hodges, Watson, Kessler, & Opdyke, 1996; Wiederhold, Jang, Kim, & Wiederhold, 2002). Preliminary research suggests that virtual reality technology also may be a useful tool in treating driving phobia (Wald & Taylor, 2003), public speaking (Harris, Kemmerling, & North, 2002), panic disorders (Botella et al., 2004), and posttraumatic stress disorder (Difede & Hoffman, 2002). However, to date the results of such research are not conclusive.

Aversion Therapy: We Won't Do Something if We Dislike It

Application ⟫

Do you bite your nails? As a child, did you suck your thumb? Did loved ones try to get you to stop such behaviors? Many parents put a foul-tasting or spicy liquid such as Tabasco sauce on their child's nails or thumb to stop nail-biting or thumb-sucking. These parents unknowingly are performing aversion therapy, another example of a behavior therapy relying on classical conditioning principles. **Aversion therapy** involves pairing an unpleasant stimulus (foul or spicy taste) with a specific behavior such as biting one's fingernails. Ideally, the aversive stimulus becomes associated with the undesirable response such that the person is less likely to engage in the response again.

aversion therapy a behavior therapy technique in which a specific behavior is paired with an unpleasant stimulus in order to reduce its occurrence

Aversive conditioning occurs frequently in everyday life. Food poisoning is another example. If a particular food has ever made you sick, normally it is months or even years before you will touch that food again. The food (stimulus) becomes associated with being sick (response) such that you avoid it at all costs. Therapists use this knowledge to treat a variety of undesirable habits and behaviors. For example, an aversion therapy method for treating alcoholism involves taking a drug called Antabuse (Cannon & Baker, 1981). Antabuse interacts with alcohol, causing nausea and vomiting. If an alcoholic drinks when using Antabuse it makes him or her ill. The unwanted stimulus (alcohol) becomes associated with the response of feeling ill and nauseated. The alcoholic learns to avoid alcohol in order to avoid the associated unpleasant response. Unfortunately, the alcoholic can also simply avoid taking the medication, thereby nullifying the effectiveness of the procedure.

Aversion therapy also has been used to eliminate a variety of other behaviors, including compulsive hair pulling, gambling, smoking tobacco, marijuana, or crack cocaine, and maladaptive sexual behaviors such as pedophilia (child molestation) and fetishism (Emmelkamp, 1994; Laws, 2001). For instance, one common aversion therapy method for cigarette addiction is rapid smoking (Lichtenstein, 1982). In this method, clients are told to smoke continuously, one cigarette after another, until they are miserable, nauseated, or even sick. By this time, the sight of a cigarette and the idea of smoking one repulse many clients. Existing studies provide insufficient evidence to determine the effectiveness of rapid smoking (Hajek & Stead, 2004). However, the relapse rate for former smokers is exceedingly high regardless of which stop-smoking technique has been used. Roughly, one half of those who quit smoking begin again within a year.

At this point, you may be disturbed by the knowledge that therapists use such unpleasant procedures in treatment. Keep in mind, though, that therapists are ethically bound to get informed consent from clients. Clients are informed of the procedure and must agree before such a method can be used. An alternative and less disturbing form of aversion therapy is called **covert sensitization therapy.** In this procedure, graphic imagery is used to create unpleasant associations with specific stimuli. For example, a smoker may have to repeatedly imagine black and diseased lungs when faced with the stimulus of a cigarette.

Application

covert sensitization therapy   a milder form of aversion therapy in which graphic imagery is used to create unpleasant associations with specific stimuli

Operant Conditioning Techniques

While systematic desensitization and aversion therapy rely on classical conditioning principles, some behavior therapies rely on the principles of operant conditioning outlined in Chapter 5. Briefly, operant conditioning focuses on the consequences of a behavior. It assumes that reinforced behavior will be maintained and punished behavior will be extinguished. For instance, in the previous example in which one of the authors developed a fear of large dogs, recall that following the dog-biting episodes she responded by avoiding large dogs whenever possible. The consequence of this response was reinforcing—it reduced her fear. The next time she encountered a large dog she learned that avoiding it would quickly rid her of any anxiety. This example illustrates how operant conditioning principles often operate to maintain problem behaviors.

Changing undesirable behavior, therefore, involves changing the consequences of a behavior. These changes can be accomplished in a variety of ways (Thorpe & Olson, 1997):

1. *Positive reinforcement.* Positive reinforcement is used to encourage or maintain a behavior. For example, every time a child complies with a parental request, verbal praise follows. After the compliance of the child increases, verbal praise need not occur every single time.

2. *Nonreinforcement and extinction.* To discourage unwanted behavior, any reinforcers of the behavior are removed. If a reinforcer does not follow a behavior, the behavior will occur less frequently. Eventually the behavior will be eliminated or extinguished. However, keep in mind that oftentimes the unwanted behavior will increase before it goes away because a person is expecting the reinforcer. Consequently, the person will at first engage in the behavior even more to get the reinforcer. Also, consider the powerful effect of attention and approval. Misbehavior may continue because all subtle forms of reinforcers have not been eliminated.

For example, consider what happens when a child acts up in school. Although the teacher may scold or reprimand the child, the child still receives a form of attention and therefore the behavior may not subside. Even if the teacher ignores the child's misbehavior, classmates may reinforce the behavior by laughing and paying attention to him or her.

3. *Punishment.* Sometimes punishment is used to decrease undesirable behaviors. Recall that punishment is when an undesired behavior is immediately followed by a negative or aversive consequence. Yet, remember the side effects of punishment. It can produce negative emotions such as anger, fear, or escaping the situation altogether. For these reasons, punishment is used sparingly.

4. *Shaping.* Recall from Chapter 5 that shaping involves positively reinforcing each successive attempt at a behavior. It is used to teach a person new, desired behaviors. For example, shaping may be used to teach autistic children how to speak. If the child makes a "t" sound to say toy, this attempt is rewarded. Shaping also has been successfully used to teach people with mental retardation self-help skills, such as washing their face or brushing their teeth.

5. *Token economy.* A **token economy** involves rewarding people with tokens, or symbolic rewards, for desired behavior. Because not everyone is influenced by the same reward, tokens—such as chips, points, or stars—are given each time a person engages in a desired behavior. The person's tokens can then be exchanged for a variety of reinforcers such as food, privileges, goods, phone time, and so on.

You may recall having had a treasure chest or a goody box in elementary school. Students who had acquired a certain number of points or tokens could visit the prize box at the end of the week. Today, your consumer behavior unknowingly may be reinforced by a token economy. Many credit card companies offer points for purchases. These points can then be exchanged for a variety of merchandise. Airlines do the same thing with frequent flyer points. Their aim is to increase your consumption of their services.

The same principle can be used in hospital settings, halfway houses, prisons, and other institutional settings. People earn tokens for desired behavior and constructive activities, and then exchange them for passes, free time, meals, access to television, or private rooms. Recall that Emily's behavior in Riggs sanitarium was monitored in a similar fashion. To receive privileges, she had to get her work-jobs done and go to bed at the appropriate time. In some institutions, patients may even lose or be charged tokens for undesired behavior such as fighting, noncompliance, or not completing their chores. A token economy can be a very effective tool for managing behavior in a group setting (Adams, Girolami, Joseph, Sauvageot, & Slater, 2002; Comaty, Stasio, & Advokat, 2001; Morisse, Batra, Hess, & Silverman, 1996; Mottram & Berger-Gross, 2004; Petry et al., 2004; Sullivan & O'Leary, 1990).

Application

Application

token economy a behavioral therapy technique in which people are rewarded with tokens for desired behavior; the tokens can then be exchanged for what is reinforcing to them

Although the behavior therapies have been very successful in treating a variety of psychological problems, particularly in children, they do not address thoughts and perceptions that often accompany behavior. For this reason, behavioral strategies have been increasingly used in conjunction with cognitive therapy (Wilson, Hayes, & Gifford, 1997), our next topic of discussion.

Let's Review!

This section described the aim of behavior therapy approaches and the ways in which classical and operant conditioning techniques are used to change behavior. For a quick check of your understanding, answer these questions.

1. Behavior therapies change behavior by:
   a. uncovering unconscious conflicts such that the client can gain insight into the source of his or her problems.
   b. uncovering negative cognitive patterns that impede the client's ability to function.
   c. examining and then changing the environmental circumstances that seem to elicit negative behavior.
   d. providing the client with a safe environment for self-exploration and facilitating the journey toward self-fulfillment.

2. Celia goes to a therapist to try to reduce her fear of driving. The therapist teaches Celia how to relax and then has her imagine those aspects of driving that make her fearful while maintaining her relaxed mode. Celia is most likely undergoing:
   a. aversion therapy.   c. systematic desensitization.
   b. a token economy.   d. client-centered therapy.

3. Which of the following is *not* a therapy approach based on the principles of operant conditioning?
   a. token economies   c. positive reinforcement
   b. shaping   d. aversion therapy

ANSWERS
1. c 2. c 3. d

Cognitive Therapies: >
Thinking Through Problems

What do cognitive therapists do? We saw in Chapter 15 that many psychological problems such as anxiety and depression may stem from negative and distorted thought patterns. *Cognitive therapies* focus on changing these maladaptive patterns of thinking and perceiving, and replacing them with more adaptive ways of interpreting events. Two of the most widely used cognitive therapies are Albert Ellis's rational-emotive therapy and Aaron Beck's cognitive therapy.

LEARNING OBJECTIVE

Describe the aim of cognitive therapy approaches, and distinguish between rational-emotive therapy and Beck's cognitive therapy.

Ellis's Rational-Emotive Therapy

Developed by Albert Ellis (1973, 1995), **rational-emotive therapy** is based on the premise that many psychological problems stem from how people think about and interpret events in their lives. It is not the actual event that causes the emotional upset, but rather the individual's *interpretation* of the event that results in emotional distress. Specifically, it identifies the client's faulty or irrational beliefs that lead to self-defeating behaviors, anxiety, depression, anger, or other psychological problems. Several studies support Ellis's notion that people who think more irrationally evidence more psychological distress (Solomon, Arnow, Gotlib, & Wind, 2003; Ziegler & Leslie, 2003; Ziegler & Smith, 2004).

rational-emotive therapy a cognitive therapy approach created by Albert Ellis that focuses on changing the irrational beliefs that people hold that are believed to impede healthy psychological functioning

Rose is Rose © reprinted by permission of United Feature Syndicate, Inc.

Albert Ellis developed rational-emotive therapy to deal with clients' faulty or irrational beliefs that lead to self-defeating behaviors such as anxiety, depression, or anger.

Ellis identified common irrational beliefs (1991) that often impede people's functioning, as listed in Table 16.2 ◆. Identifying such irrational beliefs is the first step in rational-emotive therapy. For example, one client may have an excessive need for approval because she believes that she "must be loved by everyone." Another client may irrationally believe that there is a "right" solution for every problem and become frustrated or depressed because a problem reoccurs. Once these beliefs have been identified, the therapist challenges their validity. The therapist confronts and disputes these fallacies in a logical and persuasive manner to push the client to recognize that such beliefs are irrational and unhealthy. The therapist might make statements such as "What evidence do you have to support this belief?" or "In what other ways could this evidence be interpreted?" Additionally, the client may be asked "What is the worst thing that could happen?" and "If that happened, what could you do?" Asking such questions forces the client to consider alternative viewpoints, face his fears and anxieties, and explore possible problem-solving methods. After a client's irrational beliefs have been recognized and refuted, they then can be replaced with more realistic and rational beliefs. These beliefs may be reflected in such statements as "Not everyone will like me, but that is okay and not a measure of my worth" or "There are several ways to solve a problem and if I fail I can try another approach."

Rational-emotive therapy is a very direct and confrontational approach. Admitting that our way of thinking is irrational and unhealthy, and radically changing our interpretation of events in our lives is not an easy task. Yet despite these obstacles, rational-emotive therapy generally has been effective in treating depression, social phobias, and other anxiety disorders (Gould et al., 1997; Lewinsohn, Clark, Hops & Andrews, 1990; Robinson, Berman, & Neimeyer, 1990).

Beck's Cognitive Therapy

cognitive therapy a therapy created by Aaron Beck that focuses on uncovering negative automatic thought patterns that impede healthy psychological functioning

A second illustration of focusing on thought patterns in therapy is Aaron Beck's **cognitive therapy.** Initially trained as a psychoanalyst, Beck noticed that many of his depressed patients expressed a negative view of themselves and the world almost

◆ **Table 16.2**

Examples of Irrational Assumptions

1. I must be loved by or approved of by everyone.

2. I must be competent and achieving in all things I do; otherwise I am worthless.

3. Some people are bad and should be severely blamed and punished for it. I should be extremely upset over the wrongdoings of others.

4. It is awful and upsetting when things are not the way I would like them to be.

5. Unhappiness is caused by external events, and I cannot control my bad feelings and emotional reactions.

6. If something unpleasant happens, I should dwell on it.

7. Avoiding difficulties, rather than facing them, will make you happy.

8. Always rely on someone who is stronger than you.

9. Your past will indefinitely affect your present life.

10. There is a perfect solution for every problem, and it is awful and upsetting if this solution is not found.

habitually. Beck abandoned the psychoanalytic assumption that psychological problems are caused by unconscious conflicts and instead turned his attention to the role cognitions play in emotional distress. He developed a cognitive therapy based on the principle that distorted thinking in the form of **cognitive distortions** and negative, automatic thought patterns lead to depression, anxiety, and low self-esteem (Beck, Rush, Shaw, & Emery, 1979). For example, do you ever notice that you make critical remarks to yourself such as "Oh, I am so stupid" or "I am such an idiot"? Such personal negative statements depress mood and lower self-esteem. Beck believed that such maladaptive patterns could be identified and changed, resulting in more adaptive behavior. Table 16.3 ◆ illustrates some of the more common cognitive distortions that Beck identified in depressed people.

Unlike rational-emotive therapy, Beck's cognitive therapy is not as confrontational in its approach. Rather, Beck (1991) saw the client and therapist as a collaborative team, working together to identify and evaluate the accuracy and biases of the client's thought patterns. At first, the therapist teaches the client how to recognize and keep track of her negative automatic thoughts such as "I never do anything right" or "I always fail at whatever I do." The therapist and client then work together to test the validity or accuracy of these thoughts. For example, a client may be asked to list all the tasks assigned to him in a week and then indicate whether each task was completed or not. The therapist hopes that such an exercise will not only point out the inaccuracy of the client's beliefs, but also train him how to evaluate negative automatic thoughts in the future. We saw that as a part of therapy, Dr. Farber would often highlight Emily's negative thought patterns as a way of improving her self-image.

Cognitive therapy, like rational-emotive therapy, has been very effective in treating depression and anxiety disorders (Resick, Nishith, Weaver, Astin, & Feuer, 2002; Wampold, Minami, Baskin, & Callen Tierney, 2002). In some studies, it has been just as effective as drugs (Abramowitz, 1997; Gould et al., 1997). More important, clients who have adopted new and more adaptive patterns of thinking are less likely to become depressed in the future—a benefit that drugs cannot provide (G. A. Fava, Grandi, Zielezny, & Rafanelli, 1996; Jarrett et al., 2001; Teasdale et al., 2001). Cognitive therapy also has been shown to be highly effective in treating a variety of other disorders including eating disorders and substance abuse (Dobson, Backs-Dermott, & Dozois, 2000).

cognitive distortion   distorted thinking patterns, such as overgeneralization or all-or-none thinking, that according to Beck lead to depression, anxiety, and low self-esteem

 Application

Aaron Beck developed cognitive therapy based on the principle that distorted thinking and negative, automatic thought patterns lead to depression, anxiety, and low self-esteem.

Courtesy of Beck Institute for Cognitive Therapy and Research

◆ **Table 16.3**

Examples of Cognitive Distortions

Cognitive Error	Description	Example
All-or-nothing thinking	Each event is seen as completely good or bad, right or wrong, or as a success or failure.	"If I don't get this job, I am a failure."
Arbitrary inference	Concluding that something negative will happen or is happening even though there is no evidence to support it.	"My neighbor did not say hello to me. She must be mad at me."
Disqualifying the positive	Rejecting positive experiences.	"Anyone can paint. It's no big deal."
Emotional reasoning	Assuming that negative emotions are accurate without questioning them.	"I feel fat, so I must be fat."
Labeling	Placing a negative, global label on a person or situation.	"I can't do anything right, so why should I try?"
Magnification and minimization	Overestimating the importance of negative events and underestimating the impact of positive events.	"In my job evaluation, my boss said I need to work on my time-management skills. She only said I was a productive worker and good team manager to be nice."
Overgeneralization	Applying a negative conclusion of one event to other unrelated events and areas of one's life.	"I messed up on my math test, so I won't do well in history or Spanish. I should drop out of school."
Personalization	Attributing negative events to oneself without reason.	"My parents are in a bad mood because they have an idiot for a son."
Selective abstraction	Focusing on a single, irrelevant, negative aspect of a situation, while ignoring the more relevant and important aspects of the situation.	"It doesn't matter that I got a raise and promotion. I have to go to work an hour earlier."

Let's Review!

This section detailed the aim of cognitive therapy approaches and described Ellis's rational-emotive therapy and Beck's cognitive therapy. For a quick check of your understanding, answer these questions.

1. Svetlana goes to a therapist who focuses on her negative automatic statements. Svetlana is most likely undergoing what type of therapy?

   a. rational-emotive therapy
   b. cognitive therapy
   c. systematic desensitization
   d. client-centered therapy

2. The goal of cognitive therapy approaches is to change behavior by:

   a. uncovering unconscious conflicts such that the client can gain insight into the source of his or her problems.

   b. uncovering negative cognitive patterns that impede the client's ability to function.

   c. examining and then changing the environmental circumstances that seem to elicit negative behavior.

   d. providing the client with a safe environment for self-exploration and facilitating the journey toward self-fulfillment.

3. The cognitive therapies have been most effective in treating which type of disorders?

   a. schizophrenia
   b. personality disorders
   c. depression
   d. autism

ANSWERS

1.b; 2.b; 3.c

Group Therapy Approaches: > > > > > > > > > > > > Strength in Numbers

The psychotherapies we have detailed so far have focused on a one-to-one relationship between a client and a therapist. This is known as individual psychotherapy. However, therapy can be administered to many people at one time with one or more therapists, in a process called **group therapy**. Group therapy approaches often are used in psychiatric facilities, group homes, addiction centers, and mental institutions. They also are frequently offered by community mental health centers and outpatient treatment programs. Emily attended many group meetings, not only at the hospital as an inpatient but also as an outpatient at the community center. Group therapy often centers on one type of problem (such as addiction or depression) or is offered for a specific type of client (such as battered women, teenagers, or sex offenders). Group therapy may be administered by any of the different types of professionals discussed at the beginning of this chapter.

LEARNING OBJECTIVE

Describe the advantages and disadvantages of group therapy approaches.

group therapy therapy that is administered to more than one person at a time

The Benefits of Group Therapy

Is group therapy better than individual therapy? Group therapy has several distinct advantages over individual therapy (Dies, 1993; Yalom, 1995). First, group therapy tends to be less expensive than individual therapy. The cost of one or more therapists is shared by several people. However, clients do receive less one-on-one, or individualized treatment, in a group therapy setting. Second, group

© Baby Blues Partnership. Reprinted with permission of King Features.

David Harry Stewart/Getty Images

Group therapy can be a less expensive alternative to individual psychotherapy.

therapy offers therapists a view into the client's social interactions with others. Because many people receive therapy to address interpersonal problems, group therapy offers a safe mini-environment to explore new social behaviors or to understand how our interactions with others may be impeding our psychological health. Group therapy also enables clients to recognize that they are not the only ones struggling with difficulties. Group members also can offer acceptance, trust, and support for someone who is having problems. They can offer ideas or suggestions for solving problems and learn from one another. Such features often are not found in individual therapy. Studies on group therapy have found it to be generally effective for specific disorders (Forsyth & Corazzini, 2000).

The Nature and Types of Group Therapy

What happens in group therapy? Group therapy, like individual psychotherapy, can take many forms. Any one of the four approaches previously described can be used for treating groups of people (Alonso & Swiller, 1993). For example, group behavior therapy can be used to reduce people's fear of flying. Group psychoanalysis or group cognitive therapy can be adapted to work with people who are depressed or to improve interpersonal relations. Three unique forms of group therapy include family therapy, couple therapy, and self-help groups.

Family Therapy: The Whole System

In **family therapy,** the family unit is the group. Often families come to therapy with an "identified patient," such as a misbehaving or rebellious teenager. Yet the focus of family therapy is not on the functioning of the individual, but rather on the functioning of the family as a whole system. The goal of family therapy is to create balance and restore harmony within this family system to improve its functioning. If one person in the family is having problems, these problems are seen as a symptom of disharmony within the family unit (Lebow & Gurman, 1995).

Think of your own family for a moment. Each person in a family has roles, expectations, or labels placed on them, usually at a very young age. One member of the family may be considered "the brain." Another family member may be viewed as "the peacemaker." These roles are not spoken but rather are communicated within the interactions we have with our family members. If a family member does not conform to his or her assigned role, then the rest of the family system will be disrupted. Many times we try the best we can to make family members behave in a way that is consistent with our expectations of their perceived roles. Do you ever feel that your family does not know the "real" you? Have you ever tried to step out of your assigned role, only to find family members so concerned or shaken by your new behavior that it is just easier to go back to your old pattern of behaving? If so, you have experienced the power of the family system.

Family therapists view the "identified patient" as merely the scapegoat for the problems in the family system. As such, they explore and analyze the interactions and communications between family members. They address sources of conflict and note how unspoken rules or expected roles may be interfering with healthy family functioning. Recall Emily's case presented at the beginning of this chapter. Although Emily never underwent family therapy, she understands how a family therapist may have viewed her situation: "A family therapist would have identified me as the family scapegoat, the child designated to 'act out' the conflicts between my tense, driven father and my incipiently alcoholic mother . . ." (p. 63).

Couple Therapy: Improving Communication

Couple therapy focuses on improving communication and intimacy between two people in a committed relationship. The unspoken rules that we use to communicate

family therapy therapy that focuses on creating balance and restoring harmony to improve the functioning of the family as a whole system

Application

couple therapy therapy that focuses on improving communication and intimacy between two people in a committed relationship and the ways in which couples miscommunicate are identified and addressed. The couple therapist then replaces ineffective or unhealthy patterns of communicating with more adaptive ones (Gurman & Jacobson, 2002). For example, couples are encouraged to paraphrase what their partner has said to confirm that they heard the correct message. Criticism and derogatory labels or names are discouraged in communications. These are just two examples of the "new rules" therapists use to improve communication and intimacy among couples.

Self-Help Groups: Helping Each Other Cope

Self-help groups are comprised of people who share the same problem who meet to help one another. Self-help groups differ from other forms of group therapy in that they are organized and led by nonprofessionals. Self-help organizations are becoming increasingly popular, and you, a family member, or a friend may have attended one of their meetings. It is estimated that as many as 20 million people belong to one of these groups and that perhaps 2–3% of the U.S. population is involved in a self-help group at any one time (Borkman, 1997). Self-help groups can be found for anything from addictions and eating disorders, to people who have undergone a medical procedure such as a mastectomy or open-heart surgery. The main purpose of these groups is to offer social support and help one another cope, but they often provide useful information and advice as well.

There is a lot of variability in the format and purpose of self-help groups. For example, the group meetings may be highly structured or conducted more loosely. Yet mental health professionals often encourage clients to participate in such groups to receive additional emotional support and encouragement. They can increase a patient's adherence to treatment and reduce the severity of psychological symptoms (Depression and Bipolar Support Alliance, 2002; Magura, Laudet, Mahmood, Rosenblum, & Knight, 2002). Some research suggests that self-help groups can be just as effective as therapy with a mental health professional (Christensen & Jacobson, 1994). However, research still has been unable to detail what elements of self-help groups make them effective or what types of people they may most benefit.

self-help group group comprised of people who share the same problem who meet to help one another

Let's Review!

This section described group therapy approaches and discussed the advantages and disadvantages of such approaches. For a quick check of your understanding, answer these questions.

1. Which of the following is *not* an advantage of group therapy approaches?
   a. less expensive
   b. more individual attention
   c. focus on interpersonal interactions
   d. none of the above

2. The goal of family therapy is to:
   a. fix the person with the most problems.
   b. improve communication between the parents.
   c. create harmony and balance within the family unit.
   d. understand the past problems of the family.

3. Many self-help groups such as Alcoholics Anonymous or Narcotics Anonymous assume that _____ is a critical factor in improving one's psychological health.
   a. social support
   b. physical health
   c. financial status
   d. medication

ANSWERS

1.b; 2.c; 3.a

» **LEARNING** < < < < < < < <
» **OBJECTIVE**
Examine the effectiveness of psychotherapy, detailing those factors
that contribute to effective therapy.

Effective Psychotherapy: What Treatments Work?

After reading about all these different forms of psychotherapy, you may be asking your-self, "Does psychotherapy work? And if it does work, which approach is the best?" All approaches seem to be helpful and effective in treating some disorders. Researchers an-alyzing the effectiveness of therapy have asked themselves similar questions. As we shall soon see, the answers to these questions are neither simple nor straightforward. Many factors influence and contribute to the effectiveness of therapy.

Which Type of Psychotherapy Is Best?

To answer the question "Does psychotherapy work?" outcome research typically com-pares clients who are receiving therapy with clients who are receiving a placebo treat-ment or no treatment at all. Over the past 25 years, comparisons of hundreds of out-come studies have generally shown that the different approaches—psychodynamic, humanistic, behavioral, and cognitive—produce relatively equivalent results in terms of client improvement (Chambless & Ollendick, 2001; Kopta, Lueger, Saunders, & Howard, 1999; Lambert & Bergen, 1994; Nathan, Stuart, & Dolan, 2000; Robinson et al., 1990; Smith & Glass, 1977; Smith, Glass, & Miller, 1980; Wampold et al., 1997). Thus, it appears that psychotherapy has positive effects and is better than a placebo treatment or no treatment at all. Analyses of over 475 published studies that compared at least one therapy group with a control group showed that on average, the person who receives therapy is better off than about 80% of those in the control groups. These benefits usually develop within 8 weeks to 6 months and tend to endure after the therapy has ended (Assay & Lambert, 1999; Shapiro & Shapiro, 1982; Smith, Glass, & Miller, 1980).

Are all psychotherapies equally effective? Some reviews suggest that the standard psychotherapies have very similar success rates (Kopta et al., 1999; Nathan et al., 2000; Wampold et al., 2002; Wampold et al., 1997). However, other research questions the equivalence of treatment approaches. Such reviews suggest that certain forms of ther-apy work better for certain types of disorders (Chambless & Ollendick, 2001; Crits-Christoph, 1997; Engels, Garnefski, & Diekstra, 1993; Lambert & Bergen, 1994). For example, panic disorder may respond best to cognitive therapy, whereas phobias may respond best to behavioral methods (Chambless & Ollendick, 2001; Hollon & Beck, 1994; Seligman, 1995).

Such mixed results underscore the complexity of conducting research on therapy effectiveness. Think about the selection of participants for such a study. It is hard to find people who all have the same disorder to the same degree. Such differences in symptoms introduce potential sampling problems into the research. Second, think about the administration of the independent variable. In an experiment, therapists would be trained to deliver a very specific type of therapy. To ensure consistency among therapists, deviations from these methods would not be allowed. As you might imagine, this is much different from the way treatment is administered in the real world (Chambless & Hollon, 1998). In addition, it is difficult to design a "no treat-ment" control group. Add to these issues the problem of defining what a good outcome is and how it will be measured (the dependent variable; Hollon, 1996). Do we rely on the therapist's judgment of improvement, the client's self-report of well-being, or some other measure? How long should the client be free of symptoms to consider his or her treatment effective? Although you may not feel that such research questions are im-portant to you, the results of such studies are important to health insurance companies. They use such research to determine the most cost-effective and efficient means of treatment. Consequently, such research may indirectly impact you or a loved one in the future as the competition between therapies increases.

Perhaps a more appropriate question to ask about therapy is "Which treatment is most effective for this person, with this problem, under these circumstances?" Such a personalized approach to treatment is becoming more common as many therapists are adopting an eclectic approach to treatment (Kopta et al., 1999). An **eclectic approach** involves an integrated and diverse use of therapeutic methods. For example, a therapist may combine cognitive therapy with specific psychoanalytic and client-centered methods to help a depressed client. We have seen throughout this chapter that Emily's eventual success in therapy may be attributed in part to the eclectic methods used by Dr. Farber. He combined the free association and interpretation methods of psychoanalysis with the genuineness and unconditional regard of humanism. For Emily and her problems at her age, such an approach proved successful.

eclectic approach   therapy that incorporates an integrated and diverse use of therapeutic methods

Factors That Contribute to Effective Psychotherapy

Although research has provided mixed results to the question "Which psychotherapy is best?" evidence does suggest that all successful psychotherapies share common elements, even when the specific methods used in such approaches may differ greatly. Over the last decade, the term **therapeutic alliance** has surfaced to describe the interactive and collaborative relationship between the client and the therapist. The nature and development of this relationship impact the effectiveness of therapy (Barber, Connolly, Crits-Christoph, Gladis, & Siqueland, 2000; Kozart, 2002; Martin, Garske, & Davis, 2000).

therapeutic alliance   the interactive and collaborative relationship between the client and the therapist

Therapists contribute to a successful alliance in many ways. First, they establish a positive relationship with the client. This involves an atmosphere of mutual respect and trust. Clients who trust their therapist are more likely to believe that they will benefit from therapy. The clients, therefore, are more likely to engage in the therapy process by revealing important information about themselves and by trying the new skills, behaviors, or techniques that the therapist suggests. Effective therapists also are empathetic and warm, evidencing a caring attitude toward the client and the ability to listen (Beutler et al., 1994; Crits-Christoph, Baranackie, Kurcias, & Beck, 1991; Teyber & McClure, 2000). Successful therapists also offer an explanation or interpretation of why the client is having a problem and encourage clients to confront painful emotions (Garfield, 1992; Ingram, Hayes, & Scott, 2000; Snyder, Ilardi, Michael, & Cheavens, 2000). Finally, effective therapists are sensitive to any cultural differences between them and their clients, as the following It's a Diverse World highlights (Yutrzenka, 1995).

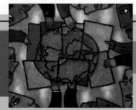

IT'S A DIVERSE WORLD

Culture and Therapy

Culture defines who we are and how we live. Therefore, culture is a crucial component of therapy that can strengthen traditional psychological perspectives. Since the days of Freud, therapy has been delivered within a Euro-American context, often ignoring or only paying scant attention to cultural values important to other non-mainstream groups. Given that most providers of psycho-

logical services come from the majority culture and most clients are members of minority cultures, the success of therapy will be influenced by how sensitive counselors are to cultural differences between them and their clients (Pedersen, 2002).

Recall that successful therapy is very much dependent on the trust that is established between a therapist and a client. Many therapists develop such trust by being

(continued)

Culture and Therapy, *continued*

empathetic, or understanding, of the other person's situation and point of view. Yet if the cultural differences between a client and a therapist are wide, empathy and thereby trust are more difficult to achieve (Draguns, 2002). Therefore, it is important to the success of therapy that counselors acknowledge and understand the experiences and values of ethnocultural populations in the United States.

Counselors working with Native American Indians, for example, must be aware of the specific traditions and customs of the tribes, villages, or communities where the mental health services will be provided as Native Americans comprise many different groups with different languages, traditions, and orientations. Moreover, Native American clients may have a view of "counselor" that differs from the typical therapist–client relationship. They may view counselors as "healers" and thereby seek counseling for a multitude of issues such as financial problems, spiritual guidance, or the problems of other family members as Native Americans tend to be very family-oriented (Trimble & Thurman, 2002). For example, alcohol treatment approaches for Native Americans that incorporate spirituality as well as sensitivity to cultural issues seem to enhance the effectiveness of treatment (Garrett & Carroll, 2000).

Similarly, counselors need to understand several basic cultural values that may be operating when working with Asian American populations. For example, high respect for

and obedience to parents is a strong value that may influence Asian Americans to comply with family wishes rather than their own desires. Such a value illustrates the Asian American emphasis on consensus, belongingness, and togetherness rather than the U.S. model of individualism. Asian Americans tend to value self-control and inconspicuousness and avoid being the center of attention or asserting themselves (Maki & Kitano, 2002). However, as with most culture groups, Asian Americans differ widely among themselves. Therefore a therapist should be careful not to overemphasize traditional cultural expectations just because of the client's nationality.

Given such findings, is successful therapy dependent on the therapist and client sharing the same racial or ethnic background? Not necessarily. Research suggests that a good match between the counselor's and client's beliefs and value systems is of prime importance (Gamst, Dana, Der-Karaberian, & Kramer, 2000). Training in multicultural counseling will be necessary for many therapists to achieve such sensitivity and knowledge. The need for such sensitivity has encouraged academic programs in the United States to incorporate training on multicultural issues into their curriculum. Some states require psychologists to complete such training before they can become licensed. Until such cultural differences are understood, ethnic minorities—a growing segment of the U.S. population—will continue to receive inadequate mental health services.

Therapist characteristics are not the only determinant of a successful alliance. Client attitudes and behaviors of the clients also make a difference (Garfield, 1994; Leon, Kopta, Howard, & Lutz, 1999). Clients who are motivated and committed to therapy tend to experience more positive results. Those who are actively involved in the therapy process and optimistic about the benefits of therapy also fare better. Moreover, clients who can express their feelings and thoughts and who are more psychologically mature experience more gains from therapy. Clients who have no previous history of psychological disorders also tend to benefit more. The social environment of the client also is important. Clients who have supportive loved ones and stable, rather than chaotic, living conditions tend to benefit more from therapy.

Application

Notice that none of these characteristics is specific to any one of the therapy approaches we have described. Consequently, if you or a loved one is in need of a therapist, it is important to find a therapist and an approach that makes you comfortable. If you are more comfortable with the philosophy behind psychoanalysis, find a warm and caring psychoanalyst. If you lean more toward a cognitive approach, seek a therapist who is trained in cognitive methods. Believing in the therapist and his or her approaches will establish a positive therapeutic alliance, thereby enhancing the effectiveness of your therapy.

Modern Delivery Methods of Therapy: Computer Technology and Cybertherapy

In recent years, the rapid development of computer technology and the Internet has started to influence psychotherapy (Taylor & Luce, 2003). Computer-based programs can now be used to administer psychological assessments such as the MMPI-2 to clients. Personal digital assistants (PDAs) can be used to collect data from clients on their thoughts, behaviors, and mood, allowing clinicians to analyze a client's behavior across many situations. Effective computer programs have been developed to reduce symptoms in people with anxiety and depressive disorders (Kenardy et al., 2003; Proudfoot, 2004; Selmi, Klein, Griest, Sorrell & Erdman, 1990). Videoconferencing can provide clients who live too far away a link to therapists. These are just some of the computer tools that can enhance the delivery of psychotherapy.

Are there online psychological services? You bet! The Internet has produced psychological treatment by e-mail, real-time online counseling, professionally assisted chat rooms, self-help groups, and mental health information and education sites. However, Internet-based interventions present a number of professional and ethical issues (Hsiung, 2001; Humphreys, Winzelberg, & Klaw, 2000). Online psychological services lack the close, personal contact of face-to-face interactions. Establishing a therapeutic alliance is more difficult when you cannot hear the tone of someone's voice or read his or her body language and facial expressions. "Cybershrinks" may or may not have adequate training or be appropriately licensed (Bloom, 1998). Client confidentiality is of great concern because information on the Internet can be easily accessed. Moreover, the effectiveness of these programs has not been demonstrated. Controlled studies are needed to evaluate all the benefits and disadvantages of these new communication tools. At this time, technology and the Internet appear to be valuable resources that can be added to traditional psychotherapy (Castelnuovo, Gaggioli, Mantovani, & Riva, 2003). However, caution should be exercised if they are the only type of treatment used.

Let's Review!

This section detailed the effectiveness of psychotherapy and described those factors that contribute to effective therapy. As a quick check of your understanding, answer these questions.

1. Which of the following statements about the effectiveness of psychotherapy is true?
   a. Cognitive therapy is considerably more effective than other forms of therapy.
   b. Psychoanalysis is considerably more effective than other forms of therapy.
   c. The main types of therapy appear to be equally effective.
   d. Receiving therapy appears to be no more effective than no therapy.

2. Which of the following is an element associated with successful therapy?
   a. free association
   b. chaotic living conditions of the client
   c. being forced to receive therapy
   d. a positive therapist–client relationship

3. An eclectic approach to therapy refers to:
   a. an integrated and diverse use of therapeutic methods.
   b. a reliance on free association and interpretation.
   c. a mutual bond of respect and warmth between the therapist and client.
   d. deepening the client's knowledge of psychology.

ANSWERS
1.c; 2.d; 3.a

> ⌄ **LEARNING** < < < < < < < <
> ⌄ **OBJECTIVE**
> ⌄ Describe the aim of biological thera-
> ⌄ pies, and distinguish among the
> ⌄ varying drug therapies.
> ⌄

Biological and Medical Therapies: Changing the Chemistry

Now that we have described psychological treatments for mental health disorders, it is time to turn our attention to biological approaches. Recall that biological therapies are medical treatments designed to treat psychological disorders. Treating psychological disorders with medical treatments is not new. Biological therapies actually predate the psychotherapy approaches. Recall from Chapter 15 (p.659) that prehistoric societies used trephining (drilling holes in the skull) to cure mental illness. During the Renaissance, mentally ill people were chained to walls, heavily restrained, or blood was drawn to treat mental illness. In the 1930s, physicians used insulin coma therapy for people with schizophrenia. These patients were administered massive doses of insulin until they went into a coma in an attempt to alleviate psychotic symptoms. A more positive side of biological therapy did not emerge until the 1950s when the drug *chlorpromazine* was discovered as an effective treatment for schizophrenia. Such a discovery produced a drug revolution in society that continues today. The two dominant biological approaches include drug therapy and electroconvulsive therapy (ECT). Far less used, but still a dramatic last resort, is psychosurgery.

Drug Therapies

Today, the most common biological therapy used to treat mental health problems is medications. You will recall from earlier in this chapter that medications must be prescribed by a physician or a psychiatrist and are generally not prescribed by psychologists. As with any prescribed medication, side effects can occur and must be considered in any treatment plan. Medication cannot cure a mental health disorder. Rather, they reduce the symptoms of the disorder while the person is taking the medication. Often, therefore, medications are prescribed jointly with psychotherapy. The medication sufficiently stabilizes the person such that psychological issues can be addressed. Chapter 4 outlined the major classes of drugs and their effects. Here we review the major types of medications that are prescribed for specific psychological disorders.

Antianxiety Drugs

antianxiety medication minor tranquilizers such as Valium that are prescribed to reduce tension and anxiety

As the name implies, **antianxiety medications** are minor tranquilizers prescribed to reduce tension and anxiety (Table 16.4 ◆). The best-known antianxiety drugs are the *benzodiazepines* such as Valium and Xanax. These medications reduce tension, relax the muscles, and promote sleep by depressing the central nervous system. They influence the functioning of three neurotransmitters: GABA, serotonin, and norepinephrine. They are fast-acting drugs, calming feelings of anxiety within an hour or so. These medications are useful in treating people who are diagnosed with generalized anxiety disorder, panic disorder, posttraumatic stress disorder, agoraphobia, and insomnia (Barlow, 2002; Greenblatt, Harmatz, & Shader, 1993). Unfortunately, the benzodiazepines have three major disadvantages.

What are the side effects of antianxiety medications? The benzodiazepines are highly addictive if taken over a long period. People quickly build up a tolerance to these medications, requiring higher and higher dosages to achieve a reduction in anxiety. If physical dependence does occur, the person must be gradually weaned from the drug because abrupt withdrawal is life threatening. The withdrawal symptoms are quite unpleasant and can include tremors, irritability, insomnia, tingling sensations, a return of intense anxiety, and in rare cases even seizures and paranoia. A second drawback of taking benzodiazepines is the effect on cognitive and motor functioning. As a depres-

◆ **Table 16.4**

Antianxiety Drugs

Generic Name	Trade Name	Common Side Effects
BENZODIAZEPINES		
Alprazolam	Xanax	Dizziness, drowsiness, hypotension, blurred vision
Chlordiazepoxide	Librium	Dizziness, drowsiness, hypotension, blurred vision
Diazepam	Valium	Dizziness, drowsiness, hypotension, blurred vision
Triazolam	Halcion	Headache, tiredness, drowsiness
NONBENZODIAZEPINES		
Buspirone	BuSpar	Dizziness, headache, depression, insomnia, nervousness, numbness, tremors, nausea, dry mouth, diarrhea, constipation, heart palpitations, sore throat, blurred vision, nasal congestion, muscle pain and weakness, rash, sweating

Reprinted from Skidmore-Roth, Mosby's Nursing Drug Reference, copyright © 2005, with permission from Elsevier.

sant drug, the benzodiazepines reduce coordination, alertness, and reaction time (van Laar, Volkerts, & Verbaten, 2001). These impairments can affect a person's ability to drive a car or perform tasks at work or school. These effects are even more severe when an individual combines alcohol with these medications. Finally, *relapse rates* for patients taking benzodiazepines are high. This means that many of the patients taking these drugs experience the anxiety symptoms again when they discontinue treatment or are taken off of the drugs. Consequently, these drugs appear to provide only a short-term relief from anxiety symptoms. Long-term benefits are more likely when benzodiazepine treatment is combined with cognitive-behavioral therapies (Spiegel, 1998).

Because of the serious disadvantages of benzodiazepine treatment, a new nonbenzodiazepine drug, called *buspirone* (trade name BuSpar), is being more widely prescribed to treat anxiety (Asnis, Kohn, Henderson, & Brown, 2004; Laakmann et al., 1998; Rickels et al., 2000; Varley & Smith, 2003). A modest success, buspirone has a lower risk of physical dependence, but it takes considerably longer for the drug to reduce anxiety. The person must take this medication for several days or weeks before a noticeable reduction in anxiety symptoms is achieved.

Antipsychotic Drugs

Over the centuries, many physical treatments had been unsuccessful in treating psychotic symptoms, especially in people diagnosed with schizophrenia. Such treatments included brain surgery (lobotomy), insulin injections, and shock treatment. Because these treatments were ineffective, most people with schizophrenia were merely warehoused in mental hospitals. Yet, in the 1950s, *chlorpromazine* (trade name Thorazine) was discovered as an effective drug in treating psychosis, or a loss of touch with reality. Thorazine and the numerous drugs that followed, such as Mellaril and Haldol, are antipsychotic medications. **Antipsychotic medications** are major tranquilizers prescribed to relieve psychotic symptoms such as agitation, delusions, disordered thinking, and hallucinations (Table 16.5 ◆). They may be prescribed for people with schizophrenia, bipolar depression, or major depression when such individuals have lost touch with reality. These drugs appear to work by reducing the action of the neurotransmitter dopamine in the brain (Sanyal & vanTol, 1997). You will recall from Chapter 15 (p. 688) that dopamine has long been suspected as a major link in understanding the cause of schizophrenia.

antipsychotic medication   major tranquilizers such as Haldol that are prescribed to relieve psychotic symptoms such as delusions and hallucinations

◆ **Table 16.5**

Antipsychotic Drugs

Generic Name	Trade Name	Common Side Effects
TYPICAL ANTIPSYCHOTICS		
Chlorpromazine	Thorazine	Hypotension, dry mouth, nausea, vomiting, constipation, rash, pseudoparkinsonism, tardive dyskinesia, headache
Fluphenazine	Prolixin	Hypotension, dry mouth, nausea, vomiting, constipation, rash, drowsiness, headache, pseudoparkinsonism, tardive dyskinesia
Haloperidol	Haldol	Hypotension, dry mouth, nausea, vomiting, constipation, rash, drowsiness, headache, pseudoparkinsonism, tardive dyskinesia
Thioridazine	Mellaril	Dry mouth, nausea, vomiting, constipation, rash, pseudoparkinsonism, tardive dyskinesia, headache
ATYPICAL ANTIPSYCHOTICS		
Aripiprazole	Abilitat	Drowsiness, insomnia, agitation, anxiety, headache, nausea
Clozapine	Clozaril	Sedation, salivation, dizziness, headache, tremors, sleep problems, fever, sweating, confusion, fatigue, insomnia, drooling, constipation, nausea, abdominal discomfort, vomiting, diarrhea, hypotension, hypertension, urinary abnormalities
Risperidone	Risperdal	Drowsiness, insomnia, agitation, anxiety, headache, pseudoparkinsonism, tardive dyskinesia, nausea, constipation

Reprinted from Skidmore-Roth, Mosby's Nursing Drug Reference, *copyright © 2005, with permission from Elsevier.*

Although antipsychotic drugs decreased dramatically the number of patients in mental hospitals, they also have shortcomings. Antipsychotic medications do not cure schizophrenia. The drugs must be taken all the time—even when the person is not psychotic—to prevent future episodes of symptoms. Moreover, antipsychotic medication does not work for all people with schizophrenia. It is more effective in treating the positive symptoms of schizophrenia than the negative symptoms (see Figure 15.2). These drugs in some cases can even make negative symptoms worse (Miller, Perry, Cadoret, & Andreasen, 1994). Consequently, about 20% of people with schizophrenia do not respond to this treatment (Tamminga, 1997).

What are the side effects of antipsychotic medications? Even more disturbing are the significant side effects that these drugs produce: sleepiness, dry mouth, blurred vision, weight change, drooling, constipation, sexual dysfunction, and depression. Motor side effects also occur including tremors, spasms, frozen facial expressions, and motor agitation, causing people with schizophrenia to pace. These motor side effects often look like Parkinson's disease. This should not be surprising given that Parkinson's disease has been related to a reduced functioning of dopamine in the brain, precisely the effect of antipsychotic medications.

Long-term use of such drugs can lead to an irreversible motor disorder called tardive dyskinesia. **Tardive dyskinesia** involves involuntary motor movements of the mouth, tongue, and face. People experiencing this side effect may repeatedly smack their lips, stick out their tongues, puff out their cheeks, or make other odd facial movements. It is estimated that this serious side effect occurs in 15–20% of people with long-term use of antipsychotic drugs (Chakos, Alvir, Woerner, & Koreen, 1996; Morgenstern & Glazer, 1993).

Such serious side effects often cause people to want to stop taking these drugs. This has created what is referred to as a "revolving door" hospitalization pattern in people with schizophrenia. When a person with schizophrenia is acutely psychotic,

tardive dyskinesia a side effect of antipsychotic medications involving involuntary motor movements of the mouth, tongue, and face

Biological and Medical Therapies: Changing the Chemistry **733**

he or she is hospitalized and then treated with these drugs. Once stabilized, the patient leaves the hospital and then, due to either the serious side effects of the drug and/or inadequate medical follow-up, the person stops taking the drug. Psychotic symptoms return, forcing the patient through the "revolving door" again (Paul & Menditto, 1992).

Recently, new drugs have renewed our hope in successfully treating schizophrenia. These new drugs, called *atypical antipsychotics*, influence the action of serotonin and dopamine in the brain and cause less serious side effects. They are effective in reducing both the positive and negative symptoms of schizophrenia (Bondolfi et al., 1998; Buchanan, Breier, Kirkpatrick, Ball, & Carpenter, 1998; Stahl, 2001a, 2001b). Side effects such as sedation, nausea, seizures, and dizziness may occur, but for those people who did not respond to the traditional antipsychotic medications, these newer drugs can be a lifesaver. Examples of such drugs include *clozapine*, *risperidone*, and *aripiprazole* (see Table 16.5).

Antidepressants

Antidepressants are prescribed to alter mood and alleviate the symptoms of major depression: sadness, guilt, reduced attention and concentration, and changes in sleep, appetite, and energy. Newly developed antidepressants also have been effective in treating people with obsessive-compulsive disorders, panic disorders, eating disorders, and cigarette cravings (Barlow, 2002). As shown in Table 16.6 ◆, there are three main classes of antidepressants: tricyclics, MAO inhibitors, and selective serotonin reuptake inhibitors.

> **antidepressant** medication prescribed to alleviate the symptoms of depression, eating disorders, and some anxiety disorders

Tricyclics Tricyclic antidepressants, such as Tofranil and Elavil, elevate mood and thereby reduce the symptoms of depression by influencing the action of norepinephrine and serotonin in the brain (Stahl, 1998). However, it takes anywhere from 4 to 8 weeks on such medication before a noticeable relief from depression occurs. Tricyclics are effective in relieving depressive symptoms in 60–85% of depressed people (Fawcett, 1994; Guze & Gitlin, 1994). As with any drug, tricyclics do have a number of side effects, such as dry mouth, weight gain, dizziness, blurred vision, constipation, and sexual dysfunction. The tricyclics also can be fatal in overdose amounts, which is why they are seldom prescribed to suicidal patients.

MAO Inhibitors The monoamine oxidase (MAO) inhibitors are a class of antidepressants that elevate mood by increasing the monamine neurotransmitters in the brain (Stahl, 1998). They are just as effective as the tricyclic antidepressants but are less frequently prescribed because of their more serious side effects (M. Fava & Rosenbaum, 1995). These include lowered blood pressure, liver damage, and weight gain. These drugs also interact with substances high in an amino acid called *tyramine*. Tyramine is present in common foods such as cheese, smoked meats, and chocolate, liquids such as beer and wine, and even over-the-counter medications. This interaction can produce a sudden rise in blood pressure that is potentially fatal. Simply check the caution statements on the back of any over-the-counter cold medication and you will notice that it is not to be used by a person who is taking a MAO inhibitor. Yet, MAO inhibitors may be more effective in the treatment of severe depression than the newer antidepressants (Parker, Roy, Wilhelm, & Mitchell, 2001).

 **≪** Application

Selective Serotonin Reuptake Inhibitors (SSRIs) Currently, the most frequently prescribed antidepressant medications are the **selective serotonin reuptake inhibitors (SSRIs)** such as Prozac and Zoloft. Recall from Chapter 2 (p. 58) that reuptake is the process whereby the neurotransmitters that are left over in the synapse of the neuron are recycled back into the terminal button. SSRIs elevate mood by leaving the neuro-

> **selective serotonin reuptake inhibitor (SSRI)** a type of antidepressant drug that inhibits the reuptake of the neurotransmitter serotonin, thereby improving mood

◆ **Table 16.6**

Antidepressant Drugs

Generic Name	Trade Name	Common Side Effects
TRICYCLIC ANTIDEPRESSANTS		
Amitriptyline	Elavil	Dizziness, drowsiness, constipation, dry mouth, urinary retention, hypotension, blurred vision
Desipramine	Norpramin, Pertofrane	Dizziness, drowsiness, dry mouth, hypotension, headache, increased appetite/weight, nausea, unusual tiredness, unpleasant taste
Doxepin	Adepin, Sinequan	Dizziness, drowsiness, diarrhea, dry mouth, urinary retention, hypotension, blurred vision
Imipramine	Tofranil	Dizziness, drowsiness, diarrhea, dry mouth, urinary retention, hypotension
Nortriptyline	Aventyl, Pamelor	Dizziness, drowsiness, constipation, dry mouth, urinary retention, hypotension, blurred vision
MAO INHIBITORS		
Phenelzine	Nardil	Dizziness, drowsiness, change in appetite, hypotension, hypertension, dysrhythmias
Tranylcypromine	Parnate	Dizziness, drowsiness, change in appetite, hypotension, hypertension, dysrhythmias
SELECTIVE SEROTONIN REUPTAKE INHIBITORS (SSRIs)		
Fluoxetine	Prozac	Headache, insomnia, drowsiness, tremor, dizziness, fatigue, poor concentration, abnormal dreams, agitation, nausea, diarrhea, dry mouth, change in appetite, constipation, cramps, vomiting, flatulence, sweating, rash, nasal congestion, cough, heart palpitations, muscle pain, decreased sexual desire, increased urinary frequency
Paroxetine	Paxil	Nausea, prolonged sleepiness, headache, dry mouth, constipation, dizziness, insomnia, diarrhea, sweating
Sertraline	Zoloft	Insomnia or prolonged drowsiness, dizziness, headache, tremor, fatigue, male sexual dysfunction, diarrhea, nausea, constipation, change in appetite, dry mouth, vomiting, flatulence
OTHER ANTIDEPRESSANTS		
Bupropion	Wellbutrin, Zyban	Headache, agitation, dizziness, confusion, insomnia, tremors, hypertension, nausea, vomiting, dry mouth, constipation, menstrual irregularities, rash, sweating, blurred vision, weight loss or gain

Reprinted from Skidmore-Roth, Mosby's Nursing Drug Reference, *copyright © 2005, with permission from Elsevier.*

transmitter serotonin in the synapse longer. SSRIs are equally as effective as the other classes of antidepressants (Mulrow et al., 2000; Thase, 2003; Thase, Jindal, & Howland, 2002; Thase & Kupfer, 1996) and have several advantages.

The SSRIs alleviate depression more quickly than the tricyclics or the MAO inhibitors, providing relief from symptoms within a few weeks. Their side effects also are less severe and are not fatal in overdose. The side effects of SSRIs include increased nervousness, headaches, insomnia, nausea, stomach cramps, decreased sexual drive, and sexual dysfunction (Fisher, Kent, & Bryant, 1995; Michelson, Bancroft, Targum,

Kim, & Tepner, 2000). Some of these side effects may diminish after a few weeks of treatment, however. As stated previously, the SSRIs also are useful in treating other disorders besides depression, such as anxiety and eating disorders (Abramowitz, 1997; Bell & Nutt, 1998; Hudson et al., 1998). For all of these reasons, the SSRIs are quite popular. Moreover, other new antidepressants, such as Zyban and Wellbutrin that are similar to the SSRIs but influence the norepinephrine and dopamine systems, are also being prescribed (Stahl, 1998). These antidepressants do not decrease one's sexual drive and are therefore sometimes used in conjunction with SSRI drugs.

However, antidepressant medication has been associated with an increased risk of suicidal thoughts and behaviors in children and adolescents, especially in the first few months of treatment (FDA Public Health Advisory, 2004). In October 2004, the Food and Drug Administration directed that manufacturers of antidepressants include a "black box" warning—the FDA's strongest—on all antidepressant medication.

Antimanics

The **antimanic medications** are prescribed to alleviate manic symptoms of bipolar depression. The most effective and commonly prescribed antimanic is **lithium,** a naturally occurring mineral salt. Lithium has the advantage of controlling both manic and depressive symptoms in people with bipolar disorder, although it is far more effective in treating mania (Barondes, 1993; Kahn, 1995). For this reason, people with bipolar disorder may be prescribed antidepressant drugs in addition to lithium to stabilize their moods. Lithium achieves its effect by influencing several neurotransmitters in the brain: glutamate, serotonin, and dopamine (Dixon & Hokin, 1998; Lenox & Manji, 1995). It is taken even when people have no symptoms of mania to prevent future manic episodes. This has led to the saying "Once on lithium, always on lithium."

How effective is lithium in treating mania? Research on the effectiveness of lithium is controversial. Some research reports a success rate of 80–90%, whereas other research indicates a considerably lower level of success (30–50%; Goodwin & Jamison, 1990; Moncrieff, 1997; Shou, 1993). This controversy in success rate may be related to the extreme variability in people's absorption of lithium. Some people absorb lithium rather quickly and can therefore tolerate only small dosages, whereas others absorb the chemical more slowly. Lithium dosage amounts, therefore, vary considerably from one person to the next. Too little lithium can lead to manic episodes, whereas too much can lead to lithium poisoning involving vomiting, nausea, slurred speech, and impaired muscle coordination. For any one person, the difference between the correct, or "therapeutic," amount of lithium and a toxic amount is a very fine line. For this reason, lithium levels must be carefully monitored in people with bipolar disorder.

The effectiveness of lithium is further complicated by patient compliance. That is, some people with bipolar disorder who take lithium miss the euphoric feelings of the manic state and, against the advice of their physicians, go off lithium when they are feeling better. They often believe that they can control their symptoms without the assistance of lithium. Unfortunately, manic symptoms often return, thus requiring a recalibration of appropriate lithium levels (Cookson, 1997).

What are the side effects of lithium? Lithium, like all the drugs discussed so far, also has side effects, including nausea, vomiting, diarrhea, blurred vision, reduced concentration, weight gain, and increased risk of diabetes and kidney problems (Maj, Pirozzi, Magliano, & Bartoli, 1997). It also can lead to birth defects if taken by pregnant women during their first trimester. For those people with bipolar disorder who do not respond to lithium or who cannot tolerate its side effects, other drug options are available (Table 16.7 ◆). For example, *anticonvulsant drugs* such as Tegretol and Depakote are effective in treating severe mania and produce fewer side effects than lithium. However, they can still cause birth defects when taken by pregnant women.

antimanic medication drugs that are prescribed to alleviate manic symptoms of bipolar disorder

lithium a naturally occurring mineral salt prescribed to control manic symptoms in people with bipolar disorder. It influences several neurotransmitters in the brain including glutamate, serotonin, and dopamine

◆ **Table 16.7**

Antimanic Drugs

Generic Name	Trade Name	Common Side Effects
LITHIUM		
Lithium carbonate		Headache, drowsiness, dizziness, dry mouth, change in appetite, nausea, vomiting, diarrhea, hypotension
ANTICONVULSANTS		
Carbamazepine	Tegretol	Drowsiness, nausea, constipation, diarrhea, rash
Divalproex sodium	Depakene and Valproate	Drowsiness, nausea, vomiting, constipation, diarrhea, change in appetite, rash
Valproic acid	Depakote	Drowsiness, nausea, vomiting, constipation, diarrhea, change in appetite, rash
TYPICAL ANTIPSYCHOTICS		
Haloperidol	Haldol	Hypotension, dry mouth, nausea, vomiting, constipation, rash, drowsiness, pseudoparkinsonism, tardive dyskinesia, headache
CALCIUM CHANNEL BLOCKERS		
Nimodipine		Low blood pressure, nausea, irregular heartbeat, flushing, light-headedness, rash
Verapamil		Fluid retention, nausea, constipation, headache, drowsiness

Reprinted from Skidmore-Roth, Mosby's Nursing Drug Reference, *copyright © 2005, with permission from Elsevier.*

Their long-term effectiveness also has not been firmly established (Post et al., 1998). When a person with bipolar disorder experiences a manic state that progresses to the point of psychosis, antipsychotic medications may be prescribed (discussed previously). Most recently, drugs called *calcium channel blockers* have proven effective in treating manic symptoms in some cases (Goodnick, 2000; Levy & Janicak, 2000; Post et al., 1998; Yingling, Utter, Vengalil, & Mason, 2002). Although their effectiveness is questionable, these drugs are advantageous in that they have fewer side effects and do not lead to birth defects when taken by pregnant women.

Electroconvulsive Therapy (ECT)

electroconvulsive therapy (ECT) a series of treatments in which electrical current is passed to the brain. It is used to alleviate severe depression

Before the birth of drug therapy in the 1950s, the most common form of biological therapy consisted of administering electrical shocks to the brains of patients to induce seizures. This procedure, called **electroconvulsive therapy (ECT),** was a routine therapy approach used on people with schizophrenia. It was believed that producing a seizure would calm the hallucinations, agitation, and delusions that people with schizophrenia experience. Such an effect did not occur. It was not effective in treating people with schizophrenia. However, for reasons that aren't clear, it can be effective in treating people with severe depression.

How is ECT administered? Although still highly controversial, today ECT consists of a series of treatments, usually performed in a hospital, in which electrical current is passed to the brain causing a seizure. After administration of anesthesia and a muscle relaxant, metal electrodes are placed on the head of the now-unconscious patient. A current of 70–130 volts is passed through one side of the brain for roughly $\frac{1}{2}$ of a second. A seizure occurs in the brain, causing the patient to have muscle tremors for about 1 minute. Violent convulsions do not occur due to the administration of the muscle relaxant prior to the procedure. The patient undergoes this procedure about every other day for 6 to 12 sessions. It is a quick and painless medical procedure.

Many students are abhorred and even frightened by ECT. It seems so archaic and primitive. These are natural and common reactions. However, keep in mind that ECT is not the first treatment for depression, but rather a last resort. It is administered to patients who are depressed and are not responding to psychotherapy or drug therapy and remain in a severely depressed state. These patients may be suicidal or even psychotic. For these patients, ECT may be the only form of treatment that is effective (Barlow & Durand, 2005). Imagine that a close friend or relative of yours was deeply depressed. This loved one may be imagining that he or she is the devil, or he or she may be suicidal. Psychotherapy has not been effective. Drug therapy has not helped. So what do you do? Your loved one can continue suffering—or try ECT.

Is ECT effective? Yes. It is effective for 50–80% of people who are severely depressed, and it is very effective in treating psychotic depression (Coryell, 1998; Maxmen & Ward, 1995; Parker, Roy, Wilhelm, & Mitchell, 2001). It also relieves depression faster than drug therapy. Most patients improve within a few days. How does ECT work? We currently don't understand how ECT lifts depression. It is speculated that the seizure may alter the functioning of brain structures. Alternatively, the seizure may alter the functioning of neurotransmitters in the brain (O'Connor, 1993). Identifying the precise effect of shock on all brain functions is rather like finding a needle in a haystack. So we continue to investigate the power of ECT on depression.

What are the side effects of ECT? ECT does have its drawbacks. It can lead to cognitive impairments, such as memory loss, learning difficulties, or disturbances in verbal abilities. In the past, ECT was administered to both sides of the brain, causing severe memory loss and cognitive impairments. Today, it is commonly administered only to one side of the brain, thus causing fewer side effects. Typically, it is administered to the right side of the brain as this hemisphere plays less of a role in learning and memory.

A second concern in using ECT is the high relapse rate. As many as 85% of ECT patients relapse into depression. This relapse may occur as soon as 4 months after treatment. Consequently, the effects of ECT seem to be short-lived (Swartz, 1995). Despite ECT's short-term effectiveness, these concerns— as well as people's fears about administering electrical shock to the brain—continue to make ECT a very controversial treatment approach.

◀◀ **Application**

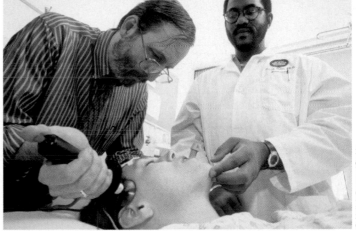

Electroconvulsive therapy (ECT) is a last-resort treatment option administered to patients who are depressed and are not responding to psychotherapy or drug therapy and remain in a severely depressed state.

© Najlah Feanny/Corbis

Psychosurgery

A dramatic last resort for the treatment of psychological disorders is psychosurgery. **Psychosurgery** involves surgically altering the brain to alleviate symptoms in someone with a mental health disorder. First introduced in the 1940s and 1950s, probably the best-known psychosurgery is the *prefrontal lobotomy*, in which the nerves connecting the frontal lobe to the rest of the brain were surgically disconnected. However, with the rise and success of drug therapies, psychosurgery declined considerably as lobotomies were generally ineffective and produced seizures and a loss in intellectual functioning (Swayze, 1995).

Is psychosurgery still used today? Yes. Many neurosurgeons continue to use psychosurgery for treating people with mental illness who do not respond to conventional biomedical or psychological treatments. Today, psychosurgery methods are more precise due to recent improvements in surgical techniques. For example, a neurosurgeon

psychosurgery   a biological treatment approach involving neurosurgery to alleviate symptoms in someone with a mental health disorder may lesion (destroy) a small target area of the brain to reduce symptoms of obsessive-compulsive disorder. Research suggests that approximately 25%–30% of patients who have undergone this procedure significantly improve (Baer et al., 1995; Dougherty et al., 2002; Jenike et al., 1991). Since 1993, neurosurgeons have been implanting deep brain stimulators in people who have Parkinson's disease (Benabid et al., 2001). It is the most commonly practiced surgical treatment for this disease, improving motor function by at least 60%, leading to a significant improvement in the quality of life for people with Parkinson's (Ashcan, Wallace, Bell, & Benabid, 2004). Yet keep in mind that such operations are performed very infrequently and only as a last resort. Psychosurgery continues to be a controversial biomedical technique (Anderson & Arciniegas, 2004).

Let's Review!

This section described biological approaches to therapy including drug therapies, electroconvulsive therapy, and psychosurgery. For a quick check of your understanding, answer these questions.

1. Electroconvulsive therapy is most effective for the treatment of:
   a. schizophrenia.
   c. severe depression.
   b. panic attacks.
   d. bipolar disorder.

2. Which of the following is the most serious side effect of taking typical antipsychotic medication?
   a. rebound anxiety
   c. hallucinations
   b. physical dependence
   d. tardive dyskinesia

3. Prozac is what type of antidepressant drug?
   a. SSRI
   c. tricyclic
   b. MAO inhibitor
   d. benzodiazepine

ANSWERS

1.c; 2.d; 3.a

Are You Getting the Big Picture?

This chapter outlined the major types of psychotherapies and biological therapies. We have seen that each therapeutic approach stems from one of the main psychological perspectives introduced in the beginning of this textbook: biological, psychoanalytic, cognitive, behavioral, and humanistic. We also have seen that therapy is generally effective, regardless of the specific techniques endorsed. Of course, the effectiveness of therapy will be directly related to the characteristics of the therapist and the client.

As you study the material in this chapter, keep in mind how the knowledge you gained from previous chapters directly relates to your understanding of the focus and techniques of these varying therapy approaches. For example, if you are having difficulty understanding the behavioral techniques, review Chapter 5 on learning. It presents the basic principles under-

lying their use of conditioning to modify behavior. Similarly, Chapter 2 on biology may further your understanding of how medications work to alleviate psychological distress. If you are unsure which chapter to refer to, the index at the end of the textbook is a valuable resource. Looking up a particular term will refer you to all the pages in which that idea is presented.

We hope that you have enjoyed your journey through psychology. Moreover, we hope that you have found the material relevant to your life. Being aware of the complex interaction among biological, psychological, and social variables will further your understanding of not only your behavior but the behavior of those around you. Good luck!

STUDYING THE CHAPTER

Key Terms

therapy (704)
psychotherapy (705)
biological therapy (705)
psychoanalysis (709)
free association (709)
dream analysis (709)
interpretations (710)
resistance (710)
transference (710)
psychodynamic therapy (710)
client-centered therapy (712)
empathy (712)
genuineness (713)
unconditional positive regard (713)

behavior therapy (714)
systematic desensitization (715)
anxiety hierarchy (715)
aversion therapy (716)
covert sensitization therapy (717)
token economy (718)
rational-emotive therapy (719)
cognitive therapy (720)
cognitive distortions (721)
group therapy (723)
family therapy (724)
couple therapy (724)
self-help group (725)
eclectic approach (727)

therapeutic alliance (727)
antianxiety medication (730)
antipsychotic medication (731)
tardive dyskinesia (732)
antidepressant (733)
selective serotonin reuptake
    inhibitor (SSRI) (733)
antimanic medication (735)
lithium (735)
electroconvulsive therapy
    (ECT) (736)
psychosurgery (737)

Test Yourself!

Concept Check

Test your knowledge of the chapter concepts by matching the type of therapy with the statement that best describes it. For a more comprehensive review, visit the book Web site (http://psychology.wadsworth.com/pastorinole/) for online quizzes, flashcards, crosswords, and Internet links.

_____ **1.** The therapist uses techniques such as free association and hypnosis to uncover hidden conflicts.

_____ **2.** The therapist uses systematic desensitization to treat a person with phobic disorder.

_____ **3.** The therapist challenges the irrational beliefs of the client.

_____ **4.** A client takes antidepressants to treat her mood disorder.

_____ **5.** The therapist expresses genuineness and empathy to her client.

_____ **6.** The therapist interprets the client's information and behavior so as to provide insight into his problems.

_____ **7.** The therapist reinforces appropriate client behavior and ignores inappropriate behavior.

_____ **8.** The therapist reflects the client's thoughts and feelings so that the therapist can better understand the client's problems.

_____ **9.** A therapist pairs an unpleasant stimulus with the behavior in the hopes of reducing its occurrence.

_____ **10.** The therapist teaches the client how to recognize negative automatic thought patterns.

a. cognitive therapies

b. psychoanalysis

c. behavior therapies

d. biological therapies

e. humanistic therapies

Answers:

1. b; 2. c; 3. a; 4. d; 5. e; 6. b; 7. c; 8. e; 9. c; 10. a

Critical Thinking About the Chapter

1. Compare and contrast psychoanalysis and client-centered therapy. What qualities do they have in common? What are their major differences?

2. Which psychotherapy approach do you find the most appealing, and why? Which psychotherapy approach do you find the least appealing, and why?

3. What can the critical components of therapy effectiveness teach us about resolving our own problems? How might these components be useful in group therapy approaches?

4. What are the advantages and disadvantages of using medication to treat mental health problems?

Applying Psychology. Think about a behavior or problem that you have had or are having. Choose a behavior therapy method to change this behavior. What would the behavior and the method be, and how would you go about changing the behavior?

Critical Thinking for Integration

1. Design an experiment (Chapter 1) that would test the effectiveness of a drug therapy versus a psychotherapy. Be sure to carefully define your dependent measure of effectiveness.

2. Refer to the conditioning of Little Albert's fear of a white rat in Chapter 5 and design a therapy approach to reduce Albert's fear.

3. How might some of the psychotherapy techniques described in this chapter promote problem-focused coping styles in response to stress (Chapter 13)?

Chapter Study Resources

Suggested Readings

1. Gordon, E. F. (2000). *Mockingbird years: A life in and out of therapy.* New York: Basic Books.
Emily Fox Gordon's riveting account of receiving various forms of therapy both in and out of different mental health facilities.

2. Yalom, I. D. (2000). *Momma and the meaning of life: Tales of psychotherapy.* New York: Basic Books.
Psychiatrist and psychotherapist Irvin D. Yalom recounts six entertaining and thoughtful stories drawn from his own clinical experience that illustrate the nature of therapy.

3. Beutler, L. E., Bongar, B., & Shurkin, J. N. (1998). *Am I crazy or is it my shrink?* New London: Oxford University Press.
An easy-to-read guide about finding the therapy that is right for you.

5. For additional readings, visit InfoTrac College Edition, your online library of archived journals and periodicals. Go to http://www.infotrac-college.com/wadsworth and use the passcode from the card that came with your book. For this chapter, search using these keywords:

cognitive therapy

antidepressants

group therapy

virtual reality exposure therapy

unconditional positive regard

Web Links for Further Study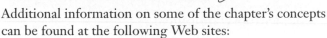

Additional information on some of the chapter's concepts can be found at the following Web sites:

1. The American Psychoanalytic Association contains articles and scientific programs related to psychoanalysis.
http://www.apsa.org/

2. Links to behavior analysis resources are listed at this site.
http://www.cocdu.usf.edu/behavior/bares.htm

3. About Psychotherapy provides general information on the types of psychotherapy and choosing a psychotherapist.
http://www.aboutpsychotherapy.com/

4. MedWeb is a resource by Emory University providing information on mental health, psychiatry, and psychology. Click on Mental Health to access links to mental health disorders and treatment options.
http://www.medweb.emory.edu/MedWeb/

5. The Health Square site offers information on drugs prescribed for various health and mental health disorders.
http://www.healthsquare.com/drugmain.htm

Student Study Guide

To help organize your learning, work through Chapter 16 of the *What Is Psychology? Student Study Guide*. The study guide includes learning objectives, a chapter summary, fill-in review, key terms, a practice test, and activities.

Psychology Now™

PsychologyNow is a Web-based, personalized study system that provides you with a pretest and a posttest for each chapter, quizzes you by chapter, and provides a personalized study plan, pointing you to elements in the text or in individual learning modules that will help you to achieve 80% mastery. Check out the learning module that relates to this chapter: cognitive-behavioral therapy.

PsychNow CD-ROM, Version 2.0

Go to the PsychNow CD-ROM for further study of the concepts in this chapter. The CD-ROM includes learning modules with videos, animations, and quizzes, as well as simulations of psychological phenomena. Each module follows a consistent Explore, Lesson, and Apply structure that allows you to experience the concept or principle, learn more about it, and then apply it. You and your friends can participate in a team-based Quiz Game that makes learning fun. Learning modules include: 7b. Major Psychological Theories.

What Therapies Are Used to Treat Psychological Problems?

Therapy consists of techniques that are used to help people with psychological or interpersonal problems.

PROVIDING PSYCHOLOGICAL ASSISTANCE

• Psychotherapy assumes that psychological factors such as emotions, cognitions, behaviors, or relationships underlie mental health disorders and interpersonal problems.

• Psychotherapy is administered by clinical psychologists, licensed counselors, social workers, or therapists.

• Psychotherapists abide by ethical standards of confidentiality, competent treatment, informed consent, and appropriate interactions.

• You do not have to be suffering from a psychological disorder in order to benefit from therapy, but should consider therapy if you feel helpless, sad, or nervous for a prolonged period of time or if such feelings do not improve despite several efforts to change them.

TYPES OF PSYCHOTHERAPY

• The goal of traditional psychoanalysis is to have clients gain insight into the real source of their problems. Free association, resistance, dream analysis, transference, and interpretation are typical methods that are used to uncover critical issues from long-standing unconscious conflicts.

• Modern psychodynamic therapy approaches continue to rely on the therapist's interpretations of the client's feelings and behaviors yet place more emphasis on the client's current problems and interpersonal relations and focus less on the client's past.

• The goal of humanistic therapies, such as client-centered therapy, is to connect with and understand the client's worldview. The therapist offers the client genuineness, empathy, and unconditional positive regard to encourage self exploration and self-fulfillment.

• Behavior therapies directly focus on changing current problem behaviors by using learning principles to change environmental circumstances that seem to elicit maladaptive behavior. In classical conditioning therapies, such as systematic desensitization, virtual reality technology, and aversion therapy, the client's responses to stimuli are changed. In operant conditioning therapies such as shaping, extinction, positive reinforcement, and token economies, the consequences of a client's behavior are changed.

• In cognitive therapies, maladaptive patterns of thinking and perceiving are replaced with more adaptive ways of interpreting events. For example, in rational-emotive therapy, the therapist confronts, questions, and challenges the validity of client's irrational beliefs. In Beck's cognitive therapy, the therapist identifies and tracks negative automatic thoughts and has the client test the accuracy of these cognitive distortions.

GROUP THERAPY

• The goal of group therapy is to improve the functioning and interactions among individuals, families, couples, or other groups.

• Group therapy tends to be less expensive than individual therapy and offers a safe mini-environment to explore new social behaviors or to understand how our interactions with others may be impeding our psychological health.

EFFECTIVE PSYCHOTHERAPY

• Generally, the different psychotherapy approaches produce relatively equivalent results in terms of clients improving. Yet successful psychotherapy depends on several variables including qualities of the therapist, client, and the client's environment to establish a positive therapeutic alliance.

• A personalized approach to treatment is becoming more common as many therapists are adopting an eclectic approach to treatment. An eclectic approach involves an integrated and diverse use of therapeutic methods.

• Modern delivery methods of therapy include computer technology and cybertherapy. However, the effectiveness of these new communication tools has not been demonstrated.

BIOLOGICAL AND MEDICAL THERAPIES

• Biological therapies assume that biological factors underlie mental health problems. These therapies are administered by psychiatrists and other medical professionals.

• The most common biological therapy used to treat mental health problems is medications. Drug therapies influence brain neurotransmitters to alter behavior.
— Antianxiety medications such as the benzodiazepines influence GABA, serotonin, and norepinephrine levels in the brain. They are prescribed to reduce tension and anxiety.
— Antipsychotic drugs such as Haldol reduce the action of the neurotransmitter dopamine in the brain and are prescribed to relieve psychotic symptoms such as agitation, delusions, disordered thinking, and hallucinations.
— Antidepressant medications that are prescribed for mood and anxiety disorders influence dopamine, serotonin, norepinephrine, or monamine neurotransmitters.
— Antimanic drugs are used primarily to treat mania and influence glutamate, serotonin, and dopamine neurotransmitters.

• More controversial biological therapies include electroconvulsive therapy (ECT) and psychosurgery. In ECT a seizure is created in the brain to treat severe depression. Psychosurgery involves surgically altering the brain to alleviate severe symptoms of Parkinson's disease and obsessive-compulsive disorder.

Statistical Appendix

Statistics in Psychology > > > > > > > > > > > > > > > >

As you learned in Chapter 1, psychology is the scientific study of behavior and mental processes. As such, psychologists develop hypotheses about behavior and mental processes and then test these hypotheses using experiments, case studies, surveys, naturalistic observations, or other research methods. In the course of their research, psychologists collect a variety of information, or **data,** from their research participants.

For example, many people believe that when it comes to romance, opposites attract. Is this really true, or is it just a bit of ill-conceived folk wisdom? A psychologist would rely on science to answer this question. One way to test this idea would be to collect data from couples concerning each partner's personal characteristics and then examine these data to see whether couples tend to be more similar or dissimilar on these characteristics. After numerous studies that have taken this scientific approach to romance (for a review, see Aronson, Wilson, & Akert, 2004, pp. 342–344), psychologists have concluded that the folk wisdom of "opposites attract" does *not* seem to be true. Rather, when seeking romantic partners, we tend to gravitate toward those who are similar to us. Without scientific data to point us in the right direction, it would be impossible to separate fact from fiction in the world.

In another example of how a scientist might use data, imagine that you are a health psychologist interested in whether or not the legal drinking age in a country affects the rate of underage drinking in that society. More specifically, you might ask questions like "Does having a lower legal drinking age encourage drinking among 15-year-olds?" "And if so, does legal drinking age equally affect both male and female 15-year-olds?" To see whether such relationships exist, you must first collect data on the number of 15-year-olds who drink in particular countries along with each country's legal drinking age.

Obviously, it would be impractical for any researcher to survey the entire **population** of 15-year-olds in the world. So, instead of trying to collect data from the entire population, you would measure the characteristics of a subset, or **sample,** of the population. However, if your sample is to be useful in answering your questions, you must use a **representative sample,** or a sample in which the participants are representative of the entire population about which you are trying to draw conclusions. For instance, you would not wish to sample and test only 15-year-olds from wealthy families. Likewise, it would be a mistake to limit your sample to White 15-year-olds or to those growing up in rural areas. So, how can you ensure that your sample of 15-year-olds is representative and accurately reflects the behavior of the entire population of 15-year-olds?

One way to do this is to use **random selection** when choosing participants for your study. Random selection involves selecting participants so that each person in the population has an equal chance of being chosen to participate in the study. By randomly selecting 15-year-olds in each country you are studying, it is highly unlikely that your sample will be limited to any specific type of 15-year-old. Therefore your sample will be unbiased and representative of the whole population. This is important because only a representative sample will allow you to draw conclusions about the entire population—not just those 15-year-olds who participated in your study. Table A.1 ◆ shows data from a representative sample of male and female 15-year-olds for 28 selected countries.

Take a moment to look at the data in Table A.1. By just looking at the table, can you tell whether a relationship exists between the percentage of 15-year-old students who drink and a country's minimum legal drinking age? If you cannot, don't feel bad. You are in good company—it's impossible to tell from just a table whether the data support one's hypothesis. Instead, psychologists must use a type of applied mathematics, called **statistics,** to describe and analyze their data. Only then can a researcher determine what the data say about her hypothesis.

LEARNING OBJECTIVES

≫ Define the terms data and statistics, and explain how they are used in science.
≫ Explain the difference between samples and populations, as well as the importance of obtaining representative samples through random selection.

data information gathered in scientific studies

population all the members of a group that we wish to draw inferences about in a scientific study

sample the subset of the population that is actually studied in a piece of research

representative sample a sample or subset, of the population that is representative of the entire population (i.e., the participants in the sample have the same characteristics as the larger population from which they are taken)

random selection a method of obtaining a representative sample from a population in which all members of the population have an equal chance of being selected to be in the sample

statistics a type of applied mathematics used to describe data and test hypotheses

◆ **Table A.1**

Percent of Students Who Report Drinking Alcohol Weekly at Age 15, Selected Countries

Country	Minimum Legal Drinking Age	Males	Females
Austria	16	39	23
Belgium	16	38	22
Canada	18	22	17
Czech Republic	18	32	19
Denmark	15	46	38
England	18	47	36
Estonia	18*	21	10
Finland	18	11	8
France	16	31	15
Germany	16	29	22
Greece	16*	52	31
Greenland	18	13	10
Hungary	16	29	11
Ireland	18	27	12
Israel	18	26	10
Latvia	18	28	12
Lithuania	21	16	9
Northern Ireland	18	33	20
Norway	18	16	12
Poland	18	20	8
Portugal	16	29	9
Russia	18	28	24
Scotland	18	37	33
Slovakia	18	32	16
Sweden	18	17	11
Switzerland	16	19	9
United States	21	23	15
Wales	18	53	36

Except where noted, data taken from: Kaul, C. (2002). Statistical Handbook on the World's Children, (p. 447). Westport, CT: Oryx Press.

*These data taken from: http://www2.potsdam.edu/alcohol-info/ LegalDrinkingAge.html#worlddrinkingages on 11/6/03

LEARNING OBJECTIVES

- Interpret the different types of graphs and distributions used in statistical analyses, including frequency distributions, frequency polygons, histograms, and scatter plots.
- Calculate and interpret the different measures of central tendency and variability used in statistics—the mean, median, mode, range, sample variance, and standard deviation.
- Explain what a normal and standard normal distribution are.
- Calculate and interpret a z score and the correlation coefficient.

Using Statistics to Describe Data

Graphs: Depicting Data Visually

Take another look at the data in Table A.1. Where would you start if you wanted to see whether the legal drinking age is related to drinking rates among 15-year-olds? Well, have you ever heard that *a picture is worth a thousand words?* One way to start would be to create a **graph,** or pictorial representation of the data. Psychologists use many different types of graphs to help analyze their data. One of the more common graphs is a **frequency distribution.** A graph of a frequency distribution is a two-dimensional illustration that plots how frequently certain events occur. For example, it might be useful to see the frequency, or rate at which countries have set certain minimum drinking ages. This information could be depicted using several types of graphs to illustrate the frequency distribution, but two of the more common ones are **frequency polygons** (a line graph) and **histograms** (a bar graph). Figures A.1a and A.1b show the frequency distribution of legal drinking age depicted with both a frequency polygon and a histogram. By looking at these graphs, we can see that most of these selected governments have set their minimum drinking age below 21, with the most commonly set drinking age at 18.

graph   a visual depiction of data

frequency distribution   a graph of data that plots the frequency of data points on the *y*-axis and the data points themselves on the *x*-axis

frequency polygon   a line graph that is used to illustrate a frequency distribution

histogram   a bar graph that is used to illustrate a frequency distribution

scatter plot   a graph of data that plots pairs of data points, with one data point on the *x*-axis and the other on the *y*-axis

An even more useful type of graph for this investigation would be a **scatter plot.** In a scatter plot, two variables are plotted as a function of each other. For example, we could plot the percentage of 15-year-old drinkers as a function of the country's minimum drinking age. Figure A.2a shows such plots for males and females. By looking at the scatter plots in Figure A.2a, you can get a *very crude* picture of the relationship between drinking age and the rate of underage drinking at age 15. Looking at Figure A.2a, as the minimum drinking age decreases, does the rate of underage drinking increase? Do these data confirm or discount our hypothesis that lowering the drinking age encourages underage drinking? Although it is true that countries with a minimum drinking age of 16 or younger have relatively high levels of underage drinking, there are also a number of countries with a minimum drinking age of 18 that have even higher levels of underage drinking by 15-year-olds. Similarly, Figure A.2b seems to show that male and female rates of drinking are related. It appears that as more males drink, more females also engage in drinking—but if you look closely at the scatter plot, this isn't always true. Therefore, these plots only give us a crude picture of the relationship between our variables. It's impossible to say for sure whether our hypotheses about teenage drinking have merit by simply looking at these plots. To truly examine our hypothesis, we will have to delve deeper into our statistical analysis.

Measures of Central Tendency: Means, Medians, and Modes

To get to the heart of the matter, we are going to have to use **descriptive statistics.** Descriptive statistics are numerical values that are calculated on the data to summarize and describe the data as a whole. For example, you could calculate the percent-

descriptive statistics   statistics that are calculated to summarize or describe certain aspects of a data set

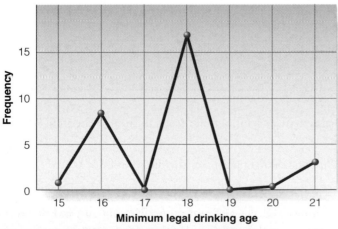

Figure A.1a Frequency Distribution (Shown Using a Frequency Polygon) for the Minimum Drinking Age in the 28 Countries Listed in Table A.1

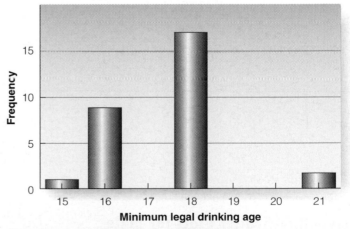

Figure A.1b Frequency Distribution (Shown Using a Histogram) for the Minimum Drinking Age in the 28 Countries Listed in Table A.1

Figure A.2b Scatter Plot of the Percentage of Males and Percentage of Females Who Drink Alcohol Weekly at Age 15 for the 28 Selected Countries

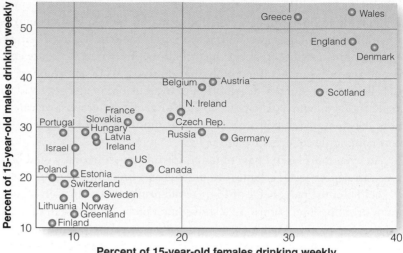

age of the 28 countries that have a minimum drinking age of 18 or higher. This percentage would be 19 of the 28 countries, or 67.9%. Or you could calculate the percentage of countries with a minimum drinking age under 18 in which more than 25% of their male sample indicate that they drank weekly (i.e., 8 out of 9, countries, or 88.9%). Although such percentages can sometimes be helpful, there are other, better statistical methods to use in this situation.

Some of the most useful descriptive statistics are those that describe the average, or most typical, entry in a data set; in other words, a statistic that shows what a *typical* country's legal drinking age is. These measures are collectively referred to as **measures of central tendency** in that they tell us something about the center of the frequency distribution (i.e., what minimum drinking age is most common, or most typical). Look again at Figures A.1a and A.1b. What do you think is the most common minimum drinking age? To answer this question, we have three different measures of central tendency: the *mean*, *mode*, and *median*.

The **mean** is synonymous with the average of a distribution. To calculate the mean, you add up all of the data points and divide the total by the number of data points. This formula can be expressed with the equation:

$$\bar{X} = \sum X/N$$

Where

$\bar{X}$ is the symbol for the mean

Σ is a mathematical symbol that means to sum up the items that follow it

X = the individual data points in the distribution

N = the total number of data points or scores in the distribution

The calculation of the average minimum drinking age and the average percentages of males and females that drink weekly at age 15 is shown in Table A.2 ◆.

Another measure of central tendency is the **median,** or the score that is at the center of the frequency distribution of the scores. To find the median, you must first list all of the scores in ascending order.

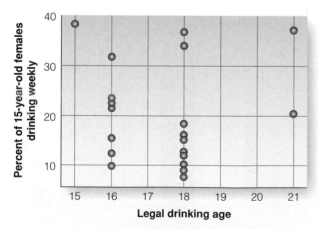

Figure A.2a Scatter Plots for Male and Female Drinking at Age 15 as a Function of Minimum Legal Drinking Age for the 28 Selected Countries

◆ **Table A.2**

Average Minimum Drinking Age and Average Percent of Students Who Report Drinking Alcohol Weekly at Age 15, Selected Countries

Country	Minimum Legal Drinking Age	Males	Females
Austria	16	39	23
Belgium	16	38	22
Canada	18	22	17
Czech Republic	18	32	19
Denmark	15	46	38
England	18	47	36
Estonia	18*	21	10
Finland	18	11	8
France	16	31	15
Germany	16	29	22
Greece	16*	52	31
Greenland	18	13	10
Hungary	16	29	11
Ireland	18	27	12
Israel	18	26	10
Latvia	18	28	12
Lithuania	21	16	9
Northern Ireland	18	33	20
Norway	18	16	12
Poland	18	20	8
Portugal	16	29	9
Russia	18	28	24
Scotland	18	37	33
Slovakia	18	32	16
Sweden	18	17	11
Switzerland	16	19	9
United States	21	23	15
Wales	18	53	36
ΣX	491	814	498
$\bar{X} = \Sigma X/N$	491/28 = 17.5	814/28 = 29.1	498/28 = 17.8

Except where noted, data taken from: Kaul, C. (2002). Statistical Handbook on the World's Children. (p. 447). Westport, CT: Oryx Press.

*These data taken from: http://www2.potsdam.edu/alcohol-info/LegalDrinkingAge .html#worlddrinkingages on 11/6/03

measures of central tendency descriptive statistics that describe the most central, or typical, data points in the frequency distribution

mean a descriptive statistic that describes the most average, or typical, data point in the distribution

median A descriptive statistic that identifies the center of the frequency distribution; the median is the point at which 50% of the scores are above and 50% are below this point in the distribution

Once this is done, the median can be found by finding the score that is at the center of this ordered list of scores. The calculation of the median legal drinking age can be found in Figure A.3. As you can see in Figure A.3, the median and the mean are not the same number. This shows one advantage of the median over the mean. The mean is highly affected by unusual scores, or **outliers** in the distribution. In this case, one country, Denmark, has an unusually low drinking age of 15. Although Denmark's minimum drinking age of 15 does not differ that much from the other countries that set their limit at 16, Denmark is the only country to set the age this low, and this outlying score works to lower the mean somewhat. However, because the median is simply

outliers unusual data points that are at the extremes of the frequency distribution and either far above or below the mean

First take all of the minimum legal drinking ages for the countries and list them in ascending order:

15, 16, 16, 16, 16, 16, 16, 16, 16, 18, 18, 18, 18, 18, 18, 18, 18, 18, 18, 18, 18, 18, 18, 18, 18, 18, 21, 21

Now find the score at the center of this distribution. In this case, because there is an even number of scores ($N = 28$) the center of this distribution would be between the 14th and 15th score in the list above. Therefore, to find the median or X_{50}, we would average the 14th and 15th score:

$$(18 + 18)/2 = 18$$
$$X_{50} = 18$$

Figure A.3 Calculation of the Median Legal Drinking Age

the center score of the distribution, it is unaffected by unusual scores. So, whereas the mean drinking age is 17.5, the median drinking age is somewhat higher at 18.

When a distribution contains outliers, the median is the better choice for measuring central tendency. This is especially true in situations in which the outliers are even more outlying than those in our drinking-age example. For instance, assume that in a class of 10 students, 9 students score a 75 on an exam, and 1 student scores a 15. The mean for the class would be 69, but the median would be 75. That's a difference of over half a letter grade between these two measures of central tendency, with the median more accurately reflecting how most of the students scored on the exam.

mode a measure of central tendency that identifies the most common, or frequent, score in the distribution

The final measure of central tendency is the **mode,** or the most *frequent* score in the distribution. If you look again at Figure A.1a (or Figure A1.b), you will see that the most frequent, or most common, drinking age is 18. Therefore, like the median, the mode is also 18. The mode is an especially useful measure of central tendency when the data being examined are not numerical (e.g., the most typical car color in the student parking lot).

Measures of central tendency tell us something about the most representative scores at the center of the frequency distribution, but they do not tell us anything about the range, or breadth, of the scores in the distribution. To determine this characteristic of the distribution, we will have to look at *measures of variability*.

Measures of Variability: Analyzing the Distribution of Data

Variability refers to the degree to which the individual scores of the distribution tend to *differ* from the central tendency of the distribution. In other words, variability measures how spread out the frequency distribution is. Look back at Figure A.1a. As we just saw, the mean drinking age is 17.5. As you would expect, most of the scores in the frequency distribution are clustered around 18, but that does not mean that *all* of the scores are close in value to 18. Some scores are as low as 15, and some are as high as 21. Measures of variability tell us about the degree to which these more extreme scores differ from the mean. The simplest measure of variability is the **range** of the distribution, or the difference between the highest and lowest values in the distribution. In this case, the range of drinking ages would be $21 - 15 = 6$ years.

range a measure of variability that is the difference between the high score and the low score of the distribution

Although the range is a measure of variability, it is fairly crude in that it doesn't really tell us how much the average score differs from the mean. Another measure of variability, called **sample variance,** takes into account the difference between the individual scores of the distribution and the mean of the distribution. The first step to calculating the sample variance is to calculate the mean of the distribution. The next step is to calculate the **sums of squares** of the distribution. Here, *squares* refers to the difference between each score in the distribution and the mean of the distribution, with this difference being taken to the second power. So, the sums of the squares (SS) can be calculated using the following equation:

$$SS = \sum (X - \bar{X})^2$$

Once you have calculated the SS, the sample variance (S^2) is simply calculated by the following formula:

$$S^2 = \sum (X - \bar{X})^2 / N$$

Another measure of variability is the **standard deviation** (S), or the square root of the sample variance:

$$S = \sqrt{\sum (X - \bar{X})^2 / N}$$

All three measures of variability indicate the degree to which the scores in the distribution are dispersed. The higher these measures are, the more dispersion, or spread, there is among the scores. Although it may be difficult to see why you would want to know the variability of a distribution, one reason is that you can use the standard deviation as a ruler, or guideline, for judging how atypical or typical a score in the distribution is. To see how this works, take a look at Figure A.4. Figure A.4 shows the calculation of the standard deviation for the male drinking percentages across the 28 countries. As you can see, the standard deviation for the distribution of male drinking scores is 11.03. We can use this figure to gauge how unusual a specific score in the distribution is. Using the standard deviation and the mean of the distribution, we can calculate a **z score.** A z score expresses the degree to which an individual score differs from the mean of the distribution in terms of the standard deviation of the distribution.

$$Z = (X - \bar{X}) / S$$

For example, in Germany, 29% of 15-year-old males drink weekly. This means that Germany's score would be:

$$Z = (29 - 29.1)/11.03 = -.009$$

Germany's z score indicates that the percentage of German 15-year-old boys who drink is far less than one standard deviation below the mean of 29.1 for all of the 28 countries (Figure A.5).

On the other hand, look at the figure reported for Wales. In Wales, 53% of the 15-year-old males surveyed were drinking. Wales's z score of 2.17 indicates that their score of 53% is more than 2 standard deviations above the mean. This indicates that Wales's experience is not very typical of the average country's experience with male underage drinking at age 15. Wales *seems* to have a bigger problem with this issue than the average country does, but is this deviation from the mean enough of a problem to worry about? To answer this, we have to assess the probability that a given country would have a particular percentage of its young men drinking alcohol on a weekly basis. Luckily, we might be able to do this.

Many variables, such as height, weight, IQ, and so on follow a **normal distribution.** In other words, if you measured these characteristics for a very large number of people and plotted them in a frequency distribution, the resulting graph would be bell-shaped and symmetrical (Figure A.6). If we assume that drinking behavior is normally distributed, then we can also assume that if we calculated the z scores for all of the different countries and plotted them in a frequency distribution, that distribution of z

sample variance   a measure of variability that shows on average how much the scores vary from the mean

sums of squares   the sum of the squared errors, or deviations, from the mean for the scores in the distribution; the numerator of the sample variance equation

standard deviation   a measure of variability equal to the square root of the sample variance; the standard deviation is often used to gauge the degree to which an individual score deviates from the mean of a distribution

z score   a measure of relative standing that measures the distance of a score from the mean of the distribution in standard deviation units

normal distribution   a bell-shaped, symmetric frequency distribution

Figure A.4 Calculation of the Standard Deviation for the Percentage of Males Drinking Weekly at Age 15

Country N = 28	X = Percent of 15-Year-Old Males Drinking	X − X̄ = X − 29.1	(X − X̄)² = (X − 29.1)²
Austria	39	9.9	98.01
Belgium	38	8.9	79.21
Canada	22	− 7.1	50.41
Czech Republic	32	2.9	8.41
Denmark	46	16.9	285.61
England	47	17.9	320.41
Estonia	21	− 8.1	65.61
Finland	11	−18.1	327.61
France	31	1.9	3.61
Germany	29	− .1	.01
Greece	52	22.9	524.41
Greenland	13	−16.1	259.21
Hungary	29	− .1	.01
Ireland	27	− 2.1	4.41
Israel	26	− 3.1	9.61
Latvia	28	− 1.1	1.21
Lithuania	16	−13.1	171.61
Northern Ireland	33	3.9	15.21
Norway	16	−13.1	171.61
Poland	20	− 9.1	82.81
Portugal	29	− .1	.01
Russia	28	− 1.1	1.21
Scotland	37	7.9	62.41
Slovakia	32	2.9	8.41
Sweden	17	−12.1	146.41
Switzerland	19	−10.1	102.01
United States	23	− 6.1	37.21
Wales	53	23.9	571.21
	$\Sigma X = 814$		$\Sigma(X - \bar{X})^2 =$ 3407.88
	$\bar{X} = \Sigma X/N =$ 814/28 = 29.1		$S^2 = \Sigma(X - \bar{X})^2 / N =$ 3407.88/28 = 121.71
			$S = \sqrt{\Sigma(X - \bar{X})^2 / N} =$ $\sqrt{121.71} = 11.03$

Legend: $\bar{X}$ = the mean; S^2 = the sample variance; S = the standard deviation; Σ = a symbol that means sum up the items that follow; N = the total number of scores or data points

standard normal distribution a bell-shaped, symmetric distribution ($\bar{X} = 0$; and $S^2 = 1$) for which we know the exact area under the curve

scores would also be a normal distribution, with $\bar{X} = 0$ and $S = 1$. When a distribution of z scores is normal in shape, it is referred to as the **standard normal distribution.** The great thing about the standard normal distribution is that we know exactly what percentage of the distribution falls between any two scores (again, see Figure A.6). As you can see from Figure A.6, 68.26% of the z scores should be within

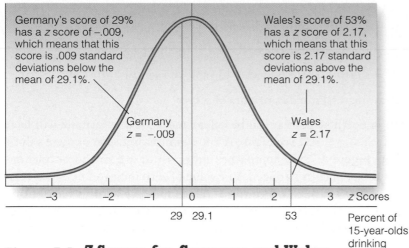

Figure A.5 *Z Scores for Germany and Wales*

The average or mean percentage of 15-year-old males who drank was 29.1% and the standard deviation was 11.03 across the 28 countries. This figure shows the individual *z* scores for the percentage of 15-year-old males drinking in Germany and Wales. *Z* scores indicate how many standard deviations away from the mean a particular score falls. As you can see, Germany has a slightly below average percentage of 15-year-old male drinkers, with a raw score of 29% and a *z* score of −.009. Wales is quite a bit above average in its underage drinking, with a raw score of 53% and a *z* score of 2.17.

the range of z scores from -1 to $+1$, whereas only .26% of the scores will be above a z score of $+3$ or below a z score of -3. This means that the probability that Wales would have a z score of $+2.17$ or higher is on the order of a mere 1.5%. So, indeed, Wales seems to have some possible cause for concern here because the number of 15-year-old boys consuming alcohol on a weekly basis is unusual compared to other countries.

The Correlation Coefficient: Measuring Relationships

Take a look again at Figure A.2b, the scatterplot for underage drinking in males and females from the 28 countries. Do you notice anything interesting about this scatterplot? Don't the data points of the scatterplot tend to fall along a line that slopes up to the right of the graph? Doesn't this seem to indicate that there might be a linear relationship between the percentage of 15-year-old males and females drinking alcohol in a country? As one sex drinks more, doesn't the other seem to generally follow suit? To examine the degree to which such a relationship might exist, psychologists would use yet another statistic to describe these data—the **correlation coefficient.** Simply put, the correlation coefficient measures the degree to which pairs of data points fall along a straight line on a scatterplot. The formula for the correlation coefficient is:

$$r = \sum z_x z_y / N$$

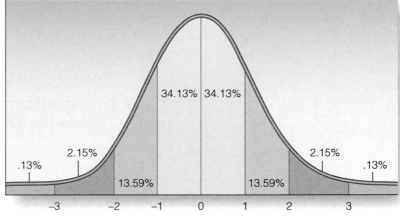

Figure A.6   **The Standard Normal Distribution of *Z* Scores**

The standard normal distribution is a symmetric, bell-shaped distribution of *z* scores with $\overline{X} = 0$ and $S = 1$. The *z* score is the number of standard deviations from the mean that the score is.

correlation coefficient   the average product of *z* scores calculated on pairs of scores; the correlation coefficient describes the degree to which the scores in the pairs are linearly related

Where:

r = the correlation coefficient

z_x = the z score for one of the variables in a pair

z_y = the z score for the other variable of the pair

N = the total number of pairs of scores

The correlation coefficients that can be calculated with this formula will have a possible range of $-1 \leq r \leq +1$. See Figure A.7 for an interpretation of these values. As you can see from Figure A.7, as r approaches either $+1$ or -1, the linear relationship between the two variables is stronger. An r value of zero indicates no linear relationship between the two variables. Positive r values indicate a *direct* relationship between the variables—in other words one variable increases with the other. Negative r values indicate an *indirect* relationship between the variables—in other words one variable increases whereas the other decreases.

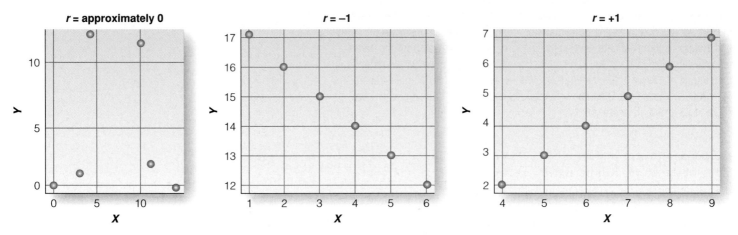

Figure A.7 Depictions of Different Values of the Correlation Coefficient, *r*

So let's return to our question of a relationship between the percentage of males and females in a country who at age 15 drink weekly. Figure A.8 shows the calculation of the correlation coefficient for these data. As you can see, there is a strong positive correlation between the percentage of males and females who drink alcohol weekly at age 15. This makes sense, because one might expect many of the factors that influence male underage drinking in a country to influence females similarly. One might think that one of these factors would be the legal drinking age in the country—that countries with a younger drinking age would have the highest percentage of 15-year-olds drinking alcohol illegally.

The data, however, do not fully support this hypothesis. In our sample, the correlation between legal drinking age and the percentage of males drinking at 15 is $r = -.412$. This moderately negative correlation indicates that countries with a lower legal drinking age tend to also have higher rates of males drinking illegally at age 15. However, such a clear relationship for females was not found. Therefore, we can conclude that having a lower drinking age is *related* to higher rates of drinking at age 15 for males only. Recall from Chapter 1 that correlation does not imply causation here. We cannot say that lowered drinking age *causes* males to drink at 15. We can only say that the two variables are related in a linear fashion.

Country	Percent of Males	z score for Percent of Males	Percent of Females	z score for Percent of Females	$z_{male}z_{female}$
Austria	39	.90027	23	.56263	.50652
Belgium	38	.80961	22	.45464	.36808
Canada	22	–.64098	17	–.08531	.05468
Czech Republic	32	.26564	19	.13067	.03471
Denmark	46	1.53490	38	2.18251	3.34994
England	47	1.62557	36	1.96652	3.19671
Estonia	21	–.73164	10	–.084125	.61549
Finland	11	–1.63826	8	–1.05724	1.73203
France	31	.17498	15	–.30130	–.05272
Germany	29	–.00635	22	.45464	–.00289
Greece	52	2.07888	31	1.42657	2.96565
Greenland	13	–1.45694	10	–.84125	1.22565
Hungary	29	–.00635	11	–.73326	.00465
Ireland	27	–.18767	12	–.62527	.11734
Israel	26	–.27833	10	–.84125	.23415
Latvia	28	–.09701	12	–.62527	.06066
Lithuania	16	–1.18495	9	–.94924	1.12481
Northern Ireland	33	.35630	20	.23866	.08504
Norway	16	–1.18495	12	–.62527	.74091
Poland	20	–.82230	8	–1.05724	.86937
Portugal	29	–.00635	9	–.94924	.00602
Russia	28	–.09701	24	.67063	–.06506
Scotland	37	.71895	33	1.64255	1.18091
Slovakia	32	.26564	16	–.19330	–.05135
Sweden	17	–1.09429	11	–.73326	.80240
Switzerland	19	–.91296	9	–.94924	.86663
United States	23	–.55032	15	–.30130	.16581
Wales	53	2.16954	36	1.96652	4.26644
					$\sum z_{male}z_{female} =$ 24.403
					$r = \sum z_{male}z_{female} / N$ $= 24.403/28 = .8715$

Figure A.8 Calculation of the Correlation Coefficient for the Percentage of Males and Females, Who Drink Alcohol Weekly in 28 Select Countries

Recall that the formula for a z score is: $z = (X - \bar{X})/S$, where $\bar{X} =$ the mean and S = the standard deviation.

Inferential Statistics >

Inferential statistics are statistics that psychologists use to test hypotheses about their data. In short, inferential statistics help psychologists judge whether or not observed differences in their data are large enough to be **significant** or meaningful. To illustrate this issue, let's look at the difference in the average rate of drinking for males and females across the 28 countries (see Figure A.2). The mean percentage of males drinking at 15 is 29.1%, but the mean percentage of females who report drinking at 15 is only 17.8%. Thus, it appears that males and females are not equally likely to drink at

LEARNING OBJECTIVE

Explain the logic behind inferential statistics, hypothesis testing, and statistical significance.

inferential statistics statistics that psychologists use in hypothesis testing to tell them when they should reject or accept their hypotheses about the population.

significant results are considered significant when we find that there is a very small chance (usually less than 5%) of finding our results given the assumption that our null hypothesis is true

null hypothesis (H$_0$) the hypothesis that contains a statement of what we do *not* believe is true about our variables in the population

alternative hypothesis (H$_1$) the hypothesis that contains a statement of what we do believe is true about our variables in the population

age 15. But is this difference $(29.1 - 17.8 = 11.3)$ large enough to convince us that males really differ from females in their underage drinking? Is it possible that these data are merely a fluke or coincidence? How big of a difference must we see between the sexes before we can say that our results are *significant?* These are the questions that inferential statistics tackle for us.

The first step to understanding inferential statistics is to understand the nature of hypotheses. In all studies that use inferential statistics, there are two hypotheses set forth by the researcher. The first one, called the **null hypothesis (H$_0$),** is a statement of what the researcher does *not* believe to be true about the variables. The second one, called the **alternative hypothesis (H$_1$),** is a statement of what the researcher *does* believe to be true about the variables. In our example, these would be:

$$H_0: \mu_{males} = \mu_{females}$$
$$H_1: \mu_{males} \neq \mu_{females}$$

Where:

μ_{males} = the mean percent of males drinking in the entire population of all 15-year-old males

$\mu_{females}$ = the mean percent of females drinking in the entire population of all 15-year-old females

So, in other words, we do *not* believe that the rate of drinking is the same for males and females across the world at age 15. Rather, we believe that 15-year-old males drink at a different rate than 15-year-old females. Although it may seem odd, the way that scientists proceed from this point is to try to show that the null hypothesis is correct. Rather than directly testing the notion set forth in the alternative hypothesis, we will instead test the hypothesis that contains the statement of what we do *not* believe to be true about our variables. So for the moment, we will assume that there is no difference between the rates of drinking for males and females at age 15, and we will analyze our data to see whether they support this notion or whether we must reject this null hypothesis in favor of the alternative hypothesis that at age 15, males and females do indeed differ in their rates of drinking alcohol.

To test the null hypothesis, we must determine the probability of finding our results (that 29.1% of males and 17.8% of females were drinking), given the *assumption* that there is no real difference between the males and females when it comes to drinking at age 15. This is where a standard distribution comes in handy. If we can calculate a statistic on our data for which we know the distribution and the probabilities of obtaining certain values of the statistic, then we can determine how likely or unlikely it would be to get our results simply by accident or fluke. In a sense, we did this earlier when we looked at the probability of finding that Wales had a rate of drinking for males that was 2.17 standard deviations above the mean. When we found that the probability of a country having a *z* score of 2.17 was only 1.5%, we were then fairly confident that the rate of male drinking in Wales was significantly different from most of the other countries. So, how low of a probability is low enough for us to say that our results are significant? Generally speaking, psychologists are comfortable dealing with results that have probabilities less than 5% although in some cases, this significance level might be placed at a lower percentage.

Back to our current example, the question for us now is this: "Is there a 5% or less probability of finding that 29.1% of males and 17.8% of the females in our sample drink, if there is indeed *no* difference among 15-year-old males and females in the population at large?" If we do find that the probability of obtaining our results is less than 5%, then we can safely conclude that our null hypothesis is likely incorrect, and we should *reject* it in favor of the alternative hypothesis. If we find that the probability of obtaining our results is greater than 5%, then we must accept our null hypothesis and admit that we were likely wrong in formulating our alternative hypothesis.

So how do we go about finding the probability of our results? Unfortunately, a detailed explanation of how we would determine this probability is beyond the scope of this text. If you ever take a statistics class, you will learn how this number is determined. However, so as not to leave you in suspense, we will tell you how the story ends. If the null hypothesis is true and there is no difference between male and female drinking in the population, the probability of finding our results (i.e., that 29.1% of males and 17.8% of females drink at age 15) is almost equal to zero. This means that it is highly unlikely that males and females drink equally at age 15, and we can safely reject our null hypothesis in favor of the alternative hypothesis.

Summary

We hope that this appendix has helped you get a very basic understanding of how psychologists use statistics. Statistics are the major tool through which we as scientists judge the validity of our experimental results. Without statistics, we would have no way to separate the flukes and coincidences of life from the true, meaningful differences that exist in the world. We use statistics to describe our data, and in doing so, we use *graphs* or *plots* to visually depict data. We also use measures of *central tendency*, such as the *mean*, *median*, and *mode* to describe the center, or most typical, score in a *frequency distribution*. We also use measures of *variability*, such as the *range*, *sample variance*, or *standard deviation* to describe the dispersion, or spread, of the scores within the frequency distribution.

Another descriptive statistic that is commonly used is the *correlation coefficient*. The correlation coefficient describes the degree to which two variables are linearly related. A linear relationship between variables indicates that as one variable changes in magnitude, the other variable also experiences some change. The range of the correlation coefficient is $-1 \leq r \leq +1$. Positive correlations indicate a *direct* relationship between the variables in that as one variable increases, so does the other. Negative correlations indicate an *indirect* relationship between the variables in that as one variable increases, the other tends to decrease. As the correlation coefficient approaches -1 and $+1$, the described relationship between the variables is stronger or more linear.

Statistics are also used to test hypotheses about variables in the *population* being studied using a representative *sample*. When statistics are used to test hypotheses and thus to draw inferences about the population, they are referred to as *inferential statistics*. In testing hypotheses, researchers always set up two competing hypotheses in their studies. The *null hypothesis* contains a statement of what the researcher does *not* believe about the variables. The *alternative hypothesis* contains a statement of what the researcher believes to be true about the variables. The researcher then uses inferential statistics to test the null hypothesis.

To do this, the researcher must calculate some statistic on the data in the sample, and this statistic must be one for which we know what its distribution looks like. For instance, if the variable being studied is normally distributed in the population, then one could calculate z scores on her data and know that the distribution of these z scores in the population would be the *standard normal distribution*. The standard normal distribution is a bell-shaped, symmetric curve that has a mean of 0 and a variance of 1. Because we know the shape, mean, and variance of the standard normal distribution, we also know exactly how much area exists in the distribution between any two z scores in the distribution. This allows us to determine exactly the probability of obtaining any particular z score in our data.

In practice, *z* scores are not used very often to test hypotheses because psychologists frequently study more than one variable, and *z* scores can help us determine only the probability of obtaining a single data point in a sample. Therefore, psychologists often use other inferential statistics. The principle is still the same, however. You calculate an inferential statistic with a known distribution on your sample data. Next, you use the distribution to determine the probability of obtaining this particular value of the statistic, given the assumption that the null hypothesis is true. If the probability of obtaining this value of the inferential statistic when the null hypothesis is true is less than 5%, then you can safely say that within an acceptable margin of error, it appears that the null hypothesis is not true and it should be rejected in favor of the alternative hypothesis. In other words, your results are *significant*, and your data support your theory.

In conclusion, please realize that this appendix has just skimmed the surface of what statistics is all about. All psychologists must undergo fairly extensive training in statistics prior to completing their degrees so that they have all the tools they need to discover the true nature of mental processes and behavior.

Key Terms

data (p. 745)
population (p. 745)
sample (p. 745)
representative sample (p. 745)
random selection (p. 745)
statistics (p. 747)
graph (p. 746)
frequency distribution (p. 746)
frequency polygon (p. 747)
histogram (p. 747)

scatter plot (p. 747)
descriptive statistics (p. 747)
measures of central tendency (p. 748)
mean (p. 748)
median (p. 748)
outliers (p. 749)
mode (p. 750)
range (p. 750)
sample variance (p. 751)
sums of squares (p. 751)

standard deviation (p. 751)
z score (p. 751)
normal distribution (p. 751)
standard normal distribution (p. 752)
correlation coefficient (p. 753)
inferential statistics (p. 755)
significant (p. 745)
null hypothesis (p. 756)
alternative hypothesis (p. 756)

Test Yourself!

Concept Check

Test your knowledge of the appendix concepts by completing the following fill-in-the-blank exercise. For a more comprehensive review, go to the book Web site (http://psychology.wadsworth.com/pastorinole/) for online quizzing, flashcards, crosswords, and Internet links.

(1) _____ are bits of information gathered in scientific studies. (2) The statistic that describes the degree to which two variables are linearly related is the _____ _____. (3) The mean, median, and mode are all measures of _____ _____. (4) A very unusual score in a distribution is called a(n) _____. (5) The mean of the standard normal distribution is equal to _____. (6) If you are doing a scientific study, it is important to use _____ _____ when selecting your participants to ensure that your sample is representa-

tive of the population. (7) A *z* score of 2.33 means that the raw score in question is _____ standard deviations above the mean of the distribution. (8) The hypothesis that contains a statement of what the research believes to be true about the world is called the _____ hypothesis. (9) In doing research, scientists actually test the _____ hypothesis. (10) A(n) _____ distribution is a bell-shaped, symmetric frequency distribution.

Answers:

1. Data, 2. correlation coefficient, 3. central tendency; 4. outlier; 5. 0; 6. random selection; 7. 2.33, 8. alternative; 9. null, 10. normal.

References

Abad, V.C., & Guilleminault, C. (2004). Review of rapid eye movement behavior sleep disorders. *Current Neurology Neuroscience Reports, 4,* 157–163.

Abkevich, V., Camp, N. J., Hensel, C. H., Neff, C. D., Russell, D. L., Hughes, D. C., et al. (2003). Predisposition locus for major depression at chromosome 12q22-12q23.2. *American Journal of Human Genetics, 73,* 1271–1281.

Abramov, I., & Gordon, J. (1994). Color appearance: On seeing red—or yellow, or green, or blue. *Annual Review of Psychology, 45,* 451–485.

Abramowitz, J. S. (1997). Effectiveness of psychological and pharmacological treatments for obsessive-compulsive disorder: A quantitative review. *Journal of Consulting & Clinical Psychology, 65,* 44–52.

Abrams, D. B., & Wilson, G. T. (1983). Alcohol, sexual arousal, and self-control. *Journal of Personality and Social Psychology, 45,* 188–198.

Abramson, L. Y., Alloy, L. B., Hankin, B. L., Haeffel, G. J., MacCoon, D. G., & Gibb, B. E. (2002). Cognitive vulnerability—stress models of depression in a self-regulatory and psychobiological content. In I. H. Gotlib & C. L. Hammen (Eds.), *Handbook of depression* (pp. 268–294). New York: Guilford Press.

Adams, C. D., Girolami, P. A., Joseph, K. E., Sauvageot, S. A., & Slater, H. (2002). Use of a token reinforcement system to promote appropriate behavior at a pediatric burn summer camp. *Journal of Burn and Care Rehabilitation, 23,* 297–305.

Adams, J. (1976). *Conceptual blockbusters* (2nd ed.). New York: Norton.

Adan, A. & Natale. V. (2002). Gender differences in morningness-eveningness preference. *Chronobiology International, 19,* 709–720.

Ader, R. (2001). Psychoneuroimmunology. *Current Directions in Psychological Science, 10,* 94–98.

Aderibigbe, Y. A., Bloch, R. M., & Walker, W. R. (2001). Prevalence of depersonalization and derealization experiences in a rural population. *Social Psychiatry & Psychiatric Epidemiology, 36,* 63–69.

Adler, A. (1928). *Understanding human nature.* London: Allen & Unwin.

Adler, J., & Rosenberg, D. (1994, December 19). The endless binge. *Newsweek,* p. 72.

Adolphs, R. (2002). Neural systems for recognizing emotion. *Current Opinion in Neurobiology, 12,* 169–177.

Adolphs, R., Tranel, D., & Damasio, A. R. (1998). The human amygdala in social judgment. *Nature, 393,* 470–474.

Aghajanian, G. K. (1994). Serotonin and the action of LSD in the brain. *Psychiatric Annals, 24,* 137–141.

Ahern, J., Galea, S., Resnick, H., & Vlahov, D. (2004). Television images and probable posttraumatic stress disorder after September 11th: The role of background characteristics, event exposures, and perievent panic. *Journal of Nervous and Mental Disorders, 192,* 217–226.

Aiken, L. R. (1996). *Personality assessment methods and practices* (2nd ed.). Seattle: Hogrefe & Huber.

Ainsworth, M. D., Blehar, M. C., Waters, E., & Wall, S. (1978). *Patterns of attachment.* Hillsdale, NJ: Erlbaum.

Air travel remains safe. (1999, November 5). *Salt Lake City Tribune,* p. A12.

Alan Guttmacher Institute. (2001). Facts in brief: Teenagers' sexual and reproductive behavior, developed countries. Retrieved September 6, 2004, from http://www.agi-usa.org/pubs/fb_teens.html

Alderidge, M.A., Stillman, R. D., & Bower, T. G. R. (2001). Newborn categorization of vowel-like sounds. *Developmental Science, 4,* 220–232.

Alexander, G. M. (2003). An evolutionary perspective on sex-typed toy preferences: Pink, blue, and the brain. *Archives of Sexual Behavior, 32,* 7–14.

Alexander, M. G., & Fisher, T. D. (2003). Truth and consequences: Using the bogus pipeline to examine sex differences in self-reported sexuality. *Journal of Sex Research, 40,* 27–35.

Allen, L. S., & Gorski, R. A. (1991). Sexual dimorphism of the anterior commissure and the massa intermedia of the human brain. *Journal of Comparative Neurology, 312,* 97–104.

Alloy, L. B., Abramson, L. Y., & Francis, E. L. (1999). Do negative cognitive styles confer vulnerability to depression? *Current Directions in Psychological Science, 8,* 128–132.

Allport, G. W. (1961). *Pattern and growth in personality.* New York: Holt, Rinehart, & Winston.

Allport, G. W. (1979). *The nature of prejudice.* Reading, MA: Addison-Wesley. (Original work published 1954)

Allport, G. W., & Postman, L. (1965). *The psychology of rumor.* New York: Russell & Russell. (Originally published 1947.)

Alonso, A., & Swiller, H. I. (1993). Introduction: The case for group therapy. In A. Alonso & H. I. Swiller (Eds.), *Group therapy in clinical practice.* Washington, DC: American Psychiatric Press.

Alsaker, F. D. (1995). Timing of puberty and reactions to pubertal changes. In M. Rutter (Ed.), *Psychosocial disturbances in young people* (pp. 37–82). New York: Cambridge University Press.

Alter-Reid, K., Gibbs, M. S., Lachenmeyer, J. R., Sigal, J., & Massoth, N. A. (1986). Sexual abuse of children: A review of the empirical findings. *Clinical Psychology Review, 6,* 249-266.

Alvarez, F. J., Delrio, M. C., & Prado, R. (1995). Drinking and driving in Spain. *Journal of Studies on Alcohol, 56*(4), 403–407.

Amato, P. R. (1993). Children's adjustment to divorce: Theories, hypotheses, and empirical support. *Journal of Marriage and the Family, 55,* 23–38.

Amato, P. R. (1996). Explaining the intergenerational transmission of divorce. *Journal of Marriage and the Family, 58,* 628–640.

Amato, P. R. (2000). The consequences of divorce for adults and children. *Journal of Marriage and the Family, 62,* 1269–1287.

Amato, P. R., & Booth, A. (1996). A prospective study of divorce and parent-child relationships. *Journal of Marriage and the Family, 58,* 356–365.

Amato, P. R., & DeBoer, D. D. (2001). The transmission of marital instability across generations: Relationship skills or commitment to marriage? *Journal of Marriage and Family, 63,* 1038–1051.

Amato, P. R., & Rogers, S. J. (1997). A longitudinal study of marital problems and subsequent divorce. *Journal of Marriage and the Family, 59,* 612–624.

Amato, P. R., Johnson, D. R., Booth, A., & Rogers, S. J. (2003). Continuity and change in marital quality between 1980 and 2000. *Journal of Marriage and the Family, 65,* 1–22.

American Psychiatric Association, (2000). *Diagnostic and statistical manual of mental disorders* (4th ed., Text Revision). Washington, DC: Author.

American Psychiatric Association. (1994). *Diagnostic and statistical manual of mental disorders* (4th ed.). Washington DC: Author.

American Psychological Association. (1984). *Behavioral research with animals.* Washington, D.C.: Author.

American Psychological Association. (1997). *Visions and transformations.* Washington D.C: APA's Commission on Ethnic Minority Recruitment, Retention and Training in Psychology.

American Psychological Association. (2000a). *Psychology careers for the twenty-first century.* Washington D.C.: Author.

American Psychological Association. (2000b). *Women in academe: Two steps forward, one step back.* Washington, D.C.: Author.

American Psychological Association. (2002). Ethical principles of psychologists and code of conduct. *American Psychologist, 57,* 1060–1073.

Amir, Y. (1976). The role of intergroup contact in change of prejudice and ethnic relations. In P. Katz (Ed.), *Toward the elimination of racism.* New York: Pergamon Press.

Amoore, J. E. (1970). *Molecular basis of odor.* Springfield, IL: Thomas.

Amoore, J. E. (1977). Specific anosmia and the concept of primary odors. *Chemical Senses and Flavor, 2,* 267–281.

Anderson, C. (2003). Social stress and support factors in susceptibility to the common cold. *APS Observer, 16,* 37.

Anderson, C. A., & Arciniegas, D. B. (2004). Neurosurgical interventions for neuropsychiatric syndromes. *Current Psychiatry Reports, 6,* 355–363.

Anderson, C. A., & Bushman, B. J. (2002). Human aggression, *Annual Review of Psychology,* 27–51.

Anderson, C. A., Benjamin, A. J., & Barthlow, B. D. (1998). Does the gun pull the trigger? Automatic priming effects of weapon pictures and weapon names. *Psychological Science, 9,* 308–314.

Anderson, J. R. (1974). Verbatim and propositional representation of sentences in immediate and long-term memory. *Journal of Verbal Learning and Verbal Behavior, 13,* 149–162.

Anderson, J. R. (2000). *Cognitive psychology and its applications* (5th ed). New York: Worth.

Anderson, J. R., & Gower, G. H. (1973). *Human associative memory.* Washington, D.C.: Winston.

Anderson, R. N., & Smith, B. L. (2003). Deaths: Leading causes for 2001. *National Vital Statistics Reports,* (Vol. 52, No. 9). Maryland: National Center for Health Statistics.

Andreasen, N. (2001). Neuroimaging and neurobiology of schizophrenia. In K. Miyoshi, C. M. Shapiro, M. Gaviria, & Y. Morita (Eds.), *Contemporary neuropsychiatry* (pp. 265–271). Tokyo: Springer-Verlag.

Andreasen, N. C., Arndt, S., Alliger, R., Miller, D., & Flaum, M. (1995). Symptoms of schizophrenia. *Archives of General Psychiatry, 52,* 341–351.

Andreasen, N. C., Rezai, K., Alliger, R., & Swayze, V. W. (1992). Hypofrontality in neuroleptic-naïve patients and in patients with chronic schizophrenia: Assessment with xenon 133 single-photon emission computed tomography and the Tower of London. *Archives of General Psychiatry, 49,* 943–958.

Andreasen, N. C., Swayze, V. W., Flaum, M., & Alliger, R. (1990). Ventricular abnormalities in affective disorder: Clinical and demographic correlates. *American Journal of Psychiatry, 147,* 893–900.

Andresen, J. (2000). Meditation meets behavioural medicine: The story of experimental research on meditation. *Journal of Consciousness Studies, 7*(11–12), 17–73.

Angelou, M. (1977). *Gather together in my name.* New York: Bantam.

Angst, J., & Sellaro, R. (2000). Historical perspectives and natural history of bipolar disorder. *Biological Psychiatry, 48,* 445–457.

Ankey, C. D. (1992). Sex differences in relative brain size: The mismeasure of woman, too? *Intelligence, 16,* 329–336.

Anshel, M. H. (1995). Effect of chronic aerobic exercise and progressive relaxation on motor performance and affect following acute stress. *Behavioral Medicine, 21*(4), 186–196.

Antonioni, D. (2003). Leading with responsibility. *Industrial Management, 45,* 8–15.

Antony, M. M., & Barlow, D. H. (Eds.). (2002). *Handbook of assessment and treatment planning for psychological disorders.* New York: Guilford Press.

APA Research Office. (2001). *2000–2001 Faculty salaries survey.* Washington, D.C.: American Psychological Association.

Applbaum, K. D. (1995). Marriage with the proper stranger: Arranged marriage in metropolitan Japan. *Ethnology, 34,* 37–51.

Appleby, D. (1997). *The handbook of psychology.* New York: Longman.

Arborelius, L., Owens, M. J., Plotsky, P. M., & Nemeroff, C. B. (1999). The role of corticotropin-releasing factor in depression and anxiety disorders. *Journal of Endocrinology, 160,* 1–12.

Archer, J., Birring, S. S., & Wu, F. C. W. (1998). The association between testosterone and aggression in young men: Empirical findings and a meta-analysis. *Aggressive Behavior, 24,* 411–420.

Ardelt, M. (1997). Wisdom and life satisfaction in old age. *Journal of Gerontology: Psychological Sciences and Social Sciences, 52,* P15–P27.

Arias, E., Anderson, R. N., Kung, H. C., Murphy, S. L., & Kockanek, K. D. (2003). Deaths: Final data for 2001. *National Vital Statistics Reports,* (Vol. 52, No. 3). Maryland: National Center for Health Statistics.

Armitage, R. (1995). The distribution of EEG frequencies in REM and NREM sleepstages in healthy young adults. *Sleep, 18*(5), 334–341.

Aronson, E. (1998). Dissonance, hypocrisy, and the self-concept. In E. Harmon-Jones & J. S. Mills, *Cognitive dissonance theory: Revival with revisions and controversies.* Washington, DC: American Psychological Association.

Aronson, E. (2000). The jigsaw strategy. *Psychology Review, 7,* 2.

Aronson, E., & Mills, J. (1959). The effects of severity of initiation on liking for a group. *Journal of Abnormal and Social Psychology, 59,* 177–181.

Aronson, E., Wilson, T. D., & Akert, R. M. (1999). *Social psychology,* 3rd ed. New York: Longman.

Aronson, E., Wilson, T. D., & Akert, R. M. (2004). *Social Psychology,* 4th ed. Upper Saddle River, NJ: Prentice Hall, 745.

Aronson, E., Wilson, T. D., & Akert, R. M. (2005). *Social Psychology* (5th ed.). Englewood Cliffs, NJ: Prentice Hall.

Arrindell, W. A., Eisemann, M., Richter, J., Oei, T. P. S., Caballo, V. E., van der Ende, J., et al. (2003). Masculinity-femininity as a national characteristic and its relationship with national agoraphobic fear levels: Fodor's sex role hypothesis revitalized. *Behaviour Research and Therapy, 41,* 795–807.

Asay, T. P., & Lambert, M. J. (1999). The empirical case for the common factors in therapy: Quantitative findings. In M. A. Hubble, B. L. Duncan, & S. D. Miller (Eds.), *The heart and soul of change: What works in therapy.* Washington, DC: American Psychological Association.

Asch, S. E. (1951). Effects of group pressure upon modification and distortion of judgments. In H. Guetzkow (Ed.), *Groups, leadership, and men.* Pittsburgh: Carnegie.

Ashcan, K., Wallace, B., Bell, B. A., & Benabid, A. L. (2004). Deep brain stimulation of the subthalamic nucleus in Parkinson's disease 1993–2003: Where are we ten years on? *British Journal of Neurosurgery, 18,* 19–34.

Asnis, G. M., Kohn, S. R., Henderson, M., & Brown, N. L. (2004). SSRIs versus non-SSRIs in post-traumatic stress disorder: An update with recommendations. *Drugs, 64,* 383–404.

Assor, A., Roth, G., & Deci, E. L. (2004). The emotional costs of parents' conditional regard: A self-determination theory analysis. *Journal of Personality, 72,* 47–88.

Astin, J. A. (2004). Mind-body therapies for the management of pain. *Clinical Journal of Pain, 20,* 27–32.

Atkinson, J. W. (1983). Towards experimental analysis of human motivation in terms of motives, expectancies, and incentives. In J. W. Atkinson (Ed.), *Personality, motivation, and action: Selected papers* (pp. 81–97). New York: Praeger. (Original work published 1958)

Atkinson, R. C., & Shiffrin, R. W. (1968). Human memory: A proposed system and its control processes. In K. Spence & J. Spence (Eds.), *The psychology of learning and motivation* (Vol. 2). New York: Academic Press.

Auster, C. J., & Ohm, S. C. (2000). Masculinity and femininity in contemporary American society: A reevaluation using the Bem Sex-Role Inventory. *Sex Roles, 43,* 499–528.

Axinn, W. G., & Barber, J. S. (1997). Living arrangements and family formation attitudes in early adulthood. *Journal of Marriage and the Family, 59,* 595–611.

Aylesworth, A. B., Goodstein, R. C., & Kalra, A. (1999). Effect of archetypal embeds on feelings: An indirect route to affecting attitudes? *Journal of Advertising, 28,* 73–81.

Azar, B. (1998). A genetic disposition for certain tastes may affect people's food preferences. *The American Psychological Association Monitor* [On line], *29.* Available from http://www.apa.org/monitor/jan98/food.html

Azjen, I., & Fishbein, M. (1977). Attitude-behavior relations: A theoretical analysis and review of empirical research. *Psychological Bulletin, 84,* 888–918.

Bach, A. K., Wincze, J. P., & Barlow, D. H. (2001). Sexual dysfunction. In D. H. Barlow (Ed.), *Clinical handbook of psychological disorders: A step-by-step treatment manual* (3rd ed., pp. 562-608). New York: Guilford Press.

Bachrach, H. M., Galatzer-Levy, R., Skolnikoff, A., & Waldron, S. (1991). On the efficacy of psychoanalysis. *Journal of the American Psychoanalytic Association, 39,* 871–916.

Baddeley, A. D. (1986). *Working memory.* Oxford: Claredon Press.

Baddeley, A. D. (1992). Working memory, *Science, 255,* 556–559.

Baddeley, A. D., & Hitch, G. J. (1974). Working memory. In G. H. Bower (Ed.), *The psychology of learning and motivation* (Vol. 8). London: Academic Press.

Baddeley, A. D., Logie, R., Bressi, S., Della Sala, S., & Spinnler, H. (1986). Dementia and working memory. Special Issue: Human Memory. *Quarterly Journal of Experimental Psychology: Human Experimental Psychology, 38*(4-A), 603–618.

Baer, L., Rauch, S. L., Ballantine, T., Martuza, R., Cosgrove, R., Cassem, E., Giriunas, I., Manzo, P. A., Domino, C., & Jenike, M. A. (1995). Cingulotomy for intractable obsessive-compulsive disorder. *Archives of General Psychiatry, 52,* 384–392.

Bagshaw, S. M., Jr. (1985). The desensitisation of chronically motion sick aircrew in the Royal Air Force. *Aviation Space Environmental Medicine, 56,* 1144–1151.

Bahrick, H. P. (1984). Semantic memory content in permastore: Fifty years of memory for Spanish learned in school. *Journal of Experimental Psychology: General, 113,* 1–24.

Bailargeon, R., & DeVos, J. (1992). Object permanence in young infants: Further evidence. *Child Development, 62*(6), 1227–1246.

Bailey, J. M., & Pillard, R. C. (1991). A genetic study of male sexual orientation. *Archives of General Psychiatry, 48,* 1089–1096.

Bailey, J. M., Pillard, R. C., Neale, M. C., & Agyei, Y. (1993). Heritable factors influence female sexual orientation in women. *Archives of General Psychiatry, 50,* 217-223.

Baird, A. A., Gruber, S. A., Fein, D. A., Maas, L. C., Steingard, R. J., Renshaw, P. F., Cohen, B. M., & Yurgelun-Todd, D. A. (1999). Functional magnetic resonance imaging of facial affect recognition in children and adolescents. *Journal of the American Academy of Child and Adolescent Psychiatry, 38,* 195–209.

Ball, E. M. (1997). Sleep disorders in primary care. *Comprehensive Therapy, 23,* 25–30.

Balota, D. A., Dolan, P. O., & Duchek, J. M. (2000). Memory changes in healthy older adults. In E. Tulving & F. I. M. Craik (Eds.), *The Oxford handbook of memory* (pp. 395–409). Oxford, England: Oxford University Press.

Balter, M. (1996). New clues to brain dopamine control, cocaine addiction. *Science, 271,* 909.

Baltes, P. B. (1997). On the incomplete architecture of human ontogeny: Selection, optimization, and compensation as foundation of developmental theory. *American Psychologist, 52,* 366–380.

Baltes, P. B., & Staudinger, U. M. (1993). The search for a psychology of wisdom. *Current Directions in Psychological Science, 2,* 75–80.

Bandura, A. (1965). Influence of model's reinforcement contingencies on the acquisition of imitative responses. *Journal of Personality and Social Psychology, 1,* 589–595.

Bandura, A. (1977). *Social learning theory.* Englewood Cliffs, NJ: Prentice Hall.

Bandura, A. (1986). *Social foundations of thought and action: A social cognitive theory.* Englewood Cliffs, NJ: Prentice Hall.

Bandura, A. (1997). *Self-efficacy: The exercise of control.* New York: W. H. Freeman.

Bandura, A., Grusec, J. E., & Menlove, F. L. (1966). Observational learning as a function of symbolization and incentive set. *Child Development, 37,* 499–506.

Bandura, A., Ross, D., & Ross, S. A. (1961). Transmission of aggression through imitation of aggressive models. *Journal of Abnormal and Social Psychology, 63,* 575–582.

Bandura, A., Ross, D., & Ross, S. (1963). Imitation of film-mediated aggressive models. *Journal of Abnormal and Social Psychology, 66,* 3–11.

Banich, M. T., & Heller, W. (1998). Evolving perspectives on lateralization of function. *Current Directions in Psychological Science, 74,* 1–2.

Barbee, J. G. (1993). Memory, benzodiazepines, and anxiety: Integration of theoretical and clinical perspectives. *Journal of Clinical Psychiatry, 54* (Suppl. 10), 86–101.

Barber, J. P., Connolly, M. B., Crits-Christoph, P., Gladis, L., & Siqueland, L. (2000). Alliance predicts patients' outcome beyond in-treatment change in symptoms. *Journal of Consulting & Clinical Psychology, 68,* 1027–1032.

Bardone, A. M., Vohs, K. D., Abramson, L. Y., Heatherton, T. F., & Joiner, T. E., Jr. (2000). The confluence of perfectionism, body dissatisfaction, and low self-esteem predicts bulimic symptoms: Clinical implications. *Behavior Therapy, 31,* 265–280.

Barlow, D. H. (2000). Unraveling the mysteries of anxiety and its disorders from the perspective of emotion theory. *American Psychologist, 55,* 1247–1263.

Barlow, D. H. (2002). *Anxiety and its disorders: The nature and treatment of anxiety and panic* (2nd ed.). New York: Guilford Press.

Barlow, D. H., & Durand, V. M. (2005). *Abnormal psychology: An integrative approach* (4th ed.). Belmont, CA: Wadsworth/Thomson Learning.

Baron, R. A., & Richardson, D. R. (1992). *Human aggression* (2nd ed.) New York: Plenum.

Barondes, S. H. (1993). *Molecules and mental illness.* New York: Scientific American Library.

Barr, S. (1996, September). Up against the glass. *Management Review, 85*(9), 12–17.

Barringer, F. (1993a, April 1). Viral sexual diseases are found in 1 of 5 in U.S. *The New York Times,* pp. A1, B9.

Barringer, F. (1993b, June 2). School hallways as gauntlets of sexual taunts. *The New York Times,* p. B7.

Bartlett, F. C. (1932). *Remembering.* Cambridge: Cambridge University Press.

Bartlik, B., & Goldstein, M. Z. (2001). Practical geriatrics: Men's sexual health after midlife. *Psychiatric Services, 52,* 291-293.

Bartoshuk, L. M. (2000a). Comparing sensory experiences across individuals: Recent psychophysical advances illuminate genetic variation in taste perception. *Chemical Senses, 25,* 447–460.

Bartoshuk, L. M. (2000b). Psychophysical advances aid the study of genetic variation in taste. *Appetite, 34,* 105.

Bartoshuk, L. M., & Beauchamp, G. K. (1994). Chemical senses. *Annual Review of Psychology, 45,* 419–449.

Bass, B. M., & Avolio, B. J. (1994). Shatter the glass ceiling: Women may make better managers. *Human Resource Management, 33,* 549–560.

Batabyal, A. A. (2001). On the likelihood of finding the right partner in an arranged marriage. *Journal of Socio-Economics, 30,* 273–281.

Bates, B. L. (1994). Individual differences in response to hypnosis. In J. W. Rhue, S. J. Lynn, & I. Kirsch (Eds.), *Handbook of clinical hypnosis.* Washington, DC: American Psychological Association.

Bauby, J. D. (1997). *The diving bell and the butterfly.* New York: Vintage.

Baumeister, R. F., & Leary, M. R. (1995). The need to belong: The desire for interpersonal attachments as a fundamental human motivation. *Psychological Bulletin, 117,* 497–529.

Baumeister, R. F., Catanese, K. R., & Vohs, K. D. (2001). Is there a gender difference in strength of sex drive? Theoretical views, conceptual distinctions, and a review of relevant evidence. *Personality and Social Psychology Review, 5,* 242.

Baumrind, D. (1964). Some thoughts on ethics of research: After reading Milgram's "Behavioral study of obedience." *American Psychologist, 19,* 421–423.

Baumrind, D. (1967). Child care practices anteceding three patterns of preschool behavior. *Genetic Psychology Monographs, 75,* 43–88.

Baumrind, D. (1971). Current patterns of parental authority. *Developmental Psychology Monograph, 4*(No. 1, Pt. 2).

Beach, S. R. H., Sandeen, E. E., & O'Leary, K. D. (1990). Depression in marriage: A model for etiology and treatment. In D. H. Barlow (Ed.), *Treatment manuals for practitioners.* New York: Guilford Press.

Beal, C. R. (1994). *Boys and girls: The development of gender roles.* New York: McGraw-Hill.

Beardsley, T. (1996, July). Waking up. *Scientific American,* pp. 14, 18.

Beatty, W. W. (1992). Gonadal hormones and sex differences in nonreproductive behaviors. In A. A. Gerall, H. Moltz, & I. L. Ward (Eds.), *Handbook of behavioral neurobiology: Vol 11. Sexual differentiation* (pp. 85–128). New York: Plenum.

Beck, A. T. (1967). *Depression: Clinical, experimental, and theoretical aspects.* New York: Harper & Row.

Beck, A. T. (1976). *Cognitive therapy and the emotional disorders.* New York: International Universities Press.

Beck, A. T. (1991). Cognitive therapy: A 30-year retrospective. *American Psychologist, 46,* 368–375.

Beck, A. T. (1997). Cognitive therapy: Reflections. In J. K. Zeig (Ed.), *The evolution of psychotherapy: The third conference.* New York: Brunner/Mazel.

Beck, A. T., Rush, A. J., Shaw, B. F., & Emery, G. (1979). *Cognitive therapy of depression.* New York: Guilford Press.

Beck, J. G. (1993). Vaginismus. In W. O'Donohue & J. H. Geer (Eds.), *Handbook of sexual dysfunctions: Assessment and treatment* (pp. 381-397). Boston: Allyn & Bacon.

Becker, P.M., Schwartz, J.R., Feldman, N.T., & Hughes, R. J. (2004). Effect of modafinil on fatigue, mood, and health-related quality of life in patients with narcolepsy. *Psychopharmacology, 171,* 133–139.

Beeman, M. J., & Chairello, C. (1998). Complementary right- and left-hemisphere language comprehension. *Current Directions in Psychological Science, 74,* 2–8.

Beitchman, J. H., Zucker, K. J., Hood, J. E., daCosta, G. A., Akman, D., & Cassavia, E. (1992). A review of the long-term effects of child sexual abuse. *Child Abuse and Neglect, 16,* 101-118.

Békésy, G. von (1960). *Experiments in hearing.* New York: McGraw-Hill.

Bell, A. R., Weinberg, M. S., & Hammersmith, S. K. (1981). *Sexual preference: Its development in men and women.* Bloomington, IN: Indiana University Press.

Bell, C. J., & Nutt, D. J. (1998). Serotonin and panic. *British Journal of Psychiatry, 172,* 465–471.

Belsky, J., & Rovine, M. (1990). Patterns of marital change across the transition to parenthood: Pregnancy to three years postpartum. *Journal of Marriage and the Family, 52,* 5–19.

Belsky, J., Woodworth, S., & Crnic, K. (1996). Trouble in the second year: Three questions about family interaction. *Child Development, 67,* 556–578.

Benabid, A. L., Koudsie, A., Benazzouz, A., Vercueil, L., Fraix, V., Chabardes, S., Lebas, J. F., & Pollak, P. (2001). Deep brain stimulation of the corpus luysi (subthalamic nucleus) and other targets in Parkinson's disease. Extension to new indications such as dystonia and epilepsy. *Journal of Neurology, 248* (Suppl. 3), III37–III47.

Bender, E. (2004). Virtual reality treatment combats phobias, PTSD. *Psychiatric News, 39,* 45.

Bennett, A. E. (1947). Mad doctors. *Journal of Nervous and Mental Disorders, 29,* 11–18.

Bennett, W. I. (1990, December). Boom and doom. *Harvard Health Letter, 16,* 1–3.

Benson, H. (1996). *Timeless healing: The power and biology of belief.* New York: Scribner.

Benson, P. L., Sharma, A. R., & Roehlkepartain, E. C. (1994). *Growing up adopted: A portrait of adolescents and their families.* Minneapolis: Search Institute.

Berk, L. E., & Spuhl, S. T. (1995). Maternal interaction, private speech, and task performance in preschool children. *Early Childhood Research Quarterly, 10,* 145–169.

Berkowitz, L. (1990). On the formation and regulation of anger and aggression: A cognitive-neoassociationistic analysis. *American Psychologist, 45,* 494–503.

Berlyne, D. E. (1967). Novelty and curiosity as determinants of exploratory behavior. *British Journal of Psychology, 41,* 68–80.

Bernhardt, A., Morris, M., & Handcock, M. S. (1995). Women's gains or men's losses? A closer look at the shrinking gender gap in earnings. *American Journal of Sociology, 101,* 302–328.

Berrington, A., & Diamond, I. (1999). Marital dissolution among the 1958 British birth cohort: The role of cohabitation. *Population Studies, 53,* 19–38.

Berry, J. O., & Rao, J. M. (1997). Balancing employment and fatherhood: A systems perspective. *Journal of Family Issues, 18,* 386–402.

Berry, N., Jobanputra, V., & Pal, H. (2003). Molecular genetics of schizophrenia: A critical review. *Journal of Psychiatry and Neuroscience, 28,* 415–429.

Berscheid, E., Dion, K., Walster, E., & Walster, G. W. (1971). Physical attractiveness and dating choice: A test of the matching hypothesis. *Journal of Experimental Social Psychology, 7,* 173–189.

Betz, N. E. (1993). Women's career development. In F. L. Denmark & M. A. Paludi (Eds.), *Psychology of women* (pp. 627–684). Westport, CT: Greenwood Press.

Beutel, M., Willner, H., Deckhardt, R., Von Rad, M., & Weiner, H. (1996). Similarities and differences in couples' grief reactions following miscarriage: Results from a longitudinal study. *Journal of Psychosomatic Research, 40,* 245–253.

Beutler, L. E., Machado, P. P., & Neufeldt, S. A. (1994). Therapist variables. In A. E. Bergin & S. L. Garfield (Eds.), *Handbook of psychotherapy and behavior change* (4th ed.). New York: Wiley.

Bezchlibnyk-Butler, K. Z., & Jeffries, J. J. (Eds.) (1998). *Clinical handbook of psychotropic drugs,* (8th ed.). Seattle: Hogrete & Huber

Bianchi, S. M., Kilkie, M. A., Sayer, L. C., & Robinson, J. P. (2000). Is anyone doing the housework?: Trends in the gender division of household labor. *Social Forces, 79,* 191–228.

Bieber, I., Dain, H., & Dince, P. (1962). *Homosexuality: A psychoanalytic study.* New York: Basic Books.

Biederman, J., Faraone, S. V., Hirschfeld-Becker, D. R., Friedman, D., Robin, J. A., & Rosenbaum, J. F. (2001). Patterns of psychopathology and dysfunction in high-risk children of parents with panic disorder and major depression. *American Journal of Psychiatry, 158,* 49–57.

Bierut, L. J., Heath, A. C., Bucholz, K. K., Dinwiddie, S. H., Madden, P. A. F., Statham, D. J., Dunne, M. P., & Martin, N. G. (1999). Major depressive disorder in a community-based twin sample: Are there different genetic contributions for men and women? *Archives of General Psychiatry, 56,* 557–563.

Binet, A. (1890). Perceptions d'enfants. *La Révue Philosophique, 30,* 582–611.

Binet, A., & Simon, T. (1905). Méthodes nouvelles pour le diagnostics du niveau intéllectuel des anormaux. *L'Année Psychologique, 11,* 191–244.

Bivens, J. A., & Berk, L. E. (1990). A longitudinal study of elementary school children's private speech. *Merrill-Palmer Quarterly, 36,* 443–463.

Black, D.W., Blum, N., Pfohl, B., & Hale, N. (2004). Suicidal behavior in borderline personality disorder: Prevalence, risk factors, prediction, and prevention. *Journal of Personality and Disorders, 18,* 226–239.

Blagys, M. D., & Hilsenroth, M. J. (2000). Distinctive features of short-term psychodynamic-interpersonal psychotherapy: A review of the comparative psychotherapy process literature. *Clinical Psychology: Science and Practice, 7,* 167–188.

Blanchard, R., Zucker, K. J., Siegelman, M., Dickey, R., & Klassen, P. (1998). The relation of birth order to sexual orientation in men and women. *Journal of Biosocial Science, 30,* 511.519.

Blane, H. T. (1988). Prevention issues with children of alcoholics. *British Journal of Addiction, 83*(7), 793–798.

Blatt, S. J., & Shahar, G. (2004). Psychoanalysis—with whom, for what, and how? Comparisons with psychotherapy. *Journal of the American Psychoanalysis Association, 52,* 393–447.

Blazer, D. G., Kessler, R. C., McGonagle, K. A., & Swartz, M. S. (1994). The prevalence and distribution of major depression in a national community sample: The National Comorbidity Study. *American Journal of Psychiatry, 151,* 979–986.

Bless, H., Bohner, G., Schwarz, N., & Strack, F. (1990). Mood and persuasion: A cognitive response analysis. *Personality and Social Psychology Bulletin, 16,* 331–345.

Block, J. A. (1995). A contrarian view of the five-factor approach. *Psychological Bulletin, 117,* 187–215.

Bloom, F., Nelson, C. A., & Lazerson, A. (2001). *Brain, mind and behavior* (3rd ed.). New York: Worth.

Bloom, J. W. (1998). The ethical practice of WebCounseling. *British Journal of Guidance and Counselling, 26,* 53–59.

Blumberg, E. S. (2003). The lives and voices of highly sexual women. *Journal of Sex Research, 40,* 146-157.

Boden, M. (1988). *Computer models of the mind.* Cambridge: Cambridge University Press.

Bohannon, J. N., III, & Bonvillian, J. D. (1997). Theoretical approaches to language acquisition. In J. B. Gleason (Ed.), *The development of language* (4th ed., pp. 259–316). Boston: Allyn & Bacon.

Bohart, A. C. (1990). Psychotherapy integration from a client-centered perspective. In G. Lietaer (Ed.), *Client-centered and experiential psychotherapy in the nineties* (pp. 481–500). Leuven, Belgium: Leuven University Press.

Boivin, D. B., Czeisler, C. A., Dijk, D. J., Duffy, J. F., Folkard, S., Minors, D. S., Totterdell, P., & Waterhouse, J. M. (1997). Complex interaction of sleep-wake cycle and circadian phase modulates mood in healthy subjects. *Archives of General Psychiatry, 54,* 145–152.

Bolles, R. C. (1972). Reinforcement, expectancy, and learning. *Psychological Review, 79,* 394–409.

Bond, R., & Smith, P. B. (1996). Culture and conformity: A meta-analysis of studies using Asch's (1952, 1956) line judgment task. *Psychological Bulletin, 119,* 111–137.

Bondolfi, G., Dufour, H., Patris, M., May, J. P., Billeter, U., Eap, C. B., & Bauman, P. (1998). Risperidone versus clozapine in treatment-resistant chronic schizophrenia: A randomized double-blind study. *American Journal of Psychiatry, 155,* 449–504.

Bonte, M. (1962). The reaction of two African societies to the Mueller-Lyer illusion. *Journal of Social Psychology, 58,* 265–268.

Boonstra, H. (2002). Legislators craft alternative vision of sex education to counter abstinence-only drive. *Guttmacher Report, 5*(2). Retrieved September 6, 2004, from http://ww.agi-usa.org/journals/toc/gr0502toc.html

Booth, A., & Amato, P. R. (2001). Parental pre-divorce relations and offspring postdivorce well-being. *Journal of Marriage and the Family, 63,* 197–212.

Booth-Kewley, S. & Friedman, H. S. (1987). Psychological predictions of heart disease: A quantitative review. *Psychological Bulletin, 101,* 343–362.

Bootzin, R. R., & Rider, S. P. (1997). Behavioral techniques and biofeedback for insomnia. In M. R. Pressman & W. C. Orr (Eds.), *Understanding sleep: The evaluation and treatment of sleep disorders.* Washington DC: American Psychological Association.

Borkman, T. J. (1997). A selected look at self-help groups in the U.S. *U.S. Health and Scoial Care in the Community, 5,* 357–364.

Borkovec, T. D., & Mathews, A. M. (1988). Treatment of nonphobic anxiety disorders: A comparison of nondirective, cognitive, and coping desensitization therapy. *Journal of Consulting & Clinical Psychology, 56,* 877–884.

Born, J., Lange, T., Hansen, K., Molle, M., & Fehn, H. L. (1997). Effects of sleep and circadian rhythm on human circulating immune cells. *Journal of Immunology, 158,* 4454–4464.

Bornstein, M. H. (1985). On the development of color naming in young children: Data and theory. *Brain and Language, 26,* 72–93.

Bornstein, M. H., & Marks, L. E. (1982, January). Color revisionism. *Psychology Today, 16,* 64–73.

Bornstein, M. H., Selmi, A. M., Haynes, O. M., Painter, K. M., & Marx, E. S. (1999). Representational abilities and the hearing status of child/mother dyads. *Child Development, 70,* 833–852.

Bornstein, R. F. (1994). Dependency as a social cue: A meta-analytic review of research on the dependency-helping relationship. *Journal of Research in Personality, 28,* 182–213.

Bosch, J. A., de Geus, E. J., Kelder, A., Veerman, E. C., Hoogstraten, J., & Amerongen, A.V. (2001). Differential effects of active versus passive coping on secretory immunity. *Psychophysiology, 38,* 836–846.

Bosse, R., Spiro, A., III, & Kressin, N. R. (1996). The psychology of retirement. In R. T. Woods (Ed.), *Handbook of the clinical psychology of aging* (pp. 141–157). Chicester, England: Wiley.

Botella, C., Villa, H., Garcia Palacios, A., Quero, S., Banos, R. M., & Alcaniz, M. (2004). The use of VR in the treatment of panic disorders and agoraphobia. *Student Health & Technology Information, 99,* 73–90.

Bouchard, T. J. (2004). Genetic influence on human psychological traits: A survey. *Current Directions in Psychological Science, 13,* 148–151.

Bouchard, T. J., Lykken, D. T., McGue, M., Segal, N. L., & Tellegen, A. (1990). Sources of human psychological differences: The Minnesota study of twins reared apart. *Science, 250,* 223–228.

Bourin, M., Baker, G. B., & Bradwejn, J. (1998). Neurobiology of panic disorder. *Journal of Psychosomatic Research, 44,* 163–180.

Bower, B. (November 8, 2003). Forgetting to remember: Emotion robs memory while reviving it. *Science News, 164,* 293.

Bowers, K. S., & LeBaron, S. (1986). Hypnosis and hypnotizability: Implications for clinical intervention. *Hospital and Community Psychiatry, 37,* 457–467.

Bowie, W., Hammerschlag, M., & Martin, D. (1994). STIs in 1994: The new CDC guidelines. *Patient Care, 28,* 29-53.

Bowlby, J. (1960). Separation anxiety. *International Journal of Psychoanalysis, 41,* 89–113.

Bowlby, J. (1980). *Attachment and loss: Vol. 3. Loss, sadness, and depression.* New York: Basic Books.

Boyatzis, R. E., Goleman, D., & Rhee, K. S. (2000). Clustering competence in emotional intelligence: Insights from the emotional competence inventory. In R. Baron & J. D. A. Parker (Eds.), *Handbook of emotional intelligence: Theory, development, assessment, and application at home, school, and in the workplace.* San Francisco, CA: Jossey-Bass.

Boyer, C. B., Shafer, M. A., Teitle, E., Wibbelsman, C. J., Seeberg, F., & Schnachter, J. (1999). Sexually transmitted diseases in a health maintenance organization teen clinic. *Archives of Pediatrics and Adolescent Medicine, 153,* 838-844.

Bozarth, M. A., & Wise, R. A. (1984). Anatomically distinct opiate receptor fields mediate reward and physical dependence. *Science, 224,* 516–518.

Bradford, H. F. (1987). Neurotransmitters and neuromodulators. In R. L. Gregory (Ed.), *The Oxford companion to the mind* (pp. 550–560). New York: Oxford University Press.

Brady, E. C., Chrisler, J. C., Hosdale, D. C., Osowiecki, D. M., & Veal, T. A. (1991). Date rape: Expectations, avoidance strategies, and attitudes toward victims. *Journal of Social Psychology, 131,* 427-429.

Brainerd, C. J., & Reyna, V. F. (2002). Recollection rejection: How children edit their false memories. *Developmental Psychology, 38,* 156–172.

Bramlett, M. D., & Mosher, W. D. (2002). Cohabitation, marriage, divorce, and remarriage in the United

States. *Vital Health Statistics, 23* (22). Hyattsville, MD: National Center for Health Statistics.

Brannon, L., & Feist, J. (2004). *Health psychology: An introduction to behavior and health* (5th ed.). Belmont, CA: Wadsworth.

Braudy, S. O. (2003, April 13). Small kindness in the big city. *The New York Times,* p. 3.

Braungart, J. M., Plomin, R., DeFries, J. C., & Fulker, D. W. (1992). Genetic influence on tester-rated infant temperament as assessed by Bayley's Infant Behavior Record. *Developmental Psychology, 28*(1), 40–47.

Brehm, S. S. (1992). *Intimate relationships* (2nd ed.). New York: McGraw-Hill.

Brehm, S. S., Kassin, S. M., & Fein, S. (2002). *Social psychology* (5th ed.). Boston: Houghton Mifflin.

Breier, A., Schreiber, J. L., Dyer, J., & Pickar, D. (1991). National Institutes of Mental Health longitudinal study of chronic schizophrenia: Prognosis and predictors of outcome. *Archives of General Psychiatry, 48,* 239–246.

Brende, J. O. (2000). Stress effects of floods. In G. Fink (Ed.), *Encyclopedia of stress* (Vol. 2, pp. 153–157). San Diego: Academic Press.

Brent, D. A., Perper, J. A., Allman, C. J., Moritz, G. M., Wartella, M. E., & Zelenak, J. P. (1991). The presence and accessibility of firearms in the homes of adolescent suicide: A case-control study. *Journal of the American Medical Association, 266,* 2989–2995.

Breslow, N., Evans, L., & Langley, J. (1986). Comparisons among heterosexual, bisexual, and homosexual male sadomasochists. *Journal of Homosexuality, 13,* 83-107.

Brewer, M. B. (1979). In-group bias in the minimal intergroup situation; A cognitive-motivational analysis. *Psychological Bulletin, 86,* 307–324.

Brewer, M., & Campbell, D. T. (1976). *Ethnocentrism and intergroup attitudes: East African evidence.* New York: Halstead.

Brier, N. (1999). Understanding and managing the emotional reactions to a miscarriage. *Obstetrics & Gynecology, 93,* 151–155.

Bromberger, J. T., & Matthews, K. A. (1996). A longitudinal study of the effects of pessimism, trait anxiety, and life stress on depressive symptoms in middle-aged women. *Psychology & Aging, 11,* 207–213.

Brooks-Gunn, J., & Matthews, W. S. (1979). *He and she: How children develop their sex-role identity.* Englewood Cliffs, NJ: Spectrum.

Broude, G. J., & Greene, S. J. (1976). Cross-cultural codes on twenty sexual attitudes and practices. *Ethnology, 15,* 409-429.

Brown, B. (1980). Perspectives on social stress. In H. Selye (Ed.), *Selye's guide to stress research* (Vol. 1). New York: Van Nostrand Reinhold.

Brown, J. A. (1958). Some tests of the decay theory of immediate memory. *Quarterly Journal of Experimental Psychology, 10,* 12–21.

Brown, J. D., & Rogers, R. J. (1991). Self-serving attributions: The role of physiological arousal. *Personality and Social Psychology Bulletin, 17,* 501–506.

Brown, L. R., Kane, H., & Ayers, E. (1993). *Vital signs 1993: The trends that are shaping our future.* New York: Norton.

Brown, R., & Kulik, J. (1977). Flashbulb memories. *Cognition, 5,* 73–99.

Brown, S. L., Nesse, R. M., Vinokur, A. D., & Smith, D. M. (2003). Providing social support may be more beneficial than receiving it: Results from a prospective study of mortality. *Psychological Science, 14,* 320–327.

Brown, T. A., DiNardo, P. A., Lehman, C. L., & Campbell, L. A. (2001). Reliability of DSM-IV anxiety and mood disorders: Implications for the classification of emotional disorders. *Journal of Abnormal Psychology, 110,* 49–58.

Browne, A. (1993). Violence against women by male partners: Prevalence, outcomes, and policy implications. *American Psychologist, 48,* 1077–1087.

Brownell, K. (1988, January). Yo-yo dieting. *Psychology Today, 22,* 22–23.

Browning, J. R., Kessler, D., Hatfield, E., & Choo, P. (1999). Power, gender, and sexual behavior. *The Journal of Sex Research, 36,* 342–348.

Brugman, T., & Ferguson, S. (2002). Physical exercise and improvements in mental health. *Journal of Psy-*

chosocial Nursing and Mental Health Services, 40, 24–31.

Brzezinski, A. (1997). Melatonin in humans. *New England Journal of Medicine, 336,* 186–195.

Brzustowicz, L. M., Hodgkinson, K. A., Chow, E. W. C., Honer, W. G., & Bassett, A. S. (2000). Location of a major susceptibility locus for familial schizophrenia on chromosome 1q21-q22. *Science, 288,* 678–682.

Buboltz, W. C. Jr., Brown, F., & Soper, B. (2001). Sleep habits and patterns of college students: A preliminary study. *Journal of American College Health, 50,* 131–135.

Buchanan, R. W., Breier, A., Kirkpatrick, B., Ball, P., & Carpenter, W. T. (1998). Positive and negative symptom response to clozapine in schizophrenic patients with and without the deficit syndrome. *American Journal of Psychiatry, 155,* 751–760.

Buckle, L., Gallup, G. G., Jr., & Rodd, Z. A. (1996). Marriage as a reproductive contract: Patterns of marriage, divorce, and remarriage. *Ethology and Sociobiology, 17,* 363–377.

Buckley, K. W. (1989). *Mechanical man: John Broadus Watson.* New York: Guilford Press.

Buckner, J. P., & Fivush, R. (2002). Gendered themes in family reminiscing. *Memory, 8,* 401–412.

Budak, F., Llhan, A., Ozmenoglu, M., & Komsuoglu, S. S. (1994). Locked-in syndrome: A case report. *Clinical Electroencephalogram, 25,* 40–43.

Bueler, R., Griffin, D., & Ross, M. (1994). Exploring the "planning fallacy": Why people underestimate their task completion times. *Journal of Personality and Social Psychology, 67,* 366–381.

Buhler, P. M. (2003). Managing in the new millennium. *Supervision, 64,* 20–22.

Bullock, W. A., & Gilliland, K. (1993). Eysenck's arousal theory of introversion-extraversion: A converging measures investigation. *Journal of Personality and Social Psychology, 64,* 113–123.

Bumpass, L. L., & Lu, H. H. (2000). Trends in cohabitation and implications for children's family contexts in the United States. *Population Studies, 54,* 29–41.

Bunge, M. (1984). What is pseudoscience? *The Skeptical Inquirer, 9,* 36–46.

Burger, J. M. (2004). *Personality* (6th ed.). Belmont, CA: Wadsworth.

Burke, K. C., Burke, J. D., Regier, D. A., & Rae, D. S. (1990). Age at onset of selected mental disorders in five community populations. *Archives of General Psychiatry, 47,* 511–518.

Burnham, D. (1993). Visual recognition of mother by young infants: Facilitation by speech. *Perception, 22,* 1133–1153.

Bush, S. I., & Geer, J. H. (2001). Implicit and explicit memory of neutral, negative emotional, and sexual information. *Archives of Sexual Behavior, 30,* 615–631.

Bushman, B. J. (1988). The effects of apparel on compliance: A field experiment with a female authority figure. *Personality and Social Psychology Bulletin, 14,* 459–467.

Buss, D. M. (1995). Psychological sex differences. *American Psychologist, 50,* 164–168.

Buss, D. M., Larsen, R. J., Westen, D., & Semmelroth, J. (1992). Sex differences in jealousy: Evolution, physiology, and psychology. *Psychological Science, 3,* 251–255.

Bussey, K., & Bandura, A. (1999). Social cognitive theory of gender development and differentiation. *Psychological Review, 106,* 676–713.

Butler, L. D., Duran, R. E. F., Jasiukaitis, P., Koopman, C., & Spiegel, D. (1996). Hypnotizability and traumatic experience: A diathesis stress model of dissociative symptomatology. *American Journal of Psychiatry, 153,* 42–63.

Butzlaff, R. L., & Hooley, J. M. (1998). Expressed emotion and psychiatric relapse. *Archives of General Psychiatry, 55,* 547–552.

Buunk, B. P., Angleitner, A., Oubaid, V., & Buss, D. M. (1996). Sex differences in jealousy in evolutionary and cultural perspective: Tests from the Netherlands, Germany, and the United States. *Psychological Science, 7,* 359–363.

Byrne, D. (1969). Attitudes and attraction. In L. Berkowitz (Ed.), *Advances in experimental social psychology* (Vol. 4, pp. 35–89). New York: Academic Press.

Byrne, D., Gouaux, C., Griffitt, W., Lamberth, J., Murakawa, N., Prasad, M. B., Prasad, A., & Ramirez, M., III. (1971). The ubiquitous relationship: Attitude similarity and attraction: A cross-cultural study. *Human Relations, 24,* 201–207.

Byrnes, J., & Takahira, S. (1993). Explaining gender differences on SAT-math items. *Developmental Psychology, 29,* 805-810.

Cacioppo, J. T., & Petty, R. E. (1980). Sex differences in influenceability: Toward specifying the underlying processes. *Personality and Social Psychology Bulletin, 6,* 651–656.

Cacioppo, J. T., Petty, R. E., Feinstein, J., & Jarvis, B. (1996). Dispositional differences in cognitive motivation: The life and times of individuals low versus high in need for cognition. *Psychological Bulletin, 119,* 197–253.

Caetano, R. (1988). Drinking patterns and alcohol problems in a national sample of U.S. Hispanics. In National Institute on Alcohol Abuse and Alcoholism (Ed.), *Alcohol use among U.S. ethnic minorities* (Research Monograph No. 18, DHHS Publication No. 87–1435). Washington, DC: U.S. Government Printing Office.

Cain, W. S. (1977). Differential sensitivity for smell: Noise at the nose. *Science, 195,* 796–798.

Cain, W. S. (1988). Olfaction. In R. C. Atkinson, R. J. Herrnstein, G. Lindzey, & R. D. Luce (Eds.), *Steven's handbook of experimental psychology* (2nd ed., Vol. 1, pp. 409–459). New York: Wiley.

Camper, J. (1990, February 7). Drop pompom squad, U. of I. Rape study says. *Chicago Tribune* p.1.

Cannon, D. S., & Baker, T. B. (1981). Emetic and electric shock alcohol aversion therapy: Assessment of conditioning. *Journal of Consulting & Clinical Psychology, 49,* 20 33.

Cannon, T. D. (1996). Abnormalities of brain structure and function in schizophrenia: Implications for etiology and pathophysiology. *Annals of Medicine, 28,* 533–539.

Cannon, T. D. (1998). Genetic and perinatal influences in the etiology of schizophrenia: A neurodevelopmental model. In M. F. Lenzenweger (Ed.), *Origins and development of schizophrenia: Advances in experimental psychopathology,* (pp. 67–92). Washington DC: American Psychological Association.

Cannon, W. & Washburn, A. L. (1912). An explanation of hunger. *American Journal of Physiology, 29,* 441–454.

Cannon, W. B. (1927). The James-Lange theory of emotions: A critical examination and an alternative theory. *American Journal of Psychology, 39,* 106–124.

Canova, A., & Geary, N. (1991). Intraperitoneal injections of nanogram CCK-8 doses inhibits feeding in rats. *Appetite,* 221–227.

Caplan, G. A., & Brigham, B. A. (1990). Marijuana smoking and carcinoma of the tongue: Is there an association? *Cancer, 66,* 1005–1006.

Cappelletto, F. (2003). Long-term memory of extreme events: From autobiography to history. *Journal of the Royal Anthropological Institute, 9,* 241–260.

Cardozo, B. L., Bilukha, O. O., Crawford, C. A., Shaikh, I., Wolfe, M. I., Gerber, M., & Anderson, M. (2004). Mental health, social functioning, and disability in postwar Afghanistan. *The Journal of the American Medical Association. 292,* 575–584.

Carey, G., & DiLalla, D. L. (1994). Personality and psychpathology: Genetic perspectives. *Journal of Abnormal Psychology, 103,* 32–43.

Carey, G., & Goldman, D. (1997). The genetics of antisocial behavior. In D. M. Stoff, J. Breiling, & J. D. Maser (Eds.), *Handbook of antisocial personality disorder* (pp. 243–254). New York: Wiley.

Carey, M. P., Maisto, S. A., Kalichman, S. C., Forsyth, A. D., Wright, E. M., & Johnson, B. T. (1997). Enhancing motivation to reduce the risk of HIV infection for economically disadvantaged urban women. *Journal of Consulting and Clinical Psychology, 65,* 531–541.

Carlston, D. E., & Shovar, N. (1983). Effects of performance attributions on others' perceptions of the attributor. *Journal of Personality and Social Psychology, 44,* 515–525.

Carrington, P. (1993). Modern forms of meditation. In P. M. Lehrer & R. L. Woolfolk (Eds.), *Principles and practice of stress management* (2nd ed.). New York: Guilford Press.

Carroll, M. E., Morgan, A. D., Lynch, W. J., Campbell, U. C., & Dess, N. K. (2002). Intravenous cocaine and heroin self-administration in rats selectively bred fro differential saccharin intake: Phenotype and sex differences. *Psychopharmacology, 161,* 304–313.

Cartwright, R. D. (1993). Who needs their dreams? The usefulness of dreams in psychotherapy. *Journal of the American Academy of Psychoanalysis, 21,* 539–547.

Carver, C. S., Harris, S. D., Lehman, J. M., Durel, L. A., Antoni, M. H., Spencer, S. M., & Pozo-Kaderman, C. (2000). How important is the perception of personal control? Studies of early stage breast cancer patients. *Personality and Social Psychology Bulletin, 26,* 139–149.

Cascio, W. F. (1995). Whither industrial and organizational psychology in a changing world of work? *American Psychologist, 50,* 928–939.

Case, R. B., Moss, A. J., Case, N., McDermott, M., & Eberly, S. (1992). Living alone after myocardial infarction: Impact on prognosis. *Journal of the American Medical Association, 267,* 515–519.

Casey, B. J., Giedd, J. N., & Thomas, K. M. (2000). Structural and functional brain development and its relation to cognitive development. *Biological Psychology, 54,* 241–257.

Caspi, A., Bem, D. J., & Elder, G. H., Jr. (1989). Continuities and consequences of interactional styles across the life course. *Journal of Personality, 57,* 375–406.

Caspi, A., Harrington, H., Milne, B., Amell, J. W., Theodore, R. F., & Moffitt, T. E. (2003). Children's behavioral styles at age 3 are linked to their adult personality traits at age 26. *Journal of Personality, 71,* 495–513.

Castelnuovo, G., Gaggioli, A., Mantovani, F., & Riva, G. (2003). From psychotherapy to e-therapy: The integration of traditional techniques and new communication tools in clinical settings. *Cyberpsychology and Behavior, 6,* 375–382.

Cates, W., Jr. (1998). Reproductive tract infections. In R. A. Hatcher et al. (Eds.), *Contraceptive technology* (17th rev. ed., pp. 179-210). New York: Ardent Media.

Catipovic-Veselica, K., Glavas, B., Kristek, J., & Sram, M. (2001). Components of Type A behavior and two-year prognosis of patients with acute coronary syndrome. *Psychological Reports, 89,* 467–475.

Cattell, R. B. (1943). The description of personality: Basic traits resolved into clusters. *Journal of Abnormal and Social Psychology, 38,* 476–506.

Cattell, R. B. (1963). Theory of fluid and crystallized intelligence: A critical experiment. *Journal of Educational Psychology, 54,* 1–22.

Cattell, R. B. (1965). *The scientific analysis of personality.* Baltimore: Penguin.

CBS News. (2004). *Medicare to fund obesity treatment.* Available online at: http://www.cbsnews.com/stories/2004/07/16/health/printable630141.shtml

Ceci, S. J. (1995). False beliefs: Some developmental and clinical considerations. In D. L. Schacter (Ed.), *Memory distortions.* Cambridge, MA: Harvard University Press.

Centers for Disease Control and Prevention. (1996). Cigarette smoking among adults—United States, 1994. *Morbidity and Mortality Weekly Report, 45*(27), 588–590.

Centers for Disease Control and Prevention. (1998, December 11). Impaired driving. Atlanta, GA: CDC Office of Communications, Division of Medicine.

Centers for Disease Control and Prevention. (2001). *First marriage dissolution, divorce, and remarriage: United States, advanced data, Number 323.* Atlanta, GA: Department of Health and Human Services.

Centers for Disease Control and Prevention. (2001). *Tracking the hidden epidemic: Trends in STDs in the United States (2000).* Atlanta, GA: Department of Health and Human Services.

Centers for Disease Control. (2001). A glance at the HIV epidemic. Retrieved September 27, 2004, from http://www.cdc.gov.nchstp/od/news/At-a-glance.pdf

Centers for Disease Control and Prevention. (2002). Alcohol use among women of childbearing age—United States, 1991–1999. *MMWR, 51,* 273–276.

Centers for Disease Control. (2004). Mental health status of World Trade Center rescue and recovery workers and volunteers—New York City, July 2002–August 2004. *MMWR, 53,* 812–815.

Cermak, L. S., Lewis, R., Butters, N., & Goodglass, H. (1973). Role of verbal mediation in performance of motor tasks by Korsakoff patients. *Perceptual & Motor Skills, 37,* 259–262.

Cernoch, J., & Porter, R. H. (1985). Recognition of maternal axillary odors by infants. *Child Development, 56*(6), 1593–1598.

Chabas, D., Baranzini, S. E., Mitchell, D., Bernard, C.C.A., Rittling, S. R., Denhardt, D. T., Sobel, R. A., Lock, C., Karpuj, M., Pedotti, R., Heller, R., Oksenberg, J. R., & Steinman, L. (2001). The influence of the proinflammatory cytokine, oesteopontin, on autoimmune demyelinating disease (Reports). *Science, 294,* 1731–1735.

Chabris, C. F., & Kosslyn, S. M. (1998). How do the cerebral hemispheres contribute to encoding spatial relations? *Current Directions in Psychological Science, 74,* 8–14.

Chaiken, S. (1987). The heuristic model of persuasion. In M. P. Zanna, J. M. Olson, & C. P. Herman (Eds.), *Social influence: The Ontario Symposium* (Vol. 5., pp. 3–19). Hillsdale, NJ: Erlbaum.

Chaiken, S., & Baldwin, M. W. (1981). Affective-cognitive consistency and the effect of salient behavioral information on the self-perception of attitudes. *Journal of Personality and Social Psychology, 34,* 605–614.

Chakos, M. H., Alvir, J. M., Woerner, M., & Koreen, A. (1996). Incidence and correlates of tardive dyskinesia in first episode of schizophrenia. *Archives of General Psychiatry, 53,* 313–319.

Chamberlain, K., & Zika, S. (1990). The minor events approach to stress: Support for the use of daily hassles. *British Journal of Psychology, 81,* 469–481.

Chambers, D., & Reisberg, D. (1985). Can mental images be ambiguous? *Journal of Experimental Psychology: Human Perception & Performance, 11,* 317–328.

Chambers, D., & Reisberg, D. (1992). What an image depicts depends on what an image means. *Cognitive Psychology, 24,* 145–174.

Chambless, D. L., & Hollon, S. D. (1998). Defining empirically supported therapies. *Journal of Consulting & Clinical Psychology, 66,* 7–18.

Chambless, D. L., & Ollendick, T. H. (2001). Empirically supported psychological interventions: Controversies and evidence. *Annual Review of Psychology, 52,* 685–716.

Chao, R. K. (2001). Extending research on the consequences of parenting style for Chinese Americans and European Americans. *Child Development, 72,* 1832–1843.

Charney, D. S., Nagy, L. M., Bremner, J. D., Goddard, A.W., Yehuda, R., & Southwick, S. M. (2000). Neurobiologic mechanisms of human anxiety. In B. S. Fogel (Ed.), *Synopsis of neuropsychiatry* (pp. 273–288). Philadelphia: Lippincott Williams & Wilkins.

Chaves, J. F. (1989). Hypnotic control of clinical pain. In N. P. Spanos & J. F. Chaves (Eds.), *Hypnosis: The cognitive-behavioral perspective.* Buffalo, NY: Prometheus Books.

Chaves, J. F. (1994). Hypnosis in pain management. In J.W. Rhue, S. J. Lynee, & I. Kirsch (Eds.), *Handbook of clinical hypnosis.* Washington, DC: American Psychological Association.

Cheasty, M., Clare, A.W., & Collins, C. (2002). Child sexual abuse: A predictor of persistent depression in adult rape and sexual assault victims. *Journal of Mental Health, 11,* 79-84.

Check, J. V. P., & Malamuth, N. M. (1983). Sex-role stereotyping and reactions to depictions of stranger versus acquaintance rape. *Journal of Personality and Social Psychology, 45,* 344-356.

Cherlin, A. J., & Furstenberg, F. F., Jr. (1986). *The new American grandparent: A place in the family, a life apart.* New York: Basic Books.

Chess, S., & Thomas, A. (1984). *Origins and evolution of behavior disorders: From infancy to early adult life.* New York: Brunner/Mazel.

Chi, I., Lubben, J., & Kitano, H. H. L. (1989). Differences in drinking behavior among three Asian-American groups. *Journal of Studies on Alcohol, 50,* 15–23.

Chipuer, H. M., Rovine, M. J., & Polmin, R. (1990). LISREL modeling: Genetic and environmental influences on IQ revisited. *Intelligence, 14,* 11–29.

Choi, I., & Nesbitt, R. E. (1998). Situational salience and cultural differences in the correspondence bias and actor-observer bias. *Personality and Social Psychology, Bulletin, 24,* 949–960.

Chollar, S. (1989, April). Dreamchasers. *Psychology Today,* pp. 60–61.

Chomsky, N. (1957). *Syntactic structures.* The Hague: Mouton.

Chomsky, N. (1965). *Aspects of the theory of syntax.* Cambridge, MA: MIT Press.

Chory-Assad, R. M., & Tamborini, R. (2001). Television doctors: An analysis of physicians on fictional and non-fictional television programs. *Journal of Broadcasting & Electronic Media, 45,* 499–521.

Chory-Assad, R. M., & Tamborini, R. (2003). Television exposure and the public's perceptions of physicians. *Journal of Broadcasting & Electronic Media, 47,* 197–215.

Christensen, A., & Jacobson, N. S. (1994). Who (or what) can do psychotherapy: The status and challenge of nonprofessional therapies. *Psychological Science, 5,* 8–14.

Church, R. M., & Black, A. H. (1958). Latency of the conditioned heart rate as a function of the CS-US interval. *Journal of Comparative and Physiological Psychology, 51,* 478–482.

Churchland, P. S. , & Ramachandran, V. S. (1996). Filling in: Why Dennett is wrong. In K. Atkins (Ed.), *Perception.* Oxford, England: Oxford University Press.

Cialdini, R. B. (2001). *Influence: Science and practice* (4th ed.). Needham Heights, MA: Allyn & Bacon.

Cialdini, R. B., Borden, R. J., Thorne, A., Walker, M. R., Freeman, S., & Sloan, L. R. (1976). Basking in the reflected glory: Three (football) field studies. *Journal of Personality and Social Psychology, 34,* 366–375.

Cialdini, R. B., Vincent, J. E., Catalan, J., Wheeler, D., & Darby, B. L. (1975). Reciprocal concessions procedure for inducing compliance: The door-in-the-face technique. *Journal of Personality and social Psychology, 31,* 206–215.

Cibelli, J. B., Lanza, R. P., & West, M. D. (2002). The first human cloned embryo. *Scientific American, 286,* 44–51.

Clark, D. C., & Fawcett, J. (1992). Review of empirical risk factors for evaluation of the suicidal patient. In B. Bongar (Ed.), *Suicide: Guidelines for assessment, management, and treatment* (pp. 16–48). New York: Oxford University Press.

Clark, D. C., Gibbons, R. D., Fawcett, J., & Scheftner, W. A. (1989). What is the mechanism by which suicide attempts predispose to later suicide attempts? A mathematical model. *Journal of Abnormal Psychology, 98,* 42–49.

Clark, R., Anderson, N. B., Clark, V. R., & Williams, D. R. (1999). Racism as a stressor for African Americans: A biopsychosocial model. *American Psychologist, 54,* 805–816.

Clark, W. B., & Midanik, L. (Eds). (1982). *Alcohol use and alcohol problems among U.S. adults: Results of the 1979 national survey* (Research Monograph No. 1, DHHS Publication No. 82-1190). Washington, DC: U.S. Government Printing Office.

Clarke, A. C. (1952). An examination of the operation of residential propinquity as a factor in mate selection. *American Sociological Review, 17,* 17–22.

Clay, R. A. (1996, May). Modern hypnosis wins clinical respect, praise. *APA Monitor.*

Cloninger, C. R., & Gottesman, I. I. (1987). Genetic and environmental factors in antisocial behavior disorders. In S. A. Mednick, T. E. Moffitt, & S. A. Stack (Eds.), *The causes of crime: New biological approaches* (pp. 92–109). New York: Cambridge University Press.

Cloninger, C. R., Bayon, C., & Przybeck, T. (1997). Epidemiology and axis I comorbidity of antisocial personality disorder. In D. M. Stoff, J. Breiling, & J. D. Maser (Eds.), *Handbook of antisocial personality disorder* (pp. 12–21). New York: Wiley.

Coffer, C. N., & Appley, M. (1964). *Motivation: Theory and research.* New York: Wiley.

Cohan, C. L., & Kleinbaum, S. (2002). Toward a greater understanding of the cohabitation effect: Premarital cohabitation and marital communication. *Journal of Marriage and Family, 64,* 180–192.

Cohen, D. A., Farley, T. A., Taylor, S. N., Martin, D. H., & Schuster, M. A., (2002). When and where do youths have sex? The potential role of adult supervision. *Pediatrics, 110,* E66.

Cohen, J., & Servan-Schreiber, D. (1992). Context, cortex, and dopamine: A connectionist approach to behavior and biology in schizophrenia. *Psychological Review, 99,* 45–77.

Cohen, L. L., & Shotland, R. L. (1996). Timing of first sexual intercourse in a relationship: Expectations, experiences, and perceptions of others. *Journal of Sex Research, 33,* 291-299.

Cohen, N. J. (1984). Preserved learning capacity in amnesia: Evidence for multiple memory systems. In L. R. Squire & N. Butters (Eds.), *Neuropsychology of memory.* New York: Guilford Press.

Cohen, P., Cohen, J., Kasen, S., Velez, C. N., Hartmark, C., Johnson, J., Rojas, M., Brook, J., & Streuning, E. L. (1993). An epidemiological study of disorders in late adolescence: I. Age- and gender specific prevalence. *Journal of Child Psychology and Psychiatry, 6,* 851-867.

Cohen, S. (1996). Psychological stress, immunity, and upper respiratory infections. *Current Directions in Psychological Science, 5,* 86–90.

Cohen, S., Doyle, W. J., Turner, R., Alper, C. M., & Skoner, D. P. (2003). Sociability and susceptibility to the common cold. *Psychological Science, 14,* 389–395.

Cohen, S., Tyrrell, D., & Smith, A. (1991). Psychological stress and susceptibility to the common cold. *New England Journal of Medicine, 325,* 606–612.

Colapinto, J. (2000). *As nature made him: The boy who was raised as a girl.* New York: HarperCollins.

Colcombe, S., & Kramer, A. F. (2003). Fitness effects on the cognitive function of older adults: A meta-analytic study. *Psychological Science, 14,* 125–130.

Cole, W. (1992). Incest perpetrators: Their assessment and treatment. *Psychiatric Clinics of North America, 15,* 689-701.

Coleman, M., Ganong, L., & Fine, M. (2000). Reinvestigating marriage: Another decade of progress. *Journal of Marriage and the Family, 62,* 1288–1307.

Coles, B., & Stokes, F. S. (1985). *Sex and the American teenager.* New York: Harper & Row.

Coley, R. L. (2001). (In)visible men: Emerging research on low-income, unmarried, and minority fathers. *American Psychologist, 56,* 743–753.

Coley, R. L., & Chase-Lansdale, P. L. (1999). Stability and change in paternal involvement among urban African American fathers. *Journal of Family Psychology, 13,* 416–435.

Colin, V. (1996). *Human attachment.* New York: McGraw-Hill.

Colley, A., Ball, J., Kirby, N., Harvey, R., & Vingelen, I. (2002, December). Gender-linked differences in everyday memory performance: Effort makes the difference. *Sex Roles: A Journal of Research,* 577–582.

Collier, G. Hirsch, E., & Hamlin, P. H. (1972). The ecological determinants of reinforcement in the rat. *Physiology and Behavior, 9,* 705–716.

Collings, V. B. (1974). Human taste response as a function of locus of stimulation on the tongue and soft palate. *Perception & Psychophysics, 16,* 169–174.

Collins, M. W., Field, M., Lovell, M. R., Iverson, G., Johnston, K. M., Maroon, J., & Fu, F. H. (2003). Relationship between postconcussion headache and neuropsychological test performance in high school athletes. *The American Journal of Sports Medicine, 31,* 168–173.

Collins, R. L., Elliott, M. N., Berry, S. H., Kanouse, D. E., Kunkel, D., Hunter, S. B., & Miu, A. (2004). Watching sex on television predicts adolescent initiation of sexual behavior. *Pediatrics, 114,* 280-289.

Coltheart, M. (1983). Ecological necessity of iconic memory. *Behavioral & Brain Sciences, 6,* 17–18.

Coltrane, S. (2001). Research on household labor: Modeling and measuring the social embeddedness of routine family work. In R. M. Milardo (Ed.), *Understanding families in the new millennium: A decade in review* (pp. 427–452). Minneapolis: National Council on Family Relations.

Comaty, J. E., Stasio, M., & Advokat, C. (2001). Analysis of outcome variables of a token economy in a state psychiatric hospital: A program evaluation. *Research in Developmental Disabilities, 22,* 233–253.

Compas, B. E., Oppedisano, G., Connor, J. K., Herhardt, C. A., Hinden, B. R., Achenbach, T. M., & Hammen, C. (1997). Gender differences in depressive symptoms in adolescence: Comparison of national samples of clinically referred and nonreferred youths. *Journal of Consulting and Clinical Psychology, 65,* 617–626.

Compton, W. M., Helzer, J. E., Hwu, H., Yeh, E., McEvoy, L., Tipp, J. E., & Spitznagel, E. L. (1991). New methods in cross-cultural psychiatry: Psychiatric illness in Taiwan and the United States. *American Journal of Psychiatry, 148,* 1697–1704.

Conklin, H. M., & Iacono, W. G. (2002). Schizophrenia: A neurodevelopmental perspective. *Current Directions in Psychological Science, 11,* 33–37.

Conrad, R. (1964). Acoustic confusions in immediate memory. *British Journal of Psychology, 55,* 75–84.

Contrada, R. J., Ashmore, R. D., Gary, M. L., Coups, E., Egeth, J. D., Sewell, A., Ewell, K., Goyal, T. M., & Chasse, V. (2000). Ethnicity-related sources of stress and their effects on well-being. *Current Directions in Psychological Science, 9,* 136–139.

Conway, B. R. (2003). Colour vision: A clue to hue in V2. *Current Biology, 13,* R308–R310.

Conway, K., & Russell, G. (2000). Couples' grief and experience of support in the aftermath of miscarriage. *British Journal of Medical Psychology, 73,* 531–545.

Conwell, Y., & Brent, D. (1995). Suicide and aging I: Patterns of psychiatric diagnosis. *International Psychogeriatrics, 7,* 149–164.

Cook, J. L., & Cook, G. (2005). *Child development: Principles and perspectives.* Boston: Allyn & Bacon.

Cookson, J. (1997). Lithium: Balancing risks and benefits. *British Journal of Psychiatry, 171,* 113–119.

Cools, J., Schotte, D. E., & McNally, R. J. (1992). Emotional arousal and overeating in restrained eaters. *Journal of Abnormal Psychology, 69,* 390–400.

Coons, P. M. (1994). Confirmation of childhood abuse in child and adolescent cases of multiple personality disorder and dissociative disorder not otherwise specified. *Journal of Nervous & Mental Disease, 182,* 461–464.

Cooper, L. A., & Shepard, R. N. (1973). Chronometric studies of the rotation of mental images. In W. G. Chase (Ed.), *Visual information processing.* New York: Academic Press.

Cooper, M. L., Russell, M., Skinner, J. B., Frone, M. R., & Mudar, P. (1992). Stress and alcohol use: Moderating effects of gender, coping, and alcohol expectancies. *Journal of Abnormal Psychology, 101,* 139–152.

Coperhaver, S., & Grauerholz, E. (1991). Sexual victimization among sorority women: Exploring the link between sexual violence and institutional practices. *Sex Roles, 24,* 31-41.

Cordes, C. L., & Dougherty, T. W. (1993). A review and integration of research on job burnout. *Academy of Management Review, 18,* 621–656.

Coren, S. (1996). *Sleep-thieves: An eye-opening exploration into the science and mysteries of sleep.* New York: Free Press.

Coren, S., Porac, C., Aks, D. J., & Morikawa, K. (1988). A method to assess the relative contribution of lateral inhibition to the magnitude of visual-geometric illusions. *Perception & Psychophysics, 43* 551–558.

Coren, S., Ward, L. M., & Enns, J. T. (1999). *Sensation and perception* (5th ed.). Fort Worth: Harcourt Brace.

Corkin, S. (1968). Acquisition of motor skill after bilateral medial temporal-lobe excision. *Neuropsychologia, 6,* 255–265.

Corrigan, P. W., Holmes, E. P., Luchins, D., Buichan, B., & Basit, A. (1994). Staff burnout in a psychiatric hospital: A cross-lagged panel design. *Journal of Organizational Behavior, 15,* 65–74.

Corrigan, P., McCorkle, B., Schell, B., & Kidder, K. (2003). Religion and spirituality in the lives of people with serious mental illness. *Community Mental Health Journal, 39,* 487–499.

Coryell, W. (1998). The treatment of psychotic depression. *Journal of Clinical Psychiatry, 59*(Suppl. 1), 22–27.

Cosmides, L., & Tooby, J. (1996). Are humans good intuitive statisticians after all? Rethinking some conclusions from the literature on judgment under uncertainty. *Cognition, 58,* 1–73.

Costa, P. T., & McCrae, R. R. (1992). Multiple uses for longitudinal personality data. *European Journal of Personality, 6*(2), 85–102.

Costa, P. T., & McCrae, R. R. (1997). Longitudinal stability of adult personality. In R. Hogan, J. A. Johnson, & S. R. Briggs (Eds.), *Handbook of personality psychology* (pp. 269–290). San Diego, CA: Academic Press.

Costa, P. T., Terracciano, A., & McCrae, R. R. (2001). Gender differences in personality traits across cultures: Robust and surprising findings. *Journal of Personality & Social Psychology, 81,* 322–331.

Courtois, C. (2000). *Healing the incest wound.* New York: Norton.

Cowan, C. P., & Cowan, P. A. (2000). *When partners become parents: The big life change for couples.* Mahwah, NJ: Erlbaum.

Craik, F. I. M., & Lockhart, R. S. (1972). Levels of processing: A framework for memory research. *Journal of Verbal Learning & Verbal Behavior, 11,* 671–684.

Crandall, C. S. (1988). Social contagion of binge eating. *Journal of Personality and Social Psychology, 55,* 588–598.

Crandall, C. S., Preisler, J. J., & Aussprung, J. (1992). Measuring life event stress in the lives of college students: The Undergraduate Stress Questionnaire (USQ). *Journal of Behavioral Medicine, 15*(6), 627–662.

Craske, M. G., & Barlow, D. H. (2001). Panic disorder and agoraphobia. In H. H. Barlow (Ed.), *Clinical handbook of psychological disorders* (3rd ed.). New York: Guilford Press.

Crawford, H. J., Brown, A. M., & Moon, C. E. (1993). Sustained attentional and disattentional abilities: Differences between low and highly hypnotizable persons. *Journal of Abnormal Psychology, 102*(4), 534–543.

Crespo-Facorro, B., Wiser, A. K., Andreasen, N. C., O'Leary, D. S., Watkins, G. L., Ponto, L. L. B., & Hichwa, R. D. (2001). Neural basis of novel and well-learned recognition memory in schizophrenia: A positron emission tomography study. *Human Brain Mapping, 12,* 219–231.

Crews, F. (1996). The verdict on Freud. *Psychological Science, 7,* 63–68.

Crick, F., & Mitchison, G. (1995). REM sleep and neural nets. *Behavioural Brain Research, 69*(1–2), 147–155.

Crick, N. R., & Dodge, K. A. (1994). A review and reformulation of social information-processing mechanisms in children's social adjustment. *Psychological Bulletin, 115,* 74–101.

Crick, N. R., Casas, J. F., & Ku, H. C. (1999). Relational and physical forms of peer victimization in preschool. *Developmental Psychology, 35,* 376-385.

Crits-Christoph, P. (1992). The efficacy of brief dynamic psychotherapy: A meta-analysis. *American Journal of Psychiatry, 149,* 151–158.

Crits-Christoph, P. (1997). Limitations of the dodo bird verdict and the role of clinical trials in psychotherapy research: Comment on Wampold et al. (1997). *Psychological Bulletin, 122,* 216–220.

Crits-Christoph, P., & Baranackie, K., Kurcias, J. S., & Beck, A. T. (1991). Meta-analysis of therapist effects in psychotherapy outcome. *Psychotherapy Research, 1,* 81–91.

Crombag, H. S., & Robinson, T. E. (2004). Drugs, environment, brain, and behavior. *Current Directions in Psychological Science, 13,* 107–111.

Crosby, A. E., Cheltenham, M. P., & Sacks, J. J. (1999). Incidence of suicidal ideation and behavior in the United States, 1994. *Suicide and Life-Threatening Behavior, 29,* 131–140.

Cross-National Collaborative Group. (1992). The changing rate of major depression. *Journal of the American Medical Association, 268,* 3098–3105.

Crowe, R. R. (1990). Panic disorder: Genetic considerations. *Journal of Psychiatric Research, 24*(Suppl. 2), 129–134.

Crowell, T. A., Luis, C. A., Vanderploeg, R. D., Schinka, J. A., & Mullan, M. (2002). Memory patterns and executive functioning in mild cognitive impairment and Alzheimer's disease. *Aging Neuropsychology and Cognition, 9,* 288–297.

Crowley, A. E., & Hoyer, W. D. (1994). An integrative framework for understanding two-sided persuasion. *Journal of Consumer Research, 20,* 561–574.

Culbertson, F. M. (1997). Depression and gender: An international review. *American Psychologist, 52,* 25–31.

Cytowic, R. E. (1999). *The man who tasted shapes.* Cambridge, MA: MIT Press.

Dabbs, J. M., Jr., & Morris, R. (1990). Testosterone, social class, and antisocial behavior in a sample of 4,462 men. *Psychological Science, 1,* 209–211.

Daly, K. J. (1993). Reshaping fatherhood. In W. Marsiglio (Ed.), *Fatherhood: Contemporary theory, research, and social policy* (pp. 21–40). Thousand Oaks, CA: Sage.

Damak, S., Rong, M., Yasumatsu, K., Kokrashvii, Z., Varadarajan, V., Zou, S., Jiang, P., Ninomiya, Y., & Margolskee, R. F. (2003). Detection of sweet and umami taste in the absence of taste receptor T1r3. *Science, 301,* 850–851.

Damasio, H., Grabowski, T., Frank, R., Galaburda, A. M., & Damasio, A. R. (1994). The return of Phineas Gage: Clues about the brain from the skull of a famous patient. *Science, 264,* 1102–1105.

Damon, W. (1999). The moral development of children. *Scientific American, 281,* 73–78.

Darke, P. R., Chaiken, S., Bohner, G., Einwiller, S., Erb, H-P., & Hazlewood, J. D. (1998). Accuracy motivation, consensus information, and the law of large numbers: effects on attitude judgment in the absence of argumentation. *Personality & Social Psychology Bulletin, 24,* 1205–1215.

Darley, J., & Batson, C. D. (1973). "From Jerusalem to Jericho": A study of situational and dispositional variables in helping behavior. *Journal of Personality and Social Psychology, 27,* 100–108.

Darwin, C. (1859). *The origin of species.* London: John Murray.

Darwin, C. (1936). *On the origin of species by means of natural selection.* New York: Random House. (Original work published 1859)

Dasen, P. R. (1994). Culture and cognitive development from a Piagetian perspective. In W. J. Lonner & R. Malpass (Eds.), *Psychology and culture.* Boston: Allyn & Bacon.

Dasgupta, A. M., Juza, D. M., White, G. M., & Maloney, J. F. (1995). Memory and hypnosis: A comparative analysis of guided memory, cognitive interviews, and hypnotic hyperamnesia. *Imagination, Cognition, and Personality, 14*(2), 117–130.

Davidson, J. R. T. (2000). Trauma: The impact of post-traumatic stress disorder. *Journal of Psychopharmacology, 14,* S5–S12.

Davidson, R. J., Jackson, D. C., & Kalin, N. H. (2000). Emotion, plasticity, context, and regulation: Perspectives from affective neuroscience. *Psychological Bulletin, 126,* 873–889.

Davidson, R. J., Putnam, K. M., & Larson, C. L. (2000). Dysfunction in the neural circuitry of emotion regulation: A possible prelude to violence. *Science, 289,* 591–594.

Davies, C., & Williams, D. (2002). *The grandparent study 2002 report.* Washington, DC: AARP.

Davies, I. R. L. (1998). A study of colour grouping in three languages: A test of the linguistic relativity hypothesis. *British Journal of Psychology, 89,* 433–452.

Davies, P. G., Spencer, S. J., Quinn, D. M., & Gerhardstein, R. (2002). Consuming images: How television commercials that elicit stereotype threat can restrain women academically and professionally. *Journal of Personality and Social Psychology, 28,* 1615–1628.

Davies, P. T., & Cummings, E. M. (1998). Exploring children's emotional security as a mediator of the link between marital relations and child adjustment. *Child Development, 69,* 124–139.

Davies, S., & Guppy, N. (1997). Fields of study, college selectivity, and student inequalities in higher education. *Social Forces, 75*(4), 1417–1422.

Davis, K. L., Kahn, R. S., Ko, G., & Davidson, M. (1991). Dopamine in schizophrenia: A review and conceptualization. *American Journal of Psychiatry, 148,* 1474–1486.

Davis, M. H., Luce, C., & Kraus, S. J. (1994). The heritability of characteristics associated with dispositional empathy. *Journal of Personality, 60,* 369–391.

Davis, M., & Egger, M. D. (1992). Habituation and sensitization in vertebrates. In L. R. Squire, J. H. Byrne, L. Nadel, H. L. Roediger, D. L. Schacter, & R. F. Thompson (Eds.), *Encylcopedia of learning and memory* (pp. 237–240). New York: Macmillan.

Davis, P. J. (1999). Gender differences in autobiographical memory for childhood emotional experiences. *Journal of Personality and Social Psychology, 76,* 498–510.

De Benedittis, G., Lorenzetti, A., & Pieri, A. (1990). The role of stressful life events in the onset of chronic primary headache. *Pain, 40*(1), 65–75.

de Fonseca, F., Carrera, M. R. A., Navarro, M., Koob, G. F., & Weiss, F. (1997, June 27). Activation of corticotropin-releasing factor in the limbic system during cannabinoid withdrawal. *Science, 276*(5321), 2050–2054.

De Lisi, R., & Gallagher, A. M. (1991). Understanding gender stability and constancy in Argentinean children. *Merrill-Palmer Quarterly, 37,* 483–502.

Deaux, K. (1985). Sex and gender. *Annual Review of Psychology, 36,* 49-81.

Deaux, K., & Hanna, R. (1984). Courtship in the personals column: The influence of gender and sexual orientation. *Sex Roles, 11,* 363–375.

DeCasper, A. J., & Fifer, W. P. (1980). Of human bonding: Newborns prefer their mothers' voices. *Science, 208,* 1174–1176.

DeCastro, J. M., & Elmore, D. K. (1988). Subjective hunger relationships with meal patterns in the spontaneous feeing behavior of humans: Evidence for a causal relationship. *Physiology and Behavior, 43,* 159–165.

Deci, E. L. & Ryan, R. M. (1985). *Intrinsic motivation and self-determination in human behavior.* New York: Plenum Press.

Deci, E. L., Koestner, R., & Ryan, R. M. (1999). A meta-analytic review of experiments examining the effects of extrinsic rewards. *Psychological Bulletin, 125,* 627–668.

Deckers, L. (2001). *Motivation: Biological, psychological, and environmental.* Needham Heights, MA: Allyn & Bacon.

DeFrain, J., & Olson, D. H. (1999). Contemporary family patterns and relationships. In M. B. Sussman, S. K. Steinmetz, & G. W. Peterson (Eds.), *Handbook of marriage and the family* (pp. 309–326). New York: Plenum Press.

DeJoseph, J. (December 8, 2003). After the fall. *Adweek, 48,* p. 17.

DeLacoste-Utamsing, C., & Holloway, R. L. (1982). Sexual dimorphism in the human corpus callosum. *Science, 216,* 1431–1432.

DeLoache, J. (2001). The symbol-mindedness of young children. In W. W. Hartup & R. A. Weinberg (Eds.), *Child psychology in retrospect and prospect.* Mahwah, NJ: Erlbaum.

DeMaris, A., & MacDonald, W. (1993). Premarital cohabitation and marital instability: A test of the unconventionality hypothesis. *Journal of Marriage and the Family, 55,* 399–407.

DeMaris, A., & Rao, K. V. (1992). Premarital cohabitation and subsequent marital stability in the United States: A reassessment. *Journal of Marriage and the Family, 54,* 178–190.

Dement, W. (1960). The effect of dream deprivation. *Science, 131,* 1705–1707.

Dement, W., & Kleitman, N. (1957). Cyclic variations in EEG during sleep and their relation to eye movements, body motility, and dreaming. *Electroencephalography and Clinical Neurophysiology, 9,* 673–690.

Dement, W., & Vaughan, C. (1999). *The promise of sleep: A pioneer in sleep medicine explains the vital connection between health, happiness, and a good night's sleep.* New York: Delacorte.

Denis, M., & Cocude, M. (1999). On the metric properties of visual images generated from verbal descriptions: Evidence for the robustness of the mental scanning effect. *Journal of Cognitive Psychology, 9,* 353–379.

Denning, D. G., Conwell, Y., King, D., & Coz, C. (2000). Method choice, intent, and gender in completed suicide. *Suicide & Life-Threatening Behavior, 30,* 282–288.

Denollet, J. (1993). Biobehavioral research on coronary heart disease. *Journal of Behavioral Medicine, 16*(2), 115–141.

D'Eon, J. L. (1989). Hypnosis in the control of labor pain. In N. P. Spanos & J. F. Chaves (Eds.), *Hypnosis: The cognitive-behavioral perspective.* Buffalo, NY: Prometheus Books.

Depression and Bipolar Support Alliance. (2002). *National DMDA support groups: An important step on the road to wellness.* Chicago: Author.

DeSteno, D. A., & Salovey, P. (1996). Evolutionary origins of sex differences in jealousy? Questioning the "fitness" of the model. *Psychological Science, 7,* 367–372.

Deutsch, F. M. (2001). Equally shared parenting. *Current Directions in Psychological Science, 10,* 25–28.

Deutsch, J. A. (1990). Food intake. In E. M. Stricker (Ed.), *Handbook of behavioral neurobiology: Vol. 10. Neurobiology of food and fluid intake* (pp. 151–182). New York: Plenum Press.

Deutsch, J. A., Puerto, A., & Wang, M. L. (1978). The stomach signals satiety. *Science, 201,* 165–167.

DeValois, R. L., & DeValois, K. K. (1975). Neural coding of color. In E. C. Carterette & M. P. Friedman (Eds.), *Handbook of perception* (pp. 117–166). New York: Academic Press.

DeValois, R. L., & DeValois, K. K. (1993). A multistage color model. *Vision Research, 33,* 1053–1065.

Dhabhar, F. S., Miller, A. H., McEwen, B. S., & Spencer, R. L., (1995). Effects of stress on immune cell distribution. Dynamics and hormonal mechanisms. *The Journal of Immunology, 154* (10), 5511–5527.

Diamond, M. C., Scheibel, A. B., & Elson, L. M. (1985). *The human brain coloring book.* New York: Harper Perennial.

Diaz, R. M., & Berk, L. E. (Eds.). (1992). *Private speech: From social interaction to self-regulation.* Hillsdale, NJ: Erlbaum.

Diener, E., & Seligman, M. E. (2004). Beyond money: Toward an economy of well-being. *Psychological Science in the Public Interest, 5,* 1–31.

Dies, R. R. (1993). Research on group psychotherapy: Overview and clinical applications. In A. Alonso & H. I. Swiller (Eds.), *Group therapy in clinical practice.* Washington, DC: American Psychiatric Press.

Difede, J., & Hoffman, H. G. (2002). Virtual reality exposure therapy for World Trade Center posttraumatic stress disorder: A case report. *Cyberpsychology & Behavior, 5,* 529–535.

Digman, J. M. (1997). Higher-order factors of the Big Five. *Journal of Personality and Social Psychology, 73,* 1246–1256.

DiLillo, D. (2002). Interpersonal functioning among women reporting a history of childhood sexual abuse: Empirical findings and methodological issues. *Clinical Psychology Review, 21,* 553-576.

Dindia, K., & Allen, M. (1992). Sex differences in self-disclosure: A meta-analysis. *Psychological Bulletin, 112,* 106-124.

Dion, K. K., Berscheid, E., & Walster, E. (1972). What is beautiful is good. *Journal of Personality and Social Psychology, 24,* 285–290.

Dishion, T. J., & Patterson, G. R. (1997). The timing and severity of antisocial behavior: Three hypotheses within an ecological framework. In D. M. Stoff, J. Breiling, & J. D. Maser (Eds.), *Handbook of antisocial personality disorder* (pp. 205–217). New York: Wiley.

Dixon, J. F., & Hokin, L. E. (1998). Lithium acutely inhibits and chronically up-regulates and stabilizes glutamate uptake by presynaptic nerve endings in mouse cerebral cortex. *Neurobiology, 95,* 8363–8368.

Dobson, K. S., Backs-Dermott, B. J., & Dozois, D. J. A. (2000). Cognitive and cognitive-behavioral therapies. In C. R. Snyder & R. E. Ingram (Eds.), *Handbook of psychological change: Psychotherapy processes and practices for the 21st century* (pp. 409–428). New York: Wiley.

Doctor, R. M., & Doctor, J. N. (1994). Stress. *Encyclopedia of human behavior, Vol. 4.* San Diego, CA: Academic.

Doering, S., Muller, E., Kopcke, W., Pietcker, A., Gaebel, W., Linden, M., Muller, P., Muller-Spahn, F., Tegler, J., & Schussler, G. (1998). Predictors of relapse and rehospitalization in schizophrenia and schizoaffective disorder. *Schizophrenia Bulletin, 24,* 87–98.

Dohrenwend, B. P., Levav, I., Shrout, P. E., Link, B. G., Skodol, A. E., & Martin, J. L. (1987). Life stress and psychopathology: Progress on research begun with Barbara Snell Dohrenwend. *American Journal of Community Psychology, 15,* 677–715.

Dolbier, C. L., Cocke, R. R., Leiferman, J. A., Steinhardt, M. A., Schapiro, S. J., Nehete, P. N., Perlman, J. E., & Sastry, J. (2001). Differences in functional immune responses of high vs. low hardy healthy individuals. *Journal of Behavioral Medicine, 24,* 219–229.

Dollard, J., Doob, L., Miller, N., Mowrer, O. H., & Sears, R. R. (1939). *Frustration and aggression.* New Haven, CT: Yale University Press.

Dominowski, R. L., & Dallob, P. (1995). Insight and problem solving. In R. J. Sternberg & J. E. Davidson (Eds.), *The nature of insight* (pp. 33–62). Cambridge, MA: MIT Press.

Domjan, M., & Purdy, J. E. (1995). Animal research in psychology: More than meets the eye of the general psychology student. *American Psychologist, 50,* 496–503.

Dornan, W. A., & Malsbury, C. W. (1989). Neuropeptides and male sexual behavior. *Neuroscience and Biobehavioral Reviews, 13,* 1-15.

Doty, R. L. (2001). Olfaction. *Annual Review of Psychology, Annual 2001,* 423–447.

Dougherty, D. D., Baer, L., Cosgrove, G. R., Cassem, E. H., Price, B. H., Nirenberg, A. A., Jenike, M. A., & Rauch, S. L. (2002). Prospective long-term follow-up of 44 patients who received cingulotomy for treatment of refractory obsessive-compulsive disorder. *American Journal of Psychiatry, 159,* 269–275.

Draguns, J. G. (2002). Universal and cultural aspects of counseling and psychotherapy. In P. B. Pedersen, J. G. Draguns, W. J. Lonner, & J. E. Trimble (Eds.), *Counseling across cultures* (5th ed.; pp. 29–50). Thousand Oaks, CA: Sage Publications.

Driesen, N. R., & Raz, N. (1995). The influence of sex, age, and handedness on corpus callosum morphology: A meta-analysis. *Psychobiology, 23,* 240–247.

Druckman, D., & Bjork, R. A. (1994). *Learning, remembering, believing: Enhancing human performance.* Washington, DC: National Academy Press.

Dube, R., & Hebert, M. (1988). Sexual abuse of children 12 years of age: A review of 511 cases. *Child Abuse and Neglect, 12,* 321-330.

Duckitt, J. (1992). Psychology and prejudice: A historical analysis and integrative framework. *American Psychologist, 47,* 1182–1193.

Duiker, W. J., & Spielvogel, J. J. (2004). *The world history, volume II: Since 1400* (4th ed.). Belmont, CA: Wadsworth.

Duncan, L. E., & Agronick, G. S. (1995). The intersection of life stage and social events: Personality and life outcomes. *Journal of Personality & Social Psychology, 69,* 558–568.

Durston, S., Hulshoff Pol, H. E., Casey, B. J., Giedd, J. N., Buitelaar, J. K., & van Engeland, H. (2001). Anatomical MRI of the developing human brain: What have we learned? *Journal of the American Academy of Child and Adolescent Psychiatry, 40,* 1012–1020.

Dweck, C. S., Chiu, C., & Hong, Y. (1995). Implicit theories and their role in judgments and reactions: A world from two perspectives. *Psychological Inquiry, 6,* 267–285.

Eagly, A. H., & Chaiken, S. (1975). An attribution analysis of communicator characteristics on opinion change: The case of communicator attractiveness. *Journal of Personality and Social Psychology, 32,* 136–144.

Eagly, A. H., & Steffen, V. J. (1986). Gender and aggressive behavior: A meta-analytic review of the social-psychological literature. *Psychological Bulletin, 100,* 309–330.

Eagly, A. H., & Warren, R. (1976). Intelligence, comprehension, and opinion. *Journal of Personality, 44,* 226–242.

Eaton, A. H., & Resko, J. A. (1974). Plasma testosterone and male dominance in a Japanese macaque (Macca fuscata) troop compared with repeated measures of testosterone in laboratory males. *Hormones and Behavior, 5,* 251–259.

Eaton, W. W., & Keyl, P. M. (1990). Risk factors for the onset of Diagnostic Schedule/DSM-III agoraphobia in a prospective population-based study. *Archives of General Psychiatry, 47,* 819–824.

Eaton, W. W., Thara, R., Federman, E., & Tien, A. (1998). Remission and relapse in schizophrenia: The Madras longitudinal study. *Journal of Nervous & Mental Disease, 186,* 357–363.

Ebbinghaus, H. (1910). *Abriss der psychologie.* Leipzig: Veit & Company.

Ebbinghaus, H. (1913). *Memory: A contribution to experimental psychology* (H. Ruyer & C. E. Bussenius, Trans.). New York: Teachers College, Columbus University. (Original work published 1885)

Ebstein, R. P., Zohar, A. H., Benjamin, J., & Belmaker, R. H. (2002). An update on molecular genetic studies of human personality traits. *Applied Bioinformatics, 1,* 57–68.

Edelman, B. (1981). Binge eating in normal and overweight individuals. *Psychological Reports, 49,* 739–746.

Edley, N., & Wetherell, M. (1999). Imagined futures: Young men's talk about fatherhood and domestic life. *British Journal of Social Psychology, 38,* 181–194.

Eggebeen, D. J., & Knoester, C. (2001). Does fatherhood matter for men? *Journal of Marriage and Family, 63,* 381–393.

Ehlers, A. (1995). A 1-year prospective study of panic attacks: Clinical course and factors associated with maintenance. *Journal of Abnormal Psychology, 104,* 164–172.

Ehlers, A., & Breuer, P. (1992). Increased cardiac awareness in panic disorder. *Journal of Abnormal Psychology, 101,* 371–382.

Eich, J., Weingartner, H., Stillman, R. C., & Gillin, J. C. (1975). State-dependent accessibility of retrieval cues in the retention of a categorized list. *Journal of Verbal Learning and Verbal Behavior, 14,* 408–417.

Eilers, R. E., & Oiler, D. K. (1994). Infant vocalizations and the early diagnosis of severe hearing impairment. *Journal of Pediatrics, 124,* 199–203.

Eisen, S. V. (1979). Actor-observer differences in information inference and causal attribution. *Journal of Personality and Social Psychology, 37,* 261–272.

Ekman, P. (1973). Cross-cultural studies of facial expression. In P. Ekman (Ed.), *Darwin and facial expression* (pp. 169–222). New York: Academic Press.

Ekman, P., & Friesen, W. V. (1984). *Unmasking the face* (2nd ed.). Palo Alto, CA: Consulting Psychologists Press.

Elicker, J., Englund, M., & Sroufe, L. A. (1992). Predicting peer competence and peer relationships in childhood from early parent–child relationships. In R. D. Parke & G. W. Ladd (Eds.), *Family-peer relationships: Modes of linkage.* Hillsdale, NJ: Erlbaum.

Elkind, D. (1984). *All grown up and no place to go.* Reading, MA: Addison-Wesley.

Elkind, D. (1994). *A sympathetic understanding of the child: Birth to sixteen* (3rd ed.). Boston: Allyn & Bacon.

Elkind, D. (1998). *All grown up and no place to go.* Reading, MA: Perseus Books.

Elkind, D., & Bowen, R. (1979). Imaginary audience behavior in children and adolescents. *Developmental Psychology, 15,* 38–44.

Ellason, J. W., & Ross, C. A. (1997). Two-year follow up of inpatients with dissociative identity disorder. *American Journal of Psychiatry, 154,* 832–839.

Ellason, J. W., Ross, C. A., & Fuchs, D. L. (1996). Lifetime axis I and II comorbidity and childhood trauma history in dissociative identity disorder. *Psychiatry, 59,* 255–266.

Elliott, E. S., & Dweck, C. S. (1988). Goals: An approach to motivation and achievement. *Journal of Personality and Social Psychology, 54,* 5–12.

Ellis, A. (1959). Requisite conditions for basic personality change. *Journal of Consulting Psychology, 23,* 538–540.

Ellis, A. (1973, February). The no cop-out therapy. *Psychology Today, 7,* 56–60, 62.

Ellis, A. (1991). *Reason and emotion in psychotherapy.* New York: Carol Publishing.

Ellis, A. (1995). Changing rational-emotive therapy (RET) to rational-emotive behavior therapy (REBT). *Journal of Rational-Emotive & Cognitive Behavior Therapy, 13,* 85–89.

Emery, R. E., & Tuer, M. (1993). Parenting and the marital relationship. In T. Luster & L. Okagaki (Eds.), *Parenting: An ecological perspective.* Hillsdale, NJ: Erlbaum.

Emmelkamp, P. M. (1994). Behavior therapy with adults. In A. E. Bergin & S. L. Garfield (Eds.), *Handbook of psychotherapy and behavior change* (4th ed.). New York: Wiley.

Endo, T., Roth, C., Landolt, H. P., & Werth, E. (1998). Selective REM sleep deprivation in humans: Effects on sleep and sleep EEG. *American Journal of Physiology, 43,* 1186–1194.

Eng, T. R., & Butler, W. T. (1997). *The hidden epidemic: Confronting sexually transmitted diseases.* Washington, DC: National Academy Press.

Engels, G. I., Garnefski, N., & Diekstra, R. F. W. (1993). Efficacy of rational-emotive therapy: A quantitative analysis. *Journal of Consulting & Clinical Psychology, 61,* 1083–1090.

Engen, T. (1971). Psychophysics: I. Discrimination and detection. In J. W. Kling & L. A. Riggs (Eds.), *Woodworth's & Scholsberg's experimental psychology* (pp. 11–46). New York: Rinehart & Winston.

Epley, N., Savitsy, K., & Kachelski, R. A. (1999). What every skeptic should know about subliminal persuasion. *Skeptical Inquirer, 23,* 40–45.

Epping-Jordan, M. P., Watkins, S. S., Koob, G. F., & Markou, A. (1998). Dramatic decreases in brain reward function during nicotine withdrawal. *Nature, 393,* 76.

Epstein, S. (1994). Trait theory as personality theory: Can a part be as great as the whole? *Psychological Inquiry, 5,* 120–122.

Equal Employment Opportunity Commission. (2003). *Sexual harassment charges EEOC & FEPAs combined: FY 1992-2002.* Retrieved November 18, 2003, from www.eeoc.gov/stats/harass.html

Erdtmann-Vourliotis, M., Mayer, P., Ammon, S., Riechert, U., & Hollt, V. (2001). Distribution of g-protein-coupled receptor kinase (GRK) isoforms 2, 3, 5, and 6 mRNA in the rat brain. *Molecular Brain Research, 95,* 129–137.

Erel, O., & Burman, B. (1995). Interrelatedness of marital relations and parent-child relations: A meta analytic review. *Psychological Bulletin, 118,* 108–132.

Erikson, E. H. (1956). The problem of ego identity. *Journal of American Psychoanalysis Association, 4,* 56–121.

Erikson, E. H. (1958). *Young man Luther.* New York: Norton.

Erikson, E. H. (1959). Identity and life cycle. Selected papers. *Psychological Issues, 1,* 1–171.

Erikson, E. H. (1963). *Childhood and society* (2nd ed.). New York: Norton.

Erikson, E. H. (1968). *Identity, youth and crisis.* New York: Norton.

Erikson, E. H. (1980). *Identity and the life cycle* (2nd ed.). New York: Norton.

Erwin, E. (Ed.). (2002). *The Freud encyclopedia: Theory, therapy, and culture.* London: Routledge.

Escobar, J. I. (1993). Psychiatric epidemiology. In A. C. Gaw (Ed.), *Culture, ethnicity, and mental illness* (pp. 43–73). Washington, DC: American Psychiatric Press.

Escobar, J. I., Gara, M., Waitzkin, H., Cohen Silver, R., Holman, A., & Compton, W. (1998). DSM-IV hypochondriasis in primary care. *General Hospital Psychiatry, 20,* 155–159.

Espy, K. A., Riese, M. L., & Francis, D. J. (1997). Neurobehavior in preterm neonates exposed to cocaine, alcohol, and tobacco. *Infant Behavior and Development, 20,* 297–309.

Esser, J. K. (1998). Alive and well after 25 years: A review of groupthink research. *Organizational Behavior and Human Decision Processes, 73,* 116–141.

Esses, V. M., Dovidio, J. F., Jackson, L. M., & Armstrong, T. L. (2001). The immigration dilemma: The role of perceived group competition, ethnic prej-udice, and national identity. *Journal of Social Issues, 57,* 389–412.

Eysenck, H. J. (1967). *The biological basis of personality.* Springfield, IL: Charles C. Thomas.

Eysenck, H. J. (1982). *Personality, genetics, and behavior: Selected papers.* New York: Praeger.

Eysenck, H. J. (1991). Dimensions of personality: 16, 5 or 3?—Criteria for a taxonomic paradigm. *Personality and Individual Differences, 12,* 773–790.

Eysenck, H. J. (1995). *Genius: The natural history of creativity.* Cambridge, England: Cambridge University Press.

Eysenck, H. J., & Rachman, S. (1965). *The causes and cures of neurosis: An introduction to modern behavior therapy based on learning theory and the principle of conditioning.* San Diego: Knapp.

Fagot, B. I., & Kavanaugh, K. (1990). The prediction of antisocial behavior from avoidant attachment classifications. *Child Development, 61,* 864–873.

Farley, E., Loup, D., Nelson, M., Mitchell, A., Esplund, G., Macri, C., Harrison, C., & Gray, K. (1997). Neoplastic transformation of the endocervix associated with down regulation of lactoferrin expression. *Molecular Carcinography, 20,* 240-250.

Faust, K. A., & McKibben, J. N. (1999). Marital dissolution: Divorce, separation, annulment, and widowhood. In M. B. Sussman, S. K. Steinmetz, & G. W. Peterson (Eds.), *Handbook of marriage and the family* (pp. 475–502). New York: Plenum Press.

Faustman, W. O., Bardgett, M., Faull, K. F., Pfefferbaum, A., & Csernansky, J. G. (1999). Cerebrospinal fluid glutamate inversely correlates with positive symptom severity in unmedicated male schizophrenic/schizoaffective patients. *Biological Psychiatry, 45,* 68–75.

Fava, G. A., Grandi, S., Zielezny, M., & Rafanelli, C. (1996). Four-year outcome for cognitive-behavioral treatment of residual symptoms in major depression. *American Journal of Psychiatry, 153,* 945–947.

Fava, M., & Rosenbaum, J. F. (1995). Pharmacotherapy and somatic therapies. In E. E. Beckham & W. R. Leber (Eds.), *Handbook of depression* (2nd ed., pp. 280–301). New York: Guilford.

Fawcett, J. (1994). Antidepressants: Partial response in chronic depression. *British Journal of Psychiatry, 165*(Suppl. 26), 37–41.

Fazio, R. H. (1990). Multiple processes by which attitudes guide behavior: The MODE model as an integrative framework. In M. P. Zanna (Ed.), *Advances in experimental social psychology* (Vol 23). San Diego: Academic Press.

FDA Public Health Advisory. (2004, Oct 15). *Suicidality in children and adolescents being treated with antidepressant medications.* Retrieved October 23, 2004, from www.fda.gov/cder/drug/antidepressants/SS-RIPHA200410.htm

Federal Bureau of Investigation. (2002). *Uniform crime reports.* Retrieved March 17, 2004, from http://www.fbi.gov/ucr/ucr.htm

Federal Bureau of Investigation. (2003). *Uniform crime reports.* Retrieved March 17, 2004, from http://www.fbi.gov/ucr/ucr.htm

Federman, D. D. (1994). Life without estrogen. *The New England Journal of Medicine, 331,* 1088-1089.

Feingold, A. (1988). Matching for attractiveness in romantic partners and same-sex friends: A meta-analysis and theoretical critique. *Psychological Bulletin, 104,* 226–235.

Feingold, A. (1994). Gender differences in personality: A meta-analysis. *Psychological Bulletin, 116,* 429-456.

Feiring, C. (1996). Concepts of romance in 15-year-old adolescents. *Journal of Research on Adolescence, 6,* 181–200.

Feldman, R. S., & Meyer, J. (1996). *Fundamentals of neuropsychopharmacology.* Sunderland, MA: Sinauer Associates.

Fenton, W. S., & McGlashan, T. H. (1994). Antecedents, symptom progression, and long-term outcome of the deficit syndrome in schizophrenia. *American Journal of Psychiatry, 151,* 351–356.

Ferguson, C. P., & Pigott, T. A. (2000). Anorexia and bulimia nervosa: Neurobiology and pharmacotherapy. *Behavior Therapy, 31,* 237–263.

Fergusson, D. M., Horwood, L. J., & Lynskey, M. T. (1996). Childhood sexual abuse and psychiatric disorder in young adulthood II: Psychiatric outcomes of childhood sexual abuse. *Journal of the American Academy of Child & Adolescent Psychiatry, 35,* 1365–1374.

Ferrell, D. (1996, December 16). Scientists unlocking secrets of marijuana's effects. *Los Angeles Times,* p. 3.

Ferster, D., Chung, S., & Wheat, H. (1996). Orientation selectivity of thalamic input to simple cells of cat visual cortex. *Nature, 380,* 249–252.

Festinger, L. (1951). Architecture and group membership. *Journal of Social Issues, 1,* 152–163.

Festinger, L. (1957). *A theory of cognitive dissonance.* Evanston, IL: Row, Peterson.

Festinger, L., Schachter, S., & Back, K. (1950). *Social pressures in informal groups: A study of human factors in housing.* Stanford, CA: Stanford University Press.

Field, T. M., Schanberg, S. M., Scafidi, F., Bauer, C. R., Vega-Lahr, N., Garcia, R., Nystrom, J., & Kuhn, C. M. (1986). Tactile/kinesthetic stimulation effects of preterm neonates. *Pediatrics, 77,* 654–658.

Fieldman, J. P., & Crespi, T. D. (2002). Child sexual abuse: Offenders, disclosure, and school-based initiatives. *Adolescence, 37,* 151-160.

Fields, J., & Casper, L. (2001). *America's families and living arrangements: March 2000.* (Current Population Reports, P20–537). Washington, DC: U.S. Census Bureau.

Finch, C. E. (2001). Toward a biology of middle age. In M.E. Lachman (Ed.), *Handbook of midlife development* (pp. 77–108). New York: Wiley.

Fincham, F. D. (2003). Marital conflict: Correlates, structure, and context. *Current Directions in Psychological Science, 12,* 23–27.

Fink, M., & Mathias, L. (2002). *Never forget: An oral history of September 11, 2001.* New York: HarperCollins.

Finkelhor, D. (1990). Early and long-term effects of child sexual abuse: An update. *Professional Psychology: Research and Practice, 21,* 325-330.

Finn, R. (2003). Antabuse no panacea for alcoholism. *Clinical Psychiatry News, 31,* 6.

Finn, R. (2004, February 15). Functional MRI offers insights into working memory in Alzheimer's. (greater whole-brain activation). *Internal Medicine News, 37,* 29.

Fischer, A. B. (1992, September 21). When will women ever get to the top? *Fortune,* pp. 44–56.

Fischer, C., Hatzidimitriou, G., Wlos, J., Katz, J., & Ricaurte, G. (1995). Reorganization of ascending 5-HT axon projections in animals previously exposed to recreational drug 3, 4-methelenedioxymethamphetamine (MDMA, "ecstasy"). *Journal of Neuroscience, 15,* 5476–5485.

Fisher, B. S., Cullen, F. T., & Turner, M. G. (2000). *Are rapes and sexual assault part of college life?* National Institute of Justice Bureau of Justice Statistics. Retrieved September 4, 2004, from http://www.center4policy.org/violencem.html

Fisher, C. A., Hoffman, K. J., Austin-Lane, J., & Kao, T. C. (2000). The relationship between heavy alcohol use and work productivity loss in active duty military personnel: A secondary analysis of the 1995 Department of Defense Worldwide Survey. *Military Medicine, 165,* 355–361.

Fisher, L., Ames, E. W., Chisholm, K., & Savoie, L. (1997). Problems reported by parents of Romanian orphans adopted to British Columbia. *International Journal of Behavioral Development, 20,* 67–82.

Fisher, S., Kent, T. A., & Bryant, S. G. (1995). Postmarketing surveillance by patient self-monitoring: Preliminary data for sertraline versus fluoxetine. *Journal of Clinical Psychiatry, 56,* 288–296.

Fiske, M. (1980). Tasks and crises of the second half of life: The interrelationship of commitment, coping, and adaptation. In J. E. Birrent & R. B. Sloane (Eds.), *Handbook of mental health and aging.* Englewood Cliffs, NJ: Prentice Hall.

Fiske, S. T. & Taylor, S. E. (1991). *Social cognition* (2nd. ed.). New York: McGraw-Hill.

Fitzgerald, L. F. (1993). Sexual harassment: Violence against women in the workplace. *American Psychologist, 48,* 1070–1076.

Flaherty, C. F., Hamilton, L. W., Gandelman, R. J., & Spear, N. E. (1977). *Learning and memory.* Chicago: Rand McNally.

Fleeson, W. (2004). Moving personality beyond the person-situation debate. *Current Directions in Psychological Science, 13,* 83–87.

Flieller, A. (1999). Comparison of the development of formal thought in adolescent cohorts aged 10 to 15 years (1967–1996 and 1972–1993). *Developmental Psychology, 35,* 1048–1058.

Foa, E. B., & Kozak, M. J. (1995). DSM-IV field trial: Obsessive-compulsive disorder. *American Journal of Psychiatry, 152,* 90–96.

Folkman, S., & Lazarus, R. (1988). *Manual for the ways of coping questionnaire.* Palo Alto, CA: Consulting Psychologists Press.

Folkman, S., & Moskowitz, J. T. (2000). Stress, positive emotion, and coping. *Current Directions in Psychological Science, 9,* 115–118.

Follette, W. C., & Hayes, S. C. (2000). Contemporary behavior therapy. In C. R. Snyder & R. E. Ingram (Eds.), *Handbook of psychological change: Psychotherapy processes and practices for the 21st century* (pp. 381–408). New York: Wiley.

Fomon, S. J., Filer, L. J., Thomas, L. N., Rogers, R. R., & Proksch, A. M. (1969). Relationship between formula concentration and rate of growth of normal infants. *Journal of Nutrition, 98,* 241–245.

Ford, C. S., & Beach, F. A. (1951). *Patterns of sexual behavior.* New York: Harper & Row.

Forest, D. W. (1974). *Francis Galton: The life and work of a Victorian genius.* London: Paul Elek.

Forsyth, D. R., & Corazzini, J. G. (2000). Groups as change agents. In C. R. Snyder & R. E. Ingram (Eds.), *Handbook of psychological change: Psychotherapy processes and practices for the 21st century* (pp. 309–336). New York: Wiley.

Fouts, R. (1973). Capacities for language in the great apes. In S. Tax & G. C. Neuberger (Eds.), *Proceedings of the Ninth International Congress of Anthropological and Ethnological Sciences.* The Hague: Mouton.

Fowler, J., & Peterson, P. (1981). Increasing reading persistence and altering attributional style of learned helpless children. *Journal of Educational Psychology, 73,* 251–260.

Fox, P. T., Mintun, M. A., Raichle, M. E., Meizen, F. M., Allman, J. M., & Van Essen, D. C. (1986). Mapping human visual cortex with positron emission tomography. *Nature, 323,* 806–809.

Franche, R. L. (2001). Psychologic and obstetric predictors of couples' grief during pregnancy after miscarriage or perinatal death. *Obstetrics & Gynecology, 97,* 597–602.

Fredrickson, B. L. (2003). The value of positive emotions: The emerging science of positive psychology is coming to understand why it's good to feel good. *American Scientist, 91,* 330–335.

Freedman, J. L., & Fraser, S. C. (1966). Compliance without pressure: The foot-in-the-door technique. *Journal of Experimental Social Psychology, 4,* 195–203.

Freud, A. (1936). *The ego and the mechanisms of defense.* London: Hogarth Press.

Freud, S. (1900; reprinted 1980). *The interpretation of dreams* (J. Strachey, Ed. and Trans.). New York: Avon.

Freud, S. (1909). *Analysis of a phobia of a five-year-old boy* (Vol. III). New York: Basic Books.

Freud, S. (1911). *On dreams.* New York: Norton.

Freud, S. (1915). Repression. In *Freud's collected papers* (Vol. IV). London: Hogarth.

Freud, S. (1917). Mourning and melancholia. *Collected works.* London: Hogarth Press.

Freud, S. (1943). *A general introduction to psychoanalysis.* New York: Garden City.

Freud, S. (1949). *An outline of psychoanalysis.* New York: Norton.

Freud, S. (1964). An outline of psycho-analysis. In J. Strachey (Ed. and Trans.), *The standard edition of the complete psychological works of Sigmund Freud* (Vol. 23). London: Hogarth Press. (Originally published 1940)

Freund, K., & Kuban, C. (1994). The basis of the abused abuser theory of pedophilia: A further elaboration on an earlier study. *Archives of Sexual Behavior, 34,* 553-563.

Friedman, M. A., & Brownell, K. D. (1996). A comprehensive treatment manual for the management of obesity. In V. B. Van Hasselt & M. Hersen (Eds.), *Source book of psychological treatment manuals for adult disorders* (pp. 375–422). New York: Plenum.

Friedman, M. I. (1990). Body fat and the metabolic control of food intake. *International Journal of Obesity, 14,* 53–67.

Friedman, M., & Rosenman, R. (1974). *Type A behavior and your heart.* New York: Knopf.

Friedman, M., Thoresen, C. E., Gill, J. J., Powell, E. (1984). Alteration of Type A behavior and reduction in cardiac recurrences in postmyocardial infarction patients. *American Heart Journal, 108*(2), 237–248.

Friedrich, W. N., Fisher, J., Broughton, D., Houston, M., & Shafran, C. R. (1998). Normative sexual behavior in children: A contemporary sample. *Pediatrics, 101,* E9.

Friend, T. (1996, August 21). Teens and drugs. *USA Today,* p. 1A.

Funder, D. C. (1993). Explaining traits. *Psychological Inquiry, 5,* 125–127.

Furnham, A., Reeves, E., & Budhani, S. (2002). Parents think their sons are brighter than their daughters: Sex differences in parents' self-estimations and estimations of their children's multiple intelligences. *Journal of Genetic Psychology, 163,* 24–39.

Furumoto, L. (1989). The new history of psychology. In I. S. Cohen (Ed.), *The G. Stanley Hall lecture series* (Vol. 9). Washington D.C.: American Psychological Association.

Gade, D. W. (2000). II.G.13 Hogs (pigs). In K. E. Kipple & K. C. Ornelas (Series Eds.), *The Cambridge world history of food: Vol. 1* (pp. 536–542). Cambridge, UK: Cambridge University Press.

Galanter, E. (1962). Contemporary psychophysics. In R. Brown, E. Galanter, E. H. Hess, & G. Mandler (Eds.), *New directions in psychology* (pp. 87–156). New York: Holt, Rinehart, & Winston.

Galea, S., Ahern, J., Resnick, H., Kilpatrick, D., Bucuvalas, M., Gold, J., Vlahov, D. (2002). Psychological sequelae of the September 11 terrorist attacks in New York City. *New England Journal of Medicine, 346,* 982–987.

Galensky, T. L., Miltenberger, R. G., Stricker, J. M., & Garlinghouse, M. A. (2001). Functional assessment and treatment of mealtime behavior problems. *Journal of Positive Behavior Interventions, 3,* 211.

Gall, T. L., Evans, D. R., & Howard, J. (1997). The retirement adjustment process: Changes in the well-being of male retirees across time. *Journal of Gerontology: Psychological Sciences, 52,* P110–P117.

Gallagher, A. M., DeLisi, R., Holst, P. C., McGillicuddy-DeLisi, R., Marley, M., & Cahalan, C. (2000). Gender differences in advanced mathematical problem solving. *Journal of Experimental Child Psychology, 75,* 165-190.

Gallagher, A. M., Levin, J., & Cahalan, C. (2002). *GRE research: Cognitive patterns of gender differences on mathematics admission tests* (ETS Report No. 02-19). Princeton, NJ: Educational Testing Service.

Gallagher, W. (1994). *The power of place.* New York: Harper Perennial.

Gallerani, M., Manfredini, R., Dal Monte, D., Calo, G., Brunaldi, V., & Simona, C. (2001). Circadian differences in the individual sensitivity to opiate overdose. *Critical Care Medicine, 29,* 96–101.

Galliano, G. (2003). *Gender: Crossing boundaries.* Belmont, CA: Wadsworth.

Gallo, U. E., & Fontanarosa, P. B. (1989). Locked-in syndrome: Report of a case. *American Journal of Emergency Medicine, 7,* 581–583.

Gallopin, T., Luppi, P. H., Rambert, F. A., Frydman, A., & Fort, P. (2004). Effect of the wake-promoting agent modafinil on sleep-promoting neurons from the ventrolateral preoptic nucleus: An in vitro pharmacologic study. *Sleep, 27,* 19–25.

Galton, F. (1869). *Hereditary genius.* London: Macmillan.

Galton, F. (1907). *Inquires into Human Faculty and Its Development.* London: Everyman's Library. (Original work published 1883)

Gamst, G., Dana, R. H., Der-Karaberian, A., & Kramer, T. (2000). Ethnic match and client ethnicity effects on global assessment and visitation. *Journal of Community Psychology, 28,* 547–564.

Garbarino, J. (1997). The role of economic deprivation in the social context of child maltreatment. In M. E. Helfer, R. S. Kempe, & R. D. Krugman (Eds.), *The battered child* (5th ed., pp. 49–60). Chicago: University of Chicago Press.

Garcia, J. (1992). Taste aversion and preference learning in animals. In L. R. Squire, J. H. Byrne, L. Nadel, H. L. Roediger, D. L. Schacter, & R. F. Thompson (Eds.), *Encyclopedia of Learning and Memory.* (pp. 611–613). New York: Macmillan.

Garcia, J., & Koelling, R. A. (1966). Relation of cue to consequence in avoidance learning. *Psychonomic Science, 4,* 123–124.

Garcia, J., Ervin, F. R., & Koelling, R. A. (1966). Learning with prolonged delay of reinforcement. *Psychonomic Science, 5,* 121–122.

Gardiner, H. W., Mutter, J. D., & Kosmitzki, C. (1998). *Lives across cultures: Cross-cultural human development.* Needham Heights, MA: Allyn & Bacon.

Gardner, H. (1983). *Frames of mind.* New York: Basic Books.

Gardner, H. (1999). *Intelligence reframed: Multiple intelligences for the 21st century.* New York: Basic Books.

Gardner, H. (2004). *Changing minds: The art and science of changing our own and other people's minds.* Boston: Harvard Business School Press.

Garfield, S. L. (1992). Eclectic psychotherapy: A common factors approach. In J. C. Norcross (Ed.), *Handbook of psychotherapy integration* (pp. 169–201). New York: Basic Books.

Garfield, S. L. (1994). Research on client variables in psychotherapy. In A. E. Bergin & S. L. Garfield (Eds.), *Handbook of psychotherapy and behavior change* (4th ed., pp. 190–228). New York: Wiley.

Garlick, D. (2002). Understanding the nature of the general factor of intelligence: The role of individual differences in neural plasticity as an explanatory mechanism. *Psychological Review, 109,* 116–136.

Garlick, D. (2003). Integrating brain science research with intelligence research. *Current Directions in Psychological Science, 12,* 185–189.

Garpenstrand, H., Norton, N., Damberg, M., Rylander, G., Forslund, K., Mattila-Evenden, M., Gustavsson, J. P., Ekblom, J. Oreland, L., Bergman, H., Owen, M J., & Jonsson, E. G. (2002). A regulatory monoamine oxidase a promoter polymorphism and personality traits. *Neuropsychobiology, 46,* 190–193.

Garrett, M., & Carroll, J. (2000). Mending the broken circle: Treatment of substance dependence among Native Americans. *Journal of Counseling and Development, 78,* 379–388.

Gawin, F. H. (1991). Cocaine addiction: Psychology and neurophysiology. *Science,251,* 1580–1586.

Gazzaniga, M. S. (1967). The split brain in man. *Scientific American, 217,* 24–29.

Ge, X., Conger, R. D., & Elder, G. H. (1996). Coming of age too early: Pubertal influences on girls' vulnerability to psychological distress. *Child Development, 67,* 3386–3400.

Gedo, J. E. (2002). The enduring scientific contributions of Sigmund Freud. *Perspectives in Biology and Medicine, 45,* 200–212.

Gehring, W.J., Himle, J., & Nisenson, L.G. (2000). Action-monitoring dysfunction in obsessive-compulsive disorder. *Psychological Science, 11,* 1–6.

Gelade, G. (2002). Creative style, personality, and artistic endeavor. *Genetic, Social and General Psychology Monographs, 128,* 213–234.

Gelfand, S. A. (1981). *Hearing.* New York: Marcel Dekker.

Geller, E. S., Russ, N. W., & Altomari, M. G. (1986). Naturalistic observations of beer drinking among college students. *Journal of Applied Behavior Analysis, 19,* 391–396.

Gendell, M., & Siegel, J. S. (1996). Trends in retirement age in the United States, 1955–1993, by sex and race. *Journal of Gerontology: Social Sciences, 51,* S132–S139.

Gergen, K. J., & Gergen, M. M. (1988). Narrative and self as relationship. In L. Berkowitz (Ed.), *Advances in experimental social psychology* (Vol. 21, pp. 17–56). New York: Academic Press.

Gernsbacher, M. A. (1985). Surface information and loss in comprehension. *Cognitive Psychology, 17,* 324–363.

Gerrish, C. J., & Mennella, J. A. (2001). Flavor variety enhances food acceptance in formula-fed infants. *American Journal of Clinical Nutrition, 73,* 1080–1085.

Geschwind, N. (1975). The apraxias: Neural mechanisms of disorders of learned movements. *American Scientist, 63,* 188–195.

Geschwind, N., & Levitsky, W. (1968). Human brain: Left-right asymmetries in temporal speech region. *Science, 161,* 186–187.

Gibb, B. E., Alloy, L. B., Abramson, L. Y., Beevers, C. G., & Miller, I. W. (2004). Cognitive vulnerability to depression: A taxometric analysis. *Journal of Abnormal Psychology, 113,* 81–89.

Gibbs, W. W. (1996). Gaining on fat. *Scientific American, 275,* 88–94.

Gibson, E. J., & Walk, R. (1960). The visual "cliff." *Scientific American, 202,* 64–71.

Gibson, H. B. (1995, April). Recovered memories. *The Psychologist,* pp. 153–154.

Giedd, J. N. (2004). Structural magnetic resonance imaging of the adolescent brain. *Annals of the New York Academy of Sciences, 1021,* 77–85.

Giedd, J. N., Blumentahl, J., Jeffries, N. O., Castellanos, F. X., Liu, H., Zijdenbos, A., Paus, T., Evans, A. C., & Rapoport, J.L. (1999). Brain development during childhood and adolescence: A longitudinal MRI study. *Nature Neuroscience, 2,* 861–863.

Gilbert, D. G., Stunkard, M. E., Jensen, R. A., & Detwiler, F. R. J. (1996). Effects of exam stress on mood, cortisol, and immune functioning. *Personality and Individual Differences, 21*(2), 235–246.

Gilbert, M. J., & Cervantes, R. C. (1987). *Mexican Americans and alcohol.* Los Angeles: University of California Press.

Gilbert, S. (1998, June 30). Optimism's bright side: A healthy, longer life. *New York Times,* p. F7.

Gillam, B. (1980). Geometrical illusions. *Scientific American, 242,* 102–111.

Gilligan, C. F. (1982). *In a different voice.* Cambridge, MA: Harvard University Press.

Gillund, G., & Shiffrin, R. M. (1984). A retrieval model for both recognition and recall. *Psychological Review, 91,* 1–67.

Gilson, R. J., & Mindel, A. (2001). Sexually transmitted infections. *British Medical Journal, 322* (729S), 1135–1137.

Ginzberg, E. (1972). Toward a theory of occupational choice: A restatement. *Vocational Guidance Quarterly, 20,* 169–176.

Ginzberg, E. (1984). Career development. In D. Brown, L. Brooks, & Associates (Eds.), *Career choice and development.* San Francisco: Jossey-Bass.

Girandola, F. (2002). Sequential requests and organ donation. *The Journal of Social Psychology, 142,* 171–178.

Givens, B. (1995). Low doses of ethanol impair spatial working memory and reduce hippocampal theta activity. *Alcoholism: Clinical and Experimental Research, 19*(3), 763–767.

Gladue, B. (1990, November). Adolescents' sexual practices: Have they changed? *Medical Aspects of Human Sexuality,* 53-54.

Gladwell, M. (2004, September 20). Annals of psychology: Personality plus. *The New Yorker,* pp. 42–48.

Glanzer, M., & Cunitz, A. R. (1966). Two storage mechanisms in free recall. *Journal of Verbal Learning and Verbal Behavior, 5,* 351–360.

Glenberg, A. M., Smith, S. M., & Green, C. (1977). Type I rehearsal: Maintenance and more. *Journal of Verbal Learning & Verbal Behavior, 16,* 339–352.

Glik, D. C., Kronenfeld, J. J., & Jackson, K. (1996). Predictors of well role performance behaviors. *American Journal of Health Behavior, 20,* 218–228.

Godden, D. R., & Baddeley, A. D. (1975). Context dependent memory in two natural environments: On land and underwater. *British Journal of Psychology, 66,* 325–332.

Goeders, N. E. (2004). Stress, motivation, and drug addiction. *Current Directions in Psychological Science, 13,* 33–35.

Gold, M. S. (1994). The epidemiology, attitudes, and pharmacology of LSD use in the 1990's. *Psychiatric Annals, 24*(3), 124–126.

Goldbach, K. R., Dunn, D. S., Toedter, L. J., & Lasker, J. N. (1991). The effects of gestational age and gender on grief after pregnancy loss. *American Journal of Orthopsychiatry, 61,* 461–467.

Goldin-Meadow, S., & Mylander, C. (1998). Spontaneous sign systems crated by deaf children in two cultures. *Nature, 391,* 279–281.

Goldstein, I. (1998). Cited in Kolata, G. (1998, April 4). Impotence pill: Would it also help women? *The New York Times,* pp. A1, A6.

Goldstein, I., Lue, T. E., Padmap, H. H., Rosen, C. Steers, W. D., & Wicker, P. A. (1998). Oral sildenafil in the treatment of erectile dysfunction: Sildenafil study group. *New England Journal of Medicine, 338,* 1394-1404.

Goldstein, J. M. (1997). Sex differences in schizophrenia: Epidemiology, genetics, and the brain. *International Review of Psychiatry, 9,* 399–408.

Goldstein, J. M., & Lewine, R. R. J. (2000). Overview of sex differences in schizophrenia: Where have we been and where do we go from here? In D. J. Castle, J. McGrath, & J. Kulkarni (Eds.), *Women and schizophrenia* (pp. 111–141). Cambridge, UK: Cambridge University Press.

Goldstein, J. M., Seidman, L. J., Buka, S. L., Horton, N. J., Donatelli, J. L., Rieder, R. O., & Tsuang, M. T. (2000). Impact of genetic vulnerability and hypoxia on overall intelligence by age 7 in offspring at high risk for schizophrenia compared with affective psychoses. *Schizophrenia Bulletin, 26,* 323–334.

Goleman, D. (1982, March). Staying up: The rebellion against sleep's gentle tyranny. *Psychology Today,* pp. 24–35.

Goleman, D. (1995). *Emotional intelligence.* New York: Bantam.

Goleman, D. (1998). *Working with emotional intelligence.* London: Bloomsbury.

Goleman, D., Boyatzis, R. E., & McKee, A. (2002). *Primal leadership: Realizing the power of emotional intelligence.* Boston: Harvard Business School Press.

Goodnick, P. J. (2000). The use of nimodipine in the treatment of mood disorders. *Bipolar Disorders, 2,* 165–173.

Goodwin, F. K., & Jamison, K. R. (1990). *Manic-depressive illness.* New York: Oxford University Press.

Gordon, E. F. (2000). *Mockingbird years: A life in and out of therapy.* New York: Basic Books.

Gorey, K. M., & Leslie, D. R. (1997). The prevalence of child sexual abuse: Integrative review adjustment for potential response and measurement biases. *Child Abuse and Neglect, 21,* 391-398.

Gormezano, I. (1972). Investigations of defense and reward conditioning in the rabbit. In A. H. Black & W. F. Prokasy (Eds.), *Classical conditioning II: Current theory and research.* New York: Academic.

Gorsky, R. D., Schwartz, E., & Dennis, D. (1988). The mortality, morbidity, and economic costs of alcohol abuse: New Hampshire. *Preventative Medicine, 17,* 736–745.

Gottesman, I. I. (1991). *Schizophrenia genesis.* New York: W. H. Freeman.

Gottfredson, L. S. (1996). Gottfredson's theory of circumscription and compromise. In D. Brown, L. Brooks, & Associates (Eds.), *Career choice and development* (3rd ed). San Francisco: Jossey-Bass.

Gottlieb, G., Wahlsten, D., & Lickliter, R. (1998). The significance of biology for human development: A developmental psychobiological systems view. In W. Damon & R. M. Lerner (Eds.), *Handbook of child psychology* (Vol. 1). New York: Wiley.

Gottman, J. (1999a). *The seven principles of making marriage work.* New York: Crown.

Gottman, J. (1999b). *The marriage clinic.* New York: Norton.

Gould, R. A., Otto, M. W., Pollack, M. H., & Yap, L. (1997). Cognitive behavioral and pharmacological treatment of generalized anxiety disorder: A preliminary meta-analysis. *Behavior Therapy, 28,* 285–305.

Gouras, P. (1991). Precortical physiology of colour vision. In P. Gouras (Ed.), *The perception of colour* (pp. 163–178). Boca Raton, FL: CRC Press.

Graber, B. (1993). Medical aspects of sexual arousal disorders. In W. O'Donohue & J. H. Greer (Eds.), *Handbook of sexual dysfunctions: Assessment and treatment* (pp. 103-156). Boston: Allyn & Bacon.

Grados, M. A., Walkup, J., & Walford, S. (2003). Genetics of obsessive-compulsive disorders: New findings and challenges. *Brain Development, 25,* S55–S61.

Grady, C. L. (2000). Functional brain imaging and age-related changes in cognition. *Biological Psychology, 54,* 259–281.

Graf, P., & Schacter, D. L. (1985). Implicit and explicit memory for new associations in normal and amnesiac subjects. *Journal of Experimental Psychology: Learning, Memory, & Cognition, 11,* 501–518.

Graffin, N. F., Ray, W. J., & Lundy, R. (1995). EEG concomitants of hypnosis and hypnotic susceptibility. *Journal of Abnormal Psychology, 104*(1), 123–131.

Graham, K. S., Simons, J. S., Pratt, K. H., Patterson, K., & Hodges, J. R. (2000). Insights from semantic dementia on the relationship between episodic and semantic memory. *Neurpsychologia, 38,* 313–324.

Grant, J. E., & Phillips, K.A. (2004). Is anorexia nervosa a subtype of body dysmorphic disorder? Probably not, but read on. . . .*Harvard Review of Psychiatry, 12,* 123–126.

Green, R. (1987). *The "sissy boy syndrome" and the development of homosexuality: A fifteen-year prospective study.* New Haven, CT: Yale University Press.

Green, S. K., Buchanan, D. R., & Heuer, S. K. (1984). Winners, losers, and choosers: A field investigation of dating initiation. *Personality and Social Psychology Bulletin, 10,* 502–511.

Greenberg, B. D., Li, Q., Lucas, F. R., Hu, S., Sirota, L. A., Benjamin, J., Lesch, K. P., Hamer, D., & Murphy, D. L. (2000). Association between the serotonin transporter promoter polymorphism and personality traits in a primarily female population sample. *American Journal of Medical Genetics, 96,* 202–216.

Greenberg, L. S., & Rice, L. N. (1997). Humanistic approaches to psychotherapy. In P. L. Wachtel & S. B. Messer (Eds.), *Theories of psychotherapy: Origins and evolution.* Washington DC: American Psychological Association.

Greenberg, L. S., Elliot, R., & Lietaer, G. (1994). Research on humanistic and experiential psychotherapies. In A. Bergin & S. Garfield (Eds.), *Handbook of psychotherapy and behavior change* (4th ed., pp. 509–542). New York: Wiley.

Greenblatt, D., Harmatz, J., & Shader, R. I. (1993). Plasma alprazolam concentrations: Relation to efficacy and side effects in the treatment of panic disorder. *Archives of General Psychiatry, 50,* 715–732.

Greenfield, P. (1997). You can't take it with you: Why ability assessments don't cross cultures. *American Psychologist, 52,* 1115–1124.

Greenough, W. T., Wallace, C. S., Alcantara, A. A., Anderson, B. J., Hawrylak, N., Sirevaag, A. M., Weiler, I. J., & Withers, G. S. (1993). Experience affects the structure of neurons, glia, and blood vessels. In N. J. Anastasiow & S. Harel (Eds.), *At-risk infants: Interventions, family, and research* (pp. 175–185). Baltimore: Paul H. Brookes.

Greenvale, J. K., Jeen-Su, L., & Mukesh, B. (1998). The role of affect in attitude formation: A classical conditioning approach. *Academy of Marketing Science Journal, 26,* 143–152.

Greenwald, A. G., & Draine, S. C. (1997). Do subliminal stimuli enter the mind unnoticed? Tests with a new method. In J. D. Cohen & J. W. Schooler (Eds.), *Scientific approaches to consciousness: Carnegie Mellon symposia on cognition* (pp. 83–108). Mahwah, NJ: Erlbaum.

Grieger, T. A., Fullerton, C. S., & Ursano, R. J. (2004). Posttraumatic stress disorder, depression, and perceived safety 13 months after September 11th. *Psychiatric Services, 55,* 1061–1063.

Grimsley, K. D. (2001, December 13). Stress from attacks still taking workplace toll. *Washington Post,* p. E01.

Grinspoon, L., & Bakalar, J. B. (1995). Marijuana as medicine: A plea for reconsideration. *Journal of the American Medical Association, 273*(23), 1875–1876.

Grinspoon, L., Bakalar, J. B., Zimmer, L., & Morgan, J. P. (1997). Marijuana addiction. *Science, 277,* 751–752.

Grivetti, L. E. (2000). VI.13/ Food prejudices and taboos. In K. E. Kipple & K. C. Ornelas (Series Eds.), *The Cambridge world history of food: Vol. 1* (pp. 1495–1513). Cambridge, UK: Cambridge University Press.

Grossman, M. I., & Stein, L. F. (1948). Vagotomy and the hunger-producing action of insulin in man. *Journal of Applied Physiology, 1,* 263–269.

Grossman, R. P., & Till, B. D. (1998). The persistence of classically conditioned brand attitudes. *Journal of Advertising, 27,* 23–31.

Gruen, R. J. (1993). Stress and depression: Toward the development of integrative models. In L. Goldberger & S. Breznitz (Eds.), *Handbook of stress: Theoretical and clinical aspects.* New York: Free Press.

Guilford, J. P. (1967). *The nature of human intelligence.* New York: McGraw-Hill.

Guilleminault, C., Palombini, L., Pelayo, R., & Chervin, R.D. (2003). Sleepwalking and sleep terrors in prepubertal children: What triggers them? *Pediatrics, 111,* e17–25.

Gulick, W. L., Gescheider, G. A., & Frisina, R. D. (1989). *Hearing: Physiological acoustics, neural coding, and psychoacoustics.* New York: Oxford University Press.

Gur, R. E., Cowell, P., Turetsky, B. I., Gallacher, F., Cannon, T., Bilker, W., & Gur, R. C. (1998). A follow-up magnetic resonance imaging study of schizophrenia. *Archives of General Psychiatry, 55,* 145–152.

Gurman, A. S., & Jacobson, N. S. (Eds.), (2002). *Clinical handbook of couple therapy* (3rd. ed.). New York: Guilford Press.

Gustavson, C. R., & Garcia, J. (1974, August). Pulling a gag on the wily coyote. *Psychology Today,* pp. 68–72.

Guthrie, J. P., Ash, R. A., & Bendapudi, V. (1995). Additional validity evidence for a measure of morningness. *Journal of Applied Psychology, 80,* 186–190.

Guthrie, R. (1998). *Even the rat was white* (2nd ed.) Boston: Allyn & Bacon.

Gutin, J. A. C. (1993). Good vibrations. *Discover, 14,* 44–54.

Guze, B. H., & Gitlin, M. (1994). New antidepressants and the treatment of depression. *Journal of Family Practice, 38,* 49–57.

Haack, L. J., Dykman, B. M., Metalsky, G. I., & Abramson, L. Y. (1996). Use of current situational information and causal inference: Do dysphoric individuals make "unwarranted" causal inferences? *Cognitive Therapy and Research, 20,* 309–332.

Haarlander, L. (1998, November 2). Bystander sees stabbing, aids man's arrest. *The Buffalo News,* p. 5B.

Haas, L. (1999). Families and work. In M. B. Sussman, S. K. Steinmetz, & G. W. Peterson (Eds.), *Handbook of marriage and the family* (pp. 571–612). New York: Plenum Press.

Haber, D. (1994). *Health promotion and aging.* New York: Springer.

Haith, M. M., & Benson, J. B. (1998). Infant cognition. In W. Damon & R. M. Lerner (Eds.), *Handbook of child psychology* (Vol. 1). New York: Wiley.

Hajek, P., & Stead, L. F. (2004). Aversive smoking for smoking cessation. *The Cochrane Database of Systematic Reviews, 3,* Article No. CD000546.

Hall, C. S. (1984). "A ubiquitous sex difference in dreams" revisited. *Journal of Personality and Social Psychology, 46,* 1109-1117.

Hall, C. W., Davis, N. B., Bolen, L. M., & Chia, R. (1999). Gender and racial differences in mathematical performance. *Journal of Social Psychology, 139,* 677–689.

Hall, D. R., & Zhao, J. Z. (1995). Cohabitation and divorce in Canada: Testing the selectivity hypothesis. *Journal of Marriage and the Family, 57,* 421–427.

Hall, D. T., & Nougaim, K. E. (1968). An examination of Maslow's need hierarchy in an organizational setting. *Organizational Behavior and Human Performance, 3,* 12–35.

Halpern, D. (1996). Public policy implications of sex differences in cognitive abilities. *Psychology, Public Policy and Law, 2(3/4),* 564.

Halpern, D. (2004). A cognitive-process taxonomy for sex differences in cognitive abilities. *Current Directions in Psychological Science, 13,* 135-139.

Halpern, D. F. (2000). *Sex differences in cognitive abilities* (3rd ed.). Mahwah, NJ: Erlbaum.

Halpern, D. F., & LeMay, M. L. (2000). The smarter sex: A critical review of sex-differences in intelligence. *Educational Psychology Review, 12,* 229–246.

Hamel, R., & Elshout, J. (2000). On the development of knowledge during problem solving. *Journal of Cognitive Psychology, 12,* 289–322.

Hamer, D. (2002). Genetics. Rethinking behavior genetics. *Science, 298,* 71–72.

Hamilton, C. E. (2000). Continuity and discontinuity of attachment from infancy through adolescence. *Child Development, 71,* 690–694.

Hamilton, V. L., & Sanders, J. (1995). Crimes of obedience and conformity in the workplace: Surveys of Americans, Russians, and Japanese. *Journal of Social Issues, 51,* 67–88.

Hamilton, V. L., Blumenfeld, P. C., Akoh, H., & Miura, K. (1991). Group and gender in Japanese and American elementary classrooms. *Journal of Cross-Cultural Psychology, 22,* 317–346.

Hänig, D. P. (1901). Zur Psychophysik des Geschmackssinnes. *Philosophische Studien, 17,* 576–623.

Hans, S., Ray, A., Bernstein, V., & Halpern, R. (1995). *Caregiving in the inner city.* Chicago: University of Chicago and The Erikson Institute.

Hanson, G., & Venturelli, P. J. (1998). *Drugs and society* (5th ed.). Boston: Jones and Bartlett.

Hansson, R. O., DeKoekkoek, P. D., Neece, W. M., & Patterson, D. W. (1997). Successful aging at work: Annual review, 1992–1996: The older worker and transitions to retirement. *Journal of Vocational Behavior, 51,* 202–233.

Harlow, H. F., & Zimmerman, R. (1959). Affectional responses in the infant monkey. *Science, 130,* 421–432.

Harold, G. T., Fincham, F. D., Osborne, L. N., & Conger, R. D. (1997). Mom and Dad are at it again: Adolescent perceptions of marital conflict and adolescent psychological distress. *Developmental Psychology, 33,* 335–350.

Harris, C. R., & Christenfeld, N. (1996). Gender, jealousy, and reason. *Psychological Science, 7,* 364–366.

Harris, J. D. (1943). Habituatory response decrement in the intact organism. *Psychological Bulletin, 40,* 385–422.

Harris, J. R. (2000). Context-specific learning, personality, and birth order. *Current Directions in Psychological Science, 9,* 174–177.

Harris, S. R., Kemmerling, R. L., & North, M. M. (2002). Brief virtual reality therapy for public speaking. *Cyberpsychology & Behavior, 5,* 543–550.

Harrow, M., Sands, J. R., Silverstein, M. L., & Goldberg, J. F. (1997). Course and outcome for schizophrenia versus other psychotic patients: A longitudinal study. *Schizophrenia Bulletin, 23,* 287–303.

Hartmann, E. (1981, April). The strangest sleep disorder. *Psychology Today,* pp. 14, 16, 18.

Hartung, C. M., & Widiger, T. A. (1998). Gender differences in the diagnosis of mental disorders: Conclusions and controversies of the DSM-IV. *Psychological Bulletin, 123,* 260–278.

Haruki, Y. (2000). Human reinforcement: Conception of alien reinforcement. *Japanese Psychological Review, 43,* 501–518.

Haruki, Y., Shigehisa, T., Nedate, K., Wajima, M., & Ogawa, R. (1984). Effects of alien-reinforcement and its combined type on learning behavior and efficacy in relation to personality. *International Journal of Psychology, 19,* 527–545.

Hatcher, R., Trussell, J., Stewart, F., Stewart, G., Kowal, D., Guest, E., Cates, W., & Policar, M. (1994). *Contraceptive technology* (16th ed.). New York: Irvington.

Hawks, S. R., Hull, M. L., Thalman, R. L., & Richins, P. M. (1995). Review of spiritual health: Definition, role, and intervention strategies in health promotion. *American Journal of Health Promotion, 9,* 371–378.

Hayes, J. R. (1989). *The complete problem solver* (2nd ed.) Hillsdale, NJ: Erlbaum.

Hayne, H., & Rovee-Collier, C. (1995). The organization of reactivated memory in infancy. *Child Development, 66(3),* 893–906.

Hearn, J. C. (1984). The relative role of academic, ascribed, and socioeconomic characteristics in college destinations. *Sociology of Education, 57,* 22–30.

Hearn, J. C. (1990). Pathways to attendance at the elite colleges. In P. Kingston and L. Lewis (Eds.), *The high status track: Studies of elite schools and stratification.* New York: SUNY Press.

Hearn, J. C. (1991). Academic and nonacademic influences on the college destinations of 1980 high school graduates. *Sociology of Education, 64,* 158–171.

Heath, R. (1972). Pleasure and brain activity in man. *Journal of Nervous and Mental Disorders, 154,* 3–18.

Hebb, D. O. (1955). Drives and the C.N.S. (conceptual nervous system). *Psychological Review, 62,* 243–255.

Hedge, L. V., & Nowell, A. (1995). Sex differences in central tendency variability and numbers of high scoring individuals. *Science, 269,* 41-45.

Heider, F. (1946). Attitudes and cognitive organization. *Journal of Psychology, 21,* 107–112.

Heider, F. (1958). *The psychology of interpersonal relations.* New York: Wiley.

Heilman, M. E., & Kram, K. E. (1983). Male and female assumptions about colleagues' views of their competence. *Psychology of Women Quarterly, 7,* 329–337.

Heim, C., Plotsky, P. M., & Nemeroff, C. B. (2004). Importance of studying the contributions of early adverse experience to neurobiological findings in depression. *Neuropsychopharmacology, 29,* 641–648.

Heiser, P., Dickhaus, B. Schreiber, W., Clement, H. W., Hasse, C., Hennig, J., Remschmidt, H., Krieg, J. C., Wesemann, W., & Opper, C. (2000). White blood cells and cortisol after sleep deprivation and recovery sleep in humans. *European Archives of Psychiatry and Clinical Neuroscience, 250,* 16–23.

Hejmadi, A., Davidson, R. J., & Rozin, P. (2000). Exploring Hindu Indian emotion expressions. *Psychological Science, 11,* 183–187.

Helgeson, V. S. (1994). Relation of agency and communion to well-being: Evidence and potential explanations. *Psychological Bulletin, 116,* 412–428.

Helmers, K. H., Krantz, D. S., Merz, C. N. B., Klein, J., Kop, W. J., Gottdiener, J. S., & Rozanski, A. (1995). Defensive hostility: Relationship to multiple markers of cardiac ischemia in patients with coronary disease. *Health Psychology, 14,* 202–209.

Helmholtz, H. L. F. von. (1930). *The sensations of tone* (A. J. Ellis, Trans.). New York: Longmans, Green. (Original work published 1863).

Helmuth, L. (2001). From the mouths (and hands) of babes. *Science, 293,* 1758–1759.

Helson, R., & Wink, P. (1992). Personality change in women from the early 40's to the early 50's. *Psychology of Aging, 7,* 46–55.

Helwig, C. C. (1997). Making moral cognition respectable (again): A retrospective review of Lawrence Kohlberg. *Contemporary Psychology, 42,* 191–195.

Helzer, J. E., & Canino, G. J. (Eds.). (1992). *Alcoholism in North America, Europe, and Asia.* New York: Oxford University Press.

Hendrick, C., & Hendrick, S. S. (1983). *Liking, loving, & relating.* Pacific Grove, CA: Brooks/Cole.

Henning, H. (1916). Die Qualitätsreibe des geschmacks. *Zeitschrift für Psychologie, 74,* 203–219.

Henry, B., & Moffitt, T. E. (1997). Neuropsychological and neuroimaging studies of juvenile delinquency and adult criminal behavior. In D. M. Stoff, J. Breiling, & J. D. Maser (Eds.), *Handbook of antisocial personality disorder* (pp. 280–288). New York: Wiley.

Henry, W. P., Strupp, H. H., Schacht, T. E., & Gaston, L. (1994). Psychodynamic approaches. In A. E. Bergin & S. L. Garfield (Eds.), *Handbook of psychotherapy and behavior change* (4th ed.). New York: Wiley.

Hensley, L. G. (2002). Treatment of survivors of rape: Issues and interventions. *Journal of Mental Health Counseling, 24,* 331-348.

Herd, D. (1990). Subgroup differences in drinking patterns among Black and White men: Results from a national survey. *Journal of Studies on Alcohol, 51,* 221–232.

Herd, D. (1994). The effects of parental influences and respondents' norms and attitudes on Black and White adult drinking patterns. *Journal of Substance Abuse, 6,* 137–154.

Herman, L. M., & Uyeyama, R. J. (1999). The dolphin's grammatical competency: Comments on Kako (1999). *Animal Learning & Behavior, 27,* 18–23.

Herman, L. M., Kuczaj, S. A., II, & Holder, M. D. (1993). Responses to anomalous gestural sequences by a language-trained dolphin: Evidence for processing of semantic relations and syntactical information. *Journal of Experimental Psychology: General, 122,* 184–194.

Herrera, N. C., Zajonc, R. B., Wieczorkowska, G., & Cichomski, B. (2003). Beliefs about birth rank and their reflection in reality. *Journal of Personality and Social Psychology, 85,* 142–150.

Herrnstein, R., & Murray, C. (1994). *The Bell Curve.* New York: Free Press.

Heston, L. L. (1966). Psychiatric disorders in foster home reared children of schizophrenic mothers. *British Journal of Psychiatry, 112,* 819–825.

Hettema, J. M., Neale, M. C., & Kendler, K. S. (2001). A review and meta-analysis of the genetic epidemiology of anxiety disorders. *American Journal of Psychiatry, 158,* 1568–1578.

Hewlett, W. A. (2000). Benzodiazepines in the treatment of obsessive-compulsive disorder. In W. K. Goodman (Ed.), *Obsessive-compulsive disorder: Contemporary issues in treatment* (pp. 405–429). Mahwah, NJ: Erlbaum.

Hewstone, M., Rubin, M., & Willis, H. (2002). Intergroup bias (social prejudice). *Annual Review of Psychology,* 575–604.

Hikosaka, O., Nakamura, K., Sakai, K., & Nakahara, H. (2002). Central mechanisms of motor skill learning. *Current Opinion in Neurobiology, 12,* 217–222.

Hilgard, E. R. (1977). *Divided consciousness: Multiple controls in human thought and action.* New York: Wiley.

Hilgard, E. R. (1982). Hypnotic susceptibility and implications for measurement. *International Journal of Clinical and Experimental Hypnosis, 30,* 394–403.

Hilgard, E. R. (1992). Divided consciousness and dissociation. *Consciousness and Cognition, 1,* 16–31.

Hilgard, E. R., Morgan, A. H., & MacDonald, H. (1975). Pain and dissociation in the cold pressor test: A study of "hidden reports" through automatic key-pressing and automatic talking. *Journal of Abnormal Psychology, 84,* 280–289.

Hill, C. E., & Nakayama, E. Y. (2000). Client-centered therapy: Where has it been and where is it going? A comment on Hathaway (1948). *Journal of Clinical Psychology, 56,* 861–875.

Hill, P. C., & Pargament, K. I. (2003). Advances in the conceptualization and measurement of religion and spirituality. Implications for physical and mental health research. *American Psychologist, 58,* 64–74.

Hinton, G. E. (1979). Some demonstrations of the effects of structural descriptions in mental imagery. *Cognitive Science, 3,* 231–251.

Hiroto, D. S. (1974). Locus of control and learned helplessness. *Journal of Experimental Psychology, 102,* 187–193.

Hirsch, M. S., Conway, B., D'Aquila, R. T., Johnson, V. A., Brun-Vezinet, F., Clotet, B., Demeter, L. M., Hammer, S. M., Jacobsen, D. M., Kuritzkes, D. R., Loveday, C., Mellors, J. W., Vella, S., & Richman, D. D. (1998). Antiretroviral drug resistance testing in adults with HIV infection: Implications for clinical management. *Journal of the American Medical Association, 279,* 1984–1991.

Hirshfeld, J. A. (1995). The "back-to-sleep" campaign against SIDS. *American Family Physician, 51*(3), 611–612.

Hirshkowitz, M., Moore, C. A., & Minhoto, G. (1997). The basics of sleep. In M. R. Pressman & W. C. Orr (Eds.), *Understanding sleep: The evaluation and treatment of sleep disorders.* Washington, DC: American Psychological Association.

Ho, B.-C., Black, D. W., & Andreasen, N. C. (2003). Schizophrenia and other psychotic disorders. In R. E. Hales & S. C. Yudofsky (Eds.), *Textbook of clinical psychiatry* (4th ed.; pp. 379–438). Washington DC: American Psychiatric Publishing.

Hobbs, F. B. (with Damon, B. L.). (1996). *65+ in the United States.* Washington DC: U.S. Bureau of the Census.

Hobson, J. A., & McCarley, R. W. (1977). The brain as a dream state generator: An activation-synthesis hypothesis of the dream process. *American Journal of Psychiatry, 134,* 1335–1348.

Hobson, J.A., Pace-Schott, E., & Stickgold, R. (2000). Dreaming and the brain: Toward a cognitive neuroscience of conscious states. *Behavioral and Brain Sciences, 23,* 783–842.

Hoffer, T. B., Sederstrom, L., Selfa, V., Welch, M., Hess, S., Brown, S., Reyes, K., Webber, & Guzman-Barron, I. (2003). *Doctorate recipients from United States Universities: Summary Report 2002.* Chicago: National Opinion Research Center.

Hoff-Sommers, C. (2000). The war against boys. *The Atlantic Monthly, 285,* 59-74.

Hogben, M. (1998). Factors moderating the effect of televised aggression on viewer behavior. *Communication Research, 25,* 220–247.

Hoge, C. W., Castro, C. A., Messer, S. C., McGurk, D., Cotting, D. I., & Koffman, R. L. (2004). Combat duty in Iraq and Afghanistan, mental health problems, and barriers to care. *New England Journal of Medicine, 351,* 13–22.

Holcomb, D. R., Holcomb, L. C., Sondag, K. A., & Williams, N. (1991). Attitudes about date rape: Gender differences among college students. *College Student Journal, 25,* 434-439.

Holden, C. (1980, November). Twins reunited. *Science, 80,* 55–59.

Holland, A. J., Sicotte, N., & Treasure, J. (1988). Anorexia nervosa: Evidence of a genetic basis. *Journal of Psychosomatic Research, 32,* 561–571.

Holley, A. (1991). Neural coding of olfactory information. In T. V. Getchell, R. L. Doty, L. M. Bartoshuk, & J. B. Snow, Jr. (Eds.), *Smell and taste in health and disease.* (pp. 329–343). New York: Raven.

Hollon, S. D. (1996). The efficacy and effectiveness of psychotherapy relative to medications. *American Psychologist, 51,* 1025–1030.

Hollon, S. D., & Beck, A. T. (1994). Cognitive and cognitive-behavioral therapies. In A. E. Bergin & S. L. Garfield (Eds.), *Handbook of psychotherapy and behavior change* (4th ed.). New York: Wiley.

Hollos, M., & Richards, F. A. (1993). Gender-associated development of formal operations in Nigerian adolescents. *Ethos, 21,* 24–52.

Holloway, S. R. (1998). Exploring the neighborhood contingency of race discrimination in mortgage lending in Columbus, Ohio. *Annals of the Association of American Geographers, 88,* 252–276.

Holmes, D. S. (1987). The influence of meditation versus rest on physiological arousal: A second examination. In M. A. West (Ed.), *The psychology of meditation.* Oxford: Clarendon Press.

Holmes, T. H., & Rahe, R. H. (1967). The Social Readjustment Rating Scale. *Journal of Psychosomatic Research, 11,* 213–218.

Holroyd, J. (2003). The science of meditation and the state of hypnosis. *American Journal of Clinical Hypnosis, 46,* 109–128.

Holt, S., Brand, J. C., Soveny, C., & Hansky, J. (1992). Relationship of satiety to postprandial glycaemic, insulin and cholecystokinin responses. *Appetite, 18,* 129–141.

Hood, D. C., & Finkelstein, M. A. (1986). Sensitivity to light. In K. R. Boff, L. Kaufman, & J. P. Thomas (Eds.), *Handbook of perception and human performance* (pp. 5.1–5.66). New York: Wiley.

Hooley, J. M., & Hiller, J. B. (1998). Expressed emotion and the pathogenesis of relapse in schizophrenia. In M. F. Lenzenweger & R. H. Dworkin (Eds.), *Origins of the development of schizophrenia* (pp. 447–468). Washington, DC: American Psychological Association.

Horgan, D. D. (1995). *Achieving gender equity: Strategies for the classroom.* Boston: Allyn & Bacon.

Horgan, J. (1996, December). Why Freud isn't dead. *Scientific American,* 106–111.

Horn, J. L. (1982). The aging of human abilities. In B. B. Wolman (Ed.), *Handbook of developmental psychology* (pp. 847–870). Englewood Cliffs, NJ: Prentice-Hall.

Horn, J. L., Donaldson, G., & Engstrom, R. (1981). Apprehension, memory, and fluid intelligence decline through the "vital years" of adulthood. *Research on Aging, 3,* 33–84.

Hornbacher, M. (1998). *Wasted: A memoir of anorexia and bulimia.* New York: Harper Perennial.

Horne, J. A., & Staff, L. H. E. (1983). Exercise and sleep: Body-heating effects. *Sleep, 6,* 36–46.

Horney, K. (1937). *The neurotic personality of our time.* New York: Norton.

Horney, K. (1939). *New ways in psychoanalysis.* New York: Norton.

Houry, D., Feldman, K. M., & Abbott, J. (2000). Mandatory reporting laws. *Annals of Emergency Medicine, 35,* 404.

Hovland, C. I., & Weiss, W. (1951). The influence of source credibility on communication effectiveness. *Public Opinion Quarterly, 15,* 635–650.

Howe, M. L. (2000). *The rate of early memories.* Washington, DC: American Psychological Association.

Howell, M. R., Kassler, W. J., & Haddix, A. (1997). Partner notification to prevent pelvic inflammatory disease in women: Cost effectiveness of two strategies. *Sexually Transmitted Diseases, 24,* 287-292.

Howland, D. (1999, March 1). *Body of missing boy found.* Associated Press On-line News Service. Retrieved March 6, 1999, from http://dailynews .yahoo.com/headlines/ap/ap_us/story.html?s=v/ap/ 199903.../missing_boy_19.htm

Hoyert, D. L., Kochanek, K. D., & Murphy, S. L. (1999). Deaths: Final data for 1997. *National Vital Statistics Report, 47* (DHHS Publication No. 99–1120). Hyattsville, MD: National Center for Health Statistics.

Hsiung, R. C. (2001). Suggested principles of professional ethics for the online provision of mental health services. *Medinfo, 10,* 296–300.

Hsu, R. (1994). Gender differences in sexual fantasy and behavior in a college population: A ten-year replication. *Journal of Sex and Marital Therapy, 20,* 103-118.

Hubel, D. H. (1990, February). Interview. *Omni,* pp. 74–110.

Hubel, D. H. (1995). *Eye, brain, and vision.* New York: Scientific American Library.

Hubel, D. H., & Weisel, T. N. (1965). Receptive fields of single neurons in two nonstriate visual areas (18 and 19) of the cat. *Journal of Neurophysiology, 28,* 229–289.

Hubel, D. H., & Weisel, T. N. (1979). Brain mechanisms and vision. *Scientific American, 214,* 150–162.

Hudson, J. I., McElroy, S. L., Raymond, N. C., Crow, S., Keck, P. E., Carter, W. P., Mitchell, J. E., Strakowski, S. M., Pope, Jr., H. G., Coleman, B. S., & Jonas, J. M. (1998). Fluvoxamine in the treatment of binge-eating disorder: A multicenter placebo-controlled, double-blind trial. *American Journal of Psychiatry, 155,* 1756–1762.

Huesman, L. R. (1994). (Ed.). *Aggressive behavior: Current perspectives.* New York: Plenum.

Hughes, J., Smith, T. W., Kosterlitz, H. W., Fothergill, L. A., Morgan, B. A., & Morris, H. R. (1975). Identification of two related pentapeptides from the brain with potent opiate agonist activity. *Nature, 258,* 577–579.

Hull, C. L. (1943). *Principles of behavior.* New York: Appleton-Century-Crofts.

Humphreys, K., Winzelberg, A., & Klaw, E. (2000). Psychologists' ethical responsibilities in Internet-based groups: Issues, strategies, and a call for dialogue. *Professional Psychology, Research, and Practice, 31,* 493–496.

Hunt, M. (1974). *Sexual behavior in the 1970's.* Chicago: Playboy Press.

Hunt, M. (1993). *The story of psychology.* New York: Anchor Books.

Hunt, R. R. (2002). How effective are pharmacologic agents for alcoholism? *Journal of Family Practice, 51,* p577.

Hurlbert, A. (2003). Colour vision: Primary visual cortex shows its influence. *Current Biology, 13,* R270–R272.

Hurvich, L. M., & Jameson, D. (1957). An opponent-process theory of color vision. *Psychological Review, 64,* 384–404.

Huston, A. C., & Wright, J. C. (1998). Mass media and children's development. In W. Damon (Series Ed.), *Handbook of child psychology* (Vol. 4). New York: Wiley.

Huston, T. L., & Vangelisti, A. L. (1991). Socioemotional behavior and satisfaction in marital relationships: A longitudinal study. *Journal of Personality and Social Psychology, 6,* 721–733.

Huttenlocher, P. R. (2002). *Neural plasticity: The effects of environment on the development of the cerebral cortex.* Cambridge, MA: Harvard University Press.

Hyde, J. S., & Linn, M. C. (1988). Gender differences in verbal ability: A meta-analysis. *Psychological Bulletin, 104,* 53-69.

Hyde, J. S., & McKinley, N. M. (1997). Gender differences in cognition: Results from meta-analyses. In P. J. Caplan, M. Crawford, J. S. Hyde, & J. T. E. Richardson (Eds.), *Gender differences in human cognition* (pp. 30–51). New York: Oxford University Press.

Hyde, J. S., & Oliver, M. B. (2000). Gender differences in sexuality. Results from meta-analysis. In C. B. Travis & J. W. White (Eds.), *Sexuality, society, and feminism* (pp. 57-77). Washington, DC: American Psychological Association.

Hyde, J. S., & Plant, E. A. (1995). Magnitude of psychological gender differences: Another side to the story. *American Psychologist, 50,* 159-161.

Hyde, J. S., Fenneman, E., & Lamon, S. (1990). Gender differences in mathematics performance: A meta-analysis. *Psychological Bulletin, 107,* 139–155.

Hyman, S. E., & Rudorfer, M. V. (2000). Anxiety disorders. In D. C. Dale & D. D. Federman (Eds.), *Scientific American Medicine,* (Vol. 3). New York: Healtheon/WebMD Corp.

Iidaka, T., Anderson, N. D., Kapur, S., Cabeza, S., & Craik, F. I. M. (2000). The effect of divided attention on encoding and retrieval in episodic memory revealed by positron emission tomography. *Journal of Cognitive Neuroscience, 12,* 267.

Ikonomidou, C., Bittigau, P., Ishimaru, M. J., Wozniak, D. F., et al. (2000, February 11). Ethanol-induced apoptotic neurodegeneration and fetal alcohol syndrome. *Science, 287,* 1056–1060.

In demand again: The middle-age worker. (2000, January 2). *St. Petersburg Times,* p. G1.

Inciardi, J. A., Surratt, H. L., & Saum, C. A. (1997). *Cocaine-exposed infants: Social, legal, and public health issues.* Thousand Oaks, CA: Sage.

Ineichen, B. (1979). The social geography of marriage. In M. Cook & G. Wilson (Eds.), *Love and attraction.* New York: Pergamon Press.

Infante-Rivard, C., Fernandez, A., Gauthier, R., David, M., & Rivard, G. E. (1993). Fetal loss associated with caffeine intake before and during pregnancy. *Journal of the American Medical Association, 270*(24), 2940–2943.

Ingram, R. E., Hayes, A., & Scott, W. (2000). Empirically supported treatments: A critical analysis. In C. R. Snyder & R. E. Ingram (Eds.), *Handbook of psychological change: Psychotherapy processes and practices for the 21st century* (pp. 40–60). New York: Wiley.

Innis, N. K. (1979). Stimulus control of behavior during postreinforcement pause of FI schedules. *Animal Learning and Behavior, 7,* 203–210.

Inzlicht, M., & Ben-Zeev, T. (2000). A threatening intellectual environment: Why females are susceptible to experiencing problem-solving deficits in the presence of males. *Psychological Science, 11,* 365–371.

Ironsmith, M., Marva, J., Harju, B., & Eppler, M. (2003). Motivation and performance in college students enrolled in self-paced versus lecture-format remedial mathematics courses. *Journal of Instructional Psychology, 30,* 276–284.

Irwin, M., McClintick, J., Costlow, C., Fortner, M., White, J., & Gillin, J. C. (1996). Partial night sleep deprivation reduces natural killer and cellular immune responses in humans. *Journal of the Federation of American Societies for Experimental Biology, 10,* 643–653.

Isenberg, N., Silbersweig, D., Engelien, A., Emmerich, S., Malavade, K., Beattie, B., Leon, A. C., & Stern, E. (1999). Linguistic threat activates the human amygdala. *Proceedings of the National Academy of Sciences, USA, 96,* 10456–10459.

Jablensky, A. (2000). Epidemiology of schizophrenia: The global burden of disease and disability. *European Archives of Psychiatry & Clinical Neuroscience, 250,* 274–285.

Jablensky, A. (2002). The classification of personality disorders: Critical review and need for rethinking. *Psychopathology, 35,* 112–116.

Jack, D. C. (1991). *Silencing the self: Women and depression.* New York: HarperPerennial.

Jackson, J. S., Williams, D. R., & Torres, M. (1997). *Perceptions of discrimination: The stress process and physical and psychological health.* Washington, DC: National Institute for Mental Health.

Jacobs, B. L. (2004). Depression: The brain finally gets into the act. *Current Directions in Psychological Science, 13,* 103–106.

Jacobs, B. L., van Praag, H., & Gage, F. H. (2000). Adult brain neurogenesis and psychiatry: A novel theory of depression. *Molecular Psychiatry, 5,* 262–269.

Jacobsen, T., & Hofmann, V. (1997). Children's attachment representations: Longitudinal relations to school behavior and academic competency in middle childhood and adolescence. *Developmental Psychology, 33,* 701–710.

Jadack, R. A., Hyde, J. S., Moore, C. F., & Keller, M. L. (1995). Moral reasoning about sexually transmitted diseases. *Child Development, 66,* 167–177.

Jaffee, S., & Hyde, J. (2000). Gender differences in moral orientation: A meta-analysis. *Psychological Bulletin, 126,* 703–726.

James, W. (1884). What is an emotion? *Mind, 9,* 188–205.

James, W. (1890). *The principles of psychology.* New York: Holt.

James, W. (1892). *Psychology: A briefer course.* New York: Holt.

James, W. (1950). *The principles of psychology.* New York: Dover. (Original work published 1890)

Jang, K. L., Hu, S., Livesley, W. J., Angleitner, A., Riemann, R., Ando, J., Ono, Y., Vernon, P. A., & Hamer, D. H. (2001). Covariance structure of neuroticism and agreeableness: A twin and molecular genetic analysis of the role of the serotonin transporter gene. *Journal of Personality & Social Psychology, 81,* 295–304.

Janis, I. L. (1982). *Victims of groupthink* (2nd ed.). Boston: Houghton Mifflin.

Janis, I. L. (1985). Sources of error in strategic decision making. In J. M. Pennings (Ed.), *Organizational strategy and change.* San Francisco: Jossey-Bass.

Janoff-Bulman, R. (1992). *Shattered assumptions: Toward a new psychology of trauma.* New York: Maxwell Macmillan International.

Janowitz, H., & Grossman, M. (1950). Hunger and appetite: Some definitions and concepts. *Journal of Mount Sinai Hospital, 16,* 231–240.

Janus, S. S., & Janus, C. L. (1993). *The Janus report on sexual behavior.* New York: Wiley.

Jarrett, R. B., Kraft, D., Doyle, J., Foster, B. M., Eaves, G. G., & Silver, P. C. (2001). Preventing recurrent depression using cognitive therapy with and without a continuation phase. *Archives of General Psychiatry, 58,* 381–388.

Jarvik, M. E. (1995). "The scientific case that nicotine is addictive": Comment. *Psychopharmacology, 117*(1), 18–20.

Jemmott, J. B., III, Borysenko, M., McClelland, D. C., Chapman, R., & Benson, H. (1985). Academic stress, power motivation, and decrease in salivary secretory immunoglobulin: A secretion rate. *Lancet, 1,* 1400–1402.

Jenike, M. A., Baer, L., Ballantine, H. T., Martuza, R. L., Tynes, S., Giriunas, I., Buttolph, M. L., & Cassem, N. H. (1991). Cingulotomy for refractory obsessive-compulsive disorder: A long-term follow up of 33 patients. *Archives of General Psychiatry, 48,* 548–555.

Jenkins, J. G., & Dallenbach, K. M. (1924). Obliviscence during sleep and waking. *American Journal of Psychology, 35,* 605–612.

Jenkins, J. M., & Astington, J. W. (1996). Cognitive factors and family structure associated with theory of mind development in young children. *Developmental Psychology, 32,* 70–78.

Jennings, J. R., Monk, T. H., & van der Molen, M. W. (2003). Sleep deprivation influences some but not all processes of supervisory attention. *Psychological Science, 14,* 473–479.

Jensen, A. R. (1969). How much can we boost IQ and scholastic achievement? *Harvard Educational Review, 39,* 1–23.

Johnson, J. A. (1997). Units of analysis for the description and explanation of personality. In R. Hogan, J. Johnson, & S. Briggs (Eds.), *Handbook of personality psychology.* New York: Academic Press.

Johnson, J. S., & Newport, E. L. (1991). Critical period effects on universal properties of language: The status of subjacency in the acquisition of a second language. *Cognition, 39,* 215–258.

Johnson, M. K., Hashtroudi, S., & Lindsay, D. S. (1993). Source monitoring. *Psychological Bulletin, 114,* 3–28.

Johnson, M. K., Mitchell, K. J., Raye, C. L., & Greene, E. J. (2004). An age-related deficit in prefrontal cortical function associated with refreshing information. *Psychological Science, 15,* 127–132.

Johnson, S. P., & Nanez, J. E. (1995). Young infants' perception of object unity in two-dimensional displays. *Infant Behavior & Development, 18*(2), 133–143.

John-Steiner, V., & Mahn, H. (1996). Sociocultural approaches to learning and development: A Vygotskian framework. *Educational Psychologist, 31,* 191–206.

Joliot, A. E. (2001). A comparative study of body image satisfaction and attitudes among American, Israeli, Spanish, & Brazilian college women (United States). *Dissertation Abstracts International: Section B: The Sciences and Engineering, 61,* 55–67.

Jones, C. J., & Meredith, W. (1996). Patterns of personality change across the life span. *Psychology of Aging, 11,* 57–65.

Jones, E. E. (1979). The rocky road from acts to dispositions. *American Psychologist, 34,* 107–117.

Jones, E. E., & Nesbitt, R. E. (1971). *The actor and the observer: Divergent perceptions of the causes of behavior.* Morristown, NJ: General Learning Press.

Jones, M. C., Webb, R. J., Hsiao, C. Y., & Hannan, P. (1995). Relationships between socioeconomic status and drinking problems among Black and White men. *Alcoholism, Clinical and Experimental Research, 19,* 623–627.

Jones, P., & Cannon, M. (1998). The new epidemiology of schizophrenia. *Psychiatric Clinics of North America, 21,* 1–25.

Jones, R. T. (1971). Tetrahydrocannabinol and the marijuana-induced social "high" or the effects on the mind of marijuana. *Annals of the New York Academy of Sciences, 191,* 155–165.

Jones, S., Casswell, S., & Zhang, J. F. (1995). The economic costs of alcohol-related absenteeism and reduced productivity among the working population of New Zealand. *Addiction, 90,* 1455–1461.

Jones, W. P., & Emerson, S. (1994). Sexual abuse and binge eating in a nonclinical population. *Journal of Sex Education and Therapy, 20,* 47-55.

Jonsson, E. G., Burgert, E., Crocq, M. A., Gustavsson, J. P., Forslund, K., Mattila-Evenden, M., Rylander, G., Flyckt, L. K., Bjerkenstedt, L., Wiesel, F. A., Asberg, M., & Bergman, H. (2003). Association study between dopamine D3 receptor gene variant and personality traits. *American Journal of Medical Genetics, 117B,* 61–65.

Jonsson, E. G., Ivo, R., Gustavsson, J. P., Geijer, T. Forslund, K., Mattila-Evenden, M., Rylander, G., Cichon, S., Propping, P., Bergman, H., Asberg, M., & Nothen, M. M. (2002). No association between dopamine D4 receptor gene variants and novelty seeking. *Molecular Psychiatry, 7,* 18–20.

Jordan, A. S., & McEvoy, R. D. (2003). Gender differences in sleep apnea: Epidemiology, clinical presentation and pathogenic mechanisms. *Sleep Medical Review, 7,* 377–389.

Julien, R. M. (1995). *A primer of drug action.* San Francisco: Freeman.

Jung, C. (1967). *Collected works.* Princeton, NJ: Princeton University Press.

Jung, C. G. (1966). The psychology of the unconscious. In H. Read, M. Fordham, & G. Adler (Eds.), *Collected works of C. G. Jung* (Vol. 7). Princeton, NJ: Princeton University Press. (Originally published 1917)

Jung, J. (2001). *Psychology of alcohol and other drugs: A research perspective.* Thousand Oaks, CA: Sage.

Kaeser, F., DiSalvo, C., & Moglia, R. (2001). Sexual behaviors of young children that occur in schools. *Journal of Sex Education and Therapy, 25,* 277-285.

Kahn, D. A. (1995). New strategies in bipolar disorder: Part II. Treatment. *Journal of Practical Psychiatry & Behavioral Health, 3,* 148–157.

Kahneman, D. & Tversky, A. (1984). Choices, values, and frames. *American Psychologist, 39,* 341–350

Kahneman, D., & Tversky, A. (1973). On the psychology of prediction. *Psychological Review, 80,* 237–251.

Kail, R., & Salthouse, T. A. (1994). Processing speed as a mental capacity. *Acta Psychologica, 86,* 199–225.

Kaiser Family Foundation. (1998). *Sexually transmitted diseases in America: How many and at what cost?* Menlo Park, CA: Author.

Kako, E. (1999). Elements of syntax in the systems of three language-trained animals. *Animal Learning and Behavior, 27,* 1–14.

Kales, A., & Kales, J. (1973). Recent advances in the diagnosis and treatment of sleep disorders. In G. Usdin (Ed.), *Sleep research and clinical practice.* New York: Brunner/Mazel.

Kalish, R. A. (1985). The social context of death and dying. In R. H. Binstock & E. Shanas (Eds.), *Handbook of aging and the social sciences* (2nd ed., pp. 149–170). New York: Van Nostrand Reinhold.

Kamara, S., Lecours, A. R., Leroux, J.-M., Bourgouin, P., Beaudoin, G., Joubert, S., & Beauregard, M. (2002). Areas of brain activation in males and females during viewing of erotic excerpts. *Human Brain Mapping, 16,* 1–13.

Kamb, M. L., Fishbein, M., Douglas, J. M., Jr., Rhodes, F., Rogers, J., Bolan, G., Zenilman, J., Hoxworth, T., Malotte, C. K., Iatesta, M., Kent, C., Lentz, A., Graziano, S., Byers, R. H., & Peterman, T. A. (1998). Efficacy of risk-reduction counseling to prevent human immunodeficiency virus and sexually transmitted diseases: A randomized controlled trial. *Journal of the American Medical Association, 280,* 1161–1167.

Kandel, D. B. (1978). Similarity in real-life adolescent friendship pairs. *Journal of Personality and Social Psychology, 36,* 306–312.

Kanin, E. J., Davidson, D. K. D., & Scheck, S. R. (1970). A research note on male-female differentials in the experience of heterosexual love. *The Journal of Sex Research, 6,* 64–72.

Kaplan, C. A., & Simon, H. A. (1990). In search of insight. *Cognitive Psychology,22,* 374–419.

Kaplan, E., Mukherjee, P., & Shapley, R. (1993). Information filtering in the lateral geniculate nucleus. In R. Shapley & D. M.-K. Lam (Eds.), *Contrast sensitivity: Proceedings of the Retina Research Foundation Symposia* (pp. 183–200). Cambridge, MA: MIT Press.

Kaplan, H. S. (1974). *The new sex therapy: Active treatment of sexual dysfunctions.* New York: Brunner/Mazel.

Kaplan, R. M., & Saccuzzo, D. P. (1989). *Psychological testing: Principles, applications, and issues.* Pacific Grove, CA: Brooks/Cole.

Kaplan, S. J., Pelcovitz, D., Salzinger, S., Mandel, F., & Weiner, M. (1997). Adolescent physical abuse and suicide attempts. *Journal of the American Academy of Child & Adolescent Psychiatry, 36,* 799–808.

Kaplowitz, P. B., Oberfield, S. E., & the Drug and Therapeutics and Executive Committees of the Lawson Wilkins Pediatric Endocrine Society. (1999). Reexamination of the age limit for defining when puberty is precocious in girls in the United States: Implications for evaluation and treatment. *Pediatrics, 104,* 936–941.

Kapur, S., Craik, F. I. M., Tulving, E., Wilson, A. A., Houle, S., & Brown, G. M. (1994). Neuroatomical correlates of encoding in episodic memory. *Proceedings of the National Academy of Science, USA,* 91, 2008–2011.

Karabenick, S. A. (1983). Sex-relevance of context and influenceability, Sistrunk and McDavid revisted. *Personality and Social Psychology Bulletin, 9,* 243–252.

Karni, A., Tanne, D., Rubenstien, B. S., Askenasy, J. J. M., & Sagi, D. (1994). Dependence on REM sleep of overnight improvement of a perceptual skill. *Science, 265*(5172), 679–682.

Karno, M., & Golding, J. M. (1991). Obsessive compulsive disorder. In L. R. Robins & D. A. Regier (Eds.), *Psychiatric disorders in America: The Epidemiologic Catchment Area Study.* New York: Maxwell Macmillan International.

Kaslow, F. W., Hansson, K., & Lundblad, A. (1994). Long-term marriages in Sweden: And some comparisons with similar couples in the United States. *Contemporary Family Therapy, 16,* 521–537.

Katigbak, M. S., Church, A. T., Guanzon-Lapena, M. A., Carlota, A. J., del, P. (2002). Are indigenous personality dimensions culture specific? Philippine inventories and the five-factor model. *Journal of Personality and Social Psychology, 82,* 89–101.

Kato, S., Wakasa, Y., & Yanagita, T. (1987). Relationship between minimum reinforcing doses and injection speed in cocaine and pentobarbital self-administration in crab-eating monkeys. *Pharmacology, Biochemistry, and Behavior, 28,* 407–410.

Katsuragi, S., Kiyota, A., Tsutsumi, T., Isogawa, K., Nagayama, H., Arinami, T., & Akiyoshi, J. (2001). Lack of association between a polymorphism in the promoter region of the dopamine D2 receptor and personality traits. *Psychiatry Research, 105,* 123–127.

Katz, M. H., Schwarcz, S. K., Kellogg, T. A., Klausner, J. D., Dilley, J. W., Gibson, S., et al. (2002). Impact of highly active antiretroviral treatment on HIV seroincidence among men who have sex with men. *American Journal of Public Health, 92,* 388–395.

Kaufman, L. & Rock, L. (1989). The moon illusion thirty years later. In M. Hershenson (Ed.), *The moon illusion* (pp. 193–234). Hillsdale, NJ: Erlbaum.

Kaufman, R. H., Adam, E., Hatch, E. E., Noller, K. L., Herbst, A., et al. (2000). Continued follow-up of pregnancy outcomes of diethylstilbestrol-exposed offspring. *Obstetrics & Gynecology, 96,* 483–489.

Kaye, K. L., & Bower, T. G. R. (1994). Learning and intermodal transfer of information in newborns. *Psychological Science, 5,* 286–288.

Kazdin, A. E. (1977). *The token economy: A review and evaluation.* New York: Plenum.

Kedia, K. (1983). Ejaculation and emission: Normal physiology, dysfunction and therapy. In R. J. Krane, M. B., Siroky, & I. Goldstein (Eds.), *Male sexual dysfunction* (pp. 37-54). Boston: Little, Brown.

Keller, J., & Dauenheimer, D. (2003). Stereotype threat in the classroom: Dejection mediates the disrupting threat effect of women's math performance. *Personality and Social Psychology Bulletin, 29,* 371–381.

Kelsey, J. E., & Vargas, H. (1993). Medial septal lesions disrupt spatial, but not nonspatial, working memory in rats. *Behavioral Neuroscience, 107,* 565–574.

Kemeny, M. E. (2003). The psychobiology of stress. *Current Directions in Psychological Science, 12,* 124–129.

Kenardy, J. A., Dow, M. G., Johnston, D. W., Newman, M. G., Thompson, A., & Taylor, C. B. (2003). A comparison of delivery methods of cognitive-behavioral therapy for panic disorder: An international multicenter trial. *Journal of Consulting & Clinical Psychology, 71,* 1068–1075.

Kendler, K. S., McGuire, M., Gruenberg, A. M., & Walsh, D. (1994). Outcome and family study of the subtypes of schizophrenia in the west of Ireland. *American Journal of Psychiatry, 151,* 849–856.

Kendler, K. S., Neale, M. C., Kessler, R. C., Heath, A. C., & Eaves, L. J. (1992). A population-based twin study of major depression in women. *Archives of General Psychiatry, 49,* 257–266.

Kenrick, D. T., & Sheets, V. (1993). Homicidal fantasies. *Ethology and Sociobiology, 14,* 231–246.

Kerns, K. A., Klepac, L., & Cole, A. K. (1996). Peer relationships and preadolescents' perceptions of security in the child–mother relationship. *Developmental Psychology, 32,* 457–466.

Kessler, R. C., Berglund, P., Demler, O., Jin, R., Koretz, D., Merikangas, K. R. et al. (2003). The epidemiology of major depressive disorder. Results from the National Comorbidity Survey Replication (NCS-R). *Journal of the American Medical Association, 289,* 3095–3105.

Kessler, R. C., McGonagle, K. A., Zhao, S., Nelson, C. B., Hughes, M., Eshelman, S., Wittchen, H., & Kendler, K. S. (1994). Lifetime and 12-month prevalence of DSM-III-R psychiatric disorders in the United States: Results from the National Comorbidity Survey (NCS). *Archives of General Psychiatry, 51,* 8–19.

Kessler, R. C., Stein, M. B., & Berglund, P. (1998). Social phobia subtypes in the National Comorbidity Survey. *American Journal of Psychiatry, 155,* 613–619.

Kety, S. S., Wender, P. H., Jacobsen, B., Ingraham, L. J., Jansson, L., Faber, B., & Kinney, D. K. (1994). Mental illness in the biological and adoptive relative of schizophrenic adoptees: Replication of the Copenhagen study in the rest of Denmark. *Archives of General Psychiatry, 51,* 442–455.

Keverne, E. B. (1982). Chemical senses: Taste. In H. B. Barlow & J. D. Mollon (Eds.), *The senses* (pp. 428–477). Cambridge: Cambridge University Press.

Key, W. B. (1973). *Subliminal seduction.* Englewood Cliffs, NJ: Signet.

Key, W. B. (1989). *Age of manipulation: The con in confidence and the sine in sincere.* New York: Holt.

Kiecolt-Glaser, J. J., McGuire, L., Robles, T. F., & Glaser, R. (2002). Emotions, morbidity, and mortality: New perspectives from psychoneuroimmunology. *Annual Review of Psychology, 53,* 83–107.

Kiecolt-Glaser, J. K., & Glaser, R. (1992). Psychoneuroimmunology: Can psychological interventions modulate immunity? *Journal of Consulting and Clinical Psychology, 60,* 569–575.

Kiecolt-Glaser, J. K., Marucha, P. T., Malarkey, W. B., Mercado, A. M., & Glaser, R. (1995). Slowing of wound healing by psychological stress. *Lancet, 346,* 1194–1196.

Kihlstrom, J. F. (1993). The continuum of consciousness. *Consciousness and Cognition, 2,* 334–354.

Kihlstrom, J. F., Glisky, M. L., & Angiulo, M. J. (1994). Dissociative tendencies and dissociative disorders. *Journal of Abnormal Psychology, 103,* 117–124.

Killen, M., Crystal, D. S., & Watanabe, H. (2002). Japanese and American children's evaluations of peer exclusion, tolerance of differences, and prescriptions for conformity. *Child Development, 73,* 1788–1802.

Kim, J. E., & Moen, P. (2001). Moving into retirement: Preparation and transitions in late midlife. In M. E. Lachman (Ed.), *Handbook of midlife development* (pp. 487–527). New York: Wiley.

Kim, J. E., & Moen, P. (2002). Retirement transitions, gender, and psychological well-being: A life-course, ecological model. *Journal of Gerontology: Psychological Sciences, 57B,* P212–P222.

Kim, J., Mohamed, S., Andreasen, N. C., O'Leary, D. S., Watkins, G. L., Ponto, L. L. B., & Hichwa, R. D. (2000). Regional neural dysfunctions in chronic schizophrenia studies with positron emission tomography. *American Journal of Psychiatry, 157,* 542–548.

Kimball, M. M. (1986). Television and sex-role attitudes. In T. M. Williams (Ed.), *The impact of television* (pp. 265–301). New York: Academic Press.

Kimm, S. Y., & Obarzanek, E. (2002). Childhood obesity: A new pandemic of the new millennium. *Pediatrics, 110,* 1003–1007.

Kimm, S. Y., Barton, B. A., Berhane, K., Ross, J. W., Payne, G. H., & Schreiber, G. B. (1997). Self-esteem and adiposity in Black and White girls: The NHLBI growth and health study. *Annals of Epidemiology, 7,* 550–560.

Kimm, S. Y., Barton, B. A., Obarzanek, E., McMahon, R. P., Kronsberg, S. S., Waclawiw, M. A., Morrison, J. A., Schrieber, G. B., Sabry, Z. I., & Daniels, S. R. (2002). Obesity development during adolescence in a biracial cohort: The NHLBI Growth and Health Study. *Pediatrics, 110,* e54.

Kimm, S. Y., Glynn, N. W., Aston, C. E., Damcott, C. M., Poehlman, E. T., Daniels, S. R., & Ferrell, R. E. (2002). Racial differences in the relation between uncoupling protein genes and resting energy expenditure. *American Journal of Clinical Nutrition, 75,* 714–719.

Kimm, S. Y., Glynn, N. W., Aston, C. E., Poehlman, E. T., & Daniels, S. R. (2001). Effects of race, cigarette smoking, and use of contraceptive medications on resting energy expenditure in young women. *American Journal of Epidemiology, 154,* 718–724.

Kimm, S. Y., Glynn, N. W., Kriska, A. M., Barton, B. A., Kronsberg, S. S., Daniels, S. R., Crawford, P. B., Sabry, Z. I., & Liu, K. (2002). Decline in physical activity in Black girls and White girls during adolescence. *New England Journal of Medicine, 347,* 709–715.

Kimm, S. Y., Obarzanek, E., Barton, B. A., Aston, C. E., Similo, S. L., Morrison, J. A., Sabry, Z. I., Schreiber, G. B., & McMahon, R. P. (1996). Race, socioeconomic status, and obesity in 9- to 10-year-old girls: The NHLBI growth and health study. *Annals of Epidemiology, 6*, 266–275.

Kimura, D. (2000). *Sex and cognition.* Cambridge, MA: MIT Press.

Kinder, B. N., & Curtiss, G. (1988). Specific components in the etiology, assessment, and treatment of male sexual dysfunctions: Controlled outcome studies. *Journal of Sex and Marital Therapy, 14,* 40-48.

King, H. E. (1961). Psychological effects of excitation in the limbic system. In D. E. Sheer (Ed.), *Electrical stimulation of the brain* (pp. 477–486). Austin, TX: University of Texas Press.

King, N. J., Gullone, E., Tonge, B. J., & Ollendick, T. H. (1993). Self-reports of panic attacks and manifest anxiety in adolescents. *Behaviour Research and Therapy, 31,* 111–116.

King, P. M., & Kitchener, K. S. (1994). *Developing reflective judgment: Understanding and promoting intellectual growth and critical thinking in adolescents and adults.* San Francisco: Jossey-Bass.

Kinomura, S., Larsson, J., Gulyas, B., & Roland, P. E. (1996). Activation by attention of the human reticular formation and thalamic intralaminar nuclei. *Science, 271,* 512–515.

Kinsella, K., & Velkoff, V. A. (2001). *An aging world: 2001. U.S. Census Bureau, Series P95/01–1.* Washington, DC: U.S. Government Printing Office.

Kinsey, A. C., Pomeroy, W. B., & Martin, C. E. (1948). *Sexual behavior in the human male.* Philadelphia: Saunders.

Kinsey, A. C., Pomeroy, W. B., Martin, C. E., & Gebhard, P. H. (1953). *Sexual behavior in the human female.* Philadelphia: Saunders.

Kirsch, I. (1994). Cognitive-behavioral hypnotherapy. In J. W. Rhue, S. J. Lynn, & I.Kirsch (Eds.), *Handbook of clinical hypnosis.* Washington, DC: American Psychological Association.

Kirsch, I. (2000). The response set theory of hypnosis. *American Journal of Clinical Hypnosis, 42,* 274–292.

Kirsch, I., & Lynn, S. J. (1995). The altered state of hypnosis. *American Psychologist, 50*(10), 846–858.

Kirsch, I., & Lynn, S. J. (1997). Hypnotic involuntariness and the automaticity of everyday life. *American Journal of Clinical Hypnosis, 40,* 329–348.

Kirsch, I., Montgomery, G., & Sapirstein, G. (1995). Hypnosis as an adjunct to cognitive behavioral psychotherapy: A meta-analysis. *Journal of Consulting and Clinical Psychology, 63,* 214–220.

Kisilevsky, B. S., Hains, S. M., Lee, K., Xie, X., Huang, H., Ye, H. H., Zhnag, K., & Wang, Z. (2003). Effects of experience on fetal voice recognition. *Psychological Science, 14,* 220–224.

Kitterod, R. H., & Kjeldstad, R. (2002, Oct.). *A new father's role? Employment patterns among Norwegian fathers in the 1990's.* Paper presented at the IATUR conference in Lisbon, Norway.

Klass, D. (1993). Solace and immortality: Bereaved parents' continuing bond with their children. *Death Studies, 17,* 343–368.

Klatzky, R. L. (1980). *Human memory: Structures and processes* (2nd ed.). New York: W. H. Freeman.

Klatzky, R. L., Lederman, S. J., & Matula, D. E. (1985). Identifying objects by touch: An "expert system." *Perception & Psychophysics, 37,* 299–302.

Klein, D. N., Durbin, C. E., Shankman, S. A., & Santiago, N. J. (2002). Depression and personality. In J. H. Gotlib & C. L. Hammen (Eds.), *Handbook of depression* (pp. 115–140). New York: Guilford Press.

Klein, D. N., Lewinsohn, P. M., & Seeley, J. R. (2001). A family study of major depressive disorder in a community sample of adolescents. *Archives of General Psychiatry, 58,* 13–21.

Klein, S. B. (1987). *Learning.* New York: McGraw-Hill.

Kleinknecht, R. A. (1991). *Mastering anxiety: The nature and treatment of anxious conditions.* New York: Plenum.

Klonoff, E. A., & Landrine, H. (1999). Cross-validation of the schedule of racist events. *Journal of Black Psychology, 25,* 231–254.

Klonoff, E. A., Landrine, H., & Campbell, R. (2000). Sexist discrimination may account for well-known

gender differences in psychiatric symptoms. *Psychology of Women Quarterly, 24,* 93–99.

Kluft, R. P. (1999). Current issues in dissociative identity disorder. *Journal of Practical Psychology and Behavioral Health, 5,* 3–19.

Knox, D., Sturdivant, L., & Zusman, M.E. (2001). College student attitudes toward sexual intimacy. *College Student Journal, 35,* 241-243.

Knudsen, D. D. (1991). Child sexual coercion. In E. Grauerholz & M. A. Koralewski (Eds.), *Sexual coercion: A sourcebook on its nature, causes, and prevention* (pp. 17-28). Lexington, MA: Lexington Books.

Kobasa, S. C. (1982). Commitment and coping in stress resistance among lawyers. *Journal of Personality and Social Psychology, 42,* 707–717.

Kochanska, G. (1995). Children's temperament, mothers' discipline, and security of attachment: Multiple pathways to emerging internalization. *Child Development, 66,* 597–615.

Kochanska, G. (1997). Mutually responsive orientation between mothers and their young children: Implications for early socialization. *Child Development, 68,* 94–112.

Koelega, H. S. (1992). Extraversion and vigilance performance: 30 years of inconsistencies. *Psychological Bulletin, 112,* 239–258.

Koff, E., & Rierdan, J. (1995). Early adolescent girls' understanding of menstruation. *Women and Health, 22,* 1–19.

Kohlberg, L. (1969). Stage and sequence: The cognitive-developmental approach to socialization. In D. A. Goslin (Ed.), *Handbook of socialization theory and research* (pp. 347–480). Chicago: Rand McNally.

Kohlberg, L., Levine, C., & Hewer, A. (1983). *Moral stages: A current formulation and a response to critics.* Basel, Switzerland: Karger.

Köhler, W. (1925). *The mentality of apes.* New York: Harcourt Brace.

Kohn, P. M., & Macdonald, J. E. (1992). The survey of recent life experiences: A decontaminated Hassles Scales for adults. *Journal of Behavioral Medicine, 15,* 221–236.

Kolb, B. (1989). Brain development, plasticity, and behavior. *American Psychologist, 44*(9), 1203–1212.

Kolbe, L. (1998, September 18). Cited in poll shows decline in sex by high school students. *The New York Times,* p. A26.

Kolbe, L. J., Collins, J., & Cortese, P. (1997). Building the capacity of schools to improve the health of the nation. *American Psychologist, 52*(3), 256–265.

Konkol, R. J., Murphey, L. J., Ferriero, D. M., Dempsey, D. A., & Olsen, G. D. (1994). Cocaine metabolites in the neonate: Potential for toxicity. *Journal of Child Neurology, 9*(3), 242–248.

Koob, G. F., & Bloom, F. E. (1988). Cellular and molecular mechanisms of drug dependence. *Science, 242,* 715–723.

Kopelman, P. G. (2000). Obesity as a medical problem. *Nature, 404,* 635–643.

Kopta, S. M., Lueger, R. J., Saunders, S. M., & Howard, K. I. (1999). Individual psychotherapy outcome and process research: Challenges leading to greater turmoil or a positive transition? *Annual Review of Psychology, 50,* 441–469.

Koretz, J. F., & Handelman, G. H. (1988). How the human eye focuses. *Scientific American, 259,* 92–99.

Korn, S. J. (1984). Continuities and discontinuities in difficult/easy temperament: Infancy to young adulthood. *Merrill-Palmer Quarterly, 30,* 189–199.

Koskinen, S., Kalviainen, N., & Tuorila, H. (2003). Flavor enhancement as a tool for increasing pleasantness and intake of a snack product among elderly. *Appetite, 41,* 87–96.

Koslowsky, M., & Babkoff, H. (1992). Meta-analysis of the relationship between total sleep deprivation and performance. *Chronobiology International, 9,* 132–136.

Koss, M. P., & Kilpatrick, D. G. (2001). Rape and sexual assault. In E. Gerrity (Ed.), *The mental health consequences of torture* (pp. 177–193). New York: Kluwer Academic/Plenum.

Kosslyn, S. M. (1994). *Image and brain: The resolution of the imagery debate.* Cambridge, MA: MIT Press.

Kosslyn, S. M., Ball, T. M., & Reiser, B. J. (1978). Visual images preserve metric spatial information: Evidence from studies of image scanning. *Journal of Experimental Psychology: Human Perception & Performance, 4,* 47–60.

Kowalski, K. (2003). The emergence of ethnic and racial attitudes in preschool-aged children. *The Journal of Social Psychology, 143,* 677–690.

Kowalski, R. M. (1996). Complaints and complaining: Functions, antecedents, and consequences. *Psychological Bulletin, 119,* 179–196.

Kozart, M. F. (2002). Understanding efficacy in psychotherapy. *American Journal of Orthopsychiatry, 72,* 217–231.

Kraft, J. M. (1996). Prenatal alcohol consumption and outcomes for children: A review of the literature. In R. L. Parrott & C. M. Condit (Eds.), *Evaluating women's health messages: A resource book* (pp. 175–189). Thousand Oaks, CA: Sage.

Kramer, M. S., Cutler, N., Feighner, J., Shrivastava, R., Carman, J., Sramek, J. J., Reines, S. A., Guanghan, L., Snavely, D., Wyatt-Knowles, E., Hale, J., Mills, S. G., MacCoss, M., Swain, C. J., Harrison, T., Hill, R. G., Hefti, F., Scolnick, E. M., Cascieri, M. A., Chicchi, G. G., Sadowski, S., Carlson, E. J., Hargreaves, R. J., & Rupniak, N. M. J. (1998). Distinct mechanism for anti-depressant activity by blockade of central substance P receptor. *Science, 281,* 1640–1645.

Krantz, D. S., & McCeney, M. K. (2002). Effects of psychological and social factors on organic disease: A critical assessment of research on coronary heart disease. *Annual Reviews of Psychology, 53,* 341–369.

Kraut, R. E. (1982). Social presence, facial feedback, and emotion. *Journal of Personality and Social Psychology, 42,* 853–863.

Kreider, R. M., & Fields, J. M. (2002). Number, timing, and duration of marriages and divorces: Fall 1996. *Current Population Reports, P70–80.* Washington, DC: U.S. Census Bureau.

Krijn, M., Emmelkamp, P. M., Olafsson, R. P., & Biemond, R. (2004). Virtual reality exposure therapy of anxiety disorders: A review. *Clinical Psychology Review, 24,* 259–281.

Krosnick, J. A., & Alwin, D. F. (1989). Aging and susceptibility to attitude change. *Journal of Personality and Social Psychology, 57,* 416–425.

Krstic, Z. D., Smoljanic, Z., Vukanic, D., Varinac, D., & Janiic, G. (2000). True hermaphroditism: 10 years' experience. *Pediatric Surgery International, 16,* 580-583.

Krug, D., Davis, T. B., & Glover, J. A. (1990). Massed versus distributed repeated reading: A case of forgetting helping recall. *Journal of Educational Psychology, 82,* 366.371.

Kubler-Ross, E. (1969). *On death and dying.* New York: Macmillan.

Kubler-Ross, E. (1974). *Questions and answers on death and dying.* New York: Macmillan.

Kulka, R. A., Schlenger, W. E., Fairbank, J. A., et al. (1988). *Contractual report of findings from the National Vietnam veterans readjustment study.* Research Triangle Park, NC: Research Triangle Institute.

Kurdek, L. A. (1993). The allocation of household labor in gay, lesbian, and heterosexual married couples. *Journal of Social Issues, 49,* 127–139.

Kurdek, L. A. (1999). The nature and predictors of the trajectory of change in marital quality for husbands and wives over the first 10 years of marriage. *Developmental Psychology, 35,* 1283–1296.

Kurosawa, K. (1993). The effects of self-consciousness and self-esteem on conformity to a majority. *Japanese Journal of Psychology, 63,* 379–387.

Laakmann, G., Schuele, C., Lorkowski, G., Baghai, R., Kuhn, K., & Ehrentraut, S. (1998). Buspirone and lorazepam in the treatment of generalized anxiety disorder in outpatients. *Psychopharmacology, 136,* 357–366.

Lacayo, A. (1995). Neurologic and psychiatric complications of cocaine abuse. *Neuropsychiatry, Neuropsychology, & Behavioral Neurology, 8*(1), 53–60.

Laflamme, D., Pomerleau, A., & Malcuit, G. (2002). A comparison of fathers and mothers involvement in childcare and stimulation behaviors during free-play with their infants at 9 and 15 months. *Sex Roles, 47,* 507–518.

Lagana, L., McGarvey, E. L., Classen, C., & Koopman, C. (2001). Psychosexual dysfunction among gynecological cancer survivors. *Journal of Clinical Psychology in Medical Settings, 8,* 73-84.

Lakatos, K., Nemoda, Z., Birkas, E., Ronai., Kovacs, E., Ney, K., Toth, I., Sasvari-Szekely, M., & Gervai, J. (2003). Association of D4 receptor gene and serotonin transporter promoter polymorphisms with infants' response to novelty. *Molecular Psychiatry, 8,* 90–97.

Lambert, M. J., & Bergen, A. E. (1994). The effectiveness of psychotherapy. In A. E. Bergen & S. L. Garfield (Eds.), *Handbook of psychotherapy and behavior change* (4th ed., pp. 143–189). New York: Wiley.

Lambeth, G. S., & Hallett, M. (2002). Promoting healthy decision making in relationships: Developmental interventions with young adults on college and university campuses. In C. L. & D. R. Atkinson (Eds.), *Counseling across the lifespan: Prevention and treatment* (pp. 209–226). Tousand Oaks, CA: Sage.

Lancet, D. Ben-Arie, N., Cohen, S., Gat, U., Gross-Isseroff, R., Horn-Saban, S., Khen, M., Lehrach, H., Natochin, M., North, M., Seidmann, E., & Walker, N. (1993). Oflactory receptors: Transduction diviersity, human psychophysics and genome analysis. In D. Chadwick, J. Marsh, & J. Goode (Eds.), *The molecular basis of smell and taste transduction* (pp. 131–146). New York: Wiley.

Landabaso, M. A., Iraurgi, I., Sanz, J., Calle, R., Ruiz de Apodaka, J., Jimenez-Lerma, J. M., & Gutierrez-Fraile, M. (1999). *European Journal of Psychiatry, 13,* 97–105.

Landauer, T. K. (1986). How much do people remember? Some estimates of the quantity of learned information in long-term memory. *Cognitive Science, 10,* 477–493.

Landy, S. (2004). Migraine throughout the life cycle: Treatment through the ages. *Neurology, 62,* S2–S8.

Lang, A. J. & Stein, M. B. (2001). Social phobia: Prevalence and diagnostic threshold. *Journal of Clinical Psychiatry, 62*(Suppl. 1), 5–10.

Lang, A., Gottlieb, L. N., & Amsel, R. (1996). Predictors of husbands' and wives' grief reactions following infant death: The role of marital intimacy. *Death Studies, 20,* 33–57.

Langfeldt, T. (1982). Childhood masturbation. In L. L. Constantine & E. M. Martinson (Eds.), *Children and sex* (pp. 63–74). Boston: Little, Brown.

Langlois, J. H., Roggman, L. A., Casey, R. J., Ritter, J. M., Rieser-Danner, L. A., & Jenkins, V. Y. (1987). Infant preferences for attractive faces: Rudiments of a stereotype? *Developmental Psychology, 23,* 363–369.

Langreth, R. (2000, May 1). Every little bit helps: How even moderate exercise can have a big impact on your health. *Wall Street Journal,* p. R5.

Larkin, M. (1998). On the trail of human pheromones. *Lancet, 351,* 809.

Latané, B. & L'Herrou, T. (1996). Spatial clustering in the conformity game: Dynamic social impact in electronic groups. *Journal of Personality and Social Psychology, 70,* 1218–1230.

Latané, B., & Darley, J. (1969). Bystander "apathy." *American Scientist, 57,* 244–268.

Lating, J. M., Sherman, M. F., Everly, G. S., Jr., Lowry, J. L., & Peragine, T. F. (2004). PTSD reactions and functioning of American Airlines flight attendants in the wake of September 11. *Journal of Nervous and Mental Disorders, 192,* 435–441.

Laubmeier, K. K., Zakowski, S. G., & Bair, J. P. (2004). The role of spirituality in the psychological adjustment to cancer. A test of the transactional model of stress and coping. *International Journal of Behavioral Medicine, 11,* 48–55.

Laumann, E. O., Gagnon, J. H., Michael, R. T., & Michaels, S. (1994). *The social organization of sexuality: Sexual practices in the United States.* Chicago: University of Chicago Press.

Laumann, E. O., Paik, A., & Rosen, R. C. (1999). Sexual dysfunction in the United States. *Journal of the American Medical Association, 281,* 537-544.

Lavoie, C., & Desrochers, S. (2002). Visual habituation at five months: Short-term reliability of measures obtained with a new polynomial regression criterion. *Journal of Genetic Psychology, 163,* 261–271.

Lawrie, S. M., & Abukmeil, S. S. (1998). Brain abnormality in schizophrenia: A systematic and quantitative review of volumetric magnetic resonance imaging studies. *British Journal of Psychiatry, 172,* 110–120.

Laws, D. R. (2001). Olfactory aversion: Notes on procedure, with speculations on its mechanism of effect. *Sex Abuse, 13,* 275–287.

Lawson, A. (1988). *Adultery: An analysis of love and betrayal.* New York: Basic Books.

Lazarus, R. S. (1990). Theory-based stress measurement. *Psychological Inquiry, 1,* 3–13.

Lazarus, R. S. (1991). Cognition and motivation in emotion. *American Psychologist, 46,* 352–367.

Lazarus, R. S. (1993). From psychological stress to the emotions: A history of changing outlooks. In L. W. Porter and M. R. Rosenzweig (Eds.), *Annual Review of Psychology, 44,* 1–21.

Lazarus, R. S. (1995). Vexing research problems inherent in cognitive-mediational theories of emotion—and some solutions. *Psychological Inquiry, 6,* 183–197.

Lazarus, R. S., & Folkman, S. (1984). *Stress, appraisal, and coping.* New York: Springer.

Leary, W. E. (1998, September 29). Older people enjoy sex, survey says. *The New York Times,* p. F8.

LeBlanc, J., Ducharme, M. B., & Thompson, M. (2004). Study on the correlation of the autonomic nervous system response to a stressor of high discomfort with personality traits. *Physiology of Behavior, 82,* 647–652.

Lebow, J. L., & Gurman, A. S. (1995). Research assessing couple and family therapy. *Annual Review of Psychology, 46,* 27–57.

Lecanuet, J.-P., Manera, S., & Jacquet, A.-Y. (2002, April). *Fetal cardiac responses to maternal sentences, to playback of these sentences, and to their recordings by another woman's voice.* Paper presented at the XIII International Conference on Infant Studies, Toronto, Ontario, Canada.

LeDoux, J. (1998). Fear and the brain: Where have we been, and where are we going? *Biological Psychiatry, 44,* 1229–1238.

Lee, A. Y. (2001). The mere exposure effect: An uncertainty reduction explanation revisited. *Personality and Social Psychology Bulletin, 27,* 1255–1266.

Lee, H. (1996). *Still life with rice.* New York: Touchstone.

Lee, V. E., & Bryk, A. S. (1986). Effects of single-sex secondary schools on student achievement and attitudes. *Journal of Educational Psychology, 78,* 381–395.

Lefcourt, H. M. (2001). The humor solution. In C. R. Snyder (Ed.), *Coping with stress: Effective people and processes* (pp. 68–92). New York: Oxford University Press.

Lefcourt, H. M., & Davidson-Katz, K. (1991). The role of humor and the self. In C. R. Synder & D. R. Forsyth (Eds.), *Handbook of social and clinical psychology: The health perspective.* New York: Pergamon Press.

Lehrer, P. M., & Woolfolk, R. L. (1993). Specific effects of stress management techniques. In P. M. Lehrer & R. L. Woolfolk (Eds.), *Principles and practice of stress management* (2nd ed.). New York: Guilford Press.

Lehrer, P., Feldman, J., Giardino, N., Song, H. S., & Schmaling, K. (2002). Psychological aspects of asthma. *Journal of Consulting and Clinical Psychology, 70,* 691–711.

Leibowitz, S. F. (1991). Brain neuropeptide Y: An integrator of endocrine, metabolic, and behavioral processes. *Brain Research Bulletin, 27,* 333–337.

Leigh, B. C. (1989). In search of the seven dwarves: Issues of measurement and meaning in alcohol expectancy research. *Psychological Bulletin, 105,* 361–373.

Leitenberg, H., & Henning, K. (1995). Sexual fantasy. *Psychological Bulletin, 117,* 469-496.

Leitenberg, H., Greenwald, E., & Tarran, M. J. (1989). The relation between sexual activity among children during preadolescence and/or early adolescence and sexual behavior and sexual adjustment in young adulthood. *Archives of Sexual Behavior, 18,* 299-313.

Leland, J. (1997, November 17). A pill for impotence? *Newsweek,* pp. 62-68.

Lengagne, T., Jouventin, P., & Aubin, T. (1999). Findings one's mate in a king penguin colony: Efficiency of acoustic communication. *Behavior, 136,* 833–846.

Lenihan, G., Rawlins, M. E., Eberly, C. G., Buckley, B., & Masters, B. (1992). Gender differences in rape supportive attitudes before and after a date rape education intervention. *Journal of College Student Development, 33,* 331-338.

Lenox, R. H., & Manji, H. K. (1995). Lithium. In A. F. Schatzberg & C. B. Nemeroff (Eds.), *The American Psychiatric Press textbook of psychopharmacology.* Washington, DC: American Psychiatric Press.

Leon, S. C., Kopta, S. M., Howard, K. I., & Lutz, W. (1999). Predicting patients' responses to psychotherapy: Are some more predictable than others? *Journal of Consulting & Clinical Psychology, 67,* 698–704.

Leonard, C. M. (1997). Corpus callosum: Sex or size? *Cerebral Cortex, 7,* 2.

LePore, P. C., & Warren, J. R. (1997). A comparison of single-sex and coeducational Catholic secondary schooling: Evidence from the National Educational Longitudinal Study of 1988. *American Educational Research Journal, 34,* 485–511.

Lepore, S. J., Ragan, J. D., & Jones, S. (2000). Talking facilitates cognitive-emotional processes of adaptation to an acute stressor. *Journal of Personality and Social Psychology, 78,* 499–508.

Lesch, K. P., & Merschdorf, U. (2000). Impulsivity, aggression, and serotonin: A molecular psychobiological perspective. *Behavioral Sciences and the Law, 18,* 581–604.

Leshner, A. I. (1997, October 3). Addiction is a brain disease, and it matters. *Science, 278,* 45–47.

Lester, B. M., Corwin, M. J., Sepkoski, C., Seifer, R., Peucker, M., McLaughlin, S., & Golub, H. L. (1991). Neurobehavioral syndromes in cocaine-exposed newborn infants. *Child Development, 62*(4), 694–705.

Lester, D. (1992). Suicide and disease. *Loss, Grief, & Care, 6,* 173–181.

Letourneau, E., & O'Donohue, W. (1993). Sexual desire disorders. In W. O'Donohue & J. H. Geer (Eds.), *Handbook of sexual dysfunctions: Assessment and treatment* (pp. 53-81). Boston: Allyn & Bacon.

LeVay, S. (1996). *Queer science: The use and abuse of research into homosexuality.* Cambridge, MA: MIT Press.

Levenson, R. W., Carstensen, L. L., & Gottman, J. M. (1993). Long-term marriage: Age, gender, and satisfaction. *Psychology and Aging, 8,* 301–313.

Levenson, R. W., Ekman, 00, & Friesen, W. V. (1990). Voluntary facial action generates emotion-specific nervous system activity. *Psychophysiology, 27,* 363–384.

Levine, J. A., & Pittinsky, T. L. (1997). *Working fathers: New strategies for balancing work and family.* Orlando, FL: Harcourt Brace.

Levine, M., & Thompson, K. (2004). Identity, place, and bystander intervention: Social categories and helping after natural disasters. *The Journal of Social Psychology, 144,* 229–245.

Levine, R. A., & Campbell, D. T. (1972). *Ethnocentrism: theories of conflict, ethnic attitudes, and group behavior.* New York: Wiley.

Levinson, D. J. (1978). *The seasons of a man's life.* New York: Knopf.

Levinson, D. J. (1996). *The seasons of a woman's life.* New York: Knopf.

Levitt, A. G., & Utmann, J. G. A. (1992). From babbling towards the sound systems of English and French: A longitudinal two-case study. *Journal of Child Language, 19,* 19–40.

Levy, D., Kimhi, R., Barak, Y., Demmer, M., Harel, M., & Elizur, A. (1996). Brainstem auditory evoked potentials of panic disorder patients. *Neuropsychobiology, 33,* 164–167.

Levy, G. D., Taylor, M. G., & Gelman, S. A. (1995). Traditional and evaluative aspects of flexibility in gender roles, social conventions, moral rules, and physical laws. *Child Development, 66,* 515–531.

Levy, N. A., & Janicak, P. G. (2000). Calcium channel antagonists for the treatment of bipolar disorder. *Bipolar Disorders, 2,* 108–119.

Levy-Shiff, R. (1994). Individual and contextual correlates of marital change across the transition to parenthood. *Developmental Psychology, 30,* 591–601.

Lewinsohn, P. M. (1974). A behavioral approach to depression. In R. J. Friedman & M. M. Katz (Eds.), *The psychology of depression: Contemporary theory and research.* Washington, DC: Winston-Wiley.

Lewinsohn, P. M., Clark, G. N., Hops, H., & Andrews, J. (1990). Cognitive-behavioral treatment for depressed adolescents. *Behavior Therapy, 21,* 385–401.

Lewinsohn, P. M., Klein, D. N., & Seeley, J. R. (2000). Bipolar disorder during adolescence and young adulthood in a community sample. *Bipolar Disorders, 2,* 281–293.

Lewinsohn, P. M., Rohde, P., & Seeley, J. R. (1994). Psychosocial risk factors for future adolescent suicide attempts. *Journal of Consulting & Clinical Psychology, 62,* 297–305.

Lewis, C. (2000). *A man's place in the home: Fathers and families in the UK.* York: Joseph Roundtree Foundation/YPS.

Lewis, D. O. (1992). From abuse to violence: Psychophysiological consequences of maltreatment. *Journal of the American Academy of Child and Adolescent Psychiatry, 31,* 383–391.

Lewis, D. O., Picus, J. H., Feldman, M., Jackson, L., & Bard, B. (1986). Psychiatric, neurological, and psychoeducational characteristics of 15 death row inmates in the United States. *American Journal of Psychiatry, 143,* 838–845.

Li, D.K., Liu, L., & Odouli, R. (2003). Exposure to nonsteroidal anti-inflammatory drugs during pregnancy and risk of miscarriage: Population based cohort study. *BMJ, 327,* 368–372.

Li, S., Lindenberger, U., Hommel, B., Aschersleben, G., Prinz, W., & Baltes, P. B. (2004). Transformations in the couplings among intellectual abilities and constituent cognitive processes across the life span. *Psychological Science, 15,* 155–163.

Libersat, F., & Pflueger, H.-J. (2004). Monoamines and the orchestration of behavior. *BioScience, 54,* 17–25.

Lichtenstein, E. (1982). The smoking problem: A behavioral perspective. *Journal of Consulting & Clinical Psychology, 50,* 804–819.

Lieberman, J., Chakos, M., Wu, H., Alvir, J., Hoffman, E., Robinson, D., & Bilder, R. (2001). Longitudinal study of brain morphology in first episode schizophrenia. *Biological Psychiatry, 49,* 487–499.

Liebert, R. M., & Spiegler, M. D. (1998). *Personality: Strategies and issues* (8th ed.), Pacific Grove, CA: Brooks/Cole.

Lilienfeld, S. O., Wood, J. M., & Garb, H. N. (2000). The scientific status of projective techniques. *Psychological Science in the Public Interest, 1,* 27–66.

Lillard, L. A., & Panis, C. W. A. (1996). Marital status and mortality: The role of health. *Demography, 33,* 313–327.

Lino, M. (2000). *Expenditures on children by families, 1999 annual report.* Washington, DC: U.S. Department of Agriculture, Center for Nutrition Policy and Promotion. Miscellaneous Publication No. 1528–1999.

Linville, P. W., Fischer, G. W., & Salovey, P. (1989). Perceived distributions of characteristics on in-group and out-group members: Empirical evidence and a computer simulation. *Journal of Personality and Social Psychology, 57,* 165–188.

Lipsitt, L.P. (2003). Crib death: A biobehavioral phenomenon? *Current Directions in Psychological Science, 12,* 164–170.

Livesley, W. J., Jang, K. L., & Vernon, P. A. (1998). Phenotypic and genotypic structure of traits delineating personality disorder. *Archives of General Psychiatry, 55,* 941–948.

Livesley, W. J., Schroeder, M. L., Jackson, D. N., & Jang, K. L. (1994). Categorical distinctions in the study of personality disorder: Implications for classification. *Journal of Abnormal Psychology, 103,* 6–17.

Livson, N., & Peskin, H. (1980). Perspectives on adolescence from longitudinal research. In J. Adelson (Ed.), *Handbook of adolescent psychology.* New York: Wiley.

Lloyd, G., Alexander, A. A., Rice, D. G., & Greenfield, N. S. (1980). Life events as predictors of academic performance. *Journal of Human Stress, 6,* 15–26.

Lockhart, R. S., & Craik, F. I. M. (1990). Levels of processing: A retrospective commentary on a framework for memory research. *Canadian Journal of Psychology, 44,* 87–112.

Lodewijkx, H. F., & Syroit, J. E. M. M. (2001). Affiliation during naturalistic severe and mild initiations: Some further evidence against the severity-attraction hypothesis [Special Issue]. *Current Research in Social Psychology, 6,* 90–107.

Loehlin, J. C., & Nichols, R. C. (1976). *Heredity, environment, and personality.* Austin: University of Texas Press.

Loewenstein, W. R. (1960). Biological transducers. *Scientific American, 203,* 98–108.

Loftus, E. F. (1979). *Eyewitness testimony.* Cambridge, MA: Harvard University Press.

Loftus, E. F. (2000). Remembering what never happened. In E. Tulving (Ed.), *Memory, consciousness, and the brain* (pp. 106–118). Philadelphia, PA: Psychology Press.

Loftus, E. F., & Palmer, J. C. (1974). Reconstruction of automobile destruction: An example of the interaction between language and memory. *Journal of Verbal Learning and Verbal Behavior, 13,* 585–589.

Loftus, E. F., & Zanni, G. (1975). Eyewitness testimony: The influence of the wording of a question. *Bulletin of the Psychonomic Society, 5,* 86–88.

Logie, R. H. (1996). The seven ages of working memory. In J. T. E. Richardson, R.W. Engle, L. Hasher, R. H. Logie, E. R. Stoltzfus, & R. T Zacks (Eds.), *Working memory and human cognition* (pp. 31–65). Oxford: Oxford University Press.

Logie, R. H. (1999). State of the art: Working memory. *The Psychologist, 12,* 174–178.

Logue, A. W. (1979). Taste aversion and the generality of the laws of learning. *Psychological Bulletin, 86,* 276–296.

Long, B. C., & van Stavel, R. (1995). Effects of exercise training on anxiety: A meta-analysis. *Journal of Applied Sport Psychology, 7,* 167–189.

Longman, J. (2002). *Among the heroes: United Flight 93 and the passengers and crew who fought back.* New York: HarperCollins.

LoPiccolo, J., & Stock, W. E. (1986). Treatment of sexual dysfunction. *Journal of Consulting and Clinical Psychology, 54,* 158-167.

Lorenz, F. O., Simons, R. L., Conger, R. D., Elder, G. H., Jr., Johnson, C., & Chao, W. (1997). Married and recently divorced mothers' stressful events and distress: Tracing change across time. *Journal of Marriage and the Family, 59,* 219–232.

Lourenco, O., & Machado, A. (1996). In defense of Piaget's theory: A reply to 10 common criticisms. *Psychological Review, 103,* 143–164.

Lu, N. Z., Eshleman, A. J., Janowsky, A. & Bethea, C. L. (2003). Ovarian steroid regulation of serotonin reuptake transporter (SERT) binding, distribution, and function in female macaques. *Molecular Psychiatry, 8,* 353–360.

Luce, R. D. (1993). *Sound & hearing: A conceptual introduction.* Hillsdale, NJ: Erlbaum.

Luecken, L. J., & Compas, B. E. (2002). Stress, coping, and immune function in breast cancer. *Annals of Behavioral Medicine, 24,* 336–344.

Lumer, E. D., Friston, K. J., & Rees, G. (1998, June 19). Neural correlates of perceptual rivalry in the human brain. *Science, 280,* 1930–1934.

Luna, T. D., French, J., & Mitcha, J. I. (1997). A study of USAF air traffic controller shiftwork: Sleep, fatigue, activity, and mood analyses. *Aviation, Space, and Environmental Medicine, 68,* 18–23.

Luszcz, M. A., Bryan, J., & Kent, P. (1997). Predicting episodic memory performance of very old men and women: Contributions from age, depression, activity, cognitive ability, and speed. *Psychology and Aging, 12,* 340–351.

Lykken, D. T., McGue, M., Tellegen, A., & Bouchard, T. J. (1992). Emergenesis. *American Psychologist, 47,* 1565–1567.

Lynch, W. J., Roth, M. E., & Carroll, M. E. (2002). Biological basis of sex differences in drug abuse: Preclinical and clinical studies. *Psychopharmacology, 164,* 121–137.

Lynn, S. J. (1997). Automaticity and hypnosis: A sociocognitive account. *International Journal of Clinical and Experimental Hypnosis, 45,* 239–250.

Lytton, H., & Romney, D. M. (1991). Parents' differential socialization of boys and girls: A meta-analysis. *Psychological Bulletin, 109,* 267–296.

Maas, J. B. (1998). *The sleep advantage: Preparing your mind for peak performance.* New York: Villard.

Maccoby, E. E., & Jacklin, C. N. (1974). *The psychology of sex differences.* Stanford, CA: Stanford University Press.

MacIntyre, G. F. (1998). And what's keeping you from finishing your book? *Writer's Digest, 78,* 6.

Mackay, J. (2000). *The Penguin atlas of human sexual behavior: Sexuality and sexual practices around the world.* New York: Penguin Putnam.

Mackey, W. C. (1996). Fathers in the 1990's: Dr. Jekyll and Mr. Hyde. In *The American father: Biocultural and developmental aspects* (pp. 127–136). New York: Plenum Press.

MacKinnon, D., Jamison, K. R., & DePaulo, J. R. (1997). Genetics of manic depressive illness. *Annual Review of Neuroscience, 20,* 355–373.

Macmillian, N. A., & Creelman, C. D. (1991). *Detection theory: A user's guide.* Cambridge: Cambridge University Press.

Macrae, C. N., & Milne, A. B. (1992). A curry for your thoughts: Empathetic effects on counterfactual thinking. *Personality and Social Psychology Bulletin, 18,* 625–630.

Maddi, S. R., & Kobasa, S. C. (1984). *The hardy executive: Health under stress.* Homewood, IL: Dorsey Press.

Magley, V. J. (2002). Coping with sexual harassment: Reconceptualizing women's resistance. *Journal of Personality and Social Psychology, 83,* 930-946.

Magley, V. J., Hulin, C. L., Fitzgerald, L. F., & DeNardo, M. (1999). Outcomes of self-labeling sexual harassment. *Journal of Applied Psychology, 84,* 390-402.

Maguire, E. A., Gadian, D. G., Johnsrude, I. S., Good, C. D., Ashburner, J., Frackowiak, R. S. J., & Firth, C. D. (2000). Navigation-related structural change in the hippocampi of taxi drivers. *Proceedings of the National Academy of Sciences, USA, 97,* 4398–4403.

Magura, S., Laudet, A.B., Mahmood, D., Rosenblum, A., & Knight, E. (2002). Adherence to medication regimes and participation in dual-focus self-help groups. *Psychiatric Services, 53,* 310–316.

Maisonneuve, J., Palmade, G., & Fourment, C. (1952). Selective choices and propinquity. *Sociometry, 15,* 135–140.

Maj, M., Pirozzi, R., Magliano, L., & Bartoli, L. (1997). Long-term outcome of lithium prophylaxis in bipolar disorder: A 5-year prospective study of 402 patients at a lithium clinic. *American Journal of Psychiatry, 155,* 30–55.

Maki, M. T., & Kitano, H. H. (2002). Counseling Asian Americans. In P. B. Pedersen, J. G. Draguns, W. J. Lonner, & J. E. Trimble (Eds.), *Counseling across cultures* (5th ed., pp. 109–132). Thousand Oaks, CA: Sage Publications.

Maletzky, B. (1998). The paraphilias: Research and treatment. In P. E. Nathan (Ed.), *A guide to treatments that work* (pp. 472-500). New York: Oxford University Press.

Malina, R. M. (1990). Physical growth and performance during the transitional years (9–16). In R. Montemayor, G. R. Adams, & T. P. Gullotta (Eds.), *From childhood to adolescence: A transitional period?* (pp. 41–62). Newbury Park, CA: Sage.

Malone, K., & Mann, J. J. (1993). Serotonin and major depression. In J. J. Mann & D. J. Kupfer (Eds.), *Biology of depressive disorders: Part A. A systems perspective* (pp. 29–49). New York: Plenum.

Maltz, W. (2002). Treating the sexual intimacy concerns of sexual abuse survivors. *Sexual and Relationship Therapy, 17,* 321-327.

Maltz, W., & Boss, S. (2001). *Private thoughts: Exploring the power of women's sexual fantasies.* Novato, CA: New World Library.

Mann, J. (1991, March 29). Kuwaiti rape a doubly savage crime. *Washington Post,* p. C3.

Manson, S., Beals, J., O'Nell, T., Piasecki, J., Bechtold, D., Keane, E., & Jones, M. (1996). Wounded spirits, ailing hearts: PTSD and related disorders among American Indians. In A. J. Marsella, M. J. Friedman, E. T. Gerrity, & R. M. Scurfield (Eds.), *Ethnocultural aspects of posttraumatic stress disorder* (pp. 255–283). Washington DC: American Psychiatric Press.

Manuck, S. B., Flory, J. D., Ferrell, R. E., Mann, J. J., Muldoon, M. F. (2000). A regulatory polymorphism of the monoamine oxidase-A gene may be associated with the variability in aggression, impulsivity, and central nervous system serotonergic responsivity. *Psychiatry Research, 95,* 9–23.

Marañon, I., Echeburúa, E., & Grijalvo, J. (2004). Prevalence of personality disorders in patients with eating disorders: A pilot study using the IPDE. *European Eating Disorders Review, 12,* 217–222.

Marazziti, D., Rotondo, A., Presta, S., Pancioloi-Guasagnucci, M. L., Palego, L., & Conti, L. (1993). Role of serotonin in human aggressive behavior. *Aggressive Behavior, 19,* 347–353.

Marcia, J. E. (1966). Development and validation of ego identity status. *Journal of Personality and Social Psychology, 21,* 551–559.

Marcia, J. E. (1968). The case history of a construct: Ego identity status. In E. Vinache (Ed.), *Readings in general psychology.* New York: American Book.

Marcia, J. E. (1980). Identity in adolescence. In J. Adelson (Ed.), *Handbook of adolescent psychology* (pp. 159–187). New York: Wiley.

Marcia, J. E. (1993). The relational roots of identity. In J. Kroger (Ed.), *Discussions on ego identity* (pp. 101–120). Hillsdale, NJ: Erlbaum.

Marcia, J. E. (2002). Identity and psychosocial development in adulthood. *Identity, 2,* 7–28.

Mareschal, D. (2000). Object knowledge in infancy: Current controversies and approaches. *Trends in Cognitive Science, 4,* 408–416.

Marijuana as medicine: How strong is the science? (1997, May). *Consumer Reports,* pp. 62–63.

Marler, P. R., Duffy, A., & Pickert, R. (1986). Vocal communication in the domestic chicken: II. Is a sender sensitive to the presence and nature of a receiver? *Animal Behavior, 34,* 194–198.

Marsh, A. A., Elfenbein, H. A., & Ambady, N. (2003). Nonverbal "Accents": Cultural differences in facial expressions of emotion. *Psychological Science, 14,* 373–376.

Martin, C. L., & Halverson, C. F. (1981). A schematic processing model of sex typing and stereotyping in children. *Child Development, 52,* 1119–1134.

Martin, C. L., & Halverson, C. F. (1987). The role of cognition in sex role acquisition. In D. B. Carter (Ed.), *Current conceptions of sex roles and sex typing: Theory and research* (pp. 123–137). New York: Praeger.

Martin, C. L., & Ruble, D. (2004). Children's search for gender cues: Cognitive perspectives on gender development. *Current Directions in Psychological Science, 13,* 67–70.

Martin, D. J., Garske, J. P., & Davis, M. K. (2000). Relation of the therapeutic alliance with outcome and other variables: A meta-analytic review. *Journal of Consulting & Clinical Psychology, 68,* 438–450.

Martin, G. L., England, G., Kaprowy, E., Kilgour, K., & Pilek, V. (1968). Operant conditioning of kindergarten-class behavior in autistic children. *Behavior Research and Therapy, 6,* 281–294.

Martin, G., & Pear, J. (1983). *Behavior modification: What it is and how to do it.* (2nd ed.). Englewood Cliffs, NJ: Prentice Hall.

Martin, L. (1986). Eskimo words for snow: A case study on the genesis and decay of an anthropological example. *American Anthropologist, 88,* 418–423.

Martin, P. D., Specter, G., Martin, D., & Martin, M. (2003). Expressed attitudes of adolescents toward marriage and family life. *Adolescence, 38,* 359-367.

Maslach, C., Stapp, J., & Santee, R. T. (1985). Individuation: Conceptual analysis and assessment. *Journal of Social and Personality Psychology, 49,* 729–738.

Masland, R. H. (1996, February 2). Unscrambling color vision. *Science, 271,* 616–617.

Maslow, A. (1968). *Toward a psychology of being* (2nd ed.). New York: Van Nostrand.

Maslow, A. (1970). *Motivation and personality* (2nd ed.). New York: Harper & Row.

Maslow, A. (1971). *The farther reaches of human nature.* New York: Viking.

Masters, W. H., & Johnson, V. E. (1966). *Human sexual response.* Boston: Little, Brown.

Masters, W. H., Johnson, V. E., & Kolodny, R. C. (1993). *Biological foundations of human sexuality.* New York: HarperCollins.

Mathew, R., Wilson, W., Blazer, D., & George, L. (1993). Psychiatric disorders in adult children of alcoholics: Data from the epidemiologic catchment area project. *American Journal of Psychiatry, 150*(5), 793–796.

Matlin, M. W., & Foley, H. J. (1997). *Sensation and perception.* Boston: Allyn & Bacon.

Matsuda, L. A., Lolait, S. J., Brownstein, M. J., Young, A. C., & Bonner, T. I. (1990). Structure of a cannabinoid receptor and functional expression of the cloned cDNA. *Nature, 346,* 561–564.

Matsumoto, D. (1994). *People: Psychology from a cross-cultural perspective.* Pacific Grove, CA: Brooks/Cole.

Maxmen, J. S., & Ward, N. G. (1995). *Essential psychopathology and its treatment* (2nd ed.). New York: Norton.

Mayer, R. E. (1983). *Thinking, problem solving, cognition.* San Francisco: Freeman.

Mayes, L. C., Bornstein, M. H., Chawarska, K., & Haynes, O. M. (1996). Impaired regulation of arousal in 3-month-old infants exposed prenatally to cocaine and other drugs. *Development & Psychopathology, 8*(1), 29–42.

Maypole, D. (1987). Sexual harassment at work: A review of research and theory. *Affilia: Journal of Women & Social Work, 2,* 24-38.

Mays, V. M., & Cochran, S. D. (2001). Mental health correlates of perceived discrimination among lesbian, gay, and bisexual adults in the United States. *American Journal of Public Health, 91,* 1869–1876.

Maziade, M., Caron, C., Cote, R., Merette, C., Bernier, H., Laplante, B., Boutin, P., & Thivierge, J. (1990). Psychiatric status of adolescents who had extreme temperaments at age 7. *American Journal of Psychiatry, 147,* 1531–1536.

Mazure, C. M., Keita, G. P., & Blehar, M. C. (2002). *Summit on women and depression: Proceedings and recommendations.* Washington, DC: American Psychological Association.

McAndrew, F. (1986). A cross-cultural study of recognition thresholds for facial expressions of emotions. *Journal of Cross-Cultural Psychology, 17,* 211–224.

McBride, B. A., & Darragh, J. (1995). Interpreting the data on father involvement: Implications for parenting programs for men. *Families in Society, 76,* 490–497.

McBride, J. (1996). *The color of water: A black man's tribute to his white mother.* New York: Riverhead Books.

McBurney, D. H. (1978). Psychological dimensions and perceptual analysis of taste. In E. C. Carterette & M. P. Friedman (Eds.), *Handbook of perception* (pp. 125–155). New York: Academic Press.

McCabe, M. (1987). Desired and experienced levels of premarital affection and sexual intercourse during dating. *Journal of Sex Research, 23,* 23-33.

McCarley, R. W. (1998). Dreams: Disguise of forbidden wishes or transparent reflections of a distinct brain state? *Annals of the New York Academy of Sciences, 843,* 116–133.

McCarthy, B. W. (2001). Relapse prevention strategies and techniques with erectile dysfunction. *Journal of Sex and Marital Therapy, 27,* 1-8.

McClelland, D. C. (1987). *Human motivation.* Cambridge: Cambridge University Press.

McCloskey, M., Wible, C. G., & Cohen, N. J. (1988). Is there a special flashbulb-memory mechanism? *Journal of Experimental Psychology: General, 117,* 171–181.

McClure, E. B. (2000). A meta-analytic review of sex differences in facial expression processing and their development in infants, children, and adolescents. *Psychological Bulletin, 126,* 424–453.

McConkey, K. M. (1995). Hypnosis, memory, and the ethics of uncertainty. *Australian Psychologist, 30,* 1–10.

McCourt, F. (1996). *Angela's ashes.* New York: Scribner.

McCourt, F. (1999). *Tis.* New York: Scribner.

McCrae, R. R., & Costa, P. T., Jr. (1998). Personality trait structure as a human universal. *American Psychologist, 52,* 509–516.

McCrae, R. R., Costa, P. T., Jr., Pedroso de Lima, M., Simoes, A., Ostendorf, F., Angleitner, A., Marusic, I., Bratko, D., Caprara, G. V., Barbaranelli, C., Chae, J. H., & Piedmont, R. L. (1999). Age differences in personality across the adult life span: Parallels in five cultures. *Developmental Psychology, 35,* 466–477.

McCrae, R. R., Costa, P. T., Ostendorf, F., Angleitner, A., Hrebickova, M., Avia, M. D., Sanz, J., Sanchez-Bernardos, M. L., Kusdil, M. E., Woodfield, R., Saunders, P. R., & Smith, P. B. (2000). Nature over nurture: Temperament, personality, and life span development. *Journal of Personality and Social Psychology, 78,* 173–186.

McCrae, R. R., Costa, P. T., Terracciano, A., Parker, W. D., Mills, C. J., De Fruyt, F., Mervielde, I. (2002). Personality trait development from age 12 to age 18: Longitudinal, cross-sectional, and cross-cultural analyses. *Journal of Personality and Social Psychology, 83,* 1456–1468.

McCrae, S. (1997). Cohabitation: A trial run for marriage? *Sexual and Marital Therapy, 12,* 259–273.

McDonald, C., & Murphy, K. C. (2003). The new genetics of schizophrenia. *The Psychiatric Clinics of North America, 26,* 41–63.

McFalls, J. A., Jr. (1990). The risks of reproductive impairment in the later years of childbearing. *Annual Review of Sociology, 16,* 491–519.

McGehee, D. S., Heath, M. J. S., Gelber, S., Devay, P., & Role, L. W. (1995). Nicotine enhancement of fast excitation synaptic transmissions in CNS by presynaptic receptors. *Science, 269,* 1692–1696.

McGinnis, J. M., & Foege, W. H. (1993). Actual causes of death in the United States. *Journal of the American Medical Association, 270,* 2207–2212.

McGlashan, T. H. (1988). A selective review of recent North American long-term followup studies of schizophrenia. *Schizophrenia Bulletin, 14,* 515–542.

McGlashan, T. H., & Hoffman, R. E. (2000). Schizophrenia as a disorder of developmentally reduced synaptic connectivity. *Archives of General Psychiatry, 57,* 637–648.

McGrady, A. V., Bush, E. G., & Grubb, B. P. (1997). Outcome of biofeedback-assisted relaxation for neurocardiogenic syncope and headache: A clinical replication series. *Applied Psychophysiology and Biofeedback, 22,* 63–72.

McGreal, D., Evans, B. J., & Burrows, G. D. (1997). Gender differences in coping following loss of a child through miscarriage or stillbirth: A pilot study. *Stress Medicine, 13,* 159–165.

McGregor, G. 00, Desaga, J. F., Ehlenz, K., Fischer, A., Heese, F, Hegele, A., Lammer, C., Peiser, C., & Lang, R. E. (1996). Radioimmunological measurement of leptin in plasma of obese and diabetic human subjects. *Endocrinology, 137,* 1501–1504.

McGuire, A. M. (1994). Helping behaviors in the natural environment: Dimensions and correlates of helping. *Personality and Social Psychology Bulletin, 20,* 45–56.

McIntosh, D. N. (1996). Facial feedback hypotheses: Evidence, implications, and directions. *Motivation and Emotion, 20,* 121–147.

McKean, K. J. (1994). Using multiple risk factors to assess the behavioral, cognitive, and affective effects of learned helplessness. *Journal of Psychology, 128*(2), 177–183.

McKillip, J., & Reidel, S. L. (1983). External validity of matching on physical attractiveness for same and opposite sex couples. *Journal of Applied Social Psychology, 13,* 328–337.

McKim, W. A. (1997). *Drugs and behavior.* Upper Saddle River, NJ: Prentice Hall.

McKnight Investigators. (2003). Risk factors for the onset of eating disorders in adolescent girls: The results of the McKnight longitudinal risk factor study. *American Journal of Psychiatry, 160,* 248–254.

McMillen, D. L., Smith, S. M., & Wells-Parker, E. (1989). The effects of alcohol, expectancy, and sensation seeking on driving risk taking. *Addictive Behaviors, 14,* 477–483.

McNaughton, P. A. (1990). The light response of photoreceptors. In C. Blakemore (Ed.), *Vision: Coding and efficiency* (pp. 65–73). Cambridge: Cambridge University Press.

McSweeney, F. K., & Swindell, S. (2002). Common processes may contribute to extinction and habituation. *The Journal of General Psychology, 129,* 364–400.

Mediascope, Inc. (1996). *National television violence study.* Studio City, CA: Author.

Medin, D. L. (1989). Concepts and conceptual structure. *American Psychologist, 44,* 1469–1481.
Mednick, S. A., Machon, R. A., Huttunen, M. O., & Bonett, D. (1988). Adult schizophrenia following prenatal exposure to an influenza epidemic. *Archives of General Psychiatry, 45,* 189–192.
Mednick, S. A., Watson, J. B., Huttunen, M., Cannon, T. D., Katila, H., Machon, R., Mednick, B., Hollister, M., Parnas, J., Schulsinger, F., Sajaniemi, N., Voldsgaard, P., Pyhala, R., Gutkind, D., & Wang, X. (1998). A two-hit working model of the etiology of schizophrenia. In M. F. Lenzenweger & R. H. Dworkin (Eds.), *Origins of the development of schizophrenia* (pp. 27–66). Washington, DC: American Psychological Association.
Meissner, J. S., Blanchard, E. B., & Malamood, H. S. (1997). Comparison of treatment outcome measures for irritable bowel syndrome. *Applied Psychophysiology and Biofeedback, 22,* 55–62.
Melke, J., Landen, M., Baghei, F., Rosmond, R., Holm, G., Bjorntorp, P., Westberg, L., Hellstrand, M., & Eriksson, E. (2001). Serotonin transporter gene polymorphisms are associated with anxiety-related personality traits in women. *American Journal of Medical Genetics, 105,* 458–463.
Melzack, R., & Wall, P. D. (1988). *The challenge of pain* (2nd. ed.). London: Penguin.
Memmler, R. L., Cohen, B. J., & Wood, D. (1992). *Structure and function of the human body* (5th ed.). Philadelphia: J. B. Lippincott.
Mennella, J. A., & Beauchamp, G. K. (1991). Maternal diet alters the sensory qualities of human milk and nursling's behavior. *Pediatrics, 88,* 737–744.
Menon, V., Mackenzie, K., Rivera, S. M., & Reiss, A. L. (2002). Prefrontal cortex involvement in processing incorrect arithmetic equations: Evidence from event-related fMRI. *Human Brain Mapping, 16,* 119–130.
Menzies, R. G., & Clark, J. C. (1993). A comparison of *in vivo* and vicarious exposure in the treatment of childhood water phobia. *Behaviour Research & Therapy, 31,* 9–15.
Mergenhagen, P. (1996). Her own boss. *American Demographics, 18,* 36–41.
Merritt, J. M., Stickgold, R., Pace-Schott, E., Williams, J., & Hobson, J. A. (1994). Emotion profiles in the dreams of men and women. *Consciousness & Cognition, 3*(1), 46–60.
Meschke, L. L., Bartholomae, S., & Zentall, S. R. (2000). Adolescent sexuality and parent-adolescent processes: Promoting healthy teen choices. *Family Relations, 49,* 143-155.
Meston, C. M., Trapnell, P. D., & Gorzalka, B. B. (1996). Ethnic and gender differences in sexuality: Variations in sexual behavior between Asian and non-Asian university students. *Archives of Sex Behavior, 25,* 33-71.
Meyer, L. (1999). Hostile classrooms. *The Advocate, 32*(1), 33-35.
Michael, G. A., Boucart, M., Degreef, J. F., & Goefroy, O. (2001). The thalamus interrupts top-down attentional control for permitting exploratory shiftings to sensory signals. *Neuroreport, 12,* 2041–2048.
Michael, R. T., Gagnon, J. H., Lauman, E. O., & Kolata, G. (1994). *Sex in America: A definitive survey.* Boston: Little, Brown.
Michelson, D., Bancroft, J., Targum, S., Kim, Y., & Tepner, R. (2000). Female sexual dysfunction associated with antidepressant administration: A randomized, placebo-controlled study of pharmacological intervention. *American Journal of Psychiatry, 157,* 239–243.
Mignot, E. (1997). Behavioral genetics '97: Genetics of narcolepsy and other sleep disorders. *American Journal of Human Genetics, 60,* 1289–1302.
Milgram, S. (1963). Behavioral study of obedience. *Journal of Abnormal and Social Psychology, 67,* 371–378.
Milgram, S. (1965). Some conditions of obedience and disobedience to authority. *Human Relations, 18,* 57–76.
Milgram, S. (1974). *Obedience to authority: An experimental view.* New York: Harper & Row.
Millar, M. (2002). The effectiveness of the door-in-the-face compliance strategy on friends and strangers. *The Journal of Social Psychology, 142,* 295–305.
Millar, M. G., & Tessar, A. (1986). Effects of affective and cognitive focus on the attitude-behavior relation. *Journal of Personality and Social Psychology, 51,* 270–276.
Miller, D. D., Perry, P. J., Cadoret, R. J., & Andreasen, N. C. (1994). Clozapine's effect on negative symptoms in treatment-refractory schizophrenics. *Comprehensive Psychiatry, 35,* 8–15.
Miller, D. T., & Ross, M. (1975). Self-serving biases in the attribution of causality: Fact or fiction? *Psychological Bulletin, 82,* 213–225.
Miller, E. (1999). The pheromone androsterol: Evolutionary considerations. *Mankind Quarterly, 39,* 455–466.
Miller, G. A. (1956). The magical number seven, plus or minus two: Some limits on our capacity for processing information. *Psychological Review, 63,* 81–97.
Miller, I. J., Jr., & Bartoshuk, L. M. (1991). Taste perception, taste bud distribution, and spatial relationships. In T. V. Gethell, R. L. Doty, L. M. Bartoshuk, & J. B. Snow, Jr. (Eds.), *Smell and taste in health and disease* (pp. 205–233). New York: Raven.
Miller, L. C., & Fishkin, S. A. (1997). On the dynamics of human bonding and reproductive success: Seeking windows on the adapted-for human-environmental interface. In J. A. Simpson & D. T. Kenrick (Eds.), *Evolutionary social psychology* (pp. 197-236). Hillsdale, NJ: Erlbaum.
Miller, N. S., & Gold, M. S. (1994). LSD and Ecstasy: Pharmacology, phenomenology, and treatment. *Psychiatric Annals, 24,* 131–133.
Miller, R. B., Hemesath, K., & Nelson, B. (1997). Marriage in middle and later life. In T. D. Hargrave & S. M. Hanna (Eds.), *The aging family: New visions in theory, practice, and reality* (pp. 178–198). New York: Brunner/Mazel.
Miller, T. Q., Smith, T. W., Turner, C. W., Guijarro, M. L., & Hallet, A. J. (1996). A meta- analytic review of research on hostility and physical health. *Psychological Bulletin, 119,* 322–348.
Miller, T. Q., Turner, C. W., Tindale, R. S., Posavac, E. J., & Dugoni, B. L. (1991). Reasons for the trend toward null findings in research on Type A behavior. *Psychological Bulletin, 110,* 469–485.
Miller, W. R., & Seligman, M. E. P. (1975). Depression and learned helplessness in man. *Journal of Abnormal Psychology, 84,* 228–238.
Miller, W. R., & Thoresen, C. E. (2003). Spirituality, religion, and health. An emerging research field. *American Psychologist, 58,* 24–35.
Milner, B. (1962). Les troubles de la memoire accompagnant des lesions hippocampiques bilaterales. In P. Passonant (Ed.), *Physiologie de l'hippocampe.* Paris: Centre National de la Récherche Scientifique.
Milton, C., & Pasley, K., (1996). Fathers' parenting role identity and father involvement: A comparison of nondivorced and divorced, nonresident fathers. *Journal of Family Issues, 17,* 26–45.
Mindell, J. A. (1997). Children and sleep. In M. R. Pressman & W. C. Orr (Eds.), *Understanding sleep: The evaluation and treatment of sleep disorders.* Washington DC: American Psychological Association.
Mischel, W., & Shoda, Y. (1995). A cognitive-affective system theory of personality: Reconceptualizing situations, dispositions, dynamics, and invariance of personality structure. *Psychological Review, 102,* 246–268.
Miselis, R. R., & Epstein, A. N. (1970). Feeding induced by 2-deoxy-D-glucose injections into the lateral ventrical of the rat. *Physiologist, 13,* 262.
Miyaoka, Y., Sawada, M., Sakaguchi, T., & Shingai, T. (1987). Sensation of thirst in normal and laryngectomized man. *Perceptual and Motor Skills, 64,* 239–242.
Moffitt, T. E., Brammer, G. L., Caspi, A., Fawcet, J. P., Raleigh, M., Yuwiler, A., & Silva, P. A. (1998). Whole blood serotonin relates to violence in an epidemiological study. *Biological Psychiatry, 43,* 446–457.
Mohr, C. (1964, March 28). Apathy is puzzle in Queens killing. *The New York Times,* pp. 21, 40.
Molero, F., Navas, M. S., Gonzalez, J. L., Aleman, P., & Cuadrado, I. (2003). Paupers or riches: The perception of immigrants, tourists and ingroup members in a sample of Spanish children. *Journal of Ethnic and Migration Studies, 29,* 501–517.
Moncrieff, J. (1997). Lithium: Evidence reconsidered. *British Journal of Psychiatry, 171,* 113–119.
Money, J., & Ehrhardt, A. (1972). *Man and woman, boy and girl.* Baltimore: Johns Hopkins University Press.
Monteith, M., & Winters, J. (2002, May–June). Why we hate; we may not admit it, but we are plagued with xenophobic tendencies. Our hidden prejudices run so deep, we are quick to judge, fear and even hate the unknown. *Psychology Today, 35,* 44–51.
Monti-Bloch, L., Diaz-Sanchez, V., Jennings-White, C., & Berliner, D. L. (1998). Modulation of serum testosterone and autonomic function through stimuluation of the male human vomeronasal organ (VNO) with pregna-4, 20-diene-3, 6-dione. *The Journal of Steroid Biochemistry and Molecular Biology, 65,* 237–242.
Mooney, D. K., Fromme, K., Kivlahan, D. R., & Marlatt, G. A. (1987). Correlates of alcohol consumption: Sex, age, and expectancies relate differentially to quantity and frequency. *Addictive Behaviors, 12,* 235–240.
Moore, E. G. J. (1986). Family socialization and the IQ test performance of traditionally and transracially adopted black children. *Developmental Psychology, 22,* 317–326.
Moore, S. M. (1995). Girls' understanding and social constructions of menarche. *Journal of Adolescence, 18,* 87–104.
Morales, A. (2003). Erectile dysfunction: An overview. *Clinical Geriatric Medicine, 19,* 529-538.
Moreland, R. L., & Zajonc, R. B. (1977). Is stimulus recognition a necessary condition for the occurrence of mere exposure effects? *Journal of Personality and Social Psychology, 35,* 191–199.
Morgan, W. P. (1987). Reduction of state anxiety following acute physical activity. In W. P. Morgan & S. E. Golston (Eds.), *Exercise and mental health* (pp. 105–109). Washington, D.C.: Hemisphere.
Morgenstern, H., & Glazer, W. M. (1993). Identifying risk factors for tardive dyskinesia among long-term outpatients maintained with neuroleptic medications. Results of the Yale Tardive Dyskinesia Study. *Archives of General Psychiatry, 50,* 723–733.
Morisse, D., Batra, L., Hess, L., & Silverman, R. (1996). A demonstration of a token economy for the real world. *Applied & Preventive Psychology, 5,* 41–46.
Morokoff, P. J. (1993). Female sexual arousal disorder. In W. O'Donohue & J. H. Greer (Eds.), *Handbook of sexual dysfunctions: Assessment and treatment* (pp. 157-199). Boston: Allyn & Bacon.
Morrill, A. C., Ickovics, J. R., Golubchikov, V. V., Beren, S. E., & Rodin, J. (1996). Safer sex: Social and psychological predictors of behavioral maintenance and change among heterosexual women. *Journal of Consulting and Clinical Psychology, 64,* 819–828.
Mortensen, M. E., Sever, L. E., & Oakley, G. P. (1991). Teratology and the epidemiology of birth defects. In S. G. Gabbe, J. R. Niebyl, & J. L. Simpson (Eds.), *Obstetrics: Normal and problem pregnancies.* New York: Churchill Livingstone.
Morzorati, S. L., Ramchandani, V. A., Flury, L., Li, T.-K., & O'Connor, S. (2002). Self-reported subjective perception of intoxication reflects family history of alcoholism when breath alcohol levels are constant. *Alcoholism: Clinical and Experimental Research, 26,* 1299–1306.
Mottram, L., & Berger-Gross, P. (2004). An intervention to reduce disruptive behaviors in children with brain injury. *Pediatric Rehabilitation, 7,* 133–143.
Mowen, J. C., & Cialdini, R. B. (1980). On implementing the door-in-the-face compliance technique in a business context. *Journal of Marketing Research, 17,* 253–258.
Muehlenhard, C., & McCoy, M. L. (1991). Double standard/double bind: The sexual double standard and women's communication about sex. *Psychology of Women Quarterly, 15,* 447-461.
Mulrow, C. D., Williams, J. W., Jr., Chiquette, E., Aguilar, C., Hitchcock-Noel, P., Lee, S., Cornell, J., & Stamm, K. (2000). Efficacy of newer medications for treating depression in primary care patients. *American Journal of Medicine, 108,* 54–64.
Mumford, M. D. (2003). Where have we been, where are we going? Taking stock in creativity research. *Creativity Research Journal, 15,* 107–120.

Mumme, D. L., & Fernald, A. (2003). The infant as onlooker: Learning from emotional reactions observed in a television scenario. *Child Development, 74*, 221–237.

Murdoch, B. B., Jr. (1962). The serial position effect of free recall. *Journal of Experimental Psychology, 64*, 482–288.

Murphy, M., Glaser, K., & Grundy, E. (1997). Marital status and long-term illness in Great Britain. *Journal of Marriage and the Family, 59*, 156–164.

Murphy, S. T., & Zajonc, R. B. (1993). Affect, cognition, and awareness: Affective priming with optimal and suboptimal stimulus exposures. *Journal of Personality and Social Psychology, 64*, 723–739.

Murray, C. J., & Lopez, A. D. (Eds.). (1996). *Summary: The global burden of disease: A comprehensive assessment of mortality and disability from diseases, injuries, and risk factors in 1990 and projected to 2020.* Cambridge, MA: Harvard University Press.

Murray, H. A. (1938). *Explorations in personality.* New York: Oxford University Press.

Murray, L., Fiori-Cowley, A., Hooper, R., & Cooper, P. (1996). The impact of postnatal depression and associated adversity on early mother–infant interactions and later infant outcome. *Child Development, 67*, 2512–2526.

Murray, R. M., O'Callaghan, E., Castle, D. J., & Lewis, S. W. (1992). A neurodevelopmental approach to the classification of schizophrenia. *Schizophrenia Bulletin, 18*, 319–332.

Murray, S. O., Olshausen, B. A., & Woods, D. L. (2003). Processing shape, motion, and three-dimensional shape-from-motion in the human cortex. *Cerebral Cortex, 13*, 508–516.

Murray, T., & Williams, S. (1999). *APA Research Office: Analysis of data from graduate study in psychology: 1997–98.* Washington D.C.: American Psychological Association.

Muurahainen, N. E., Kisileff, H. R., Lachaussee, J., & Pi-Sunyer, F. X. (1991). Effect of a soup preload on reduction of food intake by cholecystokinin in humans. *American Journal of Physiology, 260*, R672–R680.

Myers, D. G. (2000). The funds, friends, and faith of happy people. *American Psychologist, 55*, 56–67.

Naegele, B., Thouvard, V., Pepin, J. L., Levy, P., Bonnet, C., Perret, J. E., Pellat, P., & Feuerstein, C. (1995). Deficits of cognitive functions in patients with sleep apnea syndrome. *Sleep, 18*(1), 43–52.

Nakano, K. (1996). Application of self-control procedure to modifying Type A behavior. *Psychological Record, 46*(4), 595–606.

Narrow, W. E., Rae, D. S., & Regier, D. A. (1998). *NIMH epidemiology note: Prevalence of anxiety disorders. One-year prevalence best estimates calculated from ECA and NCS data.* Unpublished.

Narrow, W. E., Rae, D. S., Robins, L. N., & Regier, D. A. (2002). Revised prevalence estimates of mental disorders in the United States: Using a clinical significance criterion to reconcile two survey estimates. *Archives of General Psychiatry, 59*, 115–123.

Narrow, W. E., Regier, D. A., Rae, D., Manderscheid, R. W., & Locke, B. Z. (1993). Use of services by persons with mental and addictive disorders. *Archives of General Psychiatry, 50*, 95–107.

Nasar, S. (1998). *A beautiful mind: A biography of John Forbes Nash, Jr.* New York: Simon & Schuster.

Nash, M. (1987). What, if anything, is regressed about hypnotic age regression? A review of the empirical literature. *Psychological Bulletin, 102*, 42–52.

Nathan, P. E., Stuart, S. P., & Dolan, S. L., (2000). Research on psychotherapy efficacy and effectiveness: Between Scylla and Charybdis? *Psychological Bulletin, 126*, 964–981.

Nathans, J., Merbs, S. L., Sung, C. H., Weitz, C. J., & Wang, Y. (1992). Molecular genetics of human visual pigments. *Annual Review of Genetics, 26*, 403–424.

National Center for Health Statistics. (2001). *Percent of high school students who smoked cigarettes in the past 30 days.* Retrieved September 27, 2004, from http://www.cdc.gov/nchs/fastats/smoking.htm

National Center for Health Statistics. (2003). *Current smoking among adults: 1997–2003.* Retrieved September 27, 2004, from http://www.cdc.gov/nchs/fastats/smoking.htm

National Gay and Lesbian Task Force. (2004). *Hate crime laws in the United States.* Retrieved September 4, 2004, from http://www.ngltf.org/issues/maps.cfm?issueID=12

National Institute of Mental Health. (2002). *Suicide facts.* Retrieved May 9, 2004, from http//www.nimh.nih.gov/research/suifact.htm

National Institute on Drug Abuse (NIDA) (1997). *Monitoring the Future Study.* Washington DC: U.S. Department of Health & Human Services.

National Institute on Mental Health Genetics Workgroup. (1998). *Genetics and mental disorders.* NIH Publication No. 98–4268. Rockville, MD: National Institute of Mental Health.

National Institutes of Health (2000). *The practical guide: Identification, evaluation, and treatment of overweight and obesity in adults* (NIH Publication No. 00-4084). Washington, DC: Author.

Navarro, M. (1995, Dec. 9). Drugs sold abroad by prescription becomes widely abused in U.S. *The New York Times,* pp. 1, 9.

Navarro, M., Carrera, M. R. A., Fratta, W., Valverde, O., Cossu, G., Fattore, L., Chowen, J. A., Gomez, R., del Arco, I., Villanua, M. A., Maldonado, R., Koob, G. F., & de Fonseca, F. R. (2001). Functional interaction between opioid and cannabinoid receptors in drug self-administration. *Journal of Neuroscience, 21*, 5344–5350.

Neher, A. (1991). Maslow's theory of motivation: A critique. *Journal of Humanistic Psychology, 31*, 89–112.

Neitz, J., Neitz, M., & Jacobs, G. H. (1993). More than three different cone pigments among people with normal color vision. *Vision Research, 33*, 117–122.

Neitz, J., Neitz, M., & Kainz, P. M. (1996, November 1). Visual pigment gene structure and severity of color vision defects. *Science, 274*, 801–804.

Nelson, C. A., Thomas, K. M., de Haan, M., & Wewerka, S. S. (1998). Delayed recognition memory in infants and adults as revealed by event-related potentials. *International Journal of Psychophysiology, 29*, 145–165.

Nelson, R. (1988). Nonoperative management of impotence. *Journal of Urology, 139*, 2-5.

Neuberg, S. L. (1988). Behavioral implications of information presented outside of awareness: The effect of subliminal presentations of trait information on behavior in the Prisoner's Dilemma game. *Social Cognition, 6*, 207–230.

Neugebauer, R. (2003). Depressive symptoms at two months after miscarriage: Interpreting study findings from an epidemiological versus a clinical perspective. *Depression & Anxiety, 17*, 152–161.

Neumark-Sztainer, D., Croll, J., Story, M., Hannan, P. J., French, S. A., & Perry, C. (2002). Ethnic/racial differences in weight-related concerns and behaviors among adolescent girls and boys: Findings from Project-EAT. *Journal of Psychosomatic Research, 53*, 963–974.

Nevid, J. S., Rathus, S. A., & Greene, B. A. (2000). *Abnormal psychology in a changing world* (4th ed.). Upper Saddle River, NJ: Prentice Hall.

Newby, R. W., & Davis, J. B. (2004). Relationships between locus of control and paranormal beliefs. *Psychological Reports, 94*, 1261–1266.

Newcomb, T. M. (1961). *The acquaintance process.* New York: Holt, Rinehart & Winston.

Newland, M. C., & Rasmussen, E. B. (2003). Behavior in adulthood and during aging is affected by contaminant exposure in utero. *Current Directions in Psychological Science, 12*, 212–217.

Newman, J. L. (2000). V. E. 1 Africa south from the Sahara. In K. E. Kipple & K. C. Ornelas (Series Eds.), *The Cambridge world history of food: Vol. 2* (pp. 1330–1339). Cambridge, UK: Cambridge University Press.

Newman, S. D., & Tweig, D. (2001). Differences in auditory processing of words and pseudowords: An fMRI study. *Human Brain Mapping, 14*, 39–47.

Niccols, G. A. (1994). Fetal alcohol syndrome: Implications for psychologists. *Clinical Psychology Review, 14*, 91–111.

Nicholson, I. R., & Neufield, R. W. J. (1993). Classification of the schizophrenias according to symptomatology: A two factor model. *Journal of Abnormal Psychology, 102*, 259–270.

Niedzwienska, A. (2003). Gender differences in vivid memories. *Sex Roles: A Journal of Research, 49*, 321–331.

Niemi, R. G., Mueller, J., & Smith, T. W. (1989). *Trends in public opinion: A compendium of survey data.* New York: Greenwood Press.

Nikcevic, A. V., Tunkel, S. A., Kuczmierczyk, A. R., & Nicolaides, K. H. (1999). Investigation of the cause of miscarriage and its influence on women's psychological distress. *British Journal of Obstetrics & Gynecology, 106*, 808–813.

Nisbett, R. (1995). Race, IQ, and scientism. In Steven Fraser (Ed.), *The bell curve wars: Race, intelligence, and the future of America.* New York: Basic Books.

Noah, T. & Robinson, L. (1997, March 31). OK, OK, cigarettes do kill. *U.S. News & World Report,* pp. 29, 32.

Noble, M., & Harding, G. E. (1963). Conditioning of rhesus monkeys as a function of the interval between CS and US. *Journal of Comparative and Physiological Psychology, 56*, 220–224.

Nolan, R. P., Spanos, N. P., Hayward, A. A., & Scott, H. A. (1995). The efficacy of hypnotic and nonhypnotic response-based imagery for self-managing recurrent headache. *Imagination, Cognition, and Personality, 14*(3), 183–201.

Nolen-Hoeksema, S. (2001). Gender differences in depression. *Current Directions in Psychological Science, 10*, 173–176.

Nolen-Hoeksema, S. (2002). Gender differences in depression. In I. H. Gotlib & C. L. Hammen (Eds.), *Handbook of depression* (pp. 492–509). New York: Guilford Press.

Nolen-Hoeksema, S., Larson, J., & Grayson, C. (1999). Explaining the gender difference in depressive symptoms. *Journal of Personality & Social Psychology, 77*, 1061–1072.

Nolen-Hoeksema, S., Parker, L. E., & Larson, J. (1994). Ruminative coping with depressed mood following loss. *Journal of Personality & Social Psychology, 67*, 92–104.

Nordin, S., Razani, J. L., Markison, S., & Murphy, C. (2003). Age-associated increases in intensity discrimination for taste. *Experimental Aging Research, 29*, 371–381.

Norman, R. M., & Malla, A. K. (1993). Stressful life events and schizophrenia: II. Conceptual and methodological issues. *British Journal of Psychiatry, 162*, 166–174. Hormones and behavior at puberty. In J. Bancroft & J. M. Reinisch (Eds.), *Adolescence and puberty* (pp. 88–123). New York: Oxford University Press.

Nottlemann, E. D., Inoff-Germain, G., Susman, E. J., & Chrousos, G. P. (1990). Hormones and behavior at puberty. In J. Bancroft & J. M. Reinisch (Eds.), *Adolescence and puberty* (pp. 88–123). New York: Oxford University Press."

Nowell, P. D., Buysse, D. J., Morin, C. M., Reynolds, C. F., III, & Kuper, D. J. (1998). Effective treatments for selected sleep disorder. In P. E. Nathan (Ed.), *A guide to treatments that work* (pp. 531–543). New York: Oxford University Press.

Nurnberger, J. (1993). Genotyping status report for affective disorder. *Psychiatric Genetics, 3,* 207–214.

O'Brien, M. (1996). Child-rearing difficulties reported by parents of infants and toddlers. *Journal of Pediatric Psychology, 21*, 433–446.

O'Connor, M. K. (1993). Hypotheses regarding the mechanism of action of electroconvulsive therapy, past and present. *Psychiatric Annals, 23*, 15–18.

O'Connor, T. G., Marvin, R. S., Rutter, M., Olrick, J. T., & Britner, P. A. (2003). Child–parent attachment following early institutional deprivation. *Developmental Psychopathology, 15*, 19–38.

Ohlsson, S. (1992). Information processing explanations of insight and related phenomena. In M. T. Keane & K. J. Gihooly (Eds.), *Advances in the psychology of thinking.* London: Harvester Wheatsheaf.

O'Keefe, D. J., & Figge, M. (1997). A guilt-based explanation of the door-in-the-face influence strategy. *Human Communication Research, 24*, 64–81.

Olds, J., & Milner, P. (1954). Positive reinforcement produced by electrical stimulation of the septal area and other regions of the rat brain. *Journal of Comparative and Physiological Psychology, 47*, 419–428.

O'Leary, A. (1990). Stress, emotion, and human immune function. *Psychological Bulletin, 108,* 363–382.

Oliver, M. B., & Hyde, J. S. (1993). Gender differences in sexuality: A meta-analysis. *Psychological Bulletin, 114,* 29-51.

Ondersma, S. J., & Walker, C. E. (1998). Elimination disorders. In T. H. Ollendick & M. Hersen (Eds.), *Handbook of child psychopathology* (pp. 355–380). New York: Plenum.

O'Neill, B. (April 19, 2004). Britain debates: To spank or not to spank. *The Christian Science Monitor,* p. 9.

Ornish, D. (1998). *Love and survival.* New York: HarperCollins.

Ornstein, S., & Isabella, L. (1990). Age versus stage models of career attitudes of women: A partial replication and extension. *Journal of Vocational Behavior, 36,* 1–19.

Ortony, A., & Turner, T. J. (1990). What's basic about basic emotions? *Psychological Review, 97,* 315–331.

Osborne, J. (2001). Testing stereotype threat: Does anxiety explain race and sex differences in achievement? *Contemporary Educational Psychology, 26,* 291–310.

Osborne, R. H., Sali, A., Aaronson, N. K., Elsworth, G. R., Mdzewski, B., & Sinclair, A. J. (2004). Immune function and adjustment style: Do they predict survival in breast cancer? *Psychooncology, 13,* 199–210.

Osher, Y., Hamer, D., & Benjamin, J. (2000). Association and linkage of anxiety-related traits with a functional polymorphism of the serotonin transporter gene regulatory region in Israeli sibling pairs. *Molecular Psychiatry, 5,* 216–219.

Osterman, K., Bjorkqvist, K., Lagerspertz, K. M. J., Kaukianainen, A., Huesman, L. W., & Fraczek, A. (1994). Peer and self-estimated aggression and victimization in 8-year-old children from five ethnic groups. *Aggressive Behavior, 20,* 411–428.

Osvold, L. L., & Sodowsky, G. R. (1993). Eating disorders of White American, racial and ethnic minority American, and international women. Special issue: Multicultural health issues. *Journal of Multicultural Counseling & Development, 21,* 143–154.

Overman, W. H., Bachevalier, J., Schuhmann, E., & Ryan, P. (1996).Cognitive gender differences in very young children parallel biologically based cognitive gender differences in monkeys. *Behavioral Neuroscience, 110,* 673–684.

Overmier, J. B., & Seligman, M. E. (1967). Effects of inescapable shock upon subsequent escape and avoidance responding. *Journal of Comparative & Physiological Psychology, 63,* 28–33.

Owens, W. A., Jr. (1953). Age and mental abilities: A longitudinal study. *Genetic Psychology Monographs, 48,* 3–54.

Ozturk, L., Pelin, Z., Karadeniz, D., Kaynak, H., Cakar, L., & Gozukirmizi, E. (1999). Effects of 48 hours sleep deprivation on human immune profile. *Sleep Research Online* [electronic resource], 2, 107–111.

Ozturk, R., Niazi, S., Stessman, M., & Rao, S. S. (2004). Long-term outcome and objective changes of anorectal function after biofeedback therapy for faecal incontinence. *Aliment Pharmacology Therapy, 20,* 667–674.

Painter, K. (1997, August 15–17). Doctors have prenatal test for 450 genetic diseases. *USA Today.*

Paivio, A. (1971). *Imagery and verbal processes.* New York: Holt, Rinehart, and Winston.

Paivio, A. (1982). The empirical case for dual coding. In J. Yuille (Ed.), *Imagery, cognition, and memory.* Hillsdale, NJ: Erlbaum.

Paivio, A. (1986). *Mental representations: A dual coding approach.* New York: Oxford University Press.

Pakkenberg, B., & Gundersen, H. J. G. (1997). Neocortical neuron number in humans: Effect of sex and age. *Journal of Comparative Neurology, 384,* 312–320.

Pallier, G. (March, 2003). Gender differences in the self-assessment of accuracy on cognitive tasks. *Sex Roles: A Journal of Research, 265–276.*

Palmer, J. R., Hatch, E. E., Rao, R. S., Kaufman, R. H., Herbst, A., et al. (2001). Infertility among women exposed prenatally to diethylstilbestrol. *American Journal of Epidemiology, 154,* 316–321.

Palmer, J. R., Hatch, E. E., Rosenberg, C. L., Hartge, P., Kaufman, R. H., Titus-Ernstoff, L., et al. (2002). Risk of breast cancer in women exposed to diethylstilbe-

strol in utero: Preliminary results (United States). *Cancer Causes Control, 13,* 753–758.

Palmore, E. B., Burchett, B. M., Fillenbaum, G. G., George, L. K., & Wallman, L. M. (1985). *Retirement: Causes and consequences.* New York: Springer.

Pankratz, H. (1999, March 5). Samaritan sounds off in court: Victim's colorful words recall attack. *The Denver Post,* p. B1.

Parasuraman, R., Masalonis, A. J., & Hancock, P. A. (2000). Fuzzy signal detection theory: Basic postulates and formulas for analyzing human and machine performance. *Human Factors, 42,* 636–672.

Parasuraman, S., & Greenhaus, J. H. (1997). The changing world of work and family. In S. Parasuraman & J. H. Grennhaus (Eds.), *Integrating work and family.* Westport, CT: Quorum Books.

Parke, R. D., & Buriel, R. (1998). Socialization in the family: Ethnic and ecological perspectives. In W. Damon (Ed.), *Handbook of child psychology* (Vol. 3). New York: Wiley.

Parker, E. S., Birnbaum, I. M., & Noble, E. P. (1976). Alcohol and memory: Storage and state dependency. *Journal of Verbal Learning and Verbal Behavior, 15,* 691–702.

Parker, G. B., & Brotchie, H. L. (2004). From diathesis to dimorphism: The biology of gender differences in depression. *Journal of Nervous and Mental Disorders, 192,* 210–216.

Parker, G., Roy, K., Wilhelm, K., & Mitchell, P. (2001). Assessing the comparative effectiveness of antidepressant therapies: A prospective clinical practice study. *Journal of Clinical Psychiatry, 62,* 117–125.

Parker-Pope, T. (2002, August 27). A new reason for teens to avoid sex: It could be harmful to their health. *Wall Street Journal,* D1.

Parkes, C. M. (1986). *Bereavement: Studies of grief in adult life* (2nd ed.). London: Tavistock.

Parkes, C. M. (1991). Attachment, bonding, and psychiatric problems after bereavement in adult life. In C. M. Parkes, J. Stevenson-Hinde, & P. Marris (Eds.), *Attachment across the life cycle.* London: Tavistock/Routledge.

Parkin, A. J., & Leng, N. R. C. (1993). *Neruopsychology of the amnesic syndrome.* Hove, UK: Psychology Press.

Parnas, J., Cannon, T., Jacobsen, B., Schulsinger, H., Schulsinger, F., & Mednick, S. (1993). Lifetime DSM-III-R diagnostic outcomes in the offspring of schizophrenic mothers. *Archives of General Psychiatry, 50,* 707–714.

Pasquet, P., Obeerti, B., Ati, J. El, & Hladik, C. M. (2002). Relationships between threshold-based PROP sensitivity and food preferences of Tunisians. *Appetite, 39,* 167–173.

Pate, J. E., Pumariega, A. J., Hester, C., & Garner, D. M. (1992). Cross-cultural patterns in eating disorders: A review. *Journal of the American Academy of Child & Adolescent Psychiatry, 31,* 802–809.

Patel, V. L., & Ramoni, M. F. (1997). Cognitive models of directional inference in expert medical reasoning. In P. J. Feltovich, K. M. Ford, et al. (Eds.), *Expertise in context: Human and machine* (pp. 67–99). Cambridge, MA: MIT Press.

Paul, G. L., & Menditto, A. A. (1992). Effectiveness of inpatient treatment programs for mentally ill adults in public psychiatric facilities. *Applied & Preventive Psychology, 1,* 41–63.

Paulus, P. B. (Ed.). (1989). *Psychology of group influence.* (2nd ed.). Hillsdale, NJ: Erlbaum.

Pavlov, I. P. (1960). *Conditioned reflexes: An investigation of the physiological activity of the cerebral cortex.* (G. V. Anrep, Trans.). New York: Dover. (Original work published 1927)

Payte, J. T. (1997). Methadone maintenance treatment: The first thirty years. *Journal of Psychoactive Drugs, 29,* 149–153.

Pearlin, L. I. (1993). The social contexts of stress. In L. Goldberger & S. Breznitz (Eds.), *Handbook of stress: Theoretical and clinical aspects* (2nd ed., pp. 303–315). New York: Free Press.

Pedersen, D. M., & Wheeler, J. (1983). The Müller-Lyer illusion among Navajos. *Journal of Social Psychology, 121,* 3–6.

Pedersen, P. B. (2002). Ethics, competence, and other professional issues in culture-centered counseling. In

P. B. Pedersen, J. G. Draguns, W. J. Lonner, & J. E. Trimble (Eds.), *Counseling across cultures* (5th ed., pp. 3–28). Thousand Oaks, CA: Sage Publications.

Pekkanen, J. (1982, June). Why do we sleep? *Science, 82,* 86.

Pelleymounter, M. A., Cullen, M. J., Baker, M. B., Hecht, R., Winters, D. Boone, T., & Collins, F. (1995). Effects of the obese gene product on body weight regulation in ob/ob mice. *Science, 269,* 540–543.

Pelzer, D. (1995). *A child called "it."* Deerfield Beach, FL: Health Communications.

Pelzer, D. (1997). *The lost boy.* Deerfield Beach, FL: Health Communications.

Pelzer, D. (1999). *A man named Dave.* New York: Dutton.

Penley, J. A., Tomaka, J., & Wiebe, J. S. (2002). The association of coping to physical and psychological health outcomes: A meta-analytic review. *Journal of Behavioral Medicine, 25,* 551–603.

Peplau, L. A. (2003). Human sexuality: How do men and women differ? *Current Directions in Psychological Science, 12,* 37-40.

Pepperberg, I. M. (1991). A communicative approach to animal cognition: A study of conceptual abilities of an African gray parrot. In C. A. Ristau (Ed.), *Cognitive ethology.* Hillsdale, NJ: Erlbaum.

Pepperberg, I. M. (1993). Cognition and communication in an African gray parrot (*Psittacus erithacus*): Studies on a nonhuman, nonprimate, nonmammilian, subject. In H. L. Roitblat, L. M. Herman, & P. E. Nachtigall (Eds.), *Language and communication: Comparative perspectives.* Hillsdale, NJ: Erlbaum.

Pepperberg, I. M. (1999). Rethinking syntax: A commentary on E. Kako's "Elements of syntax in the systems of three language-trained animals." *Animal Learning & Behavior, 27,* 15–17.

Perez, M., Joiner, T. E., Jr., & Lewisohn, P. M. (2004). Is major depressive disorder or dysthymia more strongly associated with bulimia nervosa? *International Journal of Eating Disorders, 36,* 55–61.

Perina, K. (2002). Hot on the trail of flashbulb memory. *Psychology Today, 35,* 15–16.

Perlini, A. H., Bertolissi, S., & Lind, D. L. (1999). The effects of women's age and physical appearance on evaluations of attractiveness and social desirability. *The Journal of Social Psychology, 139,* 343–344.

Perry, C. (1997). Admissibility and per se exclusion of hypnotically elicited recall in American courts of law. *International Journal of Clinical and Experimental Hypnosis, 45,* 266–279.

Perry, E., Walker, M., Grace, J., & Perry, R. (1999). Acetylcholine in mind: A neurotransmitter correlate of consciousness? *Trends in Neurosciences, 22,* 273–280.

Perry, W. G., Jr. (1981). Cognitive and ethical growth. In A. Chickering (Ed.), *The modern American college* (pp. 76–116). San Francisco: Jossey-Bass.

Person, E. S. (1990). The influence of values in psychoanalysis: The case of female psychology. In C. Zanardi (Ed.), *Essential papers in psychoanalysis* (pp. 305–325). New York: University Press.

Pesant, N., & Zadra, A. (2004). Working with dreams in therapy: What do we know and what should we do? *Clinical Psychology Review, 24,* 489–512.

Peskin, H. (1973). Influence of the developmental schedule of puberty on learning and ego functioning. *Journal of Youth and Adolescence, 2,* 273–290.

Peters, A., & Liefbroer, A. C. (1997). Beyond marital status: Partner history and well- being in old age. *Journal of Marriage and the Family, 55,* 687–699.

Petersen, S. E., Fox, P. T., Synder, A. Z., & Raichle, M. E. (1990). Activation of extrastriate and frontal cortical areas by visual words and word-like stimuli. *Science, 249,* 1041–1044.

Peterson, C. (2000). The future of optimism. *American Psychologist, 55,* 44–55.

Peterson, C., & Bossio, L. M. (2001). Optimism and physical well-being. In E. C. Chang (Ed.), *Optimism and pessimism: Implications for theory, research, and practice* (pp. 127–146). Washington, DC: American Psychological Association.

Peterson, C., & Seligman, M. E. (1984). Causal explanations as a risk factor for depression: Theory and evidence. *Psychological Review, 91,* 347–374.

Peterson, C., & Seligman, M. E. (2003). Character strengths before and after September 11. *Psychological Science, 14,* 381–384.

Peterson, C., Maier, S. F., & Seligman, M. E. P. (1993). *Learned helplessness: A theory for the age of personal control.* New York: Oxford University Press.

Peterson, L. R., & Peterson, M. J. (1959). Short-term retention of individual verbal items. *Journal of Experimental Psychology, 58,* 193–198.

Petri, H. L. (1996). *Motivation: Theory, research, and applications* (4th ed.) Pacific Grove, CA: Brooks/Cole.

Petrides, K. V., Furnham, A., & Martin, G. N. (2004). Estimates of emotional and psychometric intelligence: Evidence for gender-based stereotypes. *The Journal of Social Psychology, 144,* 149–162.

Petry, N. M., Tedford, J., Austin, M., Nich, C., Carroll, K. M., & Rounsaville, B. J. (2004). Prize reinforcement contingency management for treating cocaine users: How low can we go, and with whom? *Addiction, 99,* 349–360.

Petty, R. E., & Brock, T. C. (1981). Thought disruption and persuasion: Assessing the validity of attitude change experiments. In R. E. Petty, T. M. Ostrom, & T. C. Brock (Eds.), *Cognitive responses in persuasion* (pp. 55–79). Hillsdale, NJ: Erlbaum.

Petty, R. E., & Cacioppo, J. T. (1986). *Communication and persuasion: Central and peripheral routes to attitude change.* New York: Springer-Verlag.

Petty, R. E., Cacioppo, J. T., & Goldman, R. (1981). Personal involvement as a determinant of argument-based persuasion. *Journal of Personality and Social Psychology, 41,* 847–855.

Petty, R. E., Wegener, D. T., & Fabrigar, L. R. (1997). Attitude and attitude change. *Annual Review of Psychology, 48,* 609–647.

Pfann, K. D., Penn, R. D., Shannon, K. M., & Corcos, D. M. (1998). Pallidotomy and bradykinesia: Implications for basal ganglia function. *Neurology, 51,* 796–803.

Pfizer. (2002). *Pfizer global study of sexual attitudes and behaviors.* Retrieved September 4, 2004, from http://pfizerglobalstudy.com

Phares, E. J. (1991). *Introduction to personality* (3rd ed.). New York: HarperCollins.

Phillips, M. R., Li, X., & Zhang, Y. (2002). Suicide rates in China, 1995–99. *Lancet, 359,* 835–840.

Phillipson, O. T. (1987). Catecholamines. In R. L. Gregory (Ed.), *The Oxford companion to the mind* (pp. 126–127). New York: Oxford University Press.

Piaget, J. (1929). *The child's conception of the world.* New York: Harcourt Brace.

Piaget, J. (1952). *The origins of intelligence in children.* New York: International Universities Press. (Original work published 1936)

Pickerell, J. (2003, July 8). Urine vision? How rodents communicate with UV light. *National Geographic News.* Retrieved on January, 19, 2004, from http://news.nationalgeographic.com/news/2003/07/07 08_030708_ultravioletmammals.html

Pidoplichko, V. I., DeBiasi, M., Williams, J. T., & Dani, J. A. (1997). Nicotine activates and desensitizes midbrain dopamine neurons. *Nature, 390,* 401–404.

Pinel, J. P. J. (1997). *Biopsychology* (3rd ed.). Boston: Allyn & Bacon.

Pinker, S. (1994). *The language instinct: How the mind creates language.* New York: Morrow.

Pion, G. M. (1991). Psychologists wanted: Employment trends over the last decade. In R. R. Kilburg (Ed.), *How to manage your career in psychology* (pp. 229–246). Washington, DC: American Psychological Association.

Plazzi, B., Corsini, R., Provini, R., Pierangeli, G., Martinelli, P., Montagna, P., Lugaresi, E., & Cortelli, P. (1997). REM sleep behavior disorders in multiple system atrophy. *Neurology, 48,* 1094–1097.

Pleck, E. H., & Pleck, J. H. (1997). Fatherhood ideals in the United States: Historical dimensions. In M. E. Lamb (Ed.), *The role of the father in child development* (3rd ed., pp. 33–48). New York: Wiley.

Plomin, R., DeFries, J. C., McClearn, G. E., & McGuffin, P. (2001). *Behavioral genetics* (4th ed.). New York: Worth.

Plutchik, R. (1984). Emotions: A general psychoevolutionary theory. In K. R. Scherer & P. Ekman (Eds.), *Approaches to emotion.* Hillsdale, NJ: Erlbaum.

Podd, J. (1990). The effects of memory load and delay on facial recognition. *Applied Cognitive Psychology, 4,* 47–59.

Poldrack, R. A., Desmond, J. E., Glover, G. H., & Gabrieli, J. D. E. (1996). The neural bases of visual skill: An fMRI study of mirror reading. *Society of Neuroscience, 22,* 719.

Polmin, R. (1994). The Emanuel Miller Memorial Lecture 1993: Genetic research and identification of environmental influences. *Journal of Child Psychology and Psychiatry, 35,* 817–834.

Pomeroy, W. (1965, May). Why we tolerate lesbians. *Sexology,* 652-654.

Poore, A. G., Gagne, F., Barlow, K. M., Lydon, J. E., Taylor, D. M., & Wright, S. C. (2002). Contact and the personal/group discrimination discrepancy in an Inuit community. *The Journal of Psychology, 136,* 371–382.

Pope, H. D., Jr., Oliva, P. S., Hudson, J. I., Bodkin, J. A., & Gruber, A. J. (1999). Attitudes toward DSM-IV dissociative disorders diagnoses among board-certified American psychiatrists. *American Journal of Psychiatry, 156,* 321–323.

Pope, H. G., & Yurgelun-Todd, D. (1996). The residual cognitive effects of heavy marijuana use in college students. *Journal of the American Medical Association, 275*(7), 521–527.

Porkka-Heiskanen, T., Strecker, R. E., Thakkar, M., Bjorkum, A. A., Greene, R. W., & McCarley, R. W. (1997). Adenosine: A mediator of the sleep-inducing effects of prolonged wakefulness. *Science, 276,* 1265–1268.

Porte, H. S., & Hobson, J. A. (1996). Physical motion in dreams: One measure of three theories. *Journal of Abnormal Psychology, 105,* 329–335.

Post, R., Frye, M., Denicoff, K. Leverich, G., Kimbrell, T., & Dunn, R. (1998). Beyond lithium in the treatment of bipolar illness. *Neuropsychopharmacology, 19,* 206–219.

Potter, W. J., Warren, R., Vaughan, M., Howley, K., Land, A., & Hagemeyer, J. (1997). Antisocial acts in reality programming on television. *Journal of Broadcasting and Electronic Media, 41,* 69–89.

Powell, E. (1996). *Sex on your terms.* Boston: Allyn & Bacon.

Powell, L. H., Shahabi, L., & Thoresen, C. E. (2003). Religion and spirituality. Linkages to physical health. *American Psychologist, 58,* 36–52.

Pratkanis, A. R. (1992). The cargo-cult science of subliminal persuasion. *The Skeptical Inquirer, 16,* 260–272.

Prescott, C. A., Hewitt, J. K., Truett, K. R., Heath, A. C., Neale, M. C., & Eaves, L. J. (1994). Genetic and environmental influences on alcohol-related problems in a volunteer sample of older twins. *Journal of Studies on Alcohol, 55,* 184–202.

Price, W. F., & Crapo, R. H. (2002). *Cross-cultural perspectives in introductory psychology.* Belmont, CA: Wadsworth.

Proctor, F., Wagner, N., & Butler, J. (1974). The differentiation of male and female orgasm: An experimental study. In N. Wagner (Ed.), *Perspectives on human sexuality.* New York: Behavioral Publications.

Proudfoot, J. G. (2004). Computer-based treatment for anxiety and depression: Is it feasible? Is it effective? *Neuroscience Biobehavior Review, 28,* 353–363.

Prutkin, J., Duffy, V. B., Etter, L., Fast, K., Gardner, E., Lucchina, L. A., Snyder, D. J., Tie, K., Weiffenbach, J., & Bartoshuk, L. M. (2000). Genetic variation and inferences about perceived taste intensity in mice and men. *Physiology and Behavior, 69,* 161–173.

Pullman, G. K. (1989). The great Eskimo vocabulary hoax. *National Language and Linguistic Theory, 7,* 275–281.

Purcell, P., & Stewart, L. (1990). Dick and Jane in 1989. *Sex Roles, 22,* 177–185.

Purves, D., Augustine, G. J., Fitzpatrick, D., Katz, L., LaMantia, A. S., & McNamara, J. O. (1997). *Neuroscience.* Sunderland, MA: Sinauer.

Putnam, F. W., Guroff, J. J., Silberman, E. K., & Barban, L. (1986). The clinical phenomenology of multiple personality disorder: Review of 100 recent cases. *Journal of Clinical Psychiatry, 47,* 285–293.

Quatrone, G. A., & Jones, E. E. (1980). The perception of variability within ingroups and outgroups: Implications for the law of small number. *Journal of Personality and Social Psychology, 38,* 141–152.

Querido, J. G., Warner, T. D., & Eyberg, S. M. (2002). Parenting styles and child behavior in African American families of preschool children. *Journal of Clinical Child and Adolescent Psychology, 31,* 272–277.

Quinn, D. M., & Spencer, S. J. (2001). The interference of stereotype threat with women's generation of mathematical problem-solving strategies. *Journal of Social Issues, 57,* 55–71.

Rabkin, J. G., & Ferrando, S. (1997). A "second life" agenda. *Archives of General Psychiatry, 54,* 1049–1053.

Rabkin, S. W., Boyko, E., Shane, F., & Kaufert, J. (1984). A randomized trial comparing smoking cessation programs utilizing behavior modification, health education, or hypnosis. *Addictive Behaviors, 9,* 157–173.

Raichle, M. E. (1987). Images of the brain in action. In R. L. Gregory (Ed.), *The Oxford companion to the mind* (pp. 347–353). New York: Oxford University Press.

Raichle, M. E. (1994). Visualizing the mind. *Scientific American, 270,* 58–64.

Raine, A. (1997). Antisocial behavior and psychophysiology: A biological perspective. In D. M. Stoff, J. Breiling, & J. D. Maser (Eds.), *Handbook of antisocial personality disorder* (pp. 289–304). New York: Wiley.

Raine, A. Lencz, T., Bihrle, S., LaCasse, L., & Colletti, P. (2000). Reduced prefrontal gray matter volume and reduced autonomic activity in antisocial personality disorder. *Archives of General Psychiatry, 57,* 119–127.

Rainville, P., & Price, D. D. (2003). Hypnosis phenomenology and the neurobiology of consciousness. *International Journal of Clinical and Experimental Hypnosis, 51,* 105–129.

Rainville, P., Duncan, G. H., Price, D. D., Carrier, B., & Bushnell, M. C. (1997). Pain affect encoded in human anterior cingulate but not somatosensory cortex. *Science, 277,* 968–971.

Rakic, P. (1991). Plasticity of cortical development. In S. E. Brauth, W. S. Hall, & R. J. Dooling (Eds.), *Plasticity of Development.* Cambridge, MA: Bradford/MIT Press.

Raloff, J. (1997). FDA can regulate tobacco as a device. *Science News, 151,* 268.

Rando, T. A. (1995). Grief and mourning: Accommodating to loss. In H. Wass & R. A. Neimeyer (Eds.), *Dying: Facing the facts* (3rd ed., pp. 211–241). Washington, DC: Taylor & Francis.

Rank, M. R. (2000). Poverty and economic hardship in families. In D. H. Demo, K. R. Allen, & M. A. Fine (Eds.), *Handbook of family diversity* (pp. 293–315). New York: Oxford University Press.

Rauch, S. L., Savage, C. R., Alpert, N. M., Dougherty, D., Kendrick, A., Curran, T., Brown, H. D., Manzo, P., Fischman, A. J., & Jenike, M. A. (1997). Probing striatal function in obsessive-compulsive disorder: A PET study of implicit sequence learning. *Journal of Neuropsychiatry & Clinical Neuroscience, 9,* 568–573.

Ravenna, H., Jones, C., & Kwan, V. S. (2002). Personality change over 40 years of adulthood: Hierarchial linear modeling analyses of two longitudinal samples. *Journal of Personality & Social Psychology, 83,* 752–766.

Ray, O., & Ksir, C. (1990). *Drugs, society, and human behavior* (5th ed.). St. Louis: Times Mirror/Mosby.

Reedy, M. N. (1983). Personality and aging. In D. S. Woodruff & J. E. Birren (Eds.), *Aging: Scientific perspectives and social issues* (2nd ed.). Monterey, CA: Brooks/Cole.

Regier, D. A., Narrow, W. E., Rae, D. S., Manderscheid, R. W., Locke, B. Z., & Goodwin, F. K. (1993). The de facto U.S. mental and addictive disorders service system: Epidemiologic Catchment Area prospective 1-year prevalence rates of disorders and services. *Archives of General Psychiatry, 50,* 85–94.

Reinisch, J. M. (1991). *The Kinsey Institute new report on sex: What you must know to be sexually literate.* New York: St. Martin's Press.

Reisenzein, R. (1983). The Schachter theory of emotion: Two decades later. *Psychological Bulletin, 94,* 239–264.

Reissing, E. D., Binik, Y. M., & Khalife, S. (1999). Does vaginismus exist? *Journal of Nervous & Mental Disease, 187,* 261-274.

Rescorla, R. A. (1967). Pavlovian conditioning and its proper control procedures. *Psychological Review, 74,* 71–80.

Resick, P. A., Nishith, P., Weaver, T. L., Astin, M. C., & Feuer, C. A. (2002). A comparison of cognitive-processing therapy with prolonged exposure and a waiting condition for the treatment of chronic post-traumatic stress disorder in female rape victims. *Journal of Consulting & Clinical Psychology, 70,* 867–879.

Ress, D., & Heeger, D. J. (2003). Neuronal correlates of perception in early visual cortex. *Nature Neuroscience, 6,* 414–420.

Reynold, C. R., & Brown, R. T. (Eds.) (1984). *Perspectives on bias in mental testing.* New York: Plenum Press.

Reynolds, S., Stiles, W. B., Barkham, M., & Shapiro, D. A. (1996). Acceleration of changes in session impact during contrasting time-limited psychotherapies. *Journal of Consulting & Clinical Psychology, 64,* 577–586.

Rhodes, N., & Wood, W. (1992). Self-esteem and intelligence affect influencability: The mediating role of message reception. *Psychological Bulletin, 111,* 156–171.

Rice, F. P. (1992). *Intimate relationships, marriages, and families.* Mountain View, CA: Mayfield.

Rice, V. H. (Ed.). (2000). *Handbook of stress, coping and health.* Thousand Oaks, CA: Sage.

Richardson, G. E., & Day, N. L. (1994). Detrimental effects of prenatal cocaine exposure: Illusion or reality. *Journal of the American Academy of Child and Adolescent Psychiatry, 33,* 28–34.

Richardson, J. T. E., Engle, R. W., Hasher, L., Logie, R. H., Stoltzfus, E. R., & Zacks, R. T. (1996). *Working memory and human cognition.* Oxford: Oxford University Press.

Richardson-Klavehn, A., & Bjork, R. A. (1988). Measures of memory. *Annual Review of Psychology, 39,* 475–543.

Rich-Edwards, J., Krieger, N., Majzoub, J., Zierler, S., Lieberman, E., & Gillman, M. (2001). Maternal experiences of racism and violence as predictors of preterm birth: Rationale and study design. *Pediatric and Perinatal Epidemiology, 15,* 124–135.

Rickels, K., DeMartinis, N., Garcia-Espana, F., Greenblatt, D. J., Mandos, L. A., & Rynn, M. (2000). Imipramine and buspirone in treatment of patients with generalized anxiety disorder who are discontinuing long-term benzodiazepine therapy. *American Journal of Psychiatry, 157,* 1973–1979.

Ridley, M. (2003). What makes you who you are: Which is stronger, nature or nurture? *Time, 161*(22), 54-62.

Rigotti, N. A., Lee, J. E., & Wechsler, H. (2000). U.S. college students' use of tobacco products: Results of a national survey. *Journal of the American Medical Association, 284,* 699–705.

Riley, W. T., Trieber, F. A., & Woods, M. G. (1989). Anger and hostility in depression. *Journal of Nervous & Mental Disease, 177,* 668–674.

Rind, B., Tromovitch, P., & Bauseman, R. (1998). A meta-analytic examination of assumed properties of child sexual abuse using college samples. *Psychological Bulletin, 124,* 22-53.

Rine, R. M., Schubert, M. C., & Balkany, T. J. (1999). Visual-vestibular habituation and balance training for motion sickness. *Physical Therapy, 79,* 949–957.

Riskind, J. H., Williams, N. L., Gessner, T. L., Chrosniak, L. D., & Cortina, J. M., (2000). The looming maladaptive style: Anxiety, danger, and schematic processing. *Journal of Personality and Social Psychology, 79,* 837–852.

Rivers, P. C. (1994). *Alcohol and human behavior.* Englewood Cliffs, NJ: Prentice Hall.

Roach, M. (1996). Can you laugh your stress away? *Health, 10*(5), 92–97.

Roberts, B. W., & DelVecchio, W. F. (2000). The rank-order consistency of personality traits from childhood to old age: A quantitative review of longitudinal studies. *Psychological Bulletin, 126,* 3–25.

Roberts, B. W., Caspi, A., & Moffitt, T. E. (2001). The kids are alright: Growth and stability in personality development from adolescence to adulthood. *Journal of Personality & Social Psychology, 81,* 670–683.

Roberts, S. M. (1995). Applicability of the goodness-of-fit hypothesis to coping with daily hassles. *Psychological Reports, 77*(3, Pt. 1), 943–954.

Robins, L. N., & Regier, D. A. (Eds.). (1991). *Psychiatric disorders in America: The Epidemiologic Catchment Area Study.* New York: The Free Press.

Robins, R. W., Fraley, R. C., Roberts, B. W., & Trzesniewski, K. H. (2001). A longitudinal study of personality change in young adulthood. *Journal of Personality, 69,* 617–640.

Robinson, J., & Godbey, G. (1998). No sex, please. We're college graduates. *American Demographics, 20,* 18-23.

Robinson, L. A., Berman, J. S., & Neimeyer, R. A. (1990). Psychotherapy for the treatment of depression: A comprehensive review of controlled outcome research. *Psychological Bulletin, 109,* 30–49.

Robinson, N. M., Abbott, R. D., Berninger, V. W., & Busse, J. (1996). The structure of abilities in math-precocious young children: Gender similarities and differences. *Journal of Educational Psychology, 88,* 341–352.

Rodriguez, L. J. (1994). *Always running: Mi vida loca, gang days in L.A.* New York: Simon & Schuster.

Rogers, C. R. (1942). *Counseling and psychotherapy.* Boston: Houghton Mifflin.

Rogers, C. R. (1951). *Client-centered therapy: Its current practice, implications, and theory.* Boston: Houghton Mifflin.

Rogers, C. R. (1959). A theory of therapy, personality, and interpersonal relationships, as developed in the client-centered framework. In S. Koch (Ed.), *Psychology: A study of science,* (Vol. 3). New York: McGraw-Hill.

Rogers, C. R. (1961). *On becoming a person.* Boston: Houghton Mifflin.

Rogers, C. R. (1970). *Carl Rogers on encounter groups.* New York: Harper & Row.

Rogers, C. R. (1980). *A way of being.* Boston: Houghton Mifflin.

Rogers, C. R. (1986). Client-centered therapy. In I. L. Kutash & A. Wolf (Eds.), *Psychotherapists' casebook.* San Francisco: Jossey-Bass.

Rogers, N. L., Szuba, M. P., Staab, J. P., Evans, D. L., & Dinges, D. F. (2001). Neuroimmunologic aspects of sleep and sleep loss. *Seminars in Clinical Neuropsychiatry, 6,* 295–307.

Rogers, T. B. (1995). *The psychological testing enterprise: An introduction.* Pacific Grove, CA: Brooks/Cole.

Rogoff, B., & Chavajah, P. (1995). What's become of research on the cultural basis of cognitive development? *American Psychologist, 50,* 859–873.

Rohan, M. J., & Zanna, M. P. (1996). Value transmission in families. In C. Seligman & J. M. Olson (Eds.), *The psychology of values: The Ontario symposium* (Vol. 8). Mahwah, NJ: Erlbaum.

Rokicki, L. A., Holroyd, K. A., France, C. R., Lipchik, G. L., France, J. L., & Kvaal, S. A. (1997). Change mechanisms associated with combined relaxation/EMG biofeedback training for chronic tension headache. *Applied Psychophysiology and Biofeedback, 22,* 21–41.

Rollins, B. C. & Feldman, H. (1975, February). Marital satisfaction over the life cycle. *Journal of Marriage and the Family, 32,* 25.

Rolls, E. T. (2000). The representation of umami tastes in the taste cortex. *Journal of Nutrition, 130,* 960–965.

Rooney, N. J., Bradshaw, J. W. S., & Robinson, I. H. (2001). Do dogs respond to play signals given by humans? *Animal Behavior, 61,* 715–722.

Rosch, E. (1973a). Natural categories. *Cognitive Psychology, 4,* 328–350.

Rosch, E. (1973b). On the internal structure of perceptual and semantic categories. In T. E. Moore (Ed.), *Cognitive development and the acquisition of language.* New York: Academic Press.

Rosch, E., Mervis, C. B., Gray, W. D., Johnson, D. M., & Boyes-Braem, P. (1976). Basic objects in natural categories. *Cognitive Psychology, 8,* 382–439.

Rose, D. (April 16, 2003). Spy aided rescue of Jessica. *New York Daily News.* Retrieved April 18, 2003, from http://story.news.yahoo.com/news?tmpl=story&u=/kr/20030416/lo_krnewyork/spy_aided_rescue_of_jessica

Rose, R. J. (1995). Genes and human behavior. *Annual Review of Psychology, 46,* 625–654.

Rose, S. A. (1980). Enhancing visual recognition memory in preterm infants. *Developmental Psychology, 16,* 85–92.

Rosen, J. B. (2004). The neurobiology of conditioned and unconditioned fear: A neurobehavioral system analysis of the amygdale. *Behavior and Cognitive Neuroscience Reviews, 3,* 23–41.

Rosenblith, J. F. (1992). *In the beginning.* Newbury Park, CA: Sage.

Rosenhan, D. L. (1969). Some origins of the concerns for others. In P. Mussen & M. Covington (Eds.), *Trends and issues in developmental psychology.* New York: Holt, Rinehart, & Winston.

Rosenhan, D. L. (1973). On being sane in insane places. *Science, 179,* 250–258.

Ross, C. A. (1997). *Dissociative identity disorder: Diagnosis, clinical features, and treatment of multiple personality.* Toronto: Wiley.

Ross, M. W. (1980). Retrospective distortion in homosexual research. *Archives of Sexual Behavior, 9,* 523-531.

Roth, S., & Cohen, J. L. (1986). Approach, avoidance, and coping with stress. *American Psychologist, 41,* 813–819.

Roth, W. F. (1991). *Work and rewards: Redefining our work-life reality.* New York: Praeger.

Rothbart, M. K., Ahadi, S. A., & Evans, D. E. (2000). Temperament and personality: Origins and outcomes. *Journal of Personality and Social Psychology, 78,* 122–135.

Rothbaum, B. O., Hodges, L. F., Kooper, R., Opdyke, D., & Williford, J. (1995). Effectiveness of computer-generated (virtual reality) graded exposure in the treatment of acrophobia. *American Journal of Psychiatry, 152,* 626–628.

Rothbaum, B. O., Hodges, L., Watson, B. A., Kessler, G. D., Opdyke, D. (1996). Virtual reality exposure therapy in the treatment of fear of flying: A case report. *Behavior Research & Therapy, 34,* 477–481.

Rothbaum, F., Schneider Rosen, K. S., Pott, M., & Beatty, M. (1995). Early parent-child relationships and later problem behavior: A longitudinal study. *Merrill-Palmer Quarterly, 41,* 133–151.

Rothenberg, A., & Wyshak, G. (2004). Family background and genius. *Canadian Journal of Psychiatry, 49,* 185–191.

Rotter, J. (1982). *The development and application of social learning theory.* New York: Praeger.

Rowe, D. C. (1990). *The limits of family influence.* New York: Guilford.

Rubin, K. H., Lynch, D., Coplan, R., Rose-Krasnor, L., & Booth, C. L. (1994). "Birds of a feather . . .": Behavioral concordances and preferential personal attraction in children. *Child Development, 65,* 1778–1785.

Rubin, S. S. (1993). The death of a child is forever: The life course impact of child loss. In M. Stroebe, W. Stroebe, & R. O. Hansson (Eds.), *Handbook of bereavement: Theory, research, and intervention.* Cambridge: Cambridge University Press.

Rubinstein, R. L., Alexander, R. B., Goodman, M., & Luborsky, M. (1991). Key relationships of never married, childless older women: A cultural analysis. *Journal of Gerontology: Social Sciences, 46,* S270–S277.

Rubonis, A.V., & Bickman, L. (1991). Psychological impairment in the wake of disaster: The disaster-psychopathology relationship. *Psychological Bulletin, 109,* 384–399.

Ruderman, A. J. (1985). Dysphoric mood and overeating: A test of restraint theory's disinhibition hypothesis. *Journal of Abnormal Psychology, 94,* 78–85.

Rudgley, R. (1998). *The encyclopedia of psychoactive substances.* New York: Little, Brown.

Ruffin, C. L. (1993). Stress and health: Little hassles vs. major life events. *Australian Psychologist, 28*(3), 201–208.

Rumelhart, D. E. (1980). Schemata: The basic building blocks of cognition. In R. Spiro, B. Bruce, & W. Brewer (Eds.), *Theoretical issues in reading comprehension.* Hillsdale, NJ: Erlbaum.

Rush, M. C., Schoel, W. A., & Barnard, S. M. (1995). Psychological resiliency in the public sector: "Hardiness" and pressure for change. *Journal of Vocational Behavior, 46*(1), 17–39.

Rushton, W. A. H. (1958). Kinetics of cone pigments measured objectively in the living fovea. *Annals of the New York Academy of Sciences, 74,* 291–304.

Rushton, W.A.H. (1975). Visual pigments and color blindness. *Scientific American, 232,* 64–74.

Russell, R. J. H., & Wells, P. A. (1994). Predictors of happiness in married couples. *Personality and Individual Differences, 17,* 313–321.

Rutherford, W. (1886). A new theory of hearing. *Journal of Anatomy and Physiology, 21, 166–168.*

Rutkowski, G. K., Gruder, C. L., & Romer, D. (1983). Group cohesiveness, social norms, and bystander intervention. *Journal of Personality and Social Psychology, 44,* 542–552.

Rutter, M. (1981). *Maternal deprivation revisited* (2nd ed.). New York: Penguin Books.

Rutter, M., & O'Connor, T. G. (2004). Are there biological programming effects for psychological development? Findings from a study of Romanian adoptees. *Developmental Psychology, 40,* 81–94.

Sacks, O. W. (1985). *The man who mistook his wife for a hat and other clinical tales.* New York: HarperPerennial.

Sadker, M., & Sadker, D. (1986). Questioning skills. In J. Cooper (Ed.), *Classroom teaching skills* (3rd ed.; pp. 143–180). Lexington, MA: D. C. Heath.

Sadker, M., & Sadker, D. (1994). *How America's schools cheat girls.* New York: Scribners.

Sadler, W. A. (2000). *The third age: Six principles for growth and renewal after forty.* New York: Perseus.

Sah, P., Faber, E. S. L., Lopez De Armentia, M., & Power, J. (2003). The aymgdaloid complex: Anatomy and physiology. *Physiological Reviews, 83* 803–834.

Sakari, M. M. (1975). Small group cohesiveness and detrimental conformity. *Sociometry, 38,* 340–357.

Salend, S. J. (2001). *Creating inclusive classrooms: Effective and reflective practices* (4th ed.). Upper Saddle River, NJ: Prentice Hall.

Salkovskis, P. M., Westbrook, D., Davis, J., Jeavons, A., & Gledhill, A. (1997). Effects of neutralizing on intrusive thoughts: An experiment investigating the etiology of obsessive-compulsive disorder. *Behaviour Research & Therapy, 35,* 211–219.

Salthouse, T. A. (1994). The aging of working memory. *Neuropsychology, 8,* 535–543.

Salthouse, T. A. (2004). What and when of cognitive aging. *Current Directions in Psychological Science, 13,* 140–144.

Samarel, N. (1995). The dying process. In H. Wass & R. A. Neimeyer (Eds.), *Dying: Facing the facts* (3rd ed.; pp. 89–116). Washington, DC: Taylor & Francis.

Samuels, J., & Nestadt, G. (1997). Epidemiology and genetics of obsessive-compulsive disorder. *International Review of Psychiatry, 9,* 61–72.

Sanborn, F. (2003). September 11 and the pursuit of evil. *APS Observer, 16*(1), 20.

Sanders, S. K., & Shekhar, A. (1995). Regulation of anxiety by GABA-sub(A) receptors in the rat amygdala. *Pharmacology, Biochemistry, & Behavior, 52,* 701–706.

Sanderson, A., & Dugoni, B. (1999). *Summary report 1997: Doctorate recipients from United States universities.* Chicago: National Opinion Research Center.

Sanderson, C. A., & Cantor, N. (1995). Social dating goals in late adolescence: Implications for safer sexual activity. *Journal of Personality and Social Psychology, 68,* 1121–1134.

Sanes, J. N., Dimitrov, B., & Hallett, M. (1990). Motor learning in patients with cerebellar dysfunction. *Brain, 113,* 103–120.

San Jose Mercury News, (1996, September 6). Western states battle methamphetamine.

Sanyal, S., & vanTol, H. M. (1997). Review the role of dopamine D4 receptors in schizophrenia and antipsychotic action. *Journal of Psychiatric Research, 31,* 219–232.

Sapolsky, R. M. (2000). The possibility of neurotoxicity in the hippocampus in major depression: A primer on neuron death. *Biological Psychiatry, 48,* 755–765.

Saskin, P. (1997). Obstructive sleep apnea: Treatment options, efficacy, and effects. In M. R. Pressman & W. C. Orr (Eds.), *Understanding sleep: The evaluation and treatment of sleep disorders.* Washington DC: American Psychological Association.

Saudino, K. J., McQuire, S., Reiss, D. Heatherington, E. M., & Plomin, R. (1995). Parent ratings of EAS temperaments in twins, full siblings, half siblings, and step siblings. *Journal of Personality and Social Psychology, 68,* 723–733.

Savage-Rumbaugh, E..S., McDonald, K., Sevcik, R., Hopkins, W., & Rupert, E. (1986). Spontaneous symbol acquisition and communicative use by pygmy chimpanzees (*Pan paniscus*). *Journal of Experimental Psychology: General, 115,* 211–235.

Savage-Rumbaugh, S. (1987). Communication, symbolic communication and language: Reply to Seidenberg and Petitto. *Journal of Experimental Psychology: General, 116,* 288–292.

Saxena, S., Brody, A. L., Schwartz, J. M., & Baxter, L. R. (1998). Neuroimaging and frontal-subcortical circuitry in obsessive-compulsive disorder. *British Journal of Psychiatry, 173* (Suppl. 35), 26–37.

Schachter, S. (1951). Deviation, rejection, and communication. *Journal of Abnormal and Social Psychology, 46,* 190–207.

Schachter, S., & Singer, J. E. (1962). Cognitive, social, and physiological determinants of emotional state. *Psychological Review, 69,* 379–399.

Schacter, D. L. (1996). *Searching for memory.* New York: Basic Books.

Schacter, D. L., Alpert, N. M., Savage, C. R., Rauch, S. L., & Alpert, M. S. (1996). Conscious recollection and the hippocampal formation: Evidence from positron emission tomography. *Proceedings of the National Academy of Science, USA, 93,* 321–325.

Schafran, L. H. (1995, August 26). Rape is still underreported. *The New York Times,* p. A19.

Schaie, K. W. (1983). The Seattle longitudinal study: A 21-year exploration of psychometric intelligence in adulthood. In K. W. Schaie (Ed.), *Longitudinal studies of adult psychological development.* New York: Guilford.

Schaie, K. W. (1994). The course of adult intellectual development. *American Psychologist, 49,* 304–313.

Schaie, K. W. (1996). *Intellectual development in adulthood. The Seattle longitudinal study.* New York: Cambridge University Press.

Schaie, K. W., & Willis, S. L. (2000). A stage theory model of adult cognitive development revisited. In B. Rubinstein, M. Moss, & M. Kleban (Eds.), *The many dimensions of aging: Essays in honor of M. Powell Lawton* (pp. 173–191). New York: Springer.

Schaller, S. (1995). *A man without words.* Berkeley, CA: University of California Press.

Scharf, B., & Buus, S. (1986). Audition I. In K. R. Boff, L. Kaufman, & J. P. Thomas (Eds.), *Handbook of perception and human performance* (pp. 14.1–14.71). New York. Wiley.

Scheir, M. F., & Carver, C. S. (1992). Effects of optimism on psychological and physical well-being: Theoretical overview and empirical update. *Cognitive Therapy and Research, 16,* 201–228.

Scherrer, J. F., True, W. R., Xian, H., Lyons,. M. J., Eisen, S. A., Goldberg, J., Lin, N., & Tsuang, M. T. (2000). Evidence for genetic influences common and specific to symptoms of generalized anxiety and panic. *Journal of Affective Disorders, 57,* 25–35.

Scheutte, R. A., & Fazio, R. H. (1995). Attitude accessibility and motivation as determinants of biased processing: A test of the MODE model. *Personality and Social Psychology Bulletin, 21,* 704–710.

Schielser-Stropp, B. (1984). Bulimia: A review of the literature. *Psychological Review, 95,* 247–257.

Schiffman, S. S., Graham, B. G., Sattley-Miller, E. A., Zervakis, J., & Welsh-Bohmer, K. (2002). Taste, smell and neuropsychological performance of individuals at familial risk for Alzheimer's disease. *Neurobiology of Aging, 23,* 397–404.

Schinka, J. A., Letsch, E. A., & Crawford, F. C. (2002). DRD4 and novelty seeking: Results of meta-analyses. *American Journal of Medical Genetics, 114,* 643–648.

Schleifer, S. J., Keller, S. E., Camerino, M., Thornton, J. C., & Stein, M. (1983). Suppression of lymphocyte stimulation following bereavement. *Journal of the American Medical Association, 250,* 374–377.

Schleifer, S. J., Keller, S. E., McKegney, F. P., & Stein, M. (1979). The influence of stress and other psychosocial factors on human immunity. Paper presented at the 36th Annual Meeting of the American Psychosomatic Society.

Schlenger, W. E., Caddell, J. M., Ebert, L., Jordan, B. K., Rourke, K. M., Wilson, D., Thalji, L., Dennis, J. M., Fairbank, J. A., & Kulka, R. A. (2002). Psychological reactions to terrorist attacks: Findings from the National Study of Americans' Reactions to September 11. *Journal of the American Medical Association, 288,* 581–588.

Schlosser, E. (1994, August). Reefer madness. *Atlantic,* p. 45.

Schmidt-Hieber, C., Jonas, P., & Bischofberger, J. (2004). Enhanced synaptic plasticity in newly generated granule cells of the adult hippocampus. *Nature, 429,* 184–187.

Schooler, J. W., & Engstler-Schooler, T. Y. (1990). Verbal overshadowing of visual memories: Some things are better left unsaid. *Cognitive Psychology, 22,* 36–71.

Schott, R. L. (1995). The childhood and family dynamics of transvestites. *Archives of Sexual Behavior, 24,* 309-327.

Schrader, E. (2000, August 2). Vast meth supply network broken, U.S. says 10-ton seizure of chemical used to make speed. *Los Angeles Times, p. 3.*

Schuckit, M. A. (1998). Biological, psychological, and environmental predictors of the alcoholism risk: A longitudinal study. *Journal of Studies on Alcohol, 59,* 485–494.

Schuckit, M. A., & Smith, T. L. (1997). Assessing the risk for alcoholism among sons of alcoholics. *Journal of Studies on Alcohol, 58,* 141–145.

Schuh, K. J., & Griffiths, R. R. (1997). Caffeine reinforcement: The role of withdrawal. *Psychopharmacology, 130,* 320–326.

Schultz, D. P., & Schultz, S. E. (2000). *A history of modern psychology,* (7th ed.). Fort Worth, TX: Harcourt Brace.

Schultz, D. P., & Schultz, S. E. (2005). *Theories of personality* (8th ed.). Belmont, CA: Thomson Learning.

Schwartz, I. M. (1999). Sexual activity prior to coitus initiation: A comparison between males and females. *Archives of Sexual Behavior, 28,* 63-69.

Schwartz, J. E., Friedman, H. S., Tucker, J. S., Tomlinson-Keasey, C., Wingard, D. L., & Criqui, M. H. (1995). Sociodemographic and psychosocial factors in childhood as predictors of adult mortality. *American Journal of Public Health, 85,* 1237–1245.

Schwarzwald, J., Bizman, A., & Raz, M. (1983). The foot-in-the-door paradigm: Effects of second request size on donation probability and donor generosity. *Personality and Social Psychology Bulletin, 9,* 443–450.

Scott, S. K., Young, A. W., Calder, A. J., & Hellawell, D. J. (1997). Impaired auditory recognition of fear and anger following bilateral amygdala lesions. *Nature, 385,* 254–257.

Scott, T. R., & Plata-Salaman, C. R. (1991). Coding of taste quality. In T. V. Gethell, R. L. Doty, L. M. Bartoshuk, & J. B. Snow, Jr. (Eds.), *Smell and taste in health and disease* (pp. 345–368). New York: Raven.

Scoville, W. B., & Milner, B. (1957). Loss of recent memory after bilateral hippocampal lesions. *Journal of Neurology, Neurosurgery, and Psychiatry, 20,* 11–19.

Scully, J. A., Tosi, H., & Banning, K. (2000). Life events checklist: Revisiting the social readjustment rating scale after 30 years. *Educational & Psychological Measurement, 60,* 864–876.

Seeman, P. (1999). Brain development, X: Pruning during development. *American Journal of Psychiatry, 156,* 168.

Segal, M. W. (1974). Alphabet and attraction: An unobtrusive measure of the effect of propinquity in a field setting. *Journal of Personality and Social Psychology, 30,* 654–657.

Segal, N. L. (1993). Twin, sibling, and adoption methods: Tests of evolutionary hypotheses. *American Psychologist, 48,* 943–956.

Segerstrom, S. C. (2000). Personality and the immune system: Models, methods, and mechanisms. *Annals of Behavioral Medicine, 22,* 180–190.

Segerstrom, S. C., Taylor, S. E., Kemeny, M. E., & Fahey, J. L., (1998). Optimism is associated with mood, coping, and immune change in response to stress. *Journal of Personality and Social Psychology, 74,* 6.

Segraves, R. T. (1988). Drugs and desire. In S. Leiblum & R. Rosen (Eds.), *Sexual desire disorders.* New York: Guilford Press.

Segrin, C., & Nabi, R. L. (2002). Does television viewing cultivate unrealistic expectations about marriage? *Journal of Communication, 52,* 247–263.

Seidler, R. D., Purushotham, A., Kim, S.-G., Ugurbil, K., Willingham, D., & Ashe, J. (2002). Cerebellum activation associated with performance change but not after motor learning. *Science* (Washington), *296,* 2043–2046.

Seidman, S. N., & Rieder, R. O. (1994). A review of sexual behavior in the U.S. *American Journal of Psychiatry, 151,* 330-341.

Seiffert, A. E., Somers, D. C., Dale, A. M., & Tootell, R. B. H. (2003). Functional MRI studies of human visual motion perception: Texture, luminance, attention, and after-effects. *Cerebral Cortex, 13,* 340–349.

Seligman, L. (1994). *Developmental career counseling and assessment* (2nd ed.). Thousand Oaks, CA: Sage.

Seligman, M. E. P. (1970). On the generality of laws of learning. *Psychological Review, 77,* 406–418.

Seligman, M. E. P. (1974). Depression and learned helplessness. In R. J. Friedman & M. M. Katz (Eds.), *The psychology of depression: Contemporary theory and research.* Washington, DC: Winston-Wiley.

Seligman, M. E. P. (1989). *Helplessness.* New York: Freeman.

Seligman, M. E. P. (1995). The effectiveness of psychotherapy: The *Consumer Reports* Study. *American Psychologist, 50,* 965–974.

Seligman, M. E. P., & Maier, S. F. (1967). Failure to escape traumatic shock. *Journal of Experimental Psychology, 74,* 1–9.

Selling, L. H. (1940). *Men against madness.* New York: Greenberg.

Selmi, P. M., Klein, M. H., Greist, J. H., Sorrell, S. P., & Erdman, H. P. (1990). Computer-administered cognitive-behavioral therapy for depression. *American Journal of Psychiatry, 147,* 51–56.

Seltzer, J. A. (2001). Families formed outside of marriage. In R. M. Milardo (Ed.), *Understanding families into the new millennium: A decade in review* (pp. 466–487). Minneapolis: National Council on Family Relations.

Selye, H. (1976). *The stress of life.* New York: McGraw-Hill.

Sen, S., Burmeister, M., & Ghosh, D. (2004). Meta-analysis of the association between a serotonin transporter promoter polymorphism (5-HTTLPR) and anxiety–related personality traits. *American Journal of Medical Genetics, 127,* 85–89.

Sen, S., Villafuerte, S., Nesse, R., Stoltenberg, S. F., Hopcian, J., Gleiberman, L., Weder, A., & Burmeister, M. (2004). Serotonin transporter and GABA(A) alpha 6 receptor variants are associated with neuroticism. *Biological Psychiatry, 55,* 244–249.

Senghas, A., & Coppola, M. (2001). Children creating language: How Nicaraguan sign language acquired a spatial grammar. *Psychological Science, 12,* 323–328.

Seto, M. C., & Barbaree, H. E. (1995). The role of alcohol in sexual aggression. *Clinical Psychology Review, 15,* 545–566.

Sexton, J. (1995, July 25). Reviving Kitty Genovese case, and its passions. *The New York Times,* pp. B1, B5.

Seyman, R. M., Albakry, A., Ghobish, A., Arif, H., Dandash, K., & Rashwan, H. (2003). Prevalence of erectile dysfunction and its correlates in Egypt: A community-based study. *International Journal of Impotence Research, 15,* 237-245.

Shafer, M., & Crichlow, S. (1996). Antecedents of groupthink: A quantitative study. *Journal of Conflict Resolution, 40,* 415–435.

Shallenberger, R. S. (1993). *Taste chemistry.* London: Blackie.

Shallice, T., & Warrington, E. K. (1970). Independent functioning of verbal memory stores: A neuropsychological study. *Quarterly Journal of Experimental Psychology, 22,* 261–273.

Shallice, T., & Warrington, E. K. (1974). The dissociation between long-term retention of meaningful sounds and verbal material. *Nueropsychologica, 12,* 553, 555.

Shanker, S. G., Savage-Rumbaugh, E. S., & Taylor, T. J. (1999). Kanzi: A new beginning. *Animal Learning & Behavior, 27,* 24–25.

Shapiro, D. A., & Shapiro, D. (1982). Meta-analysis of comparative therapy outcome studies: A replication and refinement. *Psychological Bulletein, 92,* 581–604.

Share, D. L., & Silva, P. A. (2003). Gender bias in IQ-discrepancy and post-discrepancy definitions of reading disability. *Journal of Learning Disabilities, 36,* 4–14.

Shaw, J. L., Borough, H. W., & Fink, M. I. (1994). Perceived sexual orientation and helping behavior by males and females: The wrong number technique. *Journal of Psychology and Human Sexuality, 6,* 73–81.

Sheldon, K. M., Arndt, J., & Houser-Marko, L. (2003). In search of the orgasmic valuing process: The human tendency to move towards beneficial goal choices. *Journal of Personality, 71,* 835–869.

Sheline, Y. I. (2000). 3D MRI studies of neuroanatomic changes in unipolar major depression: The role of stress and medical comorbidity. *Biological Psychiatry, 48,* 791–800.

Shen, B. J., McCreary, C. P., & Myers, H. F. (2004). Independent and mediated contributions of personality, coping, social support, and depressive symptoms to physical functioning outcome among patients in cardiac rehabilitation. *Journal of Behavioral Medicine, 27,* 39–62.

Shenon, P. (1994, May 15). The world: Asia's having one huge nicotine fit. *New York Times, 4,* p. 1.

Shepard, R. N. (1978). The mental image. *American Psychologist, 33,* 125–137.

Sherif, M. (1966). *In common predicament: Social psychology of intergroup conflict and cooperation.* Boston: Houghton Mifflin.

Sherif, M., Harvey, O. J., White, J., Hood, W., & Sherif, C. (1961). *Intergroup conflict and cooperation: The Robber's Cave experiment.* Norman, OK: University of Oklahoma Press.

Sherman, F. T. (2001). How to predict your patient's future: Mnemonic serves as a quick screening device for treatable late-life disability. *Geriatrics, 56,* 3.

Sherman, S. J., Beike, D. R., & Ryalls, K. R. (1999). Dual-process accounts of inconsistencies in responses to general and specific cases. In S. Chaiken & Y. Trope (Eds.), *Dual-process theories in social psychology.* New York: Guilford.

Sherwin, B. B., & Gelfand, M. M. (1987). The role of androgen in the maintenance of sexual functioning in oophorectomized women. *Psychosomatic Medicine, 49,* 397-409.

Shields, M. (2004). Stress, health and the benefit of social support. *Health Reports, 15,* 9–38.

Shimoff, E., Catania, A. C., & Matthews, B. A. (1981). Unstructured human responding: Sensitivity to low-rate performance to schedule contingencies. *Journal of Experimental Analysis of Behavior, 36,* 207–220.

Shiner, R. L., Masten, A. S., & Roberts, J. M. (2003). Childhood personality foreshadows adult personality and life outcomes two decades later. *Journal of Personality, 71,* 1145–1170.

Shintani, T., Hughes, C., Beckham, S., & O'Connor, H. (1991). Obesity and cardiovascular risk intervention through the ad libitum feeding of traditional Hawaiian diet. *American Journal of Clinical Nutrition, 53,* 1647S–1651S.

Shneidman, E. S. (1987, March). At the point of no return. *Psychology Today,* pp. 54–58.

Shou, M. (1993). *Lithium treatment of manic-depressive illness: A practical guide* (5th ed.). Basel, Switzerland: Karger.

Shulman, S., Scharf, M., Lumer, D., & Maurer, O. (2001). Parental divorce and young adult children's romantic relationships: Resolution of the divorce experience. *American Journal of Orthopsychiatry, 71,* 473–478.

Siegel, J. M. (2001). The REM sleep-memory consolidation hypothesis. *Science, 294,* 1058–1063.

Siegel, L. S., & Hodkin, B. (1982). The garden path to the understanding of cognitive development: Has Piaget led us into the poison ivy? In S. Modgil & C. Modgil (Eds.), *Jean Piaget: Consensus and controversy.* New York: Praeger.

Siegelman, M. (1987). Empirical input. In L. Diamant (Ed.), *Male and female homosexuality: Psychological approaches* (pp. 33-79). Washington, DC: Hemisphere.

Siever, L. J., & Koenigsberg, H. W. (2000). The frustrating no-mans-land of borderline personality disorder. *Cerebrum, The Dana Forum on Brain Science, 2*(4).

Signorielli, N., & Bacue, A. (1999). Recognition and respect: A content analysis of prime-time television characters. *Sex Roles, 40,* 527–544.

Signorielli, N., & Lears, M. (1992). Children, television, and conceptions about chores: Attitudes and behavior. *Sex Roles, 27,* 157–170.

Silva, C. E., & Kirsch, I. (1992). Interpretive sets, expectancy, fantasy proneness, and dissociation as predictors of hypnotic response. *Journal of Personality and Social Psychology, 63,* 847–856.

Sim, H. (2000). Relationship of daily hassles and social support to depression and antisocial behavior among early adolescents. *Journal of Youth & Adolescence, 29,* 647–659.

Simon, H. A. (1974). How big is a chunk? *Science, 183,* 482–488.

Simonson, K., & Subich, L. M. (1999). Rape perceptions as a function of gender-role traditionality and victim-perpetrator association. *Sex Roles, 40,* 617-634.

Simpson, G., & Yinger, J. M. (1985). *Racial and cultural minorities.* New York: Plenum.

Sinclair, S. (1985). *How animals see.* New York: Facts on File Publications.

Singer, B. (Ed.). (1998). *42 Up.* New York: The New Press.

Singh, S., & Darroch, J. E. (1999). Trends in sexual activity among adolescent American women: 1982-1995. *Family Planning Perspectives, 31,* 211.219.

Sinnott, J. D. (1998). *The development of logic in adulthood: Postformal thought and its applications.* New York: Plenum.

Sistrunk, F., & McDavid, J. W. (1971). Sex variable in conformity behavior. *Journal of Social and Personality Psychology, 17,* 200–207.

Skager, R., Frifth, S. L., & Maddahian, E. (1989). *Biennial survey of drug and alcohol use among California students in Grades 7, 9, and 11: Winter 1987–1988.* Sacramento, CA: Office of the Attorney General, Crime Prevention Center.

Skinner, B. F. (1938). *The behavior of organisms.* New York: Appleton-Century-Crofts.

Skinner, B. F. (1953). *Science and human behavior.* New York: Macmillan.

Slameka, N. J. (1966). Differentiation versus unlearning of verbal associations. *Journal of Experimental Psychology, 71,* 822–828.

Sleep Foundation Organization (2001). *Sleep in America Poll.* Retrieved November 13, 2003, from www.sleepfoundation.org/publications/poll2001

Sloan, R. P., & Bagiella, E. (2002). Claims about religious involvement and health outcomes. *Annals of Behavioral Medicine, 24,* 14–21.

Smith, A. D. (1996). Memory. In J. E. Birrent & K. W. Schaie (Eds.), *Handbook of the psychology of aging* (4th ed., pp. 236–250). San Diego, CA: Academic Press.

Smith, A. D., & Earles, J. L. K. (1996). Memory changes in normal aging. In F. Blanchard-Fields & T. M. Hess (Eds.), *Perspectives on cognitive change in adulthood and aging.* New York: McGraw-Hill.

Smith, A. M., Rosenthal, D. A., & Reichler, H. (1996). High schoolers' masturbatory practices: Their relationship to sexual intercourse and personal characteristics. *Psychological Reports, 79,* 499-509.

Smith, C. (1995). Sleep states and memory processes. *Behavioural Brain Research, 69*(1–2), 137–145.

Smith, D. C. (1993). The terminally ill patient's right to be in denial. *Omega, 27,* 115–121.

Smith, D. E., & Cogswell, C. (1994). A cross-cultural perspective on adolescent girls' body perception. *Perceptual and Motor Skills, 78,* 744–746.

Smith, J. W., Frawley, P. J., & Polissar, N. L. (1997). Six- and twelve-month abstinence rates in inpatient alcoholics treated with either faradic aversion or chemical aversion compared with matched inpatients from a treatment registry. *Journal of Addictive Diseases, 16,* 5–24.

Smith, J., & Baltes, P. B. (1990). Wisdom-related knowledge: Age/cohort differences in responses to life-planning problems. *Developmental Psychology, 26,* 494–505.

Smith, J., Staudinger, U. M., & Baltes, P. B. (1994). Occupational settings facilitating wisdom-related knowledge: The sample case of clinical psychologists. *Journal of Consulting and Clinical Psychology, 66,* 989–999.

Smith, M. C., Coleman, S. R., & Gormezano, I. (1969). Classical conditioning of the rabbit's nictitating membrane response at backward, simultaneous, and forward, CS-US intervals. *Journal of Comparative and Physiological Psychology, 69,* 226–231.

Smith, M. L., & Glass, G. V. (1977). Meta-analysis of psychotherapy outcome studies. *American Psychologist, 32,* 752–760.

Smith, M. L., Glass, G. V., & Miller, T. I. (1980). *The benefits of psychotherapy.* Baltimore: Johns Hopkins University Press.

Smith, P. (1991). Introduction: The study of grandparenthood. In P. K. Smith (Ed.), *The psychology of grandparenthood: An international perspective* (pp. 1–16). London: Routledge.

Smith, R. A. (2002). Race, gender, and authority in the workplace: Theory and research. *Annual Review of Sociology,* 509–542.

Smock, P. J. (2000). Cohabitation in the United States: An appraisal of research themes, findings, and implications. *Annual Review of Sociology, 26,* 1–20.

Smyth, J., Litcher, L., Hurewitz, A., & Stone, A. (2001). Relaxation training and cortisol secretion in adult asthmatics. *Journal of Health Psychology, 6,* 217–227.

Snarey, J. (1995). In a communitarian voice: The sociological expansion of Kohlbergian theory, research, and practice. In W. M. Kurtines & J. L. Gewirtz (Eds.), *Moral development: An introduction* (pp.109–134). Boston: Allyn & Bacon.

Snibbe, A. C. (2003). Cultural psychology: Studying the exotic other. *APS Observer, 16*(1), 30–32.

Snyder, C. R., Ilardi, S., Michael, S. T., & Cheavens, J. (2000). Hope theory: Updating a common process for psychological change. In C. R. Snyder & R. E. Ingram (Eds.), *Handbook of psychological change: Psychotherapy processes and practices for the 21st century* (pp. 128–153). New York: Wiley.

Soares, J. C., & Mann, J. J. (1997). The functional neuroanatomy of mood disorders. *Journal of Psychiatric Research, 31,* 393–432.

Solberg, E. E., Halvorsen, R., & Holen, A. (2000). Effect of meditation on immune cells. *Stress Medicine, 16,* 185–190.

Soloff, P. H., Lis, J. A., Kelly, T., Cornelius, J., & Ulrich, R. F. (1994). Self-mutilation and suicidal behavior in borderline personality disorder. *Journal of Personality Disorders, 8,* 257–267.

Solomon, A., Arnow, B. A., Gotlib, I. H., & Wind, B. (2003). Individualized measurement of irrational beliefs in remitted depressives. *Journal of Clinical Psychology, 59,* 439–455.

Solomon, R. L. (1980). The opponent process theory of acquired motivation: The costs of pleasure and the benefits of pain. *American Psychologist, 35,* 691–712.

Somers, V. K., Phil, D., Dyken, M. E., Mark, A. L., & Abboud, F. M. (1993). Sympathetic-nerve activity during sleep in normal subjects. *New England Journal of Medicine, 328,* 303–307.

Sommers, C. H. (2000). *The war against boys: How misguided feminism is harming our young men.* New York: Simon & Schuster.

Sonstroem, R. J., & Bernardo, P. (1982). Intraindividual pregame state anxiety and basketball performance: A re-examination of the inverted-U curve. *Journal of Sport Psychology, 4,* 235–245.

Sonuga-Barke, E. J. S., Dalen, L., & Remington, B. (2003). Do executive deficits and delay aversion make independent contributions to preschool attention-deficit/hyperactivity disorder symptoms? *Journal of the American Academy of Child and Adolescent Psychiatry, 42,* 1335–1342.

Soper, B., Milford, G. E., & Rosenthal, G. T. (1995). Belief when evidence does not support theory. *Psychology & Marketing, 12,* 415–422.

Sowell, E. R., Thompson, P. M., Tessner, K. D., & Toga, A. W. (2001). Mapping continued brain growth and gray matter density reduction in dorsal frontal cortex: Inverse relationships during postadolescent brain maturation. *Journal of Neuroscience, 21,* 8819–8829.

Spanos, N. P. (1996). *Multiple identities and false memories: A sociocognitive perspective.* Washington, DC: American Psychological Association.

Spanos, N. P., Burnley, M. C. E., & Cross, P. A. (1993). Response expectancies and interpretations as determinants of hypnotic responding. *Journal of Personality and Social Psychology, 65*(6), 1237–1242.

Spark, R. F. (2000). *Sexual health for men: The complete guide.* Cambridge, MA: Perseus.

Spearman, C. (1904). The proof and measurement of association between two things. *American Journal of Psychology, 15,* 72–101.

Spector, I., & Carey, M. (1990). Incidence and prevalence of the sexual dysfunctions: A "critical" review of the empirical literature. *Archives of Sexual Behavior, 19,* 389–408.

Spence, J. T., & Buckner, C. E. (2000). Instrumental and expressive traits, trait stereotypes, and sexist attitudes: What do they signify? *Psychology of Women Quarterly, 24,* 44–62.

Spencer, J. A., & Fremouw, W. J. (1979). Binge eating as a function of restraint and weight classification. *Journal of Abnormal Psychology, 88,* 262–267.

Sperling, G. (1960). The information that is available in brief visual presentations. *Psychological Monographs, 74* (Whole No. 498), 1–29.

Spiegel, D. A. (1998). Efficacy studies of alprazolam in panic disorder. *Psychopharmacology Bulletin, 43,* 191–195.

Squire, L. R. (1992). Memory and the hippocampus: A synthesis from findings with rats, monkeys, and humans. *Psychological Review, 99,* 195–232.

Squire, L. R., Knowlton, B., & Musen, G. (1993). The structure and organization of memory. *Annual Review of Psychology, 44,* 453–495.

Squire, L. R., Ojemann, J. G., Miezin, F. M., Petersen, S. E., Videen, T. O., & Raichle, M. E. (1992). Activation of the hippocampus in normal humans: A functional anatomical study of memory. *Proceedings of the National Academy of Science, USA, 89,* 1837–1841.

Srivastava, S., John, O. P., Gosling, S. D., & Potter, J. (2003). Development of personality in early and middle adulthood: Set in plaster or persistent change? *Journal of Personality and Social Psychology, 84,* 1041–1053.

Stagner, R. (1985). Aging in industry. In J. E. Birren & K. W. Schaie (Eds.), *Handbook of the psychology of aging* (pp. 789–817). New York: Van Nostrand Reinhold.

Stahl, S. M. (1996). *Essential psychopharmacology.* New York: Cambridge University Press.

Stahl, S. M. (1998). Basic psychopharmacology of antidepressants: Part I. Antidepressants have seven distinct mechanisms of action. *Journal of Clinical Psychiatry, 59*(Suppl. 4), 5–14.

Stahl, S. M. (2001a). Dopamine system stabilizers, aripiprazole, and the next generation of antipsychotics, Part I: "Goldilocks" actions at dopamine receptors. *Journal of Clinical Psychiatry, 62,* 841–842.

Stahl, S. M. (2001b). Dopamine system stabilizers, aripiprazole, and the next generation of antipsychotics, Part II: Illustrating their mechanism of action. *Journal of Clinical Psychiatry, 62,* 923–924.

Stanovich, K. E., & West, R. F. (1998). Individual differences in rational thought. *Journal of Experimental Psychology: General, 127,* 161–188.

Stanton, J. L. (2004). The end of TV advertising: Technologies allow consumers to miss what once were the bedrock of consumer product advertising. *Food Processing, 65,* 26.

Starr, C., & Taggart, R. (1989). *Biology: The unity and diversity of life* (5th ed.). Pacific Grove, CA: Wadsworth.

Starrels, M. E. (1994). Husbands' involvement in female gender-typed household chores. *Sex Roles, 31,* 473–491.

Statham, D. J., Heath, A. C., Madden, P., Bucholz, K. Bierut, L., Dinwiddie, S. H., Slutske, W. S., Dunne, M. P., & Martin, N. G. (1998). Suicidal behavior: An epidemiological study. *Psychological Medicine, 28,* 839–855.

Staudinger, U. M., Smith, J., & Baltes, P. B. (1992). Wisdom-related knowledge in a life review task: Age differences and the role of professional specialization. *Psychology and Aging, 7,* 271–281.

Steadman, H. J., Mulvey, E. P., Monahan, J., Robbins, P. C., Applebaum, P. S., Grisso, T., Roth, L., & Silver, F. (1998). Violence by people discharged from acute psychiatric inpatient facilities and by others in the same neighborhoods. *Archives of General Psychiatry, 55,* 393–401.

Stear, S. (2003). Health and fitness series—1. The importance of physical activity on health. *Journal of Family Health Care, 13,* 10–13.

Steele, C. M. (1997). A threat in the air: How stereotypes shape the intellectual identities and performance of women and African-Americans. *American Psychologist, 52,* 613–629.

Steele, C. M., & Aronson, J. (1995). Stereotype threat and the intellectual test performance of African Americans. *Journal of Personality and Social Psycholoty, 69,* 797–811.

Steele, J., James, J. B., & Barnett, R. C. (2002). Learning in a man's world: Examining the perceptions of undergraduate women in male-dominated academic areas. *Psychology of Women Quarterly, 26,* 46–50.

Stefflre, V., Castillo-Vales, V., & Morley, L. (1966). Language and cognition in Yucatan: A cross-cultural replication. *Journal of Personality & Social Psychology, 4,* 112–115.

Stein, J. H., & Reiser, L. W. (1994). A study of white middle-class adolescent boys' responses to "semenarche" (the first ejaculation). *Journal of Youth and Adolescence, 23,* 373–384.

Steinberg, L., & Morris, A. S. (2001). Adolescent development. *Annual Reviews of Psychology, 52,* 83–110.

Steinberg, L., Lamborn, S. D., Dornbusch, S. M., & Darling, N. (1992). Impact of parenting practices on adolescent achievement: Authoritative parenting, school involvement, and encouragement to succeed. *Child Development, 63,* 1266–1281.

Steiner, M., & Born, L. (2000). Diagnosis and treatment of premenstrual dysphoric disorder: An update. *International Clinical Psychopharmacology, 15*(Suppl. 3) s5–s17.

Steiner, M., Dunn, E., & Born, L. (2003). Hormones and mood: From menarche to menopause and beyond. *Journal of Affective Disorders, 74,* 67–83.

Steinhausen, H. C., & Vollrath, M. (1993). The self-image of adolescent patients with eating disorders. *International Journal of Eating Disorders, 13,* 221–229.

Stephan, K. E., Marshall, J. C., Friston, K. J., Rowe, J. B., Ritzl, A., Zilles, K., & Fink, G. R. (2003). Lateralized cognitive processes and lateralized task control in the human brain. *Science, 301,* 384–386.

Stephens, C. E., Pear, J. J., Wray, L. D., & Jackson, G. C. (1975). Some effects of reinforcement schedules in teaching picture names to retarded children. *Journal of Applied Behavior Analysis, 8,* 435–447.

Stephens, E. A. (2000). H. G. 3/ Camels. In K. E. Kipple & K. C. Ornelas (Series Eds.) *The Cambridge world history of food: Vol. 1* (pp. 467–480). Cambridge, UK: Cambridge University Press.

Stephens, R. S., Roffman, R. A., & Simpson, E. E. (1994). Treating adult marijuana dependence: A test of the relapse prevention model. *Journal of Consulting and Clinical Psychology, 62*(1), 92–99.

Stephenson, M. T., Benoit, W. L., & Tschida, D. A. (2001). Testing the mediating role of cognitive responses in the elaboration likelihood model. *Communication Studies, 52,* 324–337.

Steriade, M., & McCarley, R. W. (1990). *Brainstem control of wakefulness and sleep.* New York: Plenum.

Stern, G. S., McCants, T. R., & Pettine, P. W. (1982). Stress and illness: Controllable and uncontrollable life events' relative contributions. *Personality and Social Psychology Bulletin, 8,* 140–143.

Stern, K. N., & McClintock, M. K. (1998). Regulation of ovulation by human pheromones. *Nature, 392,* 177-179.

Sternbach, R. A. (1963). Congenital insensitivity to pain: A review. *Psychological Bulletin, 60,* 252–264.

Sternberg, R. J. (1999). *Handbook of creativity.* Cambridge, England: Cambridge University Press.

Sternberg, R. S. (1985). *Beyond IQ: A triarchic theory of human intelligence.* New York: Cambridge University Press.

Sternberg, R. S. (1997a). *Successful intelligence.* New York: Plume.

Sternberg, R. S. (1997b). The concept of intelligence and its role in lifelong learning and success. *American Psychologist, 52,* 1030–1037.

Stevens, A., & Coupe, P. (1978). Distortions in judged spatial relations. *Cognitive Psychology, 10,* 422–437.

Stevenson, H. W., & Lee, S. (1990). Contexts of achievement: A study of American, Chinese, and Japanese children. *Monographs of the Society for Research in Child Development, 55* (Serial No. 221, Nos. 1–2).

Stine-Morrow, E. A. L., & Soederberg Miller, L. M. (1999). Basic cognitive processes. In J. C. Cavanaugh & S. K. Whitbourne (Eds.), *Gerontology: An interdisciplinary perspective.* New York: Oxford University Press.

Stock, W. E. (1991). Feminist explanations: Male power, hostility, and sexual coercion. In E. Grauerholz & M. A. Koralewski (Eds.), *Sexual coercion: A sourcebook on its nature, causes, and prevention* (pp. 61-73). Lexington, MA: Lexington Books.

Stoel-Gammon, C., & Otomo, K. (1986). Babbling development of hearing impaired and normal subjects. *Journal of Speech and Hearing Disorders, 51,* 33–41.

Storms, M. D. (1973). Videotape and the attribution process: Reversing actors' and observers' points of view. *Journal of Personality and Social Psychology, 27,* 165–175.

Stoyva, J. M., & Budzynski, T. H. (1974). Cultivated low arousal—an anti-stress response? In L. V. DiCara (Ed.), *Recent advances in limbic and autonomic nervous systems research.* New York: Plenum Press.

Strassberg, D. S., & Lockerd, L. K. (1998). Force in women's sexual fantasies. *Archives of Sexual Behavior, 27,* 403-415.

Strassberg, D. S., Mahoney, J. M., Schaugaard, M., & Hale, V. E. (1990). The role of anxiety in premature ejaculation: A psychophysiological model. *Archives of Sexual Behavior, 19,* 251-257.

Strassberg, Z., Dodge, K., Pettit, G. S., & Bates, J. E. (1994). Spanking in the home and children's subsequent aggression toward kindergarten peers. *Development and Psychopathology, 6,* 445–461.

Strassman, R. J. (1995). Hallucenogenic drugs in psychiatric research and treatment: Perspectives and prospects. *Journal of Nervous and Mental Diseases, 183,* 127–138.

Streissguth, A. P., Treder, R. P., Barr, H. M., Shepard, T. H., Bleyer, W. A., Sampson, P. D., & Martin, D. C. (1987). Aspirin and acetaminophen use by pregnant women and subsequent child IQ and attention decrements. *Teratology, 35*(2), 211–219.

Strickland, B. R. (1989). Internal-external control expectancies: From contingency to creativity. *American Psychologist, 44,* 1–12.

Stroebe, W., & Stroebe, M. (1987). *Bereavement and health.* New York: Cambridge University Press.

Stroebe, W., & Stroebe, M. S. (1993). Determinants of adjustment to bereavement in younger widows and widowers. In M. S. Stroebe, W. Stroebe, & R. O. Hansson (Eds.), *Handbook of bereavement* (pp. 208–226). New York: Cambridge University Press.

Stryer, L. (1987). The molecules of visual excitation. *Scientific American, 257,* 42–50.

Stull, D. E., & Scarisbrick-Hauser, A. (1989). Nevermarried elderly: A reassessment with implications for long-term care policy. *Research on Aging, 11,* 124–139.

Stunkard, A. (1997). Eating disorders: The last 25 years. *Appetite, 29,* 181–190.

Substance Abuse and Mental Health Services Administrations (2002). *National Household Survey on Drug Abuse.* (retrieved on June 7, 2003) www.drugabusestatistics.samhsa.gov

Suddath, R. L., Christison, G. W., Torrey, E. F., & Casanova, M. F. (1990). Anatomical abnormalities in the brains of monozygotic twins discordant for schizophrenia. *New England Journal of Medicine, 322,* 789–794.

Sullivan, J. W., & Horowitz, F. D. (1983). The effects of intonation on infant attention: The role of the rising intonation contour. *Journal of Child Language, 10,* 521–534.

Sullivan, M. A., & O'Leary, S. G. (1990). Maintenance following reward and cost token programs. *Behavior Therapy, 21,* 139–149.

Sullivan, P. F., Neale, M. C., & Kendler, S. K. (2000). Genetic epidemiology of major depression: Review and meta-analysis. *American Journal of Psychiatry, 157,* 1552–1562.

Super, D. E. (1957). *The psychology of careers.* New York: Harper & Row.

Super, D. E. (1976). *Career education and the meanings of work.* Washington, DC: U.S. Offices of Education.

Super, D. E. (1980). A life-span, life-space approach to career development. *Journal of Vocational Behavior, 16,* 282–298.

Super, D. E. (1991). A life-span, life-space approach to career development. In D. Brown, L. Brooks, & Associates (Eds.), *Career choice and development: Applying contemporary theories to practice* (2nd ed.). San Francisco: Jossey-Bass.

Swaab, D. F., & Hofman M. A. (1995). Sexual differentiation of the human hypothalamus in relation to gender and sexual orientation. *Trends in Neurosciences, 18,* 264–270.

Swain, I. U., Zelazo, P. R., & Clifton, R. K. (1993). Newborn infants' memory for speech sounds retained over 24 hours. *Developmental Psychology, 29*(2), 312–323.

Swan, G. E., & Carmelli, D. (2002). Impaired olfaction predicts cognitive decline in nondemented older adults. *Neuroepidemiology, 21,* 58–67.

Swanson, S. (2002, November 14). Anti-Muslim crimes peaked after 9/11. *Chicago Tribune,* p.11.

Swartz, C. (1995). Setting the ECT stimulus. *Psychiatric Times, 12*(6), 33–34.

Swartz, M., Blazer, D., George, L., & Winfield, I. (1990). Estimating the prevalence of borderline personality disorder in the community. *Journal of Personality Disorders, 4,* 257–272.

Swayze, V.W. (1995). Frontal leucotomy and related psychosurgical procedures in the era before antipsychotics (1935–1954): A historical overview. *American Journal of Psychiatry, 152,* 505–515.

Symons, C. S., & Johnson, B. T. (1997). The self-reference effect in memory: A meta-analysis. *Psychological Bulletin, 121,* 371–394.

Szasz, T. S. (1987). *Insanity: The idea and its consequences.* New York: Wiley.

Szkrybalo, J., & Ruble, D. N. (1999). "God made me a girl": Sex-category constancy judgments and explanations revisited. *Developmental Psychology, 35,* 392–402.

Tager-Flusberg, H. (1997). Putting words together: Morphology and syntax in the preschool years. In J. B. Gleason (Ed.), *The development of language* (4th ed., pp. 159–209). Boston: Allyn & Bacon.

Tajfel, H. (1982). *Social identity and intergroup relations.* Cambridge, England: Cambridge University Press.

Talamini, J. (1982). *Boys will be girls: The hidden world of the heterosexual male transvestite.* Lanham, MD: University Press of America.

Tamminga, C. A. (1997). The promise of new drugs for schizophrenia treatment. *Canadian Journal of Psychiatry, 42,* 264–273.

Tan, A. (2003). *The opposite of fate: A book of musings.* New York: Penguin Books.

Tang, C. S., Critelli, J. W., & Porter, J. F. (1995). Sexual aggression and victimization in dating relationships among Chinese college students. *Archives of Sexual Behavior, 24,* 47-53.

Tankova, I., Adan, A., & Buela-Casal, G. (1994). Circadian typology and individual differences. A review. *Personality and Individual Differences, 16,* 671–684.

Task Force on Infant Sleep Position and Sudden Infant Death (2000). Report at year 2000. *Pediatrics: American Academy of Pediatrics, 105,* 650–656.

Taylor, C. B., & Luce, K. H. (2003). Computer- and Internet-based psychotherapy interventions. *Current Directions in Psychological Science, 12,* 18–22.

Taylor, E. J., & Outlaw, F. H. (2002). Use of prayer among persons with cancer. *Holistic Nursing Practices, 16,* 46–60.

Taylor, H. (2002). Poor people and African Americans suffer the most stress from the hassles of daily living. *The Harris Poll No. 66.*

Taylor, S. E. (2003). *Health psychology* (5th ed.). New York: McGraw-Hill.

Teachman, J. (2003). Premarital sex, premarital cohabitation and the risk of subsequent marital dissolution among women. *Journal of Marriage and Family, 65,* 444–455.

Teachman, J. D., Tedrow, L. M., & Crowder, K. D. (2000). The changing demography of America's families. *Journal of Marriage and Family, 62,* 1234–1246.

Teasdale, J. D., & Russell, M. L. (1983). Differential effects of induced mood on the recall of positive, negative, and neutral words. *British Journal of Clinical Psychology, 22,* 163–171.

Teasdale, J. D., Scott, J., Moore, R. G., Hayhurst, H., Pope, M., & Paykel, E. S. (2001). How does cognitive therapy prevent relapse in residual depression? Evidence from a controlled trial. *Journal of Consulting and Clinical Psychology, 69,* 347– 357.

Teicher, M. H. (2002). Scars that won't heal: The neurobiology of child abuse. *Scientific American, 286,* 68–75.

Teitelbaum, P., & Epstein, A. N. (1962). The lateral hypothalamic syndrome: Recovery of feeding and drinking after lateral hypothalamic lesions. *Psychological Review, 69,* 74–90.

Teitelbaum, P., & Stellar, E. (1954). Recovery from failure to eat produced by hypothalamic lesions. *Science, 120,* 894–895.

Temoshok, L. (1992). *The Type C connection: The behavioral links to cancer and your health.* New York: Random House.

Terman, L. M. (1916). *The measurement of intelligence.* Boston: Houghton Mifflin.

Ternent, M. A., & Garshelis, D. L. (1999). Taste-aversion conditioning to reduce nuisance activity by black bears in a Minnesota military reservation. *Wildlife Society Bulletin, 27,* 720–728.

Terr, L. C. (1983). Chowchilla revisited: The effects of psychic trauma four years after a school-bus kidnapping. *American Journal of Psychiatry, 140,* 1543–1550.

Teyber, E., & McClure, F. (2000). Therapist variables. In C. R. Snyder & R. E. Ingram (Eds.), *Handbook of psychological change: Psychotherapy processes and practices for the 21st century* (pp. 62–87). New York: Wiley.

Thase, M. E. (2003). Effectiveness of antidepressants: Comparative remission rates. *Journal of Clinical Psychiatry, 64*(Suppl. 2), 3–7.

Thase, M. E., & Kupfer, D. J. (1996). Recent developments in the pharmacotherapy of mood disorders. *Journal of Consulting & Clinical Psychology, 64,* 646–659.

Thase, M. E., Jindal, R., & Howland, R. H. (2002). Biological aspects of depression. In H. Gotlib & C. L. Hammen (Eds.), *Handbook of depression* (pp. 192–218). New York: Guilford Press.

Thelen, E. (1995). Motor development: A new synthesis. *American Psychologist, 50,* 79–95.

Thelen, M., Farmer, J., Mann, L., & Pruitt, J. (1990). Bulimia and interpersonal relationships: A longitudinal study. *Journal of Counseling Psychology, 37,* 85–90.

Thomas, A., & Chess, S. (1977). *Temperament and development.* New York: Brunner/Mazel.

Thomas, A., & Chess, S. (1986). The New York longitudinal study: From infancy to early adult life. In R. Plomin & J. Dunn (Eds.), *The study of temperament: Changes, continuities, and challenges.* Hillsdale, NJ: Erlbaum.

Thomlison, B., Stephens, M., Cunes, J. W., & Grinnell, R. M. (1991, Fall). Characteristics of Canadian male and female child sexual abuse victims. Special Issue: Child sexual abuse. *Journal of Child and Youth Care,* 65-76.

Thompson, P. M., Giedd, J. N., Woods, R. P., MacDonald, D., Evans, A. C., & Togo, A. W. (2000, March 9). Growth patterns in the developing human brain detected by using continuum-mechanical tensor maps. *Nature, 404,* 190–193.

Thompson, V. L. (1996). Perceived experiences of racism as stressful life events. *Community Mental Health Journal, 32,* 223–233.

Thomson, E., & Colella, U. (1992). Cohabitation and marital stability: Quality or commitment. *Journal of Marriage and the Family, 54,* 259–267.

Thorndike, E. L. (1898). Animal intelligence: An experimental study of associative process in animals. *Psychological Review Monograph,* No. 8.

Thorndike, E. L. (1905). *The elements of psychology.* New York: Seiler.

Thorpe, G. L., & Olson, S. L. (1997). *Behavior therapy: Concepts, procedures, and applications* (2nd ed.). Boston, MA: Allyn & Bacon.

Thurber, C. A. (1995). The experience and expression of homesickness in preadolescent and adolescent boys. *Child Development, 66,* 1162–1178.

Thurstone, L. L. (1938). *Primary mental abilities.* Chicago: University of Chicago Press.

Tienari, P., Wynne, L. C., Laksy, K., Moring, J., Nieminen, P., Sorri, A., Lahti, I., & Wahlberg, K. E. (2003). Genetic boundaries of the schizophrenia spectrum: Evidence from the Finnish Adoptive Family Study of Schizophrenia. *American Journal of Psychiatry, 160,* 1567–1594.

Tjaden P., & Thoennes, N. (1998). Prevalence, incidence and consequences of violence against women. *Findings from the National Violence Against Women study. Research in Brief,* U.S. Department of Justice, NCJRS, 17283.

Tollison, C. D., & Adams, H. E. (1979). *Sexual disorders: Treatment, theory, and research.* New York: Gardner Press.

Tolman, E. C., & Honzik, C. H. (1930). "Insight" in rats. *University of California Publications in Psychology, 4,* 215–232.

Tomasello, M. (2000). Culture and cognitive development. *Current Directions in Psychological Science, 9,* 37–40.

Tomasello, M., Call, J., Nagell, K., Olguin, R., & Carpenter, M. (1994). The learning and use of gestural signals by young chimpanzees: A trans-generational study. *Primates, 35,* 137–154.

Touris, M., Kromelow, S., & Harding, C. (1995). Mother–firstborn attachment and the birth of a sibling. *American Journal of Orthopsychiatry, 65,* 293–297.

Trafimow, D., Armendariz, M. L., & Madsen, L. (2004). A test of whether attributions provide for self-enhancement or self-defense. *Journal of Social Psychology, 144,* 453–463.

Treas, J., & Lawton, L. (1999). Family relations in adulthood. In M. B. Sussman, S. K. Steinmetz, & G. W. Peterson (Eds.), *Handbook of marriage and the family* (pp. 425–438). New York: Plenum Press.

Tremblay, R. E., Pihl, R. O., Vitaro, F., & Dobkin, P. (1994). Predicting early onset of male antisocial behavior from preschool behavior. *Archives of General Psychiatry, 51,* 732–739.

Tremblay, R. E., Schaal, B., Boulerice, B., Arseneault, L., Soussignan, R. G., Paquette, D., & Laurent, D. (1998). Testosterone, physical aggression, dominance, and physical development in early adolescence. *International Journal of Behavioral Development, 22,* 753–777.

Triandis, H. C. (1994). *Culture and Social Behavior.* New York: McGraw-Hill.

Triesman, A. M. (1964). Verbal cues, language, and meaning in selective attention. *American Journal of Psychology, 77,* 206–219.

Trimble, J. E., & Thurman, P. J. (2002). Ethnocultural considerations and strategies for providing counseling services to Native American Indians. In P. B. Pedersen, J. G. Draguns, W. J. Lonner, & J. E. Trimble (Eds.), *Counseling across cultures* (5th ed., pp. 53–92). Thousand Oaks, CA: Sage.

Troisi, J. R., II. (2003). Spontaneous recovery during, but not following, extinction of the discriminative stimulus effects of nicotine in rats: Reinstatement of stimulus control. *The Psychological Record, 53,* 579–592.

Trosclair, A., Husten, C., Pederson, L., & Dhillon, I. (2002). Cigarette smoking among adults, United States, 2000. *MMWR Weekly, 51,* 642–645.

Tsai, G., & Coyle, J. T. (2002). Glutamatergic mechanisms in schizophrenia. *Annual Review of Pharmacological Toxicology, 42,* 165–179.

Tsai, G., Gastfriend, D. R., & Coyle, J. T. (1995). The glutamatergic basis of human alcoholism. *American Journal of Psychiatry, 152,* 332–340.

Tseng, W. (1973). The development of psychiatric concepts in traditional Chinese medicine. *Archives of General Psychiatry, 29,* 569–575.

Tsuang, M. T., Fleming, J. A., & Simpson, J. C. (1999). Suicide and schizophrenia. In D. G. Jacobs (Ed.), *The Harvard Medical School guide to suicide assessment and intervention* (pp. 287–299). San Francisco: Jossey-Bass.

Tsuang, M. T., Stone, W. S., & Faraone, S. V. (2001). Genes, environment and schizophrenia. *British Journal of Psychiatry, 178*(Suppl. 40), s18–s24.

Tugrul, C., & Kabakci, E. (1997). Vaginismus and its correlates. *Sexual and Marital Therapy, 12,* 23-34.

Tulving, E. (1972). Episodic and semantic memory. In E. Tulving & W. Donaldson (Eds.), *Organisation of memory.* London: Academic Press.

Tulving, E. (1974). Cue-dependent forgetting. *American Scientist, 62,* 74–82.

Tulving, E. (1983). *Elements of episodic memory.* Oxford: Oxford University Press.

Turati, C. (2004). Why faces are not special to newborns: An alternative account of the face preference. *Current Directions in Psychological Science, 13,* 5–8.

Turati, C., & Simion, F. (2002). Newborns' recognition of changing and unchanging aspects of schematic faces. *Journal of Experimental Child Psychology, 83,* 239–261.

Turk, C. L., Heimberg, R. G., & Hope, D. A. (2001). Social anxiety disorder. *Clinical handbook of psychological disorders: A step-by-step treatment manual* (3rd ed., pp. 114–153). New York: Guilford Press.

Turk, D. C., Meichenbaum, D. H., & Nerman, W. H. (1979). Application of biofeedback for the regulation of pain: A critical review. *Psychological Bulletin, 110,* 392–405.

Turner, A. J., & Ortony, A. (1992). Basic emotions; can conflicting criteria converge? *Psychological Review, 99,* 566–571.

Turner, P. J., & Gervai, J. (1995). A multidimensional study of gender typing in preschool children and their parents: Personality, attitudes, preferences, behavior, and cultural differences. *Developmental Psychology, 31,* 759–772.

Turner-Bowker, D. M. (1996). Gender stereotyped descriptors in children's picture books: Does "Curious Jane" exist in the literature? *Sex Roles, 35,* 461–488.

Tversky, A., & Kahneman, D. (1974). Judgment under uncertainty: Heuristics and biases. *Science, 185,* 1124–1131.

Tversky, A., & Kahneman, D. (1980). Causal schemas in judgments under uncertainty. In M. Fishbein (Ed.), *Progress in social psychology.* Hillsdale, NJ: Erlbaum.

Tversky, B. (1981). Distortions in memory for maps. *Cognitive Psychology, 13,* 407–433.

Twenge, J. M., Zhang, L., & Im, C. (2004). It's beyond my control: A cross-temporal meta-analysis of increasing externality in locus of control, 1960–2002. *Personality and Social Psychology Review, 8,* 308–319.

Twitchell, G. R., Hanna, G. L., Cook, E. H., Fitzgerald, H. E., Little, K. Y., & Zucker, R. (1998). Overt behavior problems and serotonergic function in middle childhood among male and female offspring of alcoholic fathers. *Alcoholism, Clinical and Experimental Research, 22,* 1340–1348.

U.S. Bureau of Justice Statistics. (1995). *National crime victimization survey.* Washington, DC: U.S. Department of Justice.

U. S. Census Bureau. (1998). *Statistical abstract of the United States* (120th ed.). Washington, DC: U.S. Government Printing Office.

U.S. Census Bureau. (1996). *Statistical abstract of the United States* (118th ed.). Washington, DC: U.S. Government Printing Office.

U.S. Census Bureau. (2000). *Statistical abstract of the United States* (122nd ed.). Washington, DC: U.S. Government Printing Office.

U.S. Census Bureau. (2002). *U.S. Summary: 2000.* Washington, DC: U.S. Department of Commerce, Economics and Statistics Administration.

U.S. Department of Education. (1995). *Digest of educational statistics, 1995.* Washington DC: Government Printing Office.

U.S. Department of Education. (2001). *The Condition of Education 2001* (NCES 2001-072). Washington, DC: U.S. Government Printing Office.

U.S. Department of Health and Human Services. (1991). *What you can do about drug use in America.* Retrieved December 22, 2004, from http://www.health.orggovpubs/PHDS87/ Public Health Document (PHD587).

U.S. Department of Health and Human Services. (1998). *Tobacco use among U.S. racial/ethnic minority groups—African Americans, American Indians and Alaska Natives, Asian Americans and Pacific Islanders, and Hispanics: A report of the Surgeon General.* Atlanta, GA: U.S. Department of Health and Human Services, Centers for Disease Control and Prevention, National Center for Chronic Disease Prevention and Health Promotion, Office on Smoking and Health.

Uchino, B. N., Cacioppo, J. T., & Kiecolt-Glaser, J. K. (1996). The relationship between social support and physiological processes: A review with emphasis on underlying mechanisms and implications for health. *Psychological Bulletin, 119,* 488–531.

Ultan, R. (1969). Some general characteristics of interrogative systems. *Working Papers in Language Universals (Stanford University), 1,* 41–63.

Upchurch, D. M., Aneshensel, C. S., Sucoff, C. A., & Levy-Storm, L. (1999). Neighborhood and family contexts of adolescent sexual activity. *Journal of Marriage and the Family, 61,* 920-933.

Ursu, S., Stenger, A., Shear, M. K., Jones, M. R., & Carter, C. S. (2003). Overactive action-monitoring in obsessive-compulsive disorder: Evidence from functional magnetic resonance imaging. *Psychological Science, 14,* 347–353.

Valenza, E., Simion, F., Cassia, V. M., & Umilta, C. (1996). Face preference at birth. *Journal of Experimental Psychology, 33,* 711–723.

Van de Castle, R. L. (1994). *Our dreaming mind.* New York: Ballantine.

Van Goozen, S., Frijda, N., & de Poll, N. V. (1994). Anger and aggression in women: Influence of sports choice and testosterone administration. *Aggressive Behavior, 20,* 213–222.

Van Heteren, C. F., Boekkooi, P. F., Jongsma, H. W., & Nijhuis, J. G. (2000). Fetal learning and memory. *Lancet, 356,* 9236–9237.

van Ijzendoorn, M. H., & Kroonenberg, P. (1988). Cross-cultural patterns of attachment: A meta-analysis of the Strange Situation. *Child Development, 59,* 147–156.

van Laar, M., Volkerts, E., & Verbaten, M. (2001). Subcronic effects of the GABA-agonist lorazepam and the 5-HT2A/2C antagonist ritanserin on driving performance, slow wave sleep and daytime sleepiness in healthy volunteers. *Psychopharmacology, 154,* 189–197.

Van, P. (2001). Breaking the silence of African American women: Healing after pregnancy loss. *Health Care Women International, 22,* 229–243.

Vance, E. B., & Wagner, N. N. (1976). Written descriptions of orgasms: A study of sex differences. *Archives of Sexual Behavior, 5,* 87-98.

vanReekum, C., Johnstone, T., Etter, A., Wehrle, T., & Scherer, K. (2004). Psychophysiological response to appraisal dimensions in a computer game. *Cognition and Emotion, 18,* 663–688.

Varley, C. K., & Smith, C. J. (2003). Anxiety disorders in the child and teen. *Pediatric Clinics of North America, 50,* 1107–1138.

Vartanian, O., Martindale, C., & Kwiatkowski, J. (2003). Creativity and inductive reasoning: The relationship between divergent thinking and performance on Wason's 2-4-6 task. *The Quarterly Journal of Experimental Psychology, 56A,* 641–655.

Vaughn, B. E., Stevenson-Hinde, J., Waters, E., Kotsaftis, A., Lefever, G., Shouldice, A., Trudel, M., & Belsky, J. (1992). Attachment security and temperament in infancy and early childhood: Some conceptual clarifications. *Developmental Psychology, 28,* 463–473.

Vendel, C. (1998, September 4). Frantic rescue for girl trapped underwater. *The Kansas City Star,* p. A1.

Verhaeghen, P., Marcoen, A., & Goosens, L. (1993). Facts and fiction about memory aging: A quantitative integration of research findings. *Journal of Gerontology: Psychological Sciences, 48,* P157–P171.

Virgile, R. S. (1984). Locked-in syndrome: Case and literature review. *Clinical Neurology and Neurosurgery, 86,* 275–279.

Vitaliano, P. P., Scanlon, J. M., Ochs, H. D., Syrjala, K., Siegler, I. C., & Snyder, E. A. (1998). Psychosocial stress moderates the relationship of cancer history with natural killer cell activity. *Annals of Behavioral Medicine, 20,* 199–208.

Vitaliano, P. P., Young, H. M., & Zhang, J. (2004). Is caregiving a risk factor for illness? *Current Directions in Psychological Science, 13,* 13–16.

Voderholzer, U., Al-Shajlawi, A., Weske, G., Feige, B., & Riemann, D. (2003). Are there gender differences in objective and subjective sleep measures? A study of insomniacs and healthy controls. *Depression & Anxiety, 17,* 162–172.

Vogeltanz-Holm, N. D., Wonderlich, S. A., Lewis, B. A., Wilsnack, S. C., Harris, T. R., Wilsnack, R. W., & Kristjanson, A. F. (2000). Longitudinal predictors of binge eating, intense dieting, and weight concerns in a national sample of women. *Behavior Therapy, 31,* 221–235.

Volkow, N. D., Gillespie, H., Mullani, N., & Tancredi, L. (1996). Brain glucose metabolism in chronic marijuana users at baseline and during marijuana intoxication. *Psychiatry Research: Neuroimaging, 67*(1), 29–38.

Voyer, D., Voyer, S., & Bryden, M. P. (1995). Magnitude of sex differences in spatial abilities: A meta-analysis and consideration of critical variables. *Psychological Bulletin, 117,* 250-270.

Vygotsky, L. S. (1978). *Mind in society: The development of higher mental process.* Cambridge, MA: Harvard University Press.

Vygotsky, L. S. (1986). *Thought and language.* Cambridge, MA: MIT Press.

Vygotsky, L. S. (1987). Thinking and speech. In R. W. Reiber, A. S. Carton (Eds.), *The collected works of L. S. Vygotsky: Volume I. Problems of general psychology* (pp. 37–285). New York: Plenum. (Original work published 1934)

Wadden, T. A., & Stunkard, A. J. (1987). Psychopathology and obesity, *Annals of the New York Academy of Sciences, 499,* 55–65.

Wagner, G. C., Beuving, L. J., & Hutchinson, R. R. (1980). The effects of gonadal hormone manipulations on aggressive target-biting in mice. *Aggressive Behavior, 6,* 1–7.

Wakefield, J. C. (1992). The concept of mental disorder: On the boundary between biological facts and social values. *American Psychologist, 47,* 373–388.

Wald, G. (1964). The receptors of human color vision. *Science, 145,* 1007–1017.

Wald, J., & Taylor, S. (2003). Preliminary research on the efficacy of virtual reality exposure therapy to treat driving phobia. *Cyberpsychology & Behavior, 6,* 459–465.

Waldron-Hennessey, R., & Sabatelli, R. M. (1997). The parental comparison level index: A measure for assessing parental rewards and costs relative to expectations. *Journal of Marriage and the Family, 59,* 824–833.

Walker, L. (1995). Sexism in Kohlberg's moral psychology? In W. M. Kurtines & J. L. Gewirtz (Eds.), *Moral development: An introduction* (pp. 83–107). Boston: Allyn & Bacon.

Walker, L. J. (1989). A longitudinal study of moral reasoning. *Child Development, 60,* 157–166.

Walker, L. J., & Taylor, J. H. (1991). Stage transitions in moral reasoning: A longitudinal study of developmental processes. *Developmental Psychology, 27,* 330–337.

Wallace, J. Schneider, T., & McGuffin, P. (2002). Genetics of depression. In I. H. Gotlib & C. L. Hammen (Eds.), *Handbook of depression* (pp. 169–191). New York: Guilford Press.

Walster, E., Aronson, E., Abrahams, D., & Rottman, L. (1966). Importance of physical attractiveness in dating behavior. *Journal of Personality and Social Psychology, 4,* 508–516.

Wampold, B. E., Minami, T., Baskin, T. W., & Callen Tierney, S. (2002). A meta-(re)analysis of the effects of cognitive therapy versus other therapies for depression. *Journal of Affective Disorders, 68,* 159–165.

Wampold, B. E., Mondin, G. W., Moody, M., Stich, F., Benson, K., & Ahn, H. (1997). A meta-analysis of outcome studies comparing bona fide psychotherapies: Empirically, "All must have prizes." *Psychological Bulletin, 122,* 203–215.

Wanner, H. E. (1968). *On remembering, forgetting, and understanding sentences. A study of the deep structure hypothesis.* Unpublished doctoral dissertation, Harvard University.

Warburton, D. M. (1995). Effects of caffeine on cognition and mood without caffeine abstinence. *Psychopharmacology, 119,* 66–70.

Ward, C. (1994). Culture and altered states of consciousness. In W. J. Lonner, & R. S. Malpass (Eds.), *Psychology and culture.* Boston: Allyn & Bacon.

Ward, J. (2003). State of the art synaesthesia. *Psychologist, 16,* 196–199.

Ward, R., Logan, J., & Spitze, G. (1992). The influence of parent and child needs on coresidence in middle and later life. *Journal of Marriage and the Family, 54,* 209–221.

Warr, P. B. (1992). Age and occupational well-being. *Psychology and Aging, 7,* 37–45.

Warr, P. B. (1994). Age and employment. In M. D. Dunnette, L. Hough, & H. Triandis (Eds.), *Handbook of industrial and organizational psychology* (pp. 485–550). Palo Alto, CA: Consulting Psychologists Press.

Warrington, E. K., & Shallice, A. (1972). Neuropsychological evidence of visual storage in short-term memory tasks. *Quarterly Journal of Experimental Psychology, 24,* 30–40.

Waschbusch, D. A., Sellers, D. P., LeBlanc, M., & Kelley, M. L. (2003). Helpless attributions and depression in adolescents: The roles of anxiety, event valence, and demographics. *Journal of Adolescence, 26,* 169–183.

Wasserman, E. A., & Miller, R. R. (1997). What's elementary about associative learning? *Annual Review of Psychology, 48,* 573–607.

Wasserman, G. S. (1978). *Color vision: An historical introduction.* New York: Wiley.

Waterman, J., & Lusk, R. (1986). Scope of the problem. In K. MacFarlane et al. (Eds.), *Sexual abuse of young children: Evaluation and treatment* (pp. 3-14). New York: Guilford Press.

Watkins, D., Cheng, C., Mpofu, E., Olowu, S., Singh-Sengupta, S., & Regmi, M. (2003). Gender differences in self-construal: How generalizable are Western findings? *Journal of Social Psychology, 143,* 501-519.

Watson, J. B., & Raynor, R. (1920). Conditioned emotional reactions. *Journal of Experimental Psychology, 3,* 1–14.

Webb, W. B. (1983). Theories in modern sleep research. In A. Mayes (Ed.), *Sleep mechanisms and functions.* Wokingham, England: Van Nostrand Reinhold.

Webb, W. B., & Campbell, S. S. (1983). Relationships in sleep characteristics of identical and fraternal twins. *Archives of General Psychiatry, 40,* 1093–1095.

Wechsler, D. (1939). *The measurement of adult intelligence.* Baltimore: Williams & Wilkins.

Weiner, B. (1980). A cognitive (attribution) emotion-action model of motivated behavior: An analysis of judgments of helping. *Journal of Personality and Social Psychology, 39,* 186–200.

Weinrich, J. D. (1994). Homosexuality. In V. L. Bullough & B. Bullough (Eds.), *Human sexuality: An encyclopedia* (pp. 277-283). New York: Garland.

Weisner, T. S., & Wilson-Mitchell, J. E. (1990). Nonconventional family lifestyles and sex typing in six-year-olds. *Child Development, 61,* 1915–1933.

Weiss, R. D., & Mirin, S. M. (1987). *Cocaine.* Washington, DC: American Psychiatric Press.

Weissman, M. M. (1993). The epidemiology of personality disorders: A 1990 update. *Journal of Personality Disorders* (Spring Suppl. 1), 44–62.

Weissman, M. M., Bland, R. C., Canino, G. J., Greenwald, S., Hwu, H. G., Joyce, P. R., Karem, E. G., Lee, C. K., Lellouch, J., Lepine, J. P., Newman, S. C., Rubio-Stipec, M., Wells, J. E., Wickramaratne, P. J., Wittchen, H. U., & Yeh, E. K. (1999). Prevalence of suicide ideation and suicide attempts in nine countries. *Psychological Medicine, 29,* 9–17.

Weissman, M. M., Markowitz, J. C., & Klerman, G. I. (2000). *Comprehensive guide to interpersonal psychotherapy.* New York: Basic Books.

Weissman, M., & Olfson, M. (1995). Depression in women: Implications for health care research. *Science, 269,* 799–801.

Weizenbaum, J. (1966). ELIZA-A computer program for the study of the natural language communication between man and machine. *Communication Associates Computing Machinery, 9,* 36–45.

Welch, S. S. (2001). A review of the literature on the epidemiology of parasuicide in the general population. *Psychiatric Services, 52,* 368–375.

Welford, A. T. (1987). Ageing. In R. L. Gregory (Ed.), *The Oxford companion to the mind* (pp. 13–14). Oxford: Oxford University Press.

Wellman, H. M., Cross, D., & Watson, J. (2001). Meta-analysis of theory of mind development: The truth about false-belief. *Child Development, 72,* 655–684.

Wells, G. L., Olson, E. A. (2003). Eyewitness testimony. *Annual Review of Psychology, Annual 2003,* 277–295.

Welte, J. W., & Barnes, G. M. (1987). Alcohol use among adolescent minority groups. *Journal of Studies on Alcohol, 48,* 329–336.

Wender, P. H., Kety, S. S., Rosenthal, D., Schulsinger, F., Ortmann, J., & Lunde, I. (1986). Psychiatric disorders in the biological and adoptive families of adopted individuals with affective disorders. *Archives of General Psychiatry, 43,* 923–929.

Wertheimer, M. (1923). Principles of perceptual organization (Abridged trans. by M. Wertheimer). In D. S. Beardslee & M. Wertheimer (Eds.), *Readings in perception* (pp. 115–137). Princeton, NJ: Van Nostrand-Reinhold. (Originally published 1923, *Psychologishe Forschung, 41,* 301–350)

Weston, S. C., & Siever, L. J. (1993). Biologic correlates of personality disorders. *Journal of Personality Disorders* (Suppl. 1), 129–148.

Wever, E. G. (1970). *Theory of hearing.* New York: Wiley. (Original work published 1949).

Weyant, J. M. (1996). Application of compliance techniques to direct-mail requests for charitable donations. *Psychology and Marketing, 13,* 157–170.

Wheeler, M. A., Stuss, D. T., & Tulving, E. (1997). Toward a theory of episodic memory: The frontal lobes and autonoetic consciousness. *Psychological Bulletin, 121,* 331–354.

Wheeler, M. D. (1991). Physical changes of puberty. *Endocrinology and Metabolism Clinics of North America, 20,* 1–14.

Whitbourne, S. K. (1985). *The aging body: Physiological changes and psychological consequences.* New York: Springer-Verlag.

Whitbourne, S. K. (1996). *The aging individual.* New York: Springer.

Whitbourne, S. K. (2001). The physical aging process in midlife: Interactions with psychological and sociocultural factors. In M.E. Lachman (ed.), *Handbook of midlife development* (pp. 109–155). New York: Wiley.

Whitbourne, S. K., Zuschlag, M. K., Elliot, L. B., & Waterman, A. D. (1992). Psychosocial development in adulthood: A 22-year sequential study. *Journal of Personality & Social Psychology, 63,* 260–271.

White, L. K., & Rogers, S. J. (1997). Strong support but uneasy relationships: Coresidence and adult children's relationships with their parents. *Journal of Marriage and the Family, 59,* 62–76.

White, L., & Edwards, J. N. (1990). Emptying the nest and parental well-being: An analysis of national panel data. *American Sociological Review, 55,* 235–242.

Whiting, B., & Edwards, C. P. (1988). *Children in different worlds*. Cambridge, MA: Harvard University Press.

Whorf, B. L. (1956). *Language, thought, and reality: Selected writings of Benjamin Lee Whorf*. New York: Wiley.

Wickelgren, I. (1997). Marijuana: Harder than thought? *Science, 276,* 1967–1968.

Widiger, T. A. (1998). Invited essay: Sex differences in the diagnosis of personality disorders. *Journal of Personality Disorders, 12,* 95–118.

Widiger, T. A. (2003). Personality disorder and Axis I psychopathology: The problematic boundary of Axis I and Axis II. *Journal of Personality Disorders, 17,* 90–108.

Widiger, T. A., & Chaynes, K. (2003). Current issues in the assessment of personality disorders. *Current Psychiatry Reports, 5,* 28–35.

Widom, C. S. (1999). Posttraumatic stress disorder in abused and neglected children grown up. *American Journal of Psychiatry, 156,* 1223–1229.

Wiebe, D. J. (1991). Hardiness and stress moderation: A test of proposed mechanisms. *Journal of Personality and Social Psychology, 60,* 89–99.

Wiebe, D. J., & Smith, T. W. (1997). Personality and health: Progress and problems in psychosomatics. In R. Hogan, J. Johnson, & S. Briggs (Eds.), *Handbook of personal psychology*. New York: Academic Press.

Wiederhold, B. K., Jang, D. P., Kim, S. I., & Wiederhold, M. D. (2002). Physiological monitoring as an objective tool in virtual reality therapy. *Cyberpsychology & Behavior, 5,* 77–82.

Wiest, W. (1977). Semantic differential profiles of orgasm and other experiences among men and women. *Sex Roles, 3,* 399.

Wiggins, J. S. (1997). In defense of traits. In R. Hogan, J. Johnson, & S. Briggs (Eds.), *Handbook of personality psychology*. New York: Academic Press.

Wijdicks, E. F. M., Atkinson, J. L. D., & Okazaki, H. (2001). Isolated medulla oblongata function after severe traumatic brain injury. *Journal of Neurology, Neurosurgery, and Psychiatry, 70,* 127.

Wilder, D. A. (1984). Intergroup contact: The typical member and the exception to the rule. *Journal of Experimental Psychology, 20,* 177–194.

Wilder, D. A. (1986). Social categorization: Implications for creation and reduction of intergroup bias. In L. Berkowitz (Ed.), *Advances in experimental social psychology* (Vol. 19, pp. 291–355). New York: Academic Press.

Wiley, W. (1999, January 10). Heroic rescue in face of flames. *Sacramento Bee,* p. B1.

Williams, D. R., Yu, Y., Jackson, J. S., & Anderson, N. B. (1997). Racial differences in physical and mental health: Socioeconomic status, stress and discrimination. *Journal of Health Psychology, 2,* 335–351.

Williams, J. E., Paton, C. C., Siegler, I. C., Eigenbrodt, M. L., Nieto, F. J., & Tyroler, H. A. (2000). Anger proneness predicts coronary heart disease risk: Prospective analysis from the Atherosclerosis Risk in Communities (ARIC) study. *Circulation, 101,* 2034–2039.

Williams, R. (1993). *Anger kills.* New York: Times Books.

Willis, S. L., & Schaie, K. W. (1999). Intellectual functioning in midlife. In S. L. Willis & J. D. Reid (Eds.), *Life in the middle: Psychological and social development in middle age* (pp. 233–247). San Diego, CA: Academic Press.

Wills, T. A., & Fegan, M. (2001). Social networks and social support. In A. Baum, T. A. Revenson, & J. E. Singer (Eds.), *Handbook of health psychology* (pp. 209–234). Mahwah, NJ: Erlbaum.

Wilmut, I., Schnieke, A. E., McWhir, J., Kind, A. J., & Campbell, K. H. S. (1997). Viable offspring derived from fetal and adult mammalian cells. *Nature, 385,* 810–813.

Wilson, J. (1998, November 29). Bystander's quick response saves man from drowning. *St. Petersburg Times,* p. 3.

Wilson, J. P., & Petruska, R. (1984). Motivation, model attributes, and prosocial behavior. *Journal of Personality and Social Psychology, 46,* 458–468.

Wilson, K. G., Hayes, S. C., & Gifford, E. V. (1997). Cognition in behavior therapy: Agreements and differences. *Journal of Behavior Therapy & Experimental Psychiatry, 28,* 53–63.

Wilson, R.S., & Bennett, D.A. (2003). Cognitive activity and risk of Alzheimer's disease. *Current Directions in Psychological Science, 12,* 87–91.

Wilson, W. R. (1979). Feeling more than we can know: Exposure effects without learning. *Journal of Personality and Social Psychology, 37,* 811–821.

Wink, P., & Helson, R. (1993). Personality change in women and their partners. *Journal of Personality & Social Psychology, 65,* 597–605.

Winokur, G., Coryell, W., Keller, M., Endicott, J., & Leon, A. (1995). A family study of manic-depressive (Bipolar I) disease. *Archives of General Psychiatry, 52,* 367–373.

Wise, S. M. (2000). *Rattling the cage: Toward legal rights for animals.* Cambridge, MA: Perseus Books.

Wise, T. N., & Meyer, J. K. (1980). The border area between transvestism and gender dysphoria: Transvestitic applicants for sex reassignment. *Archives of Sexual Behavior, 9,* 327-342.

Wiseman, C. V., Gray, J. J., Mosimann, J. E., & Ahrens, A. H. (1992). Cultural expectations of thinness in women: An update. *International Journal of Eating Disorders, 11,* 85–89.

Wiseman, S., & Tulving, E. (1976). Encoding specificity: Relations between recall superiority and recognition failure. *Journal of Experimental Psychology: Human Learning & Memory, 2,* 349–361.

Wissler, C. (1901). The correlation of mental and physical tests. *Psychological Review, 3,* (Monograph Suppl. 16.)

Wolfe, J., Erickson, D. J., Sharkansky, R. J., King, D. W., & King, L. A. (1999). Course and predictors of post-traumatic stress disorder among Gulf War veterans: A prospective analysis. *Journal of Consulting & Clinical Psychology, 67,* 520–528.

Wolitzky, D. L. (1995). The theory and practice of traditional psychoanalytic psychotherapy. In A. S. Gurman (Ed.), *Essential psychotherapies: Theory and practice* (pp. 12–54). New York: Guilford Press.

Woll, S. (1986). So many to choose from: Decision strategies in video dating. *Journal of Social and Personal Relationships, 3,* 43–52.

Wolpe, J. (1958). *Psychotherapy by reciprocal inhibition.* Stanford, CA: Stanford University Press.

Woman freed after look-alike is named as suspect. (1995, April 17). *The New York Times,* p. B8.

Won, J., Mair, E. A., Bolger, W. F., & Conran, R. M. (2000). The vomeronasal organ: An objective anatomic analysis of its prevalence. *Ear, Nose, and Throat Journal, 79,* 800.

Wood, W. (2000). Attitude change: Persuasion and social influence. *Annual Review of Psychology,* 539–570.

Woods plays down Augusta row. (2002, November 19). *Golf.*

Woody, J. D., Russel, R., D'Souza, H. J., & Woody, J. K. (2000). Non-coital sex among adolescent virgins and nonvirgins. *Journal of Sex Education and Therapy, 25,* 4, 261-268.

Woodzicka, J. A., & LaFrance, M. (2001). Real versus imagined gender harassment. *Journal of Social Issues, 57,* 15-30.

World Health Organization. (1998) *Facts and figures about STIs.* Geneva, Switzerland: Author.

Wright, I. C., Rabe-Hesketh,, S., Woodruff, P. W., David, A. S., Murray, R. M., & Bullmore, E. T. (2000). Meta-analysis of regional brain volumes in schizophrenia. *American Journal of Psychiatry, 157,* 16–25.

Wrightsman, L. S. (1988). *Personality development in adulthood.* Newbury Park, CA: Sage.

Wrightsman, L. S. (1994). *Adult personality development: Vol 1. Theories and concepts.* Thousand Oaks, CA: Sage.

Wulsin, L. R., Vaillat, G. E., & Wells, V. E. (1999). A systematic review of the mortality of depression. *Psychosomatic Medicine, 61,* 6–17.

Wundt, W. (1904). *Principles of physiological psychology* (5th ed.). E. Titchener (Ed.), New York Macmillan. (Original work published 1874)

Wyatt, G. (1997). *Stolen women: Reclaiming your sexuality, taking back your lives.* New York: Wiley.

Wyatt, G. E., Loeb, T. B., Solis, B., Carmona, J. V., & Romero, G. (1999). The prevalence and circumstances of child sexual abuse: Changes across a decade. *Child Abuse and Neglect, 23,* 45-60.

Wyatt, J. W., Posey, A., Welker, W., & Seamonds, C. (1984). Natural levels of similarities between identical twins and between unrelated people. *The Skeptical Inquirer, 9,* 62–66.

Xiao, Y., Wang, Y., & Felleman, D. J. (2003). A spatially organized representation of colour in macaque cortical area V2. *Nature, 421,* 535–539.

Xiaohe, X., & Whyte, M. K. (1990). Love matches and arranged marriages. *Journal of Marriage and the Family, 52,* 709–722.

Yackinous, C. A., & Guinard, J. (2002). Relation between PROP (6-n-propylthiouracil) taster status, taste anatomy and dietary intake measures for young men and women. *Appetite, 38,* 201–209.

Yalom, I. D. (1989). *Love's executioner and other tales of psychotherapy.* New York: HarperCollins.

Yalom, I. D. (1995). *The theory and practice of group therapy* (4th ed.). New York: Basic Books.

Yerkes, R. M. (1921). Psychological examining in the U.S. Army. *Memoirs: National Academy of Science, 15,* 1–890.

Yeung, W. J., Sandberg, J. F., Davis-Kean, P. E., & Hofferth, S. L. (2001). Children's time with fathers in intact families. *Journal of Marriage and Family, 63,* 136–154.

Yi, H., Stinson, F. S., Williams, G. D., & Dufour, M. C. (1999). *Surveillance report #53: Trends in alcohol-related fatal traffic crashes, United States, 1977–1998.* Rockville, MD: National Institute on Alcohol Abuse and Alcoholism.

Yingling, D. R., Utter, G., Vengali, S., & Mason, B. (2002). Calcium channel blocker, nimodipine, for the treatment of bipolar disorder during pregnancy. *American Journal of Obstetrics & Gynecology, 187,* 1711–1712.

York, J. L., & Welte, J. W. (1994). Gender comparisons of alcohol consumption in alcoholic and nonalcoholic populations. *Journal of Studies on Alcohol, 55(6),* 743–750.

Young, E., & Korzun, A. (1998). Psychoneuroendocrinology of depression: Hypothalmic-pituitary-gonadal axis. *Psychiatric Clinics of North America, 21,* 309–323.

Young, N. K. (1997). Effects of alcohol and other drugs on children. *Journal of Psychoactive Drugs, 29,* 23–42.

Yunker, G. W., & Yunker, B. D. (2002). Primal leadership (book). *Personnel Psychology, 55,* 1030–1033.

Yutrzenka, B. A. (1995). Making a case for training in ethnic and cultural diversity in increasing treatment efficacy. *Journal of Consulting & Clinical Psychology, 63,* 197–206.

Zaalberg, R., Manstead, A. S. R., & Fischer, A. H. (2004). Relations between emotions, display rules, social motives, and facial behaviors. *Cognition and Emotion, 18,* 183–207.

Zadina, J. E., Hackler, L., Ge, L. J., & Kastin, A. J. (1997). A potent and selective endogenous agonist for the u-opiate receptor. *Nature, 386,* 499–502.

Zahn-Waxler, C., & Robinson, J. (1995). Empathy and guilt: Early origins of feelings of responsibility. In J. P. Tangney & K. W. Fischer (Eds.), *Self-conscious emotions* (pp. 143–173). New York: Guilford.

Zajonc, R. B. (1968). Attitudinal effects of mere exposure. *Journal of Personality and Social Psychology, 9,* 1–27.

Zajonc, R. B. (1980). Feeling and thinking: Preferences need no inferences. *American Psychologist, 35,* 151–175.

Zajonc, R. B., Adelmann, P. K., Murphy, S. T., & Neidenthal, P. M. (1987). Convergence in the physical appearance of spouse. *Motivation and Emotion, 11,* 335–346.

Zajonc, R. B., Murphy, S. T., & Inglehart, M. (1989). Feeling and facial efference: Implications of the vascular theory of emotions. *Psychological Review, 96,* 395–416.

Zanarini, M. C. (2000). Childhood experiences associated with the development of borderline personality disorder. *Psychiatric Clinics of North America, 23,* 89–101.

Zanarini, M. C., & Frankenburg, F. R. (1997). Pathways to the development of borderline personality disorder. *Journal of Personality Disorders, 11,* 93–104.

Zanarini, M. C., Skodol, A. E., Bender, D., Dolan, R., Sanislow, C., Schaefer, E., Morey, L., Grilo, C. M., Shea, M. T., McGlashan, T. H., & Gunderson, G. (2000). The Collaborative Longitudinal Personality Disorders Study: Reliability of Axis I and II diagnoses. *Journal of Personality Disorder, 14,* 291–299.

Zani, B. (1993). Dating and interpersonal relationships in adolescence. In S. Jackson & H. Rodriguez-Tome (Eds.), *Adolescence and its social worlds* (pp. 95–119). Hillsdale, NJ: Erlbaum.

Zettle, R. D. (2003). Acceptance and commitment therapy (ACT) vs. systematic desensitization in treatment of mathematics anxiety. *The Psychological Record, 53,* 197–215.

Ziegler, D. J., & Leslie, Y. M. (2003). A test of the ABC model underlying rational-emotive behavior therapy. *Psychological Reports, 92,* 235–240.

Ziegler, D. J., & Smith, P. N. (2004). Anger and the ABC model underlying rational-emotive behavior therapy. *Psychological Reports, 93,* 1009–1014.

Zimmer, L., & Morgan, J. P. (1997). *Marijuana myths, marijuana fact: A review of scientific evidence.* New York: Lindesmith Center.

Zorrilla, L. T., Cannon, T. D., Kronenberg, S., Mednick, S. A., Schulsinger, F., Parnas, J., Praestholm, J., & Vestergaard, A. (1997). Structural brain abnormalities in schizophrenia: A family study. *Biological Psychiatry, 42,* 1080–1086.

Zuckerman, M. (1978). The search for high sensation. *Psychology Today, 11,* 38–99.

Zuckerman, M. (1994). *Behavioral expressions and biosocial bases of sensation seeking.* Cambridge: Cambridge University Press.

Zuckerman, M., Eysenck, S. B. G., & Eysenck, H. J. (1978). Sensation seeking in England and America: Cross-cultural, age and sex comparisons. *Journal of Clinical Psychology, 46,* 139–149.

Credits

Chapter 1

xxx: © Robert Essel NYC/Corbis;
2: Entire book cover (Harper Perennial edition) from *Among the Heroes: United Flight 93 & the Passengers & Crew Who Fought* Back by Jere Longman. © 2002 Jere Longman. Reprinted by permission of HarperCollins Publishers;
3: AP Photo/Kathy Willens;
5: © Douglas Kirkland/Corbis;
9: top, © Bettmann/Corbis; bottom, © Bettmann/Corbis;
10: top, © Bettmann/Corbis; bottom, © Topham/The Image Works;
11: left, Archives of the History of American Psychology, University of Akron, Akron, Ohio; right, © Bettmann/Corbis;
12: © Bettmann/Corbis;
19: © Shmuel Thaler/Index Stock Imagery;
21: David Buffington/Getty Images;
22: both, Archives of the History of American Psychology, University of Akron, Akron, Ohio;
28: © Ariel Skelley/Corbis;
33: © Charles Gupton/Corbis;
37: From the film *Obedience* © 1965 by Stanley Milgram and distributed by Penn State Media Sales. Reprinted by permission of Alexandra Milgram;
42: top, AP Photo/Kathy Willens; center left, © Bettmann/Corbis; center right, © Bettmann/Corbis; bottom left, © Topham/The Image Works; bottom right, © Bettmann/Corbis;
43: top, David Buffington/Getty Images; center (both), Archives of the History of American Psychology, University of Akron, Akron, Ohio; bottom, © Charles Gupton/Corbis.

Chapter 2

44: Mehau Kulyk/Photo Researchers, Inc.;
46: From *The Diving Bell and the Butterfly* by Jean Dominique-Bauby, copyright © 1997 by Editions Robert Laffont, S.A., Paris. Used by permission of Alfred A. Knopf, a division of Random House, Inc.,
48: Courtesy J.S. Brooks;
50: © Reuters/Corbis;
55: top, © Robert Maass/Corbis; bottom, © Network Productions/Index Stock Imagery;
58: © Network Productions/Index Stock Imagery;
60: © Custom Medical Stock Photo;
61: left, © Ron Sachs/CNP/Corbis; right, © Frank Trapper/Corbis;
62: © Mark Adams/SuperStock;
64: Courtesy J.S. Brooks;
65: left, © Renee Lynn/Corbis; right, © Dave Bartruff/Corbis
68: © Peter Hvizdak/The Image Works;
69: © Jose Luis Pelaez, Inc./Corbis;
71: © Corbis;
72: left, © Leestma/Custom Medical Stock Photo; right, Reproduced with permission from an image(s) by Wally Welker (University of Wisconsin-Madison) at http://www.brainmuseum.org, supported by the US National Science Foundation Division of Integrative Biology and Neuroscience, Grant # 0131028;
81: top row, left to right, © Custom Medical Stock Photo; © Custom Medical Stock Photo; S&I/Photo Researchers, Inc; bottom row, left to right, Tim Beddow/Photo Researchers, Inc; © Lester Lefkowitz/Corbis;
82: © Custom Medical Stock Photo;
87: left, Dr. M.A. Ansary/Photo Researchers, Inc.; right, © Lester V. Bergman/Corbis;
89: left, © Dana Tynan/Corbis; right, Gary Parker/Photo Researchers, Inc.;
91: © Niall Benvie/Corbis;
96: © Michael Keller/Corbis;
97: Courtesy of Lisa Torri.

Chapter 3

98: Richard Dobson/Getty Images;
101: Reprinted by permission of MIT Press; cover art used by permission of Haydn Cornner;
102: © Jim Corwin/Picturequest;
104: Matthew McVay/Getty Images;
106: GDT/Getty Images;
111: top, Ray Hendley/Indexstock; center, © ISM/Phototake; center right, Omikron/Photo Researchers, Inc.;
113: © IFA/Picturequest;
115: © Corbis;
116: Martin Barraud/Getty Images;
118: both, © Corbis;
122: © Gage/Custom Medical Stock Photo;
123: Ryan McVay/Getty Images;
130: © Rolf Bruderer/Corbis;
131: © Michael Newman/Photo Edit;
132: top, © Corbis; bottom, © Cary Wolinsky/IPN;
133: Bill Losh/Getty Images;
135: © Joe McDonald/Visuals Unlimited;
137: © Corbis;
139: left, © Novastock/Index Stock Imagery, Inc.; right, Getty Images;
143: top to bottom, © Robert Estall/Corbis; © Richard T. Nowitz/Corbis; © W. Cody/Corbis; © Corbis; Sylvain Grandadam/Getty Images; © Corbis; Steven Lam/Getty Images;
145: © Corbis;
147: Thinkstock/Getty Images;
148: © Jim Wark/Lonely Planet Images;
154: GDT/Getty Images;
155: © Corbis.

Chapter 4

156: © Ellen Pastorino;
158: Reprinted by permission of Health Communications Inc.;
159: © Shannon Wilsey;
160: © Tom Carter/Photo Edit;
165: © Superstock/Picturequest;
166: © Jonathan Nourok/Photo Edit;
174: AP Photo/News Tribune, Stephen Brooks;
176: © Rachel Epstein/Photo Edit;
177: © Tony Freeman/Photo Edit;
180: © David Young-Wolff/Photo Edit;
181: © Corbis;
186: top, AP/Jack Kustron; bottom, AP/Wide World Photos;
188: Penny Tweedie/Getty Images;
189: left, © Pacha/Corbis; right, © Reuters/Corbis;
191: all, © McCann, Lowe and Ricuarte. From *The Neuroscientist,* Issue 3, pp. 399–411, © 1997. Reprinted by permission of Sage Publications, Inc.
198: © Jonathan Nourok/Photo Edit;
199: top, AP Photo/News Tribune, Stephen Brooks; bottom, © Corbis.

Chapter 5

200: Walter Hodges/Getty Images;
202: Copyright © 1998 *42 Up* edited by Bennett Singer. Reprinted by permission of The New Press. www.thenewpress.com; cover image used by permission of ITV/Granada Media;
204: top left, © LWA-Sharie Kennedy/Corbis; top right, © Mitch Tobias/Masterfile; bottom left, Ryan McVay/Getty Images;
207: © Tom & Dee Ann McCarthy/Corbis;
214: top, Archives of the History of American Psychology, University of Akron, Akron, Ohio; bottom, © Spencer Grant/PhotoEdit;
216: © Reuters/Corbis;
218: © Martyn F. Chillmaid/Photo Researchers, Inc.;
226: both, Photo Researchers, Inc.;
229: © Bob Daemmrich/IPNStock;
231: © Bonnie Kamin/Photo Edit;
233: © Lowell Georgia/Corbis;
235: Ryan McVay/Getty Images;
240: all, © Albert Bandura;
242: © Jennie Woodcock; Reflections Photolibrary/Corbis;
248: top left, © Mitch Tobias/Masterfile; top right, © LWA-Sharie Kennedy/Corbis; bottom, Archives of the History of American Psychology, University of Akron, Akron;
249: top (both), Photo Researchers, Inc; center, © Bonnie Kamin/Photo Edit; bottom, © Albert Bandura.

Chapter 6

250: © David Turnley/Corbis;
254: © Yoshi Ohara/Corbis;
258: Ryan McVay/Getty Images;
259: © Peter Turnley/Corbis;
263: © Buddy Mays/Corbis;
269: © David Butow/Corbis Saba;
271: © Bank of New Zealand Kiwi Recovery Trust;
272: © Steve Joester/Corbis;
273: Rachel Weill/Getty Images;
277: © Jose Luis Pelaez, Inc./Corbis;
282: © Steve McCurry/Magnum Photos;
284: LWA-Dann Tardif/Corbis;
294: © Buddy Mays/Corbis;
295: top, © Bank of New Zealand Kiwi Recovery Trust; bottom, © LWA-Dann Tardif/Corbis.

Chapter 7

296: © Helen King/Corbis;
298: Reprinted by permission of University of California Press; cover image: *The Hands of Georgia O'Keeffe* by Alfred Stieglitz/© 2005 The Georgia O'Keeffe Foundation/Artists Rights Society (ARS), New York;
304: left to right, © Athol Franz/Gallo Images/Corbis; © Paul Poplis/FoodPix; © Corbis;
307: © Paul Barton/Corbis;
314: © Cardinale Stephane/Corbis Sygma;
322: © Michael Nichols/Magnum Photos;
323: © Rick Friedman/Corbis;
328: © Bob Daemmrich/The Image Works;
340: top, © Paul Poplis/FoodPix; bottom, © Paul Barton/Corbis;
341: © Michael Nichols/Magnum Photos.

Chapter 8

342: © Wally McNamee/Corbis;
344: Entire book cover (Harper Perennial edition) from *Wasted: A Memoir of Anorexia and Bulimia* by Marya Hornbacher-Beard, © Marya Hornbacher-Beard. Reprinted by permission of Harper Collins Publishers;
347: © Ashley Cooper/Corbis;
350: David Madison/Getty Images;
352: © Bill Aron/PhotoEdit;
354: left, © Polak Matthew/Corbis Sygma; right, © Jason Reed/Reuters/Corbis;
359: © Richard Howard;
362: © T. Garcha/Masterfile;
363: © SuperStock/PictureQuest;
366: © AP Photo/The Grand Island Independent, Barrett Stinson;
367: top right, Kevin Winter/Getty Images; top row, left to right, Hulton Archive/Stringer/Getty Images; © Bettmann/Corbis; Getty Images; bottom row, left to right, jackhollingsworth.com/Alamy; © Buddy Mays/Corbis; Greer & Associates, Inc./Alamy;
368: © Neal Preston/Corbis;
369: left to right, © David Young-Wolff/Photo Edit; Jack Star/PhotoLink/Getty Images; SPL/Photo Researchers, Inc.;

374: © LA Daily News / David Crane / Corbis Sygma;
379: all, © P. Ekman & W. Friesen, "Unmasking the Face", 2nd Edition 1984. Used by permission of Ekman;
384: top, © Ashley Cooper / Corbis; center, © AP Photo / The Grand Island Independent, Barrett Stinson; bottom right, © Neal Preston / Corbis;
385: top left, © David Young-Wolff / Photo Edit; top right, Jack Star / PhotoLink / Getty Images; bottom (all), © P. Ekman & W. Friesen, "Unmasking the Face", 2nd Edition 1984. Used by permission of Ekman.

Chapter 9
386: Andy Cox / Getty Images;
388: Reprinted with the permission of Scribner, an imprint of Simon & Schuster Adult Publishing Group, from *Angela's Ashes* by Frank McCourt. Copyright © 1996 by Frank McCourt, cover image reprinted with the permission of Culver Pictures, Inc.;
391: © Tom Stewart / Corbis;
392: © Norbert Schaefer / Corbis;
396: top left, Don W. Fawcett / Photo Researchers, Inc.; top right, Claude Edelmann / Photo Researchers, Inc; bottom left, Anatomical Travelogue / Photo Researchers, Inc.; bottom right, Neil Bromhall / Photo Researchers, Inc.;
401: Juergen Berger, Max-planck Institute / Photo Researchers, Inc.;
404: © Mark Richards / Photo Edit;
406: Bill Anderson / Photo Researchers, Inc.;
408: both, © Laura Dwight / Photo Edit;
411: Archives of the History of American Psychology, University of Akron, Akron, Ohio;
414: © Bettmann / Corbis;
416: © Ellen Pastorino;
419: both, Courtesy of Harlow Primate Lab, University of Wisconsin–Madison;
422: © Corbis Sygma;
425: Archives of the History of American Psychology, University of Akron, Akron, Ohio;
432: top, Claude Edelmann / Photo Researchers, Inc.; bottom, © Laura Dwight / Photo Edit;
433: top, © Bettmann / Corbis; center, Courtesy of Harlow Primate Lab, University of Wisconsin-Madison; bottom, Archives of the History of American Psychology, University of Akron, Akron, Ohio.

Chapter 10
434: Wilfried Krecichwost / Getty Images;
436: Book cover for Touchstone Books paperback edition of *Still Life with Rice: A Young American Woman Discovers the Life and Legacy of Her Korean Grandmother* by Helie Lee. (New York: Touchstone Books / Simon & Schuster, 1997). Cover used by permission of Simon & Schuster Adult Publishing Group;
440: Greg Ceo / Getty Images;
444: Myrna Suarez / Getty Images;
446: © Corbis;
449: Nick Dolding / Getty Images;
454: © Kim Kulish / Corbis;
455: © Ed Bock / Corbis;
456: © John Henley / Corbis;
459: top, © Corbis; bottom, PNC / Getty Images;
461: © Susan Van Etten / Photo Edit;
463: Barbara Peacock / Getty Images;
466: © Ronnie Kaufman / Corbis;
468: © Peter Beck / Corbis;
469: Benelux Press / Picturequest;
472: Photodisc Collection / Getty Images;
473: © Mark Richards / Photo Edit;
478: top, Greg Ceo / Getty Images; bottom, © Corbis;
479: top, © Susan Van Etten / Photo Edit; center left, Photodisc Collection / Getty Images; center right, © Peter Beck / Corbis.

Chapter 11
480: Robert Daly / Getty Images;
482: From *I Know Why the Caged Bird Sings* (jacket cover) by Maya Angelou, copyright © 1983 by Random House, Inc. Used by permission of Bantam Books, a division of Random House, Inc.;
483: © Gary Hershorn / Reuters / Corbis;
486: © Corbis;
487: © Reuters / Corbis;
490: © Reuters / Corbis;
491: © Bettmann / Corbis;
493: © Michael Keller / Corbis;
497: top, © Reuters / Corbis; bottom, Thinkstock / Getty Images;
498: © Monika Graff / The Image Works;
500: © Gallo Images / Corbis;
501: top, © Steve Prezant / Corbis; bottom, © Bettmann / Corbis;
504: Carol Ford / Getty Images;
507: Thomas Hoeffgen / Getty Images;
510: © Dan Lamont / Corbis;
512: © Ed Andreski / Associated Press / Pool / Corbis;
514: Stuart McClymont / Getty Images;
516: top, © A. Ramey / Photo Edit; bottom, Eye of Science / Photo Researchers, Inc.;
520: top, © Corbis; center, © Michael Keller / Corbis; bottom, Thinkstock / Getty Images;
521: Eye of Science / Photo Researchers, Inc.

Chapter 12
522: © Chuck Savage / Corbis;
524: Reprinted with the permission of Simon & Schuster from *Always Running: La Vida Loca, Gang Days in L.A.* by Luis J. Rodriguez. (N.Y.: Simon & Schuster, 1994);
527: © Mark Richards / Photo Edit;
529: © Colin Young-Wolff / Photo Edit;
532: © Ramin Talaie / Corbis;
539: © Mark Peterson / Corbis;
544: Tim Boyles / Getty Images;
546: © David Butow / Corbis Saba;
547: left to right, © Tim Pannell / Corbis; James Connelly / Corbis; Ryan McVay / Getty Images; © Corbis;
548: left to right, Andy Levin / Photo Researchers, Inc.; Inc, MedioImages / IndexStock; © Corbis;
550: © Joseph Sohm; ChromoSohm Inc. / Corbis;
553: © Anthony Redpath / Corbis;
556: © Susan Van Etten / Photo Edit;
562: © Ariel Skelley / Corbis;
564: © PHOTICK / IndexStock;
566: © Tom Stewart / Corbis;
574: top, © Mark Richards / Photo Edit; bottom, © Mark Peterson / Corbis;
575: top, © Tim Pannell / Corbis; center left, © Susan Van Etten / Photo Edit; center right, © David Butow / Corbis Saba; bottom, Ariel Skelley / Corbis.

Chapter 13
576: © Ellen Pastorino;
578: © Ellen Pastorino;
580: © Streetstock Images / Corbis;
584: © Tony Arruza / Corbis;
585: © Michael Newman / Photo Edit;
594: © David Madison / Corbis;
597: © Tom Stewart / Corbis;
600: © Picturequest;
604: © Bradley Smith / Corbis;
606: © Bill Aron / Photo Edit;
607: © Scott Houston / Corbis Sygma;
608: © Rufus F. Folkks / Corbis;
614: top, © Streetstock Images / Corbis; center left, © Michael Newman / Photo Edit;
615: top, © Picturequest; bottom, © Bill Aron / Photo Edit.

Chapter 14
616: © David Young-Wolff / Photo Edit;
618: Cover copyright © 1996 by Honi Werner, from *The Color of Water* by James McBride. Used by permission of Riverhead Books, an imprint of Penguin Group (USA) Inc.;
619: © Michael Newman / Photo Edit;
620: Getty Images;
624: Ryan McVay / Getty Images;
625: © Strauss / Curtis / Corbis;
626: top, © Bettmann / Corbis; bottom, © Bettmann / Corbis;
627: © Bettmann / Corbis;
630: © Courtesy of Cattell Family;
632: Mel Yates / Getty Images;
636: Archives of the History of American Psychology, University of Akron, Akron, Ohio;
639: © Corbis Sygma;
640: © Roger Ressmeyer / Corbis;
647: Zigy Kaluzny / Getty Images;
652: top, Getty Images; bottom, Mel Yates / Getty Images;
653: top, © Roger Ressmeyer / Corbis; bottom, Zigy Kaluzny / Getty Images.

Chapter 15
654: Jean-Noel Reichel / Getty Images;
656: top left, Cover, © 2003 by Amy Tan, from *The Opposite of Fate* by Amy Tan. Used by permission of G.P. Putnam's Sons, a division of Penguin Group (USA) Inc; bottom left, Book cover for Touchstone Books paperback edition of *A Beautiful Mind* by Silvia Nasar (New York: Touchstone Books / Simon & Schuster, 2001). Cover used by permission of Simon & Schuster Adult Publishing Group; cover photo, © Universal Studios. All Rights Reserved; right, Diane Freed / Getty Images;
658: © Michael Macor / San Francisco Chronicle / Corbis;
660: © Bettmann / Corbis;
662: © Frank Trapper / Corbis;
667: © Creatas / Picturequest;
669: © Barbara Stitzer / Photo Edit;
671: © Najlah Feanny / Corbis Saba;
676: Benelux Press / Getty Images;
685: © Jean-Michel Girand / Photo Researchers, Inc.;
686: © Grunnitus Studio / Photo Researchers, Inc.;
695: © Corbis Sygma;
700: top, Jean-Noel Reichel / Getty Images; bottom, © Creatas / Picturequest;
701: top, Benelux Press / Getty Images; center, © Grunnitus Studio / Photo Researchers, Inc.; bottom, © Corbis Sygma.

Chapter 16
702: © Jose Luis Pelaez, Inc. / Corbis;
704: From *Mockingbird Years* by Emily Fox Gordon. © 2000 by Emily Fox Gordon. Reprinted by permission of Basic Books, a member of Perseus Books, L.L.C.;
709: © Jose Luis Pelaez, Inc. / Corbis;
712: © Tom Stewart / Corbis;
715: © Will Burgess / Reuters / Corbis;
720: Courtesy of Ellis Institute;
721: Courtesy of Beck Institute for Cognitive Therapy and Research;
723: David Harry Stewart / Getty Images;
737: © Najlah Feanny / Corbis;
742: top, © Nancy Sheehan / Photo Edit; bottom, © Tom Stewart / Corbis;
743: top, David Harry Stewart / Getty Images; center, © Jose Luis Pelaez, Inc. / Corbis; bottom, © Najlah Feanny / Corbis.

Name Index

Subject Index

Page numbers in **bold** indicate terms defined in the margins.